Learning Microsoft® Office 2016: Level 2

Joyce J. Nielsen

Catherine Skintik

Faithe Wempen

Pearson

Boston • Columbus • Indianapolis • New York • San Francisco
Amsterdam • Cape Town • Dubai • London • Madrid • Milan • Munich • Paris • Montréal • Toronto
Delhi • Mexico City • São Paulo • Sydney • Hong Kong • Seoul • Singapore • Taipei • Tokyo

Pearson

330 Hudson Street, New York, NY 10013

Hardcover ISBN 10: 0-13-444657-7

Hardcover ISBN 13: 978-0-13-444657-8

2 17

Table of Contents

Microsoft Word 2016

Microsoft Excel 2016

Chapter 6 Managing Large Workbooks 286

Chapter 7 Creating Charts, Shapes, and Templates 340

Chapter 8 Creating Macros and Using Data Analysis Tools 406

Chapter 9 Analyzing Data............. 468

Chapter 10 Collaborating with Others and Preparing a Final Workbook for Distribution 570

Microsoft Access 2016

Chapter 4 Customizing Tables and Databases 618

Chapter 5 Developing Advanced Queries 652

Chapter 6 Customizing Forms and Reports 684

Chapter 7 Securing, Integrating, and Maintaining Data 748

Microsoft PowerPoint 2016

Chapter 5 Working with Masters, Handouts, and Text 780

Chapter 6 Working with Graphic Objects and Media 828

Chapter 7 Finalizing and Sharing a Presentation 884

Index 921

Introduction

Microsoft Office 2016 is Microsoft's suite of application software. The Standard version includes Word, Excel, Outlook, and PowerPoint. Other editions may also include Access, Publisher, OneNote, and InfoPath. This book covers Word (the word processing tool), Excel (the spreadsheet tool), PowerPoint (the presentation tool), and Access (the database tool). Because Microsoft Office is an integrated suite, the components can all be used separately or together to create professional-looking documents and to manage data.

How the Book Is Organized

Learning Microsoft Office 2016: Level 2 continues building on the skills introduced in ***Learning Microsoft Office 2016: Level 1***. The book is made up of four sections:

- **Word 2016.** With Word you can create letters, memos, Web pages, newsletters, and more.
- **Excel 2016.** Excel, Microsoft's spreadsheet component, is used to organize and calculate data, track financial data, and create charts and graphs.
- **Access 2016.** Access is Microsoft's powerful database tool. Using Access you will learn to store, retrieve, and report on information.
- **PowerPoint 2016.** Create dynamic onscreen presentations with PowerPoint, the presentation graphics tool.

Chapters are comprised of short lessons designed for using Microsoft Office 2016 in real-life business settings. Each lesson is made up of six key elements:

- **What You Will Learn.** Each lesson starts with an overview of the learning objectives covered in the lesson.
- **Words to Know.** Key terms are included and defined at the start of each lesson, so you can quickly refer back to them. The terms are then highlighted in the text.
- **What You Can Do.** Concise notes for learning the computer concepts.
- **Try It.** Hands-on practice activities provide brief procedures to teach all necessary skills.
- **Practice.** These projects give students a chance to create documents, spreadsheets, database objects, and presentations by entering information. Steps provide all the how-to information needed to complete a project.
- **Apply.** Each lesson concludes with a project that challenges students to apply what they have learned through steps that tell them what to do, without all the how-to information. In the Apply projects, students must show they have mastered each skill set.
- Each chapter ends with two assessment projects: **Critical Thinking** and **Portfolio Builder**, which incorporate all the skills covered throughout the chapter.

Working with Data and Solution Files

As you work through the projects in this book, you'll be creating, opening, and saving files. You should keep the following instructions in mind:

- For many of the projects, you will use data files. The data files can be accessed from the Navigate IT Web site (www.pearsonhighered.com/navigateit). Select "Student" and browse for "Learning Microsoft Office 2016: Level 2."
- The data files are used so that you can focus on the skills being introduced—not on keyboarding lengthy documents.
- When the project steps tell you to open a file name, you open the data file provided.
- All the projects instruct you to save the files created or to save the project files under a new name. This is to make the project file your own and to avoid overwriting the data file in the storage location. Throughout this book, when naming files and folders, replace *xx* with your name or initials as instructed by your teacher.
- Follow your instructor's directions for where to access and save the files on a network, local computer hard drive, or portable storage device such as a USB drive.
- Many of the projects also provide instructions for including your name in a header or footer. Again, this is to identify the project work as your own for grading and assessment purposes.
- Unless the book instructs otherwise, use the default settings for text size, margin size, and so on when creating a file. If someone has changed the default software settings for the computer you're using, your exercise files may not look the same as those shown in this book. In addition, the appearance of your files may look different if the system is set to a screen resolution other than 1024 × 768.

Navigating the Textbook

Software Skills

Each lesson begins with an introduction to the computer skills that will be covered in the lesson.

Words to Know

Vocabulary terms are listed at the start of each lesson for easy reference and appear in bold in the text on first use.

What You Can Do

The technology concepts are introduced and explained.

168 | Chapter 8 | Word | **Learning Microsoft Office 2016**

Lesson 54

Working with Outlines

➤ **What You Will Learn**

Creating an Outline
Managing an Outline
Numbering an Outline

WORDS TO KNOW

Body text
Outline text that is not formatted with a heading-level style.

Collapse
To hide subtopics in an outline.

Demote
To move down one level in an outline.

Expand
To show subtopics in an outline.

Outline
A document that lists levels of topics.

Promote
To move up one level in an outline.

Software Skills Create an outline to organize ideas for any document that covers more than one topic, such as an article, a report, a presentation, or a speech. For example, you might create an outline to list the chapters or headings in a report or to arrange main subjects for a presentation. The outline serves as a map you can follow as you complete the entire document.

What You Can Do

Creating an Outline

- Use Outline view to create and edit an **outline**.
- When you switch to Outline view, the Outlining tab becomes available on the ribbon.
- An outline is similar to a multilevel list (refer to Word, Lesson 7). Outline topics are formatted in levels, which may be called headings: Level 1 is a main heading, Level 2 is a subheading, Level 3 is a sub-subheading, and so on up to 9 heading levels.
- By default, text you type in an outline is formatted as **Level 1**. You use the tools in the Outline Tools group on the Outlining tab of the ribbon to **promote** or **demote** paragraphs to different levels.
- Headings in an outline are preceded by one of three outline symbols:
  - Levels that have sublevels under them are preceded by a circle with a plus sign in it ⊕.
  - Levels that do not have sublevels are preceded by a circle with a minus sign in it ⊖.
  - **Body text** that is not formatted as a heading level is preceded by a small circle ○.
- Note that although outline levels print as expected, the indentation does not appear onscreen in Print Layout view or on the Print tab in the Backstage view.

Try It!

Short, hands-on activities give students the opportunity to practice the software features in a sample document.

Illustrations

Illustrations throughout the text can be used as guidelines for visual learners.

Learning Microsoft Office 2016 | Word | Chapter 8 179

Try It! Modifying a Page Border

1. In the W55Try_xx file, position the insertion point at the beginning of page 2.
2. Click Design > Page Borders.
3. Click the Page Border tab, if necessary.
4. Click the Art drop-down arrow and click the first option, apples.
5. Under Width, use the increment arrows to set the Width to 20 pt.
6. In the Preview area, click the top, left, and right borders in the diagram to remove them.
7. Click the Apply to drop-down arrow and click This section.
8. Click the Options button.
9. Under Margin, use the increment arrows to set the Bottom margin to 30 pt.
10. Click OK.
11. Click OK.
12. Save the changes to W55Try_xx, and leave it open to use in the next Try It.

Hiding or Displaying White Space

- By default, in Print Layout view, Word displays white space. In this context, the term "white space" refers to the space between the bottom of one page and the top of the next page, as well as the header and footer.
- You can hide white space by double-clicking the top or bottom edge of any page in the document.

✓ *Word also hides any page borders applied to the document.*

- When white space is hidden, a gray line marks the location where one page ends and the next begins.
- To display white space, double-click the gray line between pages. If your document has only one page, double-click the top or bottom edge of the page.
- You can also select or clear the Show white space between pages in Print Layout view check box on the Display tab in the Word Options dialog box.

Try It! Hiding or Displaying White Space

1. In the W55Try_xx file, click View > Print Layout to change to Print Layout view, if necessary.
2. Scroll down so you can see the bottom of the first page and the top of the second page onscreen at the same time.
3. Position the mouse pointer over the bottom edge of page 1. The pointer changes to resemble arrows pointing up and down.
4. Double-click.
5. Position the mouse pointer on the gray line between the pages. Double-click again.
6. Leave the file open to use in the next Try It.

Display white space between pages

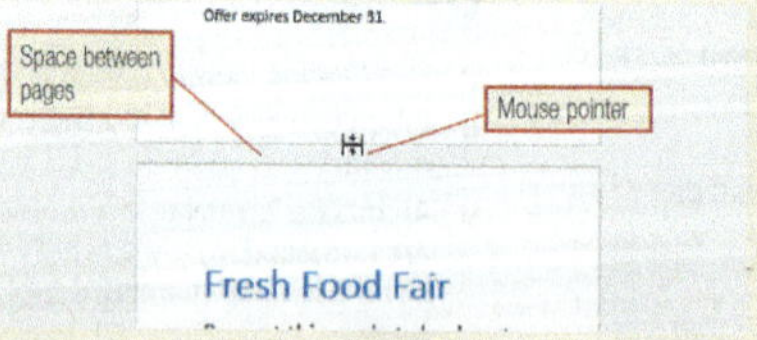

Word 2016, Windows 10, Microsoft Corporation

Hide white space between pages

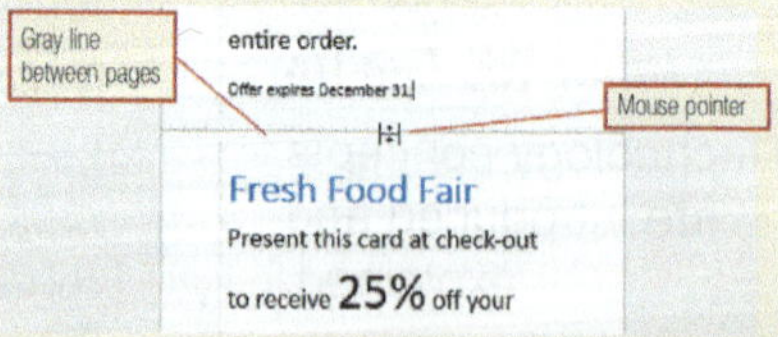

Word 2016, Windows 10, Microsoft Corporation

Lesson 37—Practice

The Clifton Community Center (CCC) runs a presentation on a screen in the lobby to keep community members up to date with the latest events in the community and at the center for a given month. The CCC is committed to serving a diverse population with information for and about different cultures. In this project, you begin work on the November presentation. You use the Translator and the Smart Lookup task pane to locate information about a November event and define a word.

DIRECTIONS

1. Start PowerPoint, if necessary, and open **P37Practice** from the data files for this lesson.
2. Save the presentation as **P37Practice_xx** in the location where your teacher instructs you to store the files for this lesson.
3. Display slide 2.
4. Click at the end of the bullet item, press ENTER, and type **The dictionary defines mincemeat as follows:**
5. Double-click the word *mincemeat* that you just typed, and then click **Review** > **Smart Lookup** to open the Smart Lookup task pane.
6. Click **Define** near the top of the task pane.
7. Under the heading *noun: mincemeat*, drag over the definition (*a mixture of spiced* . . .), and press CTRL + C.
8. On the slide, press ENTER at the end of the second bullet item, press TAB, and then press CTRL + V to paste the definition.
9. Remove the bullet formatting from the definition, change the first letter to a capital *A*, and then drag the left indent marker on the ruler to create a **1"** left indent. Your slide should look similar to Figure 37-1.

Figure 37-1

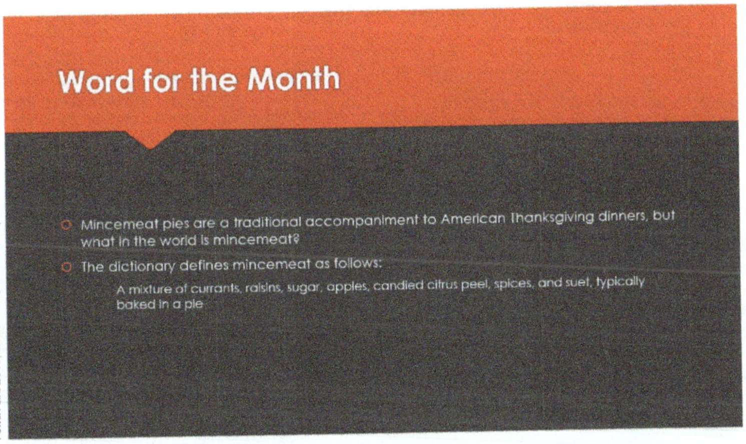

PowerPoint 2016, Windows 10, Microsoft Corporation

End-of-Lesson Projects

Each lesson includes two hands-on projects where students can use all of the skills that they have learned in the lesson.

End-Result Solutions

Students can refer to solution illustrations to make sure that his or her work is on track.

End-of-Chapter Activities

Topics include a variety of business, career, and college-readiness scenarios. Critical-thinking skills are required to complete the project.

Directions

Projects challenge students to apply what they have learned through steps that tell what needs to be done, without all the how-to information.

---

824 Chapter 5 | PowerPoint | **Learning Microsoft Office 2016**

End-of-Chapter Activities

➤ PowerPoint Chapter 5—Critical Thinking

Communicating with Coworkers and Clients

You and your colleagues at Restoration Architecture work with clients every day. Some recent misunderstandings and miscommunications have convinced you that the staff could benefit from a presentation that reviews how to communicate effectively not only with clients but also with coworkers.

In this project, working alone or in teams, you will research effective workplace communication. Your research should cover the following topics:

- Communicating effectively with colleagues and clients.
- Recognizing the difference between verbal and nonverbal forms of communication.
- Understanding how both verbal and nonverbal behaviors help you communicate with coworkers and clients.
- Employing active listening to help you understand issues.
- Employing strategies that will help you communicate with clients and colleagues from diverse backgrounds.
- Understanding how to resolve conflicts that might arise within a diverse workforce and client base.
- Avoiding behaviors that could be considered sexual harassment.

As part of this project, you should prepare support materials that will enhance the presentation.

DIRECTIONS

1. Start a new presentation, and save it as **PCT05A_xx** in the location where your teacher instructs you to store the files for this chapter.
2. Insert the title **Effective Workplace Communication**. In the subtitle placeholder, type **A Presentation by** and then insert your first and last name.
3. Apply a theme and variant of your choice. In Slide Master view, customize the background of at least one slide layout with a gradient, picture, or texture.
4. Change the font on the title slide to a heavy, bold font and apply advanced text formatting such as a fill, outline, and effect.
5. Add a slide to the presentation with the title **Sources**. Use this slide to record the Web addresses of sites you use to find information for this presentation.
6. **With your teacher's permission,** use the Smart Lookup task pane to research the topics listed above. Use valid and reputable sites for your research, and copy site information to your Sources slide.
7. When your research is complete, organize your material into topics and plan how to use the material in your presentation. You may use a storyboard, if desired. Select slide layouts suitable for the type of information you find. Add illustrations as desired, using online pictures or other graphics.
8. Use at least one slide for each topic. Use additional slides to expand the topic as necessary.
9. On one slide, define the word *communication* using a source from the Smart Lookup task pane. Adjust indents as desired to present the definition clearly.
10. Check spelling.
11. Apply transitions to enhance the presentation's effectiveness.

Learning Microsoft® Office 2016: Level 2

Chapter 5

(Courtesy Yuri Arcurs/Shutterstock)

Using Advanced Formatting, Lists, and Charts

Lesson 36
Inserting Text Files and Blank Pages

- Inserting a File in a Document
- Inserting a Blank Page or a Cover Page
- Setting Up an Employment Portfolio

Lesson 37
Creating and Editing Styles

- Creating a Style
- Editing a Style
- Reapplying Direct Formatting
- Setting a Default Style Set
- Using the Navigation Pane

Lesson 38
Managing Style Formatting

- Revealing Style Formatting
- Applying Advanced Font and Paragraph Attributes
- Tracking Formatting Inconsistencies
- Managing Style Conflicts
- Copying Styles Using the Organizer
- Attaching a Template to a Document

Lesson 39
Working with Multilevel Lists

- Formatting a Multilevel List
- Customizing a Multilevel List
- Creating and Deleting a Multilevel List Style

Lesson 40
Inserting Charts

- Inserting a Chart
- Modifying a Chart
- Formatting a Chart

End-of-Chapter Activities

Lesson 36

Inserting Text Files and Blank Pages

➤ What You Will Learn

Inserting a File in a Document
Inserting a Blank Page or a Cover Page
Setting Up an Employment Portfolio

WORDS TO KNOW

Cover page
The first page of a document that usually displays such information as the document title and subtitle, the author's name, and the date.

Electronic portfolio
A collection of digital information and documents that illustrates your abilities and achievements.

Employment portfolio
A collection of documents that illustrates the qualities and abilities of a job candidate.

Reflection
The act of thinking critically about items in a portfolio and communicating the importance of each item to others.

Software Skills Word has many features that help you save time by reusing existing content. You can insert a file into another file to save time retyping existing text. You can also insert a blank page anywhere in a document, or select a preformatted cover page design from a gallery to insert at the beginning of your document.

What You Can Do

Inserting a File in a Document

- You can insert one file into another file to incorporate the first file's contents into the second file.
- The entire contents of the inserted first file are saved as part of the second file.
- The first file remains unchanged.
- The command for inserting a file is available on the Object menu in the Text group on the Insert tab of the ribbon.

Try It! Inserting a File in a Document

1. Start Word, and open **W36TryA** from the data files for this lesson.
2. Save the file as **W36TryA_xx** in the location where your teacher instructs you to store the files for this lesson.

   ✓ *Replace xx with your own name or initials as instructed by your teacher.*
3. Display nonprinting characters, if they are not already displayed. Position the insertion point on the last line of the document, below the last text paragraph.
4. Click the Insert tab.
5. Click the Object drop-down arrow > Text from File.
6. Navigate to the location where the data files for this lesson are stored.
7. Click **W36TryB**.
8. Click Insert.
9. Save the changes to **W36TryA_xx**, and leave it open to use in the next Try It.

Inserting a Blank Page or a Cover Page

- Use commands in the Pages group on the Insert tab of the ribbon to insert a blank page or **cover page**.
- When you insert a blank page at the beginning of a document or a cover page, Word inserts a hard page break after the new page.
- When you insert a blank page in the body of the document, Word inserts hard page breaks before and after the new page.
- Word includes a gallery of preformatted cover pages that include page layout and design features as well as content controls for standard text, such as the document title and the author's name.
- You replace the sample text by typing new text or by selecting data from the content control's drop-down list.
- You can remove a cover page at any time.

Try It! Inserting a Blank Page or a Cover Page

1. In the **W36TryA_xx** file, position the insertion point at the beginning of the paragraph you inserted in the previous Try It.
2. On the Insert tab, click the Blank Page button.
3. On the Insert tab, click the Cover Page button to display the gallery of cover page styles, and click Facet.
4. Click the Cover Page button again, and click Remove Current Cover Page.
5. Click the Cover Page button to display the gallery of cover page styles, and click Filigree.
6. On the cover page, click [DOCUMENT TITLE], and type **NUTRITION CLASS SCHEDULE**.
7. Right-click [Document subtitle], and click Remove Content Control on the shortcut menu.
8. Click [DATE], click the drop-down arrow, and click the Today button on the calendar.
9. Click [COMPANY NAME], and type your name.
10. Right-click [Company address], and click Remove Content Control on the shortcut menu.
11. Save and close the file.

(continued)

Try It! **Inserting a Blank Page or a Cover Page** *(continued)*

Cover page gallery

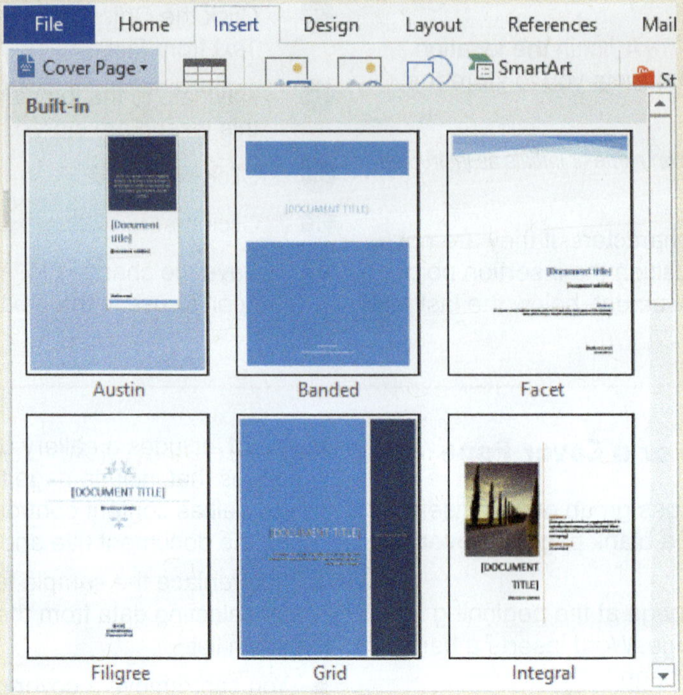

Word 2016, Windows 10, Microsoft Corporation

Setting Up an Employment Portfolio

- Set up an **employment portfolio** to organize information about yourself that you can use as a reference while looking for a job.
- An employment portfolio may be as simple as a binder in which you store printed documents and a Windows folder in which you store digital documents.
- Printed documents should be placed in the binder in plastic sleeves for protection and to maintain a professional appearance when you take the binder to interviews or meetings.
- Documents are usually organized by category or type. For example, store letters of recommendation together, certifications together, and examples of achievement together.
- An effective employment portfolio illustrates the progress you make in school and in your career and helps you stay on track to achieve your educational and career goals.
- There are three types of portfolios, but most portfolios are a combination of all three.
  - A *development portfolio* shows the progress of skills over a period of time.
  - An *assessment portfolio* demonstrates competency.
  - A *showcase portfolio* highlights achievements and the quality of work.
- Most employment portfolios include a resume, transcripts, letters of application, lists of references, letters of recommendation, copies of certifications, samples of your work, and examples of achievement. You may wish to include teacher evaluations in your portfolio. If you've received any scholarships, they could be included as part of your portfolio as well.
- An effective portfolio also includes comments or explanations that describe the importance of each item, help define goals, and map a path or plan to achieve those goals. This is often called a **reflection**, or self-reflection, because the owner of the portfolio must think critically about each item and communicate its value to others.
- Throughout your career, you should maintain and update your employment portfolio so that it is always ready if you need it.

- An **electronic portfolio** is a collection of digital information and documents. An electronic portfolio should include an abstract, or summary, of your accomplishments.
- All pieces of a portfolio must use proper grammar and be free of punctuation, capitalization, and spelling errors.

Lesson 36—Practice

In this project, you will insert a cover page, insert a blank page, and insert text from an existing document using the skills you learned in this lesson.

DIRECTIONS

1. Start Word, click **Blank document**, and save the document as **W36PracticeA_xx** in the location where your teacher instructs you to store the files for this lesson.
2. Apply the **Metropolitan** theme and the **Minimalist** style set, then type the following paragraphs using the default Normal style:

   Roses are prized by gardeners around the world. While some roses have a reputation as being difficult to grow or care for, many variations exist that are resistant to disease, offer beautiful blooms and fragrances, and blend easily into different landscapes.

   Other considerations include the size of the garden, the growing conditions, and how much time you want to spend caring for the plants. Drawing a garden plan can help you determine the number of plants you will need and how the colors and shapes of the blooms will relate to the other plants in the garden. Whether you have container pots on a balcony or a large suburban yard, with a little thought and preparation, you can select and grow magnificent roses.
3. Position the insertion point at the beginning of the second paragraph.
4. Click **Insert** > **Blank Page**.
5. On the Insert tab, click the **Object** drop-down arrow Object > **Text from File**.
6. Navigate to the location where the data files for this lesson are stored.
7. Click **W36PracticeB** > **Insert**.
8. Reposition the insertion point at the beginning of the document.
9. On the Insert tab, click **Cover Page**.
10. Scroll down the Cover Page gallery, and click **Whisp**.
11. Click **[Date]**, click the drop-down arrow, and click the **Today** button on the calendar.
12. Click **[Document title]**, and type **Selecting Roses**.
13. Click **[Document subtitle]**, and type **A Buyer's Guide**.
14. Click the **Author** content control, and type your full name.
15. Right-click the **Company name** content control, and click **Remove Content Control** on the shortcut menu.
16. Reposition the insertion point on the blank line above the Page Break on page 2 of the document.
17. On the Insert tab, click **Pictures**, navigate to the location where the data files for this lesson are stored, click **W36PracticeC**, and click **Insert**.
18. Reposition the insertion point on the blank line above the Page Break on page 3 of the document.
19. On the Insert tab, click **Pictures**, navigate to the location where the data files for this lesson are stored, click **W36PracticeD**, and click **Insert**.
20. Delete the blank line above the picture you just inserted.
21. Check and correct the spelling and grammar in the document. Proofread the document and correct any errors in capitalization or punctuation. Save the document.
22. **With your teacher's permission**, print the document. Page 1 should look similar to Figure 36-1 on the next page.
23. Save and close the document, and exit Word.

Figure 36-1

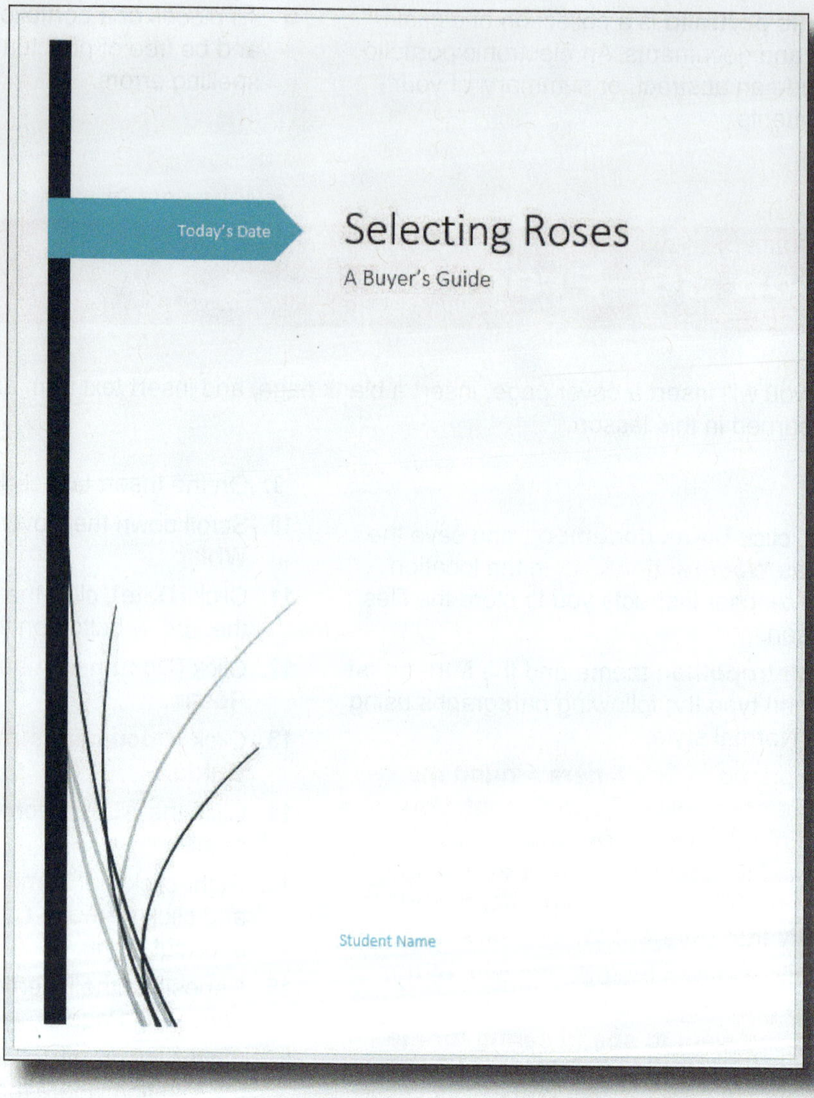

Word 2016, Windows 10, Microsoft Corporation

Lesson 36—Apply

Liberty Blooms, a flower shop, has asked you to develop a customer handout about selecting rose plants. You have missing content in an existing document, which you can insert on a blank page in the brochure. You will also insert a cover page.

DIRECTIONS

1. Start Word, and open **W36ApplyA** from the data files for this lesson.
2. Save the file as **W36ApplyA_xx** in the location where your teacher instructs you to store the files for this lesson.
3. Remove the current cover page.
4. Change the theme to **Wisp**, and the style set to **Lines (Simple)**.
5. Position the insertion point at the end of the last sentence in the second to last paragraph and insert a blank page.
6. On the new blank page, insert the text from the file **W36ApplyB**.

7. Insert a cover page in the **Semaphore** style.
8. In the Company Name content control, replace the sample text with the text **Liberty Blooms**.
9. Edit the brochure title to **How to Select Roses**.
10. Edit the brochure subtitle to **Your Guide to Buying Quality Blooms**.
11. Replace the sample author name with your own name, and enter today's date.
12. Remove the **Company address** content control
13. Reposition the insertion point on the blank line above the Page Break on page 3 of the document.
14. Insert the **W36ApplyC** picture file on the page.
15. Check and correct the spelling and grammar in the document, and save the document.
16. **With your teacher's permission**, print the document. Page 1 should look similar to Figure 36-2.
17. Save and close the document, and exit Word.

Figure 36-2

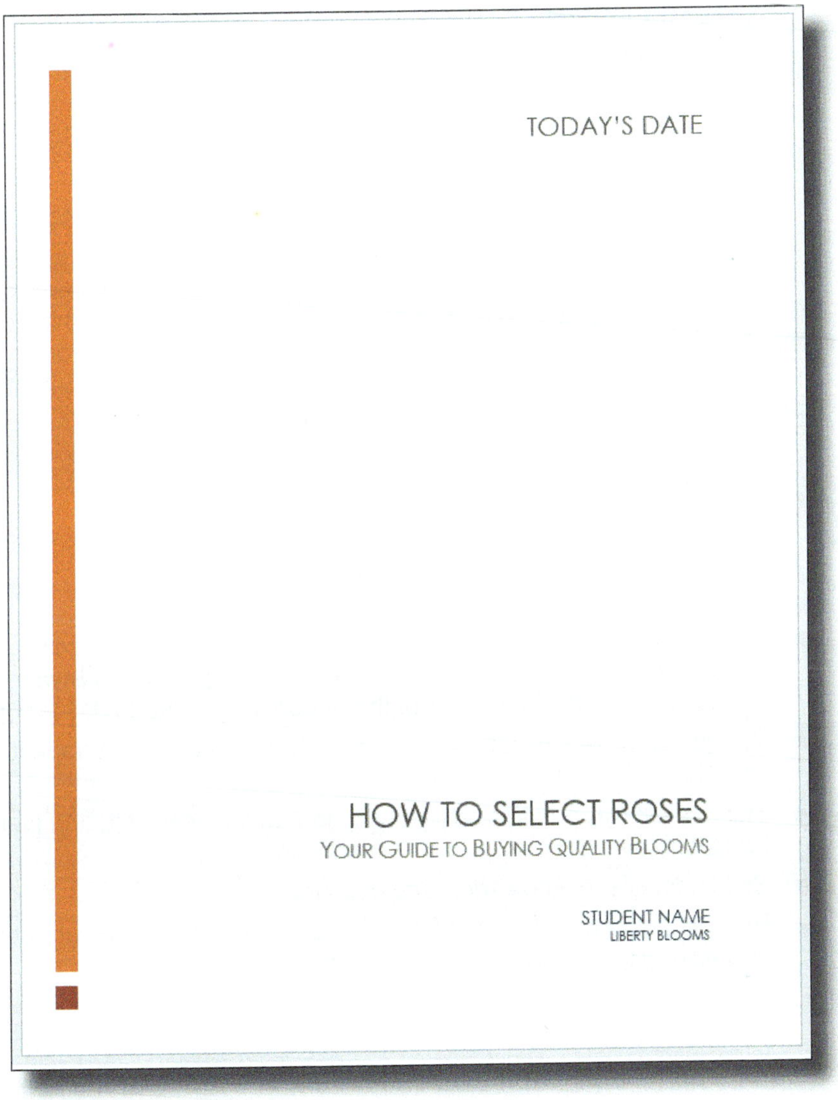

Word 2016, Windows 10, Microsoft Corporation

Lesson 37

Creating and Editing Styles

➤ What You Will Learn

Creating a Style
Editing a Style
Reapplying Direct Formatting
Setting a Default Style Set
Using the Navigation Pane

WORDS TO KNOW

Direct formatting
Individual font or paragraph formatting settings applied directly to text, as opposed to a collection of settings applied with a style.

Navigation Pane
A separate pane with a Headings area that displays a list of headings in the document.

Software Skills When Word's built-in styles do not provide the look you need, you can create your own styles or modify existing styles. You can use direct formatting to fine-tune or customize the appearance of your documents. Word 2016 provides tools to navigate and track your place within a document.

What You Can Do

Creating a Style

- Recall that you use styles to apply a collection of formatting settings to paragraphs all at once, and that Quick Styles display in the Styles gallery in the Styles group on the Home tab of the ribbon, and in the Styles task pane.
- You can create a new Quick Style to apply font and/or paragraph formatting to your documents.
- The easiest way to create a style is to format text, select it, and then assign the formatting a style name.
- Style names should be short and descriptive.
- By default, the new style is added to the style sheet for the current document and displays in the Quick Styles gallery.

Try It! Creating a Style

1. Start Word, and open **W37Try** from the data files for this lesson.
2. Save the file as **W37Try_xx** in the location where your teacher instructs you to store the files for this lesson.
3. Select the first line of text and format it in 24 point Arial, Dark Red, and center it horizontally.
4. On the Home tab, in the Styles group, click the Quick Styles gallery More button.
5. Click Create a Style. The Create New Style from Formatting dialog box appears.
6. In the Name box, type **Headline** to replace the sample style name.
7. Click OK to create the style and add it to the Quick Styles gallery.
8. Click in the paragraph beginning *Class size is limited*.

Create New Style from Formatting dialog box

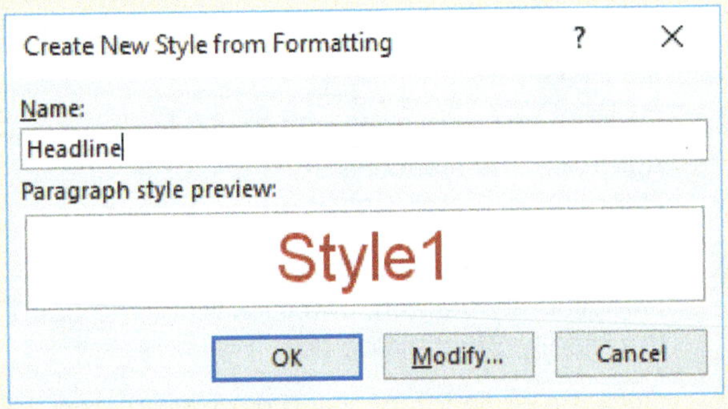

Word 2016, Windows 10, Microsoft Corporation

9. In the Quick Styles gallery, click the Headline style to apply it.
10. Save the **W37Try_xx** file, and leave it open to use in the next Try It.

Editing a Style

- You can edit, modify, or delete an existing style.
- Note that you can also remove a style from the Quick Styles gallery, but that does not delete the style.
- When you modify a style that has already been applied to text in the document, the formatting is updated to reflect the changes to the style.
- If you modify a style and give it a new name, it becomes a new style; the original style remains unchanged.
- You can quickly modify a style by changing the formatting and then updating the style in the Quick Styles gallery.
- When you want to modify any or all of the style properties at the same time, you can use the Modify Style dialog box.
- You can use the Modify Style dialog box to set advanced paragraph and character attributes and assign a shortcut key to a style.

Try It! Editing a Style

1. In the **W37Try_xx** file, select the first line of text and apply the Gradient Fill - Gray text effect style (first option on the second row in the Text Effects gallery).
2. On the Home tab, in the Quick Styles gallery, right-click the Headline style and click Update Headline to Match Selection.
3. In the Quick Styles gallery, right-click the Headline style again, and click Modify to open the Modify Style dialog box.
4. Click the Style for following paragraph drop-down arrow and click Normal.
5. Under Formatting, click the Font drop-down arrow and click Times New Roman.
6. Click OK to save the changes to the style.
7. On the Home tab, click the Styles group dialog box launcher to display the Styles task pane.
8. Click the Headline style drop-down arrow and then click Delete Headline.
9. Click Yes in the confirmation dialog box to delete the style.

✓ *Note that you can also remove a style from the Quick Styles gallery, but that does not delete the style.*

Modify Style dialog box

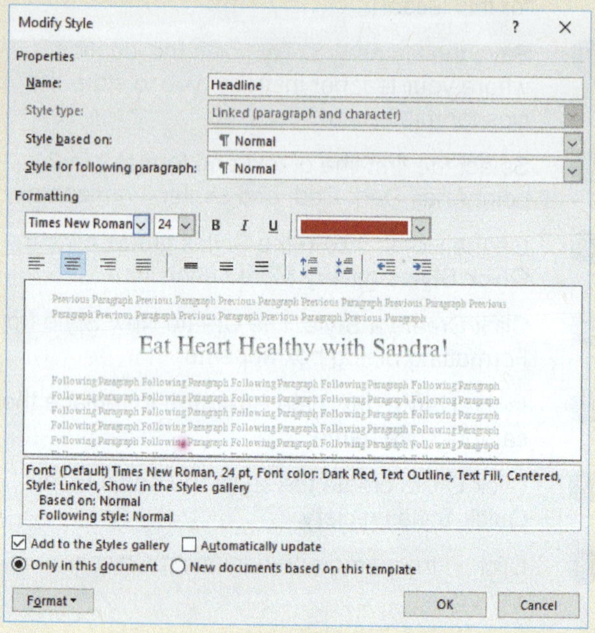

Word 2016, Windows 10, Microsoft Corporation

10. Save the **W37Try_xx** file, and leave it open to use in the next Try It.

Reapplying Direct Formatting

- By default, Word does not display information about **direct formatting** in the Styles task pane.
- You can select to display direct formatting so that you can reapply it to different text without saving it as a style.
- This feature is similar to the Format Painter, but instead of scrolling through the document to copy the formatting, you can select the direct formatting in the Styles task pane.

Try It! Reapplying Direct Formatting

1. In the Styles task pane in the **W37Try_xx** file, click Options to open the Style Pane Options dialog box.
2. Click to select the Paragraph level formatting, Font formatting, and Bullet and numbering formatting check boxes.
3. Click OK.

Style Pane Options dialog box

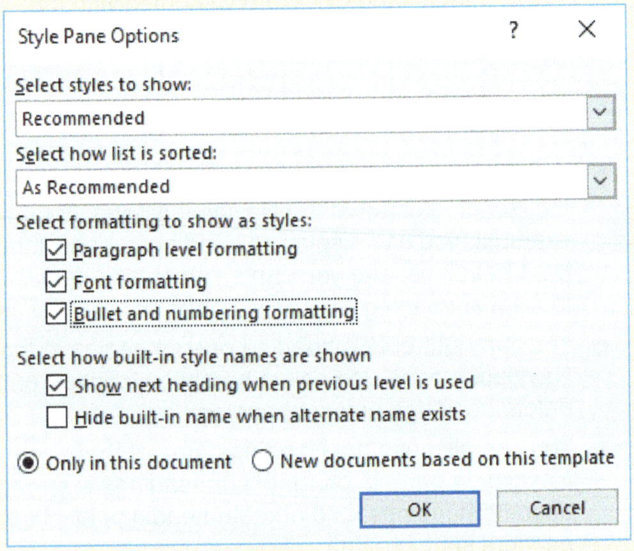

Word 2016, Windows 10, Microsoft Corporation

4. Select the first line of text and apply the Heading 1 style.
5. Increase the font size to 24 points and change the font color to Red.
6. Select the paragraph beginning *Class size is limited*.
7. In the Styles task pane, click Heading 1 + 24 pt, Red to reapply the direct formatting to the selected text, and then close the Styles task pane.
8. Save and close **W37Try_xx**, but leave Word open to use in the next Try It.

View direct formatting in the Styles task pane

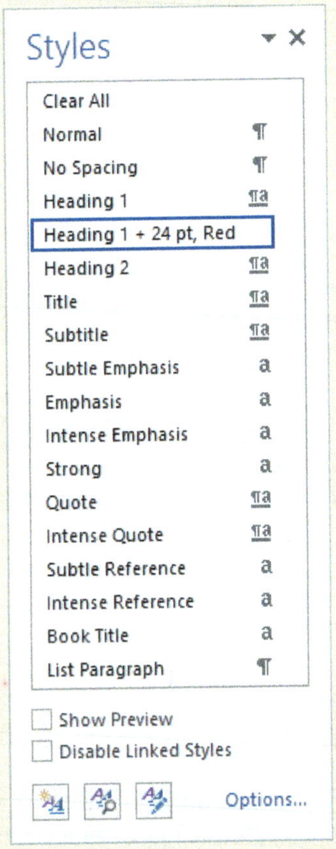

Word 2016, Windows 10, Microsoft Corporation

Setting a Default Style Set

- Recall that a style set is a collection of styles that use coordinated font formatting.
- A style set also contains options for +Body and +Heading fonts.
- Most templates have a built-in default style set. For example, the default style set for the Normal template is Word.
- You can change the default style set so that all new documents based on the template are created using the new style set.
- You can restore the original style set as the default.
- Take care when changing the Normal template's default style set because the changes will affect all new, blank documents.

Try It! Setting a Default Style Set

1. In Word, create a new blank document.
2. Click the Design tab, and in the Document Formatting group, click the More button ▾ to display the Style Set gallery.
3. In the gallery, click Basic (Simple).
4. In the Document Formatting group, click Set as Default.
5. Click Yes to apply this setting to all new blank documents.
6. Click File > Close > Don't Save to close the file without saving.
7. Create a new blank document, and click the Design tab. Notice that the styles use the new default style set—Basic (Simple).
8. In the Document Formatting group, click the More button ▾ to display the Style Set gallery, and click Word.
9. In the Document Formatting group, click Set as Default to restore the original default style set.
10. Click Yes to apply this setting to all new blank documents, and exit Word without saving the document.

Using the Navigation Pane

- You can use the Headings area of the **Navigation pane** to quickly navigate within your document and keep track of your location within it.
- You can access this feature from the Navigation Pane option in the Show group on the View tab.
- Click a heading in the Navigation pane to navigate to the corresponding heading in your document.
- The Navigation pane displays the selected heading at the top of the document window.
- You can choose the level of detail to display in the Headings area of the Navigation pane. For example, you can display all headings or only top-level headings, and you can show or hide details for individual headings.
- You can right-click a heading or subheading in the Navigation pane and select an option to insert and delete headings and subheadings.
- You can also use the Headings area of the Navigation pane to promote subheadings to become headings, and demote headings to become subheadings.

Try It! Using the Navigation Pane

1. Start Word, and open **W37Try_xx** from the location where your teacher instructs you to store the files for this lesson.
2. Click View > Navigation Pane. The Navigation pane appears.
3. Click the heading beginning *Class size is limited*. Notice that the document window displays the selected heading at the top of the page.
4. Click the Close button × on the Navigation pane to close it.
5. Close the document without saving the changes.

Headings in the Navigation pane

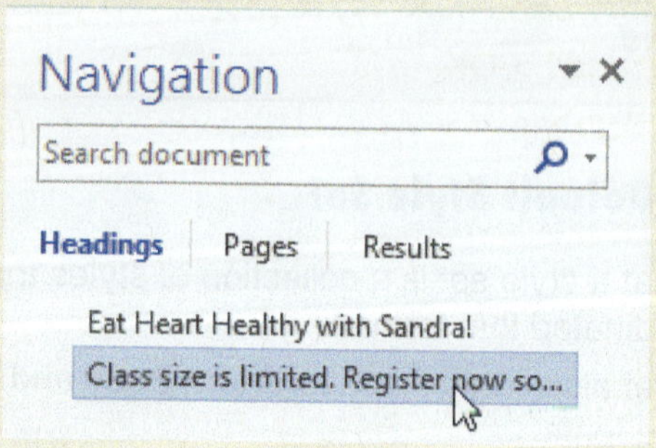

Word 2016, Windows 10, Microsoft Corporation

Lesson 37—Practice

In this project, you will format a training schedule for Restoration Architecture. You will use styles and direct formatting, and navigate the document using the Navigation pane.

DIRECTIONS

1. Start Word, and open **W37Practice** from the data files for this lesson.
2. Save the file as **W37Practice_xx** in the location where your teacher instructs you to store the files for this lesson.
3. Double-click in the header, and type your full name and today's date on two lines. Click **Close Header and Footer**.
4. Click the Design tab and in the Document Formatting group, in the Style Set gallery, click **Lines (Stylish)**.
5. On the Design tab, in the Document Formatting group, click **Set as Default** > **Yes**.
6. Click the Home tab, and click the **Styles** group dialog box launcher to display the Styles task pane.
7. In the Styles task pane, click **Options**.
8. In the Style Pane Options dialog box, click to select the **Paragraph level formatting**, **Font formatting**, and **Bullet and numbering formatting** check boxes, and click **OK**.
9. Apply the **Heading 1** style to the company name.
10. Select the company address and phone number, and change the font size to **10 points** and the font color to **Dark Red**.
11. With the address still selected, click the Quick Styles gallery **More** button > **Create a Style**.
12. Type **Subhead1** > **OK**.
13. Apply the **Subhead1** style to the text *Training Schedule*.
14. With the text *Training Schedule* still selected, change the font size to **12 points**, apply bold, and increase the spacing after to **30 pt**.
15. In the Styles task pane, click the **Subhead1** drop-down arrow > **Update Subhead1 to Match Selection**.
16. Select the text *January*.
17. Change the font to **18 point Times New Roman**.
18. Select the course name *Microsoft Word 1*, and in the Styles task pane, click **Times New Roman, 18 pt** to apply the direct formatting you applied in step 17.
19. Click **View** > **Navigation Pane**.
20. In the Navigation pane, click **Restoration Architecture** to navigate to the top of the document.
21. Close the Navigation pane.
22. Check and correct the spelling and grammar in the document, and save the document.
23. **With your teacher's permission**, print the document. It should look similar to Figure 37-1 on the next page.
24. In the Styles task pane, click the **Subhead1** drop-down arrow, click **Delete Subhead1**, and click **Yes** at the prompt to delete the **Subhead1** style.
25. Apply the **Subtitle** style to the company address and phone number and the text *Training Schedule*, and close the **Styles** task pane.
26. Click **Design** > **Word**.
27. In the Document Formatting group, click **Set as Default** > **Yes**.
28. Save and close the document, and exit Word.

Figure 37-1

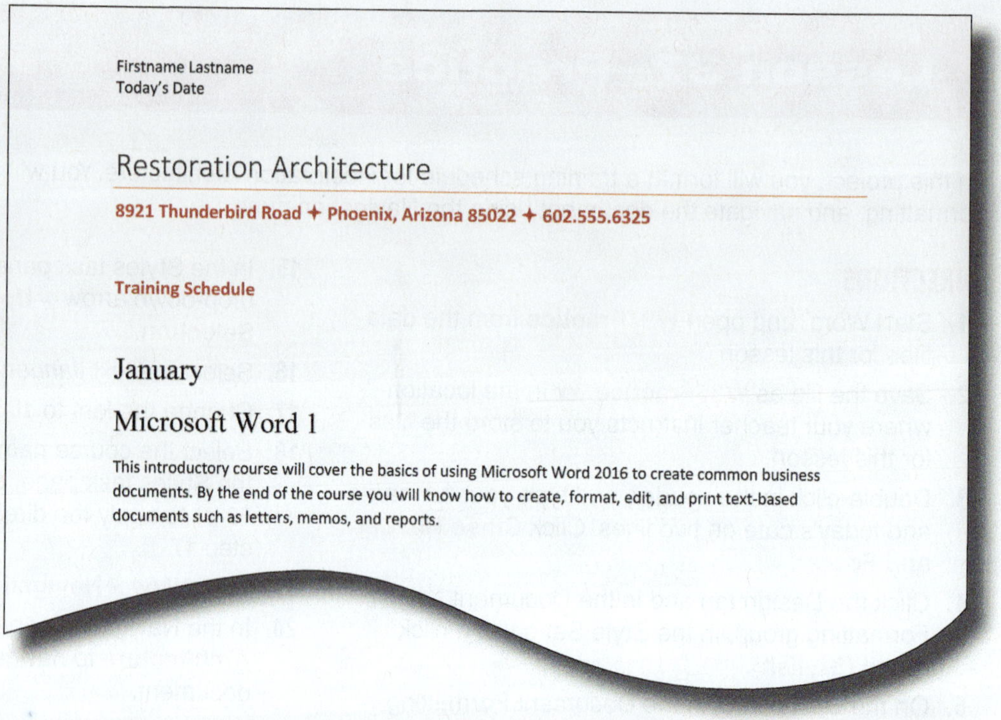
Firstname Lastname
Today's Date

Restoration Architecture

8921 Thunderbird Road ✦ Phoenix, Arizona 85022 ✦ 602.555.6325

Training Schedule

January

Microsoft Word 1

This introductory course will cover the basics of using Microsoft Word 2016 to create common business documents. By the end of the course you will know how to create, format, edit, and print text-based documents such as letters, memos, and reports.

Lesson 37—Apply

Restoration Architecture has contracted with a training company to provide computer training for employees. You have been asked to prepare a document listing the courses that will be available for the first three months of the year. In this project, you will use styles and direct formatting to apply consistent formatting to the document.

DIRECTIONS

1. Start Word, and open **W37Apply** from the data files for this lesson.
2. Save the file as **W37Apply_xx** in the location where your teacher instructs you to store the files for this lesson.
3. Double-click in the header, and type your full name and today's date on two lines. Click **Close Header and Footer**.
4. Change the default style set to **Minimalist**.
5. Apply the **Heading 1** style to the company name.
6. Select the text *Training Schedule* and change the formatting to **24 point bold Arial**, centered horizontally.
7. Save the formatting as a new Quick Style named **Subhead1**.
8. Apply the **Subhead1** style to the names of all three months.
9. Modify the **Subhead1** style to be left-aligned with a solid underline.
10. Select the course name *Microsoft Word 1*, change the font size to **14 points**, and center it.
11. Reapply the formatting you applied in step 10 to the names of the other two courses.
12. Format the paragraph describing the Word 1 course in **14 point Arial**, indented **0.5"** from both the left and the right, with **0 pt** of space before and **6 pt** of space after.
13. Create a style named **Course Description** based on the formatting of the course description.
14. Apply the **Course Description** style to the other two course descriptions.
15. Modify the **Course Description** style to change the font size to **12 points**.
16. Check and correct the spelling and grammar in the document, and save the document.

17. **With your teacher's permission**, print the document. It should look similar to Figure 37-2.
18. Delete the **Course Description** style.
19. Point to the **Subhead1** style in the Styles task pane, and click the down arrow. Click **Revert to Subtitle**, and click **Yes** at the prompt to delete the **Subhead1** style.
20. Close the **Styles** task pane.
21. Change the default style set to **Word**.
22. Save and close the document, and exit Word.

Figure 37-2

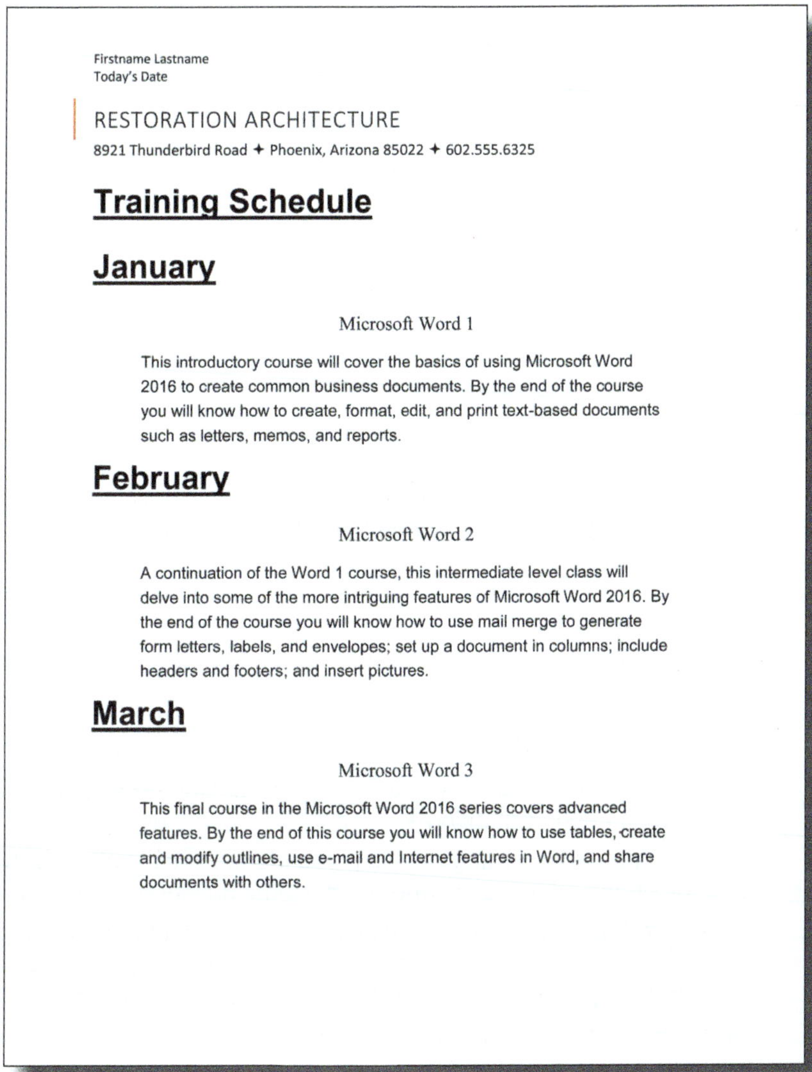

Firstname Lastname
Today's Date

RESTORATION ARCHITECTURE

8921 Thunderbird Road ✦ Phoenix, Arizona 85022 ✦ 602.555.6325

Training Schedule

January

Microsoft Word 1

This introductory course will cover the basics of using Microsoft Word 2016 to create common business documents. By the end of the course you will know how to create, format, edit, and print text-based documents such as letters, memos, and reports.

February

Microsoft Word 2

A continuation of the Word 1 course, this intermediate level class will delve into some of the more intriguing features of Microsoft Word 2016. By the end of the course you will know how to use mail merge to generate form letters, labels, and envelopes; set up a document in columns; include headers and footers; and insert pictures.

March

Microsoft Word 3

This final course in the Microsoft Word 2016 series covers advanced features. By the end of this course you will know how to use tables, create and modify outlines, use e-mail and Internet features in Word, and share documents with others.

Word 2016, Windows 10, Microsoft Corporation

Lesson 38

Managing Style Formatting

➤ What You Will Learn

- Revealing Style Formatting
- Applying Advanced Font and Paragraph Attributes
- Tracking Formatting Inconsistencies
- Managing Style Conflicts
- Copying Styles Using the Organizer
- Attaching a Template to a Document

WORDS TO KNOW

Character style
A collection of formatting settings that can be applied all at once to a single character or multiple characters.

Kerning
The process of adjusting the spacing between characters.

Paragraph style
A collection of formatting settings that can be applied all at once to a single paragraph or multiple paragraphs.

Organizer
A feature in Word that manages styles and macros.

Template
A document that contains formatting, styles, and sample text that you can use to create new documents.

Software Skills Consistent formatting ensures that your documents look professional and are easy to read. Microsoft Word 2016 includes tools, such as the Style Inspector, to help you monitor and track inconsistent formatting. You can use the Style Organizer to copy and manage styles and attach a template to a document.

What You Can Do

Revealing Style Formatting

- Use Word's Style Inspector and Reveal Formatting task panes to display specific information about formatting applied to the current text.
- Revealing style formatting can help you identify inconsistent formatting in order to improve the appearance and professional quality of your documents.
- The Style Inspector task pane displays details about the current paragraph and text level formatting, such as the name of the current **paragraph style** and/or **character style**, as well as any direct formatting that has been manually applied.
- You can move the insertion point with the Style Inspector task pane open in order to reveal formatting for different text.
- In the Reveal Formatting task pane, you can view specific details about font formatting, paragraph formatting, and page setup.
- You can also compare the formatting of two selections to display differences between the two.

Try It! Revealing Style Formatting

1. Start Word, and open **W38TryA** from the data files for this lesson.
2. Save the document as **W38TryA_xx** in the location where your teacher instructs you to store the files for this lesson.
3. Click on the word *Eat* in the heading *Eat Heart Healthy with Sandra!*
4. On the Home tab, click the Styles group dialog box launcher to display the Styles task pane.
5. Click the Style Inspector button to display the Style Inspector task pane, and then close the Styles task pane.

Style Inspector task pane

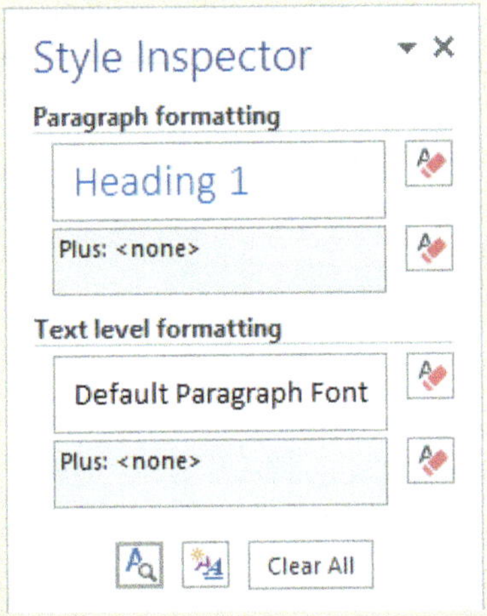

Word 2016, Windows 10, Microsoft Corporation

6. In the Style Inspector task pane, click the Reveal Formatting button to display the Reveal Formatting task pane.
7. In the Reveal Formatting task pane, click to select the Compare to another selection check box.
8. In the document, click on the word *left* in the sentence *Register now so you won't be left out!* The differences between the formatting of the two selections display in the task pane.
9. Close the Reveal Formatting task pane and then close the Style Inspector task pane.
10. Save the **W38TryA_xx** file, and leave it open to use in the next Try It.

Reveal Formatting task pane

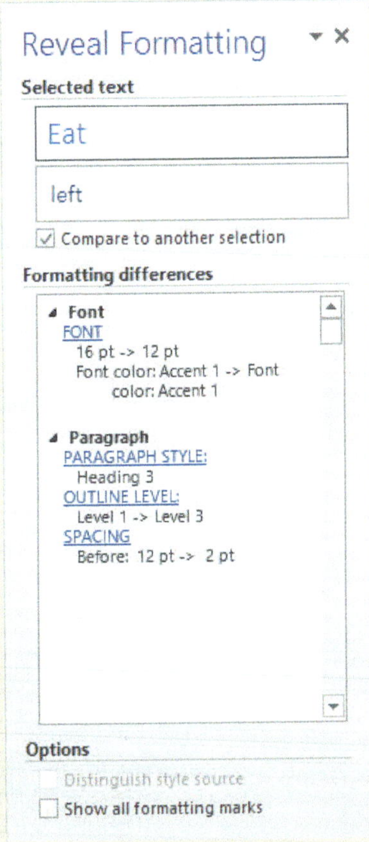

Word 2016, Windows 10, Microsoft Corporation

Applying Advanced Font and Paragraph Attributes

- You can use advanced font and paragraph attributes to enhance the formatting of your document.
- Use the Advanced tab of the Font dialog box to control advanced font attributes.
  - You can set the character spacing to be expanded or condensed to emphasize text.
  - You can set the **kerning** to adjust the spacing between letters.
- You can use advanced paragraph attributes to sort paragraphs, headings, or fields within a document.
- You can use the Set As Default button to change the default font for all new documents to the current settings.

Try It! Applying Advanced Font Attributes

1. In the W38TryA_xx file, select the text *Eat Heart Healthy with Sandra!*.
2. On the Home tab, in the Font group, click the Font dialog box launcher.
3. In the Font dialog box, click the Advanced tab.
4. In the Character Spacing group, next to Spacing, click the drop-down arrow, and select Expanded.
5. In the By box next to Spacing, change the point spacing to 6 pt. Click OK.
6. Select the paragraph heading that begins with *Class size is limited*.
7. On the Home tab, in the Font group, click the Font dialog box launcher.
8. In the Font dialog box, on the Advanced tab, in the Character Spacing group, click the Kerning for fonts check box, and click OK. Notice that the characters are now slightly closer together.
9. Save the changes to W38TryA_xx, and leave it open to use in the next Try It.

Advanced tab of Font dialog box

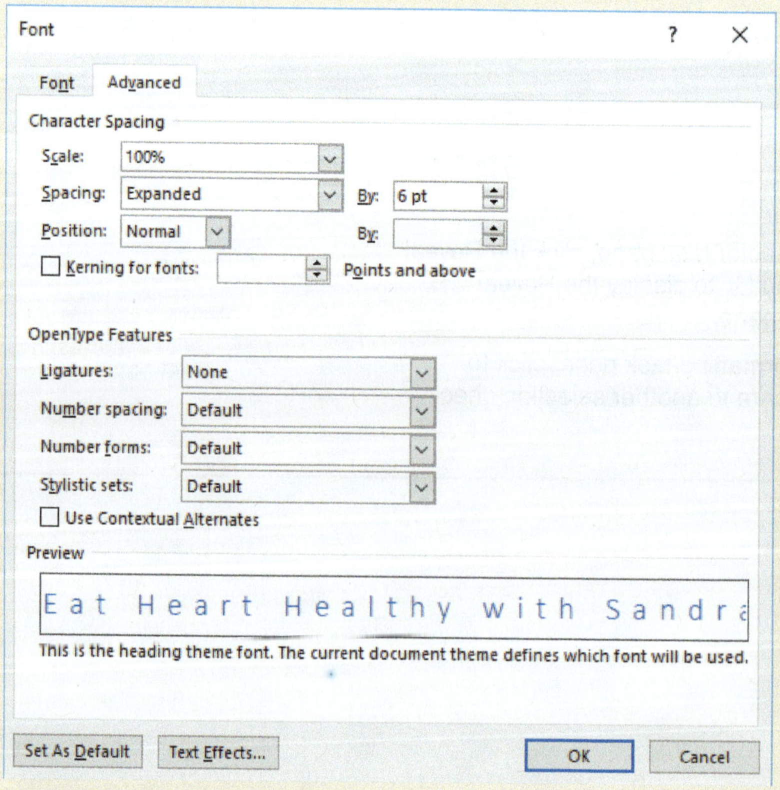

Word 2016, Windows 10, Microsoft Corporation

Try It! Sorting Paragraphs

1. In the **W38TryA_xx** file, select the four bullet points of text.
2. On the Home tab, in the Paragraph group, click Sort.
3. In the Sort Text dialog box, make sure Paragraphs is selected in the Sort by box, Text is selected in the Type box, and the Ascending option button is selected.
4. Click OK.
5. Save the changes to **W38TryA_xx**, and leave it open to use in the next Try It.

Tracking Formatting Inconsistencies

- You can set Word to check formatting while you work in much the same way that it checks spelling and grammar.
  - For example, Word can mark formatting such as a one-point decrease in font size that appears accidental.
- If the instances of similar formatting are not distinct enough, then Word cannot identify an inconsistency.
  - For example, Word will not mark distinct formatting, such as Arial 12 point and Arial 14 point, because the larger font size could be used for a heading.
- If Word identifies a formatting inconsistency, it marks it with a wavy blue underline.
  - For example, if you change the formatting of an item in a bulleted list without changing the formatting of other items in the list, Word identifies the formatting as inconsistent.
- You can ignore the blue lines and keep typing, or you can use a shortcut menu to correct the formatting error.
- The automatic format checker is off by default; you must turn it on to use it. It remains on in all documents until you turn it off.

Try It! Tracking Formatting Inconsistencies

1. In **W38TryA_xx**, click File > Options > Advanced.
2. In the Editing options group, click the Keep track of formatting check box, and click the Mark formatting inconsistencies check box.
3. Click OK.
4. Reposition the insertion point at the end of the document, and press ENTER to start a new line.
5. On the Home tab, click the Bullets button, and type the following list, pressing ENTER to start a new line between each item: **Carbs**, **Sugar**, **Fat**, **Protein**.

   ✓ *If the default bullet list formatting on your system has been modified, lists may display differently from those in the figures.*

6. Select the word *Sugar* and click the Decrease Font Size button. Word applies a blue wavy underline to the word, indicating that the formatting is inconsistent.
7. Right-click the word *Sugar* to display a shortcut menu.
8. On the shortcut menu, click Ignore Once.
9. Click File > Options > Advanced, click to clear the Mark formatting inconsistencies check box, and click to clear the Keep track of formatting check box.
10. Click OK.
11. Save the **W38TryA_xx** file, and leave it open to use in the next Try It.

(continued)

Try It! Tracking Formatting Inconsistencies *(continued)*

Tracking formatting

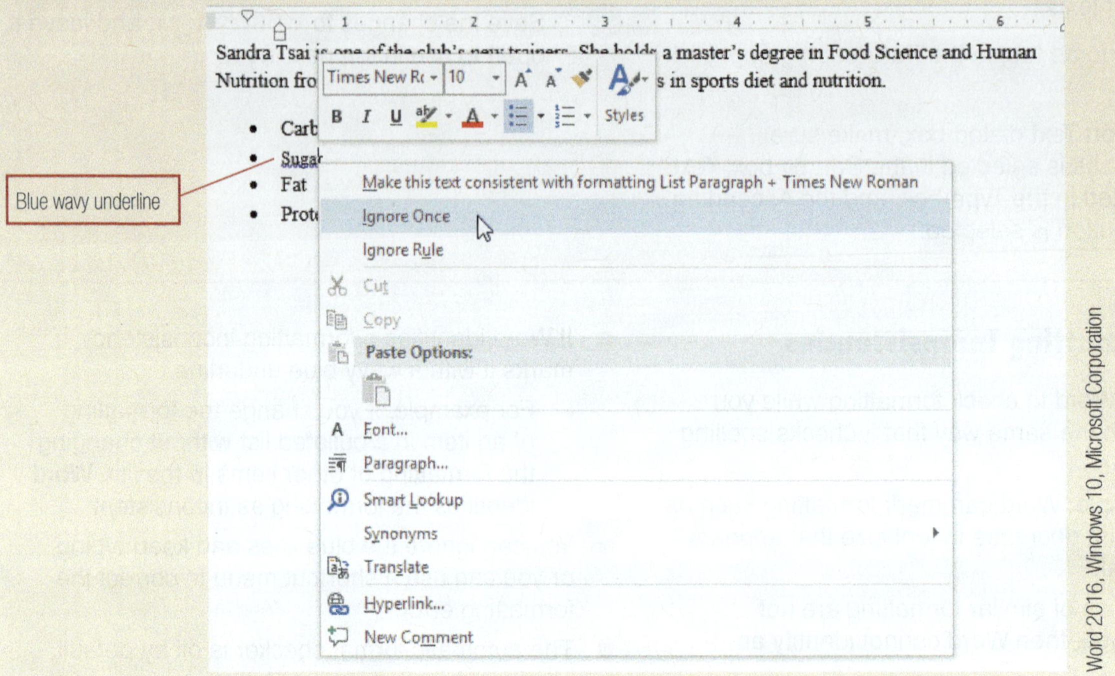

Managing Style Conflicts

- When you copy and paste text between documents, the styles of the pasted text may conflict with the styles in your document.
- You can manage style conflicts after you have pasted your text by selecting a paste option.
  - Use the Keep Text Only paste option to remove styles from the pasted text.
  - Click the Use Destination Styles paste option to apply destination styles to the pasted text.
- You can also use the Styles task pane to manage style conflicts.
  - You can apply the styles in your document to the pasted text.
  - You can delete styles that might have been brought into your document when you pasted text.

Try It! Managing Style Conflicts

1. In the **W38TryA_xx** file, reposition the insertion point at the beginning of the document.
2. On the Home tab, in the Styles group, click the Styles dialog box launcher. The Styles task pane appears.

   ✓ *Drag the Styles task pane to the left for easier viewing.*
3. Browse to the data files for this lesson, open **W38TryB**, and select the two paragraphs of text.
4. On the Home tab, click Copy.
5. In the **W38TryA_xx** file, on the Home tab, click Paste.

(continued)

Try It! Managing Style Conflicts *(continued)*

6. Click the Paste Options icon (Ctrl) > Use Destination Styles. Notice that the second line of text is now formatted as the Heading 3 style in the current document.
7. Select the text *Your health is important!*
8. In the Styles task pane, hover the mouse pointer over the paragraph mark to the right of the Centered Heading style.
9. Click the down arrow > Delete Centered Heading.
10. Click Yes to confirm the deletion.

    ✓ *Notice that the text* Your health is important! *returns to the Normal style.*

11. Close the **W38TryB** file without saving the changes.
12. Save the changes to **W38TryA_xx**, and leave it open to use in the next Try It.

Delete a style from the Styles task pane

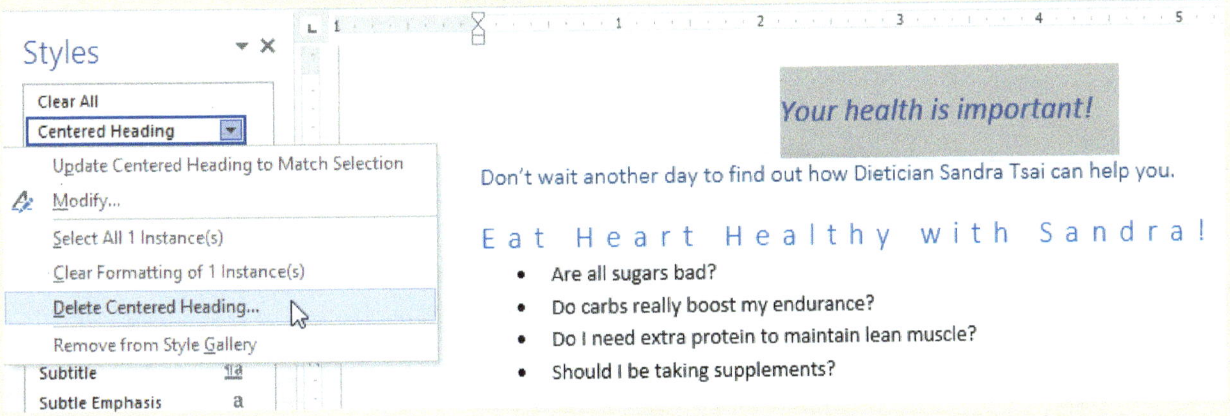

Word 2016, Windows 10, Microsoft Corporation

Copying Styles Using the Organizer

- Copying a style into a document can be easier than creating a new style or reformatting an existing style.
- You can use the **Organizer** to copy, delete, or rename styles in a document or **template**.
- You can also use the Organizer to copy, delete, or rename macros in a document or template.

  ✓ *You learn about using the Organizer with macros in Lesson 65.*

- To access the Organizer, open the Styles task pane, click the Manage Styles button, and click the Import/Export button Import/Export... .
- When you open the Organizer, Word displays the Styles tab by default.
- The Organizer displays the styles in the current document on the left and the styles in the Normal template on the right.
- You can copy styles from one document to another, or from one template to another.
- You can toggle the Close File button to an Open File button to select a different document or template from which to copy styles.

Try It! Copying Styles Using the Organizer

1. In the **W38TryA_xx** file, in the Styles task pane, click the Manage Styles button. The Manage Styles dialog box appears.

   ✓ *If necessary, on the Home tab, in the Styles group, click the Styles dialog box launcher to display the Styles task pane.*

2. In the Manage Styles dialog box, click the Import/Export button Import/Export... . The Organizer dialog box appears.
3. On the In **W38TryA_xx** side, in the Styles available in box, check that the **W38TryA_xx** (Document) is selected.
4. On the In Normal side, click the Close File button Close File . Notice that the button becomes an Open File button.
5. Click the Open File button Open File... . The Open dialog box appears.
6. Click All Word Templates > Word Documents.
7. Browse to the location of the data files for this lesson, click **W38TryB**, and click Open.
8. In the To W38TryB box, click Centered Heading.
9. Click Copy.
10. Click Close Close .
11. Select the text *Your health is important!*, and click the Centered Heading style in the Styles task pane.
12. Save the changes to **W38TryA_xx**, and leave it open to use in the next Try It.

The Organizer dialog box

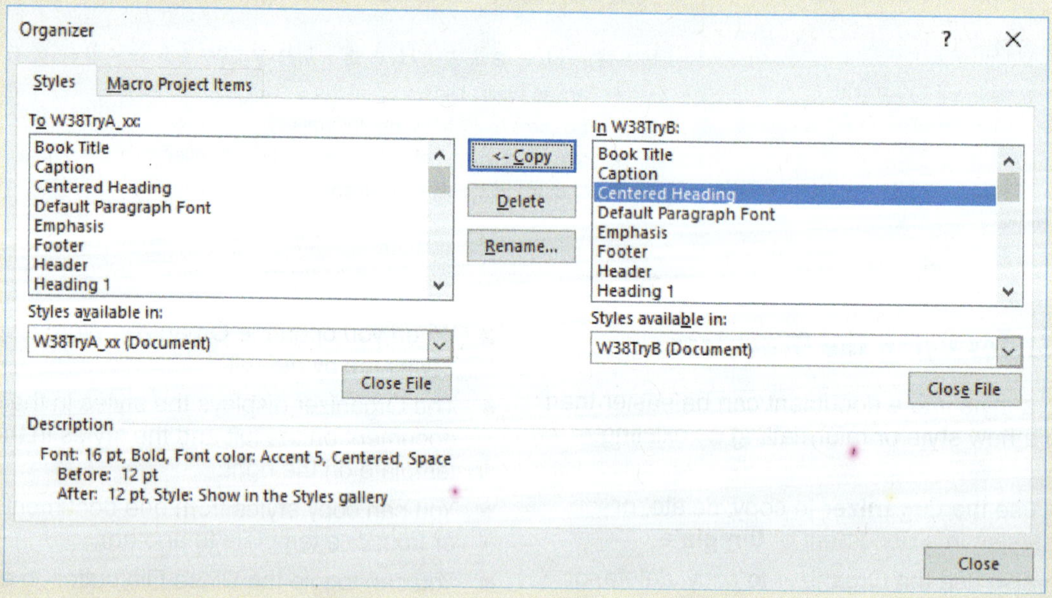

Word 2016, Windows 10, Microsoft Corporation

Attaching a Template to a Document

- You can change the styles and theme of a document by attaching a template.
- The template you attach must be saved in a location to which you can browse.

  ✓ *To attach an online template, you must first save it to your computer.*

- Use the Document Template button on the Developer tab to attach a template.

  ✓ *To view the Developer tab, click File > Options > Customize Ribbon > Developer > OK.*

- You can automatically update the document styles in the Templates and Add-ins dialog box.
- After you have attached a template to your document, you can choose that template's theme to use the template's style set.

Try It! Attaching a Template to a Document

1. In the **W38TryA_xx** file, click File > Options > Customize Ribbon > Developer > OK. The Developer tab appears on the ribbon.
2. Click the Developer tab.
3. In the Templates group, click Document Template. The Templates and Add-ins dialog box appears.
4. Click Attach. The Attach Template dialog box appears.
5. Browse to the data files for this lesson, click **W38TryC**, and click Open.
6. Click to select the Automatically update document styles check box.
7. Click OK.
8. Click Design > Themes > Ion.
9. Follow the steps in Step 1 to remove the Developer tab from the ribbon.
10. Save and close the file, and exit Word.

The Templates and Add-ins dialog box

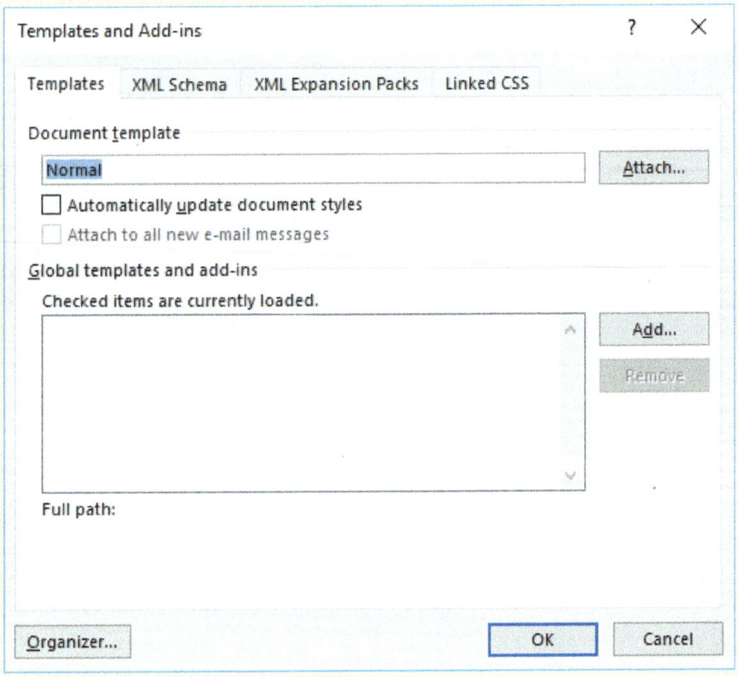

Lesson 38—Practice

You are preparing a document for the Liberty Blooms flower shop that lists programs and events the shop is sponsoring in the coming months. However, the document does not appear to be formatted consistently. In this project, you will turn on the check formatting and mark formatting features, and you will reveal style formatting in order to identify and correct formatting inconsistencies.

DIRECTIONS

1. Start Word, click **Blank document**, and save the document as **W38Practice_xx** in the location where your teacher instructs you to store the files for this lesson.
2. Double-click in the header, and type your full name and today's date on two lines. Click **Close Header and Footer**.
3. Apply the **Ion** theme and the **Shaded** style set.
4. Click **File** > **Options** > **Advanced**.
5. In the Word Options dialog box, click to select the **Keep track of formatting** check box, and click to select the **Mark formatting inconsistencies** check box.
6. Click **OK**.
7. On the first line of the document, type **Liberty Blooms**, and format it using the **Heading 1** style.
8. Press ENTER, type **Upcoming Programs**, and format it using the **Heading 2** style.
9. Press ENTER, click the **Bullets** button to apply bullet list formatting, and type the following list, pressing ENTER between each item to start a new line:

   Flower Arranging

   All about Herbs

   Water Gardens

   Edible Plants

   Roses
10. Select the second item in the list and increase the font size to **14 points**. (Word should mark the item as inconsistently formatted.)
11. Click the **Styles** group dialog box launcher.
12. In the Styles task pane, click the **Style Inspector** button.
13. Close the Styles task pane.
14. Click the company name to display its formatting in the Style Inspector task pane.
15. In the Style Inspector task pane, click the **Reveal Formatting** button.
16. Click the text **Arranging** in the first item in the bullet list.
17. In the Reveal Formatting task pane, click to select the **Compare to another selection** check box.
18. In the document, click the text **Herbs** in the second item in the bullet list. Note the formatting difference.
19. Select the second item in the bulleted list and change the font size to **10 points**.
20. Close the **Reveal Formatting** task pane, and close the **Style Inspector**.
21. Check and correct the spelling and grammar in the document, and save the document.
22. **With your teacher's permission**, print the document. It should look similar to Figure 38-1 on the next page.
23. Click **File** > **Options** > **Advanced**, click to clear the **Mark formatting inconsistencies**, and click to clear the **Keep track of formatting** check box.
24. Click **OK**.
25. Save and close the document, and exit Word.

Figure 38-1

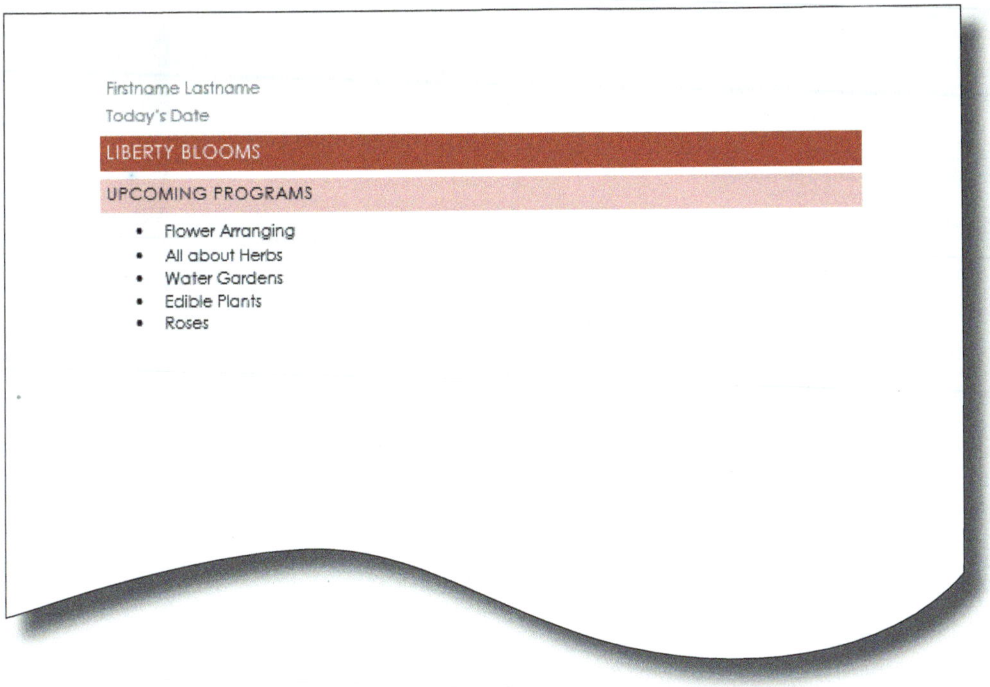

Firstname Lastname

Today's Date

LIBERTY BLOOMS

UPCOMING PROGRAMS

- Flower Arranging
- All about Herbs
- Water Gardens
- Edible Plants
- Roses

Word 2016, Windows 10, Microsoft Corporation

Lesson 38—Apply

You are working with a document for the upcoming programs that Liberty Blooms flower shop is sponsoring this year. However, you have been told that the company's template has changed and now you need to apply the new company template to the document. In this project, you will attach the new template to the document.

DIRECTIONS

1. Start Word, and open **W38Apply** from the data files for this lesson.
2. Save the file as **W38Apply_xx** in the location where your teacher instructs you to store the files for this lesson.
3. Double-click in the header, and type your full name and today's date on two lines. Click **Close Header and Footer**.
4. Click the **Developer** tab.

   ✓ *If necessary, activate the Developer tab by clicking File > Options > Customize Ribbon > Developer > OK.*

5. Click **Document Template** > **Attach**.
6. Browse to the data files for this lesson, and attach the **Liberty Blooms Template**.
7. Click **File** > **Options** > **Customize Ribbon** > **Developer** > **OK**. This will deactivate the Developer tab.
8. Check and correct the spelling and grammar in the document, and save the document.
9. **With your teacher's permission**, print the document. It should look similar to Figure 38-2 on the next page.
10. Save and close the document, and exit Word.

Figure 38-2

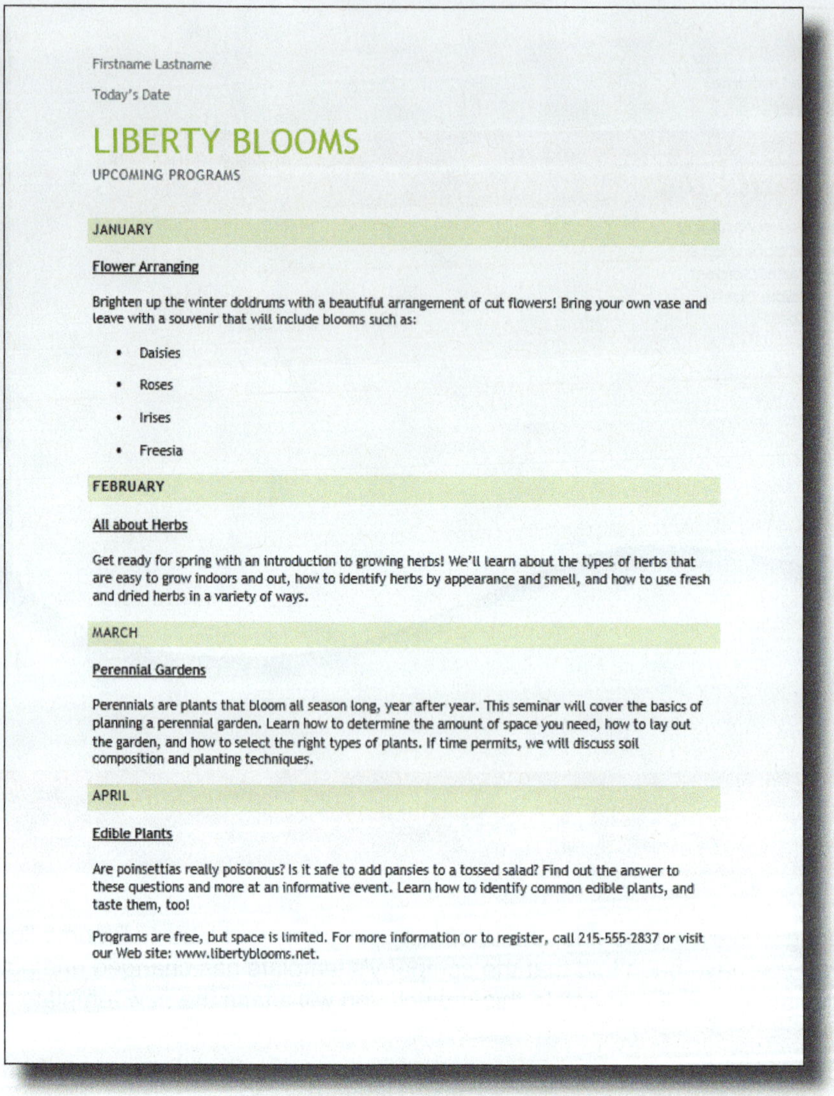

Firstname Lastname

Today's Date

LIBERTY BLOOMS

UPCOMING PROGRAMS

JANUARY

Flower Arranging

Brighten up the winter doldrums with a beautiful arrangement of cut flowers! Bring your own vase and leave with a souvenir that will include blooms such as:

- Daisies
- Roses
- Irises
- Freesia

FEBRUARY

All about Herbs

Get ready for spring with an introduction to growing herbs! We'll learn about the types of herbs that are easy to grow indoors and out, how to identify herbs by appearance and smell, and how to use fresh and dried herbs in a variety of ways.

MARCH

Perennial Gardens

Perennials are plants that bloom all season long, year after year. This seminar will cover the basics of planning a perennial garden. Learn how to determine the amount of space you need, how to lay out the garden, and how to select the right types of plants. If time permits, we will discuss soil composition and planting techniques.

APRIL

Edible Plants

Are poinsettias really poisonous? Is it safe to add pansies to a tossed salad? Find out the answer to these questions and more at an informative event. Learn how to identify common edible plants, and taste them, too!

Programs are free, but space is limited. For more information or to register, call 215-555-2837 or visit our Web site: www.libertyblooms.net.

Lesson 39

Working with Multilevel Lists

➤ What You Will Learn

Formatting a Multilevel List
Customizing a Multilevel List
Creating and Deleting a Multilevel List Style

Software Skills Some lists—such as outlines or test questions—require the use of different levels that display different number or bullet formatting. You can easily format multilevel lists using the styles in Word's Multilevel List gallery. If none of the styles in the Multilevel List gallery are what you want, you can define a new multilevel list, or create a new list style.

WORDS TO KNOW

Multilevel list
A list that has a hierarchical structure that indicates the relationship between items in the list.

What You Can Do

Formatting a Multilevel List

- Use Word's **multilevel list** styles to format items into a list that has more than one level.
- Each level in the list has different formatting so you can clearly see the relationship between items.
- To apply multilevel list formatting, select the list style from the gallery of Multilevel List styles, and then type the list.
- Decrease the level of an item by pressing TAB or by clicking the Increase Indent button on the Home tab.
- Increase the level by pressing ENTER twice, by pressing SHIFT + TAB, or by clicking the Decrease Indent button.
- You can change the style of a multilevel list by selecting the list and clicking a different style in the List Library.

Try It! Formatting a Multilevel List

1. Start Word, and save a new blank document as **W39Try_xx** in the location where your teacher instructs you to store the files for this lesson.
2. On the Home tab, in the Paragraph group, click the Multilevel List button.
3. In the List Library, click the middle style in the first row.
4. Type **Microsoft Office 2016** and press ENTER.
5. Press TAB, type **Microsoft Word**, and press ENTER.
6. Click the Increase Indent button, type **Word processing** and press ENTER.
7. Press SHIFT + TAB, type **Microsoft Excel**, and press ENTER.
8. Type **Microsoft PowerPoint** and press ENTER three times to end the list.
9. Select all items in the list, click the Multilevel List button, and click the first style in the second row.
10. Save the changes to **W39Try_xx**, and leave it open to use in the next Try It.

Format a multilevel list

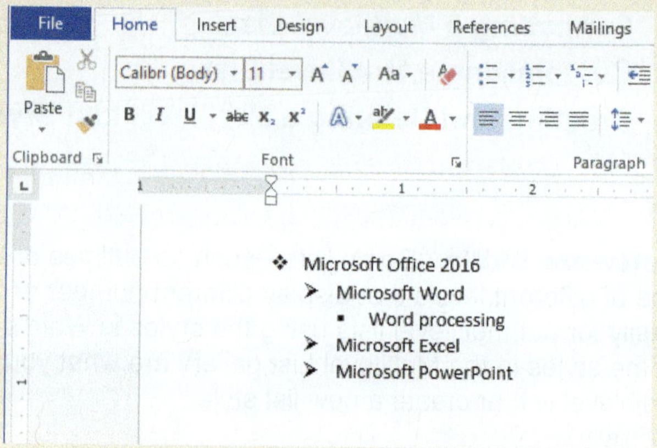

Word 2016, Windows 10, Microsoft Corporation

Customizing a Multilevel List

- You can customize a multilevel list to meet your own needs. For example, you might want to combine bullets and numbers in the same list.
- When you define a customized multilevel list, Word adds it to the Multilevel List gallery under Lists in Current Documents; the list formatting is only available when the document in which you created it is open.
- Keep in mind that a multilevel list style includes formatting for all levels in the list. You do not have to create a style for each individual level.
- You can sort a multilevel list by selecting the items beneath the level 1 list style.
  - For example, if you have a multilevel list with three level 1 list styles, select the items beneath the first level 1 list style, and sort these items.
  - Then select the items beneath the second level 1 list style and sort.
  - Repeat the above steps to sort the items in the rest of the level 1 lists.

Try It! Customizing a Multilevel List

1. In the **W39Try_xx** file, select all items in the multilevel list.
2. In the Paragraph group, click the Multilevel List button, and click Define New Multilevel List to open the Define new Multilevel list dialog box. Level 1 is selected by default.
3. Click the Number style for this level drop-down arrow, scroll to the top of the list, and click 1, 2, 3,.... This sets the number style for level 1.
4. Click in the Enter formatting for number box, position the insertion point to the right of the number, and type a period.

(continued)

Try It! Customizing a Multilevel List *(continued)*

5. In the Click level to modify list, click 2.
6. Click the Number style for this level drop-down arrow, scroll down, and click the first basic round, black bullet.
7. In the Click level to modify list, click 3.
8. Click the Number style for this level drop-down arrow, scroll up, and click a, b, c.
9. Click in the Enter formatting for number box, position the insertion point to the right of the number, and type a close parenthesis—**)**.

   ✓ *You can repeat these steps to customize additional levels.*

10. Click OK. Word applies the list style and adds the new style to the Multilevel List gallery.
11. Save the changes to **W39Try_xx**, and leave it open to use in the next Try It.

Define new Multilevel list dialog box

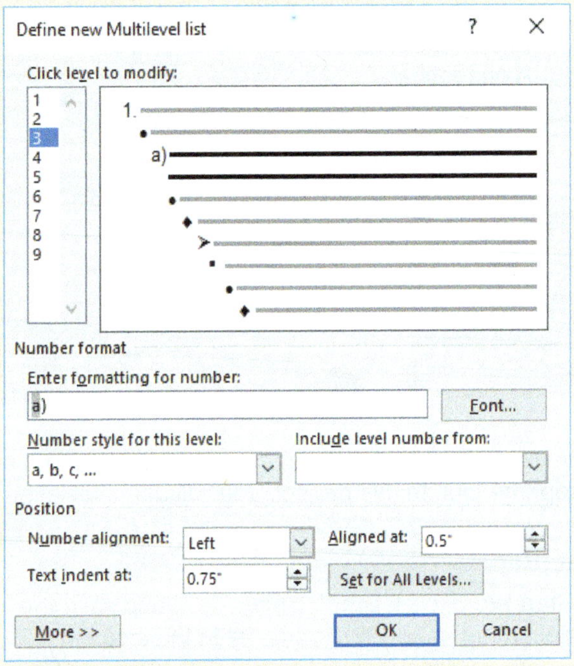

Word 2016, Windows 10, Microsoft Corporation

Creating and Deleting a Multilevel List Style

- Use the Define New List Style command to create a multilevel list style that you can use in the current document only, or make available in any document.
- When you make a new list style available in any document, Word adds it to the Multilevel List gallery under List Styles.
- The easiest way to create a new multilevel list style is to define a customized list and then use the Define New List Style dialog box to give it a name.
- You can also change formatting options in the Define New List Style dialog box to create a new style.
- Again, keep in mind that formatting for all levels in the list are part of a single style; you do not create a style for each individual level.
- To delete a multilevel list style, use the Manage Styles dialog box.

Try It! Creating and Deleting a Multilevel List Style

1. In the **W39Try_xx** file, select the multilevel list.
2. In the Paragraph group, click the Multilevel List button , and click Define New List Style to open the Define New List Style dialog box.
3. In the Name box, type **Multilevel List 1** to replace the sample name.
4. Click the Font Color drop-down arrow > Red.
5. Click the New documents based on this template option button > OK.

   ✓ *To make the new style available only in the current document, select the Only in this document option button.*

6. On the Home tab, click the Styles group dialog box launcher to open the Styles task pane.

(continued)

Try It! **Creating and Deleting a Multilevel List Style** *(continued)*

7 Click the Manage Styles button to open the Manage Styles dialog box.

8 Click the Sort order drop-down arrow > Alphabetical.

9 Click the New documents based on this template option button.

10 In the Select a style to edit list, scroll down, and click Multilevel List 1.

11 Click Delete, click Yes in the confirmation dialog box, and click OK to close the Manage Styles dialog box.

12 Save and close the file, and exit Word.

Lesson 39—Practice

For Voyager Travel Adventures, you are developing a questionnaire to help potential customers select an appropriate tour. In this project, you will use multilevel list formatting to prepare the questionnaire.

DIRECTIONS

1. Start Word, click **Blank document**, and save the document as **W39Practice_xx** in the location where your teacher instructs you to store the files for this lesson.
2. Double-click in the header, and type your full name and today's date on two lines. Click **Close Header and Footer**.
3. On the first line of the main document, type **Voyager Travel Adventures Questionnaire**, and format it with the **Title** style.
4. Press ENTER and type: **What type of adventure is right for you? How can you decide? At Voyager Travel Adventures, we know that not everyone wants the same travel experience. To help you pick the tour that's right for you, we developed this brief series of questions. Once you complete the form, we'll recommend an adventure we think you'll love.**
5. Press ENTER.
6. On the Home tab, in the Paragraph group, click the **Multilevel List** button, and click the style in the middle of the first row.
7. Type **How do you feel about camping?**, and press ENTER.
8. Press TAB and type **I am comfortable in a camper as long as it has electricity and running water.**
9. Press ENTER and type **I am comfortable in a tent as long as there are restroom facilities nearby.**
10. Press ENTER and type **I love wilderness camping.**
11. Press ENTER and type **I will not camp.**
12. Select all of the items in the multilevel list.
13. In the Paragraph group, click the **Multilevel List** button > **Define New Multilevel List**.
14. Click the **Number style for this level** drop-down arrow, and click **I, II, III,....**
15. Click in the **Enter formatting for number** box, delete the close parenthesis, and type a period.
16. In the Click level to modify list, click **2**.
17. Click the **Number style for this level** drop-down arrow, scroll down if necessary, and click **A, B, C,....**
18. Click **OK**.
19. Check and correct the spelling and grammar in the document, and save the document.
20. **With your teacher's permission,** print the document. It should look similar to Figure 39-1 on the next page.
21. Save and close the document, and exit Word.

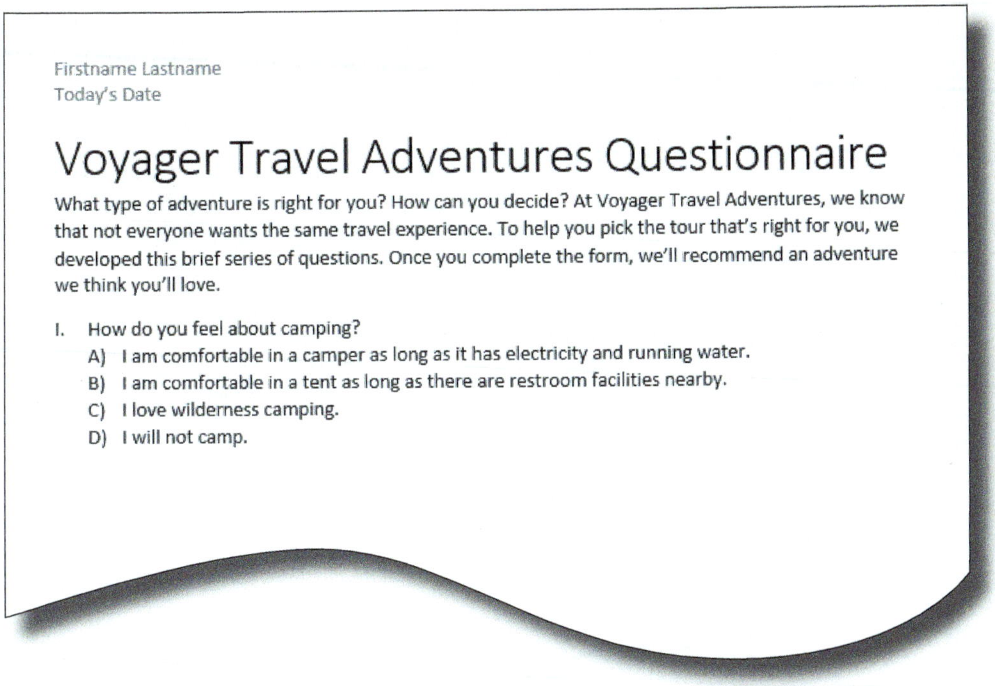
Firstname Lastname
Today's Date

Voyager Travel Adventures Questionnaire

What type of adventure is right for you? How can you decide? At Voyager Travel Adventures, we know that not everyone wants the same travel experience. To help you pick the tour that's right for you, we developed this brief series of questions. Once you complete the form, we'll recommend an adventure we think you'll love.

I. How do you feel about camping?
A) I am comfortable in a camper as long as it has electricity and running water.
B) I am comfortable in a tent as long as there are restroom facilities nearby.
C) I love wilderness camping.
D) I will not camp.

Word 2016, Windows 10, Microsoft Corporation

Figure 39-1

Lesson 39—Apply

You continue to develop the tour questionnaire for Voyager Travel Adventures. You want to add more questions with multilevel list formatting to the questionnaire to make it easy to read. In this project, you will create and modify multilevel list formatting and create a new list style.

DIRECTIONS

1. Start Word, and open **W39Apply** from the data files for this lesson.
2. Save the file as **W39Apply_xx** in the location where your teacher instructs you to store the files for this lesson.
3. Double-click in the header, and type your full name and today's date on two lines. Click **Close Header and Footer**.
4. Select all of the text beginning with *I am comfortable in a tent* and apply the Multilevel List format that uses **1.** for level 1, **1.1.** for level 2, and **1.1.1.** for level 3.
5. Position the insertion point at the beginning of the text *Wild animals are*, and click **Layout** > **Breaks** > **Column** to insert a column break.
6. Adjust the levels in the list as shown in Figure 39-2 on the next page.
7. Modify the current multilevel list formatting for all items in the document so level 1 uses an Arabic (standard) numeral followed by a close parenthesis and level 2 uses uppercase letters followed by a period.
8. Create a new list style named **Form List 1** based on the current formatting. Change the color of level 1 to purple, and the color of level 2 to red. Make the style available in the current document only.
9. Check and correct the spelling and grammar in the document, and save the document.
10. **With your teacher's permission**, print the document. It should look similar to Figure 39-3 on the next page.
11. Save and close the document, and exit Word.

Figure 39-2

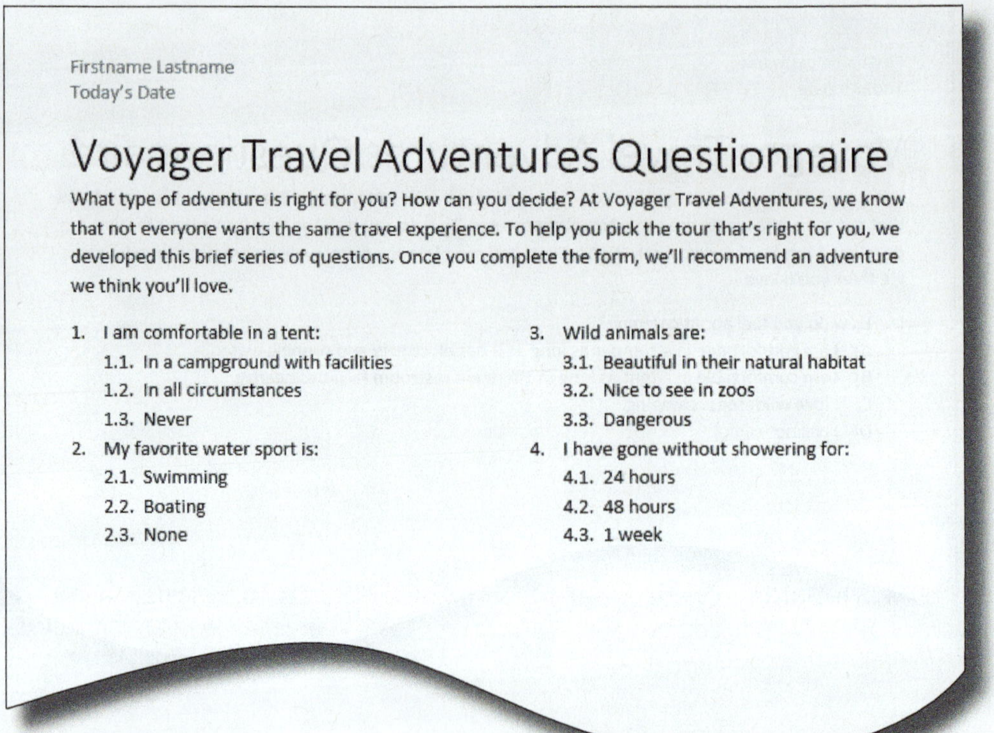
Firstname Lastname
Today's Date

Voyager Travel Adventures Questionnaire

What type of adventure is right for you? How can you decide? At Voyager Travel Adventures, we know that not everyone wants the same travel experience. To help you pick the tour that's right for you, we developed this brief series of questions. Once you complete the form, we'll recommend an adventure we think you'll love.

1. I am comfortable in a tent:
   1.1. In a campground with facilities
   1.2. In all circumstances
   1.3. Never
2. My favorite water sport is:
   2.1. Swimming
   2.2. Boating
   2.3. None
3. Wild animals are:
   3.1. Beautiful in their natural habitat
   3.2. Nice to see in zoos
   3.3. Dangerous
4. I have gone without showering for:
   4.1. 24 hours
   4.2. 48 hours
   4.3. 1 week

Figure 39-3

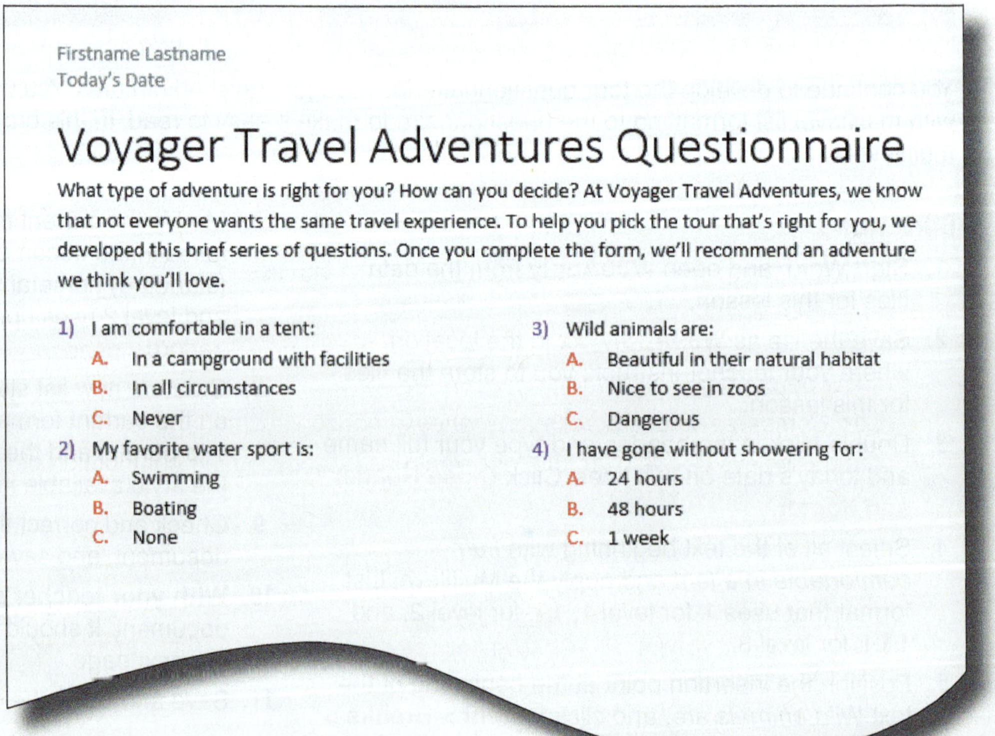
Firstname Lastname
Today's Date

Voyager Travel Adventures Questionnaire

What type of adventure is right for you? How can you decide? At Voyager Travel Adventures, we know that not everyone wants the same travel experience. To help you pick the tour that's right for you, we developed this brief series of questions. Once you complete the form, we'll recommend an adventure we think you'll love.

1) I am comfortable in a tent:
   A. In a campground with facilities
   B. In all circumstances
   C. Never
2) My favorite water sport is:
   A. Swimming
   B. Boating
   C. None
3) Wild animals are:
   A. Beautiful in their natural habitat
   B. Nice to see in zoos
   C. Dangerous
4) I have gone without showering for:
   A. 24 hours
   B. 48 hours
   C. 1 week

Lesson 40

Inserting Charts

➤ What You Will Learn

Inserting a Chart
Modifying a Chart
Formatting a Chart

Software Skills Charts are an effective way to illustrate numeric data and trends. For example, you can use charts to plot sales over time, compare projected income to actual income, or show a breakdown in revenue sources.

What You Can Do

Inserting a Chart

- Word comes with a Chart tool that lets you use Microsoft Excel charting features to embed a **chart object** in a Word document.
- To create a **chart**, use the Chart button in the Illustrations group on the Insert tab of the ribbon.
- You can select a chart type and/or subtype in the Insert Chart dialog box.
- Some common chart types include:
  - Column: Compares values across categories in vertical columns.
  - Line: Displays trends over time or categories.
  - Pie: Displays the contributions of each value to a total value. Often used to show percentages of a whole.
  - Bar: Compares values across categories in horizontal bars.
  - Area: Displays trends over time or categories by showing the contribution of each value to the whole.
  - XY (Scatter): Compares pairs of values.
- When you insert a chart, Word creates the chart object in the document, and then displays an Excel worksheet with sample data.
- To create your own chart, you replace the sample data by typing the actual **data series** you want to plot. You may have to increase or decrease the chart **data range**, depending on the amount of data you are entering.
- Charts are linked to the data you enter in the Excel worksheet, so when you edit the worksheet, the chart changes too.
- You can also create a chart by copying data from a Word table, an Excel worksheet, or an Access table.

WORDS TO KNOW

Chart
A visual representation of information.

Chart object
A chart embedded in a Word document.

Chart title
The name of the chart.

Data axis
The scale used to measure the data in the chart. The Y axis shows the vertical scale, and the X axis shows the horizontal scale.

Data label
Text that identifies the units plotted on the chart, such as months or dollar values.

Data range
A range of cells in which you may enter data.

Data series
A range of values plotted in a chart.

Legend
The key that identifies what each color or symbol in the chart represents.

Plot area
The area of the chart where the data series are displayed.

Try It! Inserting a Chart

1. Start Word, open **W40Try** from the data files for this lesson, and save it as **W40Try_xx** in the location where your teacher instructs you to store the files for this lesson.
2. Click Insert > Chart.
3. In the left pane of the Insert Chart dialog box, click Bar.

Insert Chart dialog box

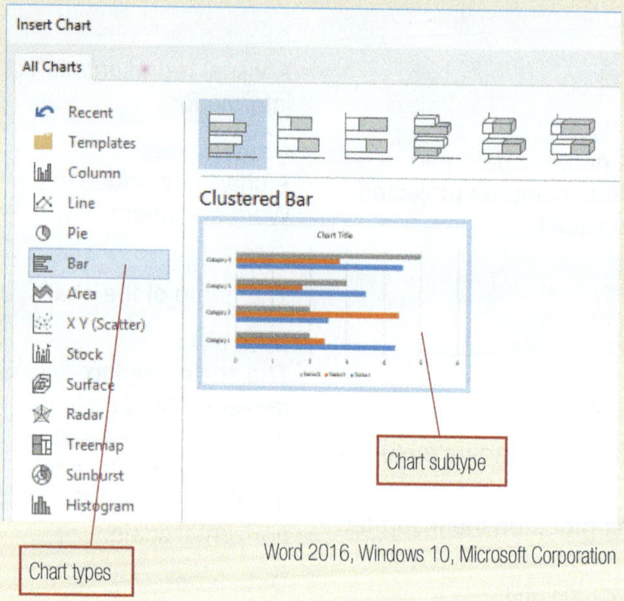

Word 2016, Windows 10, Microsoft Corporation

4. Click OK. Word creates a bar chart in the document using sample data and displays an Excel workbook named Chart in Microsoft Word.
5. Replace the sample data with the following, as shown in the graphic below:

	Northeast	Southeast	Midwest
January	32	19	61
February	43	22	45
March	22	35	22
April	52	45	65

✓ *To enter data in a worksheet, click the cell and type.*

6. Close the Excel program window.
7. In the Word document, select row 2 of the table below the chart, and click Home > Copy.
8. Click the selection frame around the chart object to select the entire chart.
9. Click the Chart Tools Design tab, and in the Data group, click the Edit Data button to display the worksheet again.
10. Drag the lower right corner of the chart data range down one row, so the data range includes A1:D6.
11. Click cell A6 and then press CTRL + V to paste the data.
12. Close the Excel workbook. Save the changes to **W40Try_xx**, and leave it open to use in the next Try It.

Create a chart in Word

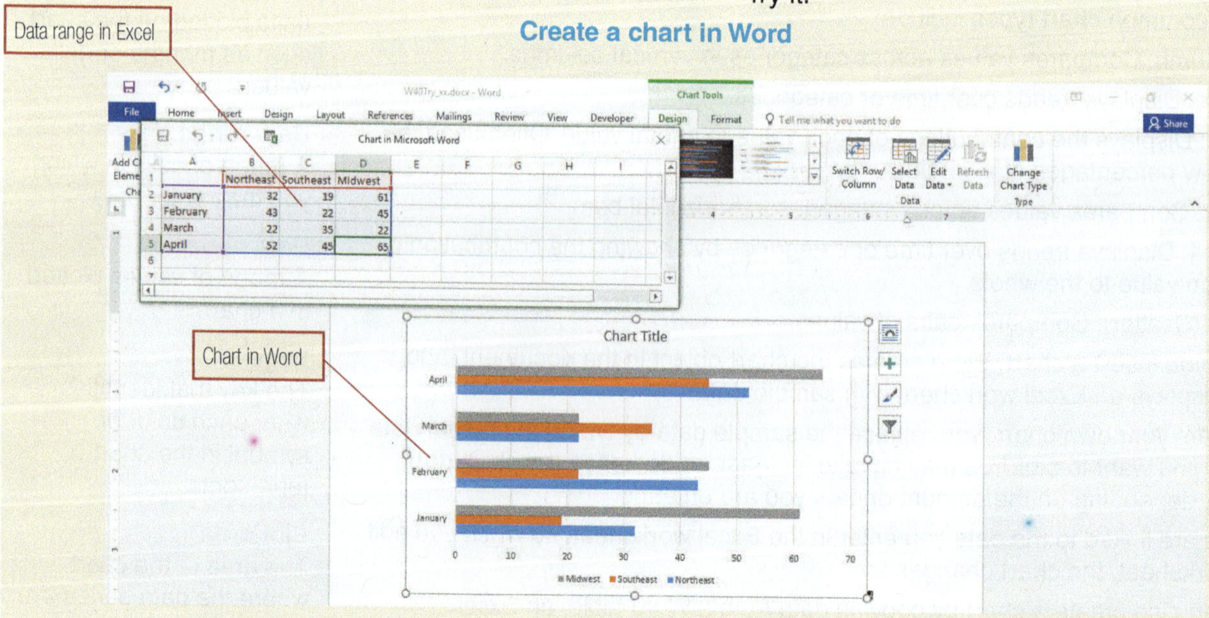

Word 2016, Windows 10, Microsoft Corporation

Modifying a Chart

- You can change the chart type by selecting a different type in the Change Chart Type dialog box.
- The Change Chart Type button, the Chart Styles gallery, and the Quick Layout button are on the Chart Tools Design tab on the ribbon.
- You can apply a chart layout to control the way chart elements such as the **chart title**, **data axis** titles, data axes, **legend**, gridlines, **plot area**, and **data labels** are positioned in the chart.
- You can use the Chart Elements button located to the right of a selected chart to display and position individual chart elements.
- You can use the Add Chart Element button to add chart elements.

Try It! Modifying a Chart

1. In the **W40Try_xx** file, click the selection frame around the chart to select it, if necessary.
2. On the Chart Tools Design tab, click the Change Chart Type button.
3. In the left pane of the Change Chart Type dialog box, click Column.
4. In the right pane of the Change Chart Type dialog box, click 3-D Clustered Column (the fourth option from the left in the first row) > OK.
5. On the Chart Tools Design tab, click Quick Layout > Layout 9.
6. On the chart, click the text *Chart Title* to select the Chart Title element, and replace the sample text by typing **Sales**.
7. Click the text *Axis Title* on the vertical, or Y-axis (left side of the chart), and type **Dollars (in thousands)**.
8. Click the text *Axis Title* on the horizontal, or X-axis (bottom of chart), and type **Month**.
9. Click the selection frame around the chart to select the chart. The chart shortcut buttons appear to the right of the chart.
10. Click the Chart Elements shortcut button, and click the Data Labels check box to select it.
11. Save the changes to **W40Try_xx**, and leave it open to use in the next Try It.

Formatting a Chart

- You can resize, position, and format a chart object the same way you do other graphics objects in a Word document. For example, you can set text wrapping to integrate the chart with the document text, or you can apply an outline or shadow effect to the object.
- You can apply a chart style to format the chart elements with color and effects.
- You can select a style for individual chart elements.
- You can select and format individual chart elements using standard formatting commands, the Chart Elements shortcut button, or the commands in the Format task pane.

✓ *The Format task pane name changes depending on the selected element.*

Try It! Formatting a Chart

1. In the **W40Try_xx** file, click the selection frame around the chart to select it, if necessary.
2. Click the Chart Tools Format tab. In the Current Selection group, click the Chart Elements drop-down arrow, and click Walls.
3. Click Shape Fill [Shape Fill] > Blue, Accent 5, Lighter 60%.
4. On the Chart Tools Format tab, in the Current Selection group, click the Chart Elements drop-down arrow, and click Series "Midwest."
5. Click the Format Selection button to display the Format Data Series task pane.
6. Click Fill & Line, click the Fill arrow, and click Solid fill.
7. Click the Fill Color button, and click Purple. Close the Format Data Series task pane.
8. Click the selection frame around the chart to select it, and on the Chart Tools Format tab, in the Size group, change the value in the Shape Height box to 4".
9. In the Arrange group, click the Position button, and in the With Text Wrapping group, click Position in Bottom Center with Square Text Wrapping (the middle option in the third row).
10. Save and close the document, and exit Word.

Format a chart in Word

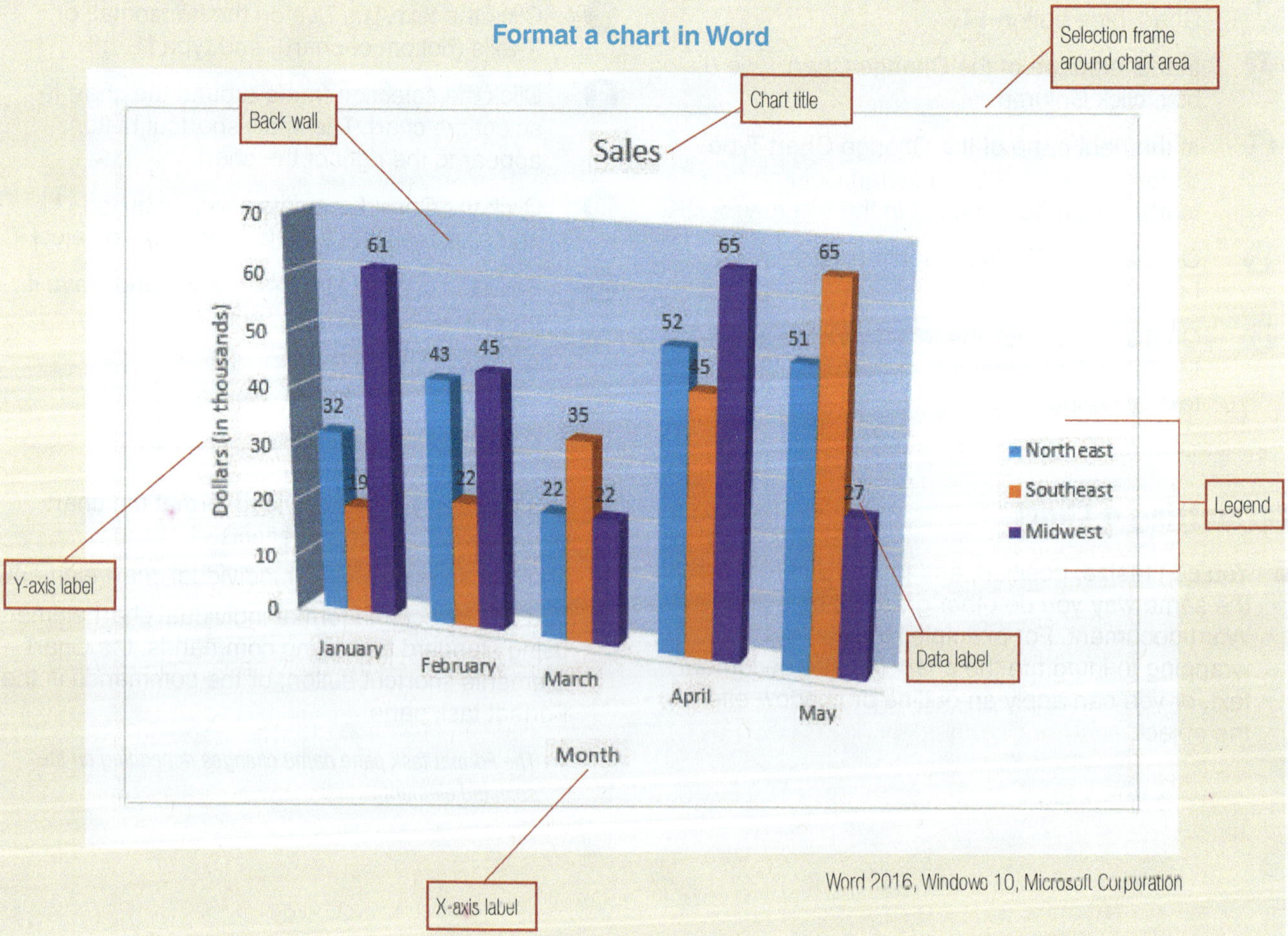

Word 2016, Windows 10, Microsoft Corporation

Lesson 40—Practice

You are investigating the possibility of home delivery service for Fresh Food Fair, a natural food store. In this project you will create a chart to illustrate the results of a customer survey.

DIRECTIONS

1. Start Word, click **Blank document**, and save the document as **W40Practice_xx** in the location where your teacher instructs you to store the files for this lesson.
2. Double-click in the header, and type your full name and today's date on two lines. Click **Close Header and Footer**.
3. Position the insertion point on the first line of the document.
4. Click **Insert** > **Chart** .
5. Verify that the selected chart type is **Column** and the subtype is **Clustered Column**, and click **OK**.
6. Replace the sample data in the worksheet with the following survey results:

	Responses
No	10
Maybe	38
Yes	49
Don't Know	3

7. Select columns C and D headers, right-click, and click **Delete**.
8. Resize the data range to include only the cells that contain data (A1:B5), if necessary.
9. Close the Excel window.
10. Click **Chart Tools Design** > **Change Chart Type** > **Pie** > **3-D Pie** subtype > **OK**.
11. Double-click the chart title text **Responses** and change the font size to **12 points**.
12. With the chart title still selected, type **Likely to Purchase Home Delivery**.
13. Click the selection frame around the chart to select it > **Chart Elements** > **Legend** to hide the chart legend.
14. In the Chart Elements shortcut menu, hover the mouse pointer over **Data Labels**, click the arrow, and click **Outside End** to display the data labels outside the chart.
15. Click **Chart Tools Format** > **Chart Elements** drop-down arrow and click **Series "Responses" Data Labels**.
16. Click **Format Selection** to display the Format Data Labels task pane.
17. Click to select the **Category Name** and **Percentage** check boxes, and, if necessary, click to clear the **Series Name** and **Value** check boxes. Close the **Format Data Labels** task pane.
18. Click **Chart Tools Design** > **Edit Data** to display the worksheet. Click cell **B3**, and type **30**. Click cell **B4**, type **57**, and click ENTER .
19. Close the Excel window.
20. Click the selection frame around the chart to select it, click **Chart Tools Format**, change the value in the **Shape Height** box to **2.5"** and the value in the **Shape Width** box to **4"**.
21. Check and correct the spelling and grammar in the document, and save the document.
22. **With your teacher's permission**, print the document. It should look similar to Figure 40-1 on the next page.
23. Save and close the document, and exit Word.

Figure 40-1

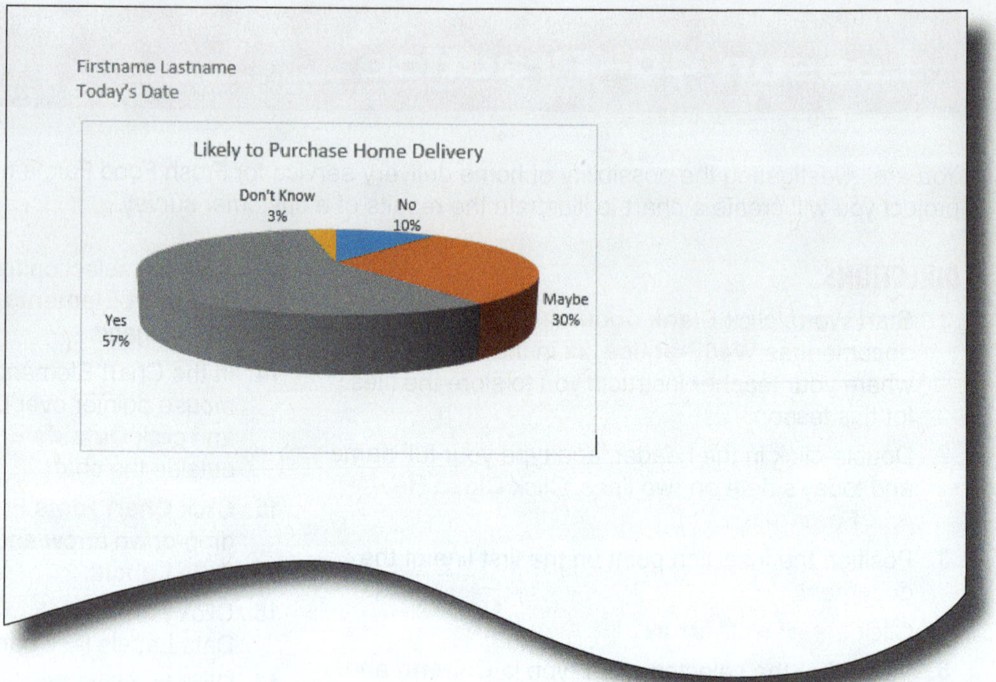

Word 2016, Windows 10, Microsoft Corporation

Lesson 40—Apply

You are continuing to investigate the possibility of home delivery service for Fresh Food Fair. In this project, you will create charts illustrating the results of two customer surveys and include them in a memo to the company owner.

DIRECTIONS

1. Start Word, and open **W40ApplyA** from the data files for this lesson.
2. Save the file as **W40ApplyA_xx** in the location where your teacher instructs you to store the files for this lesson.
3. Replace the sample text *Student's Name* with your own name and *Today's Date* with today's date.
4. Position the insertion point on the last line of the document.
5. Insert a **Clustered Column** chart.
6. Start Excel and open the workbook file **W40ApplyB** from the data files for this lesson.
7. Copy the data in cells **A4:E8** to the Clipboard, and exit Excel without saving any changes.

   ✓ *To copy the data, click cell A4, press and hold Shift, click cell E8, and click Copy.*

8. Click cell **A1** in the Chart in the Microsoft Word worksheet, and paste the data from the Clipboard.

   ✓ *To paste the data, press and hold Ctrl, and press V.*

9. Close the Excel window.
10. Resize the chart to **2.5"** high by **4"** wide.
11. Apply **Chart Layout 3**.
12. Change the chart title to **Product Preferences by Area**.
13. Apply **Chart Style 8** to the clustered column chart.
14. Apply **Chart Style 7** to the pie chart.
15. Change the font size of the chart titles of both charts to **12 points**.
16. Reposition the chart title of the pie chart higher in the chart area.

    ✓ *Click the chart title to select it, press and hold the mouse pointer, and drag the chart title up slightly.*

17. Change the Chart Area color of both charts to a **solid fill Blue, Accent 5, Darker 50%**.
18. Check and correct the spelling and grammar in the document, and save the document.
19. **With your teacher's permission**, print the document. It should look similar to Figure 40-2.
20. Save and close the document, and exit Word.

Figure 40-2

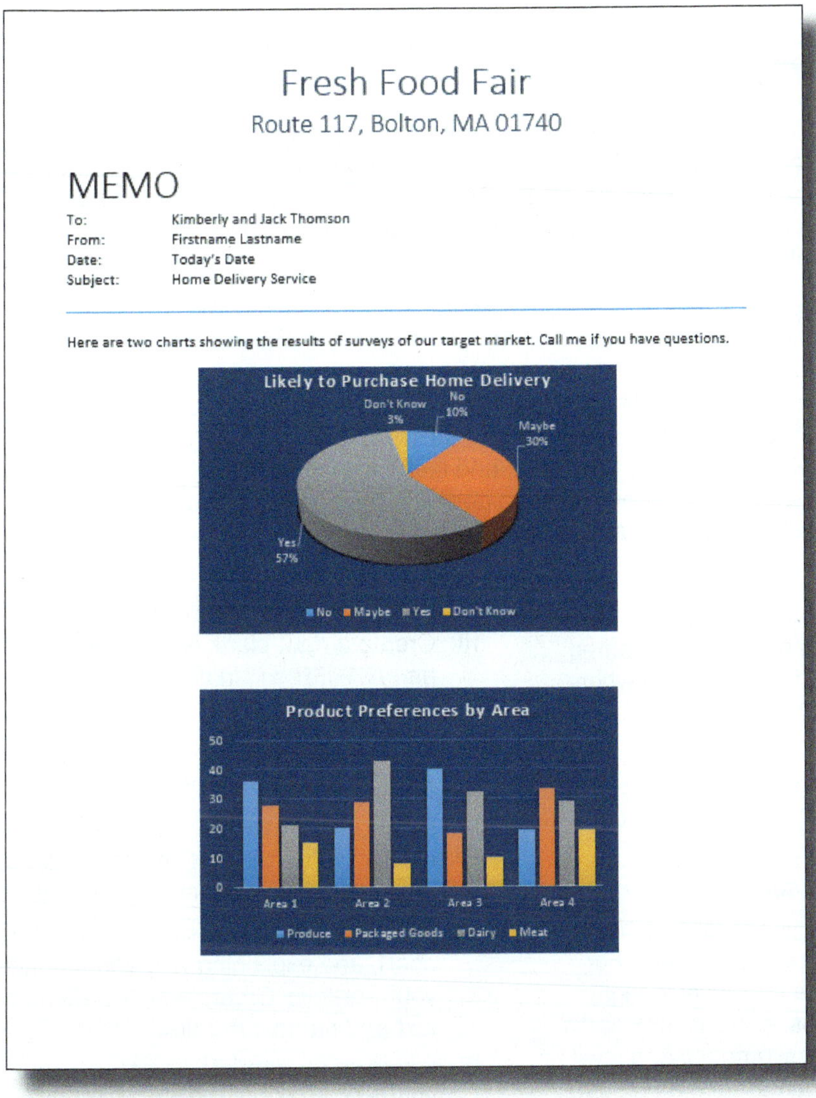

End-of-Chapter Activities

➤ Word Chapter 5—Critical Thinking

Employment Portfolio

Use the skills you have learned in this chapter to set up an employment portfolio. You can create a digital portfolio by creating a folder on a removable storage device, and you can use a manila or an accordion folder to store printed copies of documents. In this project, set up the folder and create a multilevel list describing the contents of your portfolio.

It is not necessary to have all of the documents now; you can use the multilevel list as a guide for items you plan to include. Create at least one document that uses a chart to illustrate information you think a potential employer might find useful. For example, you might chart improvement in your grades over time, or your performance in athletics. You might also include an abstract detailing your accomplishments, samples of your work, and teacher evaluations. You may also copy or move existing documents into the portfolio, such as a resume, sample cover letters, or a list of recommendations.

DIRECTIONS

1. Use File Explorer to create a new folder named **WChapter5_portfolio_xx** in the location where your teacher instructs you to store the files for this chapter.
2. Start Word, click **Blank document**, and save the document as **WCT05A_xx** in the folder you created in step 1.
3. Apply a theme and a style set.
4. Set up an outline-style multilevel list that includes the items you plan to store in the portfolio. For example, level 1 might be a title, level 2 might be main categories of items, such as job search materials or academic achievements, and level 3 might be specific documents, such as resume, references, or school transcripts.
5. Choose one of the built-in multilevel list styles, or define your own for use in this document only. Use direct formatting to indicate documents you have already created and added to the portfolio compared to documents you plan to create in the future.
6. Insert a cover page for the outline, and include a title, your name, and the date.
7. Check and correct the spelling and grammar in the document, and save the document.
8. **With your teacher's permission**, print the document, and put the printed document in your portfolio.
9. Save and close the document.
10. Create a new, blank document in Word and save it as **WCT05B_xx**, in the folder you created in step 1.
11. Type your name and the date in the document header.
12. Apply a theme and a style set.
13. Decide what information you want to chart, and type a title on the first line of the document. Create a new style for the title and name it **Portfolio Title**.
14. Type a paragraph describing the information in the chart, and explaining why you are including it in your portfolio. Create a new style for the paragraph text and name it **Portfolio Text**.
15. Insert an appropriate chart type and enter the information. Modify and format the chart to make it easy to read and visually appealing.
16. Check and correct the spelling and grammar in the document, and save the document.
17. When you are satisfied with the document, ask a classmate to review it and make comments or suggestions that will help you improve it.
18. Make changes and corrections, as necessary.
19. **With your teacher's permission**, print the document, and put the printed document in your portfolio.
20. Save and close the document, and exit Word.

➤ Word Chapter 5—Portfolio Builder

Expansion Proposal

In response to a customer survey, Liberty Blooms flower shop has asked you to draft a proposal for expanding the business. In this project, you will create an outline for the proposal, which you will format as a multilevel list. You will insert text from an existing file, create a style, and include a chart illustrating the results of the survey and a cover page. If time allows, compile your portfolio information into a presentation and present it to all interested stakeholders.

DIRECTIONS

1. Start Word, click **Blank document**, and save the document as **WPB05A_xx** in the location where your teacher instructs you to store the files.
2. Apply the **Organic** theme and the **Basic (Elegant)** style set.
3. Type your name and the date in the document header.
4. Set Word to track formatting inconsistencies.
5. Define a new multilevel list using the following formatting for each level:
   - Level 1 None (with no punctuation)
   - Level 2 Uppercase letters followed by a period
   - Level 3 Arabic numbers followed by a period
   - Level 4 Lowercase letters followed by a close parenthesis
6. On the first line of the document, press SHIFT + TAB to make the line level 1, type **Liberty Blooms Flower Shop Proposal Outline**, and press ENTER.
7. Press TAB, and type **Introduction**.
8. Press ENTER, and type **Background**.
9. Continue applying indents and typing to create the outline shown in Illustration A on the next page.
10. Select the first line of the text, increase the font size to **18 points**, and apply a solid underline.
11. Create a new Quick Style with the name **Proposal Title**. Set the **Style for following paragraph** to **Normal**.
12. Insert a new page at the end of the document.
13. Type **Customer Survey Results**, and format it with the **Proposal Title** style.
14. Reveal the style formatting, and examine it closely. Note that it includes list formatting.
15. Remove the list formatting, and update the style to match the selection.

    ✓ *Hint: Click Multilevel List, and select None from the List Library.*

16. Close all open task panes.
17. Position the insertion point on the line below the second page heading, and clear all formatting.
18. Insert the text from the **WPB05B** file from the data files for this chapter, and apply the **Normal** style.
19. Apply bold to the text *Most Favorable* and *Least Favorable*.
20. On a line below the inserted paragraph, insert a pie chart using the following data:

	Average Rank
Expand the current store	3.2
Open a new store downtown	9.3
Open a new store at the mall	1.6
Open a new store in the next town	7.8
Don't change a thing	6.6

21. Apply the **Chart Layout 6** and the **Chart Style 3**.
22. Change the chart subtype to **3-D Pie**.
23. Format the Chart Area fill to a solid **Blue-Gray, Accent 3, Lighter 60%**.
24. Edit the Chart Title to **Average Customer Rankings**.
25. Center the chart object on the page horizontally.
26. Set Word to not track formatting.
27. Insert the **Austin** style Cover Page. Replace the content controls as follows:
    - Abstract: **This proposal examines the pros and cons of expanding the Liberty Blooms flower shop business.**
    - Document title: **Liberty Blooms Expansion Proposal**
    - Subtitle: *Today's date*
    - Author: *Your full name*

28. Check and correct the spelling and grammar in the document, and save the document.

29. **With your instructor's permission**, print the document. Page 2 should look similar to Illustration 5A, and page 3 should look similar to Illustration 5B on the next page.

30. Save and close the document, and exit Word.

Illustration 5A

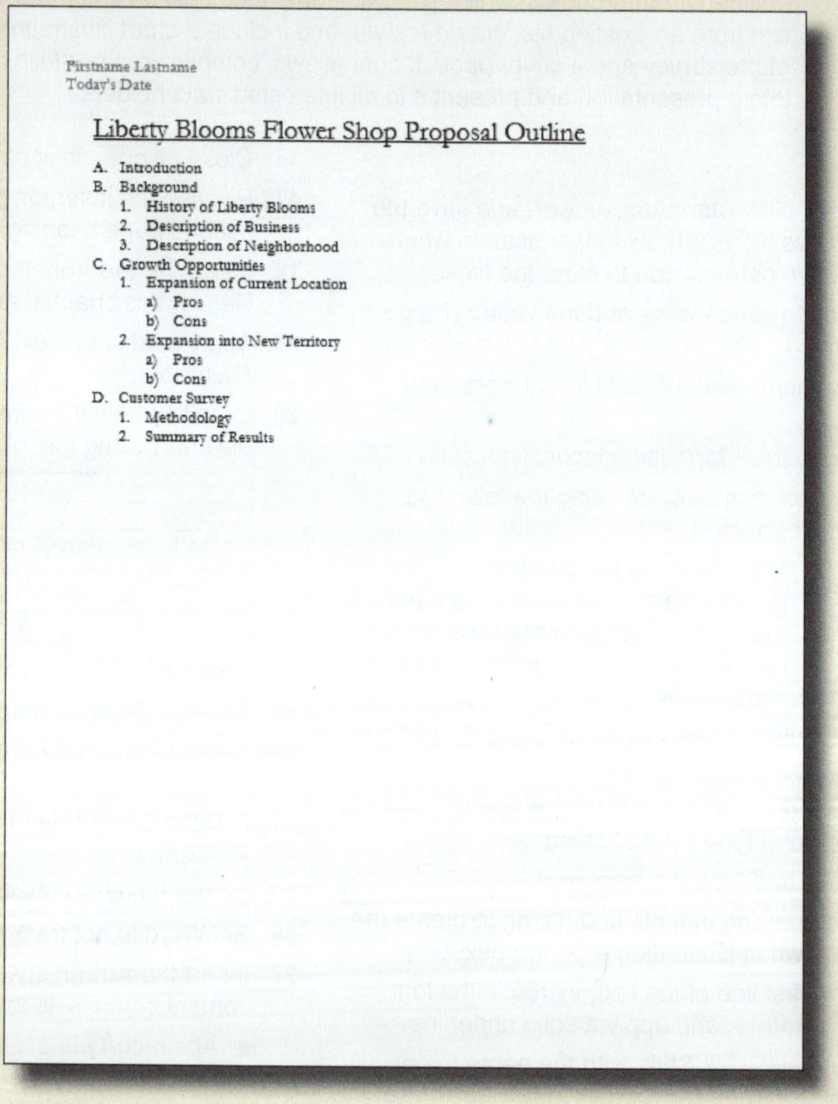

Firstname Lastname
Today's Date

Liberty Blooms Flower Shop Proposal Outline

A. Introduction
B. Background
1. History of Liberty Blooms
2. Description of Business
3. Description of Neighborhood
C. Growth Opportunities
1. Expansion of Current Location
a) Pros
b) Cons
2. Expansion into New Territory
a) Pros
b) Cons
D. Customer Survey
1. Methodology
2. Summary of Results

Word 2016, Windows 10, Microsoft Corporation

Illustration 5B

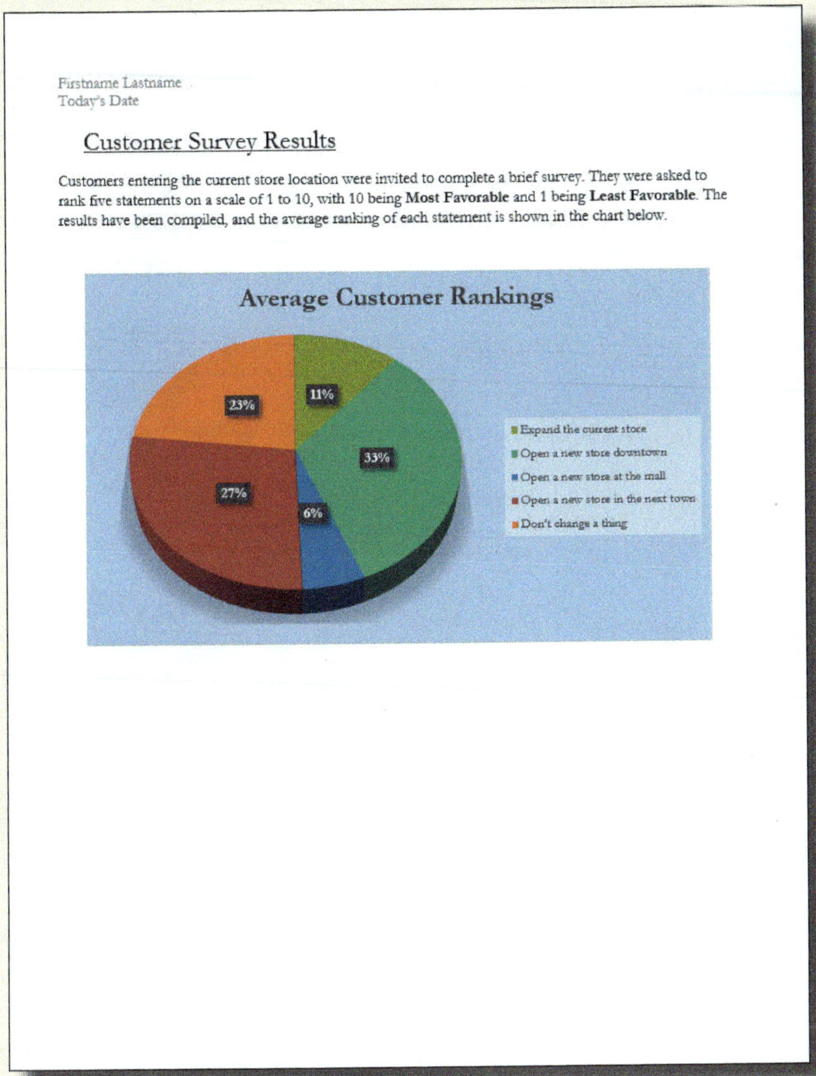

Firstname Lastname
Today's Date

Customer Survey Results

Customers entering the current store location were invited to complete a brief survey. They were asked to rank five statements on a scale of 1 to 10, with 10 being **Most Favorable** and 1 being **Least Favorable**. The results have been compiled, and the average ranking of each statement is shown in the chart below.

Chapter 6

(Courtesy Yuri Arcurs/Shutterstock)

Using Reusable Content and Markup Tools

Lesson 41 Customizing Language and Word Options

- Analyzing Effective Communication
- Translating Text
- Using Accessibility Features
- Customizing the Quick Access Toolbar
- Customizing the Ribbon
- Locating the Default Save Options
- Personalizing Your User Name and Initials
- Adding and Removing Document Metadata
- Customizing the View for Opening E-Mail Attachments

Lesson 42 Using Advanced Find and Replace

- Analyzing Conflict
- Collecting Images and Text from Multiple Documents
- Using the Navigation Task Pane
- Finding and Replacing Formatting
- Using Wildcard Characters in Find and Replace
- Understanding Projects and Project Management

Lesson 43 Using Building Blocks

- Inserting a Built-In Building Block
- Creating a Custom Building Block
- Using the Building Blocks Organizer

Lesson 44 Inserting Fields from Quick Parts

- Inserting a Field from Quick Parts
- Setting Field Display Options
- Analyzing Employment Packages

Lesson 45 Creating Custom Templates, Themes, and Style Sets

- Creating and Saving a Custom Template
- Modifying a Custom Template
- Creating a New Document from a Custom Template
- Deleting a Custom Template
- Creating a Custom Theme
- Applying, Resetting, and Deleting a Theme
- Creating a Style Set
- Applying, Resetting, and Deleting a Style Set
- Demonstrating Professional Standards of Behavior

Lesson 46 Tracking Changes

- Tracking Changes
- Customizing Revision Marks
- Accepting and Rejecting Changes

Lesson 47 Comparing Documents

- Viewing Documents Side by Side
- Managing Document Versions
- Comparing Documents
- Combining Documents

Lesson 48 Restricting Access to Documents

- Setting and Removing Restrictions in a Document
- Changing a Password in a Protected, Encrypted Document
- Using Online Word Processing Technologies

End-of-Chapter Activities

Lesson 41

Customizing Language and Word Options

➤ What You Will Learn

Analyzing Effective Communication
Translating Text
Using Accessibility Features
Customizing the Quick Access Toolbar
Customizing the Ribbon
Locating the Default Save Options
Personalizing Your User Name and Initials
Adding and Removing Document Metadata
Customizing the View for Opening E-Mail Attachments

WORDS TO KNOW

Accessibility
The ability to make documents easier for people with disabilities to use.

Accessibility Checker
A feature in Word that checks for and displays issues in a document that might be challenging for a user with a disability.

Active listening
Paying attention to a message, hearing it, and interpreting it correctly.

Alternative text (alt text)
Text that appears when you move the mouse pointer over a picture or object.

Software Skills Effective communication skills are essential for succeeding in any business or career. Microsoft Word 2016 provides tools to help you get your message across, including the ability to translate text to and from English. Customize Word Options, the ribbon, and the Quick Access Toolbar so you have easy access to the tools and features you use most often.

What You Can Do

Analyzing Effective Communication

- In business, it is important to make sure all **communication** is clear and effective in speeches, e-mails, blogs, and Web posts, as well as more traditional letters, memos, and reports.
- Effective communication is when the receiver interprets the message the way the sender intended.
- Ineffective communication is when the receiver misinterprets the message.
- Talking is usually a very effective form of **verbal communication**. When you write, you lose some of the context, which can make the communication less effective.
- **Nonverbal communication** includes visual messages that the receiver can see, such as a smile. It also includes physical messages, such as a pat on the back, and aural, or sound, messages, such as your tone of voice.

- Nonverbal communication also includes the use of visual aids, such as pictures and charts, which can help clarify your message and put it in context.
- **Active listening** is a sign of respect. It shows you are willing to communicate and that you care about the speaker and the message. When you listen actively, the other person is more likely to listen when you speak, too.
- It is also important that a communicator considers his or her audience and that global content standards are considered so that the material is accessible to the audience.

Translating Text

- You can use Microsoft Word 2016 to **translate** document text between languages.
- Right-click a word and click Translate on the shortcut menu to display the translation in the Research task pane.
- Use the Translate button in the Language group on the Review tab of the ribbon to display all translation commands or to set translation options.
  - Use the Translate Selected Text command to display the translation in the Research task pane. You can select the languages you want to translate from and to.
  - Use the Mini Translator to display a pop-up translation. The Mini Translator also includes buttons for opening the Research task pane, copying the text, playing an audio file of the text in its current language, or displaying help.
  - If you have access to an online translation service, you can select the Translate Document command to transmit the entire document to the service.
- By default, Word uses the online dictionary if there is a connection to the Internet. Otherwise, only the languages for which you have bilingual dictionaries installed will be available for translation.
- Translation options are not the same as Office Language Preferences.
- You can customize the Office Language Preferences on the Language tab of the Word Options dialog box to set the default language of text entry and editing and for displaying Help and ScreenTips.
  - For example, you can set the default language for editing and for displaying Help and ScreenTips.
  - Office Language Preferences affect all Word documents globally, so be sure that you want any customization to apply to all your documents.

Communication
The exchange of information between a sender and a receiver.

Document properties
Details about a document, such as author, subject, and title.

Nonverbal communication
The exchange of information without using spoken words.

Translate
To change text from one language into another.

User name
A name assigned to someone who uses a computer system or program that identifies the user to the system.

Verbal communication
The exchange of information by speaking.

Try It! Translating Text

1. Start Word, and open **W41Try** from the data files for this lesson.
2. Save the file as **W41Try_xx** in the location where your teacher instructs you to store the files for this lesson.
3. Select the sentence **My mother went home.**, right-click, and click Translate to display the Research task pane.

✓ *If the Translate Selected Text dialog box displays, click Yes to proceed.*

4. In the Research task pane, click the To drop-down arrow and click Italian (Italy). The English to Italian translation displays in the Research task pane.
5. Click the Review tab, and in the Language group, click Translate.

(continued)

Try It! Translating Text *(continued)*

6. Click Choose Translation Language to display the Translation Language Options dialog box.

Translation in the Research task pane

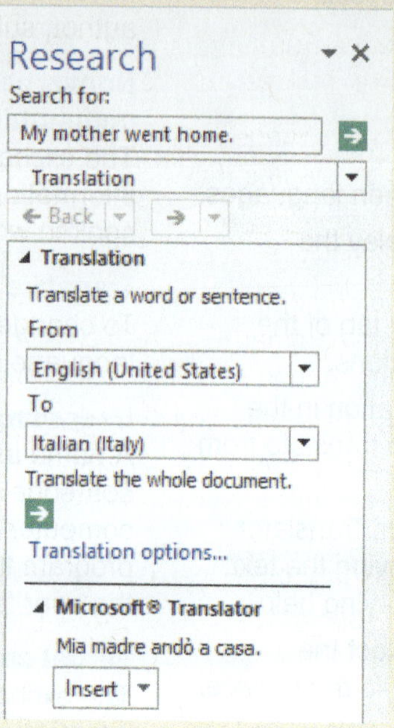

Word 2016, Windows 10, Microsoft Corporation

7. Under Choose Mini Translator language, click the Translate to: drop-down arrow, click French (France), and click OK.

8. On the Review tab, click the Translate button and click Mini Translator. In the Mini Translator dialog box, click Yes to proceed. This toggles the feature on; it remains on until you toggle it off.

9. Click anywhere in the document to deselect the sentence. Rest the mouse pointer on the word *mother*. A dim Mini Translator displays.

10. Move the mouse pointer over the Mini Translator to make it display clearly.

✓ *The options may differ depending on whether you are working from an online or an installed dictionary.*

11. On the Review tab, click Translate > Mini Translator to toggle the feature off.

12. Close the Research task pane.

13. Save the changes to **W41Try_xx**, and leave it open to use in the next Try It.

The Mini Translator

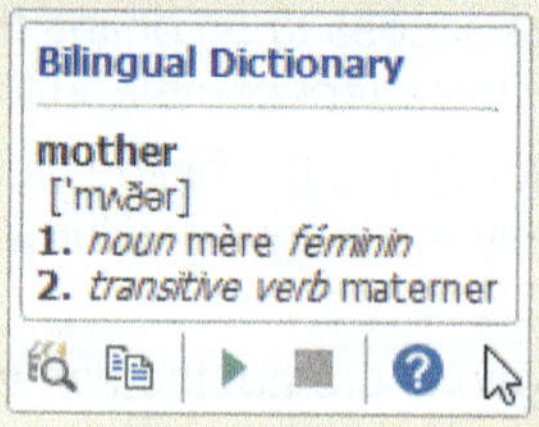

Word 2016, Windows 10, Microsoft Corporation

Using Accessibility Features

- You can use **accessibility** features in Word 2016 to make documents more accessible to users with disabilities.
- **Alternative text**, or **alt text**, is an accessibility feature that helps people who use screen readers to understand the content of a picture in a document.

✓ *Alt text may not work with touch-screen or mobile devices.*

- When making a document accessible, you should include alt text for objects such as pictures, embedded objects, charts, and tables.
- You can add alt text from the Layout & Properties group of the Format Picture task pane.
- When you use a screen reader to view a document, or save it to a file format such as HTML, alt text appears in most browsers when the picture doesn't display.

✓ *You may have to adjust the computer's browser settings to display alt text.*

- Screen readers and other assistive technologies read the tab order of objects from left to right starting at the top of the page and moving down to the bottom of the page.
- You can change the tab order by moving and reordering the text, pictures, and graphics on the page.
- You can use the **Accessibility Checker** to check and correct a document for possible issues that might make it hard for a user with a disability to read and interpret the content.
- You access the Accessibility Checker from the Info tab on the File tab.

Try It! Using Accessibility Features

1. In the W41Try_xx file, click File.
2. On the Info tab, click Check for Issues > Check Accessibility. Note the Missing Alt Text error in the Accessibility Checker task pane.
3. Right-click the picture of the globe, and click Format Picture to display the Format Picture task pane.
4. Click Layout & Properties > Alt Text.
5. In the Title box, type **Globe**.
6. In the Description box, type **A picture of planet earth**. The Accessibility Checker Inspection Results now finds no accessibility issues.
7. Close the Format Picture and Accessibility Checker task panes.
8. Save the changes to W41Try_xx, and leave it open to use in the next Try It.

Customizing the Quick Access Toolbar

- By default, there are three buttons on the Quick Access Toolbar: Save, Undo, and Repeat.

  ✓ *The Repeat button changes to Redo after you use the Undo command.*

- Use the Customize Quick Access Toolbar button to display a menu of common commands to add or remove from the toolbar, or to choose to display the Quick Access Toolbar below the ribbon.
- To add a command to the Quick Access Toolbar, locate the command on the ribbon, right-click it, and select Add to Quick Access Toolbar.
- You can also select any command from a list of all available commands using the Quick Access Toolbar tab in the Word Options dialog box.
- You can rearrange the order of buttons on the Quick Access Toolbar, and you can reset the Quick Access Toolbar to its default configuration.

Try It! Customizing the Quick Access Toolbar

1. In the W41Try_xx document, click the Customize Quick Access Toolbar button to display a menu of common commands.

   ✓ *A check mark indicates the command is already on the Quick Access Toolbar.*

2. Click Quick Print on the menu. The Quick Print button is added to the Quick Access Toolbar.
3. Click Customize Quick Access Toolbar > Show Below the Ribbon.
4. Click Customize Quick Access Toolbar > Show Above the Ribbon.
5. Click Home, right-click the Bold button **B**, and click Add to Quick Access Toolbar.
6. Click Customize Quick Access Toolbar, and click More Commands to display the Quick Access Toolbar tab in the Word Options dialog box.
7. Click the Choose commands from drop-down arrow > File Tab.
8. In the list of commands, click Close File, and click the Add button Add >>.
9. In the list of commands on the Quick Access Toolbar, click Bold, and click the Remove button << Remove.
10. In the list of commands on the Quick Access Toolbar, click Close File, and click Move Up twice.
11. In the list of commands on the Quick Access Toolbar, click the Redo button > Move Down > OK.
12. Click Customize Quick Access Toolbar > More Commands.

(continued)

Try It! Customizing the Quick Access Toolbar *(continued)*

13. Click Reset > Reset only Quick Access Toolbar.
14. Click Yes in the confirmation dialog box > OK.
15. If necessary, click Customize Quick Access Toolbar > Show Above the Ribbon.
16. Save the changes to **W41Try_xx**, and leave it open to use in the next Try It.

Customized Quick Access Toolbar

Word 2016, Windows 10, Microsoft Corporation

Customizing the Ribbon

- In Word 2016 you can customize the ribbon by adding commands you use frequently or removing commands you rarely use.
- You can create new groups on a ribbon tab, and you can create a new tab with new groups.
- Commands for customizing the ribbon are on the Customize Ribbon tab of the Word Options dialog box.

Try It! Customizing the Ribbon

1. In the **W41Try_xx** document, right-click the ribbon, and click Customize the Ribbon.
2. On the right side of the Word Options dialog box, under Main Tabs, click to clear the check mark to the left of Insert, and click OK. Notice that the ribbon no longer displays the Insert tab.
3. Right-click the ribbon, and click Customize the Ribbon.
4. Under Main Tabs, click Home to deselect the check box, and click New Tab. Word creates a new tab with one new group.
5. Click New Tab (Custom) > Rename > type **Documents** > OK.
6. Click New Group (Custom) > Rename > type **Management** > OK.
7. Click the Choose commands from: drop-down arrow > File Tab.
8. In the list of commands, click Close File > Add.
9. In the list of commands, click New from Template > Add.
10. In the list of commands, click Save As > Add.
11. Click OK, and click the Documents tab on the ribbon to view the new group of commands.
12. Right-click on the ribbon > Customize the Ribbon.
13. Click Reset > Reset all customizations.
14. Click Yes in the confirmation dialog box > OK.
15. Save the changes to **W41Try_xx**, and leave it open to use in the next Try It.

Customized tab on the ribbon

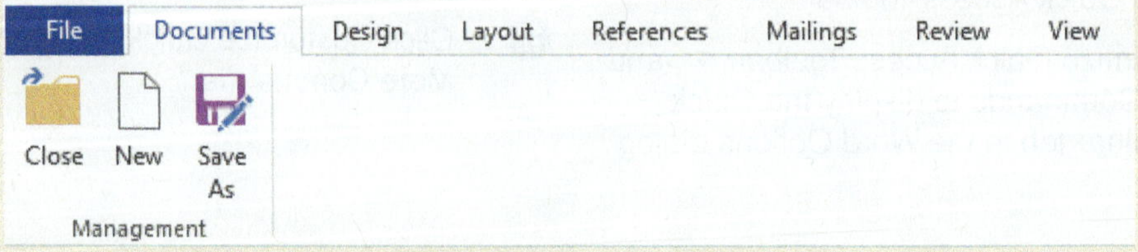

Word 2016, Windows 10, Microsoft Corporation

Locating the Default Save Options

- Word 2016 is set to save files using default options.
- By default, Word 2016 saves documents in the Word Document (*.docx) format, in the Documents folder.
- Word saves AutoRecover information every 10 minutes.
- You can change the default save options on the Save tab in the Word Options dialog box.
- Additional save options are available on the Advanced tab in the Word Options dialog box. For example, you can select a default folder for storing specific file types, such as images and templates.
- Your system may have been customized to use different save options. For example, files may be saved on a network.

Try It! Locating the Default Save Options

1. In the W41Try_xx document, click File > Options to display the Word Options dialog box.
2. In the left pane, click Save.
3. Examine the Save options.
4. In the left pane, click Advanced, and scroll down to the General group in the dialog box.
5. Click the File Locations button to view the storage locations for specific file types.
6. Click Close.
7. Click Cancel to close the Word Options dialog box without making any changes.
8. Save the changes to W41Try_xx, and leave it open to use in the next Try It.

Personalizing Your User Name and Initials

- When you set up Microsoft Word 2016 on your computer, you enter a **user name** and initials.
- Word uses this information to identify you as the author of new documents that you create and save, and as the editor of existing documents that you open, modify, and save.
- In addition, your user name is associated with revisions that you make when you use the Track Changes feature, and the initials are associated with comments that you insert.
- You can change the user name and initials using options in the General group in the Word Options dialog box.

Try It! Personalizing Your User Name and Initials

1. In the W41Try_xx document, click File > Options to display the Word Options dialog box.
2. On the General tab, under Personalize your copy of Microsoft Office, view the current User name and Initials.
3. Click Cancel to close the Word Options dialog box without making any changes.
4. Save the changes to W41Try_xx, and leave it open to use in the next Try It.

Adding and Removing Document Metadata

- You can add information, such as a title and subject, to the document properties of your document.
- Document properties can also include information that is automatically maintained by Office programs, such as the name of the person who authored a document, the date when a document was created, and the document location.
- You can access the document properties from the Properties area on the Info tab of the File tab.
- You can also click the Properties drop-down menu and select Advanced Properties to add and edit additional properties in the Properties dialog box.

Try It! Adding and Removing Document Metadata

1. In the **W41Try_xx** file, click File > Info.
2. On the right side of the Info tab, click Properties > Advanced Properties. The Properties dialog box appears.
3. On the Summary tab, in the Author box, type your name.
4. Click OK.
5. Save the changes to **W41Try_xx**, and leave it open to use in the next Try It.

Customizing the View for Opening E-Mail Attachments

- By default, when you open a document that you receive as an attachment to an e-mail message, it displays in Full Screen Reading view.
- You can use the Word Options dialog box to disable the feature so that the document opens in Print Layout view.

Try It! Customizing the View for Opening E-Mail Attachments

1. In the **W41Try_xx** document, click File > Options to display the Word Options dialog box.
2. On the General tab, under Start up options, click to clear the **Open e-mail attachments and other uneditable files in reading view** check box, if necessary.
3. Click **Cancel** to close the Word Options dialog box without making any changes.
4. Save and close the file, and exit Word.

Lesson 41—Practice

A Fresh Food Fair store wants to post a sign with the company slogan in Spanish. In this project, you will translate the slogan from English to Spanish to create the sign. You will also practice customizing and personalizing Word 2016 options.

DIRECTIONS

1. Start Word, if necessary, click **Blank document**, and save the document as **W41Practice_xx** in the location where your teacher instructs you to store the files for this lesson.
2. Double-click in the header, and type your full name and today's date. Click **Close Header and Footer**.
3. Apply the **Slice** theme and the **Shaded** style set.
4. Click **Customize Quick Access Toolbar** > **Spelling & Grammar** to add the button to the Quick Access Toolbar.
5. Click **Insert** > right-click **Online Pictures** > **Add to Quick Access Toolbar**.
6. Click **Layout** > **Orientation** > **Landscape**.
7. Click **View** > **Page Width**.
8. On the first line of the document, type **Fresh Food Fair**, and format it with the **Title** style. Select the text, click in the **Font Size** box, type **50**, and press ENTER to increase the font size to 50 points.
9. Click at the end of the line, press ENTER, type **Organic and Locally Grown for You**, and format it with the **Heading 1** style. Increase the font size to **16 points**.
10. Click at the end of the last line and press ENTER to start a new line at the end of the document.
11. Select the text Organic and Locally Grown for You.
12. Right-click the selection > **Translate**. If you see the Translate Selected Text dialog box, click Yes to proceed.
13. In the Research task pane, click the To drop-down arrow, and click Spanish (Spain). The text is translated to *Orgánicos y cultivados localmente para usted*.
14. Position the mouse pointer on the blank line at the end of the document, and click the Insert button below the translated text in the Research task pane.

    ✓ *To insert the á character if it isn't already displayed, select the "a" in the first word of the translated text, click Insert > Symbol > More Symbols, click the character, click the Insert button, and click Close.*
15. Format the Spanish text with the **Heading 2** style.
16. Close the Research task pane.
17. Reposition the mouse pointer at the top of the document, and on the Quick Access Toolbar, click **Online Pictures**. Use the Insert Pictures dialog box to search for a photograph of vegetables, such as the one shown in Figure 41-1, and insert it into the document.

    ✓ *If you cannot find a suitable online picture, insert the file **W41Practice_picture.jpg** from the data files for this lesson.*
18. Click the picture to select it if necessary, click **Picture Tools Format**, and resize it to **3"** high. The width should adjust automatically.
19. On the Picture Tools Format tab, click **Position**, and click **Position in Top Left with Square Text Wrapping** (the first item in the first row of the With Text Wrapping group).
20. Open the Properties dialog box, and add your full name to the Author box and **Fresh Food Fair** to the Title box.
21. On the Quick Access Toolbar, click the **Spelling & Grammar** button. Check and correct the spelling and grammar in the document—ignoring the errors in the Spanish, and save the document.
22. **With your teacher's permission,** print the document. It should look similar to Figure 41-1 on the next page.
23. Click **Customize Quick Access Toolbar** > **More Commands**.
24. In the Word Options dialog box, click **Reset** Reset > **Reset only Quick Access Toolbar**.
25. Click **Yes** in the Reset Customizations confirmation dialog box, and click **OK**.
26. Save and close the document, and exit Word.

Figure 41-1

Lesson 41—Apply

A Fresh Food Fair store wants to post signs with the company slogan in English, Spanish, and Brazilian Portuguese. In this project, you will translate the slogan from English to Spanish and from English to Portuguese to create the signs. You will also practice customizing and personalizing Word 2016 options.

DIRECTIONS

1. Start Word, if necessary, and open **W41Apply** from the data files for this lesson.
2. Save the document as **W41Apply_xx** in the location where your teacher instructs you to store the files for this lesson.
3. Double-click in the header, and type your full name and today's date. Click **Close Header and Footer**.
4. Apply the **Wisp** theme and the **Shaded** style set to the document.
5. Add the **Print Preview and Print** button to the Quick Access Toolbar.
6. Customize the ribbon to create a new ribbon tab named **Photos**, with a group named **Formatting**.
7. Add the following buttons for working with pictures to the new group: **Insert Picture**, **Position**, **Wrap Text**, **Height**, and **Width**.
8. Change the page orientation to **Landscape**, and set the zoom to **Page Width**.
9. Format the first line of text in the **Title** style, increase the Font Size to **50 points**, and center it horizontally.
10. Format the second line of text in the **Heading 1** style, increase the Font Size to **22 points**, and center it horizontally.
11. Format the third line of text in the **Heading 3** style, increase the Font Size to **22 points**, and center it horizontally.
12. Insert a new line at the end of the document.
13. Set the Mini Translator to translate to **Portuguese (Brazil)**, and toggle the Mini Translator feature on.
14. Select the text **Organic and Locally Grown for You**, and rest the mouse pointer over the selection.
15. Move the mouse pointer over the Mini Translator so you can see the translation, and on the Mini Translator, click **Copy**.
16. Position the insertion point on the last line of the document, and click **Home** > **Paste**.

17. Delete the text **Microsoft® Translator**, and any blank lines in the document.
18. Format the Portuguese translation with the **Heading 3** style, increase the Font Size to **22 points**, and center it horizontally.
19. Insert a new line at the end of the document. Use the Photos tab on the ribbon to insert the picture **W41Apply_picture** from the data files for this lesson. Resize the picture so it is **3"** high (the width should adjust automatically), and position it in the **Bottom Center with Square Text Wrapping**.
20. Add the alt text **Fresh Vegetables** in the Title box and **A display of organic, locally grown produce** in the Description box of the picture.
21. Use the Accessibility Checker to check the document for accessibility issues. Ignore the picture and heading level warnings.
22. Close the Format Picture and Accessibility Checker task panes.
23. Check and correct the spelling and grammar in the document—ignoring any flagged errors in the Spanish and Portuguese text, and save the document.
24. **With your teacher's permission,** print the document. It should look similar to Figure 41-2.
25. Reset all customizations, and toggle off the Mini Translator.
26. Save and close the document, and exit Word.

Figure 41-2

Lesson 42

Using Advanced Find and Replace

➤ What You Will Learn

Analyzing Conflict
Collecting Images and Text from Multiple Documents
Using the Navigation Task Pane
Finding and Replacing Formatting
Using Wildcard Characters in Find and Replace
Understanding Projects and Project Management

WORDS TO KNOW

Bias
An opinion based on something you think you know, not necessarily based on the truth.

Conflict
A disagreement between two or more people who have different ideas.

Diversity
People of many cultures, backgrounds, and abilities living and working together.

Prejudice
A negative bias.

Problem
Something that blocks you from achieving a goal.

Project
An activity with a starting date and an ending date designed to produce a product, service, or specific result.

Project management
Using resources such as time, money, and people to plan, organize, and complete a project.

Software Skills Use the Office Clipboard to collect images and text from multiple documents. Use Advanced Find and Replace features to locate and replace existing formatting throughout a document. Use wildcard characters with Find and Replace when you are not sure what text you want to find. Conflict with others can make it difficult to achieve goals. You can manage conflict by being open, honest, and respectful, and by working with others to compromise and find solutions.

What You Can Do

Analyzing Conflict

- **Conflict** with others can interfere with your ability to complete tasks and achieve goals.
- There is a **problem** at the root of all conflict. You may be able to use a problem-solving process to find a solution that will resolve the conflict.
- Managing conflict does not always mean eliminating the conflict completely. It means that you are able to recognize what is causing the conflict, and that you can cope with it in an honest and respectful way.
- Sometimes, **diversity** can cause conflict. Focusing on the common goals you and others share will help you see past the differences.
- Understanding the differences between people makes it easier to communicate. It does not mean you have to always agree with people who have different opinions. It just means that you are willing to listen to them and show respect.
- You might have a **bias** about people who are different from you, even before you meet them. When a bias is negative, it is called **prejudice**. There is no place for prejudice at work or anywhere else.

- You can work and communicate effectively in a diverse workplace by developing the qualities of tolerance, cooperation, respect, and understanding.
- **Sexual harassment** can be another source of conflict in a workplace. It can consist of inappropriate jokes or language in verbal or written communications, unwanted touching, staring, requests for dates, or offensive remarks about one sex in general.
- Understanding what may be offensive to others in the workplace will help to prevent conflicts from arising.

Project manager
The person responsible for overseeing the project.

Sexual harassment
Unwanted sexual advances, requests for sexual favors, or verbal or physical conduct of a sexual nature that creates a hostile or uncomfortable work environment.

Wildcard character
A typed character such as an asterisk (*) that represents one or more other characters in a string of text.

Collecting Images and Text from Multiple Documents

- Use the Microsoft Office Clipboard with the Cut or Copy commands to collect images and text from multiple documents.
- Recall that the Copy command stores a duplicate of the selection on the Clipboard, leaving the original selection unchanged, and that the Cut command deletes the selection from its original location, and stores it on the Clipboard.
- You can then use the Paste command to paste a selection from the Clipboard to the insertion point location in the same file or a different file.
- You can store up to 24 items on the Clipboard task pane at a time.

Try It! Collecting Images and Text from Multiple Documents

1. Start Word, click Blank document, and save as **W42TryA_xx** in the location where your teacher instructs you to store the files for this lesson.
2. Click the Clipboard group dialog box launcher to display the Clipboard task pane.
3. In the task pane, click the Clear All button to delete any selections currently on the Clipboard.
4. Open **W42TryB** from the data files for this lesson.
5. Press CTRL + A to select all of the text in **W42TryB**, click Copy to place the selection on the Clipboard, and close **W42TryB** without saving changes.
6. Open **W42TryC** from the data files for this lesson, select all of the text in the document, click Copy, and close **W42TryC** without saving changes.
7. Open **W42TryD** from the data files for this lesson, right-click the picture, click Copy on the shortcut menu, and close **W42TryD** without saving changes.
8. Double-click in the header of **W42TryA_xx**, and click the third selection listed in the Clipboard task pane.
9. Close the header area, and click the second selection listed in the Clipboard task pane.
10. Position the insertion point at the beginning of the text *Mission Statement*, and click the first selection listed in the Clipboard task pane.
11. Close the Clipboard task pane.
12. Save the changes to **W42TryA_xx**, and leave it open to use in the next Try It.

Three selections on the Clipboard

Word 2016, Windows 10, Microsoft Corporation

Using the Navigation Task Pane

- You can use Word's Navigation task pane to search for text or other document content such as graphics, tables, equations, footnotes, and comments.
- You can access the Navigation task pane using the Find button in the Editing group on the Home tab.
- To search for text, click in the Search document box, and type the text.
  - Word displays the results in the Results tab.
  - You can click a result in the Results tab to go to it in your document.
- To search for other document content, such as a graphic, use the magnifying glass in the Search document box.
  - Word displays the results in the Pages or Headings tab.
  - Use Headings to view the results by heading. Word colors a heading yellow if the text under that heading contains a search result.
  - Use Pages to view only the pages that contain the search results.
- When you're done searching, click the × in the Search document box to end your search and remain at the selected search result.

Try It! Using the Navigation Task Pane

1. In the **W42TryA_xx** document, on the Home tab, in the Editing group, click Find to open the Navigation task pane.
2. In the Search document box, click the magnifying glass.
3. Click Graphics.
4. Click Pages to view a thumbnail picture of the page that contains the graphic.
5. Click Results to view the result of the graphic search.
6. In the Search document box, click × to end the search.
7. Close the Navigation task pane.
8. Save the changes to **W42TryA_xx**, and leave it open to use in the next Try It.

Navigation task pane search result

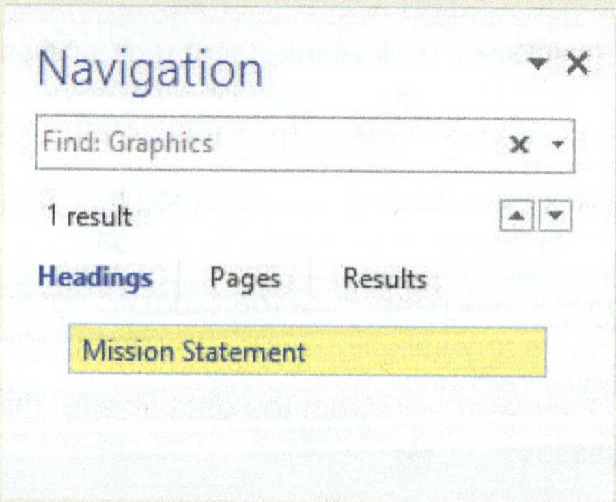

Word 2016, Windows 10, Microsoft Corporation

Finding and Replacing Formatting

- Use options in the Find and Replace dialog box to find and/or replace text formatting.
- Open the Find and Replace dialog box using the Find drop-down list or the Replace button in the Editing group on the Home tab of the ribbon.
- For example, you can find text formatted with the Small caps effect and replace the formatting with the All caps effect.

Try It! Finding and Replacing Formatting

1. In the **W42TryA_xx** document, on the Home tab, in the Editing group, click Replace.
2. In the Find what text box, type **Michigan Avenue Athletic Club**.
3. Click the More button to expand the dialog box.
4. Click the Format button, and click Font.
5. In the Font style list, click Bold, and click OK.
6. In the Replace with text box, type **Michigan Avenue Athletic Club**.
7. Click Format > Font. Under Effects, click to select Small caps, and click OK.
8. Click Replace All. When the process is complete, click OK to close the confirmation dialog box.
9. Close the Find and Replace dialog box.
10. Save the changes to **W42TryA_xx**, and leave it open to use in the next Try It.

Find and replace formatting

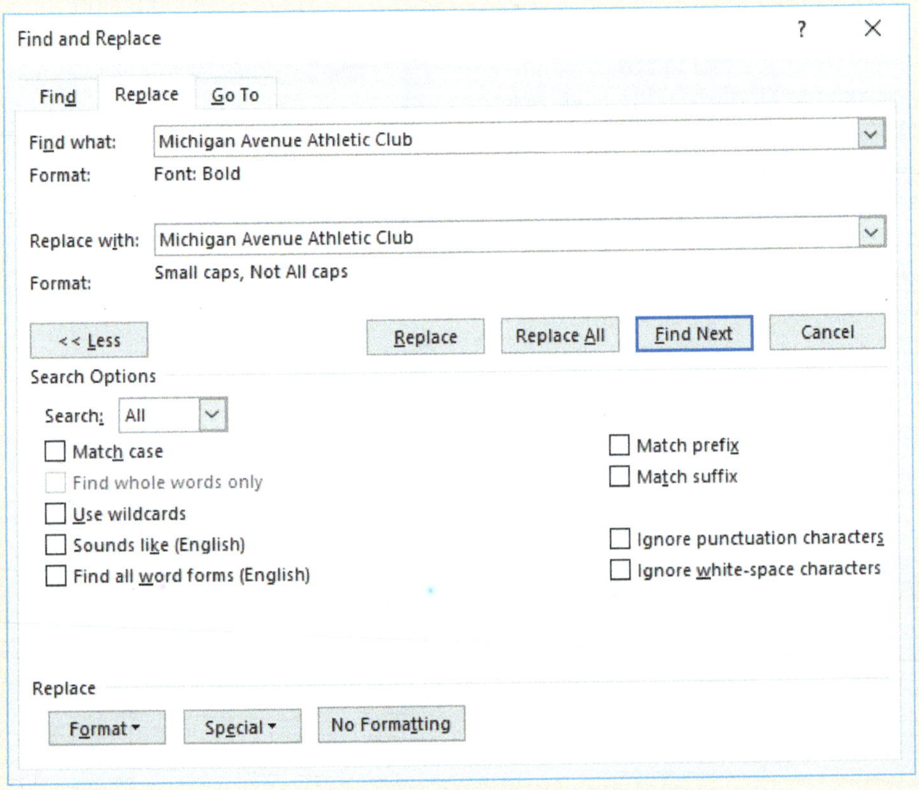

Word 2016, Windows 10, Microsoft Corporation

Using Wildcard Characters in Find and Replace

- Use **wildcard characters** with Find and/or Replace when you are not sure what text you want to find.
- For example, you may want to find all occurrences of someone's last name in a document, but you are not sure if the name is Olden, Oldheimer, or Oldsman. By using wildcard characters, you can find the name, no matter which spelling is used.
- You can use wildcard characters in the Find and Replace dialog box or in the Navigation pane.
- Click the Special button in the Find and Replace dialog box to access special characters that you can find and replace in the document, such as a manual line break or an em dash.
- You can use the Reading Highlight button to have Word apply a text highlight color to text matching your criteria.
- Table 42-1 on the next page lists common wildcard characters available for find and replace searches.

Table 42-1 Common Wildcard Characters

Character	Description	Example
?	Any single character	b?d finds bad, bid, bud, and bed
*	Any string of characters	b*d finds all of the above plus bold, build, and bartered
<	The beginning of a word	<inter finds interesting and interdepartmental but not splintered or winter
>	The end of a word	ent> finds sent and represent but not presents or enter

Try It! Using Wildcard Characters in Find and Replace

1. In the **W42TryA_xx** document, on the Home tab, click the Find drop-down arrow, and click Advanced Find.
2. In the Find and Replace dialog box, click the Find tab, click in the Find what box, and click the No Formatting button.
3. Click the More button, if necessary.
4. Click to select the Use wildcards check box.
5. In the Find what box, type **Peters?n**.
6. Click Find Next.
7. Click the Reading Highlight button, and click Highlight All.
8. Click the Replace tab.
9. In the Replace with box, type **Petersun**. Click the No Formatting button, if necessary.
10. Click Replace All.
11. Click OK to confirm the replacement.
12. In the Find and Replace dialog box, click to clear the Use wildcards check box.
13. Click the Less button.
14. Clear the text from the Find what and Replace with boxes.
15. Click Close to close the Find and Replace dialog box.
16. Save and close **W42TryA_xx**, and exit Word.

Find and replace using wildcards

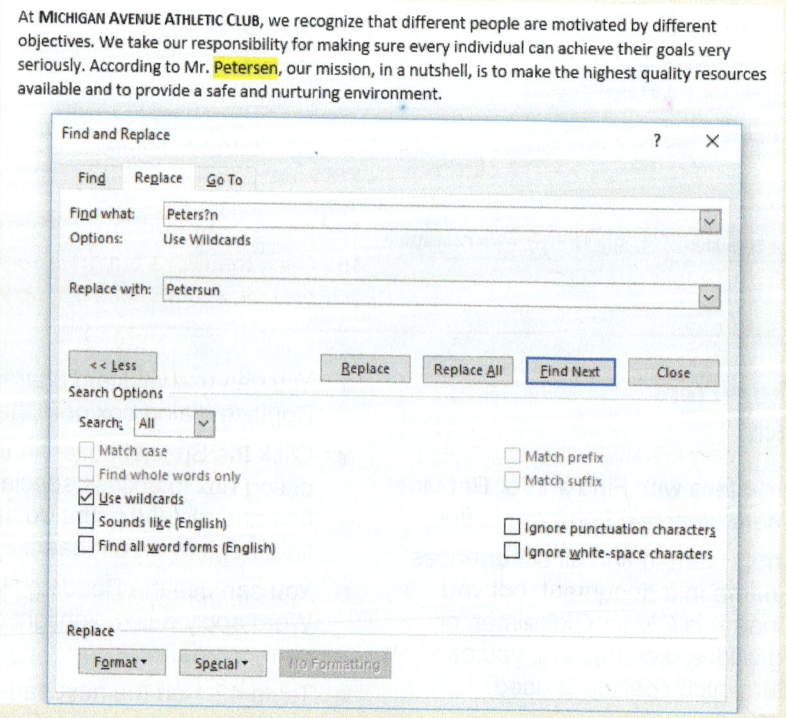

Word 2016, Windows 10, Microsoft Corporation

Understanding Projects and Project Management

- In order to successfully complete a project, it is important to use project management processes and techniques.
- Project management is a process used to take a project from conception to execution to close. It helps you design and implement processes for monitoring and controlling the project, such as tracking trends, setting timelines, and evaluating progress so you can make improvements, as well as providing the documentation for when it is time to close a project.
- Many companies use emerging project management software for scheduling, organizing, controlling, and closing projects. Several of the emerging technologies for project management include Microsoft Project and Smart Sheets. Many use Microsoft Excel, which offers pivot tables and data analysis. You will learn more about the Excel tools later in this text.
- A well-managed project is completed on schedule and within budget, and achieves the stated goals.
- An effective project manager is a strong leader who can use project management processes to plan, execute, control, and close a business project, and who can guide team members to successfully meet common goals.

Lesson 42—Practice

Two sales representatives from Long Shot, Inc. were observed laughing at a disabled golfer while on company business. The legal department has instructed you, a human resources assistant, to draft a letter of apology to the disabled golfer. In this project, you will use text and images from multiple documents and advanced Find and Replace features to create the letter.

DIRECTIONS

1. Start Word, if necessary, click **Blank document**, and save as **W42PracticeA_xx** in the location where your teacher instructs you to store the files for this lesson.
2. Click the Clipboard group dialog box launcher to display the Clipboard task pane.
3. In the task pane, click Clear All.
4. Open **W42PracticeB** from the data files for this lesson.
5. Select all the text in the header, click **Copy**, and close **W42PracticeB** without saving changes.
6. Open **W42PracticeC** from the data files for this lesson, right-click the logo picture, click Copy on the shortcut menu, and close **W42PracticeC** without saving changes.
7. In **W42PracticeA_xx**, double-click in the header area, and click the last selection in the Clipboard task pane, to insert the company letterhead.
8. Click **Header & Footer Tools Design** > **Go to Footer**, and click the first selection in the Clipboard task pane to insert the logo image.
9. Click the image to select it, and click the **Picture Tools Format** tab.
10. Resize the picture to 1.5" high by 2" wide, and center it horizontally in the footer.
11. Close the header and footer area, and close the Clipboard task pane.
12. Type the letter shown in Figure 42-1 on the next page, replacing the sample text *Today's Date* with the actual date and *Student's Name* with your own name. Use the **No Spacing** style and proper page setup and spacing for a full-block business letter.
13. Click **Home** > **Replace**.
14. In the Find what text box, type **Special O*s**.
15. Click the **More** button to expand the dialog box, and click to select the **Use wildcards** check box.
16. Click in the **Replace with** box, and delete any text.
17. Click the **Format** button, and click **Font**.
18. In the Font style list, click **Bold**, and click **OK**.
19. Click **Replace All**, and click **OK** in the confirmation dialog box.
20. In the Find and Replace dialog box, click to clear the **Use wildcards** check box.
21. Click in the **Replace with** box, and click **No Formatting**.
22. Click **Close**.

23. Check and correct the spelling and grammar in the document, and save the document.

24. **With your teacher's permission,** print the document.

25. Save and close the document, and exit Word.

Figure 42-1

Long Shot, Inc.

234 Simsbury Drive ⁞ Ithaca, NY 14850 ⁞ 607.555.9191 ⁞ mail@longshot.net

Today's Date

Mr. John Smith
1001 Main Street
Pine Ridge, NY 11111

Dear Mr. Smith,

I am writing on behalf of the entire Long Shot, Inc. organization to express my deepest apologies for the conduct of the two sales representatives last month at the Pine Ridge Golf Club. Please believe me when I say that they do not represent the attitudes of other Long Shot employees.

At Long Shot, Inc. we have a great respect for diversity. We work very hard to insure an open, honest, and respectful environment, and we have a zero tolerance policy for prejudice and discrimination in any form. In accordance with that policy, we have terminated the contracts of the two offending employees.

I want to assure you that we are reviewing our corporate policies, and plan to conduct additional sensitivity training for all employees. We take this responsibility very seriously. In addition, we are making a sizable donation to the Special Olympics, and plan to provide equipment and ongoing support for the Special Olympics golf team. We are also implementing a partnership program between our employees and Special Olympian athletes.

As a token of our goodwill, we are sending you a full set of golf clubs, customized to accommodate your special needs. The package will include other accessories, as well.

Again, we are all deeply sorry for any pain or humiliation you experienced. Feel free to contact me at any time, for any reason.

Sincerely,

Firstname Lastname

Cc: Legal department

LSI

Lesson 42—Apply

As the human resources assistant for Long Shot, Inc., a golf supply company, you have assumed responsibility for an ongoing project to improve relations within the company and with the community. In this project, you will write an internal memo reinforcing the company's position on diversity. You will use text and images collected from multiple documents and advanced Find and Replace features.

DIRECTIONS

1. Start Word, if necessary, and open **W42ApplyA** from the data files for this lesson.
2. Save the file as **W42ApplyA_xx** in the location where your teacher instructs you to store the files for this lesson.
3. Replace the sample text *Student's Name* with your own name and *Today's Date* with the actual date.
4. Display the Clipboard task pane, and clear all currently stored selections.
5. Open **W42ApplyB** from the data files for this lesson and copy the text beginning with *To reinforce...* through the end of the numbered list to the Clipboard.
6. Close **W42ApplyB** without saving changes.
7. Open **W42ApplyC** from the data files for this lesson, and on the Home tab, click Find to open the Navigation task pane.
8. In the Search document box, click the magnifying glass .

   ✓ *If necessary, clear any text from the Search document box.*
9. Click Graphics.
10. Click Pages, and click the thumbnail picture of the page that contains the graphic.
11. In the document, right-click on the graphic, and copy it to the Clipboard.
12. In the Search document box, click ✕ to end the search.
13. Close the Navigation task pane, and close **W42ApplyC** without saving changes.
14. Insert the text copied from **W42ApplyB** between the two paragraphs of the memo body (refer to Figure 42-2 on the next page).

    ✓ *If necessary, insert a blank line above or below the pasted text.*
15. Insert the logo image in the document. Position it in the **Bottom Center with Square Text Wrapping**, and resize it to 2" high by 2.75" wide. Close the Clipboard task pane.
16. Use Find and Replace with wildcard characters to apply bold formatting to all occurrences of the text *Special Olympics* and *Special Olympian athletes*.
17. Reset the Find and Replace options to clear the options for using wildcard characters and formatting.
18. Check and correct the spelling and grammar in the document, and save the document.
19. **With your teacher's permission,** print the document. It should look similar to Figure 42-2 on the next page.
20. Save and close the document, and exit Word.

Figure 42-2

Long Shot, Inc.

234 Simsbury Drive ⁞ Ithaca, NY 14850 ⁞ 607.555.9191 ⁞ mail@longshot.net

MEMORANDUM

To: All Employees
From: Firstname Lastname
Date: Today's Date

By now you are all aware of the unpleasant incident that took place at the Pine Ridge Golf Club last month. You should also all be aware of the fact that the two employees involved in the incident have been let go. There should be no doubt that we have a zero tolerance policy for prejudice and discrimination in any form, and that we will administer that policy if necessary.

To reinforce our policies, we will be conducting sensitivity training classes throughout the coming year. Every employee will be required to participate. There will be no exceptions.

Two positive changes will occur in response to the incident.

1. Long Shot, Inc. will make a significant financial contribution to the **Special Olympics**, including the donation of equipment and ongoing support to the golf team.
2. Long Shot, Inc. will implement a partnership program with the **Special Olympics** designed to bring Long Shot employees together with **Special Olympian athletes** as mentors, coaches, and friends.

Information about the training classes and programs with the **Special Olympics** will be posted on the company's Web site. You may also contact the Human Resources Department to learn more.

Thank you.

LSI

Lesson 43

Using Building Blocks

➤ What You Will Learn

Inserting a Built-In Building Block
Creating a Custom Building Block
Using the Building Blocks Organizer

Software Skills Use built-in and custom building blocks to design and save common parts of a document so you can insert them in any document at any time. Use the Building Blocks Organizer to modify, view, insert, or delete a building block.

WORDS TO KNOW

AutoText
A category of building block displayed in the AutoText gallery.

Building block
A feature of Microsoft Office 2016 that lets you insert reusable pieces of content such as headers, footers, or tables created from saved text and graphics.

What You Can Do

Inserting a Built-In Building Block

- A **building block** is a feature of Microsoft Office 2016 designed to make it easy to save content so you can insert it into any document at any time.
- Word 2016 comes with many built-in building blocks which display in galleries you can access using commands on the ribbon.
- For example, there are building block galleries for bibliographies, cover pages, headers, footers, equations, page numbers, tables of contents, tables, text boxes, and watermarks.
- Some of the building block galleries are called Quick galleries because they enable you to quickly insert a formatted object. For example, you use the Quick Tables gallery to insert a table building block.
- Click a building block in a gallery to insert it in a document, then adjust formatting as necessary.

Try It! **Inserting a Built-In Building Block**

1. Start Word, open **W43Try** from the data files for this lesson, and save the file as **W43Try_xx** in the location where your teacher instructs you to store the files for this lesson.
2. Position the insertion point on the blank line at the end of the document.
3. Click Insert > Text Box. A gallery of built-in text box building blocks displays.
4. Click the Austin Quote building block.
5. Type **Building Blocks are one way Word 2016 makes it easy to create professional-looking documents.**
6. Save the changes to **W43Try_xx**, and leave it open to use in the next Try It.

Creating a Custom Building Block

- You can save any selection of text and graphics as a custom building block.
- Use the Create New Building Block dialog box to enter properties for the building block, such as a name and a description.
- The Gallery setting determines in which gallery the building block will display. For example, if you are creating a header building block, it displays in the Headers gallery.
- If the building block does not fit in a particular category, you can select the **AutoText** gallery.
- Open the Create New Building Block dialog box from the gallery where you want to store the new building block. For example, use the Page Numbers gallery when you want to create a Page Number building block.
- You can save a custom building block as a Quick Part, which is an object such as a document property or field you insert from a gallery.

✓ *Using Quick Parts is covered in Lesson 44.*

- When you exit Word after creating or modifying a building block, the program asks if you want to save the changes to the Building Blocks template.

Try It!

Creating a Custom Building Block

1. In **W43Try_xx**, select the table.
2. Click Insert > Table > Quick Tables to display the gallery of built-in table building blocks.
3. Click Save Selection to Quick Tables Gallery to display the Create New Building Block dialog box.
4. Verify that the Gallery is Tables, the Category is General, the Save in option is Building Blocks, and Options is set to Insert content in its own paragraph. If necessary, select these options.
5. In the Name box, type **Weekly Class Schedule**.
6. In the Description box, type **High School Class Schedule**, and click OK.
7. Position the insertion point on the blank line just below the table and press ENTER.
8. On the Insert tab, click Table > Quick Tables, and scroll down to the bottom of the Quick Tables gallery.
9. Under the heading General, click the Weekly Class Schedule building block to insert it into the document.
10. Save the changes to **W43Try_xx**, and leave it open to use in the next Try It.

Create a new building block

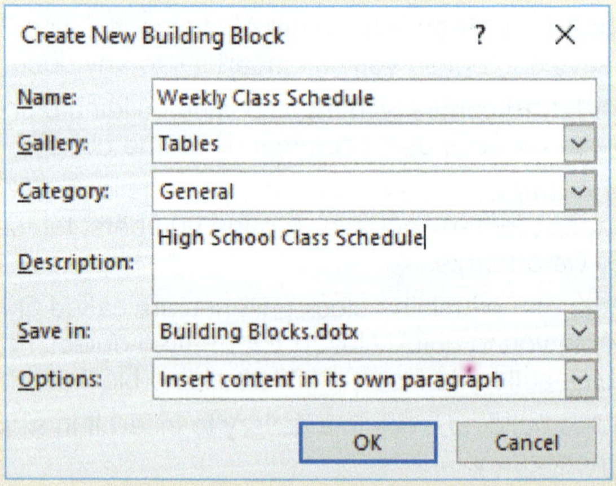

Word 2016, Windows 10, Microsoft Corporation

Using the Building Blocks Organizer

- Use the Building Blocks Organizer dialog box to edit, insert, view, or delete a building block.
- Open the Building Blocks Organizer from the Quick Parts drop-down menu on the Insert tab of the ribbon, or by right-clicking a building block in any gallery and clicking Organize and Delete on the shortcut menu.

- By default, building blocks are listed by gallery. Click a heading at the top of the list to change the sort order.
- Click a building block to preview it on the right side of the Building Blocks Organizer dialog box, or to select it for insertion, editing, or deletion.
- You can use the Edit Properties button to open the Modify Building Block dialog box to change the properties.
- To display the gallery where the building block is stored, right-click the building block, and click Edit Properties on the shortcut menu.
- Building blocks can be moved between documents.

Try It! Using the Building Blocks Organizer

1. In **W43Try_xx**, on the Insert tab, in the Text group, click Quick Parts.
2. On the Quick Parts drop-down menu, click Building Blocks Organizer.
3. In the list of Building Blocks, click the Name heading to sort the list by building block name.
4. Scroll down the list, and click the Weekly Class Schedule Table building block. Notice the category is General—the default for custom building blocks.

   ✓ *The name and description display below the preview of a building block in the Building Blocks Organizer.*

5. Click the Edit Properties button to open the Modify Building Block dialog box for the selected building block.
6. Edit the name to Class Schedule, then click OK. Click Yes in the confirmation dialog box.
7. Scroll down the list and click the Class Schedule Tables building block, then click the Delete button.
8. Click Yes in the confirmation dialog box, click the Gallery heading to sort the list by gallery, and click Close to close the Building Blocks Organizer.
9. Save and close **W43Try_xx**, and exit Word.
10. Click Save in the confirmation dialog box to save the changes to the Building Blocks template.

The Building Blocks Organizer

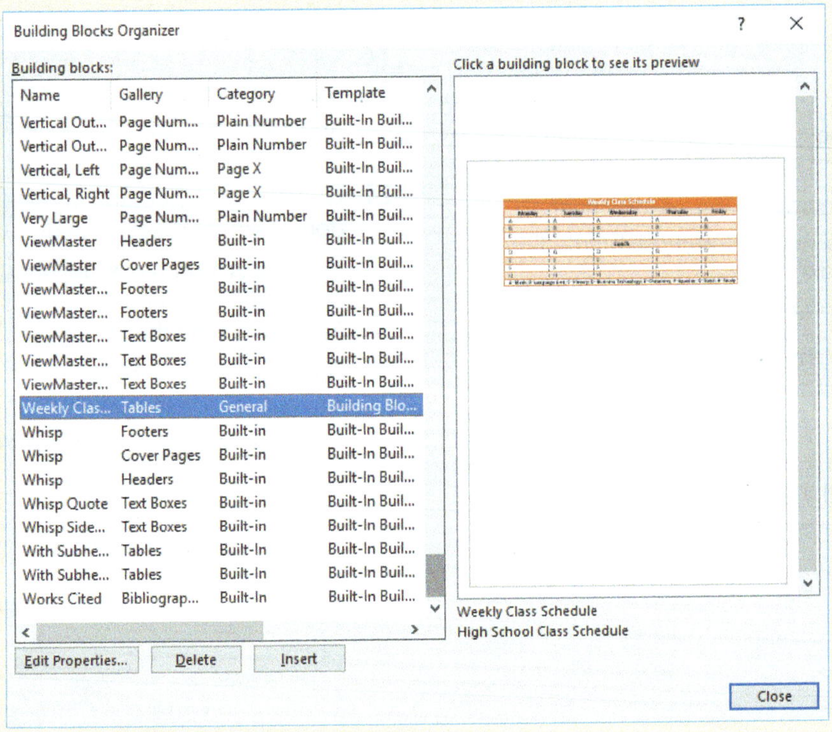

Lesson 43—Practice

You work in the publications department for Long Shot, Inc. You need to create a new letterhead. You will design a header with a logo and create a custom header building block.

DIRECTIONS

1. Start Word, if necessary, click **Blank document**, and save as **W43Practice_xx** in the location where your teacher instructs you to store the files for this lesson.
2. Apply the **Integral** theme and the **Lines (Simple)** style set.
3. Double-click in the header and apply the **No Spacing** style. Set the horizontal alignment to **Center**.
4. Click **Insert** > **Pictures**, then insert **W43Practice_logo** from the data files for this lesson. Resize the picture height to **1"**. The width should adjust automatically.
5. Reposition the insertion point to the right of the picture, increase the font size to **36 points** and type **Long Shot, Inc.**
6. Press SHIFT + ENTER to insert a line break. Change the font size to **10 points** and type **234 Simsbury Drive, Ithaca, NY 14850 - 607.555.9191 - mail@longshot.net**.
7. Select the hyphen after the address, click **Insert** > **Symbol** > **More Symbols**, and use the Symbol dialog box to replace the hyphen character with the Wingdings symbol number 80—a golf flag (refer to Figure 43-1 on the next page).
8. Repeat step 7 to replace the second hyphen with the Wingdings symbol number 80. Select the picture and the text.
9. Select the picture and the text.

   ✓ *Click to the left of the picture to select the first line, then press and hold the mouse pointer, and drag down to select the second line.*
10. Click **Insert** > **Text Box** > **Draw Text Box** to draw a text box around the picture and the text.
11. Click the **Drawing Tools Format** tab, click the **Shape Outline** drop-down arrow, and click **No Outline**.
12. Click **Align Objects** > **Align to Page**.
13. Click **Align Objects** again > **Align Center**.
14. Click **Align Objects** again > **Align Top**.
15. Click **Design** > **Page Borders** > **Borders**.
16. In the Style list, click the default single line. Click the **Color** drop-down arrow, and under Standard Colors click **Dark Blue**. Click the **Width** drop-down arrow, and click **2 ¼ pt**.
17. In the Preview area, click the **Bottom Border** button, and click **OK**.
18. With the text box selected, click **Insert** > **Header** > **Save Selection to Header Gallery**.

    ✓ *You could also save the selection to the Text Box Gallery.*
19. In the Create New Building Block dialog box, verify that the Gallery is Headers, the category is General, Save in is set to Building Blocks, and Options are set to Insert content only.
20. In the Name text box, type **LSI Letterhead**.
21. In the Description text box, type **Company letterhead with logo and address**.
22. Click **OK**.
23. Make the footer active and type your full name and today's date, then close the header and footer area.
24. Check and correct the spelling and grammar in the document, and save the document.
25. **With your teacher's permission,** print the document. The header should look similar to Figure 43-1 on the next page.
26. Save and close the document, and exit Word. Click **Save** in the confirmation dialog box to save the changes to the Building Blocks template.

Figure 43-1

Word 2016, Windows 10, Microsoft Corporation

Lesson 43—Apply

The publications manager for Long Shot, Inc. asks you to send a press release about the company's commitment to the Special Olympics. You need to format the document by adding a header and footer. You will insert the header building block you created in the previous project and insert a built-in footer building block.

DIRECTIONS

1. Start Word, if necessary, and open **W43Apply** from the data files for this lesson.
2. Save the file as **W43Apply_xx** in the location where your teacher instructs you to store the files for this lesson.
3. Apply the **Integral** theme and the **Lines (Simple)** style set.
4. Replace the sample text *Today's Date* with the actual date and *Student Name* with your own name.
5. Insert the **LSI Letterhead** header building block.
   a. Click **Insert** > **Header**.
   b. Scroll to and click **LSI Letterhead**.
6. Click **Insert** > **Quick Parts** > **Building Blocks Organizer**.
7. Sort the list by Name.
8. Scroll to and select the **LSI Letterhead** building block.
9. Click **Edit Properties**, and change the name to **Long Shot Header**.
10. Click **OK**, and click **Yes** to redefine the building block.
11. Delete the **Long Shot Header** building block.
12. Sort the building block list by Gallery, and close the Building Blocks Organizer dialog box.
13. In the document, insert the built-in **Semaphore** footer building block.
14. Check and correct the spelling and grammar in the document, and save the document.
15. **With your teacher's permission,** print the document. It should look similar to Figure 43-2 on the next page.
16. Save and close the document, and exit Word.
17. Click **Save** in the confirmation dialog box to save the changes to the Building Blocks template.

Figure 43-2

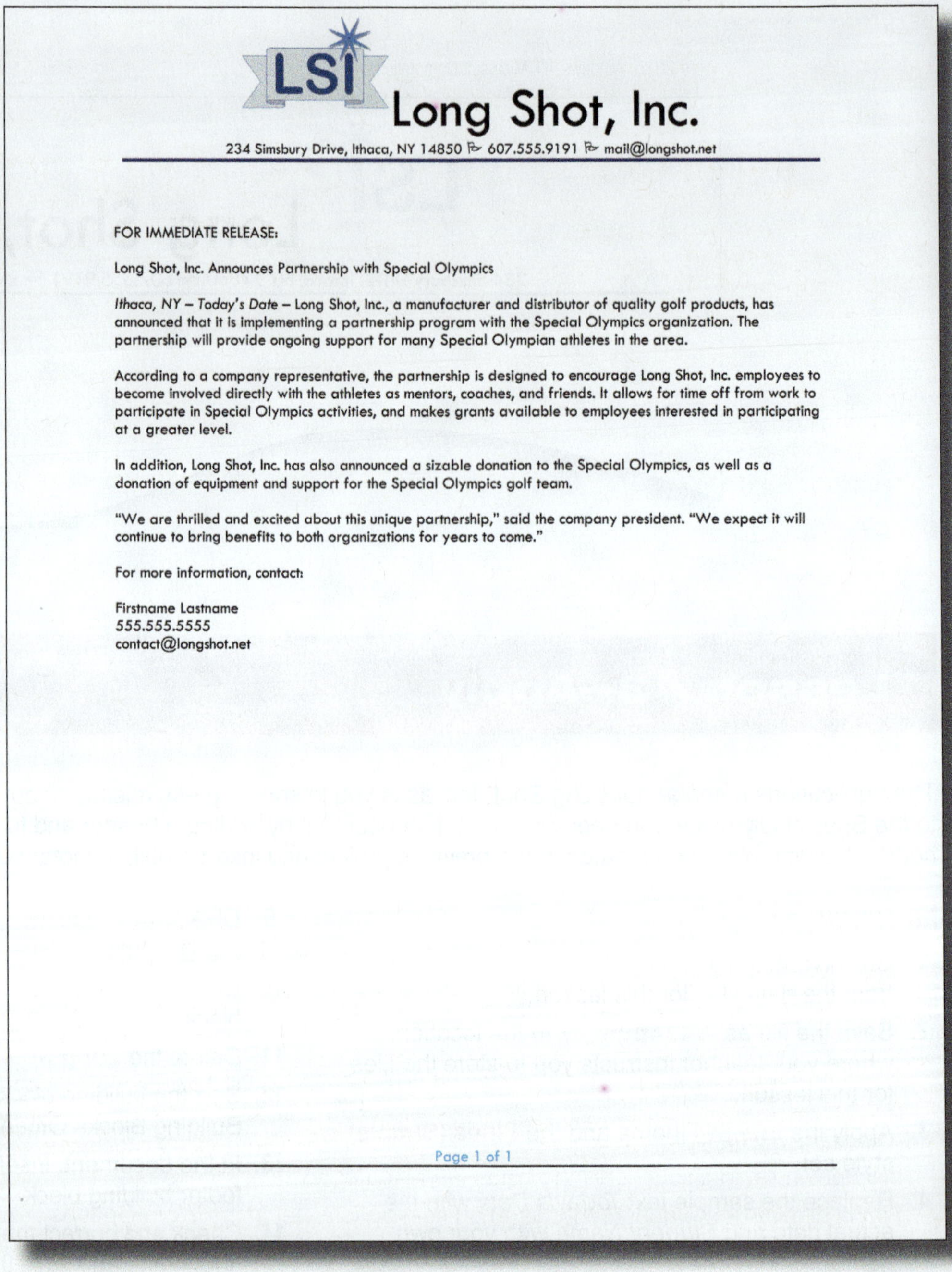

Long Shot, Inc.

234 Simsbury Drive, Ithaca, NY 14850 ▷ 607.555.9191 ▷ mail@longshot.net

FOR IMMEDIATE RELEASE:

Long Shot, Inc. Announces Partnership with Special Olympics

Ithaca, NY – Today's Date – Long Shot, Inc., a manufacturer and distributor of quality golf products, has announced that it is implementing a partnership program with the Special Olympics organization. The partnership will provide ongoing support for many Special Olympian athletes in the area.

According to a company representative, the partnership is designed to encourage Long Shot, Inc. employees to become involved directly with the athletes as mentors, coaches, and friends. It allows for time off from work to participate in Special Olympics activities, and makes grants available to employees interested in participating at a greater level.

In addition, Long Shot, Inc. has also announced a sizable donation to the Special Olympics, as well as a donation of equipment and support for the Special Olympics golf team.

"We are thrilled and excited about this unique partnership," said the company president. "We expect it will continue to bring benefits to both organizations for years to come."

For more information, contact:

Firstname Lastname
555.555.5555
contact@longshot.net

Page 1 of 1

Lesson 44

Inserting Fields from Quick Parts

➤ What You Will Learn

Inserting a Field from Quick Parts
Setting Field Display Options
Analyzing Employment Packages

Software Skills Insert a field into a document as a placeholder for data that might change, such as a date, results of a calculation, or a page number. Access the available fields using Word's Quick Parts menu to locate the field, enter field options, and insert the field at the desired location.

What You Can Do

Inserting a Field from Quick Parts

- Use Word's Quick Parts menu to insert a **field** into a document.
- The available fields are listed alphabetically in the left pane of the Field dialog box.
- Field properties display in the middle pane and options, if any, display in the right pane.
- By default, all fields are listed; you can select a category from the Categories drop-down list to display only the fields in that category.
- Fields display in the document based on field options set in the Word Options dialog box. The default setting is to display the **field value**.

✓ *Setting field options is covered in the next section.*

- If the field value changes, you can update the field to display the current value.
- Most of the fields can also be inserted using other Word features and commands.
- For example, you can insert the date and time using the Date and Time dialog box, which can be opened from the Text group on the Insert tab of the ribbon.

WORDS TO KNOW

Employment package
Compensation offered to employees by an employer, usually including salary, insurance, and other benefits.

Field
A placeholder used to insert information that changes, such as the date, the time, a page number, or the results of a calculation.

Field code
A code that represents the data that Word will display in a document.

Field value
The data displayed in a field.

Try It! Inserting a Field from Quick Parts

1. Start Word, click Blank document, and save the document as **W44Try_xx** in the location where your teacher instructs you to store the files for this lesson.
2. Click Insert > Quick Parts to display the Quick Parts drop-down menu.
3. Click Field.
4. In the left pane of the Field dialog box, click the Categories drop-down arrow, and click User Information.
5. In the list of Field names, click UserName.
6. In the Format list, click Uppercase > OK. Word inserts the field and displays the name currently entered as the user name, in all uppercase characters.
7. Save the changes to **W44Try_xx**, and leave it open to use in the next Try It.

Field dialog box

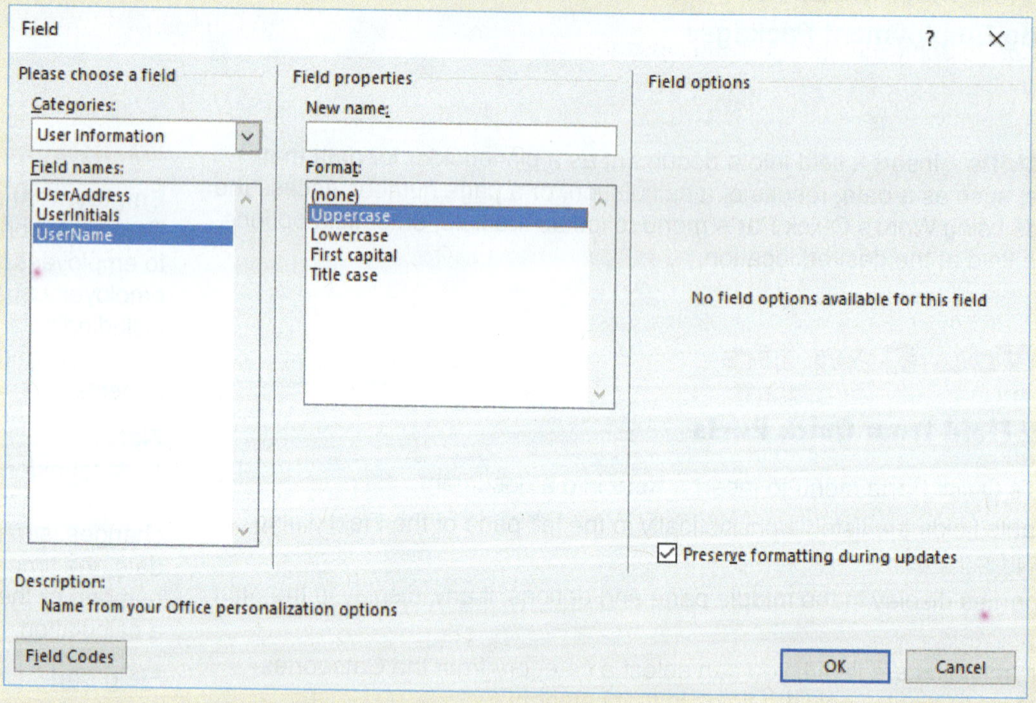

Word 2016, Windows 10, Microsoft Corporation

Setting Field Display Options

- In the Advanced tab of the Word Options dialog box, you can select options for how fields display in a document.
- You can select to display **field codes** instead of field values.
- When a field is selected, Word displays shading by default.
- You can choose to always or never display shading when a field is selected.

Try It! Setting Field Display Options

1. In the W44Try_xx document, click the user name. By default, field shading displays when the field is selected.
2. Move the insertion point off the user name. The field is no longer shaded.
3. Click File > Options > Advanced to display the Advanced tab of the Word Options dialog box.
4. Under Show document content, click to select the Show field codes instead of their values check box.
5. Click the Field shading drop-down arrow, and click Always.
6. Click OK to apply the changes and close the dialog box. The field code displays in place of the field value, and shading displays.
7. Click File > Options > Advanced.
8. Under Show document content, click to clear the Show field codes instead of their values check box, click the Field shading drop-down arrow, and click When selected.
9. Click OK.
10. Save and close W44Try_xx, and exit Word.

Display field codes and shading

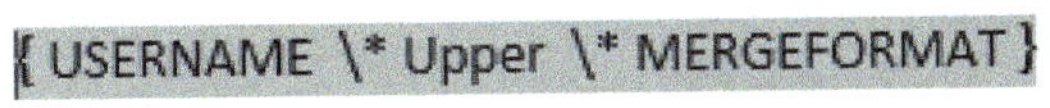

Word 2016, Windows 10, Microsoft Corporation

Analyzing Employment Packages

- When you are offered a job, the company offers an **employment package** that includes benefits as well as salary.
- Most employment packages include some level of health insurance as well as a pension or retirement plan. They usually include vacation time, holidays, and sick/personal days.
- Other benefits that may be offered include:
  - Life insurance
  - Disability insurance
  - Transportation assistance
  - Cafeteria plan
  - Tax-sheltered annuities
  - Fitness assistance
  - Tuition reimbursement
  - Dependent care
- When evaluating an employment package, prospective employees should consider factors such as:
  - The value of the offered benefits.
  - The amount the employee must contribute for benefits and whether the contribution is deducted "pre-tax."
  - Whether the benefits cover family members.
  - Whether benefits are available immediately, or if there is a waiting period.
  - Whether there is flexibility in selecting or changing benefit coverage.

Lesson 44—Practice

You are an administrative assistant at Executive Recruitment Resources, Inc., a job search and recruitment agency. You need to create a newsletter to explain the types of benefits often included in employment packages. In this project, you will use fields from Quick Parts and save a nameplate for the top of the newsletter as an AutoText building block.

DIRECTIONS

1. Start Word, if necessary, click **Blank document**, and save as **W44Practice_xx** in the location where your teacher instructs you to store the files for this lesson.
2. Apply the **Integral** theme.
3. Apply the **No Spacing** style, and then type the following three lines of text, pressing ENTER at the end of each line (after the company name, the address, and the Web site URL):

   Executive Recruitment Resources, Inc.

   8921 Thunderbird Road – Phoenix, Arizona – 85022

   Phone: 602-555-6325 – Fax: 602-555-6425 – www.errinc.net

   ✓ *If necessary, right-click the Web site URL, and click* ***Remove Hyperlink****.*
4. Format the first line of text with the **Small caps** font effect, and increase the font size to **22 points**.
5. Increase the font size of the second line of text to **14 points**.
6. Click **Insert** > **Symbol** Ω > **More Symbols**, and use the Symbol dialog box to replace the hyphen characters in the second and third lines with the Wingdings symbol number 118 (refer to Figure 44-1 on the next page).
7. Select the three lines of text, and click **Design** > **Page Borders** > **Shading**.
8. Under Patterns, click the **Style** drop-down arrow and click **12.5%**.
9. Click the **Borders** tab, and, in the Style list, click the default single line. Click the **Color** drop-down arrow and, under Theme Colors, click **Blue, Accent 2, Darker 50%.** Click the **Width** drop-down arrow, and click **3 pt**.
10. In the Preview area, click the **Bottom Border** button, and click **OK**.
11. With the three lines of text still selected, click **Insert** > **Quick Parts** > **AutoText** > **Save Selection to AutoText Gallery**.
12. In the Name text box, type **ERR Nameplate**.
13. In the Description text box, type **Company name and address**, and click **OK**.
14. Double-click in the Header, and click **Insert** > **Quick Parts** > **Field**.
15. If necessary, click the **Categories** drop-down arrow > **User Information**.
16. In the Field names list, click **UserName**, and, in the Format list, click **First capital**.
17. Click **OK**.
18. Press ENTER, and click **Insert** > **Quick Parts** > **Field**, again.
19. Click the **Categories** drop-down arrow > **Date and Time**.
20. In the Field names list, click **Date**, and, in the Format list, click the third format in the list: **MMMM d, yyyy**.
21. Click **OK**.
22. Click **File** > **Options** > **Advanced**.
23. Under Show document content, click to select the **Show field codes instead of their values** check box.
24. Click the **Field shading** drop-down arrow, click **Always** > **OK**.
25. Close the header and footer, and check and correct the spelling and grammar in the document.
26. **With your teacher's permission,** print the document. It should look similar to Figure 44-1 on the next page.
27. Save and close the document, and exit Word.

Figure 44-1

Word 2016, Windows 10, Microsoft Corporation

Firstname Lastname
Today's Date

EXECUTIVE RECRUITMENT RESOURCES, INC.
8921 Thunderbird Road ❖ Phoenix, Arizona ❖ 85022
Phone: 602-555-6325 ❖ Fax: 602-555-6425 ❖ www.errinc.net

Lesson 44—Apply

As an administrative assistant at Executive Recruitment Resources, Inc., you are completing a newsletter explaining the types of benefits often included in employment packages. In this project, you will use fields from Quick Parts to complete a newsletter. You will also insert a nameplate at the top of the newsletter using an AutoText building block.

DIRECTIONS

1. Start Word, if necessary, and open **W44Apply** from the data files for this lesson.
2. Save the file as **W44Apply_xx** in the location where your teacher instructs you to store the files for this lesson.
3. Apply the **Integral** theme.
4. Set fields to display values and field shading to display only when the field is selected.
5. Position the insertion point at the beginning of the document, and insert the **ERR Nameplate** AutoText building block.
6. With the insertion point still at the beginning of the heading *What Is an Employment Package?*, insert a continuous section break.
7. Set the spacing before the heading to **10 pt**.
8. Format the second section into two newsletter-style columns, and set the width of the gutter between columns to **0.25"**.

   ✓ *Hint: Set gutter spacing by clicking Layout, Columns drop-down arrow, More Columns.*
9. Reposition the insertion point to the beginning of the heading *Evaluating an Employment Package*, and insert a column break.
10. Set the spacing before the heading to **18 pt** so it is visually aligned with the heading in the left column.
11. Insert a new paragraph at the end of the first column, insert the picture file **W44Apply_picture** from the data files for this lesson, and set the text wrapping to **Square**. Change the height of the image to **1.85"** (the width adjusts automatically).
12. Flush left in the footer, type **Prepared by:** and then insert the **UserName** field with **uppercase** formatting.
13. Centered in the footer, type **Date:** and a space, and insert the **Date** field in the **m/d/yy** format.
14. Flush right in the footer, type **Time:** and a space, and insert the **Time** field in the **HH:mm** format.
15. Delete the **ERR Nameplate** building block.
16. Check and correct the spelling and grammar in the document, and save the document.
17. **With your teacher's permission,** print the document. It should look similar to Figure 44-2.
18. Save and close the document, and exit Word.

Figure 44-2

EXECUTIVE RECRUITMENT RESOURCES, INC.

8921 Thunderbird Road ❖ Phoenix, Arizona ❖ 85022

Phone: 602-555-6325 ❖ Fax: 602-555-6425 ❖ www.errinc.net

What Is an Employment Package?

An employment package—which is sometimes called a benefits package—is all of the compensation that an employer provides for an employee. It includes monetary compensation, such as salary, overtime, and commissions, as well as other benefits, such as insurance coverage.

Benefits and non-monetary compensation have value. Therefore, it is important that everyone who is looking for employment, or who is considering accepting a new position, understands the concept of an employment package. It is also important to know how to evaluate and compare different packages.

An overview of the standard employment package should be discussed during the interview process. A prospective employer should provide a complete, written explanation of the employment package at the time he or she makes a job offer to the prospective employee. It is also advisable for the prospective employee to sit down and discuss the package with a human resources professional or recruitment counselor. The HR professional should be able to answer all questions, and explain the package in detail.

Evaluating an Employment Package

Medical Insurance: Consider the type of plan, what is covered, the amount of the deductibles, co-payments, exclusions, and whether it includes coverage for family members. Also, consider whether there is separate coverage for dental and orthodontic care, as well as for vision and eye care.

Life Insurance: Consider the amount and type of coverage, and whether it is possible to purchase additional coverage.

401(k) plan: A 401 (k) is a tax-deferred retired account. Many companies are replacing pension plans with 401 (k) plans. Consider the maximum amount you can contribute, whether the employer matches your contributions, and conditions for transferring the account if you change employers.

Pension plan: Some organizations, particularly government agencies, still offer pension plans for retirement savings. Consider the length of time it takes to become eligible, how the account is managed, and the age at which you can start claiming benefits.

Vacation/holiday/sick/personal days: Consider the number of days for each, when you become eligible, and whether you are paid your full salary for time off. Some companies allow you to carry over unused days from one year to the next.

Other benefits to consider include cafeteria plans which subsidize meals, transportation assistance which subsidizes mileage or public transportation costs incurred while traveling to and from work, and tuition reimbursement for work-related education.

Prepared by: FIRSTNAME LASTNAME   Today's Date   Time: 13:25

Lesson 45

Creating Custom Templates, Themes, and Style Sets

➤ What You Will Learn

- Creating and Saving a Custom Template
- Modifying a Custom Template
- Creating a New Document from a Custom Template
- Deleting a Custom Template
- Creating a Custom Theme
- Applying, Resetting, and Deleting a Theme
- Creating a Style Set
- Applying, Resetting, and Deleting a Style Set
- Demonstrating Professional Standards of Behavior

Software Skills Word comes with built-in templates, themes, and style sets you can use to apply consistent formatting to your documents. You can create custom templates, themes, and style sets to personalize your documents, and save them to use again. For example, you can create a custom template that also includes a custom theme and a custom style set to ensure that your documents will be consistent and professional-looking. You can restore a custom theme or style set to its original settings. You can modify and manage a custom theme or style set to keep the formatting fresh and modern.

WORDS TO KNOW

Acceptable use policy
A set of rules governing how a network or the Internet may be used.

Agenda
A list or schedule of activities or topics to be accomplished or discussed.

Ethical
Conforming to accepted standards of social or professional behavior.

Integrity
Adherence to a strict moral or ethical code.

Style set
A collection of styles that have coordinated colors and fonts.

Template
A document that contains formatting, styles, and sample text that you can use to create new documents.

Theme
A set of coordinated colors, fonts, and effects that can be applied to Office 2016 documents.

What You Can Do

Creating and Saving a Custom Template

- A **template** includes settings for formatting, styles, and sample text that you can use to create new documents.
- You can use Word's built-in templates, or you can create and save your own.

✓ *Template files in recent versions of Word have a .dotx file extension, and template files from versions of Word prior to 2007 have a .dot file extension.*

- You can create a custom template by creating a document and saving it as a template.
- You can also create a custom template by modifying a built-in template, and saving it with a different file name.
- Word stores custom templates in the Custom Office Templates folder. The file path is C:\Users\Username\Documents\Custom Office Templates.

✓ *Based on your computer's configuration, your file path may be different than the one given here.*

- You can save a template in another location, but then you cannot access the template from the template gallery using File > New.
- You can delete a template by using File Explorer to browse to the folder with the file, right-clicking the file, and selecting Delete.
- You must close all documents using a template before you can delete the template file.

Try It! Creating and Saving a Custom Template

1. Start Word, and open **W45TryA** from the data files for this lesson.
2. Click File > Save As > Browse.
3. In the Save as type drop-down box, select Word Template. Notice that Word selects the Custom Office Templates location on your computer.
4. In the File name box, type **W45TryA_xx**, and click Save.
5. Close the file and exit Word.

The Custom Office Templates location

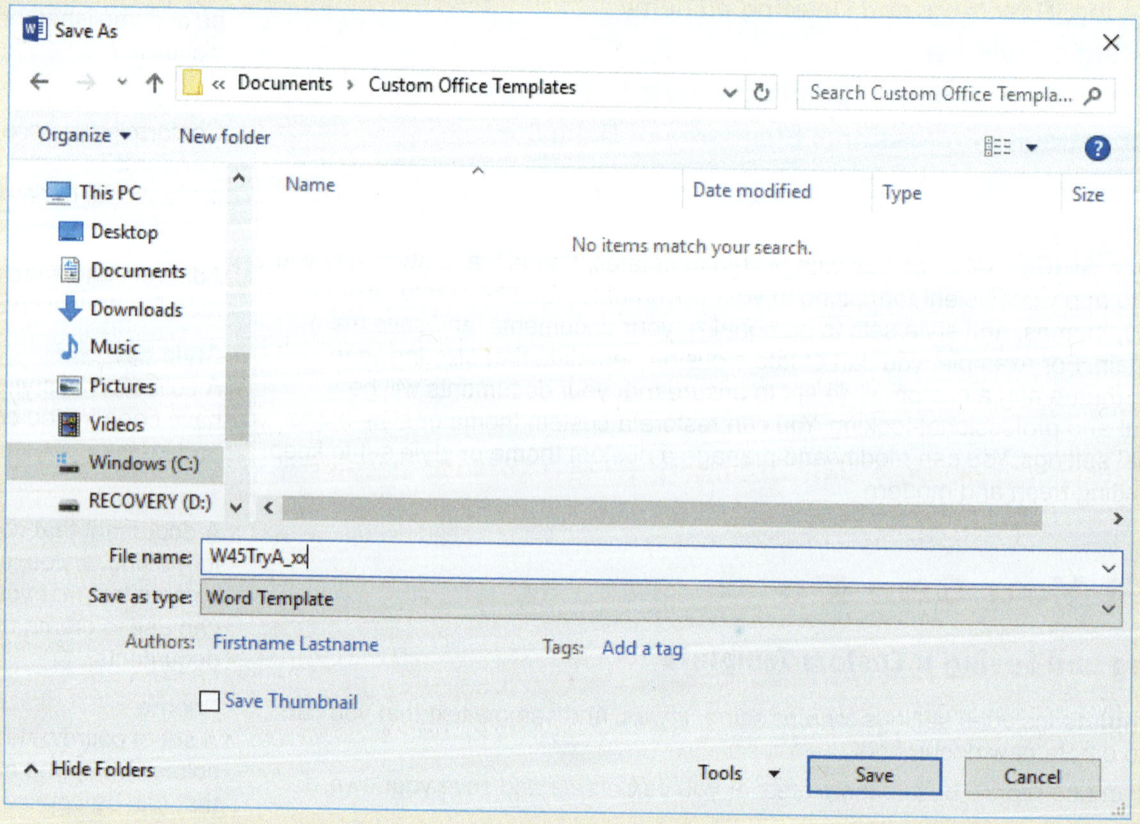

Word 2016, Windows 10, Microsoft Corporation

Modifying a Custom Template

- You can modify a custom template that you have saved to your computer.
- For example, you can change the sample text or graphics, the formatting options, and the page layout settings.
- You must open a template file to modify it.
- To open a custom template, browse to the file using the following file path: C:\Users\Username\Documents\Custom Office Templates.
- In the open template file, you can make changes, and then save the modified template.

Try It! Modifying a Custom Template

1. Start Word, and click Open Other Documents > This PC > Browse.
2. Browse to the file path C:\Users\Username\Documents\Custom Office Templates.

   ✓ *Your file path may be different than the one given here; check with your teacher for the correct file path.*
3. Click the **W45TryA_xx** template file, and click Open.
4. Reposition the mouse pointer at the end of the document, and type **Heading 4**.
5. Select the text Heading 4, click the Styles More button, and click **Heading 4**.
6. Click at the end of the selected text, press ENTER, and type **Normal with Subtle Emphasis**.
7. Select the text *Normal with Subtle Emphasis*, click the Styles More button, and click Subtle emphasis.
8. Save the changes to the **W45TryA_xx** file.
9. Click File, click Save As, and save the **W45TryA_xx** file in the location where your teacher instructs you to store the files for this lesson.
10. Close the document, and close Word.

Creating a New Document from a Custom Template

- You can create a new, blank document from a custom template, just as you would from one of Word's built-in templates.
- You can select and preview a custom template in the Backstage view.
- Access the template gallery by clicking the File tab, and then clicking the New tab.
- Use the PERSONAL tab on Word's New start screen to access the custom templates in your personal template gallery.
- You can also use File Explorer to browse to a template file, and double-click it to create a new document based on that template.

Try It! Creating a New Document from a Custom Template

1. Start Word, and click the PERSONAL template tab. The PERSONAL template gallery displays.
2. Click the **W45TryA_xx** template file. Word opens a new document based on the custom template you created.
3. Save the file as **W45TryB_xx** in the location where your teacher instructs you to store the files for this lesson.
4. Close the **W45TryB_xx** file, and leave Word open to use in the next Try It.

(continued)

Try It! Creating a New Document from a Custom Template (continued)

The PERSONAL template gallery

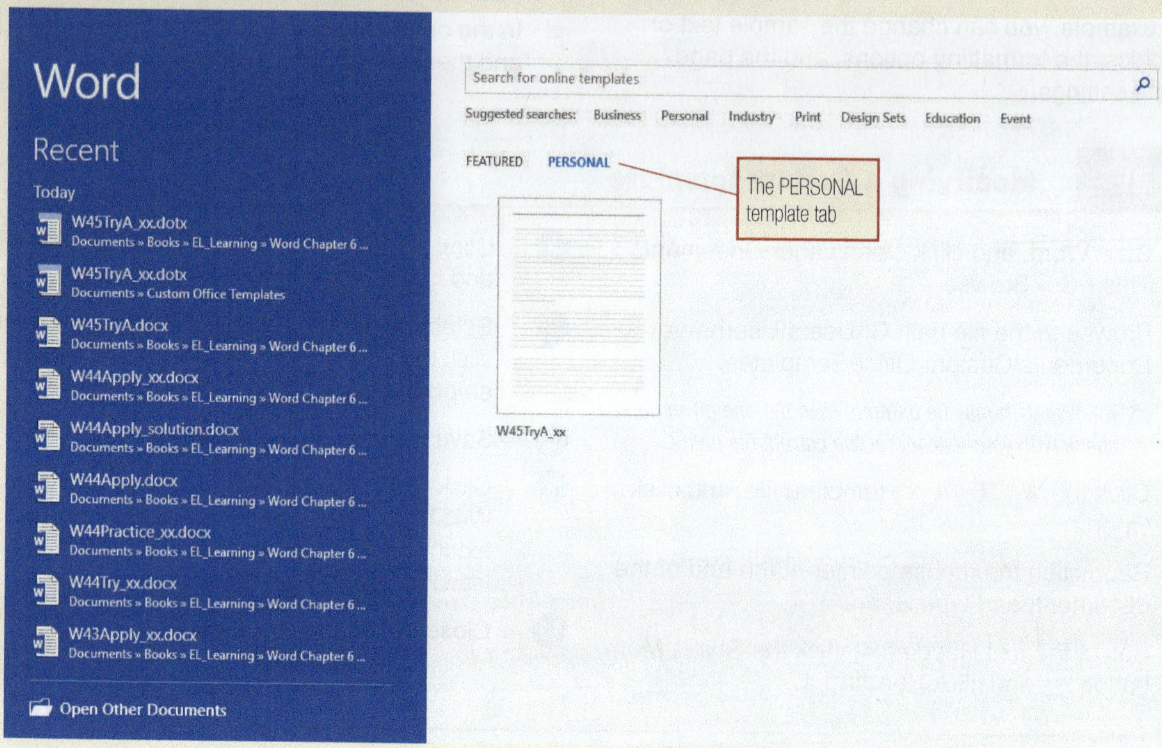

Word 2016, Windows 10, Microsoft Corporation

Deleting a Custom Template

- You can delete a template by using File Explorer to browse to the folder with the file, right-clicking the file, and selecting Delete.
- You must close all documents using a template before you can delete the template file.
- Recall that Word stores custom templates in the Custom Office Templates folder. The file path is C:\Users\Username\Documents\Custom Office Templates.

✓ *Based on your computer's configuration, your file path may be different than the one given here.*

Try It! Deleting a Custom Template

1. Start File Explorer, and browse to the file path C:\Users\Username\Documents\Custom Office Templates.

   ✓ *Your file path may be different than the one given here; check with your teacher for the correct file path.*

2. Right-click the **W45TryA_xx** template file, and click Delete. If you see a message asking to confirm the deletion, click Yes.
3. Close File Explorer.
4. Start Word, if necessary, and open the **W45TryB_xx** file. Notice that the **W45TryB_xx** file still uses the styles from **W45TryA_xx** even though the template has been deleted.
5. Leave **W45TryB_xx** open to use in the next Try It.

Creating a Custom Theme

- A **theme** includes settings for fonts, colors, and effects.
- You can create and save a custom theme by selecting colors, fonts, and/or effects using the galleries accessed from the Document Formatting group on the Design tab of the ribbon.
- Word comes with built-in sets of theme colors, theme fonts, and theme effects.
- If you do not want to use a built-in theme, you can create and save your own.
- Word stores custom themes in the Document Themes folder.
- Word stores custom templates in the Custom Office Templates folder with the following file path: C:\Users\Username\Documents\Custom Office Templates.

✓ *Based on your computer's configuration, your file path may be different than the one given here.*

- A saved custom theme displays at the top of the Themes Gallery under the heading Custom.
- You can apply a custom theme to a document or a template.
- In addition to creating custom themes, you can create custom theme color sets and theme font sets.
- Click the Colors button on the Design tab and click Customize Colors to choose custom theme colors.
- Click the Fonts button on the Design tab and click Customize Fonts to choose custom theme fonts.

Try It! Creating a Custom Theme

1. In the **W45TryB_xx** file, click the Design tab, and click the Colors button to display a gallery of coordinated theme colors.
2. Click Red to apply that set of built-in colors.
3. On the Design tab, in the Document Formatting group, click the Fonts button to display a gallery of coordinated theme fonts.
4. Click Customize Fonts to display the Create New Theme Fonts dialog box.
5. Click the Heading font drop-down arrow, and click Arial.
6. Click the Body font drop-down arrow, and click Century.
7. Click in the Name text box, type **Theme Fonts 1**, and click Save.
8. Click the Effects button, and click Banded Edge.
9. Click the Themes button, and click Save Current Theme.
10. In the File name box, type **W45TryB**, and click Save.
11. Save and close **W45TryB_xx**.
12. Leave Word open to use in the next Try It.

Custom themes display at the top of the Themes gallery

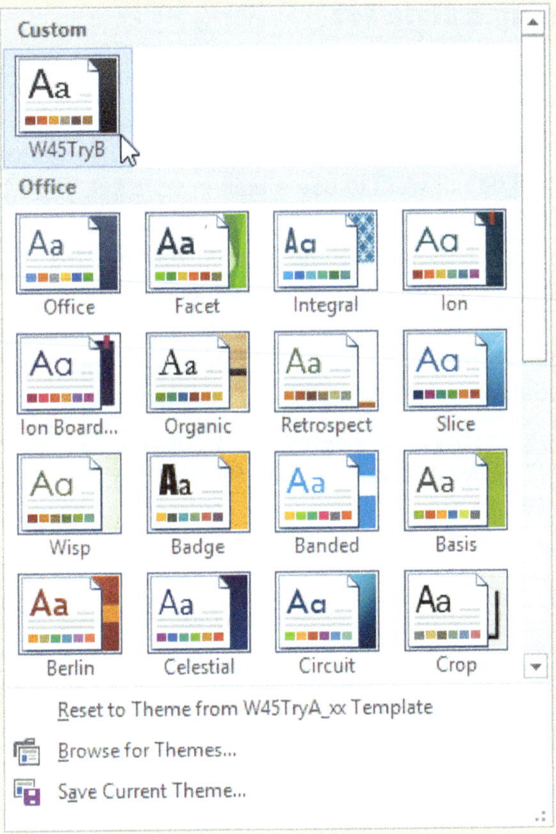

Applying, Resetting, and Deleting a Theme

- Most templates have a built-in, default theme. For example, the default theme for the Normal template is Office.
- You can reset, or restore, the default template theme, even if you apply a different theme, or a custom theme.
- You can delete a custom theme that you no longer need. Deleting a custom theme does not affect existing documents formatted with that theme.

Try It! Applying, Resetting, and Deleting a Theme

1. In Word, create a new blank document, and save it as **W45TryC_xx** in the location where your teacher instructs you to store the files for this lesson.
2. On the Design tab, click Themes to display the Themes gallery.
3. Under Custom, at the top of the gallery, click **W45TryB** to apply the theme to the template.
4. Type your full name, and format it with the Title style.
5. Save the changes to the **W45TryC_xx** file.
6. On the Design tab, click Themes, and click Reset to Theme from Template to restore the default Normal template theme.
7. Click Themes, right-click the **W45TryB** theme, click Delete on the shortcut menu, and click Yes in the confirmation dialog box.
8. Click Fonts.
9. Under Custom, right-click Theme Fonts 1, click Delete, and click Yes in the confirmation dialog box.
10. Save and close the file, and exit Word.

Creating a Style Set

- A **style set** includes settings for font and paragraph properties.
- Word comes with built-in style sets.
- If you do not want to use a built-in style set, you can create and save your own.
- You can access the Style Sets gallery from the Document Formatting group of the Design tab of the ribbon.
- You can modify a style in the document, and update the style using the Styles task pane.

✓ *Recall that you can access the Styles task pane from the Styles dialog box launcher in the Styles group on the Home tab.*

- Word stores a custom style set file as a template file in the QuickStyles folder with the following file path:

  C:\Users\Username\AppData\Roaming\Microsoft\QuickStyles

✓ *Based on your computer's configuration, your file path may be different than the one given here.*

- When you save a custom style set, you change the template file of the current document.
- A saved style set displays at the top of the Style Sets Gallery under the heading Custom.

Try It! Creating a Style Set

1. Start Word, and open **W45TryB_xx** from the location where your teacher instructs you to store the files for this lesson.
2. Select the text *Title*, and, on the Home tab, in the Paragraph group, click Center ≡.
3. Click the Styles dialog box launcher ↘ to display the Styles task pane.
4. In the Styles task pane, point to the style type indicator at the right end of the Title style. Notice that the style type indicator changes to a down arrow.
5. Click the down arrow of the Title style, and click Update Title to Match Selection.
6. Click the Design tab.
7. In the Document Formatting group, click the More button ▾ of the Style Sets gallery.
8. Click Save as a New Style Set.
9. In the File name box type **W45TryB_xx**, and click Save.
10. Close the **W45TryB_xx** file.
11. Leave Word open to use in the next Try It.

Custom style sets display at the top of the Style sets gallery

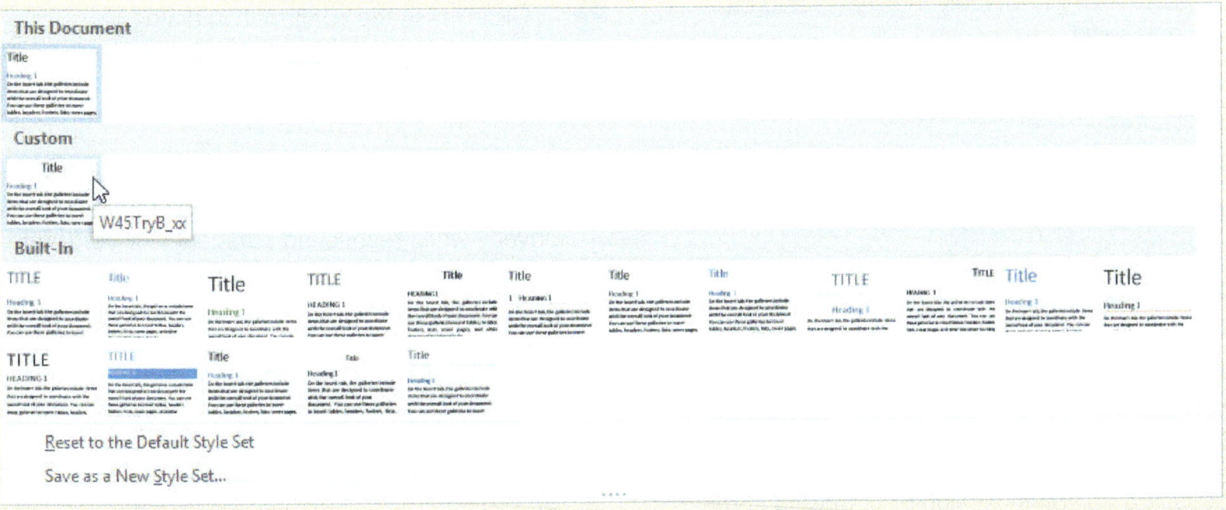

Word 2016, Windows 10, Microsoft Corporation

Applying, Resetting, and Deleting a Style Set

- Most templates have a built-in, default style set. For example, the default style set for the Normal template is Office.
- You can apply a style set to a document or a template.
- You can restore, or reset, the default template style set, even if you apply a different style set, or a custom style set.
- Reset a style set using the command on the More menu of the Style Sets gallery.
- Delete a style set by right-clicking the style set in the Style Set gallery, and selecting Delete.

Try It! Applying, Resetting, and Deleting a Style Set

1. Open the **W45TryC_xx** file, from the location where your teacher instructs you to store the files for this lesson.
2. On the Design tab, click the More button ▾ to display the Style Sets gallery.
3. Under Custom, at the top of the gallery, click **W45TryB_xx** to apply the style set to the document.
4. Click the More button ▾, and click Reset to the Default Style Set.
5. Save the changes to the **W45TryC_xx** file.
6. Click the More button ▾, and right-click the **W45TryB_xx** style set, click Delete on the shortcut menu.
7. Click Yes in the confirmation dialog box.
8. Save and close the file, and exit Word.

Demonstrating Professional Standards of Behavior

- Employees and employers should conduct themselves in a professional and **ethical** manner, with honesty and **integrity**, according to legal and corporate policies.
- Most companies and organizations establish an **acceptable use policy** (AUP) that specifies rules for using the corporate network or the Internet. Usually, a person must sign or otherwise agree to the policy before he or she is allowed access.
- Typically, an AUP describes the most important aspects of what a person may or may not do when using the network, and what the punishments for breaking the rules will be. For example, there may be rules for what data you can share between departments, or between the company and outside companies.
- Some rules that are typically found on an AUP cover issues such as the following:
  - Use of appropriate language while online.
  - Participation in illegal activities.
  - Disruption of others' work.
  - Release of personal information.
  - Dissemination of obscene or defamatory material.
  - Plagiarism and other copyright infringements.
- These policies address the legal and social aspects of computer use and are designed to protect privacy while respecting personal and corporate values and adhering to federal and local laws.
- As an employee of any company, you will also be expected to demonstrate a professional attitude by behaving in a way appropriate for your workplace; displaying a positive and productive work ethic; and complying with the rules, laws, and regulations that are applicable in your workplace.
- Professional behavior also includes demonstrating time-management skills by tending to goal-relevant activities in a way that uses time wisely and optimizes efficiency and results. This means setting priorities, focusing on the tasks for which you are responsible, and meeting deadlines. It also means arriving on time, leaving on time, and not using time at work for personal business.
- Time management techniques include figuring out exactly how you currently spend your time, creating a schedule, making to-do lists, and ranking list items in order of importance. You can use technology tools, such as calendar programs, tasks and to-do lists, and Microsoft Office applications to automate many time-management tasks in order to optimize your efficiency and results.

Lesson 45—Practice

The Horticultural Shop Owner's Association is running a two-day conference. As the organization's secretary, you must prepare the **agenda**. In this project, you will create a custom theme and a custom style set, and use them to format the agenda for the first day. You will also practice deleting a custom theme and a custom style set.

DIRECTIONS

1. Start Word, if necessary, click **Blank document**, and save as **W45Practice_xx** in the location where your teacher instructs you to store the files for this lesson.
2. Apply the **Basic (Elegant)** style set.
3. On the first line of the document apply the **Title** style, and type **Agenda**.
4. Press ENTER, apply the **Heading 1** style, and type **Horticultural Shop Owner's Association, Day One**.
5. Press ENTER, apply the **No Spacing** style, and apply the **Strong** style.
6. Type today's date, press ENTER, and type **9:00 a.m. to 5:00 p.m.**
7. Click **Layout**, set the spacing after to **54 pt**, and press ENTER.
8. Apply the **No Spacing** style.
9. Insert a table with five rows and three columns, and enter the following data (refer to Figure 45-1):
10. Click in the table > **Table Tools Design** > **Table Styles More**.
11. Click the **Grid Table 2 - Accent 2** style.
12. Click to clear the **Header Row** check box.
13. Set the horizontal alignment for column 3 to **Right**.
14. Reposition the insertion point to the line below the table, and press ENTER.
15. Apply the Normal style, type **For more information, contact:**, press ENTER, and type your full name.
16. Save the document.
17. Click **Design** > **Colors** > **Blue Green**.
18. Click **Fonts** > **Arial**.
19. Click **Themes** > **Save Current Theme**.
20. In the File name box, type **W45Practice**, and click **Save**.
21. Select the text **Agenda**, and change the font size to **28 pt**.
22. Click the **Styles dialog box launcher** to display the **Styles** task pane.

9:00 a.m. – 10:00 a.m.	Introduction Continental Breakfast Welcome Speaker: James Keefe, President	River View Room
10:00 a.m. – Noon	Session 1 Marketing Expanding	Conference Room A Conference Room B
Noon – 1:00 p.m.	Lunch	River View Room
1:00 p.m. – 3:00 p.m.	Session 2 Recordkeeping Legal Issues	Conference Room A Conference Room B
3:00 p.m. – 5:00 p.m.	Demonstrations Wedding Arrangements Valentine's Day Bouquets	Conference Room A Conference Room B

23. Update the Title style to match the selection, and close the **Styles** task pane.
24. On the Design tab, click the **More** button of the Style Sets gallery, and click **Save as a New Style Set**.
25. In the File name box, type **W45Practice**, and click **Save**.
26. Check and correct the spelling and grammar in the document, and save the document.
27. **With your teacher's permission,** print the document.
28. On the Design tab, click **Themes** > **Reset to Theme from Template**. The agenda should look similar to Figure 45-1.
29. Click **More** > **Reset to the Default Style Set.**
30. Delete the **W45Practice** custom theme.
31. Delete the **W45Practice** custom style set.
32. Save and close the document, and exit Word.

Figure 45-1

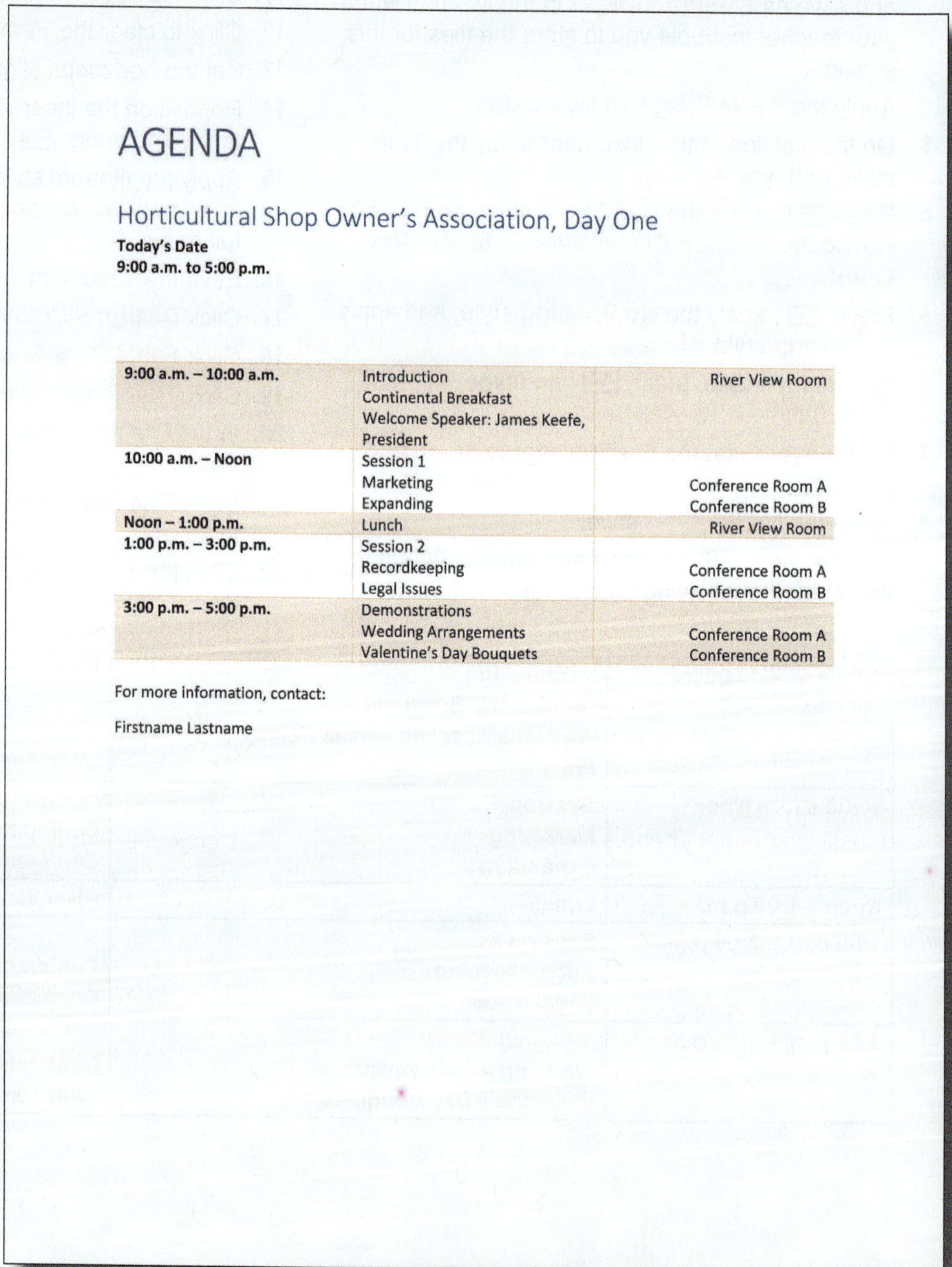

AGENDA

Horticultural Shop Owner's Association, Day One

Today's Date
9:00 a.m. to 5:00 p.m.

9:00 a.m. – 10:00 a.m.	Introduction Continental Breakfast Welcome Speaker: James Keefe, President	River View Room
10:00 a.m. – Noon	Session 1 Marketing Expanding	 Conference Room A Conference Room B
Noon – 1:00 p.m.	Lunch	River View Room
1:00 p.m. – 3:00 p.m.	Session 2 Recordkeeping Legal Issues	 Conference Room A Conference Room B
3:00 p.m. – 5:00 p.m.	Demonstrations Wedding Arrangements Valentine's Day Bouquets	 Conference Room A Conference Room B

For more information, contact:

Firstname Lastname

Word 2016, Windows 10, Microsoft Corporation

Lesson 45—Apply

As the secretary of the Horticultural Shop Owner's Association, you must prepare the agenda for a two-day conference. In this project, you will create a custom template with a custom theme and a custom style set. You will create a new document from the custom template, and complete the agenda for the second day.

DIRECTIONS

1. Start Word, if necessary, and open **W45Apply** from the data files for this lesson.
2. Save the file as a Word Template named **W45Apply_xx** in the default Custom Office Templates folder.
3. Apply the **Basic (Stylish)** style set to the document.
4. Format line 1 with the **Title** style.
5. Format line 2 with the **Heading 1** style, underline the text, and update the style to match the selection.
6. Save the custom style set as **W45Apply** in the default QuickStyles folder.
7. Replace the word *One* with the word **Two**.
8. Replace the text *Today's Date* with today's date and *Student's Name* with your own name.
9. Format lines 3 and 4 with the **No Spacing** style and the **Strong** style.
10. Set the spacing after line 4 to **54 pt**.
11. Select the table. On the Table Tools Design tab, click to clear the **Header Row** check box.
12. Apply the **Grid Table 2 - Accent 6** table style to the table.
13. Change the Fonts to **Cambria**.
14. Save the custom theme as **W45Apply** in the default Document Themes folder.
15. Save and close the template. Leave Word open.
16. Create a new document based on the **W45Apply_xx** template, and save as **W45Apply_xx** in the location where your teacher instructs you to store the files for this lesson.
17. Edit the time from *5:00 p.m.* to **4:00 p.m.**
18. Replace the data in the table with the data in the table at the top of the next page.
19. Check and correct the spelling and grammar in the document, and save the document.
20. **With your teacher's permission,** print the document. It should look similar to Figure 45-2 on the next page.
21. Close the **W45Apply_xx** document, and leave Word open.
22. **With your teacher's permission**, conduct research on the Internet to learn about professional standards of behavior for office workers. Include in your research standard policies for ethical treatment of clients and work colleagues; acceptable use policies for corporate workplaces; rules governing legal and social aspects of computer use and adherence to federal and local laws; and professional attitudes such as appropriate behavior for an office workplace, demonstrating a positive and productive work ethic, and use of time management skills to accomplish tasks in a timely and efficient manner.
23. Create a one-page document to record your results, and format it using the **W45Apply** theme and style set.
24. Save the document as directed and follow your teacher's instructions for printing. Then close the document.
25. Open a new, blank document.
26. Delete the **W45Apply** custom theme.
27. Delete the **W45Apply** custom style set.
28. Use File Explorer to browse to the **W45Apply_xx** template file, and delete it.

   ✓ *The default file path is C:\Users\Username\Documents\Custom Office Templates. Check with your teacher for the correct file path.*

29. Close File Explorer, and exit Word.

9:00 a.m. – 10:00 a.m.	State of the Association Continental Breakfast Speaker: Stephanie Moore, Treasurer	River View Room
10:00 a.m. – Noon	Keynote Address Maryellen Rubinsky, Author	Jewel Room
Noon – 1:00 p.m.	Lunch	River View Room
1:00 p.m. – 3:00 p.m.	Workshops Holiday Arrangements Living Wreaths	Conference Room A Conference Room B
3:00 p.m. – 4:00 p.m.	Farewell Reception	River View Room

Figure 45-2

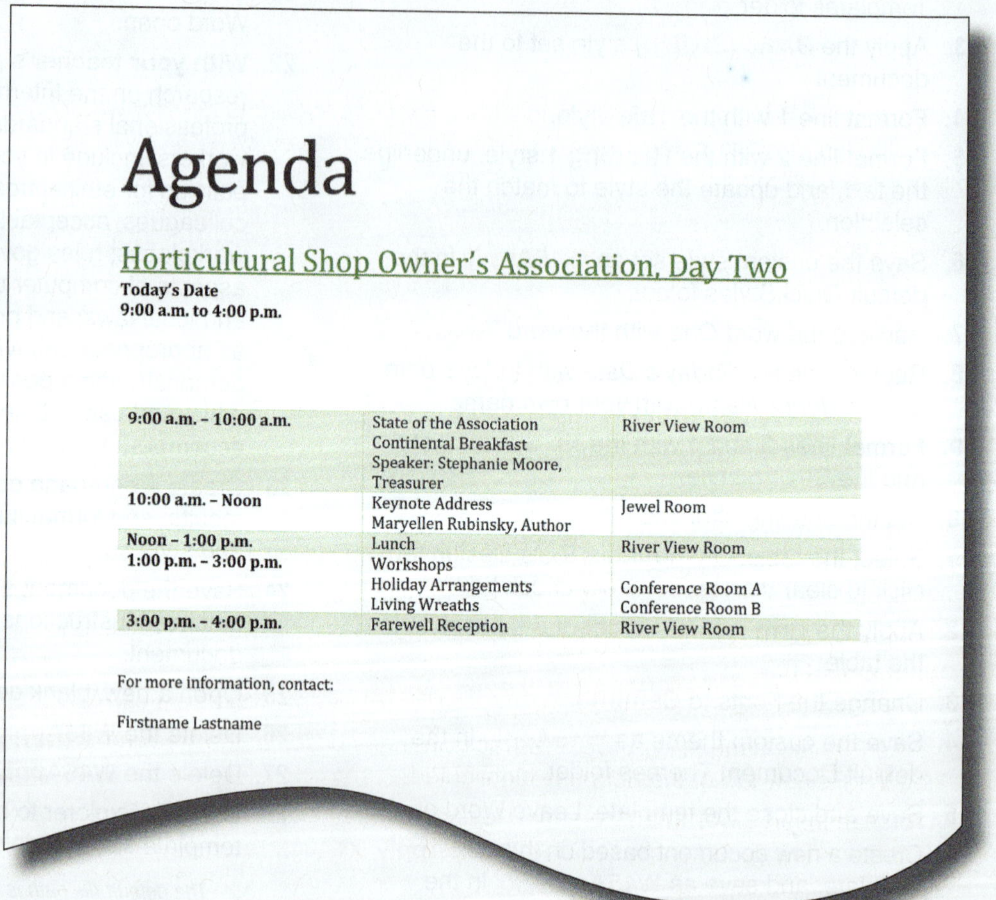

Agenda

Horticultural Shop Owner's Association, Day Two

Today's Date
9:00 a.m. to 4:00 p.m.

9:00 a.m. – 10:00 a.m.	State of the Association Continental Breakfast Speaker: Stephanie Moore, Treasurer	River View Room
10:00 a.m. – Noon	Keynote Address Maryellen Rubinsky, Author	Jewel Room
Noon – 1:00 p.m.	Lunch	River View Room
1:00 p.m. – 3:00 p.m.	Workshops Holiday Arrangements Living Wreaths	Conference Room A Conference Room B
3:00 p.m. – 4:00 p.m.	Farewell Reception	River View Room

For more information, contact:

Firstname Lastname

Lesson 46

Tracking Changes

➤ What You Will Learn

Tracking Changes
Customizing Revision Marks
Accepting and Rejecting Changes

Software Skills You can use Word's track changes feature to monitor when and how edits are made to a document. Tracking changes lets you consider revisions before incorporating them into a document. If you agree with a change, you can accept it, but if you disagree with a change, you can reject it. You can track changes made by one person or by many people, which is useful when you are collaborating on a document with others.

WORDS TO KNOW

Comment
A note attached to a document for reference.

Ink annotations
Comments, notes, and other marks added to a document using a tablet PC or other type of pen device.

Revision marks
Formatting applied to text in a document to identify where insertions, deletions, and formatting changes have been made.

What You Can Do

Tracking Changes

- Turn on Word's Track Changes feature to apply **revision marks** to all insertions, deletions, formatting changes, and **ink annotations** in a document.

  ✓ *You can only add ink annotations on a tablet PC.*

- The commands for tracking changes are in the Tracking group on the Review tab of the ribbon.
- The Track Changes feature is a toggle; it remains on until you turn it off.
- When Track Changes is active, the Track Changes button in the Tracking group on the Review tab of the ribbon is highlighted.
- You can insert a **comment** to annotate text, communicate with readers, or to attach reminders or questions to a document.

  ✓ *You learned about using comments in Lesson 32.*

- By default, Word inserts a vertical line in the left margin of any changed line to indicate where revisions occur in the document.
- You can click the vertical line to toggle the display of the change on and off. The vertical line displays as red when you click it, or when you are in Simple Markup view.
- The way that revisions are marked onscreen depends on the selected Display for Review and Show Markup options.
- You can use the Display for Review options to control how insertions, deletions, and formatting changes display in a document.

- The Display for Review button provides four options:
  - Simple Markup displays the document with a red vertical line in the left margin of a line with a revision. Insertions, deletions, comments, and formatting changes display as they would look in the final document if the changes are accepted. This is the default option.
  - All Markup displays the document with all insertions, deletions, and comments marked. Formatting changes display as they look in the final document if the changes are accepted.
  - No Markup displays the document as it would look if all revisions are accepted.
  - Original displays the document as it would look if all revisions are rejected.
- Revisions are color coded by reviewer.
- You can view descriptions of all revisions in the Reviewing Pane.
- You can view a deletion by resting the mouse pointer on the revision to display a ScreenTip.
- You can select Track Changes > Lock Tracking to assign a password so that others reviewing a document cannot turn off the Track Changes feature.

Try It! Tracking Changes

1. Start Word, and open **W46Try** from the data files for this lesson.
2. Save the file as **W46Try_xx** in the location where your teacher instructs you to store the files for this lesson.
3. Click the Review tab, and click the Track Changes button.
4. Click the Display for Review drop-down arrow Simple Markup, and click Simple Markup, if necessary.
5. Double-click the word *outstanding* in the first paragraph, and press DEL.
6. Click the red vertical line in the left margin of the line you changed. Word displays the deleted text in red, with a strikethrough.
7. Click the vertical line again to display the change as it would look if you accepted the change.
8. Position the insertion point after the word *personal* in the first paragraph, and type **, physical,**. Word displays the change with another red vertical line in the left margin.
9. Double-click the word *harmony* at the end of the first paragraph, and click Home > Italic. Notice that Word displays the change as it would look if you accepted the change.
10. Click the Review tab, click the Display for Review drop-down arrow, and click All Markup to display all of the changes.
11. Click the Display for Review drop-down arrow, and click Original to display the document without changes.
12. Click the Display for Review drop-down arrow, and click No Markup.
13. Click the Reviewing Pane drop-down arrow, and click Reviewing Pane Vertical to display the Reviewing Pane. Notice that Word displays all changes, including the formatting change in the Reviewing Pane.
14. Click the Display for Review drop-down arrow, and click All Markup.
15. Save the changes to **W46Try_xx**, and leave it open to use in the next Try It.

Using revision marks to track changes

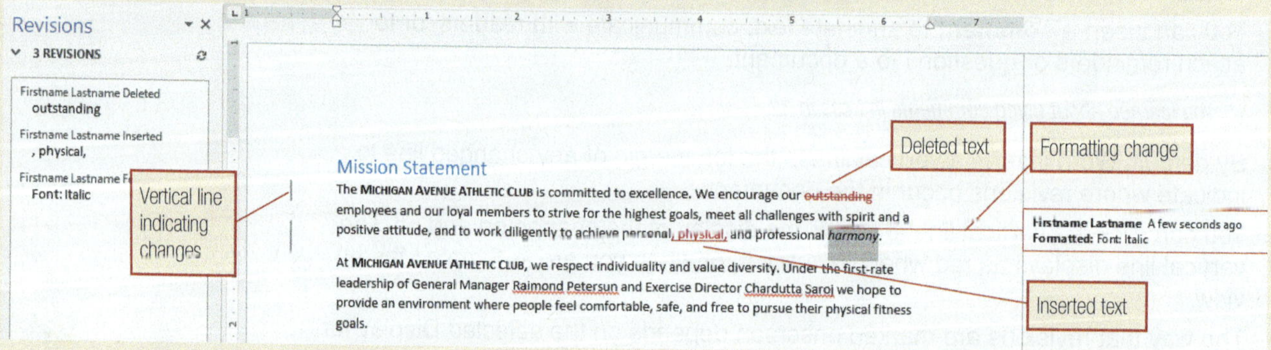

Word 2016, Windows 10, Microsoft Corporation

Customizing Revision Marks

- You can customize revision marks using options in the Track Changes Options dialog box.
- For example, you can select the formatting used to indicate changes. You can mark formatting changes with a double-underline, or insertions with color only instead of color and an underline.
- You can select the colors you want to use to mark changes.
- You can customize the location and color of the vertical bar used to mark changes.
- You can also customize the way balloons are displayed in a document.
- From the Show Markup drop-down menu, you can select which changes you want displayed onscreen. For example, you can display insertions and deletions, but not formatting.
- You can set Word to show only the changes made by one reviewer at a time.

Try It! Customizing Revision Marks

1. In the **W46Try_xx** document, on the Review tab, click the Show Markup button, and click to uncheck the Formatting option. Word hides the formatting revision marks.
2. Click the Show Markup button, click Balloons, and click Show Revisions in Balloons. Word displays the deletion revision marks in balloons.

   ✓ *When you display the All Markup Display for Review option, insertion revision marks display in balloons.*
3. Click Show Markup > Balloons > Show All Revisions Inline.
4. Click Show Markup > Formatting to display formatting revisions again.
5. Click Show Markup > Balloons > Show Only Comments and Formatting in Balloons.
6. Click the Track Changes dialog box launcher to display the Track Changes Options dialog box.
7. Click Advanced Options to display the Advanced Track Changes Options dialog box.
8. Click the Insertions drop-down arrow and click Color only, then click the Insertions Color drop-down arrow and click Blue.
9. Click the Deletions drop-down arrow and click Double strikethrough, then click the Deletions Color drop-down arrow and click Bright Green.
10. Click to clear the Show lines connecting to text check box, and click OK to apply the changes and close the dialog box. Notice the changes onscreen.
11. In the Track Changes Options dialog box, click Advanced Options to open the Advanced Track Changes Options dialog box.
12. Click the Insertions drop-down arrow and click Underline, then click the Insertions Color drop-down arrow and click By author.
13. Click the Deletions drop-down arrow and click Strikethrough, then click the Deletions Color drop-down arrow and click By author.
14. Click to select the Show lines connecting to text check box, and click OK to close the Advanced Track Changes Options dialog box.
15. Click OK to close the Track Changes Options dialog box.
16. Save the changes to **W46Try_xx**, and leave it open to use in the next Try It.

(continued)

Try It! Customizing Revision Marks *(continued)*

Tracked changes in the Reviewing pane

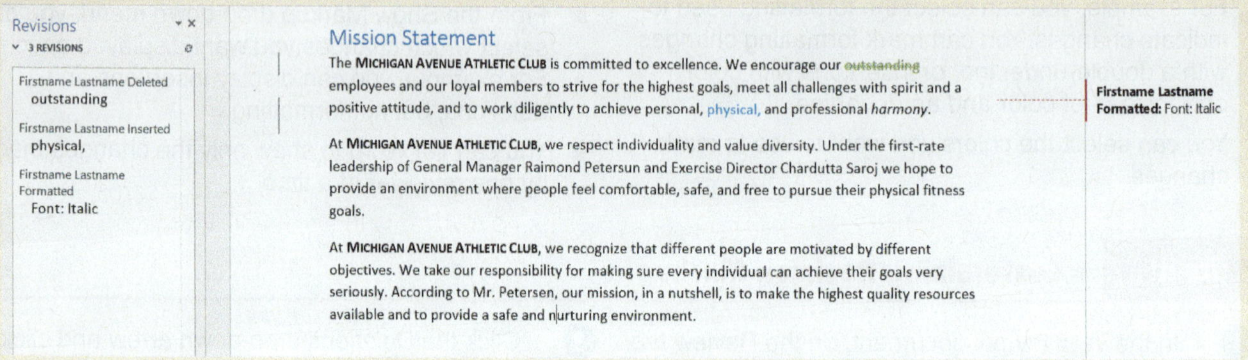

Word 2016, Windows 10, Microsoft Corporation

Accepting and Rejecting Changes

- Revision marks remain stored as part of a document until the changes are either accepted or rejected.
- The commands for accepting, rejecting, and navigating to changes are in the Changes group on the Review tab of the ribbon.
- To incorporate edits into a document file, accept the changes.
- To cancel the edits and erase them from the file, reject the changes.
- You can navigate to a previous change or the next change.
- You also can display only changes made by specific reviewers and then accept or reject all changes currently shown in the document.
- To finalize all changes in a document, you can accept all changes and stop tracking.
- When you accept all changes in a document, you must review and address comments separately.
- You can manage comments similar to the way you navigate to and delete changes.

Try It! Accepting and Rejecting Changes

1. In the **W46Try_xx** document, press CTRL + HOME to move the insertion point to the beginning of the document.
2. On the Review tab, in the Changes group, click the Next Change button to move to the next marked change.
3. Click the Next Change button again.
4. Click the Reject drop-down arrow Reject, and click Reject and Move to Next.

   ✓ *You can also right-click the revision marks and click Reject Insertion, or simply click the Reject button.*
5. In the Changes group, click the Previous Change button.
6. Click the Accept drop-down arrow Accept, and click Accept This Change.

   ✓ *You can also right-click the revision marks and click Accept Deletion, or click the Accept button.*
7. Click the Undo button on the Quick Access Toolbar, click the Accept drop-down arrow Accept, and click Accept All Changes and Stop Tracking.
8. Close the Revisions task pane.
9. Save and close the file, and exit Word.

Lesson 46—Practice

The Director of Training at Restoration Architecture has asked you to review a document listing in-house training courses. In this project, you will use the Track Changes feature while you review and edit the document. You will then update the document by accepting or rejecting the changes.

DIRECTIONS

1. Start Word, if necessary, and open **W46Practice** from the data files for this lesson.
2. Save the document as **W46Practice_xx** in the location where your teacher instructs you to store the files for this lesson.
3. Double-click in the header, and type your full name and today's date. Click **Close Header and Footer**.
4. Click **Review** > **Track Changes** to turn on the track changes feature. Click the **Display for Review** drop-down arrow > **Simple Markup**, if necessary.
5. Click the **Track Changes dialog box launcher**, and click **Advanced Options**.
6. Click the **Insertions** drop-down arrow and click **Bold**, then click the **Insertions Color** drop-down arrow and click **Red**.
7. Click the **Deletions Color** drop-down arrow, and click **Blue**.
8. Click the **Margin** drop-down arrow, and click **Left**.
9. Click **OK** > **OK** to apply the changes and close the dialog boxes.
10. Click the Display for Review drop-down arrow, and click All Markup.
11. On the Review tab, in the Tracking group, click **Show Markup** > **Balloons** > **Show Revisions in Balloons**.
12. In the document, on the address line, select one of the diamond symbols, and click **Home** > **Copy** to copy it to the Clipboard.
13. Position the insertion point at the end of the address line, press SPACE, click **Home** > **Paste**, press SPACE, and type **www.rarc.net**.
14. Select the entire address line and decrease the font size to **10 pt**.
15. In the description of the Microsoft Word 1 course, select the text *will cover*, and type **covers**.
16. In the same sentence, select the text *2013* and type **2016**.
17. In the description of the Microsoft Word 2 course, select the text *2013*, and type **2016.** Apply the same change in the description of the Microsoft Word 3 course.
18. At the end of the description of the Microsoft Word 3 course, type the following sentence: **Open only to those who have completed the Word 1 and Word 2 courses.**
19. Select the last line in the document, and remove the italic formatting. Your document should look similar to Figure 46-1 on the next page.
20. Click **File** > **Print** to display the Print tab in the Backstage view.
21. Click the **Print All Pages** drop-down arrow, and check that **Print Markup** is selected.
22. **With your teacher's permission,** print the document with the markup.
23. Press CTRL + HOME to move the insertion point to the beginning of the document.
24. Click **Review** > **Next Change**.
25. Click **Reject** to reject the formatting change and move to the next change.
26. Click **Reject** multiple times as necessary, to reject the remaining formatting changes to the address line and the insertion of the Internet address and move to the next change.
27. Click **Reject** twice to reject the change to *will cover*.
28. On the Review tab, in the Tracking group, click **Show Markup** > **Balloons** > **Show Only Comments and Formatting in Balloons**.
29. Click the **Accept** drop-down arrow Accept > **Accept All Changes and Stop Tracking**.
30. Check and correct the spelling and grammar in the document, and save the document.
31. **With your teacher's permission,** print the document.
32. Save and close the document, and exit Word.

Figure 46-1

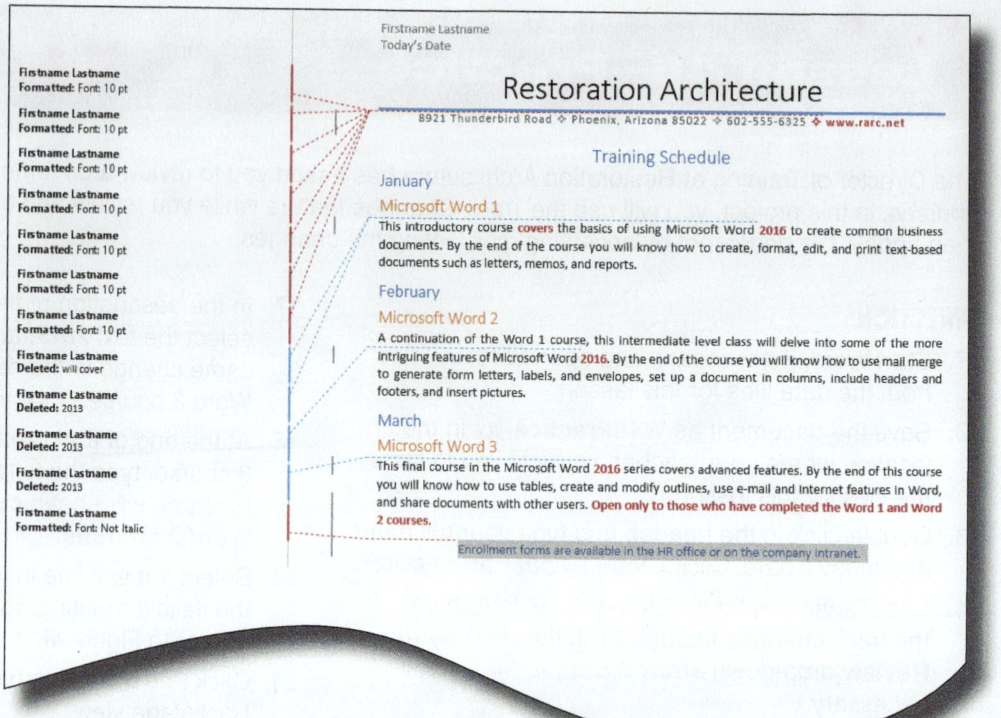

Word 2016, Windows 10, Microsoft Corporation

Lesson 46—Apply

The Director of Training at Restoration Architecture has asked you to update another version of the in-house training document you previously revised. In this project, you will use the Track Changes feature while you review and edit the document. You will then update the document by accepting or rejecting the changes.

DIRECTIONS

1. Start Word, if necessary, and open **W46Apply** from the data files for this lesson.
2. Save the file as **W46Apply_xx** in the location where your teacher instructs you to store the files for this lesson.
3. Type your full name and today's date in the document header. Click **Close Header and Footer**.
4. Turn on the Track Changes feature, and set tracking options to display insertions underlined in pink and deletions with a strikethrough in bright green. Display balloons in the markup area along the right margin of the page.
5. Show only comments and formatting in balloons, and set the display for review to **Simple Markup**.
6. Change the font of the address and phone number line to **Times New Roman**.
7. Replace the text *January* with **June**, *February* with **July**, and *March* with **August**.
8. Add the following sentence to the end of the Microsoft Word 2 course description: **If there is enough time, the course will also include basic desktop publishing concepts.**
9. Display the Reviewing pane vertically.
10. **With your teacher's permission,** print the document with the markup. It should look similar to Figure 46-2 on the next page.

11. Change the display for review to **All Markup**.
12. Accept the formatting changes in the document.
13. Accept the changes to the names of the months.
14. Reject all remaining changes in the document, and turn off the Track Changes feature.
15. Close the Reviewing Pane.
16. Set the insertion and deletion colors to **By author**.
17. Check and correct the spelling and grammar in the document, and save the document.
18. **With your teacher's permission,** print the document.
19. Save and close the document, and exit Word.

Figure 46-2

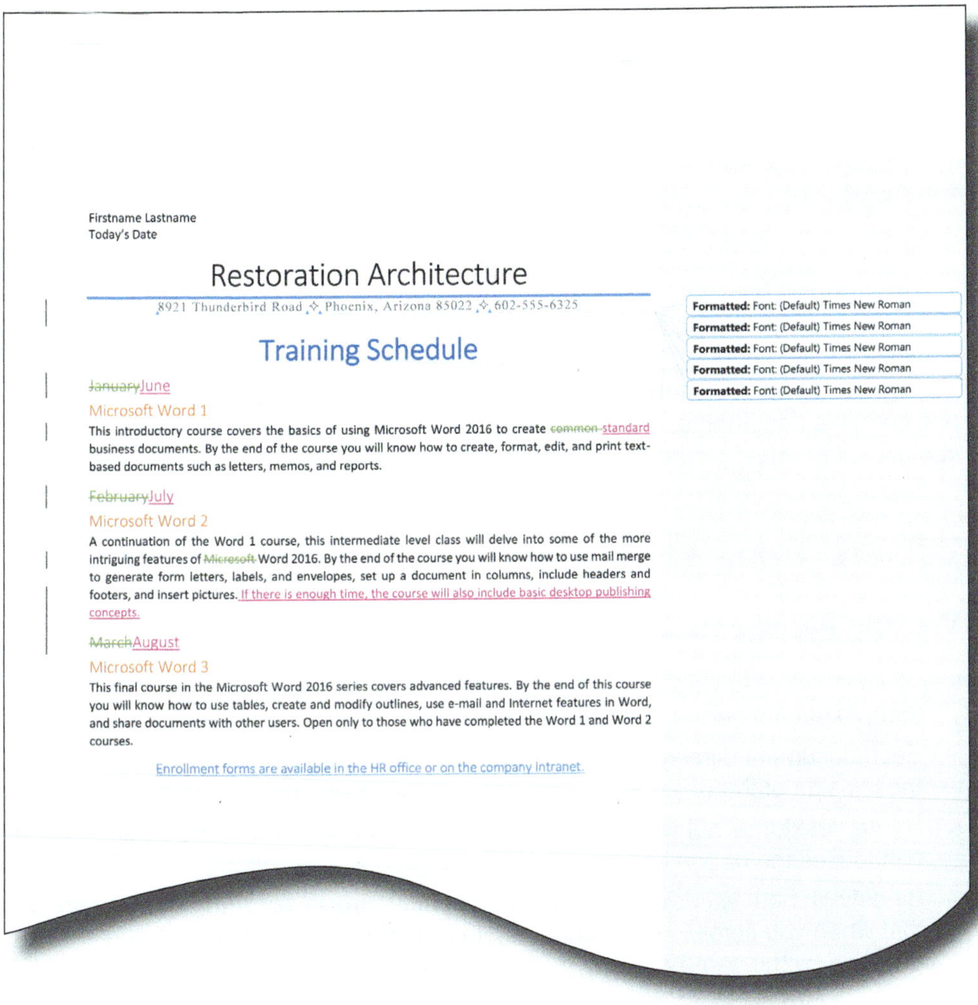
Firstname Lastname
Today's Date

Restoration Architecture

8921 Thunderbird Road ✧ Phoenix, Arizona 85022 ✧ 602-555-6325

Training Schedule

~~January~~June

Microsoft Word 1

This introductory course covers the basics of using Microsoft Word 2016 to create ~~common~~ standard business documents. By the end of the course you will know how to create, format, edit, and print text-based documents such as letters, memos, and reports.

~~February~~July

Microsoft Word 2

A continuation of the Word 1 course, this intermediate level class will delve into some of the more intriguing features of ~~Microsoft~~ Word 2016. By the end of the course you will know how to use mail merge to generate form letters, labels, and envelopes, set up a document in columns, include headers and footers, and insert pictures. If there is enough time, the course will also include basic desktop publishing concepts.

~~March~~August

Microsoft Word 3

This final course in the Microsoft Word 2016 series covers advanced features. By the end of this course you will know how to use tables, create and modify outlines, use e-mail and Internet features in Word, and share documents with other users. Open only to those who have completed the Word 1 and Word 2 courses.

Enrollment forms are available in the HR office or on the company intranet.

Formatted: Font: (Default) Times New Roman
Formatted: Font: (Default) Times New Roman
Formatted: Font: (Default) Times New Roman
Formatted: Font: (Default) Times New Roman
Formatted: Font: (Default) Times New Roman

Lesson 47

Comparing Documents

➤ What You Will Learn

Viewing Documents Side by Side
Managing Document Versions
Comparing Documents
Combining Documents

WORDS TO KNOW

Independent scrolling
The ability to scroll a window without affecting the display in other open windows.

Synchronous scrolling
A feature that links the scroll bars in two windows so that when you scroll in one window the other window scrolls as well.

Software Skills View documents side by side to compare the differences between similar versions. You can recover or delete document versions using the Manage Documents button on the Info tab in Backstage view. When you compare and combine documents, differences between the two are marked as revisions. You can accept or reject changes to incorporate revisions.

What You Can Do

Viewing Documents Side by Side

- You can select to view two open documents side by side so you can compare them to each other.
- Each document displays in a separate window; the active document displays on the left side of the desktop and the second document displays on the right.
- If your desktop is not wide enough when viewing documents side by side, Word condenses the ribbon commands for some groups into buttons.
- By default, both windows are set to use **synchronous scrolling**, which means that when you scroll in one document, the other document scrolls in the same direction by the same amount.
- You can turn off synchronous scrolling to use **independent scrolling**.
- Changes you make to the view in one window affect the other window as well.
  - For example, if you zoom in on one document, the other document zooms in by the same amount.
- The View Side by Side and Synchronous Scrolling commands are located in the Window group on the View tab of the ribbon.
- You can only view two documents side by side at a time. If more than two documents are open in Word when you select the View Side by Side command, the Compare Side by Side dialog box displays so you can select the second document to view.

Try It! Viewing Documents Side by Side

1. Start Word, and open **W47TryA** from the data files for this lesson.
2. Save the file as **W47TryA_xx** in the location where your teacher instructs you to store the files for this lesson.
3. Open **W47TryB** from the data files for this lesson.
4. Save the file as **W47TryB_xx** in the location where your teacher instructs you to store the files for this lesson.
5. Click the View tab.
6. In the Window group, click the View Side by Side button. Word arranges the document windows side by side, and turns synchronous scrolling on.
7. In the **W47TryA_xx** document window on the right side of the screen, click the scroll down arrow three times. Notice that the other document scrolls down as well.
8. Press CTRL + END. Both documents scroll down to the end of the document.
9. Click in the **W47TryB_xx** window, and click the Zoom In button on the status bar. Notice that the other document zooms in as well.
10. In the **W47TryB_xx** window, on the View tab, click the Synchronous Scrolling button to toggle the feature off.
11. Press CTRL + HOME. Only the active document scrolls.
12. In the **W47TryB_xx** window, on the View tab, click the View Side by Side button. Both windows are restored; the active window displays on top.
13. Close both **W47TryB_xx** and **W47TryA_xx**, and leave Word open to use in the next Try It.

View documents side by side with synchronous scrolling

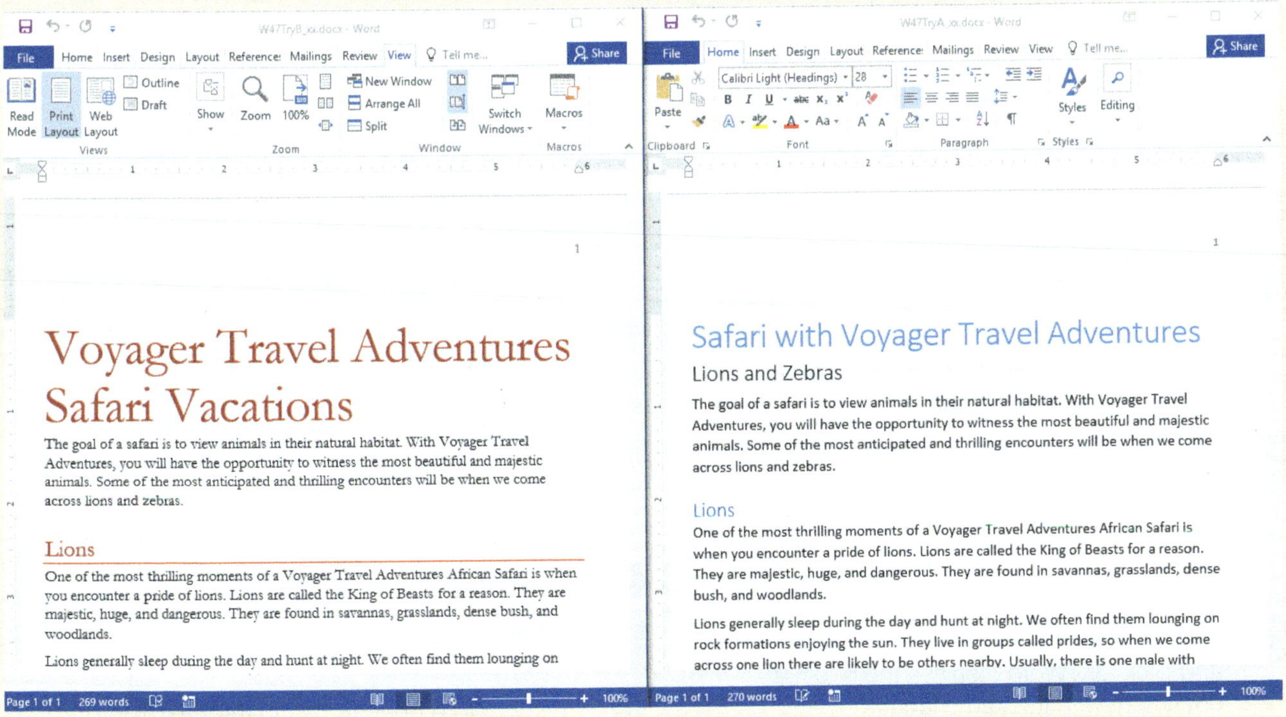

Word 2016, Windows 10, Microsoft Corporation

Managing Document Versions

- Word can automatically save versions of your document as you work on it when the AutoRecover option is enabled on the Save tab in the Word Options dialog box.
- Use the Manage Document button on the Info tab in Backstage view to access commands that allow you to recover or delete unsaved documents.
- To recover a file that you didn't previously save, click File > Info > Manage Document > Recover Unsaved Documents. Select the file you want to recover and then click Open. Click the Save As button to save the file.
- To recover an earlier version of a Word document if you've saved the file, click File > Info > Manage Document and then click the file labeled *(when I closed without saving)*. Then click Restore to overwrite previously unsaved versions or click Compare to compare the file versions.
- To delete all recent copies of unsaved files, click File > Info > Manage Document > Delete All Unsaved Documents.
- You can change the frequency used by Word to save AutoRecover data. On the Save tab of the Word Options dialog box, adjust the setting in the minutes box. The default setting is to save every 10 minutes.

Comparing Documents

- You can compare two documents to mark the differences between them.
- To compare documents, you select the original document and the revised document; Word displays the original document with revision marks showing the differences between the two.
- You can choose to show the original document with tracked changes, the revised document with tracked changes, or both. Word creates a new document named Compare Result 1 and uses revision marks to indicate the differences between the original and revised documents.
- If you show both, Word displays all three documents onscreen, along with the Reviewing pane.
- By default, the user name of the author of the revised document is used to mark the revisions, but you can use different initials or text.
- Comparing documents is useful if you have more than one version of a document and need to see what changes have been made, or if someone has edited a document without using track changes.
- You can also select the types of differences to compare. For example, you can choose to compare formatting, but not headers and footers.

Try It! Comparing Documents

1. In Word, click the Review tab, click the Compare button, and click Compare.
2. Click the Original document drop-down arrow and click **W47TryA_xx**.

   ✓ *If the document you want is not listed, click the Browse button and navigate to locate it.*
3. Click the Revised document drop-down arrow and click **W47TryB_xx**.
4. Under the Revised document box, click in the Label changes with box, and type your full name.
5. Click the More button to view additional options, and click OK. Word displays the original document with tracked changes.
6. Click the Compare button, click Show Source Documents, and click Show Both. Word displays all three documents and the Reviewing pane.
7. Click the Close button in the Original document, and click the Close button in the Revised document. Only the Compare Result 1 document remains open, with the Reviewing pane displayed.
8. Click the Accept drop-down arrow, and click Accept All Changes and Stop Tracking.
9. Close the Revisions task pane.
10. Save the document as **W47TryC_xx**, and close it.
11. Leave Word open to use in the next Try It.

(continued)

Try It! Comparing Documents *(continued)*

Compare differences between two documents

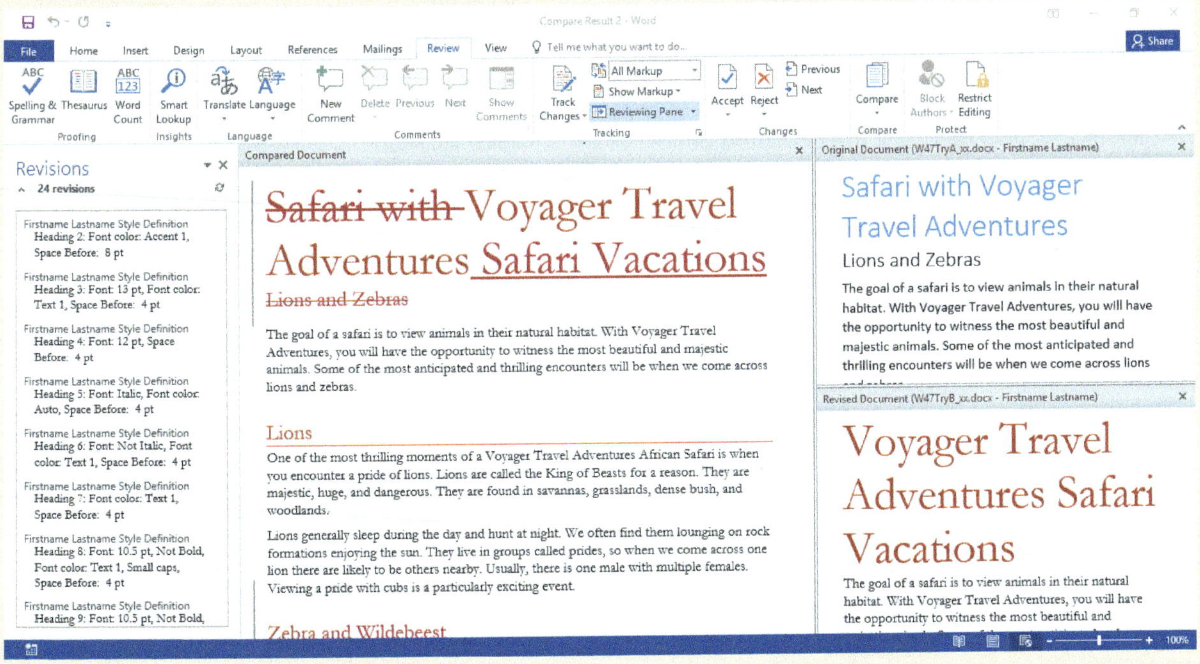

Word 2016, Windows 10, Microsoft Corporation

Combining Documents

- Use the Combine feature to combine revisions made by more than one reviewer into a single document.
- Word merges the two documents into a final document.
- Word can only store one set of formatting changes in the final document. If necessary, it prompts you to select which formatting changes to keep.
- By default, Word marks the changes made in the combined document with the user name of the document author.
- You can manage draft versions of the documents by changing the names of the document authors.

Try It! Combining Documents

1. In Word, open **W47TryD** from the data files for this lesson, save it as **W47TryD_xx** in the location where your teacher instructs you to store the files for this lesson, and close it. Leave Word open.
2. Click the Review tab, click the Compare button, and click Combine.
3. Click the Original document drop-down arrow, and click **W47TryC_xx**.

   ✓ *If the document you want is not listed, click the Browse button and navigate to locate it.*
4. Your name should display in the Label unmarked changes with box for the original document. If not, click in the box, and type your full name.
5. Click the Revised document drop-down arrow, and click **W47TryD_xx**.
6. Click in the Label unmarked changes with box for the revised document, and type **Reviewer Two**.
7. Click the Less button to hide the options, and click OK. Word displays the final document with revisions marked.
8. On the Review tab, in the Tracking group, click the Display for Review drop-down arrow, and click All Markup, if necessary.
9. On the Review tab, in the Tracking group, click the Show Markup button, and click Formatting to deselect it.
10. Click the Compare button, click Show Source Documents, and click Show Both. Word displays all three documents and the Reviewing pane. The marked changes indicate the changes made by Reviewer Two in the combined document.
11. Click the Accept drop-down arrow, and click Accept All Changes.
12. Click the Reviewing Pane button to close the Revisions task pane.
13. Save the document as **W47TryE_xx**, and close the document.
14. Exit Word.

Combine two versions of a document

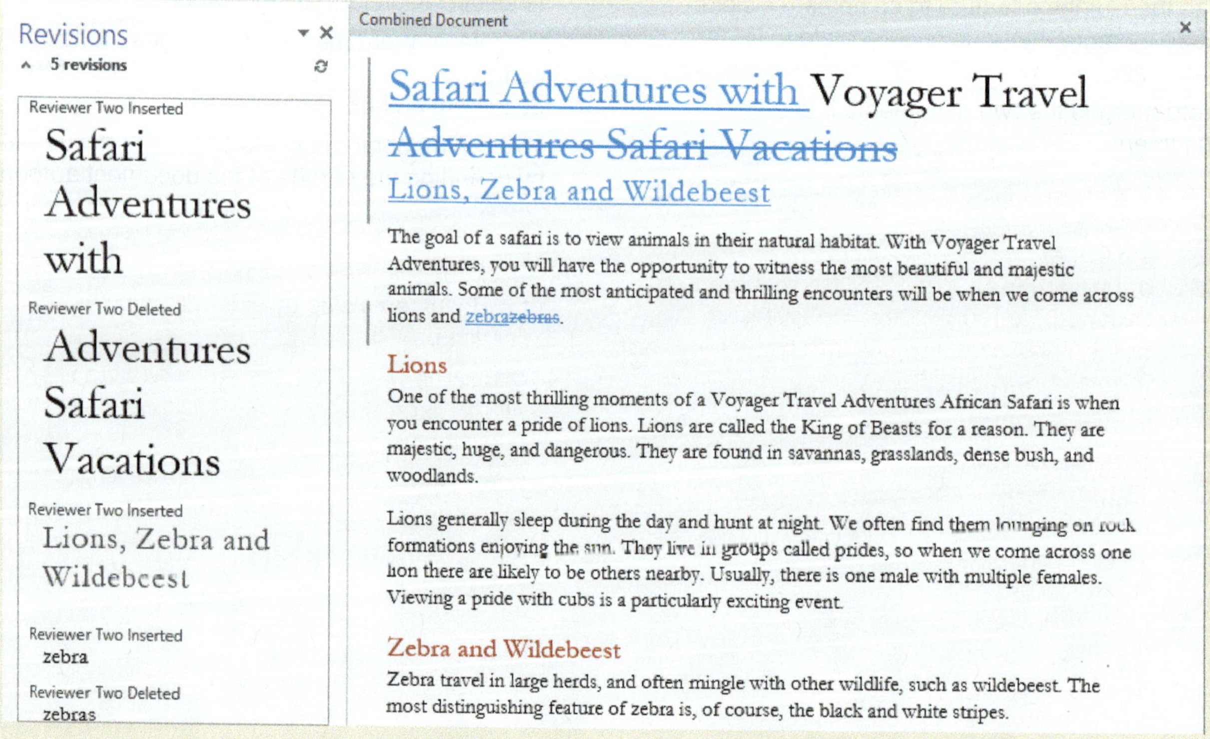

Lesson 47—Practice

You have been working on a newsletter about the value of employment benefits for Executive Recruitment Resources, Inc., a job search and recruitment agency. You will create the newsletter for your manager to review. Your manager sends you a version of the newsletter which she edited without using revision marks. You will view the two documents side by side to verify that they are not the same. You will then compare the documents and highlight the differences.

DIRECTIONS

1. Start Word, if necessary, and open **W47PracticeA** from the data files for this lesson.
2. Save the file as **W47PracticeA_xx** in the location where your teacher instructs you to store the files for this lesson.
3. Double-click in the header, type your full name and today's date, and close the header.
4. On the first line of the document, type the following headings and paragraphs:

   Career Planning

   An important aspect of career planning is identifying career opportunities that meet your needs and fit your skills, interests, and abilities. Here at Executive Recruitment Resources, we provide access to many job search resources, which are tools designed to help you find career opportunities. We also provide training and support to help you build your own job search resources.

   Occupational Outlook Handbook

   The U.S. Bureau of Labor Statistics (BLS) is a government agency that tracks information about jobs and workers. BLS publishes the Occupational Outlook Handbook in printed and online editions. The Handbook describes more than 200 occupations, including responsibilities, working conditions, education requirements, salary ranges, and job outlook.

   Networking

   Employers like to hire people who come with a recommendation from someone they know and trust. That's why networking is one of the best ways to find a job. Networking is when you share information about yourself and your career goals with people you know already or new people you meet. One of these contacts might know of a job opening, or be able to introduce you to someone in a field that interests you.

   Networking is more than just chatting with others. It requires you to be focused and organized. It works best if you keep track of all the people you meet and talk to, and if you follow up by e-mail or phone.
5. With the insertion point in the second section of the document, click **Layout** > **Columns** > **Two** to format the text in two newsletter-style columns.
6. Position the insertion point at the beginning of the heading Networking, and click **Layout** > **Breaks** > **Column** to insert a column break.
7. Apply the **Heading 1** style to the three headings (Career Planning, Occupational Outlook Handbook, and Networking).
8. Change the spacing before the Networking heading to **20 pt** so it visually aligns with the Career Planning heading.
9. Check and correct the spelling and grammar in the document, and save the document.
10. Open **W47PracticeB** from the data files for this lesson.
11. Save the file as **W47PracticeB_xx** in the location where your teacher instructs you to store the files for this lesson, type your full name and today's date in the header, and close the header.
12. Click **View** > **View Side by Side** to arrange the documents side by side with synchronous scrolling.
13. Adjust the view using the zoom and scroll controls so you can easily see the left column in both documents.
14. Compare the text in the left column of each document.
15. Highlight in yellow the differences in the **W47PracticeB_xx** document.

    ✓ *To highlight text, select the text, click Home > Text Highlight Color .*

16. Adjust the view using the zoom and scroll controls so you can easily see the right columns of each document.
17. Compare the text in the right column of each document, and highlight in yellow the differences you find in **W47PracticeB_xx**.
18. In **W47PracticeB_xx**, click **View** > **View Side by Side**.
19. Save and close **W47PracticeB_xx**, and save and close **W47PracticeA_xx**. Leave Word open.
20. In Word, click **Review** > **Compare** > **Compare**.
21. Click the **Original document** drop-down arrow, and click **W47PracticeB_xx**.

   ✓ *If the document you want is not listed, click the Browse button and navigate File Explorer to locate it.*

22. Click the **Revised document** drop-down arrow, and click **W47PracticeA_xx**.
23. Click in the **Label changes with** box, and type your full name, if necessary.
24. Click **OK**.
25. Click **Review** > **Display for Review** drop-down arrow > **All Markup**.
26. Save the Compare Result document as **W47PracticeC_xx** in the location where your teacher instructs you to store the files for this lesson.
27. **With your teacher's permission,** print the document with markup. It should look similar to Figure 47-1.
28. Save and close the document, and exit Word.

Figure 47-1

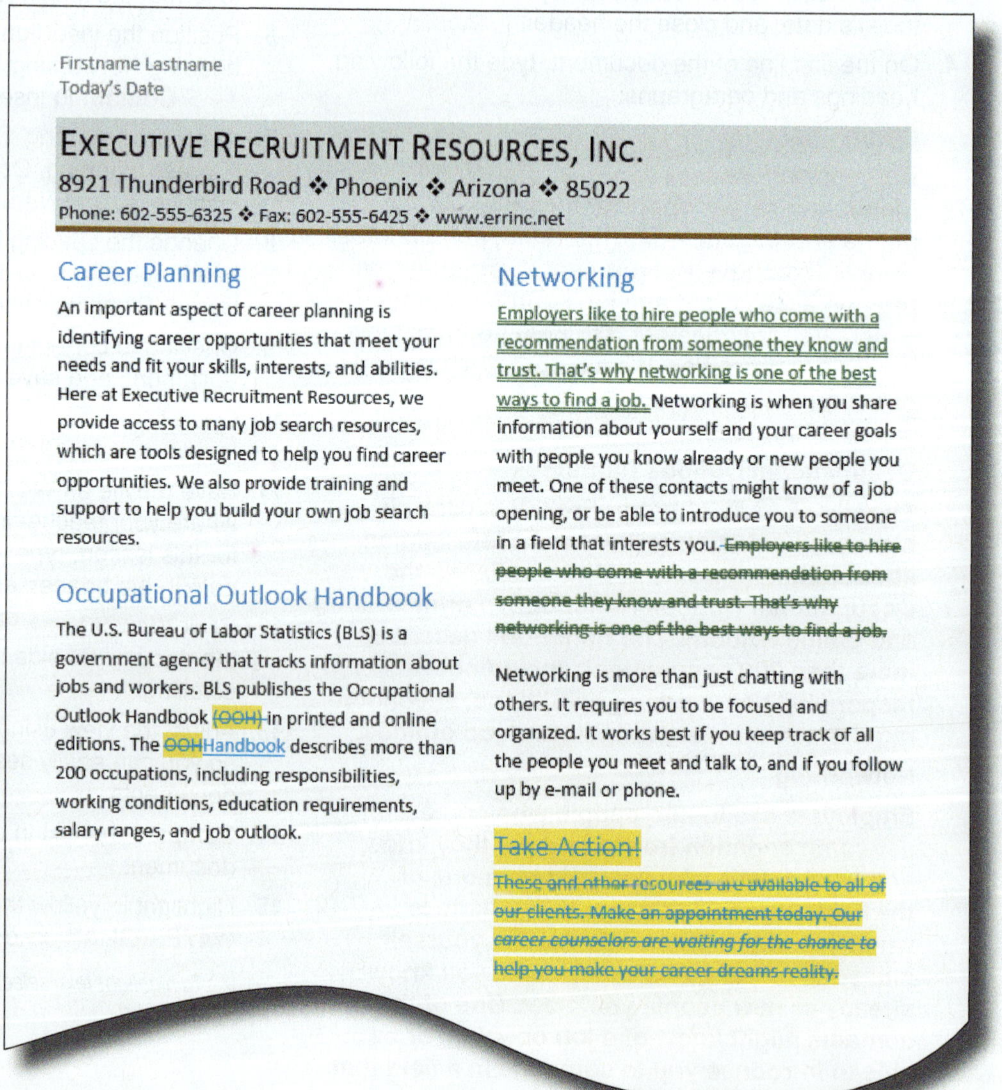
Firstname Lastname
Today's Date

EXECUTIVE RECRUITMENT RESOURCES, INC.
8921 Thunderbird Road ❖ Phoenix ❖ Arizona ❖ 85022
Phone: 602-555-6325 ❖ Fax: 602-555-6425 ❖ www.errinc.net

Career Planning

An important aspect of career planning is identifying career opportunities that meet your needs and fit your skills, interests, and abilities. Here at Executive Recruitment Resources, we provide access to many job search resources, which are tools designed to help you find career opportunities. We also provide training and support to help you build your own job search resources.

Occupational Outlook Handbook

The U.S. Bureau of Labor Statistics (BLS) is a government agency that tracks information about jobs and workers. BLS publishes the Occupational Outlook Handbook ~~(OOH)~~ in printed and online editions. The ~~OOH~~Handbook describes more than 200 occupations, including responsibilities, working conditions, education requirements, salary ranges, and job outlook.

Networking

Employers like to hire people who come with a recommendation from someone they know and trust. That's why networking is one of the best ways to find a job. Networking is when you share information about yourself and your career goals with people you know already or new people you meet. One of these contacts might know of a job opening, or be able to introduce you to someone in a field that interests you. ~~Employers like to hire people who come with a recommendation from someone they know and trust. That's why networking is one of the best ways to find a job.~~

Networking is more than just chatting with others. It requires you to be focused and organized. It works best if you keep track of all the people you meet and talk to, and if you follow up by e-mail or phone.

~~Take Action!~~

~~These and other resources are available to all of our clients. Make an appointment today. Our career counselors are waiting for the chance to help you make your career dreams reality.~~

Word 2016, Windows 10, Microsoft Corporation

Lesson 47—Apply

You work in the publications department of Executive Recruitment Resources, Inc. Your manager sent you a copy of the newsletter that she edited without using revision marks. You will compare your manager's copy of the newsletter and the one on which you are working. In this project, you will combine the revisions and create a final newsletter.

DIRECTIONS

1. Start Word, if necessary, and open **W47ApplyA** from the data files for this lesson.
2. Save the file as **W47ApplyA_xx** in the location where your teacher instructs you to store the files for this lesson.
3. Type your full name and today's date in the header, and close the header.
4. Open **W47ApplyB** from the data files for this lesson.
5. Save the file as **W47ApplyB_xx** in the location where your teacher instructs you to store the files for this lesson.
6. Type your full name and today's date in the header, and close the header.
7. View the documents side by side and use synchronous scrolling to compare the content to identify differences.
8. Remove the side-by-side display, then save and close both documents. Leave Word open.
9. Combine the two documents, using the following options:
   a. Use **W47ApplyA_xx** as the original document.
   b. Use **W47ApplyB_xx** as the revised document.
   c. Label unmarked changes in the original document with your full name, and unmarked changes in the revised document with your initials.
   d. Choose to show the changes in the revised document.

   ✓ *Click the More button in the Combine Documents dialog box and, under Show changes in, click the Revised document option button.*
10. If necessary, click **Review** > **Display for Review** drop-down arrow > **All Markup**.
11. Check and correct the spelling and grammar in the document.
12. Save the changes to **W47ApplyB_xx**.
13. **With your teacher's permission,** print the document with markup. It should look similar to Figure 47-2 on the next page.
14. Close the Revisions task pane, if necessary.
15. Save and close the document, and exit Word.

Figure 47-2

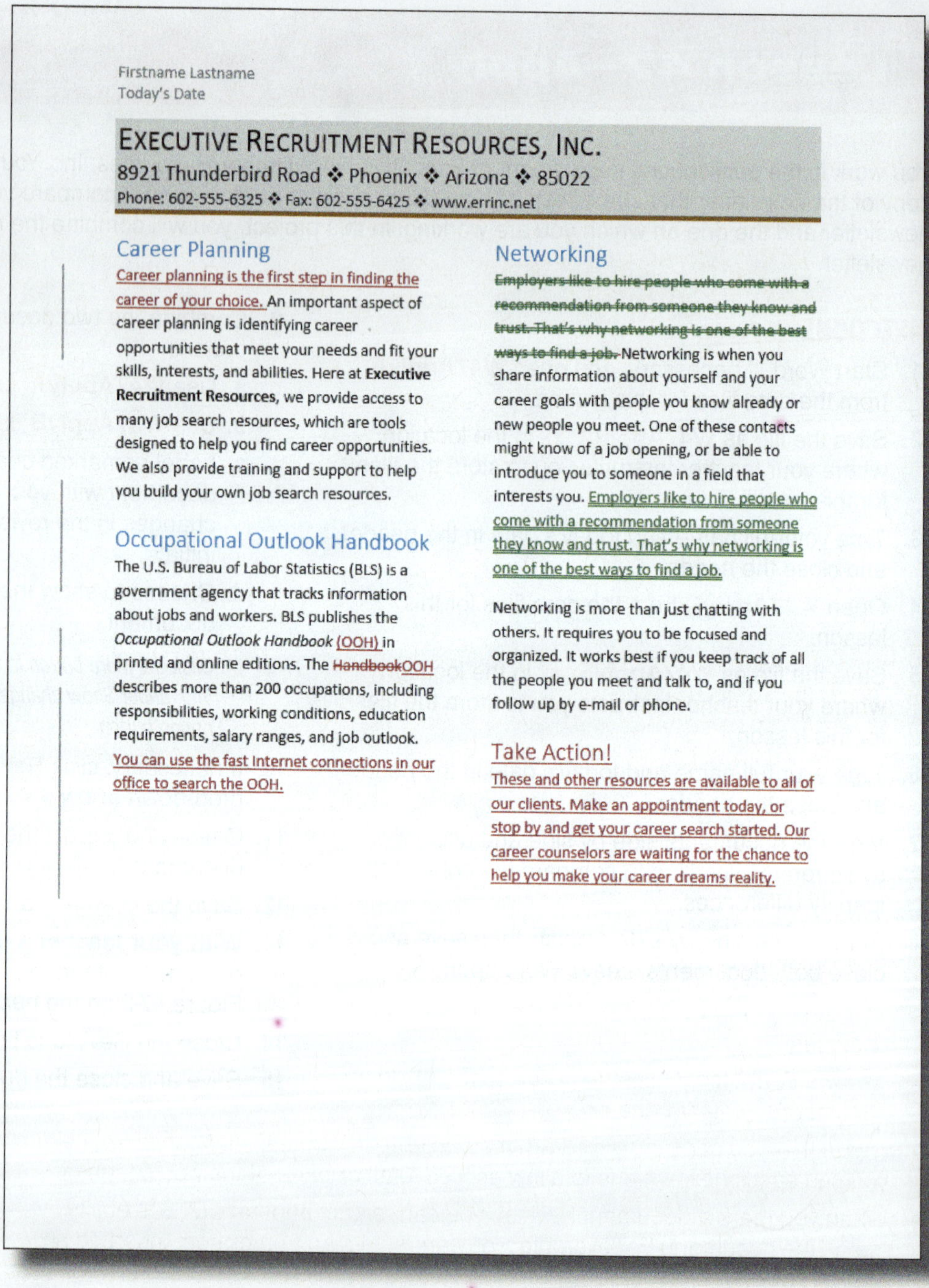
Firstname Lastname
Today's Date

EXECUTIVE RECRUITMENT RESOURCES, INC.
8921 Thunderbird Road ❖ Phoenix ❖ Arizona ❖ 85022
Phone: 602-555-6325 ❖ Fax: 602-555-6425 ❖ www.errinc.net

Career Planning

Career planning is the first step in finding the career of your choice. An important aspect of career planning is identifying career opportunities that meet your needs and fit your skills, interests, and abilities. Here at **Executive Recruitment Resources**, we provide access to many job search resources, which are tools designed to help you find career opportunities. We also provide training and support to help you build your own job search resources.

Occupational Outlook Handbook

The U.S. Bureau of Labor Statistics (BLS) is a government agency that tracks information about jobs and workers. BLS publishes the *Occupational Outlook Handbook* (OOH) in printed and online editions. The ~~Handbook~~OOH describes more than 200 occupations, including responsibilities, working conditions, education requirements, salary ranges, and job outlook. You can use the fast Internet connections in our office to search the OOH.

Networking

~~Employers like to hire people who come with a recommendation from someone they know and trust. That's why networking is one of the best ways to find a job.~~ Networking is when you share information about yourself and your career goals with people you know already or new people you meet. One of these contacts might know of a job opening, or be able to introduce you to someone in a field that interests you. Employers like to hire people who come with a recommendation from someone they know and trust. That's why networking is one of the best ways to find a job.

Networking is more than just chatting with others. It requires you to be focused and organized. It works best if you keep track of all the people you meet and talk to, and if you follow up by e-mail or phone.

Take Action!

These and other resources are available to all of our clients. Make an appointment today, or stop by and get your career search started. Our career counselors are waiting for the chance to help you make your career dreams reality.

Lesson 48

Restricting Access to Documents

➤ What You Will Learn

Setting and Removing Restrictions in a Document
Changing a Password in a Protected, Encrypted Document
Using Online Word Processing Technologies

Software Skills In Word, you can restrict the ability of authors to format, edit, or digitally sign a document. You can limit the number of authors that can revise a document. You can protect and encrypt a document with a password to limit unauthorized access to a document.

What You Can Do

Setting and Removing Restrictions in a Document

- You can restrict another author's ability to format and edit a document.
- You can restrict whether an author can apply a different theme or style set to a document.
- Use the Formatting Restrictions dialog box to block authors from switching the document's contents to a different format.
- Recall that you can set formatting, read only, or comments restrictions, and that you can specify exceptions to allow access to all or parts of the document.
- When you mark a document as final, you can restrict another author's ability to edit the document. For example, you can restrict an author from inserting a **digital signature**.
- You can use a Microsoft Account to restrict permissions for specific users.
  - You can add permissions with the Restrict Access feature.
  - You can apply permissions using a template used by your organization.
- You must protect a document to enforce restrictions.
- Remove restrictions and protection to enable unlimited editing.
- Recall that restrictions apply to documents even when they are copied or saved with a new name.

WORDS TO KNOW

Authenticated
Checked and verified as real or legitimate.

Digital signature
An electronic, encryption-based, secure stamp of authentication on a macro or document.

Encryption
Scrambling so as to be indecipherable.

Password
A string of characters used to authenticate the identity of a user, and to limit unauthorized access.

Try It! Setting and Removing Restrictions in a Document

1. Start Word, and open **W48Try** from the data files for this lesson.
2. In the Password box, type **Try?W?48!**, and click OK.
3. Save the file as **W48Try_xx** in the location where your teacher instructs you to store the files for this lesson.
4. Click Review > Restrict Editing.
5. In the Restrict Editing task pane, click Stop Protection, and in the Unprotect Document dialog box type **Try?W?48!**. Click OK.
6. In the Restrict Editing pane, under Formatting restrictions, click to select the Limit formatting to a selection of styles check box, and click Settings to display the Formatting Restrictions dialog box.
7. In the Formatting Restrictions dialog box, under Formatting, click the Block Theme or Scheme switching and the Block Quick Style Set switching check boxes, and click OK.
8. In the warning dialog box, click No.
9. In the Restrict Editing pane, under Editing restrictions, click to uncheck the Allow only this type of editing in the document check box.
10. In the warning dialog box, click Yes to remove the ignored exceptions.
11. Under Start enforcement click Yes, Start Enforcing Protection, and click OK without entering a password.
12. Click File > Protect Document > Mark as Final.
13. Click OK > OK.
14. Click the Back button. Notice that the editing options, including the ability to insert a digital signature, are disabled.
15. Close the document. Leave Word open to use in the Try It.

Restricted formatting

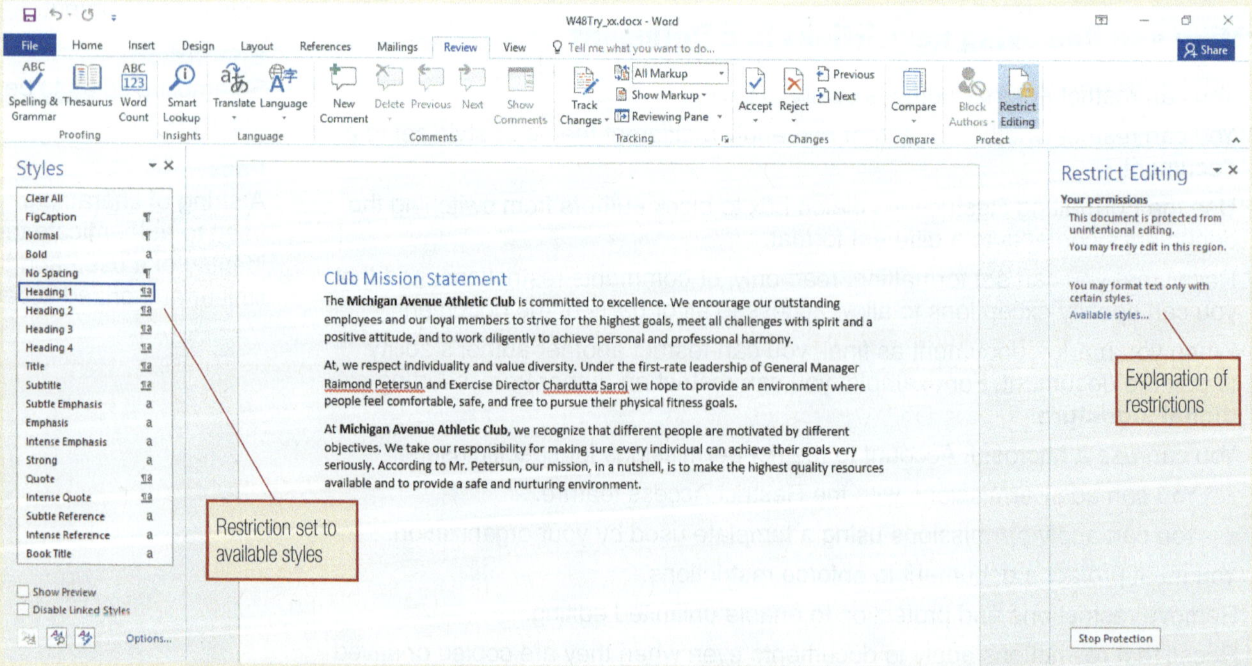

Word 2016, Windows 10, Microsoft Corporation

Changing a Password in a Protected, Encrypted Document

- You can use a **password** and **encryption** to ensure that users cannot remove or change restriction settings.
- If you are an **authenticated** owner of the document, you can remove the document's protection and change the assigned password.
- You must know the current password and remove the document protection before you can change the password.
- You can reassign a password and re-encrypt a document at the same time using options on the Info tab in the Backstage view.
- Be careful to select a password you can remember. If you do not enter the correct password, you will not be able to open the document.
- Recall that the password protection applies to documents even when they are copied or saved with a new name.

Try It! Changing a Password in a Protected, Encrypted Document

1. Open the **W48Try_xx** file from the location where your teacher instructs you to store the files for this lesson.
2. In the Password dialog box, type **Try?W?48!**, and click OK.
3. In the MARKED AS FINAL bar, click Edit Anyway.
4. Click File > Protect Document > Encrypt with Password.
5. In the Password box, delete the existing password, and type **Try?W?48!New**. Click OK.
6. In the Reenter Password dialog box, click in the Enter new password box, and type **Try?W?48!New**. Click OK.
7. Click the Back button.
8. Save and close the document, and exit Word.

Using Online Word Processing Technologies

- Word Online is a free version of Microsoft Word available to anyone with a Microsoft or a school account.
- You can log in from any device with an Internet connection.
- Word Online does not include all the features of the desktop version of Microsoft Word or Word 365, which is the online app available to subscribers who pay a yearly fee.
- You can save documents created with Word Online on OneDrive or you can download them to a storage device connected to your computer.

Try It! Using Word Online

1. Go to https://office.live.com/start/Word.aspx and sign in with a Microsoft or school account. Word Online opens in your browser.
2. Click New blank document.
3. Type your name and today's date.
4. Click File > Save As > Download a Copy.
5. Click Click here to download your document. Your browser downloads the document.
6. Open the downloaded document and save it as **W48Try2_xx** in the location where your teacher instructs you to store the files for this lesson.
7. Close the document, exit Word, and exit your browser.

Lesson 48—Practice

The research and development department at Long Shot, Inc., is working on an exciting new product. It is important that all information related to the product remain confidential and out of the hands of business competitors. The department manager has asked you to generate a memo to all team members explaining the importance of confidentiality with regard to this project, and what problems might arise from a breach of confidentiality. In this project, you will create the document and set restrictions so that it cannot be changed.

DIRECTIONS

1. Start Word, if necessary.
2. Create a new blank document and save it as **W48Practice_xx** in the location where your teacher instructs you to store the files for this lesson.
3. Display the rulers and nonprinting characters, if necessary.
4. Set paragraph spacing **Before** to **24** points and paragraph spacing **After** to **36** points.
5. Set the line spacing at **Single**.
6. Type **MEMO**, and press ENTER.
7. Apply the **No Spacing** style, and set a left tab stop at **0.75"** on the horizontal ruler.
8. Type **To:**, press TAB, and type **Team Members**. Press ENTER.
9. Type **From:**, press TAB, and type your own name. Press ENTER.
10. Type **Date:**, press TAB, and type or insert today's date. Press ENTER.
11. Type **Subject:**, press TAB, and type **Confidentiality**. Press ENTER twice.
12. Apply the **Normal** style and type the following paragraphs.

    As you all know, we are working on a new and exciting product which the company expects will completely revolutionize the golf equipment industry. This memo is simply a reminder of the Long Shot, Inc., corporate policy on confidentiality and ethical behavior.

    Confidentiality in business refers to the protection of proprietary and secret information. In some businesses, the information belongs to a client, and it is the responsibility of the business to make sure no one else can access the information. In our case, the information belongs to the corporation, and it is our responsibility to make sure no one outside the company gains access.
13. Check and correct the spelling and grammar in the document, and save the changes.
14. Click **Review** > **Restrict Editing**.
15. In the Restrict Editing pane, under *Formatting restrictions*, click to select the **Limit formatting to a selection of styles** check box, and click **Settings**.
16. In the Formatting Restrictions dialog box, click **Recommended Minimum** > **OK**.
17. If necessary, in the warning dialog box, click **No**.
18. In the Restrict Editing pane, under *Editing restrictions*, click to select the **Allow only this type of editing in the document** check box, click the drop-down arrow, and click **Comments**.
19. In the document, select the last paragraph.
20. In the Restrict Editing task pane, under *Exceptions (optional)*, click to select the **Everyone** check box.
21. Under *Start enforcement* click **Yes, Start Enforcing Protection**.
22. In the Start Enforcing Protection dialog box, in the Enter new password (optional) box, type **!48?Project&**.
23. In the Reenter password to confirm box, type **!48?Project&**, and click **OK**.
24. Select the text *MEMO*, and try to apply the Title style.
25. Select the first paragraph, and press DEL.
26. Click **Review** > **New Comment** and type **What about the code of conduct?**
27. Click outside the comment balloon, then in the task pane, click **Find Next Region I Can Edit** to select the last paragraph, and apply the **No Spacing** style.
28. Save the document.

29. **With your teacher's permission**, print the document. It should look similar to Figure 48-1.

30. Save and close the document, and exit Word.

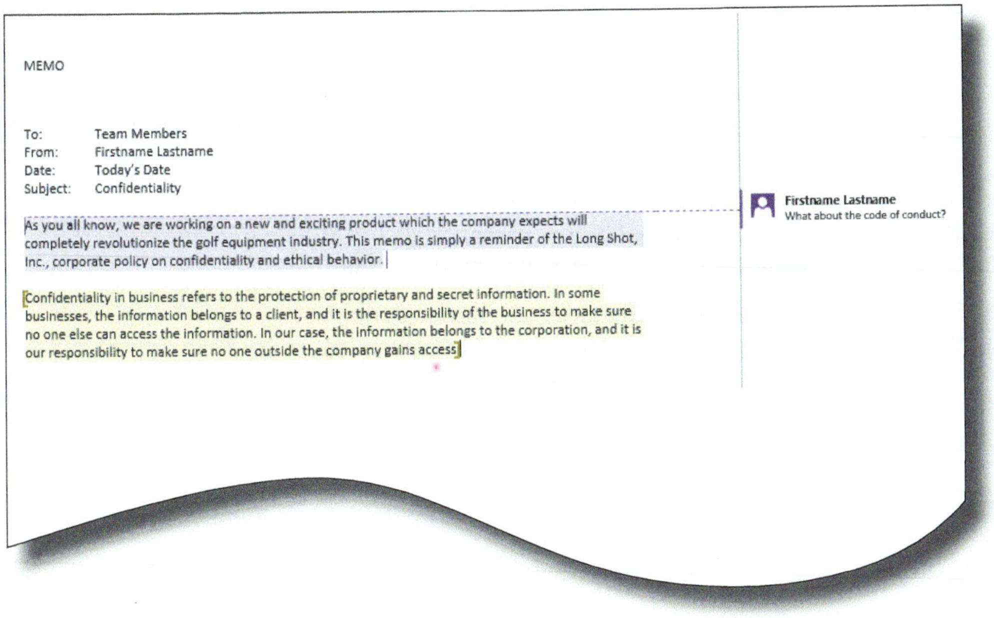
MEMO

To: Team Members
From: Firstname Lastname
Date: Today's Date
Subject: Confidentiality

As you all know, we are working on a new and exciting product which the company expects will completely revolutionize the golf equipment industry. This memo is simply a reminder of the Long Shot, Inc., corporate policy on confidentiality and ethical behavior.

Confidentiality in business refers to the protection of proprietary and secret information. In some businesses, the information belongs to a client, and it is the responsibility of the business to make sure no one else can access the information. In our case, the information belongs to the corporation, and it is our responsibility to make sure no one outside the company gains access.

Word 2016, Windows 10, Microsoft Corporation

Figure 48-1

Lesson 48—Apply

You have created a restricted document for Long Shot, Inc. so that product information will remain confidential. Your department manager has approved the memo and asked you to prepare the document so that the legal department can review and revise. In this project, you will restrict editing in the document to track changes and encrypt the document.

DIRECTIONS

1. Start Word, if necessary, and open **W48Apply** from the data files for this lesson.
2. Save it as **W48Apply_xx** in the location where your teacher instructs you to store the files for this lesson.
3. Replace the sample text *Student's Name* with your own name, and *Today's Date* with the actual date.
4. In the last line of the document, insert a signature line with the following instructions to the signer: **Before signing this document, verify that you have read the content you are signing.**

   ✓ *Hint: Click Insert > Signature Line.*
5. Set options so users cannot apply any styles to the document, but do not remove existing styles.
6. Restrict editing to tracked changes, and start enforcement. Do not apply a password.
7. Close the Restrict Editing task pane.
8. Use the Info tab in Backstage view to encrypt the document with the password **&LSI?48**.
9. Save and close the document. Leave Word open.
10. Open the document using the correct password.
11. **With your teacher's permission,** print the document.
12. Save and close the document, and exit Word.

End-of-Chapter Activities

➤ Word Chapter 6—Critical Thinking

Directory

A directory is a book containing an alphabetical list of names and descriptions of items in a category or group. The items might be people, such as the students in your class, or things, such as companies, countries, sports teams, or books.

Working as a team with other classmates, use skills you have learned in this chapter to create a directory of items in a category approved by your teacher. Each team member will write one page for the directory, and you will collaborate to combine the pages into a professional-quality, multi-page booklet. Enhance the booklet by using a custom theme and a logo saved as a building block.

DIRECTIONS

1. As a team, work together to select a topic that your teacher approves, and decide who will write each page.
2. Collaborate by designing a custom theme that will give your directory a unique look.
3. Also work together to design a logo you can use on each page, and then save the logo as a building block that you can all access.
4. Design a cover page for your directory using the theme and the building block. Enter all team members' names and the current date on the cover.
5. Individually, start Word, click **Blank document**, and save as **WCT06_xx** in the location where your teacher instructs you to store the files for this chapter.
6. Apply the custom theme your team designed, and insert the logo building block somewhere on the page.
7. In the footer, insert the user name and date fields from Quick Parts.
8. Write your directory page. It should have a title, be at least two paragraphs long, and may include a picture or other type of illustration.
9. Use Word's Translation tools to translate your page title into at least one other language.
10. Exchange documents with a teammate and use revision marks and comments to review the document and make suggestions for improvement.
11. When you receive your own document back, accept and reject changes, or compare and combine the documents to create the final document.
12. Check and correct the spelling and grammar in the document, and save the document.
13. When you are satisfied with the document, ask a classmate to review it and make comments or suggestions that will help you improve it.
14. Make changes and corrections, as necessary.
15. **With your teacher's permission,** print the document.
16. Restore all default settings, and delete custom themes and building blocks you will no longer need.
17. Save and close the document.
18. Arrange the printed documents in alphabetical order, and staple them together with the cover page to create the booklet.

Word Chapter 6—Portfolio Builder

Information Sheet

You and a co-worker at Fresh Food Fair have been collaborating on a document explaining the benefits of organic farming. In this project, you will start by comparing and combining the two versions of the document. You will then use the skills you have learned in this chapter including translating text, advanced find and replace, building blocks, Quick Parts, comments, and revision marks to complete the document. You will also save the finished document as a template.

Design a Building Block and a Custom Theme

1. Start Word, click **Blank document**, and save as **WPB06_xx** in the location where your teacher instructs you to store the files for this chapter.
2. In the header, type **Fresh Food Fair** and format it in **48 point Times New Roman**. Select the text, and draw a text box around it.
3. Format the text box to have no fill or outline, and resize it to **1"** high by **4.5"** wide. Align the text box with the top of the page and with the left margin.
4. To the right of the text box, insert an image of vegetables. If you cannot find a suitable image, insert **WPB06_picture** from the data files for this chapter.
5. Size the image to **0.8"** high and **1.14"** wide, set the text wrapping to **Square**, and align it with the text box and the right margin.
6. Select the text box and the image and then save the selection as a building block in the Headers Gallery with the name **WPB06 Header** and the description **Header for Fresh Food Fair**.
7. Customize the theme with the **Green** theme colors and the **Cambria** theme fonts.
8. Save the custom theme with the name **WPB06 Theme**.
9. Close the document without saving changes. Leave Word open.

Compare and Combine Documents

1. In Word, open **WPB06A** from the data files for this chapter. This is the original document.
2. Save the file as **WPB06A_xx** in the location where your teacher instructs you to store the files for this chapter.
3. Type your full name and today's date in the footer, close the footer, and scroll to the top of the document.
4. Open **WPB06B** from the data files for this chapter. This is the revised document.
5. Save the file as **WPB06B_xx** in the location where your teacher instructs you to store the files for this chapter.
6. Type your full name and today's date in the footer, close the footer, and scroll back to the top of the document.
7. View the documents side by side, and use synchronous scrolling to compare the content to identify differences.
8. When you identify a difference, insert a comment in the revised document (**WPB06B_xx**) describing the difference. For example, insert a comment to identify the different title, and to note that terms beginning with the word organic are italicized.
9. When you complete the comparison, remove the side-by-side display, and save and close both documents. Leave Word open.
10. Combine the two documents, using the following options:
    - Use **WPB06A_xx** as the original document.
    - Use **WPB06B_xx** as the revised document.
    - Label unmarked changes in the original document with your full name, and unmarked changes in the revised document with your initials.
    - Choose to show the changes in the original document.
    - Unselect the Formatting option to keep formatting changes from the revised document.
11. Save the changes to **WPB06A_xx**.
12. Save the document as **WPB06C_xx** in the location where your teacher instructs you to store the files for this chapter.

Finalize the Document

1. In the **WPB06C_xx** document, delete all comments.
2. Show all revisions inline, and display the Reviewing pane vertically.
3. Accept the changes to the title.
4. Reject the changes to the first heading.
5. Reject the changes to the first sentence.
6. Accept all the remaining changes in the document.
7. Close the Reviewing pane, and set Word to Show Only Comments and Formatting in Balloons.
8. Save the changes to the document.
9. Use Find and Replace to find and match the case of **ly-** in the document, and replace with **ly** —with a space after the letters.

   ✓ *Hint: Click More > Match case.*
10. Clear the match case formatting options, and close the Find and Replace dialog box.
11. Insert the **WPB06 Header** building block.
12. Apply the **WPB06 Theme** custom theme.

   ✓ *If necessary, adjust the indent of the title line so it fits on one line, as shown in Illustration 6A.*
13. Use Word's translation features to translate the last line of text into Spanish (Spain), then insert a new line at the end of the document, and type the translated text. Format both lines with the **Heading 3** style, centered.

   ✓ *Remove hyperlink formatting, if necessary.*
14. Flush right in the footer, insert the **UserInitials** field with **Uppercase** format and the **Time** field in **HH:mm:ss** format.
15. Check and correct the spelling and grammar in the document, and save the document.
16. **With your teacher's permission,** print the document. It should look similar to Illustration 6A on the next page.
17. Delete the **WPB06 Header** building block, and the **WPB06 Theme** custom theme.
18. Save the document, and exit Word. Save the building blocks template.
19. Start Word, and open **WPB06C_xx**.
20. Save the **WPB06C_xx** document as a Word Template with the file name **WPB06C_Template_xx** in the location where your teacher instructs you to store the files for this chapter.
21. Close the **WPB06C_Template_xx** template, and exit Word.

Illustration 6A

Fresh Food Fair

Organic Farming Information Sheet

What Is Organic Farming?

Organic farming is an ecological management system that promotes and enhances biodiversity, biological cycles, and soil biological activity. This system is based on management practices that restore, maintain, and enhance biological harmony. Organic farmers fertilize and build healthy soils by using compost and other biologically based soil modifications. This produces healthy plants which are better able to resist disease and insects.

Standards of Quality

Organic farmers follow a set of strict standards set by the U.S. Department of Agriculture (USDA). Essentially, the organic standards offer a national definition for the term "organic." The standards also state that all agricultural products labeled "organic" must originate from farms or handling operations certified by a state or private agency accredited by the USDA.

For products to carry the label "Made with Organic Ingredients," at least 70% of their ingredients must be organic. Furthermore, the standards provide information for consumers by requiring manufacturers to state the exact percentage of organic ingredients on the chief display panel of the product.

Benefits and Drawbacks

Because organic farming systems do not use toxic chemical pesticides or fertilizers, organic foods are not exposed to these toxins. Organic foods are also minimally processed to maintain the integrity of the food without artificial ingredients, preservatives, or irradiation, which some people believe makes them taste better.

Generally, organic foods cost more than conventional foods. This is because the prices for organic foods reflect many of the same costs as conventional foods in terms of growing, harvesting, transportation, and storage, but there are added costs as well. Organically produced foods must meet stricter regulations so the process is often more labor and management intensive, which costs more. Also, organic farms tend to be smaller, which increases costs.

Where to Find Organic Foods

Organic foods can be found at natural food stores, organic farm stands, as well as in the health food and produce departments of most supermarkets. Many restaurant chefs are using organic products because of its growing popularity, as well as its reputation for having superior quality and taste.

Available in Spanish at www.freshfoodfair.org
Disponible en español en www.freshfoodfair.org

Firstname Lastname
Today's Date

FL
13:49:10

Chapter 7

(Courtesy auremar/Shutterstock)

Using Advanced Tables and Graphics

Lesson 49
Customizing Table Styles

- Creating a Custom Table Style
- Modifying and Deleting a Table Style
- Adding a Caption to a Table

Lesson 50
Using Advanced Table Features

- Inserting Graphics in a Table Cell
- Inserting a Nested Table
- Creating a Repeating Header Row
- Splitting a Table
- Inserting an Excel Worksheet in a Word Document
- Copying Excel Data to Word and Converting a Table to Text

Lesson 51
Using Advanced Graphics

- Using Document Gridlines
- Using Advanced Sizing Features
- Using Advanced Position Features
- Adjusting Objects
- Cropping a Picture

Lesson 52
Linking Text Boxes

- Aligning an Object with Another Object
- Linking Text Boxes
- Compressing a Picture
- Removing a Picture Background

Lesson 53
Creating WordArt and Watermarks

- Creating WordArt
- Creating a Watermark

End-of-Chapter Activities

Lesson 49

Customizing Table Styles

➤ What You Will Learn

Creating a Custom Table Style
Modifying and Deleting a Table Style
Adding a Caption to a Table

WORDS TO KNOW

Caption
A text label that identifies an illustration such as a figure, table, or picture.

Software Skills You can create a table style when none of the built-in table styles are suitable for your document. Add a caption to a table to help readers identify the table you are referring to in the document text.

What You Can Do

Creating a Custom Table Style

- Use the options in the Create New Style from Formatting dialog box to create and save a custom table style.
- As you select formatting, you can specify whether the formatting should apply to the whole table or to parts of the table.
- You can choose to include formatting for Table Style Options, such as a header row, banded rows, or banded columns.
- You can select to make the style available in all new documents based on the current template or only in the current document.
- The style becomes available in the Table Styles gallery so you can use it to format other tables.

Try It! Creating a Custom Table Style

1. Start Word, and open **W49Try** from the data files for this lesson.
2. Save the document as **W49Try_xx** in the location where your teacher instructs you to store the files for this lesson.
3. Click anywhere in the table. Click the Table Tools Design tab, click the Table Styles More button, and click New Table Style to open the Create New Style from Formatting dialog box.
4. In the Name text box, type **W49Try**.
5. Click the Border Style drop-down arrow, and click the triple line style.
6. Click the Borders drop-down arrow, and click Outside Borders.
7. Click the Fill Color drop-down arrow and click Blue, Accent 1, Lighter 80%.
8. Verify that the Only in this document option button is selected, and click OK.
9. Click the Table Styles More button. Under Custom, click the W49Try table style to apply it to the table in the document.
10. Save the changes to **W49Try_xx**, and leave it open to use in the next Try It.

Create New Style from Formatting dialog box

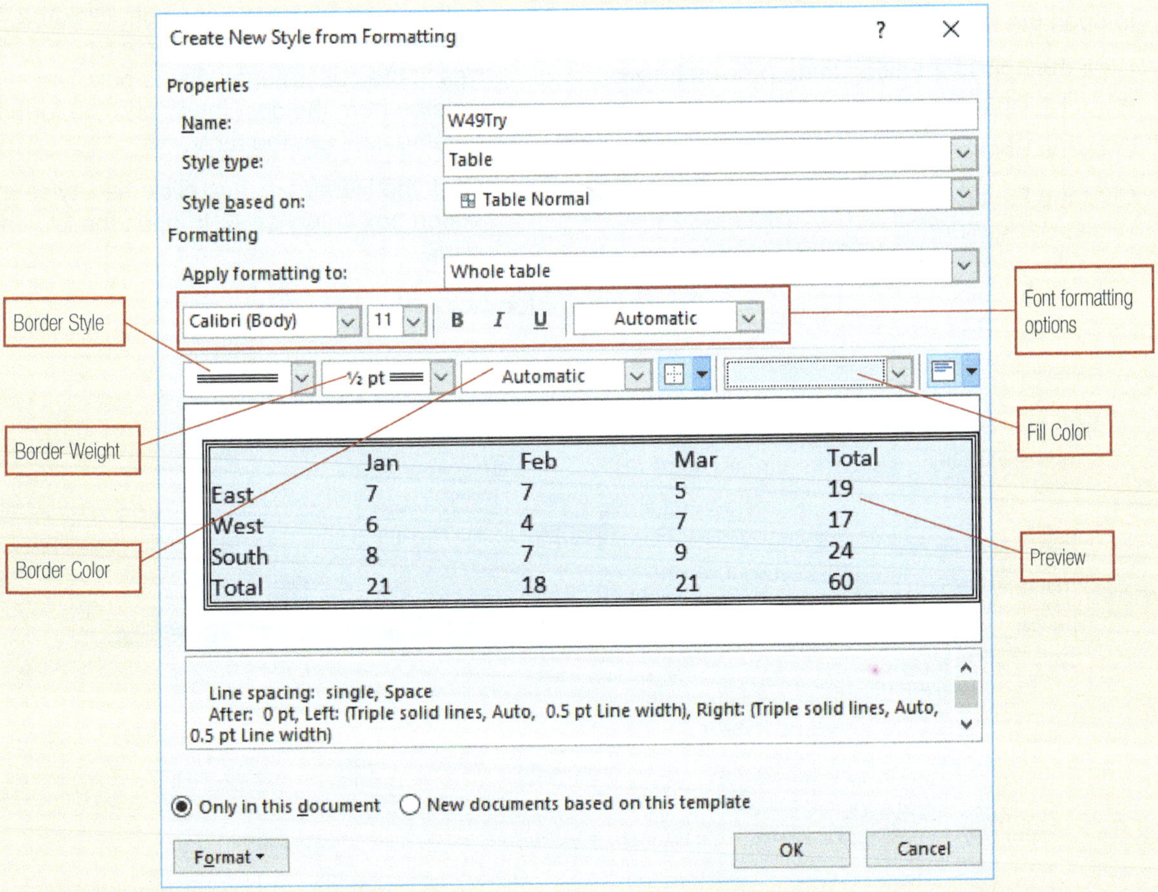

Word 2016, Windows 10, Microsoft Corporation

Modifying and Deleting a Table Style

- You can modify a custom table style or a built-in table style.
- All tables formatted with the modified style are updated to show the modified formatting.
- When you delete a custom style, the style is removed from the Table Styles gallery, and the formatting is removed from all tables formatted with that style.
- When you delete a modified built-in style, the formatting is removed from tables, but the original style remains available in the gallery.
- To delete a table style stored with the current template not just the current document, you must delete it from the template file using the Style Organizer.

Try It! Modifying and Deleting a Table Style

1. In the **W49Try_xx** file, make sure the insertion point is in the table, and click the Table Tools Design tab, if necessary.
2. In the Table Styles gallery, right-click the W49Try custom table style, and click Modify Table Style to open the Modify Style dialog box.
3. Click the Apply formatting to drop-down arrow, and click Header row.
4. Click the Bold button **B** .
5. Click the Font Color drop-down arrow, and click White, Background 1.
6. Click the Fill Color drop-down arrow and click Dark Blue.
7. Click the New documents based on this template option button, and then click OK.
8. In the Table Styles gallery, right-click the W49Try custom style, click Delete Table Style, and click Yes in the confirmation dialog box. The style is deleted from the document, and the formatting is removed from the table.
9. Click the Home tab, and click the Styles group dialog box launcher to open the Styles task pane.

Organizer dialog box

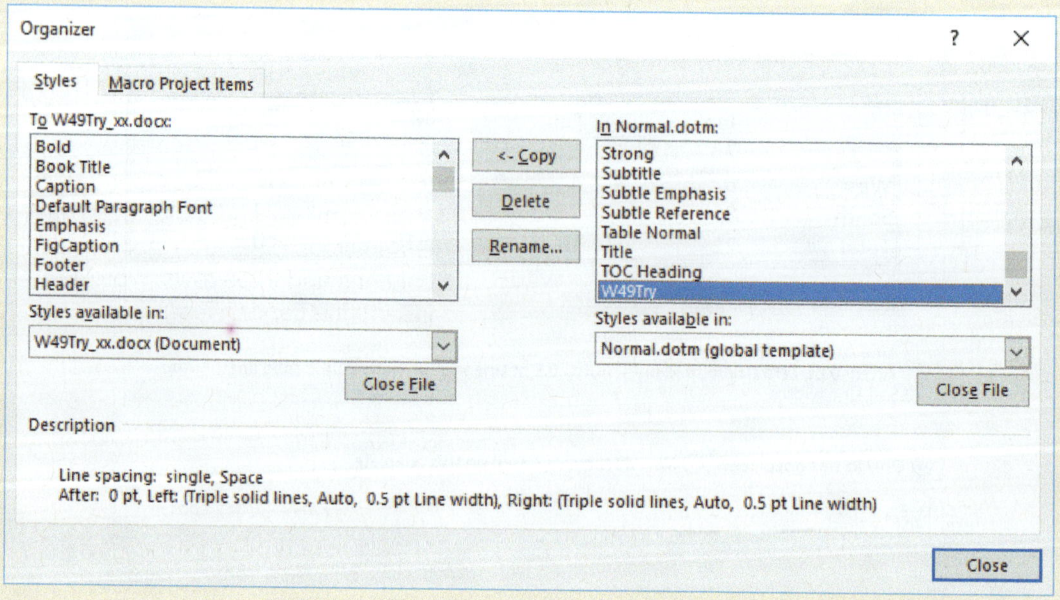

Word 2016, Windows 10, Microsoft Corporation

(continued)

Try It! Modifying and Deleting a Table Style *(continued)*

10. Click the Manage Styles button, to open the Manage Styles dialog box, and click the Import/ Export button to display the Organizer dialog box.
11. On the right side, under In Normal, click the W49Try style, and click Delete.
12. Click Yes in the confirmation dialog box, and click Close.
13. Close the Styles task pane, and save the changes to **W49Try_xx**. Leave the document open to use in the next Try It.

Adding a Caption to a Table

- Insert a **caption** to label a table so a reader can identify the table referenced in the main text.
- Each caption includes a text label and a number field.
- You can customize or edit the label as you would any text.
- By default, Word uses Arabic numbers and positions the captions below the table. You can customize the number format and select to position the caption above the table.
- Word automatically updates the numbers for each caption entered; however, if you delete or move a caption, you must manually update the remaining captions.
- You can insert a caption manually or set Word to automatically insert captions. Once you enable automatic captions, the feature remains on until you turn it off.

Try It! Adding a Caption to a Table

1. In the **W49Try_xx** file, position the insertion point in the table.
2. Click the References tab, and, in the Captions group, click the Insert Caption button to open the Caption dialog box.
3. Click the Position drop-down arrow, and click Below selected item.

Caption dialog box

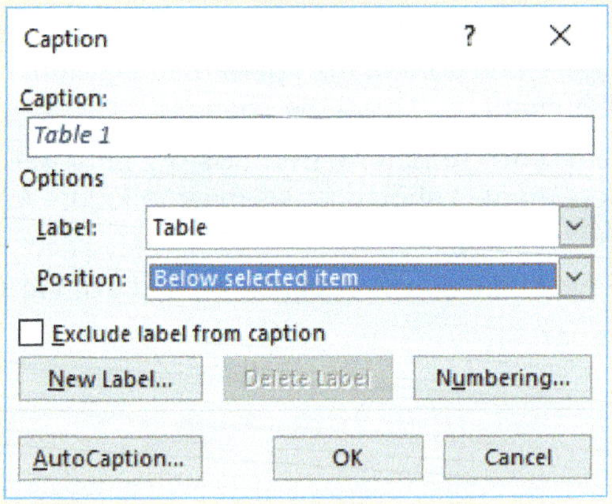

Word 2016, Windows 10, Microsoft Corporation

4. Click OK to insert the caption.
5. Click the Insert Caption button, and click AutoCaption.
6. In the Add caption when inserting box, scroll down, click to select the check box to the left of Microsoft Word Table, and click OK.
7. In the document, move the insertion point to the last line, and click Insert > Table. Drag across the grid to insert a table with five columns and three rows. Word automatically inserts the caption *Table 2*.
8. Click References > Insert Caption > AutoCaption.
9. Click to clear the check box to the left of Microsoft Word Table, and click OK.
10. Save and close the document, and exit Word.

Lesson 49—Practice

As the executive assistant to the president of Long Shot, Inc., you are responsible for planning his business trips. In this project, you prepare an itinerary for a meeting with a client, in which you include a table that you format by creating a custom table style and a caption.

DIRECTIONS

1. Start Word, if necessary, click **Blank document**, and save the document as **W49Practice_xx** in the location where your teacher instructs you to store the files for this lesson.
2. Apply the **Damask** theme, double-click in the header, and type your full name and today's date.
3. On the first line of the document, type **Long Shot, Inc.**, and format it with the **Title** style.
4. Press ENTER, apply the **No Spacing** style, and type **Itinerary for Mr. Lombardi**.
5. Press ENTER and type **Customer Meeting in Chicago, Illinois**.
6. Apply the **Normal** style, press ENTER and type the following paragraph:

   You are traveling to Chicago on Wednesday, October 11, to meet with representatives of Golf Equipment, LLC. Refer to Table A for your departure flight information.
7. Press ENTER, and insert a table with two columns and five rows.
8. Enter the following information in the table:

Departure Flight Information	
Date:	**October 11, 2017**
Airline/Flight Number:	**SouthernWest/191**
Scheduled Departure Time:	**9:40 a.m. EST**
Scheduled Arrival Time:	**10:10 a.m. CST**

9. Merge the cells in the first row.
10. Click **Table Tools Design** > **Table Styles More** > **New Table Style**.
11. In the Name text box, type **W49Practice**.
12. Click the **Border Style** drop-down arrow and click the single line border style.
13. Click the **Borders** drop-down arrow, and click **Outside Borders**.
14. Click the **Borders** drop-down arrow again, and click **Inside Horizontal Border**.
15. Click the **Fill Color** drop-down arrow No Color, and click **Dark Blue, Text 2, Lighter 80%**.
16. Click the **Apply formatting to** drop-down arrow, and click **First column**.
17. Click the **Fill Color** drop-down arrow No Color, and click **Dark Blue, Text 2, Lighter 60%**.
18. Click the **Apply formatting to** drop-down arrow, and click **Header row**.
19. Click **Bold** **B**.
20. Click the **Alignment** drop-down arrow, and click **Align Center**.
21. Click to select the **New documents based on this template** option button, and click **OK**.
22. In the Table Styles gallery, click the **W49Practice** table style to apply it to the departure flight information table.
23. Click **References** > **Insert Caption**.
24. In the Caption dialog box, click the **Numbering** button.
25. In the Caption Numbering dialog box, click the **Format** drop-down arrow, click **A, B, C, ...**, and click **OK**.
26. Click the **Label** drop-down arrow, and click **Table**, if necessary.
27. Click the **Position** drop-down arrow, click **Above selected item**, and click **OK**.
28. Check and correct the spelling and grammar in the document, and save the changes.
29. **With your teacher's permission**, print the document. It should look similar to Figure 49-1 on the next page.
30. Save and close the document, and exit Word.

Figure 49-1

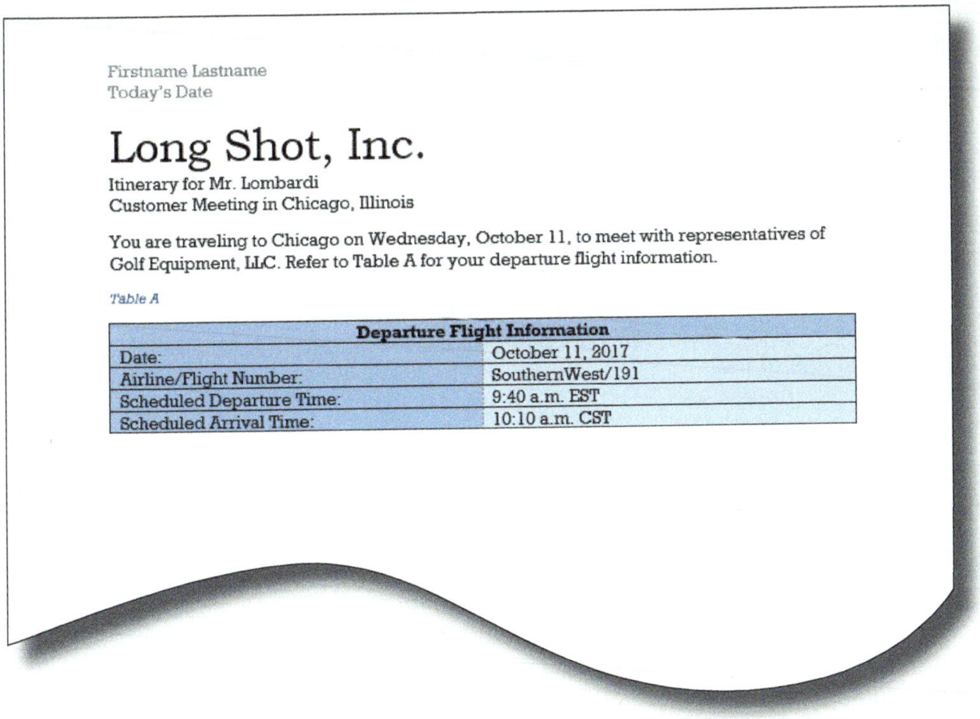
Firstname Lastname
Today's Date

Long Shot, Inc.

Itinerary for Mr. Lombardi
Customer Meeting in Chicago, Illinois

You are traveling to Chicago on Wednesday, October 11, to meet with representatives of Golf Equipment, LLC. Refer to Table A for your departure flight information.

Table A

Departure Flight Information	
Date:	October 11, 2017
Airline/Flight Number:	SouthernWest/191
Scheduled Departure Time:	9:40 a.m. EST
Scheduled Arrival Time:	10:10 a.m. CST

Lesson 49—Apply

You are the executive assistant to the president of Long Shot, Inc. The president has asked you to plan a business trip to Chicago, Illinois. In this project, you prepare an itinerary for a meeting with a client, in which you include tables that you format by creating a custom table style, and captions.

DIRECTIONS

1. Start Word, if necessary, and open **W49Apply** from the data files for this lesson.
2. Save the file as **W49Apply_xx** in the location where your teacher instructs you to store the files for this lesson.
3. Double-click in the header, and type your full name and today's date. Close the header.
4. Click in Table A, and click the **Table Tools Design** tab.
5. In the Table Styles gallery, right-click the **W49Apply** custom table style, and click **Modify Table Style**.
6. Modify the formatting for the whole table to change the single line borders to double lines.
7. Change the formatting for the first column and the header row to make the text bold and White, Background 1, and to change the fill color to Blue-Gray, Text 2, Lighter 40%.
8. Save the changes for all new documents based on the current template.
9. Turn on the **AutoCaption** feature, set to apply the text label Table followed by uppercase letters (A, B, C, ...) above the table.

10. On the last line of the document, insert a new table with two columns and five rows and enter the following information:

Return Flight Information	
Date:	October 11, 2017
Airline/Flight Number:	SouthernWest/392
Scheduled Departure Time:	5:30 p.m. CST
Scheduled Arrival Time:	8:15 p.m. EST

11. Merge the cells in the first row, and format the table using the **W49Apply** custom table style.
12. Position the insertion point on the last line of the document, press ENTER, insert a table with three columns and five rows, and enter the following:

Meeting Agenda		
Attendees:	Mr. George Lombardi Ms. Kate Sunderland Mr. Philip Katz	President, Long Shot, Inc. President, Golf Equipment, LLC Vice President of Sales, Golf Equipment, LLC
Location:	Golf Equipment, LLC Headquarters	1187 NW 151st Street, Chicago, Illinois
Time:	11:00 a.m. – 4:00 p.m.	Lunch included
Topic:	Joint marketing venture	

13. Merge the cells in the first row, and apply the **W49Apply** custom table style.
14. Apply the **No Spacing** style to the text in Table C.
15. Adjust the width of each table to AutoFit the contents (**Table Tools Layout** > **AutoFit** > **AutoFit Contents**).
16. Check and correct the spelling and grammar in the document, and save the document.
17. **With your teacher's permission**, print the document. It should look similar to Figure 49-2 on the next page.
18. Turn off **AutoCaption**.
19. Delete the **W49Apply** custom table style from the Normal.dotm template. Do not delete it from the document.
20. Save and close the document, and exit Word.

Figure 49-2

Firstname Lastname
Today's Date

Long Shot, Inc.

Itinerary for Mr. Lombardi
Customer Meeting in Chicago, Illinois

You are traveling to Chicago on Wednesday, October 11, to meet with representatives of Golf Equipment, LLC. Refer to Table A for your departure flight information. Refer to Table B for your return flight information. Refer to Table C for the meeting agenda.

Table A

Departure Flight Information	
Date:	October 11, 2017
Airline/Flight Number:	SouthernWest/191
Scheduled Departure Time:	9:40 a.m. EST
Scheduled Arrival Time:	10:10 a.m. CST

Table B

Return Flight Information	
Date:	October 11, 2017
Airline/Flight Number:	SouthernWest/392
Scheduled Departure Time:	5:30 p.m. CST
Scheduled Arrival Time:	8:15 p.m. EST

Table C

Meeting Agenda		
Attendees:	Mr. George Lombardi	President, Long Shot, Inc.
	Ms. Kate Sunderland	President, Golf Equipment, LLC
	Mr. Philip Katz	Vice President of Sales, Golf Equipment, LLC
Location:	Golf Equipment, LLC Headquarters	1187 NW 151st Street, Chicago, Illinois
Time:	11:00 a.m. – 4:00 p.m.	Lunch included
Topic:	Joint marketing venture	

Lesson 50

Using Advanced Table Features

➤ What You Will Learn

Inserting Graphics in a Table Cell
Inserting a Nested Table
Creating a Repeating Header Row
Splitting a Table
Inserting an Excel Worksheet in a Word Document
Copying Excel Data to Word and Converting a Table to Text

WORDS TO KNOW

Nested table
A table created inside the cell of another table.

Separator character
A keyboard character such as a tab, comma, or hyphen used to separate text into columns.

Software Skills You can insert graphics in a table cell to add visual interest. You can nest tables to create a table within a table. Create a repeating header row to ensure that a header row will show when a table breaks across a page. Use advanced table features, such as splitting, sorting, and calculating, to make the data in a table easier to read and analyze. With Excel features in Word, you can create a worksheet, or copy and paste Excel data into a Word document as a table. You can link inserted data from an Excel or Access file. Finally, you can convert a table to text when you want the content to display in paragraph format rather than in columns and rows.

What You Can Do

Inserting Graphics in a Table Cell

- You can insert a graphics object into a table cell so it stays positioned relative to other objects and text on the page.
- Use the same commands to insert a graphic into a table cell that you use to insert a graphic in any Word document.
- For example, use the Insert > Pictures command to insert a picture, or Insert > Online Pictures to insert online images.
- By default, the cell automatically adjusts in size to fit the dimensions of the graphic.
- You can set the table properties to keep the cell size constant and adjust the size of the graphic to fit.
- If you increase the size of the graphic after inserting it, Word automatically crops the portion that is outside the boundaries of the cell.

Try It! Inserting Graphics in a Table Cell

1. Start Word, and save a new blank document as **W50TryA_xx** in the location where your teacher instructs you to store the files for this lesson.
2. Insert a table with three columns and three rows, and move the insertion point to the second cell in the first column.
3. Click Insert > Pictures, and insert **W50Try_picture** from the data files for this lesson. Notice that the cell resizes automatically to fit the picture.
4. Click the Undo button on the Quick Access Toolbar.
5. Click the Table Tools Layout tab and, in the Table group, click the Properties button.
6. In the Table Properties dialog box, on the Table tab, click the Options button, click to clear the Automatically resize to fit contents check box, and click OK.
7. In the Table Properties dialog box, click the Row tab.
8. Under Row 2 Size, click to select the Specify height check box, and use the increment arrows to set the row height to 1.5".
9. Click the Row height is drop-down arrow, click Exactly, and click OK.
10. Click Insert > Pictures, and insert the **W50Try_picture** file from the data files for this lesson.
11. With the picture selected, drag the lower-right sizing handle down about 0.5". Notice that Word crops the picture so you only see the portion that still fits within the cell boundaries.
12. Click the Undo button on the Quick Access Toolbar, save the changes to **W50TryA_xx**, and leave it open to use in the next Try It.

Inserting a Nested Table

- Insert a **nested table** when you need to create a table within a cell of an existing table.
- For example, you might use a table to set up an agenda, and then use a nested table within the agenda to list events occurring in a particular time slot.
- You can use any method of inserting a table to create a nested table, including the Insert > Table command, Draw Table command, or copying and pasting a table from a different location.
- Nested tables make it easy to position and align data relative to other data on a page.
- You can format a nested table independently from the primary table. For example, you can apply a style to the primary table, and a different style to the nested table.

Try It! Inserting a Nested Table

1. In the **W50TryA_xx** file, position the insertion point in the cell in the lower-right of the table.
2. Click Insert > Table and drag across the grid to insert a table with three columns and four rows. The insertion point displays in the first cell in the nested table.
3. Type **Date**, press TAB, type **Name**, press TAB, and type **Age**.
4. Press TAB. The insertion point moves to the first cell in the second row of the nested table.
5. Select the main table. On the Table Tools Design tab, in the Table Styles gallery, click the More button, and click Grid Table 3 - Accent 1 table style.

(continued)

Try It! Inserting a Nested Table *(continued)*

6. Select the nested table, and in the Table Styles gallery click the Grid Table 5 Dark - Accent 2 table style. Click outside the main table.

7. Save the changes to **W50TryA_xx**, and leave it open to use in the next Try It.

Nested table in a table cell

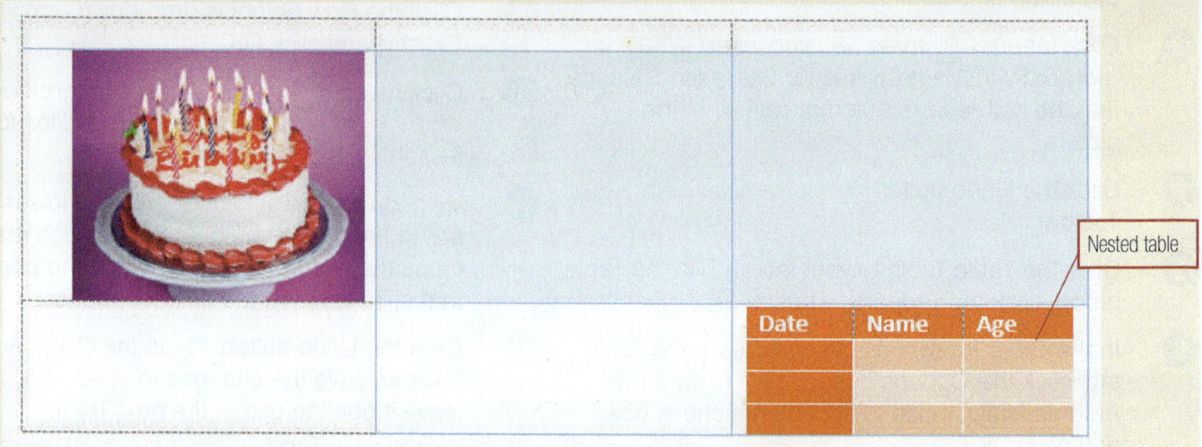

Word 2016, Windows 10, Microsoft Corporation

Creating a Repeating Header Row

- You can create a repeating header row in a table so that the header row will display again when a table breaks across a page.
- Use the Properties button in the Table group on the Table Tools Layout tab to display the Table Properties dialog box, and then use the Row tab to access the Rows Options.
- In the Table Properties dialog box, the Repeat as header row option is available only for the first row of a table.
- You can select multiple rows to repeat as header rows using the Repeat Header Rows command in the Data group on the Table Tools Layout tab.
- You can also create single or multiple header rows in a nested table.

Try It! Creating a Repeating Header Row

1. In the **W50TryA_xx** file, right-click in the first row of the nested table.
2. Click Table Properties to display the Table Properties dialog box.
3. Click the Row tab.
4. Under Options, click to select the Repeat as header row check box.
5. Click OK.
6. Save the changes to **W50TryA_xx**, and leave it open to use in the next Try It.

(continued)

Try It! Creating a Repeating Header Row *(continued)*

Set the Repeat as header row table option

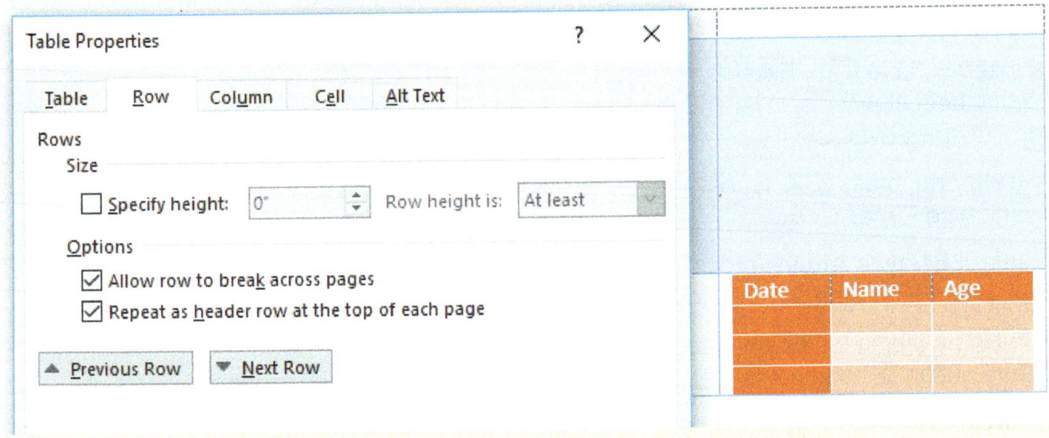

Word 2016, Windows 10, Microsoft Corporation

Splitting a Table

- You can split a table, or a nested table, in much the same way as you split a cell.
- Place the insertion point on the row which you want to become the first row of the split table.
- Use the Split Table command in the Merge group on the Table Tools Layout tab.
- You can also split a nested table.

Try It! Splitting a Table

1. In the **W50TryA_xx** file, place the insertion point in the third row of the nested table.
2. Click the Table Tools Layout tab.
3. In the Merge group, click the Split Table button. The nested table splits between the second and third rows.
4. Save the changes to **W50TryA_xx**, and leave it open to use in the next Try It.

Inserting an Excel Worksheet in a Word Document

- There may be times when you want more advanced spreadsheet functions than a Word table provides.
- You can use the Insert > Table > Excel Spreadsheet command to create an Excel worksheet object in your document.
- Like a chart, the worksheet data is not saved in an Excel file; it is only saved as part of the Word document.

✓ *Refer to Word, Lesson 40 for information on creating charts in Word.*

- When you double-click the worksheet object, the Excel ribbon becomes available so you can use the Excel tools and commands to enter, edit, and format the data.

✓ *For information on working with Excel, refer to the Excel chapters in this book.*

- You can also insert an Excel worksheet in a Word document and link to the data in the original Excel file. When you change the data in the Excel file, the data in the linked Excel worksheet will change.

✓ *For information on linking and embedding objects saved in a separate file, refer to the lessons in Word, Chapter 9.*

Try It! Inserting an Excel Worksheet in a Word Document

1. In the **W50TryA_xx** file, insert another blank paragraph below the table and position the insertion point on the last blank paragraph.
2. Click Insert > Table > Excel Spreadsheet. The worksheet object displays, and the Excel ribbon becomes available.
3. Type **Balloons**, press ENTER, type **Cake**, press ENTER, and type **Paper Goods**.
4. Click in cell B1, type **$15.99**, press ENTER, type **$19.99**, press ENTER, type **$12.99**, and press ENTER.
5. On the Home tab, in the Editing group, click the AutoSum button Σ, and press ENTER.
6. Click anywhere outside the worksheet object to deselect it. The Word ribbon and tools become available again.
7. Click the worksheet object to select it, and click Home > Center to center the object horizontally.
8. Double-click the worksheet object. The Excel tools become available.
9. Double-click the border between column A and column B in the worksheet frame to automatically adjust the width of column A to display all contents.
10. Select the cell range A1:B4, and drag the sizing handle of the worksheet object in the lower-right corner up and to the left so that only the range A1:B4 displays.

    ✓ *After resizing the object, you may have to scroll the worksheet to display the correct range.*

11. With the cell range A1:B4 still selected, on the Home tab, in the Styles group, click Cell Styles (or the More arrow, if applicable), and click 20% - Accent 1.
12. Click anywhere outside the worksheet object.
13. Save the changes to **W50TryA_xx**, and leave it open to use in the next Try It.

Insert an Excel worksheet in a document

Word 2016, Windows 10, Microsoft Corporation

Copying Excel Data to Word and Converting a Table to Text

- If you have existing data in an Excel worksheet, you can copy and paste it as a table into a Word document.
- The pasted table has the same formatting it had in the Excel worksheet, but you can edit and reformat it using Word commands.
- You can convert an entire table or selected table rows into regular document text.
- Word inserts the specified **separator character** into the text at the end of each column and starts a new paragraph at the end of each row.
- If document text is set to wrap around a table, when you convert the table to text, Word inserts the text in a text box.

Try It! Copying Excel Data to Word and Converting a Table to Text

1. In the **W50TryA_xx** file, toggle on nonprinting characters, and insert two blank paragraphs below the worksheet object. Position the insertion point on the last blank paragraph, and click the Align Left button.
2. Start Excel, and open **W50TryB** from the data files for this lesson.
3. Select the cell range A1:C4.
4. On the Home tab in the Clipboard group, click Copy, and exit Excel without saving any changes.
5. In Word, click Home > Paste to paste the Excel data as a Word table.
6. Click the table selection handle of the table you pasted in step 5, right-click the table, and then click AutoFit > AutoFit to Window.
7. Click the Table Tools Layout tab and, in the Data group, click the Convert to Text button to open the Convert Table To Text dialog box.
8. Verify that the Tabs option button is selected, and click OK. Word converts the table to text, separating the columns with tabs.
9. Toggle off the nonprinting characters.
10. Save and close **W50TryA_xx**, and exit Word.

Convert a table to text

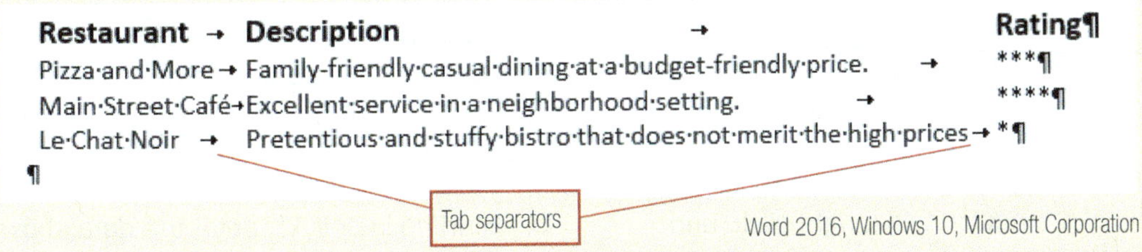

Word 2016, Windows 10, Microsoft Corporation

Lesson 50—Practice

The Horticultural Shop Owner's Association has asked you to create a purchase order for gifts that will be handed out to attendees at a national meeting. In this project, you will use nested tables, graphics, and Excel worksheet data to create the purchase order. You will also convert a table to text, create a repeating header row, split the tables, and sort the data to make the document visually appealing.

DIRECTIONS

1. Start Word, if necessary, click **Blank document**, and save the default blank document as **W50Practice_xx** in the location where your teacher instructs you to store the files for this lesson.
2. Insert a table with five columns and seven rows. Rest the mouse pointer over the table and click the **Table Selector** button to select the entire table.
3. On the **Table Tools Design** tab, click the **Borders** drop-down arrow > **No Border**. If table gridlines are not displayed, click **Table Tools Layout** > **View Gridlines**.
4. Select the first row, click **Table Tools Layout** > **Merge Cells**.

5. Position the insertion point in the first cell of the third row, and enter the data (shown in Table 50-1 at the bottom of this page) in the third and fourth rows, replacing the sample text *Today's Date* with the actual date and *Student's Name* with your own name.
6. Select the fifth row, and on the Table Tools Layout tab, in the Merge group, click **Merge Cells**.
7. In the third column of the seventh row, type **Authorized by:**, press TAB, type your name, press TAB, and type today's date.
8. Position the insertion point in the top-left cell in the table, and click **Insert** > **Table**.
9. Drag across the grid to insert a nested table with three columns and three rows.
10. Click the Table Selector button of the nested table to select the entire nested table. Format the nested table with **No Border**.
11. Select the top row of the nested table and merge the cells.
12. In the top row of the nested table, type **PURCHASE ORDER**, and format the text with the **Heading 1** style.
13. Position the insertion point in the first cell in the second row of the nested table, right-click, and click **Table Properties**.
14. In the Table Properties dialog box, click the **Row** tab, and specify a row height of exactly **2.5"**.
15. Click **OK** to apply the changes and close the Table Properties dialog box.
16. With the insertion point still in the first cell in the second row of the nested table, click **Insert** > **Pictures**, and insert **W50Practice_picture** from the data files for this lesson.
17. Merge the middle and right cells in the second row of the nested table.
18. Type the following five lines of text:

    Horticultural Shop Owner's Association

    452 Cathedral Street

    Baltimore, MD 21201

    555.555.5555

    hsoamail@hsoassoc.net
19. Format the first line with the **Heading 1** style, and click **Table Tools Layout** > **Align Top Right**.
20. In the third row of the nested table, type the data shown in Table 50-2 at the bottom of this page.
21. Position the insertion point in the fifth row of the main table (that you merged in step 6), and click **Insert** > **Table** > **Excel Spreadsheet**.
22. Starting in cell A1, enter the data shown in Table 50-3 at the bottom of this page.

✓ *If Excel marks cell E5 as containing an error, click the error warning button drop-down arrow, and click Ignore Error.*

Table 50-1

P.O. Date	Ordered By	Shipped Via	F.O.B. Point	Terms
Today's Date	*Student's Name*	Ground	Shipping	Net 30

Table 50-2

To: Swag Manufacturing	Ship To: HSOA	P.O. Number: 11001

Table 50-3

QTY	UNIT	DESCRIPTION	UNIT PRICE	TOTAL
250	Shirt	Blue T with logos	$3.12	=D2*A2
250	Mug	Blue coffee with logos	$3.49	=D3*A3
			SUBTOTAL	=SUM(E2:E3)
			SALES TAX	=E4*.05
			TOTAL	=SUM(E4:E5)

23. Format the cell range **E2:E6** with the Accounting number format.
24. Adjust the column widths to display all data, and resize the Excel worksheet so that only the cell range A1:E6 displays.
25. Select the cell range **A1:E1**, and apply the **Accent1** cell style.
26. Select the range **A2:E6**, and apply the **20% - Accent1** cell style.
27. Click outside the worksheet object, click the worksheet object in the document to select it, and center it.
28. Insert a second blank paragraph below the main table, and position the insertion point on the last blank paragraph.
29. Start Excel, and open **W50PracticeB** from the data files for this lesson.
30. Select the range **A3:A6**, click **Home** > **Copy**, and exit Excel without saving.
31. In Word, click **Home** > **Paste** to paste the Excel data as a Word table.
32. Select the table you pasted in step 31, and click **Table Tools Layout** > **Convert to Text**.
33. Verify that the **Paragraph marks** option button is selected, and click **OK**. Word converts the table to text, separating the rows with paragraph marks.
34. With the converted text still selected, click **Home** > **Numbering**.
35. At the end of the last line, type your name followed by a period.
36. Adjust the width of the two cells where you entered your name in the main table so the text fits on a single line.
37. Click in the third row of the main table (with the text *P.O. Date* in the first cell), and on the Table Tools Layout tab, click **Split Table**.
38. Select the first two rows of the new second table, click **Table Tools Layout** > **Repeat Header Rows**.
39. Select the second table, and on the Table Tools Layout tab, click **Sort**.
40. In the Sort by box, click the drop-down arrow, and select **P.O. Date**. In the Then by box, click the drop-down arrow, select **Ordered By**, and click **OK**.
41. Check and correct the spelling and grammar in the document, and save the document.
42. **With your teacher's permission**, print the document. It should look similar to Figure 50-1 on the next page.
43. Save and close the document, and exit Word.

Figure 50-1

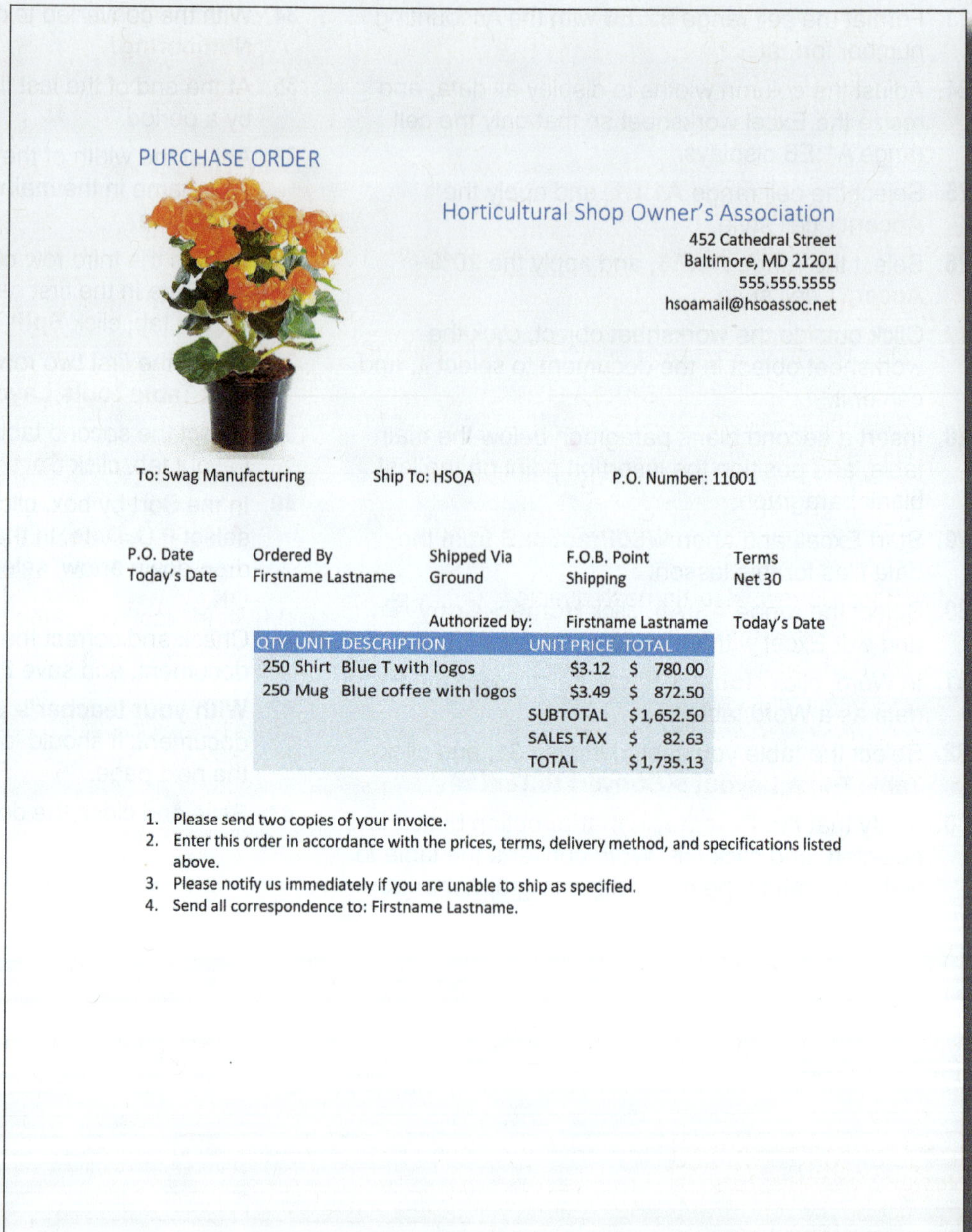

PURCHASE ORDER

Horticultural Shop Owner's Association
452 Cathedral Street
Baltimore, MD 21201
555.555.5555
hsoamail@hsoassoc.net

To: Swag Manufacturing | Ship To: HSOA | P.O. Number: 11001

P.O. Date	Ordered By	Shipped Via	F.O.B. Point	Terms
Today's Date	Firstname Lastname	Ground	Shipping	Net 30
		Authorized by:	Firstname Lastname	Today's Date

QTY	UNIT	DESCRIPTION	UNIT PRICE	TOTAL
250	Shirt	Blue T with logos	$3.12	$ 780.00
250	Mug	Blue coffee with logos	$3.49	$ 872.50
			SUBTOTAL	$1,652.50
			SALES TAX	$ 82.63
			TOTAL	$1,735.13

1. Please send two copies of your invoice.
2. Enter this order in accordance with the prices, terms, delivery method, and specifications listed above.
3. Please notify us immediately if you are unable to ship as specified.
4. Send all correspondence to: Firstname Lastname.

Lesson 50—Apply

The purchase order for gifts that you created for The Horticultural Shop Owner's Association was handed out to attendees at a national meeting and resulted in a sale. Now you need to create an invoice for the first gift order. In this project, you will use nested tables, graphics, and Excel worksheet data to create an invoice for the sale items.

DIRECTIONS

1. Start Word, if necessary, and open **W50ApplyA** from the data files for this lesson.
2. Save the file as **W50ApplyA_xx** in the location where your teacher instructs you to store the files for this lesson.
3. Select the table and apply the **Grid Table 6 Colorful - Accent 1** table style.
4. In the top row, insert a nested table with two columns and three rows. Remove all borders from the nested table.
5. Merge the cells in row 1 of the nested table and type **INVOICE**. Format the text with the **Title** style.
6. Set the row height of row 2 of the nested table to exactly **1.75"**.
7. In the left cell of row 2 of the nested table, type the following five lines:

   SWAG Manufacturing Co.

   779 Industrial Avenue

   Marlborough, MA 01752

   555.555.5555

   mail@swagmftg.net
8. Format the company name with the **Heading 1** style.
9. Insert **W50Apply_picture** from the data files for this lesson into the right cell of row 2 in the nested table, and align it with the top right of the cell.
10. Type the data (shown in Table 50-4 at the bottom of this page) in row 3 in the nested table, replacing the sample text *Student's Name* with your own name and *Today's Date* with the date.
11. In the last row of the main table, insert an Excel spreadsheet and enter the data (shown in Table 50-5 at the bottom of this page) starting in cell A1:

    ✓ *If Excel marks cell D5 as containing an error, click the error warning button drop-down arrow and click Ignore Error.*
12. Format the cell range **D2:D6** with the **Accounting** number format.
13. Adjust the column widths to display all data, and adjust the size of the object to display only the range **A1:D6**.
14. Format the range **A1:D1** with the **Accent4** cell style, and format the range **A2:D6** with the **20% - Accent4** cell style.

Table 50-4

Invoice # HOSA-2C **Invoice Date:** ***Today's Date***	**Ship To:** ***Student's Name*** **Horticultural Shop Owner's Association** **452 Cathedral Street** **Baltimore, MD 21201**

Table 50-5

QTY	DESCRIPTION	UNIT PRICE	TOTAL
250	T-shirts with logos	$3.12	=C2*A2
250	Mugs with logos	$3.49	=C3*A3
		SUBTOTAL	=SUM(D2:D3)
		SALES TAX	=D4*.05
		TOTAL	=SUM(D4:D5)

15. Center the worksheet object horizontally in the Word table.
16. Start Excel, and open **W50ApplyB** from the data files for this lesson.
17. Copy and paste the data from cells **A3:A5** to a blank line below the main table (insert a new blank line, if necessary) in **W50ApplyA_xx**, and exit Excel without saving.
18. Replace the sample text *Student's Name* in the copied Excel data with your own name, and convert the copied Excel data to text separated by paragraph marks.
19. Center the last line.
20. Check and correct the spelling and grammar, and save the document.
21. **With your teacher's permission**, print the document. It should look similar to Figure 50-2.
22. Save and close the document, and exit Word.

Figure 50-2

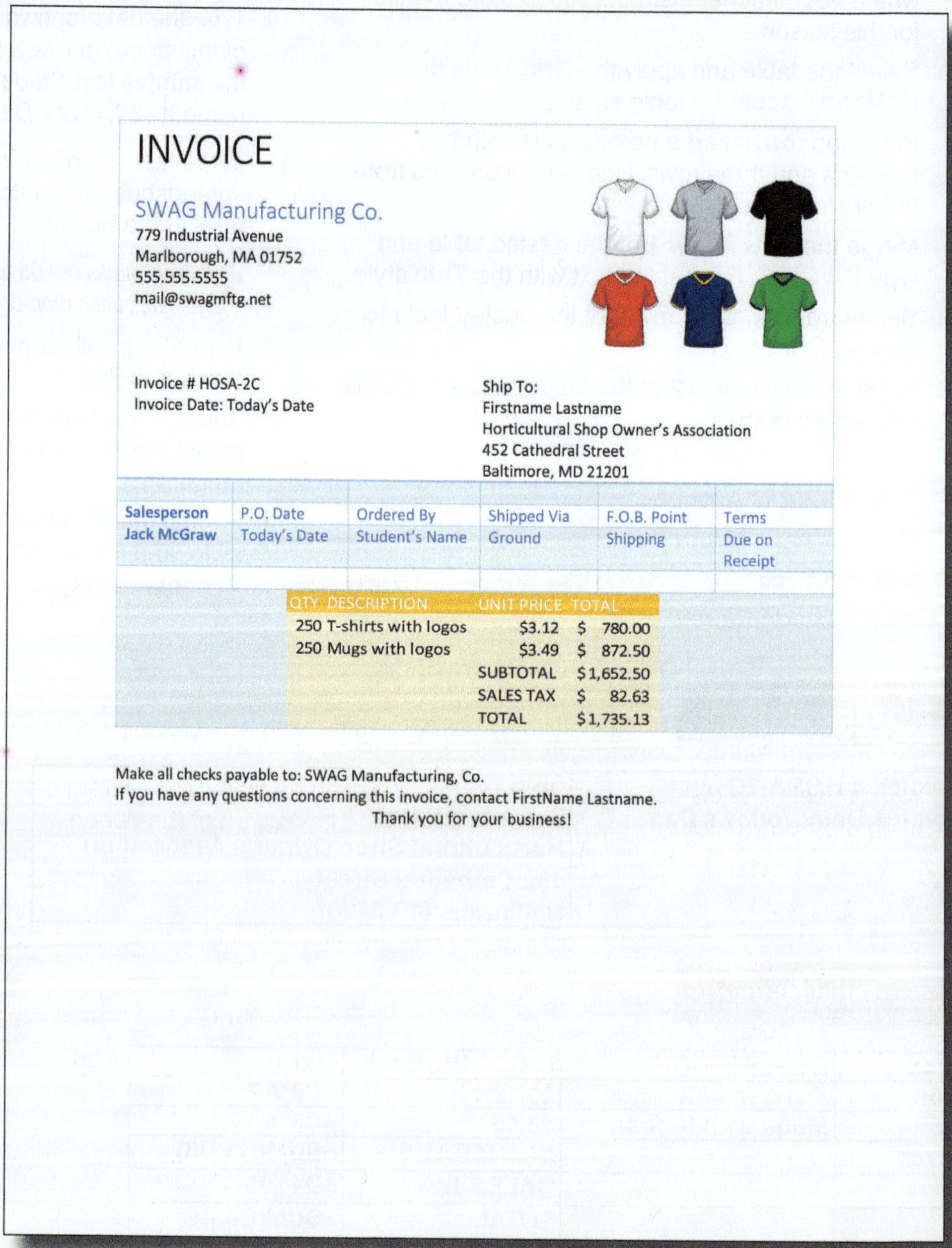

INVOICE

SWAG Manufacturing Co.
779 Industrial Avenue
Marlborough, MA 01752
555.555.5555
mail@swagmftg.net

Invoice # HOSA-2C
Invoice Date: Today's Date

Ship To:
Firstname Lastname
Horticultural Shop Owner's Association
452 Cathedral Street
Baltimore, MD 21201

Salesperson	P.O. Date	Ordered By	Shipped Via	F.O.B. Point	Terms
Jack McGraw	Today's Date	Student's Name	Ground	Shipping	Due on Receipt

QTY	DESCRIPTION	UNIT PRICE	TOTAL
250	T-shirts with logos	$3.12	$ 780.00
250	Mugs with logos	$3.49	$ 872.50
		SUBTOTAL	$1,652.50
		SALES TAX	$ 82.63
		TOTAL	$1,735.13

Make all checks payable to: SWAG Manufacturing, Co.
If you have any questions concerning this invoice, contact FirstName Lastname.
Thank you for your business!

Lesson 51

Using Advanced Graphics

➤ What You Will Learn

Using Document Gridlines
Using Advanced Sizing Features
Using Advanced Position Features
Adjusting Objects
Cropping a Picture

Software Skills Using the advanced graphics options in Word 2016, you can integrate graphics objects with text and white space on the page to create professional-looking documents. You can apply precise settings for sizing and positioning objects, change a picture by adjusting or cropping, and add a caption to help describe an illustration.

What You Can Do

Using Document Gridlines

- **Document gridlines** display between the margins to help you size and position objects on a page.
- By default the gridlines are spaced 0.13" apart horizontally and vertically. You can change the spacing in the Grid and Guides dialog box.
- You can also select the number of gridlines to display, and whether objects should **snap to** the grid or to other objects.
- You can select to display the gridlines on the View tab on the ribbon or from the Align drop-down menu in the Arrange group on the Layout tab of the ribbon.

WORDS TO KNOW

Adjustment handle
A small yellow square used to alter the most prominent feature of a shape. The mouse pointer is an arrowhead when resting on an adjustment handle.

Anchor
An element in a document, such as the margin or the page itself, relative to which you can position an object.

Aspect ratio
The relative horizontal and vertical sizes of an object, or the ratio of width to height.

Crop
Trim or hide one or more edges of a picture.

Document gridlines
Nonprinting horizontal and vertical lines that you can display on the page to help you align and position objects.

Outcrop
Use the cropping tool to add a margin around an object.

Scale
Adjust the size of an object based on a percentage of its original size.

Snap to
Align evenly with.

Try It! Using Document Gridlines

1. Start Word, and open **W51Try** from the data files for this lesson.
2. Save the file as **W51Try_xx** in the location where your teacher instructs you to store the files for this lesson.
3. Click the View tab. In the Show group, click to select the Ruler check box and the Gridlines check box.
4. Click the Layout tab. In the Arrange group, click the Align button, and click Grid Settings to display the Grid and Guides dialog box.
5. Under Object Snapping, click to clear the Snap objects to other objects check box.
6. Under Grid settings, set both the Horizontal spacing and Vertical spacing to 0.25", and click OK.
7. In the document, click the heart shape, and drag it about 1" to the left. Notice that it snaps to each vertical gridline as you drag.
8. On the Layout tab, click Align > Grid Settings.
9. Click to select the Snap objects to other objects check box, and click OK.
10. Save the changes to **W51Try_xx**, and leave it open to use in the next Try It.

Display document gridlines

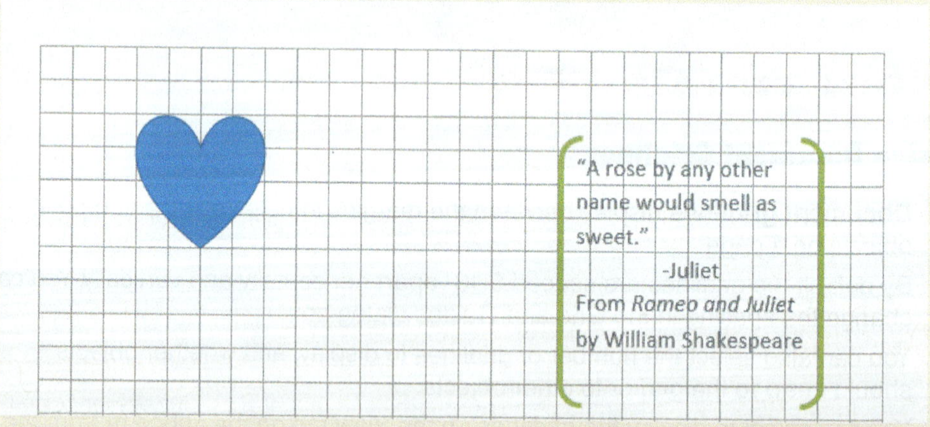

Word 2016, Windows 10, Microsoft Corporation

Using Advanced Sizing Features

- You can easily resize the height and/or width of an object by dragging a sizing handle or entering a precise measurement in the Height or Width boxes in the Size group on the Format tab.
- Use advanced sizing features to fine tune the size of an object.
- By default, the **aspect ratio** of most picture objects is locked, so when you adjust one dimension, either height or width, the other dimension adjusts automatically.

- You can lock or unlock the aspect ratio for any object.
- **Scale** an object when you want to adjust its size based on a percentage of its current or original size. For example, scale an object by 50% to make it half its original size.
- Set a relative size for a drawing object when you want to size it relative to the page or margins.
- Some sizing options are available only for certain types of objects. For example, you cannot set a relative size for a picture, but you can reset a picture to its original size.

Try It! Using Advanced Sizing Features

1. In the W51Try_xx file, click to select the heart shape.
2. Click the Drawing Tools Format tab, and click the Size group dialog box launcher to display the Size tab of the Layout dialog box. (You may have to click the Size group button to display the dialog box launcher.)
3. Under Scale, set the Height value to 200%, and click OK. The shape height doubles, but the width remains the same.
4. Click Undo on the Quick Access Toolbar.
5. Click the Size group dialog box launcher.
6. Under Scale, click to select the Lock aspect ratio check box, and set the Height value to 200%.
7. Click OK to resize the shape.
8. Save the changes to W51Try_xx, and leave it open to use in the next Try It.

Using Advanced Position Features

- Use Word's advanced position features to position or align an object precisely.
- You access these features by clicking More Layout Options on the Position drop-down menu on the Drawing Tools Format tab of the ribbon.
- You can also access these features by clicking the See more option on the Layout Options shortcut menu that appears to the right of the object.
- You can position or align the object relative to an **anchor**, such as a column, page, or margin.
- You can lock the anchor to keep the object from moving when you add or delete text.
- Object anchors display with other nonprinting characters.

Try It! Using Advanced Position Features

1. In the W51Try_xx file, display nonprinting characters if they are not already displayed.
2. Click to select the picture. Notice the object anchor in the upper-left margin.
3. Click the Picture Tools Format tab, click the Position button, and click More Layout Options to display the Position tab of the Layout dialog box.
4. Under Horizontal, click the Alignment option, verify that the Alignment position box is Left, click the relative to drop-down arrow, and click Page.
5. Under Vertical, enter 2.5" in the Absolute position measurement box, and verify that the below box is Margin.
6. Click OK.
7. Save the changes to W51Try_xx, and leave it open to use in the next Try It.

(continued)

Try It! Using Advanced Position Features *(continued)*

Position an object precisely

Word 2016, Windows 10, Microsoft Corporation

Adjusting Objects

- Some—but not all—drawing objects have one or more **adjustment handles** that display as a yellow square.
- You can drag the adjustment handle to alter the most prominent feature of the shape.
- For example, you can drag an adjustment handle on a block arrow shape to change the width of the arrow body or the length of the arrowhead.
- When the mouse pointer touches an adjustment handle, it looks like an arrowhead.

Try It! Adjusting Objects

1. In the W51Try_xx file, click to select the text box. Notice the adjustment handle just below the upper-left sizing handle.
2. Drag the adjustment handle down and to the right about 0.5", and release the mouse button. (You can use the gridlines to estimate the distance.) The text box border adjusts to a rounder, more curved shape.
3. Increase the width of the text box to 2.5" so all the text displays within the box.
4. Save the changes to W51Try_xx, and leave it open to use in the next Try It.

Adjust an object's most prominent feature

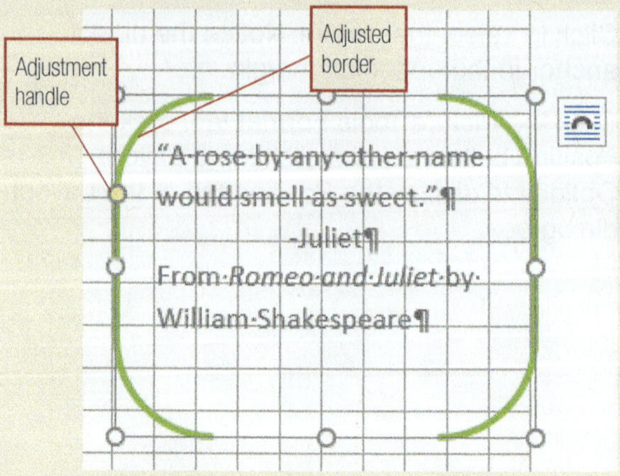

Word 2016, Windows 10, Microsoft Corporation

Cropping a Picture

- **Crop** a picture to remove or trim one or more of the edges.
- You can crop from the left, right, top, and/or bottom.
- Cropping hides the edges, but does not permanently delete them.

  ✓ *You can permanently delete cropped edges when you compress a picture. You learn about compressing pictures in Word, Lesson 52.*

- You can access the Crop command from the Picture Tools Format tab, or by right-clicking the picture.
- Crop handles appear as thick black lines at the edges of the picture.
- When you select a crop handle, the mouse pointer takes on the shape of the crop handle.
- You can reset a cropped picture to its original appearance.
- If you want to add a margin around a picture, you can **outcrop** it by dragging a cropping handle out, away from the picture area.

Try It! Cropping a Picture

1. In the W51Try_xx file, click the picture to select it.
2. Click the Picture Tools Format tab, and in the Size group, click the Crop button. Crop handles display on the picture.
3. Position the mouse pointer over the center crop handle on the left side of the picture. Click, hold, and drag the crop handle half an inch to the right, and release the mouse button.
4. Position the mouse pointer over the crop handle in the upper-right corner of the picture, and click and drag down and to the left three-quarters of an inch (one gridline down and three gridlines to the left).
5. Click outside the picture to complete the crop.
6. Click the picture to select it, and click the Crop drop-down arrow to display a menu of cropping options.
7. Point to Crop to Shape to display the Shapes palette. Under Basic Shapes, click Oval.
8. Click the Layout Options shortcut menu > See more.
   a. Under Horizontal, click the Alignment option, verify the Alignment box is Left, click the relative to drop-down arrow, and click Margin.
   b. Under Vertical, in the Absolute position box, enter 3", verify that the below box is Margin.
   c. Click OK.
9. Click View > Gridlines to hide the gridlines.
10. Save and close the document, and exit Word.

Lesson 51—Practice

Business owners and managers must continually look for ways to bring in customers, improve products, and develop opportunities. At Liberty Blooms, this means creating newsletters, sponsoring classes, and hosting events. In this project, you will create a recipe flier using advanced graphic features to hand out to customers interested in growing and using herbs.

DIRECTIONS

1. Start Word, if necessary, click **Blank document**, and save the document as **W51Practice_xx** in the location where your teacher instructs you to store the files for this lesson.
2. Double-click in the header, and type your full name and today's date. Click **Close Header and Footer**.
3. On the first line of the document, type **Recipe Showcase**, and format it with the **Title** style.
4. Press ENTER, type **Chicken with Tomatoes and Herbs**, and format it with the **Heading1** style.
5. Press ENTER, type **Yield: Four Servings**, and format it with the **Heading 2** style.
6. Press ENTER, type **Ingredients**, and format it with the **Heading 3** style.
7. Press ENTER and type the following eight lines using the **No Spacing** style:

   8 boneless chicken pieces

   1 tablespoon olive oil

   10 ½ ounces canned diced tomatoes, drained

   ¾ cup chicken stock

   2 teaspoons mixed herbs, chopped

   1 ½ ounces black olives, chopped

   1 teaspoon sugar

   Fresh basil to garnish
8. Press ENTER, type **Directions**, and format it with the **Heading 3** style.
9. Press ENTER, click the **Numbering** button and type the following list:

   Heat oil in large skillet.

   Add chicken pieces and cook until browned on all sides.

   Add the tomatoes, stock, and mixed herbs and simmer for 30 minutes or until chicken is cooked through.

   Add the olives and sugar and simmer for an additional 5 minutes.

   Garnish with fresh basil and serve with rice or pasta.
10. Click **View**, and in the Show group, click to select the **Gridlines** check box.
11. Click **Layout** > **Align** > **Grid Settings**.
12. In the Grid and Guides dialog box, click **Snap objects to other objects** to clear the check box > **OK**.
13. Click **Insert** > **Shapes** > **5-Point Star** (under Stars and Banners). Click in the upper-right part of the document to insert the shape.
14. Click **Drawing Tools Format**, and in the Shape Styles gallery, click the **Subtle Effect - Blue, Accent 1** style.
15. On the Drawing Tools Format tab, click the **Size** group dialog box launcher. (You may have to click the Size group button to display the dialog box launcher.)
16. In the Layout dialog box, on the Size tab, under Scale, click the **Lock aspect ratio** check box, and set the Height value to **250%**.
17. Click **OK** to resize the shape.
18. Right-click the star, and click **Add Text**. Type **From the Liberty Blooms Kitchen!**
19. With the shape still selected, click **Drawing Tools Format** > **Position** > **More Layout Options**.
20. In the Layout dialog box, on the Position tab, under Horizontal, click to select the **Alignment** option, click the **Alignment** drop-down arrow, and click **Right**. Click the **relative to** drop-down arrow and click **Margin**.
21. Under Vertical, click the **Absolute position** option, enter **1"** in the measurement box, click the **below** drop-down arrow, and click **Margin**.
22. Click to select the **Lock anchor** check box, and click **OK**.
23. With the shape still selected, click, hold, and drag the **adjustment handle** up and to the right about 0.25" (use the gridlines to judge the distance), and release the mouse button.
24. Select the text in the shape and increase the font size to **14 points**.
25. Click outside the shape to deselect it, and save the document.

26. Position the insertion point at the end of the document, click **Insert** > **Pictures**, and insert **W51Practice_picture** from the data files for this lesson.
27. With the picture selected, click **Picture Tools Format** > **Wrap Text** > **Square**.
28. Click the **Layout Options** shortcut menu > **See more**.
29. Under Horizontal, click to select the **Absolute position** option, set the value to **1.5"**, click the **to the right of** drop-down arrow, and click **Page**.
30. Under Vertical, click to select the **Absolute position** option, set the value to **5.12"**, click the **below** drop-down arrow, and click **Margin**.
31. Click to select the **Lock anchor** check box, and click **OK**.
32. With the picture still selected, right-click the picture, and click **Crop**.
33. Drag the lower-right corner **crop handle** up and to the left to crop out as much of the dish handle as possible, and click outside the shape to complete the crop.
34. Click the picture to select it, on the Picture Tools Format tab click the **Crop** drop-down arrow, and point to **Crop to Shape**.
35. On the Shapes palette, under Basic Shapes, click **Oval**.
36. Click **View**, and click to clear the **Gridlines** check box.
37. Check and correct the spelling and grammar, and save the document.
38. **With your teacher's permission**, print the document. It should look similar to Figure 51-1.
39. Save and close the document, and exit Word.

Figure 51-1

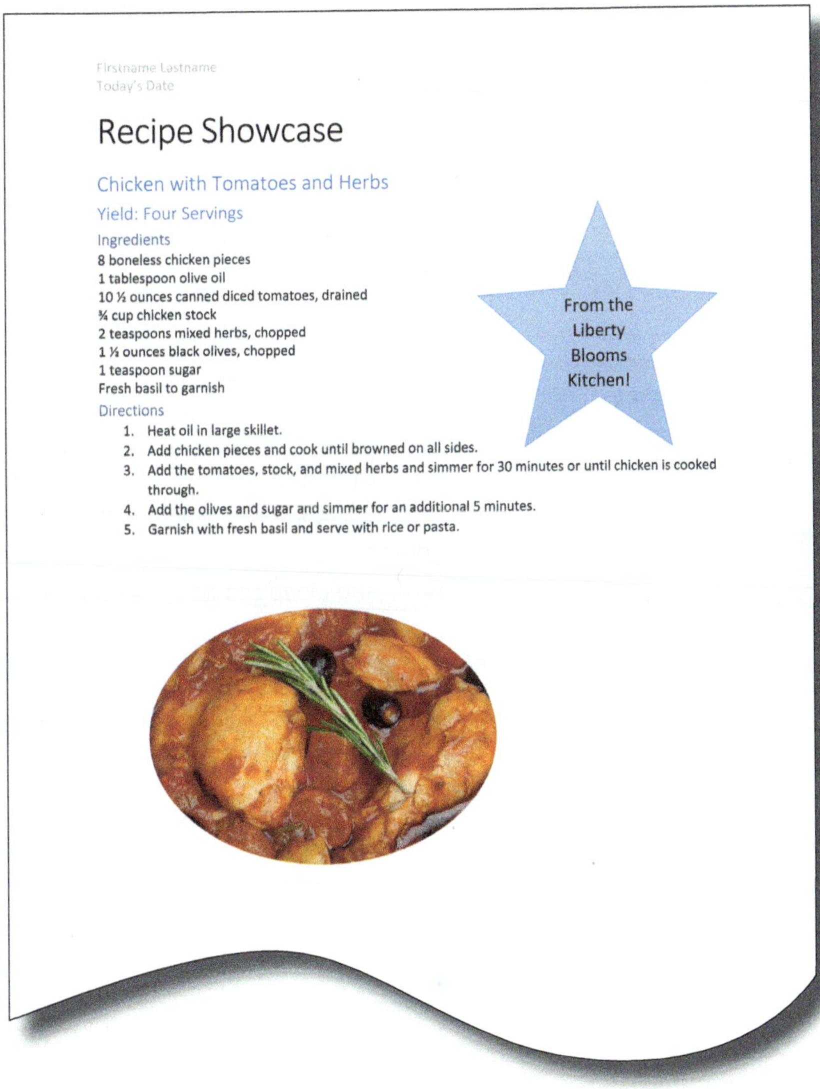
Firstname Lastname
Today's Date

Recipe Showcase

Chicken with Tomatoes and Herbs

Yield: Four Servings

Ingredients

8 boneless chicken pieces
1 tablespoon olive oil
10 ½ ounces canned diced tomatoes, drained
¾ cup chicken stock
2 teaspoons mixed herbs, chopped
1 ½ ounces black olives, chopped
1 teaspoon sugar
Fresh basil to garnish

From the Liberty Blooms Kitchen!

Directions

1. Heat oil in large skillet.
2. Add chicken pieces and cook until browned on all sides.
3. Add the tomatoes, stock, and mixed herbs and simmer for 30 minutes or until chicken is cooked through.
4. Add the olives and sugar and simmer for an additional 5 minutes.
5. Garnish with fresh basil and serve with rice or pasta.

Lesson 51—Apply

You work in the publicity department of Liberty Blooms. In this project, you will use advanced graphics features to enhance a newsletter to customers interested in growing and using herbs.

DIRECTIONS

1. Start Word, if necessary, and open **W51Apply** from the data files for this lesson.
2. Save the file as **W51Apply_xx** in the location where your teacher instructs you to store the files for this lesson.
3. Type your name and today's date in the header, and apply the **Facet** theme.
4. Position the insertion point at the beginning of the line *News in Brief*, and insert a continuous section break.
5. Insert another continuous section break at the beginning of the line *Recipe Showcase*.
6. Format section 2 into two columns of equal width.
7. Insert a column break at the beginning of the line *Classes and Seminars*. Note that the headings in the left and right columns do not align.
8. Display gridlines.
9. Set the spacing before the heading *News in Brief* to **10 pt**, and set the spacing before the heading *Classes and Seminars* to **18 pt**. The headings should now align with each other.
10. Set the spacing before the heading *Recipe Showcase* to **18 pt**.
11. Insert an Austin Quote text box, and type **Introducing Recipe Showcase, a new feature designed to bring your garden into your kitchen.**
12. Change the width of the text box to 2.75".
13. Position the text box horizontally at 4" to the right of the Margin and vertically -0.5" below the Margin (type a minus sign or hyphen to enter the negative value), click to deselect the **Move object with text** checkbox, if necessary, and lock the anchor.
14. Set the text wrapping for the text box to **In front of text**.
15. Position the insertion point at the end of the heading *Recipe Showcase*, and insert **W51Apply_picture** from the data files for this lesson.
16. Scale the picture to 65% of its original size, and set the text wrapping to **Square**.
17. Crop about 0.5" from the right side of the picture (refer to Figure 51-2 on the next page).
18. Position the picture horizontally aligned Left relative to the Margin and vertically 5.25" below the Margin.
19. Check and correct the spelling and grammar, and save in the document.
20. **With your teacher's permission**, print the document. It should look similar to Figure 51-2 on the next page.
21. Set objects to snap to other objects, and hide the gridlines.
22. Save and close the document, and exit Word.

Figure 51-2

Firstname Lastname
Today's Date

Liberty Blooms News

"The newsletter that brings your garden to life!"

Introducing Recipe Showcase, a new feature designed to bring your garden into your kitchen.

News in Brief

Plans are progressing on the store expansion. Thanks to everyone who completed a survey.

Spring-planting bulbs are in! Get them in the ground now so you can enjoy a summer of colorful blooms.

We offer a range of natural pest control products. Ask for details.

Classes and Seminars

There is always something going on at 345 Chestnut Street. We try to fill the calendar with interesting and informative activities that the whole family will enjoy.

The following events are scheduled for the coming months. Some events require registration, so please call ahead for more information.

- Edible Gardens May 13
- Flower Arranging May 21
- Water Gardens June 3
- Potpourri Designs June 11

Recipe Showcase

Chicken with Tomatoes and Herbs Yield: Four Servings

Ingredients

8 boneless chicken pieces
1 tablespoon olive oil
10 ½ ounces canned diced tomatoes, drained
¾ cup chicken stock
2 teaspoons mixed herbs, chopped
1 ½ ounces black olives, chopped
1 teaspoon sugar
Fresh basil to garnish

Directions

1. Heat oil in large skillet.
2. Add chicken pieces and cook until browned on all sides.
3. Add the tomatoes, stock, and mixed herbs and simmer for 30 minutes or until chicken is cooked through.
4. Add the olives and sugar and simmer for an additional 5 minutes.
5. Garnish with fresh basil and serve with rice or pasta.

Lesson 52

Linking Text Boxes

➤ What You Will Learn

Aligning an Object with Another Object
Linking Text Boxes
Compressing a Picture
Removing a Picture Background

WORDS TO KNOW

Compress
Reduce in size. A compressed picture has a reduced color format which results in a smaller file size.

Link (text boxes)
Establish a connection between text boxes so that text which does not fit within the borders of the first text box flows into the next, linked text box.

Text box chain
A series of linked text boxes.

Software Skills Using text boxes makes it possible to position and format text independently from the rest of the document. You can link text boxes so that the text flows from one to another. Align objects to improve the appearance of the document. Copy objects to save time and ensure consistency among similar objects in a document. Compress a picture to reduce the file size. You can remove the background from a picture to create a more interesting graphic.

What You Can Do

Aligning an Object with Another Object

- A truly professional-looking document contains objects properly aligned on the page and with each other.
- You can align multiple objects on a page horizontally and vertically relative to each other. For example, you can align the tops of text boxes relative to each other.
- Aligning objects with each other can also help you design graphics. For example, if you want to center a star shape over a circle, you can align the centers and middles of the shapes.
- When you select more than one object, Word activates the Align Selected Objects option so you can align the objects with each other.
- Options for aligning objects are on the Align drop-down menu in the Arrange group on the Layout tab or the Format tab.

Try It! Aligning an Object with Another Object

1. Start Word, and open **W52Try** from the data files for this lesson.
2. Save the file as **W52Try_xx** in the location where your teacher instructs you to store the files for this lesson.
3. Click the heart shape, press and hold SHIFT, and click the circle shape to select both objects.
4. Click the Drawing Tools Format tab, and click Align. Notice that the Align Selected Objects option is selected.
5. Click Align Center. The centers of the shapes are aligned vertically.
6. Click Align > Align Middle. The middles of the shapes are aligned horizontally, and the heart shape is now centered over the circle.
7. Click the text box on the left, press and hold SHIFT, and click the text box on the right.
8. On the Drawing Tools Format tab, click Align > Align Top. The tops of the text boxes are aligned.
9. Save the changes to **W52Try_xx**, and leave it open to use in the next Try It.

Align objects relative to each other

Word 2016, Windows 10, Microsoft Corporation

Linking Text Boxes

- You can **link** text boxes in a document so that text which does not fit within the first text box automatically flows into the next linked text box.
- To link one text box with another, select the first text box, click the Create Link button in the Text group on the Drawing Tools Format tab of the ribbon, and click the next text box.
- The second text box must not contain text when you establish the link.
- Text flows through a **text box chain** in the order in which you link the text boxes, not in the order in which the text boxes appear in the document, or in the order in which the text boxes were created.
- Use the Break Link button to break the link and move all text into the first text box.

Try It! Linking Text Boxes

1. In the **W52Try_xx** file, click the text box on the left.
2. Resize it to 1.5" high by 1.5" wide.
3. On the Drawing Tools Format tab, in the Text group, click Create Link. The mouse pointer changes to resemble a pitcher with an arrow on it.
4. Position the mouse pointer over the blank text box on the right (the mouse pointer changes to a pouring pitcher), and click. The text boxes are linked, and overflow text from the first box displays in the second box.
5. Click in the text box on the left, and on the Drawing Tools Format tab, click Break Link to break the link and remove the overflow text from the second text box.
6. Click Undo to create the link again.
7. Save the changes to **W52Try_xx**, and leave it open to use in the next Try It.

Compressing a Picture

- Picture files may be large and therefore take up a lot of disk space or take a long time to transmit electronically.
- You can **compress** a picture to make its file size smaller.
- Compressing reduces the color format of the image, which makes the color take up fewer bits per pixel. In most cases, you do not notice a difference in image quality.
- You can select options to control the final resolution of the compressed picture. For example, if you plan to print the picture, you can select a higher resolution than if you plan to display the picture on-screen or send the picture by e-mail.
- You can also choose to delete cropped areas at the same time that you compress the pictures.
- You can compress the selected picture or all pictures in the document.
- The tool for compressing pictures is in the Adjust group on the Picture Tools Format tab of the ribbon.

Try It! Compressing a Picture

1. In the **W52Try_xx** file, click the picture to select it.
2. Click the Picture Tools Format tab, and in the Adjust group, click the Compress Pictures button to display the Compress Pictures dialog box.
3. Click to select the Print (220 ppi): excellent quality on most printers and screens option button, and click OK.
4. Save the changes to **W52Try_xx**, and leave it open to use in the next Try It.

Removing a Picture Background

- You can remove the background from a picture when you want to eliminate details or highlight a focal point.
- The Remove Background tool is in the Adjust group on the Picture Tools Format tab of the ribbon.
- When you start the removal process, Word displays the Background Removal tab on the ribbon, providing the tools you need to complete the process.
- Word applies a magenta overlay to everything in the background of the picture, and leaves the foreground unchanged. It also displays a selection box.
- By adjusting the size and position of the selection box, you can affect the areas Word identifies as background.
- You can fine tune the removal by marking areas you want to keep and areas you want to remove.
- Because compressing a picture may change its appearance, you should compress pictures and save the file before removing a background.
- Use Undo to reverse the background removal if you are not satisfied with the results.
- Combine background removal with other picture effects, such as cropping and picture styles, to create an interesting graphic.

Try It! Removing a Picture Background

1. In the **W52Try_xx** file, click the picture to select it.
2. Click the Picture Tools Format tab, and in the Adjust group click the Remove Background button. Word displays the Background Removal tab on the ribbon, and highlights the picture background in magenta. Note that some foreground areas that you might want to keep—such as the tip of the rhino's horn—are magenta.
3. Drag the right center sizing handle to the right about 0.25". Word distinguishes the horn as foreground and removes the magenta. The only area marked for removal that you might want to keep is the tail and part of the hind leg.
4. On the Background Removal tab, click the Mark Areas to Keep button. The mouse pointer changes to a pencil.
5. Click and drag to draw a line along the left edge of the tail covered in magenta. (If necessary, you can draw more than one line.) Each line is marked by a circle with a plus sign in it, indicating the area is foreground.
6. On the Background Removal tab, click the Mark Areas to Remove button, and click anywhere on the grass beneath the larger rhino. The area is marked by a circle with a minus sign in it, indicating the area is background.
7. On the Background Removal tab, click the Keep Changes button ✓. Word removes the magenta areas identifying the background.
8. Save and close the document, and exit Word.

Marking the background for removal

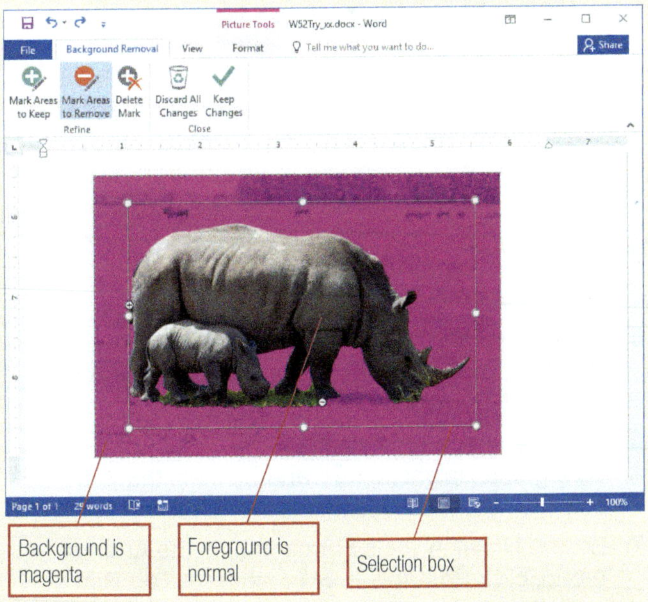

Word 2016, Windows 10, Microsoft Corporation

Lesson 52—Practice

New Media Designs, a Web site design and management company, wants to inspire local students to pursue careers in computer information systems and technology. It is sponsoring a communications contest for students in middle school to encourage them to learn more about the available opportunities. In this project, you will create a flier to advertise the contest. You will use pictures and text boxes to make the flier visually appealing and informative.

DIRECTIONS

1. Start Word, if necessary, click **Blank document**, and save the document as **W52Practice_xx** in the location where your teacher instructs you to store the files for this lesson.
2. Double-click in the header, and type your full name and today's date. Click **Close Header and Footer**.
3. Set the font to **Arial**, set the font size to **28 points**, and type the following, pressing ENTER after each line:

   New Media Designs

   Proudly Announces

   Its First Ever

   Communications Contest

   Topic:

   The Future of Computer Technology
4. On the last blank line, change the font size to **14 points**, and type **Grand Prize winner will receive a $2,500.00 scholarship and a tablet computer, similar to the one shown in Illustration A. Other prizes include gift certificates, computer accessories, and more. For more information and for an entry form, consult New Media's Web site: www.nmd.com.**
5. Click **Insert** > **Shapes**. Under Stars and Banners, click **Explosion 1**, and click in the upper-right part of the document.
6. With the shape still selected, enter **3"** in the Size group Height box and **2.75"** in the Width box.
7. On the Drawing Tools Format tab, in the Arrange group, click **Position** > **Position in Top Right with Square Text Wrapping**.
8. Right-click the shape, and click **Add Text**.
9. Change the font size to **16 points**, and type **Middle Division: Grades 5-8**.
10. Click **Insert** > **Text Box** > **Draw Text Box**, and then click and drag below the line *The Future of Computer Technology* to insert a text box approximately 0.75" high by 1.75" wide. (You can set the exact height and width once the object is on the page.)

    ✓ *If nonprinting characters are displayed, the object's anchor should display to the left of the line The Future of Computer Technology.*
11. On the Drawing Tools Format tab, click **Wrap Text** > **Top and Bottom**.
12. Click the **Layout Options** shortcut menu > **See more**.
13. Under Horizontal, click the **Alignment** option button, verify that the **Alignment** position box is **Left**, click the **relative to** drop-down arrow, and click **Margin**.
14. Under Vertical, in the Absolute position box enter **0.5"**, and verify that the **below** drop-down box is **Paragraph**.
15. Click to select the **Lock anchor** check box, and click **OK**.
16. Select the text box, click **Home** > **Copy** to copy it to the Clipboard, and click **Paste** twice to create two copies of the text box. There should be three text boxes in total, overlapping each other.
17. With the top text box selected, click **Drawing Tools Format** > **Position** > **More Layout Options**. Under Horizontal, click the **Alignment** option, click the **Alignment** drop-down arrow, and click **Right**, click the **relative to** drop-down arrow > **Margin** > **OK**.
18. Select the second text box you created, click **Drawing Tools Format** > **Position** > **More Layout Options**. Under Horizontal, click the **Alignment** option, click the **Alignment** drop-down arrow, click **Centered**, verify the **relative to Margin**, and click **OK**.

19. Press and hold SHIFT, and click to select all three text boxes.
20. On the Drawing Tools Format tab, in the Arrange group, click **Align** > **Align Top**.
21. Click in the text box on the left, apply the **No Spacing** style, set the font size to **14 points**, and set the horizontal alignment to **Center**.
22. Type the following six lines of text, pressing ENTER between each line (you will not be able to view all of the text within the text box).

    Category 1

    Writing

    Category 2

    Graphic Design

    Category 3

    Oral Presentation
23. Click **Drawing Tools Format** > **Create Link**, and click in the middle text box.
24. Click **Create Link** again, and click in the right text box.
25. Position the insertion point at the end of the document. and press ENTER to insert a blank line. (Right-click the Web URL and click **Remove Hyperlink**, if necessary.)
26. Click **Insert** > **Pictures**, and insert **W52Practice_picture** from the data files for this lesson.
27. Resize the picture height to **2"**. The width should adjust automatically.
28. With the picture selected, click **References** > **Insert Caption**.
29. In the Caption dialog box, click **New Label**, in the New Label dialog box, type **Illustration**, and click **OK**.
30. In the Caption dialog box, click **Numbering**, in the Caption Numbering dialog box click the **Format** drop-down arrow > **A, B, C, ...** > **OK**.
31. In the Caption dialog box, click the Position box drop-down arrow, click **Above selected item** > **OK**.
32. Click the picture to select it, and click **Picture Tools Format** > **Compress Pictures** > **OK**.
33. In the Adjust group, click **Remove Background**.
    a. Use the sizing handles to resize the selection box so it is the same size as the picture.
    b. On the Background Removal tab, click **Mark Areas to Keep**.
    c. Click and drag a line through areas inside the tablet that you want to keep.
    d. On the Background Removal tab, click Mark Areas to Remove.
    e. Mark areas above and below the tablet to remove.
    f. On the Background Removal tab, click **Keep Changes**.
34. Check and correct the spelling and grammar, and save the document.
35. **With your teacher's permission**, print the document. It should look similar to Figure 52-1 on the next page.
36. Save and close the document, and exit Word.

Figure 52-1

Firstname Lastname
Today's Date

New Media Designs
Proudly Announces
Its First Ever
Communications
Contest

Middle
Division:
Grades 5-8

Topic:
The Future of Computer Technology

Category 1 Writing	Category 2 Graphic Design	Category 3 Oral Presentation

Grand Prize winner will receive a $2,500.00 scholarship and a tablet computer, similar to the one shown in Illustration A. Other prizes include gift certificates, computer accessories, and more. For more information and for an entry form, consult New Media's Web site: www.nmd.com.

Illustration A

Lesson 52—Apply

You work in the publicity department of New Media Designs, a Web site design and management company. You are in charge of a campaign to inspire local students to pursue careers in computer information systems and technology. In this project, you will create a flier to advertise a contest for high school students. You will use pictures and text boxes to make the flier visually appealing and informative.

DIRECTIONS

1. Start Word, if necessary, and open **W52Apply** from the data files for this lesson.
2. Save the file as **W52Apply_xx** in the location where your teacher instructs you to store the files for this lesson.
3. Double-click in the header, type your full name and today's date, and close the header.
4. Insert an **Explosion 2** shape. Size it to **2"** high by **2.5"** wide, and add the text **High School Division!** in **14 point Arial**.
5. Position the object in the top left part of the document relative to the margins, and set the text wrapping to **Behind Text**.
6. Insert an **Explosion 1** shape. Size it to **2.5"** high by **2.5"** wide, and add the text **Winners announced June 1!** in **14 point Arial**.
7. Set the text wrapping to **Behind Text**, and align it with the top right margin.
8. Apply the **Subtle Effect - Green, Accent 6** shape style to both shapes.
9. Use the Selection Pane to select the objects, and align the middles of the shapes relative to each other.
10. Position the insertion point in the left text box, set the style to **No Spacing**, set the font size to **14 points**, and set the alignment to **Center**.
11. Type the following six lines:

    Category 1

    Video Presentation

    Category 2

    Web Page Design

    Category 3

    Essay Writing
12. Link the left text box to the middle text box, and the middle text box to the right text box.
13. Format the text boxes on the left and right with the **Moderate Effect - Blue, Accent 1** shape style and the text box in the middle with the **Moderate Effect - Orange, Accent 2** shape style.
14. Insert a blank line at the end of the document (remove the hyperlink from the URL, if necessary), and insert **W52Apply_picture**.
15. Set text wrapping to **Square**, resize the picture to **1.5"** wide, position it **0.25"** below the blank line, and center the picture horizontally.
16. Add a caption below the picture using the label Figure and Arabic numbers.
17. Compress the picture, and remove its background and other areas as necessary so it looks similar to the picture in Figure 52-2 on the next page.
18. Check and correct the spelling and grammar, and save the document.
19. **With your teacher's permission**, print the document.
20. Save and close the document, and exit Word.

Figure 52-2

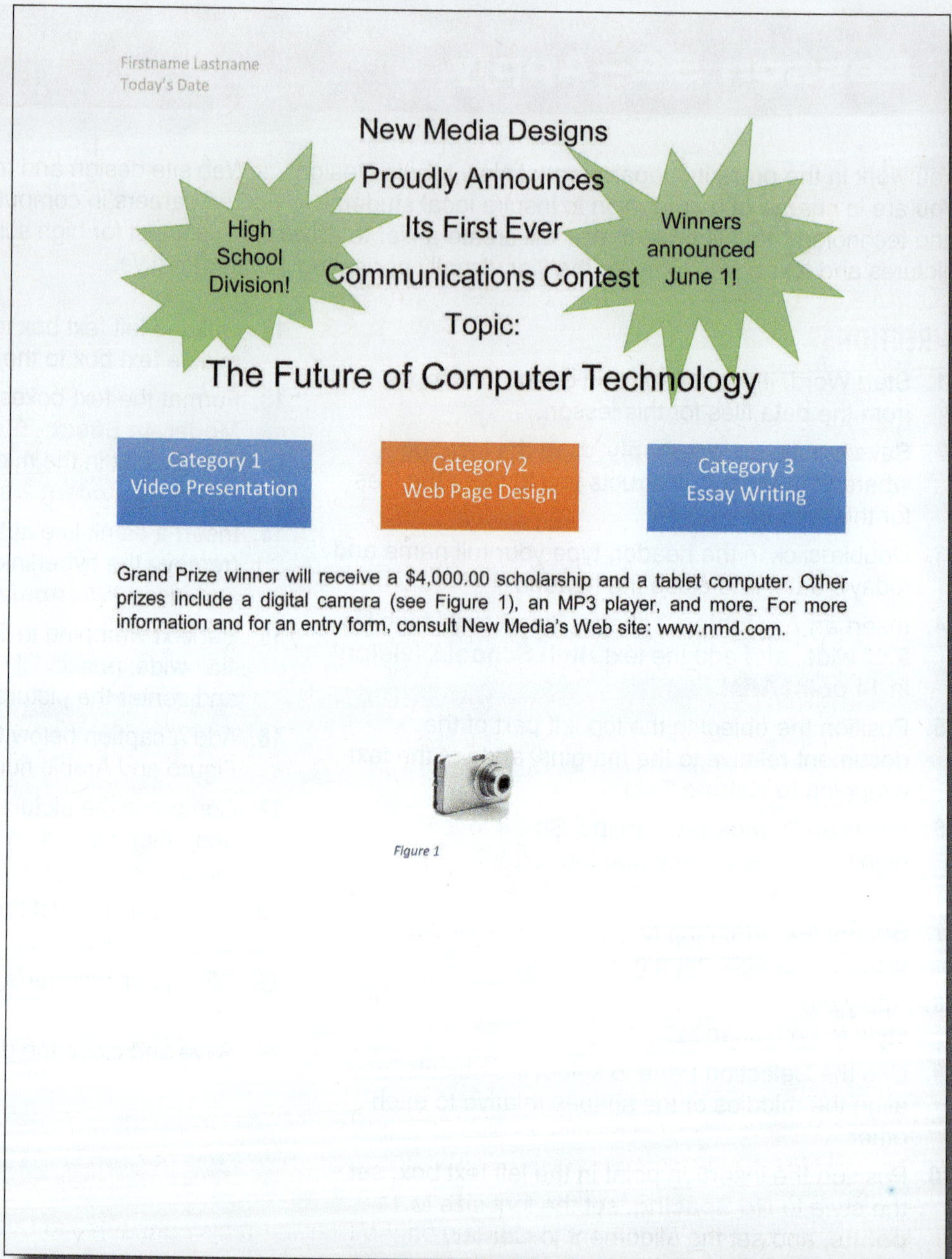

Firstname Lastname
Today's Date

High School Division!

New Media Designs
Proudly Announces
Its First Ever
Communications Contest
Topic:
The Future of Computer Technology

Winners announced June 1!

Category 1
Video Presentation

Category 2
Web Page Design

Category 3
Essay Writing

Grand Prize winner will receive a $4,000.00 scholarship and a tablet computer. Other prizes include a digital camera (see Figure 1), an MP3 player, and more. For more information and for an entry form, consult New Media's Web site: www.nmd.com.

Figure 1

Lesson 53

Creating WordArt and Watermarks

➤ What You Will Learn

Creating WordArt
Creating a Watermark

Software Skills Use WordArt to transform text into artwork for letterheads, logos, brochures, and other documents. WordArt lets you create special effects using any text that you type. You can stretch characters, rotate them, reverse direction, and even arrange the text in shapes such as circles, waves, or arcs. Place a watermark on a document to make an impression on readers, convey an idea, or provide a consistent theme. For example, a watermark on corporate stationery can communicate a corporate identity.

WORDS TO KNOW

Watermark
A pale or semitransparent graphics object positioned behind text in a document.

WordArt
A feature of Word used to transform text into a drawing object.

What You Can Do

Creating WordArt

- **WordArt** is an Office feature similar to text effects that you use to transform text into a drawing object.
- You create WordArt by selecting a style from the WordArt gallery.
- The WordArt text is inserted in a text box which you can size and position on the page.
- Use the tools in the WordArt Styles group on the Drawing Tools Format tab to customize the WordArt text.
- For example, you can apply text effects to transform the shape of the text, or to add a glow, reflection, or 3-D effect.
- You can also use the standard tools for formatting the text box, such as fill, outline, text wrapping, size, position, and alignment.
- The command for creating WordArt is in the Text group on the Insert tab of the ribbon.

Try It! Creating WordArt

1. Start Word, click Blank document, and save the document as **W53Try_xx** in the location where your teacher instructs you to store the files for this lesson.
2. Click Insert, and in the Text group click the WordArt button to display the WordArt gallery.
3. Click the fourth style in the first row—Fill - White, Outline - Accent 1, Shadow. Word creates the WordArt in a text box using sample text.
4. Type **Adventure!** to replace the sample text. Click the border surrounding the WordArt.
5. On the Drawing Tools Format tab, in the WordArt Styles group, click the Text Effects button to display a menu of text effects options.
6. Point to Transform to display a gallery of transform styles. Under Warp, point to the first option in the fourth row—Curve Up—to see how it affects the WordArt.
7. Scroll down to the bottom of the Transform gallery and click the first style in the last row—Slant Up.
8. In the WordArt Styles group, click the Text Fill drop-down arrow, and click Gold, Accent 4.
9. In the Arrange group, click Position, and click Position in Top Center with Square Text Wrapping.
10. Save the changes to **W53Try_xx**, and leave it open to use in the next Try It.

WordArt

Word 2016, Windows 10, Microsoft Corporation

Creating a Watermark

- Insert text or graphics objects as a **watermark** to provide a background image for text-based documents.
- Word 2016 comes with built-in watermark styles that you can select from the Watermark gallery in the Page Background group on the Design tab.
- You can also create a custom watermark using the options in the Printed Watermark dialog box.
- A watermark may be a graphics object, such as an image, a text box, WordArt, or a shape.
- You can also create a watermark from text.
- Watermarks are usually inserted into the document header so that they automatically appear on every page, and so that they are not affected by changes made to the document content.
- To remove a watermark, click the Watermark button and click Remove Watermark, or make the header active, select the watermark, and press DEL.
- You can add a watermark to a template so that every document based on the template will display the same watermark.

Try It! Creating a Watermark

1. In the **W53Try_xx** file, adjust the zoom to display the entire page.
2. Click Design, and in the Page Background group click Watermark to display the Watermark gallery.
3. Click the CONFIDENTIAL 1 style. Word inserts the watermark on the page.
4. Click the Undo button on the Quick Access Toolbar to remove the watermark.
5. Click Watermark, and click Custom Watermark to display the Printed Watermark dialog box.
6. Click the Picture watermark option button, and click Select Picture.
7. In the Insert Pictures dialog box, click the Browse link next to From a file, navigate to the location where the data files for this lesson are stored, and insert **W53Try_picture**.
8. In the Printed Watermark dialog box, click OK.
9. Click Undo on the Quick Access Toolbar to remove the watermark, click Watermark, and click Custom Watermark to display the Printed Watermark dialog box.
10. Click the Text watermark option button, select the text in the Text box, type **Adventure!**, and click OK.
11. Save and close the document, and exit Word.

Lesson 53—Practice

Long Shot, Inc. is growing by leaps and bounds. To fill job vacancies, it is hosting an open house and career fair. In this project, you will use WordArt and a watermark to create a notice to announce the event.

DIRECTIONS

1. Start Word, if necessary, click **Blank document**, and save the document as **W53Practice_xx** in the location where your teacher instructs you to store the files for this lesson.
2. Double-click in the header, and type your full name and today's date. Click **Close Header and Footer**.
3. Position the insertion point on the first line of the document, set the font to **72 point Arial**, and type **SOAR**. Center the line horizontally.
4. Press ENTER, decrease the font size to **20 points**, type **to new heights with**, and press ENTER.
5. Click **Insert**, and in the Text group click **WordArt**.
6. Click the **Gradient Fill - Blue, Accent 1, Reflection** style (second style in the second column).
7. In the WordArt text box, type **Long Shot, Inc.**
8. On the Drawing Tools Format tab, in the WordArt Styles group, click **Text Effects**, point to **Transform**, and under Warp, click **Inflate** (first style in the sixth row).
9. With the WordArt text box selected, click **Wrap Text** > **Top and Bottom**.
10. Click **Position** > **More Layout Options**.
11. Under Horizontal, click the **Alignment** option, click the **Alignment** drop-down arrow, click **Centered**, click the **relative to** drop-down arrow, and click **Margin**.
12. Under Vertical, click the **Absolute position** option, in the **Absolute position** box enter **3.25"**, click the **below** drop-down arrow, and click **Page**.
13. Click to select the **Lock Anchor** check box, and click **OK**.

14. Position the insertion point on the last line of the document, set the spacing before to **132 pt**, and press ENTER.
15. Type **Please Come to Our** and press ENTER.
16. Set the spacing before to **0 pt**, and type the following five lines, pressing ENTER between each line:

    Open House and Career Fair

    Saturday, April 15th and Sunday, April 16th

    10:00 a.m. – 3:00 p.m.

    234 Simsbury Drive

    Ithaca, NY 14850

17. Click **Design** > **Watermark**.
18. Click **Custom Watermark** to open the Printed Watermark dialog box.
19. Click the **Picture watermark** option, click **Select Picture**, click **From a file**, browse to the location where the data files for this lesson are stored, and insert **W53Practice_picture**.
20. In the Printed Watermark dialog box, click **OK**.
21. Check and correct the spelling and grammar, and save the document.
22. **With your teacher's permission**, print the document. It should look similar to Figure 53-1.
23. Save and close the document, and exit Word.

Figure 53-1

Firstname Lastname
Today's Date

SOAR

to new heights with

Long Shot, Inc.

Please Come to Our

Open House and Career Fair

Saturday, April 15th and Sunday, April 16th

10:00 a.m – 3:00 p.m.

234 Simsbury Drive

Ithaca, NY 14850

Lesson 53—Apply

You work for the publicity department of Long Shot, Inc. You are in charge of the publications for an open house and career fair. In this project, you will use WordArt and a watermark to create a handout for attendees.

DIRECTIONS

1. Start Word, if necessary, and open **W53Apply** from the data files for this lesson.
2. Save the file as **W53Apply_xx** in the location where your teacher instructs you to store the files for this lesson.
3. Double-click in the header, and type your full name and today's date. Click **Close Header and Footer**.
4. Insert a WordArt object using the **Fill - Gold, Accent 4, Soft Bevel** style.
5. In the WordArt text box, type **234 Simsbury Drive**, press ENTER, type **Long Shot, Inc.**, press ENTER, and type **Ithaca, NY**.
6. Resize the WordArt text box to **3.5"** high by **4.5"** wide.
7. Click **Text Effects** > **Transform**, and under Follow Path click **Button**.
8. Set the word wrap for the WordArt object to **Top and Bottom**, position it horizontally centered on the page and **3"** below the page, and lock the anchor.
9. Create a picture watermark using the **W53Apply_picture** file from the data files for this lesson.
10. Check and correct the spelling and grammar, and save the document.
11. **With your teacher's permission**, print the document. It should look similar to Figure 53-2 on the next page.
12. Save and close the document, and exit Word.

Figure 53-2

Firstname Lastname
Today's Date

Welcome

to our Open House and Career Fair

234 Simsbury Drive

Long Shot, Inc.

Ithaca, NY

Career Opportunities are available in:

- ✓ Manufacturing
- ✓ Marketing
- ✓ Design

Department managers are stationed in the cafeteria to provide additional information. Please complete a job application to submit along with your resume, letter of introduction, and list of references. We appreciate your interest in working at Long Shot, Inc.

End-of-Chapter Activities

➤ Word Chapter 7—Critical Thinking

Travel Itinerary

In this project, create an itinerary for yourself and three or four traveling companions. They might be your friends, family, or a club or organization to which you belong. You might start by looking up sample itineraries online, or searching online for itinerary templates to use to create the document.

Include the following information:

- The names of everyone who will be traveling.
- The locations, dates, and times of departure and arrival for all legs of the trip.
- The method of transportation, including schedule and flight, train, or bus numbers. You may choose to include the cost information, as well.
- Information about accommodations at the destination, such as hotel name, address, and telephone number, and the number of nights.
- A schedule of activities or sightseeing options.

Create the itinerary using the advanced tables and graphics skills you have learned in this chapter, including table styles, nested tables, advanced graphics sizing and positioning, captions, WordArt, and watermarks.

DIRECTIONS

1. Start Word, if necessary, and save a new, blank document or the itinerary template of your choice as **WCT07_xx** in the location where your teacher instructs you to store the files for this chapter.
2. Type your name and today's date in the document header, and apply a theme and style set.
3. Design the itinerary using tables and graphics. For example, you might use a large table to organize the page into columns, then insert a graphic image of your destination in one of the table cells. You might insert a nested table in a cell to enter the names of the travelers and the travel information.
4. Design and save a custom table style to give your tables a unique look.
5. Embellish and enhance the document by including shapes and pictures, and format the objects using advanced graphics features. Use document gridlines to help you make sure objects are aligned evenly on the page, and with each other.
6. When you have completed a first draft, exchange documents with a classmate, make suggestions for improvement, and then exchange back.
7. Make the improvements to your document.
8. Check and correct the spelling and grammar, and save the document.
9. **With your teacher's permission**, print the document.
10. When you are satisfied with the document, ask a classmate to review it and make comments or suggestions that will help you improve it.
11. Make changes and corrections, as necessary.
12. Restore all default settings, and delete custom styles.
13. Save and close the document, and exit Word.

➤ Word Chapter 7—Portfolio Builder

Invitation

You have been asked to design an invitation to a luncheon honoring the winners of New Media Design's Communications contest. You will use tables, graphics objects, WordArt, and a watermark to create an effective, eye-catching document.

DIRECTIONS

1. Start Word, if necessary, and save a new, blank document as **WPB07_xx** in the location where your teacher instructs you to store the files for this chapter.
2. Insert your name and today's date in the document header, and apply the **Integral** theme.
3. Use the following steps to create the document shown in Illustration 7A.
4. Insert a WordArt object using the **Fill - Turquoise, Accent 3, Sharp Bevel** style.
5. Type the text **New Media Designs**, and apply the **Chevron Up** transform text effect.
6. Resize the WordArt text box to **1"** high by **5"** wide, set the text wrapping to **Top and Bottom**, center it horizontally on the page, and position it along the top margin.
7. Insert a text box sized to **1"** high by **3"** wide. Position it horizontally aligned with the left margin and vertically **3"** below the page.
8. Set the style to **No Spacing**, set the font size to **16 points**, and type the following seven lines:

   You are invited to celebrate the winners of our first ever Communications Contest!

   Please join us for lunch.

   Friday, October 20

   12:30 p.m.

   New Media Designs

   Highway 73

   Cambridge, WA 53523
9. Draw a second text box of the same size. Position it centered horizontally and vertically **4"** below the page.
10. Draw a third text box of the same size. Position it horizontally aligned with the right margin and vertically **5"** below the page.
11. Link the left text box to the middle box and the middle box to the right box.
12. Apply the **Subtle Effect - Turquoise, Accent 3** shape style to the left text box, the **Subtle Effect - Blue, Accent 2** shape style to the middle text box, and the **Subtle Effect - Green, Accent 4** shape style to the right text box.
13. Insert a table with four columns and five rows, and drag it down near the bottom of the page (refer to Illustration 7A). Merge the cells in the top row. Enter the following data in the first two rows:

Communications Contest Winners			
Middle (5–8)	Category 1	Category 2	Category 3

14. In the second cell of the third row, insert a nested table with two columns and three rows and enter the following data:

1st	Alex Grogan
2nd	Michaela Jackson
3rd	Jaclyn Brown

15. In the third cell of the third row, insert a nested table with two columns and three rows and enter the following data:

1st	Jill Kline
2nd	Sam Lapp
3rd	Dinesh Patel

16. In the fourth cell of the third row, insert a nested table with two columns and three rows and enter the following data:

1st	Matt O'Toole
2nd	Chris White
3rd	Liz Jones

17. In the fourth row, enter the following data:

High School	Category 1	Category 2	Category 3

18. In the second cell of the fifth row, insert a nested table with two columns and three rows and enter the following data:

1st	Keith Feeney
2nd	Brady Kim
3rd	Olivia Tombola

19. In the third cell of the fifth row, insert a nested table with two columns and three rows and enter the following data:

1st	June Tsai
2nd	Leah Gold
3rd	George Wei

20. In the fourth cell of the fifth row, insert a nested table with two columns and three rows and enter the following data:

1st	Jen LeBlanc
2nd	Robbie Maltz
3rd	Jim Shepard

21. Apply the **List Table 3** table style to the main table. Increase the font size in the first row to **14 points**, and center the text horizontally and vertically.
22. Apply the **Grid Table 5 Dark - Accent 2** table style to all six nested tables. Adjust the column widths, as needed (refer to Illustration 7A).
23. Click outside the table, and insert **WPB07_picture1** from the data files for this chapter.
24. Resize the image to **2.5"** high.
25. Set the text wrapping to **In Front of Text**, and position the picture **0.5"** to the right of the margin horizontally and **4"** below the margin vertically.
26. Insert a caption below the picture that says: **1 Grand Prize Winner, Middle School**. Adjust the caption width and height, as needed.
27. Insert **WPB07_picture2** from the data files for this chapter, and resize it to **2.5"** high.
28. Set the text wrapping to **In Front of Text**, and position it **4"** to the right of the margin horizontally, and **1"** below the margin vertically.
29. Insert a caption below the picture that says: **2 Grand Prize Winner, High School**. Adjust caption width and height, as needed.
30. Compress all of the pictures in the document, and remove the backgrounds.
31. Create a picture watermark using the file **WPPB07_picture3** from the data files for this chapter.
32. Check and correct the spelling and grammar, and save the document.
33. **With your teacher's permission**, print the document.
34. Restore all default settings, and delete custom styles.
35. Save and close the document, and exit Word.

Illustration 7A

Firstname Lastname
Today's Date

New Media Designs

You are invited to celebrate the winners of our first ever Communications Contest!

Please join us for lunch.
Friday, October 20
12:30 p.m.

New Media Designs
Highway 73
Cambridge, WA 53523

2 Grand Prize Winner, High School

1 Grand Prize Winner, Middle School

Communications Contest Winners							
Middle (5-8)	Category 1		Category 2		Category 3		
	1st	Alex Grogan	1st	Jill Kline	1st	Matt O'Toole	
	2nd	Michaela Jackson	2nd	Sam Lapp	2nd	Chris White	
	3rd	Jaclyn Brown	3rd	Dinesh Patel	3rd	Liz Jones	
High School	Category 1		Category 2		Category 3		
	1st	Keith Feeney	1st	June Tsai	1st	Jen LeBlanc	
	2nd	Brady Kim	2nd	Leah Gold	2nd	Robbie Maltz	
	3rd	Olivia Tombola	3rd	George Wei	3rd	Jim Shepard	

Word 2016, Windows 10, Microsoft Corporation

Chapter 8

(Courtesy lightpoet/Shutterstock)

Working with Long Documents

Lesson 54
Working with Outlines

- Creating an Outline
- Managing an Outline
- Numbering an Outline

Lesson 55
Advanced Layout Options

- Setting Paper Size
- Creating and Modifying a Page Border
- Hiding or Displaying White Space
- Adjusting Character Spacing
- Inserting a Non-Breaking Space

Lesson 56
Working with Master Documents

- Creating a Master Document
- Managing a Master Document
- Revising a Master Document

Lesson 57
Creating Custom Headers and Footers, Bookmarks, and Cross-References

- Customizing Headers and Footers
- Inserting Bookmarks
- Inserting a Cross-Reference

Lesson 58
Creating an Index

- Marking Index Entries
- Using an Index AutoMark File
- Generating an Index
- Modifying an Index

Lesson 59
Managing Source Information and Generating Special Tables

- Using the Research Task Pane
- Sharing Sources Between Documents
- Editing Shared Sources
- Using Multiple Footnote Formats in a Document
- Adding Styles to a Table of Contents
- Creating a Table of Figures
- Creating a Table of Authorities

End-of-Chapter Activities

Lesson 54

Working with Outlines

➤ What You Will Learn

Creating an Outline
Managing an Outline
Numbering an Outline

WORDS TO KNOW

Body text
Outline text that is not formatted with a heading-level style.

Collapse
To hide subtopics in an outline.

Demote
To move down one level in an outline.

Expand
To show subtopics in an outline.

Outline
A document that lists levels of topics.

Promote
To move up one level in an outline.

Software Skills Create an outline to organize ideas for any document that covers more than one topic, such as an article, a report, a presentation, or a speech. For example, you might create an outline to list the chapters or headings in a report or to arrange main subjects for a presentation. The outline serves as a map you can follow as you complete the entire document.

What You Can Do

Creating an Outline

- Use Outline view to create and edit an **outline**.
- When you switch to Outline view, the Outlining tab becomes available on the ribbon.
- An outline is similar to a multilevel list (refer to Word, Lesson 7). Outline topics are formatted in levels, which may be called headings: Level 1 is a main heading, Level 2 is a subheading, Level 3 is a sub-subheading, and so on up to 9 heading levels.
- By default, text you type in an outline is formatted as **Level 1**. You use the tools in the Outline Tools group on the Outlining tab of the ribbon to **promote** or **demote** paragraphs to different levels.
- Headings in an outline are preceded by one of three outline symbols:
  - Levels that have sublevels under them are preceded by a circle with a plus sign in it ⊕.
  - Levels that do not have sublevels are preceded by a circle with a minus sign in it ⊖.
  - **Body text** that is not formatted as a heading level is preceded by a small circle ○.
- Note that although outline levels print as expected, the indentation does not appear onscreen in Print Layout view or on the Print tab in the Backstage view.

Try It! Creating an Outline

1. Start Word, and save a new blank document as **W54Try_xx** in the location where your teacher instructs you to store the files for this lesson.
2. On the View tab, in the Views group, click the Outline button to change to Outline view.
3. On the first line of the document, type **Packing for International Travel** and press ENTER.
4. In the Outline Tools group, click the Demote button →, type **Travel Documents**, and press ENTER.

   ✓ *You can also press TAB to demote a paragraph.*
5. Click the Demote button →, type **Itinerary**, press ENTER, type **Passport**, and press ENTER.
6. In the Outline Tools group, click the Promote button ←, type **Boarding Documents**, and press ENTER.

   ✓ *You can also press SHIFT + TAB to promote a paragraph.*
7. Click the Demote button →, type **ID**, press ENTER, type **Airline tickets**, press ENTER, type **Boarding pass**, and press ENTER.
8. Click the Demote to Body Text button and type **Print boarding pass 24 hours in advance**.
9. Save the changes to **W54Try_xx**, and leave it open to use in the next Try It.

An outline in Outline view

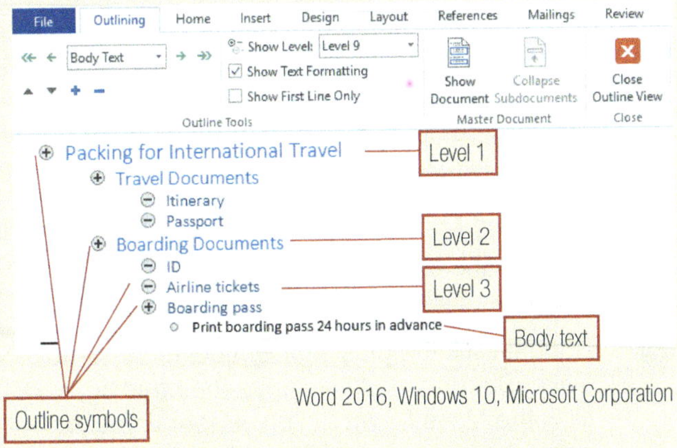

Word 2016, Windows 10, Microsoft Corporation

Managing an Outline

- When you want to work with only some heading levels at a time, you can **collapse** the outline.
- Collapsing an outline hides lower-level headings.
- A gray line appears under a collapsed heading to indicate that there are subheadings that are not displayed.
- You can also select to show only headings above a certain level in the outline, hiding the lower-level headings.
- To see hidden or collapsed levels, you can **expand** the outline.
- You can also move headings and subheadings up or down to reorganize the outline.
- You can edit an outline using the same techniques you use to edit regular document text. For example, you can insert and delete text at any location.
- Word automatically applies different styles to different levels in an outline. By default, Word displays the formatting in the document, but you can toggle it off.
- By default, Word displays all body text that you type in the document. If you have multiple lines of body text, you can select to show only the first line. An ellipsis at the end of the line indicates the remaining lines are hidden.

Try It! Managing an Outline

1. In the **W54Try_xx** file, double-click the plus sign symbol to the left of *Boarding Documents*. This collapses—or hides—the levels below.
2. Double-click the symbol again to expand the outline.
3. Click on the text *Boarding pass* and click the Collapse button ▬ in the Outline Tools group. This is an alternative method of collapsing an outline.
4. In the Outline Tools group, click the Show Level drop-down arrow and click Level 2. Only the Level 1 and Level 2 headings are displayed.
5. Click the Show Level drop-down arrow, and click All Levels.
6. Click on the text *ID* and click the Move Up button ▲.
7. Double-click the plus sign symbol to the left of *Travel Documents* to collapse the heading, and click the Move Down button ▼ four times to move the heading and its subheadings to the end of the outline.
8. Position the insertion point after the Body Text *Print boarding pass 24 hours in advance*, press SPACE, and type **and verify seating as well as special meals.**
9. In the Outline Tools group, click to select the Show First Line Only check box.
10. Click to clear the Show Text Formatting check box.
11. Click to select the Show Text Formatting check box and to clear the Show First Line Only check box.
12. Save the changes to **W54Try_xx**, and leave it open to use in the next Try It.

An outline with no style formatting

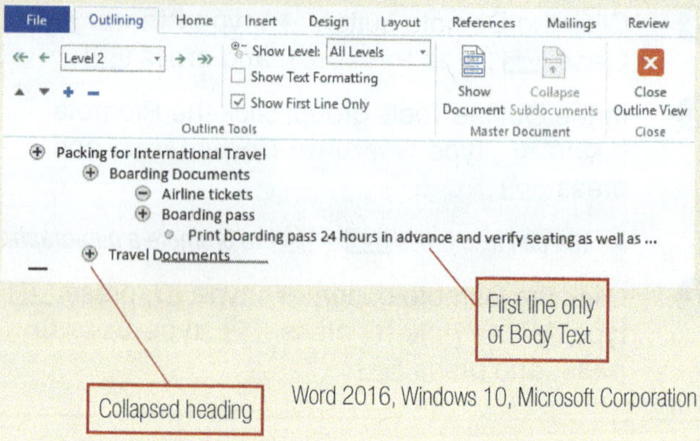

Word 2016, Windows 10, Microsoft Corporation

Numbering an Outline

- Use a multilevel list to number an outline.

  ✓ *Refer to Word, Lesson 7 for more on multilevel lists.*

- Traditionally, outlines are numbered using a I., A., 1., a) numbering style.
- You can apply numbering to an outline before you start typing the text, or you can apply numbering to an existing outline.
- Work in Print Layout view to select multilevel list formatting, then return to Outline view to view or edit the outline.
- Once you number an outline, the outline levels appear in Print Layout view and on the Print tab in the Backstage view.

Try It! Numbering an Outline

1. In the **W54Try_xx** file, on the Outlining tab, in the Close group, click the Close Outline View button.
2. Click in the text *Packing for International Travel*.
3. On the Home tab, in the Paragraph group, click the Multilevel List button to display the gallery of multilevel list styles.
4. Under List Library, click the style on the left end of the bottom row.
5. Save and close the file, and exit Word.

Use a multilevel list style to number an outline

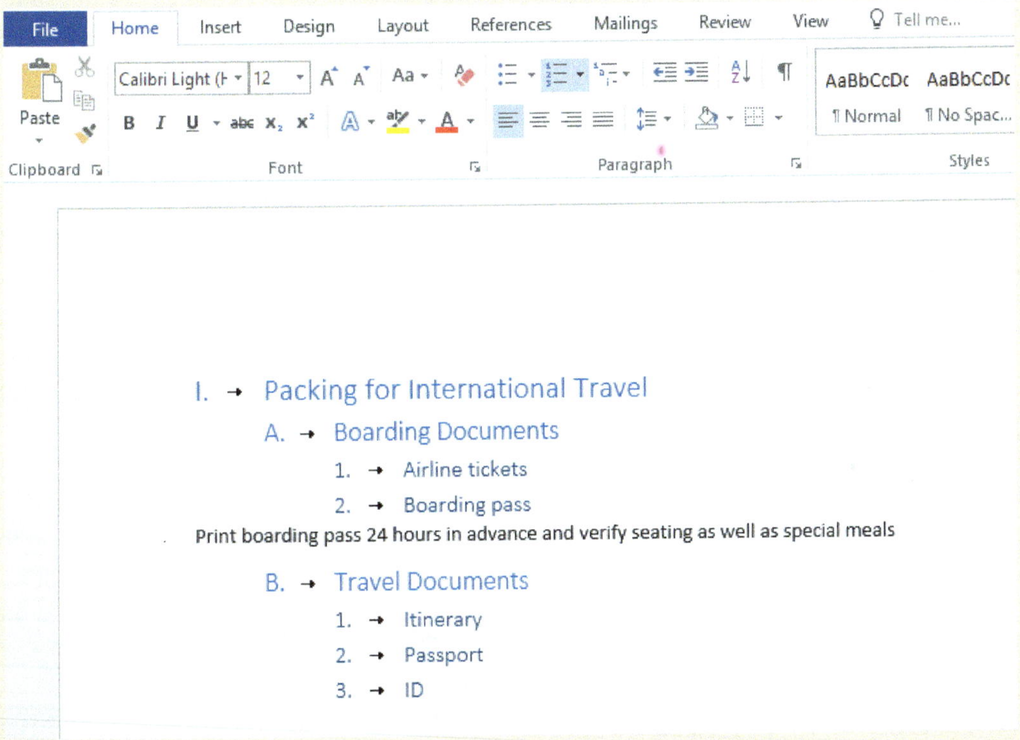

Word 2016, Windows 10, Microsoft Corporation

Lesson 54—Practice

You work in the publishing department of the Michigan Avenue Athletic Club and want to publish a document describing some of the benefits of regular exercise. In this project, you will create an outline for that document.

DIRECTIONS

1. Start Word, if necessary, and save a new blank document as **W54Practice_xx** in the location where your teacher instructs you to store the files for this lesson.
2. In the header, type your full name and today's date. Close the header and footer.
3. Click **View** > **Outline**.
4. On the first line, type **Exercise for Life** and press ENTER.
5. In the Outline Tools group, click the **Demote** button →, type **Introduction**, and press ENTER.
6. Click the **Demote to Body Text** button »», type **Studies have shown that people who exercise regularly live longer, are healthier, and enjoy a better quality of life than those who do not exercise.** Press ENTER.
7. Click the **Promote** button ←, type **Getting Started**, press ENTER, click the **Demote** button →, type **Safety**, and press ENTER.
8. Click the **Demote** button →, type **Doctor Supervision**, press ENTER, type **Proper Equipment**, press ENTER, type **Preparation**, and press ENTER.
9. Click the **Promote** button ←, type **Tips**, press ENTER, type **Instruction**, and press ENTER.
10. Click the **Demote** button →, type **Using a Personal Trainer**, press ENTER, click the **Demote** button →, type **Certification**, press ENTER, type **References**, and press ENTER.
11. Click the **Promote** button ← three times and type **Conclusion**.
12. Click the **Show Level** drop-down arrow and click **Level 2**.
13. Double-click the **plus sign symbol** to the left of the text *Getting Started* to expand the heading.
14. Double-click the **plus sign symbol** to the left of the text *Instruction* to collapse the heading.
15. Click the **Move Up** button ▲ to move the *Instruction* heading and all its subheadings above the heading *Tips*.
16. Click to clear the **Show Text Formatting** check box.
17. Click to select the **Show First Line Only** check box.
18. Click the **Show Level** drop-down arrow and click **All Levels**.
19. Click **Outlining** > **Close Outline View**.
20. Click in the text *Exercise for Life*.
21. Click **Home** > **Multilevel List** to display the gallery of multilevel list styles.
22. Under List Library, click the style on the left end of the bottom row to number the outline.
23. Check and correct the spelling and grammar in the document, and save the document.
24. Click **View** > **Outline**.
25. Click to select the **Show Text Formatting** check box and to clear the **Show First Line Only** check box.
26. **With your teacher's permission**, print the document. It should look similar to Figure 54-1 on the next page.
27. Save and close the document, and exit Word.

Figure 54-1

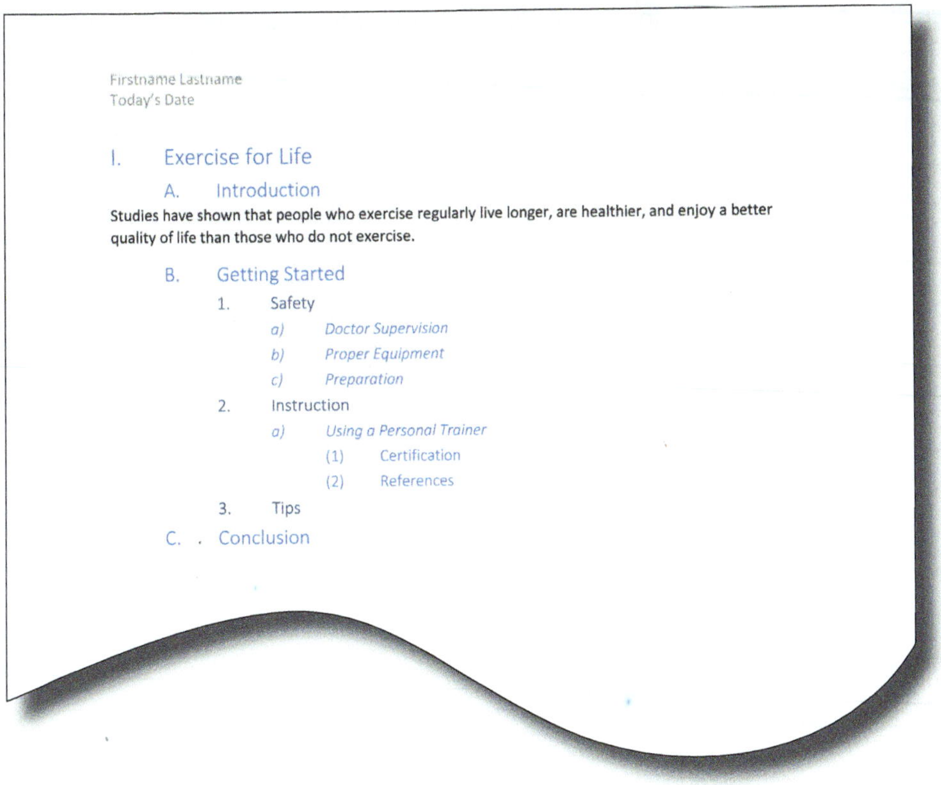
Firstname Lastname
Today's Date

I. Exercise for Life

A. Introduction

Studies have shown that people who exercise regularly live longer, are healthier, and enjoy a better quality of life than those who do not exercise.

B. Getting Started

1. Safety

a) *Doctor Supervision*

b) *Proper Equipment*

c) *Preparation*

2. Instruction

a) *Using a Personal Trainer*

(1) Certification

(2) References

3. Tips

C. . Conclusion

Lesson 54—Apply

You hold a brainstorming session with your colleagues, which results in an expanded list of topics for your document about exercise. In this project, you will turn the list into an outline, reorganize some of the topics, and add a new topic.

DIRECTIONS

1. Start Word, if necessary, and open **W54Apply** from the data files for this lesson.
2. Save the file as **W54Apply_xx** in the location where your teacher instructs you to store the files for this lesson.
3. In the header, type your full name and today's date. Close the header and footer.
4. Change to **Outline** view.
5. Promote and demote headings to create the outline shown in Figure 54-2 on the next page.
6. Hide text formatting and show the first line of Body Text only.
7. Move the Level 2 heading *Getting Started* and all of its subheadings above the Level 2 heading *Health Benefits*.
8. Promote the Level 3 heading *Tips* to Level 2, and move it down after the last subheading in the *Health Benefits* section, above the Level 2 heading *Conclusion*.
9. Add a new Level 4 heading, **Heart Disease**, between *Diabetes* and *Osteoporosis* under *Reduce Symptoms of Existing Conditions*.
10. Apply the **I., A., 1., a), (1)** multilevel list numbering style to the outline.
11. Set the spacing before and after all paragraphs to **0**.

12. Check and correct the spelling and grammar in the document, and save the document.
13. Select to display text formatting and to show all lines of Body Text paragraphs.
14. **With your teacher's permission**, print the document. It should look similar to Figure 54-3 on the next page.
15. Save and close the document, and exit Word.

Figure 54-2

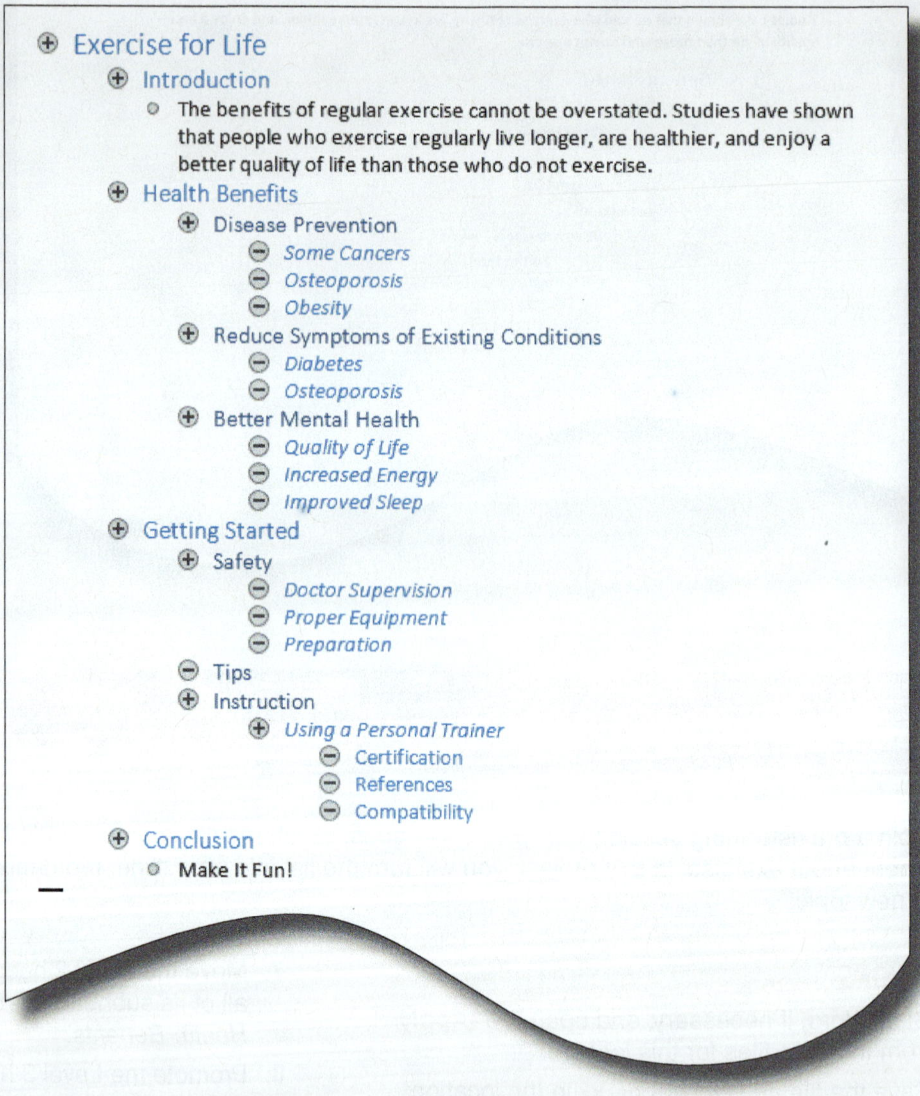

Figure 54-3

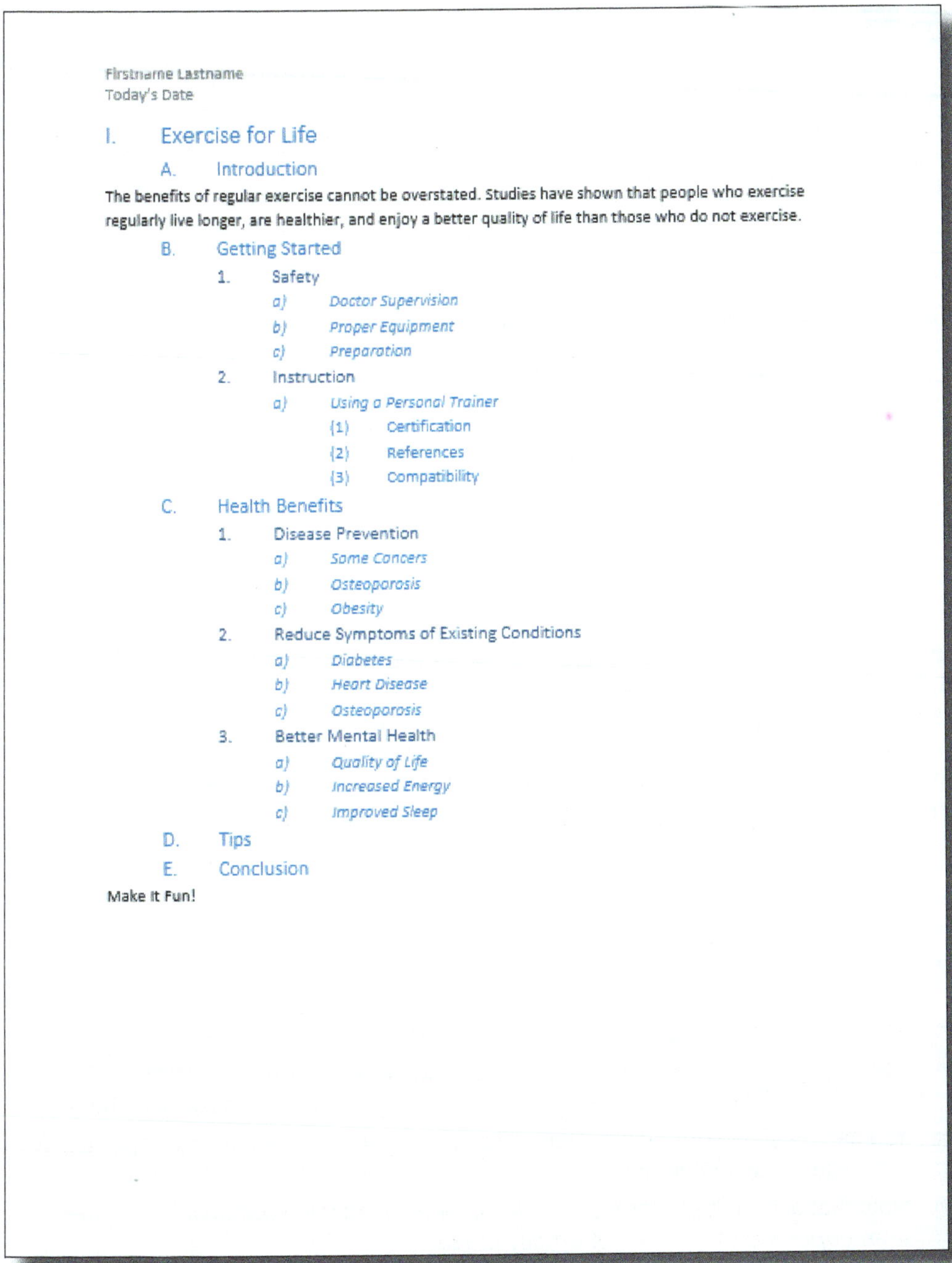

Firstname Lastname
Today's Date

I. Exercise for Life

A. Introduction

The benefits of regular exercise cannot be overstated. Studies have shown that people who exercise regularly live longer, are healthier, and enjoy a better quality of life than those who do not exercise.

B. Getting Started
1. Safety
a) *Doctor Supervision*
b) *Proper Equipment*
c) *Preparation*
2. Instruction
a) *Using a Personal Trainer*
(1) Certification
(2) References
(3) Compatibility

C. Health Benefits
1. Disease Prevention
a) *Some Cancers*
b) *Osteoporosis*
c) *Obesity*
2. Reduce Symptoms of Existing Conditions
a) *Diabetes*
b) *Heart Disease*
c) *Osteoporosis*
3. Better Mental Health
a) *Quality of Life*
b) *Increased Energy*
c) *Improved Sleep*

D. Tips

E. Conclusion

Make It Fun!

Lesson 55

Advanced Layout Options

➤ What You Will Learn

Setting Paper Size
Creating and Modifying a Page Border
Hiding or Displaying White Space
Adjusting Character Spacing
Inserting a Non-Breaking Space

WORDS TO KNOW

Kerning
Spacing between pairs of characters.

Page size
The dimensions of a finished document page.

Paper size
The dimensions of the sheet of paper on which a document is printed. Also called sheet size.

Software Skills Select a paper size when you want to print on a specific piece of paper. Create a page border to add visual interest to graphical documents, such as marketing and promotional materials. Hide white space in Print Layout view to see more of the content of your document on the screen. Set character spacing to make text easier to read and improve the appearance of a published document. Insert non-breaking spaces when you want to keep words together on a line.

What You Can Do

Setting Paper Size

- The default **paper size** in Word 2016 is Letter, which is 8.5 inches by 11 inches.
- You can select from a list of different sizes such as A5 (5.83 inches by 8.27 inches), B5 (7.17 inches by 10.12 inches), or Legal (8.5 inches by 14 inches).
- You can also set your own custom size by using the options on the Paper tab of the Page Setup dialog box.
- Note that although the term *page size* is often used interchangeably with the term *paper size*, they are not exactly the same.
  - **Page size** is the dimensions of a finished document page.
  - Paper size is the dimensions of the sheet of paper on which the document is printed.
- It is sometimes useful to combine custom margins with custom paper sizes. For example, when you are printing on a small paper size, you may want to use narrower margins.

Try It! Setting Paper Size

1. Start Word, and open **W55Try** from the data files for this lesson.
2. Save the file as **W55Try_xx** in the location where your teacher instructs you to store the files for this lesson.
3. Click View > One Page so you can see the entire page on your screen.
4. On the Layout tab, in the Page Setup group, click the Size button to display the gallery of built-in paper sizes.
5. In the gallery, click 5x7in. If you don't see 5x7 in the list, select any other size. Word changes the paper size to the size you selected.
6. Click the Size button again and click More Paper Sizes to display the Paper tab of the Page Setup dialog box.

   ✓ *You can also open the Page Setup dialog box by clicking the dialog box launcher in the Page Setup group on the ribbon.*
7. Under Paper size, use the increment arrows to set the Width to 3.5".
8. Use the increment arrows to set the Height to 3.5" and click OK.
9. Click Layout > Margins and click Narrow.
10. Save the changes to **W55Try_xx**, and leave it open to use in the next Try It.

Set a custom paper size

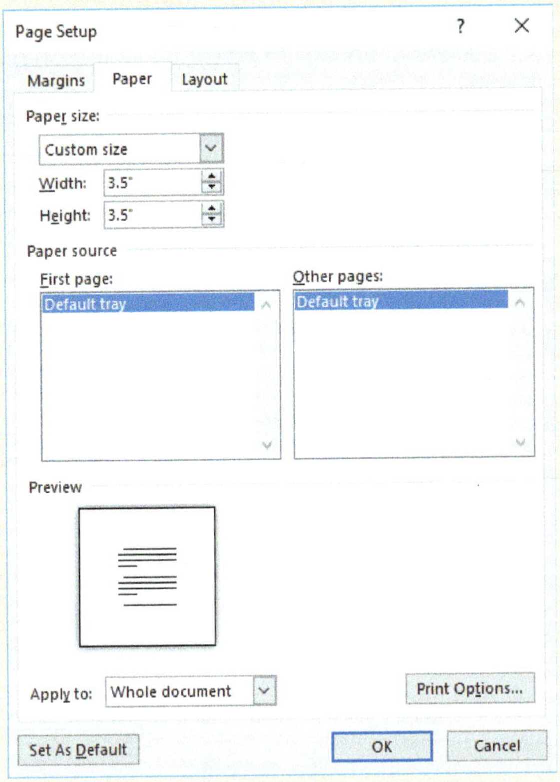

Word 2016, Windows 10, Microsoft Corporation

Creating and Modifying a Page Border

- You can apply a border to pages in a document to enhance visual interest.
- Page border commands are on the Page Border tab of the Borders and Shading dialog box. You can access the dialog box by clicking the Page Borders button on the Design tab.
- In the Preview area of the Page Border tab, you can click the diagram or buttons to apply borders. Likewise, you can click the diagram or buttons to remove borders.
- Using the Apply to drop-down menu, you can apply the borders to all pages of your document, to all pages in only a section of your document, to only the first page of a section, or to all pages of a section except the first page.
- Clicking the Options button on the Page Border tab opens the Border and Shading Options dialog box, where you can adjust margins and other settings to refine the position of the border.

Try It! Creating a Page Border

1. In the **W55Try_xx** file, adjust the zoom to 100%.
2. Press CTRL + A to select all text.
3. Press CTRL + C to copy the text.
4. Position the insertion point at the end of the document and insert a next page section break.

   ✓ *To insert a next page section break, click Layout > Breaks. Click Next Page under Section Breaks.*

5. Press CTRL + V to paste the text you copied in step 3. Press BACKSPACE to delete the blank paragraph and page 3.
6. On page 2, change the text *10%* to **25%**.
7. On the Design tab, in the Page Background group, click the Page Borders button.
8. Click the Page Border tab, if necessary.

Use the Preview area to apply a border

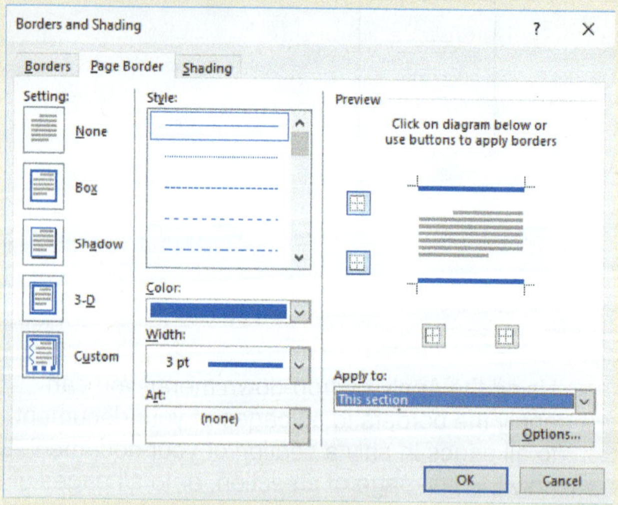

Word 2016, Windows 10, Microsoft Corporation

9. Click the Color drop-down arrow and, under Standard Colors, click Blue.
10. Click the Width drop-down arrow and click 3 pt.
11. In the Preview area, click the top of the diagram to add a border to the top of the page.
12. Click the bottom of the diagram to add a border to the bottom of the page.
13. Click the Apply to drop-down arrow and click This section.
14. Click OK. The borders appear on page 2 only.
15. Save the changes to **W55Try_xx**, and leave it open to use in the next Try It.

Apply a border to a document section

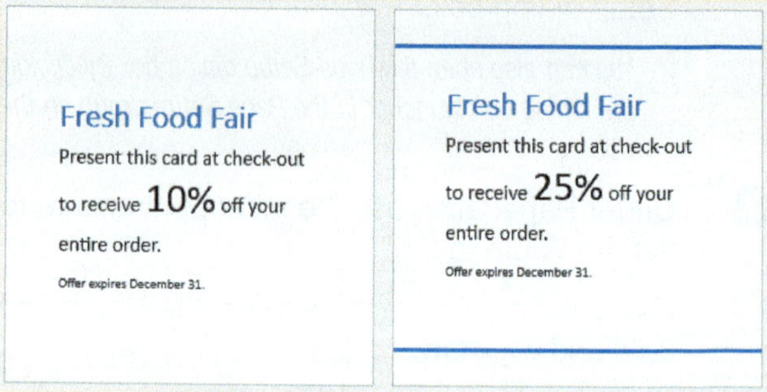

Word 2016, Windows 10, Microsoft Corporation

Try It! Modifying a Page Border

1. In the W55Try_xx file, position the insertion point at the beginning of page 2.
2. Click Design > Page Borders.
3. Click the Page Border tab, if necessary.
4. Click the Art drop-down arrow and click the first option, apples.
5. Under Width, use the increment arrows to set the Width to 20 pt.
6. In the Preview area, click the top, left, and right borders in the diagram to remove them.
7. Click the Apply to drop-down arrow and click This section.
8. Click the Options button.
9. Under Margin, use the increment arrows to set the Bottom margin to 30 pt.
10. Click OK.
11. Click OK.
12. Save the changes to W55Try_xx, and leave it open to use in the next Try It.

Hiding or Displaying White Space

- By default, in Print Layout view, Word displays white space. In this context, the term "white space" refers to the space between the bottom of one page and the top of the next page, as well as the header and footer.
- You can hide white space by double-clicking the top or bottom edge of any page in the document.

✓ *Word also hides any page borders applied to the document.*

- When white space is hidden, a gray line marks the location where one page ends and the next begins.
- To display white space, double-click the gray line between pages. If your document has only one page, double-click the top or bottom edge of the page.
- You can also select or clear the Show white space between pages in Print Layout view check box on the Display tab in the Word Options dialog box.

Try It! Hiding or Displaying White Space

1. In the W55Try_xx file, click View > Print Layout to change to Print Layout view, if necessary.
2. Scroll down so you can see the bottom of the first page and the top of the second page onscreen at the same time.
3. Position the mouse pointer over the bottom edge of page 1. The pointer changes to resemble arrows pointing up and down.
4. Double-click.
5. Position the mouse pointer on the gray line between the pages. Double-click again.
6. Leave the file open to use in the next Try It.

Display white space between pages

Word 2016, Windows 10, Microsoft Corporation

Hide white space between pages

Word 2016, Windows 10, Microsoft Corporation

Adjusting Character Spacing

- Use character spacing to improve the readability of the text, as well as to control the amount of text that fits on a line or on a page.
- In Word, the amount of space between characters is determined by the current font set.
- When certain characters that are wider than other characters in a font set are next to each other, they may appear to run together.
- Character spacing options are available on the Advanced tab of the Font dialog box.
- Set the **kerning** to automatically adjust the space between selected characters, when the characters are larger than a particular point size.
- You can also adjust spacing between characters by changing the scale, the spacing, or the position.
  - Set the scale to stretch or compress selected text based on a percentage. For example, set the character spacing scale above 100% to stretch the text, or below 100% to compress the text.
  - Set the spacing to expand or condense the spacing between all selected characters by a specific number of points.
  - Set the position to raise or lower characters relative to the text baseline by a specific number of points.

Try It! Adjusting Character Spacing

1. In the **W55Try_xx** file, select the text *Fresh Food Fair* on page 1.
2. On the Home tab, click the Font group dialog box launcher.
3. In the Font dialog box, click the Advanced tab.
4. Under Character Spacing, click the Spacing drop-down arrow and click Condensed.
5. Use the Spacing By box increment arrows to change the value to 2 pt and click OK.

   ✓ *To see how the change affects the selected text, Undo the change and then Redo it.*
6. On page 1, with the text *Fresh Food Fair* still selected, click the Font group dialog box launcher.
7. On the Advanced tab in the Font dialog box, click to clear the Kerning for fonts check box and click OK.
8. Open the Font dialog box again and click to select the Kerning for fonts check box and click OK.
9. Select the text *10%*, and click the Font group dialog box launcher.
10. On the Advanced tab in the Font dialog box, click the Scale drop-down arrow and click 150%. Click the Position drop-down arrow, click Lowered, and click OK.
11. Select the last line of text on page 1, and click the Font group dialog box launcher.
12. On the Advanced tab in the Font dialog box, click the Spacing drop-down arrow, click Expanded, and set the value to 2.5 pt. Click OK.
13. Save the changes to **W55Try_xx**, and leave it open to use in the next Try It.

Inserting a Non-Breaking Space

- When Word wraps text from one line to the next, it breaks the line at a space or—if hyphenation is on—at a hyphen.
- Insert a non-breaking space to keep two words together on the same line.
- A non-breaking space is a nonprinting character that looks like a small superscript o between two words.

Try It! Inserting a Non-Breaking Space

1. In the **W55Try_xx** file, click Home > Show/Hide ¶ ¶ to toggle on the display of nonprinting characters, if necessary.
2. On page 1, select the space between the words *your* and *entire*.
3. Press CTRL + SHIFT + SPACE to replace the selected space with a non-breaking space.

   ✓ *You can also select a non-breaking space on the Special Characters tab in the Symbol dialog box.*
4. Save and close the document, and exit Word.

Insert a non-breaking space

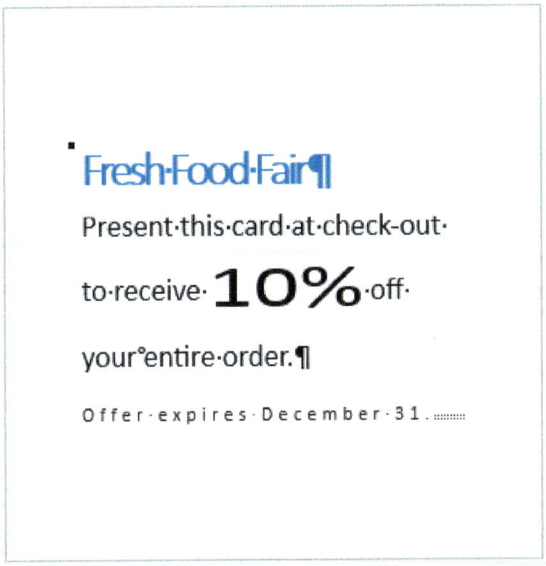

Word 2016, Windows 10, Microsoft Corporation

Lesson 55—Practice

You work at Liberty Blooms, a flower shop. The owner has asked you to create discount cards that will be placed at the cashier station for customers to take. In this project, you will create a discount card using custom paper size, page border, and character spacing options.

DIRECTIONS

1. Start Word, if necessary, and save a new blank document as **W55Practice_xx** in the location where your teacher instructs you to store the files for this lesson.
2. Apply the **Retrospect** theme and the **Shaded** style set.
3. In the header, type your full name and today's date. Select the two lines in the header and adjust the Spacing before to **0 pt**. Close the header and footer.
4. Position the mouse pointer on the top edge of the page, so it changes to look like this ⊞. Double-click to hide white space.
5. Click **Layout** > **Size** ▯, and click **More Paper Sizes**.
6. On the **Paper** tab in the Page Setup dialog box, under Paper size, use the **Width** increment arrows to set the paper width to **4"**.
7. Use the **Height** increment arrows to set the paper height to **4.5"**, and click **OK**.
8. In the Page Setup group, click the **Margins** button ▯ and click **Narrow**.
9. On the first line of the document, type **Liberty Blooms' Annual Fall Sale**. Format it with the **Title** style and center it horizontally.
10. Press ENTER and type **September 15 through October 10**. Format it with the **Heading 1** style and center it horizontally.

11. Press [ENTER], click the **Bullets** button and type the following three items:

    Perennials, including various types of ground cover and shade-loving plants

    Spring Bulbs, such as daffodils, hyacinths, crocuses, lilies of the valley, and tulips

    Shrubbery and more!

12. Press [ENTER] twice to end bullet list formatting and type **Present this coupon to receive 10% off.**
13. Select the text *Fall* in the title, click the Font group dialog box launcher, and click the **Advanced** tab. Click the **Position** drop-down arrow, click **Lowered**, and click **OK**.
14. Select all bulleted items and click the Font group dialog box launcher. Click the **Spacing** drop-down arrow, click **Expanded**, and click **OK**.
15. If necessary, adjust the Spacing after all bulleted items to **0 pt**.
16. Select the text *10%* and click the Font group dialog box launcher. Click the **Scale** drop-down arrow, click **150%**, and click **OK**.
17. Select the last line of text and click the Font group dialog box launcher. Click the **Spacing** drop-down arrow and click **Condensed**.
18. In the Spacing By box, change the value to **0.5 pt** and click **OK**.
19. Click **Home** > **Show/Hide ¶** to toggle on the display of nonprinting characters, if necessary.
20. In the second bulleted item, select the space between the words *the* and *valley*.
21. Press [CTRL] + [SHIFT] + [SPACE].
22. Position the mouse pointer on the top edge of the page, so it changes to look like this. Double-click to display white space.
23. On the Design tab, in the Page Background group, click the **Page Borders** button.
24. Click the **Page Border** tab, if necessary.
25. Under Style, click the first double line in the list.
26. Click the **Color** drop-down arrow and click **Brown, Accent 3**.
27. Click the **Options** button.
28. Under Margin, change the Top, Bottom, Left, and Right values to **18 pt**. Click **OK**.
29. Click **OK** to close the Borders and Shading dialog box.
30. Check and correct the spelling and grammar in the document.
31. **With your teacher's permission**, print the document. It should look similar to Figure 55-1.

    ✓ *You can cut paper to the selected size, or print on standard letter paper.*

32. Save and close the document, and exit Word.

Figure 55-1

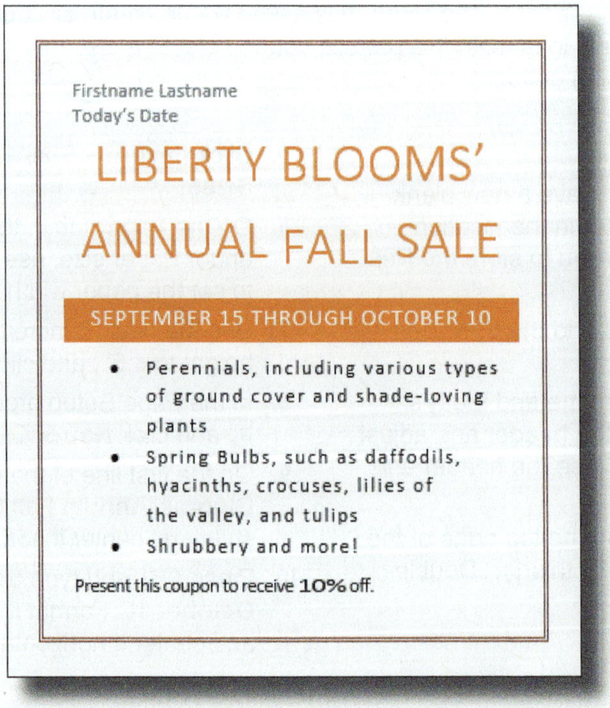
Firstname Lastname
Today's Date

LIBERTY BLOOMS'
ANNUAL FALL SALE

SEPTEMBER 15 THROUGH OCTOBER 10

- Perennials, including various types of ground cover and shade-loving plants
- Spring Bulbs, such as daffodils, hyacinths, crocuses, lilies of the valley, and tulips
- Shrubbery and more!

Present this coupon to receive 10% off.

Word 2016, Windows 10, Microsoft Corporation

Lesson 55—Apply

The owner of Liberty Blooms wants you to create a special discount card for loyal shoppers. In this project, you will create two designs for the owner to choose from.

DIRECTIONS

1. Start Word, if necessary, and open **W55Apply** from the data files for this lesson.
2. Save the file as **W55Apply_xx** in the location where your teacher instructs you to store the files for this lesson.
3. In the header, type your full name and today's date. Close the header and footer.
4. Hide white space.
5. Apply the **Depth** theme and the **Basic (Elegant)** style set.
6. Set the paper size to **5"** wide by **5"** high.
7. Set the margins to **Narrow**.
8. Expand the spacing of the first paragraph of body text by **2 pt**.
9. Scale the percentages in the three bullet items to **150%**.
10. Condense the spacing of the last paragraph by **0.5 pt**.
11. Raise the position of the word *Flower* in the heading by **5 pt**.
12. Insert a non-breaking space between the words *at* and *Liberty* in the main paragraph.
13. Display white space.
14. Change the width of the page border to **3 pt** and remove the top and bottom borders.
15. Copy all text in the document.
16. Insert a next page section break at the end of the document.
17. Paste the text you copied in step 15.
18. On page 2, center the headings *LIBERTY BLOOMS FLOWER SHOP* and *LOYAL SHOPPER DISCOUNTS*.
19. On page 2, change the page border setting to **Box** and the border color to **Aqua, Accent 1.**
20. Check and correct the spelling and grammar in the document.
21. **With your teacher's permission**, print the document. It should look similar to Figure 55-2.

    ✓ *You can cut paper to the selected size, or print on standard letter paper.*
22. Save and close the document, and exit Word.

Figure 55-2

Word 2016, Windows 10, Microsoft Corporation

Lesson 56

Working with Master Documents

➤ What You Will Learn

Creating a Master Document
Managing a Master Document
Revising a Master Document

WORDS TO KNOW

Master document
A document that contains a set of related documents.

Subdocument
A document contained in a master document.

Software Skills When you need to organize and manage long documents, you can create a master document with subdocuments. For example, use a master document to manage a book that has multiple chapters, or a report that has many sections.

What You Can Do

Creating a Master Document

- Use a **master document** to organize and manage a long document by dividing it into **subdocuments**.
- To create a master document, change to Outline view and use the tools in the Master Document group on the Outlining tab of the ribbon to designate headings as subdocuments.
- When you save the master document, Word automatically saves each designated heading, its subheadings, and its body text as a separate document.
- Word names each subdocument file based on the text in the subdocument heading.
- You can view and edit the subdocuments in the master document, or you can open a subdocument separately.
- Once you create subdocuments, the master document outline appears in Master Document view.
- Word inserts section breaks between subdocuments and displays a gray border around each subdocument.

- A subdocument icon appears to the left of each subdocument in Master Document view.
  - Click the subdocument icon to select the entire subdocument.
  - Double-click the subdocument icon to open the subdocument in a separate window.
- You can create a master document in a new document before typing any text, or convert an existing document into a master document.

Try It! Creating a Master Document

1. Start Word, and open **W56TryA** from the data files for this lesson.
2. Save the file as **W56TryA_xx** in the location where your teacher instructs you to store the files for this lesson.
3. Display nonprinting characters, if necessary, and click View > Outline to display the document in Outline view.

   ✓ *Note that the heading Selecting Roses is Level 1, Judging Rose Quality and Types of Roses are Level 2, and Grafted Roses and Bare-Root and Potted Roses are Level 3.*

4. On the Outlining tab, in the Outline Tools group, click the Show Level drop-down arrow and click Level 3 to show the headings and hide the Body Text.
5. On the Outlining tab, in the Master Document group, click Show Document to display the Master Document tools.
6. Select all Level 2 and 3 headings in the outline, and click the Create button.

   ✓ *Word creates the subdocuments. When you save the changes, Word saves the subdocument files and stores them in the same location as the master document.*

7. Click the Show Level drop-down arrow and click All Levels to display the contents of the master document.
8. Click to select the Show Text Formatting and Show First Line Only check boxes, if necessary.
9. Save the changes to **W56TryA_xx**, and leave it open to use in the next Try It.

A master document with subdocuments in Master Document view

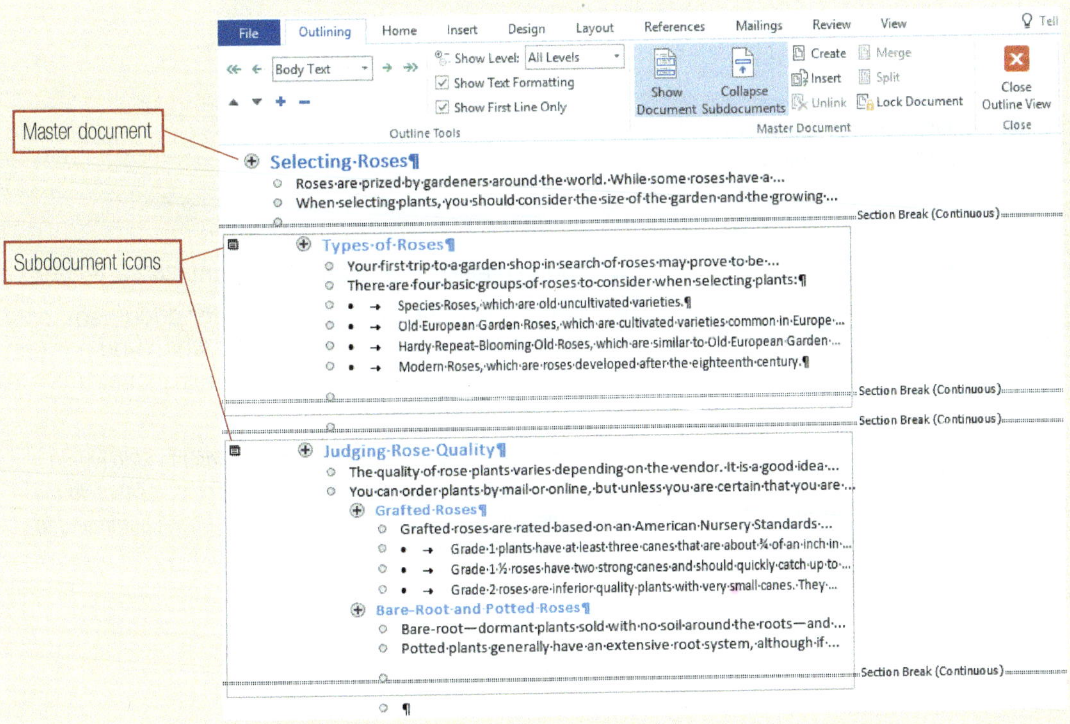

Word 2016, Windows 10, Microsoft Corporation

Managing a Master Document

- You can lock a master document to display it in Read-Only mode.
- You must use the Save As command to save changes to a Read-Only file with a new name, or in a new location.
- You can also collapse subdocuments to protect them from editing.

✓ *When subdocuments are collapsed, a lock icon appears under the subdocument icon, indicating that they cannot be edited.*

- Collapsed subdocuments appear as hyperlinks to the stored files. Press CTRL and click the hyperlink to open the subdocument file for editing.
- When subdocuments are expanded, you can use the tools in the Outline Tools group to rearrange subdocuments.
- You can also use the tools in the Outline Tools group to rearrange headings within a subdocument.

Try It! Managing a Master Document

1. In the **W56TryA_xx** file, move the insertion point to the beginning of the document.
2. Click Outlining > Lock Document. Note in the title bar that the document is now in Read-Only mode.
3. Click the Lock Document button again to toggle off protection.
4. Press CTRL + END to move the insertion point to the end of the master document.
5. Insert a Continuous section break.
6. On the Outlining tab, click to clear the Show First Line Only check box, if necessary.
7. Click Outlining > Collapse Subdocuments. Click OK in the confirmation dialog box to save changes, if necessary. Notice that the two subdocuments now appear as hyperlinks.
8. Click Outlining > Expand Subdocuments.
9. In the *Judging Rose Quality* subdocument, select the Level 3 heading *Bare-Root and Potted Roses* and the two Body Text paragraphs below it. Do not select the blank paragraphs or section breaks.
10. In the Outline Tools group, click the Move Up button ▲ five times to move the heading and its Body Text paragraphs above the *Grafted Roses* heading.
11. Save the changes to **W56TryA_xx**, and leave it open to use in the next Try It.

Revising a Master Document

- You can insert an existing document into an existing master document as a subdocument.
- You can edit and format subdocuments in the master document the same way you do any Word document.
- It is a good idea to save copies or back up the original subdocument files before editing, as changes you save in the master document are saved in the individual subdocument files as well.
- You can also open a subdocument file for editing.
- When you print a collapsed master document, only the subdocument link text prints; when you print an expanded master document, all subdocuments are printed as well.

✓ *Note that you can also use the Split command to create a new subdocument from the insertion point location to the end of the master document, and the Unlink command to merge the current subdocument into the master document.*

Try It! Revising a Master Document

1. With the **W56TryA_xx** file open in Master Document view, click the Show Level drop-down arrow and click All Levels, if necessary. Click to clear the Show First Line Only check box, if necessary.
2. Under the Level 3 heading *Bare-Root and Potted Roses*, delete the last sentence, *If so, they may be young and have an immature root system.* Save the changes to the master document.
3. Double-click the subdocument icon to the left of the Level 2 heading *Judging Rose Quality*. The subdocument file opens. Notice that the sentence you deleted in the master document has been deleted in the subdocument file as well.
4. Edit the Level 2 heading to **Judging the Quality of Roses**. Save and close the document. Note the change to the heading in the master document file as well.

   ✓ *Also note that Word does not change the name of the saved subdocument file.*

5. In the Outline Tools group, click to select the Show First Line Only check box. Click File > New > Blank document to create a new blank document and save it as **W56TryB_xx** in the location where your teacher instructs you to store the files for this lesson.
6. Apply the Heading 2 style, type **The Rose as Symbol**, and press ENTER .
7. Type **Throughout history, roses have been used to symbolize many things.**
8. Save and close the document.
9. In the **W56TryA_xx** master document, press CTRL + END to move the insertion point to the end of the document, below the second subdocument.
10. Click Outlining > Insert . Navigate to the location where you are storing the files for this lesson. Click **W56TryB_xx** and click Open. If you are prompted to rename a style, click Yes. The **W56TryB_xx** file becomes the third subdocument in the master document.
11. Save and close the document, and exit Word.

The revised master document

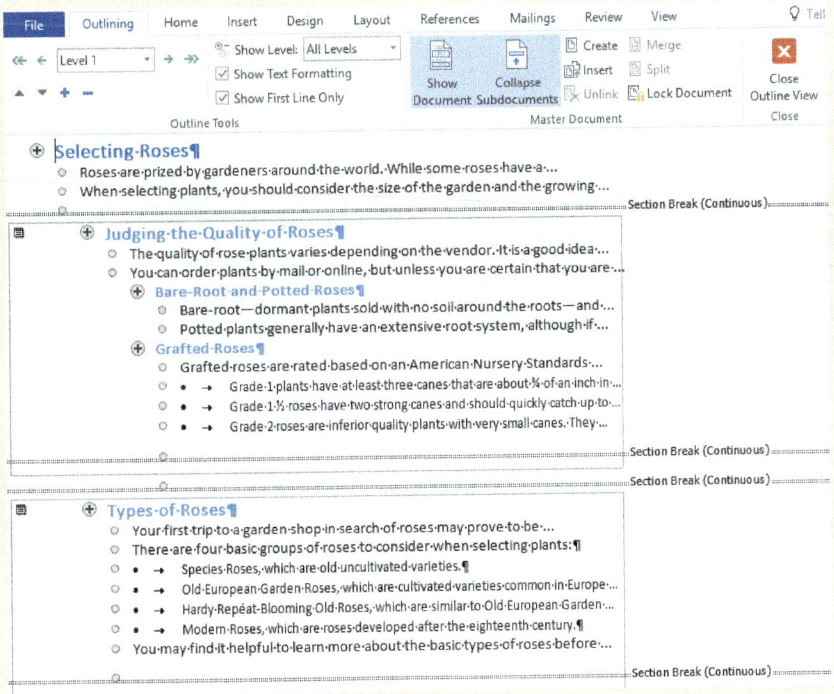

Lesson 56—Practice

You work in the marketing group at Fox Footwear. The marketing director has asked you to write a lengthy report about the history of footwear. You are just getting started on the project and have decided that using a master document will help you stay organized. In this project, you will create a master document and edit subdocuments.

DIRECTIONS

1. Start Word, if necessary, and save a new blank document as **W56Practice_xx** in the location where your teacher instructs you to store the files for this lesson.
2. In the header, type your full name and today's date. Close the header and footer.
3. Display nonprinting characters, if necessary, and click **View** > **Outline** to change to Outline view.
4. In Outline view, assign levels and type text as follows:

   Level 1: **Step in Time: A Footwear History**

   Level 2: **Ancient Footwear**

   Level 3: **The First Army Boots**

   Level 3: **Materials**

   Level 2: **Shoes as Necessity**

   Level 2: **Shoes as Fashion**

   Level 3: **Form vs. Function**
5. On the Outlining tab, in the Master Document group, click the **Show Document** button.
6. Select all Level 2 and 3 headings in the outline.
7. In the Master Document group, click the **Create** button

   ✓ *Word creates three subdocuments in the master document.*
8. Save the changes to the document. Click to clear the Show First Line Only check box, if necessary.

   ✓ *Word saves the subdocument files in the same location as the master document files.*
9. Position the insertion point on the blank Body Text line below the subdocument heading *Shoes as Necessity*, and type

   Shoes were probably developed as a means to protect the foot from bad weather and rough terrain.
10. Double-click the **subdocument icon** to the left of the subdocument heading *Ancient Footwear* to open the Ancient Footwear subdocument file.
11. In the header, type your name and today's date.
12. Position the insertion point at the end of the heading *The First Army Boots*, press ENTER and type

    Romans devised military-style footwear which enabled their legions to travel the empire on foot. These original "army boots" were sturdy, thick-soled, heavy leather sandals with an upper covering.
13. Save and close the Ancient Footwear document.
14. Double-click the **subdocument icon** to the left of the subdocument heading *Shoes as Necessity* to open the subdocument file, type your name and today's date in the header, and save and close the file.
15. Double-click the **subdocument icon** to the left of the subdocument heading *Shoes as Fashion* to open the subdocument file, type your name and today's date in the header, and save and close the file.
16. In the master document, drag over the Level 3 heading **Materials** in the Ancient Footwear subdocument to select just the heading.
17. In the Outline Tools group, click the **Move Up** ▲ button twice to move the selected heading above the Level 3 heading *The First Army Boots*.
18. Check and correct the spelling and grammar in the master document. It should look similar to Figure 56-1 on the next page.
19. **With your teacher's permission**, print the master document outline.
20. Click **Outlining** > **Collapse Subdocuments**. Click **OK** to save changes in the confirmation dialog box, if necessary,
21. **With your teacher's permission**, print the collapsed master document.
22. Save and close the document, and exit Word.

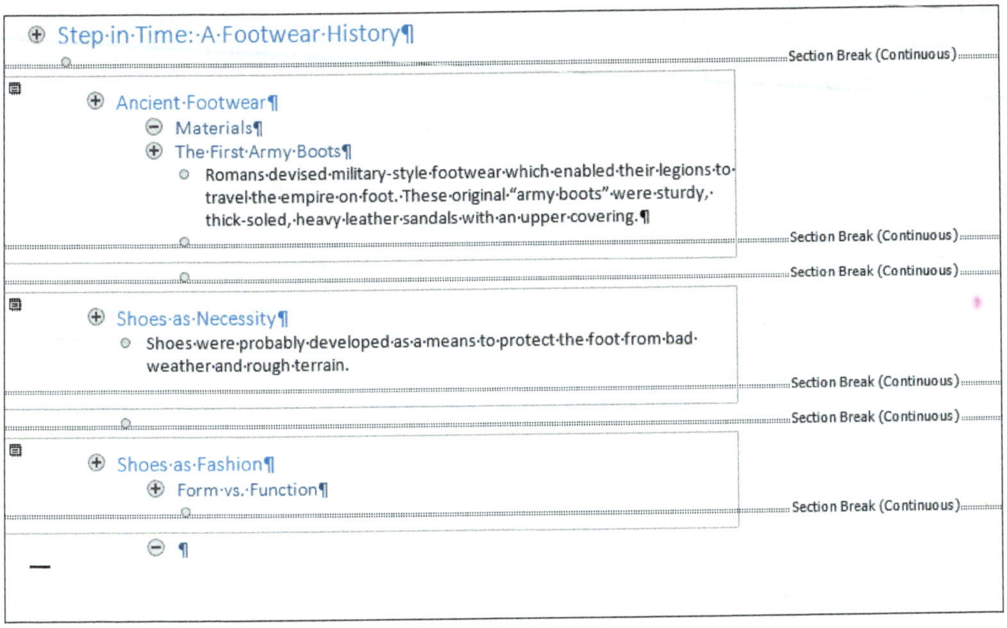

Figure 56-1

Word 2016, Windows 10, Microsoft Corporation

Lesson 56—Apply

The marketing director at Fox Footwear has asked you to show the rest of the marketing group how to create a master document. In this project, you will create a master document from an existing outline, insert an additional subdocument into the master document, and edit subdocuments.

DIRECTIONS

1. Start Word, if necessary, and open **W56ApplyA** from the data files for this lesson.
2. Save the file as **W56ApplyA_xx** in the location where your teacher instructs you to store the files for this lesson.
3. In the header, type your full name and today's date. Close the header and footer.
4. Display nonprinting characters, if necessary, and change to **Outline** view.
5. Collapse the outline to show only Levels 1 and 2 and create subdocuments from the Level 2 headings.
6. Save the master document.
7. Clear the Show First Line Only check box, if necessary.
8. Collapse the subdocuments, and open the *Why Were Shoes Developed?* subdocument. Type your name and today's date in the header.
9. Position the insertion point at the end of the last sentence (before the section break), press ENTER, apply the **Heading 3** style, and type **Specialized Shoes**.
10. Press ENTER and type

    Footwear designed for a specific purpose is a relatively modern concept, sparked in large part by the sports industry. Beginning in the 1800s, shoes were developed specifically for use in running and croquet. Now, there are shoes designed for all manner of athletics, such as basketball, baseball, and wrestling.
11. Check and correct the spelling and grammar in the document. Save and close the document.
12. Expand the subdocuments and display all levels in the outline.
13. Within the *Why Were Shoes Developed?* subdocument, move the *Specialized Shoes* heading and its Body Text above the *Shoes as Military Strategy* heading.

14. Open the *Prehistoric Footwear* subdocument, type your name and today's date in the header, and edit the heading from *Prehistoric Footwear* to **Early Footwear**. Save the document and close it.
15. Open the *The Fashion of Footwear* subdocument, type your name and today's date in the header, edit the heading from *The Fashion of Footwear* to **Footwear Fashion**. Save the document and close it.
16. Open **W56ApplyB** from the data files for this lesson, and save it as **W56ApplyB_xx** in the location where your teacher instructs you to store the files for this lesson. Type your name and today's date in the header. Save and close the document.
17. Insert **W56ApplyB_xx** as a subdocument at the end of the master document. If you are prompted to rename a style, click **Yes**.
18. Display the first line only of body text. The document should look similar to Figure 56-2.
19. Check and correct the spelling and grammar in the master document.
20. **With your teacher's permission**, print the document with collapsed subdocuments and with expanded subdocuments.
21. Save and close the document, and exit Word.

Figure 56-2

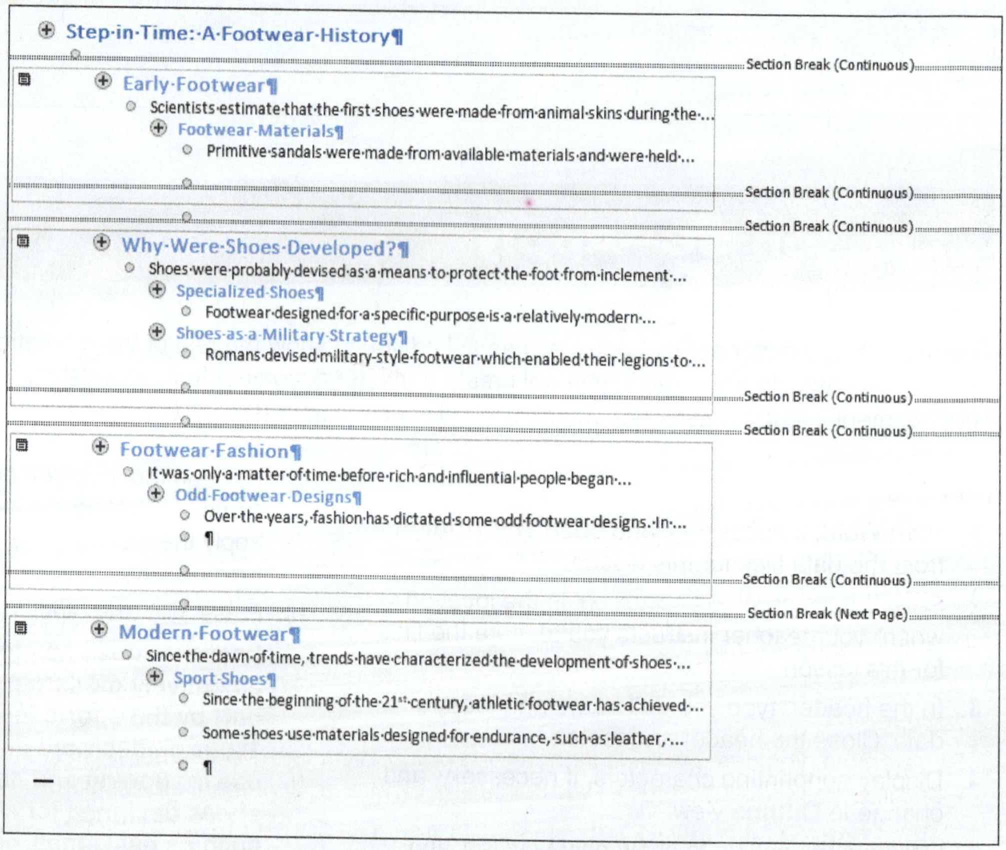

Word 2016, Windows 10, Microsoft Corporation

Lesson 57

Creating Custom Headers and Footers, Bookmarks, and Cross-References

➤ What You Will Learn

Customizing Headers and Footers
Inserting Bookmarks
Inserting a Cross-Reference

Software Skills When none of the built-in header and footer styles suit your needs, you can customize them and even save them as building blocks. For example, you can insert the current date and time, and create different headers for odd and even pages. Insert a bookmark so you can jump directly to a specific location in a document, and insert a cross-reference to refer a reader from one location to another related location.

WORDS TO KNOW

Bookmark
A nonprinting character that you insert and name so that you can quickly find a particular location in a document.

Cross-reference
Text that refers a reader to a different location in a document.

What You Can Do

Customizing Headers and Footers

- Use the tools on the Header & Footer Tools Design tab to customize headers or footers.
- For example, you can use tools in the Insert group to insert the date and/or time, a building block from the Quick Parts gallery, a picture, or document information.
- You can use the tools in the Options group to display a different header/footer on the first page of a document, to display different headers/footers on odd pages than on even pages, and to hide the document text when you are working in the header/footer area.

✓ *Note that when you insert a cover page, Word automatically selects the option for using a different header on the first page.*

- You can use the tools in the Position group to move the header closer or nearer to the top of the page, or to move the footer closer or nearer to the bottom of the page.
- If your document has sections, by default, a header/footer is linked to the header/footer in the previous section so that they display the same information.

- You can break the link so that you can enter a different header/footer in each section in a document.
- On the Header & Footer Tools Design tab, click the Link to Previous button to break a link. Click the button again to create a link.
- You can set a page value to continue the numbering from the previous section, or you can specify a different starting number or format.
- Word automatically restarts page numbering on the first page of each section. You can set a page value to continue the numbering from the previous section.

Try It! **Customizing Headers and Footers**

1. Start Word, and open **W57Try** from the data files for this lesson.
2. Save the file as **W57Try_xx** in the location where your teacher instructs you to store the files for this lesson.
3. Double-click in the footer at the bottom of the second page.
4. On the Header & Footer Tools Design tab, in the Insert group, click the Date & Time button to open the Date and Time dialog box.
5. In the list of Available formats, click the fourth format—m/d/yy—and click OK.
6. Scroll through the document. You can see that the same footer now appears on every page.
7. Click Header & Footer Tools Design > Different First Page check box.
8. Click Header & Footer Tools Design > Previous to move the insertion point to the First Page Footer – Section 1 footer, which is now blank.
9. Press TAB. On the Header & Footer Tools Design tab, in the Insert group, click the Pictures button. Navigate to the location where the data files for this lesson are stored and insert **W57Try_image**. Resize the image so that its height is 1.5".
10. On the Header & Footer Tools Design tab, in the Options group, click to select the Different Odd & Even Pages check box. Click the Next button twice to move the insertion point to the Even Page Footer – Section 1 footer.
11. Press TAB twice and type your name. Click the Next button to move the insertion point to the Even Page Footer – Section 2 footer.
12. In the Navigation group, click the Link to Previous button to toggle off the link. Delete your name and type **Computer Technology Report** in its place.
13. In the Navigation group, click the Go to Header button to move the insertion point to the Even Page Header –Section 2 header.
14. Click the Page Number button, point to Top of Page, and click the Brackets 1 style.
15. Right-click the page number field in the header and click Format Page Numbers on the shortcut menu to open the Page Number Format dialog box.
16. Click the Continue from previous section option button and click OK.
17. Click the Previous button to move the insertion point to the Odd Page Header – Section 2 header, click the Page Number button, point to Top of Page, and click the Brackets 1 style.
18. On the Header & Footer Tools Design tab, use the increment arrows to set the Header from Top value to 0.3".
19. Click the Close Header and Footer button, and scroll through the document to view the different headers and footers.
20. Save the changes to **W57Try_xx**, and leave it open to use in the next Try It.

(continued)

Try It! Customizing Headers and Footers *(continued)*

Customized headers and footers

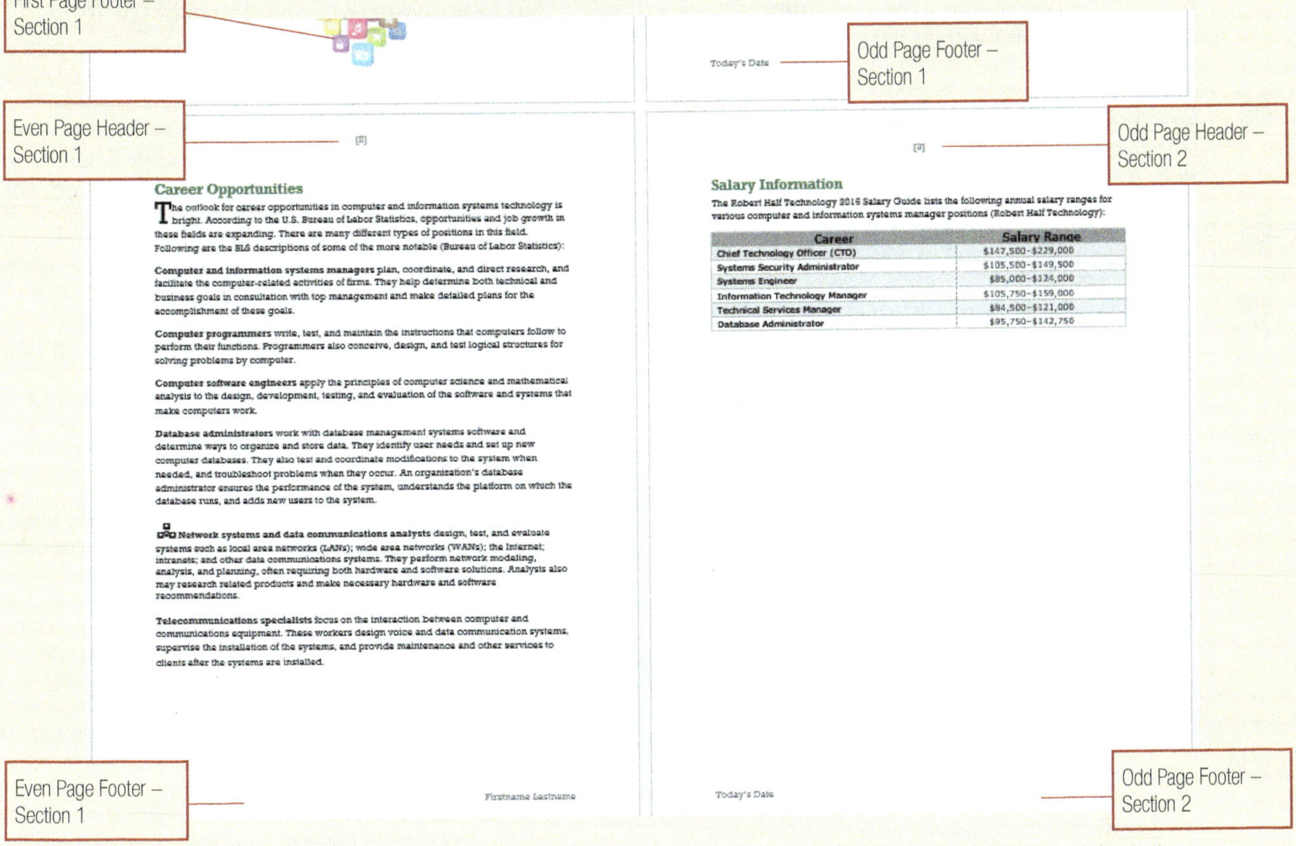

Word 2016, Windows 10, Microsoft Corporation

Inserting Bookmarks

- Insert a **bookmark** to mark a specific location in a document, such as where you stopped working or where you need to insert information.
- Then use Go To to quickly move the insertion point to the bookmark location.
- You can also create a cross-reference to a bookmark.

✓ *Cross-references are covered in the next Try It.*

- Use descriptive bookmark names to make it easier to identify the bookmark location that you want.
- You cannot use spaces in bookmark names.
- Bookmarks are nonprinting characters that look like an I-beam [I] when displayed onscreen. If you want to see them in your document, select the Show bookmarks check box on the Advanced tab of the Word Options dialog box.

Try It! Inserting Bookmarks

1. In the **W57Try_xx** file, position the insertion point at the beginning of the text *Computer programmers* on the third page of the document (numbered page 2).
2. On the Insert tab, in the Links group, click the Bookmark button to open the Bookmark dialog box.
3. In the Bookmark name box, type **Programmers**. Click Add. Word inserts the bookmark.
4. Click File > Options > Advanced. Under Show document content, click to select the Show bookmarks check box. Click OK. The bookmark character appears at the insertion point location.
5. Press CTRL + HOME to move the insertion point to the beginning of the document.
6. On the Home tab, in the Editing group, click the Find drop-down arrow and click Go To to display the Go To tab of the Find and Replace dialog box.
7. In the Go to what list, click Bookmark. Verify that *Programmers* is displayed in the Enter bookmark name box, and click Go To. Word moves the insertion point to the bookmark.

   ✓ *You can also move the insertion point to the bookmark by clicking Go To in the Bookmark dialog box.*
8. In the Find and Replace dialog box, click Close.
9. Click File > Options > Advanced. Under Show document content, click to clear the Show bookmarks check box. Click OK.
10. Save the changes to **W57Try_xx**, and leave it open to use in the next Try It.

Mark and Go To a location using a bookmark

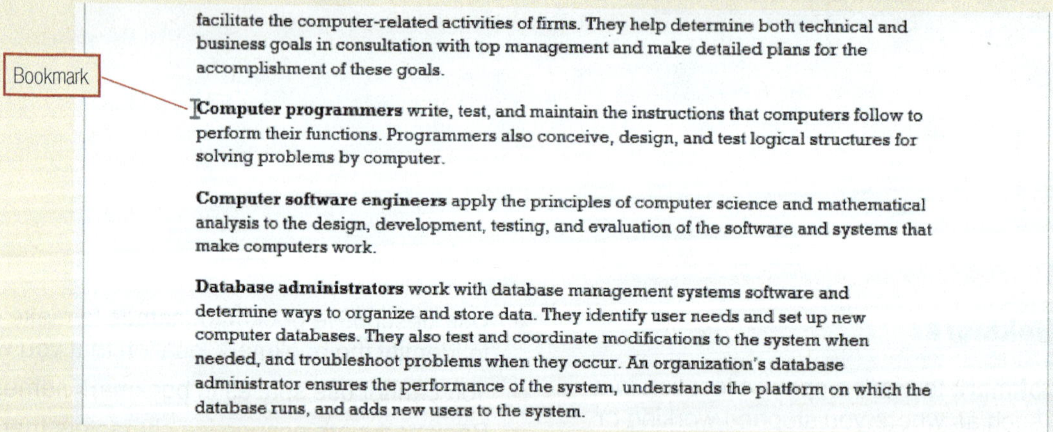

facilitate the computer-related activities of firms. They help determine both technical and business goals in consultation with top management and make detailed plans for the accomplishment of these goals.

Computer programmers write, test, and maintain the instructions that computers follow to perform their functions. Programmers also conceive, design, and test logical structures for solving problems by computer.

Computer software engineers apply the principles of computer science and mathematical analysis to the design, development, testing, and evaluation of the software and systems that make computers work.

Database administrators work with database management systems software and determine ways to organize and store data. They identify user needs and set up new computer databases. They also test and coordinate modifications to the system when needed, and troubleshoot problems when they occur. An organization's database administrator ensures the performance of the system, understands the platform on which the database runs, and adds new users to the system.

Word 2016, Windows 10, Microsoft Corporation

Inserting a Cross-Reference

- Insert a **cross-reference** to direct a reader to another location in the same document for more information. For example, "For more information, see page 22" is a cross-reference.
- To create a cross-reference, you type the text you want to use to direct the reader—such as, *For more information, see.*
- You then select the object to which you are referring, and whether you want Word to reference it by page number, text, or paragraph.
- Word inserts the cross-reference in a field, so it can be updated if necessary. This means that if you reference a heading and then move the heading to another location in the document, you can update the cross-reference to reflect the change.

- You can create cross-references to existing headings, footnotes, bookmarks, numbered paragraphs, tables, and figures, as well as to endnotes and equations.
- By default, Word inserts a cross-reference as a hyperlink. When you are viewing a document onscreen, press CTRL and click the cross-reference to jump to the specified destination.
- You can change the setting if you do not want the cross-reference inserted as a hyperlink.
- If the cross-reference field code is displayed in your document instead of the field value, you must deselect the Show field codes instead of their values option in the Advanced group in the Word Options dialog box.

Try It! Inserting a Cross-Reference

1. In the **W57Try_xx** file, position the insertion point at the end of the paragraph under the subheading *Information Systems* on the second page in the document (numbered page 1).
2. Press SPACE and type **(See Salary Information on page .)**. Be sure to leave a space between the last word and the period.
3. Position the insertion point to the left of the period you just typed. On the Insert tab, in the Links group, click the Cross-reference button to open the Cross-reference dialog box.
4. Click the Reference type drop-down arrow and click Heading.
5. Click the Insert reference to drop-down arrow and click Page number.
6. In the For which heading list, click Salary Information.
7. Click Insert, and then click Close.
8. Press and hold CTRL and click the cross-reference field. Word moves the insertion point to the Salary Information heading on the fourth page of the document (numbered page 3).
9. Save and close the document, and exit Word.

Cross-reference dialog box

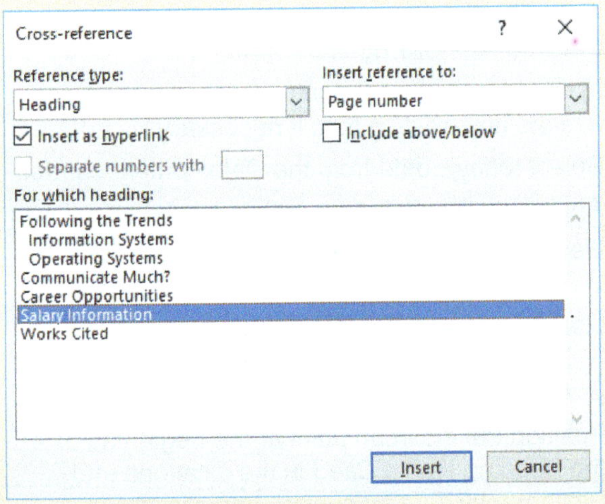

Word 2016, Windows 10, Microsoft Corporation

Lesson 57—Practice

You work in the publishing department at the Michigan Avenue Athletic Club and are writing a report describing some of the benefits of regular exercise. In this project, you will add customized headers and footers to the report. You will also add a bookmark and a cross-reference to help readers find the information they need.

DIRECTIONS

1. Start Word, if necessary, and open **W57Practice** from the data files for this lesson.
2. Save the file as **W57Practice_xx** in the location where your teacher instructs you to store the files for this lesson.
3. Click **Insert** > **Cover Page** > **Sideline**.
4. In the Company content control, type **Michigan Avenue Athletic Club**.
5. In the Title content control, type **Exercise for Life**.
6. In the Subtitle content control, type **A Report on the Benefits of Physical Activity**.
7. In the Author content control, type your name. (Delete any existing text, if necessary.)
8. Select today's date from the Date content control.
9. Apply heading styles (or outline levels) as follows:

   Heading level 2: **Introduction**, **The Impact on Your Health**, **Getting Started**, and **Conclusion.**

   Heading level 3: **Disease Control**, **Mental Health**, **Weight Control**, **Safety**, and **Doctor Supervision**.
10. Position the insertion point at the beginning of the heading *Works Cited* in the Citations and Bibliography content control, and click **Layout** > **Breaks** > **Next Page** to insert a next page section break.
11. Click **Insert** > **Header** > **Edit Header**.
12. On the Header & Footer Tools Design tab, click to select the **Different Odd & Even Pages** check box.

    ✓ *The Different First Page check box should be selected, because you inserted a cover page in step 3.*
13. Click **Header & Footer Tools Design** > **Previous** twice to display the Odd Page Header – Section 1 header.
14. Type your name, then press TAB twice. Click **Header & Footer Tools Design** > **Date & Time** .
15. In the Date and Time dialog box, click to select the third format in the list of available formats, and click **OK**.
16. Click **Header & Footer Tools Design** > **Next** to move the insertion point to the Even Page Header – Section 1 header. Type **Exercise for Life**, press TAB twice, and type **Michigan Avenue Athletic Club**.
17. Click the **Next** button to move the insertion point to the First Page Header – Section 2 header. Click **Link to Previous** to toggle off the link. Type your name, press TAB twice, and type **Works Cited**.
18. In the Navigation group, click the **Go to Footer** button , and click the **Previous** button twice to move the insertion point to the Odd Page Footer – Section 1 footer.
19. In the Header & Footer group, click **Page Number** > **Bottom of Page** > **Plain Number 2** to insert page numbers in the center of the footer on the odd pages in section 1.
20. Click the **Next** button to move the insertion point to the Even Page Footer – Section 1 footer, and click **Page Number** > **Bottom of Page** > **Plain Number 2** to insert page numbers in the center of the footer on the even pages in section 1.
21. Click the **Next** button to move the insertion point to the First Page Footer – Section 2 footer, and click **Page Number** > **Bottom of Page** > **Plain Number 2**.
22. Right-click the page number on the last page and click **Format Page Numbers** on the shortcut menu.
23. Click to select the **Continue from previous section** option button, and click **OK**.
24. Click the **Close Header and Footer** button , and save the changes to the document.
25. Position the insertion point at the beginning of the last sentence under the heading *Conclusion*.

26. Click **Insert** > **Bookmark**.
27. In the Bookmark name box, type **ContactInfo**, and click **Add**.
28. Click **File** > **Options** > **Advanced**. Under Show document content, click to select the **Show bookmarks** check box. Click **OK**. The bookmark character appears.
29. Position the insertion point after the last sentence in the Introduction and type **For contact information, see page .**
30. Position the insertion point to the left of the period you just typed. On the Insert tab, in the Links group, click the **Cross-reference** button.
31. Click the **Reference type** drop-down arrow and click **Bookmark**.
32. Click the **Insert reference to** drop-down arrow and click **Page number**.
33. Verify that the **ContactInfo** bookmark is selected in the For which bookmark list, click **Insert**, and click **Close**.
34. Press and hold CTRL and click the cross-reference field. Word moves the insertion point to the **ContactInfo** bookmark.
35. Check and correct the spelling and grammar in the document.
36. **With your teacher's permission**, print the document. Pages numbered 2 and 3 should look similar to Figure 57-1.
37. Save and close the document, and exit Word.

Figure 57-1

Word 2016, Windows 10, Microsoft Corporation

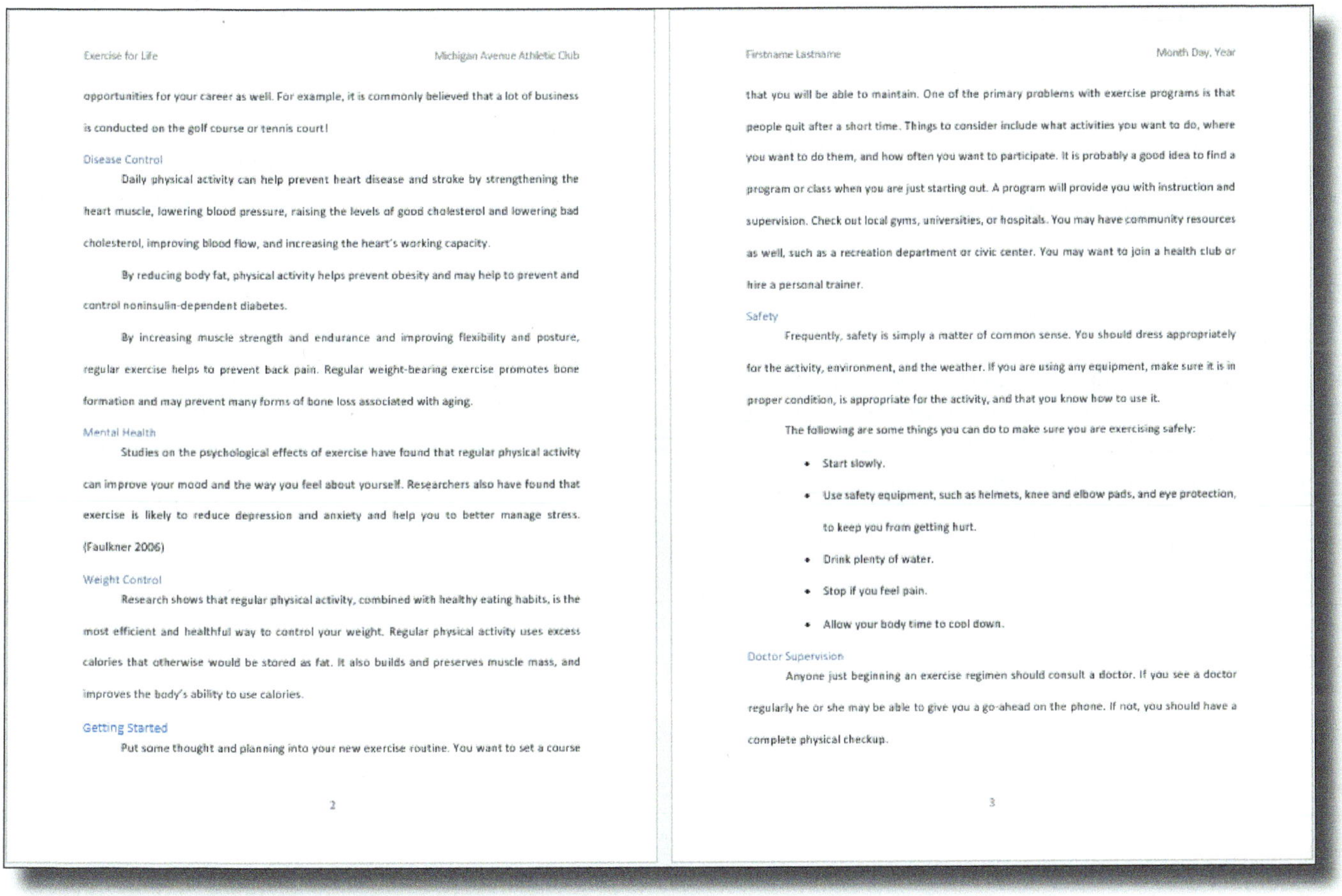

Exercise for Life Michigan Avenue Athletic Club

opportunities for your career as well. For example, it is commonly believed that a lot of business is conducted on the golf course or tennis court!

Disease Control

Daily physical activity can help prevent heart disease and stroke by strengthening the heart muscle, lowering blood pressure, raising the levels of good cholesterol and lowering bad cholesterol, improving blood flow, and increasing the heart's working capacity.

By reducing body fat, physical activity helps prevent obesity and may help to prevent and control noninsulin-dependent diabetes.

By increasing muscle strength and endurance and improving flexibility and posture, regular exercise helps to prevent back pain. Regular weight-bearing exercise promotes bone formation and may prevent many forms of bone loss associated with aging.

Mental Health

Studies on the psychological effects of exercise have found that regular physical activity can improve your mood and the way you feel about yourself. Researchers also have found that exercise is likely to reduce depression and anxiety and help you to better manage stress. (Faulkner 2006)

Weight Control

Research shows that regular physical activity, combined with healthy eating habits, is the most efficient and healthful way to control your weight. Regular physical activity uses excess calories that otherwise would be stored as fat. It also builds and preserves muscle mass, and improves the body's ability to use calories.

Getting Started

Put some thought and planning into your new exercise routine. You want to set a course

2

Firstname Lastname Month Day, Year

that you will be able to maintain. One of the primary problems with exercise programs is that people quit after a short time. Things to consider include what activities you want to do, where you want to do them, and how often you want to participate. It is probably a good idea to find a program or class when you are just starting out. A program will provide you with instruction and supervision. Check out local gyms, universities, or hospitals. You may have community resources as well, such as a recreation department or civic center. You may want to join a health club or hire a personal trainer.

Safety

Frequently, safety is simply a matter of common sense. You should dress appropriately for the activity, environment, and the weather. If you are using any equipment, make sure it is in proper condition, is appropriate for the activity, and that you know how to use it.

The following are some things you can do to make sure you are exercising safely:

- Start slowly.
- Use safety equipment, such as helmets, knee and elbow pads, and eye protection, to keep you from getting hurt.
- Drink plenty of water.
- Stop if you feel pain.
- Allow your body time to cool down.

Doctor Supervision

Anyone just beginning an exercise regimen should consult a doctor. If you see a doctor regularly he or she may be able to give you a go-ahead on the phone. If not, you should have a complete physical checkup.

3

Lesson 57—Apply

You continue to work on your report about exercise for the Michigan Avenue Athletic Club. In this project, you will add customized headers and footers to each section, add bookmarks, find a location in the document by its bookmark, and add a cross-reference.

DIRECTIONS

1. Start Word, if necessary, and open **W57Apply** from the data files for this lesson.
2. Save the file as **W57Apply_xx** in the location where your teacher instructs you to store the files for this lesson.
3. On the cover page, type your name in the Author content control and select today's date from the Date content control.
4. In section 2, insert a footer with the section heading **Introduction** flush left and today's date flush right.
5. In section 3, turn off **Link to Previous** and insert a footer with the section heading **Getting Started** flush left and today's date flush right.
6. In section 4, turn off **Link to Previous** and insert a footer with the section heading **Works Cited** flush left and today's date flush right.
7. On every page except the cover page, insert a header with page numbers in the **Accent Bar 2** style flush right. Add your name flush left as follows: place the insertion point before the word *Page*, type your name, and press TAB twice. Number the pages continuously starting on the second page (not on the cover page).
8. Save the document, and close the header and footer.
9. Insert a bookmark named **MentalHealth** at the beginning of the *Mental Health* heading.
10. Insert a bookmark named **SafetyEquipment** at the beginning of the second item in the bulleted list under the heading *Safety*.
11. Use **Go To** to move the insertion point to the **ContactInfo** bookmark, and edit the last four digits in the telephone number to **3521**.
12. Position the insertion point between the second and third sentences in the last paragraph of the introduction and type **It is imperative that you consult your physician before starting a new exercise routine. (See Doctor Supervision on page .)**
13. To the left of the period you just typed, insert a hyperlinked cross-reference to the page number where the heading *Doctor Supervision* is located.
14. Check and correct the spelling and grammar in the document.
15. Set options to hide the display of bookmark characters onscreen.
16. **With your teacher's permission**, print the document. Pages numbered 2 and 3 should look similar to Figure 57-2 on the next page.
17. Save and close the document, and exit Word.

Figure 57-2

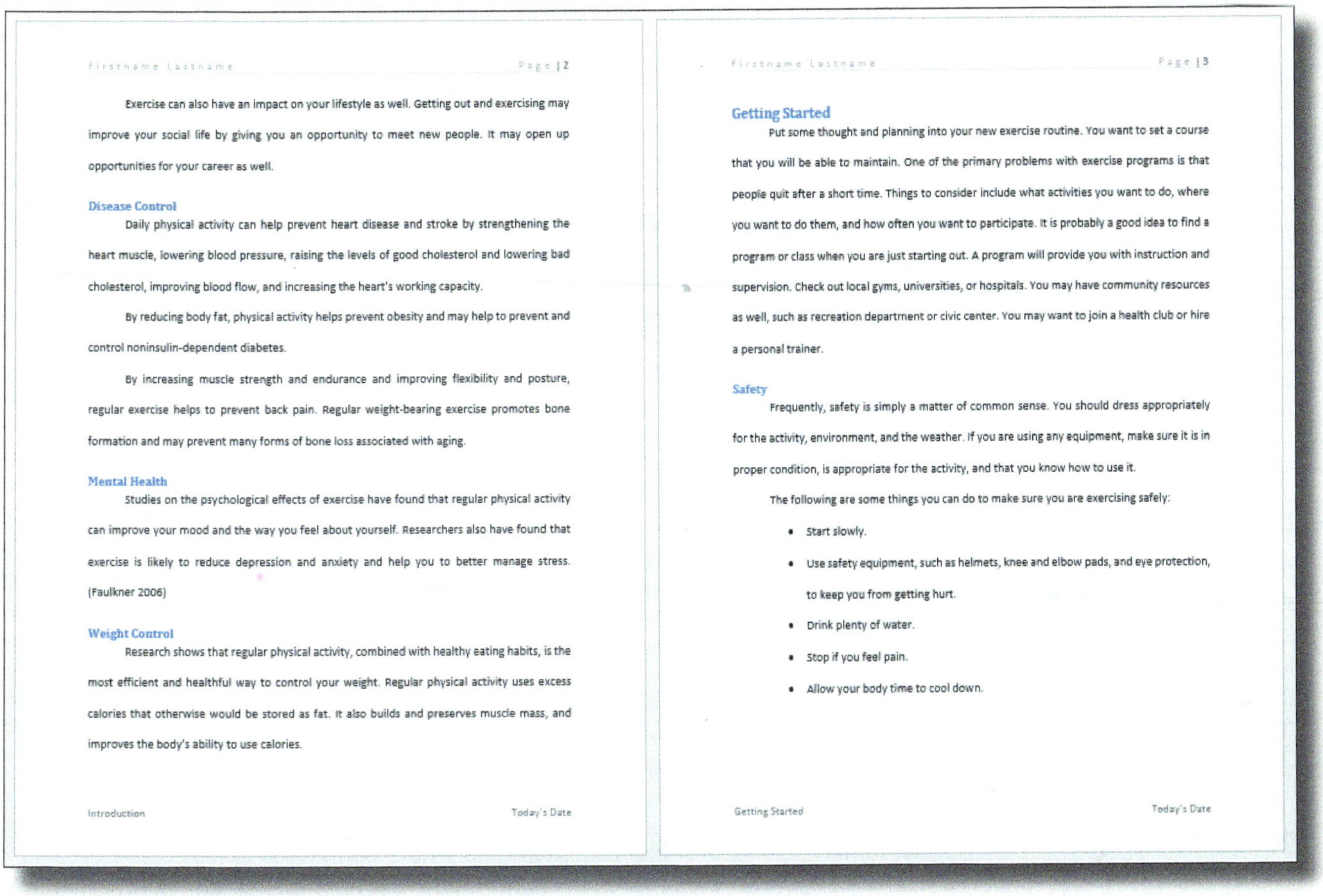
Firstname Lastname Page | 2

Exercise can also have an impact on your lifestyle as well. Getting out and exercising may improve your social life by giving you an opportunity to meet new people. It may open up opportunities for your career as well.

Disease Control

Daily physical activity can help prevent heart disease and stroke by strengthening the heart muscle, lowering blood pressure, raising the levels of good cholesterol and lowering bad cholesterol, improving blood flow, and increasing the heart's working capacity.

By reducing body fat, physical activity helps prevent obesity and may help to prevent and control noninsulin-dependent diabetes.

By increasing muscle strength and endurance and improving flexibility and posture, regular exercise helps to prevent back pain. Regular weight-bearing exercise promotes bone formation and may prevent many forms of bone loss associated with aging.

Mental Health

Studies on the psychological effects of exercise have found that regular physical activity can improve your mood and the way you feel about yourself. Researchers also have found that exercise is likely to reduce depression and anxiety and help you to better manage stress. (Faulkner 2006)

Weight Control

Research shows that regular physical activity, combined with healthy eating habits, is the most efficient and healthful way to control your weight. Regular physical activity uses excess calories that otherwise would be stored as fat. It also builds and preserves muscle mass, and improves the body's ability to use calories.

Introduction Today's Date

Firstname Lastname Page | 3

Getting Started

Put some thought and planning into your new exercise routine. You want to set a course that you will be able to maintain. One of the primary problems with exercise programs is that people quit after a short time. Things to consider include what activities you want to do, where you want to do them, and how often you want to participate. It is probably a good idea to find a program or class when you are just starting out. A program will provide you with instruction and supervision. Check out local gyms, universities, or hospitals. You may have community resources as well, such as recreation department or civic center. You may want to join a health club or hire a personal trainer.

Safety

Frequently, safety is simply a matter of common sense. You should dress appropriately for the activity, environment, and the weather. If you are using any equipment, make sure it is in proper condition, is appropriate for the activity, and that you know how to use it.

The following are some things you can do to make sure you are exercising safely:

- Start slowly.
- Use safety equipment, such as helmets, knee and elbow pads, and eye protection, to keep you from getting hurt.
- Drink plenty of water.
- Stop if you feel pain.
- Allow your body time to cool down.

Getting Started Today's Date

Word 2016, Windows 10, Microsoft Corporation

Lesson 58

Creating an Index

➤ What You Will Learn

Marking Index Entries
Using an Index AutoMark File
Generating an Index
Modifying an Index

WORDS TO KNOW

Index
An alphabetical list of topics and/or subtopics in a document along with the page numbers where they appear.

Tab leaders
Characters inserted to the left of text aligned with a tab stop, such as page numbers in an index.

Software Skills Create an index in long or complex documents to help readers locate the specific information that they need. You identify the topics and subtopics, and Word automatically inserts the correct page number.

What You Can Do

Marking Index Entries

- You can use Word to generate an **index,** which is a list of topics contained in a document, along with the page numbers where each topic appears.
- Readers can use an index to locate the page where they can find information on a topic of interest.
- The first step in creating an index in Word is to mark all of the items you want to include using the Mark Index Entry dialog box. The dialog box remains open until you close it, so you can mark as many entries as you want.
- Main topics are called main entries, and subtopics are called subentries. For example, *Pets* may be the main entry, and *Cats, Dogs*, and *Goldfish* may be subentries.
- Index entries can cross-reference a different index entry. For example, *Cats, see Pets* is a cross-referenced index entry.
- You can mark a single character, a word, a phrase, or a topic that spans multiple pages.
- You select the text to mark in the document; the selected text appears in the Main entry box in the Mark Index Entry dialog box, and is the text that will appear in the index.
- You can use the selected text as is, or edit it in the Main entry dialog box. For example, you may want to change the capitalization or tense of the selected text.

- Clicking the Mark button marks only the single occurrence of the selected text. Clicking the Mark All button marks the first occurrence of the text in each paragraph. Word marks only occurrences of exactly the same text. That means it marks only the occurrences that have the same capitalization, tense, etc. For example, if you select the text *Pet* and then choose to mark all occurrences, Word will not mark occurrences of the words *pet* or *Pets*.
- Word inserts an Index Entry field after each marked item in the document.
- When nonprinting characters are displayed, you see the Index Entry fields in the document. This makes the document appear longer than it will be when printed. To see the document as it will print, hide nonprinting characters or preview the document on the Print tab in the Backstage view.

Try It! Marking Index Entries

1. Start Word, and open **W58TryA** from the data files for this lesson.
2. Save the file as **W58TryA_xx** in the location where your teacher instructs you to store the files for this lesson.
3. Click Home > Show/Hide ¶ ¶ to display nonprinting marks, if necessary.
4. In the first paragraph of the document, select the phrase *casual Friday* (do not select the quotation marks).
5. On the References tab, in the Index group, click the Mark Entry button. Note that the selected text appears in the Main entry box.
6. In the Mark Index Entry dialog box, click Mark. Word inserts an Index Entry field code for the text, and the Mark Index Entry dialog box remains open.
7. In the next sentence in the document, select the text *business attire*, and click in the Main entry box in the Mark Index Entry dialog box.
8. In the Mark Index Entry dialog box, click Mark All. Word marks all occurrences of the text *business attire* with Index Entry field codes.
9. In the same sentence, select the text *traditional*, and click in the Main entry box. In the Main entry box, delete the text *traditional*, and type **business attire**.
10. Click in the Subentry box and type **traditional**, and click Mark All.
11. In the same sentence, select the text *general*, and click in the Main entry box. Delete the text *general*, and type **business attire**.
12. Click in the Subentry box and type **general**, and click Mark All.
13. In the same sentence, select the text *business casual*, and click in the Main entry box. Delete the text *business casual*, and type **business attire**.
14. Click in the Subentry box and type **business casual**, and click Mark All.
15. In the document, in the last paragraph under the heading *Traditional Business Attire*, select the text *formalwear*. Click in the Main entry box, and click Mark.
16. In the next sentence, select the text *black-tie*. In the Mark Index Entry dialog box, click to select the Cross-reference: option button. The insertion point moves into the Cross-reference box, after the word *See*.
17. Type **formalwear**, and click Mark.
18. In the Mark Index Entry dialog box, click the Close button.
19. Save the changes to **W58TryA_xx**, and leave it open to use in the next Try It.

(continued)

Try It! Marking Index Entries *(continued)*

Mark Index Entry dialog box

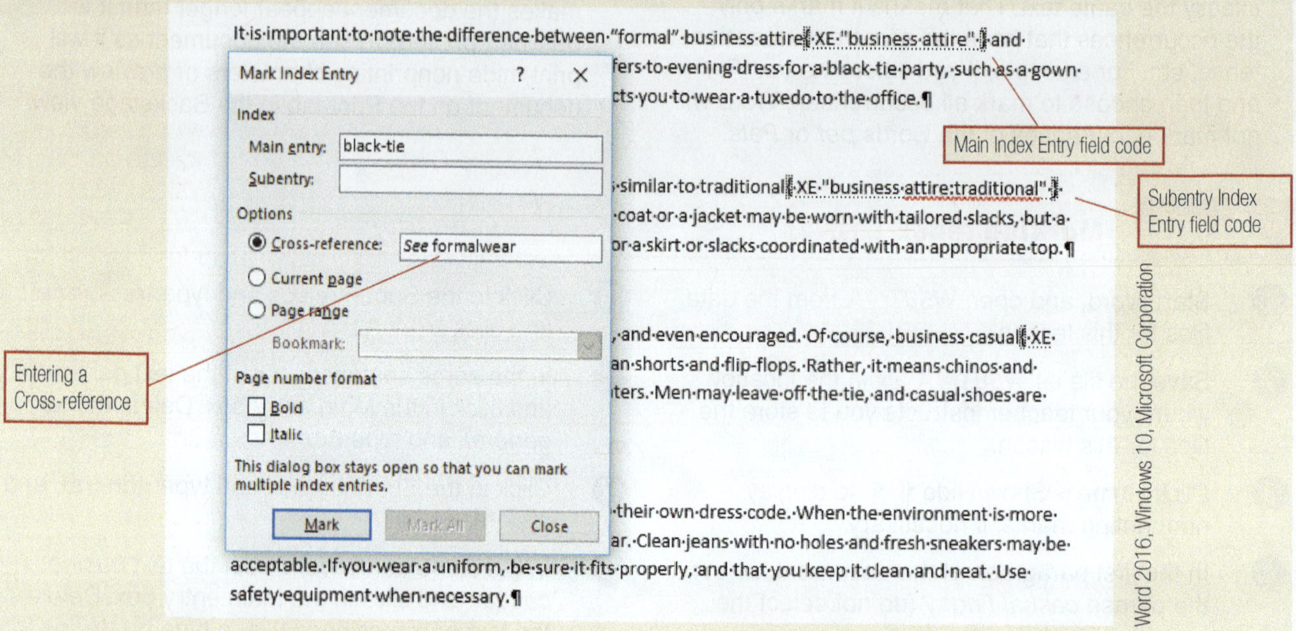

Using an Index AutoMark File

- In the previous section, you learned how to use the Mark All feature to mark index entries. Another way to accomplish this task is to create an AutoMark file.
- An AutoMark file is a separate Word document that contains the text that you want to mark and the corresponding text that you want the index to display.
- You can use an AutoMark file to mark all index entries in a document, or you can use the file to add index entries to a document that already contains entries.
- To create an AutoMark file, you create a new blank document and insert a two-column table. In the left column, enter the term that you want to mark. In the right column, enter the text that you want the index to display as the term's main entry. If the term is a subentry, enter the main-entry text, a colon, and the subentry text in the right column. For example, ***Pets:Cats***.

  ✓ *If the right column is blank, the index will display the term in the left column as a main entry.*

- Enter all the terms you want to mark, one term per row.
- After you have saved the AutoMark file, you return to the document that you want to mark, and open the AutoMark file through the Open Index AutoMark File dialog box. Word then marks all occurrences of the terms listed in the AutoMark file. If a term appears more than once in a paragraph, Word marks only the first occurrence of the term in that paragraph.

Try It! Using an Index AutoMark File

1. In Word, save a new blank document as W58TryB_xx in the location where your teacher instructs you to store the files for this lesson.
2. Insert a table with two columns and three rows.
3. Type text into the table as shown below (ensure that all text appears in lowercase):

suit	clothing:suit
skirt	clothing:skirt
jeans	clothing:jeans

4. Save and close the document.
5. In the W58TryA_xx file, click References > Insert Index.
6. In the Index dialog box, click the AutoMark button.
7. In the Open Index AutoMark File dialog box, navigate to the location where you are storing the files for this lesson, select W58TryB_xx, and click Open. Word marks all occurrences of the text suit, skirt, and jeans with Index Entry field codes.
8. Save the changes to W58TryA_xx, and leave it open to use in the next Try It.

Generating an Index

- Once you have marked all index entries, use the Insert Index command to generate the index.
- Word automatically inserts the entries in an alphabetical list, with the number of the page(s) where the entry appears.
- Word has a selection of index styles that you select from the Formats drop-down list on the Index tab in the Index dialog box.
- By default, the index contains two columns, with indented text.
- You can change the number of columns and choose to run-in the text, if you want.
- You can also choose to right-align page numbers and to precede page numbers with **tab leaders**.

Try It! Generating an Index

1. In the W58TryA_xx file, press CTRL + END to move the insertion point to the end of the document.
2. Press ENTER to start a new line, apply the Heading 1 style, type **Index**, and press ENTER twice.
3. Click References > Insert Index, and click OK. Word generates the index including the entries, subentries, and cross-referenced entry you marked in the previous Try It exercises.
4. On the Quick Access Toolbar, click the Undo button to remove the index.
5. Click References > Insert Index.
6. Click the Formats drop-down arrow and click Modern.
7. Click to select the Right align page numbers check box.
8. Click the Tab leader drop-down arrow and click the dotted line.
9. In the Columns box, change the value to 1.
10. Click OK to generate the index.
11. Save the changes to W58TryA_xx, and leave it open to use in the next Try It.

(continued)

Try It! Generating an Index *(continued)*

Index dialog box

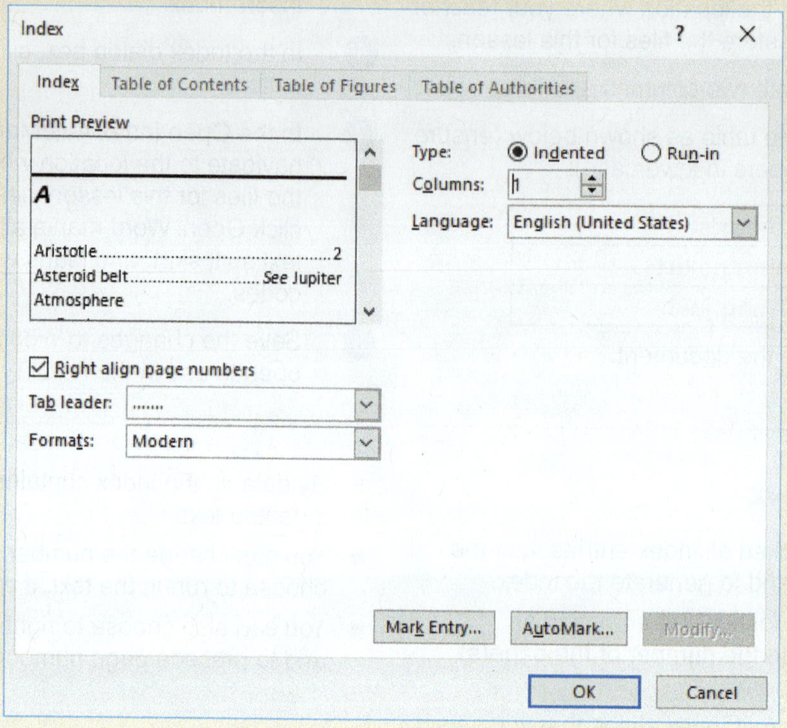

Word 2016, Windows 10, Microsoft Corporation

Modifying an Index

- Word inserts the entire index as a field that you can update if you add or remove entries, or if the page numbers change.
- You can add index entries to an existing index.
- You can edit the text that appears in an existing index entry by editing the text in the Index Entry field.
- To delete an index entry, delete the Index Entry field.
- Use the Update Index button in the Index group on the References tab to update a modified index, or press F9.

Try It! Modifying an Index

1. In the **W58TryA_xx** file, scroll up to the top of the document, and delete the field code { XE "casual Friday" } following the text *casual Friday* in the first paragraph.
2. At the end of that paragraph, select the text *respect*, click References > Mark Entry, click Mark, and click Close.
3. Position the insertion point at the beginning of the heading *General Business Attire*, and press CTRL + ENTER to insert a hard page break.
4. Scroll down to the end of the document and click anywhere within the index.
5. On the References tab, in the Index group, click the Update Index button. Word updates the index. Note the changes, including the new entry, *respect*, and the new page numbers.
6. Save and close the document, and exit Word.

Lesson 58—Practice

The Liberty Blooms flower shop has hired you to prepare a report about roses. In this project, you will create an index to help readers locate specific topics in the report quickly and easily.

DIRECTIONS

1. Start Word, if necessary, and open **W58Practice** from the data files for this lesson.
2. Save the file as **W58Practice_xx** in the location where your teacher instructs you to store the files for this lesson.
3. In the header, type your full name and today's date. Close the header and footer.
4. Select the text *roses* in the first sentence of the first paragraph.

   ✓ *Note that to help you identify the text to mark in the following steps, it is formatted in italics. However, the text in the document is formatted according to the current and appropriate paragraph formatting.*

5. Click **References** > **Mark Entry** .
6. Click **Mark All**.
7. In the same sentence, select the text *symbol*. Click in the **Mark Index Entry** dialog box and click **Mark All**.
8. Under the heading The Rose in Use, in the first sentence, select the text *ornamental decorations*.
9. Click in the **Mark Index Entry** dialog box. Replace the text in the Main entry box with the word **usage**, click in the **Subentry** box, type **ornamental decoration**, and click **Mark**.
10. In the next sentence, select the text *confetti*, replace the text in the Main entry box with the word **usage**, click in the **Subentry** box, type **confetti**, and click **Mark**.
11. In the next sentence, select the name *Cleopatra*, click in the **Mark Index Entry** dialog box and click **Mark**.
12. Under the heading The Rose as Symbol, select the text *Shakespeare*. Click in the **Mark Index Entry** dialog box and click **Mark**.
13. In the same paragraph, select the text *white rose*, and click to select the **Cross-reference** option button in the Mark Index Entry dialog box.
14. Type **symbol** and click **Mark**.
15. In the same paragraph, select the text *red rose*, click to select the **Cross-reference** option button in the Mark Index Entry dialog box, type **symbol**, and click **Mark**.
16. In the first sentence under the heading Judging Rose Quality, select the text *quality*. Click in the **Mark Index Entry** dialog box, and click **Mark All**.
17. In the Mark Index Entry dialog box, click **Close**.
18. Press CTRL + END to move the insertion point to the end of the document, and press CTRL + ENTER to insert a page break.
19. Apply the **Heading 1** style, type **Index**, and press ENTER twice.
20. Click **References** > **Insert Index** .
21. Click the **Formats** drop-down arrow and click **Fancy**.
22. Click to select the **Right align page numbers** check box.
23. Click the **Tab leader** drop-down arrow and click the dashed line.
24. In the Columns box, change the value to **2**, if necessary.
25. Click **OK** to generate the index.
26. Check and correct the spelling and grammar in the document.
27. **With your teacher's permission**, print the last page of the document. It should look similar to Figure 58-1 on the next page.
28. Save and close the document, and exit Word.

Figure 58-1

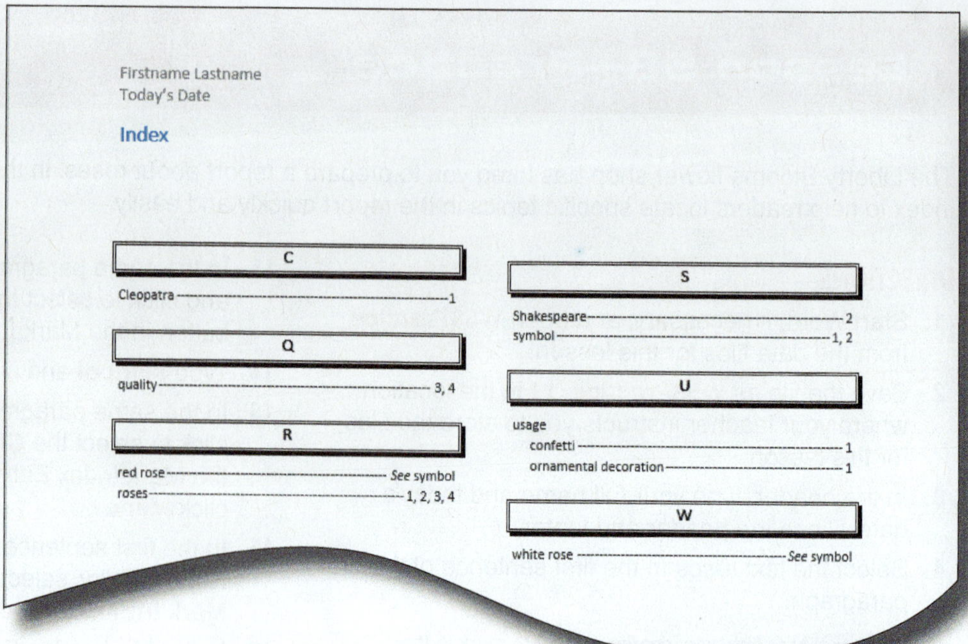

Word 2016, Windows 10, Microsoft Corporation

Lesson 58—Apply

In this project, you will continue to index the report about roses for the Liberty Blooms flower shop. You will mark additional index entries by selecting text within the document and by using an AutoMark file. You will also add a cross-reference.

DIRECTIONS

1. Start Word, if necessary, and open **W58ApplyA** from the data files for this lesson.
2. Save the file as **W58ApplyA_xx** in the location where your teacher instructs you to store the files for this lesson.
3. In the header, type your full name and today's date. Close the header and footer.
4. Mark all occurrences of the text **cultivation**, **varieties**, and **hybrids**.
5. Mark the phrases **bare-root plants** and **potted plants** as subentries for the main entry *quality*.
6. Mark the text **perfume**, **medicine**, and **currency** as subentries for the main entry *usage*.
7. Mark all occurrences of the words **diseases** and **Insects**. Edit the Main entry text so there are no initial capital letters.
8. Select the first occurrence of the word **pests**, and add a cross-reference to the Main entry *insects*.
9. When you have finished marking the entries, close the Mark Index Entry dialog box.
10. Open **W58ApplyB** from the data files for this lesson.
11. Save the file as **W58ApplyB_xx** in the location where your teacher instructs you to store the files for this lesson.
12. In the header, type your full name and today's date. Close the header and footer.
13. Add a third row to the table, type **American Nursery Standards** in the left column, and leave the right column blank.
14. Save and close the document.
15. In the **W58ApplyA_xx** file, click **References** > **Insert Index** > **AutoMark**.

16. In the Open Index AutoMark File dialog box, open **W58ApplyB_xx**.
17. Create a new page at the end of the document, type the heading **Index**, format it with the **Heading 1** style, press ENTER, and insert the index using the **Classic** format, right-aligned page numbers with dotted tab leaders, in two columns.
18. Mark the following as subentries to the main entry *diseases*: **blackspot**, **powdery mildew**, **stem cankers**, **botrytis blight**, **mosaic**, and **crown gall**.
19. Mark the first occurrence of the word **colors** as a subentry to the main entry *roses*.
20. Update the index.
21. Check and correct the spelling and grammar in the document.
22. **With your teacher's permission**, print the last page of the document. It should look similar to Figure 58-2.
23. Save and close the document, and exit Word.

Figure 58-2

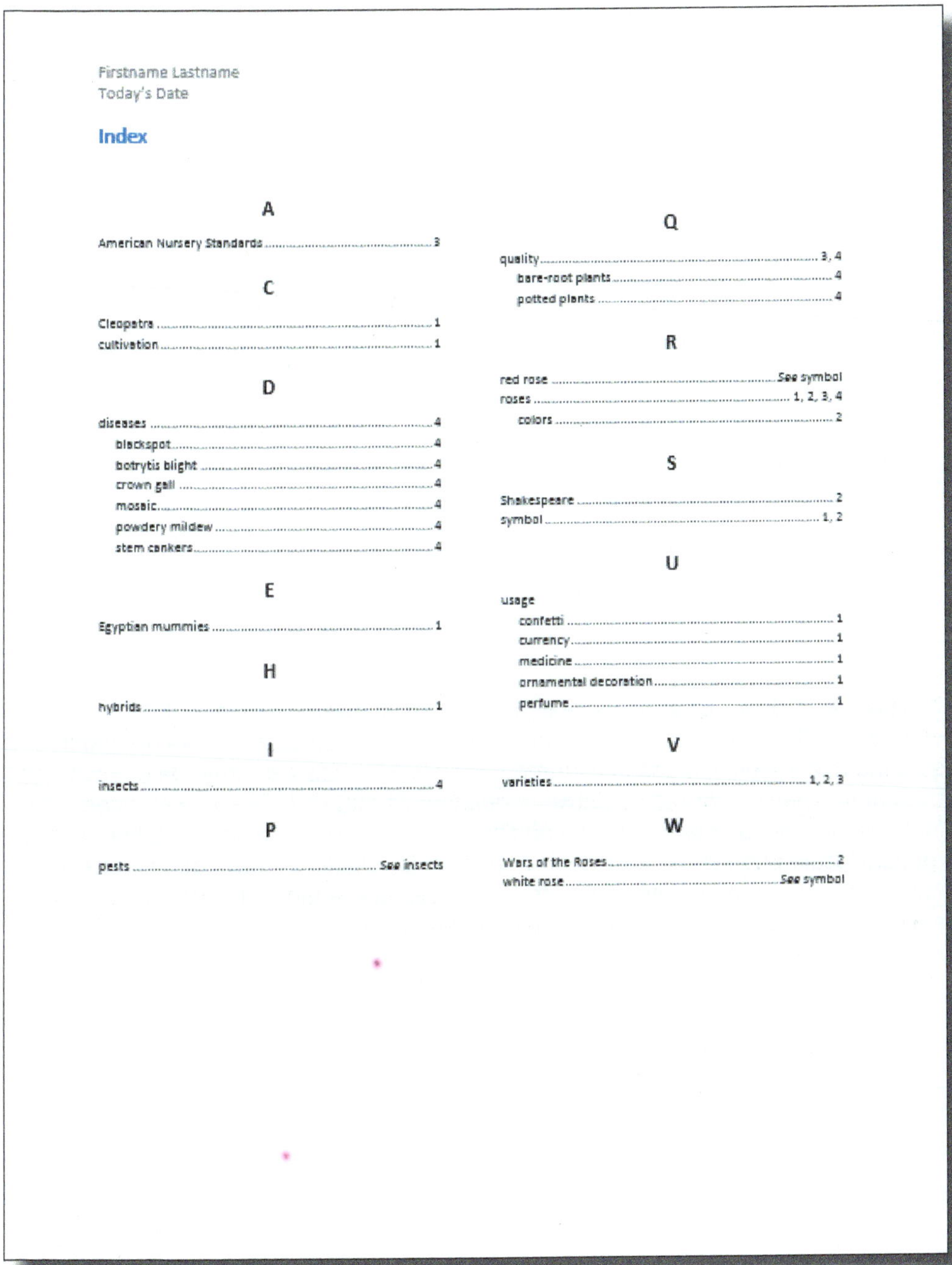

Firstname Lastname
Today's Date

Index

A

American Nursery Standards 3

C

Cleopatra 1
cultivation 1

D

diseases 4
  blackspot 4
  botrytis blight 4
  crown gall 4
  mosaic 4
  powdery mildew 4
  stem cankers 4

E

Egyptian mummies 1

H

hybrids 1

I

insects 4

P

pests .... See insects

Q

quality 3, 4
  bare-root plants 4
  potted plants 4

R

red rose .... See symbol
roses 1, 2, 3, 4
  colors 2

S

Shakespeare 2
symbol 1, 2

U

usage
  confetti 1
  currency 1
  medicine 1
  ornamental decoration 1
  perfume 1

V

varieties 1, 2, 3

W

Wars of the Roses 2
white rose .... See symbol

Lesson 59

Managing Source Information and Generating Special Tables

WORDS TO KNOW

Citation
A reference to a published or unpublished source (not always the original source).

Passim
A word used in citations of cases, articles, or books in a legal document to indicate that the reference is found in many places within the work.

Table of authorities
A list of citations in a legal document, usually accompanied by the page numbers where the references occur.

Table of figures
A list of figures in a document, usually accompanied by the page numbers where the figures are located.

➤ What You Will Learn

Using the Research Task Pane
Sharing Sources Between Documents
Editing Shared Sources
Using Multiple Footnote Formats in a Document
Adding Styles to a Table of Contents
Creating a Table of Figures
Creating a Table of Authorities

Software Skills Use the Research task pane to search online for information you need to include in your document. Manage your source information to make sure the references you use in your research are accurate and up-to-date. Save time by sharing source information between documents that use the same sources. Add footnotes to cite sources or provide additional information. Use special tables to help readers locate information and identify sources. By building a table of contents from styles, you can refine the items that the table displays. A table of figures lists figures such as tables or pictures, and a table of authorities is used in a legal document to identify references such as cases, statutes, and rules. Word automatically generates the tables, and you can update them when necessary.

What You Can Do

Using the Research Task Pane

- Use the Research task pane to search through online reference sources, such as dictionaries, encyclopedias, and translation services.
- You can search for a keyword, term, or phrase.
- You can locate information such as definitions, synonyms, encyclopedia entries, and even links to relevant Web pages.
- For best results, you must have a live connection to the Internet.
- You can select the specific reference tool or service to search from a list of available sources.
- Note that some research services require that you sign up for a subscription.
- The results of the search are displayed in the Research task pane.
- Some results also display a link to a relevant Web page; click a link to go to the destination.

Try It! Using the Research Task Pane

1. Start Word, and open **W59TryA** from the data files for this lesson.
2. Save the file as **W59TryA_xx** in the location where your teacher instructs you to store the files for this lesson.
3. Press and hold ALT and click anywhere in the document to display the Research task pane.
4. In the task pane, in the Search for box, select the existing text and type **what is videoconferencing**.
5. In the box under the Search for box, click the drop-down arrow and click All Research Sites.
6. Click the Start searching button. Word displays links to the available search engine sites and their results.
7. If you have an Internet connection, click the link to the Wikipedia article to open that page in your Web browser, and then close your Web browser.
8. Close the Research task pane.
9. Save the changes to **W59TryA_xx**, and leave it open to use in the next Try It.

Use Word's Research pane to search the Web

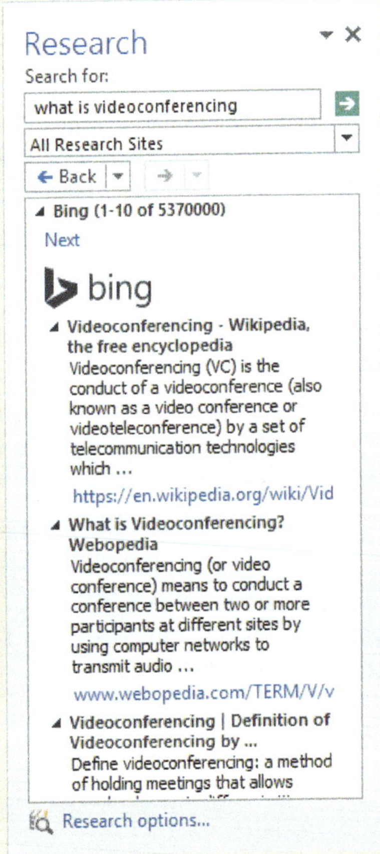

Word 2016, Windows 10, Microsoft Corporation

Sharing Sources Between Documents

- Sharing sources can save you from having to enter the same source information repeatedly when working with documents that use the same sources.
- Add sources you want to share to the Master List in the Source Manager.
- In an open document, copy sources from the Master List to the Current List to make them available for use.
- Note that the source information displayed in the Master List is actually stored in a separate file called Sources.xml.
- By default, Word stores the Sources.xml file on your local drive. You can click the Browse button in the Source Manager to see where the file is stored.
- A document's Master List changes when you view it on a different computer because the Master List is displaying the contents of the Sources.xml file on that computer's local drive.
- If you are working on multiple computers and want your documents to access the same Sources.xml file, you can save the file to a central location, such as a network drive or USB drive. Use the Browse button in the Source Manager to open the file and access the sources you need.

Try It! Sharing Sources Between Documents

1. In the **W59TryA_xx** file, click the References tab. In the Citations & Bibliography group, click Manage Sources.
2. In the Source Manager dialog box, under Current List, click the first source. Press and hold the SHIFT key and click the last source, so that all sources are selected. Release the SHIFT key.
3. Click Copy to copy all sources to the Master List.
4. Click Close.
5. Open **W59TryB** from the data files for this lesson.
6. Save the file as **W59TryB_xx** in the location where your teacher instructs you to store the files for this lesson.
7. On the References tab, click Manage Sources.
8. Under Master List, click the *Robert Half Technology* source and click Copy. The source appears in the Current List.
9. Click Close.
10. In the sentence under the heading *Salary Information: Canada*, position the insertion point between the word *Canada* and the period.
11. On the References tab, click the Style drop-down arrow Style: APA and click MLA Seventh Edition.
12. Click the Insert Citation button and click Robert Half Technology.
13. Press CTRL + END to move the insertion point to the end of the document, and press CTRL + ENTER to insert a page break.
14. On the References tab, click the Bibliography button and click References to insert a list of sources used in the document.
15. Save and close **W59TryB_xx**.
16. Save the changes to **W59TryA_xx**, and leave it open to use in the next Try It.

(continued)

Try It! Sharing Sources Between Documents *(continued)*

Copy source information from the Master List to the Current List

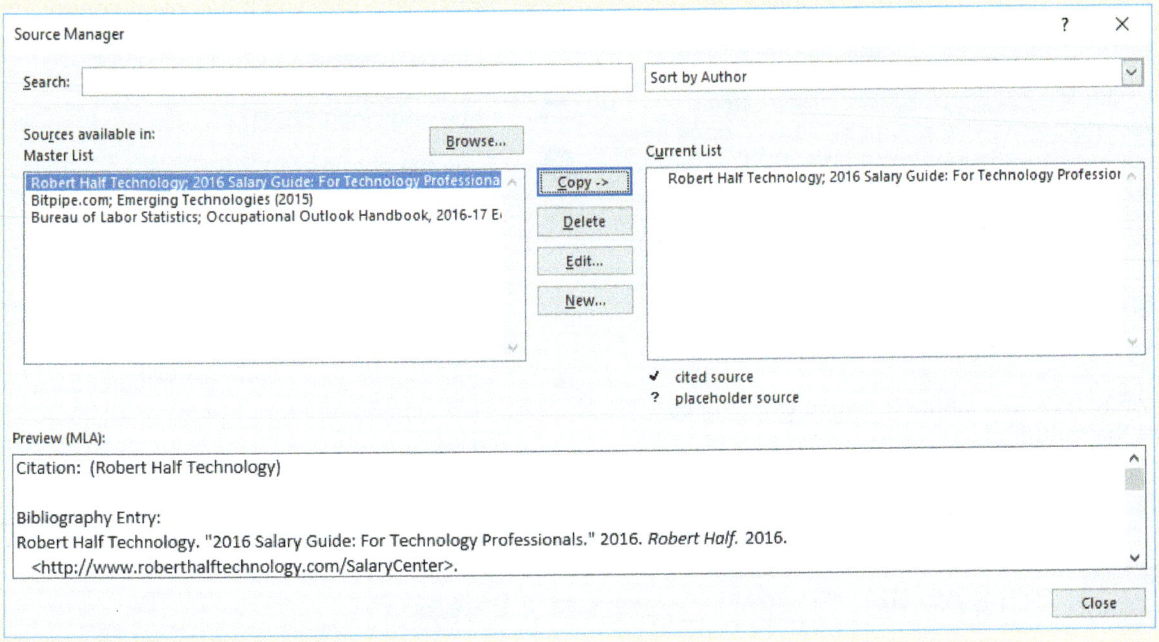

Word 2016, Windows 10, Microsoft Corporation

Editing Shared Sources

- To edit a shared source, open the Source Manager and edit the source in the Master List.
- If the Current List also contains that source, Word displays a dialog box that asks whether you want to update both lists. Clicking Yes updates both lists. Clicking No updates only the Master List.
- You can update an existing version of the source in another document by copying the updated source from the Master List to the document's Current List. Word overwrites the existing source.

Try It! Editing Shared Sources

1. In the **W59TryA_xx** file, press CTRL + END to move the insertion point to the end of the document, and press CTRL + ENTER to insert a page break.
2. On the References tab, click the Bibliography button and click References to insert a list of sources used in the document.
3. Click References > Manage Sources.
4. Under Master List, click the *Robert Half Technology* source and click Edit.
5. In the Edit Source dialog box, click to select Show All Bibliography Fields.
6. In the Year Accessed field, type **2017** and click OK.
7. Click Yes to update both the master list and the current document.
8. Click Close.
9. Click anywhere in the heading References to select the content control, and then click Update Citations and Bibliography on the content control handle.

(continued)

Try It! Editing Shared Sources *(continued)*

10. Open **W59TryB_xx** from the location where you are storing the files for this lesson.
11. Click References > Manage Sources.
12. Under Master List, click the *Robert Half Technology* source and click Copy to copy the updated source to this document. Click Yes to overwrite the existing source. Click Close.
13. On page 2, click anywhere in the heading References to select the content control, and then click Update Citations and Bibliography on the content control handle.
14. Save and close **W59TryB_xx**.
15. Save the changes to **W59TryA_xx**, and leave it open to use in the next Try It.

Using Multiple Footnote Formats in a Document

- In the Footnote and Endnote dialog box, you can adjust the format of footnotes.
- You can mark footnotes with one of the provided number formats or a custom mark.
- To specify a custom mark, type in the Custom mark box or select a symbol.
- You can divide your document into sections and apply a different number format or custom mark to each section.

Try It! Using Multiple Footnote Formats in a Document

1. In the **W59TryA_xx** file, position the insertion point at the start of the heading *Salary Information*, and insert a Continuous section break.
2. In the first paragraph of the Communications section, position the insertion point at the end of the word *conferencing*.
3. Click References > Insert Footnote.
4. Type **For more information about video conferencing, go to www.wisegeek.org/what-is-video-conferencing.htm.**
5. Right-click the note text you just typed and then click Note Options to display the Footnote and Endnote dialog box.
6. In the Format section of the dialog box, click the Number format drop-down arrow and select the symbol format that begins with an asterisk.
7. Click Apply. The note mark changes from a 1 to an asterisk.
8. In the table in the Salary Information section, position the insertion point at the end of the word *Range*.
9. On the References tab, click the Footnotes dialog box launcher.
10. In the Format section of the Footnote and Endnote dialog box, type ** (two asterisks) in the Custom mark box.
11. Click Insert to insert the footnote.
12. Type **National averages in the United States.**
13. Save the changes to **W59TryA_xx**, and leave it open to use in the next Try It.

Adding Styles to a Table of Contents

- In the Table of Contents Options dialog box, you can specify the styles that you want to include in the table of contents.
- The dialog box displays a list of all styles used in the current document.
- The TOC level column displays numbers, which correspond to the levels at which styles will appear in the table of contents. If the TOC level box is blank for a particular style, that style will not appear in the table of contents.
- To add a style to the table of contents, type a number from 1 to 9 in the TOC level box next to that style.
- To remove a style from the table of contents, delete the number in the corresponding TOC level box.
- You might choose to customize a table of contents with styles in a document that uses custom styles for headings.

Try It! Adding Styles to a Table of Contents

1. In the **W59TryA_xx** file, press CTRL + END to position the insertion point at the end of the document, and press CTRL + ENTER to insert a page break.
2. Apply the Title style, and type **Appendix**.
3. Select the text *Appendix* and change the font size to 14 pt.
4. On the Home tab, in the Styles group, click the Quick Styles gallery More button.
5. Click Create a Style. The Create New Style from Formatting dialog box appears.
6. In the Name box, type **Heading With Line** to replace the sample style name, and click OK.
7. On page 1, position the insertion point at the end of the subtitle *A Guide to Emerging Technologies and Career Opportunities*, and press ENTER.
8. Apply the Heading With Line style, type **Contents**, and press ENTER.
9. Apply the Normal style to the new paragraph.
10. Click References > Table of Contents, and click Custom Table of Contents to display the Table of Contents dialog box.
11. Under General, click the Formats drop-down arrow and click Distinctive.
12. Change the value in the Show levels box to 2.
13. Click the Tab leader drop-down arrow and click the dotted line.
14. Click the Options button. The Table of Contents Options dialog box appears.
15. In the TOC level box next to *Heading With Line*, type **1**. Click OK.
16. Click OK to insert the table. The headings *Contents* and *Appendix* appear in the table with the other headings.
17. Apply the TOC Heading style to the heading *Contents* (the title of the table of contents).
18. Click anywhere in the table of contents, and click References > Update Table.
19. In the Update Table of Contents dialog box, click to select the Update entire table option button, and then click OK. Word removes *Contents* from the table.
20. Save the changes to **W59TryA_xx**, and leave it open to use in the next Try It.

Table of contents in document

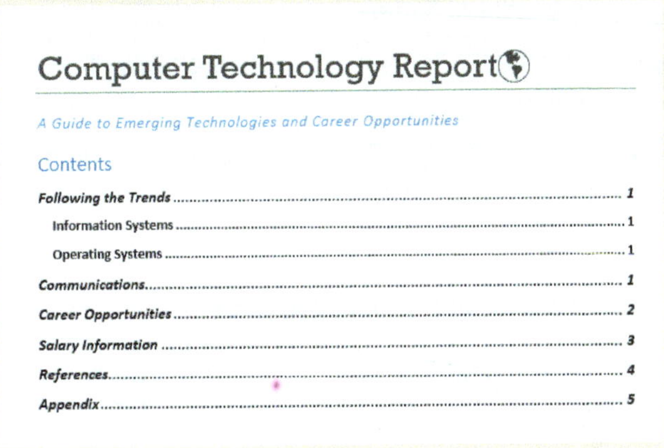
Computer Technology Report

A Guide to Emerging Technologies and Career Opportunities

Contents

Word 2016, Windows 10, Microsoft Corporation

Creating a Table of Figures

- Use a **table of figures** to list the caption and page number of tables, equations, or pictures in a document.
- The figure must include a caption to be included in the table.
- You must create a separate table for each type of figure. That means one table for all captioned tables, one for all captioned equations, and one for all captioned pictures.
- To create the table, use the options in the Table of Figures dialog box to select the type of figure you want to include, and style options similar to those for a table of contents, such as format and whether or not to include page numbers or hyperlinks.
- Word creates the table of figures at the insertion point location; you can update it if you add, remove, or reposition the figures in the document.
- Place the table of figures at the location in the document where it will best help the reader. You may want to place it after the table of contents, or at the end of the document. You may also want to create a separate table of figures for each chapter.

Try It! Creating a Table of Figures

1. In the W59TryA_xx file, insert a new line between the table of contents and the heading *Following the Trends*.
2. Format the new line with the TOC Heading style, type Table of Figures, and press ENTER.
3. Click References > Insert Table of Figures to open the Table of Figures dialog box.
4. Click the Formats drop-down arrow and click Distinctive.
5. Click the Caption label drop-down arrow and click Table. Verify that the Include label and number check box is selected.
6. Click the Tab leader drop-down arrow and click the dotted line, if necessary.
7. Click to clear the Use hyperlinks instead of page numbers check box, and click OK. Word inserts the table of figures.
8. Update the page numbers in the table of contents.
9. Save and close the document. Leave Word open to use in the next Try It.

Table of Figures dialog box

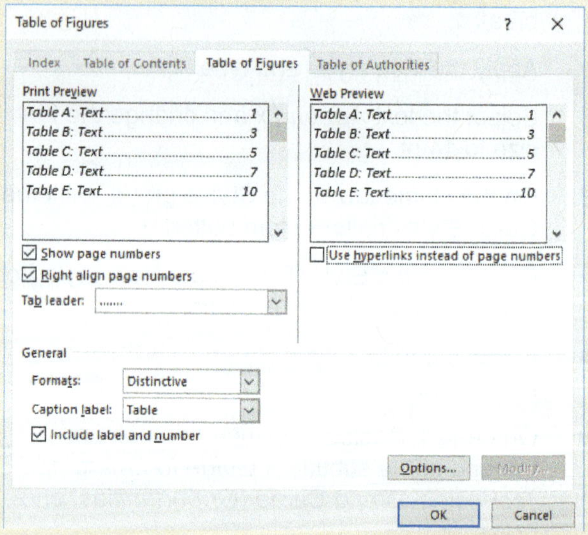

Word 2016, Windows 10, Microsoft Corporation

Creating a Table of Authorities

- Create a **table of authorities** to list **citations** in a legal document, along with the page numbers where the references are located.
- Word comes with built-in categories of common citations, such as cases, statutes, regulations, and rules.
- Use the Mark Citation dialog box to mark each citation in the document with a table of authorities field code. The process is similar to marking items for an index. For example, you can mark a single occurrence, or all occurrences.

✓ *For information on creating an index, refer to Word, Lesson 58.*

- You can locate citations to mark manually by scrolling through the document, or let Word automatically find citations by searching for the text.
- If a citation appears on five or more pages, you may select to substitute the word **passim** for the page numbers.
- You may select the category of citation, such as case, statute, rule, or regulation.
- By default, Word uses the selected text as a short citation. You can type a long citation using proper legal style, if necessary.
- When all items are marked, use the Table of Authorities dialog box to select options and generate the table at the insertion point location.
- A table of authorities is usually placed at the beginning of the document.

Try It! Creating a Table of Authorities

1. Open **W59TryC** from the data files for this lesson, and save it as **W59TryC_xx** in the location where your teacher instructs you to store the files for this lesson.

   ✓ *This is a legal document that includes citations.*

2. On page 2 of the document, select the text *Philbrick v. Andrews*.
3. On the References tab, in the Table of Authorities group, click the Mark Citation button to open the Mark Citation dialog box.
4. In the Mark Citation dialog box, click Mark. Word inserts the table of authorities field code for the citation.
5. In the Mark Citation dialog box, click Next Citation to automatically move the insertion point to the next citation—the *v.* between the names *Asher* and *Sekofsky*.
6. In the document, select the text *Asher v. Sekofsky*, click in the Mark Citation dialog box, and click Mark.
7. Click Next Citation. In the document, select the text *Wiss v. Stewart*. In the Mark Citation dialog box, click Mark.
8. In the Mark Citation dialog box, click Close.
9. Press CTRL + HOME to move the insertion point to the beginning of the document, type Table of Authorities, and press ENTER.
10. Click References > Insert Table of Authorities button to open the Table of Authorities dialog box.
11. Click the Formats drop-down arrow and click Classic, and then click OK to insert the table.
12. Save and close the document, and exit Word.

Use a table of authorities to list legal citations

Table of Authorities

CASES

Asher v. Sekofsky 2
Philbrick v. Andrews 2
Wiss v. Stewart 2

Word 2016, Windows 10, Microsoft Corporation

Lesson 59—Practice

You continue to work on the roses report for Liberty Blooms. In addition to the report, Liberty Blooms has asked you to create a quick reference guide based on some of the information in your report. In this project, you will generate a table of contents and a table of figures for the roses report. You will also copy a source from the report to the quick reference guide.

DIRECTIONS

1. Start Word, if necessary, and open **W59PracticeA** from the data files for this lesson.
2. Save the file as **W59PracticeA_xx** in the location where your teacher instructs you to store the files for this lesson.
3. In the header, type your full name and today's date. Close the header and footer.
4. Click **References** > **Manage Sources**.
5. In the Source Manager, under Current List, select the **Christopher** source and click **Copy** to copy the source to the Master List.
6. Click **Close**.
7. Open **W59PracticeB** from the data files for this lesson.
8. Save the file as **W59PracticeB_xx** in the location where your teacher instructs you to store the files for this lesson.
9. In the header, type your full name and today's date. Close the header and footer.
10. Click **References** > **Manage Sources**.
11. In the Source Manager, under Master List, select the **Christopher** source and click **Copy** to copy the source to the Current List.
12. Click **Close**.
13. Press CTRL + END to move the insertion point to the end of the document.
14. On the References tab, click the Bibliography button and click **References**.
15. **With your teacher's permission**, print the document. It should look similar to Figure 59-1 on the next page.
16. Save and close **W59PracticeB_xx**.
17. On page 5 of the **W59PracticeA_xx** file, apply the **Index Title** style to the heading *Index*.
18. Press CTRL + HOME to move the insertion point to the beginning of the document.
19. Click **References** > **Table of Contents**.
20. In the gallery of table of contents styles, under Built-In, click **Automatic Table 2**.
21. Click anywhere in the table of contents, and click **References** > **Table of Contents** > **Custom Table of Contents**.
22. In the Table of Contents dialog box, click the **Formats** drop-down arrow and click **Formal**.
23. Change the value in the Show levels box to **3**, if necessary.
24. Click the **Tab leader** drop-down arrow and click the dotted line.
25. Click the **Options** button.
26. In the Table of Contents Options dialog box, scroll down, and type **1** in the TOC level box for the Index Title style. Click **OK**.
27. Click **OK** in the Table of Contents dialog box. In the confirmation dialog box, click **OK** to replace the table of contents.
28. Insert a blank line above the document title, apply the **TOC Heading** style, type **Table of Figures**, and press ENTER.
29. Click **References** > **Insert Table of Figures**.
30. Click the **Formats** drop-down arrow and click **Formal**.
31. Click the **Caption label** drop-down arrow and click **Table**. Click **OK**.
32. Check the spelling and grammar in the document. If there are errors, correct them. Update the entire table of contents again.
33. **With your teacher's permission**, print the first page of the document. It should look similar to Figure 59-2 on the next page.
34. Save and close the document, and exit Word.

Figure 59-1

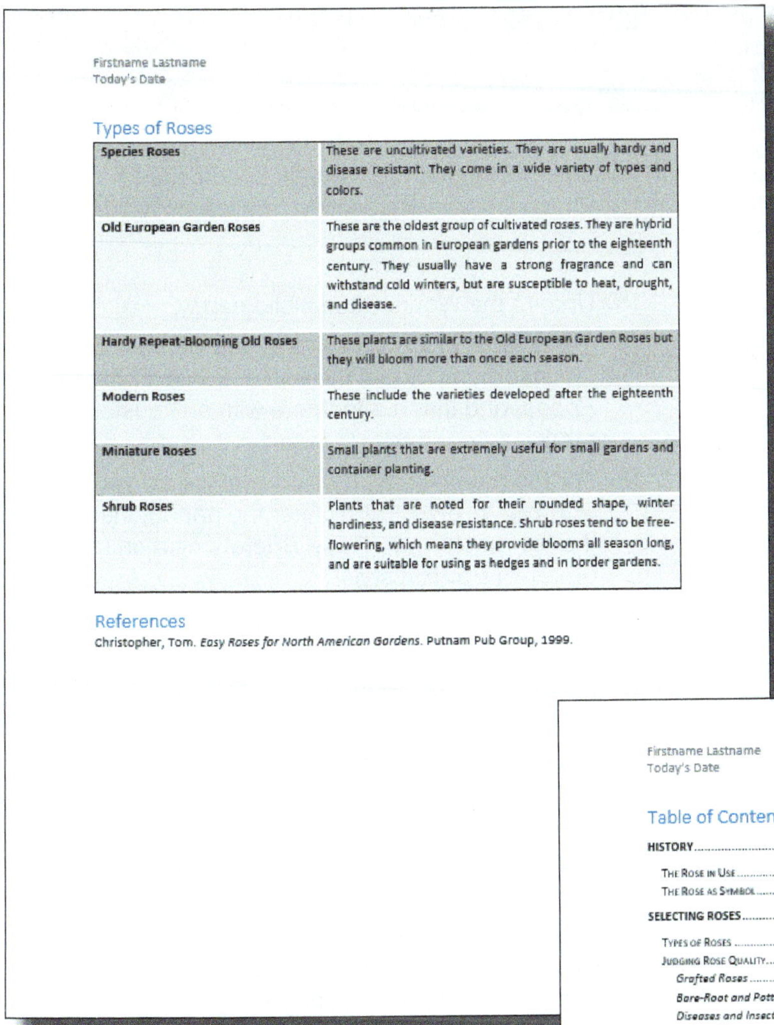
Firstname Lastname
Today's Date

Types of Roses

Species Roses	These are uncultivated varieties. They are usually hardy and disease resistant. They come in a wide variety of types and colors.
Old European Garden Roses	These are the oldest group of cultivated roses. They are hybrid groups common in European gardens prior to the eighteenth century. They usually have a strong fragrance and can withstand cold winters, but are susceptible to heat, drought, and disease.
Hardy Repeat-Blooming Old Roses	These plants are similar to the Old European Garden Roses but they will bloom more than once each season.
Modern Roses	These include the varieties developed after the eighteenth century.
Miniature Roses	Small plants that are extremely useful for small gardens and container planting.
Shrub Roses	Plants that are noted for their rounded shape, winter hardiness, and disease resistance. Shrub roses tend to be free-flowering, which means they provide blooms all season long, and are suitable for using as hedges and in border gardens.

References

Christopher, Tom. *Easy Roses for North American Gardens*. Putnam Pub Group, 1999.

Word 2016, Windows 10, Microsoft Corporation

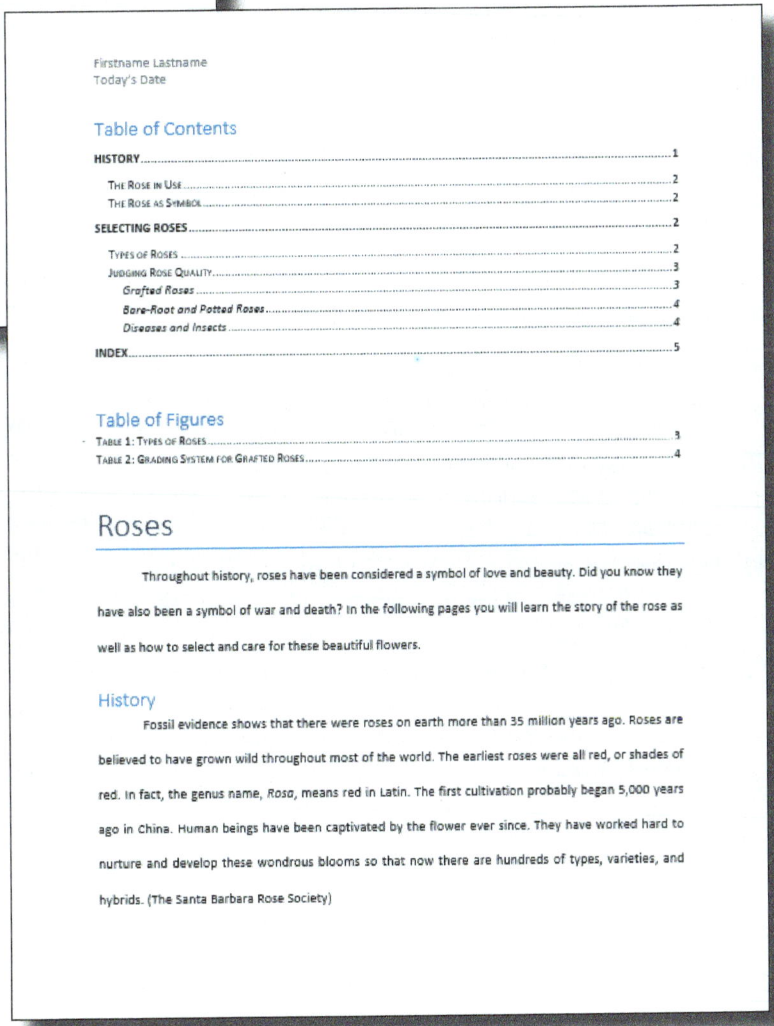
Firstname Lastname
Today's Date

Table of Contents

Table of Figures

Roses

Throughout history, roses have been considered a symbol of love and beauty. Did you know they have also been a symbol of war and death? In the following pages you will learn the story of the rose as well as how to select and care for these beautiful flowers.

History

Fossil evidence shows that there were roses on earth more than 35 million years ago. Roses are believed to have grown wild throughout most of the world. The earliest roses were all red, or shades of red. In fact, the genus name, *Rosa*, means red in Latin. The first cultivation probably began 5,000 years ago in China. Human beings have been captivated by the flower ever since. They have worked hard to nurture and develop these wondrous blooms so that now there are hundreds of types, varieties, and hybrids. (The Santa Barbara Rose Society)

Word 2016, Windows 10, Microsoft Corporation

Figure 59-2

Lesson 59—Apply

In this project, you will continue to work on the roses report for Liberty Blooms. You will edit a source, add a footnote, customize a table of contents and a table of figures, and add a reference section. You will copy the edited source into the quick reference guide.

DIRECTIONS

1. Start Word, if necessary, and open **W59ApplyA** from the data files for this lesson.
2. Save the file as **W59ApplyA_xx** in the location where your teacher instructs you to store the files for this lesson.
3. In the header, type your full name and today's date. Close the header and footer.
4. Press CTRL + HOME to make sure the insertion point is at the beginning of the document.
5. Click **Insert** > **Blank Page**, and move the insertion point to the top of the new blank page. Clear all formatting from the line.
6. Apply the **TOC Heading** style, type **Table of Contents**, and press ENTER.
7. Insert a custom table of contents that uses the **Formal** style, shows page numbers right-aligned with a solid line tab leader, and shows 3 levels. Use page numbers instead of hyperlinks. Show the Index Title style as TOC level 1.
8. Save the changes to the document.
9. On a blank line after the table of contents, apply the **TOC Heading** style, type **Table of Figures**, center the line horizontally, and press ENTER.
10. Insert a table of figures to list the table captions. Use the **Centered** format, and show page numbers as hyperlinks.
11. Position the insertion point on a blank line after the table of figures and insert a bibliography using the **Works Cited** style.
12. In the Source Manager, type **New York** in the City field of the Christopher source. Update both the Master List and the Current List, and close the Source Manager.
13. Update the Works Cited bibliography.
14. In the table in the Types of Roses section, position the insertion point at the end of the text *Modern Roses*, and insert a footnote with a ** custom mark.
15. For the note text, type **Accounts for about 80% of roses grown today.** After the period, insert the **Santa Barbara Rose Society** citation in **MLA Seventh Edition** style.
16. Insert a page break before the heading *Grafted Roses*.
17. Insert a line before the last body paragraph of the document (before the Index), type **Conclusion**, and format it with the **Heading 1** style.
18. Update the entire table of contents and the page numbers in the table of figures.
19. Check and correct the spelling and grammar in the document.
20. **With your teacher's permission**, print the first page of the document. It should look similar to Figure 59-3 on the next page.
21. Open **W59ApplyB** from the data files for this lesson.
22. Save the file as **W59ApplyB_xx** in the location where your teacher instructs you to store the files for this lesson.
23. In the header, type your full name and today's date. Close the header and footer.
24. Copy the **Christopher** source from the Master List to the Current List, overwriting the existing source.
25. Update the References bibliography.
26. **With your teacher's permission**, print the document. It should look similar to Figure 59-4 on the next page.
27. Save and close both documents, and exit Word.

Figure 59-3

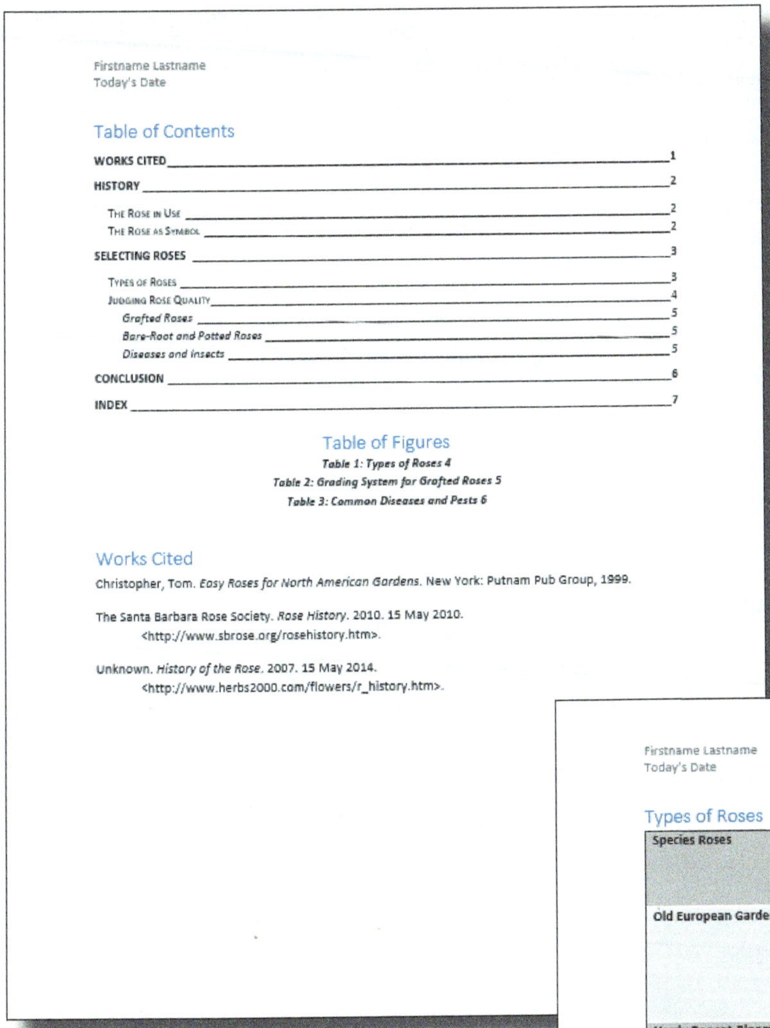

Firstname Lastname
Today's Date

Table of Contents

Table of Figures

Works Cited

Christopher, Tom. *Easy Roses for North American Gardens*. New York: Putnam Pub Group, 1999.

The Santa Barbara Rose Society. *Rose History*. 2010. 15 May 2010. <http://www.sbrose.org/rosehistory.htm>.

Unknown. *History of the Rose*. 2007. 15 May 2014. <http://www.herbs2000.com/flowers/r_history.htm>.

Word 2016, Windows 10, Microsoft Corporation

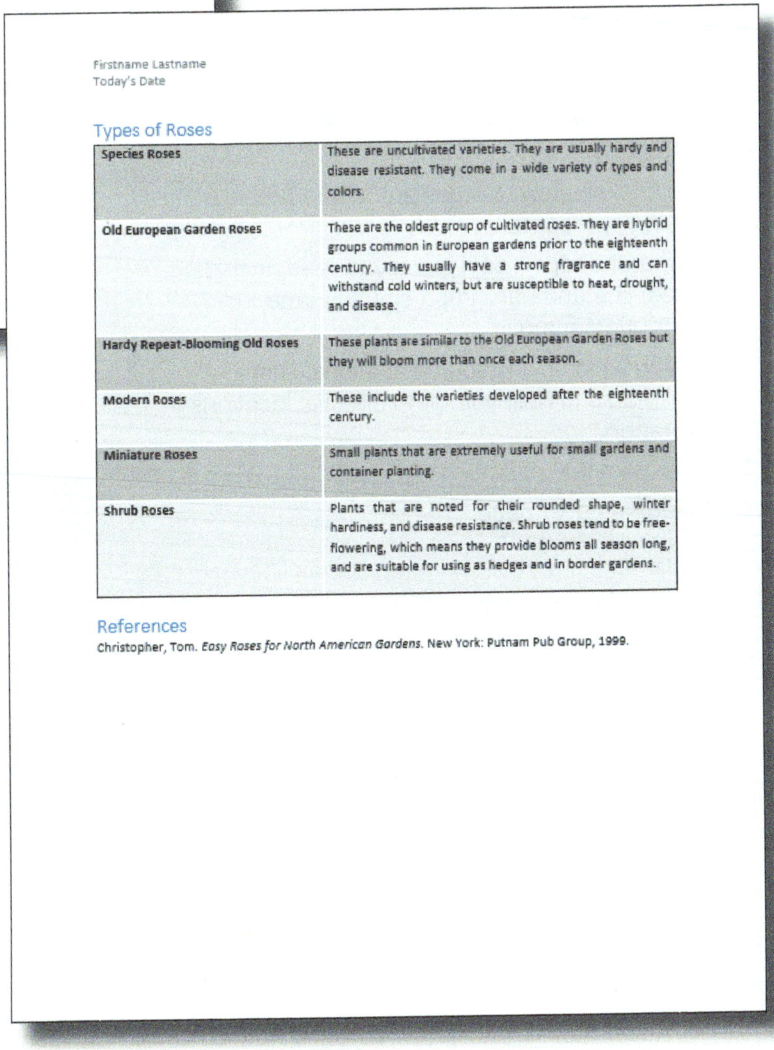

Firstname Lastname
Today's Date

Types of Roses

Species Roses	These are uncultivated varieties. They are usually hardy and disease resistant. They come in a wide variety of types and colors.
Old European Garden Roses	These are the oldest group of cultivated roses. They are hybrid groups common in European gardens prior to the eighteenth century. They usually have a strong fragrance and can withstand cold winters, but are susceptible to heat, drought, and disease.
Hardy Repeat-Blooming Old Roses	These plants are similar to the Old European Garden Roses but they will bloom more than once each season.
Modern Roses	These include the varieties developed after the eighteenth century.
Miniature Roses	Small plants that are extremely useful for small gardens and container planting.
Shrub Roses	Plants that are noted for their rounded shape, winter hardiness, and disease resistance. Shrub roses tend to be free-flowering, which means they provide blooms all season long, and are suitable for using as hedges and in border gardens.

References

Christopher, Tom. *Easy Roses for North American Gardens*. New York: Putnam Pub Group, 1999.

Word 2016, Windows 10, Microsoft Corporation

Figure 59-4

End-of-Chapter Activities

➤ Word Chapter 8—Critical Thinking

Research Report

In this project, research and write a report on a topic of your choice. Use the skills you have learned in this chapter for organizing, managing, and developing a multipage report, including outlining, specialized tables, and an index.

DIRECTIONS

1. Pick a topic for your report, and have it approved by your teacher.
2. Begin researching the topic using reputable sources on the Internet and in your school library.
3. Take notes and record source information so you can cite the sources in your report.
4. When you are ready to begin developing the report, start Word and create a new document. Save it as **WCT08_xx** in the location where your teacher instructs you to store the files for this chapter.
5. Use Outline view to organize headings and body text in your report.
6. Format the report so it is easy to read, including styles, line and paragraph spacing, and appropriate margins.
7. As you write, insert source citations. Use bookmarks to help you go to specific locations in the report.
8. Insert footnotes as necessary.
9. Include a cover page.
10. Create customized headers and footers that include your name, the report title, the date, and page numbers.
11. Include figures or tables with captions.
12. Proofread the report as you work, checking the spelling and grammar and correcting errors.
13. Ask a classmate to review the report and make suggestions for how you might improve it. If you agree, make the suggested changes.
14. Mark items for an index. Include subentries and cross-references as necessary.
15. Generate a table of contents, table of figures, works cited page or bibliography, and an index.
16. If you make changes to the report, update all tables and the index.
17. When you are satisfied with the document, ask a classmate to review it and make comments or suggestions that will help you improve it.
18. Make changes and corrections, as necessary.
19. **With your teacher's permission**, print the report.
20. Save and close the document, and exit Word.

➤ Word Chapter 8—Portfolio Builder

Eye Care Report

In this project, you will modify and format a multipage document about eye care for seniors. You will start by organizing an existing document into outline levels. You will then insert cross-references, add source citations, and create customized headers and footers. You will create a table of figures, an index, a table of contents, and a works cited page.

DIRECTIONS

1. Start Word, if necessary, and open **WPB08** from the data files for this chapter.
2. Save the file as **WPB08_xx** in the location where your teacher instructs you to store the files for this chapter.
3. Apply outline heading levels as follows:

   Level 1 **Overview**, **Common Eye Ailments**, **Maintaining Eye Health**, **Eyesight and Medication**, **Conclusion**

   Level 2 **Presbyopia**, **Cataracts**, **Glaucoma**, **Macular Degeneration**, **Nutrition**, **Lifestyle Choices**
4. Under the heading *Eyesight and Medication*, move the paragraph beginning with the text *The U.S. Department of Agriculture,* and the list that follows it, to the end of the section under the heading *Nutrition*.
5. At the end of the text under the heading *Presbyopia*, type **For a list of symptoms refer to .** To the left of the period, insert a hyperlinked cross-reference to the label and number of table 2.
6. Repeat step 5 to insert the same cross-reference at the end of the text under the headings *Cataracts* and *Macular Degeneration*, and before the last sentence under the heading *Glaucoma*.
7. Select the heading *Overview* and expand the character spacing by 1 pt.
8. Create a new style called **Heading 1 Expanded** based on the format of the *Overview* heading.
9. Apply the **Heading 1 Expanded** style to the headings **Overview**, **Common Eye Ailments**, **Maintaining Eye Health**, **Eyesight and Medication**, and **Conclusion**.
10. Select the options to display different headers and footers on the first page and on odd and even pages.
11. Remove the first page footer.
12. In the Even Page Header, insert your name flush left and the date flush right. On the ruler, drag the right tab to 6.5", if necessary.
13. In the Odd Page Header, insert the report title flush left and your name flush right.
14. In both the Odd and Even Page Footers, insert the page number flush right, using the **Bold Numbers 3** style.
15. Open the Source Manager. For all four sources in the Current List, show all bibliography fields, and update the Year Accessed to **2017**.
16. Set the citation style to **Turabian Sixth Edition**.
17. Under the heading *Common Eye Ailments*, after the first sentence, insert the **American Academy of Ophthalmology** source citation.
18. Under the heading *Common Eye Ailments*, after the last sentence, insert the **Family Vision Care Center** source citation.
19. Under the heading *Cataracts*, at the end of the first sentence, insert the **Burcham Eyecare Center** source citation.
20. Under the heading *Glaucoma*, after the last bullet item, insert the **University of Illinois** source citation.
21. Mark the following items as index entries:

    American Academy of Ophthalmology

    blindness *(mark all)*

    reversible *as a subentry for* **blindness**

    blurred vision

    The first instance of **common eye ailments**

    The headings **Presbyopia**, **Cataracts**, **Glaucoma**, *and* **Macular Degeneration** *as subentries of* **common eye ailments**; *lowercase the subentry text*

The first instances of **Presbyopia**, **cataracts**, *and* **glaucoma** *in the text (not the heading or tables), with a cross-reference to* **common eye ailments**; *lowercase the index entry for Presbyopia*

depression

diet *(mark all)*

Double vision *(lowercase the index entry and mark all)*

effects of aging

eye exam *(mark all)*

eyesight

macular degeneration, *with a cross-reference to* **common eye ailments**

The first instance of **medications**

over-the-counter, **prescription** *(in the text, not the table), and the first instance of* **side effects** *as subentries of* **medications**

nutrition *(mark all)*

physical fitness

quality of life

smoking

22. At the beginning of the document, start a new line, apply the **TOC Heading** style, type **Table of Contents**, and press ENTER.
23. Insert a custom table of contents using the **Formal** format. Show three levels and include the Heading 1 Expanded style as TOC level 1.
24. Insert a page break after the table of contents.
25. Insert a page break after the conclusion, type **Table of Figures**, format it with the **Heading 1 Expanded** style, and press ENTER.
26. Insert a table of figures using the **Formal** format and Table label and number.
27. Insert a **Works Cited** bibliography after the table of figures. Apply the **Heading 1 Expanded** style to the Works Cited heading.
28. On a new page at the end of the document (after the Works Cited table), type **Index** and format it with the **Heading 1 Expanded** style.
29. On the next line, insert an index using the **Formal** format.
30. Insert the **Sideline** cover page and type your school name in the Company content control. Type the report title, **Eye Care for Seniors**, in the Title content control, and **How Aging Affects the Health of Our Eyes** in the Subtitle content control. Type your name in the Author content control and select today's date in the Date Picker. Remove the blank line below the date, if it is interfering with the Table of Contents heading.
31. Set page numbering to start on the second page of the document (table of contents), if necessary.
32. Check the spelling and grammar in the document and correct errors.
33. Update the entire table of contents.
34. **With your teacher's permission**, print the report. Page 1 of 7 should look similar to Illustration 8A; Page 6 of 7 should look similar to Illustration 8B; Page 7 or 7 should look similar to Illustration 8C.
35. Save and close the document, and exit Word.

Illustration 8A

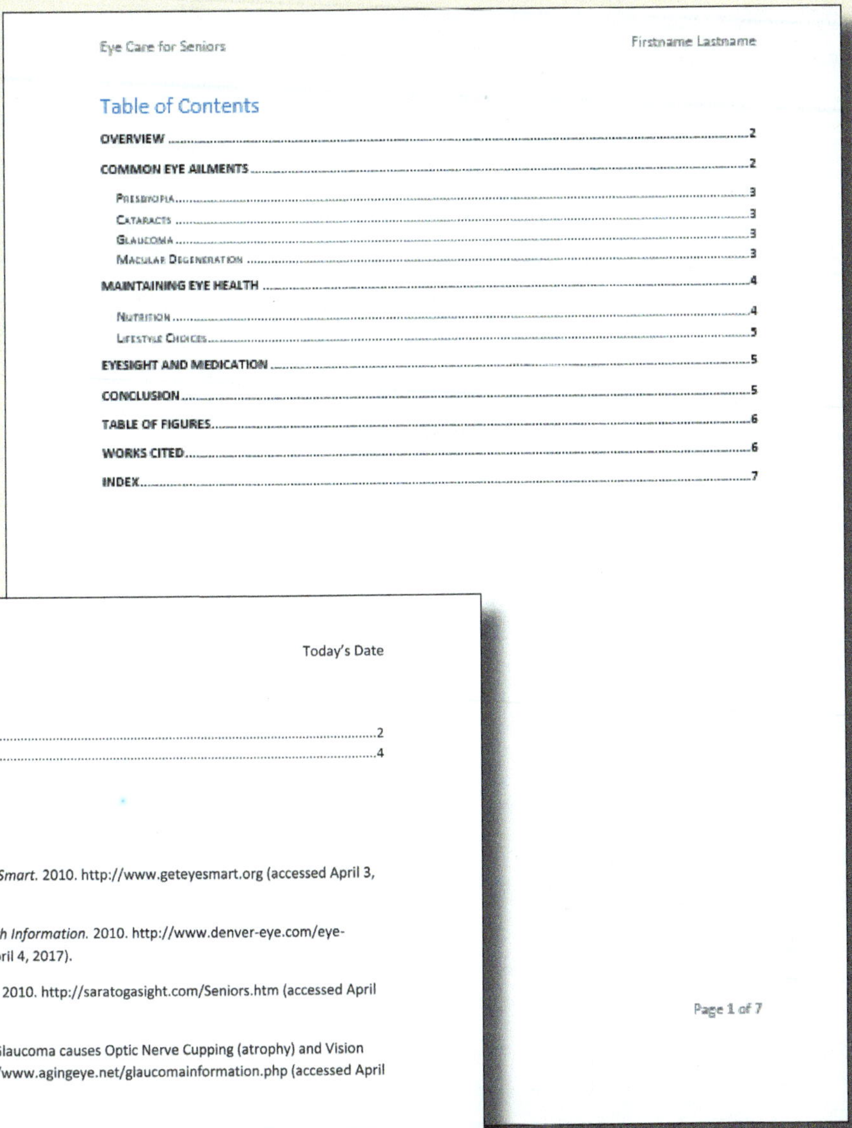

Eye Care for Seniors Firstname Lastname

Table of Contents

Page 1 of 7

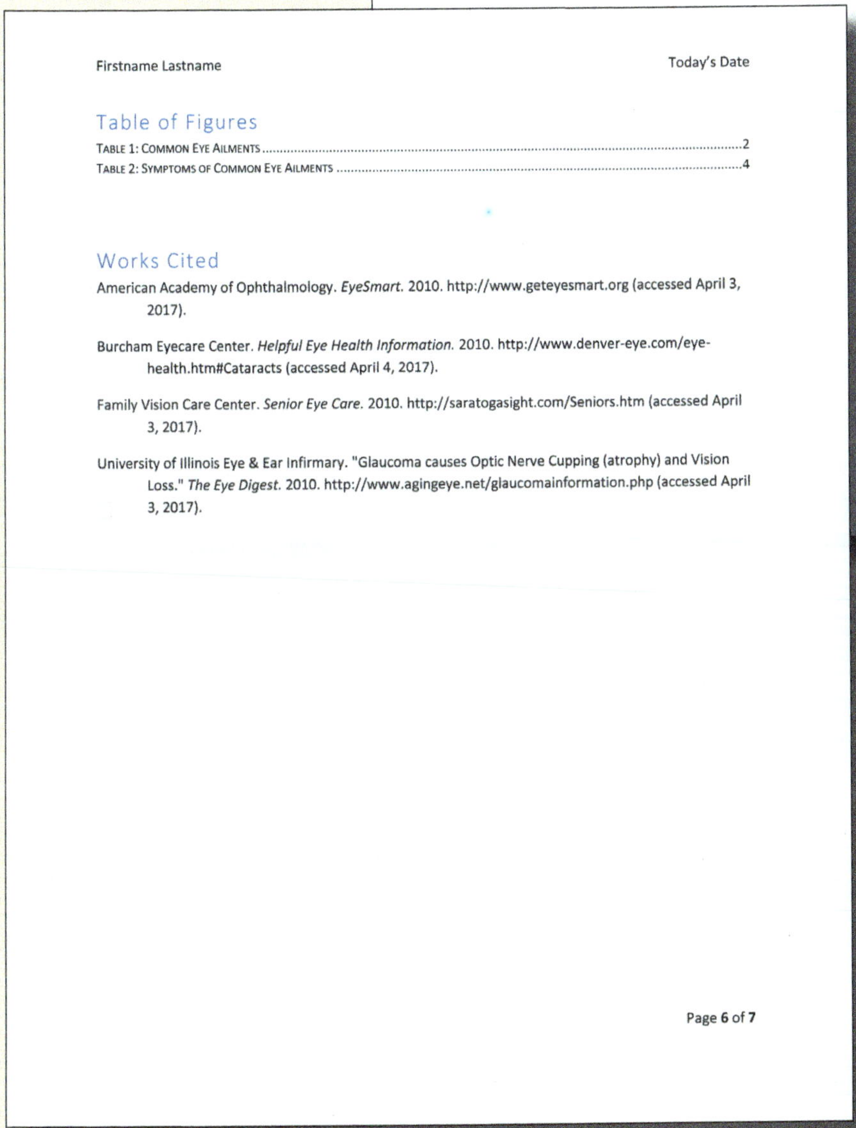

Firstname Lastname Today's Date

Table of Figures

Works Cited

American Academy of Ophthalmology. *EyeSmart*. 2010. http://www.geteyesmart.org (accessed April 3, 2017).

Burcham Eyecare Center. *Helpful Eye Health Information*. 2010. http://www.denver-eye.com/eye-health.htm#Cataracts (accessed April 4, 2017).

Family Vision Care Center. *Senior Eye Care*. 2010. http://saratogasight.com/Seniors.htm (accessed April 3, 2017).

University of Illinois Eye & Ear Infirmary. "Glaucoma causes Optic Nerve Cupping (atrophy) and Vision Loss." *The Eye Digest*. 2010. http://www.agingeye.net/glaucomainformation.php (accessed April 3, 2017).

Page 6 of 7

Illustration 8B

Illustration 8C

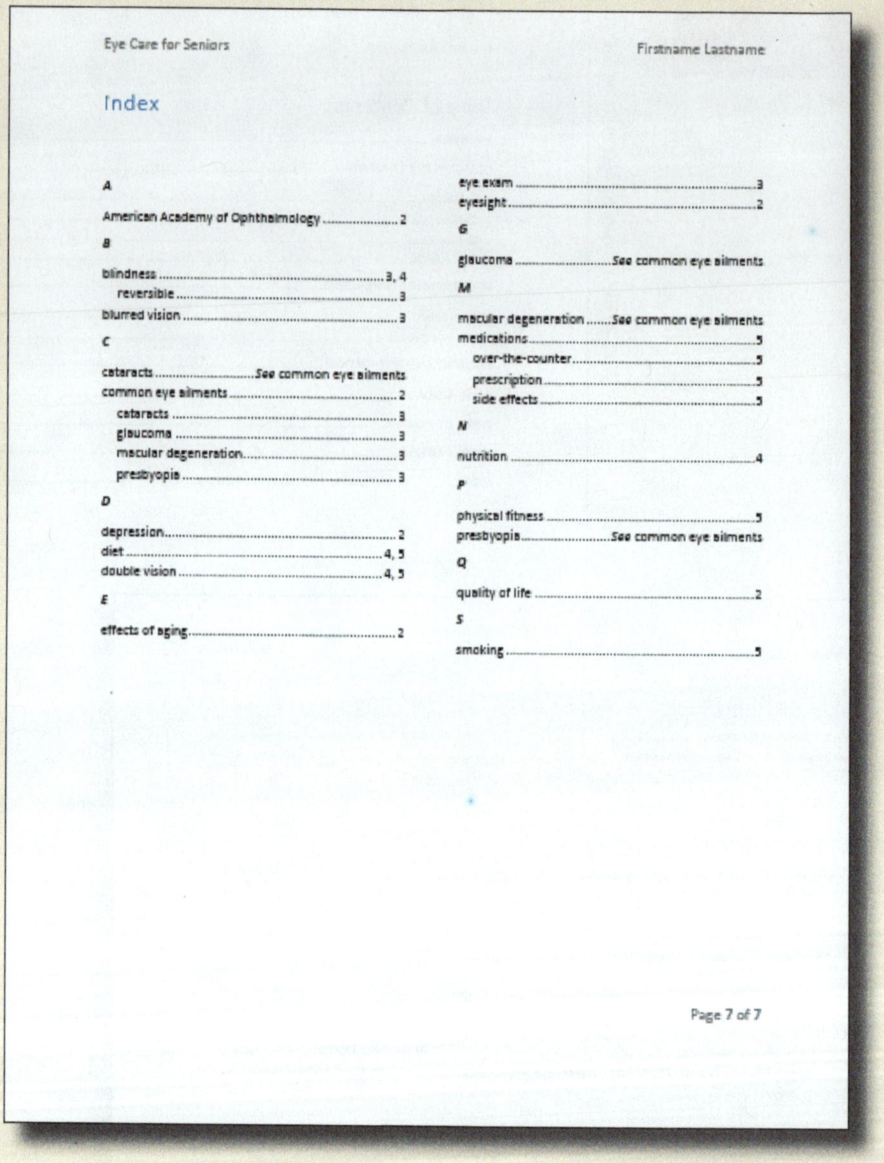

Eye Care for Seniors Firstname Lastname

Index

Page 7 of 7

Chapter 9

(Courtesy lightpoet/Shutterstock)

Embedding and Linking Objects, Using Mail Merge, and Creating Macros

Lesson 60
Copying, Moving, and Embedding Data and Objects

- Copying and Moving Data from One Office Document to Another
- Embedding Objects
- Editing Embedded Objects
- Pasting Content with Specific Formatting

Lesson 61
Linking Files and Objects

- Linking Files
- Editing a Linked Object
- Updating Links

Lesson 62
Integrating Word and PowerPoint

- Pasting PowerPoint Slides As Graphics
- Embedding a PowerPoint Slide in a Word Document
- Exporting PowerPoint Slides and Notes to a Word Document
- Exporting PowerPoint Text to a Word Document
- Using a Word Outline to Create a PowerPoint Presentation

Lesson 63
Using Merge to Create Letters, Envelopes, Labels, and E-mail

- Reviewing the Mail Merge Process
- Merging Letters Using the Mail Merge Wizard
- Merging Envelopes
- Creating Mailing Labels
- Creating an E-mail Merge
- Filtering Recipients
- Applying Rules to a Merge

Lesson 64
Creating a Directory with Mail Merge

- Creating a Directory Merge
- Adding Formatting to a Field Code
- Sorting Records in the Data Source
- Selecting Specific Records
- Customizing Fields in an Address List

Lesson 65
Working with Macros

- Recording a Macro
- Running a Macro
- Deleting and Re-recording a Macro
- Editing a Macro with VBA
- Assigning a Shortcut Key to an Existing Macro
- Copying a Macro Using the Organizer
- Managing Macro Security

End-of-Chapter Activities

Lesson 60

Copying, Moving, and Embedding Data and Objects

➤ What You Will Learn

Copying and Moving Data from One Office Document to Another
Embedding Objects
Editing Embedded Objects
Pasting Content with Specific Formatting

WORDS TO KNOW

Active window
The window in which you are currently working.

Destination file
The file where the data is pasted.

Embed
To insert an object in a file. The embedded object is not linked to a source file, but it is linked to the source application. You edit the object using the source application, but changes do not affect the source file data.

Source file
The file that contains the data to be copied.

Software Skills You may find it necessary to work with more than one Office application at a time and to share data between them. For example, you might want to create a report detailing your department's decreased costs by combining a Word document with an Excel spreadsheet or a table from Access. You can easily copy and embed all types of data among applications.

What You Can Do

Copying and Moving Data from One Office Document to Another

- You can open multiple program windows at the same time. This is useful for comparing the data in different files, as well as for exchanging data between files.
- Only one window can be active at a time. The **active window** appears on top of other open windows. Its title bar is a different color than the title bars of other open windows, and its taskbar button is highlighted.
- You can use Windows to switch among open windows to make a different window active. For example, you can press ALT + TAB to cycle between open windows, or click a window's taskbar button.

- To copy or move content between applications, you can either use the Windows Clipboard or drag-and-drop items from the **source file** to the **destination file**.
- Data pasted into a destination file becomes part of the destination file. There is no link to the source file.
- Different types of content are pasted into Word as different object types than the original in some cases. For example, when you paste Excel cells into Word, they are converted to a table. When you paste a PowerPoint slide into Word, it is converted to a graphic.

Try It! Copying and Moving Data from One Office Document to Another

✓ *This Try It assumes you know how to locate and select data in an Excel worksheet. If you do not, ask your teacher for more information.*

1. Start Word, and open **W60TryA** from the data files for this lesson. Save the file as **W60TryA_xx** in the location where your teacher instructs you to store the files for this lesson.
2. Start Excel, and open **W60TryB**.
3. In Excel, select the cells B12:J18. Press CTRL + C to copy the range to the Clipboard.
4. Switch to Word and select the text *Copy data here.* Do not select the paragraph mark after the period.
5. Press CTRL + V to paste the data from the Clipboard into Word, replacing the selected text.
6. Save the changes to the Word document. Do not save the Excel workbook. Leave both files open to use in the next Try It.

Embedding Objects

- **Embedding** an object places it into a different application, like copying does, but it retains a connection to the source application. This is useful because it enables you to edit the object later in its original application.
- For example, if you copy data from Excel into Word, the data is converted into a Word table. Word "forgets" that the data came from Excel. However, if you embed the same data into Word, the embedded cells remain Excel cells, and you can edit them using Excel's tools and commands.
- Embedding does not retain a link between the data and its source file—only the source application. Therefore, if you make changes to the original source file, they are not reflected in the copy.

✓ *Linking, which you will learn about in Lesson 61, does retain a link to the source file, so that the copy is automatically updated.*

- To embed rather than simply paste data, copy or cut the object as you would normally, but instead of using the Paste command (CTRL + V), use the Paste Special command in the Clipboard group on the Home tab.
- In the Paste Special dialog box, select a paste format that includes the word "object" in it, such as Microsoft Excel Worksheet Object. Only then will the object be embedded; otherwise, it will simply be pasted in the chosen format (covered later in this lesson).

Try It! Embedding Objects

1. With **W60TryB** open in Excel, select cells A22:J31.
2. Press CTRL + C to copy the range.
3. In **W60TryA_xx**, select the text *Embed object here.* Do not select the paragraph mark after the period.
4. On the Home tab, click the down arrow on the Paste button, and click Paste Special. The Paste Special dialog box opens.
5. In the Paste Special dialog box, select Microsoft Excel Worksheet Object and click OK. The range appears in Word, overrunning the document margins.
6. Drag a corner selection handle of the pasted object toward the inside of the worksheet to resize it to fit on the page.
7. If necessary, delete the text *Embed object here.*
8. In Word, save the changes to **W60TryA_xx**. Leave both files open in Word and Excel for the next Try It.

The Paste Special dialog box

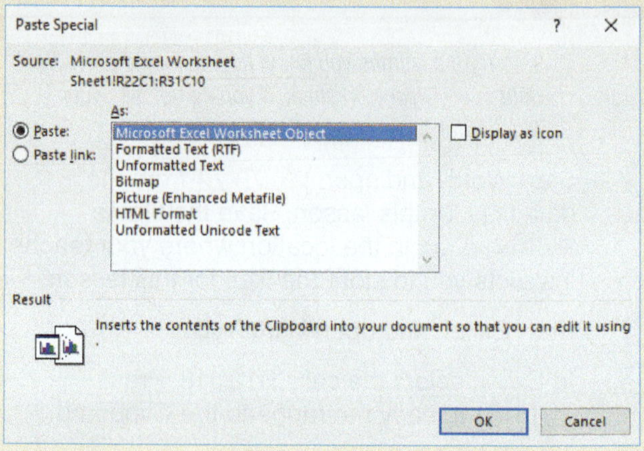

Word 2016, Windows 10, Microsoft Corporation

Editing Embedded Objects

- You can edit and format embedded objects using the source program.
- Double-click an embedded object to open the tools from its source program. Depending on the application, the source program's tools may appear within Word itself, or the object may open in a separate window in the source program.
- Changes you make to the embedded copy do not affect the original file from which the data came.

Try It! Editing Embedded Objects

1. In the **W60TryA_xx** file in Word, double-click the embedded Excel object.

   ✓ *Excel commands become available in Word.*
2. Click in cell D23 and type **60**, changing the value there.
3. Click on the Word document, outside the Excel object. The Word ribbon reappears.
4. Using Windows, switch to the Excel program, where the original data is still open. Notice that the change you made to the object in Word did not affect the value in D23 of the original worksheet.
5. Exit Excel. If you are prompted to save changes to **W60TryB**, click No.
6. Save and close **W60TryA_xx**.

(continued)

Try It! Editing Embedded Objects *(continued)*

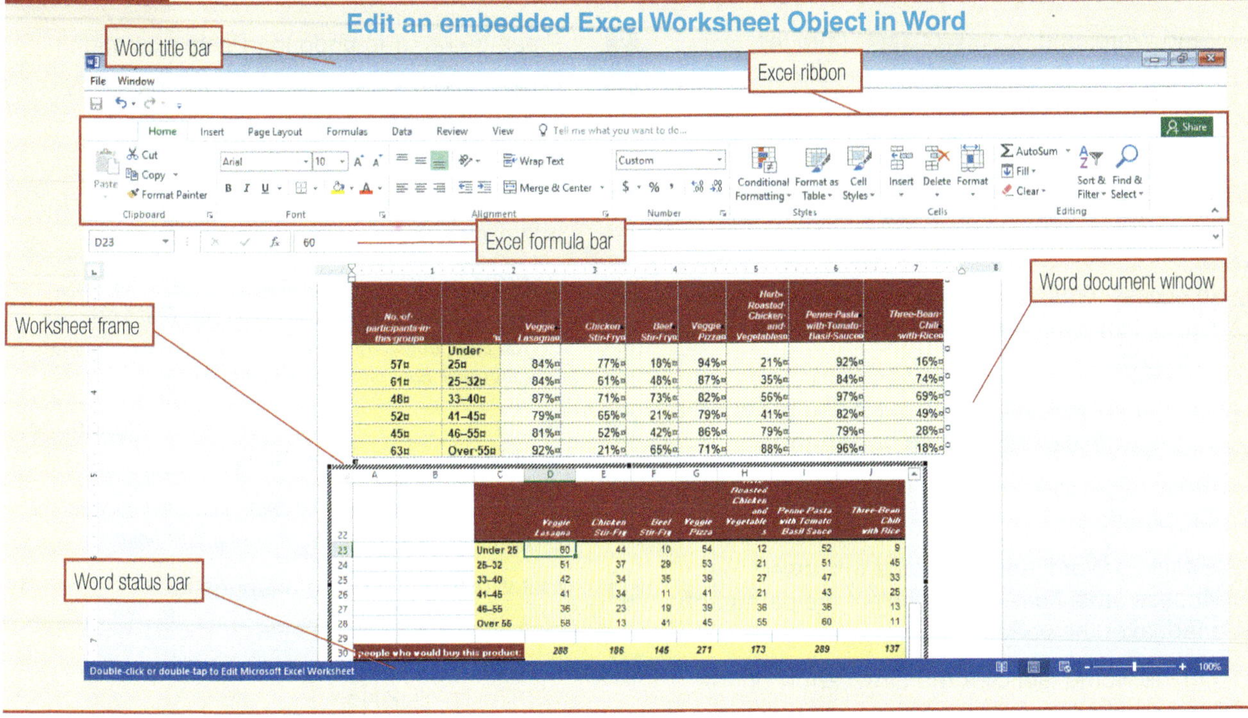

Word 2016, Windows 10, Microsoft Corporation

Pasting Content with Specific Formatting

- As you saw in the previous section, Paste Special can be used to embed objects in Word. It can also be used in other ways, such as to insert content in a specific format or insert content with or without its original formatting.
- The Paste button's drop-down list contains a menu that includes the Paste Special command, as you saw in the previous section. It also includes several shortcut buttons that you can use to specify the formatting for the paste operation. Figure 60-1 shows the paste options for an Access table.
- The buttons shown depend on the type of content being pasted. For example, Figure 60-2 shows the options for a range of Excel cells.
- These buttons are shortcuts for some of the commands and options you find in the Paste Special dialog box when you choose Paste Special from the menu (as you did in the previous section when embedding).

Figure 60-1

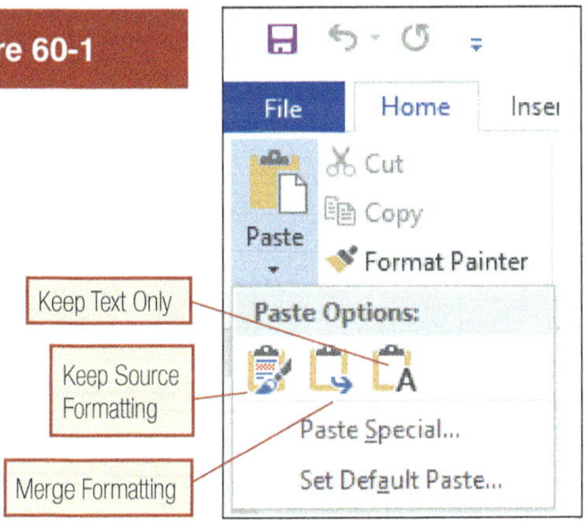

Word 2016, Windows 10, Microsoft Corporation

Figure 60-2

Word 2016, Windows 10, Microsoft Corporation

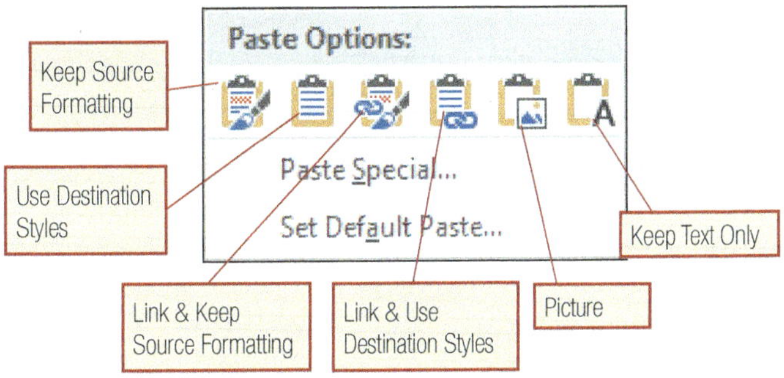

Try It! Pasting Content with Specific Formatting

1. Start Word, and open **W60TryC** from the data files for this lesson. Save the file as **W60TryC_xx** in the location where your teacher instructs you to store the files for this lesson.
2. Start Access, and open **W60TryD** from the data files for this lesson. If you see a security warning bar, click Enable Content.
3. In Access, double-click tblClients in the Navigation pane on the left. The table opens in a datasheet.
4. Click anywhere in the datasheet and press CTRL + A to select the entire datasheet.
5. Press CTRL + C to copy the datasheet to the Clipboard.
6. Switch to Word, and select the text *Insert Access table here*. Do not select the paragraph mark after the period.
7. On the Home tab, click the down arrow on the Paste button. A menu opens, as shown in Figure 60-1.
8. Click the Keep Source Formatting button. The table is pasted into the document with default Access formatting retained.
9. Press CTRL + Z to undo the Paste operation.
10. Click the down arrow again on the Paste button and click Paste Special. The Paste Special dialog box opens.
11. Click HTML Format if it is not already selected, and click OK.

    ✓ *Notice that for an Access table, there is no "object" option in the Paste Special dialog box. That's because you can't embed Access content into Word using the Clipboard, nor can you link to it that way.*

12. To confirm that the datasheet is not embedded, double-click anywhere within it.

    ✓ *Access does not open the datasheet. The imported content is in a normal Word table at this point.*

13. Exit Word, saving your changes to **W60TryC_xx**.
14. Exit Access. If prompted to save changes to **W60TryD**, click No.

Choose HTML format in which to paste the copied content

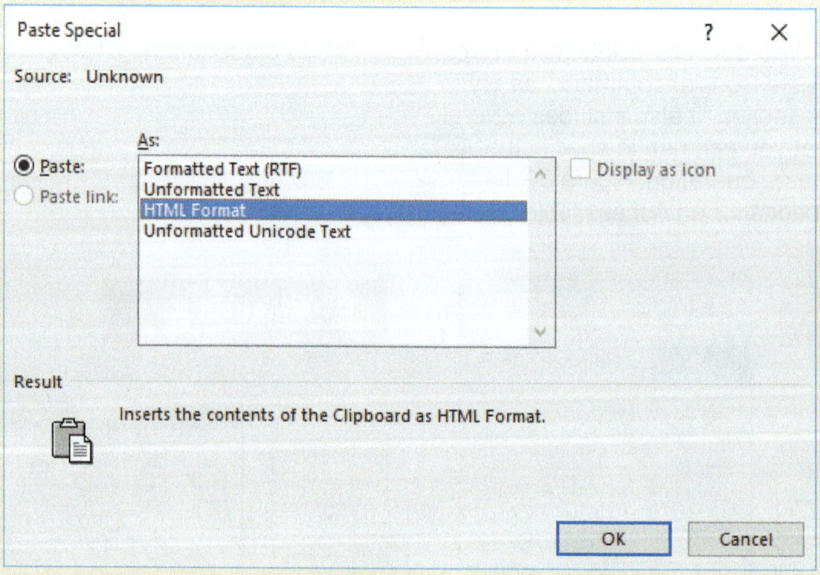

Word 2016, Windows 10, Microsoft Corporation

Lesson 60—Practice

You are the business development manager at Fresh Food Fair, a small chain of organic grocery stores. The company's owners are thinking about starting a home delivery service and have asked you to analyze the costs of such a venture. You have collected cost information in an Excel worksheet and have prepared a memo in Word to present your findings. In this project, you will copy some of the data from the worksheet to the memo.

DIRECTIONS

1. Start Word, if necessary, and open **W60PracticeA** from the data files for this lesson. Save the file as **W60PracticeA_xx** in the location where your teacher instructs you to store the files for this lesson.
2. Replace the text **Your Name** with your own name.
3. Replace the text **Today's date** with the current date.
4. Position the insertion point on the blank line at the end of the document.
5. Start Excel, and open the file **W60PracticeB** in Excel.
6. Select cells **A4:B9**.

   ✓ *To select cells, you can drag across them, or you can click in the upper left cell (A4) and hold down SHIFT as you press the arrow keys to extend the selection to B9.*

7. Press CTRL + C to copy the selected cells to the Clipboard.

   ✓ *You can use any other copy method if you prefer, such as the Home > Copy command or right-clicking the selection and choosing Copy.*

8. Switch to the Word window.
9. On the **Home** tab, click the down arrow on the **Paste** button.
10. Click the **Use Destination Styles** button on the menu that appears.

    ✓ *The cells are copied into Word and are formatted to match the Word document's formatting. The document should look similar to Figure 60-3 on the next page.*

11. **With your teacher's permission**, print the document.
12. Close Excel without saving changes to the workbook.
13. Save and close the document, and exit Word.

Figure 60-3

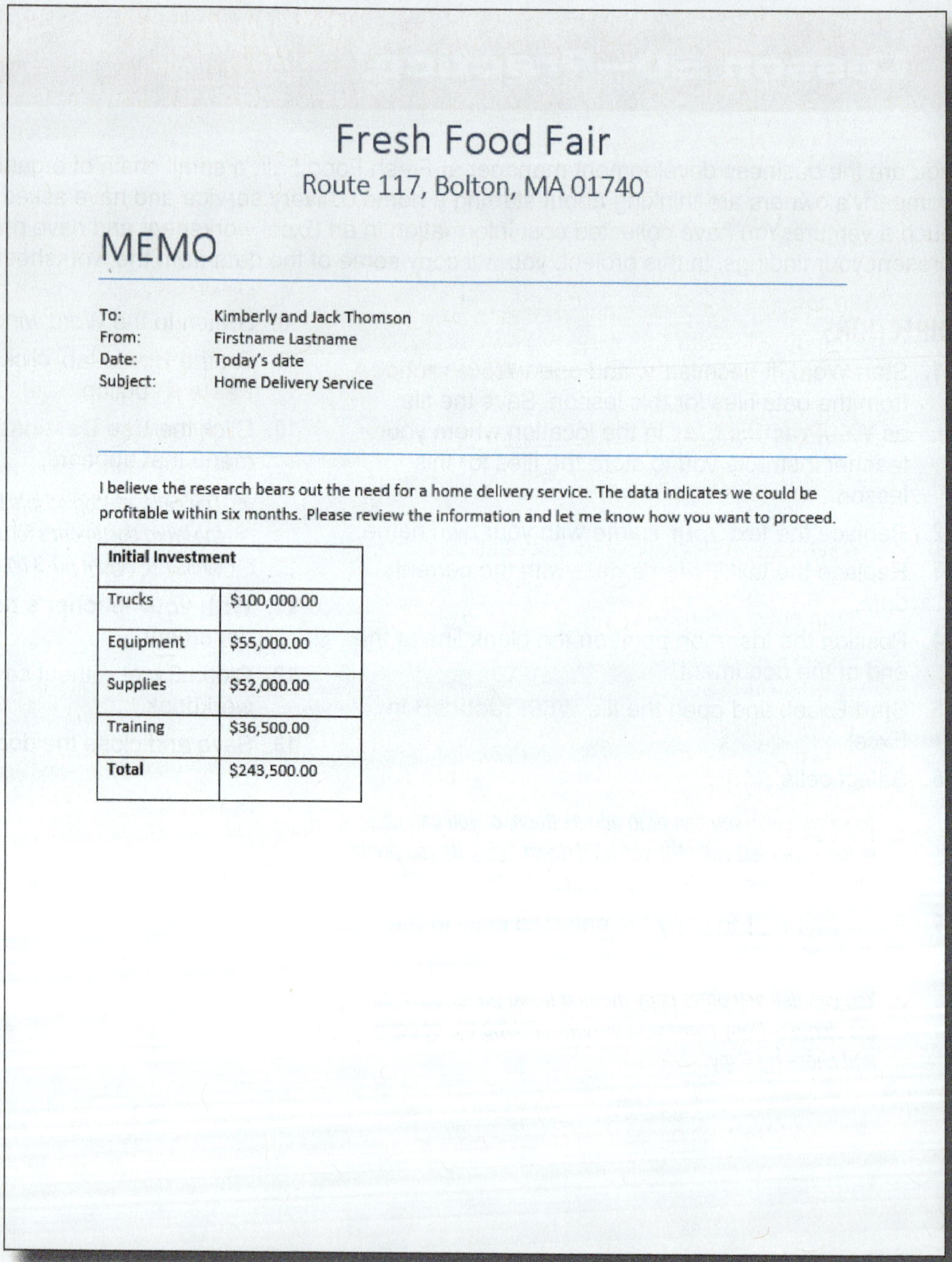

Fresh Food Fair

Route 117, Bolton, MA 01740

MEMO

To: Kimberly and Jack Thomson
From: Firstname Lastname
Date: Today's date
Subject: Home Delivery Service

I believe the research bears out the need for a home delivery service. The data indicates we could be profitable within six months. Please review the information and let me know how you want to proceed.

Initial Investment	
Trucks	$100,000.00
Equipment	$55,000.00
Supplies	$52,000.00
Training	$36,500.00
Total	$243,500.00

Lesson 60—Apply

In this project, you will continue to work on the memo for the owners of Fresh Food Fair. You will embed Excel data in the memo. You will also copy a chart from a PowerPoint presentation and paste it into the memo as a picture.

DIRECTIONS

1. Start Word, if necessary, and open **W60ApplyA** from the data files for this lesson. Save the file as **W60ApplyA_xx** in the location where your teacher instructs you to store the files for this lesson.
2. Replace the text **Your Name** with your own name.
3. Replace the text **Today's date** with the current date.
4. Open **W60ApplyB** in Excel, and select cells **E4:F11**.
5. Copy the cells to the Clipboard.
6. Switch to Word and move the insertion point to the end of the document.
7. Press ENTER and type **The estimated monthly expenses are as follows:**. Then press ENTER again to start a new paragraph.
8. Using **Paste Special**, embed the copied cells into the Word document.

   ✓ *Use the Microsoft Excel Worksheet Object data type in the Paste Special dialog box.*
9. Switch back to Excel, and close it. Do not save changes to **W60ApplyB**.
10. Edit the embedded cells to change the Gas cost to **$3000**.
11. Edit the embedded cells to match the font, font size, and cell borders of the other table in the Word document.

    ✓ *If you have not already studied Excel formatting, you may not know how to do step 11; ask your teacher for help if needed.*
12. Move the insertion point in Word to the right of the embedded Excel data, and press the spacebar a few times to create extra space there.
13. Open **W60ApplyC** in PowerPoint, and select the chart on slide 7.
14. Copy the chart to the Clipboard.
15. Switch to Word, and paste the chart as a picture at the end of the Word document.
16. Resize the chart so that it fits next to the embedded Excel data, as shown in Figure 60-4 on the next page.
17. **With your teacher's permission**, print the document.
18. Close PowerPoint without saving changes to the presentation.
19. Save your changes in Word, and exit Word.

Figure 60-4

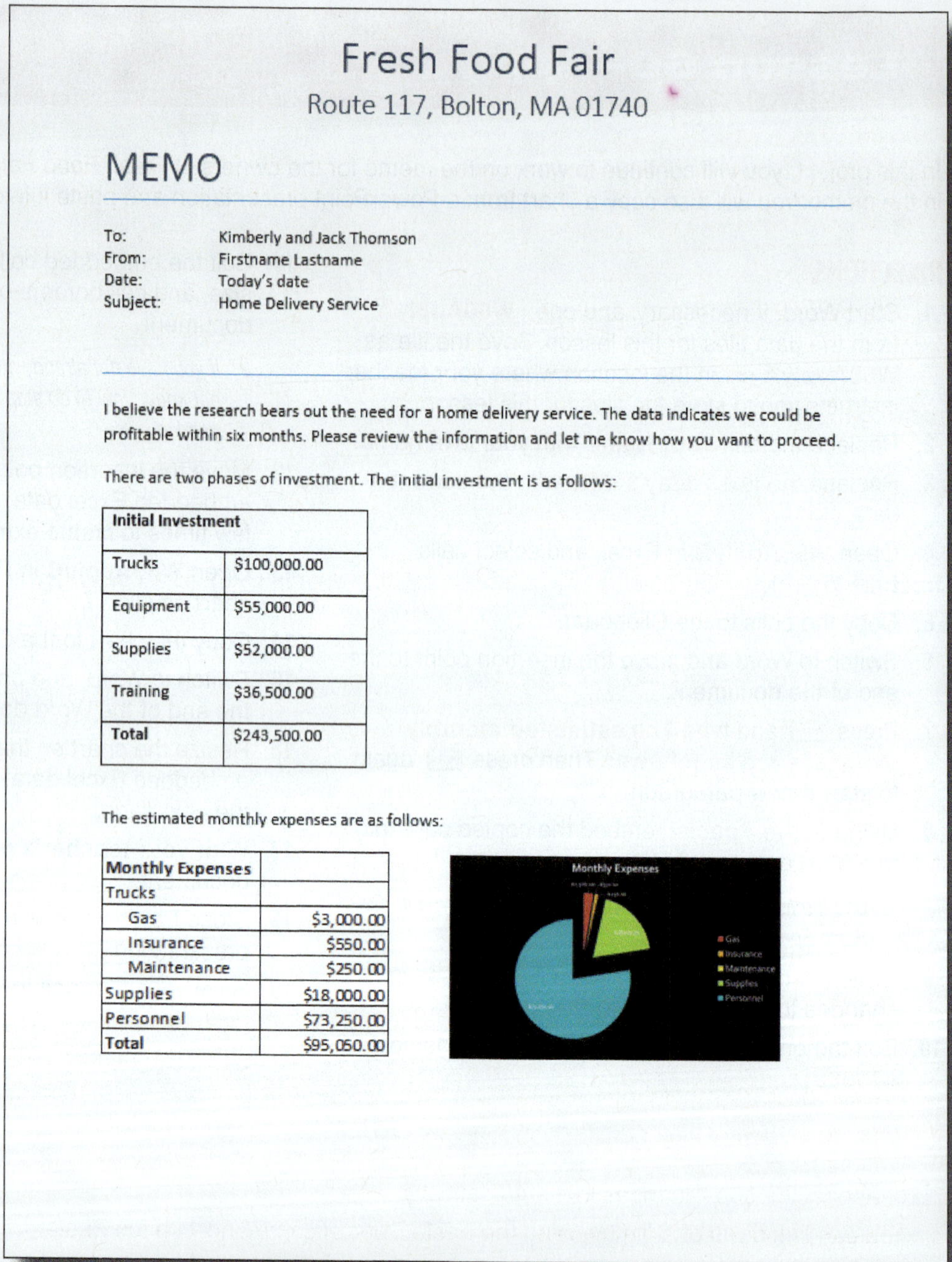

Fresh Food Fair

Route 117, Bolton, MA 01740

MEMO

To: Kimberly and Jack Thomson
From: Firstname Lastname
Date: Today's date
Subject: Home Delivery Service

I believe the research bears out the need for a home delivery service. The data indicates we could be profitable within six months. Please review the information and let me know how you want to proceed.

There are two phases of investment. The initial investment is as follows:

Initial Investment	
Trucks	$100,000.00
Equipment	$55,000.00
Supplies	$52,000.00
Training	$36,500.00
Total	$243,500.00

The estimated monthly expenses are as follows:

Monthly Expenses	
Trucks	
Gas	$3,000.00
Insurance	$550.00
Maintenance	$250.00
Supplies	$18,000.00
Personnel	$73,250.00
Total	$95,050.00

Lesson 61

Linking Files and Objects

➤ What You Will Learn

Linking Files
Editing a Linked Object
Updating Links

Software Skills Link files when you have existing data in one file that you want to use in one or more other files. Whenever the original data is changed, the link ensures that it will be updated in all other files. Linking lets you maintain data in a single file location, yet use it in other files as well.

WORDS TO KNOW

Link
To insert a link to an object in another file, so that when the original is edited, the linked copy also changes.

What You Can Do

Linking Files

- When you want to reference data from another file that might change later, you might want to link to it. A **link** is a pointer to another data file; when you open a document that contains a link, Word retrieves the latest version of the linked data.
- Linked content is different from embedded content. Embedded content retains a memory of the application it came from, but the data itself is stored only within the document in which it is embedded. There is no connection between the embedded data and the original.
- In contrast, linked data maintains information about not only the application it came from, but also the data file it came from. That way when the original changes, the copy changes too, automatically.
- You can link parts of a file by using the Paste Special command with the Paste link option enabled.
- In the Paste Special dialog box, you can also select how you want to format the selected object. The choices depend on the source program.
- Another way to link to content from an external file in Word is to click the Object arrow on the Insert tab, and select Text from File. Next, select the file (and range, if the source is an Excel file), click the Insert button arrow, and select Insert as Link.

Try It! Linking Files

1. Start Word, and open **W61TryA** from the data files for this lesson. Save the file as **W61TryA_xx** in the location where your teacher instructs you to store the files for this lesson.
2. Start Excel, and open **W61TryB**. Save the file as **W61TryB_xx** in the location where your teacher instructs you to store the files for this lesson.
3. In Excel, select the cell range A22:J31. Then press CTRL + C to copy.
4. Switch to Word, and select the text *Insert link here*. Do not select the paragraph mark after the period.
5. On the Home tab, click the down arrow on the Paste button and click Paste Special.
6. In the Paste Special dialog box, click Paste link.
7. Select *Microsoft Excel Worksheet Object*.
8. Click OK.

   ✓ *Word inserts the selected cells in the Word document.*

9. Resize the object in the Word document so it fits in the document.
10. Exit Excel, saving the changes if prompted. In Word, save the changes to **W61TryA_xx**, and leave it open to use in the next Try It.

Choose Paste link in the Paste Special dialog box

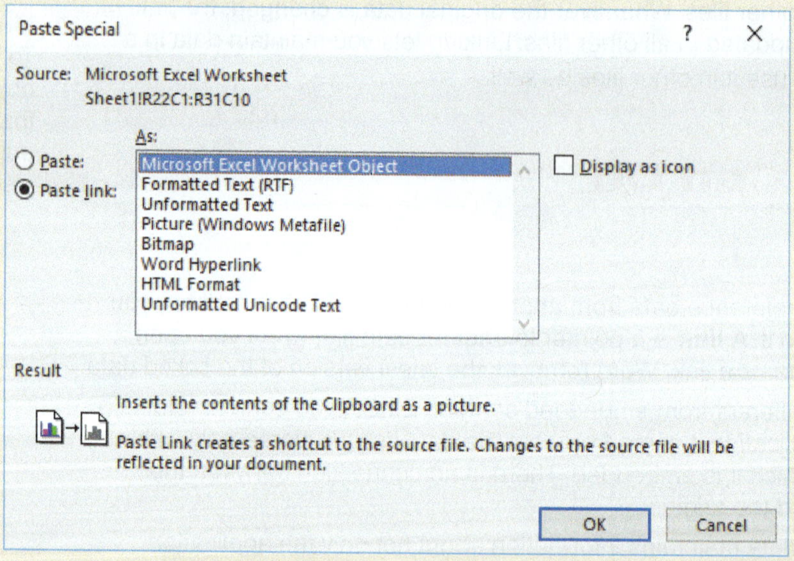

Word 2016, Windows 10, Microsoft Corporation

Editing a Linked Object

- You can edit a linked object by opening it via the link in Word, or you can open the source file separately outside of Word. Either way, the same file is being edited. The copy in Word is not a separate copy; it is a pointer to the original.
- When you double-click a linked object in Word, the source program and file open so you can edit the source file directly.
- If you open the source file separately outside of Word, the changes that you make to it are reflected in the linked copy in Word the next time the links are updated.

  ✓ *You will learn about link updating in the next section.*

Try It! Editing a Linked Object

1. With W61TryA_xx open in Word, double-click the linked worksheet object. The original copy opens in Excel.

   ✓ *Unlike with an embedded object, in this case an entirely separate Excel window opens for editing the file; Excel's ribbon and tools do not appear within Word.*

2. In Excel, change the value in cell J23 to 11.
3. Exit Excel, saving the changes.
4. In Word, right-click the linked worksheet object. Click Update Link. The change is reflected.
5. Save the changes to W61TryA_xx, and leave it open to use in the next Try It.

Updating Links

- By default, links update whenever a file is opened or printed.
- If Word cannot locate the source file (for example, if it has been deleted, renamed, or moved), it will display a warning message telling you that it cannot update the link. You can use the Links dialog box to break the link or to change the location of the source file.
- If there are many links in a file, automatic updating can slow down the process of opening the file. For that reason, you might choose to turn off automatic updating.
- The Links dialog box enables you to manage the links in various ways:
  - You can break a link, leaving the object in the document without a link to the source document.
  - You can change the source file for the link (for example, if the name or location of the source file changed).
  - You can switch between automatic and manual updating.
  - You can lock an individual link to prevent it from updating.

Try It! Switching Between Manual and Automatic Updating

1. With W61TryA_xx open in Word, double-click the linked object to reopen it in Excel.
2. In Excel, change the value in cell J23 to 15, and save the workbook.
3. Switch back to Word, and right-click the linked worksheet object. Click Update Link.
4. Right-click the linked worksheet object again, point to Linked Worksheet Object, and click Links. The Links dialog box opens.
5. Click Manual update and click OK.
6. Switch back to Excel, and change the value in cell J23 to 7.
7. Exit Excel, saving the changes.
8. Switch back to Word, and note that the value has not updated. Leave the file open for the next Try It.

   ✓ *You may need to resize the table object; it may have reverted to its original inserted dimensions.*

(continued)

Try It! Switching Between Manual and Automatic Updating *(continued)*

Manage links in the Links dialog box

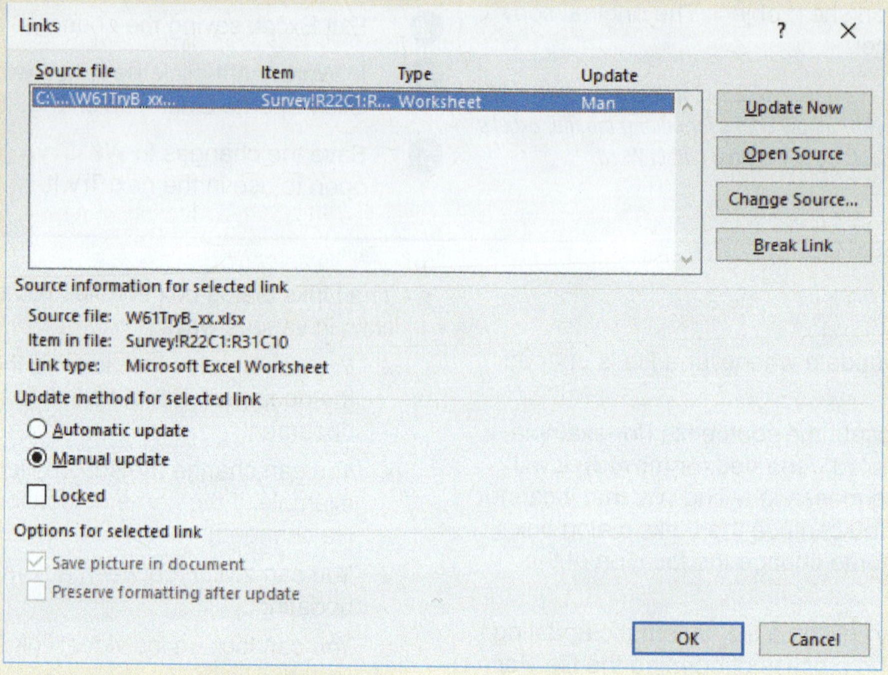

Word 2016, Windows 10, Microsoft Corporation

Try It! Manually Updating a Link

1. In the **W61TryA_xx** file, right-click the linked worksheet object > Linked Worksheet Object > Links. The Links dialog box opens.
2. Click Update Now.
3. Click Close to close the dialog box. Note that the value is now updated.

   ✓ *You may need to resize the table object; it may have reverted to its original inserted dimensions.*

4. Save the changes to **W61TryA_xx**, and leave it open to use in the next Try It.

Try It! Breaking a Link

1. In the **W61TryA_xx** file, right-click the linked worksheet object > Linked Worksheet Object > Links.
2. Click Break Link.
3. Click Yes to confirm.

   ✓ *You may need to resize the table object; it may have reverted to its original inserted dimensions.*

4. Double-click the object.

   ✓ *It no longer opens in Excel; instead picture tools appear on the ribbon. When you broke the link, you converted the object to a picture.*

5. Save and close the document, and exit Word.

Lesson 61—Practice

As the new training director at Long Shot, Inc., you have been asked to submit the department's expenses for the first quarter to the Director of Human Resources. However, you have only preliminary data available. In this project, you will link the preliminary data stored in an Excel worksheet into a Word memo.

DIRECTIONS

1. Start Word, if necessary, and open **W61PracticeA** from the data files for this lesson. Save the file as **W61PracticeA_xx** in the location where your teacher instructs you to store the files for this lesson.
2. Replace the text **Your Name** with your own name.
3. Replace the text **Today's date** with the current date.
4. Position the insertion point at the end of the document.
5. Open **W61PracticeB** in Excel, and save the file as **W61PracticeB_xx** in the location where your teacher instructs you to store the files for this lesson.
6. In Excel, select **A5:E13**.
7. Press CTRL + C to copy the cells to the Clipboard.
8. Switch to Word.
9. On the **Home** tab, click the down arrow on the **Paste** button and click **Paste Special**.
10. In the Paste Special dialog box, click **Paste link**.
11. Click **Microsoft Excel Worksheet Object**.
12. Click **OK**. The object is pasted and linked.
13. **With your teacher's permission**, print the document.
14. Save and close the document, and exit Word.
15. Exit Excel, saving your changes if prompted.

Lesson 61—Apply

In this project, you will continue to work on the memo for the Director of Human Resources at Long Shot, Inc. You will change the data to reflect actual expenses, and update the link to update the data in the Word document.

DIRECTIONS

1. Start Word, if necessary, and open **W61ApplyA** from the data files for this lesson. When prompted to update the links, click No.

   ✓ *There is no need to update this link now.*
2. Save the file as **W61ApplyA_xx** in the location where your teacher instructs you to store the files for this lesson.
3. Replace the text **Your Name** with your own name.
4. Replace the text **Today's date** with the current date.
5. Start Excel, and open the workbook **W61ApplyB** from the data files for this lesson. Save the file as **W61ApplyB_xx** in the location where your teacher instructs you to store the files for this lesson.
6. Switch to Word, and change the link in the document to refer to **W61ApplyB_xx**.

   ✓ *Use the Change Source command in the Links dialog box.*
7. Make the following changes to the linked object:
   a. Change the value in cell **C12** to **$350**.
   b. Change the value in cell **C9** to **$2000**.
8. Save the changes in Excel and exit the program.
9. Update the link in the Word document if the changes you made do not immediately appear.

   ✓ *To update the link, you can right-click the object and click Update Link.*
10. **With your teacher's permission**, print the document. It should look similar to Figure 61-1 on the next page.
11. Save and close the document, and exit Word.

Figure 61-1

Long Shot, Inc.

INTERDEPARTMENTAL MEMORANDUM

To: Director of Human Resources
From: Firstname Lastname
Date: Today's date
Re: Training Department Expenses

Per your request, here are the preliminary expense figures for the training department for the first quarter of the year. I will update the figures as soon as I receive the actual amounts.

Long Shot, Inc.
Training Department
First Quarter Expenses

	January	February	March	Total
Salaries	$135,000.00	$135,000.00	$135,000.00	$405,000.00
Overtime	$30,000.00	$32,000.00	$29,000.00	$91,000.00
Entertainment	$1,500.00	$1,750.00	$1,200.00	$4,450.00
Facility rentals	$2,000.00	$2,000.00	$1,500.00	$5,500.00
Books	$500.00	$250.00	$500.00	$1,250.00
Supplies	$250.00	$150.00	$375.00	$775.00
Miscellaneous	$350.00	$350.00	$300.00	$675.00
Total	$169,600.00	$171,500.00	$167,875.00	$508,975.00

Lesson 62

Integrating Word and PowerPoint

➤ What You Will Learn

Pasting PowerPoint Slides As Graphics
Embedding a PowerPoint Slide in a Word Document
Exporting PowerPoint Slides and Notes to a Word Document
Exporting PowerPoint Text to a Word Document
Using a Word Outline to Create a PowerPoint Presentation

Software Skills Sharing information between two applications can save you time and work and provide consistency between documents. If you have a PowerPoint presentation, for example, you can use the presentation information in a Word document. You can embed PowerPoint slides in a Word document as graphics objects, or you can export text and graphics from a PowerPoint presentation into a Word document.

WORDS TO KNOW

Export
To send data from its source file to a different file, usually in a different format.

What You Can Do

Pasting PowerPoint Slides As Graphics

- When you paste slides from PowerPoint into Word, the pasted copies become graphics, like any other graphic you would insert.

Try It! Pasting PowerPoint Slides As Graphics

1. Start Word, and open **W62TryA** from the data files for this lesson. Save the file as **W62TryA_xx** in the location where your teacher instructs you to store the files for this lesson.
2. Start PowerPoint, and open **W62TryB**. Save the file as **W62TryB_xx** in the location where your teacher instructs you to store the files for this lesson.
3. Select slide 4 in the thumbnail pane (on the left) and press CTRL + C to copy it.
4. Switch to Word, and click to move the insertion point to the bottom of the document.
5. Press CTRL + V to paste the slide. It is pasted as a graphic.
6. Double-click the slide graphic. Picture formatting tools appear in the ribbon.
7. Select the slide graphic and press DEL to remove it from the document.
8. Leave the document open for the next Try It. Leave the PowerPoint presentation open also.

Embedding a PowerPoint Slide in a Word Document

- You can embed a PowerPoint slide in a Word document. As with other embedding, the slide object remains associated with PowerPoint, so you can double-click to edit it with PowerPoint's own tools at any time.

Try It! Embedding a PowerPoint Slide in a Word Document

1. In **W62TryB_xx** in PowerPoint, select slide 4 and press CTRL + C to copy it.
2. Switch to Word, where **W62TryA_xx** should already be open, and click to move the insertion point to the bottom of the document.
3. On the Home tab, click the down arrow on the Paste button and click Paste Special.
4. Click Microsoft PowerPoint Slide Object.
5. Click OK. The slide is embedded.
6. Double-click the embedded object. It opens in PowerPoint within Word.
7. Click away from the embedded object. The Word ribbon reappears.
8. Close Word, saving your changes. Leave PowerPoint and **W62TryB_xx** open for the next Try It.

Embed the slide as a PowerPoint object

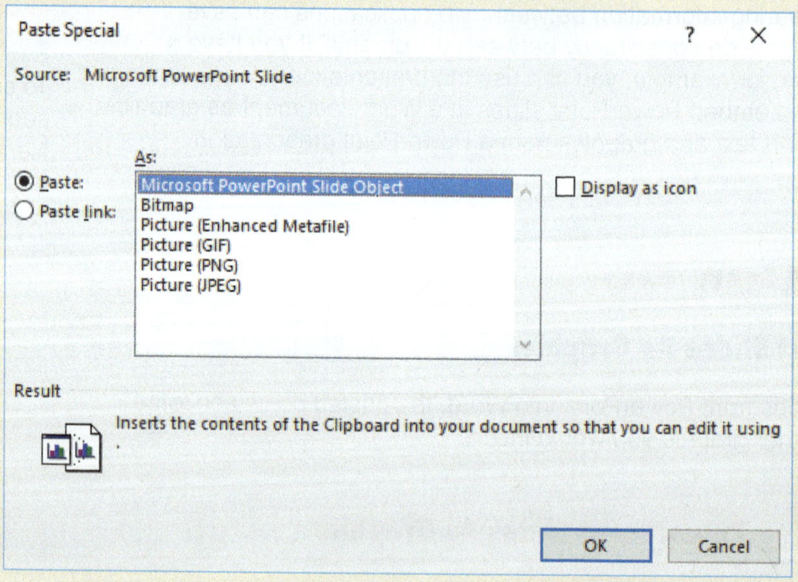

Word 2016, Windows 10, Microsoft Corporation

Exporting PowerPoint Slides and Notes to a Word Document

- For more precise control over the formatting of PowerPoint presentation handouts, you can **export** them to Word. The resulting exported handouts show miniature versions of each slide along with either your speaker notes or blank lines for writing handwritten notes or comments.
- You can optionally link the slides in the Word document to the source presentation, so when you change the source presentation, Word updates the linked slides automatically.

Try It! Exporting PowerPoint Slides and Notes to a Word Document

1. In **W62TryB_xx** in PowerPoint, click File > Export > Create Handouts > Create Handouts. The Send to Microsoft Word dialog box opens.

2. Click Blank lines next to slides.

   ✓ *Notice the Paste link option at the bottom of the dialog box. This exercise does not use it, but you can choose that option to link to the presentation if desired.*

3. Click OK. Word opens, with the handouts as a new document.

4. Close the Word document without saving it. Leave PowerPoint and **W62TryB_xx** open for the next Try It.

Choose a layout to send to Word

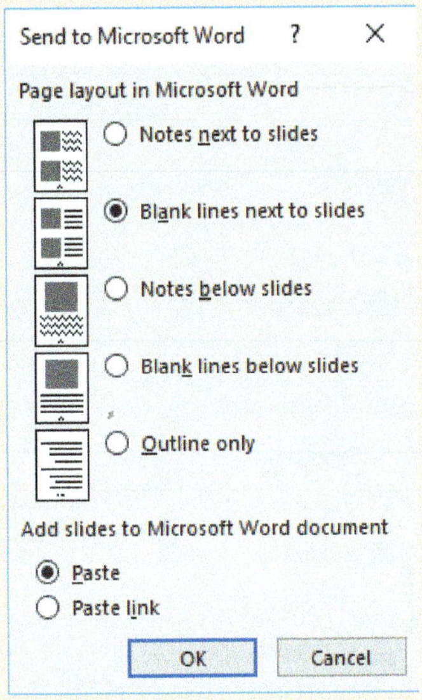

Word 2016, Windows 10, Microsoft Corporation

Exporting PowerPoint Text to a Word Document

- You can export the text from a PowerPoint presentation to Word. In Word, the text appears as an outline, using outline heading levels.
- One way to do this is with the Send to Microsoft Word dialog box, as in the previous section, but choose Outline only instead of one of the other layouts.
- Another way is to save the PowerPoint presentation as an Outline/RTF document. RTF stands for Rich Text Format, a generic word processing format. The following steps show that method.

Try It! Exporting PowerPoint Text to a Word Document

1. In **W62TryB_xx** in PowerPoint, click File > Save As.

2. Navigate to the location where your teacher instructs you to store the files for this lesson.

3. In the Save As dialog box, open the Save as type drop-down list and click Outline/RTF.

4. In the File name box, type **W62TryC_xx**.

5. Click Save.

6. Close PowerPoint without saving changes.

7. Open Word, and open **W62TryC_xx**. If a Convert File dialog box opens, click OK to accept the default of RTF and open the document.

   ✓ *This dialog box might not appear, depending on your settings.*

8. Click View > Outline to see the presentation in outline format.

9. Close Word without saving changes.

(continued)

Try It! Exporting PowerPoint Text to a Word Document *(continued)*

Save in Outline/RTF format

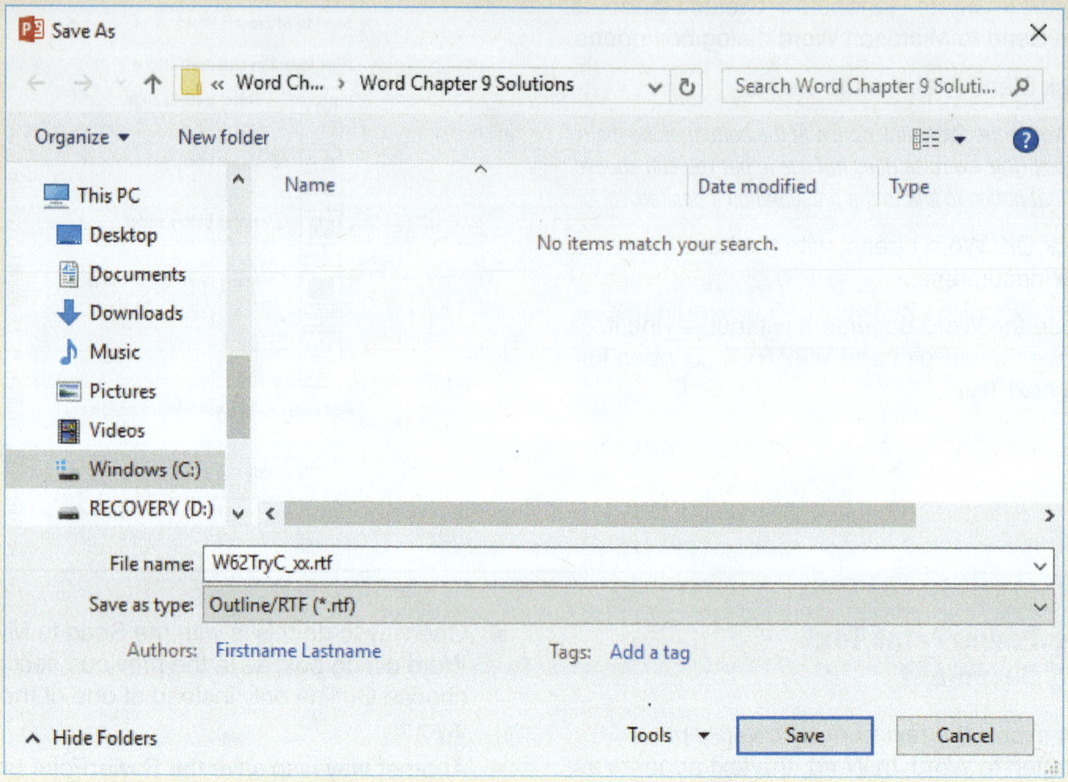

Word 2016, Windows 10, Microsoft Corporation

Using a Word Outline to Create a PowerPoint Presentation

- You can also go the other way between Word and PowerPoint: you can start with a Word outline and convert it to a PowerPoint presentation.
- The first-level headings in the outline form the slide titles, and the subheadings form the slide content.
- Be sure to reset each slide by clicking Home > Reset. Otherwise, the slides will continue to show Word styles and colors even after a new design has been applied.
- Apply the correct layouts to the slides, for example, the Title and Content layout.

Try It! Using a Word Outline to Create a PowerPoint Presentation

1. Start PowerPoint, and click Open Other Presentations.
2. Navigate to the location containing the data files for this lesson.
3. In the Open dialog box, change the file type to All Outlines.
4. Select **W62TryD.docx** and click Open to open the outline in PowerPoint as a presentation.
5. Press and hold the SHIFT key and click the last slide in the thumbnail pane (on the left) to select all four slides. Release the SHIFT key.
6. Click Home > Reset.
7. Click Home > Layout and select Title and Content.
8. Save your work in PowerPoint as **W62TryD_xx** and exit PowerPoint.

Lesson 62—Practice

You are the business development manager at Fresh Food Fair and have completed a study on the benefits and costs of starting a new home delivery service. You have been asked to present your findings at a company meeting. You already have a PowerPoint presentation about the study. You can use pieces of the presentation to create documents to distribute as a package at the meeting. In this project, you will create a cover page for the package using a slide from the PowerPoint presentation.

DIRECTIONS

1. Start Word, if necessary, and open **W62PracticeA** from the data files for this lesson. Save the file as **W62PracticeA_xx** in the location where your teacher instructs you to store the files for this lesson.
2. Replace the text **Your Name** with your own name.
3. Replace the text **Today's Date** with the current date.
4. Click to move the insertion point to the bottom of the document.
5. Start PowerPoint, and open **W62PracticeB.pptx** from the data files for this lesson.
6. Select slide 1 and press CTRL + C to copy it to the Clipboard.
7. Switch to Word.
8. On the **Home** tab, click the down arrow on the **Paste** button, and click **Paste Special**.
9. Click **Paste link**.
10. Click **Microsoft PowerPoint Slide Object**.
11. Click **OK**.
12. Center the pasted slide horizontally, and resize the slide so it fits attractively on the page and is approximately 6" in width.
13. **With your teacher's permission**, print the document.
14. Save and close the document, and exit Word.
15. Close PowerPoint without saving changes.

Lesson 62—Apply

In this project, you will continue to work on the documents that you will distribute at your presentation. You will export the entire presentation to a Word document to use as a handout, leaving blank lines for writing notes. You will also export the text from the presentation as an outline to use as a table of contents for the handout package.

DIRECTIONS

1. Start PowerPoint, and open **W62ApplyA.pptx** from the data files for this lesson.
2. Create handouts in Word that use the **Blank lines below slides** layout. Save that document as **W62ApplyB_xx**.
3. In that document, type your full name and today's date in the Header area.
4. **With your teacher's permission**, print the document.
5. Save and close the document, and exit Word.
6. Switch back to PowerPoint, and create handouts in Word that use the **Outline only** layout. Save that document as **W62ApplyC_xx**.
7. In that document, type your full name and today's date in the Header area.
8. Select the entire document (CTRL + A). Remove the bullets and change the font size to 12-point.
9. **With your teacher's permission**, print the document.
10. Save and close the document, and exit Word.
11. Close the PowerPoint presentation without saving changes, and exit PowerPoint.

Lesson 63

Using Merge to Create Letters, Envelopes, Labels, and E-mail

➤ What You Will Learn

Reviewing the Mail Merge Process
Merging Letters Using the Mail Merge Wizard
Merging Envelopes
Creating Mailing Labels
Creating an E-mail Merge
Filtering Recipients
Applying Rules to a Merge

WORDS TO KNOW

Criteria
Specific conditions used to match a record or entry in a data source file or list.

Filter
To apply one or more criteria to data and exclude data that does not match the criteria.

MAPI
A Microsoft standard that allows messaging programs to work together.

Merge document
The customized document resulting from a merge.

Software Skills Use Mail Merge to customize mass mailings such as letters and e-mails. You type the letter or message text you want each recipient to read, and insert merge fields to customize or personalize the message. Create merged envelopes or labels to send letters by mail. Word can automatically use your e-mail program to send merged e-mail messages. Filter the recipient list to quickly select the records you want to use.

What You Can Do

Reviewing the Mail Merge Process

- Use Mail Merge to create mass mailings, envelopes, labels, or e-mail messages.
- During the merge, Word generates a series of **merge documents** in which the variable information from the data source replaces the merge fields entered in the main document.
- You may use the commands on the Mailings tab of the ribbon to conduct a merge or use the Mail Merge Wizard.

Merging Letters Using the Mail Merge Wizard

- The Mail Merge Wizard prompts you through the step-by-step process of selecting the type of merge, choosing recipients, inserting fields, and previewing letters.
- When inserting a standard field such as <<AddressBlock>>, you will probably want to remove extra line spacing between paragraphs. You can perform this task before the final merge.
- You can merge directly to the printer, but this may result in wasted paper if there is an error in the merge operation.
- A more conservative approach is to merge to a new document, examine the merged copies, and then either print them or make changes to them.
- After merging to a new document, you can also save the new document as a regular Word file, to be printed later, rather than printing immediately.

Try It! Merging Letters Using the Mail Merge Wizard

1. Start Word, and open **W63TryA** from the data files for this lesson.
2. Save the document as **W63TryA_xx** in the location where your teacher instructs you to store the files for this lesson.
3. Click Mailings > Start Mail Merge > Step-by-Step Mail Merge Wizard. The Mail Merge task pane opens.
4. At the bottom of the task pane, click Next: Starting document.
5. Click Next: Select recipients.
6. Under Use an existing list in the task pane, click Browse. Navigate to the location where the data files for this lesson are stored, and click **W63TryB**.
7. Click Open. In the Mail Merge Recipients dialog box, click OK.
8. Click Next: Write your letter at the bottom of the task pane.
9. Click to place the insertion point on the second blank paragraph below the date.
10. In the task pane, click Address block. The Insert Address Block dialog box appears. Click OK.

The Mail Merge Recipients dialog box

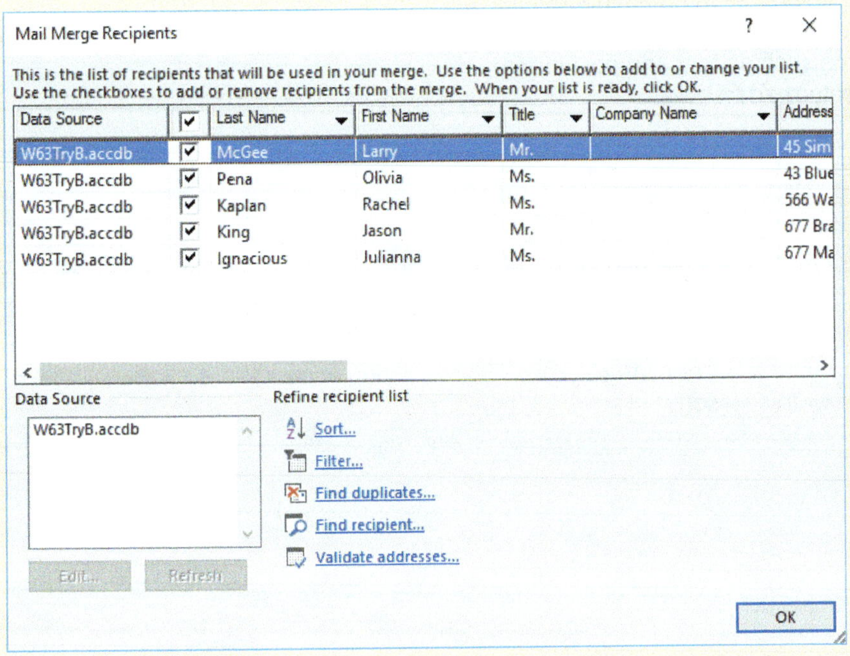

Word 2016, Windows 10, Microsoft Corporation

(continued)

Try It! Merging Letters Using the Mail Merge Wizard *(continued)*

11. Click to place the insertion point immediately before the colon that follows *Dear*.
12. In the task pane, click More items. The Insert Merge Field dialog box opens.
13. Click First Name and click Insert. Then, click Close.
14. Click the <<AddressBlock>> code to move the insertion point into that paragraph.
15. Click Home > Line and Paragraph Spacing > Remove Space After Paragraph (see figure at right).
16. Click Mailings > Preview Results to check that the address block no longer produces extra vertical space.
17. Click Mailings > Finish & Merge > Edit Individual Documents. The Merge to New Document dialog box opens.
18. Click OK.

Remove the space following the paragraph that contains the address block

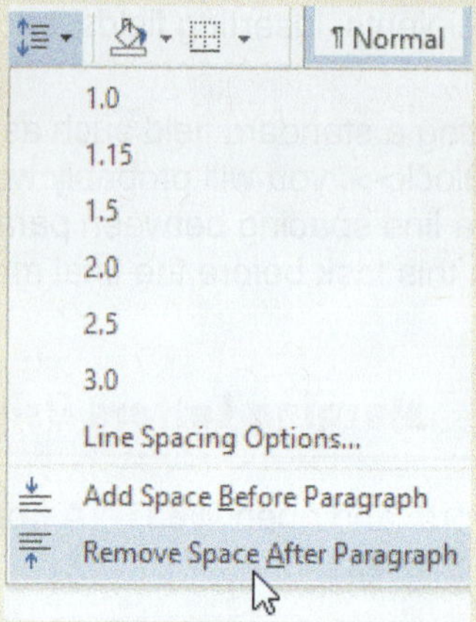

Word 2016, Windows 10, Microsoft Corporation

19. Scroll through the new document, examining the copies for errors.
20. Close the new document without saving changes. Close **W63TryA_xx**, saving changes, and leave Word open for the next Try It.

Merging Envelopes

- To create mail merged envelopes, you follow many of the same steps as when creating form letters.
- Instead of selecting letter as the main document, select envelopes. Then, select the envelope size and specify options such as font and position for the delivery and return addresses.
- You can use the Step-by-Step Mail Merge Wizard or commands on the Mailings tab to merge envelopes manually.

Try It! Merging Envelopes

1. In Word, click File > New and then click Blank document.
2. Save the document as **W63TryC_xx** in the location where your teacher instructs you to store the files for this lesson.
3. Click Mailings > Start Mail Merge > Envelopes.
4. In the Envelope Options dialog box, click OK to accept the default settings.

(continued)

Try It! Merging Envelopes *(continued)*

Envelope Options dialog box

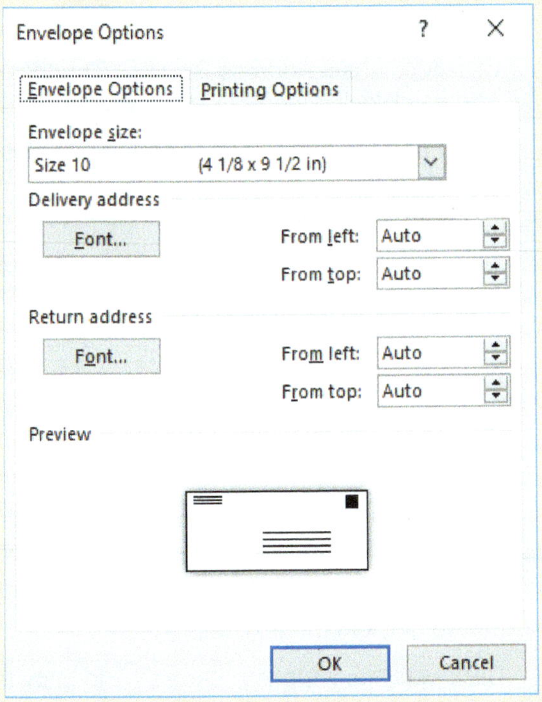

5. Click Mailings > Select Recipients > Use an Existing List.
6. Navigate to the location where the data files for this lesson are stored, and click **W63TryB**.
7. Click Open.
8. At the location of the insertion point, type your full name, press SHIFT + ENTER, type your school address, press SHIFT + ENTER, and type your city or town, state, and ZIP code.
9. Click near the center of the envelope until you see a text box with a single paragraph in it.
10. Click Mailings > Address Block. Click OK.
11. Click Mailings > Preview Results to check your envelope addresses. Use the Next Record button in the Preview Results group to scroll through each envelope and address.
12. Click Mailings > Finish & Merge > Edit Individual Documents. The Merge to New Document dialog box opens.
13. Click OK.
14. Scroll through the new document, examining the envelopes for errors.
15. Close the new document without saving changes. Close **W63TryC_xx**, saving changes, and leave Word open for the next Try It.

Creating Mailing Labels

- Creating mail merged labels is very similar to creating merged envelopes.
- After choosing labels as the merge option, you select the label type and size that match the actual labels on which you will print.
- Insert the merge block or merge fields on the first label.
- Once the first label is complete, you update the remaining labels to match.
- For labels, it is easiest to use the <<AddressBlock>> merge block, which includes all fields for a standard mailing address.
- If you insert individual fields, such as first name, last name, City, State, and ZIP Code, you must type the required punctuation, such as the comma between the city and state.
- Preview the labels the same way you learned earlier in this lesson.
- You can then merge the labels to a new document, if desired, or print them from the merge document.

Try It! Creating Mailing Labels

1. In Word, start a new blank document and save it as **W63TryD_xx** in the location where your teacher instructs you to store the files for this lesson.
2. Click Mailings > Start Mail Merge > Labels.
3. In the Label Options dialog box (see figure below), click the Label vendors drop-down arrow and click Avery US Letter.

   ✓ *Avery is a company that sells mailing labels; you would select the type of label you have on which to print.*

4. In the Product number list, click 5660 Easy Peel Address Labels, and then click OK. Word creates a table that has cells the same size and in the same layout as the labels you selected.

   ✓ *If you cannot see the cells in the document, click the Table Tools Layout tab and, in the Table group, click View Gridlines.*

5. Click Mailings > Select Recipients > Use an Existing List.
6. Navigate to the location where the data files for this lesson are stored, and click **W63TryB**.
7. Click Open.
8. Click in the first paragraph of the first label.
9. Click Mailings > Address Block. The Insert Address Block dialog box displays.
10. Verify that the Insert recipient's name in this format check box is selected and that *Mr. Joshua Randall Jr.* is highlighted in the list.
11. Click to clear the Insert company name check box.
12. Verify that the Insert postal address check box is selected and that the Only include the country/region if different than option button is selected.
13. Verify that the Format address according to the destination country/region check box is selected.
14. Click OK. Word inserts the <<AddressBlock>> merge block in the first cell.
15. Click Mailings > Update Labels to copy the layout from the first cell to the remaining cells.

Label Options dialog box

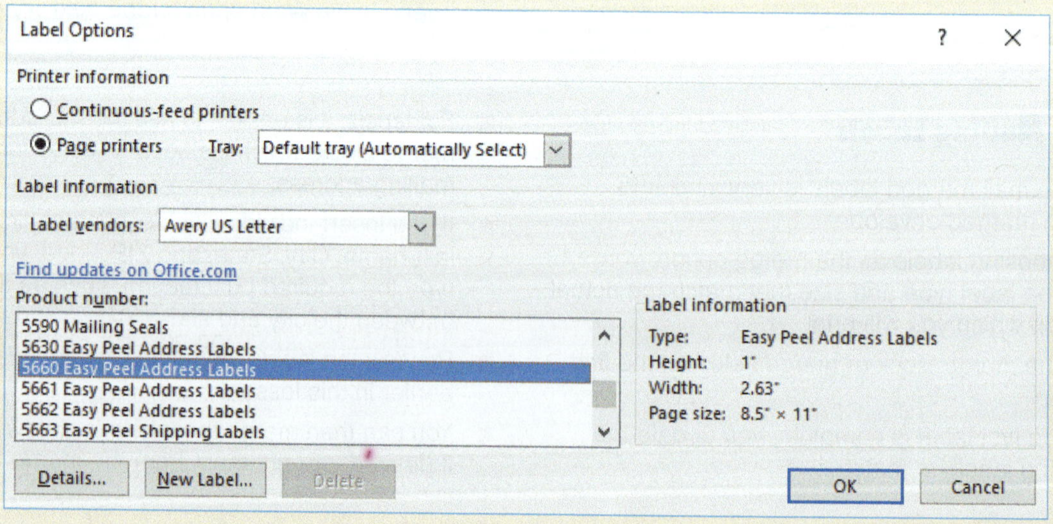

Word 2016, Windows 10, Microsoft Corporation

(continued)

Try It! Creating Mailing Labels *(continued)*

16 Click Mailings > Preview Results .Word displays the label document with the actual addresses in place of the merge block fields. Note that the text in the labels with four lines does not fit within the cell.

17 Click Preview Results to return to the merge codes.

18 Select the first table cell, click the Layout tab, and use the Spacing Before increment arrows to set the spacing to 0.

19 On the Mailings tab, click Update Labels .

20 Preview the labels to make sure the spacing change worked.

21 Click Finish & Merge .

22 **With your teacher's permission**, click Print Documents. The Merge to Printer box displays.

23 Click OK to print the labels.

✓ *You can print the labels on plain paper.*

24 Close W63TryD_xx, saving changes, and leave Word open for the next Try It.

Insert Address Block dialog box

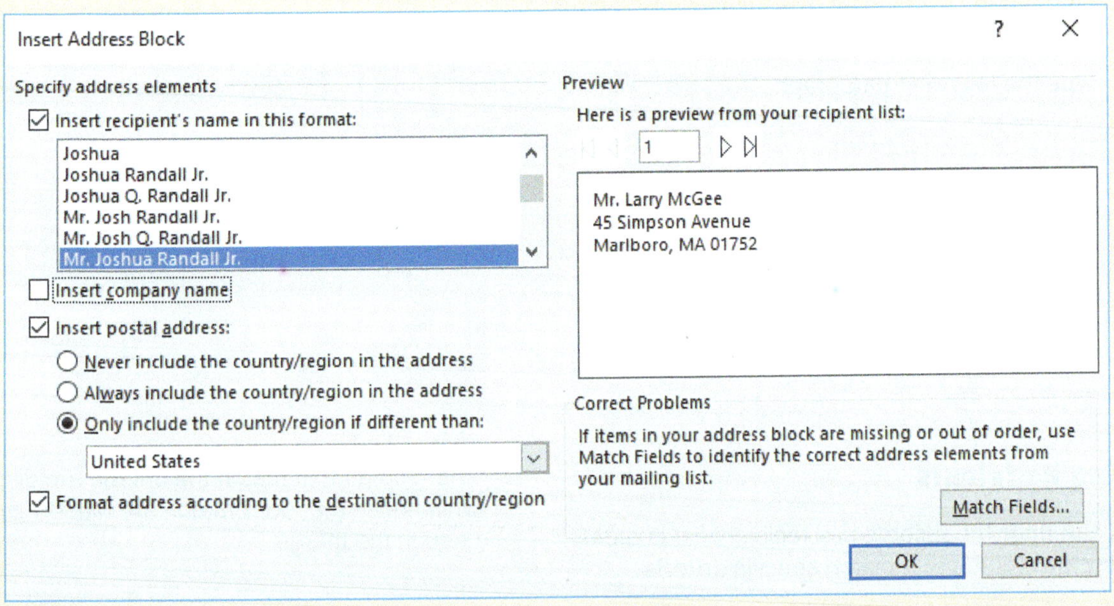

Word 2016, Windows 10, Microsoft Corporation

Creating an E-mail Merge

- Another way to use Mail Merge to customize communications is to set up and complete a merge using e-mail messages as the main document.
- The data source must contain a field that contains the e-mail addresses.
- You type the message text as if it were any normal Word document. You can optionally insert merge fields in the message body.
- You do not have to insert the e-mail address field in the main document; Word will ask for it when you complete the merge.
- You select options for merging to e-mail in the Merge to E-mail dialog box. For example, you may enter the text that will be displayed in the Subject field of the message header, and select the format to use for the message—either HTML, plain text, or as an attachment.
- When you merge to e-mail, Word does not create a merge document as it does when you merge letters, envelopes, or labels. Instead, the messages are created and sent to your e-mail program's Outbox.
- To successfully complete a merge to e-mail, you must have a **MAPI**-compatible e-mail program, such as Microsoft Office Outlook, installed and set up for use with Word.

Try It! Creating an E-mail Merge

1. In Word, start a new blank document and save it as **W63TryE_xx** in the location where your teacher instructs you to store the files for this lesson.
2. Click Mailings > Start Mail Merge > E-mail Messages.
3. Click Select Recipients > Use an Existing List.
4. Navigate to the location where the data files for this lesson are stored and click **W63TryF**.
5. Click Open.
6. Type **Dear** and press SPACE.
7. Click Insert Merge Field > First_Name. Type a colon (**:**) after «*First_Name*» and press ENTER.
8. Type the following paragraph:

   I hope you will join me in the conference room at 3:00 p.m. for the quarterly project review.
9. Click Mailings > Finish & Merge > Send Email Messages.
10. In the Merge to E-mail dialog box, click the To drop-down arrow and select Email_Address. Then, in the Subject line box, type **Quarterly review**.
11. **With your teacher's permission**, click OK to send the e-mail; otherwise, click Cancel.
12. Save the changes to **W63TryE_xx**, and leave it open to use in the next Try It.

Set e-mail sending options

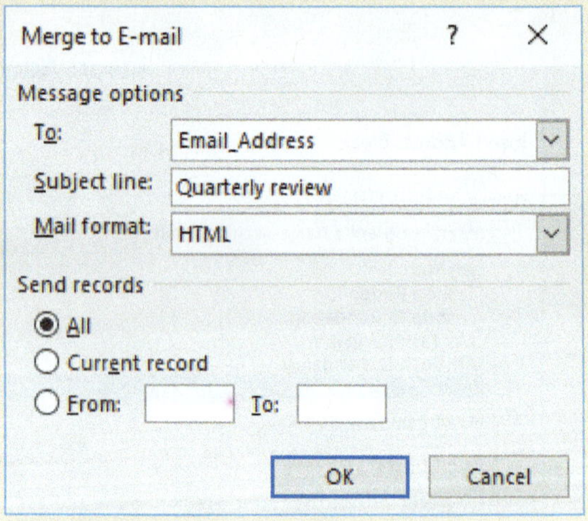

Word 2016, Windows 10, Microsoft Corporation

Filtering Recipients

- You can **filter** the records in a recipient list in order to display records that match specific **criteria**.
- The records that match the criteria are displayed, while those that don't match are hidden and not used in the merge.

Try It! Filtering Recipients

1. In the **W63TryE_xx** file, click Mailings > Edit Recipient List.
2. Click the Filter hyperlink. The Filter and Sort dialog box appears with the Filter Records tab displayed.
3. Open the Field drop-down list, and click State.
4. Click in the Compare to text box, or press TAB twice, and type **IN**.
5. Click OK to close the Filter and Sort dialog box. Only the record where the State is IN appears.

   ✓ *Notice that with a filter, unwanted records are hidden altogether, not just unchecked.*
6. Click the Filter hyperlink again.
7. Click Clear All.
8. Click OK to close the Filter and Sort dialog box.

(continued)

Try It! Filtering Recipients *(continued)*

9. Click OK to close the Mail Merge Recipients dialog box.

10. Save the changes to **W63TryE_xx**, and leave it open to use in the next Try It.

Filter records based on one or more criteria

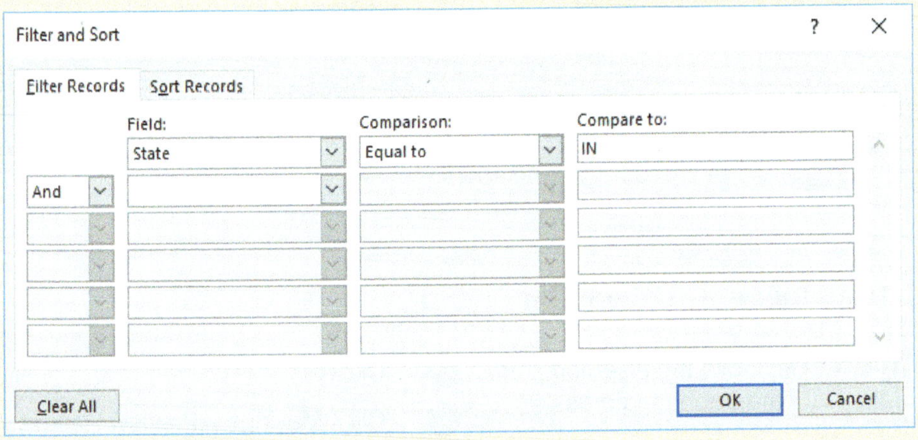

Word 2016, Windows 10, Microsoft Corporation

Applying Rules to a Merge

- Rules are special codes that you can insert in a mail merge main document. For example, <<FILLIN>> is one of these codes. You can use it to prompt the user for input each time the merge is run, to insert information that may change each time.
- Another rule code is <<IF…>>, which enables you to create logical conditions for a merge, and insert certain content only if the conditions are met.

Try It! Prompting the User for Input in a Merge

1. In the **W63TryE_xx** file, delete *3:00 p.m.* Do not delete the space before it or after it.

2. Click Mailings > Rules > Fill-in. The Insert Word Field: Fill-in dialog box opens.

3. In the Prompt box, type **What time is the meeting?**.

Set up to prompt the user for information

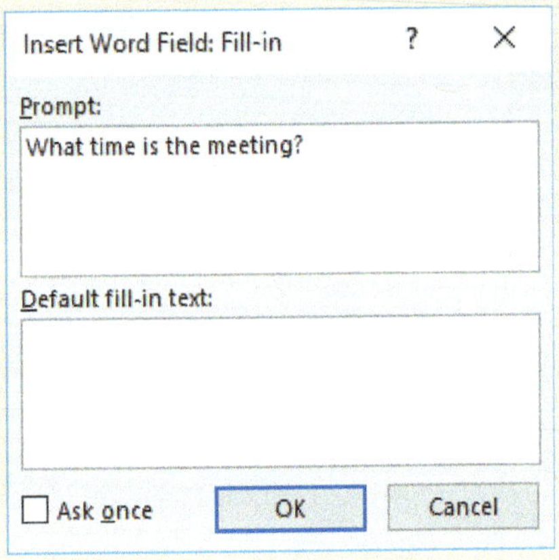

Word 2016, Windows 10, Microsoft Corporation

(continued)

Try It! Prompting the User for Input in a Merge *(continued)*

4. Click OK. A prompt appears for the time.
5. Type **4:00 p.m.** and click OK.
6. Save the changes to **W63TryE_xx**, and leave it open to use in the next Try It.

When prompted, enter the meeting time

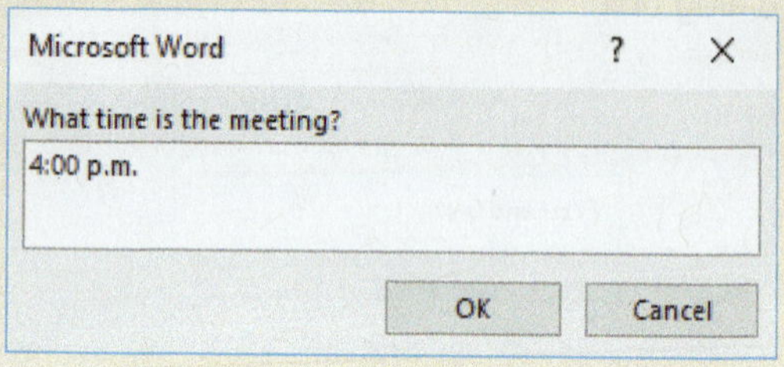

Word 2016, Windows 10, Microsoft Corporation

Try It! Setting Up an If... Condition

1. In the **W63TryE_xx** file, move the insertion point to the end of the last paragraph, and press SPACE.
2. Click Mailings > Rules > If…Then…Else.
3. Open the Field name drop-down list, and click City.
4. Open the Comparison drop-down list, and click Not equal to.
5. In the Compare to text box, type **Boston**.
6. In the Insert this text box, type the following:

   Those who are not in the Boston office may attend via video teleconferencing by dialing into the Conference Center and entering code 4432.

7. Click OK.
8. Click Mailings > Preview Results. The first record includes the added paragraph.
9. On the Mailings tab, in the Preview Results group, click the Next Record button. The next record does not include the added paragraph.
10. Save and close the document, and exit Word.

Lesson 63—Practice

A letter inviting Michigan Avenue Athletic Club members to join a volleyball team becomes a simple task using the Mail Merge feature. The form letter will be personalized with each person's name and address. In this project, you will create the letter document, merge with a data source to generate the letters, and then create merged envelopes.

DIRECTIONS

1. In Windows, copy **W63PracticeA** from the data files for the lesson. Paste the copy in the location where your teacher instructs you to store the files for this lesson. Name the copy **W63PracticeA_xx**.
2. Start Word, if necessary, and in a new blank document, type the text shown in Figure 63-1 on the next page. Substitute today's date for *Today's Date*.
3. Type your full name and today's date in the header area.
4. Save the document as **W63PracticeB_xx** in the location where your teacher instructs you to store the files for this lesson.
5. Click **Mailings** > **Start Mail Merge** > **Letters**.
6. Click **Select Recipients** > **Use an Existing List**.
7. Navigate to the location where you are storing files for this lesson, click **W63PracticeA_xx**, and click **Open**.
8. Click to move the insertion point to the line immediately below today's date.
9. Click **Mailings** > **Address Block**.
10. Click **OK** to accept the default address block settings.
11. With the insertion point in the <<AddressBlock>> paragraph, click **Home** > **Line and Paragraph Spacing** > **Remove Space After Paragraph**.
12. Move the insertion point to the blank line below <<AddressBlock>>.
13. Type **Dear**, and press SPACE once.
14. Click **Mailings** > **Insert Merge Field** > **First_Name**.
15. Type a colon (**:**).
16. Click **Mailings** > **Preview Results**. Repeat to return to viewing the merge codes.
17. Insert a blank paragraph below the <<AddressBlock>>, and remove space below the blank paragraph.
18. **With your teacher's permission**, click **Finish & Merge** > **Edit Individual Documents** to merge the letters to a new document and then print them. Close the merged letter document without saving it, if applicable.
19. Close the **W63PracticeB_xx** document, saving changes, and leave Word open.
20. In Word, create a new document and save it as **W63PracticeC_xx**.
21. Click **Mailings** > **Start Mail Merge** > **Envelopes**.
22. Click **OK** to accept the default envelope options.
23. Click **Select Recipients** > **Use an Existing List**.
24. Navigate to the location where you are storing files for this lesson, click **W63PracticeA_xx**, and click **Open**.
25. At the location of the insertion point, type your full name, your school address, and your city or town, state, and ZIP Code.
26. Click near the center of the envelope to locate the paragraph for the delivery address, and then click **Mailings** > **Address Block**.
27. Click **OK**.
28. Click **Preview Results** and preview all envelopes.
29. **With your teacher's permission**, click **Finish & Merge** > **Edit Individual Documents** to merge the envelopes to a new document and then print them. Close the merged envelope document without saving it, if applicable.
30. Close the **W63PracticeC_xx** document, saving changes, and exit Word.

Figure 63-1

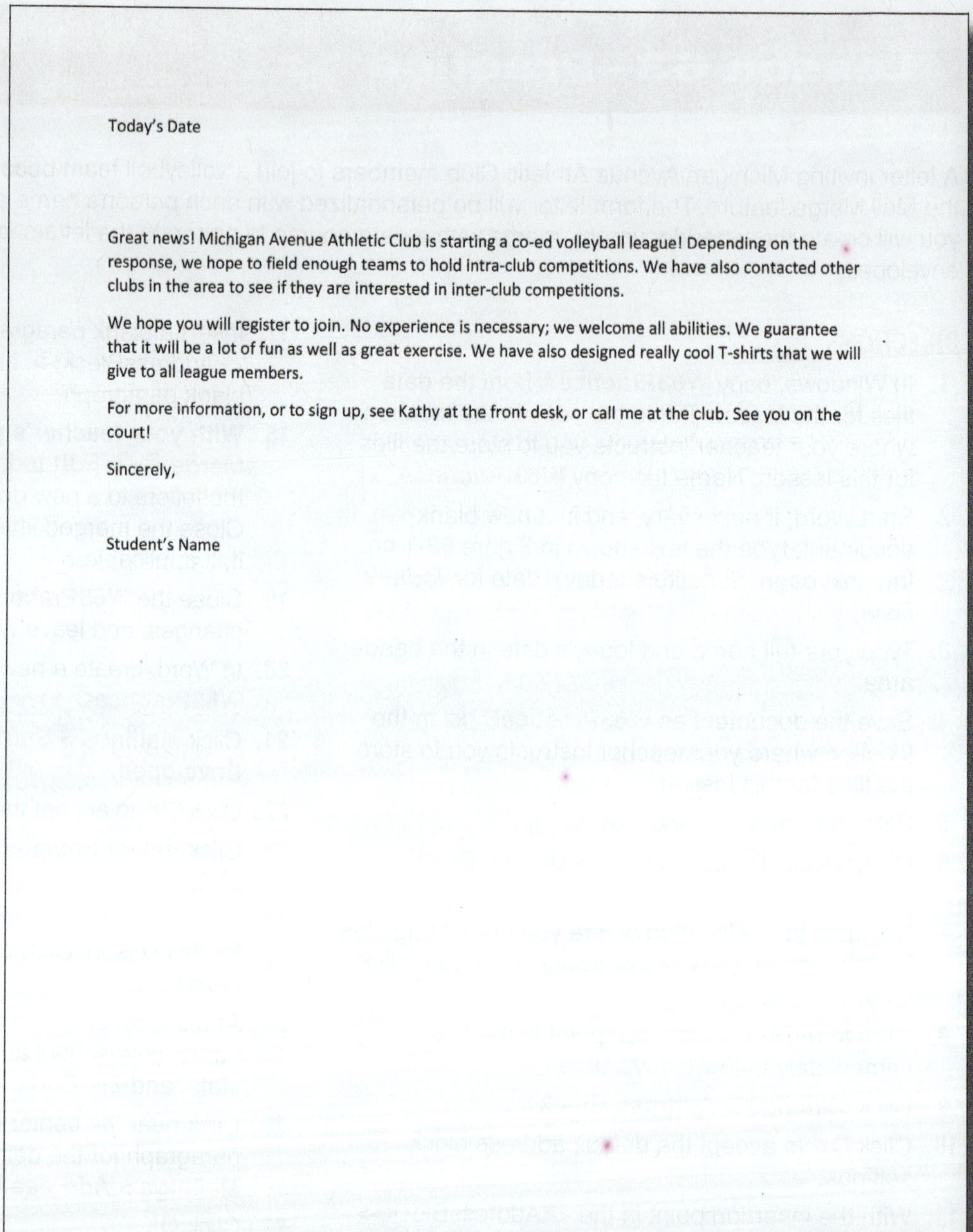

Today's Date

Great news! Michigan Avenue Athletic Club is starting a co-ed volleyball league! Depending on the response, we hope to field enough teams to hold intra-club competitions. We have also contacted other clubs in the area to see if they are interested in inter-club competitions.

We hope you will register to join. No experience is necessary; we welcome all abilities. We guarantee that it will be a lot of fun as well as great exercise. We have also designed really cool T-shirts that we will give to all league members.

For more information, or to sign up, see Kathy at the front desk, or call me at the club. See you on the court!

Sincerely,

Student's Name

Word 2016, Windows 10, Microsoft Corporation

Lesson 63—Apply

You must notify all Michigan Avenue Athletic Club exercise instructors that there is an important meeting tomorrow. In this project, you will use Mail Merge to create an e-mail message about the meeting, and you will filter an existing data source file to select only exercise instructors as recipients. You will use a rule to customize messages to water aerobics instructors and other instructors.

DIRECTIONS

1. In Windows, copy **W63ApplyA** from the data files for the lesson. Paste the copy in the location where your teacher instructs you to store the files for this lesson. Name the copy **W63ApplyA_xx**.
2. Start Word, and open **W63ApplyB** from the data files for this lesson.
3. Save the file as **W63ApplyB_xx** in the location where your teacher instructs you to store the files for this lesson.
4. In the header, type your full name and today's date. Close the header and footer.
5. Start a Mail Merge for e-mail messages.
6. Select **W63ApplyA_xx** as the data source.
7. At the insertion point, insert the First_Name merge field and then type **:**.
8. Filter the recipients so that the list includes only those whose Position is **Exercise Instructor**.
9. Use an If...Then...Else rule to create a condition where if the Specialty is **Water Aerobics**, the following sentence appears immediately before the last sentence:

   Please bring a current copy of the pool schedule.

   Otherwise the following sentence should appear in that same position:

   Please bring a current copy of your room schedule.

   ✓ *See Figure 63-2 for guidance on setting up the rule.*
10. Merge to a new document. Save the new document as **W63ApplyC_xx** in the location where your teacher instructs you to store the files for this lesson.
11. Save and close all files, and exit Word.

Figure 63-2

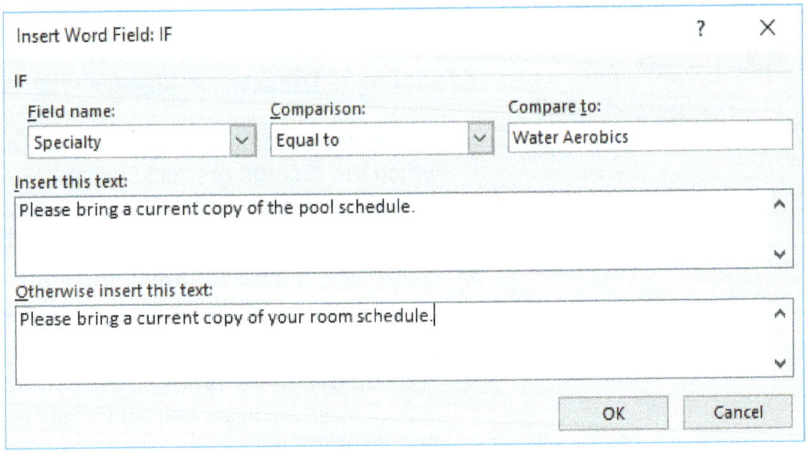

Word 2016, Windows 10, Microsoft Corporation

Lesson 64

Creating a Directory with Mail Merge

➤ What You Will Learn

- Creating a Directory Merge
- Adding Formatting to a Field Code
- Sorting Records in the Data Source
- Selecting Specific Records
- Customizing Fields in an Address List

WORDS TO KNOW

Directory
A single document listing multiple records from a data source file.

Switch
A backslash (\) followed by a code that specifies an option. Switches are used with merge field codes in Word, and also in some programming languages and operating systems.

Software Skills You can use Mail Merge to create a directory, such as a telephone directory, an address list, or a customer directory. You can customize a Word data source file by adding, deleting, renaming or moving fields. Mail Merge makes it easy to select records in your data source file, so you can include only specific recipients in a merge. You can also sort the data source file so that the merge documents are generated in alphabetical or numerical order. Use formatting options, such as switches and field properties, to create documents that are accurate and attractive.

What You Can Do

Creating a Directory Merge

- A **directory** merge is a type of mail merge in which the records are all listed, one-by-one, in a single copy of the document, as shown in Figure 64-1.
- Unlike with a label merge, the records are not separated into separate table cells; they appear as a list on a normal Word page.
- You can use many types of data source files, including an address list, an Excel file, or an Access database.
- You arrange the layout for the first entry in the directory; Mail Merge uses that layout for all entries.

Figure 64-1

NATURA LAMB AND RICE CAT FOOD
Weight: 10 lb
Price: $22.50

NATURA KITTEN FOOD
Weight: 10 lb
Price: $22.50

NATURA ADULT CAT FOOD
Weight: 10 lb
Price: $22.50

NATURA SENIOR CAT FOOD
Weight: 10 lb
Price: $22.50

Word 2016, Windows 10, Microsoft Corporation

- You may type text, spacing, and punctuation, and you can include formatting. For example, you can apply bold, italic, or underline formatting to any merge field code.
- In the merge field properties, you can specify additional formatting, such as uppercase, lowercase, first capital, or title case.

Try It! Starting a Directory Merge with an Existing Access Database

1. Start Word, and save a new blank document as **W64TryA_xx** in the location where your teacher instructs you to store the files for this lesson.
2. Click Mailings > Start Mail Merge > Directory.
3. Click Mailings > Select Recipients > Use an Existing List.
4. Navigate to the location where the data files for this lesson are stored and select **W64TryB**. Click Open.
5. Save the changes to **W64TryA_xx**, and leave it open to use in the next Try It.

Try It! Inserting Merge Fields

1. In the **W64TryA_xx** file, click Mailings > Insert Merge Field > Product.
2. Position the insertion point immediately following <<*Product*>>, and press SHIFT + ENTER.

   ✓ *SHIFT + ENTER inserts a line break without a paragraph break.*
3. Type **Weight:** and press SPACE. Click Insert Merge Field > Weight.
4. Press SHIFT + ENTER to move to the next line.
5. Type **Price:** and press SPACE. Click Insert Merge Field > Price.
6. Press ENTER twice.
7. Drag across <<*Product*>> to select it, and press CTRL + B to make it bold.
8. Right-click <<*Product*>> and click Edit Field.
9. Under Field properties, click Uppercase in the Format box.
10. Click to mark the Preserve formatting during updates check box.
11. Click OK.

The main document contains a combination of typed text and inserted merge fields

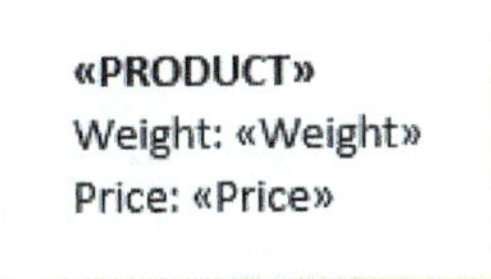

Word 2016, Windows 10, Microsoft Corporation

12. Save the changes to **W64TryA_xx**, and leave it open to use in the next Try It.

Try It! Previewing and Merging the Directory

1. In the **W64TryA_xx** file, click Mailings > Preview Results. Click Preview Results again to return to viewing fields.

   ✓ *When previewing, only one record appears. This is normal. You will see all the records when you actually perform the merge.*
2. Click Mailings > Finish & Merge > Edit Individual Documents. Click OK. The merged directory appears.
3. Close the merged document without saving.
4. Save the changes to **W64TryA_xx**, and leave it open to use in the next Try It.

Adding Formatting to a Field Code

- You may have noticed that in your results in the preceding Try It the prices were not formatted as currency.
- To format a merge field code, you manually edit the field code to include switches. A **switch** is a backslash \ followed by a code that indicates a certain option.
- The numeric format switch is \#. It is followed by a pattern that indicates the formatting you want, plus any symbols, such as $, that should be included.
- An example of a switch for currency with two decimal places is \# $#,##0.00. The first # symbol is for numeric format. The following # symbols represent optional number places. The 0s represent required number places.
- There are many more specialty options available for this switch; see the Word 2016 Help system for details.

Try It! Adding Formatting to a Field Code

1. In the **W64TryA_xx** file, right-click <<*Price*>> and click Edit Field.
2. In the Field dialog box, click the Field Codes button.

   ✓ *In the Field codes text box, MERGEFIELD Price appears.*
3. In the Field codes text box, click to move the insertion point after *Price*.
4. Press SPACE once and type **\# "$,0.00"**.
5. Click to mark the Preserve formatting during updates check box.
6. Click OK.
7. Save your work.
8. Click Mailings > Finish & Merge > Edit Individual Documents. Click OK.

   ✓ *The merged directory appears. This time the prices are formatted as currency.*
9. Close the merged document without saving.
10. Save the changes to **W64TryA_xx**, and leave it open to use in the next Try It.

Add the switch to the end of the field code text

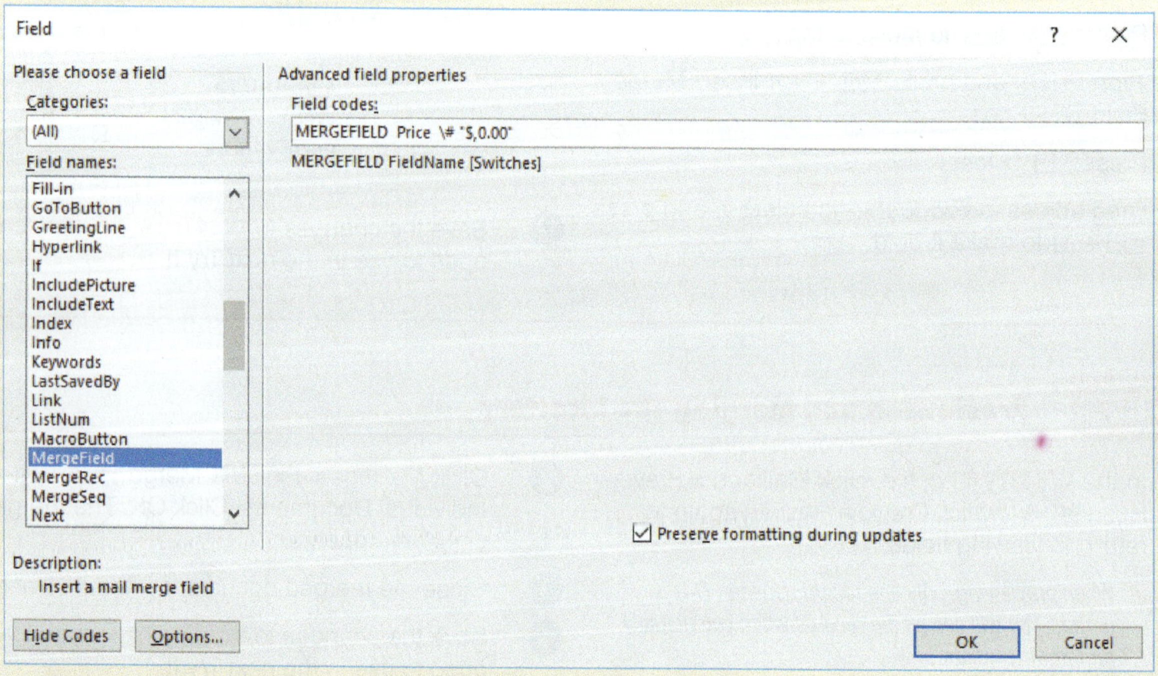

Word 2016, Windows 10, Microsoft Corporation

Sorting Records in the Data Source

- You can quickly change the order of records in a recipient list based on the data entered in any column in the list.
- Simply click any column heading in the Mail Merge Recipients dialog box to sort the records into ascending order.
- Click the column heading again to sort the records into descending order.

Try It! Sorting Records in the Data Source

1. In the **W64TryA_xx** file, click Mailings > Edit Recipient List.
2. Click the Product column heading. The list of records becomes sorted by that field.
3. Click the Product column heading again. The list becomes sorted in the reverse order.
4. Click the Sort hyperlink below the records. The Filter and Sort dialog box opens.
5. Open the Sort by drop-down list, and click Weight.
6. Click the Ascending option button next to Weight.
7. Open the Then by drop-down list, and click Product.
8. Click OK.
9. Click OK to close the Mail Merge Recipients dialog box.
10. Save the changes to **W64TryA_xx**, and leave it open to use in the next Try It.

Click a column heading to sort by that field

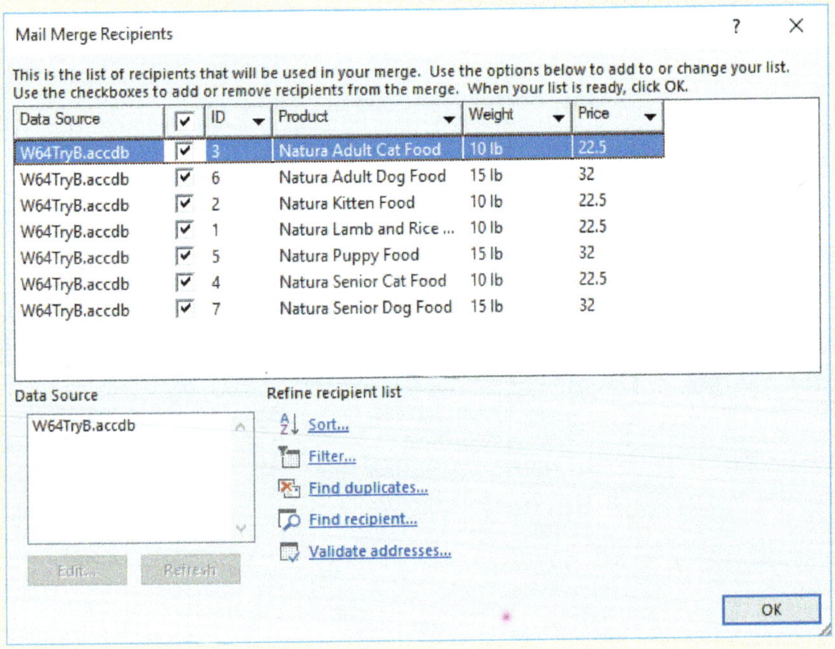

Word 2016, Windows 10, Microsoft Corporation

To sort by more than one field, use the Filter and Sort dialog box

Word 2016, Windows 10, Microsoft Corporation

Selecting Specific Records

- By default, all the records in the data source are selected to be included in a merge.
- You can select the specific records you want to include. For example, you might want to send letters only to the people who live in a specific town, or list products less than a certain dollar amount.

✓ *You learned about filtering records in Lesson 63.*

- To indicate that a recipient is selected, Word displays a check in the check box at the left end of the recipient's row in the Mail Merge Recipients dialog box.
- You click the check box to clear the check, or click the empty box to select the recipient again.

Try It! Selecting Specific Records

1. In the **W64TryA_xx** file, click Mailings > Edit Recipient List.
2. Drag the divider between the Product and Weight column headings to the right so that no entries in the Product column are truncated.
3. Click the check box in the top-most row (the row that contains the column headings). All the check boxes for the individual records are cleared.
4. Click the check boxes for the records that contain the word *Cat* or *Kitten* in the product name.
5. Click OK.
6. Save and close the document. Leave Word open to use in the next Try It.

Only certain records are selected

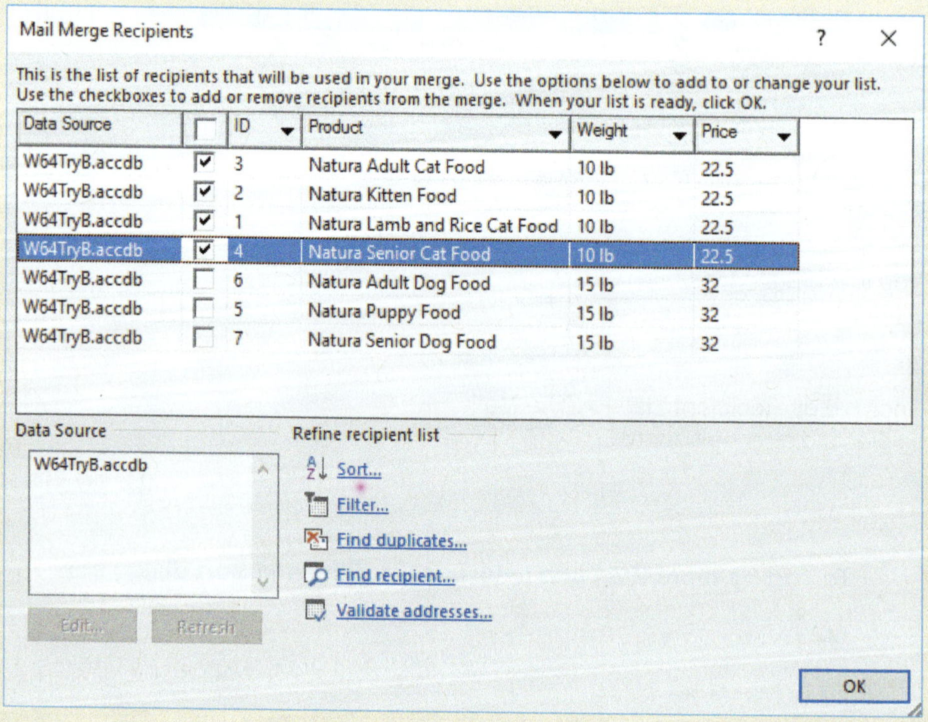

Word 2016, Windows 10, Microsoft Corporation

Customizing Fields in an Address List

- An address list is a simple data source that you can create in Word.

  ✓ *You learned how to create an address list in Word, Lesson 26.*

- You can customize the fields in an address list to change field names, delete unused fields, or add fields specific to your needs.
- You can also move fields up or down in the field list.
- To create a new address list, click Type a New List in the Select Recipients drop-down list.
- To customize fields in the new list, click the Customize Columns button in the New Address List dialog box.
- To customize fields in an existing list, click the Customize Columns button in the Edit Data Source dialog box.

Try It! Copying a Data File in Windows

✓ *This procedure is necessary because you will be making changes to a data file, but there is no way of making a copy of it via Word as you normally would with Word documents.*

1. In File Explorer, navigate to the location where the data files for this lesson are stored, and select **W64TryC**.
2. Press CTRL + C to copy the file.
3. Navigate to the location where your teacher instructs you to store the files for this lesson and press CTRL + V to paste the file.
4. Select the copied file and press F2 to rename it. Type **W64TryC_xx**, and press ENTER .
5. Close File Explorer.

Try It! Customizing Fields in an Address List

1. In Word, open **W64TryD** from the data files for this lesson. Save the file as **W64TryD_xx** in the location where your teacher instructs you to store the files for this lesson.
2. Click Mailings > Select Recipients > Use an Existing List.
3. Navigate to the location where your teacher instructs you to store the files for this lesson, and click **W64TryC_xx**.
4. Click Open.
5. Click Mailings > Edit Recipient List . The Mail Merge Recipients dialog box opens.
6. Under Data Source near the bottom of the dialog box, click the name of the data source.
7. Click Edit. The Edit Data Source dialog box opens.
8. Click Customize Columns. If prompted to save changes, click Yes.
9. Click the Last Name field to select it.

   ✓ *The new field will appear after the selected field.*

Customize fields in an address list

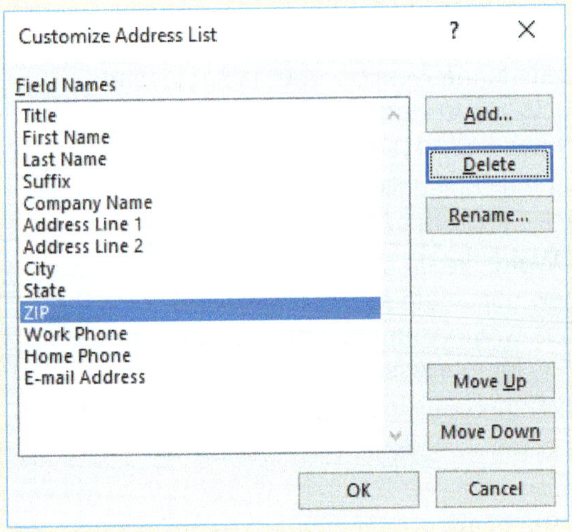

Word 2016, Windows 10, Microsoft Corporation

10. Click Add.
11. Type **Suffix** and click OK.
12. Click the Work Phone field, and click Move Up.
13. Click the ZIP Code field, and click Rename.
14. Type **ZIP**, and click OK.

(continued)

Try It! **Customizing Fields in an Address List** *(continued)*

15 Click Country or Region, and click Delete. Click Yes to confirm.

16 Click OK to close the Customize Address List dialog box.

17 Click OK to close the Edit Data Source dialog box. Click Yes to confirm saving the changes.

18 Click OK to close the Mail Merge Recipients dialog box.

19 Save and close the document, and exit Word.

Lesson 64—Practice

You work in the Human Resources department at the Michigan Avenue Athletic Club and have been asked to create a directory of the club's personal trainers to give out to members. You have an existing address list file that lists all trainers and exercise instructors. In this project, you will start a directory merge, select the existing address list as the data source, and insert and format merge fields.

DIRECTIONS

1. In Windows, navigate to the location where the data files for this lesson are stored, and select **W64PracticeA**.
2. Press CTRL + C to copy the file.
3. Navigate to the location where your teacher instructs you to store the files for this lesson, and press CTRL + V to paste the file.
4. Select the copied file and press F2 to rename it. Type **W64PracticeA_xx**, and press ENTER.
5. Start Word, create a blank document, and save the new document as **W64PracticeB_xx** in the location where your teacher instructs you to store the files for this lesson.
6. Click **Mailings** > **Start Mail Merge** > **Directory**.
7. Click **Mailings** > **Select Recipients** > **Use an Existing List**.
8. Navigate to the location where you placed the copy in step 3, and select **W64PracticeA_xx**.
9. Click **Open**.
10. Type **Name:** and press SPACE once.
11. Click **Mailings** > **Insert Merge Field** > **First_Name**.
12. Press SPACE once.
13. Click **Insert Merge Field** > **Last_Name**. Press ENTER.
14. Right-click <<*First_Name*>> and click **Edit Field**.
15. Under Field properties, click **Uppercase** in the Format box.
16. Click to mark the **Preserve formatting during updates** check box.
17. Click **OK**.
18. Right-click <<*Last_Name*>> and click **Edit Field**.
19. Under Field properties, click **Uppercase** in the Format box.
20. Click to mark the **Preserve formatting during updates** check box.
21. Click **OK**.
22. In the header, type your full name and today's date. Close the header and footer.
23. Save and close the document, and exit Word.

Lesson 64—Apply

In this project, you will continue to work on the directory of personal trainers at the Michigan Avenue Athletic Club. You will select the records you need from the data source. You will also sort the list before generating the directory.

DIRECTIONS

1. In Windows, copy **W64ApplyA** from the data files for the lesson. Paste the copy in the folder where your teacher instructs you to store the files for this lesson. Name the copy **W64ApplyA_xx**.
2. Start Word, and open **W64ApplyB** from the data files for this lesson.
3. Save the document as **W64ApplyB_xx** in the location where your teacher instructs you to store the files for this lesson.
4. In the header, type your full name and today's date. Close the header and footer.
5. Select **W64ApplyA_xx** as the data source.
6. Sort the records by **Position**.
7. Exclude records from the merge where the Position is **Exercise Instructor** by clearing the check boxes for each of those records.

   ✓ *Sorting the records by Position (step 6) makes it easier to find the records to exclude (step 7).*
8. Sort all records in A to Z order by **Last_Name**.
9. Edit the data source as follows:
   a. After the Specialty field, add a new field called **Accepting New Clients**.
   b. For each personal trainer, type **Yes** in the **Accepting New Clients** field.
10. Position the insertion point after <<*Specialty*>> and press SHIFT + ENTER.
11. Type **Accepting New Clients:**, bold the text, and press SPACE once.
12. Insert the **Accepting_New_Clients** field.
13. Merge to a new document. The finished document should resemble Figure 64-2 on the next page.
14. Save the new document as **W64ApplyC_xx** in the location where your teacher instructs you to store the files for this lesson.
15. **With your teacher's permission**, print one copy of the new document.
16. Save and close all documents, and exit Word.

Figure 64-2

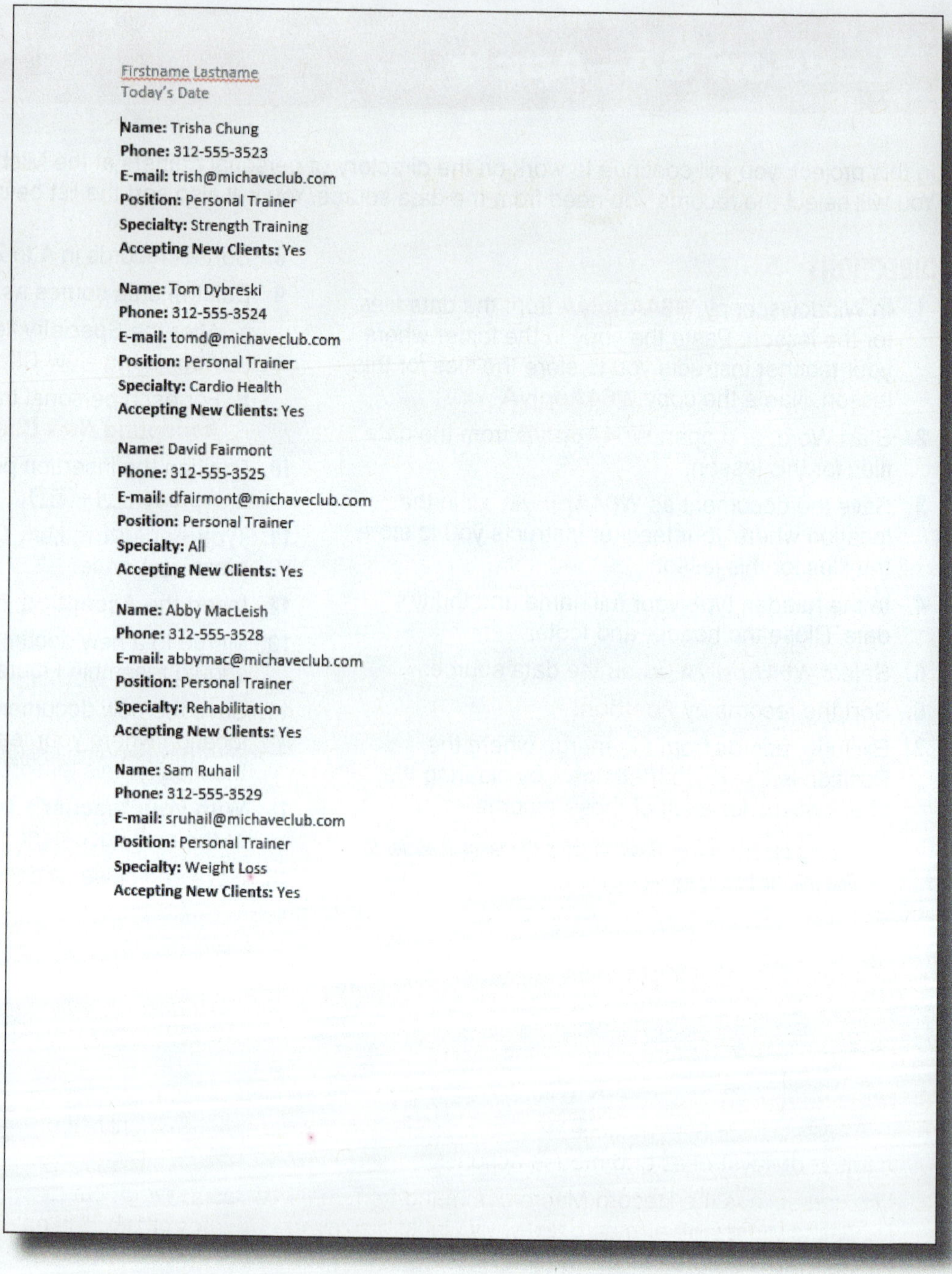

Firstname Lastname
Today's Date

Name: Trisha Chung
Phone: 312-555-3523
E-mail: trish@michaveclub.com
Position: Personal Trainer
Specialty: Strength Training
Accepting New Clients: Yes

Name: Tom Dybreski
Phone: 312-555-3524
E-mail: tomd@michaveclub.com
Position: Personal Trainer
Specialty: Cardio Health
Accepting New Clients: Yes

Name: David Fairmont
Phone: 312-555-3525
E-mail: dfairmont@michaveclub.com
Position: Personal Trainer
Specialty: All
Accepting New Clients: Yes

Name: Abby MacLeish
Phone: 312-555-3528
E-mail: abbymac@michaveclub.com
Position: Personal Trainer
Specialty: Rehabilitation
Accepting New Clients: Yes

Name: Sam Ruhail
Phone: 312-555-3529
E-mail: sruhail@michaveclub.com
Position: Personal Trainer
Specialty: Weight Loss
Accepting New Clients: Yes

Lesson 65

Working with Macros

➤ What You Will Learn

Recording a Macro
Running a Macro
Deleting and Re-recording a Macro
Editing a Macro with VBA
Assigning a Shortcut Key to an Existing Macro
Copying a Macro Using the Organizer
Managing Macro Security

Software Skills Macros enable you to simplify tasks that ordinarily require many keystrokes or commands, such as creating a header or footer or changing line spacing and indents for a paragraph. Once you record a macro, you can run it at any time to repeat the recorded actions. You can use macros for tasks as simple as opening and printing a document, or for more complicated tasks such as creating a new document, inserting a table, entering text, and applying formatting.

WORDS TO KNOW

Developer tab
An optional ribbon tab that contains commands for advanced users, such as commands for creating and managing macros.

Macro security
A macro setting that enables or disables macros when the document is opened. The default security setting is to disable macros.

Module
A container for VBA code.

What You Can Do

Recording a Macro

- Record a macro to automate tasks or actions that you perform frequently. Macros can save time and help eliminate errors. A single macro can store an unlimited number of keystrokes and mouse actions.
- You can access the Record Macro command from the View tab in Word, but for access to Word's other macro tools, you must display the **Developer tab**. It is not displayed by default, but can be enabled via the Word Options dialog box.
- Before recording the macro, you provide a name for it, and you choose where it will be stored. You also can optionally assign a **shortcut key** combination and a Quick Access Toolbar button for running it.
- A macro can be stored either in an individual document or in the Normal template (where it is available to all documents that use that template).

Shortcut key
A combination of keys (including Alt, Ctrl, and Shift and a regular keyboard key) that you can assign to run a macro.

Visual Basic for Applications (VBA)
A version of the Visual Basic programming language designed for use within Microsoft Office applications. Macros are stored and edited using this language.

...an individual document, the document must be in ...locm) rather than the regular Word format (.docx). You ...mand to save the document as the needed file type.

...rding, almost every mouse and keyboard action is

...tions that select commands on the ribbon or in dialog ...ot record mouse actions that select text or position the

...e way you want, you can delete it and record it again, or ...l Basic for Applications editor provided with Word.

Try It! Enabling the Developer Tab on the Ribbon

1. Start Word, and create a new blank document.
2. Click File > Options. The Word Options dialog box opens.
3. Click Customize Ribbon.
4. In the list at the right, click to place a checkmark next to Developer if it does not already appear.
5. Click OK. The Developer tab appears on the ribbon.
6. Leave the file open to use in the next Try It.

Enable the Developer tab on the ribbon

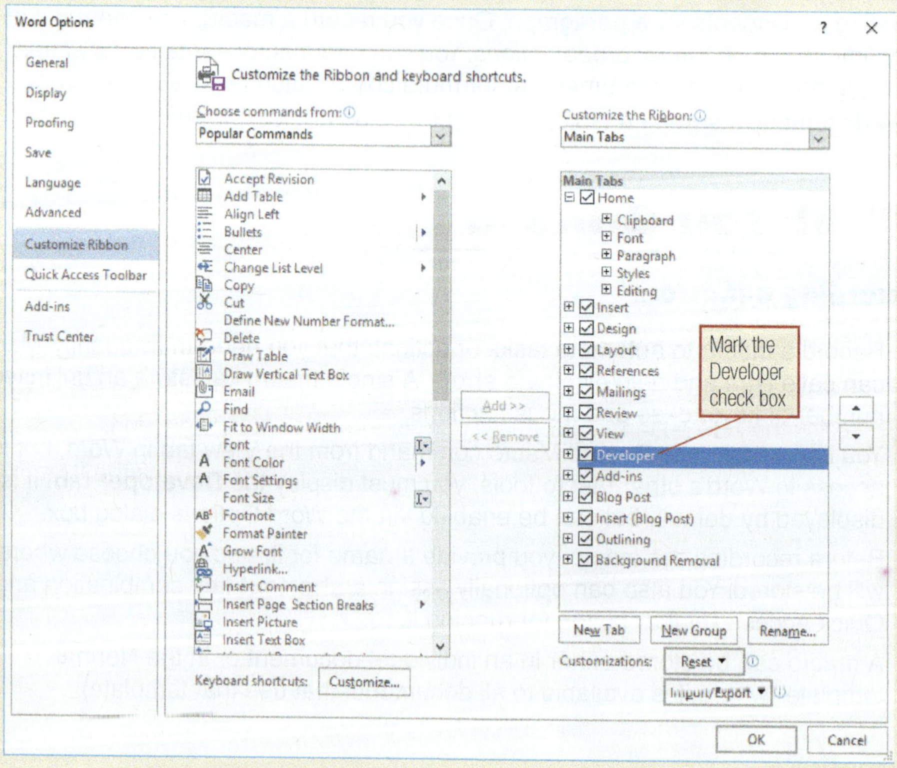

Word 2016, Windows 10, Microsoft Corporation

Try It! Saving a Document in a Macro-Enabled Format

1. With the blank document from the previous exercise open in Word, click File > Save As.
2. Navigate to the location where your teacher instructs you to store the files for this lesson.
3. In the Save As dialog box, open the Save as type drop-down list and click Word Macro-Enabled Document (*.docm).
4. In the File name box, type **W65TryA_xx**.
5. Click Save and leave the file open to use in the next Try It.

Try It! Recording a Macro

1. In the **W65TryA_xx** file, type your first name and last name.
2. Double-click your first name to select it.
3. Click View > Macros arrow > Record Macro. The Record Macro dialog box opens.

   ✓ *Alternatively you can click Developer > Record Macro, or you can click the Record Macro button on the status bar.*

4. In the Macro name box, type **Name_ Formatting**.
5. Open the Store macro in drop-down list and click the document's name.
6. In the Description, type **Arial 12-point red italics**.
7. Click Button. The Word Options dialog box opens, with the Quick Access Toolbar options displayed.
8. On the list at the left, click Project.NewMacros. Name_Formatting.
9. Click the Add button to add the macro to the list on the right.

Create a new macro

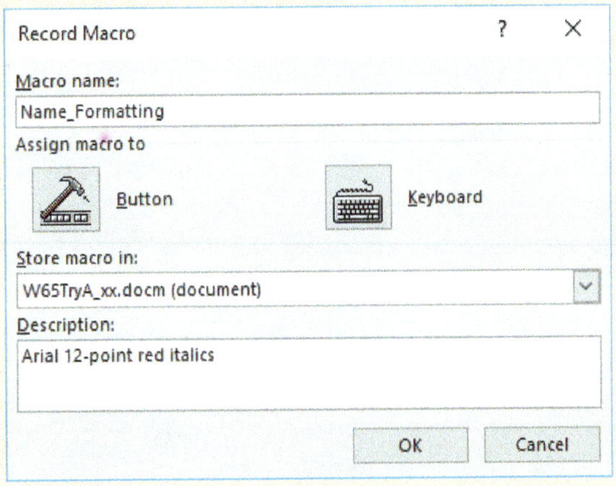

Word 2016, Windows 10, Microsoft Corporation

10. Click OK. The macro recording begins.
11. Click the Home tab. Then open the Font drop-down list Calibri (Body) and click Arial.
12. Open the Font Size drop-down list 11 and click 12.
13. Open the Font Color button's drop-down list and click the Red square in the Standard Colors section.
14. Click the Italic *I* button.

(continued)

Try It! Recording a Macro *(continued)*

15 Click the Stop Recording button on the status bar.

16 Save the changes to **W65TryA_xx**, and leave it open to use in the next Try It.

Assign the macro's button to the Quick Access Toolbar

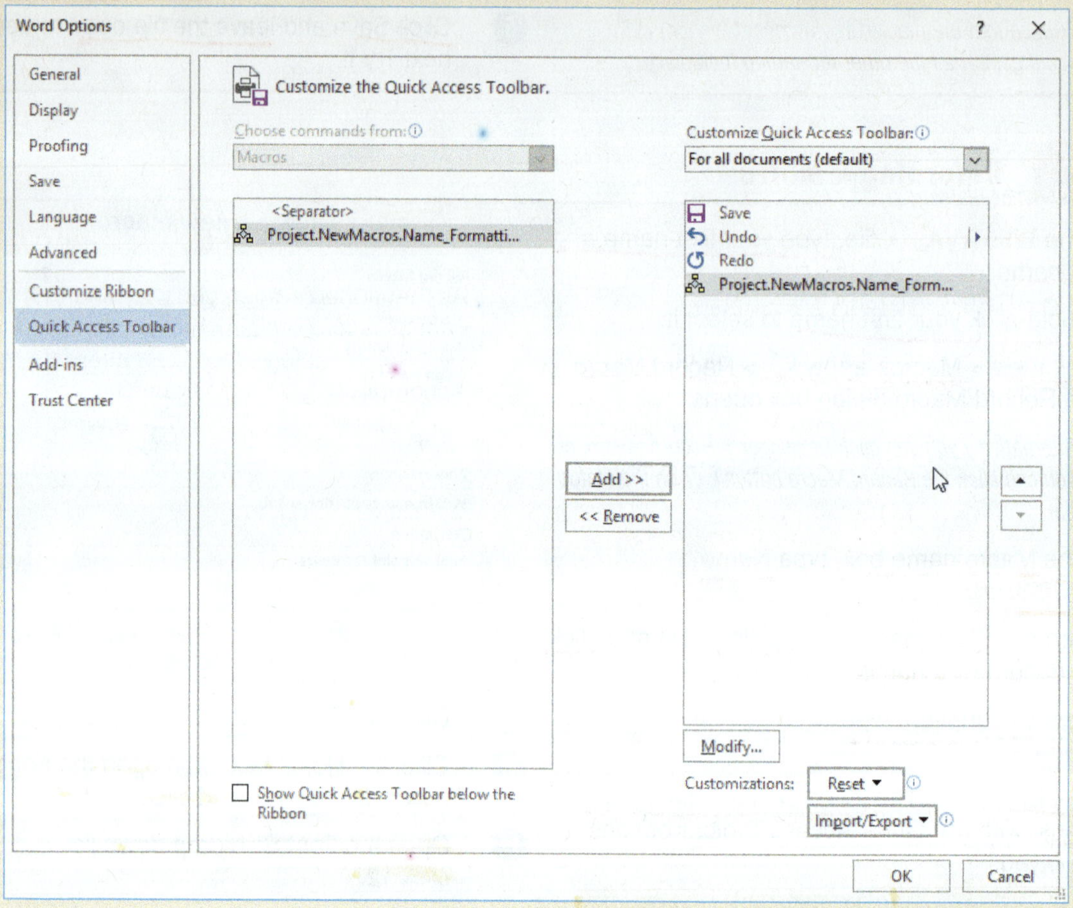

Word 2016, Windows 10, Microsoft Corporation

Running a Macro

- Once you have recorded a macro, you can run it at any time. The only requirement is that the document or template in which it is stored be open. If you attached the macro to the specific document that you were working with, as in the preceding steps, it will be available only when that document is open.
- On the other hand, if you attached it to the Normal template, it will always be available.

✓ *Even if you added a button for the macro to the toolbar, you still won't be able to run the macro unless the document or template that contains it is open. The button on the toolbar will still appear, but will not function.*

- When you run a macro, Word executes the recorded commands and actions in the current document.
- If the macro is designed to act upon selected text, make sure you select some text first before running it.

Try It! Running a Macro from a Toolbar Button

1. In the **W65TryA_xx** file, double-click your last name to select it.
2. Click the macro's button on the Quick Access Toolbar to run the macro.

   ✓ *Notice that the macro did not record the font color change, but all the other formatting took place. Some commands cannot be recorded; sometimes you can perform the action in a different way, and Word will record it the alternate way. You will see how this works in the next section.*

3. Select your first and last names and press CTRL + SPACE to strip the formatting from the text.
4. Re-run the macro to test it.
5. Save the changes to **W65TryA_xx**, and leave it open to use in the next Try It.

Deleting and Re-recording a Macro

- If a macro doesn't work the way you want, you can delete it and record it again.

  ✓ *Another alternative is to edit the existing macro in the Visual Basic for Applications editor, which is explained in the next section.*

- As mentioned earlier, you may find that Word cannot record certain commands. In this case, you may be able to record an alternate method of accomplishing the same task.

Try It! Deleting a Macro

1. In the **W65TryA_xx** file, click Developer > Macros. The Macros dialog box opens.
2. Under Macro name, click Name_Formatting.
3. Click Delete, and click Yes to confirm.
4. Click Close.
5. Right-click the macro's button on the Quick Access Toolbar and click Remove from Quick Access Toolbar.
6. Save the changes to **W65TryA_xx**, and leave it open to use in the next Try It.

Delete a recorded macro from the Macros dialog box

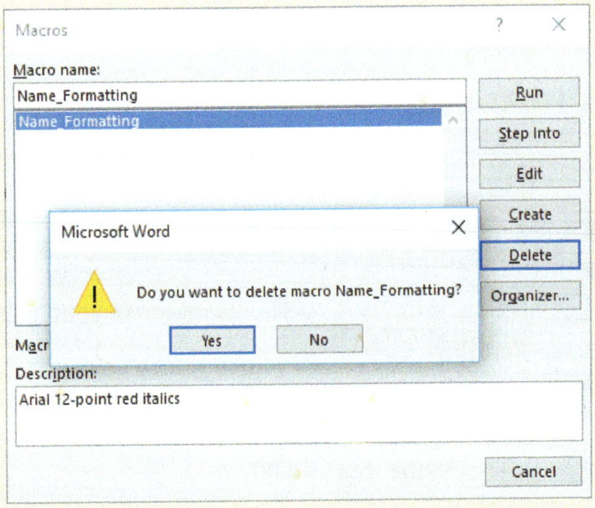

Word 2016, Windows 10, Microsoft Corporation

Try It! Re-recording a Macro

1. In the W65TryA_xx file, select your full name and press CTRL + SPACE to strip any existing formatting from it.
2. Double-click your first name to select it.
3. Click View > Macros arrow > Record Macro. The Record Macro dialog box opens.
4. In the Macro name box, type **Name_Formatting**.
5. Open the Store macro in drop-down list and click the document's name.
6. In the Description, type **Arial 12-point red italics**.
7. Click OK. The macro recording begins.
8. Click the Home tab. Then open the Font drop-down list Calibri (Body) and click Arial.
9. Open the Font Size drop-down list 11 and click 12.
10. Click the dialog box launcher in the bottom right corner of the Font group on the Home tab. The Font dialog box opens.
11. Open the Font color drop-down list in the dialog box and click the Red square.
12. In the Font style section of the dialog box, click Italic.
13. Click OK.
14. Click the Stop Recording button on the status bar.
15. Save the changes to W65TryA_xx, and leave it open to use in the next Try It.

Use the Font dialog box to set the font color

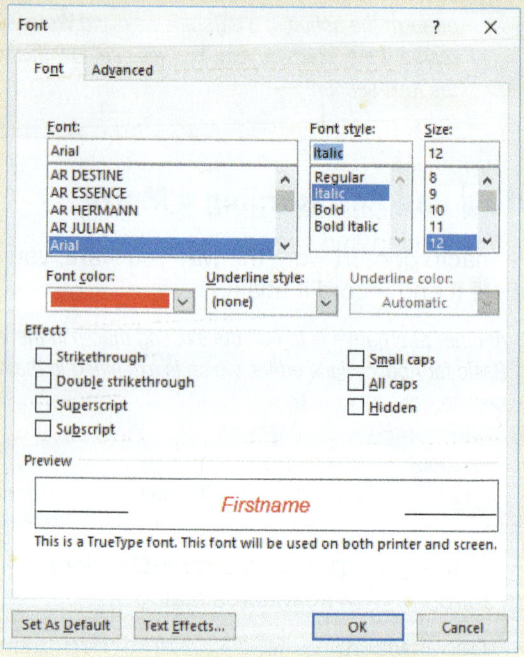

Word 2016, Windows 10, Microsoft Corporation

Try It! Running a Macro from the Macros Dialog Box

1. In the W65TryA_xx file, double-click your last name to select it.
2. Click Developer > Macros. The Macros dialog box opens.
3. Click Name_Formatting.
4. Click Run. The macro runs.

   ✓ *This time the font changes to red. The alternate method of recording font color worked.*
5. Save the changes to W65TryA_xx, and leave it open to use in the next Try It.

Editing a Macro with VBA

- **Visual Basic for Applications (VBA)** is the language in which Word writes macros. Word includes a simple VBA editor as part of its tools.
- To make extensive edits to a macro in VBA, you need to know Visual Basic programming. However, to rename a macro, remove a command, or edit a description, you do not need any special knowledge.

✓ *When you rename a macro, the link between the macro and its Quick Access Toolbar button or shortcut key is lost. After changing a macro's name, you must remove the existing button and add a new button via the Quick Access Toolbar tab in the Word Options dialog box (you can find the macro in the Macros category of commands). You must also assign its shortcut key again as described in the next section.*

Try It! Editing a Macro with VBA

1. In the **W65TryA_xx** file, click Developer > Macros.
2. In the Macros dialog box, click Name_Formatting and change the description to **Arial 10-point red italics**.
3. Click Edit. The macro appears in the Microsoft Visual Basic for Applications window.
4. In the macro code, find each reference to the macro's name (that is, each instance of Name_Formatting) and change it to **Name_Formatting_Red**.

   ✓ *There are two instances of Name_Formatting in the code. Change them both.*

5. In the macro code, find each reference to the font size (that is, each instance of 12) and change it to **10**.

   ✓ *There are three instances of the number 12 in the code. Change them all.*

6. Close the Microsoft Visual Basic for Applications window.
7. Select your full name and press CTRL + SPACE to strip any existing formatting from it.
8. Run the macro again on your full name (both first and last names) to confirm that it now changes the text to 10-point.
9. Save the changes to **W65TryA_xx**, and leave it open to use in the next Try It.

Assigning a Shortcut Key to an Existing Macro

- You can assign a shortcut key to an existing macro by using the commands in the Customize Keyboard dialog box.

  ✓ *The shortcut key must be different from any shortcut key Word has already assigned to another action. If you choose a shortcut key that Word has already assigned to another action, the macro will override the other action in this document.*

- You can access the Customize Keyboard dialog box from the Customize Ribbon tab of the Word Options dialog box.

Try It! Assigning a Shortcut Key to an Existing Macro

1. In the **W65TryA_xx** file, click File > Options. The Word Options dialog box opens.
2. Click Customize Ribbon.
3. At the bottom of the dialog box, click the Customize button next to Keyboard shortcuts. The Customize Keyboard dialog box opens.
4. Open the Save changes in drop-down list and click the name of the document.
5. Scroll down the Categories list and click Macros.
6. In the Macros list, click Name_Formatting_Red.
7. Click in the Press new shortcut key box and then press [ALT] + [1]. The text *Alt+1* appears in the box. Below the Current keys box, the text *Currently assigned to: [unassigned]* appears to indicate that the shortcut key is not assigned to any other action.
8. Click Assign. The shortcut key text *Alt+1* moves to the Current keys list.
9. Click Close.
10. Click OK to close the Word Options dialog box.
11. In the document, select your full name and press [CTRL] + [SPACE] to strip any existing formatting from it.
12. Press [ALT] + [1]. The macro runs.
13. Save the changes to **W65TryA_xx**, and leave it open to use in the next Try It.

Assign a shortcut key to an existing macro

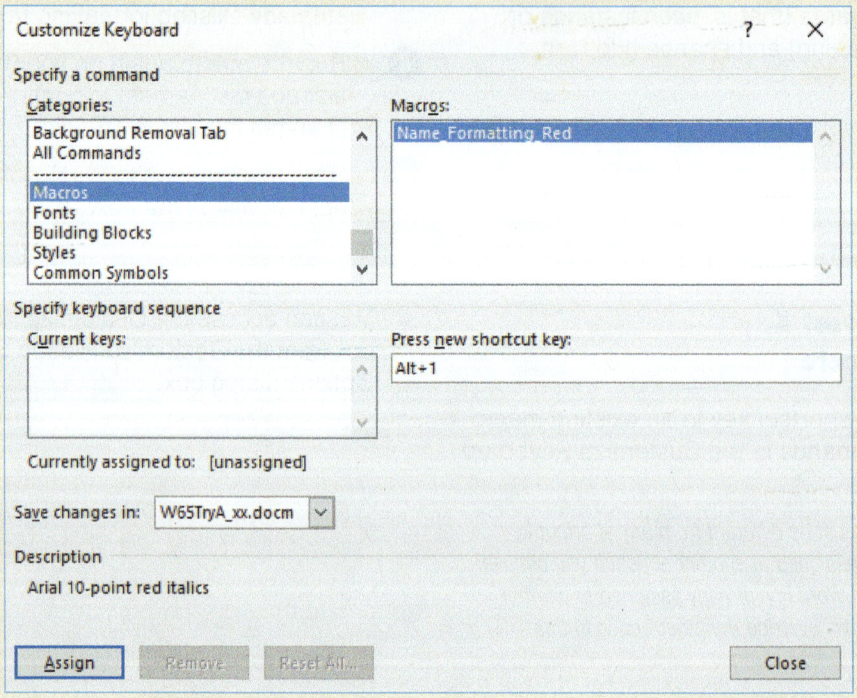

Word 2016, Windows 10, Microsoft Corporation

Copying a Macro Using the Organizer

- Macro code is stored in a **module** within the file.
- You can access VBA modules in the Microsoft Visual Basic for Applications window from the Visual Basic button on the Developer tab.
- You can open a module like a file and edit its content.
- By default, all macros in a document are stored in one module called NewMacros.
- Each time you create a new macro in the document, Word adds it to the NewMacros module.
- You can copy a module to another macro-enabled Word document to make the macros in the module available for use in that document.
- You can edit or delete individual macros in a document.

✓ *When you copy a macro from one document to another, Word does not copy its shortcut key. You will need to reassign the shortcut key by editing the macro.*

Try It! Copying a Macro Using the Organizer

1. In Word, create a new blank document.
2. Save the new document as a macro-enabled Word document called **W65TryB_xx** in the location where your teacher instructs you to store the files for this lesson.
3. Switch to the **W65TryA_xx** file, and click Developer > Macros.
4. In the Macros dialog box, click Organizer. The Organizer dialog box opens, with the Macro Project Items tab displayed.
5. On the right side of the tab, click Close File and then click Open File.
6. In the Open dialog box, change the file type to All Files (*.*).
7. Navigate to the location where you are storing the files for this lesson.
8. Click **W65TryB_xx** and click Open.
9. On the left side of the tab, confirm that W65TryA_xx.docm is selected in the Macro Project Items available in drop-down box.
10. Click NewMacros and click Copy to copy the module to the list on the right.
11. Click Close, and click Save if prompted.
12. Switch to **W65TryB_xx**, and type your full name.
13. Select your full name and click Developer > Macros.
14. Click Name_Formatting_Red and click Run. The macro runs.
15. Save and close **W65TryA_xx** and **W65TryB_xx**, and exit Word.

Copy the NewMacros module from one document to another

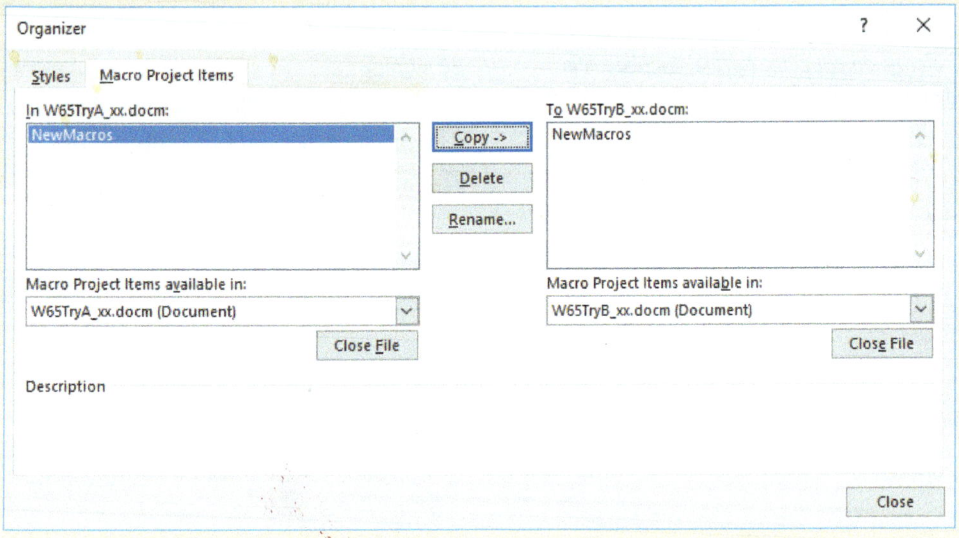

Word 2016, Windows 10, Microsoft Corporation

Managing Macro Security

- To minimize the risk of a macro virus or other malware threat contained in a macro, Word has a **macro security** feature.
- To view or change these settings, click the Developer tab, and then click Macro Security.
- Word's default setting is to disable all macros, and to display a notification option when working with a file that contains macros.
- When you open a macro-enabled document, you can click Enable Content in the security warning notification to enable the macros.

Lesson 65—Practice

As an administrative assistant at Michigan Avenue Athletic Club, you frequently have to format reports by changing the margins to 1.25". In this project, you will create a macro for setting the margins and run the macro to make sure it works.

DIRECTIONS

1. Start Word, if necessary, and create a new blank document.
2. Save the new document as a macro-enabled Word document called **W65Practice_xx** in the location where your teacher instructs you to store the files for this lesson.
3. In the header, type your full name and today's date. Close the header and footer.
4. Click **View** > **Macros arrow** > **Record Macro**.
5. In the **Macro name** box, type **Page_Setup**.
6. In the **Description** box, type **Set all margins to 1.25"**.
7. Open the **Store macro in** drop-down list and click the document name.

   ✓ *If you were recording this macro for use on your own PC, you might prefer to store it in the Normal template. It is being stored in the document in this exercise for grading purposes.*
8. Click **Keyboard**.
9. Press ALT + M.
10. Open the **Save changes in** drop-down list and click the document name.
11. Click **Assign**.
12. Click **Close**. The macro begins recording.
13. Click **Layout** > **Margins** > **Custom Margins**.
14. In the Page Setup dialog box, in the Top text box, type **1.25** and press TAB. The insertion point moves to the Bottom text box.
15. Type **1.25** and press TAB. The insertion point moves to the Left text box.
16. Type **1.25** and press TAB. The insertion point moves to the Right text box.
17. Type **1.25**.
18. Click **OK**.
19. Click the **Stop Recording** button on the status bar.
20. Click **Layout** > **Margins** > **Narrow** to set the margins to a different setting.
21. Press ALT + M to run the macro.
22. Save and close the document, and exit Word.

Lesson 65—Apply

Your manager at the Michigan Avenue Athletic Club has asked you to adjust the margins and paragraph formatting in a report. In another document, you have stored a macro that sets the appropriate margins. In this project, you will copy that macro and run it in the current report. Then you will create and run a new macro that adjusts the paragraph formatting.

DIRECTIONS

1. Start Word, if necessary, and open **W65ApplyA** from the data files for this lesson. Save the file as a macro-enabled Word document called **W65ApplyA_xx** in the location where your teacher instructs you to store the files for this lesson.
2. In the header, type your full name at the left and today's date at the right. Close the header and footer.
3. Open **W65ApplyB** from the data files for this lesson.
4. Use the Organizer to copy the **NewMacros** module from **W65ApplyB** to **W65ApplyA_xx**. Save changes to **W65ApplyA_xx**, if prompted.
5. Close **W65ApplyB** without saving changes.
6. In **W65ApplyA_xx**, run the Page_Setup macro.
7. Select the first body paragraph of the document, and record a macro called **Body_Format** that formats the paragraph as follows:
   a. **Single-spaced** lines within the paragraph.
   b. **12 points** of space after the paragraph.
   c. First line of paragraph **not indented**.
8. Run the macro on each of the other paragraphs in the document. If you get any errors or it doesn't work as expected, troubleshoot by deleting and re-recording the macro applying the formatting in different ways (for example, with dialog boxes).
9. Open the **Body_Format** macro in the Microsoft Visual Basic for Applications window.
10. Change the name of the macro to **Report_Body_Format** and set the amount of space after the paragraph to **9 points**.
11. Close the Microsoft Visual Basic for Applications window.
12. Assign a shortcut key of [ALT] + [T] to the **Report_Body_Format** macro.
13. Re-run the macro on all the body paragraphs in the document.
14. **With your teacher's permission**, print the document. It should resemble Figure 65-1 on the next page.
15. Save and close the document, and exit Word.

skip

4. Devel Tab → Macro – Organizer
Close file
Open File
Navigate to Name Folder
Select ALL Files
select W65ApplyA
Copy from B to A

5. Close Apply B w/out saving
6. in apply A click Develop → Macros → run Page-Setup
7. don't forget to click arrow store Macro in: & select Apply A
a, b, c, goes in description box
after done recording click grey box on status bar to Turn off Macro.

Figure 65-1

Firstname Lastname Today's Date

IS A PERSONAL TRAINER RIGHT FOR YOU?

Almost everyone could benefit from the services of a personal trainer. In addition to designing a personalized workout program, a good trainer provides motivation and encouragement. He or she helps you understand how to fit exercise into your life and teaches you how to make the most out of your exercise time. The lessons you learn from a trainer help ensure a safe, effective workout, even when you are exercising on your own.

Working with a trainer should be a satisfying and rewarding experience. There are many different reasons for hiring a personal trainer. Some people want the motivation of a workout partner, others require specialized services for rehabilitation, and still others are interested in achieving weight loss goals. Before hiring a trainer, make sure he or she has experience helping people with goals similar to your own. Ask for references, and then contact at least three. You should also interview the trainer to find out if you are compatible. You should feel comfortable talking and working together, and you should trust the trainer to respect your time and efforts.

Verify that the trainer is certified by a nationally recognized organization such as the American Council on Exercise, the American College of Sports Medicine, or the National Strength and Conditioning Association. Many trainers have degrees in subjects such as sports medicine, physical education, exercise physiology, or anatomy and physiology.

For more information about personal trainers, contact Candace at extension 765.

End-of-Chapter Activities

➤ Word Chapter 9—Critical Thinking

Research Project

You are working on a group project in an English Literature class about the life of Emily Dickinson. Your classmates have prepared data in Excel, Word, and PowerPoint, and now it's up to you to assemble the different pieces of information into a coherent whole.

DIRECTIONS

1. Open and examine **WCT09A.docx** in Word, **WCT09B.pptx** in PowerPoint, and **WCT09C.xlsx** in Excel to familiarize yourself with the information you have to work with. Then close each application.
2. Start Word, and save a new blank document as **WCT09D_xx** in the location where your teacher instructs you to store the files for this chapter.
3. In the header, type your full name and today's date. Close the header and footer.
4. Confirm that the document margins are **1"** on all sides.
5. Link all the text from **WCT09A.docx** into **WCT09D_xx**. Use the **Formatted Text (RTF)** object type.
6. Format the text attractively. For example, you may want to add space after each paragraph to increase readability, change the font and/or font size, and so on.
7. Embed slides 2 and 3 from the PowerPoint presentation **WCT09B** into the document at appropriate spots where the text in the main discussion matches the content of the slide. Resize the slides as needed.
8. At the end of the Word document, add the following text: **Here is an example of her work:**.
9. Open **WCT09C** in Excel, and use the hyperlinks to navigate to Web pages where the corresponding poems can be read. Read several poems, and select the one you like best.
10. Copy and paste the poem from the Web site to the end of the Word document on the line following the text you typed in step 8. Use the **Keep Text Only** paste option so that the formatting from the Web page is not copied. Then format the poem attractively using Word. (For example, you could indent the poem ½" from the left margin and italicize its text.)
11. Using the Links dialog box, break the link between the document text and **WCT09A**.
12. When you are satisfied with the document, ask a classmate to review it and make comments or suggestions that will help you improve it.
13. Make changes and corrections, as necessary.
14. **With your teacher's permission**, print the document. Illustration 9A on the next page shows the first page of one possible version, but yours may look different depending on your formatting choices.
15. Save and close the document, and exit all open applications.

Illustration 9A

Firstname Lastname
Today's Date

Emily Dickinson (1830–1886)

Emily Elizabeth Dickinson was born on December 10, 1830, in the quiet community of Amherst, Massachusetts, the second daughter of Edward and Emily Norcross Dickinson. Emily, Austin (her older brother) and her younger sister Lavinia were nurtured in a quiet, reserved family headed by their authoritative father Edward. Throughout Emily's life, her mother was not "emotionally accessible," the absence of which might have caused some of Emily's eccentricity. Being rooted in the puritanical Massachusetts of the 1800s, the Dickinson children were raised in the Christian tradition, and they were expected to take up their father's religious beliefs and values without argument. Later in life, Emily would come to challenge these conventional religious viewpoints of her father and the church, and the challenges she met with would later contribute to the strength of her poetry.

The Dickinson family was prominent in Amherst. In fact, Emily's grandfather, Samuel Fowler Dickinson, was one of the founders of Amherst College, and her father served as lawyer and treasurer for the institution. Emily's father also served in powerful positions on the General Court of Massachusetts, the Massachusetts State Senate, and the United States House of Representatives. Unlike her father, Emily did not enjoy the popularity and excitement of public life in Amherst, and she began to withdraw. Emily did not fit in with her father's religion in Amherst, and her father began to censor the books she read because of their potential to draw her away from the faith.

Being the daughter of a prominent politician, Emily had the benefit of a good education and attended the Amherst Academy. After her time at the academy, Emily left for the South Hadley Female Seminary (currently Mount Holyoke College) where she started to blossom into a delicate young woman—"her eyes lovely auburn, soft and warm, her hair lay in rings of the same color all over her head with her delicate teeth and skin." She had a demure manner that was almost fun with her close friends, but Emily could be shy, silent, or even depreciating in the presence of strangers. Although she was successful at college, Emily returned after only one year at the seminary in 1848 to Amherst where she began her life of seclusion.

➤ Word Chapter 9—Portfolio Builder

Travel Planning

The Horticultural Shop Owners' Association is sponsoring a trip to tour the Botanical Gardens in Montreal, Canada. The president of the association has asked you to create an information packet to send to members. She has sent you an Excel worksheet with financial information, a PowerPoint presentation about the trip, and an Access database of members' contact information. In this exercise, you will export the PowerPoint presentation to create a Word document.

You will add a cover page to the document, and you will add another page to the document on which you will embed financial information as an Excel worksheet object. You will also include a form. Finally, you will use the Access database as a data source to create e-mail messages to the members.

DIRECTIONS

1. Start PowerPoint and open the presentation file **WPB09A.pptx** from the data files for this chapter. Save the file as **WPB09A_xx** in the location where your teacher instructs you to store the files for this chapter.
2. Publish the file as handouts in Word using the layout that leaves blank lines next to each slide. Do not create a link.
3. Exit PowerPoint and switch to Word.
4. In Word, adjust the table column sizes as needed so that the lines next to each slide do not wrap to additional lines. See Illustration 9B on the next page.
5. Save the Word document as **WPB09B_xx**.
6. In the header, type your full name and today's date. Close the header and footer.
7. Use the **Insert** > **Cover Page** command to insert a cover page that uses the **Semaphore** design.
8. Fill in the information on the cover page as follows:

   Pick the date: **Today's date**

   Document title: **Tour the Botanical Gardens of Montreal**

   Document subtitle: **A Four-Day Deluxe Tour**

   Author: **Your name**

   Company: **Horticultural Shop Owners' Association**

   Company address: Delete this placeholder.
9. Move the insertion point to the end of the document and press ENTER.
10. Type **Breakdown of Costs for Montreal Trip** and format it with the **Heading 1** style.
11. Press ENTER to start a new paragraph. Set the paragraph formatting to leave 24 points of space before the paragraph.
12. Open **WPB09C.xlsx** in Excel from the data files for this chapter. Save the file as **WPB09C_xx** in the location where your teacher instructs you to store the files for this chapter.
13. Select cells **A4:D8** and copy the selection to the Clipboard.
14. Switch back to **WPB09B_xx** and paste a link to the data as a Microsoft Excel Worksheet Object.
15. Switch back to Excel, and close it, saving changes if prompted.
16. Switch to Word. **With your teacher's permission**, print the document.
17. Save and close **WPB09B_xx**.
18. Start a new blank Word document and save it as **WPB09D_xx**.
19. In the header, type your full name and today's date. Close the header and footer.
20. Use Mail Merge to create e-mail messages using the **WPB09E.accdb** Access database.
21. In the **WPB09D_xx** file, insert the **First_Name** field, type a colon, and press ENTER.

Illustration 9B

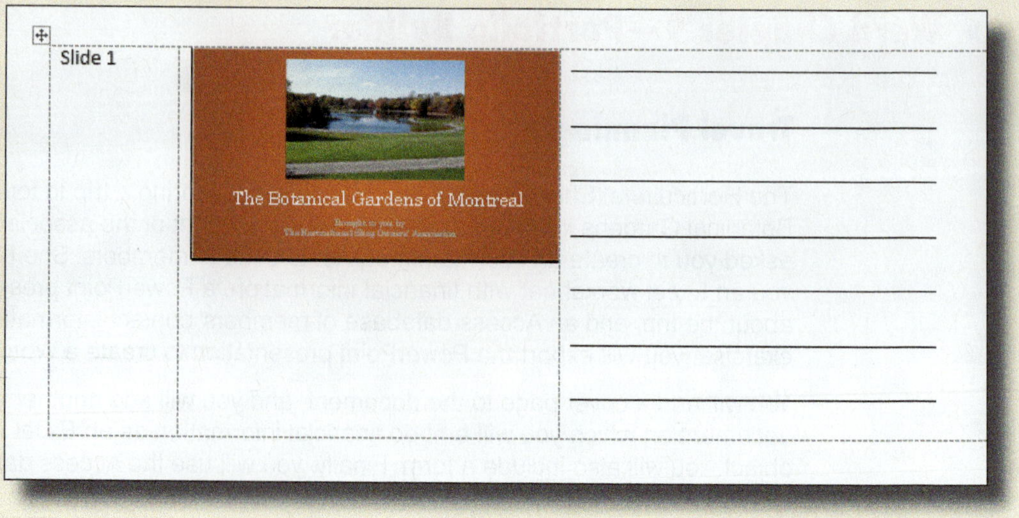

Word 2016, Windows 10, Microsoft Corporation

22. Type the following paragraphs:

    Join the Horticultural Shop Owners' Association on an exciting four-day trip to the Botanical Gardens in Montreal, Canada. Last year, twenty members of the association joined a similar tour. When asked whether they were pleased with the experience, the overwhelming majority answered with a resounding "YES!"

    Please fill out the following form and return it to the HSOA to help us plan our trip.

23. Press ENTER and insert a table with 2 columns and 4 rows. Insert a form in the table as follows:
    a. Display the Developer tab if necessary.
    b. In the left column of the first row, type **Your full name**.
    c. In the right column of the first row, insert a **Rich Text Content Control** from the Controls group on the Developer tab.
    d. In the left column of the second row, type **Are you interested in the trip?**
    e. In the right column of the second row, type **Yes**, insert a space, and then insert a **Check Box Content Control**.
    f. Click to the right of the check box control. Press SPACEBAR three times, and then type **No**. Insert a space, and then insert a **Check Box Content Control**.
    g. In the left column of the third row, type **Lodging preference**.
    h. In the right column of the third row, insert a **Drop-Down List Content Control**.
    i. In the left column of the fourth row, type **Food preference**.
    j. In the right column of the fourth row, insert a **Drop-Down List Content Control**.

24. Change the field control properties as follows:
    a. Select the *Lodging preference* drop-down list control, and then select **Properties** on the Developer tab.
    b. In the Drop-Down List Properties section of the Content Control Properties dialog box, click **Add**.
    c. In the Add Choice dialog box, type **Single occupancy** in the Display Name box, and then click **OK**.
    d. Click **Add**, type **Double occupancy**, and click **OK** twice.
    e. Select the *Food preference* drop-down list control, and then select **Properties** on the Developer tab.
    f. In the Drop-Down List Properties section of the Content Control Properties dialog box, click **Add**.
    g. In the Add Choice dialog box, type **I'll eat anything** in the Display Name box, and then click **OK**.
    h. Click **Add**, type **Vegetarian, please**, and click **OK**.
    i. Click **Add**, type **Strictly vegan**, and click **OK** twice.

25. Reduce the width of the left column to fit contents, and then apply the **Grid Table 3 - Accent 1** table style. Turn off formatting for the header row. Your form should look like Illustration 9C.
26. Click **Mailings** > **Finish & Merge** > **Edit Individual Documents**.
27. Click **OK**.
28. Save the new document as **WPB09F_xx**.
29. Save and close all Word documents, and exit Word.

Illustration 9C

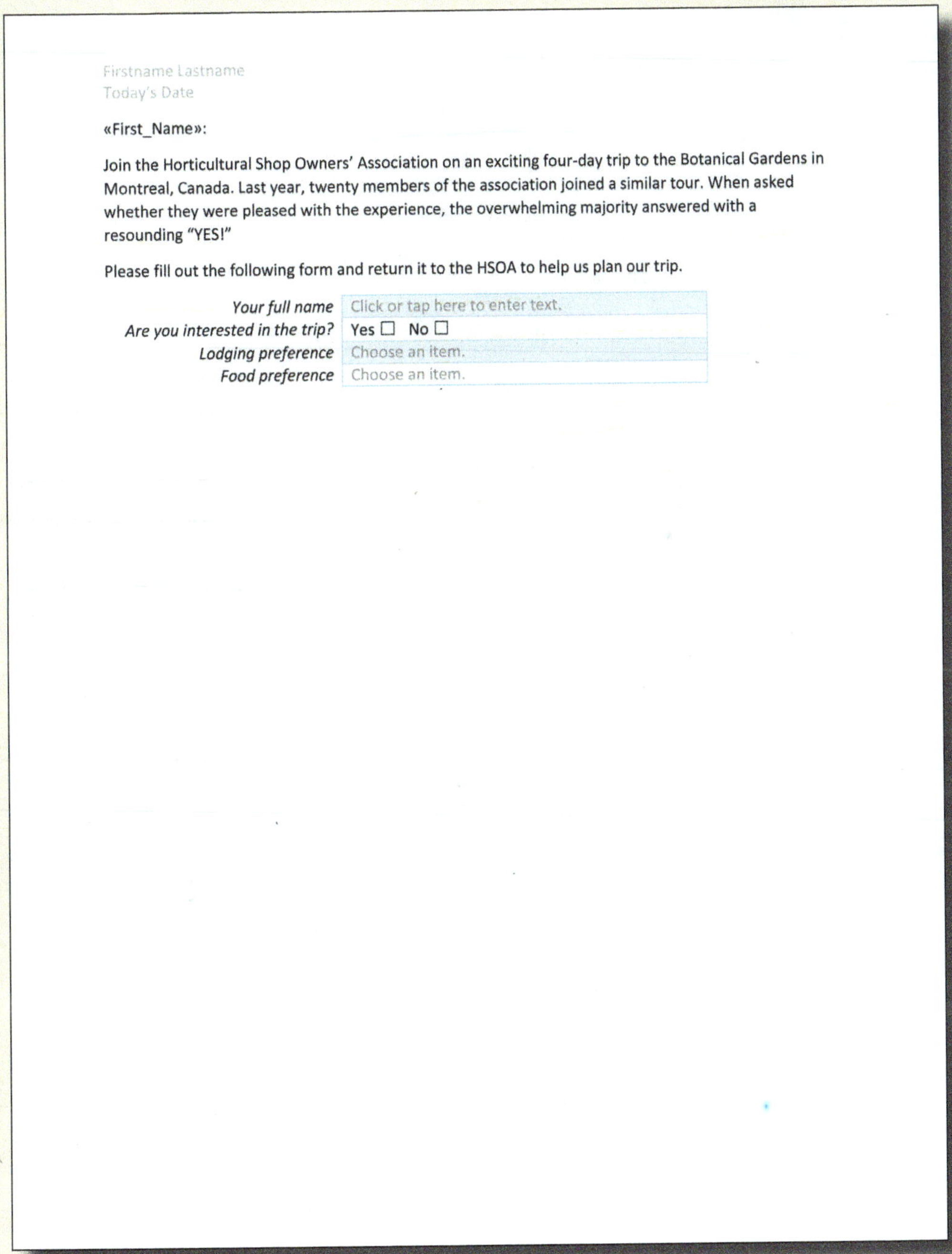

Firstname Lastname
Today's Date

«First_Name»:

Join the Horticultural Shop Owners' Association on an exciting four-day trip to the Botanical Gardens in Montreal, Canada. Last year, twenty members of the association joined a similar tour. When asked whether they were pleased with the experience, the overwhelming majority answered with a resounding "YES!"

Please fill out the following form and return it to the HSOA to help us plan our trip.

Your full name	Click or tap here to enter text.
Are you interested in the trip?	Yes ☐ No ☐
Lodging preference	Choose an item.
Food preference	Choose an item.

Chapter 6

(Courtesy Brocreative/Shutterstock)

Managing Large Workbooks

Lesson 47
Customizing the Excel Interface and Converting Text

- Customizing the Quick Access Toolbar
- Customizing the Ribbon
- Customizing Excel Options
- Converting Text to Columns

Lesson 48
Formatting Cells

- Using Advanced Formatting of Dates and Times
- Creating Custom Number Formats
- Clearing Formatting from a Cell

Lesson 49
Conditional Formatting and Internationalization

- Creating Custom Conditional Formatting Rules
- Creating Conditional Formatting Rules That Use Formulas
- Managing Conditional Formatting Rules
- Applying Multiple Conditional Format Rules
- Using Additional Languages
- Working with Currency in International Formats
- Working with Text in International Formats

Lesson 50
Customizing Styles and Themes

- Customizing a Workbook Theme
- Customizing a Cell Style
- Merging Cell Styles
- Customizing a Table Style

Lesson 51
Customizing Data Entry

- Entering Labels on Multiple Lines
- Entering Fractions and Mixed Numbers
- Using Form Controls
- Populating Cells with Advanced Fill Series Options

End-of-Chapter Activities

Lesson 47

Customizing the Excel Interface and Converting Text

➤ What You Will Learn

Customizing the Quick Access Toolbar
Customizing the Ribbon
Customizing Excel Options
Converting Text to Columns

Software Skills Like other Office programs, Excel is designed to be customized to your needs. You can customize Excel Options, the ribbon, and the Quick Access Toolbar to have easy access to the tools and features you use most often.

What You Can Do

Customizing the Quick Access Toolbar

- The Quick Access Toolbar (QAT) appears at the top-left corner of the Excel window. It provides a set of quick shortcuts to the most common functions and features.
- You can choose to show the Quick Access Toolbar below the ribbon.
- By default the Quick Access Toolbar contains three buttons: Save, Undo, and Redo. You can also customize it by adding shortcuts to most other Excel features.
- To add any button to the Quick Access Toolbar, right-click it and select Add to Quick Access Toolbar.
- To remove a button from the Quick Access Toolbar, right-click it and choose Remove from Quick Access Toolbar.
- You can use the Quick Access Toolbar section of the Excel Options dialog box to add Excel features that don't appear on the tabs of the ribbon.
- You can also use the Quick Access Toolbar section of the Excel Options dialog box to remove features or to reset any customizations.

Try It! Customizing the Quick Access Toolbar

1. Start Excel, and create a new, blank workbook.
2. Click the Review tab, right-click Spelling, and click Add to Quick Access Toolbar.
3. Click Customize Quick Access Toolbar > Sort Ascending.
4. Click File > Options > Quick Access Toolbar.
5. Click the Choose commands from drop-down arrow, and click Formulas Tab.
6. In the list of commands, click Average, and click the Add button Add >>.
7. In the list below the Customize Quick Access Toolbar box, select Average, and click the Remove button << Remove.
8. Click the Reset button Reset > Reset only Quick Access Toolbar.
9. Click Yes in the confirmation dialog box, and click OK. The Quick Access Toolbar is reset.
10. Leave the blank workbook and Excel open for the next Try It.

Customizing the Quick Access Toolbar

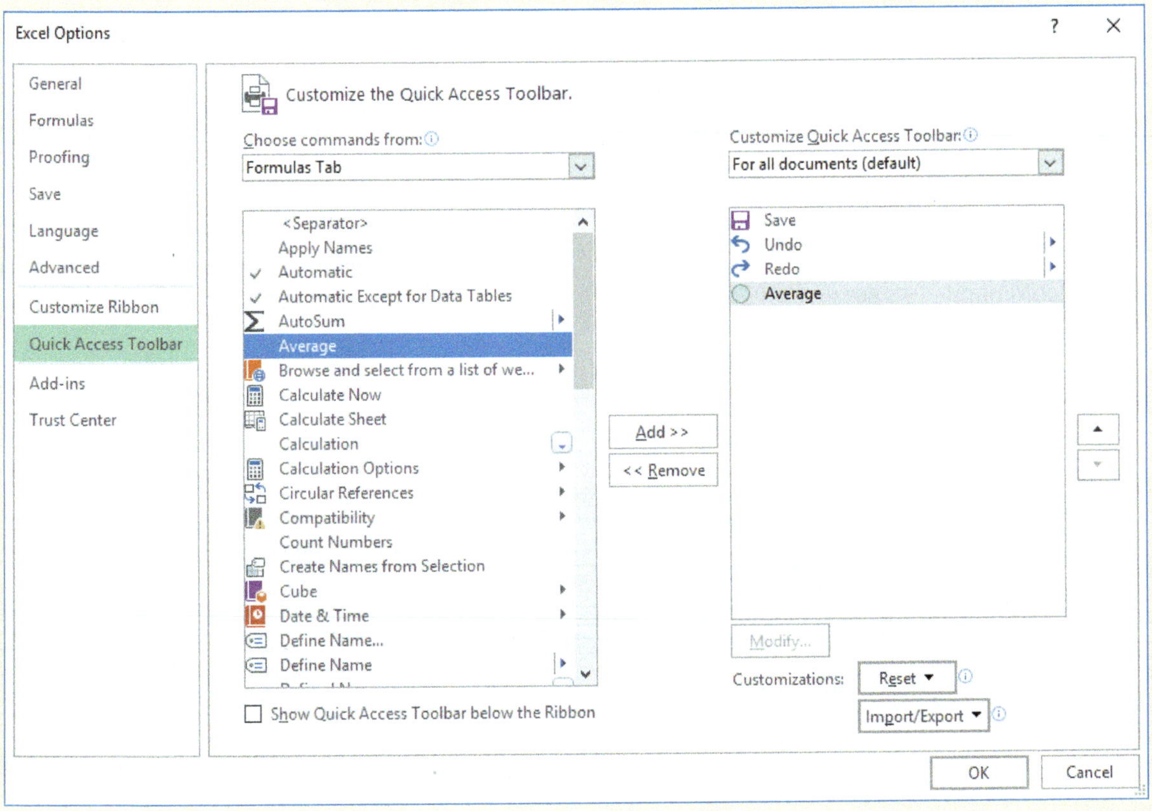

Excel 2016, Windows 10, Microsoft Corporation

Customizing the Ribbon

- In Excel 2016 you can customize the ribbon by adding commands that you use frequently or removing those commands that you don't use.
- You can create new groups on a ribbon tab, and you can create a new tab with new groups.
- Commands for customizing the ribbon are on the Customize Ribbon tab of the Excel Options dialog box.
- You can also use the Customize Ribbon section of the Excel Options dialog box to remove features or to reset any customizations.

Try It! Customizing the Ribbon

1. In Excel, click File > Options to open the Excel Options dialog box.
2. Click Customize Ribbon.
3. On the right side of the dialog box, under Main Tabs, click to clear the check mark to the left of Page Layout.
4. Click the New Tab button [New Tab].
5. In the Main Tabs box, click New Group (Custom).
6. Click the Rename button [Rename...], in the Display name box type **Learning Excel**, and click OK.
7. Click the Choose commands from drop-down arrow, and click Commands Not in the ribbon.
8. In the commands list, scroll down, click Zoom In, and click the Add button [Add >>].
9. In the commands list, click Zoom Out, and click the Add button [Add >>].
10. Click OK to apply the change and close the Excel Options dialog box. Notice that the Page Layout tab no longer appears on the ribbon and that the new tab named New Tab displays.
11. Click New Tab to view the Learning Excel group of commands.
12. Click File > Options > Customize Ribbon.
13. Click the Reset button [Reset ▾] > Reset all customizations.
14. Click Yes in the confirmation dialog box, and click OK. The Quick Access Toolbar and Ribbon are reset to the default settings.
15. Leave the blank workbook and Excel open to use in the next Try It.

Modified Ribbon

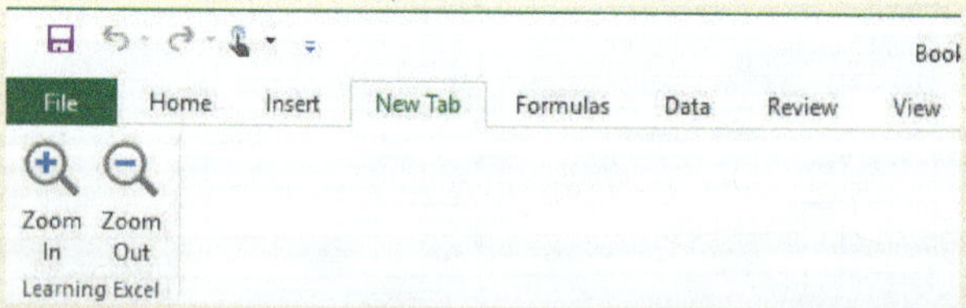

Excel 2016, Windows 10, Microsoft Corporation

Customizing Excel Options

- There are more than 100 different options and settings that you can use to control the way Excel operates.
- Excel options are organized in categories, such as Formulas, Proofing, Save, and Add-Ins.
- You can view and set program options in the Excel Options dialog box accessed from the Backstage view.
- When you set up Microsoft Excel 2016 on your computer, you enter a user name and initials.
- Excel uses this information to identify you as the author of new workbooks that you create and save, and as the editor of existing workbooks that you open, modify, and save.

- In addition, your user name is associated with revisions that you make when you use the Track Changes features, and the initials are associated with comments that you insert.
- You can change the user name and initials using options in the General group in the Excel Options dialog box.

Try It! Customizing Excel Options

1. In Excel, in the blank workbook, click File > Options.
2. On the General tab, under Personalize your copy of Microsoft Office, in the User name box, type your full name.
3. In the list on the left side of the dialog box, click Save to display the Save options.
4. Click Proofing to display the Proofing options.
5. Click Advanced, and scroll through the options.
6. Under Display options for this workbook, clear Show sheet tabs.
7. Under Display options for this worksheet, click the Gridline color button .
8. Select Blue (last color on the last row).
9. Click Cancel to close the Excel Options window without saving the changes.
10. Close the blank workbook without saving the changes, and leave Excel open to use in the next Try It.

Excel's advanced display options

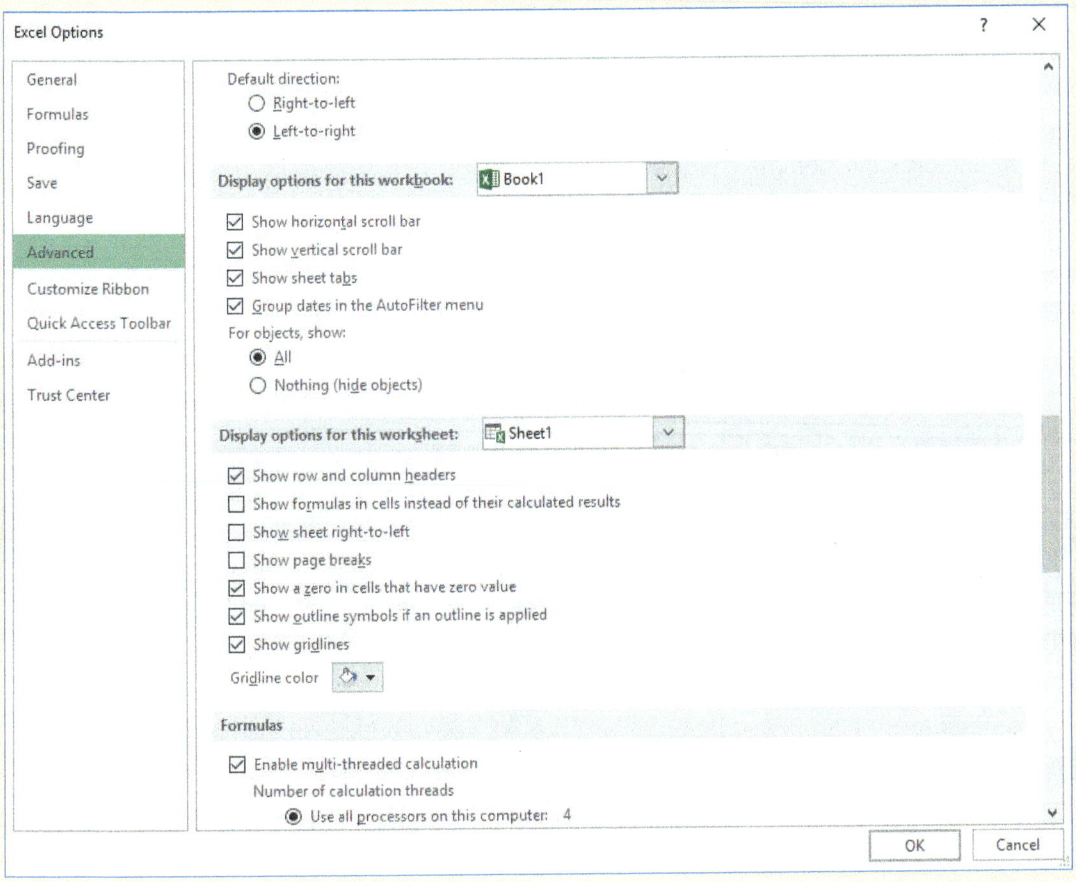

Excel 2016, Windows 10, Microsoft Corporation

Converting Text to Columns

- When working with large amounts of text data in Excel, pre-planning is often critical.
  - For example, when creating a long list of customers, it's useful to place first names in one column and last names in another so that you can sort on the column with last names and arrange the customer list alphabetically.
- It is useful to separate out the parts of a customer's address into different columns—one each for street address, city, state, and ZIP Code—so the customer list can be sorted by state or ZIP Code.
- You can split the contents of one cell across several cells.
- You can split the contents of a single cell, a range, or an entire column in one step.

Try It! Converting Delimited Text to Columns

1. In Excel, open the **E47Try** file from the data files for this lesson.
2. Save the file as **E47Try_xx** in the location where your teacher instructs you to store the files for this lesson.
3. Select the cell range I6:I57.
4. Click Data > Text to Columns to display the Convert Text to Columns Wizard.
5. Verify that the Delimited option is selected, and click Next.
6. Under Delimiters, click the Tab check box to deselect it, and click the Comma check box to select it.

   ✓ *After selecting the correct delimiter, the fields in the selected cell, range, or column will appear in the Data preview pane, separated by vertical lines.*
7. To skip empty columns, click the Treat consecutive delimiters as one check box, and click Next.
8. In the Data preview window, click the last column to select it.
9. Under Column data format, click the Text option.
10. Click Finish.
11. Save the changes to the file, and leave it open to use in the next Try It.

Try It! Converting Fixed Width Text to Columns

1. In the **E47Try_xx** file, select the cell range F6:F57.
2. On the Data tab, click Text to Columns.
3. Click the Fixed width option, and click Next.
4. In the Data preview window, click 10 on the ruler.
5. Drag the line to the end of the first five digits, and click Next.
6. In the Data preview window, click the second column.
7. Under Column data format, click Do not import column (skip).
8. Click Finish.
9. Save and close the file, and exit Excel.

Lesson 47—Practice

Your manager at The Little Toy Shoppe wants you to create a newsletter to inform clients of new products and to entice them to return to the store on special sales days. Rob the intern has been keeping track of customer names and addresses in a new worksheet, but the worksheet is not formatted correctly. Unfortunately, Rob doesn't know the first thing about creating a workable database. In this project, you will take Rob's list and convert the data into usable columns.

DIRECTIONS

1. Start Excel, if necessary, and open **E47Practice** from the data files for this lesson.
2. Save the file as **E47Practice_xx** in the location where your teacher instructs you to store the files for this lesson.
3. Add a header to the worksheet that has your name at the left, the date code in the center, and the page number code at the right, and change back to **Normal** view.
4. Select the column headers for columns C and D, right-click the headers, and select **Insert** from the shortcut menu.
5. In cell **B5**, replace the text by typing **First Name**; type **Last Name** in cell **C5**.
6. Select the cell range **B6:B57**.
7. Click **Data** > **Text to Columns**.
8. Verify that the **Delimited** option is selected, and click **Next**.
9. Under Delimiters, click the **Space** check box to select it, click to clear any other check boxes that are selected, and click **Next**.
10. Click the first column in the Data preview window, and under Column data format, click the **Text** option.
11. Click the second column in the Data preview window, and under Column data format, click the **Text** option.
12. Click **Finish**.
13. Click **OK** in the confirmation dialog box.
14. Click the **Customize Quick Access Toolbar** button, and click **Spelling**.
15. Click the **Customize Quick Access Toolbar** button, and click **Spelling** to remove it.
16. **With your teacher's permission**, print the worksheet. It should look similar to Figure 47-1 on the next page.
17. Save and close the file, and exit Excel.

Figure 47-1

The Little Toy Shoppe

Customer Database

Title	First Name	Last Name		Address	City-State-Zip	Phone
Mrs.	Barbara	Adamson		7770 Dean Road	Cincinnati, OH 33240	844-1589
Mr.	Carlos	Altare		4125 Fairlinks Ave.	Carmel, IN 46231	298-1212
Mrs.	Diana	Bond		10208 E. Ridgefield Drive	Indian Blade, IN 46236	899-1712
Mrs.	Jan	Borough		7556 Hilltop Way	Cincinnati, OH 33254	291-3678
Mr.	Adam	Bounds		4943 Windridge Drive	Indianapolis, IN 42626	542-8151
Mrs.	Mary	Jane	Brink	704 Fairway Drive	Cincinnati, OH 33250	255-1655
Mr.	Shakur	Brown		5648 Hydcort	Indianapolis, IN 46250	842-8819
Mrs.	Rafiquil	Damir		14559 Senator Way	Indianapolis, IN 46226	844-9977
Mrs.	Diana	Dogwood		6311 Douglas Road	Wayne's Town, OH 33502	251-9052
Mrs.	Lucy	Fan		5784 N. Central	Indianapolis, IN 46268	255-6479
Mr.	Joshua	Fedor		1889 E. 72nd Street	Indian Blade, IN 46003	251-4796
Mrs.	Michele	Floyd		3203 Wander Wood Ct	Indianapolis, IN 46220	291-2510
Mrs.	Jennifer	Flynn		9876 Wilshire Ave.	Cincinnati, OH 33240	975-0909
Ms.	Katerina	Flynn		4984 Wander Wood Lane	Indianapolis, IN 42626	542-0021
Mr.	Eram	Hassan		8123 Maple Ave.	Cincinnati, OH 33250	722-1487
Mrs.	Betty	High		7543 Newport Bay Drive	Cincinnati, OH 33250	722-1043
Mrs.	Addie	Howard		7960 Susan Drive, S.	Westland, IN 46215	849-3557
Mr.	Tyrell	Johnson		11794 Southland Ave.	Wayne's Town, OH 33505	846-9812
Mr.	Michael	Jordain		4897 Kessler Ave.	Indianapolis, IN 46220	255-1133
Mrs.	Ashley	Kay		8738 Log Run Drive, S.	Carmel, IN 46234	299-6136
Mrs.	Rhoda	Kuntz		567 W. 72nd Street	Indian Blade, IN 46003	251-6539
Ms.	Verna	Latinz		14903 Senator Way	Indianapolis, IN 46226	844-4333
Mr.	Wu	Lee		6467 Riverside Drive	Carmel, IN 46220	257-1253
Mr.	Chu	Lee		5821 Wilshire Ave.	Cincinnati, OH 33240	975-0484

Excel 2016, Windows 10, Microsoft Corporation

Lesson 47—Apply

You are creating a newsletter to inform clients of new products and to entice them to return to the store on special sales days. You are working with a worksheet of customer names and addresses created by Rob the intern. However, the worksheet data is not in the most usable format. In this project, you will prepare the data and convert it into usable columns.

DIRECTIONS

1. Start Excel, if necessary, and open **E47Apply** from the data files for this lesson.
2. Save the file as **E47Apply_xx** in the location where your teacher instructs you to store the files for this lesson.
3. Add a header to the worksheet that has your name at the left, the date code in the center, and the page number code at the right, and change back to **Normal** view.
4. Notice that two of the names use all three columns; these names have two-part first names. Fix the names to appear in the correct columns.
   a. Type **Mary Jane** in cell **B11**, and type **Brink** in cell **C11**.
   b. Type **Chu Gi** in cell **B34**, and type **Nguyen** in cell **C34**.
   c. Delete column **D**.
5. Insert two columns between columns E and F.
6. Type **City** in cell **E5**, type **State** in cell **F5**, and type **ZIP Code** in cell **G5**.

7. Split the addresses in column E into two columns.
    a. Select the cell range **E6:E57**.
    b. Click **Data** > **Text to Columns**.
    c. Select the **Delimited** option and **Comma** as the delimiter used.
    d. Select **Text** as the format for first column.
8. Split the state and ZIP Codes in column F into two columns.
    a. Select the cell range **F6:F57**.
    b. Click **Data** > **Text to Columns**.
    c. Select the **Fixed Width** option.
    d. Add a delimiting line at the beginning of the ZIP codes in the Data preview window.
    e. Select **Text** as the format for first column, and **General** for the second column.
9. Adjust the column widths as needed.
10. Customize the Quick Access Toolbar with the features of your choices.
11. Customize the ribbon with the tabs and commands of your choice.
12. **With your teacher's permission**, print page 1 of the worksheet in landscape orientation. It should look similar to Figure 47-2.
13. Reset the Quick Access Toolbar and the ribbon to their default settings.
14. Save and close the file, and exit Excel.

Figure 47-2

The Little Toy Shoppe

Customer Database

Title	First Name	Last Name	Address	City	State	ZIP Code	Phone
Mrs.	Barbara	Adamson	7770 Dean Road	Cincinnati	OH	33240	844-1589
Mr.	Carlos	Altare	4125 Fairlinks Ave.	Carmel	IN	46231	298-1212
Mrs.	Diana	Bond	10208 E. Ridgefield Drive	Indian Blade	IN	46236	899-1712
Mrs.	Jan	Borough	7556 Hilltop Way	Cincinnati	OH	33254	291-3678
Mr.	Adam	Bounds	4943 Windridge Drive	Indianapolis	IN	42626	542-8151
Mrs.	Mary Jane	Brink	704 Fairway Drive	Cincinnati	OH	33250	255-1655
Mr.	Shakur	Brown	5648 Hydcort	Indianapolis	IN	46250	842-8819
Mrs.	Rafiquil	Damir	14559 Senator Way	Indianapolis	IN	46226	844-9977
Mrs.	Diana	Dogwood	6311 Douglas Road	Wayne's Town	OH	33502	251-9052
Mrs.	Lucy	Fan	5784 N. Central	Indianapolis	IN	46268	255-6479
Mr.	Joshua	Fedor	1889 E. 72nd Street	Indian Blade	IN	46003	251-4796
Mrs.	Michele	Floyd	3203 Wander Wood Ct	Indianapolis	IN	46220	291-2510
Mrs.	Jennifer	Flynn	9876 Wilshire Ave.	Cincinnati	OH	33240	975-0909
Ms.	Katerina	Flynn	4984 Wander Wood Lane	Indianapolis	IN	42626	542-0021
Mr.	Eram	Hassan	8123 Maple Ave.	Cincinnati	OH	33250	722-1487
Mrs.	Betty	High	7543 Newport Bay Drive	Cincinnati	OH	33250	722-1043
Mrs.	Addie	Howard	7960 Susan Drive, S.	Westland	IN	46215	849-3557
Mr.	Tyrell	Johnson	11794 Southland Ave.	Wayne's Town	OH	33505	846-9812
Mr.	Michael	Jordain	4897 Kessler Ave.	Indianapolis	IN	46220	255-1133
Mrs.	Ashley	Kay	8738 Log Run Drive, S.	Carmel	IN	46234	299-6136
Mrs.	Rhoda	Kuntz	567 W. 72nd Street	Indian Blade	IN	46003	251-6539
Ms.	Verna	Latinz	14903 Senator Way	Indianapolis	IN	46226	844-4333
Mr.	Wu	Lee	6467 Riverside Drive	Carmel	IN	46220	257-1253
Mr.	Chu	Lee	5821 Wilshire Ave.	Cincinnati	OH	33240	975-0484

Lesson 48

Formatting Cells

➤ What You Will Learn

Using Advanced Formatting of Dates and Times
Creating Custom Number Formats
Clearing Formatting from a Cell

Software Skills Sometimes, in order to accommodate the various kinds of data in a worksheet, you have to apply various formatting techniques that you might not ordinarily use, such as adjusting the row heights, merging cells, and slanting column labels. Other refinements you may need to make include applying the proper format to data—even if that means removing existing formats and creating your own.

What You Can Do

Using Advanced Formatting of Dates and Times

- You can change the way a date or time is displayed by formatting a cell or cells before or after entering the date/time.
- You can apply several standard date and time formats. The most common ones are located on the Number Format list on the Home tab of the ribbon.
- Use the Format Cells dialog box to apply other standard date and time formats.
- You can customize the way you want dates displayed by creating a custom number format.
- After entering a date, you can change its number format as needed. For example, you can change the date 1/14/18 to display as January 14, 2018.

Try It! Formatting a Date or Time with a Standard Format

1. Start Excel, and open **E48Try** from the data files for this lesson.
2. Save the file as **E48Try_xx** in the location where your teacher instructs you to store the files for this lesson.
3. Select the cell range G6:G20.
4. On the Home tab, in the Number group, click the Number Format drop-down arrow Date, and click Short Date.
5. Select the cell range L6:M20, click the Number Format drop-down arrow Date, and click Time.
6. Save the changes to the file, and leave it open to use in the next Try It.

Try It! Formatting a Date or Time with a Custom Format

1. In the **E48Try_xx** file, select the cell range G6:G20, click the Number Format drop-down arrow Date, and click More Number Formats.
2. On the Number tab, in the Category box, click Custom.
3. In the Type box, click the d-mmm-yy option.
4. Click OK.
5. Double-click the column border between the column G and column H headings to resize the column.
6. Save the changes to the file, and leave it open to use in the next Try It.

Applying a custom date format

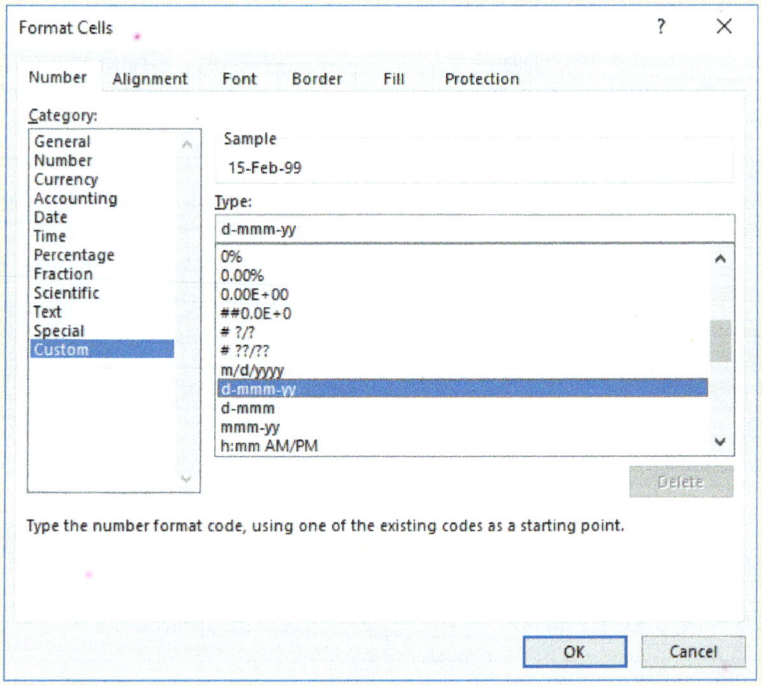

Creating Custom Number Formats

- When a number format doesn't fit your needs, you can create a custom number format:
  - Typically, you use a custom number format to preformat a column or row, prior to data entry. The custom format speeds the data entry process.
  - For example, if you need to type account numbers in the format AB-2342-CO, you can create a format that will insert the dashes for you. And if the account numbers all end in -CO, you can build that into the custom format as well.
- You create a custom number format by typing a series of special codes.

  ✓ *To speed the process, select an existing format and customize it.*
- You can specify format codes for positive numbers, negative numbers, zeros, and text:
  - If you wish to specify all four formats, you must type the codes in the order listed above.
  - If you specify only two formats, you must type a code for positive numbers and zeros first, and type a code for negative numbers second.
  - If you specify only one format, all numbers in the row or column will use that format.
  - To separate the formats, use a semicolon, as in the following custom number format: $#,##0.00;[red]($#,##0.00);"ZERO";[blue].
  - This format displays positive numbers as $0,000.00, negative numbers in red and parentheses, a zero as the word ZERO, and text in blue.
  - To specify a standard color, type any of the following in brackets: red, black, blue, white, green, yellow, cyan, and magenta.
  - The following table shows examples of codes you can use in creating a format:

#	Digit placeholder for one number
0	Zero placeholder
?	Digit placeholder for multiple digits (e.g., ?? allows two digits or one digit)
@	Text placeholder
.	Decimal point (period)
%	Percentage
,	Thousands separator (comma)
$	Dollar sign
-	Negative sign
+	Plus sign
( )	Parentheses
:	Colon
_	Underscore (skips one character width)
[color]	Type the name of a standard color (red, black, blue, white, green, yellow, cyan, or magenta)

- Custom number formats are saved with the worksheet, so if you want to use a custom format on another worksheet, use the Format Painter to copy the format.

Examples of formats you can create:

Type	To Display	Using This Code
5.56	5.5600	#.0000
5641	$5,641	$#,##0
5641 and -5641	$5,641 and ($5,641) in red	$#,##0;[red]($#,##0)
5641 and -5641	$5,641.00 and ($5,641.00) in red	$#,##0.00;[red]($#,##0.00)

Try It! Creating Custom Number Formats

1. In the **E48Try_xx** file, select the cell range N6:N20.
2. On the Home tab, click the Number group dialog box launcher ↘ to display the Format Cells dialog box.
3. In the Category box, click Custom.
4. Scroll through the Type list, and select 000-00-0000.
5. In the Type text box, place the insertion point before the first zero, and type **"AB-"**.
6. Place the insertion point after the last zero, and press BACKSPACE five times.
7. Click OK.
8. Click cell N6, type **35135**, and press ENTER. Notice the new format.
9. Save the changes to the file, and leave it open to use in the next Try It.

Creating a custom number format

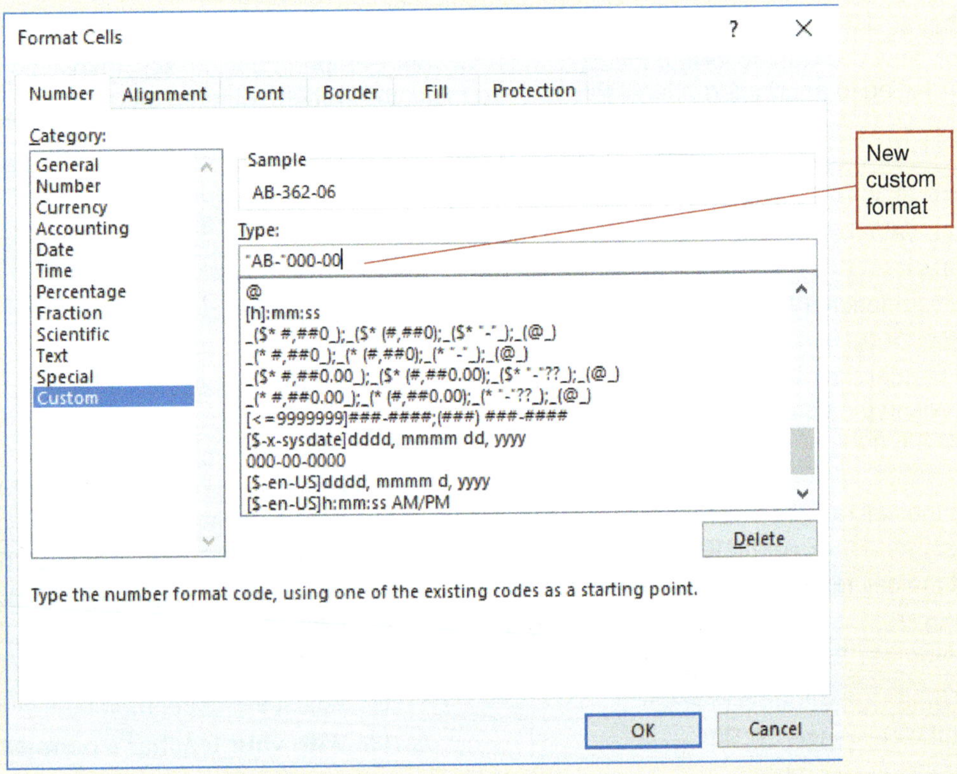

Excel 2016, Windows 10, Microsoft Corporation

Clearing Formatting from a Cell

- Sometimes, you may want to keep the data in a cell, but remove the formatting you've applied.
- Use the Clear button in the Editing group on the Home tab to clear just the format of a cell, without clearing its contents.

Try It! Clearing Formatting from a Cell

1. In the **E48Try_xx** file, select the cell range E6:E20.
2. On the Home tab, in the Editing group, click Clear .
3. Click Clear Formats.
4. Save and close the file, and exit Excel.

Lesson 48—Practice

As the owner of Giancarlo Franchetti's Go-Cart Speedrome, you're interested in using Excel to help you manage your growing business. You've created a worksheet for tracking daily admissions and receipts for your American businesses. Now you want to format the worksheet for your European businesses. In this project, you will use custom formatting to apply international formats and make the worksheet more attractive.

DIRECTIONS

1. Start Excel, if necessary, and open **E48Practice** from the data files for this lesson.
2. Save the file as **E48Practice_xx** in the location where your teacher instructs you to store the files for this lesson.
3. Add a header that has your name at the left, the date code in the center, and the page number code at the right, and change back to **Normal** view.
4. Select the cell range **C8:H8**. Click **Home** > **Orientation** > **Angle Counterclockwise.**
5. Select the cell range **B9:B20**.
6. Click the **Number Format** drop-down arrow > **More Number Formats**.
7. Click **Custom** > **d-mmm-yy** > **OK**.
8. Select the cell range **C9:D20**.
9. Click the **Number Format** drop-down arrow > **More Number Formats**. Click **Time** > **13:30:55** > **OK**.
10. Select the cell range **F21:H23**, right-click, and click **Format Cells**.
11. Click **Accounting**, click in the **Decimal places** box, and replace the zero with **2**. Click the **Symbol** drop-down arrow > **€ Euro (€ 123)** > **OK**.

    ✓ *Scroll down to about one-third in the Symbol list.*
12. Select the cell range **B21:H23**, click the **Borders** drop-down arrow > **Thick Outside Borders**.
13. Select the cell range **C9:H20**, right-click, and click **Format Cells**.
14. Click **Fill** > click the **Pattern Color** drop-down arrow > **Blue, Accent 5, Lighter 80%** (the ninth option in the second row).
15. Click the **Pattern Style** drop-down arrow > **Vertical stripe** (the second option in the second row).
16. Click **OK**.
17. Adjust the columns widths if needed.
18. **With your teacher's permission**, print the document.
19. Save and close the file, and exit Excel.

Figure 48-1

	A	B	C	D	E	F	G	H
1								
2								
3			Giancarlo Franchetti's Go-Cart Speedrome					
4								
5			Daily Admission Tracker		(Track is closed Monday & Tuesday through the racing season)			
6			Week					
7								
8			Start of Session	End of Session	Session Number	Adult	Child	Team Racers
9	Session Date	5-Oct-17	12:30:00	14:30:00		127	198	17
10		5-Oct-17	15:15:00	17:15:00		175	189	32
11		8-Oct-17	15:30:00	17:30:00		78	81	2
12		9-Oct-17	15:30:00	17:30:00		137	102	3
13		10-Oct-17	15:30:00	17:30:00		94	122	17
14		10-Oct-17	18:00:00	20:00:00		145	201	38
15		10-Oct-17	20:30:00	22:30:00		212	56	27
16		11-Oct-17	11:30:00	13:30:00		148	198	56
17		11-Oct-17	13:45:00	15:45:00		126	155	28
18		11-Oct-17	16:00:00	18:00:00		141	168	17
19		12-Oct-17	18:15:00	20:15:00		165	255	41
20		12-Oct-17	20:30:00	22:30:00		256	32	19
21		Total Admissions				€ 1,804.00	€ 1,757.00	€ 297.00
22		Admission Price				€ 10.25	€ 7.50	€ 5.00
23		Total Receipts				€ 18,491.00	€ 13,177.50	€ 1,485.00
24								

Excel 2016, Windows 10, Microsoft Corporation

Lesson 48—Apply

You are the owner of Giancarlo Franchetti's Go-Cart Speedrome, and you've created a worksheet for tracking daily admissions and receipts for your European businesses. In this project, you will use custom and conditional formatting to make the data easier to read.

DIRECTIONS

1. Start Excel, if necessary, and open **E48Apply** from the data files for this lesson.
2. Save the file as **E48Apply_xx** in the location where your teacher instructs you to store the files for this lesson.
3. Add a footer that has your name at the left, the worksheet file name in the center, and the page number code at the right, and change back to **Normal** view.
4. Apply a custom number format to the Session Number column.
    a. Select the cell range **E9:E20**.
    b. Display the **Format Cells** dialog box, and on the **Number** tab, click **Custom**.
    c. Replace the contents of the **Type** box with the following text: **00-00-"Session "0**.
    d. Click **OK**.
5. In the following cells, enter the session numbers, without dashes:

E9	**10051**
E10	**10052**
E11	**10081**
E12	**10091**
E13	**10101**
E14	**10102**
E15	**10103**
E16	**10111**
E17	**10112**
E18	**10113**
E19	**10121**
E20	**10122**

6. Clear the formatting in the title area, and reformat as shown in Figure 48-2 on the next page.
    a. Select the cell range **A1:I7**.
    b. Clear the formats in the selected range.
    c. Apply **Blue-Gray, Text 2, Lighter 40%** fill color to the selection.
    d. Apply bold formatting to the selection.
    e. Change the font size of cell **C3** to **24 pt**.
    f. Adjust the height of row 3 to **65**.
7. Apply conditional formatting to the dates.
    a. Select the cell range **B9:B20**.
    b. On the Home tab, click **Conditional Formatting**, point to **Highlight Cells Rules**, and click **Greater Than**.
    c. In the Greater Than dialog box, in the Format cells that are GREATER THAN box, replace the text with **=$B$13**.
    d. In the with box, select **Light Red Fill** and click **OK**. The dates greater than 10 Oct are formatted with light red fill.
8. Edit and manage conditional formatting you applied to the dates.
    a. On the Home tab, click **Conditional Formatting** > **Manage Rules**.
    b. Click the **Edit Rule** button.
    c. In the Edit Formatting Rule dialog box, in the middle drop-down list, click **equal to** and then click **OK**.
    d. Click **OK** to apply the changes and close the Conditional Formatting Rules Manager dialog box. The dates of 10 Oct are formatted with light red fill.
9. Adjust column widths if needed.
10. **With your teacher's permission**, adjust the page breaks and print the worksheet.
11. Save and close the file, and exit Excel.

Figure 48-2

Giancarlo Franchetti's Go-Cart Speedrome

Daily Admission Tracker (Track is closed Monday & Tuesday through the racing season)

Week

Session Date	Start of Session	End of Session	Session Number	Adult	Child	Team Racers
5-Oct-17	12:30:00	14:30:00	10-05-Session 1	127	198	17
5-Oct-17	15:15:00	17:15:00	10-05-Session 2	175	189	32
8-Oct-17	15:30:00	17:30:00	10-05-Session 1	78	81	2
9-Oct-17	15:30:00	17:30:00	10-09-Session 1	137	102	3
10-Oct-17	15:30:00	17:30:00	10-10-Session 1	94	122	17
10-Oct-17	18:00:00	20:00:00	10-10-Session 2	145	201	38
10-Oct-17	20:30:00	22:30:00	10-10-Session 3	212	56	27
11-Oct-17	11:30:00	13:30:00	10-11-Session 1	148	198	56
11-Oct-17	13:45:00	15:45:00	10-11-Session 2	126	155	28
11-Oct-17	16:00:00	18:00:00	10-11-Session 3	141	168	17
12-Oct-17	18:15:00	20:15:00	10-12-Session 1	165	255	41
12-Oct-17	20:30:00	22:30:00	10-12-Session 2	256	32	19
Total Admissions				€ 1,804.00	€ 1,757.00	€ 297.00
Admission Price				€ 10.25	€ 7.50	€ 5.00
Total Receipts				€ 18,491.00	€ 13,177.50	€ 1,485.00

Excel 2016, Windows 10, Microsoft Corporation

Lesson 49

Applying Conditional Formatting and International Settings

➤ What You Will Learn

Words to Know

Conditional formatting
Cell formatting that changes depending on the value in that cell, or in another referenced cell.

Latin characters
The alphabet characters originally used in the Latin language, also used in English, Spanish, French, Italian, and many other European languages.

Software Skills With advanced conditional formatting, you can set up logical conditions that cause data to be formatted differently. You can even create rules that use formulas, calculating the values in other cells to determine the conditions. You can also adjust settings in Excel to make it easier for users in different countries to understand and use your worksheets.

What You Can Do

Creating Custom Conditional Formatting Rules

- The basics of **conditional formatting** is that it changes the formatting of the cell depending on its content. You can set up conditional formatting by applying presets or by creating your own custom rules.
- To use a preset, click the Conditional Formatting button on the Home tab to open a menu, and then choose one of the preset types. There are presets that highlight the cells and that use a variety of symbols to mark different values, like color scales and icon sets.
- To create your own custom conditional formatting rule, use the New Rule command on the Conditional Formatting button's menu, to open the New Formatting Rule dialog box. Then create the rule using the dialog box controls.

- In the New Formatting Rule dialog box, you start by choosing a rule type; this sets the general parameters. Then you edit the rule description to define the exact conditions and the formatting to apply when the conditions are met.

✓ *You can also apply a preset conditional formatting rule and then customize it. See "Managing Conditional Formatting Rules" later in this lesson.*

Try It! Creating a Custom Conditional Formatting Rule

1. Start Excel, and open the **E49Try** file from the data files for this lesson.
2. Save the file as **E49Try_xx** in the location where your teacher instructs you to store the files for this lesson.
3. Select the cell range H6:H20.
4. Click Home > Conditional Formatting > New Rule.
5. In the Select a Rule Type list, click Format only top or bottom ranked values.
6. In the Edit the Rule Description area, click the Top drop-down arrow and click Bottom.
7. Double-click the current value in the text box and type **3** to replace it.
8. Click the Format button Format... .

New Formatting Rule dialog box

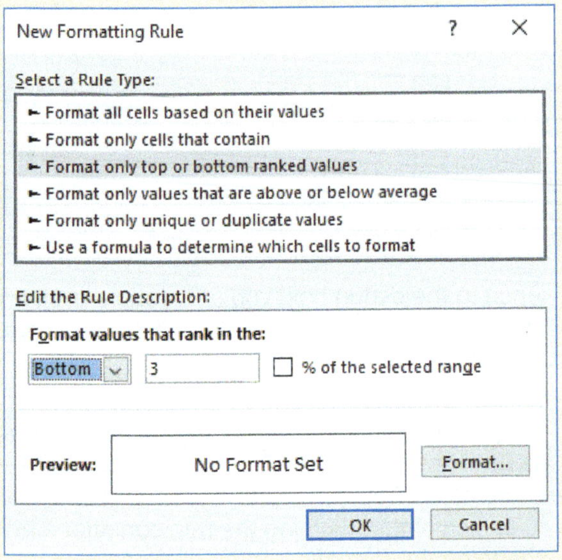

Excel 2016, Windows 10, Microsoft Corporation

9. In the Format Cells dialog box, click the Fill tab.
10. Click the Pattern Color drop-down arrow, and click the red square in the Standard Colors section.
11. Click the Pattern Style drop-down arrow, and click the 12.5% Gray square (fifth square in the top row).
12. Click OK.

Format Cells dialog box

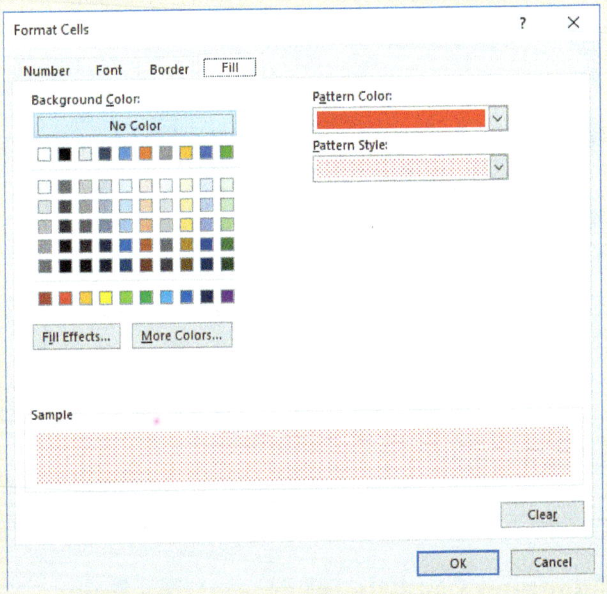

Excel 2016, Windows 10, Microsoft Corporation

13. Click OK to close the New Formatting Rule dialog box.
14. Save the changes to the file, and leave it open to use in the next Try It.

Creating Conditional Formatting Rules That Use Formulas

- Sometimes the desired condition for formatting certain cells cannot be easily expressed using any of the existing rule types. In these cases, you may want to use a formula to describe the desired condition.
- When writing a conditional formatting formula, you can reference functions and values in other cells, just like with any other formula.

✓ *When applying a conditional formatting formula to a range of cells, you can write the formula to reference the first cell in the range; the reference will adjust automatically for the other cells in the range.*

Try It! Creating Conditional Formatting Rules That Use Formulas

1. In the **E49Try_xx** file, select the cell range G6:G20.
2. Click Home > Conditional Formatting > New Rule.
3. In the Select a Rule Type list, click Use a formula to determine which cells to format.
4. Click in the Format values where this formula is true box, and type **=G6>TODAY()-1460**.
5. Click the Format button Format... .
6. Click the Fill tab.
7. Click the orange square in the Standard Colors section (the last row of colors).
8. Click OK.
9. Click OK to create the new rule.
10. Save the changes to the file, and leave it open to use in the next Try It.

✓ *This rule calculates whether the date in G6 is less than 4 years (1460 days) before today's date. The effect is to highlight hire dates for employees who have worked for the company for less than 4 years from today.*

New Formatting Rule dialog box

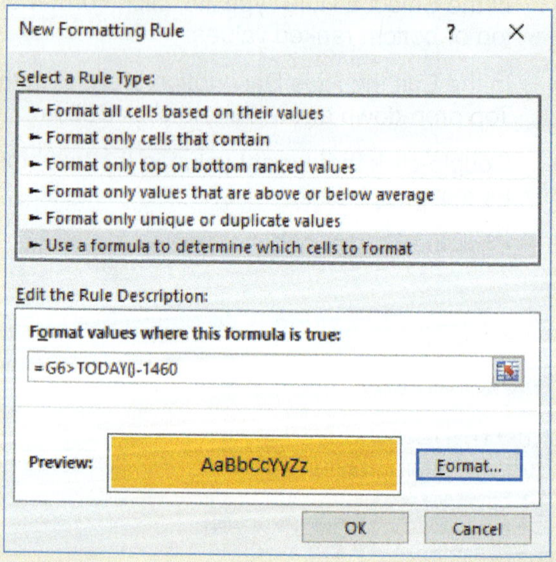

Excel 2016, Windows 10, Microsoft Corporation

Managing Conditional Formatting Rules

- You can make changes to conditional formatting rules, and even delete them entirely, from the Conditional Formatting Rules Manager dialog box. To access it, click Home > Conditional Formatting > Manage Rules.

✓ *The dialog box displays only the rules that apply to the active cell or range, so make sure you select the desired cell or range before you open the dialog box.*

- Once in the dialog box, you can double-click a rule or select it and click Edit Rule Edit Rule... to open it for editing. You can click Delete Rule Delete Rule to discard an unwanted rule.
- The Edit Formatting Rule dialog box is the same as the New Formatting Rule dialog box except for its name. You can make any changes to the rule, including redefining the rule conditions and changing the formatting to be applied.

Try It! Managing Conditional Formatting Rules

1. In the E49Try_xx file, select the cell range H6:H20.
2. Click Home > Conditional Formatting > Manage Rules.
3. Double-click the Bottom 3 rule to open it for editing.
4. Click the Bottom drop-down arrow Bottom and click Top.
5. Double-click the number 3 and type 5 to replace it.
6. Click OK.
7. Click OK to close the Conditional Formatting Rules Manager dialog box.
8. Select the cell range G6:G20.
9. Click Home > Conditional Formatting > Manage Rules.
10. Click the Formula rule to select it.
11. Click Delete Rule Delete Rule.
12. Click OK.
13. Save the changes to the file, and leave it open to use in the next Try It.

Applying Multiple Conditional Format Rules

- Conditional formatting is not always a yes/no test; you might have several possible formats to apply based on the cell content. For example, you might have different formatting for an A, B, C, D, or F in a gradebook.
- You can create your own multiple-condition formatting by creating multiple rules. There is no limit to the number of conditions you can set up.

✓ *You might not have to use multiple rules if you need to accommodate only three conditions. You can use one of the Color Scales presets, and then modify the rule as needed in the Conditional Formatting Rules Manager dialog box.*

- When there are multiple rules that apply to a certain cell or range, you have the option of stopping after the first rule that applies. For example, suppose you want to make the cell green if the value is between 90 and 100, and blue if it's between 80 and 90. You could set up the rule for green formatting, and then set it up to stop. Other rules for other color formatting will not be applicable.

Try It! Applying Multiple Conditional Format Rules

1. In the E49Try_xx file, select the cell range K6:K20.
2. Click Home > Conditional Formatting > Manage Rules.
3. Click New Rule New Rule... .
4. Click Format only cells that contain.
5. In the Edit the Rule Description section, click the Between drop-down arrow and click Greater than or equal to.
6. In the text box to the right of the drop-down list from step 5, type 3.
7. Click the Format button Format... .
8. Click the Font tab.
9. Click the Color drop-down arrow and click the red square in the Standard Colors section.
10. Click OK.
11. Click OK.
12. Click New Rule.
13. Click Format only cells that contain.
14. In the Edit the Rule Description section, click in the text box to the right of the Between drop-down list, and type 1.
15. Click in the text box to the right of the text box from step 14, and type 2.

(continued)

Try It! Applying Multiple Conditional Format Rules *(continued)*

16. Click the Format button Format... .
17. On the Font tab, click the Color drop-down arrow and click the blue square in the Standard Colors section.
18. Click OK.
19. Click OK.
20. Click to mark the Stop If True check box for the first rule.
21. Click OK. The rules are applied.
22. Save the changes to the file, and close it. Leave Excel open to use in the next Try It.

Two Rules Created for the Same Range

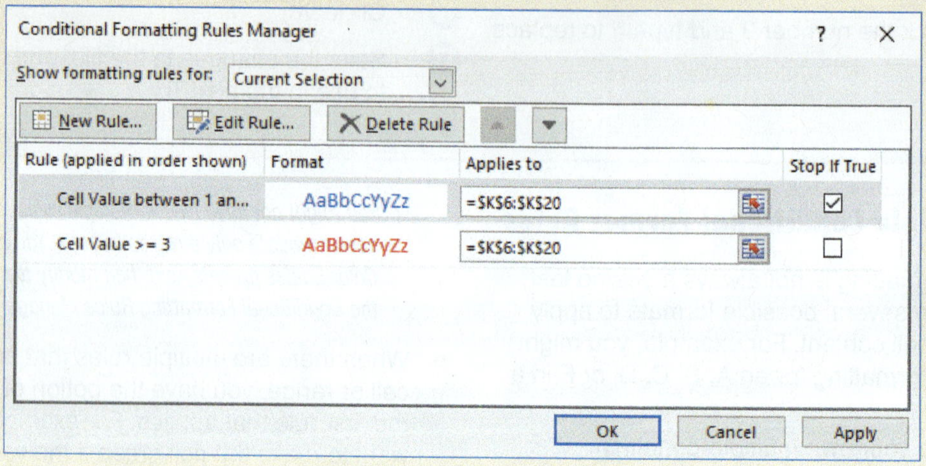

Excel 2016, Windows 10, Microsoft Corporation

Using Additional Languages

- If you are bilingual, or do work in different countries, you may want to add more editing languages. The editing language is less significant in Excel than in a more language-oriented program like Word, but it does affect the default spell check language.
- To work in another language, open the Excel Options dialog box, and then click Language. From here you can choose your default editing language and install additional editing languages. You can also choose different languages for the display (menus and dialog boxes) and for the Help system, provided you have the needed language packs installed in Windows.

Try It! Adding Support for Other Languages and Changing the Default Language

1. In Excel, click File > Options.
2. Click Language.
3. In the Choose Editing Languages section, click the Add additional editing languages drop-down arrow and click Chinese (PRC).
4. Click Add.
5. In the Choose Editing Languages section, click Chinese (PRC).
6. Click Set as Default. A message appears.
7. Click Yes.
8. Click OK. A message appears to restart Office.
9. Click OK.
10. Close Excel, and restart Excel. Leave Excel open for the next Try It.

(continued)

Try It! Adding Support for Other Languages and Changing the Default Language *(continued)*

Language options in Excel

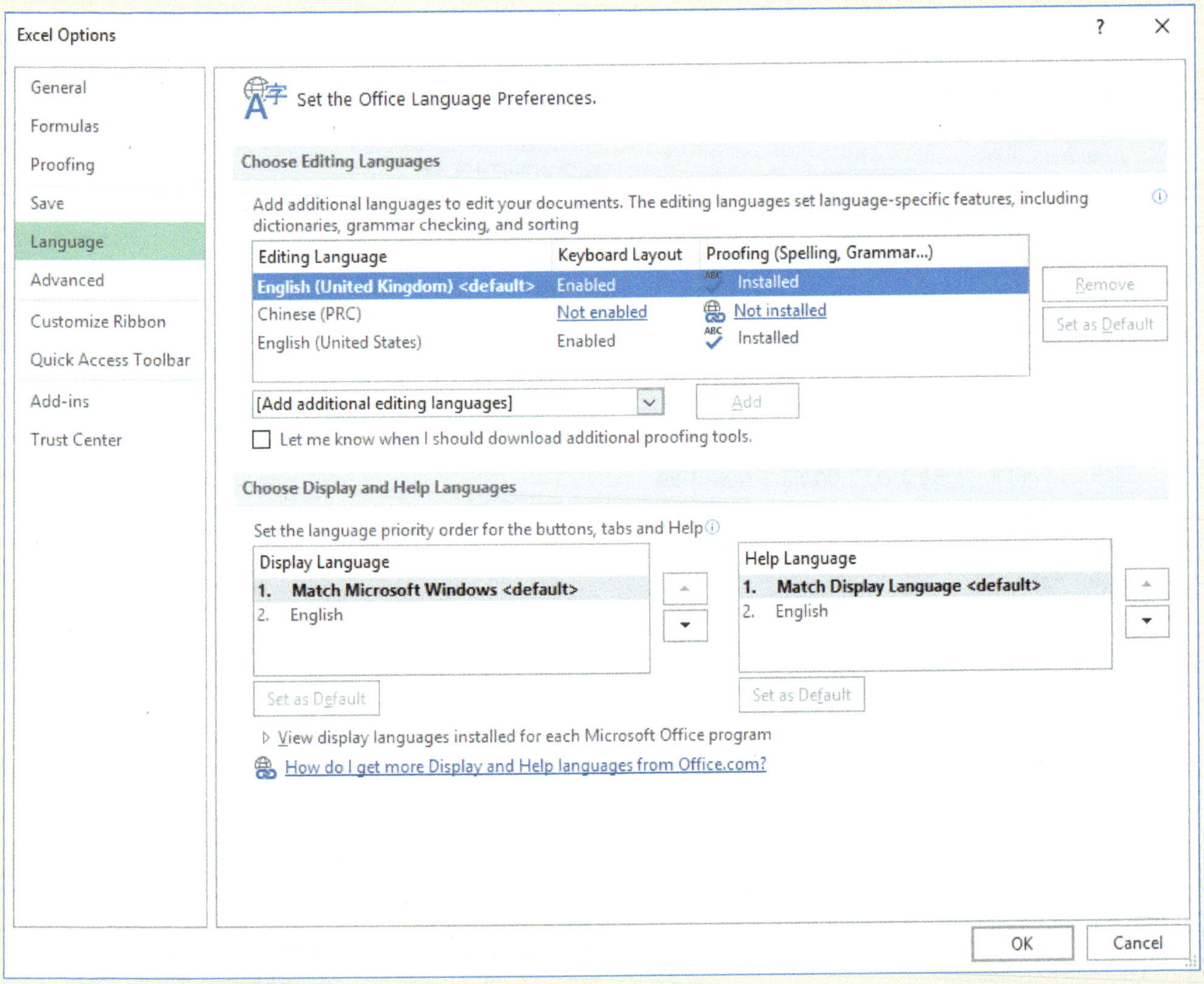

Excel 2016, Windows 10, Microsoft Corporation

Using Latin Characters

- English and many other European languages (such as Spanish and French) use the same basic character set, called **Latin characters**. Not all languages use these characters, however; for example, East Asian languages like Chinese do not.
- When you make a non-Latin language the default, you get different fonts on the Font drop-down list, including language-specific +Heading and +Body theme fonts, as shown in the following Try It exercise.

Try It! Exploring an International Interface

1. Start a new blank workbook.
2. On the Home tab, click the Font drop-down arrow to view the available fonts.
   - ✓ *Notice that there are many Chinese fonts on the list, and that the default Body and Heading theme fonts are Chinese, because of your activity in the previous Try It exercise.*
3. On the Home tab, in the Font group, click the drop-down arrow on the Show or Hide Phonetic Field button and click Phonetic Settings.
   - ✓ *The Show or Hide Phonetic Field button was not there previously; Excel added it when you made Chinese the default language in the previous Try It exercise. This is an example of an international customization of the interface.*
4. Click Cancel to close the Phonetic Properties dialog box.
5. Click Page Layout > Theme Fonts > Customize Fonts.
   - ✓ *Notice that the Create New Theme Fonts dialog box has two sections: for Latin and for East Asian. The East Asian section appears because of an East Asian language is installed (Chinese).*
6. Click Cancel to close the Create New Theme Fonts dialog box. Leave Excel open for the next Try It.

When a non-Latin language is enabled, you can have separate font themes for the languages

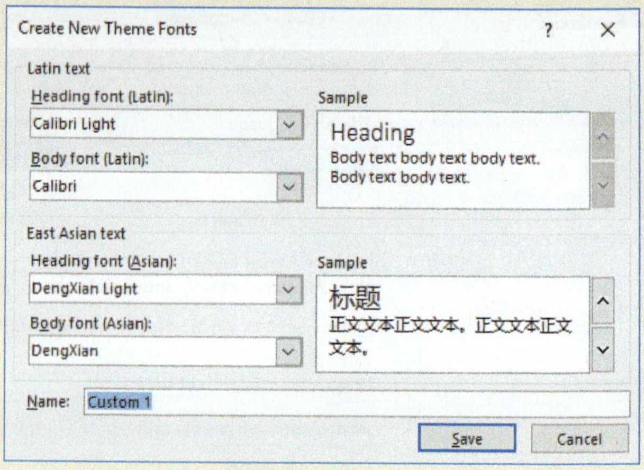

Excel 2016, Windows 10, Microsoft Corporation

Try It! Removing Additional Language Support

1. Click File > Options.
2. Click Language.
3. In the Choose Editing Languages section, click English (United States).
4. Click the Set as Default button Set as Default. A message appears.
5. Click Yes.
6. Click Chinese (PRC) and click Remove.
7. Click OK. A message appears to restart Office.
8. Click OK.
9. Close Excel and restart Excel. Start a new blank workbook.
10. Click Page Layout > Theme Fonts > Customize Fonts.
    - ✓ *Notice that the Create New Theme Fonts dialog box contains only one set of fonts now, because you removed Chinese from the editing languages.*
11. Click Cancel to close the dialog box. Leave Excel open for the next Try It.

Working with Currency in International Formats

- The most common way people need to work with international formats is through currency. You can choose an alternative currency symbol from the drop-down list on the Accounting Number Format button, which is on the Home tab in the Number group.
- If the symbol you want doesn't appear on this list, you can choose More Accounting Formats to pick from a larger list.

Try It! Working with Currency in International Formats

1. In Excel, reopen E49Try_xx.
2. Select the cell range H6:H20.
3. On the Home tab, click the drop-down arrow on the Accounting Number Format button $ ▾.
4. Click Euro.
5. Click the drop-down arrow on the Accounting Number Format button again $ ▾.
6. Click More Accounting Formats.
7. Click the Symbol drop-down arrow ⌄ and choose Korean.
8. Click OK.
9. Click the face of the Accounting Number Format button (not the arrow) to reapply the U.S. currency symbol ($).
10. Save the changes to the file, and leave it open to use in the next Try It.

Choose an alternate number format

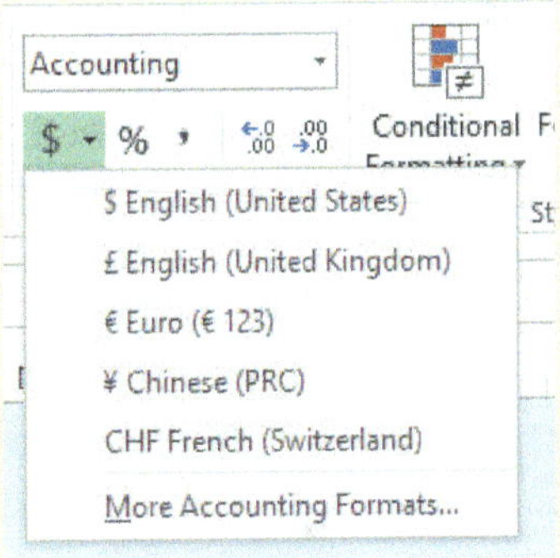

Excel 2016, Windows 10, Microsoft Corporation

Working with Text in International Formats

- If you need to enter a great deal of text in a different language, and that language requires a different keyboard layout than English, you might want to purchase a special keyboard and then switch to its layout using the Language feature in the Windows Control Panel.
- However, if you just have a few words to type in the foreign language, and the language uses Latin characters, you might be able to insert the few characters that your keyboard doesn't produce using the Insert > Symbol command. For example, you could insert a vowel with an accent mark over it, such as é.
- To use the spell-check feature for a different language, you can choose a different Dictionary language setting in the Spelling dialog box.

Try It! Inserting an Accented Letter and Spell-Checking in Another Language

1. In E49Try_xx, select cell A22 and type **Estaa informacion es confidencial**. Do not leave the cell yet.

   ✓ *That's an intentional typo in step 1. You'll fix it shortly.*

2. Select the second *o* in *informacion*.
3. Click Insert > Symbols > Symbol.
4. Click the Subset drop-down arrow and click Latin-1 Supplement.

   ✓ *Instead of step 4 you could simply scroll down through the available characters until you found the one you wanted. You aren't expected to know which subset a particular character resides in.*

5. Click ó (lowercase accented O).
6. Click Insert.
7. Click Close.
8. Click away from cell A22 to complete the data entry, and then click it again to reselect it.
9. Click Review > Spelling.
10. Click the Dictionary language drop-down arrow and click Spanish (Mexico).
11. Click Change to accept the proposed change from Estaa to Esta.
12. If you see a message asking if you want to continue checking at the beginning, click Yes.
13. Click the Dictionary language drop-down arrow and click English (United States).
14. Click Close.
15. Click OK.
16. Save the changes to the file, and exit Excel.

Select the appropriate accented letter

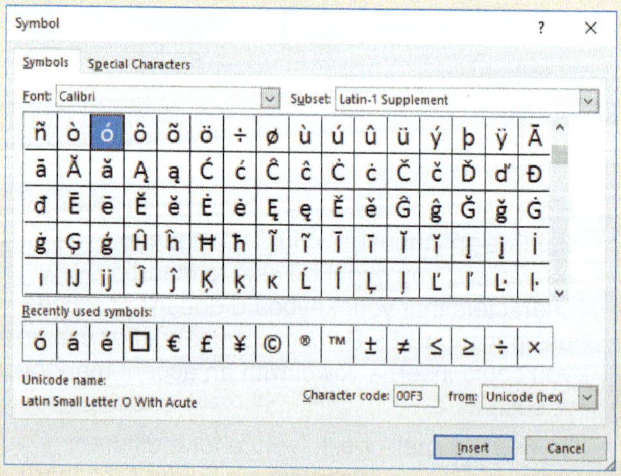

Excel 2016, Windows 10, Microsoft Corporation

Set the dictionary language appropriate to the text being checked

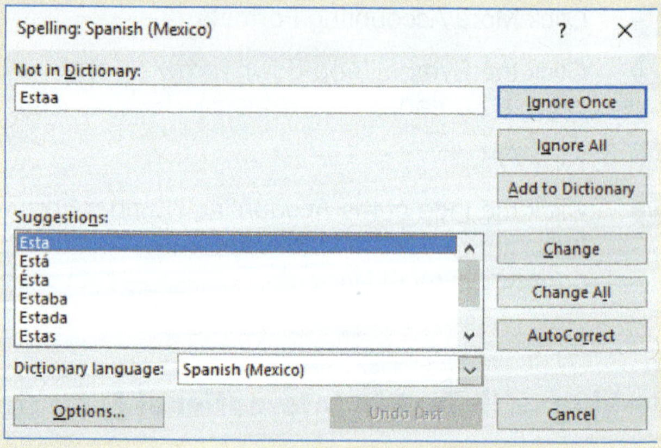

Excel 2016, Windows 10, Microsoft Corporation

Lesson 49—Practice

Giancarlo Franchetti's Go-Cart Speedrome has a track in Paris, France. The manager of that location has asked you to help him with his session-tracking worksheet. He would like to format the Sunday dates differently from the other days of the week. You will set up this conditional formatting for him, and also perform a spell-check.

DIRECTIONS

1. Start Excel, and open the **E49Practice** file from the data files for this lesson.
2. Save the workbook as **E49Practice_xx** in the location where your teacher instructs you to store the files for this lesson.
3. Insert a header that has your name at the left, the date code in the center, and the page number code at the right, and change back to **Normal** view.
4. Click in cell **A1**. Then click **Review** > **Spelling**.
5. Click the **Dictionary language** drop-down arrow and click French (France).
6. Click **Ignore Once** three times to ignore the errors generated by *Franchetti's*, *Cart*, and *Speedrome*.
7. Click **Change** to change the misspelled *sesion* to *session*.
8. Click **Change** to change *Numero* to *Numéro*.
9. Click **OK** at the Spell check complete message.
10. Select the cell range **B9:B20** and click **Home** > **Conditional Formatting** > **New Rule** New Rule... .
11. Click **Use a formula to determine which cells to format.**
12. Click in the **Format values where this formula is true** text box, and type **=WEEKDAY(B9)=1**.
13. Click the **Format** button Format... .
14. Click the **Fill** tab.
15. Click **Blue, Accent 1** (fifth color in the top row).
16. Click **OK**.
17. Click **OK**. One date appears with the new background, as shown in Figure 49-1.
18. **With your teacher's permission,** print the worksheet.
19. Save and close the file, and exit Excel.

Figure 49-1

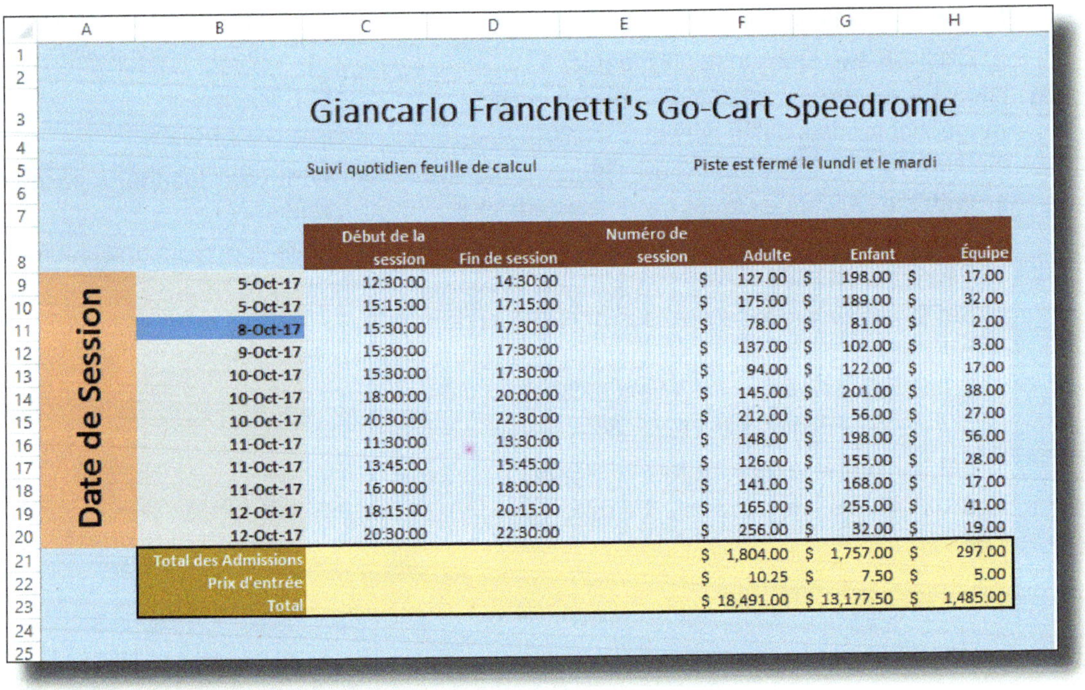

Giancarlo Franchetti's Go-Cart Speedrome

Suivi quotidien feuille de calcul — Piste est fermé le lundi et le mardi

		Début de la session	Fin de session	Numéro de session	Adulte	Enfant	Équipe
Date de Session	5-Oct-17	12:30:00	14:30:00		$ 127.00	$ 198.00	$ 17.00
	5-Oct-17	15:15:00	17:15:00		$ 175.00	$ 189.00	$ 32.00
	8-Oct-17	15:30:00	17:30:00		$ 78.00	$ 81.00	$ 2.00
	9-Oct-17	15:30:00	17:30:00		$ 137.00	$ 102.00	$ 3.00
	10-Oct-17	15:30:00	17:30:00		$ 94.00	$ 122.00	$ 17.00
	10-Oct-17	18:00:00	20:00:00		$ 145.00	$ 201.00	$ 38.00
	10-Oct-17	20:30:00	22:30:00		$ 212.00	$ 56.00	$ 27.00
	11-Oct-17	11:30:00	13:30:00		$ 148.00	$ 198.00	$ 56.00
	11-Oct-17	13:45:00	15:45:00		$ 126.00	$ 155.00	$ 28.00
	11-Oct-17	16:00:00	18:00:00		$ 141.00	$ 168.00	$ 17.00
	12-Oct-17	18:15:00	20:15:00		$ 165.00	$ 255.00	$ 41.00
	12-Oct-17	20:30:00	22:30:00		$ 256.00	$ 32.00	$ 19.00
	Total des Admissions				$ 1,804.00	$ 1,757.00	$ 297.00
	Prix d'entrée				$ 10.25	$ 7.50	$ 5.00
	Total				$ 18,491.00	$ 13,177.50	$ 1,485.00

Excel 2016, Windows 10, Microsoft Corporation

Lesson 49—Apply

The owner of The Little Toy Shoppe would like your help in organizing the store's customer database. He would like to color-code customer records according to their last order date. In this project you will implement conditional formatting that applies three different formats depending on the date. You will also correct name in the database.

DIRECTIONS

1. Start Excel, and open the **E49Apply** file from the data files for this lesson.
2. Save the workbook as **E49Apply_xx** in the location where your teacher instructs you to store the files for this lesson.
3. Insert a header that has your name at the left, the date code in the center, and the page number code at the right, and change back to **Normal** view.
4. Apply conditional formatting to the data in the Last Order Date column so that dates of 2014 or earlier appear with a red background.
   a. Select the cell range **G6:G57**.
   b. Click **Home** > **Conditional Formatting** > **New Rule**.
   c. Click **Format only cells that contain**.
   d. Set the cell value to be less than **12/31/2014**.

      ✓ *You can use the date 12/31/2014, or you can use its numeric equivalent, 42004.*

   e. Click **Format**.
   f. Set the format to be a **Red** background.
   g. Click **OK** two times to apply the rule.
5. Create a conditional formatting rule for the same range that formats dates between 1/1/2015 and 12/31/2015 with a yellow background.
   a. With the cell range **G6:G57** still selected, click **Home** > **Conditional Formatting** > **New Rule**.
   b. Click **Format only cells that contain**.
   c. Set the cell value to be between **1/1/2015** and **12/31/2015**.

      ✓ *You can use the dates 1/1/2015 and 12/31/2015 or their numeric equivalents, 42005 and 42369.*

   d. Set the format to be a **Yellow** background.
   e. Click **OK** two times to apply the rule.
6. Click a conditional formatting rule for the same range that formats dates in 2016 and later with a green background.
   a. With the cell range **G6:G57** still selected, click **Home** > **Conditional Formatting** > **New Rule**.
   b. Click **Format only cells that contain**.
   c. Set the cell value to be greater than or equal to **1/1/2016**.
   d. Set the format to be a **Green** background.

      ✓ *You can use the date 1/1/2016 or its numeric equivalent, 42370.*

   e. Click **OK** two times to apply the rule.
7. In cell **C35**, change the last name to **Nuñez** (with a tilde over the second n).
   a. Double-click in cell **C35** to move the insertion point into the cell.
   b. Delete the **i** in the name, changing it to Nunez.
   c. Select the second **n** in the name.
   d. Click **Insert** > **Symbols** > **Symbol**.
   e. Scroll down to find the **ñ** and select it.

      ✓ *That character is in the Latin-1 Supplement subset. The character code is 00F1.*

   f. Click **Insert**.
   g. Click **Close**.
8. **With your teacher's permission**, print the worksheet.
9. Save your work and exit Excel.

Figure 49-2

Excel 2016, Windows 10, Microsoft Corporation

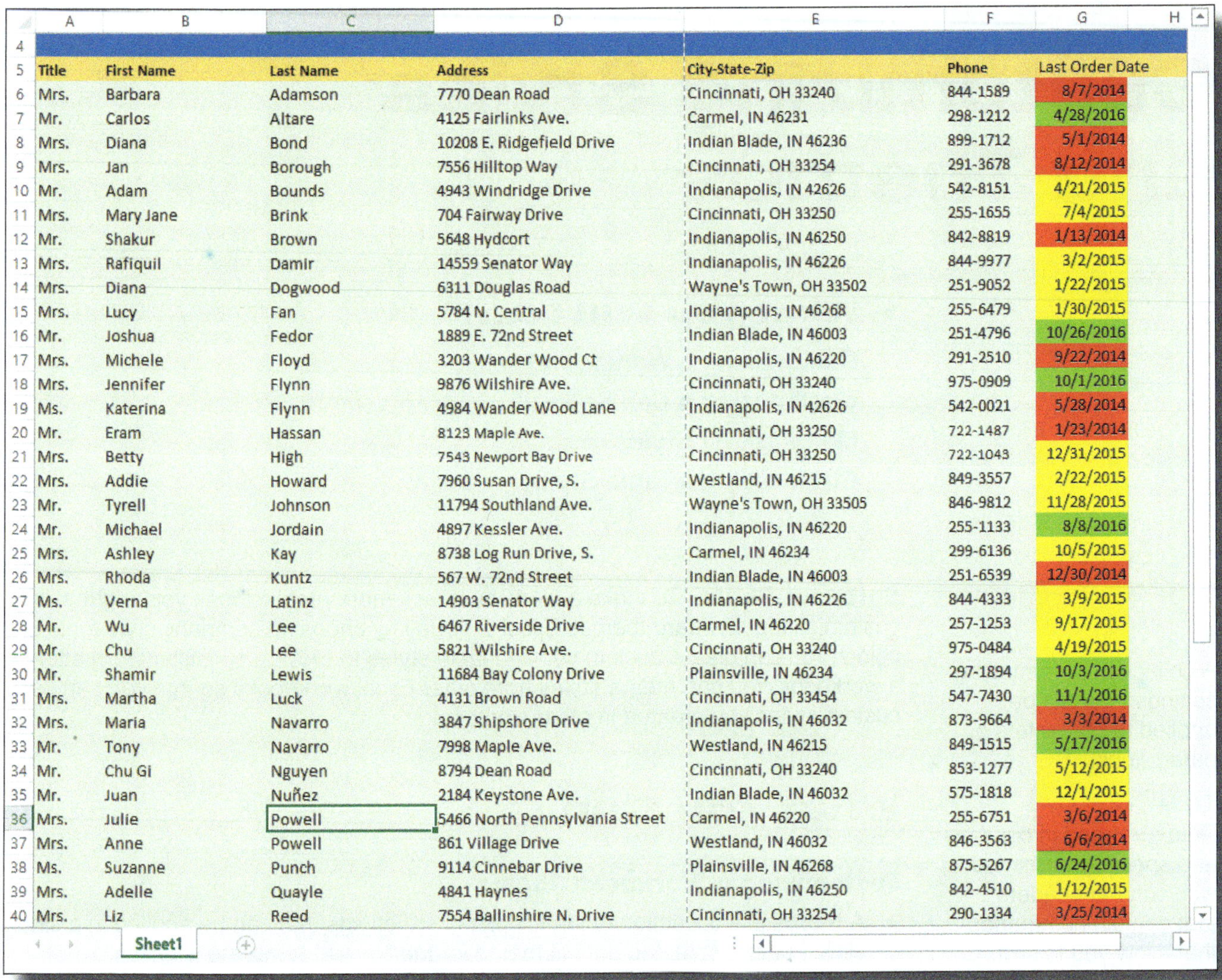

	Title	First Name	Last Name	Address	City-State-Zip	Phone	Last Order Date
6	Mrs.	Barbara	Adamson	7770 Dean Road	Cincinnati, OH 33240	844-1589	8/7/2014
7	Mr.	Carlos	Altare	4125 Fairlinks Ave.	Carmel, IN 46231	298-1212	4/28/2016
8	Mrs.	Diana	Bond	10208 E. Ridgefield Drive	Indian Blade, IN 46236	899-1712	5/1/2014
9	Mrs.	Jan	Borough	7556 Hilltop Way	Cincinnati, OH 33254	291-3678	8/12/2014
10	Mr.	Adam	Bounds	4943 Windridge Drive	Indianapolis, IN 42626	542-8151	4/21/2015
11	Mrs.	Mary Jane	Brink	704 Fairway Drive	Cincinnati, OH 33250	255-1655	7/4/2015
12	Mr.	Shakur	Brown	5648 Hydcort	Indianapolis, IN 46250	842-8819	1/13/2014
13	Mrs.	Rafiquil	Damir	14559 Senator Way	Indianapolis, IN 46226	844-9977	3/2/2015
14	Mrs.	Diana	Dogwood	6311 Douglas Road	Wayne's Town, OH 33502	251-9052	1/22/2015
15	Mrs.	Lucy	Fan	5784 N. Central	Indianapolis, IN 46268	255-6479	1/30/2015
16	Mr.	Joshua	Fedor	1889 E. 72nd Street	Indian Blade, IN 46003	251-4796	10/26/2016
17	Mrs.	Michele	Floyd	3203 Wander Wood Ct	Indianapolis, IN 46220	291-2510	9/22/2014
18	Mrs.	Jennifer	Flynn	9876 Wilshire Ave.	Cincinnati, OH 33240	975-0909	10/1/2016
19	Ms.	Katerina	Flynn	4984 Wander Wood Lane	Indianapolis, IN 42626	542-0021	5/28/2014
20	Mr.	Eram	Hassan	8123 Maple Ave.	Cincinnati, OH 33250	722-1487	1/23/2014
21	Mrs.	Betty	High	7543 Newport Bay Drive	Cincinnati, OH 33250	722-1043	12/31/2015
22	Mrs.	Addie	Howard	7960 Susan Drive, S.	Westland, IN 46215	849-3557	2/22/2015
23	Mr.	Tyrell	Johnson	11794 Southland Ave.	Wayne's Town, OH 33505	846-9812	11/28/2015
24	Mr.	Michael	Jordain	4897 Kessler Ave.	Indianapolis, IN 46220	255-1133	8/8/2016
25	Mrs.	Ashley	Kay	8738 Log Run Drive, S.	Carmel, IN 46234	299-6136	10/5/2015
26	Mrs.	Rhoda	Kuntz	567 W. 72nd Street	Indian Blade, IN 46003	251-6539	12/30/2014
27	Ms.	Verna	Latinz	14903 Senator Way	Indianapolis, IN 46226	844-4333	3/9/2015
28	Mr.	Wu	Lee	6467 Riverside Drive	Carmel, IN 46220	257-1253	9/17/2015
29	Mr.	Chu	Lee	5821 Wilshire Ave.	Cincinnati, OH 33240	975-0484	4/19/2015
30	Mr.	Shamir	Lewis	11684 Bay Colony Drive	Plainsville, IN 46234	297-1894	10/3/2016
31	Mrs.	Martha	Luck	4131 Brown Road	Cincinnati, OH 33454	547-7430	11/1/2016
32	Mrs.	Maria	Navarro	3847 Shipshore Drive	Indianapolis, IN 46032	873-9664	3/3/2014
33	Mr.	Tony	Navarro	7998 Maple Ave.	Westland, IN 46215	849-1515	5/17/2016
34	Mr.	Chu Gi	Nguyen	8794 Dean Road	Cincinnati, OH 33240	853-1277	5/12/2015
35	Mr.	Juan	Nuñez	2184 Keystone Ave.	Indian Blade, IN 46032	575-1818	12/1/2015
36	Mrs.	Julie	Powell	5466 North Pennsylvania Street	Carmel, IN 46220	255-6751	3/6/2014
37	Mrs.	Anne	Powell	861 Village Drive	Westland, IN 46032	846-3563	6/6/2014
38	Ms.	Suzanne	Punch	9114 Cinnebar Drive	Plainsville, IN 46268	875-5267	6/24/2016
39	Mrs.	Adelle	Quayle	4841 Haynes	Indianapolis, IN 46250	842-4510	1/12/2015
40	Mrs.	Liz	Reed	7554 Ballinshire N. Drive	Cincinnati, OH 33254	290-1334	3/25/2014

Lesson 50

Customizing Styles and Themes

➤ What You Will Learn

Customizing a Workbook Theme
Customizing a Cell Style
Merging Cell Styles
Customizing a Table Style

WORDS TO KNOW

Style
A collection of formatting settings that can be applied to characters or paragraphs.

Table
Data arranged in columns and specially formatted with column headers that contain commands that allow you to sort, filter, and perform other functions on the table.

Template
A document that contains formatting, styles, and sample text that you can use to create new documents.

Theme
A set of coordinated colors, fonts, and effects that can be applied to Office documents.

Software Skills To make a worksheet look more professional, you might want to customize the standard themes Excel provides by choosing company-style fonts and colors. You can create custom cell and table styles to provide consistent formatting in a workbook. You can merge styles from other Excel workbooks so that you can use custom styles you created in other workbooks.

What You Can Do

Customizing a Workbook Theme

- A **theme** is a collection of fonts, colors, and effects that can be applied in a single click. For example, the default theme for the Normal **template** is Office.
- You can select a different set of existing fonts, colors, and effects and save them in a new theme.
- You can create your own custom set of colors or fonts for use with a theme.
- Themes you create are automatically added to a Custom group in the Themes gallery on the Page Layout tab.
- When you save a custom theme, you change the template file of the current document.
- You can reset, or restore, the default template theme, even if you apply a different theme, or a custom theme.
- You can delete a custom theme that you no longer need. Deleting a custom theme does not affect existing documents formatted with that theme.

Try It! Customizing Theme Colors

1. Start Excel, and open **E50TryA** file from the data files for this lesson.
2. Save the file as **E50TryA_xx** in the location where your teacher instructs you to store the files for this lesson.
3. Click Page Layout > Colors > Customize Colors. The Create New Theme Colors dialog box displays.
4. Click the Accent 6 button, and click Blue, Accent 1, Lighter 40%.
5. Click the Accent 2 button, and click Blue, Accent 1, Darker 50%.
6. Click the Hyperlink button, and click Dark Blue, Hyperlink, Lighter 40%.
7. In the Name box, type your name, and click Save.
8. On the Page Layout tab, click Colors , right-click your custom theme, and click Delete.
9. Click Yes in the confirmation dialog box.
10. Save the changes to the file, and leave it open to use in the next Try It.

Creating a new theme color

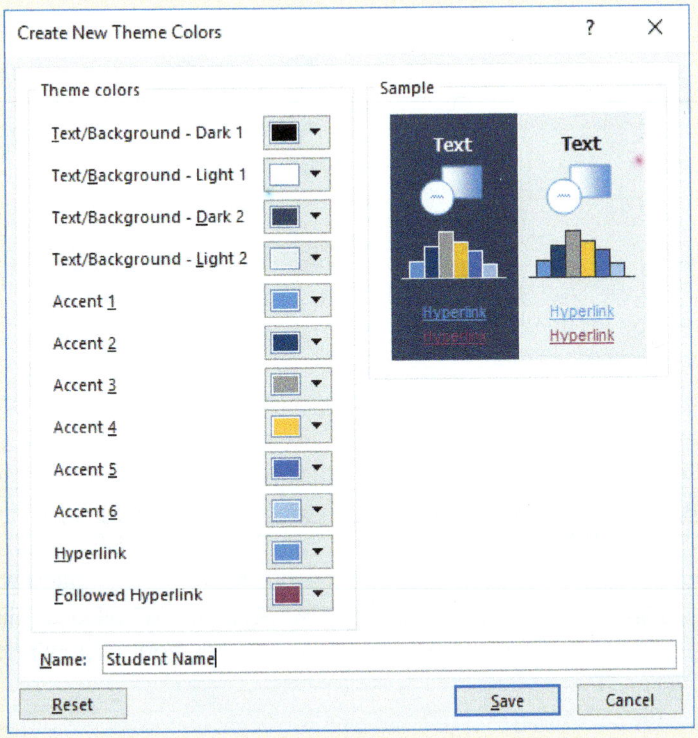

Excel 2016, Windows 10, Microsoft Corporation

Try It! Customizing Theme Fonts

1. In the E50TryA_xx file, on the Page Layout tab, click Fonts A > Customize Fonts. The Create New Theme Fonts dialog box displays.
2. Click the Heading font drop-down arrow, and click Verdana.
3. Click the Body font drop-down arrow and select Tahoma.
4. In the Name box, type your name, and click Save.
5. On the Page Layout tab, click Fonts A, right-click your custom font set, and click Delete.
6. Click Yes in the confirmation dialog box.
7. Save the changes to the file, and leave it open to use in the next Try It.

Try It! Saving and Deleting a New Theme

1. In the E50TryA_xx file, on the Page Layout tab, click Themes > Save Current Theme.
2. In the Name box, type your name, and click Save.
3. Click Themes > Facet.
4. Click Themes, and click your custom theme.
5. Click Themes, right-click your custom theme, and click Delete.
6. Click Yes in the confirmation dialog box.
7. Save the changes to the file, and leave it open to use in the next Try It.

Customizing a Cell Style

- A cell **style** includes settings for number, alignment, font border, fill, and protection properties.
- Excel comes with built-in cell styles.
- If you do not want to use a built-in cell style, you can create and save your own.
- You can access the Cell Styles gallery from the Styles group of the Home tab of the ribbon.

  ✓ *Depending on the width of your screen, you may need to click the Styles dialog box launcher to display the cell styles.*

- You can modify a cell style, and save it as a new, custom cell style.
- When you create a new cell style, it is saved in the current workbook. You can use it only in the workbook where you created it.
- Cell styles you create are automatically added to a Custom group in the Cell Styles gallery.
- You can delete a cell style that you no longer need. Deleting a custom cell style does not affect existing documents formatted with that cell style.
- To delete a cell style, access it from the Cell Style gallery, right-click it, and click Delete.

Try It! Customizing a Cell Style

1. In the **E50TryA_xx** file, click cell A3, and format it with custom formatting.
   a. On the Home tab, in the Font group, click Fill Color > Gold, Accent 4.
   b. Click the Font drop-down arrow > Arial.
   c. On the Home tab, in the Alignment group, click Center.
2. On the Home tab, in the Styles group, click the More button.

   ✓ *Depending on the width of your screen, you may need to click the Styles dialog box launcher to display the cell styles.*

3. Click New Cell Style. The Style dialog box displays.
4. In the Style name box, type your name. Verify that the cell style settings are the ones you applied.
5. Click OK.
6. Select the cell range A4:A7.
7. On the Home tab, in the Styles group, click the More button, and click your custom cell style.
8. Save the changes to the file, and leave it open to use in the next Try It.

Creating a new cell style

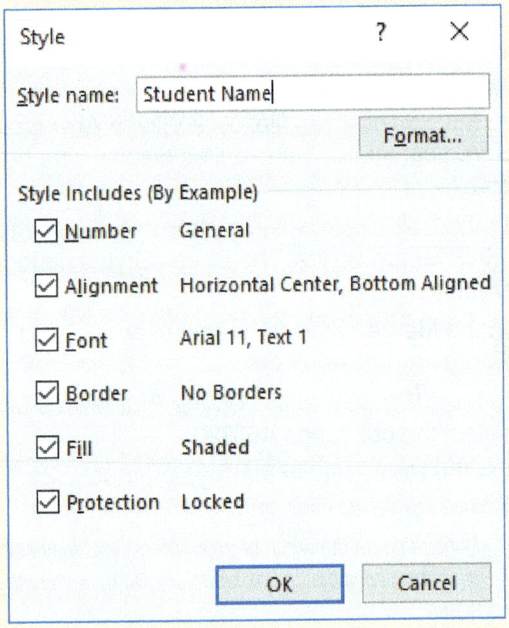

Excel 2016, Windows 10, Microsoft Corporation

Merging Cell Styles

- When you create a new cell style, you can use it only in the workbook where you created it.
- If you need to use cell styles you created in other workbooks, you can copy or merge the cell styles from the other workbooks into your current workbook.
- You can also copy or merge cell styles from other Excel templates into a current Excel template.
- The Undo command cannot reverse the effects of a cell style merge. Be sure you want to copy over all of the cell styles from the source workbook to the destination workbook.
- If the workbook into which you merge cell styles has style names that match the style names of the source workbook, the new cell styles can override the existing ones.
- You may want to delete unwanted cell styles from the source workbook before you merge styles.
- You can access the Merge Styles command at the bottom of the Cell Styles gallery in the Styles group on the Home tab of the ribbon.

Try It! Merging Cell Styles

1. Make sure that the **E50TryA_xx** file is still open from the previous Try It.
2. Open **E50TryB** from the data files for this lesson.
3. Save the file as **E50TryB_xx** in the location where your teacher instructs you to store the files for this lesson.
4. In the **E50TryB_xx** file, click View > Arrange All > Vertical > OK. The two files display side by side.
5. In the **E50TryB_xx** file, click Home > Cell Styles > Merge Styles. The Merge Styles dialog box displays.
6. In the Merge styles from box, click **E50TryA_xx.xlsx** > OK.
7. In the **E50TryB_xx** file, on the Employees tab, select the cell range A6:B20.
8. On the Home tab, in the Styles group, click Cell Styles, and click your custom cell style.

   ✓ *Depending on the width of your screen, you may need to click the Styles dialog box launcher to display the cell styles.*
9. Save the **E50TryB_xx** file, and close it.
10. Save the **E50TryA_xx** file, and leave it open to use in the next Try It.

Merging cell styles

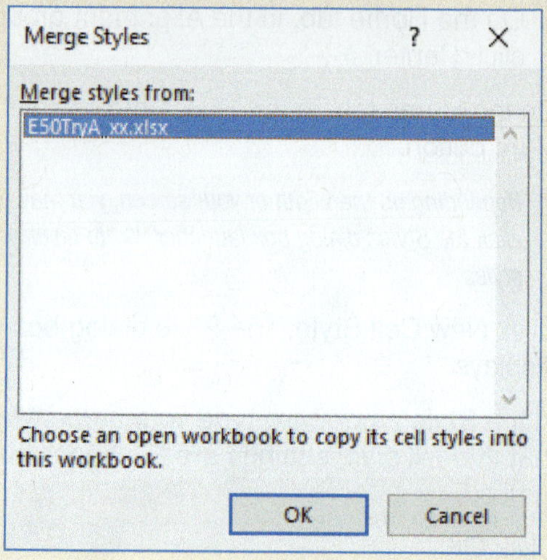

Excel 2016, Windows 10, Microsoft Corporation

Customizing a Table Style

- You can convert a list of data in Excel into a **table** using the Format as Table button on the Home tab.
- You can select an overall table format and other formatting settings on the Table Tools Design tab.
- Use one of Excel's existing table formats or create a custom table style that will appear in the Table Style gallery. You can then apply that table style to any other table.
- When you create a new table style, you can set the new table style as the default table style to be used in that workbook.
- Using the New Table Style dialog box, you can format the following table elements:
  - Whole Table: Applies a formatting choice to the entire table.
  - First Column Stripe: Applies a formatting choice to the first column in the table as well as each alternating column.
  - Second Column Stripe: Applies a formatting choice to the second column in the table as well as each alternating column.
  - First Row Stripe: Applies a formatting choice to the first row in the table as well as each alternating row.
  - Second Row Stripe: Applies a formatting choice to the second row in the table as well as each alternating row.
  - Last Column: Applies a formatting choice to the last column in a table. The last column usually contains totals.
  - First Column: Applies a formatting choice to the first column in a table. The first column usually contains headings.
  - Header Row: Applies a formatting choice to the header row in a table.

- Total Row: Applies a formatting choice to the final totals row in a table.
- First Header Cell: Applies a formatting choice to the first cell in the header row. This cell often contains no data.
- Last Header Cell: Applies a formatting choice to the final cell in the header row in a table.
- First Total Cell: Applies a formatting choice to the first cell in the total row. This cell often contains the heading "Total".
- Last Total Cell: Applies a formatting choice to the final cell in the total row. This cell often holds an overall total number.

- A new table style consists only of the formatting you apply as you create the table style. It will not automatically use any direct cell formatting you may have applied or use new cell styles you have created.

Try It! Creating a New Table Style

1. In the **E50TryA_xx** file, clear the cell formatting from the cell range A2:H2.
   a. Select the cell range A2:H2.
   b. On the Home tab, click Clear Clear > Clear Formats.
2. Select the cell range A2:H7, and format it as a table.
   a. On the Home tab, click Format as Table.
   b. Select Table Style Light 1.
   c. Verify that the data range shown in the Format As Table dialog box reflects the cell range A2:H7.
   ✓ *Excel will automatically insert absolute references. Recall that you learned about absolute references in Excel, Lesson 8.*
   d. Verify that the My table has headers check box is selected, and click OK.
   e. On the Table Tools Design tab, select the following options in the Table Style Options group: Header Row, Total Row, Last Column. Deselect any other options.
   ✓ *If your custom cell style is applied to cell A8 when you have added the Total row, click in cell A8 and then click Home > Clear > Clear Formats to remove the cell style.*
3. Click Home > Format as Table > New Table Style. The New Table Style dialog box displays.
4. In the Name box, type your name.
5. In the Table Element box, click Header Row > Format Format. The Format Cells dialog box displays.
6. Click the Fill tab, and under Background Color click Black.
7. Click the Font tab, and in the Font style list, click Bold.
8. On the Font tab, click the Color drop-down arrow, click White, Background 1, and click OK.
9. In the Table Element box, click Total Row > Format Format.
10. On the Font tab, in the Font style list, click Bold.
11. Click the Border tab, in the Style box click the double line option (last option in the second column), and under Presets click Outline.
12. Click the Fill tab, click the brighter blue in the theme colors (fifth option in the first row), and click OK.
13. In the Table Element box, scroll down, click Last Total Cell > Format Format.
14. Click the Fill tab, on the Standard colors palette click Orange, and click OK.
15. In the Table Element box, scroll up, click Whole Table > Format Format.
16. Click the Border tab, click the Color drop-down arrow, click Blue-Gray, Text 2, Lighter 40%, under Presets click Inside, and click OK.
17. Click OK to apply the changes and close the New Table Style dialog box.
18. Click inside the table, click Table Tools Design, and in the Table Styles gallery click your custom table style.
    ✓ *Depending on the width of your screen, you may need to click the Quick Styles button to display the table styles.*
19. Save and close the file, and exit Excel.

(continued)

Try It! **Creating a New Table Style** *(continued)*

Creating a table style

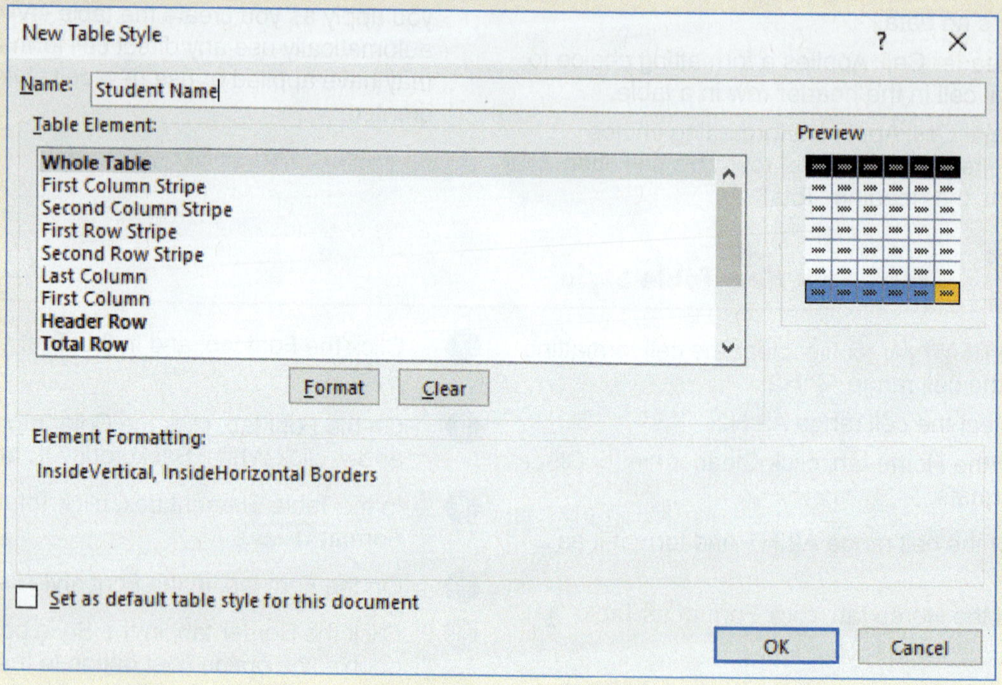

Excel 2016, Windows 10, Microsoft Corporation

Lesson 50—Practice

The worksheet you designed to track accessories sold each day at your PhotoTown store has proven very helpful, and the corporate headquarters may adopt it throughout the company. In this project, you will create a custom theme that follows the company publication standards.

DIRECTIONS

1. Start Excel, if necessary, and open **E50Practice** from the data files for this lesson.
2. Save the file as **E50PracticeA_xx** in the location where your teacher instructs you to store the files for this lesson.
3. Add a header that has your name at the left, the date code in the center, and the page number code at the right, and change back to **Normal** view.
4. Click **Page Layout** > **Colors** > **Customize Colors**.
5. Click the **Accent 5** button and select **More Colors**.
6. Set Red to **224**, Green to **183**, and Blue to **119** and click **OK**.
7. Click the **Accent 6** button, and click **More Colors**.
8. Change Red to **160**, Green to **113**, and Blue to **255**, and click **OK**.
9. In the Name box, type **PhotoTown**, and click **Save** to save the new color set.
10. Select the cell range **A6:C6**.
11. Click **Home** > **Fill Color** > **Gold, Accent 4, Lighter 40%**.
12. Click **Home** > **Font Color** > **Blue, Accent 1, Darker 25%**.

13. Click **Page Layout** > **Fonts** A > **Customize Fonts**.
14. Click the Heading font drop-down arrow, and click **Arial Rounded MT Bold**.
15. Click the Body font drop-down arrow, and click **Baskerville Old Face**.
16. In the Name box, type **PhotoTown**, and click **Save** to save the new font set.
17. Select cell range **A6:C6**, press and hold CTRL, and click cell **A2**.
18. Click **Home** > **Font** > **Arial Rounded MT Bold**. (Choose it from the Theme Fonts area at the top of the list.)
19. Click **Page Layout** > **Themes** > **Save Current Theme**.
20. Save the theme as **E50PracticeB_xx** in the location where your teacher instructs you to store the files for this lesson.
21. **With your teacher's permission**, print the worksheet. It should look similar to Figure 50-1.
22. Save and close the file, and exit Excel.

Figure 50-1

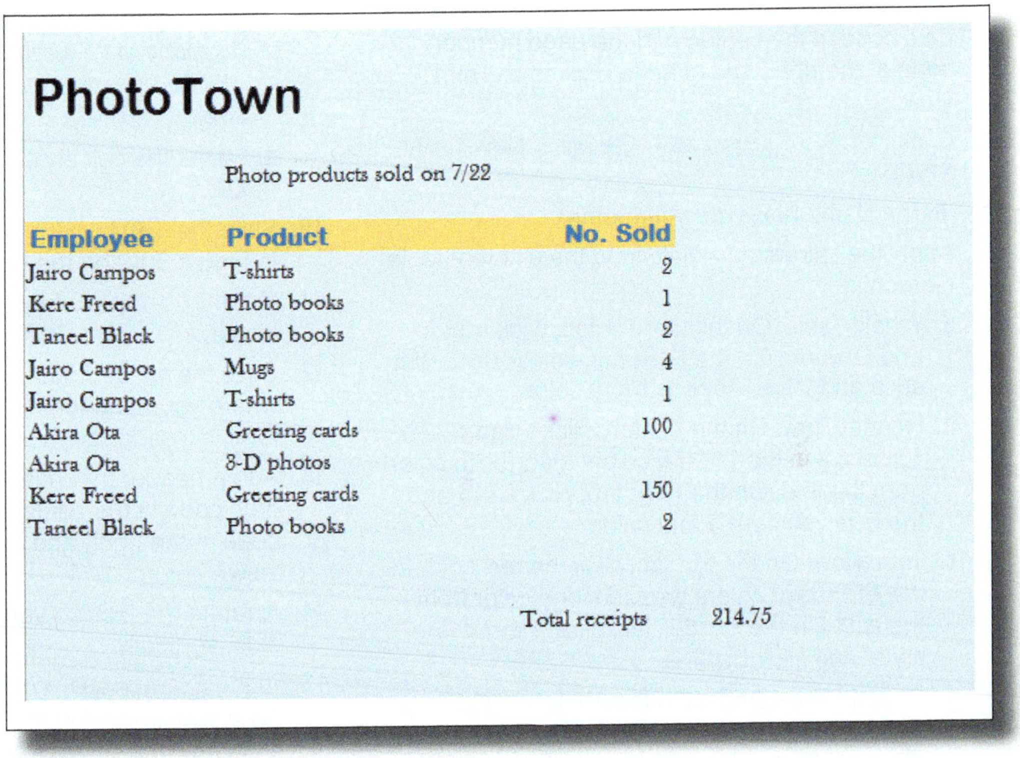
PhotoTown

Photo products sold on 7/22

Employee	Product	No. Sold
Jairo Campos	T-shirts	2
Kere Freed	Photo books	1
Taneel Black	Photo books	2
Jairo Campos	Mugs	4
Jairo Campos	T-shirts	1
Akira Ota	Greeting cards	100
Akira Ota	3-D photos	
Kere Freed	Greeting cards	150
Taneel Black	Photo books	2

Total receipts 214.75

Excel 2016, Windows 10, Microsoft Corporation

Lesson 50—Apply

PhotoTown corporate headquarters is looking to adopt the worksheet you designed throughout the company. In this project, you will create a custom table style that follows the company publication standards. You will also create a custom cell style and merge the style into another worksheet.

DIRECTIONS

1. Start Excel, if necessary, and open **E50ApplyA** from the data files for this lesson.
2. Save the file as **E50ApplyA_xx** in the location where your teacher instructs you to store the files for this lesson.
3. Add a header that has your name at the left, the date code in the center, and the page number code at the right, and change back to **Normal** view.
4. Click **Home** > **Format as Table** > **New Table Style**.
5. In the Name box, type your name.
6. Apply the following formatting to the different table elements:
   a. Whole Table: On the **Border** tab, click **Inside** and **Outline**. On the **Font** tab, select **Bold** font style and **Blue, Accent 1** font color.
   b. Header Row: On the **Fill** tab, click **Orange, Accent 2** in the **Theme** colors area (sixth color from the left). On the **Font** tab, click **Bold** and the **Blue, Accent 5** font color.
   c. Total Row: On the **Fill** tab, click the **red** color in the **Standard** colors area (second color from the left). On the **Border** tab, click a **thick line** style, and click **Outline**.
   d. Second Row Stripe: On the **Fill** tab, click **Gray 25%, Background 2** in the **Theme** colors area (third color from the left).
   e. Last Column: On the **Fill** tab, click **Blue-Gray Text 2** in the **Theme** colors area (fourth color from the left). On the **Font** tab, click **Bold**.
7. Select the cell range **A5:E14**, and format this range as a table with your new table style.
8. Click **Table Tools Design**, verify that the **Header Row** and **Banded Rows** options are checked, and click to select the **Total Row** and **Last Column** check boxes.
9. Create a new cell style.
   a. Click the cell range **A1:B1**.
   b. Format the selection with a **Black, Text 1** fill color, **White, Background 1** font color, and a **28 pt** font size.
   c. On the Table Tools Design tab, in the Styles group, click **More** > **New Cell Style**.

   ✓ *Depending on the width of your screen, you may need to click the Styles dialog box launcher to display the cell styles.*

   d. Name the cell style **PhotoTown Title**, and click **OK**.
10. Save the **E50ApplyA_xx** file. It should look similar to Figure 50-2 on the next page.
11. Open **E50ApplyB** from the data files for this lesson.
12. Save the file as **E50ApplyB_xx** in the location where your teacher instructs you to store the files for this lesson.
13. Add a header that has your name at the left, the date code in the center, and the page number code at the right, and change back to **Normal** view.
14. Arrange the files so you can view them side by side, vertically.
15. In the **E50ApplyB_xx** file, merge the custom cell style you created in the **E50ApplyA_xx** file.
    a. In the **E50ApplyB_xx** file, click **Home** > **Cell Styles** > **Merge Styles**.
    b. In the **Merge styles from** box, click **E50ApplyA_xx.xlsx** > **OK**.
16. In the **E50ApplyB_xx** file, apply the **PhotoTown Title** cell style to the cell range **A1:B1**.
17. Save the **E50ApplyB_xx** file. It should look similar to Figure 50-3 on the next page.
18. **With your teacher's permission**, print both worksheets.
19. Save and close both files, and exit Excel.

Figure 50-2

Excel 2016, Windows 10, Microsoft Corporation

PhotoTown

Photo products sold on 7/22

Employee	Product	No. Sold	Cost per Item	Total Sales
Akira Ota	T-shirts	2	10	20
Kere Freed	Photo books	1	6.25	6.25
Taneel Black	Photo books	2	6.25	12.5
Jairo Campos	Mugs	4	4	16
Jairo Campos	T-shirts	1	10	10
Akira Ota	Greeting cards	100	0.55	55
Akira Ota	3-D photos	3	2.25	6.75
Kere Freed	Greeting cards	150	0.55	82.5
Jairo Campos	Photo books	2	6.25	12.5
Total				221.5

Figure 50-3

Excel 2016, Windows 10, Microsoft Corporation

PhotoTown

Photo products sold on 7/23

Employee	Product	No. Sold	Cost per Item	Total Sales
Akira Ota	T-shirts	5	10	50
Kere Freed	Photo books	6	6.25	37.5
Taneel Black	Photo books	8	6.25	50
Jairo Campos	Mugs	0	4	0
Jairo Campos	T-shirts	2	10	20
Akira Ota	Greeting cards	80	0.55	44
Akira Ota	3-D photos	3	2.25	6.75
Kere Freed	Greeting cards	75	0.55	41.25
Jairo Campos	Photo books	2	6.25	12.5
Total				262

Lesson 51

Customizing Data Entry

➤ What You Will Learn

Entering Labels on Multiple Lines
Entering Fractions and Mixed Numbers
Using Form Controls
Populating Cells Using Advanced Fill Series Options

WORDS TO KNOW

ActiveX
Reusable software components developed by Microsoft.

Form
A document used to collect and organize information.

Format
To apply attributes to cell data to change the appearance of the worksheet.

Form controls
Tools used to create forms.

Line break
A code inserted into text that forces it to display on two different lines.

Software Skills Excel offers a variety of ways to customize data entry. When entering labels, especially long ones, you may want to display them on more than one line so the column will not need to be as wide. Entering fractions requires a special technique so they display properly. You can create a form by inserting form controls on a worksheet to make data entry even easier.

What You Can Do

Entering Labels on Multiple Lines

- If you have long column labels, you can adjust the column width to fit them.
- This doesn't always look pleasing, however, especially when the column label is much longer than the data in the column. For example, the two columns shown here are much larger than their data:

Unit Number	Total Annual Sales
2	$125,365.97

- One of the easiest ways to fix this problem is to enter the column label with **line breaks**.
- Entering line breaks between words in a cell enables you to place several lines of text in the same cell, like this next example:

Unit Number	Total Annual Sales
2	$125,365.97

- The height of the row adjusts automatically to accommodate the multiple-line column label.
- You can also use the Wrap Text command in the Alignment group of the Home tab to wrap multiple lines of text within a cell.

Try It! Entering Labels on Multiple Lines

1. Start Excel, and open **E51TryA** from the data files for this lesson.
2. Save the file as **E51TryA_xx** in the location where your teacher instructs you to store the files for this lesson.
3. Click cell C11, and type **Cases**.
4. Press ALT + ENTER to insert a line break, and type **Ordered**.
5. In cell D11, type **Price per Case**. (Do not insert a line break.)
6. In cell E11, type **Product Total Sales**. (Do not insert a line break.)
7. Click cell D11, and on the Home tab, click Wrap Text.
8. With cell D11 still selected, on the Home tab, click Format Painter, and click cell E11.
9. Click cell D11, in the formula bar, place the insertion point after Price, press ALT + ENTER, and press ENTER.
10. Save the changes to the file, and leave it open to use in the next Try It.

Enter a line break within a cell

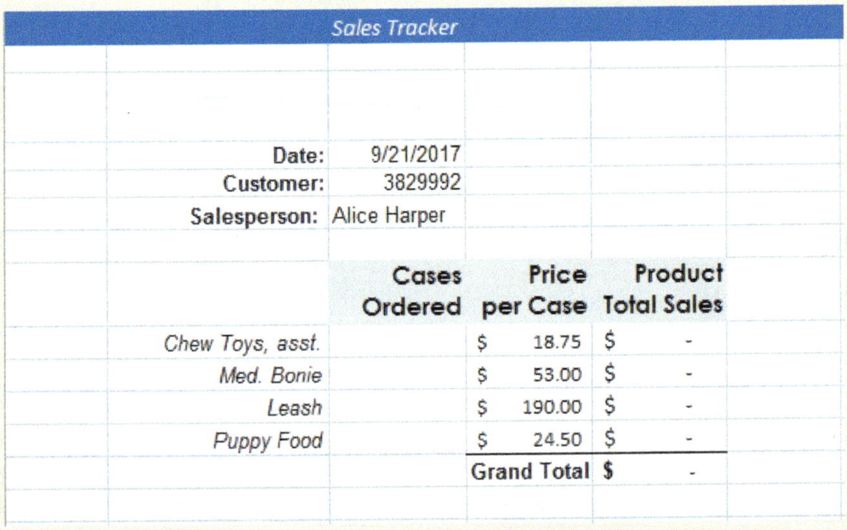

Excel 2016, Windows 10, Microsoft Corporation

Entering Fractions and Mixed Numbers

- If you type the value 1/3 into a cell with a General number format, Excel formats it as a date (in this case, January 3).
- To enter a fraction, you must precede it with a zero (0) and a space, which tells Excel that the data is a number. For example, to enter 1/3, type 0 1/3.
- When Excel recognizes the data as a fraction, it applies the Fraction number format to the cell.
- A fraction appears as a decimal value in the Formula bar. The fraction 1/3 appears as 0.333333333333333 in the Formula bar.
- When entering a mixed number (a number and a fraction), simply type it. For example, type 4, a space, and the fraction 1/2 to result in 4 1/2.
- You can **format** existing data to look like fractions using the Format Cells command.

Try It! Entering Fractions and Mixed Numbers

1. In the **E51TryA_xx** file, click cell C12 and type **0**, press SPACEBAR, type **3/4**, and press ENTER.
2. In cell C13, type **0 1/2**, and press ENTER.
3. In cell C14, type **1 1/8**, and press ENTER.
4. In cell C15 type **5 1/2**, and press ENTER.
5. Save the changes to the file, and leave it open to use in the next Try It.

Entering fractions and mixed numbers

Date:	9/21/2017			
Customer:	3829992			
Salesperson:	Alice Harper			
	Cases Ordered	**Price per Case**	**Product Total Sales**	
Chew Toys, asst.	3/4	$ 18.75	$ 14.06	
Med. Bonie	1/2	$ 53.00	$ 26.50	
Leash	1 1/8	$ 190.00	$ 213.75	
Puppy Food	5 1/2	$ 24.50	$ 134.75	
		Grand Total	**$ 389.06**	

Using Form Controls

- You can insert **form controls** in a worksheet to create a **form** for collecting information that can be stored and analyzed.
- For example, a human resources department might use a form to collect and store employee information.
- Use the commands in the Controls group on the Developer tab of the ribbon to insert form controls.

  ✓ *Recall that the Developer tab does not display by default; you must use the Excel Options to make it available.*

- Available form controls include the following:
  - Button: Performs an action, such as a running macro.
  - Combo box: Also known as a drop-down list box. You can type an entry or choose one item from the list.
  - Check box: Turns a value on or off. A check box can be selected (turned on), cleared (turned off), or mixed (allow multiple selection).
  - Spin button: Increases or decreases a value, such as a number increment, time, or date. You can also type a value directly into the cell.
  - List box: Displays a list of one or more text items from which a user can choose.
  - Option button: Allows a single choice in a set of mutually exclusive choices. An option button can be selected (turned on), cleared (turned off), or mixed (allow multiple selection). An option button is also referred to as a radio button.
  - Group box: Groups related controls into a rectangle and can include a label.
  - Label: Descriptive text (such as titles, captions, pictures) or brief instructions.
  - Scroll bar: Scrolls through a range of values.
- Some form controls are disabled by default. You can enable them by changing the **ActiveX** Settings in the Trust Center Settings on the Trust Center tab in the Excel Options; however, this may allow potentially dangerous controls to run on your computer.

  ✓ *If you need additional controls or more flexibility than form controls allow, you can insert ActiveX controls using the commands in the Controls group on the Developer tab of the ribbon.*

- Consider the form layout and the order of the form controls when inserting form controls.
- The insertion point moves from control to control based on the order in which controls are inserted in the document, not based on the order in which the controls are arranged.

Try It! Using Form Controls

1. In the **E51TryA_xx** file, click cell C9, and on the Home tab, in the Editing group, click Clear Clear ▾ > Clear All.
2. Click File > Options > Customize Ribbon.
3. Under Customize the Ribbon, click to select the Developer check box, and click OK. The Developer tab displays on the ribbon.
4. Click the Developer tab.
5. In the Controls group, click the arrow on the Insert button, and click the Combo Box form control button.
6. Position the insertion point at the top edge of cell C9.

   ✓ *The insertion pointer changes to a crosshair symbol +.*
7. Click and drag the crosshair insertion pointer across the cell range C9:D9, and release the mouse button.
8. Click the New Sheet button ⊕ to create a new sheet.
9. On Sheet1, click cell A1, type **Alice Harper**, and press ENTER.
10. Click cell A2, type **Greg Bimmel**, and press ENTER.
11. Click cell A3, type **Lucinda Diego**, and press ENTER.
12. Click the Sales Tracker tab, right-click the combo box form control, and click Format Control. The Format Control dialog box displays.
13. On the Control tab, click in the Input range text box, and type **Sheet1!A1:A3**.
14. Click OK.
15. Click the combo box drop-down arrow, and click Greg Bimmel.
16. Save and close the file. Leave Excel open for the next Try It.

A combo box form control

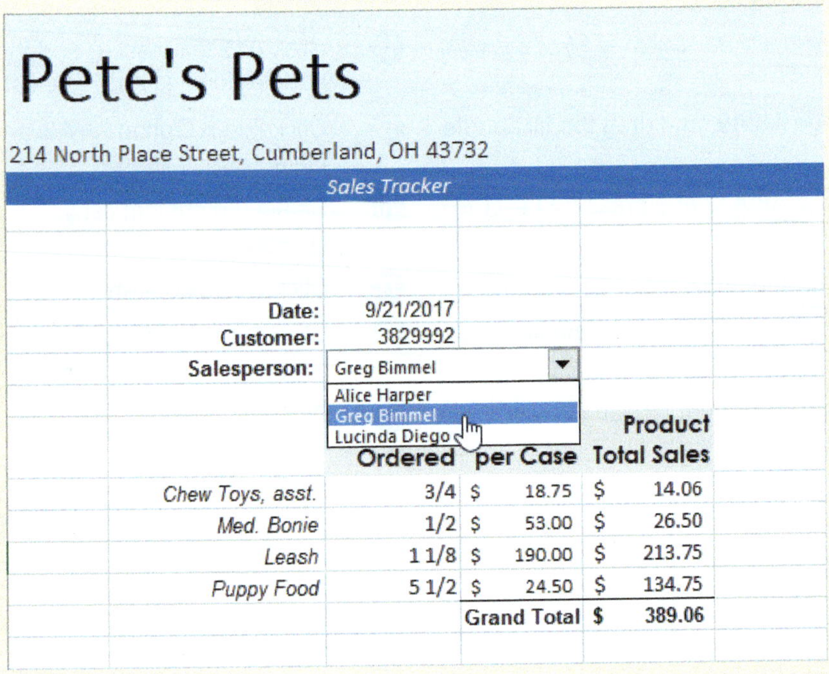

Populating Cells Using Advanced Fill Series

- Recall how you use Auto Fill to fill a series in a worksheet. For example, you can enter Monday and Tuesday in adjacent cells and then have Auto Fill complete the rest of the days of the week by dragging the fill handle.
- You can fine-tune a series fill by using the Series dialog box. From the Home tab, click Fill and then click Series to access it. This dialog box enables you to fill a series based on Linear, Growth, Date, or AutoFill patterns, and to set a step value.
- You can also create your own custom list, so that Auto Fill can use it as you are building a worksheet. To create a custom list, click File > Options > Advanced, and then in the General section, click Edit Custom Lists.

Try It! Populating Cells Using Advanced Fill Series

1. Start Excel, and open the **E51TryB** file from the data files for this lesson.
2. Save the file as **E51TryB_xx** in the location where your teacher instructs you to store the files for this lesson.
3. On the Sales sheet in cell B8, type **07/02/2018**.
4. Select the range B8:B30.
5. Click Home > Fill > Series.
6. In the Series dialog box, click Date, and then click Weekday. Click OK.

   ✓ *The series is filled with weekday dates (Monday through Friday).*
7. Select the range A8:A9, and drag the fill handle down to A12.
8. Select the range A8:A12 and press CTRL + C to copy it.
9. Click in cell A13 and press CTRL + V to paste it.
10. Select the range A8:A17, and drag the fill handle down to A30.
11. Click the Teams worksheet tab, and select A7:A11.
12. Click File > Options > Advanced. Scroll down to the General section.
13. Click Edit Custom Lists.
14. 14In the Custom Lists dialog box, click Add.
15. Confirm that $A$7:$A$11 appears in the text box, and then click Import.
16. Click OK to close the dialog box, and then OK again to close Excel Options.
17. On the Teams worksheet, in cell A15, type **Sales**.
18. Click A15 to select it, and then drag the fill handle down to A19. The list is filled in.
19. Click File > Options > Advanced > Edit Custom Lists.
20. Select the custom list you just created and click Delete.
21. Click OK to confirm.
22. Click OK twice to close the two open dialog boxes.
23. Save the changes to the file, and exit Excel.

(continued)

Try It! Populating Cells Using Advanced Fill Series *(continued)*

Custom Lists Dialog Box

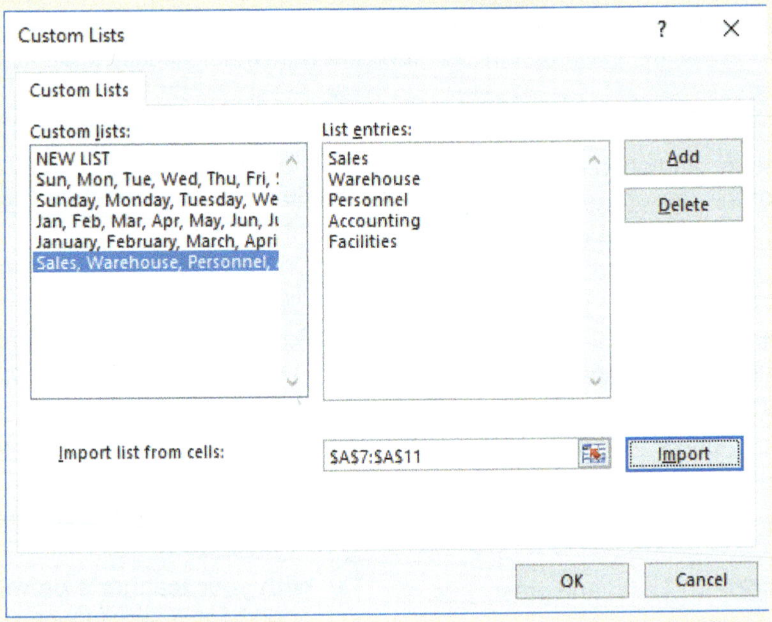

Excel 2016, Windows 10, Microsoft Corporation

Lesson 51—Practice

As assistant manager for a local PhotoTown store, you have been asked to create a weekly payroll tracker. In this project, you will use line breaks and text wrapping to make the worksheet visually appealing and easy to read.

DIRECTIONS

1. Start Excel, if necessary, and open **E51Practice** from the data files for this lesson.
2. Save the file as **E51Practice_xx** in the location where your teacher instructs you to store the files for this lesson.
3. Add a header that has your name at the left, the date code in the center, and the page number code at the right, and change back to **Normal** view.
4. In cell **E6**, type **Hourly**, press ALT + ENTER, type **Rate**, and press ENTER.
5. In cell **D6**, type **Regular Weekly Hours**, and press ENTER.
6. In cell **C6**, type **Full or Part Time**, and press ENTER.
7. Select the cell range **C6:E6**, and on the Home tab, click **Center**.
8. Select cell **C6** and then click **Home** > **Wrap Text**.
9. On the Home tab, click **Format Painter**, and click cell **D6**.
10. Select cell **C6**, and click in the formula bar. Move the insertion point to just before the **P**, and press ALT + ENTER.
11. Click cell **G24**, type **Weekly Payroll** and press ENTER.
12. Click cell **G24** and then click **Home** > **Align Right**.
13. **With your teacher's permission**, print the worksheet. It should look similar to Figure 51-1.
14. Save and close the file, and exit Excel.

Figure 51-1

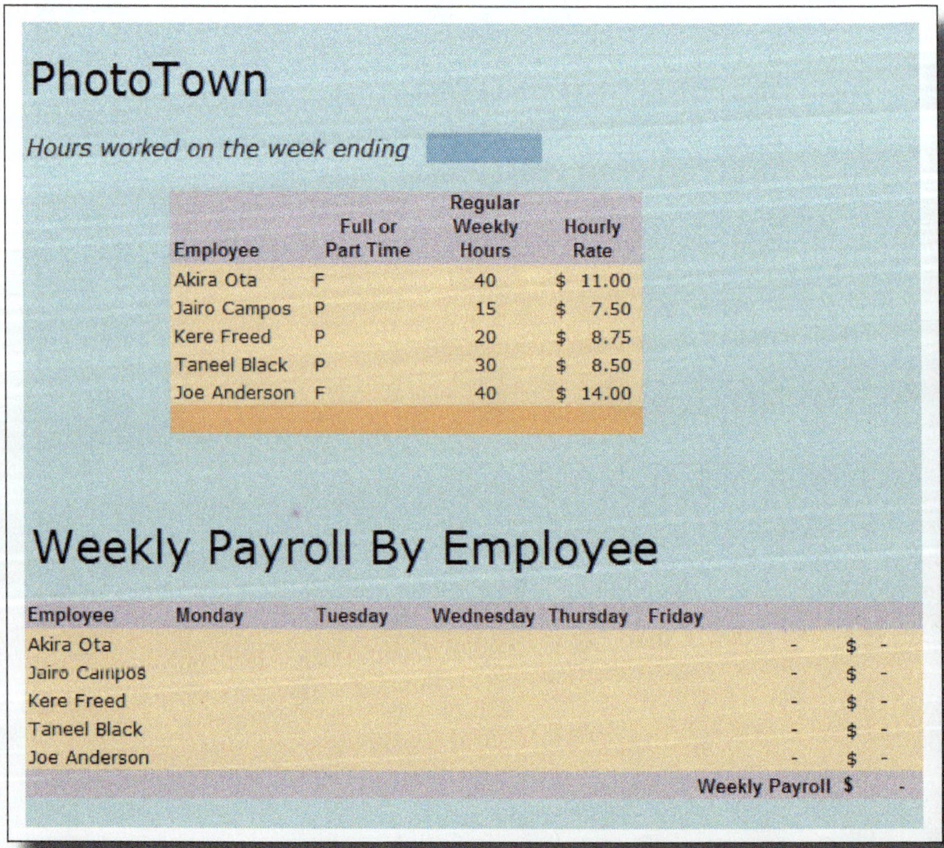

Excel 2016, Windows 10, Microsoft Corporation

Lesson 51—Apply

As assistant manager for a local PhotoTown store, you have created a weekly payroll tracker. In this project, you will calculate the total weekly hours worked for each clerk and insert a form control.

DIRECTIONS

1. Start Excel, if necessary, open **E51Apply** from the data files for this lesson.
2. Save the file as **E51Apply_xx** in the location where your teacher instructs you to store the files for this lesson.
3. Add a header that has your name at the left, the date code in the center, and the page number code at the right, and change back to **Normal** view.
4. In cell **G18**, type **Total Hours This Week**, and press ENTER.
5. In cell **H18**, type **Weekly Income**, and press ENTER.
6. Select cells **G18:H18** > **Wrap Text**.
7. Change the column width for column G to **11**, and autofit the row height for row 18 to eliminate extra space.
8. In cell **D4**, enter the fraction **8/15**, and press ENTER. Notice that Excel autmatically interprets the fraction as a date in the current year.
9. In the Weekly Payroll by Employee section, enter the following hours for the employees:

Employee	Day	Hours
Kere Freed	Monday	3/4
Taneel Black	Tuesday	4 1/2
Taneel Black	Thursday	5 1/2
Joe Anderson	Thursday	6 1/2

✓ *When entering the Monday hours, remember to type a zero followed by a space before typing the fraction.*

10. Click cell **G4** and then on the Developer tab, click **Insert**.
11. Click the **Check Box** form control button.
12. Position the insertion point at the top edge of cell **G4**, drag the crosshair insertion pointer across the cell range **G4:H4**, and release the mouse button
14. Right-click the check box form control and click **Edit Text**.
15. Replace the existing text label with **Approved by manager**, right-click the check box form control > **Exit Edit Text**.
16. Click outside of the form control, and click the check box of the form control.
17. Create a new custom Auto Fill list from the names in A19:A23.
18. Use the custom Auto Fill list to enter the employee names in A27:A31.
19. Delete the custom Auto Fill list.
20. Clear cells A27:A31.
21. **With your teacher's permission**, print the worksheet with scaling set to fit the entire sheet on one page. It should look similar to Figure 51-2 on the next page.
22. Save and close the file, and exit Excel.

Figure 51-2

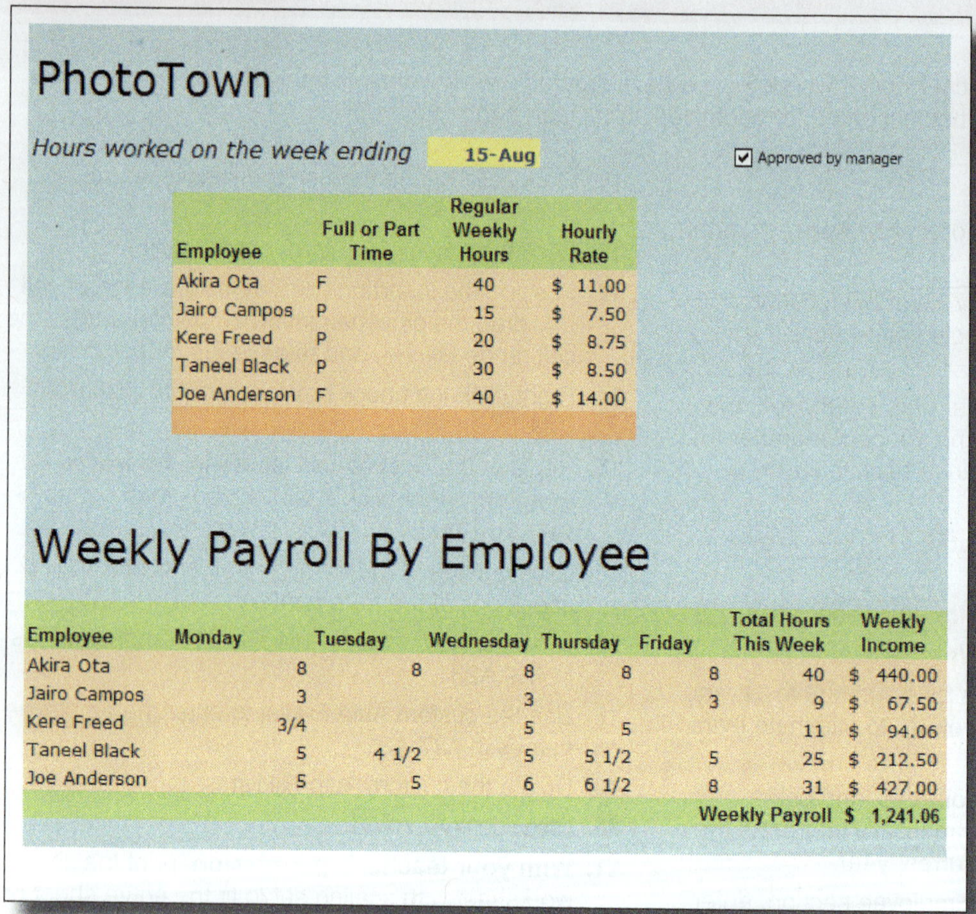

PhotoTown

Hours worked on the week ending 15-Aug

☑ Approved by manager

Employee	Full or Part Time	Regular Weekly Hours	Hourly Rate
Akira Ota	F	40	$ 11.00
Jairo Campos	P	15	$ 7.50
Kere Freed	P	20	$ 8.75
Taneel Black	P	30	$ 8.50
Joe Anderson	F	40	$ 14.00

Weekly Payroll By Employee

Employee	Monday	Tuesday	Wednesday	Thursday	Friday	Total Hours This Week	Weekly Income
Akira Ota	8	8	8	8	8	40	$ 440.00
Jairo Campos	3		3		3	9	$ 67.50
Kere Freed	3/4		5	5		11	$ 94.06
Taneel Black	5	4 1/2	5	5 1/2	5	25	$ 212.50
Joe Anderson	5	5	6	6 1/2	8	31	$ 427.00
						Weekly Payroll	$ 1,241.06

Excel 2016, Windows 10, Microsoft Corporation

End-of-Chapter Activities

➤ Excel Chapter 6—Critical Thinking

Payroll Calculations

You are the corporate payroll clerk at PhotoTown, and you've been calculating payroll checks manually ever since you were hired a month ago. Now that you're familiar with Excel, you want to use the features you have learned to complete this weekly task more easily.

DIRECTIONS

1. Start Excel, if necessary, and open **ECT06** from the data files for this chapter.
2. Save the file as **ECT06_xx** in the location where your teacher instructs you to store the files for this chapter.
3. Type the following column labels on two lines:
   a. In cell **A7**, type **Check Number**.
   b. In cell **B7**, type **Employee ID Number**.
   c. In cell **E7**, type **Hours Worked**.
   d. Adjust the column widths as needed.
4. Separate the **Name** column into **First Name** and **Last Name**.
   a. Insert a column to the right of column D.
   b. Select the cell range **D8:D37**, click **Data** > **Text to Columns**.
   c. Click the **Delimited** file type option, if necessary.
   d. Click the **Space** Delimiter option, and deselect the **Tab** Delimiter option.
   e. Format both columns as text, and set the Destination to cell $D$8.
   f. In cell **D7**, type **First Name**, and in cell **E7**, type **Last Name**.
5. Enter the hours everyone has worked as mixed fractions, as shown in Illustration A.
6. Change the theme colors to the **Slipstream** theme, and then save the customized theme as **EOC6**.
   a. Click **Page Layout** > **Colors** > **Slipstream**.
   b. Click **Page Layout** > **Themes** > **Save Current Theme**.
   c. In the File name box, type **EOC6**.
   d. Click **Save**.
7. Enter today's date in cell **H3**, and apply the Short Date format.
8. In the cell range **J2:L2**, insert a group box form control.
   a. Click **Developer** > **Insert** > **Group Box (Form Control).**
   b. Draw the group box form control over the cell range **J2:L6**.
   c. Edit the text label to be **Featured Employee**.
9. In the group box form control, in the cell **K3**, insert a label form control.
   a. On the **Developer** tab, click **Insert** > **Label (Form Control).**
   b. Draw the label box form control over cell **K3**.
   c. Edit the text label to be **Kere Freed**.
10. Format cells A1:L6 with the coloring shown in Illustration 6A on the next page.
    a. Fill rows 1–6 with the **Green, Accent 4, Lighter 40%** color.
    b. Select the cell range **A7:L7**, and use the Cell Styles gallery to apply the **Accent 5** style.
11. Use conditional formatting to fill the cells in the Net Pay column where the value is above the average of that column.
    a. Select the range **L8:L37**.
    b. Start a new conditional formatting rule.
    c. Set the rule type to use a formula.
    d. Enter the following formula: **=L8>=AVERAGE($L$8:$L$37)**.
    e. Set the formatting to fill with **Orange, Accent 5, Lighter 80%**.
    f. Apply the rule.

12. Click **Insert** > **Header & Footer**, type your name, and change back to **Normal** view.
13. **With your teacher's permission**, print the worksheet in **Full View** in landscape orientation. It should look similar to Illustration 6A.
14. Save and close the file, and exit Excel.

Illustration 6A

PhotoTown

Miller Rd

Unit #2166

Date 12/30/2018

Featured Employee

Kere Freed

Check Number	Employee ID Number	Title	First Name	Last Name	Hours Worked	Rate	Gross Pay	Fed	SS	State	Net Pay
41289	63778	Mr.	Carlos	Altare	12	$6.30	$75.60	$14.36	$5.86	$4.16	$51.22
41290	31524	Mrs.	Jan	Borough	22	$6.50	$143.00	$27.17	$11.08	$7.87	$96.88
41291	18946	Mr.	Shakur	Brown	40	$7.00	$280.00	$53.20	$21.70	$15.40	$189.70
41292	71335	Mr.	Taneed	Black	38 1/2	$7.00	$269.50	$51.21	$20.89	$14.82	$182.59
41293	22415	Mr.	Jairo	Campos	21 3/4	$7.20	$156.60	$29.75	$12.14	$8.61	$106.10
41294	20965	Mrs.	Rafiquil	Damir	10 1/2	$6.15	$64.58	$12.27	$5.00	$3.55	$43.75
41295	64121	Mrs.	Diana	Dogwood	19 3/4	$6.20	$122.45	$23.27	$9.49	$6.73	$82.96
41296	30388	Mrs.	Lucy	Fan	31 1/4	$6.55	$204.69	$38.89	$15.86	$11.26	$138.68
41297	44185	Mrs.	Jennifer	Flynn	30	$7.00	$210.00	$39.90	$16.28	$11.55	$142.28
41298	32152	Ms.	Katerina	Flynn	30	$7.10	$213.00	$40.47	$16.51	$11.72	$144.31
41299	31885	Ms.	Kere	Freed	32 1/2	$7.10	$230.75	$43.84	$17.88	$12.69	$156.33
41300	33785	Mr.	Eram	Hassan	27 1/2	$6.85	$188.38	$35.79	$14.60	$10.36	$127.62
41301	55648	Mr.	Tyrell	Johnson	22	$6.50	$143.00	$27.17	$11.08	$7.87	$96.88
41302	60219	Ms.	Verna	Latinz	12 1/2	$6.30	$78.75	$14.96	$6.10	$4.33	$53.35
41303	28645	Mr.	Wu	Lee	10 3/4	$7.00	$75.25	$14.30	$5.83	$4.14	$50.98
41304	67415	Mr.	Shamir	Lewis	20	$7.10	$142.00	$26.98	$11.01	$7.81	$96.21
41305	27995	Mrs.	Maria	Navarro	20	$6.30	$126.00	$23.94	$9.77	$6.93	$85.37
41306	32151	Mr.	Tony	Navarro	18 3/4	$6.35	$119.06	$22.62	$9.23	$6.55	$80.66
41307	28499	Mr.	Chu	Nguyen	23 1/2	$6.85	$160.98	$30.59	$12.48	$8.85	$109.06
41308	17564	Mr.	Juan	Nuniez	39 1/4	$7.00	$274.75	$52.20	$21.29	$15.11	$186.14
41309	14558	Mr.	Akira	Ota	14 1/2	$7.25	$105.13	$19.97	$8.15	$5.78	$71.22
41310	31022	Mrs.	Meghan	Ryan	31 3/4	$7.00	$222.25	$42.23	$17.22	$12.22	$150.57
41311	41885	Mrs.	Kate	Scott	23	$6.85	$157.55	$29.93	$12.21	$8.67	$106.74
41312	25448	Mr.	Jyoti	Shaw	32 1/4	$6.50	$209.63	$39.83	$16.25	$11.53	$142.02
41313	23151	Ms.	Jewel	Vidito	35	$6.55	$229.25	$43.56	$17.77	$12.61	$155.32
41314	37785	Mrs.	Corrine	Walters	35 1/2	$6.65	$236.08	$44.85	$18.30	$12.98	$159.94
41315	58945	Mrs.	Antonia	Whitney	21 1/4	$6.75	$143.44	$27.25	$11.12	$7.89	$97.18
41316	57445	Mr.	Shale	Wilson	35 3/4	$7.00	$250.25	$47.55	$19.39	$13.76	$169.54
41317	36684	Mrs.	Shiree	Wilson	39	$7.10	$276.90	$52.61	$21.46	$15.23	$187.60
41318	55412	Mrs.	Su	Yamaguchi	27 1/4	$6.30	$171.68	$32.62	$13.30	$9.44	$116.31

Excel 2016, Windows 10, Microsoft Corporation

➤ Excel Chapter 6—Portfolio Builder

Earthquake Tracking

You have been given some raw data about earthquakes that occurred worldwide during a two-week period. It is useful data, but it could be much more useful with some cleanup and formatting. In this project, you will improve the readability of the data by applying several types of formatting.

DIRECTIONS

1. Start Excel, if necessary, and open **EPB06** from the data files for this chapter.
2. Save the file as **EPB06_xx** in the location where your teacher instructs you to store the files for this chapter.
3. Add your name to the center of the header, and then change back to **Normal** view.
4. Change the page orientation to **Landscape**.
5. Change the text on the worksheet tab to **Earthquakes**.
6. Insert a new column between columns A and B.
7. Use the Text to Columns feature to split the data from the Time column into two separate columns: one for the date and one for the time. Change the column headings (row 8) to Date and Time.
8. In cell A8, type **Date**, replacing the current text. In cell B8, type **Time**.
9. Use the Text to Columns feature to split the date and time from A9:A1643 into two separate columns (A and B).
   a. Use **Fixed Width** for the delimiter.
   b. Split the columns to the right of the T in each entry.
   c. Set the data type for the Date column to **Date**.
   d. Do not assign a data type to the Time column.
10. Use a custom number format to make the dates in **A9:A1643** and in **B3:B4** appear in this format: **d-mmm**.
11. Use the PROPER function to change the labels in row 8 to capitalize the first letter.
    a. In C7, enter **=PROPER(C8)**. Then copy this formula into D7:I7.
    b. Select **C7:I7** and copy the range to the Clipboard.
    c. Select the range **C8:I8**, and then select **Paste Values** on the **Paste** button's drop-down menu.
    d. Select **C7:I7** and use the **Clear All** command to empty the selected range.
12. Move the dates from **C3:C4** to **B3:B4**.
13. Use cell styles to apply formatting, as follows:
    a. Apply the **Title style** to **A1**.
    b. Apply the **Heading 2 style** to **A2**.
    c. Apply the **Heading 4 style** to **A3:A4**.
    d. Apply the **Heading 3 style** to **A8:I8**.
14. AutoFit the column widths for columns B, C, and D.
15. Set an exact column width for **column A** to **13**.
16. Set the **Wrap Text** option to apply in the range **H9:H1643**.
17. Center the text in **A8**, and then create a new style called **Heading 3 Centered** based on that cell. Apply this new cell style to B8:I8.
18. Use **Format as Table** to apply **Table Style Medium 3** to the range **A8:I1643**.
19. Create a conditional formatting rule that formats F9:F1643 with a black fill and with bold and orange text for the top 20% of values.
20. Use the **Conditional Formatting Rules Manager** to edit the rule you just created to use a dark blue fill rather than black.
21. **With your teacher's permission**, print only the first page. It should look like Illustration 6B.
22. Save and close the file, and exit Excel.

Illustration 6B

Student Name

Worldwide Earthquakes

Magnitudes 4.5 and greater

Starting Date	1-Jan
Ending Date	14-Apr

Date	Time	Latitude	Longitude	Depth	Mag	Magtype	Place
14-Apr	T23:15:08.790Z	-7.4795	128.0844	150.75	5.7	mb	Kepulauan Barat Daya, Indonesia
14-Apr	T22:46:53.920Z	32.7956	130.7335	10	4.5	mb	1km NW of Kumamoto-shi, Japan
14-Apr	T22:29:57.090Z	32.8601	130.7389	10	4.6	mb	6km SE of Ueki, Japan
14-Apr	T22:23:28.090Z	-14.1678	166.542	10	5.2	mb	111km NNW of Port-Olry, Vanuatu
14-Apr	T21:50:26.890Z	-14.5489	166.4094	10	6.4	mww	88km NW of Port-Olry, Vanuatu
14-Apr	T20:10:37.420Z	32.7543	130.6936	10	4.7	mb	5km SW of Kumamoto-shi, Japan
14-Apr	T18:29:19.070Z	36.2495	141.8077	25.09	4.6	mb	104km ENE of Hasaki, Japan
14-Apr	T17:14:36.370Z	32.7126	130.6708	10	4.5	mb	3km N of Uto, Japan
14-Apr	T16:53:02.220Z	32.6919	130.8055	10	4.9	mb	12km SSE of Kumamoto-shi, Japan
14-Apr	T16:45:22.150Z	-20.3974	-175.1199	10	4.8	mb	81km N of Nuku`alofa, Tonga
14-Apr	T16:44:34.100Z	-0.5642	-11.611	10	5.2	mb	North of Ascension Island
14-Apr	T15:50:31.710Z	32.7411	130.7174	10	4.5	mb	5km SSW of Kumamoto-shi, Japan
14-Apr	T15:34:18.100Z	32.678	130.8189	10	4.7	mb	14km SSE of Kumamoto-shi, Japan
14-Apr	T15:25:39.580Z	34.1433	138.3282	262.98	4.5	mb	51km SSE of Oyama, Japan
14-Apr	T15:06:22.990Z	32.7284	130.7545	10	5.3	mb	6km S of Kumamoto-shi, Japan
14-Apr	T15:03:47.790Z	32.6787	130.7241	10	6	mww	5km E of Uto, Japan
14-Apr	T14:48:18.360Z	-5.7236	149.4523	154.22	4.7	mb	55km N of Kandrian, Papua New Guinea
14-Apr	T14:43:41.610Z	32.7827	130.7582	10	4.9	mb	1km ESE of Kumamoto-shi, Japan
14-Apr	T14:29:58.010Z	32.7517	130.726	10	4.6	mb	4km SSW of Kumamoto-shi, Japan
14-Apr	T14:28:13.540Z	32.7849	130.7453	10	4.5	mb	0km SSE of Kumamoto-shi, Japan
14-Apr	T14:23:05.600Z	40.3771	53.0612	43.29	4.5	mb	40km NNE of Turkmenbasy, Turkmenistan
14-Apr	T13:43:15.950Z	32.7042	130.6956	10	4.5	mb	3km NE of Uto, Japan
14-Apr	T13:38:43.640Z	32.6854	130.7106	10	4.8	mb	4km E of Uto, Japan
14-Apr	T13:22:19.310Z	32.6832	130.646	10	4.8	mb	1km W of Uto, Japan
14-Apr	T13:07:35.990Z	32.7877	130.8354	10	5.4	mb	8km E of Kumamoto-shi, Japan
14-Apr	T12:42:25.080Z	32.5779	130.6361	10	4.8	mb	8km SSW of Matsubase, Japan

Excel 2016, Windows 10, Microsoft Corporation

Chapter 7

(Courtesy NAN728/Shutterstock)

Creating Charts, Shapes, and Templates

Lesson 52
Formatting Chart Elements

- Changing Chart Elements
- Setting Data Label Options
- Setting Data Table Options
- Formatting a Data Series

Lesson 53
Formatting the Value Axis

- Creating a Stock Chart
- Modifying the Value Axis
- Formatting Data Markers
- Formatting a Legend
- Adding a Secondary Value Axis to a Chart

Lesson 54
Creating Stacked Area Charts

- Creating a Stacked Area Chart
- Formatting the Chart Floor and Chart Walls
- Displaying Chart Gridlines
- Applying a Chart Layout and Chart Styles

Lesson 55
Working with Sparklines and Trendlines

- Inserting a Line, Column, or Win/Loss Sparkline
- Formatting a Sparkline
- Inserting a Trendline
- Using a Trendline to Predict

Lesson 56
Drawing and Positioning Shapes

- Drawing Shapes
- Resizing, Grouping, Aligning, and Arranging Shapes

Lesson 57
Formatting Shapes

- Formatting Shapes
- Adding Shape Effects

Lesson 58
Enhancing Shapes with Text and Effects

- Adding Text to a Text Box, Callout, or Other Shape
- Adding 3-D Effects
- Rotating Shapes
- Inserting a Screen Capture

Lesson 59
Working with Templates

- Adding a Watermark or Other Graphics
- Formatting the Worksheet Background
- Creating a Workbook Template
- Creating a Chart Template

End-of-Chapter Activities

Lesson 52

Formatting Chart Elements

➤ What You Will Learn

Changing Chart Elements
Setting Data Label Options
Setting Data Table Options
Formatting a Data Series

WORDS TO KNOW

Categories
For most charts, a category is information in a worksheet row. If you select multiple rows of data for a chart, you'll create multiple categories, and these categories will be listed along the x-axis.

Data series
For most charts, a data series is the information in a worksheet column. If you select multiple columns of data for a chart, you'll create multiple data series. Each data series is then represented by its own color bar, line, or column.

Data table
This optional table looks like a small worksheet, and displays the data used to create the chart.

Legend key
Symbol in a legend that identifies the color or pattern of a data series in a chart.

Plot area
The area that holds the data points on a chart.

Software Skills A chart presents complex numerical data in a graphical format. Because a chart tells its story visually, you must make the most of the way your chart looks. There are many ways in which you can enhance a chart; for example, you can add color or pattern to the chart background, and format the value and category axes so that the numbers are easier to understand.

What You Can Do

Changing Chart Elements

- A chart may include some or all of the parts shown in Figure 52-1 on the next page.
- You can format various chart elements such as the data labels, data table, plot area, legend, chart title, axis titles, and the data series.
- As you move your mouse pointer over a chart, the name of the chart element appears in the ScreenTip.
- You can select specific chart elements for formatting from the Current Selection group of the Chart Tools Layout tab.
- A chart title describes the purpose of the chart. You can change the font, color, and size of the chart title as with any other text.
- The **plot area** of a chart is the element that holds the data points on a chart. You can change the plot area of the chart by modifying the border color or style, or applying a shadow or pattern to the background. You can also apply 3-D formatting effects to the plot area if a chart has a background.

Figure 52-1

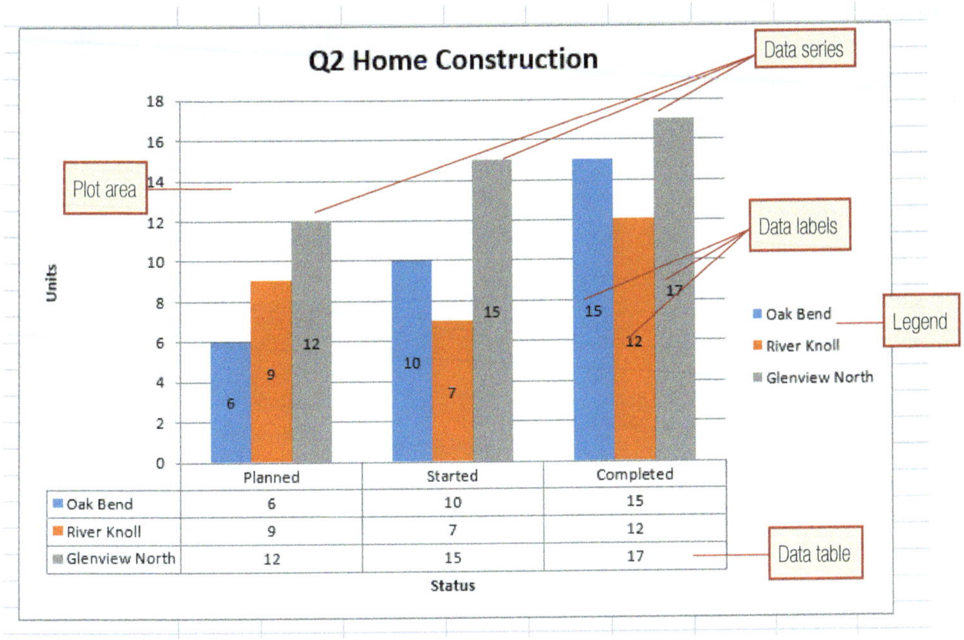

Excel 2016, Windows 10, Microsoft Corporation

Try It! Changing Chart Elements

1. Start Excel, and open **E52Try** from the data files for this lesson.
2. Save the file as **E52Try_xx** in the location where your teacher instructs you to store the files for this lesson.
3. Click the Country Antiques Q3 Sales Chart tab, if necessary.
4. Click Chart Tools Design > Add Chart Element > Chart Title > Above Chart.
5. Type **Third Quarter Sales**, and press ENTER.
6. Move the mouse pointer over the chart, and click when you see the ScreenTip for Plot Area.
7. With the plot area selected, click Chart Tools Format, and, in the Current Selection group, click Format Selection to display the Format Plot Area task pane.
8. In the task pane, click Fill > Gradient fill.
9. Click the Effects button > 3-D Format > Top bevel > Circle.
10. Click Bottom bevel > Circle.
11. In the Lighting group, in the Angle box, type **60**.
12. Close the Format Plot Area task pane.
13. Save the changes to the file, and leave it open to use in the next Try It.

The Format Plot Area task pane

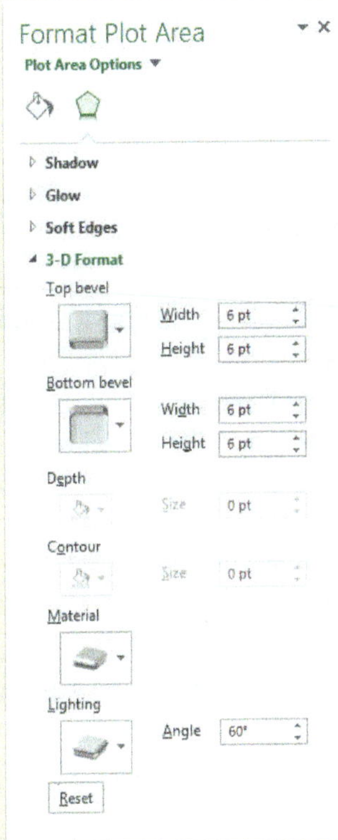

Excel 2016, Windows 10, Microsoft Corporation

Setting Data Label Options

- As shown in Figure 52-2, you can add data labels to a chart by choosing where you want the labels placed:
  - Centered on the data point(s)
  - Inside the end of the data point(s)
  - Inside the base of the data point(s)
  - Outside the end of the data point(s)

✓ *Data labels should be legible and not overlap.*

- You can choose exactly what to display in the data label, such as the:
  - Data series name
  - **Category** name
  - Data value and/or percentage
  - **Legend key**

✓ *For charts with multiple series, you have to format the data labels for each series independently.*

Figure 52-2

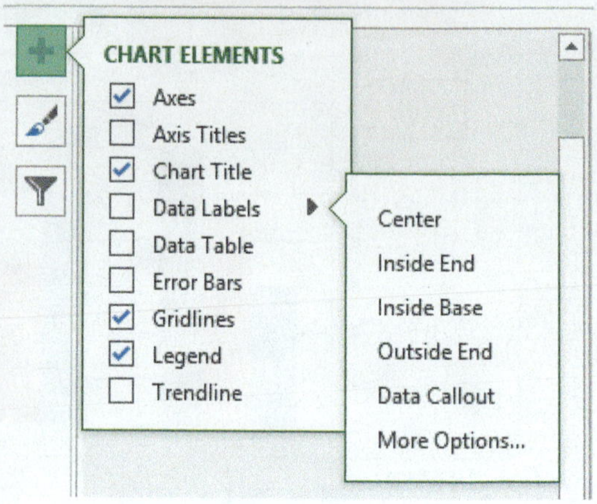

Excel 2016, Windows 10, Microsoft Corporation

Try It! Setting Data Label Options

1. In the **E52Try_xx** file, select the chart on the Country Antiques Q3 Sales Chart tab, if necessary.
2. Click the Chart Elements shortcut button +, point to Data Labels, click the Data Labels arrow that appears on the right ▶, and click Inside Base.
3. Observe the data labels. By default, Excel uses the data value as the data label. In this instance, the dollar values overlap, making them illegible.
4. In the Chart Elements shortcut menu, click Data Labels to unselect it and clear the labels.
5. In the Chart Elements shortcut menu, point to Data Labels, click the Data Labels arrow ▶ > Center. All of the data labels are centered within the data points.
6. Click one of the August data labels to select all of the August data labels.
7. Point to Data Labels, click the arrow ▶, and click More Options to display the Format Data Labels task pane.
8. In the Label Position group, click Inside End.
9. Click one of the September data labels to select all of the September data labels.

Data label options

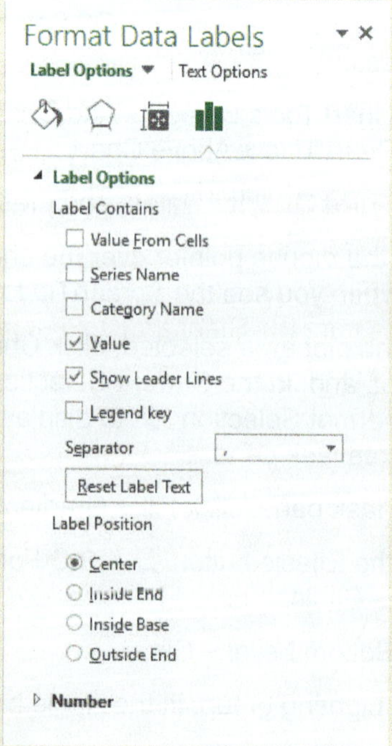

Excel 2016, Windows 10, Microsoft Corporation

(continued)

Try It! Setting Data Label Options *(continued)*

10 In the Label Contains group, click Series Name.

11 In the Label Contains group, click Legend key.

12 Notice that the gray legend key and the name September appear beside the data value in the data label.

13 Click to unselect Series Name, click to unselect Legend key, click Inside End, and close the Format Data Labels task pane.

14 Save the changes to the file, and leave it open to use in the next Try It.

Setting Data Table Options

- You can add a data table to the bottom of a chart.
- The **data table** looks like a small worksheet, and it lists the data used to create the chart.
- Adding a data table to a chart allows a viewer to easily understand the values plotted on the chart.
- Data tables have only a few basic options beyond normal formatting such as the fill and border colors.
  - You can add a border around the cells in the data table—horizontally, vertically, or around the table's outline.
  - You can choose whether or not to display the legend keys as part of the table.
- Data table formatting options, such as fill and shadow, are applied to the data inside the cells of the table, not to the table itself.

Try It! Setting Data Table Options

1 In the E52Try_xx file, click the chart on the Country Antiques Q3 Sales Chart tab to select it.

2 Click the Chart Elements shortcut button + > Data Table. A data table appears below the chart with the legend key displayed next to the data series name.

3 Click the Chart Elements shortcut button +, point to Data Table, click the Data Table arrow ▸, and click More Options.

4 In the Format Data Table task pane, click Fill & Line > Fill > Solid fill.

5 In the Fill group, click Fill Color, and click Orange from the Standard Colors group.

6 In the Fill group, click No fill, and close the Format Data Table task pane.

7 Save the changes to the file, and leave it open to use in the next Try It.

The Format Data Table task pane

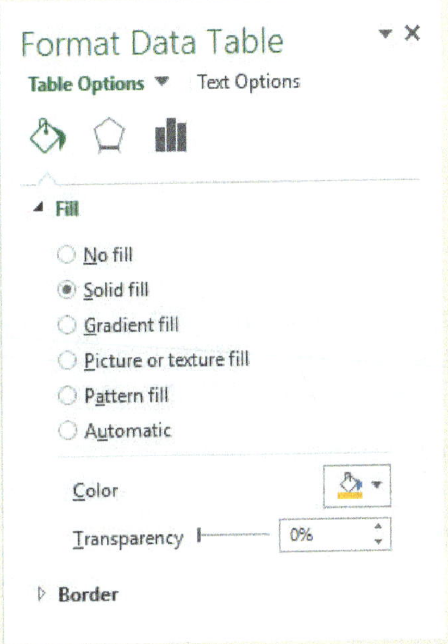

Excel 2016, Windows 10, Microsoft Corporation

Formatting a Data Series

- When you create a chart, Excel automatically assigns a color to each **data series** in the chart.
- That color appears as the bars of a column chart, the slices of a pie chart, and the legend key.
  - You may want to change the color of a particular data series to coordinate with your other business documents.
  - Even if you're printing the chart in black and white, you may want to change the color of a data series to better distinguish it from other colors in the chart that translate to a similar gray tone.
- In certain chart types, such as bar and column charts, you can adjust the amount of space between each series in a group or between each category by changing the Series Options.
- In line charts, you can change the type and look of the markers used to plot each data point.
- In pie charts, you can change the position of the first slice within the pie, and the amount of separation between the remaining slices.

Try It! **Formatting a Data Series**

1. In the **E52Try_xx** file, click the chart on the Country Antiques Q3 Sales Chart tab to select it, if necessary.
2. Click Chart Tools Format, in the Current Selection group click the Chart Elements drop-down box Chart Area, and click Series "July".
3. In the Current Selection group, click Format Selection to display the Format Data Series task pane.
4. In the Series Overlap box, type **-30%**.
5. In the Gap Width box, type **30%**, and close the Format Data Series task pane.
6. Save and close the file, and exit Excel.

Lesson 52—Practice

You're keeping the books for Special Events, the premiere party planners in your local area, and you've been asked to produce a couple of different sales charts based on last month's sales figures. The owner will choose one to use in a presentation for her bank so the stakes are high. In this project, you will format a sales chart.

DIRECTIONS

1. Start Excel, if necessary, and open **E52Practice** from the data files for this lesson.
2. Save the file as **E52Practice_xx** in the location where your teacher instructs you to store the files for this lesson.
3. For the **Chart-July Party Sales** worksheet, add a custom header that has your name at the left, the date code in the center, and the page number code at the right.

✓ *Because the chart occupies the entire tab, you may not be able to access the header the same way you learned in Lesson 42. Here is an alternate method: on the Page Layout tab, click the dialog box launcher in the Page setup group, and then on the Header/Footer tab, click Custom Header.*

4. Click the **Chart Elements** shortcut button + > **Data Table**.
5. Hover the pointer over Data Table, click the arrow ▸ > **With Legend Keys**.
6. In the Chart Elements shortcut menu, hover the pointer over Chart Title, click the **Chart Title** arrow ▸ > **Centered Overlay**.

7. Type **July Party Sales**, and press ENTER.
8. Click **Chart Tools Format** and, in the **Chart Elements** drop-down menu, in the Current Selection group, click **Plot Area**.
9. In the Chart Tools Format tab, in the Shape Styles group, click the **Shape Fill** drop-down arrow Shape Fill > **Gradient** > **Linear Diagonal – Top Right to Bottom Left** in the Light group.
10. Click **Chart Tools Format**, and, in the **Chart Elements** drop-down menu, click **Series "private"**.
11. In the **Chart Elements** shortcut menu, click **Data Labels** > **Outside End**.
12. With the series still selected, click **Format Selection** in the Current Selection group to display the Format Data Series task pane.
13. In the Series Overlap text box, type **-25%**.
14. In the Gap Width text box, type **200%**.
15. **With your teacher's permission**, print the chart. Your chart should look like Figure 52-3.
16. Save and close the file, and exit Excel.

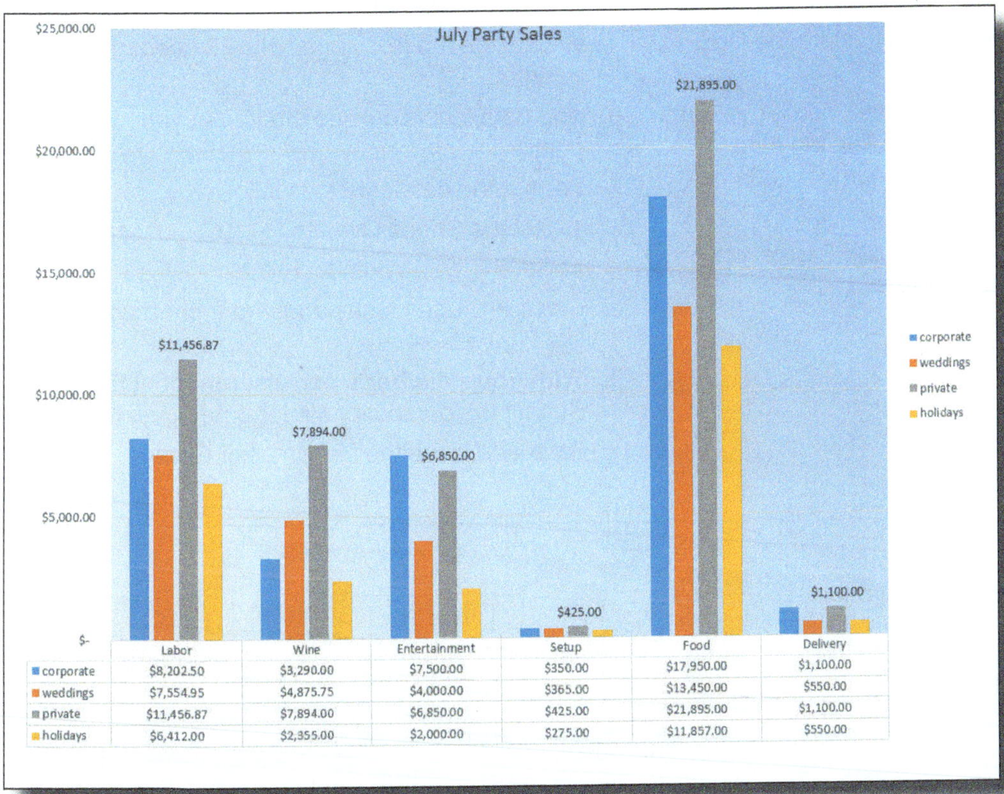

	Labor	Wine	Entertainment	Setup	Food	Delivery
corporate	$8,202.50	$3,290.00	$7,500.00	$350.00	$17,950.00	$1,100.00
weddings	$7,554.95	$4,875.75	$4,000.00	$365.00	$13,450.00	$550.00
private	$11,456.87	$7,894.00	$6,850.00	$425.00	$21,895.00	$1,100.00
holidays	$6,412.00	$2,355.00	$2,000.00	$275.00	$11,857.00	$550.00

Figure 52-3

Excel 2016, Windows 10, Microsoft Corporation

Lesson 52—Apply

You work in the accounting department for Special Events, the premiere party planners in your local area. You are preparing different sales charts based on last month's sales figures for the owner to use in a presentation for her bank. In this project, you will format another sales chart using the skills you learned in this lesson.

DIRECTIONS

1. Start Excel, if necessary, and open **E52Apply** from the data files for this lesson.
2. Save the file as **E52Apply_xx** in the location where your teacher instructs you to store the files for this lesson.
3. For the **July Party Sales** worksheet, add a custom header that has your name at the left, the date code in the center, and the page number code at the right.

   ✓ *See the tip following step 3 in Lesson 52—Practice section for help with the custom header if needed.*
4. Add a chart title, **July Party Sales**, above the chart on the July Party Sales tab.
5. Format the chart elements as follows:
   a. Add a data table and show the legend keys in the table.
   b. Apply a solid fill to the Plot Area.
   c. Change the fill color to **Blue, Accent 1, Lighter 80%**.
6. Add data labels outside the end of your data points.
7. Format the data series as follows:
   a. Set the Series Overlap to **-10%**.
   b. Set the Gap Width to **200%**.
8. Close any open task panes. Your chart should look like Figure 52-4.
9. **With your teacher's permission**, print the chart. Submit the printout or file for grading as required.
10. Save and close the file, and exit Excel.

Figure 52-4

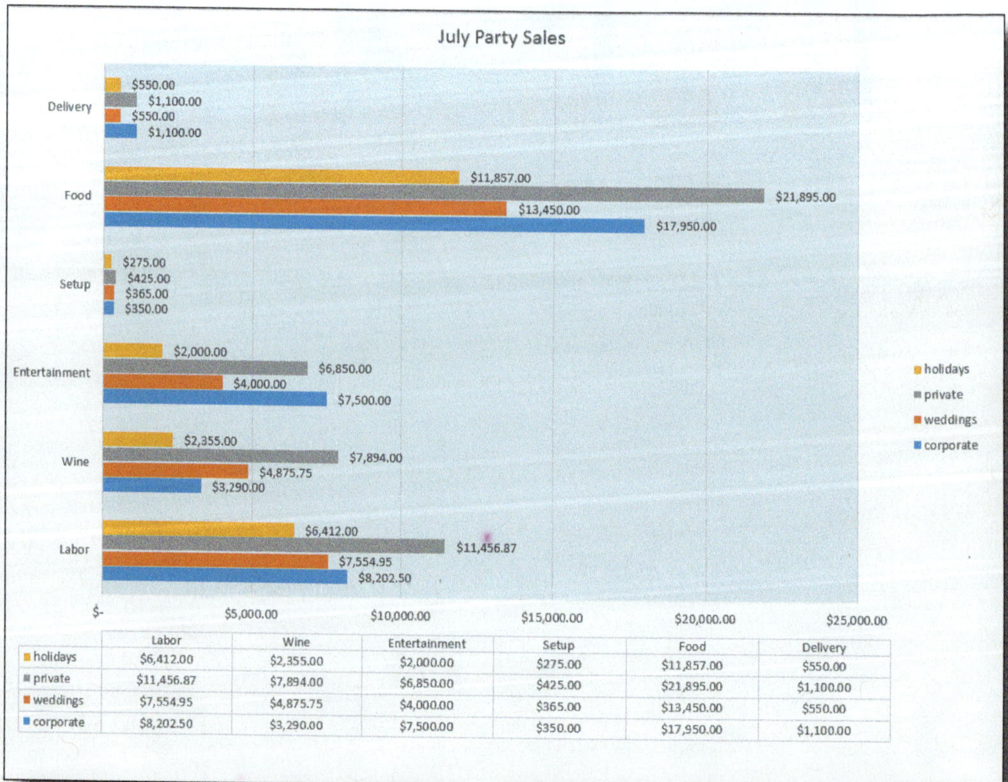

Excel 2016, Windows 10, Microsoft Corporation

Lesson 53

Formatting the Value Axis

➤ What You Will Learn

Creating a Stock Chart
Modifying the Value Axis
Formatting Data Markers
Formatting a Legend
Adding a Secondary Value Axis to a Chart

Software Skills Because Excel is used every day by thousands of investors—many of whom invest as a profession—it has to be capable of producing charts specifically tailored to the needs and expectations of those users. A stock chart is no ordinary graphical rendering, since it often has to show several related values (such as opening and closing values) on a single chart.

WORDS TO KNOW

Data marker
The symbol that appears on a stock chart to mark a specific data point.

Legend
An optional part of the chart, the legend displays a description of each data series included in the chart.

Value axis
The vertical scale of a chart on which the values from each category are plotted, sometimes called the Y axis.

What You Can Do

Creating a Stock Chart

- Charting stock data requires a special type of chart designed to handle standard stock information.
- Excel offers four different kinds of stock charts:
  - High-Low-Close
  - Open-High-Low-Close
  - Volume-High-Low-Close
  - Volume-Open-High-Low-Close
- Each chart handles a different set of data taken from this standard set of stock information:
  - Volume: the number of shares of a particular stock traded during the market day.
  - Open: the value of the stock at the time when the market opened for the day.
  - High: the highest value at which the stock was traded that day.
  - Low: the lowest value at which the stock was traded that day.
  - Close: the value of the stock when the market closed for the day.

- To create a stock chart, you must enter the data in columns or rows in the order specified by the type of stock chart you want.

  ✓ *For example, if you select the Open-High-Low-Close chart, you must enter the data in four columns (or rows) in that order: open, high, low, close.*

  - For row (or column) labels, you can use the stock symbol or name if you are going to track more than one type of stock, or you can use the date if you're tracking one stock's trading pattern over several days.

- A stock chart is also ideal for charting certain kinds of scientific data, such as temperature changes throughout the day.

Try It! Creating a Stock Chart

1. Start Excel, and open **E53Try** from the data files for this lesson.
2. Save the file as **E53Try_xx** in the location where your teacher instructs you to store the files for this lesson.
3. On the table worksheet, select the range A5:F258.
4. Create a Volume-Open-High-Low-Close stock chart on a new worksheet:
   a. Click the Insert tab, and click the Charts dialog box launcher to display the Insert Chart dialog box.
   b. Click the All Charts tab > Stock > Volume-Open-High-Low-Close > OK.
   c. On the Chart Tools Design tab, in the Location group, click Move Chart to open the Move Chart dialog box.
   d. Click New sheet, and type **Stock Chart** in the box.
   e. Click OK to move the chart to its own worksheet page.
5. Change the chart title to **Midwest Pharmaceutical Stock Tracking**.
6. Save the changes to the file, and leave it open to use in the next Try It.

The Volume-Open-High-Low-Close stock chart

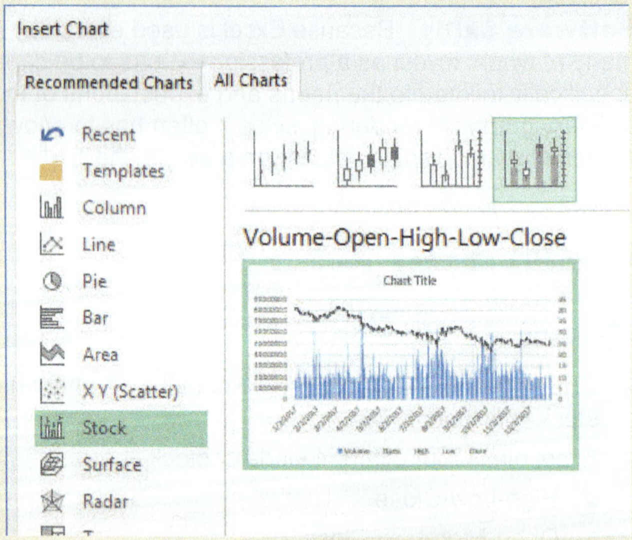

Excel 2016, Windows 10, Microsoft Corporation

Modifying the Value Axis

- The vertical, or **value axis**, provides a scale for the values of the data for most chart types.

  ✓ *For bar charts, the horizontal and vertical axes are reversed.*

- You can change the font, size, color, attributes, alignment, and placement of text or numbers along the axis.
- You can add axis titles from the Chart Elements shortcut menu.
  - You can also add axis titles from the Add Chart Element button on the Chart Tools Design tab.
- To control whether an axis should be displayed, select an axis, and click the Format Selection button from the Current Selection group on the Chart Tools Design tab.
  - In addition, you can adjust the scale used along either axis so that the numbers are easy to read.

Try It! Modifying the Value Axis

1. In the **E53Try_xx** file, select the chart on the Stock Chart tab, if necessary.
2. Click the Chart Elements shortcut button + > Axis Titles.
3. On the Chart Tools Format tab, in the Current Selection group, click the Chart Elements drop-down arrow Chart Area, click Vertical (Value) Axis Title, type **Volume (in millions)**, and press ENTER.
4. On the Chart Tools Format tab, in the Current Selection group, click the Chart Elements drop-down arrow, click Secondary Vertical (Value) Axis Title, type **Value**, and press ENTER.
5. Click the Chart Elements drop-down arrow > Vertical (Value) Axis > Format Selection.
6. In the Format Axis task pane, in the Axis Options group, under Bounds, type **10000000** in the Minimum text box, and press ENTER.
7. In the Format Axis task pane, in the Axis Options group, click the Display units drop-down arrow > Millions.
8. In the Format Axis task pane, click Number to display the number options.
9. In the Category list box click Number, in the Decimal places box type **0**, and press ENTER.

   ✓ *Because the stock exchange is not operating every day of the year, there are points along the horizontal axis with no data because Excel assumes that all dates should be included in the axis, not just the dates in your data table. You will need to modify the horizontal axis.*

10. On the Chart Tools Format tab, in the Current Selection group, click the Chart Elements drop-down arrow, click Horizontal (Category) Axis. Notice that the task pane displays the selected axis options.
11. In the Format Axis task pane, in the Axis Options group, under Axis Type, click Text axis.
12. Click the Chart Elements drop-down arrow > Secondary Vertical (Value) Axis.
13. In the Format Axis task pane, click Number, and in the Category list box click Currency to convert the stock values.
14. In the Axis Options group, under Bounds, type **20.0** in the Minimum text box, press ENTER and close the Format Axis task pane.
15. Save the changes to the file, and leave it open to use in the next Try It.

The Format Axis task pane

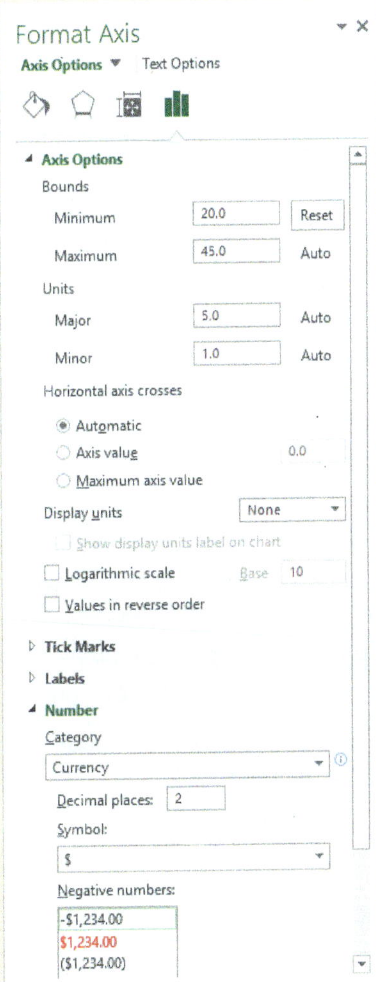

Excel 2016, Windows 10, Microsoft Corporation

Formatting Data Markers

- When you create a stock chart, Excel uses a series of standard **data markers** for the open, close, high-low, volume, close up, and close down values.
- Some of these markers may be too small, too dark, or too light to appear clearly on a printout.
- To improve the appearance of your chart, you may want to adjust the data markers used by Excel.
- You can select a series to change, and select from the Marker Options in the Format Data Series task pane.
- You can change the fill color, size, shape, outline color, and outline style of each data marker used in a stock chart.

  ✓ *You can also change the data markers used in line, xy (scatter), and radar charts.*
- You can choose to hide the data markers by selecting None in the Marker Options area of the Format Data Series task pane.

Try It! Formatting Data Markers

1. In the **E53Try_xx** file, select the chart on the Stock Chart tab, if necessary.
2. On the Chart Tools Format tab, in the Current Selection group, click the Chart Elements drop-down arrow, click Series "High," and click Format Selection.
3. In the Format Data Series task pane, click Fill & Line > Marker > Marker Options > Built-in.
4. In the Type drop-down list, choose the triangle, and in the Size box enter **4**.
5. Click Fill > Solid fill.
6. Click the Color button, and in the Standard Colors palette click Light Green.

   ✓ *The light green triangle data marker has been added to the legend.*
7. Click the Chart Elements drop-down arrow > Series "Low" > Format Selection.
8. In the Format Data Series task pane, click Fill & Line > Marker > Marker Options > Built-in.
9. In the Type drop-down list, choose the circle, and in the Size box enter **3**.
10. Under the Fill heading, click Solid fill.
11. Click the Color button, in the Standard Colors palette click Red, and close the Format Data Series task pane.

    ✓ *The red circle data marker has been added to the legend.*
12. Save the changes to the file, and leave it open to use in the next Try It.

Formatting data markers

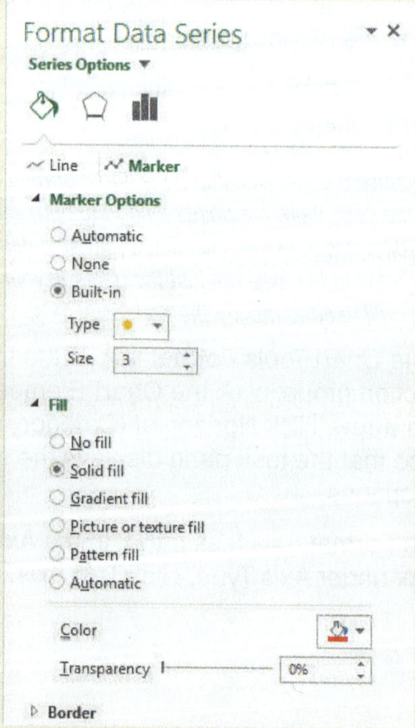

Excel 2016, Windows 10, Microsoft Corporation

Formatting a Legend

- Though a **legend** is automatically displayed when you create a chart, you can choose where you want to place it.
- You can place the legend at the top, left, bottom, or right of the chart. You can also choose to overlap the legend over the chart.
- You can access the Format Legend task pane by clicking More Options in the Chart Elements shortcut menu.
- You can change the fill color, size, border color, and outline style of a legend.

Try It! Formatting a Legend

1. In the E53Try_xx file, select the chart on the Stock Chart tab, if necessary.
2. Click the Chart Elements shortcut button + > Legend to hide the legend.
3. Click the Chart Elements shortcut button + > Legend arrow ▸ > Top.
4. Click to select the legend, and on the Chart Tools Format tab click Format Selection.
5. In the Format Legend task pane, click the Legend Options icon and then click to unselect the Show the legend without overlapping the chart option.
6. Click Fill & Line.
7. Under Fill, click the Color button, and in the Theme Colors palette click Blue, Accent 1, Lighter 80%.
8. Under Border, click Solid line.
9. Under Border, click the Color button, in the Theme Colors palette click Black, Text 1, and close the Format Legend task pane.
10. Save the changes to the file, and leave it open to use in the next Try It.

Adding a Secondary Value Axis to a Chart

- To track two related but different values, use two value axes in the chart.
- The value axes appear on opposite sides of the chart.
- For example, Excel uses two value axes for a stock chart that includes both the volume of stock trading and the value of the stock.
  - One axis plots the stock's trading volume.
  - The other axis plots the stock's value at open, close, high, and low points in the day.
- Secondary value axes are most common on stock charts and will appear automatically when Excel determines that two value axes are needed, but you can manually add a secondary axis to other types of charts as well.

Try It! Adding a Secondary Value Axis to a Chart

1. In the E53Try_xx file, select the YTD Average Table tab.
2. On the Chart Tools Design tab, click Select Data.
3. In the Select Data Source dialog box, under Legend Entries (Series), click the Add button to add a series.
4. In the Edit Series dialog box, click the Collapse Dialog button for Series name, click the YTD Table worksheet tab, click cell E5, and click the Restore Dialog button.
5. In the Edit Series dialog box, click the Collapse Dialog button for Series values, click the YTD Table worksheet tab if necessary, select the range E6:E258, and click the Restore Dialog button.

(continued)

Try It! **Adding a Secondary Value Axis to a Chart** *(continued)*

6 In the Edit Series dialog box, click OK.

7 Click OK to close the Select Data Source dialog box.

8 Right-click the orange line > Format Data Series.

9 In the Format Data Series task pane, under Series Options, click Secondary Axis.

10 On the Chart Tools Format tab, in the Current Selection group, click the Chart Elements drop-down arrow, click Secondary Vertical (Value) Axis, and click Format Selection.

11 In the Format Axis task pane, in the Axis Options group, under Bounds, type **100.00** in the Maximum text box, press ENTER, and close the Format Axis task pane.

12 Save and close the file, and exit Excel.

Lesson 53—Practice

You work in the Communications department of Midwest Pharmaceutical, and the annual shareholders' meeting is scheduled for next week. Your job is to create and format a stock chart for the CFO's presentation. You want to add axis labels, axis titles, and data markers to the stock chart using your new Excel skills.

DIRECTIONS

1. Start Excel, if necessary, and open **E53Practice** from the data files for this lesson.
2. Save the file as **E53Practice_xx** in the location where your teacher instructs you to store the files for this lesson.
3. Select the range **A3:E67**.
4. Create a **Volume-High-Low-Close** stock chart on its own worksheet tab.
   a. Click **Insert** > **Charts** dialog box launcher.
   b. Click the **All Charts** tab > **Stock** > **Volume-High-Low-Close** > **OK**.
   c. Click **Chart Tools Design** > **Move Chart** to open the Move Chart dialog box.
   d. Click **New sheet**, and in the New sheet text box type **Q1 Stock Chart**.
   e. Click **OK** to move the chart to its own worksheet page.
5. Click the chart title to select it, type **Midwest Pharmaceutical First Quarter Stock**, and press ENTER.
6. Click the **Chart Elements** shortcut button +, click the **Axis Titles** arrow ▶, and click to select the **Primary Vertical** and **Secondary Vertical** check boxes.
7. On the Chart Tools Format tab, in the Current Selection group, click the **Chart Elements** drop-down arrow Chart Area, click **Vertical (Value) Axis Title**, type **Volume (in millions)**, and press ENTER.
8. On the Chart Tools Format tab, in the Current Selection group, click the **Chart Elements** drop-down arrow, click **Secondary Vertical (Value) Axis Title**, type **Stock Price (USD)**, and press ENTER.
9. Click to select the primary vertical axis (the vertical axis on the left), and click **Format Selection**.
10. In the Format Axis task pane, in the Axis Options group, in the Display units box, click **Millions**.
11. In the Minimum text box, type **12500000**, and press ENTER.

12. Click to unselect the **Show display units label on chart** check box.

    ✓ *If you notice that the Minimum axis value does not change to 12,500,000, type 1.25E7 in the Minimum text box.*

13. Click to select the horizontal axis, and in the Axis Options group, click **Text axis**.
14. Click **Size & Properties**, and in the Text direction list click **Rotate all text 270°**.
15. Click to select the secondary vertical axis (the vertical axis on the right), and click **Axis Options**.
16. Click **Number**, and in the Category list click **Currency** to convert the stock values.
17. Under Axis Options, in the Minimum text box, type **25.0**.
18. Click the **Chart Elements** shortcut button + > **Axis Titles** arrow ▸ > **Primary Horizontal** to unselect it, if necessary.
19. Close the Format Axis task pane.
20. Add a custom header that has your name at the left, the date code in the center, and the page number code at the right.
21. **With your teacher's permission**, print the chart. The chart should look like Figure 53-1.
22. Save and close the file, and exit Excel.

Figure 53-1

Excel 2016, Windows 10, Microsoft Corporation

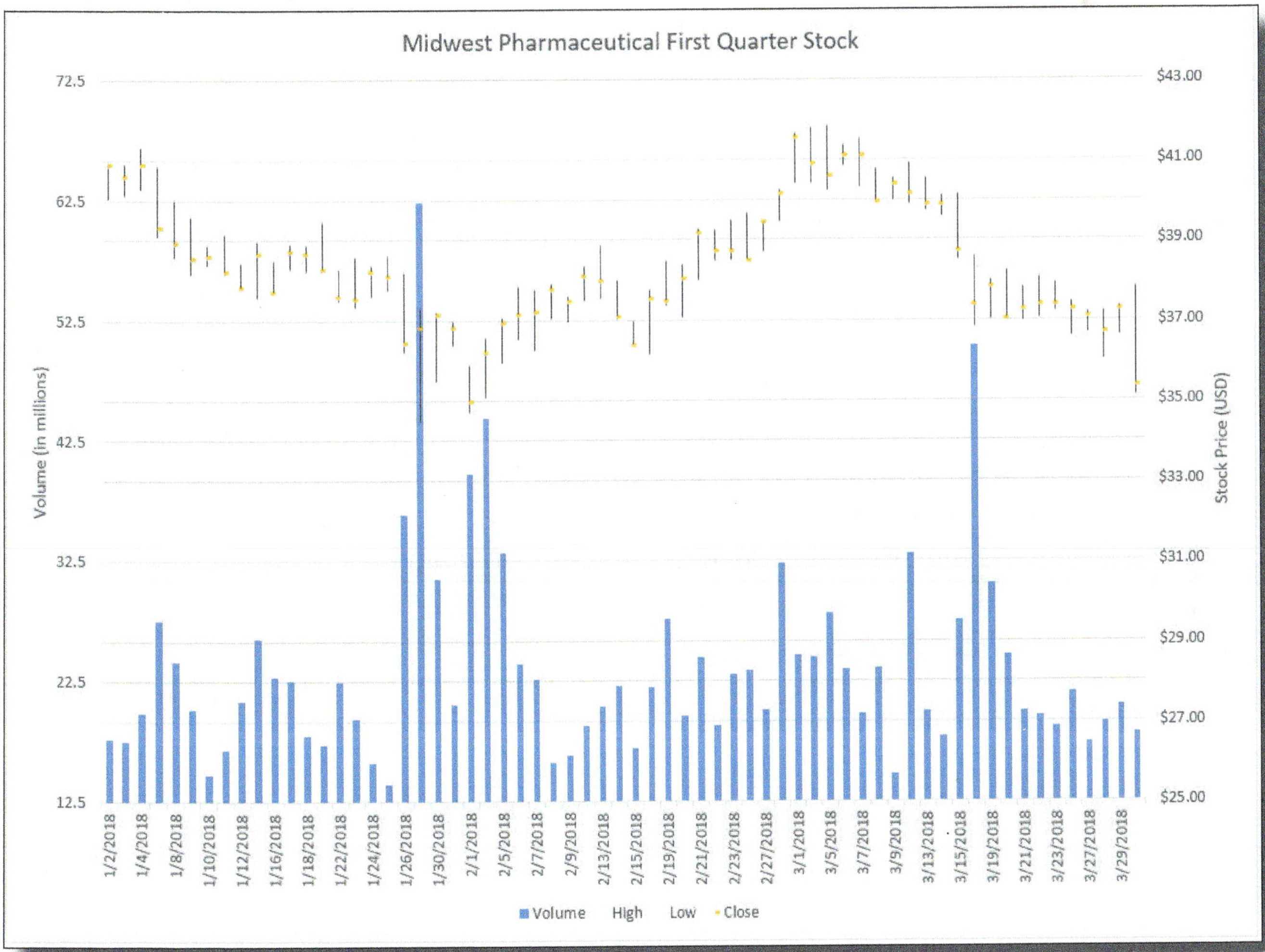

Lesson 53—Apply

You are preparing for the annual shareholders' meeting for Midwest Pharmaceutical. You have created a stock chart for the CFO's presentation, and now you want to format it so the data is clear and legible. You want to add and format data markers so that the shareholders will be able to easily see the performance of the stock.

DIRECTIONS

1. Start Excel, if necessary, and open **E53Apply** from the data files for this lesson
2. Save the file as **E53Apply_xx** in the location where your teacher instructs you to store the files for this lesson.
3. On the Q1 Stock Chart worksheet, add a custom header that has your name at the left, the date code in the center, and the page number code at the right.
4. On the **Q1 Stock Chart** worksheet, click the chart to select it, and add formatting to the "High" data series.
   a. Click **Chart Tools Format** > **Chart Elements** drop-down arrow > **Series "High"** > **Format Selection**.
   b. In the Format Data Series task pane, click **Fill & Line** > **Marker** > **Marker Options** > **Built-in**.
   c. In the **Type** drop-down list, click the triangle, and in the Size box enter **4**.
   d. Click **Fill** > **Solid fill**.
   e. Click the **Color** button, and in the Standard Colors palette click **Light Green**.
   f. Click **Border**, if necessary, and click **No line**.
5. Add formatting to the "Low" data series.
   a. On the Chart Tools Format tab, click the Chart Elements drop-down arrow > **Series "Low"** > **Format Selection**.
   b. In the Format Data Series task pane, in the Marker Options group, click **Built-in**.
   c. In the Type drop-down list, click the circle, and in the Size box enter **3**.
   d. Click **Fill** > **Solid fill**.
   e. Click the **Color** button, and in the Standard Colors palette click **Red**.
6. Add formatting to the "Volume" data series.
   a. On the Chart Tools Format tab, click the **Chart Elements** drop-down arrow > **Series "Volume"** > **Format Selection**.
   b. Click **Fill**, if necessary > **Solid fill**.
   c. Click the **Color** button, and in the Theme Colors palette click **Gold, Accent 4**.
7. Add formatting to the legend at the bottom of the chart.
   a. Click the legend to select it.
   b. In the Format Legend task pane, in the Border group, click **Solid line** > **Color** > **Gold, Accent 4**.
   c. Click **Effects** > **Shadow** > **Color** button > **Gold, Accent 4** in the Theme Colors palette.
   d. Click the **Presets** button, and in the Outer group click **Offset Diagonal Bottom Right**.
   e. Close the Format Legend task pane.
8. **With your teacher's permission**, print the chart. The chart should look like Figure 53-2 on the next page.
9. Save and close the file, and exit Excel.

Figure 53-2

Excel 2016, Windows 10, Microsoft Corporation

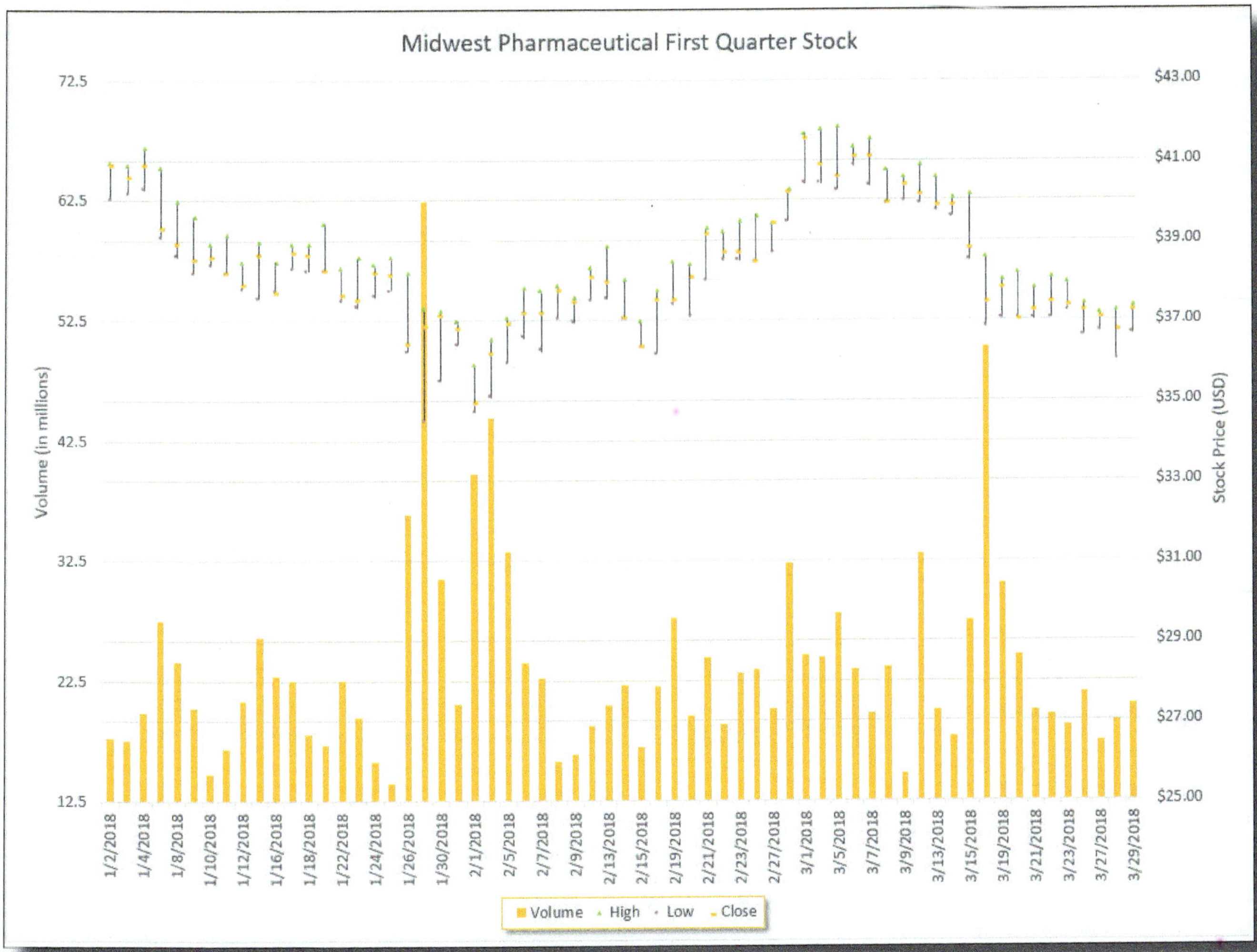

Lesson 54

Creating Stacked Area Charts

➤ What You Will Learn

Creating a Stacked Area Chart
Formatting the Chart Floor and Chart Walls
Displaying Chart Gridlines
Applying a Chart Layout and Chart Styles

WORDS TO KNOW

Chart floor
The horizontal floor below the data on a 3-D chart.

Chart wall
The vertical wall behind the data on a 3-D chart.

Gridlines
In the worksheet, gridlines are the light gray outline that surrounds each cell. In charts, gridlines are the lines that appear on a chart, extending from the value or category axes.

Stacked area chart
A special type of area chart in which the values for each data series are stacked on one another, creating one large area.

Software Skills Whether you're creating a chart for a big presentation or a printed report, you want that chart to look as good as possible. Using a 3-D chart adds a high-tech look to an otherwise ordinary presentation of the facts. As with other chart elements, basic formatting can enhance the look of your chart. You also may want to display or hide gridlines to make the values on the axes easier to read.

What You Can Do

Creating a Stacked Area Chart

- In a **stacked area chart**, the values in each data series are stacked on top of each other, creating a larger area.
  - Whereas a line chart would show the relative positions of multiple series compared to one another, a stacked area chart shows their cumulative position.
  - Each entry is stacked on top of the previous one, forming a peak that represents the sum of all series' entries together.
- Use a stacked area chart to emphasize the difference in values between two data series, while also illustrating the total of the two.

✓ *A stacked area chart can be used to track the relative contribution of each item in the data series to the cumulative total.*

- In a 100% stacked area chart, for each category, all of the series combine to consume the entire height of the chart.
- Both stacked area and 100% stacked area charts come in 2-D and 3-D versions.

Try It! Creating a Stacked Area Chart

1. Start Excel, and open **E54Try** from the data files for this lesson.
2. Save the file as **E54Try_xx** in the location where your teacher instructs you to store the files for this lesson.
3. Select the range A9:G18.
4. Click Insert > Insert Line or Area Chart > 3-D Stacked Area from the gallery.
5. On the Chart Tools Design tab, in the Location group, click Move Chart, and move the chart to a New sheet titled **Patient Care Chart**. Click OK.
6. Click the Chart Title, and type **Patient Care Chart** and press ENTER.
7. Save the changes to the file, and leave it open to use in the next Try It.

Formatting the Chart Floor and Chart Walls

- Three-dimensional charts include a **chart wall**, which forms the side and back of the chart, and the **chart floor**, which forms the bottom of the chart.

  ✓ *Because 3-D pie charts are not plotted on vertical and horizontal axes, they do not include chart walls and a floor.*

- You can apply standard formatting options, such as fill color, borders, shadows, and glows to the chart walls and floors.
- Select the element from the Chart Elements drop-down box, click Format Selection, and use the task pane to format the floor or wall.

Try It! Formatting the Chart Floor and Chart Walls

1. In the **E54Try_xx** file, select the chart on the Patient Care Chart tab, if necessary.
2. On the Chart Tools Format tab, in the Current Selection group, click the Chart Elements drop-down arrow Chart Area > Walls > Format Selection.
3. In the Format Walls task pane, click Fill > Gradient fill > Preset gradients > Bottom Spotlight - Accent 1.
4. On the Chart Tools Format tab, in the Current Selection group, click the Chart Elements drop-down arrow, and click Floor.
5. In the Format Floor task pane, under Fill, click Solid fill.
6. Click the Color button, and in the Theme Colors palette click Blue, Accent 1.
7. Close the Format Floor task pane.
8. Save the changes to the file, and leave it open to use in the next Try It.

(continued)

Try It! Formatting the Chart Floor and Chart Walls *(continued)*

Formatted chart floor and walls

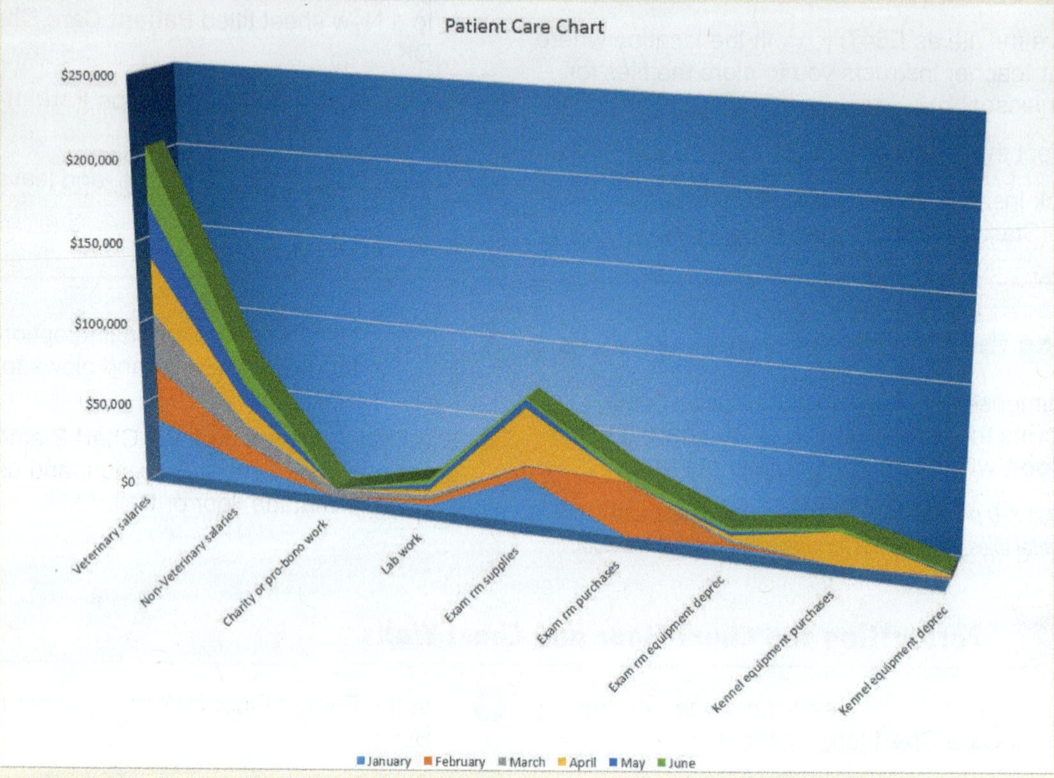

Excel 2016, Windows 10, Microsoft Corporation

Displaying Chart Gridlines

- On Excel charts, **gridlines** can help guide the eye along a given axis.
- You can access the gridlines options from the Chart Elements shortcut menu.
- You can increase the number of major gridlines by changing the point at which the gridlines recur.
- You can also display minor gridlines, which fall between major gridlines.

Try It! Displaying Chart Gridlines

1. In the E54Try_xx file, select the chart on the Patient Care Chart tab, if necessary.
2. Click the Chart Elements shortcut button +, point to Gridlines, click the Gridlines arrow ▶ > Primary Major Vertical.
3. Save the changes to the file, and leave it open to use in the next Try It.

Applying a Chart Layout and Chart Styles

- When you create a chart, Excel adds a legend and assigns default colors to each series in the chart.
- You can manually adjust the colors and placements of many items on a chart.
- Excel includes two built-in formatting features: Chart Styles and Chart Layout. These features work together to help you quickly format charts.
- You can apply a built-in chart style from the Chart Styles gallery on the Chart Tools Design tab.
  - These styles include several grayscale, monotone, and multi-colored options, and even 3-D formatting.
- You can use the Change Colors button in the Charts Styles group of the Chart Tools Design tab to apply different color schemes.
- You can use the Quick Layout button in the Chart Layouts group of the Chart Tools Design tab to format the placement of chart elements such as the legend, chart title, and the data labels.

  ✓ *The number of chart layout options available depends on the type of chart you are formatting.*

- Once these formatting features have been applied, you can still manually adjust any chart element.

Try It! Applying a Chart Layout and Chart Styles

1. In the **E54Try_xx** file, select the chart on the Patient Care Chart tab, if necessary.
2. Click Chart Tools Design > Quick Layout > Layout 2.
3. On the Chart Tools Design tab, in the Chart Styles gallery, click Style 8.

   ✓ *If you are working on a smaller screen, you can click the Quick Layouts button to access the Chart Styles gallery.*

4. Click the chart title, type **Wood Hills Patient Care Expenses**, and press ENTER.
5. Click the Home tab, and click the Increase Font Size button A twice to increase the font size of the chart title to 20 points.
6. On the Home tab, click the Font Color drop-down arrow, and in the Theme Colors palette click Orange, Accent 2.
7. Click Chart Tools Design > Switch Row/Column.
8. Click the Chart Elements shortcut button +, point to Axes, click the Axes arrow ▸, and click More Options.
9. In the Format Axis task pane, in the Axis Options group, under Axis position, click the Categories in reverse order check box to select it.
10. On the Chart Tools Format tab, in the Current Selection group, click the Chart Elements drop-down arrow > Walls.
11. In the Format Walls task pane, click Fill & Line, and in the Fill group click Gradient fill.
12. On the Chart Tools Format tab, in the Current Selection group, click the Chart Elements drop-down arrow > Floor.
13. In the Format Floor task pane, in the Fill group, click Solid fill.
14. Click the Color button, in the Theme Colors palette click Blue, Accent 1, Lighter 40%, and close the Format Floor task pane.
15. Save and close the file, and exit Excel.

(continued)

Try It! Applying a Chart Layout and Chart Styles *(continued)*

Final stacked chart

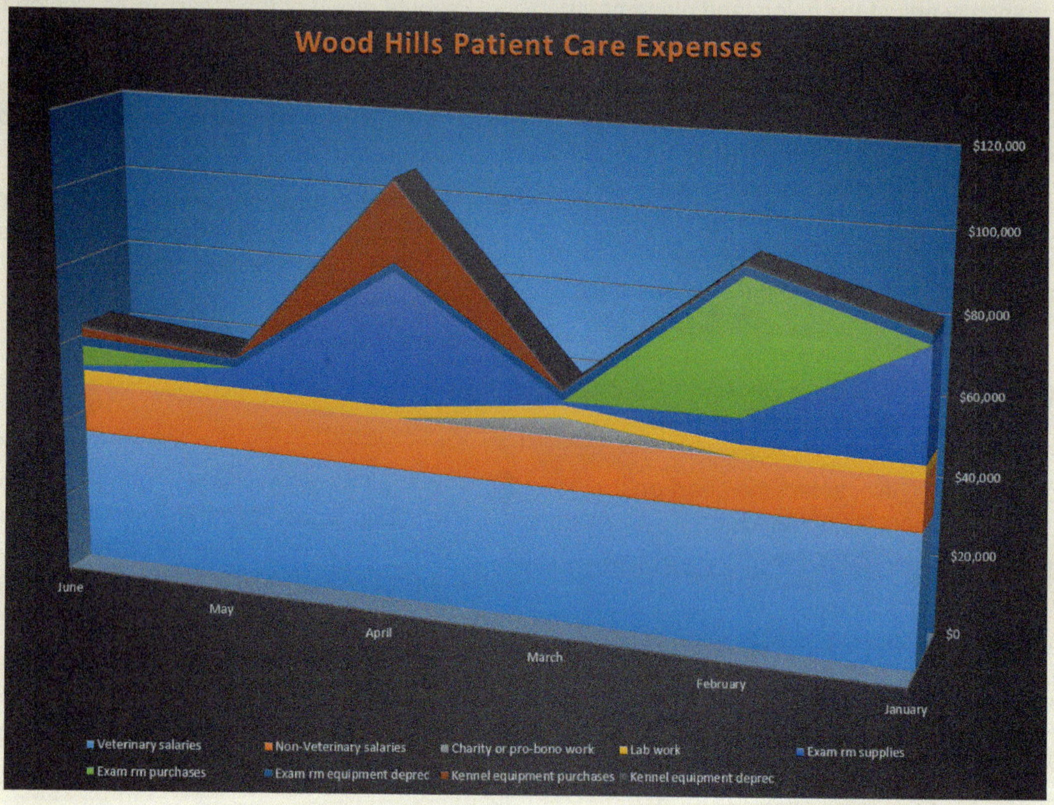

Lesson 54—Practice

You've just been hired by Premiere Formatting. The company hires recent graduates with expertise in Excel to help local businesses with their spreadsheet requirements. Your first assignment is to produce a stacked area chart for Midwest Pharmaceutical. You need to create and format a chart to show a breakdown of the company's first quarter expenses.

DIRECTIONS

1. Start Excel, if necessary, and open **E54Practice** from the data files for this lesson.
2. Save the file as **E54Practice_xx** in the location where your teacher instructs you to store the files for this lesson.
3. Select the range **A3:E10**.
4. Click **Insert** > **Insert Line or Area Chart** > **3-D Stacked Area** from the gallery.
5. On the Chart Tools Design tab, in the Location group, click **Move Chart**.
6. In the Move Chart dialog box, click **New sheet**, in the New sheet text box type **Budget Chart**, and click **OK**.
7. On the Chart Tools Design tab, click **Quick Layout** > **Layout 5** to position the chart elements.
8. Click the chart title to select it, type **First Quarter Budget**, and press ENTER.
9. Click **Home** > **Font Color** drop-down arrow.
10. In the Theme Colors palette, click **Blue, Accent 1, Darker 50%**.
11. On the Home tab, click **Increase Font Size** three times to increase the font size of the chart title to **20 points**.
12. Add a custom header that has your name at the left, the date code in the center, and the page number code at the right.
13. **With your teacher's permission**, print the chart. The chart should look like Figure 54-1.
14. Save and close the file, and exit Excel.

Figure 54-1

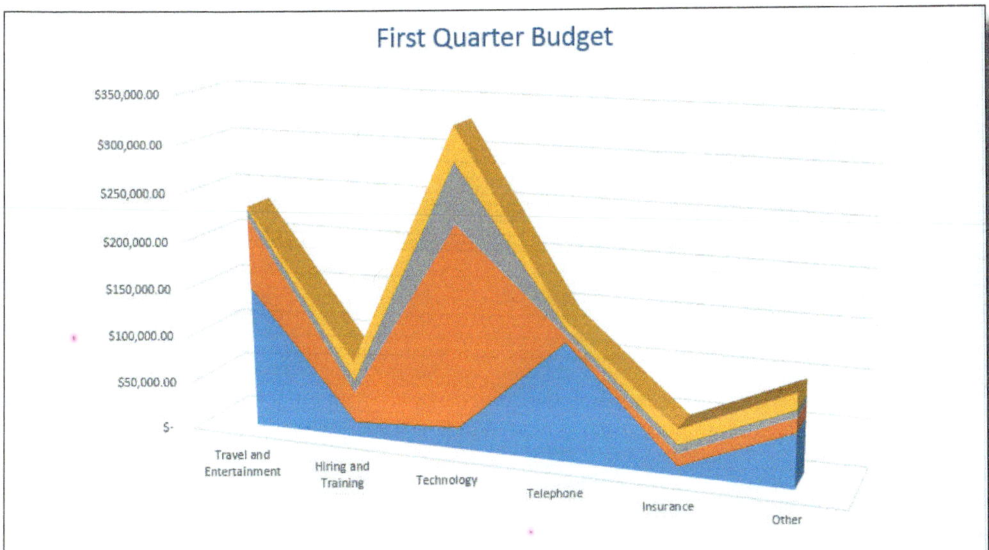

	Travel and Entertainment	Hiring and Training	Technology	Telephone	Insurance	Other
Production	$2,500.00	$19,312.50	$36,254.25	$7,350.00	$15,875.00	$16,621.88
Product Testing	$9,262.50	$12,875.00	$60,885.00	$7,350.00	$9,000.00	$7,387.50
Research & Development	$74,646.25	$32,500.00	$210,053.25	$7,350.00	$12,750.00	$15,656.58
Sales & Marketing	$148,105.00	$15,450.00	$22,383.54	$122,500.00	$9,000.00	$56,140.08

Lesson 54—Apply

You work for Premiere Formatting, and one of your first assignments is to produce stacked area charts for Midwest Pharmaceutical. The company shareholders want to see a breakdown of its first quarter expenses. In this project, you will format a 3-D budget chart by applying a chart style, formatting the chart walls and floor, and adding gridlines.

DIRECTIONS

1. Start Excel, if necessary, and open **E54Apply** from the data files for this lesson.
2. Save the file as **E54Apply_xx** in the location where your teacher instructs you to store the files for this lesson.
3. Add a custom header that has your name at the left, the date code in the center, and the page number code at the right.
4. Select the chart on the Budget Chart tab, if needed. On the Chart Tools Design tab, click **More** to open the Chart Styles gallery, and click **Style 7**.
5. Format the chart walls of the budget chart.
   a. Click **Chart Tools Format** > Chart Elements drop-down arrow Chart Area > **Walls** > **Format Selection**.
   b. In the Format Walls task pane, click **Fill** > **Solid fill** > **Color**.
   c. In the Theme Colors palette, click **Green, Accent 6, Lighter 40%**.
6. Format the chart floor of the budget chart.
   a. On the Chart Tools Format tab, click the **Chart Elements** drop-down arrow > **Floor**.
   b. In the Format Floor task pane, click **Fill** > **Solid fill** > **Color**.
   c. In the Theme Colors palette, click **Green, Accent 6, Darker 25%**.
7. Click the **Chart Elements** shortcut button +, point to Gridlines, click the Gridlines arrow ▶ > **Primary Minor Vertical**.
8. Format the data table of the budget chart.
   a. On the Chart Tools Format tab, click the **Chart Elements** drop-down arrow > **Data Table**.
   b. In the Format Data Table task pane, click **Border** > **Solid line** > **Color**.
   c. In the Theme Colors palette, click **Green, Accent 6, Darker 25%**.
9. Format the horizontal axis.
   a. On the Chart Tools Format tab, click the **Chart Elements** drop-down arrow > **Horizontal (Category) Axis**.
   b. On the Home tab, click **Decrease Font Size** A to decrease the font size to **8 points**.
10. **With your teacher's permission**, print the chart. Your chart should look like Figure 54-2 on the next page.
11. Save and close the file, and exit Excel.

Figure 54-2

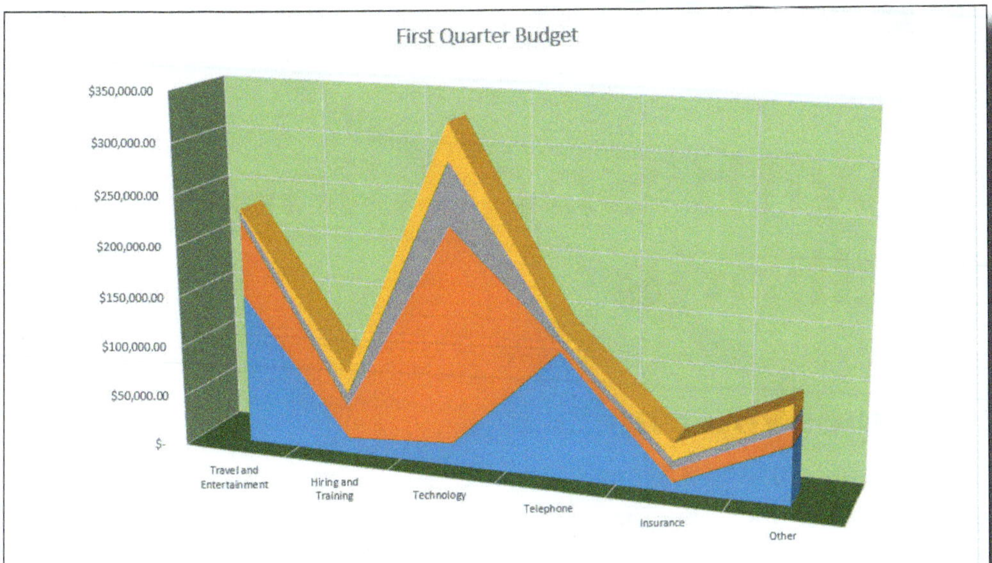

	Travel and Entertainment	Hiring and Training	Technology	Telephone	Insurance	Other
Production	$2,500.00	$19,312.50	$36,254.25	$7,350.00	$15,875.00	$16,621.88
Product Testing	$9,262.50	$12,875.00	$60,885.00	$7,350.00	$9,000.00	$7,387.50
Research & Development	$74,646.25	$32,500.00	$210,053.25	$7,350.00	$12,750.00	$15,656.58
Sales & Marketing	$148,105.00	$15,450.00	$22,383.54	$122,500.00	$9,000.00	$56,140.08

Lesson 55

Working with Sparklines and Trendlines

➤ What You Will Learn

Inserting a Line, Column, or Win/Loss Sparkline
Formatting a Sparkline
Inserting a Trendline
Using a Trendline to Predict

WORDS TO KNOW

Sparkline
Tiny charts within a worksheet cell that represent trends in a series of values.

Trendline
A line that helps determine the trend, or moving average, of your existing data.

Software Skills Trendlines can help you determine what your data means. For example, are your sales going up all year long or do they only go up in the summer? On a worksheet, a sparkline can save you the effort of creating a chart at all because it is like adding a mini chart right in your worksheet.

What You Can Do

Inserting a Line, Column, or Win/Loss Sparkline

- **Sparklines** are like mini charts placed in the worksheet itself.
- Sparklines can show trends in data, or highlight maximum and minimum values.
- Excel will automatically update the sparkline as your data changes.
- Charts are objects that sit on top of the worksheet and can be moved independent of the data. Sparklines appear as a cell background. You can add descriptive text on top of the sparkline.
- Excel includes three distinct sparkline types:
  - Line: tracks the data using a solid line.
  - Column: tracks the data using vertical bars.
  - Win/Loss: tracks the positive (win) or negative (loss) change in the data.

  ✓ *A data value equal to zero is treated as a gap in the Win/Loss sparkline.*

- You can delete a sparkline by selecting Clear Selected Sparklines from the Sparklines group in the shortcut menu when you right-click a sparkline.

Try It! Inserting a Line, Column, or Win/Loss Sparkline

1. Start Excel, and open **E55TryA** from the data files for this lesson.
2. Save the file as **E55TryA_xx** in the location where your teacher instructs you to store the files for this lesson.
3. Click to select the cell H9, and click the Insert tab.
4. In the Sparklines group, click Line.
5. Select the cell range E9:G9 to fill the Data Range box in the Create Sparklines dialog box, and click OK.
6. Expand the width of column H.

   ✓ *The sparkline will expand to fill the column width.*

7. Drag the AutoFill Handle of cell H9 down to H14 to add a sparkline to the remaining cells.
8. Save the changes to the file, and leave it open to use in the next Try It.

Sparklines in place on the worksheet

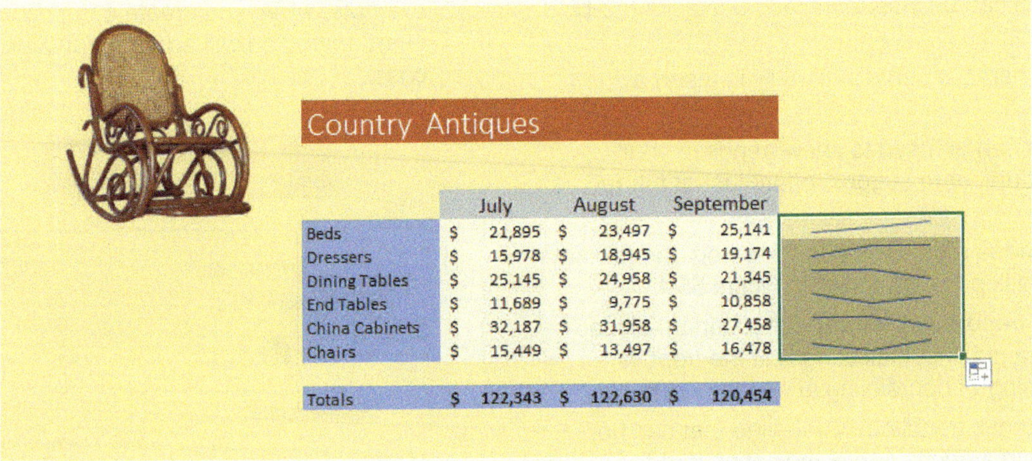

Country Antiques

	July		August		September
Beds	$	21,895	$	23,497	$ 25,141
Dressers	$	15,978	$	18,945	$ 19,174
Dining Tables	$	25,145	$	24,958	$ 21,345
End Tables	$	11,689	$	9,775	$ 10,858
China Cabinets	$	32,187	$	31,958	$ 27,458
Chairs	$	15,449	$	13,497	$ 16,478
Totals	$	122,343	$	122,630	$ 120,454

Formatting a Sparkline

- When a sparkline is inserted, the Sparkline Tools Design tab is automatically displayed on the ribbon.
  - Use the Sparkline Color button Sparkline Color to format the color of a sparkline's line.
  - Use the Marker Color button Marker Color to format the color of the data markers on a sparkline.
  - Use the Style gallery to choose one of the style formats for a sparkline.
- You can also determine which data points, such as the high point, low, first, last, or negative values, to highlight on a sparkline.

Try It! Formatting a Sparkline

1. In the E55TryA_xx file, select the cell range H9:H14, and click the Sparkline Tools Design tab, if necessary.
2. In the Show group, click High Point to add a data marker at the highest point of each sparkline.
3. Click the Sparkline Color drop-down arrow Sparkline Color, and in the Standard colors palette click Light Blue.
4. In the Style gallery, click the More button, and select Sparkline Style Accent 2, Lighter 40%.
5. Save the changes to the file, and leave it open to use in the next Try It.

Inserting a Trendline

- **Trendlines** can be inserted in any unstacked, 2-D, non-pie chart.
- Use the Chart Elements button + to insert a trendline.
- Trendlines can be used to show trends in your recorded data, or to suggest a forecast of future data.
- Excel provides six trendline options from the Format Trendline task pane, as shown in Figure 55-1.
  - Linear trendline: A trendline that can be plotted in a straight line, indicating that the trend is increasing or decreasing at a steady rate.
  - Logarithmic trendline: A trendline that can be plotted in a gentle curve, indicating that the trend increases sharply and then levels out over time.
  - Polynomial trendline: A trendline that curves following data that fluctuates in highs and lows over time.
  - Power trendline: A trendline that curves upward, indicating that the trend is increasingly moving up.
  - Exponential trendline: A trendline that is a gentle curve downward, indicating that the values rise or fall at constantly increasing rates.
  - Moving average trendline: A trendline that smoothes out fluctuations over time; it determines the average of a specified number of values at each point on the line.
- Excel uses chart animation to automatically update a chart when you change your data. For example, when you create a trendline, Excel's chart animation will add the trendline to your chart.

Figure 55-1

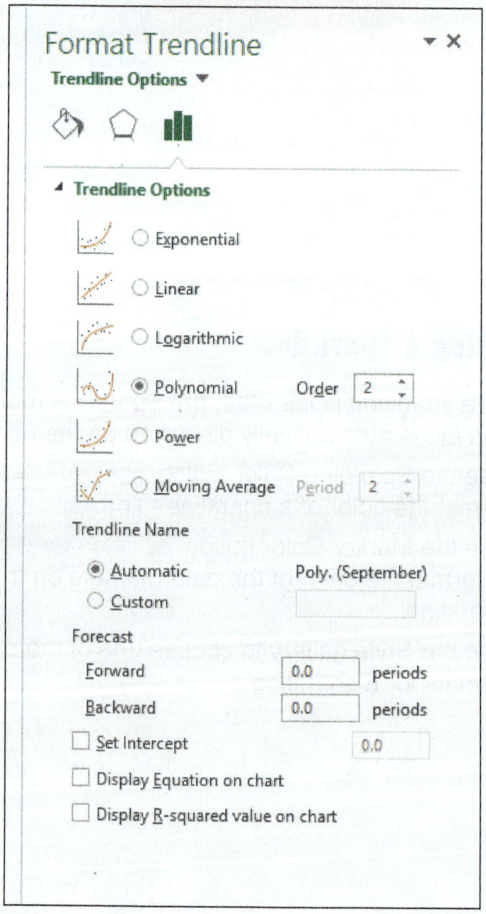

Excel 2016, Windows 10, Microsoft Corporation

Try It! Inserting a Trendline

1. In the E55TryA_xx file, select cells D8:G14.
2. Click the Insert tab > Insert Column or Bar Chart > Clustered Column Chart in the 2-D Column group.
3. Drag the chart below the worksheet data.
4. Click the Chart Elements button + > Trendline.
5. In the Add Trendline dialog box, click September > OK.
6. Click the trendline to select it, right-click, and click Format Trendline.
7. In the Format Trendline task pane, in the Trendline Options group, click Polynomial.
8. Close the Format Trendline task pane.
9. Save and close the file.
10. Leave Excel open.

Using a Trendline to Predict

- You can use trendlines to chart the trends of a set of data and to project into the future based on the slope of the curve.
- Trendlines can deal with any data over time. Income and expense reports are a good example of this type of data.

Try It! Projecting Income and Expenses with Trendlines

1. Start Excel, and open E55TryB from the data files for this lesson.
2. Save the file as E55TryB_xx in the location where your teacher instructs you to store the files for this lesson.
3. Select the data range C2:D38.
4. Click Insert > Insert Line or Area Chart.
5. Under 2-D Line, click Line. A line chart displays showing the trend.
6. Click the Chart Elements button +, hover over Trendline, click the Trendline arrow ▸, and click Linear Forecast.
7. In the Add Trendline dialog box, click Income > OK.
8. In the Chart Elements shortcut menu, hover over Trendline, click the Trendline arrow ▸, and click Linear Forecast.
9. In the Add Trendline dialog box, click Expense > OK.
10. Save and close the file, and exit Excel.

Income and expense trendlines

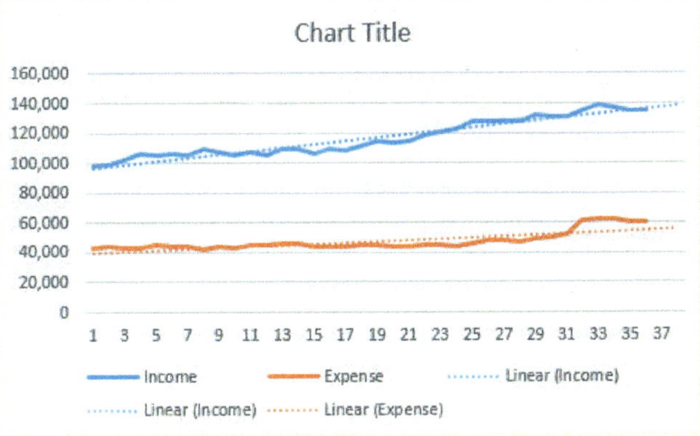

Excel 2016, Windows 10, Microsoft Corporation

Lesson 55—Practice

As the manager of PhotoTown, you are concerned that sales have fallen off lately. You decide to track each individual's gross sales for a week and try to identify a trend. In this project, you will insert a trendline. In addition, you think the employees should be selling more T-shirts than they are, so you decide to track their sales and talk to anyone you feel is underperforming.

DIRECTIONS

1. Start Excel, if necessary, and open **E55Practice** from the data files for this lesson.
2. Save the file as **E55Practice_xx** in the location where your teacher instructs you to store the files for this lesson.
3. Click the **Daily Sales** worksheet tab.
4. Create a scatter chart for employee sales.
   a. Select the cells **A4:G8**.
   b. Click **Insert** > **Insert Scatter (X, Y) or Bubble Chart** .
   c. In the Scatter group, click **Scatter**.
5. Move the new chart to its own tab.
   a. Click the chart to select it.
   b. On the Chart Tools Design tab, in the Location group, click **Move Chart**.
   c. In the New sheet box, type **Employee Sales Chart**, and click **OK**.
6. Click the **Chart Elements** button +, hover the pointer over **Trendline**, click the Trendline arrow > **Linear Forecast**.
7. In the Add Trendline dialog box, select the first employee, **Akira Ota**, and click **OK**.
8. Repeat steps 6 and 7 for each of the other three employees.
9. Highlight the data series that is trending upward.
   a. Click the **Chart Tools Format** tab, click the **Chart Elements** box Chart Area, **Series "Taneel Black" Trendline 1**.
   b. On the Chart Tools Format tab, click the **More** button to display the Shape Styles gallery.
   c. Click **Intense Line – Accent 6** from the gallery.
10. Add a chart title.
    a. On the chart, click the chart title to select it.
    b. Type **PhotoTown Daily Sales by Employee**, and press ENTER.
11. Add a header that has your name at the left, the date code in the center, and the page number code at the right.
12. **With your teacher's permission**, print the chart. Your chart should look like Figure 55-2 on the next page.
13. Save and close the file, and exit Excel.

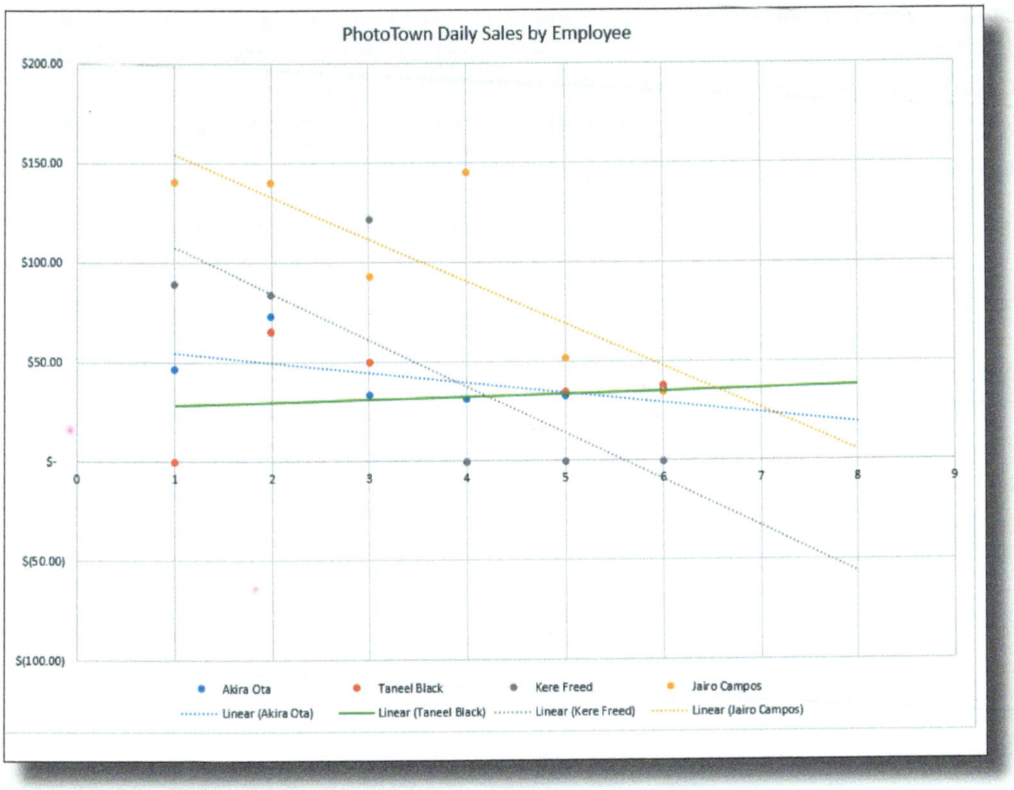

Figure 55-2

Excel 2016, Windows 10, Microsoft Corporation

Lesson 55—Apply

You are the manager of PhotoTown, and you think the employees should be selling more T-shirts than they are. Because you are concerned that sales have fallen off, you decide to track each individual's gross sales for a week to identify a trend. You need this data so that you can talk to anyone you feel is underperforming. In this project, you will insert a sparkline to track the employees' sales.

DIRECTIONS

1. Start Excel, if necessary, and open **E55Apply** from the data files for this lesson.
2. Save the file as **E55Apply_xx** in the location where your teacher instructs you to store the files for this lesson.
3. Click the **Sales by Product** worksheet tab.
4. Add sparklines to the T-shirt sales.
   a. Click cell **J5** to select it.
   b. Click **Insert** > **Line** in the Sparklines group.
   c. Select cells **B5:G5** to fill the Data Range box of the Create Sparklines dialog box, and click **OK**.
   d. Drag the AutoFill Handle down to cell **J8**.

5. With the cells still selected, on the Sparkline Tools Design tab, in the Group group, click **Ungroup**.
6. Format the sparklines based on performance.
   a. Click cell **J5** to select it.
   b. On the Sparkline Tools Design tab, click the **Sparkline Color** drop-down arrow Sparkline Color, and in the Standard Colors palette click **Red**.
   c. Click cell **J6** to select it.
   d. On the Sparkline Tools Design tab, click the **Sparkline Color** drop-down arrow Sparkline Color, and in the Standard Colors palette click **Green**.
   e. Select the cell range **J7:J8**.
   f. Click the **Sparkline Color** drop-down arrow Sparkline Color, and in the Standard Colors palette click **Yellow**.
7. Select cells **J5:J8**, and in the Show group click **High Point** to add a data marker at the point of each employee's highest sales.
8. **With your teacher's permission**, print the **Sales by Product** worksheet. Your worksheet should look like Figure 55-3.
9. Save and close the file, and exit Excel.

Figure 55-3

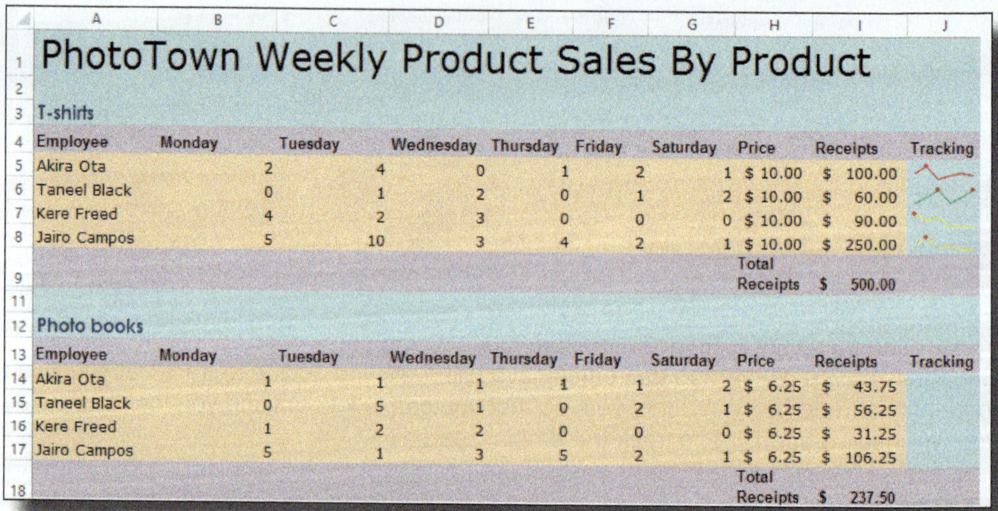

PhotoTown Weekly Product Sales By Product

T-shirts

Employee	Monday	Tuesday	Wednesday	Thursday	Friday	Saturday	Price	Receipts	Tracking
Akira Ota	2	4	0	1	2	1	$ 10.00	$ 100.00	
Taneel Black	0	1	2	0	1	2	$ 10.00	$ 60.00	
Kere Freed	4	2	3	0	0	0	$ 10.00	$ 90.00	
Jairo Campos	5	10	3	4	2	1	$ 10.00	$ 250.00	
							Total Receipts	$ 500.00	

Photo books

Employee	Monday	Tuesday	Wednesday	Thursday	Friday	Saturday	Price	Receipts	Tracking
Akira Ota	1	1	1	1	1	2	$ 6.25	$ 43.75	
Taneel Black	0	5	1	0	2	1	$ 6.25	$ 56.25	
Kere Freed	1	2	2	0	0	0	$ 6.25	$ 31.25	
Jairo Campos	5	1	3	5	2	1	$ 6.25	$ 106.25	
							Total Receipts	$ 237.50	

Lesson 56

Drawing and Positioning Shapes

➤ What You Will Learn

Drawing Shapes
Resizing, Grouping, Aligning, and Arranging Shapes

Software Skills After putting all that hard work into designing and entering data for a worksheet, of course you want it to look its best. You already know how to add formatting, color, and borders to a worksheet to enhance its appeal. To make your worksheet stand out from all the rest, you may need to do something "unexpected," such as adding your own art. You can insert predesigned shapes (such as stars or arrows) or combine them to create your own designs.

What You Can Do

Drawing Shapes

- You can use the Shapes button in the Illustrations group of the Insert tab to create many **shapes**.

  ✓ *Depending on the size of your screen, you may need to click the Illustrations button to access the Shapes button.*

- You can add lines, rectangles, arrows, equation shapes, stars and banners, and callouts as shown in Figure 56-1, on the next page, to highlight important information in your worksheet.
- You can add a text box or a callout—a shape in which you can type your own text.
- A text box or callout, like other shapes, can be placed anywhere on the worksheet.
- The Shapes button presents you with a palette of shapes sorted by category that makes it easy for you to select the shape you want to insert.
- To insert a shape, select the shape, and drag in a cell to create it—no actual drawing skills are needed.
- After inserting a shape, you can format it as needed.

WORDS TO KNOW

Adjustment handle
A yellow diamond-shaped handle that appears with some objects. You can drag this handle to manipulate the shape of the object, such as the width of a wide arrow, or the tip of a callout pointer.

Group
Objects can be grouped together so they can act as a single object. Grouping makes it easier to move or resize a drawing that consists of several objects.

Order
The position of an object with respect to other objects that are layered or in a stack.

Shape
A predesigned object (such as a banner or star) that can be drawn with a single dragging motion.

Sizing handles
Small white circles that appear around the perimeter of the active drawing object. You can resize an object by dragging one of these handles.

Stack
A group of drawing objects layered on top of one another, possibly partially overlapping. Use the Order command to change the position of a selected object within the stack.

- When you insert a shape, the Drawing Tools Format tab displays.
- You can insert more shapes from the Shapes gallery in the Insert Shapes group.

Figure 56-1

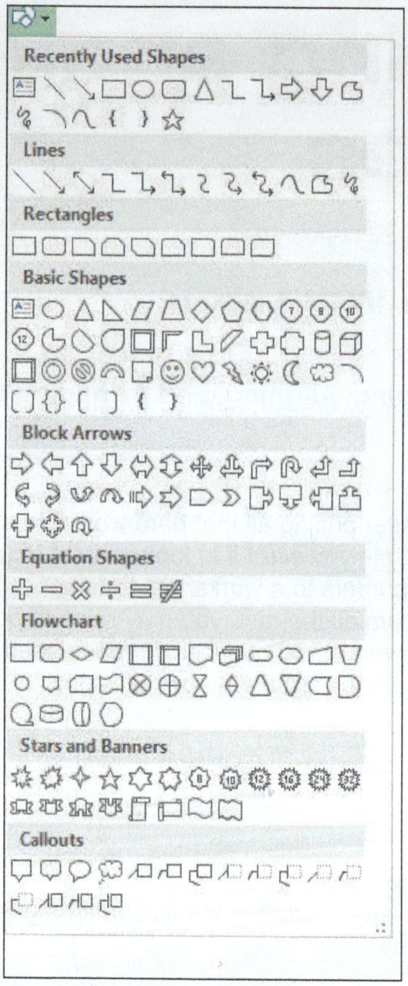

Excel 2016, Windows 10, Microsoft Corporation

Try It! Drawing Shapes

1. Start Excel, and open **E56Try** from the data files for this lesson.
2. Save the file as **E56Try_xx** in the location where your teacher instructs you to store the files for this lesson.
3. Select the P&L sheet, if necessary.
4. Click Insert > Shapes.
5. In the Rectangles group, click Rounded Rectangle (second item from the left).
6. Click and hold at the upper-left corner of cell F6, drag downward to the lower-right corner of cell J9, and release the pointer.

✓ *All shapes will appear using a default style and color.*

7. On the Drawing Tools Format tab, in the Insert Shapes group, click the More button.
8. In the Rectangles group, click Rectangle.
9. Click and hold at the upper-left corner of cell G14, drag downward to the lower-right corner of cell I16, and release the pointer.
10. Save the changes to the file, and leave it open to use in the next Try It.

Lesson 57

Formatting Shapes

➤ What You Will Learn

Formatting Shapes
Adding Shape Effects

Software Skills When shapes such as rectangles, block arrows, and banners are added to a worksheet, they originally appear in the default style—a shape with a blue outline filled with the Accent 1 color. You can change both the color and the outline style of any shape. You can also create custom colors. You can also add special effects such as shadows and soft edges.

WORDS TO KNOW

Effects
Special complex-looking formats that can be applied with a single click, such as shadows, reflection, glows, and beveled edges.

What You Can Do

Formatting Shapes

- When a shape is selected, the Drawing Tools Format tab automatically appears on the ribbon in anticipation of your need to edit it.
- Since all new shapes appear in the default style, you might want to change:
  - Shape Styles: A set of formats that include the outline color and style, edge effects, and fill.
  - Shape Fill: The color, picture, gradient, or texture that fills a shape.

    ✓ *A line shape cannot be filled. A line's color is determined by the Shape Outline settings.*

  - Shape Outline: The color, weight, and style of the border that outlines a shape.

    ✓ *You can change the color, weight, and style of a line. You can also add arrows at one or both ends.*

  - Shape Effects: Complex formats applied with a single click.
- When changing any color on a shape, either the fill or the outline, you can use the Colors dialog box to create a custom color, and even to add transparency if desired.

Try It! Formatting Shapes

1. Start Excel, and open **E57Try** from the data files for this lesson.
2. Save the file as **E57Try_xx** in the location where your teacher instructs you to store the files for this lesson.
3. Click the P&L worksheet tab > Page Layout > Selection Pane.
4. In the Selection task pane, click Rectangle 3 and then click the Drawing Tools Format tab on the ribbon.
5. In the Shape Styles group, click the Shape Fill drop-down arrow Shape Fill, and in the Theme Colors palette click Orange, Accent 2, Lighter 60%.
6. Click the Shape Outline drop-down arrow Shape Outline, and in the Standard Colors palette click Dark Red.
7. In the Selection task pane, click Right Arrow 4.
8. Click the Shape Fill drop-down arrow Shape Fill > Gradient > More Gradients.
9. In the Fill group, click Gradient fill.
10. In the Format Shape task pane, click Preset gradients > Bottom Spotlight, Accent 4.
11. In the Type list, click Linear.
12. In the Direction list, click Linear Diagonal - Top Left to Bottom Right (the first option).
13. In the Line section, click Color > Gold, Accent 4, Darker 25%.
14. In the Selection task pane, click Rounded Rectangle 2.
15. On the Drawing Tools Format tab, click the Shape Styles More button > Moderate Effect - Orange Accent 2.
16. Close the Selection and Format Shape task panes.
17. Save the changes to the file, and leave it open to use in the next Try It.

The Selection and Format Shape task panes

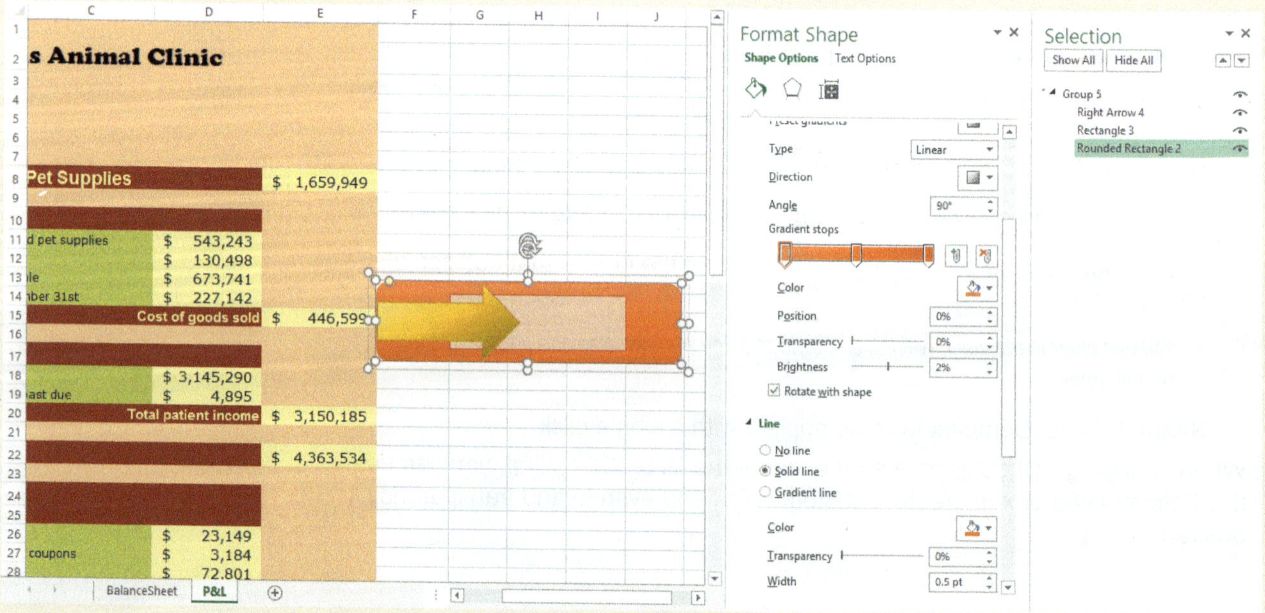

Excel 2016, Windows 10, Microsoft Corporation

Adding Shape Effects

- Shape **effects** that you can apply to a selected shape include:
  - Shadows
  - Reflections
  - Glows
  - Soft edges
  - Beveled edges
  - 3-D rotations
- Each shape effect style comes with options that allow you to customize the effect to get the look you want.
- The Preset category on the Shape Effects drop-down menu displays a set of common effects, with the options already pre-selected for you.
- Choose one of the Preset effects to change the look of a selected shape.

Try It! Adding Shape Effects

1. In the **E57Try_xx** file, on the P&L tab, click Page Layout > Selection Pane.
2. In the Selection task pane, click Rectangle 3.
3. On the Drawing Tools Format tab, in the Shape Styles group, click Shape Effects > Glow > Gold, 8 pt glow, Accent color 4.
4. In the Selection task pane, click Rounded Rectangle 2.
5. On the Drawing Tools Format tab, in the Shape Styles group, click Shape Effects > Reflection > Tight Reflection, 4 pt offset.
6. Close the Selection task pane.
7. Save and close the file, and exit Excel.

Lesson 57—Practice

As the accountant for Sydney Crenshaw Realty, you've already created a spreadsheet to track year-to-date sales and commissions with some basic shapes. Now you'd like to format the shapes with some color and dimension.

DIRECTIONS

1. Start Excel, if necessary, and open **E57Practice** from the data files for this lesson.
2. Save the file as **E57Practice_xx** in the location where your teacher instructs you to store the files for this lesson.
3. Add a header that has your name at the left, the date code in the center, and the page number code at the right
4. Click **Page Layout** > **Selection Pane**.
5. In the Selection task pane, click **Isosceles Triangle 2**.
6. Click **Drawing Tools Format**, and click the Shape Styles **More** button to open the gallery.
7. Click **Moderate Effect - Orange, Accent 2**.
8. In the Selection task pane, click **Rectangle 1**.
9. On the Drawing Tools Format tab, click the Shape Styles **More** button to open the gallery.
10. Click **Moderate Effect - Brown, Accent 3**.
11. On the Drawing Tools Format tab, in the Shape Styles group, click **Shape Effects** > **Reflection**.
12. In the Reflection Variations group, click **Tight Reflection, touching**.
13. Close the Selection task pane.
14. **With your teacher's permission**, print the worksheet. Your worksheet should look like Figure 57-1.
15. Save and close the file, and exit Excel.

Figure 57-1

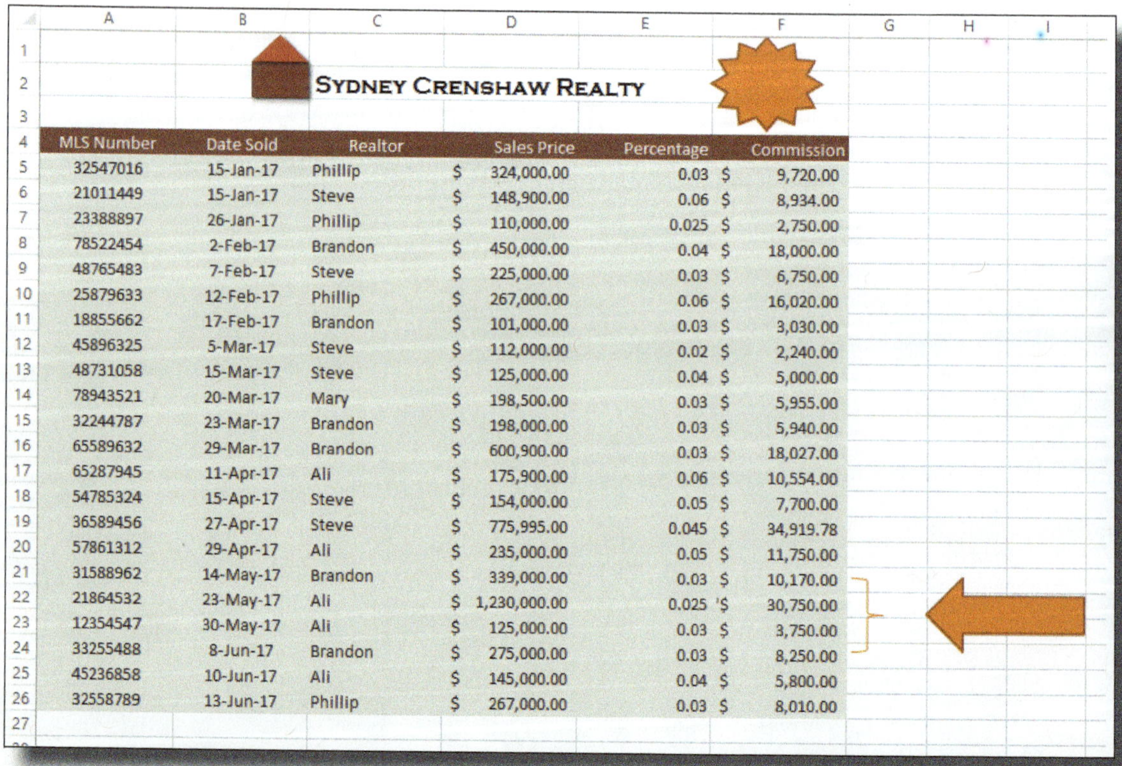

SYDNEY CRENSHAW REALTY

MLS Number	Date Sold	Realtor	Sales Price	Percentage	Commission
32547016	15-Jan-17	Phillip	$ 324,000.00	0.03	$ 9,720.00
21011449	15-Jan-17	Steve	$ 148,900.00	0.06	$ 8,934.00
23388897	26-Jan-17	Phillip	$ 110,000.00	0.025	$ 2,750.00
78522454	2-Feb-17	Brandon	$ 450,000.00	0.04	$ 18,000.00
48765483	7-Feb-17	Steve	$ 225,000.00	0.03	$ 6,750.00
25879633	12-Feb-17	Phillip	$ 267,000.00	0.06	$ 16,020.00
18855662	17-Feb-17	Brandon	$ 101,000.00	0.03	$ 3,030.00
45896325	5-Mar-17	Steve	$ 112,000.00	0.02	$ 2,240.00
48731058	15-Mar-17	Steve	$ 125,000.00	0.04	$ 5,000.00
78943521	20-Mar-17	Mary	$ 198,500.00	0.03	$ 5,955.00
32244787	23-Mar-17	Brandon	$ 198,000.00	0.03	$ 5,940.00
65589632	29-Mar-17	Brandon	$ 600,900.00	0.03	$ 18,027.00
65287945	11-Apr-17	Ali	$ 175,900.00	0.06	$ 10,554.00
54785324	15-Apr-17	Steve	$ 154,000.00	0.05	$ 7,700.00
36589456	27-Apr-17	Steve	$ 775,995.00	0.045	$ 34,919.78
57861312	29-Apr-17	Ali	$ 235,000.00	0.05	$ 11,750.00
31588962	14-May-17	Brandon	$ 339,000.00	0.03	$ 10,170.00
21864532	23-May-17	Ali	$ 1,230,000.00	0.025	$ 30,750.00
12354547	30-May-17	Ali	$ 125,000.00	0.03	$ 3,750.00
33255488	8-Jun-17	Brandon	$ 275,000.00	0.03	$ 8,250.00
45236858	10-Jun-17	Ali	$ 145,000.00	0.04	$ 5,800.00
32558789	13-Jun-17	Phillip	$ 267,000.00	0.03	$ 8,010.00

Excel 2016, Windows 10, Microsoft Corporation

Lesson 57—Apply

You are working with a spreadsheet of year-to-date sales and commissions for Sydney Crenshaw Realty. You've been enhacing the spreadsheet with basic shapes and formatting. Now you want to format the shapes with color and effects to draw attention to certain data.

DIRECTIONS

1. Start Excel, if necessary, and open **E57Apply** from the data files for this lesson.
2. Save the file as **E57Apply_xx** in the location where your teacher instructs you to store the files for this lesson.
3. Add a header that has your name at the left, the date code in the center, and the page number code at the right
4. Click **Page Layout** > **Selection Pane**.
5. In the Selection task pane, click **Group 6**.
6. On the Drawing Tools Format tab, click the **Shape Styles More** button to open the gallery, and click **Intense Effect - Orange, Accent 2**.
7. In the Selection pane, select **Right Brace 4**.
8. On the Drawing Tools Format tab, click the **Shape Styles More** button to open the gallery, and click **Subtle Line - Accent 3**.
9. In the Selection task pane, click **12-Point Star 7**.
10. On the Drawing Tools Format tab, click the **Shape Styles More** button to open the gallery, and click **Moderate Effect - Tan, Accent 5**.
11. With the shape still selected, click **Shape Effects** > **Shadow** > **Offset Diagonal Top Left** (the third item in the third row of the Outer group).
12. Close the Selection task pane.
13. **With your teacher's permission**, print the worksheet. Your worksheet should look like Figure 57-2.
14. Save and close the file, and exit Excel.

Figure 57-2

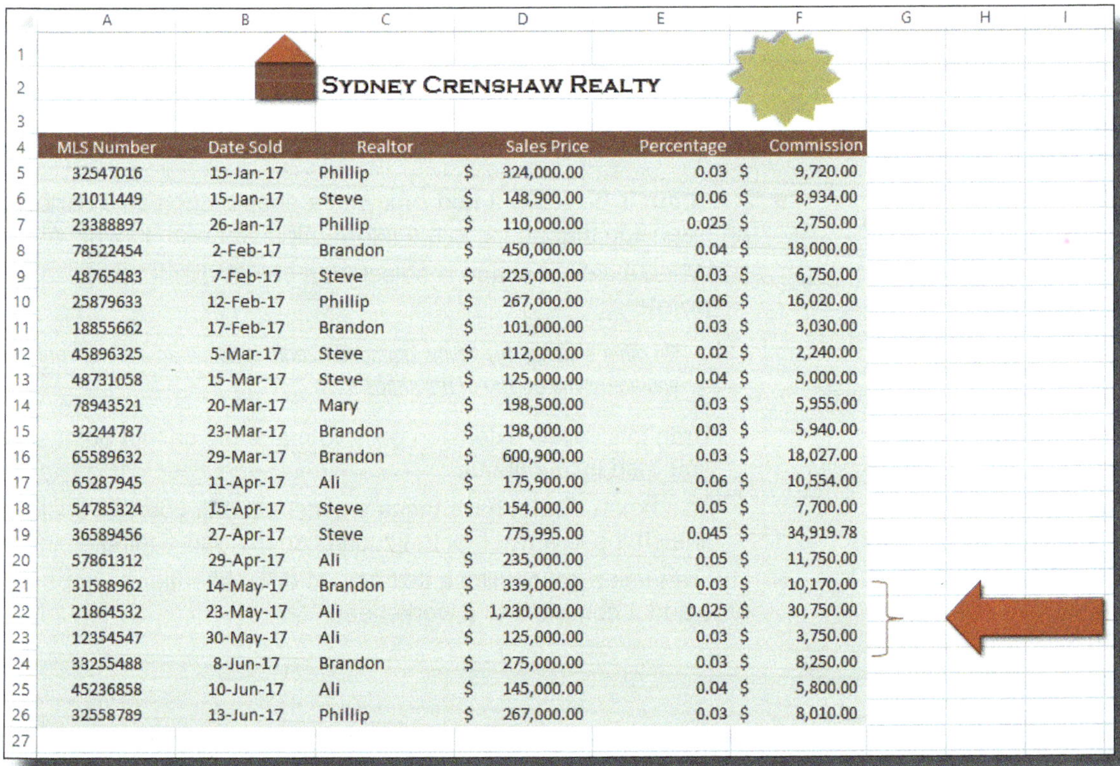

SYDNEY CRENSHAW REALTY

MLS Number	Date Sold	Realtor	Sales Price	Percentage	Commission
32547016	15-Jan-17	Phillip	$ 324,000.00	0.03	$ 9,720.00
21011449	15-Jan-17	Steve	$ 148,900.00	0.06	$ 8,934.00
23388897	26-Jan-17	Phillip	$ 110,000.00	0.025	$ 2,750.00
78522454	2-Feb-17	Brandon	$ 450,000.00	0.04	$ 18,000.00
48765483	7-Feb-17	Steve	$ 225,000.00	0.03	$ 6,750.00
25879633	12-Feb-17	Phillip	$ 267,000.00	0.06	$ 16,020.00
18855662	17-Feb-17	Brandon	$ 101,000.00	0.03	$ 3,030.00
45896325	5-Mar-17	Steve	$ 112,000.00	0.02	$ 2,240.00
48731058	15-Mar-17	Steve	$ 125,000.00	0.04	$ 5,000.00
78943521	20-Mar-17	Mary	$ 198,500.00	0.03	$ 5,955.00
32244787	23-Mar-17	Brandon	$ 198,000.00	0.03	$ 5,940.00
65589632	29-Mar-17	Brandon	$ 600,900.00	0.03	$ 18,027.00
65287945	11-Apr-17	Ali	$ 175,900.00	0.06	$ 10,554.00
54785324	15-Apr-17	Steve	$ 154,000.00	0.05	$ 7,700.00
36589456	27-Apr-17	Steve	$ 775,995.00	0.045	$ 34,919.78
57861312	29-Apr-17	Ali	$ 235,000.00	0.05	$ 11,750.00
31588962	14-May-17	Brandon	$ 339,000.00	0.03	$ 10,170.00
21864532	23-May-17	Ali	$ 1,230,000.00	0.025	$ 30,750.00
12354547	30-May-17	Ali	$ 125,000.00	0.03	$ 3,750.00
33255488	8-Jun-17	Brandon	$ 275,000.00	0.03	$ 8,250.00
45236858	10-Jun-17	Ali	$ 145,000.00	0.04	$ 5,800.00
32558789	13-Jun-17	Phillip	$ 267,000.00	0.03	$ 8,010.00

Excel 2016, Windows 10, Microsoft Corporation

Lesson 58

Enhancing Shapes with Text and Effects

➤ What You Will Learn

Adding Text to a Text Box, Callout, or Other Shape
Adding 3-D Effects
Rotating Shapes
Inserting a Screen Capture

WORDS TO KNOW

Callout
Text that's placed in a special AutoShape balloon. A callout, like a text box, "floats" over the cells in a worksheet—so you can position a callout wherever you like.

Extension point
The yellow diamond handle that indicates the position where a callout can be resized or extended.

Rotation handle
A white rotation symbol that appears just over the top of most objects when they are selected. Use this handle to rotate the object manually.

Screenshot
A screenshot is a picture of all or part of an open window, such as another application or a Web page.

Text box
A small rectangle that "floats" over the cells in a worksheet, into which you can add text. A text box can be placed anywhere you want.

Software Skills If you need to place text in some spot within the worksheet that doesn't correspond to a specific cell, you can "float" the text over the cells by creating a text box or by adding a callout. A text box or callout can be placed anywhere in the worksheet, regardless of the cell gridlines. You can add text to any shape. Add 3-D effects or rotation to shapes to really make them stand out. You can use the screen capture feature to take a picture of any open application or Web page.

What You Can Do

Adding Text to a Text Box, Callout, or Other Shape

- A **callout** is basically a **text box** with a shape, such as a cartoon balloon, with an extension that points to the information you wish to write about.
  - When a callout shape is selected, a yellow diamond indicates the **extension point**.

    ✓ *On other shapes, this yellow diamond handle is called an adjustment handle, because it lets you adjust the outline of the shape itself.*
  - Drag this yellow extension point to make the callout point precisely to the data you wish to talk about.
  - Text boxes do not have these extensions, but you can easily add an arrow or line shape to a text box to accomplish the same thing.
- You can use a callout like a text box, to draw attention to important information, or to add a comment to a worksheet.

- You can add text to any shape.
  - ✓ *If the shape already contains text, the text you type will be added to the end of the existing text. You can replace text by first selecting it, and then typing new text.*
- The border of a selected shape changes to indicate whether you're editing the object itself (solid border) or the text in the object (dashed border).
  - To move, resize, copy, or delete the object, the border must be solid.
  - To edit or add text in a text box or shape, the border must be dashed.

Try It! Adding Text to a Text Box, Callout, or Other Shape

1. Start Excel, and open **E58TryA** from the data files for this lesson.
2. Save the file as **E58TryA_xx** in the location where your teacher instructs you to store the files for this lesson.
3. Click the P&L worksheet tab > Page Layout > Selection Pane.
4. In the Selection task pane, click Rectangle 3, and type **This cost is down because of better inventory management.**
5. Select the text in the shape, and click Home.
6. Click Font Color, and in the Standard Colors palette click Dark Red.
7. With the text still selected, click te Decrease Font four times to change the font size to 8 points.
8. In the Alignment group, click Center.
9. With the rectangle still selected, right-click the rectangle, and in the shortcut menu click Format Text Effects.
10. In the Format Shape task pane, under Text Options, click Textbox. In the Left Margin box type **.5**, and in the Top margin box type **.1**.
11. Create a callout:
    a. Click Insert > Shapes and choose Rectangular Callout from the Callouts group.
    b. Draw a callout in the area of F34:I36.
    c. Type **Next year's purchases should be much lower than this.**
    d. Select the text you typed in step 11c, click Home, and click Decrease Font three times to change the font size to 9.
    e. In the Alignment group, click Center.
    f. Click the border of the callout shape.
       ✓ *Clicking the border allows you to change the format of the whole text box, not just the text.*
    g. Click Drawing Tools Format, click the Shape Styles More button, and click Intense Effect - Orange, Accent 2.
12. Click and hold the yellow extension point, and drag it until the callout tip points to cell D38.
13. Close the Selection and Format Shapes task panes.
14. Save the changes to the file, and leave it open to use in the next Try It.

Formatting the text options of a shape

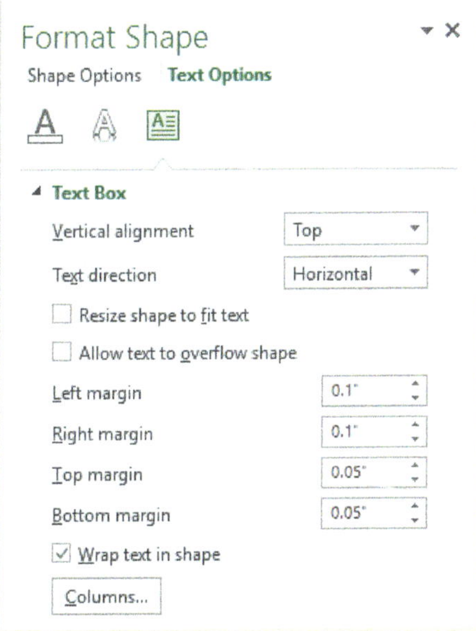

Excel 2016, Windows 10, Microsoft Corporation

Adding 3-D Effects

- When you add 3-D effects to an object, that object appears to have depth.
- You can add 3-D effects to any object, even grouped objects.
- To select a 3-D rotation style, use the Shape Effects button in the Shape Styles group on the Drawing Tools Format tab.
  - If you choose 3-D Rotation Options, the Format Shape task pane displays where you can customize the settings.
  - You can set the exact degree of rotation and other options such as whether you want the text in the shape (if any) to be rotated with the shape.
  - Objects are rotated along three axes—X (horizontal), Y (vertical), and Z (depth dimension).
- In the Format Shape task pane, shown in Figure 58-1, you can adjust the format of a 3-D shape, by selecting the depth, surface texture, and other options.
  - You can adjust the style of the edge of your 3-D shape. You can also change the color and contour of this third dimension.
  - Use the Material feature to select a surface texture—such as the apparent material used.
  - You can change how the surface is lit (both the color of the light and the angle at which it shines on the 3-D object).

Figure 58-1

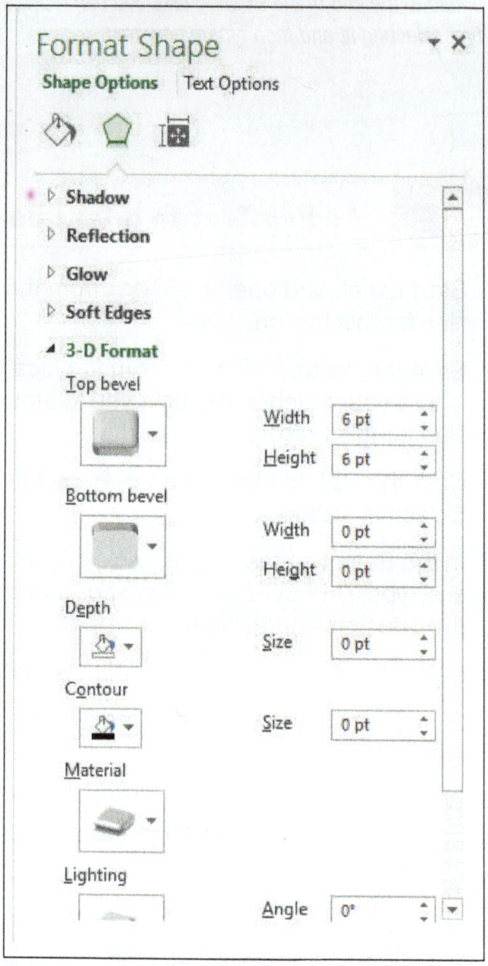

Excel 2016, Windows 10, Microsoft Corporation

Try It! Adding 3-D Effects

1. In the **E58TryA_xx** file, click the P&L tab, if necessary.
2. Click the callout shape to select it.
3. On the Drawing Tools Format, click Shape Effects, click Bevel, and in the Bevel group click Circle.
4. On the Drawing Tools Format, click Shape Effects, click 3-D Rotation, and in the Oblique group click Oblique Top Right.
5. Save the changes to the file, and leave it open to use in the next Try It.

Rotating Shapes

- A shape can be rotated around an invisible pin holding its center in place on the worksheet.
  - Use the Rotate button on the Drawing Tools Format tab to rotate a shape to the left or the right by 90 degrees.
  - You can rotate a shape by a custom amount.
  - Shapes can be manually rotated, using the **rotation handle**.
- A shape can also be flipped vertically (turning it completely upside down), or flipped horizontally (turning it backward to face the opposite direction).

Try It! Rotating Shapes

1. In the E58TryA_xx file, click the P&L tab, if necessary.
2. Click the callout shape to select it, if necessary.
3. Click and hold the rotation handle, and drag the pointer to the right to change the rotation amount of the shape so that the angle matches the figure.
4. Click and hold the yellow extension point, and drag it until the callout tip points to cell D38.
5. Save the changes to the file, and leave it open to use in the next Try It.

Manually rotating a shape

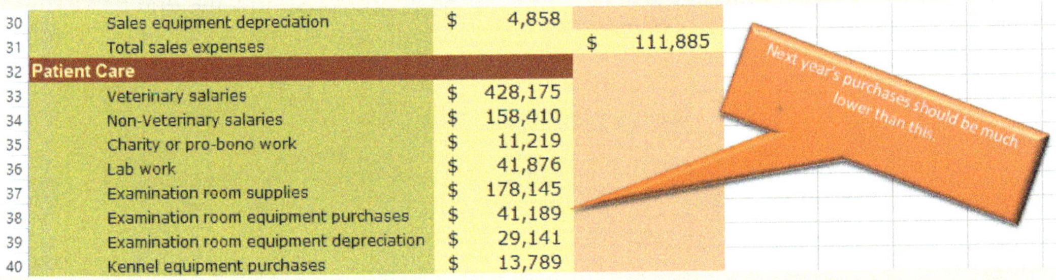

Excel 2016, Windows 10, Microsoft Corporation

Inserting a Screen Capture

- You can add a picture of any open application or Web page to your Excel worksheet.
- **Screenshots** are helpful for capturing information that will change or expire.
- Only open windows that have not been minimized to the taskbar can be captured with this tool.
- Available screenshots appear as thumbnails on the Available Windows gallery. Selecting one of the thumbnails will insert the picture of that window in your file.
- Choose Screen Clipping to insert a part of a window, such as a logo, a set of instructions, or a dialog box.
- When you click Screen Clipping, the entire screen becomes temporarily whited out. Use the mouse to outline the part of the screen that you want to capture.

Try It! Inserting a Screen Capture

1. In the **E58TryA_xx** file, select the P&L tab, if necessary.
2. Open **E58TryB.jpg** from the data files for this lesson.

   ✓ *Use File Explorer to open the folder containing your data files. Double-click on the* **E58TryB.jpg** *file to open it in your default image viewer.*
3. Minimize all open windows except Excel and your image viewer, and reposition the Excel window and the image viewer so that you can see the P&L worksheet and the image.
4. In Excel, click Insert, and in the Illustrations group click Screenshot to view your Available Windows gallery.
5. Click Screen Clipping, click and hold at the upper left corner of the image, and drag the pointer over the picture in your image viewer to select only the picture.

   ✓ *Screen Clipping whites out your screen. Dragging the mouse over the desired area of the screen restores the color to that area and highlights the portion of your screen that will be inserted into Excel.*
6. Once the screen clipping has been added to your worksheet, drag the picture to the open area of your spreadsheet between the two text boxes. Adjust the picture size as necessary to fit the area.

   ✓ *You may need to scroll down to view the screen clipping.*
7. With the screen clipping still selected, click Picture Tools Format > Picture Border drop-down arrow.
8. Click Automatic to add a border around your screenshot.
9. Save and close the file, and exit Excel. Close your image viewer application if needed.

Using screen clipping

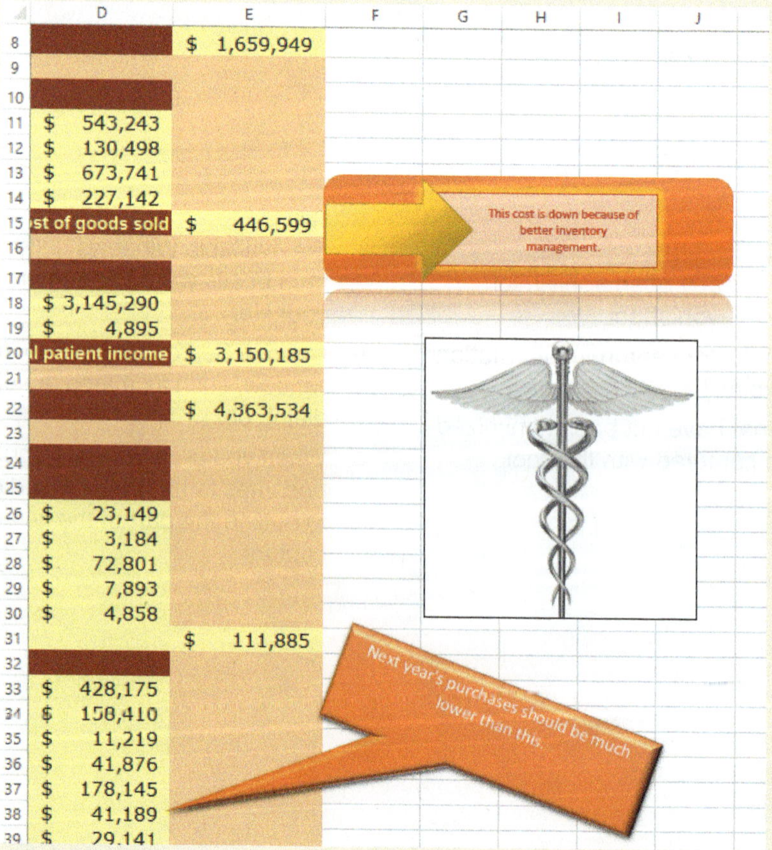

Excel 2016, Windows 10, Microsoft Corporation

Lesson 58—Practice

The year-to-date sales and commission report that you've been working on for Sydney Crenshaw Realty is coming along nicely, but you think that adding some additional text or callouts might make the information you are tracking easier to understand. In this project, you will add text to shapes, format the shapes, and insert a callout.

DIRECTIONS

1. Start Excel, if necessary, and open **E58Practice** from the data files for this lesson.
2. Save the file as **E58Practice_xx** in the location where your teacher instructs you to store the files for this lesson.
3. Add a header that has your name at the left, the date code in the center, and the page number code at the right.
4. Add text to the tan star shape.
   a. Right-click the star > **Edit Text**.
   b. Type **Rated #1**.
   c. Select the text **Rated #1**.
   d. On the Home tab click **Middle Align** > **Center**.
5. Change the text margins in the tan star shape.
   a. Right-click the star > **Format Shape**.
   b. In the Format Shape task pane, click **Text Options** > **Textbox**.
   c. In the Left margin box, type **0**.
   d. In the Right margin box, type **0**.
   e. In the Top margin box, type **0**.
   f. In the Bottom margin box, type **0**.
   g. Close the Format Shape task pane.
6. Add text to the arrow shape.
   a. Click the arrow shape, and click it again to select it in the group.
   b. Right-click the arrow > **Edit Text**.
   c. Type **Best Month**.
7. Insert a callout to bring attention to the highest commission figure.
   a. Click **Insert** > **Shapes** > **Rectangular Callout**.
   b. Draw a callout in the area of **H16:I18**.
8. **With your teacher's permission**, print the worksheet.
9. Save and close the file, and exit Excel.

Lesson 58—Apply

You have been working on the year-to-date sales and commission report for Sydney Crenshaw Realty. You want to format the shapes within the report with effects and a picture to call attention to certain data. In this project, you will use effects to format shapes and insert a screen capture to enhance the report.

DIRECTIONS

1. Start Excel, if necessary, and open **E58Apply** from the data files for this lesson.
2. Save the file as **E58Apply_xx** in the location where your teacher instructs you to store the files for this lesson.
3. Add a header that has your name at the left, the date code in the center, and the page number code at the right.
4. Add the **Preset 4** effect to the star shape.
5. Add the following text to the callout shape: **Largest commission ever paid by our firm.** Set the font size to **11**, if it is not already so.

6. Format the callout shape as follows:
   a. Shape height **0.93"**.
   b. Shape width **1.31"**.
   c. Apply the **Shape Fill - Green, Accent 6** style to the shape.
   d. Apply the **Orange, Accent 2** color to the shape outline.
7. Apply the **Circle** bevel shape effect.
8. Rotate the callout so that it looks similar to Figure 58-2.
9. Position the callout's yellow extension point on the line between F19 and G19 to indicate the larger commission figure.
10. Click **Page Layout**, and in the Sheet Options group, under Gridlines, click to unselect the **View** check box to view the worksheet without gridlines.
11. **With your teacher's permission**, print the worksheet.
12. Save and close the file, and exit Excel.

Figure 58-2

MLS Number	Date Sold	Realtor	Sales Price	Percentage	Commission
32547016	15-Jan-17	Phillip	$ 324,000.00	0.03	$ 9,720.00
21011449	15-Jan-17	Steve	$ 148,900.00	0.06	$ 8,934.00
23388897	26-Jan-17	Phillip	$ 110,000.00	0.025	$ 2,750.00
78522454	2-Feb-17	Brandon	$ 450,000.00	0.04	$ 18,000.00
48765483	7-Feb-17	Steve	$ 225,000.00	0.03	$ 6,750.00
25879633	12-Feb-17	Phillip	$ 267,000.00	0.06	$ 16,020.00
18855662	17-Feb-17	Brandon	$ 101,000.00	0.03	$ 3,030.00
45896325	5-Mar-17	Steve	$ 112,000.00	0.02	$ 2,240.00
48731058	15-Mar-17	Steve	$ 125,000.00	0.04	$ 5,000.00
78943521	20-Mar-17	Mary	$ 198,500.00	0.03	$ 5,955.00
32244787	23-Mar-17	Brandon	$ 198,000.00	0.03	$ 5,940.00
65589632	29-Mar-17	Brandon	$ 600,900.00	0.03	$ 18,027.00
65287945	11-Apr-17	Ali	$ 175,900.00	0.06	$ 10,554.00
54785324	15-Apr-17	Steve	$ 154,000.00	0.05	$ 7,700.00
36589456	27-Apr-17	Steve	$ 775,995.00	0.045	$ 34,919.78
57861312	29-Apr-17	Ali	$ 235,000.00	0.05	$ 11,750.00
31588962	14-May-17	Brandon	$ 339,000.00	0.03	$ 10,170.00
21864532	23-May-17	Ali	$ 1,230,000.00	0.025	$ 30,750.00
12354547	30-May-17	Ali	$ 125,000.00	0.03	$ 3,750.00
33255488	8-Jun-17	Brandon	$ 275,000.00	0.03	$ 8,250.00
45236858	10-Jun-17	Ali	$ 145,000.00	0.04	$ 5,800.00
32558789	13-Jun-17	Phillip	$ 267,000.00	0.03	$ 8,010.00

Excel 2016, Windows 10, Microsoft Corporation

Lesson 59

Working with Templates

➤ What You Will Learn

Adding a Watermark or Other Graphics
Formatting the Worksheet Background
Creating a Workbook Template
Creating a Chart Template

Software Skills To make a worksheet look more professional, you might want to customize the standard templates Excel provides by choosing company-style fonts and colors, adding a watermark, or applying a custom worksheet background.

Excel comes with built-in templates you can use to apply consistent formatting to your worksheets. You can create a custom workbook template to personalize your workbooks and ensure a consistent and professional look. An easy way to create a custom workbook template is to modify an existing template. You can also create a chart template to apply formatting to a new or existing chart.

WORDS TO KNOW

Template
A workbook designed for a specific purpose, complete with formatting, formulas, text, and row and column labels that you can customize.

Watermark
A faint image embedded in paper that identifies its maker. This faint image appears behind text when it's printed.

What You Can Do

Adding a Watermark or Other Graphics

- You can re-create the look of a **watermark** by placing the graphic behind your Excel data.
  - You can add the watermark graphic to either the header or footer of every page.
  - This graphic begins within either the header or footer area, and, depending on its size, extends into the data area to act as a watermark.
  - After inserting the graphic, you can adjust the size so that it fills the page.
  - You can also adjust the inserted graphic's brightness and contrast in order to make the worksheet data, which appears on top of the watermark, easier to read.
- Watermarks appear only on the worksheet on which they were added, and not every worksheet within a workbook.

Try It! Adding a Watermark or Other Graphics

1. Start Excel, and open **E59TryA** from the data files for this lesson.
2. Save the file as **E59TryA_xx** in the location where your teacher instructs you to store the files for this lesson.
3. Click the July 22 tab, if necessary.
4. Click Insert > Header & Footer.
5. Click in the middle section of the header, and in the Header & Footer Tools Design tab, in the Header & Footer Elements group, click Picture.

   ✓ *A watermark picture can be added in any of the three header sections depending on your desire to add other header elements to your page.*

6. In the Insert Pictures window, in the From a file group, click Browse.
7. Select **E59TryB.jpg** from the data files for this lesson, and click Insert.

   ✓ *In Page Layout view, an inserted picture appears as a picture code in the header or footer.*

8. On the Header & Footer Tools Design tab, in the Header & Footer Elements group, click Format Picture.
9. In the Format Picture dialog box, on the Size tab, in the Scale group, in the Height box, type **50**.
10. Click the Picture tab, and in the Image control group, in the Brightness box, type **60**.
11. On the Picture tab, in the Image control group, in the Contrast box, type **20**, and click OK.
12. Click outside of the header to view the inserted picture.
13. Save the changes to the file, and leave it open to use in the next Try It.

The Header & Footer Tools Design tab

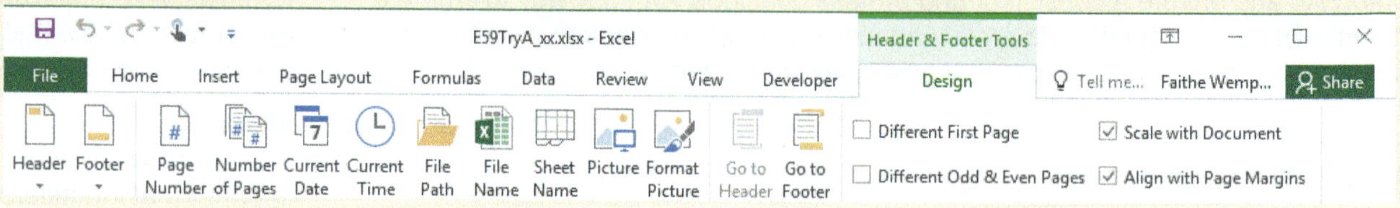

Excel 2016, Windows 10, Microsoft Corporation

Formatting the Worksheet Background

- You can add a graphic to the background of the worksheet, behind the data.
- Unlike a watermark, a background image is used for on-screen display purposes only, and does not print.
  - You might want to add a worksheet background graphic to enhance a worksheet you know will only be used in onscreen presentations.
  - Because you won't be able to adjust the brightness or contrast of your image after it's inserted, for the best effect, be sure to use a graphic that's very light in color, so that your data can still be read.

    ✓ *After inserting a graphic for use as a worksheet background, if you have trouble reading your data, you can apply a fill color to just the data cells so that the data can be more easily read.*

- The background isn't included when you create a Web page from the worksheet, unless you create the Web page from the whole workbook.
- The Show group on the View tab includes a number of options to alter the version of the worksheet you see.
  - Headings: Removes the row and column headings.
  - Gridlines: Removes the cell gridlines.
  - Ruler: Removes the horizontal and vertical rulers.
  - Formula Bar: Removes the formula bar that appears under the ribbon.

    ✓ *The options on this tab affect only the onscreen view of the worksheet and do not affect how the file prints.*

Try It! Formatting the Worksheet Background

1. In the E59TryA_xx file, click the July 23 tab to select it.
2. Click Page Layout, and in the Page Setup group click Background.
3. In the Insert Pictures window, in the From a file group, click Browse.
4. Select E59TryB.jpg from the data files for this lesson, and click Insert.

   ✓ *The background image cannot be sized or recolored. A small image will be tiled to fill the background.*

5. Select the cell range A5:C16, and click Home.
6. Click Fill Color, and in the Theme Colors palette click Gold, Accent 4, Lighter 60%.
7. Click Page Layout > Delete Background to remove the background image.
8. Save the changes to the file, and leave it open to use in the next Try It.

The Page Setup group

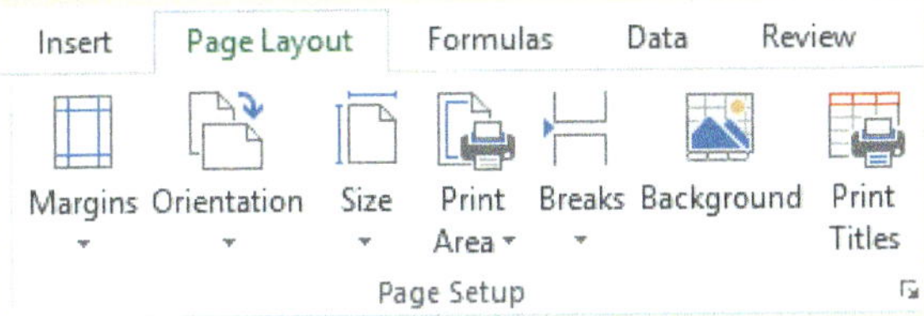

Excel 2016, Windows 10, Microsoft Corporation

Creating a Workbook Template

- If you create workbooks with a lot of similar elements—a company name and logo, similar column and row labels, and so on—create one workbook and save it as a **template**.
  - You can create a new workbook based on any existing workbook without creating a template from it first.
  - However, if you often base new workbooks on a particular workbook, you can save time by creating a template.
  - For example, with a template, you won't have to delete the data from the copied workbook before you can enter new data.
- With a template, you can quickly create new workbooks that contain the same elements.
- By default, templates are saved in the Templates folder in the following file path: C:\Users*Username*\My Documents\Custom Office Templates

  ✓ *Based on your computer's configuration, your file path may be different than the one given here.*

- Use the Personal section on Word's New screen in the Backstage view to access the custom templates in your personal template gallery.

  ✓ *If you don't see Personal under the search box on the New screen in Backstage view, click Options > Save and enter a folder in the Default personal templates location text box. You might want to create a subfolder in your Documents folder for this purpose.*

- You can create a subfolder in the Templates folder; that subfolder will appear as a folder on the Personal tab in the Backstage view.
- You can edit and modify templates that you create as well as any existing templates.
  - When saving a template, you can save it as read-only to prevent any accidental changes.

    ✓ *Template files have .xltx file name extensions. Macro-enabled template files have .xltm file extensions.*

- You can delete a template by using File Explorer to browse to the folder with the file, right-clicking the file, and selecting Delete.

Try It! Creating a Workbook Template

1. In the **E59TryA_xx** file, double-click the July 22 tab, and type **Products Sold**.
2. Modify the worksheet in the following ways:
   a. Edit cell A4 to remove the date.
   b. Switch to Sheet3, select the cell range A2:C21, and click Home > Copy.
   c. Switch to the Products Sold sheet, select cell A7, and click Paste.
   d. Remove the fill from the cells you just pasted.
   e. Click cell E4 to select it, and on the Home tab, in the Font group, click Borders > Bottom border.
   f. Click View, and deselect the Gridlines option.
3. Set up a default personal template location if needed.
   a. Click File > Options > Save.
   b. In the Default personal templates location text box, take note of the location listed. If the text box is empty, enter the desired location for saving templates. Ask your instructor what location to use if needed.
   c. Click OK.
4. Save the worksheet as a template:
   a. Click File > Save As > Browse.
   b. In the Save As dialog box, click the Save as type list > Excel Template.
   c. Click the New folder button, name the new folder **Class**, and click Open.
   d. In the File name box, type **E59TryC_xx**, and click Save.
   e. Close the template.
5. Create a new workbook using the new template:
   a. Click File > New.
   b. On the New tab in the Backstage view, click Personal, and click the Class folder.
   c. Click the **E59TryC_xx** template.
6. In cell E4 type **July 24**.
7. In cell C7 type **10**, in cell C12 type **5**, in cell C17 type **4**, and in cell C22 type **2**.
8. Save the file as **E59TryD_xx** in the location where your teacher instructs you to store the files for this lesson.
9. Save and close the file, and exit Excel.

Try It! Deleting a Workbook Template

1. Start File Explorer, and browse to the default location for personal templates. (See Step 3 in the previous Try It.)

   ✓ *Your file path may be different than the one given here; check with your teacher for the correct file path.*
2. Click the Class folder > Open.
3. Right-click the **E59TryC_xx** template file > Delete. Click Yes to confirm the deletion, if necessary.
4. Click the Back button to view the Class folder.
5. Right-click the Class folder > Delete. Click Yes to confirm the deletion, if necessary.
6. Close File Explorer.

Creating a Chart Template

- You can create a chart template from a chart that you have customized.
- Right-click the chart, and use the Save as Template command.
- A chart template is saved as a .crtx file.
- By default, Excel stores custom chart templates in the following file path: C:\Users*Username*\ My Documents\Custom Office Templates.

✓ *Based on your computer's configuration, your file path may be different than the one given here.*

- You can delete a custom chart template by using the Manage Templates feature in the Insert Chart dialog box.

Try It! Creating a Chart Template

1. Start Excel, and open the **E59TryE** file from the data files for this lesson.
2. Save the file as **E59TryE_xx** in the location where your teacher instructs you to store the files for this lesson.
3. On the Patient Care Chart chart sheet, click the chart to select it, and right-click.
4. In the shortcut menu, click Save as Template.
5. In the File name box, type **E59TryE**. Notice that Chart Template Files is already selected in the Save as type list.
6. Click Save.
7. Save the changes to the file, and leave it open to use in the next Try It.

The Save Chart Template dialog box

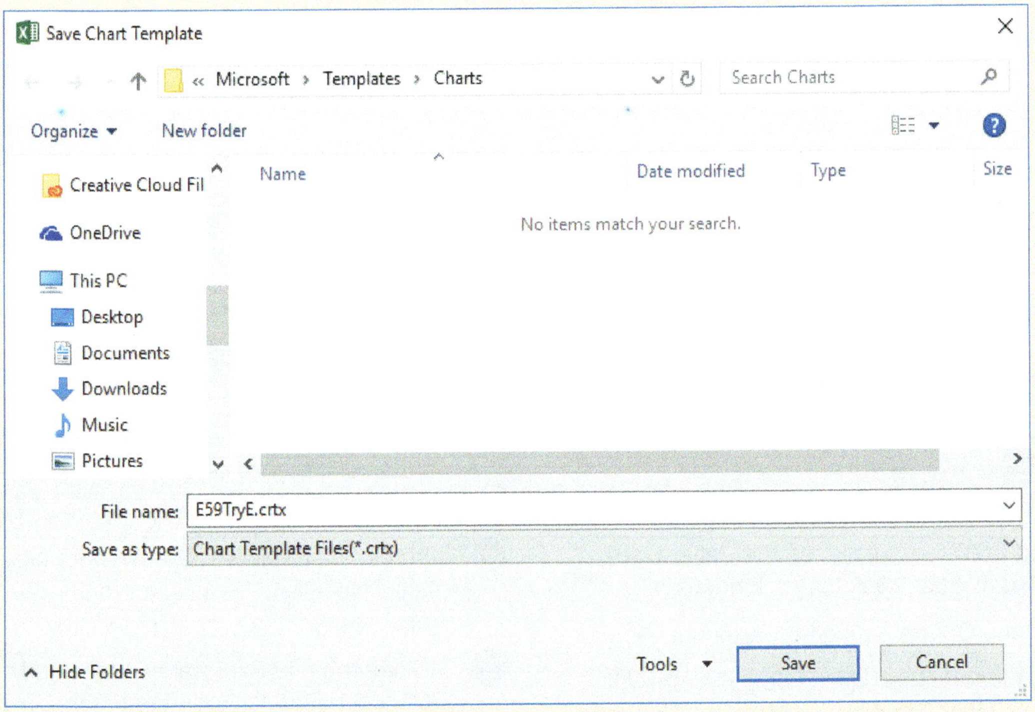

Excel 2016, Windows 10, Microsoft Corporation

Try It! Creating a Chart from a Custom Chart Template

1. In the **E59TryE_xx** file, click the Patient care breakdown tab.
2. Select the cell range B9:F18.
3. Click Insert > Charts dialog box launcher.
4. In the Insert Chart dialog box, click the All Charts tab > Templates.
5. Click the **E59TryE** chart template > OK.
6. Move the chart to below the data.
7. Save the changes to the file, and leave it open to use in the next Try It.

A custom chart template

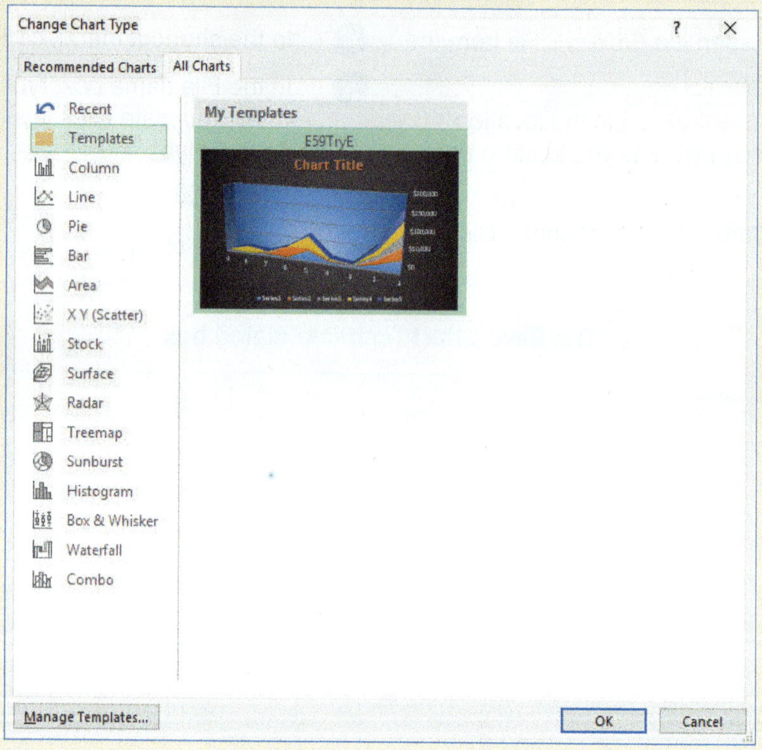

Excel 2016, Windows 10, Microsoft Corporation

Try It! Deleting a Custom Chart Template

1. In the **E59TryE_xx** file, on the Patient care breakdown tab, click Insert, if necessary.
2. Click the Charts dialog box launcher.
3. In the Insert Chart dialog box, click the All Charts tab > Templates > Manage Templates [Manage Templates...].
4. In the File Explorer window, right-click **E59TryE** > Delete. Click Yes to confirm the deletion, if necessary.
5. Close the File Explorer window, and click the Cancel button to close the Insert Chart dialog box.
6. Save and close the file, and exit Excel.

Lesson 59—Practice

The worksheet you designed to track sales each day at Pete's Pets has proven very helpful, and the corporate headquarters may adopt it throughout the company. Before you send it off for their review, you want to add some professional formatting touches. In this project, you will add a background picture and a watermark.

DIRECTIONS

1. Start Excel, if necessary, and open **E59PracticeA** from the data files for this lesson.
2. Save the file as **E59PracticeA_xx** in the location where your teacher instructs you to store the files for this lesson.
3. Add a background picture.
   a. Click **Page Layout** > **Background**.
   b. In the Insert Pictures window, in the From a file group, click **Browse**.
   c. Select **E59PracticeB.jpg** from the data files for this lesson, and click **Insert**.
4. Apply the **Orange, Accent 2, Lighter 60%** color fill to the cell range **E15:L20**.
5. Add borders to the column labels.
   a. Select the range **E15:L15**.
   b. Click **Home** > **Border**.
   c. Select **Top and Double Bottom Border**.
6. Click **View** > **Gridlines** to hide the gridlines. Your worksheet should look like Figure 59-1 on the next page.
7. Add a watermark.
   a. Click the **Watermark** worksheet tab.
   b. Click **Insert** > **Header & Footer**.
   c. Click in the middle section of the header, and on the Header & Footer Tools Design tab, click **Picture**.
   d. In the Insert Pictures window, in the From a file group, click **Browse**.
   e. Select **E59PracticeB.jpg** from the data files for this lesson, and click **Insert**.
   f. On the Header & Footer Tools Design tab, click **Format Picture**.
   g. In the Format Picture dialog box, check that the **Lock aspect ratio** check box is selected.
   h. Set the Scale Height to **190%**. (The Scale Width will automatically change to 190%.)
   i. Click the **Picture** tab, and set the Brightness to **75%**.
   j. Set the Contrast to **25%**, and click **OK**.
8. Click outside of the header > **View** > **Gridlines** to hide gridlines.
9. Select the range **E15:L20**.
10. Click **Home** > **Fill Color** > **Gold, Accent 4, Lighter 60%**. Your worksheet should look like Figure 59-2 on the next page.
11. For all worksheets, add a footer that has your name at the left, the date code in the center, and the page number code at the right.
12. **With your teacher's permission**, print the **Watermark** worksheet.
13. Save and close the file, and exit Excel.

Figure 59-1

Excel 2016, Windows 10, Microsoft Corporation

Figure 59-2

Excel 2016, Windows 10, Microsoft Corporation

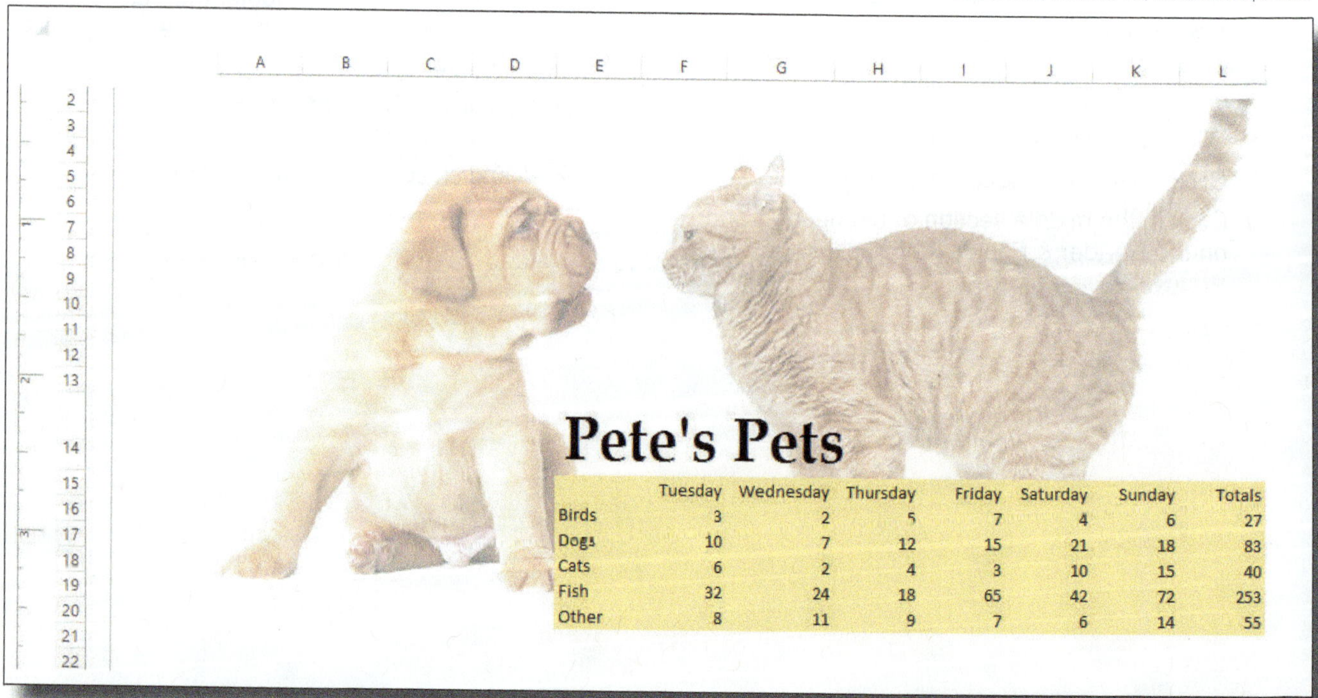

Lesson 59—Apply

You are the sales manager at Pete's Pets. Corporate headquarters has asked you to create a template from the worksheet you designed to track daily sales. You want to modify the existing worksheet to make it more usable as a template. In this project, you will create a custom workbook template from an existing worksheet. You will also create a custom chart template.

DIRECTIONS

1. Start Excel, if necessary, and open **E59ApplyA** from the data files for this lesson.
2. Save the file as **E59ApplyA_xx** in the location where your teacher instructs you to store the files for this lesson.
3. Click the **Watermark** worksheet tab.
4. Select the range **F16:K20**, and press DEL.
5. Save the changes to the **E59ApplyA_xx** file.
6. Create a template from the workbook.
   a. Click **File** > **Save As**.
   b. Click **Browse**.
   c. In the Save As dialog box, click the **Save as type** list > **Excel Template**.
   d. Save the template in the location where your teacher instructs you to store the files for this lesson.
   e. Name the template file **E59ApplyB_xx**.
7. Click the **Background** worksheet tab.
8. Create a 3-D clustered column chart on its own sheet tab.
   a. Select the cell range **E15:K20**.
   b. Click **Insert** > **Insert Column or Bar Chart** > **3-D Clustered Column Chart**.
   c. Move the chart to a new sheet titled **Daily Sales Chart**.
9. Customize the formatting on the chart:
   a. Add a chart title: **Daily Sales**.
   b. On the Chart Tools Design tab, click **Change Colors** > **Color 3**.
10. Save the changes to the **E59ApplyB_xx** template file.
11. Create a chart template.
    a. Click the chart to select it, and right-click.
    b. Click **Save as Template**.
    c. In the File name box, type **E59ApplyC_xx**.
    d. Click **Save**.
12. Save the changes to the **E59ApplyB_xx** template file.
13. Delete the **E59ApplyC** chart template.
    a. Click **Insert** > **Charts** dialog box launcher.
    b. In the Insert Chart dialog box, click the **All Charts** tab > **Templates** > **Manage Templates** Manage Templates... .
    c. Right-click **E59ApplyC_xx** > **Delete**. Click **Yes** to confirm the deletion, if necessary.
    d. Close the File Explorer window, and click the **Close** button to close the Insert Chart dialog box.
14. Add a custom footer that has your name at the left, the date code in the center, and the page number code at the right.
15. **With your teacher's permission**, print the **Daily Sales Chart** worksheet. Your worksheet should look like Figure 59-3 on the next page.
16. Save and close the file, and exit Excel.

Figure 59-3

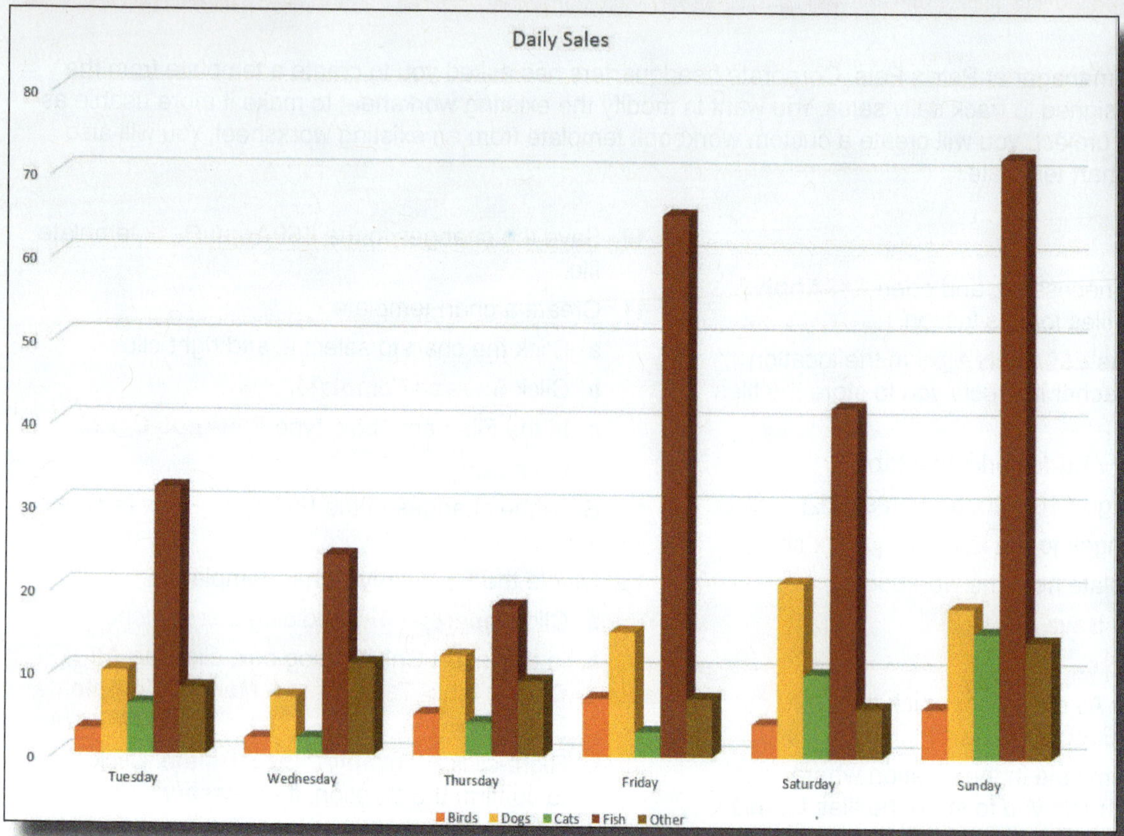

Excel 2016, Windows 10, Microsoft Corporation

End-of-Chapter Activities

➤ Excel Chapter 7—Critical Thinking

Cash Flow Projection

You are the founder of a public relations firm called Jones PR. You are looking for additional capital from angel investors and other local seed capital sources, and you need to make presentations to investors soon.

One important set of data you need to present is a Cash Flow Projection. The cash flow projection will forecast your company's future performance based on data you have captured from past performance. You need to embellish the raw data you'll present with charts that show comparisons and trends. You also want to save the workbook as a custom template to use in the future.

DIRECTIONS

1. Start Excel, if necessary, and open **ECT07A** from the data files for this chapter.
2. Save the file as **ECT07A_xx** in the location where your teacher instructs you to store the files for this chapter.
3. Apply the **Integral** theme and the **Calibri** font set to the worksheet.
4. Enter **16000** in cell **B4**. Notice that previously applied formatting rules make the entries in cells B7:C7 turn red.
5. Create and format a line chart for the title receipts.
   a. Select the range **A12:N12**, and insert a Line with Markers chart.
   b. Move the chart to its own sheet called **Comparison**.
   c. Return to the **Cash Flow** worksheet, and select and copy the cell range **A38:N38**.
   d. Return to the **Comparison** worksheet, and paste the copied data into the chart.

      ✓ *You can press CTRL + V to paste to add the copied data to the chart.*

   e. With the chart selected, click **Chart Tools Design** > **Quick Layout** > **Layout 1**.
   f. Add **Receipts vs. Cash Out** as the chart title.
   g. Edit the chart series so that the ranges **C12:N12** and **C38:N38** on the **Cash Flow** worksheet are charted.

      ✓ *Right-click the chart area, click Select Data, and edit the chart data range.*

   h. Specify the range **C6:N6** on the **Cash Flow** worksheet for the X axis labels.
   i. Edit the series name entries in the legend to draw their values from A12 and A38, respectively.
   j. Delete the vertical axis title. The finished chart should look like Illustration 7A on the next page.
6. Return to the **Cash Flow** worksheet, and select the range **A38:N38**.
7. Insert and format a Scatter chart.
   a. Create a Scatter chart from the selected range.
   b. Move the chart to its own sheet called **Trend**.
   c. Edit the chart series so that the cell range **C38:N38** on the **Cash Flow** worksheet is charted.
   d. Specify the cell range **C6:N6** on the **Cash Flow** worksheet for the X axis labels, making sure that cell **A38** on the **Cash Flow** worksheet is specified as the series name.
   e. Change the chart title to **Cash Out Trend**.
   f. Format the data labels to display on the right of the data points on the chart.
   g. Add a linear trendline to the chart to show the trend for cash out over time.
   h. Display the legend on the right side of the chart. The finished chart should look like Illustration 7B on the next page.
8. Add a custom header to the **Cash Flow** worksheet that has your name at the left, the date code in the center, and the page number code at the right.
9. Close any open task panes.
10. Save the changes to the **ECT07A_xx** workbook.

11. Save the **ECT07A_xx** workbook as an Excel template named **ECT07B_xx** in the location where your teacher instructs you to store the files for this chapter.

12. **With your teacher's permission,** print the **Comparison** and **Trend** chart worksheets.

13. Save and close the **ECT07B_xx** file, and exit Excel.

Illustration 7A

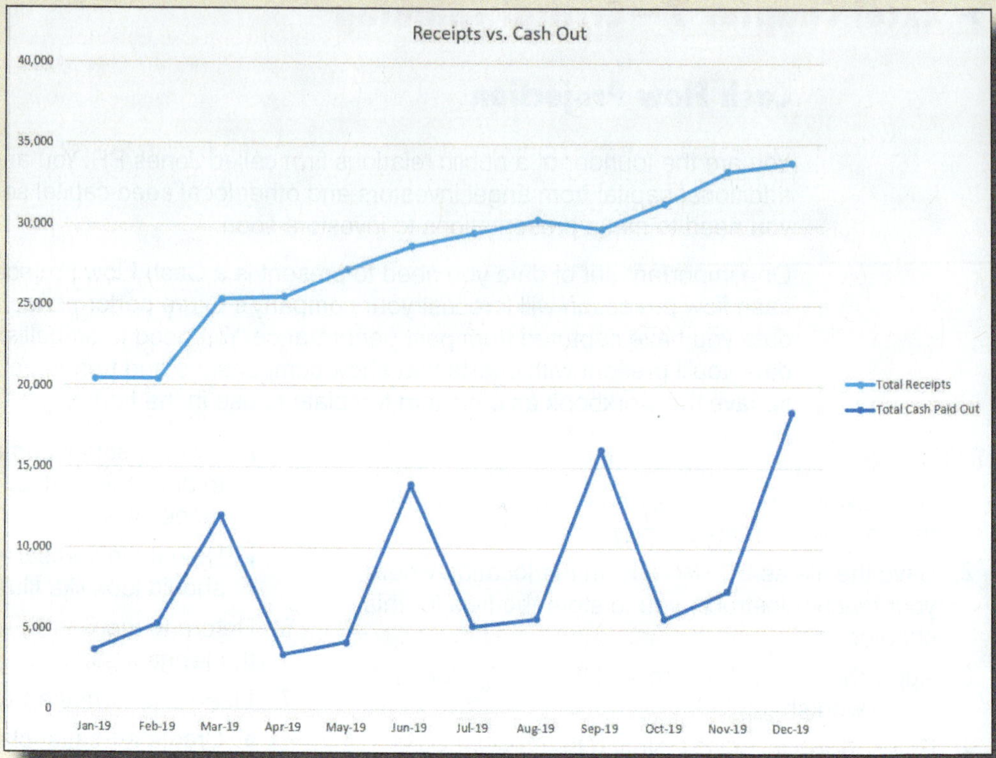

Excel 2016, Windows 10, Microsoft Corporation

Illustration 7B

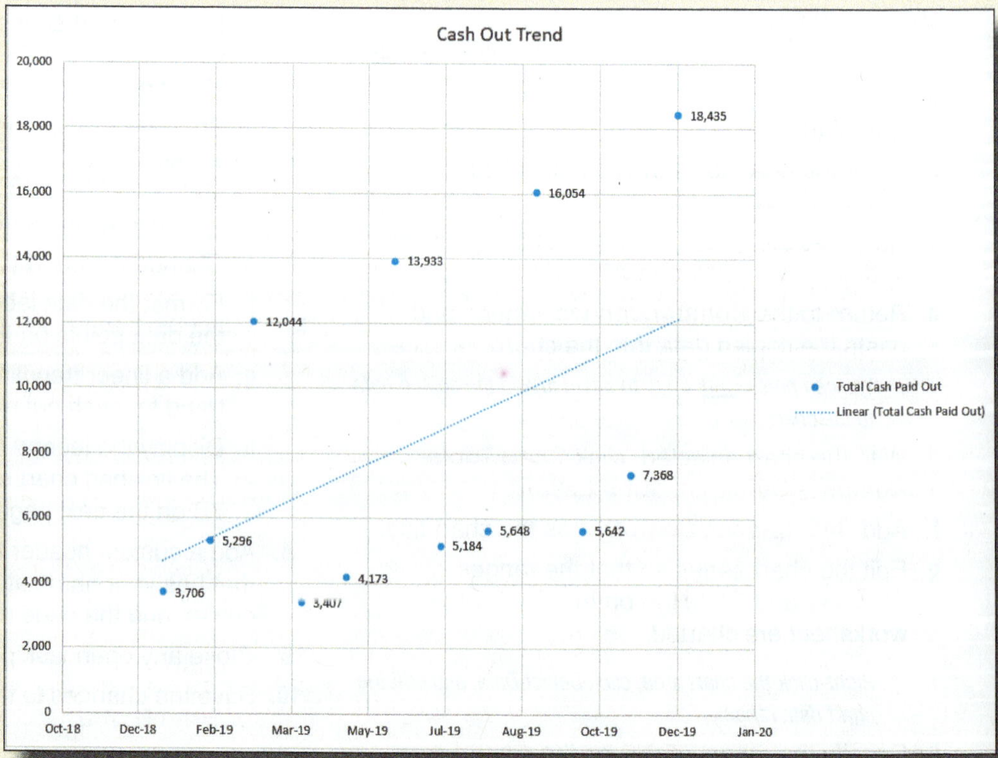

Excel 2016, Windows 10, Microsoft Corporation

➤ Excel Chapter 7—Portfolio Builder

Daily Sales Report

As assistant sales manager for Country Crazy Antiques, you've been asked to put together a collection of reports to present to the owner. You need to create a template for tracking a day's worth of sales.

The warehouse manager has also asked you to embellish the inventory report with shapes and text effects to help call attention to the pertinent information before the next meeting.

DIRECTIONS

1. Start Excel, if necessary, and open **EPB07A** from the data files for this chapter.
2. Save the file as **EPB07A_xx** in the location where your teacher instructs you to store the files for this chapter.
3. Add a custom header that has your name at the left, the date code in the center, and the page number code at the right.
4. The existing worksheet has all the necessary columns and totals, but you need to add formatting.
   a. Add the **Green, Accent 6, Lighter 80%** fill to the cell range A1:O50.
   b. Select rows **1–4**, and fill with **Gold, Accent 4, Lighter 60%**.
   c. Select cell **D2**, and apply the **Consolas** font, size **20**, in bold.
   d. Select the cell range **B8:K8**, and apply the **Gold, Accent 4, Lighter 80%** fill.
   e. Use the Format Painter to apply the **B8:K8** formatting to the cell range **B9:K33**.
   f. Select the cell range **B7:K7**, and fill with **Green, Accent 6, Darker 25%**. Increase the font size, then add a border of your choice.
5. Adjust the column widths if necessary, and save the file.The completed worksheet should look similar to Illustration 7C on the next page.
6. Create a template from the workbook, and save the file as **EPB07B_xx** in the location where your teacher instructs you to store the files for this chapter. Close the file.
7. Open **EPB07C** from the data files for this project.
8. Save the file as **EPB07C_xx** in the location where your teacher instructs you to store the files for this chapter.
9. Add a custom header that has your name at the left, the date code in the center, and the page number code at the right.
10. Create a logo for the Country Crazy Antiques store using various shapes.
    a. In the area below the table, create at least four objects, such as squares, rectangles, ovals, or any other shape of your choice.
    b. Combine the objects, overlapping at least one object, to form a pleasing logo.
11. Open the Selection task pane, and use it to select and group the individual shapes you used to create a logo for Country Crazy Antiques.
12. Apply various fill, outline, and shape effect styles to create a logo you feel represents the business.
13. Move the finished logo to the area at the left of the Country Crazy Antiques title, and resize as necessary to fit within the cell range A1:A6, as shown in Illustration 7D.
14. Insert a banner from the Stars and Banners group under the Country Crazy Antiques title in rows 4 and 5.
15. Add the text **Inventory as of 6/10/19** to the banner you created, and format the text as you like.
16. Select the banner, and format it with the **Subtle Effect - Green, Accent 6** shape style.
17. Insert a **Rounded Rectangular Callout** from the callouts group.
18. Add the following text to the callout: **End table sale was held 6/1–6/3**, and format the text as you like.
19. Apply the **Subtle Effect - Green, Accent 6** shape style.
20. Apply the **Preset 2** shape effect.
21. Resize the callout as necessary, and rotate it as shown in Illustration 7D on the next page.

22. Apply the **Gold, Accent 4, Lighter 40%** shape fill.
23. Adjust the column widths if necessary.
24. **With your teacher's permission**, print the worksheet.
25. Close the workbook, saving all changes, and exit Excel.

Illustration 7C

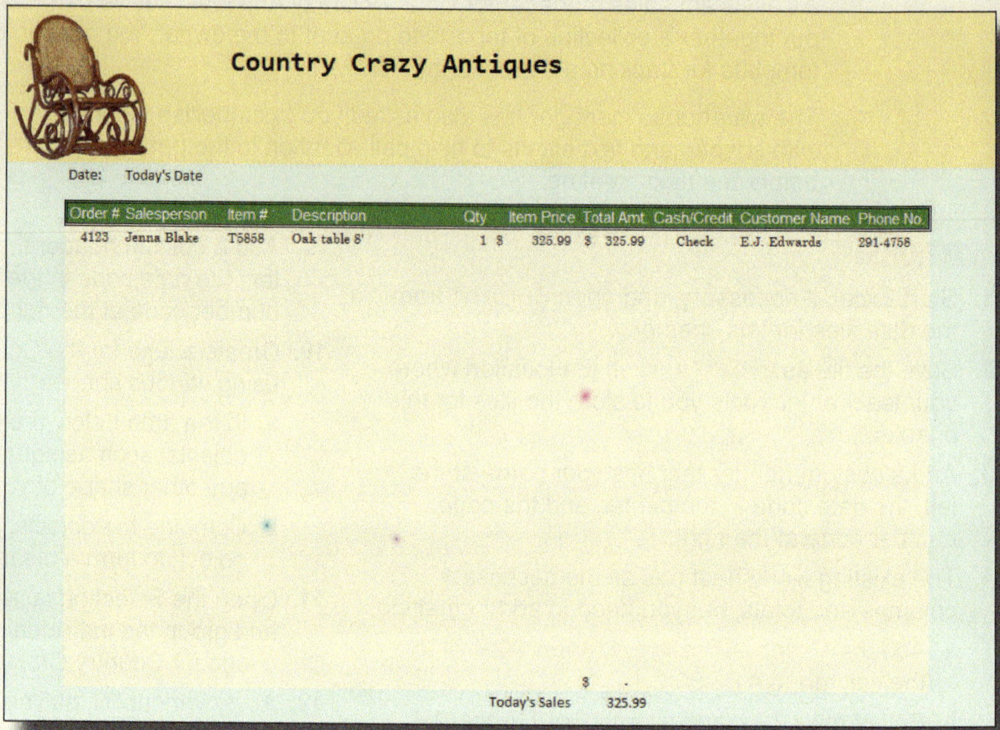

Excel 2016, Windows 10, Microsoft Corporation

Illustration 7D

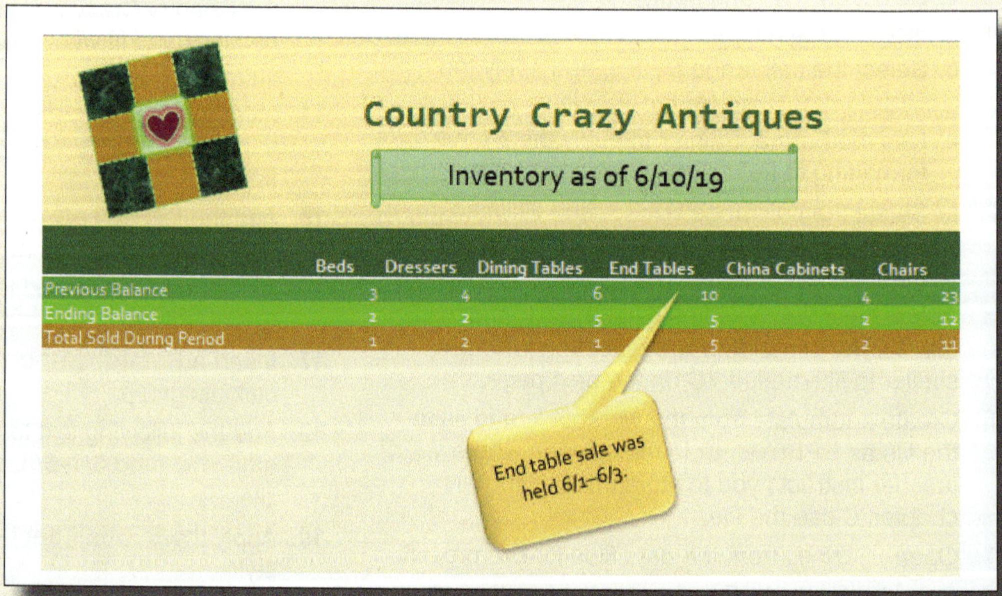

Excel 2016, Windows 10, Microsoft Corporation

Chapter 8

(Courtesy Vadym Drobot/Shutterstock)

Creating Macros and Using Data Analysis Tools

Lesson 60
Working with Macros

- Adding the Developer Tab to the Ribbon
- Setting the Macro Security Level
- Setting Trusted Locations
- Saving a Workbook That Contains Macros
- Recording a Macro
- Running a Macro
- Editing a Macro
- Copying Macros Between Workbooks

Lesson 61
Working with Logical Functions

- Using Insert Function
- Creating an IF Function
- Creating SUMIF, COUNTIF, and AVERAGEIF Functions
- Creating SUMIFS, COUNTIFS, and AVERAGEIFS Functions
- Using Logical Operations in Nested Functions
- Using AND, NOT, and OR functions

Lesson 62
Working with Date and Time Functions

- Using the TODAY and NOW Functions
- Serializing Numbers Using Date and Time Functions

Lesson 63
Working with Absolute References and Using Financial Functions

- Using Absolute, Relative, and Mixed References
- Enabling Iterative Calculations
- Using Financial Functions

Lesson 64
Creating and Interpreting Financial Statements

- Loading the Analysis ToolPak Add-On
- Calculating a Moving Average
- Calculating Growth Based on a Moving Average
- Charting the Break-Even Point with a Line Chart
- Using Goal Seek

Lesson 65
Creating Scenarios and Naming Ranges

- Creating a Scenario Using the Scenario Manager
- Naming a Range
- Creating a Scenario Summary

Lesson 66
Finding and Fixing Errors in Formulas

- Using Formula Error Checking
- Understanding Error Messages
- Showing Formulas
- Evaluating Individual Formulas
- Using the Watch Window
- Tracing Precedents and Dependents

End-of-Chapter Activities

Lesson 60

Recording a Macro

➤ What You Will Learn

- Adding the Developer Tab to the Ribbon
- Setting the Macro Security Level
- Setting Trusted Locations
- Saving a Workbook That Contains Macros
- Recording a Macro
- Running a Macro
- Editing a Macro
- Copying Macros Between Workbooks

WORDS TO KNOW

Absolute recording
A macro recording in which the cells being acted upon are referenced absolutely, so the references do not change depending on the active cell position when the macro begins running. Absolute is the default setting.

Developer tab
An optional Ribbon tab that contains commands of use to advanced users, such as commands for creating and managing macros.

Macro
A series of recorded actions that can be replayed when needed. The recorded actions are carried out automatically for the user.

Macro security
A macro setting that enables or disables macros when the workbook is opened by a person other than the person who created the file. The default security setting is to disable macros.

Software Skills You can automate the performance of a sequence of tasks in Excel by creating a macro. This automation reduces the time it takes to repeat the tasks, and increases accuracy.

What You Can Do

Adding the Developer Tab to the Ribbon

- The **Developer tab** on the ribbon contains useful commands for creating and running **macros**. The default setting is for Excel to not display the Developer tab.

✓ *You do not have to enable the Developer tab in order to record a macro because there are other ways to start a macro recording, such as the New Macro button on the status bar. However, having the Developer tab available makes the process of running and managing macros easier.*

Try It! Adding the Developer Tab to the Ribbon

1. Start Excel, and open a new, blank worksheet.
2. Click File > Options.
3. Click Customize Ribbon.
4. In the Customize the Ribbon list (on the right side of the dialog box), place a check mark next to Developer.

   ✓ *Note: The check mark may already be there if another student has already added this to the ribbon.*

5. Click OK to close the Excel Options dialog box. Notice the Developer tab appears to the right of the View tab.
6. Leave Excel open for the next Try It.

Setting the Macro Security Level

- To minimize the risk of a macro virus or other malware threat contained in a macro, Excel includes the **macro security** feature. Its default setting is to disable all macros and display a notification option when working with a file that contains macros.
- Set the protection and security levels to the level of restriction or openness according to your comfort level, or according to the policy established by the IT department where you work. You may set the security level to one of four choices:
  - Disable all macros without notification
  - Disable all macros with notification
  - Disable all macros except digitally signed macros
  - Enable all macros
- The settings on the computer you are using may be different than the default settings that are assumed for these directions. It is always advisable to check the settings and make any necessary changes.

Module
A container for VBA code.

Relative recording
A macro recording in which the cells being acted upon depend on the active cell position when the macro begins running.

Trusted location
A folder designated as a trusted location for Excel files that contain macros. Any file placed in this trusted location folder will open without the dialog box and with the macros enabled.

Visual Basic for Applications (VBA)
A version of the Visual Basic programming language designed for use within Microsoft Office applications. Macros are stored and edited using this language.

.xlsm
The file extension of an Excel 2007–2016 file that contains a macro.

Try It! Setting the Macro Security Level

1. In Excel, click File > Options > Trust Center > Trust Center Settings [Trust Center Settings...] > Macro Settings.
2. Verify that the setting is: Disable all macros with notification.

   ✓ *With this setting, a worksheet with a macro will be disabled and a warning window will display to allow you to enable the macro if you trust the source of the workbook.*

3. Click OK to close the dialog box.
4. Leave Excel open to use in the next Try It.

(continued)

Try It! Setting the Macro Security Level *(continued)*

Macro security settings

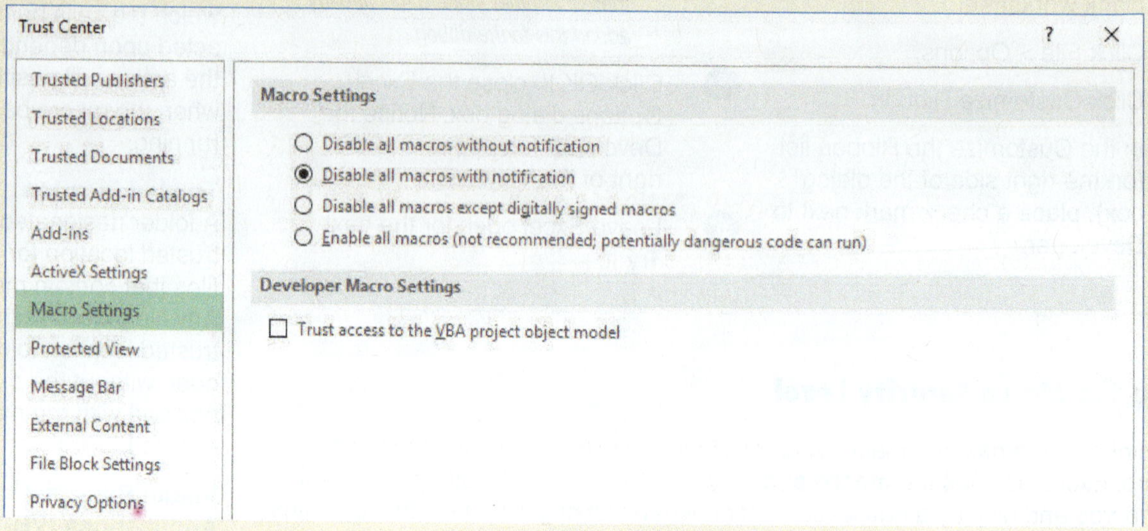

Excel 2016, Windows 10, Microsoft Corporation

Setting Trusted Locations

- In most of the Office applications (including Excel), you can define **trusted locations**. These are specific folders that you mark as safe, so that whenever you open a file from one of those locations, all of the usual safety precautions don't apply.
- For example, if you place an Excel file that contains macros in a trusted location, when you open that file, the security setting from the previous section doesn't restrict your ability to run macros.

Try It! Setting Trusted Locations

1. Click File > Options > Trust Center > Trust Center Settings [Trust Center Settings...] to open the Trust Center dialog box.
2. Click Trusted Locations.
3. Click Add new location.
4. In the Microsoft Office Trusted Location dialog box, click Browse.
5. Navigate to the folder where the data files for this class are stored, and click OK.
6. Click the Subfolders of this location are also trusted check box.
7. Click OK. The trusted location is included.
8. In the Trust Center dialog box, with the user location path you added still selected, click Remove. The trusted location is removed.
9. Click OK to close the Trust Center dialog box.
10. Click OK to close the Excel Options dialog box.
11. Close the blank workbook without saving changes, and leave Excel open to use in the next Try It.

Saving a Workbook That Contains Macros

- The default file extension for Excel 2016 is .xlsx. This file format cannot contain macros, by design, to avoid potential malware threats associated with macros.
- A workbook must be saved in **.xlsm** format in order to enable it to store macros.

  ✓ *When you save a file in .xlsm format, it does not overwrite the original file in .xlsx format.*

Try It! Saving a Workbook That Contains Macros

1. Open E60TryA from the data files for this lesson.
2. Click File > Save As and then click Browse.
3. Navigate to the location where your teacher instructs you to store the files for this lesson.
4. In the Save As dialog box, click the Save as type drop-down list > Excel Macro-Enabled Workbook.
5. In the File name box, change the file name to E60TryA_xx.
6. Click Save.
7. Leave the E60TryA_xx file open to use in the next Try It.

Recording a Macro

- The Macro Recorder records every action you take, and stores them in a macro that you can later play back to reproduce the steps.

  ✓ *Recording a macro requires planning and some practice. It is not uncommon to have to record a macro several times because errors were made in the recording process. If you make a mistake, delete the macro and record a new one.*

- By default, Excel records the actual addresses of the cells you affect when recording. For example, if the active cell happens to be cell D2 when you begin recording a macro that makes the active cell bold, the macro will always make cell D2 bold, regardless of the position of the active cell when you run that macro. This is called **absolute recording**, and it is the default behavior.
- If you go with the default setting of absolute recording, the macro begins recording your actions based on the cell that is active. When you create the macro, select the desired cell before you click Record.
- The alternative is **relative recording**, which performs the recorded action on whatever cell or range is selected before running the macro.
- On the Developer tab, click Use Relative References or Use Absolute References to switch between absolute and relative recording.
- You can name a macro to make it easier to reference; however, you cannot use spaces in a macro name.

Try It! Recording a Macro

1. In the E60TryA_xx file, click cell B2, and click the View tab.
2. Click the arrow below the Macros button, and click Record Macro.

   OR

   Click the Record Macro button on the status bar.
3. In the Record Macro dialog box, in the Macro name text box, type **TopSales**.

   ✓ *The macro name cannot have spaces.*
4. In the Shortcut key text box, type **t**.

   ✓ *This will be your shortcut key used to run the macro. If you choose a shortcut key that Excel already has assigned to another action, the macro will override the other action in this workbook.*

(continued)

Try It! Recording a Macro *(continued)*

5. In the Description text box, type **Date, sales by Z-A order, top seller**.

Define the macro before recording it

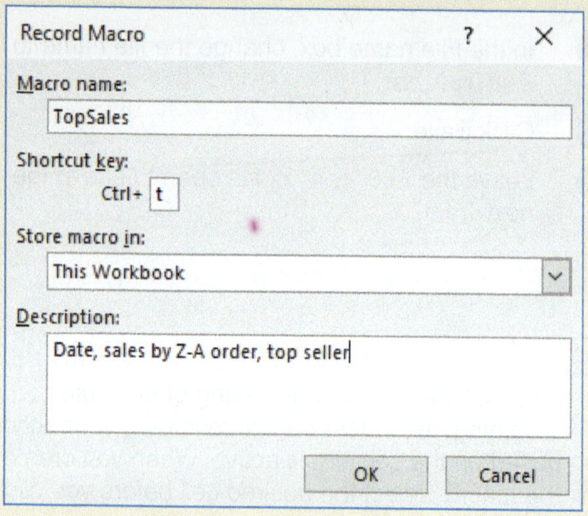

Excel 2016, Windows 10, Microsoft Corporation

6. Click OK. The recording begins.

7. Without re-clicking in cell B2, but with the cell still selected, type **=NOW()**, and press ENTER.

✓ *This will place the current date and time in this cell each time the file is opened. Notice that this cell has a date format applied to it so that only the date displays.*

8. Select cells A5:B9.

9. Click Data > Sort.

10. In the Sort dialog box, open the Sort by drop-down list and click Column B.

11. Click OK.

12. Click cell B3, type **=**, click cell A9, and press ENTER.

✓ *This will place the top sales person's name in cell B3 when the macro is run.*

13. Click View > Macros > Stop Recording ■ Stop Recording.

OR

Click the Stop Record Macro button on the status bar.

14. Save the changes to the file, and leave it open to use in the next Try It.

Running a Macro

- To run a macro, you can use the Macros command on the View tab to open a Macro dialog box from which you can select the macro you want.
- You can also use the shortcut key combination you defined when you created the macro.
- You can also assign a macro to the Quick Access Toolbar or the ribbon, and then run it from its button.

Try It! Running a Macro

1. In the **E60TryA_xx** file, select the cell range A5:B9, and click Data > Sort A to Z to re-sort the list by name, so you can test the macro.

2. Click cell B2 and press CTRL + T. The macro runs.

3. Click cell E2 and press CTRL + T again. The macro runs again.

✓ *This time the macro places =NOW() in cell E2. It does that because you did not click B2 after beginning the macro recording but before typing =NOW(). You recorded a relative reference macro that begins running at the active cell. We'll fix that later in the lesson, when you learn about editing a macro in VBA. Notice that the references to A5:B9 still work, though, because they are absolute references by default.*

(continued)

Try It! Running a Macro *(continued)*

4. Widen column E so that the content of cell E2 is visible.
5. Select cell E2, and press DEL .
6. Click cell B5, and type **5000**.
7. Click cell B2.
8. Click View > Macros to display the Macro dialog box.

✓ *The Macro dialog box provides an alternate way of running a macro. You must use this method for macros for which there is no shortcut key combination or button.*

9. Click the TopSales macro, and click Run to run the macro again.
10. Save the changes to the file, and leave it open to use in the next Try It.

Try It! Adding a Macro to the Quick Access Toolbar

1. In the **E60TryA_xx** file, click File > Options.
2. Click Quick Access Toolbar.
3. Open the Choose commands from drop-down list, and click Macros.
4. Click TopSales.
5. Click Add.
6. Click OK. A button for the macro now appears on the Quick Access Toolbar.
7. Click cell B7, and type **100**.
8. Click cell B2.
9. On the Quick Access Toolbar, click the TopSales macro button . The macro re-runs and re-sorts the list with the new value.
10. Save the changes to the file, and leave it open to use in the next Try It.

Editing a Macro

- If you make a mistake during recording, you can delete the macro, or you can edit the macro in **Visual Basic for Applications (VBA)**.
- Editing the macro requires a basic understanding of VBA, which you may not have yet. However, many of the commands are simple to figure out by their names, so that you can identify unwanted parts of the macro to delete or correct typos.

Try It! Editing a Macro

1. In the **E60TryA_xx** file, click View > Macros to open the Macro dialog box.
2. Click TopSales, and click Edit. Visual Basic for Applications opens, showing the macro code.
3. Click to place the insertion point at the beginning of the text: **ActiveCell.FormulaR1C1 = "=NOW()"**.
4. Type **Range("B2").Select**, and press ENTER .

✓ *Adding this line of code selects cell B2 as the first action in the macro.*

5. Click File > Close and Return to Microsoft Excel.
6. Save the changes to the file, and leave it open to use in the next Try It.

Try It! Deleting a Macro

1. In the **E60TryA_xx** file, click View > Macros to open the Macro dialog box.
2. Click TopSales, and click Delete.
3. Click Yes to confirm.
4. Right-click the macro button you placed on the Quick Access Toolbar earlier, and click Remove from Quick Access Toolbar.
5. Close the workbook without saving your changes to it so that macro is still in the saved copy.
6. Leave Excel open to use in the next Try It.

Copying Macros Between Workbooks

- Macro code is stored in a **module** within the file.
- You can access VBA modules in the Microsoft Visual Basic for Applications window from the Visual Basic button on the Developer tab.
- You can open a module like a file and edit its content.
- Each time you create a new macro in the worksheet, Excel adds it to the Modules folder of the Visual Basic project with the name Module1, Module2, etc.
- You can copy a module to another macro-enabled Excel workbook to make the macros in the module available for use in that workbook.

  ✓ *When you copy a macro from one workbook to another, Excel does not copy its shortcut key. You will need to reassign the shortcut key by editing the macro.*

- You can edit or delete individual macros in a workbook by using the Organizer.

Try It! Copying Macros Between Workbooks

1. In Excel, open **E60TryA_xx** from the location where your teacher instructs you to store the files for this lesson.
2. In the Security Warning bar, click Enable Content to enable the macro.
3. Create a new, blank workbook.
4. Click File > Save As. Then click Browse.
5. Navigate to the location where your teacher instructs you to store the files for this lesson.
6. In the Save As dialog box, in the File name box, type **E60TryB_xx**.
7. Click the Save as type drop-down list > Excel Macro-Enabled Workbook.
8. Click Save.
9. If the Developer tab does not already appear, enable it. To do so, click Tools > Options > Customize Ribbon, place a check mark next to Developer in the right pane, and click OK.
10. In the **E60TryB _xx** file, click Developer > Visual Basic .
11. In the Microsoft Visual Basic for Applications window, on the toolbar, click Project Explorer .

(continued)

Try It! Copying Macros Between Workbooks *(continued)*

12. Click and hold Module1, and drag it on top of the **VBAProject(E60TryB_xx.xlsm)** project. The macro is copied in a Modules folder.

13. Under **VBAProject(E60TryB_xx.xlsm)**, click the plus sign next to the Modules folder to open it and view the macro.

14. Close the Microsoft Visual Basic for Applications window.

15. Save and close the **E60TryA_xx** and **E60TryB_xx** files, and exit Excel.

Copying a macros module to another workbook

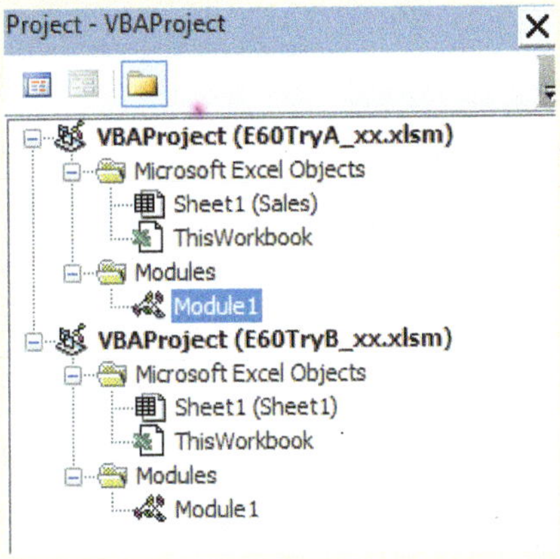

Excel 2016, Windows 10, Microsoft Corporation

Lesson 60—Practice

The Membership Chairperson for the Small Business Professional Organization is tracking attendance for the organization's quarterly meeting. She has asked you to create a worksheet to show the RSVP replies and to track who said they would come to the meeting but did not show up. In this project, you will create a macro that shows the members who said they would attend, but who did not actually attend the meeting.

DIRECTIONS

1. Start Excel, if necessary, and open **E60Practice** from the data files for this lesson.
2. Click **File** > **Save As**. Click **Browse**.
3. Navigate to the location where your teacher instructs you to store the files for this lesson.
4. In the File name box, type **E60Practice_xx**.
5. Click the **Save as type** drop-down list > **Excel Macro-Enabled Workbook**.
6. Click **Save**.
7. Add a header with your full name on the left, and today's date on the right. Return to **Normal** view.
8. Select the range **A2:G62**.
9. Click **Insert** > **Table**.
10. In the Create Table dialog box, verify that the cell range is **A2:G62**, verify that the **My table has headers** check box is selected, and click **OK**.
11. Click cell **A2** to make this the active cell.
12. Click **View** > **Macros** > **Record Macro** to display the Record Macro dialog box.
13. In the Macro Name text box, type **MeetingAttendance**. Do not put a space in the macro name.
14. In the Shortcut key box, type **t**.

    ✓ *If you receive a message telling you a macro is already assigned to that key, choose another key.*

15. In the Description box, type **People who said they would attend, but did not**.
16. In the Store macro in box, verify that This Workbook is selected, and click **OK**.
17. Click the down arrow on cell **E2**, click to clear the **No** check box, and click **OK**.

    ✓ *This shows all the people who said they would attend the meeting.*

18. Click the down arrow on cell **F2**, click to clear the **Yes** check box, and click **OK**.

    ✓ *This shows who said they would attend, but did not attend the meeting.*

19. Click **View** > **Macros** > **Stop Recording** Stop Recording.
20. Click **Data** > **Clear** to remove the filters.
21. Click **A2**.
22. Press CTRL + T to run the macro.
23. **With your teacher's permission,** print the worksheet. Your worksheet should look like the one shown in Figure 60-1.
24. Save and close the file, and exit Excel.

Figure 60-1

Student Name 4/25/2016

Small Business Professional Organization

Spring Networking Meeting

Last Name	First Name	RSVP Received	Reminder	RSVP Response	Attended
Chang	Joshua	yes		Yes	No
Copp	Seth	No	Yes	Yes	No
Devereaux	Domique	yes		Yes	No
Huang	Griffin	No	Yes	Yes	No
Klein	Nathaniel	yes		Yes	No
Nishiba	Arielle	No	Yes	Yes	No
Reisman	Sophia	yes		Yes	No

Excel 2016, Windows 10, Microsoft Corporation

Lesson 60—Apply

You are a member of the Small Business Professional Organization. The Membership Chairperson has asked you to create a chart comparing the revenue from the sales of products and services over a period of six months. Since the Membership Chairperson has asked you to do this in the past, you want to record a macro to create the chart.

DIRECTIONS

1. Start Excel, if necessary, and open **E60ApplyA** from the data files for this lesson. Notice that this file is already in a macro-enabled file format.
2. Save the file as **E60ApplyA_xx** in the location where your teacher instructs you to store the files for this lesson.
3. For all worksheets, add a header that has your name at the left, the date code in the center, and the page number code at the right, and change back to **Normal** view.
4. Prepare to record a macro that creates a chart comparing the revenue from the sales of products and services over a period of six months:

   Macro name: **Sales**

   Shortcut key: **Ctrl+s**

   Store macro in: **This Workbook**

   Description: **Sales and services revenue chart**

   ✓ *If you receive a message saying a macro is already assigned to the shortcut key, choose another key.*

5. Perform the following actions as the macro recorder records them:
   a. On the Sales tab, select the cell range **A2:C8**.
   b. Click **Insert** > **Insert Column or Bar Chart** > **3-D Clustered Column** (the first option in the 3-D Column group).
   c. Click **Chart Tools Design**, and in the Chart Styles group click **Style 4**.
6. End the recording.
7. Delete the chart from the workbook, and run the macro to re-create the chart.
8. Edit the macro in the VBA Editor to change the style applied to the chart to **Style 3**:
   a. Click **View** > **Macros**.
   b. In the Macros dialog box, click the **Macros in** drop-down arrow, and click **This Workbook**.
   c. Click **Sales**, and then click **Edit**.
   d. In the E60Apply_xx.xlsm - Module1 (Code) window, change the ActiveChart.Chartstyle to **288**.
   e. Save the macro project.
   f. Close the VBA window.
9. Delete the chart from the workbook, and run the macro to re-create the chart.
10. Reposition the chart so that the upper-left corner of the chart is at the upper-left corner of cell C10.
11. **With your teacher's permission,** print the **Sales** worksheet. Your chart should look like the one shown in Figure 60-2.
12. Copy the macro to a blank workbook:
   a. Create a new, blank workbook.
   b. Save the file as a Macro-Enabled Workbook named **E60ApplyB_xx** in the location where your teacher instructs you to store the files for this lesson.
   c. In the **E60ApplyB_xx** file, click **Developer** > **Visual Basic**. (Display the Developer tab on the Ribbon if needed.)
   d. In the Microsoft Visual Basic for Applications window, on the toolbar, click **Project Explorer** to view the Project - VBAProject pane, if necessary.
   e. Under VBAProject(E60ApplyA_xx.xlsm), click the plus sign next to the Modules folder to open it and view the Module1 macro.
   f. Click and hold **Module1**, and drag it on top of the VBAProject(E60ApplyB_xx.xlsm) project.
   g. Under VBAProject(E60ApplyB _xx.xlsm), click the plus sign next to the Modules folder to open it and view the macro.
13. Close the Microsoft Visual Basic for Applications window.
14. Save and close the **E60ApplyA_xx** and **E60ApplyB_xx** files, and exit Excel.

Figure 60-2

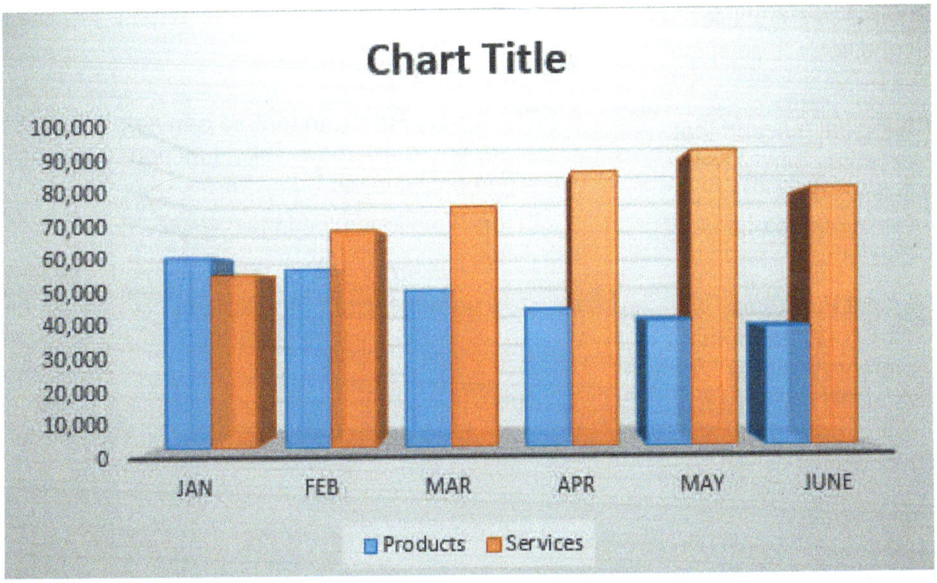

Lesson 61

Working with Logical Functions

WORDS TO KNOW

AND function
A function that checks whether all arguments are true.

AVERAGEIF function
A function that averages the values in a range that meet a certain condition.

AVERAGEIFS function
A version of AVERAGEIF that allows multiple conditions to be specified.

COUNTIF function
A function that uses a criteria to count the number of items in a range.

COUNTIFS function
A version of COUNTIF that allows multiple conditions to be specified.

IF function
A logical function that executes one of two actions depending on the outcome of a yes/no question.

Insert Function
An Excel feature that prompts the user for the required and optional arguments for a specified function.

➤ What You Will Learn

Using Insert Function
Creating an IF Function
Creating SUMIF, COUNTIF, and AVERAGEIF Functions
Creating SUMIFS, COUNTIFS, and AVERAGEIFS Functions
Using Logical Operations in Nested Functions
Using AND, NOT, and OR Functions

Software Skills Excel includes logical functions that enable you to set up conditions where a calculation is performed only if the conditions are met, such as IF, SUMIF, COUNTIF, and AVERAGEIF. Logical functions are sometimes nested inside one another, creating a complex set of conditions that may involve logical operator functions like AND, NOT, and OR. Such functions are more complex to set up than other functions, so you may prefer to construct them using Insert Function, a built-in utility in Excel that prompts you for the necessary arguments.

What You Can Do

Using Insert Function

- The **Insert Function** feature can help you construct functions in cases where either you don't know which function to use or you don't remember what arguments it takes.
- Insert Function helps in two ways:
  - It allows you to look up functions based on what they do.
  - It prompts you for the arguments needed for the chosen function.

Try It! Inserting a Function

1. Start Excel, and open **E61Try** from the data files for this lesson.
2. Save the file as **E61Try_xx** in the location where your teacher has instructed you to save your work.
3. On the IF worksheet tab, click cell A13, and type **Total**.
4. Click cell B13, and click the Insert Function *fx* button on the formula bar to open the Insert Function dialog box.

The Insert Function button

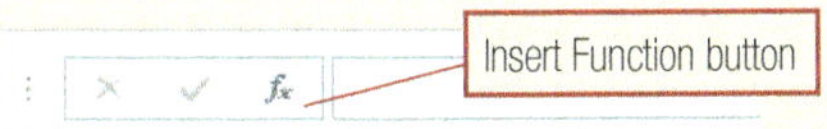

Excel 2016, Windows 10, Microsoft Corporation

5. In the Search for a function box, type **add**, and click Go.

   ✓ *We already know that we want the SUM function in this case; step 5 is just for practice.*

6. In the list of functions that appears, click SUM, and read the description of it at the bottom of the dialog box.
7. Click OK to open the Function Arguments dialog box with text boxes for each of the arguments.

   ✓ *The SUM function has only one required argument. Labels for required arguments are bold.*

8. Confirm that the Number1 argument displays B5:B12.

   ✓ *If Excel guesses at the range incorrectly, you can manually correct it, or you can select the range yourself. You can click the Collapse Dialog Box button to the right of the argument to get the dialog box out of the way, select the desired range, and then click the Expand Dialog Box button or press Enter to bring the dialog box back to full view.*

9. Click OK to display the formula result in the cell.
10. Save the changes to the file, and leave it open to use in the next Try It.

Arguments for the SUM function

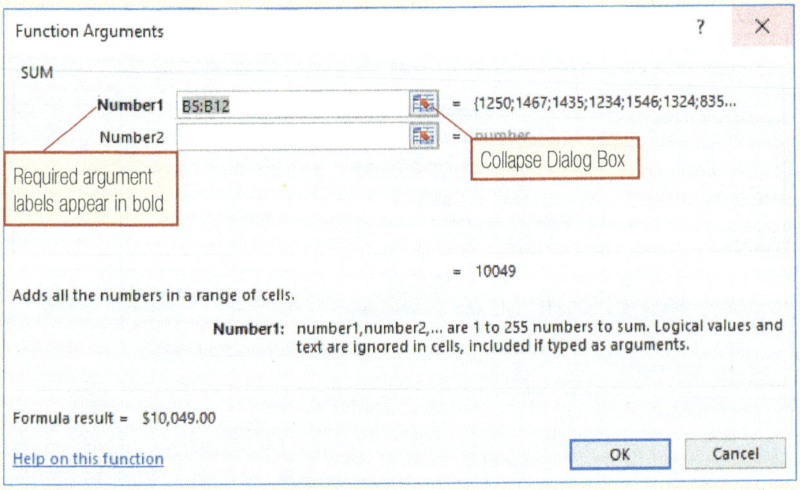

Excel 2016, Windows 10, Microsoft Corporation

Logical function
A function that evaluates a yes/no condition and then takes an action based on the result.

Nested function
A function that operates as an argument of another function.

NOT function
A function that changes false to true or vice-versa.

OR function
A function that checks whether any of the arguments are true.

SUMIF function
A function that sums the values in a range that meet a certain condition.

SUMIFS function
A version of SUMIF that allows multiple conditions to be specified.

Creating an IF Function

- **Logical functions** enable you to set up yes/no questions, and then perform one action or another based on the answer
- **IF** is the simplest of the logical functions. It has three arguments:
  - The logical condition
  - What to do if it is true
  - What to do if it is false
- For example, suppose that if cell A1 contains 100, you want cell B1 to show "Perfect Score"; otherwise, B1 should show "Thanks for Playing." To achieve this, you would place the following function in B1:

  =IF(A1=100,"Perfect Score","Thanks for Playing")
- Enclose text strings in quotation marks, and use commas to separate the arguments.
- You can use Insert Function to enter the arguments instead of typing them manually.
- Like most other functions, you can use the IF function in conjunction with other functions, such as AND or OR.
- For example, suppose you want to find out who sold item number 15634 for $150 in a range of sales data where column A contains the name of the salesperson, column B contains the item number, and column C contains the cost of the item. To achieve this, you would use the following function:

  =IF(AND(C1=150)B1=15634,A1)

Try It! Creating an IF Function

1. In the **E61Try_xx** file, on the IF worksheet tab, click cell C5.
2. Click Insert Function.
3. Click the Or select a category list > Logical.
4. In the Select a function list, click IF.
5. Click OK to open the Function Arguments dialog box.
6. In the Logical test box, type **B5>=1000**.
7. In the Value_if_true box, type **B5*0.05**.
8. In the Value_if_false box, type **B5*0.02**.
9. Click OK to place the function in cell C5.
10. Copy the function from cell C5 to the range C6:C12.

    ✓ *Use any copy method you like. You can drag the fill handle, or use the Copy and Paste commands.*
11. Save the changes to the file, and leave it open to use in the next Try It.

Arguments for the IF function

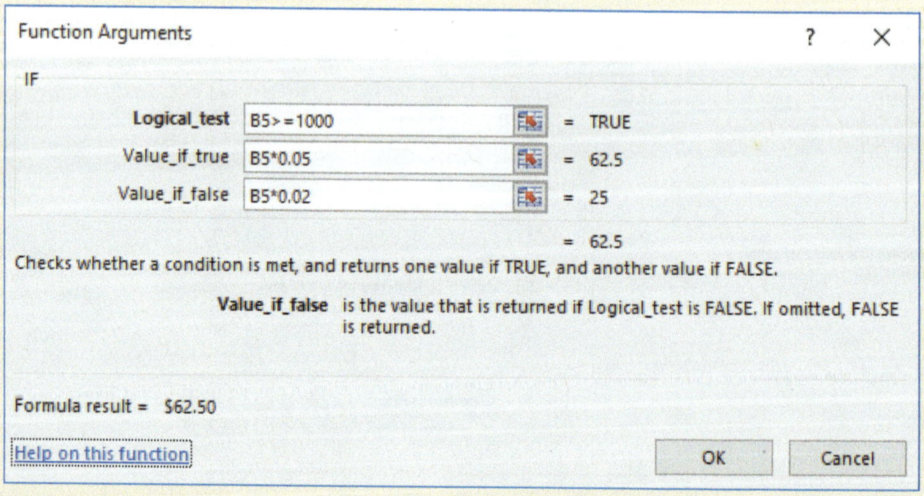

Excel 2016, Windows 10, Microsoft Corporation

Creating SUMIF, COUNTIF, and AVERAGEIF Functions

- The **SUMIF**, **COUNTIF**, and **AVERAGEIF** functions combine the IF function with either SUM, COUNT, or AVERAGE. The SUM, COUNT, or AVERAGE operation is performed upon cells within the specified range that meet a certain logical condition.
- The syntax is:

  =SUMIF(range,criteria,sum_range)
- In some cases the range to evaluate *(range)* and the range to calculate *(sum_range)* are the same. In that case, you can omit the *sum_range* argument.
- To specify that a criterion not be a certain value, precede the value with <>. For example, to exclude records where the value is 500, you would use <>500 as the criterion.
- COUNTIF and AVERAGEIF work the same way as SUMIF, with the same types of arguments.

Try It! Creating a SUMIF Function

1. In the **E61Try_xx** file, click the SUMIF worksheet tab.
2. Click cell B15 > Insert Function.
3. Type **SUMIF**, and click Go.
4. Click SUMIF in the list of functions, if necessary, and click OK.
5. In the Range box, type **D4:D13**.
6. In the Criteria box, type **Yes**.

   ✓ *Quotation marks around the criteria are required, even if the criteria are numeric. Insert Function automatically puts quotation marks around the criteria for you.*
7. In the Sum Range box, type **C4:C13**.
8. Click OK. The result ($802.00) appears in cell B15.
9. Save the changes to the file, and leave it open to use in the next Try It.

Enter the arguments for the SUMIF function

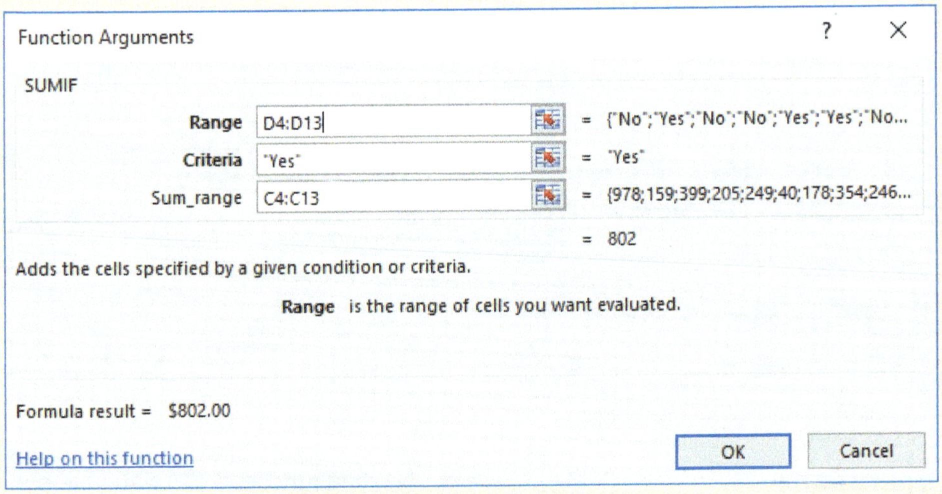

Excel 2016, Windows 10, Microsoft Corporation

Creating SUMIFS, COUNTIFS, and AVERAGEIFS Functions

- The **SUMIFS**, **COUNTIFS**, and **AVERAGEIFS** functions are the same as SUMIF, COUNTIF, and AVERAGEIF except that they allow multiple criteria.
- For the function to be evaluated as true, all the criteria must be met.
- These functions are used for statistical operations, such as finding the total, count, or average of records that meet certain criteria in a database.

Try It! Creating an AVERAGEIFS Function

1. In the **E61Try_xx** file, on the SUMIF worksheet tab, click cell A16, and type **Avg Due for Dog Items**.
2. Click cell B16 > Insert Function.
3. Type **AVERAGEIFS**, and click Go > OK.
4. In the Average_range box, type **C4:C13**.
5. In the Criteria_range1 box, type **D4:D13**.
6. In the Criteria1 box, type **No**.
7. In the Criteria_range2 box, type **E4:E13**.
8. In the Criteria2 box, type **Dog**.
9. Click OK. The function appears in the cell.
10. Save the changes to the file, and leave it open for the next Try It.

Arguments for the AVERAGEIFS function

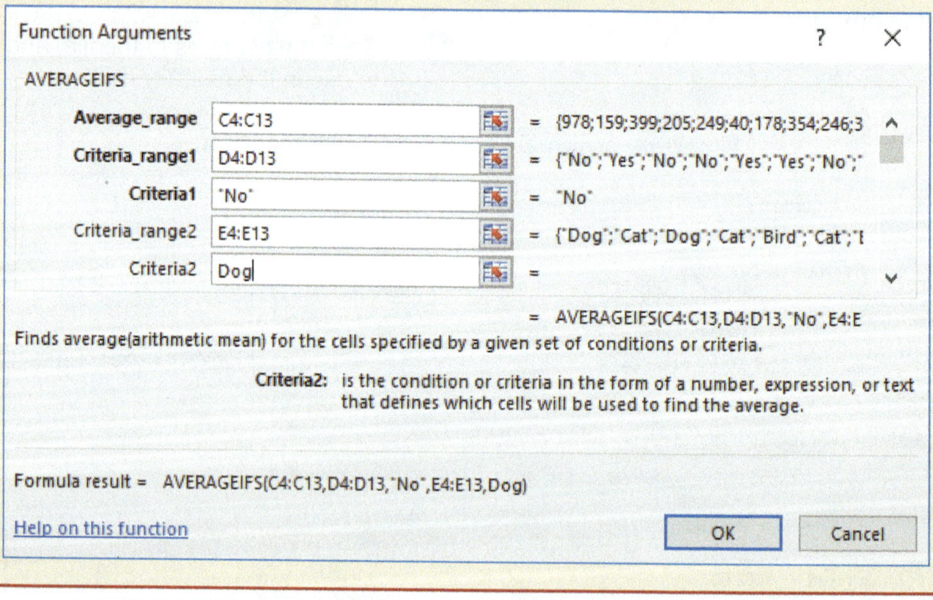

Excel 2016, Windows 10, Microsoft Corporation

Using Logical Operations in Nested Functions

- When you use one function as an argument of another function, the first one is **nested** inside the second. For example, the following function sums the range B2:B10 if G20>0, and otherwise displays N/A:

  =IF(G20>0,SUM(B2:B10),"N/A")

- Nesting functions can get quite complex in the case of multiple conditions. For example, this function from a gradebook displays a different letter depending on the value in B20: A if 90 to 100, B if 80 to 90, C if 70 to 80, D if 60 to 70, and F if less than 60. Each succeeding nested function is placed in the "if no" portion of the IF function, so it happens only if the IF function's "if yes" condition is false:

  =IF(B20>=90,"A",IF(B20>=80,"B",IF(B20>=70, "C",IF(B20>=60,"D","F"))))

Try It! Using Logical Operations in Nested Functions

1. In the **E61Try_xx** file, on the IF worksheet tab, in cell D4, type **Team Bonus**.
2. In cells A17 and A18, enter **Multiplier** and **Threshold**, respectively.
3. In cells B17 and B18, enter **0.02** and **$1200.00**, respectively.
4. Click in cell D5 and type **=IF(AVERAGE($B$5:$B$12)>=$B$18,B5*$B$17,0)**.

   ✓ *Notice the absolute references, which keep the cell references fixed when the function is copied.*

5. Copy the formula from B5 to D6:D12 using any method.
6. Change the value in B18 to $1300.00.

   ✓ *All the values in column D change to 0 because the logical condition is no longer being met.*

7. Save the changes to the file, and leave it open to use in the next Try It.

Using AND, OR, and NOT Functions

- The AND, NOT, and OR functions return only one of two values: FALSE or TRUE. They are very similar in usage.
- The AND function evaluates two conditions and returns TRUE if both are true. If neither is true, or if only one is true, it returns FALSE.
- The OR function evaluates two conditions and returns TRUE if either or both of the conditions are true. It returns FALSE only if both conditions are false.
- The NOT function inverts the value of the field used in the argument, changing false to true, or true to false. For example, if cell C1 contains TRUE, and you put =NOT(C1) in cell D1, cell D1 would display FALSE.

Try It! Evaluating Logical Conditions with AND and NOT Functions

1. In the **E61Try_xx** file, on the SUMIF worksheet tab, in cell F3, type **Preferred**.
2. Click in cell F4 and type **=AND(C4>=100,D4="Yes")**.

   ✓ *Customers are preferred if they spent $100 or more AND if they paid.*

3. In cell G3, type **Small Sale**.
4. Click in cell G4, and type **=NOT(C4>=200)**.
5. Use Format Painter to copy the formatting from D3 to F3:G3.
6. Save and close the file, and exit Excel.

Lesson 61—Practice

Your boss at Wood Hills Animal Clinic has asked you to modify the monthly sales report and create an analysis of sales based on several factors such as animal type (cat versus dog, for example) and purpose (ear infection versus flea control, for example). In this project, you will insert functions to aid in the analysis of the data.

DIRECTIONS

1. Start Excel, if necessary, and open **E61Practice** from the data files for this lesson.
2. Save the file as **E61Practice_xx** in the location where your teacher instructs you to store the files for this lesson.

3. Add a header that has your name at the left, the date code in the center, and the page number code at the right, and change back to **Normal** view.
4. Click cell D99, and type the formula **=SUM(K8:K94)** to compute the total sales revenues.
5. Use Insert Function to create a formula in cell D100 to sum the sales from dog products.
   a. Click cell **D100**.
   b. On the formula bar, click **Insert Function** *fx* to open the Insert Function dialog box.
   c. In the Search for a function box, type **SUMIF** > **Go** > **OK**.
   d. In the Function Arguments dialog box, for the Range argument, type **C8:C94**.
   e. In the Criteria argument, type **"Dog"**.

      ✓ *Typing the quotation marks is optional; if you do not type them, Excel will add them for you automatically.*

   f. In the Sum_range argument, type **K8:K94**.
   g. Click **OK**.
6. Use the process in step 5 to sum the sales of cat products in cell D101.

   ✓ *The function to be placed in cell D101 is identical to the one in cell D100 except it uses Cat rather than Dog in the criteria argument.*

7. Use Insert Function to create a formula in cell D103 to sum the sales from flea products.
   a. Click cell **D103**.
   b. On the formula bar, click **Insert Function** *fx*.
   c. Click **SUMIF** > **OK**.
   d. In the Function Arguments dialog box, for the Range argument, type **B8:B94**.
   e. In the Criteria argument, type **"Flea"**.
   f. In the Sum_range argument, type **K8:K94**.
   g. Click **OK**.
8. Use the process in step 7 to insert SUMIF functions in cells **D104** and **D105**. For cell D104, use **"Flea and Tick"** as the critieria argument. For cell D105, use **"Heartworm"** as the criteria argument.
9. Complete the functions for cells **D108:D114** using the same methods as in steps 5–8 except use **AVERAGE** and **AVERAGEIF** functions.

   ✓ *Notice that cell D108 is the average sales and D112 is the average sales of flea products.*

10. In cell **D106**, type **=D99-SUM(D103:D105)**.
11. In cell **D115**, enter an **AVERAGEIFS** function that averages the values that are not Flea, Flea and Tick, or Heartworm.
    a. Click cell **D115**.
    b. On the formula bar, click **Insert Function** *fx*.
    c. Type **AVERAGEIFS** > **Go** > **OK**.
    d. In the Average_range argument, type **K8:K94**.
    e. In the Criteria_range1 argument, type **B8:B94**.
    f. In the Criteria1 argument, type **"<>Flea"**.

       ✓ *Make sure you put the <> inside the quotation marks.*

    g. In the Criteria_range2 argument, type **B8:B94**.
    h. In the Criteria2 argument, type **"<>Flea and Tick"**.
    i. In the Criteria_range3 argument, type **B8:B94**.
    j. In the Criteria3 argument, type **"<>Heartworm"**.
    k. Click **OK**.
12. In cell L8, enter a function that displays TRUE if there are fewer than three cases left in inventory AND if the number of items sold (I8) is more than half of the number of items per case (E8).
    a. Click cell **L8**.
    b. On the formula bar, click **Insert Function** *fx*.
    c. Open the **Or select a category** list and click **Logical**.
    d. In the Select a function list, click **AND**.
    e. Click **OK**.
    f. In the Logical1 box, type **H8<E8*3**.
    g. In the Logical2 box, type **I8>E8/2**.
    h. Click **OK**.
    i. Copy the function from L8 to L94.
13. **With your teacher's permission**, print the cell range **A98:E117**. Your worksheet should look like the one shown in Figure 61-1 on the next page.
14. Save and close the file, and exit Excel.

Figure 61-1

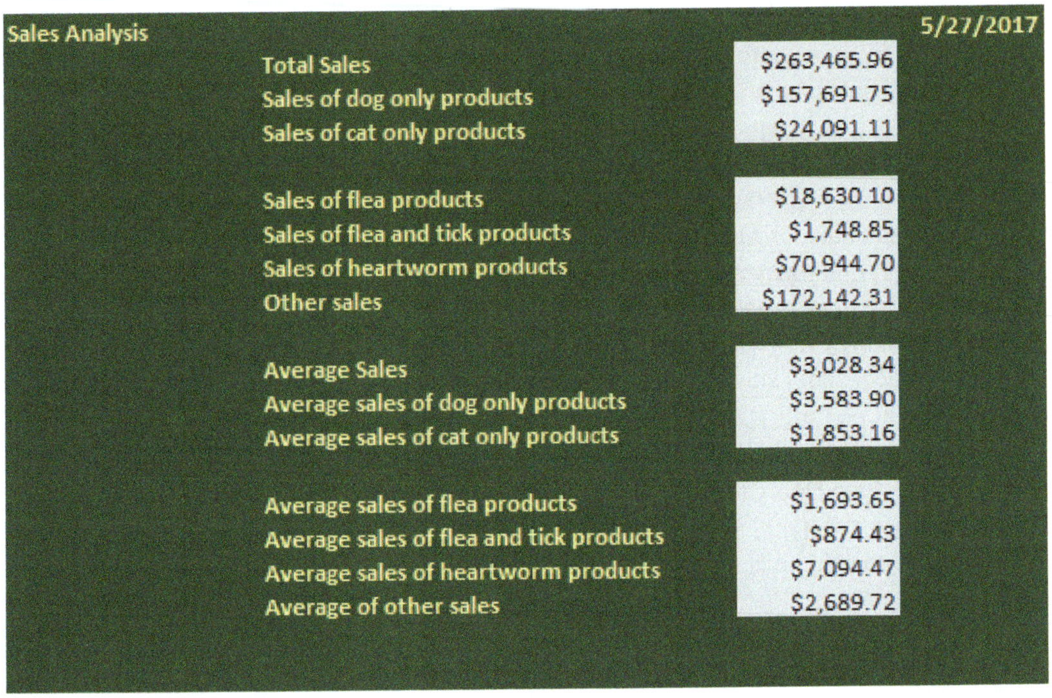

Lesson 61—Apply

You work in the sales department of Pete's Pets. Your manager has asked you to create an analysis of the store's sales based on several factors such as animal type and salesperson. Your manager also wants you to find out who sold a particular item. In this project, you will insert functions and transpose data to aid in the analysis of the sales report.

DIRECTIONS

1. Start Excel, if necessary, and open **E61Apply** from the data files for this lesson.
2. Save the file as **E61Apply_xx** in the location where your teacher instructs you to store the files for this lesson.
3. Add a header that has your name at the left, the date code in the center, and the page number code at the right, and change back to **Normal** view.
4. In cell **D54**, use the **COUNTIF** function to compute the number of **Cats** sold.
5. In cell **D55**, use the **COUNTIF** function to compute the number of **Fish** sold.
6. In cell **D62**, use the **SUMIF** function to compute the total sales for **Alice Harper**.
7. In cell **D63**, use the **SUMIF** function to compute the total sales for **Bob Cook**.
8. In cell **E62**, use the **AVERAGEIF** function to compute the average sale for **Alice Harper**.
9. In cell **E63**, use the **AVERAGEIF** function to compute the average sale for **Bob Cook**.

10. In cell **D66**, use **SUMIFS** to compute the total fish sales for **Alice Harper**.
11. In cell **D67**, use **SUMIFS** to compute the total fish sales for **Bob Cook**.
12. In cell **E66**, use **SUMIFS** to compute the total accessory sales for **Alice Harper**.
13. In cell **E67**, use **SUMIFS** to compute the total accessory sales for **Bob Cook**.
14. In cell **D70**, use **AVERAGEIFS** to calculate the average fish sale for **Alice Harper**.
15. In cell **D71**, use **AVERAGEIFS** to calculate the average fish sale for **Bob Cook**.
16. In cell **E70**, use **AVERAGEIFS** to calculate the average accessory sale for **Alice Harper**.
17. In cell **E71**, use **AVERAGEIFS** to calculate the average accessory sale for **Bob Cook**.
18. In cell **H9**, type **Dog Club**.
19. Use Format Painter to copy the formatting from column G to column H.
20. In **H10**, use an IF function to display "Eligible" if the amount in F10 is greater than 10 AND if cell D10 contains "Dog". Otherwise display nothing in H10.

    ✓ *One way to accomplish this is to start with an IF function and use an AND function to create the condition. Another way is to nest an additional IF function.*

    ✓ *To display nothing, use empty quotation marks, like this: "".*
21. Copy the function from H10 to H11:H49.
22. Apply **Accounting Format** with two decimal places to all the functions you created in this exercise, except the ones in D54 and D55.
23. Adjust the column widths as needed.
24. **With your teacher's permission**, print cells **B52:K71**. Your worksheet should look like the one shown in Figure 61-2.
25. Save and close the file, and exit Excel.

Figure 61-2

Sales Recap			
	Dogs sold	3	
	Cats sold	2	
	Fish sold	9	
	Pet sales	$ 1,696.37	
	Feed sales	$ 200.71	
	Accessories	$ 464.16	
	Salesperson	Total Sales	Average Sales
	Alice Harper	$ 1,059.37	$ 48.15
	Bob Cook	$ 1,301.87	$ 72.33
	Salesperson	Total Fish Sales	Total Accessories Sales
	Alice Harper	$ 135.15	$ 297.96
	Bob Cook	$ 17.22	$ 166.20
	Salesperson	Average Fish Sales	Average Accessories Sales
	Alice Harper	$ 22.53	$ 27.09
	Bob Cook	$ 5.74	$ 18.47

Lesson 62

Working with Date and Time Functions

➤ What You Will Learn

Showing the Current Date and Time
Serializing Numbers Using Date and Time Functions
Calculating Work Days
Determining the Day of the Week

Software Skills Excel's date and time functions can help perform calculations that are based on dates and times. This can include displaying the current date or time, using dates and times as arguments in other functions, calculating which days are workdays or weekdays, and serializing numbers using date and time functions.

What You Can Do

Showing the Current Date and Time

- Excel stores dates as sequential (serial) numbers so that they can be used in calculations using January 1, 1900 as serial number 1. For example, January 1, 2015 is serial number 42005 because it is 42,005 days after January 1, 1900.
- You can use the **TODAY function** to add today's date to a worksheet cell. The syntax for the TODAY function is: **=TODAY()**. Each time the worksheet is opened, the value is updated.
- The TODAY function retrieves today's date from Windows' clock/calendar and displays it. Although it displays the date in a human-readable date format, it internally stores the date as a serial number.
- The **NOW function** displays the current date and time on a worksheet. It can also be used to calculate a value based on the current date and time. Each time the worksheet is opened, the value is updated. The syntax for the NOW function is: **=NOW()**.

✓ *For the TODAY and NOW functions, the parentheses are mandatory, although there are no arguments in them.*

WORDS TO KNOW

DATE function
A function that converts a date represented as year, month, day to a number in Excel date-time code.

Excel date-time code
A scheme for converting dates and times to a standardized numbering system used in Excel, where January 1, 1900 equals 1.

NOW function
A function that returns the current time.

Serial date
A date represented as a numeric value.

TODAY function
A function that returns the current date.

WEEKDAY function
A function that returns the day of the week (Sunday through Saturday) that a given date falls on.

Workday
A day that falls on a Monday through Friday. This excludes weekends and holidays.

WORKDAY function
A function that calculates what date is a specified number of workdays from a given date.

Try It! Showing the Current Date and Time

1. Start Excel, and open the **E62Try** file from the data files for this lesson.
2. Save the file as **E62Try_xx** in the location where your teacher instructs you to store the files for this lesson.
3. Click in cell B3.
4. Type **=TODAY()** and press ENTER.
5. Click in cell C3.
6. Type **=NOW()** and press ENTER.

   ✓ *The NOW function shows both the date and the time by default. You can change the cell's number format to only show the time if you prefer.*
7. Click cell C3 and on the Home tab, click the drop-down arrow in the Number group and click Time.
8. Save the changes to the file, and leave it open to use in the next Try It.

Serializing Numbers Using Date and Time Functions

- To serialize a date means to convert it to **Excel's date-time code** so it can be used as a number in formulas and functions.
- Excel 2016 is very intuitive, so most of the time when you enter a date in a text format, such as January 1, 2018, Excel will automatically serialize the date for you. You might not realize this has happened because Excel displays the date in the text format in which you entered it (or something similar).
- However, in some situations, Excel may not automatically recognize a date as such. For example, if the month, day, and year are in separate columns, Excel does not see those cells collectively as a single date.
- To convert numeric values to a **serial date** in Excel, use the **DATE function.** To convert text to a date in Excel, use the DATEVALUE function. The TIME and TIMEVALUE functions are the equivalent functions when working with times.
- There are also functions for converting hours (HOUR), minutes (MINUTE), and seconds (SECOND). You might use one of these, for example, if you have calculated the difference between two times and you needed to convert the result to a number of hours, minutes, or seconds.

Try It! Serializing a Date with the DATE Function

1. In the **E62Try_xx** file, click the Holidays worksheet tab, and then click in cell C4.
2. Type **=DATE(** and then click the Insert Function button *fx* on the formula bar.
3. In the Year box, type **2018**.
4. In the Month box, type **A4**.
5. In the Day box, type **B4**.
6. Click OK.
7. Click cell C4 and then drag its fill handle down to C14 to copy the function.
8. Widen column C as needed to display the dates.
9. Save the changes to the file, and leave it open to use in the next Try It.

(continued)

Try It! Serializing a Date with the DATE Function *(continued)*

Function arguments for the DATE function

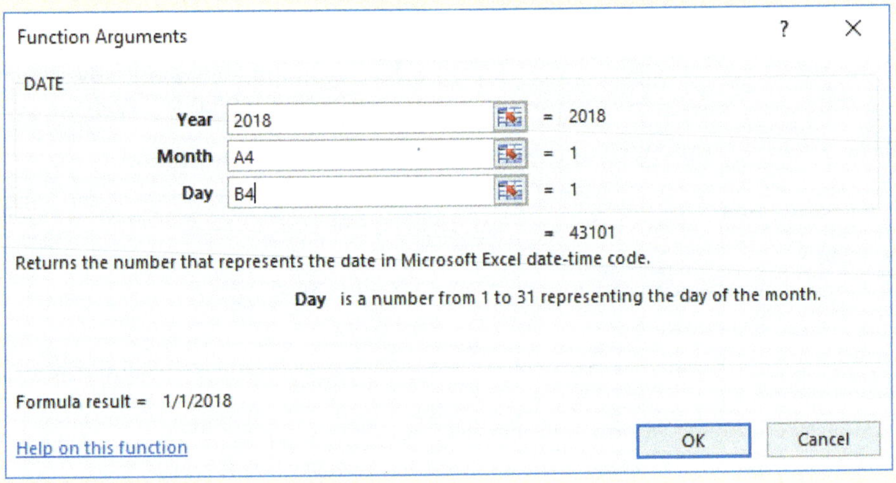

Excel 2016, Windows 10, Microsoft Corporation

Calculating Work Days

- Serialized dates and times can easily be used in calculations, just like other numbers, because they *are* numbers. For example, when two cells contain dates, subtracting one cell's value from the other returns the number of days between them.
- When you are planning a project, you might want to differentiate dates that fall on certain days of the week. For example, you might not want to schedule workers on weekends or holidays.
- The **WORKDAY function** returns the date that is a specified number of **workdays** before or after the specified date. It skips over dates that fall on a Saturday or a Sunday.
- You can optionally also have WORKDAY skip over any holiday dates. You must manually specify the holiday dates in an optional argument if you want them included.
- Not everyone's weekend is on Saturday and Sunday. You can use the WORKDAY.INTL function instead of WORKDAY if you need the weekends to be different days; this function is just like WORKDAY except it contains an additional argument for choosing the weekend days.

Try It! Calculating Work Days

1. In the **E62Try_xx** file, click the Calculator worksheet tab.
2. Click cell B4, type **1/20/2018**, and press ENTER.
3. In cell B5, type **120**, and press ENTER.
4. In cell B6, type **=WORKDAY(**, and click the Insert Function button *fx* on the formula bar.
5. In the Start_date box, type **B4**.
6. In the Days box, type **B5**.
7. Click the Select Cells icon for the Holidays box to minimize the dialog box.
8. Click the Holidays tab, select the range C4:C14, and press ENTER to return to the dialog box.

(continued)

Try It! Calculating Work Days *(continued)*

9. Click OK.
10. Click cell B6 and on the Home tab, click the drop-down arrow in the Number group and click Short Date.
11. Click cell B7 and type **14**.
12. Click cell B8, type **=B6+B7**, and press ENTER .
13. Save the changes to the file, and leave it open to use in the next Try It.

Function arguments for the WORKDAY function

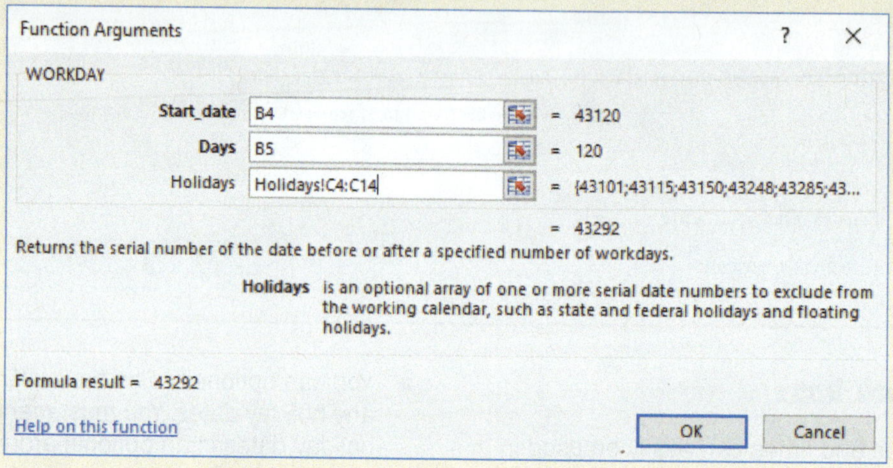

Excel 2016, Windows 10, Microsoft Corporation

Determining the Day of the Week

- It may sometimes be useful to know the day of the week that a particular date falls on. You can calculate this with the **WEEKDAY function**.
- The Weekday function returns a number between 1 and 7. By default, Sunday is represented by 1, and Saturday by 7.
- Because the text version of the days of the week is more intuitive for humans than the number, you might want to convert the number into the text equivalent for display on your worksheet.
- To show the number as a text day of the week, apply a custom format for the cell, setting the custom format to ddd (for an abbreviated version of the day, such as Mon) or dddd (for the full day, such as Monday).

Try It! Determining the Day of the Week

1. In the **E62Try_xx** file, on the Calculator worksheet, click in cell C4.
2. Type **=WEEKDAY(B4)** and press ENTER .
3. Click cell C4 and on the Home tab, click the dialog box launcher for the Number group.
4. Click Custom.
5. In the Type box, type **dddd**.
6. Click OK.
7. Click cell C4 and press CTRL + C to copy it.
8. Click cell C6 and press CTRL + V to paste the function.
9. Click cell C8 and press CTRL + V to paste the function.
10. Save the changes to the file and Exit Excel.

(continued)

Try It! Determining the Day of the Week *(continued)*

Applying a custom number format

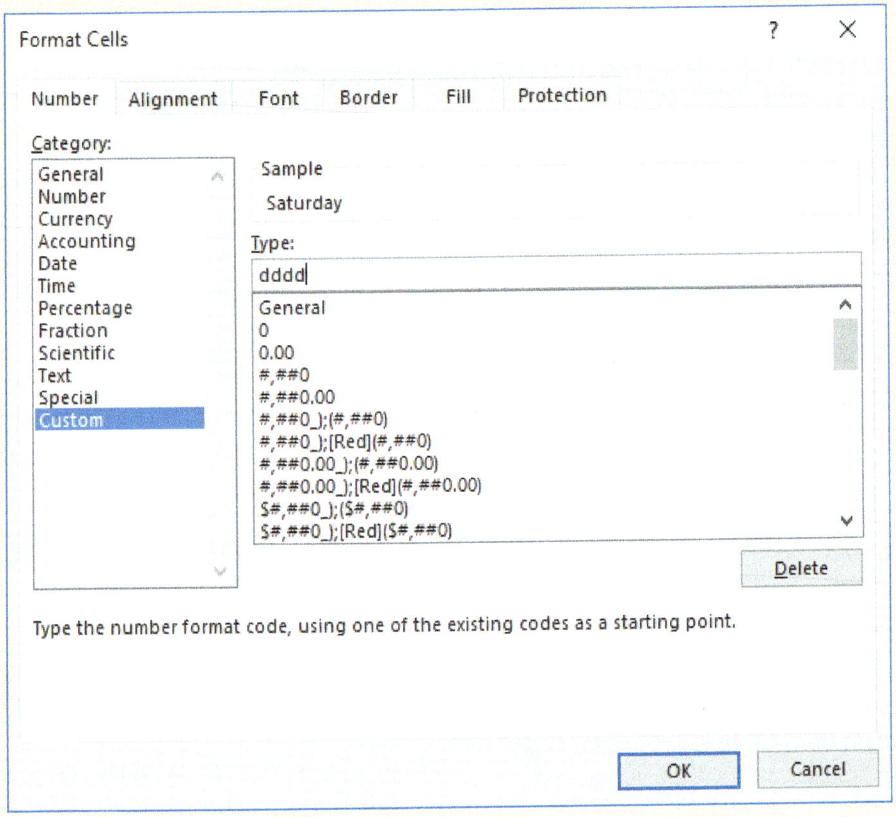

Excel 2016, Windows 10, Microsoft Corporation

Lesson 62—Practice

You have been tasked with calculating the hours worked for each employee each day at Pete's Pets for a one-week period. First, however, you must convert some of the data to serialized dates and times.

DIRECTIONS

1. Start Excel, and open the **E62Practice** file from the data files for this lesson.
2. Save the workbook as **E62Practice_xx** in the location where your teacher instructs you to store the files for this lesson.
3. Insert a header that has your name at the left, the date code in the center, and the page number code at the right, and change back to **Normal** view.
4. Click in cell **B1**. Type **=TODAY()** and press Enter.
5. Use Find and Replace to change all instances of December to 12.
   a. Press CTRL + H to open the Find and Replace dialog box.
   b. In the Find what box, type **December**.
   c. In the Replace with box, type **12**.
   d. Click **Replace All**. Then click **OK** and then **Close**.

6. Convert the months and days in columns B and C to a single Date column with serialized dates.
   a. Select column **D** and click **Home** > **Insert** to create a new column.
   b. Click in cell **D6**, and type **=DATE(2018,B6,C6)**.
   c. Copy the function from **D6** to **D7:D8**, **D10:D12**, **D14:D16**, **D18:D20**, and **D22:D24** using any method you like.
   d. Select the range **D6:D24** and press CTRL + C to copy it to the Clipboard.
   e. Click in cell **B6**.
   f. Click the down arrow on the **Paste button** on the Home tab.
   g. On the Paste button's menu, in the **Paste Values** section, click **Values & Number Formatting**.
   h. Select columns C and D and click **Home** > **Delete**.
   i. Click in **B5** and type **Date**, replacing the previous text there.
7. In column C, use the WEEKDAY function to show the days of the week represented by the dates in column B.
   a. Click in cell **C6** and type **=WEEKDAY(B6)**.
   b. Copy the function from C6 to **C7:C8**, **C10:C12**, **C14:C16**, **C18:C20**, and **C22:C24** using any method you like.
8. Apply a custom number format to C6:C24 that shows the week days in the ddd format.
   a. Select **C6:C24**.
   b. On the Home tab, click the **dialog box launcher** in the Number group.
   c. Click **Custom**.
   d. In the Type box, type **ddd**.
   e. Click **OK**.
9. Click in cell A1 and then use Find and Replace to replace all instances of a.m. with AM, and all instances of p.m. with PM so that Excel will see the entries as dates.
   a. Press CTRL + H to open the Find and Replace dialog box.
   b. In the Find what box, type **a.m**.
   c. In the Replace with box, type **AM**.
   d. Click **Replace All**.
   e. Click **OK**.
   f. In the Find what box, type **p.m**.
   g. In the Replace with box, type **PM**.
   h. Click **Replace All**.
   i. Click **OK**, and then click **Close**.
10. In column F, use the HOUR function to calculate the hours worked for each employee on each day.
    a. Click in cell **F6**, and type **=HOUR(E6-D6)** and press Enter.
    b. Copy the function from F6 to **F7:F8**, **F10:F12**, **F14:F16**, **F18:F20**, and **F22:F24** using any method you like.

    ✓ *Notice that it doesn't show the minutes as a decimal of the hour. It shows 0 rather than the expected 2.5. That's because the HOUR function deals only in whole hours.*
11. In column G, use the MINUTE function to show the number of minutes left over after calculating the hours.
    a. Click in cell **G5** and type **Minutes**.
    b. Select the range **F1:F5**, click **Home** > **Format Painter**, and drag to copy the formatting to **G1:G5**.
    c. Click in cell **G6** and type **=MINUTE(E6-D6)**.
    d. Copy the function from G6 to **G7:G8**, **G10:G12**, **G14:G16**, **G18:G20**, and **G22:G24** using any method you like. The completed worksheet should look like Figure 62-1 on the next page.
12. **With your teacher's permission**, print the worksheet.
13. Save and close the file, and exit Excel.

Figure 62-1

	A	B	C	D	E	F	G
1	Last Updated:	4/26/2016					
2	Pete's Pets						
3	Employee Schedule			Week of	12/2/2018		
4							
5	Employee	Date	Weekday	Start Time	End Time	Hours	Minutes
6	Kim Franklin	12/2/2018	Sun	9:00 AM	11:30 AM	2.0	30
7	Otto Smythe	12/2/2018	Sun	11:15 AM	5:00 PM	5.0	45
8	Gordon Pyatt	12/2/2018	Sun	4:45 PM	9:00 PM	4.0	15
9							
10	Kim Franklin	12/3/2018	Mon	8:00 AM	12:30 PM	4.0	30
11	Otto Smythe	12/3/2018	Mon	12:15 PM	5:00 PM	4.0	45
12	Rodney Plappert	12/3/2018	Mon	4:45 PM	9:00 PM	4.0	15
13							
14	Otto Smythe	12/4/2018	Tue	9:00 AM	12:30 PM	3.0	30
15	Gordon Pyatt	12/4/2018	Tue	12:15 PM	5:00 PM	4.0	45
16	Todd Dornan	12/4/2018	Tue	4:45 PM	9:00 PM	4.0	15
17							
18	Gordon Pyatt	12/5/2018	Wed	8:00 AM	12:30 PM	4.0	30
19	Rodney Plappert	12/5/2018	Wed	12:15 PM	5:00 PM	4.0	45
20	Todd Dornan	12/5/2018	Wed	4:45 PM	10:00 PM	5.0	15
21							
22	Kim Franklin	12/6/2018	Thu	9:00 AM	12:30 PM	3.0	30
23	Rodney Plappert	12/6/2018	Thu	12:15 PM	5:00 PM	4.0	45
24	Todd Dornan	12/6/2018	Thu	4:45 PM	10:00 PM	5.0	15

Lesson 62—Apply

At Marco's Bistro, the staff's "weekend" is Monday and Tuesday, the days when the restaurant is closed. As the staffing manager, you are responsible for scheduling employee work shifts. In this project you'll use several date and time functions to calculate staffing hours and determine which dates the restaurant will be open.

Directions

1. Start Excel, and open the **E62Apply** file from the data files for this lesson.
2. Save the workbook as **E62Apply_*xx*** in the location where your teacher instructs you to store the files for this lesson.
3. Insert a header that has your name at the left, the date code in the center, and the page number code at the right, and change back to **Normal** view.
4. In cells **B15:B19**, use the **HOUR** function to calculate the number of hours the restaurant is open each day, by referencing the Open and Close times in **B5:C11**.
5. In cells **D15:D19**, create formulas that multiply the hours open (column B) by the employees per hour (column C).
6. In **G5:G34**, use the **IF** function display either "Open" or "Closed" depending on the weekday represented by the corresponding date in **column F**. The sheet should look like Figure 62-2 on the next page.

✓ *There are many different ways to accomplish step 6. For example, you could nest the WEEKDAY function in the IF function to evaluate whether the day of the week represented by the date in column F is one of the days the restaurant is closed (2 or 3). You could use two IF functions, one nested inside the other, or you could use an OR function to evaluate the two conditions.*

7. **With your teacher's permission**, print the worksheet.
8. Save your work and exit Excel.

Figure 62-2

Marco's Bistro

Weekday	Open	Close
Sunday	11:00 AM	10:00 PM
Monday	CLOSED	
Tuesday	CLOSED	
Wednesday	10:00 AM	10:00 PM
Thursday	10:00 AM	10:00 PM
Friday	10:00 AM	10:00 PM
Saturday	10:00 AM	10:00 PM

	Hours Open	Employees Per Hour	Staffing Hours
Sunday	11	7	77
Wednesday	12	5	60
Thursday	12	5	60
Friday	12	8	96
Saturday	12	8	96

Date	Open/Closed
6/1/2018	Open
6/2/2018	Open
6/3/2018	Open
6/4/2018	Closed
6/5/2018	Closed
6/6/2018	Open
6/7/2018	Open
6/8/2018	Open
6/9/2018	Open
6/10/2018	Open
6/11/2018	Closed
6/12/2018	Closed
6/13/2018	Open
6/14/2018	Open
6/15/2018	Open
6/16/2018	Open
6/17/2018	Open
6/18/2018	Closed
6/19/2018	Closed
6/20/2018	Open
6/21/2018	Open
6/22/2018	Open
6/23/2018	Open
6/24/2018	Open
6/25/2018	Closed
6/26/2018	Closed
6/27/2018	Open
6/28/2018	Open
6/29/2018	Open
6/30/2018	Open

Lesson 63

Working with Absolute References and Using Financial Functions

➤ What You Will Learn

Using Absolute, Relative, and Mixed References
Enabling Iterative Calculations
Using Financial Functions

Software Skills Usually when you create a function, the cell references are relative. When you copy the function to another cell, the cell references change in relation to the new location. Sometimes, though, you may not want the cell reference to change. In cases like that, you need an absolute reference. Excel enables you to create relative, absolute, or mixed references as needed. Absolute references come in handy when you are creating functions that calculate interest rates, payments, loan periods, and other financial information.

What You Can Do

Using Absolute, Relative, and Mixed References

- When you create a formula and then copy or move the formula, a **relative reference** changes to reflect the new position.
- For example, in Figure 63-1 on the next page, cell D3 contains the formula =B3+C3. If you copy that formula to cell D4, it will automatically change to =B4+C4. It increments the row number by one because the copy is being placed one row below the original.
- Cell references are relative by default in Excel; you do not need to do anything special to create a relative cell reference.
- An **absolute reference** to a cell locks the cell's reference when the formula is moved or copied. Absolute references are created by placing a dollar sign ($) before both the row and the column of the cell reference, like this: $B$3.

WORDS TO KNOW

Absolute reference
A cell reference that remains fixed when copied to another cell.

Circular reference
When a formula in Excel refers to the cell that contains the formula, either directly or indirectly.

FV
The Future Value function. Calculates the future value of an investment when given the rate, the number of periods, and the payment amount.

Iterative calculation
A repeated calculation.

Mixed reference
A cell reference in which the row is absolute and the column is relative, or vice-versa.

NPER
The Number of Periods function. Calculates the number of payments on a loan when given the rate, payment amount, and present value.

PMT
The Payment function. Calculates a payment when given the rate, number of periods, and present value.

PV
The Present Value function. Calculates the present value of an investment when given rate, number of periods, and payment amount.

Relative reference
A cell reference that changes when copied to another cell. The default setting.

Figure 63-1

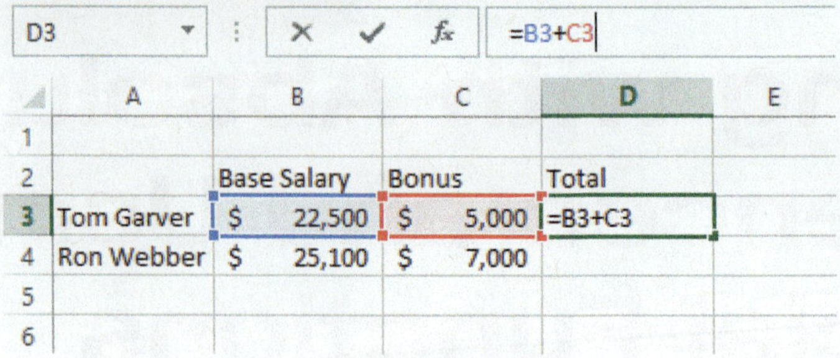

Excel 2016, Windows 10, Microsoft Corporation

- For example, in Figure 63-2, in cell C5, the following formula appears: =B5+$B$1. If you copy that formula to cell C6, the reference to B5 will change because it is relative, but the reference to B1 will not because it is absolute. The resulting formula in cell C6 will be =B6+$B$1.

Figure 63-2

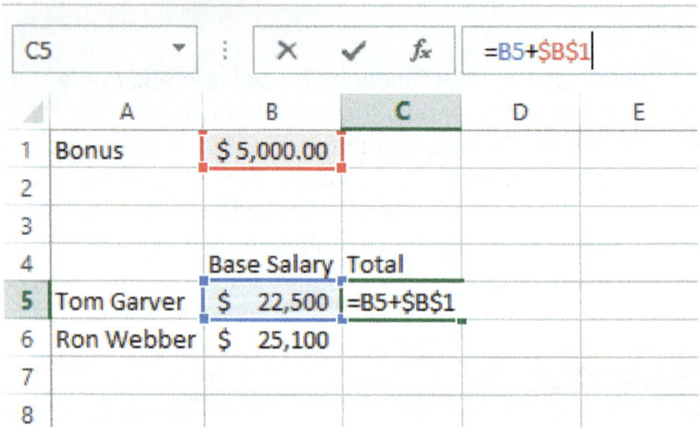

Excel 2016, Windows 10, Microsoft Corporation

- A **mixed reference** is one in which only one dimension is absolute. For example, $B1 locks the column but not the row, and B$1 locks the row but not the column.
- To create absolute or mixed references, you can manually type the dollar signs into the formulas in the appropriate places.
- You can also toggle a cell reference among all the possible combinations of absolute, relative, and mixed by pressing F4 when the insertion point is within the cell reference.

Try It! Using Absolute References

1. Start Excel, and open **E63Try** from the data files for this lesson.
2. Save the file as **E63Try_xx** in the location where your teacher instructs you to store the files for this lesson.
3. On the Taxes worksheet, click cell H3, type **=G3*$A$18**, and press ENTER.
4. Click cell H3, and press CTRL + C to copy the formula to the Clipboard.
5. Select the cell range H4:H15, and press CTRL + V to paste the formula into those cells.
6. Browse the contents of several of the pasted cells to confirm that the reference to A18 remained absolute.
7. Save the changes to the file, and leave it open to use in the next Try It.

The reference to the Total is relative; the reference to the Tax rate is absolute

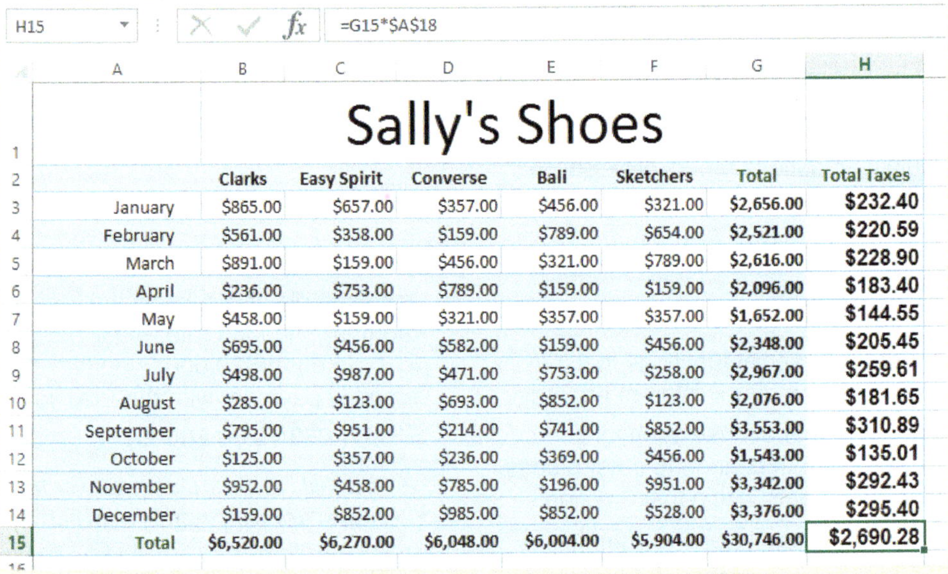

H15 =G15*$A$18

	A	B	C	D	E	F	G	H
1		Sally's Shoes						
2		Clarks	Easy Spirit	Converse	Bali	Sketchers	Total	Total Taxes
3	January	$865.00	$657.00	$357.00	$456.00	$321.00	$2,656.00	$232.40
4	February	$561.00	$358.00	$159.00	$789.00	$654.00	$2,521.00	$220.59
5	March	$891.00	$159.00	$456.00	$321.00	$789.00	$2,616.00	$228.90
6	April	$236.00	$753.00	$789.00	$159.00	$159.00	$2,096.00	$183.40
7	May	$458.00	$159.00	$321.00	$357.00	$357.00	$1,652.00	$144.55
8	June	$695.00	$456.00	$582.00	$159.00	$456.00	$2,348.00	$205.45
9	July	$498.00	$987.00	$471.00	$753.00	$258.00	$2,967.00	$259.61
10	August	$285.00	$123.00	$693.00	$852.00	$123.00	$2,076.00	$181.65
11	September	$795.00	$951.00	$214.00	$741.00	$852.00	$3,553.00	$310.89
12	October	$125.00	$357.00	$236.00	$369.00	$456.00	$1,543.00	$135.01
13	November	$952.00	$458.00	$785.00	$196.00	$951.00	$3,342.00	$292.43
14	December	$159.00	$852.00	$985.00	$852.00	$528.00	$3,376.00	$295.40
15	Total	$6,520.00	$6,270.00	$6,048.00	$6,004.00	$5,904.00	$30,746.00	$2,690.28

Excel 2016, Windows 10, Microsoft Corporation

Try It! Using Mixed References

1. In the **E63Try_xx** file, click the Area worksheet tab.
2. In cell C5, type **=$B5*C$4**, and press ENTER.
3. Click cell C5, and drag the fill handle down to fill the cell range C6:C9 with the formula.
4. Click in any filled cell, and look at the formula bar. Notice that the relative references changed, and that the absolute references remained the same.
5. Copy the formula from cell C5 into the remainder of the range (through cell F9).
6. Save the changes to the file, and leave it open to use in the next Try It.

Enabling Iterative Calculations

- Before you work with financial functions that may have a **circular reference**, it is helpful to enable **iterative calculations**. This means that you will be able to work with a formula that refers to a cell that contains that formula.
- You can access the Calculation options in the Formulas tab of the Excel Options settings.
- You can control the maximum number of iterations that Excel performs.
- You can also control the amount of acceptable change, or precision, that you need before Excel finishes the calculation.
- Be careful when setting calculation options because they will apply to all open workbooks.
- When you save a workbook, Excel saves the calculation setting that was applied when the workbook was open.
- When you open workbooks, Excel will apply the calculation settings of the first workbook you open.
- For example, if you first open workbook A (which had iteration disabled when it was last saved) and then open Workbook B (with iteration enabled when it was last saved), Excel will keep iteration disabled.

Try It! Enabling Iterative Calculations

1. In the E63Try_xx file, click File > Options.
2. In the Excel Options dialog box, click Formulas.
3. In the Calculations options group, click Enable iterative calculation to select the check box.
4. Click OK to close the Excel Options dialog box.
5. Save the changes to the file, and leave it open to use in the next Try It.

Using Financial Functions

- Excel includes a set of financial functions that can calculate variables in a loan or investment equation.
- They are considered a set because each function solves for a particular variable, and the other pieces of information are arguments within that function.

Function	Purpose	Required Arguments	Optional Arguments
PMT	Calculates a loan payment	RATE, NPER, PV,	FV, TYPE
RATE	Calculates a loan rate	NPER, PMT, PV	FV, TYPE, GUESS
NPER	Calculates the number of periods in a loan	RATE, PMT, PV	FV, TYPE
PV	Calculates the present value (beginning balance)	RATE, NPER, PMT	FV, TYPE
FV	Calculates the future value (ending balance)	RATE, NPER, PMT	PV, TYPE

- For example, if you know the loan length (60 months), the loan rate (5.9% per year), and the loan amount ($20,000), you can calculate your monthly payment with the PMT function:

  =PMT(.059/12,60,20000)

  ✓ *Note that you divide the interest rate by 12 because the interest rate is per year, and a payment is made monthly.*

- Alternatively, suppose you want to know how much money you can afford to borrow at 7% interest for 60 months if you can pay $250 a month:

  =PV(0.07/12,60,250)

- To find out how much an investment made now will be worth later, such as buying a savings bond, use the FV function. For example, suppose you buy a $10,000 savings bond that pays 5% interest, is compounded monthly, and matures in 20 years:

  =FV(0.05/12,20*12,0,10000)

  ✓ *The third argument (PMT) is 0 because you don't make any payments after the initial investment of $10,000.*

- In actual usage, you would probably want to put those values into cells, and then reference the cells in the functions rather than hard-coding the actual numbers in. That way, you could change the variables and see different results without modifying the functions themselves.

Try It! Using Financial Functions

1. In the E63Try_xx file, click the Functions worksheet tab.
2. In cell B3, type 60,000.
3. In cell B4, type .065.
4. In cell B5, type 1.
5. In cell B6, type 60.
6. In cell B8, type =PMT(B4/12,-B6,B3).

   ✓ *Notice the – preceding B6; this is to make the value negative, so the result in B8 will be positive.*

7. In cell B12, type =PV(B13/12,B15,-B17).

   ✓ *B17 is referred to as a negative so the formula result will be positive. The same is true for B26 in step 8.*

8. In cell B32, type =FV(B31,B28*B29,,-B26).

   ✓ *Notice that there are two commas in a row in this function because the PMT argument is blank.*

9. Save and close the file, and exit Excel.

Lesson 63—Practice

The manager at Sally's Shoes wants to analyze the potential revenue from various sales scenarios per month. She knows that women want to purchase shoes for a lower price, but a few people want the high-end style and are willing to pay the price for a unique designer shoe. Should the manager focus on more customers purchasing lower priced shoes, or on fewer customers purchasing higher priced shoes? You have been tasked with creating a worksheet to analyze the potential revenue from these scenarios. In this project, you will use references and formulas to calculate the data.

DIRECTIONS

1. Start Excel, if necessary, and open E63Practice from the data files for this lesson.
2. Save the file as E63Practice_xx in the location where your teacher instructs you to store the files for this lesson.
3. Add a custom header that has your name at the left, the date code in the center, and the page number code at the right.
4. Click File > Options > Formulas, and click the Enable iterative calculations check box to select it, if necessary.
5. In cell C5, type =$B5*C$4.
6. Use the Fill feature to fill in the rest of the sales data, down to cell F9.
7. Select cells A3:F9, and press CTRL + C to copy.
8. Click in cell A13, and press CTRL + V to paste.
9. Change the values in cells C14:F14 to 35, 50, 75, and 100, from left to right.
10. Edit the formula in cell C15 to =$B15*C$14.
11. Copy the formula from cell C15 into the rest of the sales data, replacing the previous values in each cell.
12. **With your teacher's permission**, print the worksheet. Your worksheet should look like the one shown in Figure 63-3.
13. Save and close the file, and exit Excel.

Figure 63-3

Sally's Shoes

	Price Points			
	$45	$65	$85	$125
50	2,250.00	3,250.00	4,250.00	6,250.00
75	3,375.00	4,875.00	6,375.00	9,375.00
100	4,500.00	6,500.00	8,500.00	12,500.00
125	5,625.00	8,125.00	10,625.00	15,625.00
150	6,750.00	9,750.00	12,750.00	18,750.00

Number of Sales

	Price Points			
	$35	$50	$75	$100
50	1,750.00	2,500.00	3,750.00	5,000.00
75	2,625.00	3,750.00	5,625.00	7,500.00
100	3,500.00	5,000.00	7,500.00	10,000.00
125	4,375.00	6,250.00	9,375.00	12,500.00
150	5,250.00	7,500.00	11,250.00	15,000.00

Number of Sales

Lesson 63—Apply

You are helping the manager at Sally's Shoes analyze the potential revenue from various sales scenarios per month. Sales have been very high so far this year and the manager is considering expanding the business. In this project, you will use financial functions to analyze loan scenarios for expanding the business.

DIRECTIONS

1. Start Excel, if necessary, and open **E63Apply** from the data files for this lesson.
2. Save the file as **E63Apply_xx** in the location where your teacher instructs you to store the files for this lesson.
3. Add a custom header that has your name at the left, the date code in the center, and the page number code at the right.
4. Click **File** > **Options** > **Formulas**, and click the **Enable iterative calculations** check box to select it, if necessary.
5. In the Payment Calculation grid, calculate what the payment would be on a four-year loan of **$30,000** with a monthly interest rate of **5.25%**. Fill the numbers for the calculation into cells **B4:B6**, and reference those cells in a function in cell **B7**.
   ✓ *Make the reference to the present value negative, so that the amount in cell B7 is positive.*
6. In the Present Value Calculation grid, calculate the present value of a loan with **$800** in monthly payments at **4.35%** interest rate for **360** months.
   ✓ *Make the reference to the payment amount negative, so that the amount in cell B11 is positive.*

7. In the Compound Interest Calculation grid, calculate the future value (FV) of an investment of **$4,000** with a **3.25%** interest rate, compounded monthly, for **5** years.

   ✓ *Make the reference to the present value amount negative, so that the amount in cell B23 is positive.*

   ✓ *The periodic interest rate is the annual interest rate (B19) divided by the number of compounding periods per year (B20).*

8. **With your teacher's permission**, print the worksheet. Your worksheet should look like the one shown in Figure 63-4.
9. Save and close the file, and exit Excel.

Figure 63-4

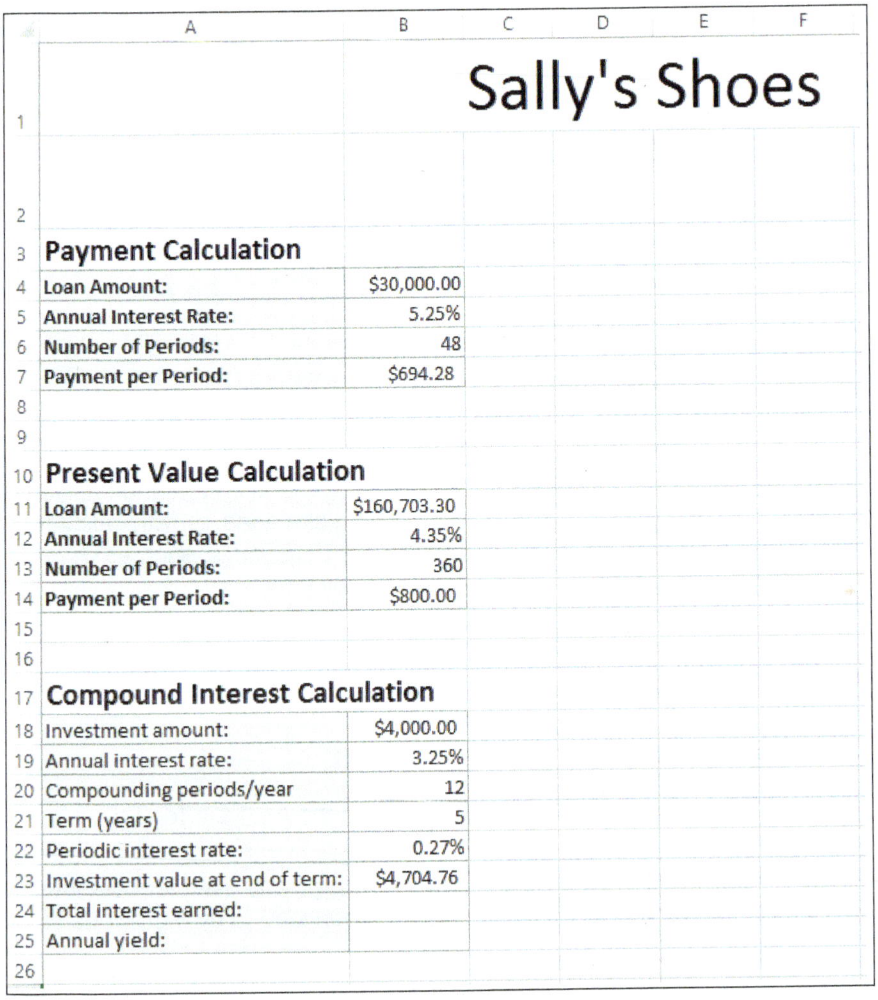

	A	B	C	D	E	F
1	Sally's Shoes					
2						
3	**Payment Calculation**					
4	**Loan Amount:**	$30,000.00				
5	**Annual Interest Rate:**	5.25%				
6	**Number of Periods:**	48				
7	**Payment per Period:**	$694.28				
8						
9						
10	**Present Value Calculation**					
11	**Loan Amount:**	$160,703.30				
12	**Annual Interest Rate:**	4.35%				
13	**Number of Periods:**	360				
14	**Payment per Period:**	$800.00				
15						
16						
17	**Compound Interest Calculation**					
18	Investment amount:	$4,000.00				
19	Annual interest rate:	3.25%				
20	Compounding periods/year	12				
21	Term (years)	5				
22	Periodic interest rate:	0.27%				
23	Investment value at end of term:	$4,704.76				
24	Total interest earned:					
25	Annual yield:					
26						

Excel 2016, Windows 10, Microsoft Corporation

Lesson 64

Creating and Interpreting Financial Statements

➤ What You Will Learn

Loading the Analysis ToolPak Add-On
Calculating a Moving Average
Calculating Growth Based on a Moving Average
Charting the Break-Even Point with a Line Chart
Using Goal Seek

WORDS TO KNOW

Break-even point
The number of units, or individual items, you must sell to begin making a profit, given your fixed costs for the unit, cost per unit, and revenue per unit.

Goal Seek
A method of performing what-if analysis in which the result (the goal) is known, but the value of a single dependent variable is unknown.

Moving average
A sequence of averages computed from parts of a data series. In a chart, a moving average corrects for the fluctuations in data, showing the pattern or trend more clearly.

Variable
An input value that changes depending on the desired outcome.

What-if analysis
Excel's term for a series of tools that perform calculations involving one or more variables.

Software Skills Excel contains more financial capabilities than just simple loan and investment calculation. You can use Excel to create and analyze financial statements and scenarios that include moving averages, growth calculations, and income and expense projections. You can use Excel tools, such as Goal Seek, to perform what-if analysis.

What You Can Do

Loading the Analysis ToolPak Add-On

- To use Excel's analysis features, you need the Analysis ToolPak, which is not loaded by default.
- If you are working on a PC in a lab that is regularly used for computer classes, the Analysis ToolPak may have already been loaded by a previous student.

Try It! Determining Whether the Analysis ToolPak Add-On Is Loaded

1. Start Excel, and open **E64Try** from the data files for this lesson.
2. Save the file as **E64Try_xx** in the location where your teacher instructs you to store the files for this lesson.
3. Click the Data tab.
4. Look for an Analysis group, with a Data Analysis command in it. If you don't see it, the Analysis Toolpak is not loaded.

Try It! Loading the Analysis ToolPak Add-On

1. In Excel, click File > Options.
2. Click Add-Ins.
3. At the bottom of the dialog box, confirm that Manage is set to Excel Add-ins, and click Go.
4. In the Add-Ins dialog box, click the Analysis ToolPak check box to select it.
5. Click OK.
6. On the Data tab, confirm that there is now an Analysis group with a Data Analysis command.
7. Leave Excel open to use in the next Try It.

Calculating a Moving Average

- A **moving average** is considered more accurate than a simple average of a set of numbers in predicting future trends. A moving average is used with data that represents changes over time to smooth out short-term fluctuations and highlight the long-term trends.
- To calculate a moving average, start with a subset of the data (for example, items 1–20 in a 100-item list) and calculate their average. That average becomes the first data point. Then you calculate the average of items 2–21 on the list, and that average becomes the second data point. You progress through the entire list until you have a complete set of data points.
- Calculating a moving average would be very labor-intensive by hand, so it makes sense to use a program like Excel to do the calculations.
- Excel's Moving Average data analysis tool makes the process easy. You can specify how many numbers to use in the averaging calculation.

Try It! Calculating a Moving Average

1. In the **E64Try_xx** file, click the Moving Average worksheet tab, if necessary.

   ✓ *This data represents the share price of mutual funds for a month.*

2. On the Data tab, in the Analysis group, click Data Analysis to open the Data Analysis dialog box.
3. In the Analysis Tools list, click Moving Average > OK.
4. In the Moving Average dialog box, in the Input Range box, type **A2:A31**.

   ✓ *You can also click the Collapse Dialog Box button next to Input Range, and select the desired range.*

(continued)

Try It! Calculating a Moving Average *(continued)*

5. In the Interval box, type **5**. This tells Excel how many numbers to average for one output.
6. In the Output Range box, type **B2:B31**.

   ✓ *You can also click the Collapse Dialog Box button next to Output Range, and select the desired range.*

7. Click the Chart Output check box to select it.
8. Click OK. A line chart is generated from the raw data and the moving average data.
9. Click in the chart area to select it, and drag a corner to make the chart larger.
10. To see how the moving average works, click cell B8. In the formula bar, the formula =AVERAGE(A4:A8) shows that the average is of the data in cells A4, A5, A6, A7, and A8.
11. Save the changes to the file, and leave it open to use in the next Try It.

Enter the specifications for the moving average calculation

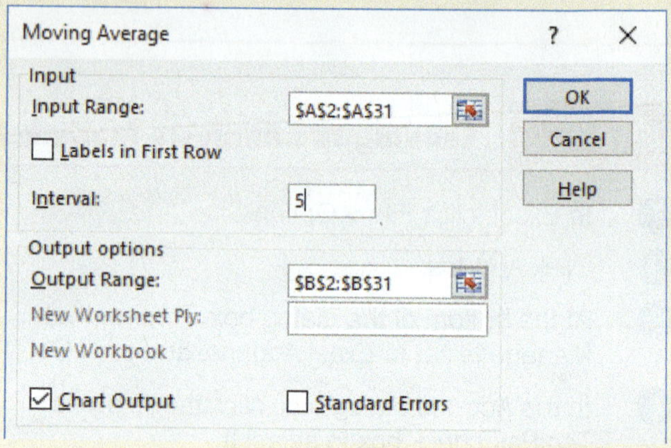

Excel 2016, Windows 10, Microsoft Corporation

Calculating Growth Based on a Moving Average

- When you have historical data, it is possible to predict what might happen in the future. You can use the GROWTH function to analyze a pattern of data from the past and create a new pattern of data for the future.
- The GROWTH function creates a statistical prediction for the future that can be used to compare actual data with what you predicted.

✓ *It is best to base the predictions you create with the GROWTH function on stable and reliable known data.*

- The GROWTH function arguments are [known-y], [known-x], [new known-x].
  - Known-x is the known original data.
  - Known-y is the past output based on the known-x values.
  - New known-x is the known new data.
- Given that information, the GROWTH function will predict the future output based on the new known-x values.

Try It! Calculating Growth Based on a Moving Average

1. In the **E64Try_xx** file, click the Growth worksheet tab.
2. Examine the data in the worksheet and note the following:
   - The data in column A represents days of the month. The cell range A2:A16 is the first half of the month (the known-x), and the cell range A19:A33 is the second half of the month (the new known-x).
   - The data in the cell range B2:B16 is moving average data for the first half of the month (the known-y).
   - The GROWTH function will be used to predict the moving averages to be placed in the cell range B19:B33.
3. Click cell B19, and type **=GROWTH(**.
4. For the first argument, drag across cells B2:B6 to select that range, and type a comma (**,**) to separate the arguments.

(continued)

Try It! Calculating Growth Based on a Moving Average *(continued)*

5. For the second argument, drag across the cell range A2:A6, and type a comma (,) to separate the arguments.
6. For the third argument, drag across the cell range A19:A23. This represents 5 days that will be used to predict future growth.
7. Press ENTER to complete the function. The final function in cell B19 should be =GROWTH(B2:B6,A2:A6,A19:A23).
8. Copy the formula in cell B19 into the cell range B20:B33.

✓ *Notice that starting at cell B30 an error message displays, #VALUE!. That's because the GROWTH formula in cell B30 refers to data in cell A34, and there is no data in cell A34.*

9. Select the cell range B30:B33, and press DEL to clear the content of those cells.

✓ *Based on the mutual fund's moving average growth experienced from the first of the month to the fifteenth of the month, you can predict that by the end of the month the mutual fund will be at the value shown in cell B29.*

10. Save the changes to the file, and leave it open to use in the next Try It.

Charting the Break-Even Point with a Line Chart

- You can enter your known costs and your projected income from sales to calculate when your revenue will exceed your costs, the **break-even point**.
- You can create a break-even line chart based on known expenses and projected income.
- This calculation can help you analyze finances to know how much you need to sell in order to make a profit, as well as how much more you need to sell in order to make a pre-determined profit amount.

Try It! Charting the Break-Even Point with a Line Chart

1. In the **E64Try_xx** file, click the Break-Even worksheet tab.
2. In cell B1, type **100**.
3. In cell B2, type **1**.
4. In cell B3, type **6**.
5. In cell B6, type **=A6*$B$2+$B$1**.

   ✓ *Notice the absolute references to cells B1 and B2.*

6. Copy the formula in cell B6 to cells B7:B30. Cell B30 should show $125.00.
7. In cell C6, type **=A6*$B$3**.
8. Copy the formula in cell C6 to cells C7:C30. Cell C30 should show $150.00.
9. In cell D6, type **=C6-B6**.
10. Copy the formula in cell D6 to cells D7:D30. Cell D30 should show $25.00.
11. Select the cell range B5:D30, and click Insert > Insert Line or Area Chart > Stacked Line (the second chart in the 2-D Line section).

    ✓ *The point where the Profit and Revenue lines cross is the break-even point.*

12. Click the chart to select it, and drag it so its top left corner aligns with cell F5.
13. Save the changes to the file, and leave it open to use in the next Try It.

Using Goal Seek

- You can use **Goal Seek** to perform **what-if analysis** when you know the result (the goal), but not the value of one of the input **variables** (the variables that create the result).
- For example, you could use Goal Seek to determine the exact amount you need to borrow at 8.25% interest to keep the payment at $1,000 per month.
- Access the Goal Seek analysis tool from the What-If Analysis button in the Data Tools group on the Data tab.
- When you input the known variables into the Goal Seek Status dialog box, the tool will show whether it found a solution and, if so, the solution. It will also change the values on the worksheet.

Try It! Using Goal Seek to Perform What-If Analysis

1. In the **E64Try_xx** file, click the Goal Seek tab.
2. Click Data > What-If Analysis > Goal Seek.
3. In the Goal Seek dialog box, in the Set cell box, type **B8**. This is the location of the input variable you know, payment per period.
4. In the To value box, type **750**. This is the value of the input variable you know; you want to pay $750 per month.
5. In the By changing cell box, type **B3**.
6. Click OK. Goal Seek finds a solution for the loan amount you need to borrow.
7. In the Goal Seek Status dialog box, click OK to accept the solution.
8. Save and close the file, and exit Excel

Entering variables in Goal Seek

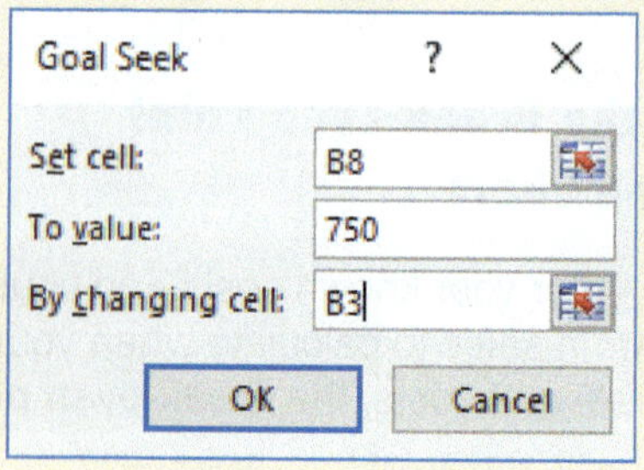

Excel 2016, Windows 10, Microsoft Corporation

Lesson 64—Practice

The owner of Best Movies Theater has asked you to analyze the attendance of his theater. He wants you to create a report to show actual and forecasted attendance. In this project, you will use Excel functions to calculate a moving average of the attendance of the theater.

DIRECTIONS

1. Start Excel, if necessary, and open **E64Practice** from the data files for this lesson.
2. Save the file as **E64Practice_xx** in the location where your teacher instructs you to store the files for this lesson.
3. Add a header that has your name at the left, the date code in the center, and the page number code at the right, and change back to **Normal** view.
4. Check that the Data Analysis command is on the Data tab, and enable the Analysis ToolPak, if necessary.
   a. Click **File** > **Options** > **Add-Ins**.
   b. Confirm that Manage is set to **Excel Add-ins**, and click **Go**.
   c. In the Add-Ins dialog box, click the **Analysis ToolPak** check box to select it, and click **OK**.
5. Select **Data** > **Data Analysis** to open the Data Analysis dialog box.

6. Click **Moving Average** > **OK**.
7. In the Input box, type **A2:A31**.
8. In the Interval box, type **7**.
9. In the Output box, type **B2:B31**.
10. Click the **Chart Output** check box, if necessary.
11. Click **OK**.
12. Drag the lower-right corner of the chart frame to enlarge the chart so it is more readable.

    ✓ *You can delete the function from cells B2:B7 when finished; they show an #N/A error rather than a value. This is expected.*

13. **With your teacher's permission,** print the chart. Your chart should look like the one shown in Figure 64-1.
14. Save and close the file, and exit Excel.

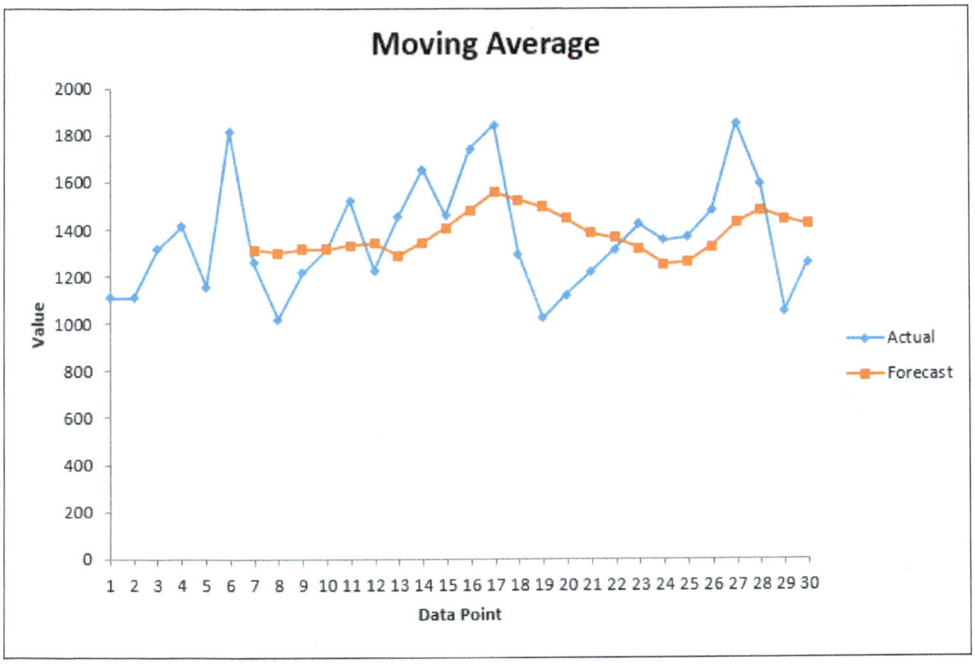

Figure 64-1

Excel 2016, Windows 10, Microsoft Corporation

Lesson 64—Apply

You are creating financial statements for the owner of several small businesses so that he can make decisions about a side seasonal business. The owner is considering expanding the business and wants you to provide the total loan amount that he can apply for given a set monthly payment. In this project, you will use Excel functions to show growth based on a moving average and show the break-even point for the business. You will also use Goal Seek to find the total loan amount for which the owner can apply.

DIRECTIONS

1. Start Excel, if necessary, and open **E64Apply** from the data files for this lesson.
2. Save the file as **E64Apply_xx** in the location where your teacher instructs you to store the files for this lesson.
3. For all worksheets, add a header that has your name at the left, the date code in the center, and the page number code at the right, and change back to **Normal** view.
4. Check that the Data Analysis command is on the Data tab, and enable the Analysis ToolPak, if necessary.

5. On the **Moving Average** worksheet tab, redo the moving average calculations in column B to change the interval from **7** data points to **5** data points, and create a line chart showing the moving average.

   ✓ *You can delete the function from cells B3:B6 when finished; they show an #N/A error rather than a value. This is expected.*

6. On the **Growth** worksheet tab, in the cell range **B19:B33**, use the **GROWTH** function to use 5 days to predict future growth based on the moving averages in the cell range **B2:B16**.

   ✓ *You can delete the function from B30:B33 when finished; they show a #VALUE error rather than a value. This is expected.*

7. On the **Break-Even** worksheet tab, fill in the **Cost**, **Revenue**, and **Profit** columns (the cell range **B6:D105**) with formulas that include absolute references to cells **B1**, **B2**, and **B3**.
8. Create a **Stacked Line** chart from the cell range **B5:D105** showing the break-even point.
9. On the **Goal Seek** worksheet tab, use the Goal Seek feature to find the loan amount of a monthly payment of **$250** for 5 years at an interest rate of 8.50%.
10. **With your teacher's permission**, print the charts from the **Moving Average** and **Break-Even** worksheets. Your charts should look like the ones shown in Figure 64-2.
11. Save and close the file, and exit Excel.

Figure 64-2

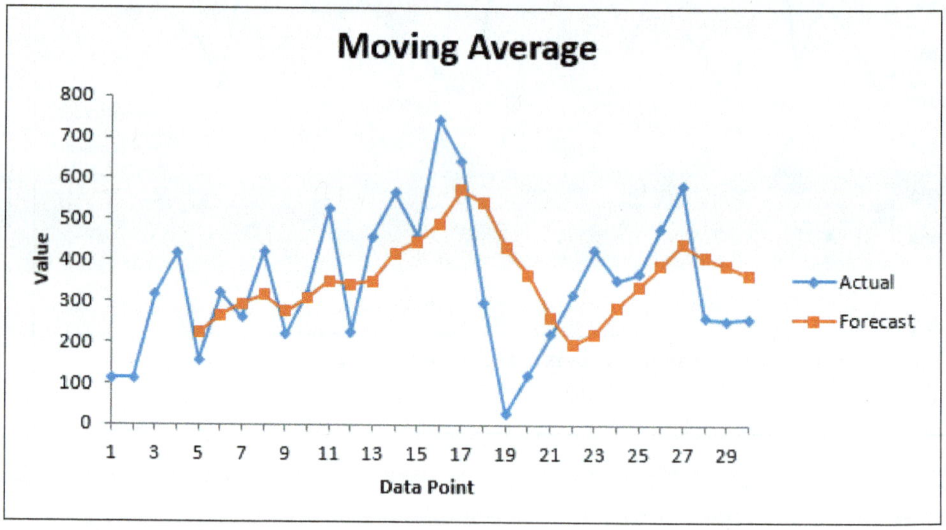

Excel 2016, Windows 10, Microsoft Corporation

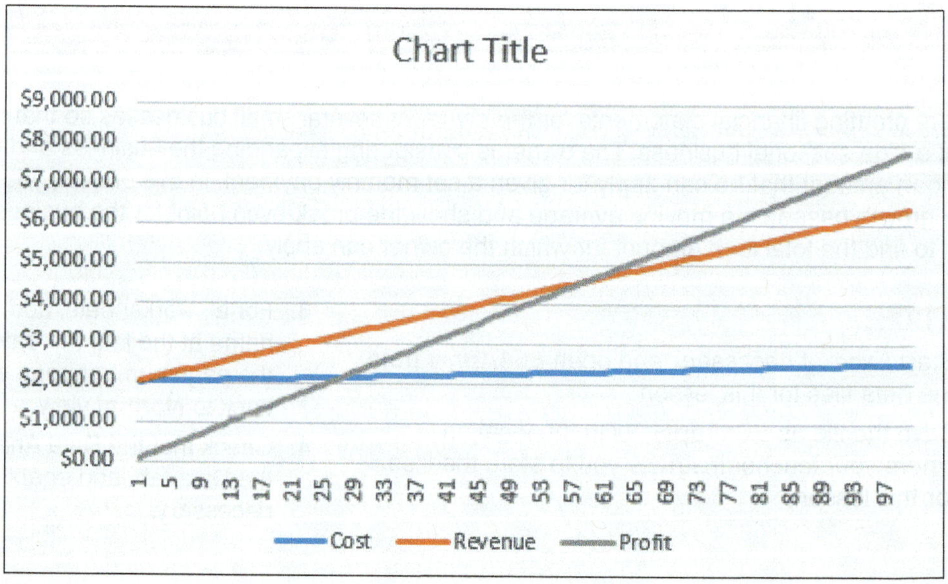

Excel 2016, Windows 10, Microsoft Corporation

Lesson 65

Creating Scenarios and Naming Ranges

➤ What You Will Learn

Creating a Scenario Using the Scenario Manager
Naming a Range
Creating a Scenario Summary

WORDS TO KNOW

Scenario
A what-if analysis tool you can use to create several versions of a worksheet, based on changing variables.

Scenario Manager
Creates named scenarios and generates reports that use outlines or pivot tables. The scenario manager can create a report that summarizes any number of input cells and result cells.

Software Skills With scenarios, you can create and save several versions of a worksheet based on "what-if" data. For example, you can create a best case, probable case, and worst case scenario for your company's annual sales. After you create your scenarios, you can use Scenario Manager to print the various versions of your data quickly.

What You Can Do

Creating a Scenario Using the Scenario Manager

- **Scenarios** help you see possible outcomes of an unpredictable future.
- You can create and save versions of your worksheet data based on changing variables.
- With the **Scenario Manager** in Excel, you can plug in the most likely values for several possible situations, and save the scenarios with the resulting worksheet data.
- Access the Scenario Manager from the What-If Analysis button in the Data Tools group on the Data tab.
- You can print and compare scenarios, save them, and switch between them.
- When you switch to a particular scenario, Excel plugs the saved values into the appropriate cells in your worksheet that represent variables and then adjusts formula results as needed.

Try It! Creating a Scenario Using the Scenario Manager

1. Start Excel, and open **E65Try** from the data files for this lesson.
2. Save the file as **E65Try_xx** in the location where your teacher instructs you to store the files for this lesson.
3. Examine the formulas in cells B9:D13 to see how the bike cost data was determined.

   ✓ *Notice that named ranges have been defined for cells B2 and B3, and the names are used in the formulas in the cell range B9:D9.*

4. Click Data > What-If Analysis > Scenario Manager.
5. Click Add to display the Add Scenario dialog box.
6. In the Scenario name text box, type **Worst Case**.
7. In the Changing cells box, type **B2:B3**.
8. In the Comment section, type **Worst case scenario**, replacing the default comment.

   ✓ *These are the cells where you will change the input data that causes the scenario to change the value in the results cells. If the hourly rate goes up, then the cost of modifying the bikes goes up.*

9. Click OK to display the Scenario Values dialog box with the current contents of cells B2 and B3.
10. In the 1: Hourly_labor_cost field, type **58**.
11. In the 2: Material_and_supplies_cost field, type **75**.
12. Click OK to display the Scenario Manager dialog box.
13. Click Show to see the results of the change.

    ✓ *Notice the negative profit.*

14. Add two more scenarios the same way, viewing each scenario's result after creating it:
    - Add a Most Likely Case in which the Hourly_labor_cost is 45 and the Material_and_supplies cost is 57.
    - Add a Best Case scenario in which the Hourly_labor_cost is 37 and the Material_and_supplies cost is 52.
15. Click Close to close the Scenario Manager dialog box.
16. Save the changes to the file, and leave it open to use in the next Try It.

Specifying the scenario's name and the cells that will change

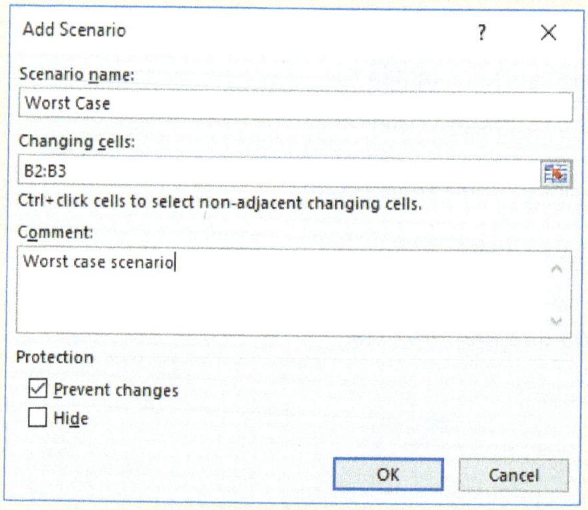

Excel 2016, Windows 10, Microsoft Corporation

Specifying the scenario values to use in the cells that will change

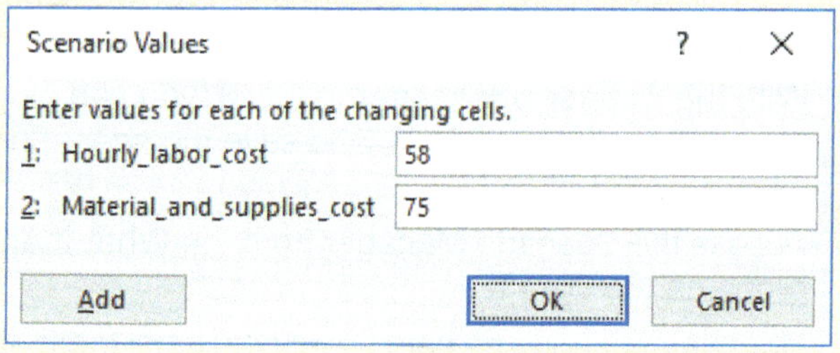

Excel 2016, Windows 10, Microsoft Corporation

Naming a Range

- It is sometimes helpful to give ranges descriptive names.
- A range can be a single cell or multiple cells.
- When a range has a name, you can use the name in formulas and functions in place of the row-and-column cell references.
- You can manually name each range by typing in the Name box on the formula bar, or you can use the naming tools on the Formulas tab.
- For example, to name cells based on the labels in adjacent cells, you can use Create from Selection.

Try It! Naming Ranges

1. In the **E65Try_xx** file, select cell B13.
2. On the far-left end of the formula bar, click in the Name box, type **Beach_cruzer_profit**, and press ENTER.

   ✓ *You can use the sizing tool on the formula bar to view the entire name of the range.*

Name the selected range

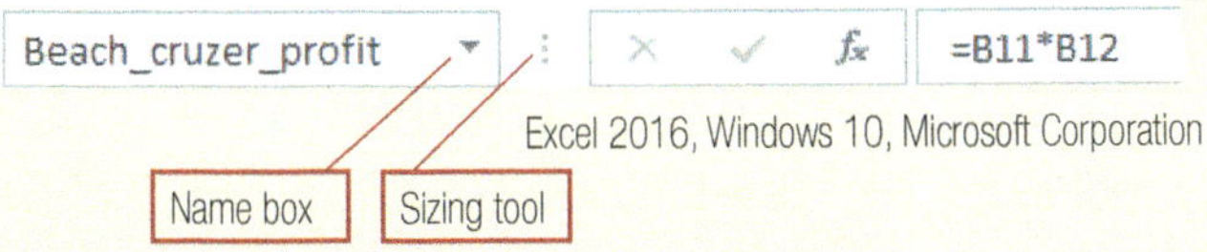

Excel 2016, Windows 10, Microsoft Corporation

3. Click cell C13, click in the Name box, type **Off_road_profit**, and press ENTER.
4. Click cell D13 click in the Name box, type **Iron_man_profit**, and press ENTER.
5. Select the cell range A15:B15.
6. Click Formulas > Create from Selection.
7. Select the Left Column check box, if necessary, and click OK to assign the name Total_Profit to cell B15.
8. Save the changes to the file, and leave it open to use in the next Try It.

Creating a Scenario Summary

- If you have created many scenarios on many different sheets, the best way to view the multiple results is to create a summary sheet of all your scenarios.
- You can create a scenario summary as a worksheet or as a PivotTable.

Try It! Creating a Scenario Summary

1. In the **E65Try_xx** file, click Data > What-If Analysis > Scenario Manager to display the Scenario Manager dialog box.
2. In the Scenarios list, click Best Case.
3. Click Summary to display the Scenario Summary dialog box.
4. In the Result cells box, type **B13,C13,D13,B15**.

Create the scenario summary

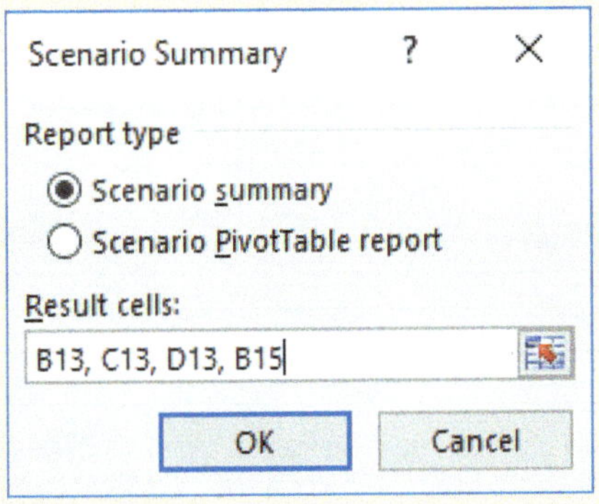

Excel 2016, Windows 10, Microsoft Corporation

(continued)

Try It! Creating a Scenario Summary *(continued)*

5. Click OK.

   ✓ *A comparison summary chart appears on a new tab. You can view each scenario and analyze the numbers to help you decide what business decisions to make. Your summary report may look like this example.*

6. Save and close the file, and exit Excel.

Scenario Summary

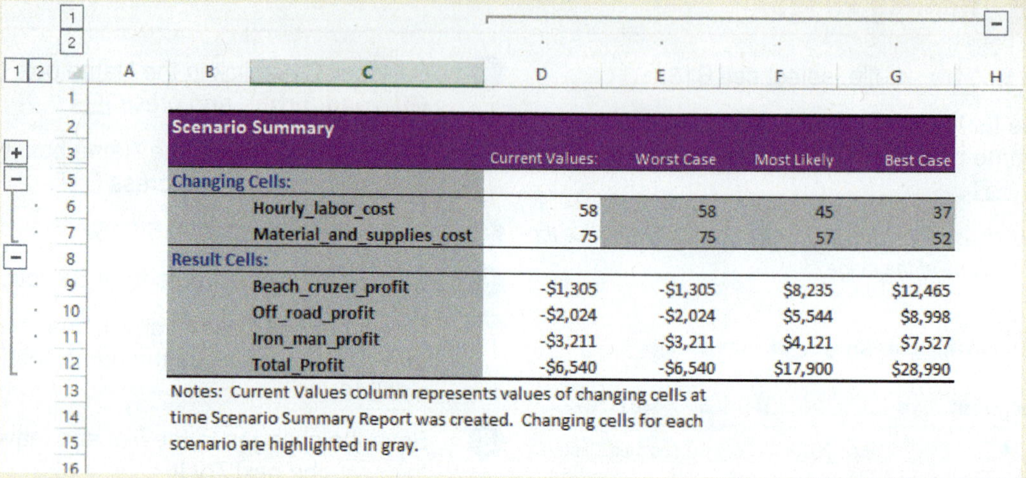

Scenario Summary	Current Values:	Worst Case	Most Likely	Best Case
Changing Cells:				
Hourly_labor_cost	58	58	45	37
Material_and_supplies_cost	75	75	57	52
Result Cells:				
Beach_cruzer_profit	-$1,305	-$1,305	$8,235	$12,465
Off_road_profit	-$2,024	-$2,024	$5,544	$8,998
Iron_man_profit	-$3,211	-$3,211	$4,121	$7,527
Total_Profit	-$6,540	-$6,540	$17,900	$28,990

Notes: Current Values column represents values of changing cells at time Scenario Summary Report was created. Changing cells for each scenario are highlighted in gray.

Excel 2016, Windows 10, Microsoft Corporation

Lesson 65—Practice

You are the owner of a theater company called The Back Street Players. Your customers have been complaining of the high ticket prices. You are considering changing the ticket prices for an upcoming show. You want to use Excel to compare the ticket price scenarios to help you compare the profit and make your decision. In this project, you will define named ranges and use them to create scenarios.

DIRECTIONS

1. Start Excel, if necessary, and open **E65Practice** from the data files for this lesson.
2. Save the file as **E65Practice_xx** in the location where your teacher instructs you to store the files for this lesson.
3. Add a header that has your name at the left, the date code in the center, and the page number code at the right, and change back to **Normal** view.
4. On the **Glass Menagerie** worksheet, select the cell range **B6:C11**, and click **Formulas** > **Create from Selection**.
5. Check that the **Left Column** check box is selected, and click **OK**. Names are assigned to cells C6:C11.
6. Select range **F6:G7**, and click **Formulas** > **Create from Selection**.
7. Check that the **Left Column** check box is selected, and click **OK**.
8. Click **Data** > **What-If Analysis** > **Scenario Manager**.
9. Click **Add**.
10. In the Add Scenario dialog box, in the Scenario Name box, type **Scenario 1**.
11. In the Changing cells text box, type **C6:C11,E5,G6:G7**.
12. Click **OK**. If you see a warning that at least one of the changing cells has a formula in it, click **OK**.
13. In the Scenario Values dialog box, click **OK** to accept the existing values as the scenario values.
14. Click **Add** to start a new scenario.
15. In the Scenario Name box, type **Scenario 2**.
16. Click **OK**. If you see a warning that at least one of the changing cells has a formula in it, click **OK**.
17. In the Scenario Values dialog box, change the value of 5: Ticket_Price to **$9.00**, and click **OK**.
18. Click **Show** to show Scenario 2.
19. Click **Close** to close the Scenario Manager dialog box.
20. **With your teacher's permission**, print the selection **A2:H15**. Your worksheet should look like the one shown in Figure 65-1.
21. Save and close the file, and exit Excel.

Figure 65-1

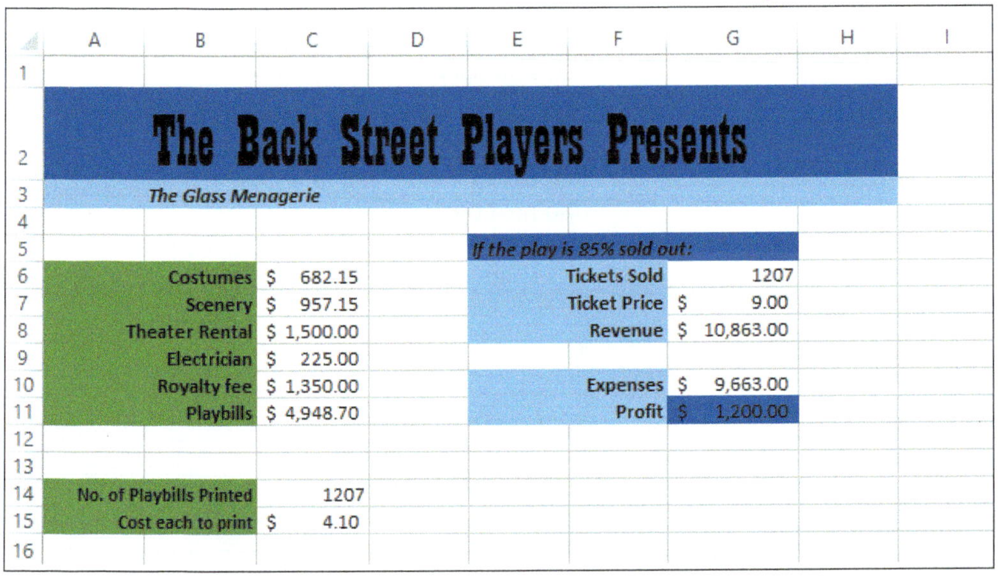

Lesson 65—Apply

You are the owner of Breakaway Bike Shop, and you are raising your labor charges in January. A customer of Breakaway Bike Shop is in a dilemma about some bike work he would like to have done. Some work is needed right away, while other parts that are showing wear could conceivably be put off until after the winter holidays. The customer needs help deciding among several scenarios—doing some of the work now and putting off the rest indefinitely, doing all of the work now, or waiting until after the winter holidays to do the work. In this project, you will use scenarios to create the reports he needs to compare the costs and make his decision.

DIRECTIONS

1. Start Excel, if necessary, and open **E65Apply** from the data files for this lesson.
2. Save the file as **E65Apply_xx** in the location where your teacher instructs you to store the files for this lesson.
3. Create a scenario called **Minimum Replacements** in which the values in the following ranges are saved as they currently appear:
   - **B26:F26**
   - **B28:F28**
   - **B37:F38**
   - **G3**
4. Create another scenario called **Recommended Replacements** in which these values change.
   - B26 **RPL**
   - C26 **2**
   - D26 **Aurens BR321**
   - E26 **1**
   - F26 **39.25**
   - B28 **RPL**
   - C28 **2**
   - D28 **Aurens BI321**
   - E28 **.10**
   - F28 **4.95**
   - B37 **RPL**
   - C37 **1**
   - D37 **Road Warrior 18F**
   - E37 **.15**
   - F37 **25.75**
   - B38 **RPL**
   - C38 **1**
   - D38 **Road Warrior 18R**
   - E38 **.25**
   - F38 **28.95**

   ✓ *Leave the value in G3 as it currently appears.*
5. Create another scenario called **All Work After January** that is identical to the Recommended Replacements scenario from step 4 except that the value of cell **G3** changes to **50.00**.

   ✓ *The simplest way to accomplish this is to first display the changed values in the worksheet. Use the Scenario Manager to display the values associated with the Recommended Replacements scenario. Then create the new scenario, and the only value you have to edit is G3.*
6. Create a summary report with **G3** as the result cell.
7. For all worksheets, add a custom header that has your name at the left, the date code in the center, and the page number code at the right, and change back to **Normal** view.
8. **With your teacher's permission**, print the **Scenario Summary** worksheet. Your worksheet should look like the one shown in Figure 65-2 on the next page.
9. Save and close the file, and exit Excel.

Figure 65-2

Scenario Summary	Current Values:	Minimum Replacements	Recommended Replacements	All Work After January
Changing Cells:				
$B$26	RPL	N/A	RPL	RPL
$C$26	2		2	2
$D$26	Aurens BR321		Aurens BR321	Aurens BR321
$E$26	1.00		1.00	1.00
$F$26	$39.25		$39.25	$39.25
$B$28	RPL	N/A	RPL	RPL
$C$28	2		2	2
$D$28	Aurens BI321		Aurens BI321	Aurens BI321
$E$28	0.10		0.10	0.10
$F$28	$4.95		$4.95	$4.95
$B$37	RPL	OK	RPL	RPL
$C$37	1		1	1
$D$37	Road Warrior 18F		Road Warrior 18F	Road Warrior 18F
$E$37	0.15		0.15	0.15
$F$37	$25.75		$25.75	$25.75
$B$38	RPL	RPL	RPL	RPL
$C$38	1	1	1	1
$D$38	Road Warrior 18R		Road Warrior 18R	Road Warrior 18R
$E$38	0.25		0.25	0.25
$F$38	$28.95		$28.95	$28.95
$G$3	$40.00	$40.00	$40.00	$50.00
Result Cells:				
$G$3	$40.00	$40.00	$40.00	$50.00

Notes: Current Values column represents values of changing cells at time Scenario Summary Report was created. Changing cells for each scenario are highlighted in gray.

Excel 2016, Windows 10, Microsoft Corporation

Lesson 66

Finding and Fixing Errors in Formulas

➤ What You Will Learn

Using Formula Error Checking
Understanding Error Messages
Showing Formulas
Evaluating Individual Formulas
Using the Watch Window
Tracing Precedents and Dependents

WORDS TO KNOW

Dependents
Formulas whose results depend on the value in a cell.

Error Checking
An information button on a cell. Error Checking options can contain information about an error in the cell contents.

Evaluate
To view the intermediate results step-by-step, as Excel solves a formula.

Precedent
A cell referenced in a formula.

Watch Window
A floating window that allows you to watch the results of formulas change as you change data.

Software Skills If you have a problem with formulas in a large or complex worksheet, working through each formula to locate the values in the cells it references and to verify that everything is all right can be a tedious, complex job unless you use Excel's error and formula auditing features.

What You Can Do

Using Formula Error Checking

- When background error checking is enabled in Excel, a small triangle in the upper-left corner of a cell indicates a possible error. When you select the cell, an **Error Checking** button appears. Click the Error Checking button to see a message explaining what the potential error is. See Figure 66-1 on the next page.

  ✓ *If errors do not appear in Error Checking options, the feature may not be enabled. Click File > Options > Formulas, and select the Enable background error checking check box.*

- Excel checks for the following errors:
  - Formulas that result in an error value, such as #DIV/0.
  - Formulas containing a text date entered using a two-digit year, such as =YEAR("02/20/27"), because it is not clear which century is being referenced.
  - Numbers stored as text rather than actual numbers, because this can cause sorting and other errors.
  - Formulas that are inconsistent with formulas in surrounding cells.

- For example, if Excel notices the pattern =SUM(A2:A10), =SUM(B2:B10) in two adjacent cells, and then sees the formula =SUM(C2:C4) in another adjacent cell, it will flag it as a possible mistake because it doesn't fit the pattern of the other formulas.
- Formulas that omit adjacent cells, as in Figure 66-1.
- An unprotected formula, if worksheet protection is enabled.

  ✓ *If you turn on worksheet protection, all cells are protected against changes by default. You can selectively unprotect the cells you want to allow others to enter data into. However, if you unprotect a cell with a formula, Excel will see that as a possible error, because it's unusual that you would want someone else to change your formulas.*

- A formula that refers to empty cells.
- Invalid data entered into a cell.
- An inconsistent formula in a calculated table column.

■ When you find an error in a formula, one way in which you might need to correct it is to change the cell(s) that the formula references. For example, you might need to change the formula =SUM(D2:D10) so that it reads =SUM(D2:D12).

■ When you click a cell with a formula, and then click in the formula bar, the cells referenced by the formula are outlined with colored borders. You can drag these colored borders and drop them on different cells, in order to change the cells used in the formula. You can also resize a colored border to make the formula reference more or fewer cells in that range.

Understanding Error Messages

■ The following is a list of some error messages you might get if you enter data or formulas incorrectly:

- **####** The cell contains an entry that's wider than the cell can display. In most cases, you can just widen the column to correct the problem.
- **#VALUE!** The wrong type of data was used in a formula. Possible causes are entering text when a formula requires a number or logical value, or entering a range in a formula or function that requires a single value.
- **#DIV/0!** A formula is attempting to divide a value by zero. For example, if the value in cell B5 in the formula =A5/B5 is zero, or if cell B5 is empty, the result will be the #DIV/0! error.
- **#NAME?** Excel doesn't recognize text in the formula. Possible causes include a misspelling or using a nonexistent range name, using a label in a formula if the Accept labels in formulas option is turned off, or omitting a colon (:) in a range reference.

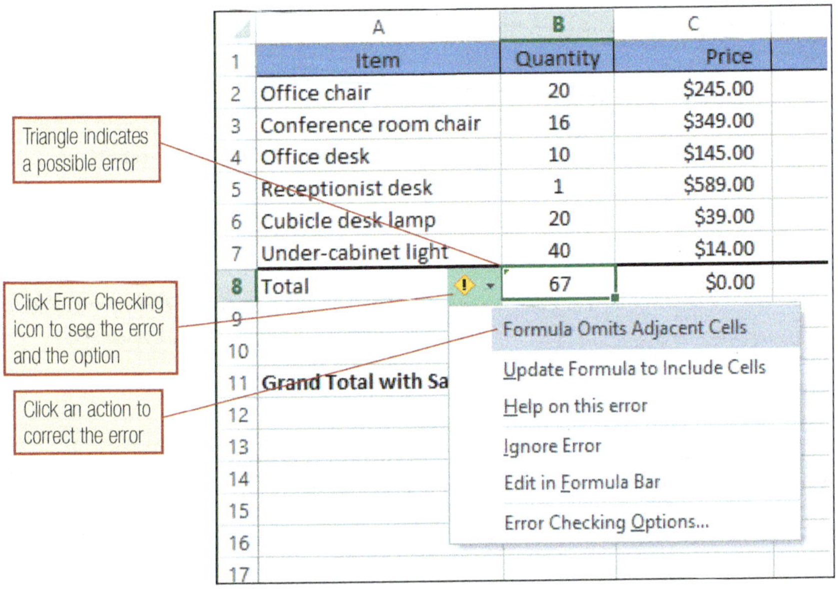

Excel 2016, Windows 10, Microsoft Corporation

Figure 66-1

- **#N/A** No value is available to the formula or function. Possible causes include omitting a required argument in a formula or function or entering an invalid argument in a formula or function.
- **#REF!** A cell reference is invalid. Possible causes include deleting cells referred to by formulas.
- **#NUM** Indicates a problem with a number in a formula or function. Possible causes include using a nonnumeric argument in a function that requires a numeric argument, or entering a formula that produces a number too large or too small for Excel to represent.
- **#NULL!** The formula contains incorrect operators or cell references using ranges in formulas. For example, if you left the comma out of the following formula, a #NULL! error would occur: SUM(A1:A6,C1:C6).

- A circular reference is a special kind of error that's caused when a formula references itself. For example, if you're adding the values of a group of cells and include the cell that contains the formula, you are creating an endless loop, which generates a circular reference error.
- When a circular reference occurs, an error message appears, followed by a Help screen filled with tips to help you correct the error.
- Until you correct a circular reference, the status bar displays the words "CIRCULAR REFERENCES" and if the worksheet with the error is displayed, the address of the cell(s) with the Circular Reference error appears after "CIRCULAR REFERENCES" in the status bar.
- You can also locate any cell(s) that contain circular references by using the Circular References option on the Error Checking button on the FORMULAS tab.

Try It! Correcting Formula Errors

1. Start Excel, and open **E66Try** from the data files for this lesson. If you see a circular reference warning, click OK.
2. Save the file as **E66Try_xx** in the location where your teacher instructs you to store the files for this lesson.
3. On the Office Items worksheet, click cell B8. An Error Checking shortcut button appears to the left.
4. Click the Error Checking shortcut button.
5. Click Update Formula to Include Cells.
6. Click Formulas > Error Checking. The Error Checking dialog box displays to point out the error in C8.
7. Click Copy Formula from Left.
8. Click OK to confirm that error checking is complete.
9. Apply the Accounting Format to cell C8.
10. Use Format Painter to copy the formatting from C8 to D8.
11. Click the Sales Tax worksheet tab.
12. Click cell B12 > Error Checking shortcut button.
13. Click Convert XX to 20XX.
14. Examine the formulas in column D to figure out why there is such a large value in cell D3 and zero values in the cell range D4:D7.

    ✓ *The formula for calculating tax is correct in cell D2. However, the formula was filled down with relative references instead of absolute references. Every row needs to reference the sales tax rate in cell B11. Fix this by making cells D2:D7 have an absolute reference to B11.*
15. Change the formula in cell D2 to **=B2*C2*$B$11**.

    ✓ *Instead of retyping the formula in cell D2, you could click in the B11 reference in the formula bar, and press F4 to cycle through the relative/absolute reference combinations until you arrive at $B$11.*
16. Copy the formula in cell D2 to the cell range D3:D7.
17. Save the changes to the file, and leave it open to use in the next Try It.

Showing Formulas

- Sometimes it can be helpful to view the actual formulas in the cells, rather than the formula results. To do this, you can either press CTRL + ` (the accent mark above the Tab key, not an apostrophe) or you can click Formulas > Show Formulas. Repeat the command to switch back to viewing the worksheet normally.

Try It! Showing Formulas

1. In the **E66Try_xx** file, click Formulas > Show Formulas to display the formulas.
2. Click Show Formulas again to toggle the feature off.
3. Save the changes to the file, and leave it open to use in the next Try It.

Evaluating Individual Formulas

- When a formula has multiple calculations in it, it can be helpful to **evaluate** each part of the formula step by step.
- You can access the Evaluate Formula command in the Formula Auditing group on the Formulas tab.

Try It! Evaluating a Formula

1. In the **E66Try_xx** file, click the Sales Tax worksheet tab, if necessary.
2. Click cell E2.
3. Click Formulas > Evaluate Formula. The Evaluate Formula dialog box opens, showing the following:

   (<u>B2</u>*C2)+D2
4. Click Evaluate. The value of the first reference appears in italic, and the second reference is underlined:

   (*20<u>C2</u>)+D2**
5. Click Evaluate. The value of the second reference appears in italic, and the portion of the formula that is in parentheses is underlined:

   (<u>*20*245*</u>)+D2
6. Click Evaluate. The portion of the formula in parentheses is calculated:

   (<u>*4900*</u>)+D2
7. Click Evaluate. The parentheses are removed and D2 becomes underlined:

   ***4900*+<u>D2</u>**
8. Click Evaluate. The value of D2 appears:

   <u>*4900+416.5*</u>
9. Click Evaluate. The final result of the formula appears:

   $5,316.50
10. Click Close.
11. Save the changes to the file, and leave it open to use in the next Try It.

Using the Watch Window

- Using the **Watch Window**, you can watch the results of your formulas change as you change other data, even if that formula is located in a cell that's out of view, on another worksheet, or located in another open workbook.
- You can watch multiple cells and their formulas.
- Access the Watch Window command in the Formula Auditing group on the Formulas tab.

Try It! Using the Watch Window

1. In the E66Try_xx file, on the Formulas tab, click Watch Window.
2. Click Add Watch.
3. On the Sales Tax worksheet, select cell E3. An absolute reference to that cell appears in the Add Watch dialog box.
4. Click Add. The cell reference appears in the Watch Window.
5. Change the value in cell B3 to 20, and press ENTER. Notice that the result for E3 changes in the Watch Window.
6. Change the value in cell B3 back to 16.
7. Click the E66Try_xx watch item in the Watch Window to select it.
8. Click Delete Watch to remove the watch.
9. Close the Watch Window.
10. Save the changes to the file, and leave it open to use in the next Try It.

Tracing Precedents and Dependents

- With the Trace Precedents button, you can trace a formula's **precedents**—cells referred to by the formula. This can help you find and fix errors that have to do with wrong cell references.
- If you are concerned about changing the value in a cell, you can trace its **dependents** with the Trace Dependents button. A dependent is a cell whose value depends on the value in another cell.
- When you trace precedents or dependents, arrows point to the related cells.

Try It! Tracing Precedents and Dependents

1. In the E66Try_xx file, click the Office Items worksheet tab.
2. Click cell D2.
3. On the Formulas tab, in the Formula Auditing group, click Trace Precedents. A line appears from cells B2 through D2 with blue dots in each field that contributes to the value in D2.
4. Click Remove Arrows.
5. Click cell D5 > Trace Precedents. Lines appear that show cell D5's precedents.
6. Click Trace Dependents. A line appears that shows cell D5's dependents.
7. Click Remove Arrows.
8. Save and close the file, and exit Excel.

Lesson 66—Practice

It looks like the sale of your old building and the purchase of a new headquarters for the Wood Hills Animal Clinic is going to go through. Before you can get final approval for your loan, however, you must prepare a balance sheet and a profit and loss statement. You've been working on the profit and loss statement, and there's just something wrong with the numbers. Your hope is that Excel's powerful formula auditing tools can help you sort out the problem.

DIRECTIONS

1. Start Excel, if necessary, and open **E66Practice** from the data files for this lesson. Click OK if the file opens with a warning notice about a circular error.
2. Save the file as **E66Practice_xx** in the location where your teacher instructs you to store the files for this lesson.
3. For all worksheets, add a header that has your name at the left, the date code in the center, and the page number code at the right, and change back to **Normal** view.
4. Look over the data on both worksheet tabs to see areas where there might be errors in formulas because data is missing or data doesn't look as expected.

   ✓ *Notice that when you are on the Balance Sheet worksheet, the status bar shows there is a circular reference, but no cell reference is given. Move to the P&L worksheet. Notice that the status bar now shows there is a circular reference in cell E57.*

5. In the **P&L** worksheet, click cell **E57**. The formula in this cell is **=SUM(E32,E43,E56,E57)**.
6. Edit this circular reference error by removing **E57** from the formula. The new formula should read **=SUM(E32,E43,E56)**.

   ✓ *Be sure to remove the last comma. If not, you will receive an error message.*

7. Click cell **E64**, and view the formula in the formula bar.

   ✓ *Cell E64 should have a calculation in it to show the earnings per share of common stock. The formula to calculate earnings per share of common stock is to divide net income by common stock shares outstanding. However, the current formula in cell E64 references E62, a blank cell.*

8. Edit this reference error by changing E62 in the formula to **E61**.
9. **With your teacher's permission**, print both worksheets.
10. Save and close the file, and exit Excel.

Lesson 66—Apply

You are the owner of Old Southern Furniture. You want to use Excel to create formulas to calculate the commission, bonuses, and earnings for each of your salespeople. Then, you want to use Excel's formula auditing tools to help ensure that your formulas are accurate and valid.

DIRECTIONS

1. Start Excel, if necessary, and open **E66Apply** from, the data files for this lesson.
2. Save the file as **E66Apply_xx** in the location where your teacher instructs you to store the files for this lesson.
3. Add a header that has your name at the left, the date code in the center, and the page number code at the right, and change back to **Normal** view.
4. Create formulas that calculate the commission and bonuses for each salesperson.
   a. In cell **C13**, create a formula that multiplies cell **B13** by an absolute reference to cell **B9**.
   b. Copy the formula from cell **C13** to the cell range **C14:C24**.
   c. In cell **D13**, use an **IF** function to show the value of cell **B10** if the value of cell **B13** is greater than **$40,000,** and otherwise to show **$0**. Refer to B10 with an absolute reference.
   d. Copy the formula from cell **D13** to the cell range **D14:D24**.
   e. Use **Format Painter** to copy the formatting from cell **C13** to the cell range **D13:D24**.
5. Create formulas that calculate the total earnings, which is the total of commissions and bonuses.
   a. In cell **E13**, use a **SUM** function to add the cell range **B13:D13**.
   b. Copy the function from cell **E13** to the cell range **E14:E24**.
6. Click any cell in the **Comm.** column, and trace the precedents. Remove the arrows.
7. Click any cell in the **Bonus** column, and trace the precedents. Remove the arrows.
8. Click any cell in the **Total Earnings** column, and trace the precedents. Remove the arrows.
9. In cell **B9**, type **0.06**, and in cell **B10**, type **$200**. Apply the **Percentage** format, zero decimal places, to cell **B9**.
10. Click cell **B9** and trace its dependents. Remove the arrows.
11. Click cell **B10** and trace its dependents. Remove the arrows.
12. Click any cell in the **Sales** column, and trace its dependents. Remove the arrows.
13. Evaluate a formula in column B.
14. Show the formulas in all cells. Adjust column widths as necessary so that all formulas are fully visible and the worksheet fits on a single page across.
15. **With your teacher's permission**, print the cell range **A9:E24** with the formulas showing. Your worksheet should look like the one shown in Figure 66-2 on the next page.
16. Return to viewing formula results in the cells, and readjust column widths as needed.
17. Save and close the file, and exit Excel.

Figure 66-2

	A	B	C	D	E
1					
2					
3					
4					
5		**Old Southern Fu**			
6		*Biweekly Earnings Review*			
7		42736			
8					
9	Commission Rate	0.06			
10	Bonus on sales over $40K	200			
11					
12	**Salesperson**	**Sales**	**Comm.**	**Bonus**	**Total Earnings**
13	Carl Jackson	44202	=B13*$B$9	=IF(B13>40000,$B$10,0)	=SUM(B13:D13)
14	Ni Li Yung	41524	=B14*$B$9	=IF(B14>40000,$B$10,0)	=SUM(B14:D14)
15	Tom Wilson	43574	=B15*$B$9	=IF(B15>40000,$B$10,0)	=SUM(B15:D15)
16	Jill Palmer	39612	=B16*$B$9	=IF(B16>40000,$B$10,0)	=SUM(B16:D16)
17	Rita Nuez	39061	=B17*$B$9	=IF(B17>40000,$B$10,0)	=SUM(B17:D17)
18	Maureen Baker	38893	=B18*$B$9	=IF(B18>40000,$B$10,0)	=SUM(B18:D18)
19	Kim Cheng	31120	=B19*$B$9	=IF(B19>40000,$B$10,0)	=SUM(B19:D19)
20	Lloyd Hamilton	41922	=B20*$B$9	=IF(B20>40000,$B$10,0)	=SUM(B20:D20)
21	Ed Fulton	45609	=B21*$B$9	=IF(B21>40000,$B$10,0)	=SUM(B21:D21)
22	Maria Alvarez	30952	=B22*$B$9	=IF(B22>40000,$B$10,0)	=SUM(B22:D22)
23	Katie Wilson	31472	=B23*$B$9	=IF(B23>40000,$B$10,0)	=SUM(B23:D23)
24	Tim Brown	44783	=B24*$B$9	=IF(B24>40000,$B$10,0)	=SUM(B24:D24)
25					

Excel 2016, Windows 10, Microsoft Corporation

End-of-Chapter Activities

➤ Excel Chapter 8—Critical Thinking

Analyzing a Business Opportunity

You are interested in purchasing a business, and you want to analyze the financial numbers of the business from the past two years to see if it is a profitable, growing company. You will analyze the raw data that the current owner has provided to make sure the business would be a good investment.

If you do purchase the business, you will need to get a small business loan. You are considering two different loans, each with different terms. You will use what you know about financial functions to determine which loan is a better deal.

DIRECTIONS

1. Start Excel, if necessary, and open **ECT08** from the data files for this chapter.
2. Save the file as **ECT08_xx** in the location where your teacher instructs you to store the files for this chapter.
3. On the **Expenses** worksheet, in cell **G5**, create a **SUMIF** function that sums the values from **D5:D124** where "Facility Rental" appears in column C.
4. Enter the appropriate **SUMIF** functions in columns **G** and **I** that summarize the data in the ways described by the labels in columns **F** and **H**. Illustration 8A shows the totals that should appear in the cells when the functions are correctly created.

   ✓ *If you apply absolute references to all the cells in the function in G5, it makes it easier to copy and paste the function into other cells and then modify the copies to meet the new criteria. For example, you can copy the function into G6 and change Facility Rental to Loan Payment.*

5. On the **Summary** tab, examine the **SUMIFS** functions in cells **C5** and **D5**.

   ✓ *Notice that in both functions, the date Jan-13 is being referenced as a general number: 40179. To determine the numeric equivalent of a date, temporarily set the cell's number format to General.*

6. Using C5 and D5 as examples, complete the rest of the functions for the cell range **C6:D28**.

   ✓ *Because the cell references are absolute, you can copy and paste the functions from cells C5 and D5 into the remaining cells, and then edit each copy.*

   ✓ *You may want to set all the dates in column A temporarily to General format to make it easier to see what numbers to use for the dates. Don't forget to set them back to the custom Date format of MMM-YY when you are finished.*

   ✓ *Another shortcut: after completing column C's functions, copy them to column D, and use Find and Replace to replace all instances of "Fixed" with "Variable."*

7. Copy the formula from cell **E5** to the cell range **E6:E28**.
8. Create a line chart from the values in column **E**, using the dates in column **A** as labels. Display the legend.
9. Add an exponential trend line to the chart.
10. Place the chart on its own sheet in the workbook. Name the sheet **Net Profit**.

    ✓ *To place the chart on its own sheet, right-click the chart border and click Move Chart.*

11. On the **Loans** sheet, use the **PMT** function to calculate the monthly payments on two different loans, both for **$2 million**:

    Loan 1: **6% APR for 60 months**

    Loan 2: **5% APR for 48 months**

12. On the **Loans** worksheet, in cell **B10**, create a formula that evaluates whether the amount in cell **B9** is less than the smallest value in column **E** of the **Summary** worksheet (hint: use the =MIN function). If it is less, display **OK**. If it is not less, display **No**. Copy the formula to cell **C10**, changing any cell references as needed.

13. Create a scenario for the current values on the **Loans** sheet, with cell **B4** as the changing cell. Name the scenario **2 Million Loan**.
14. Create another scenario in which the loan amount is **$2,500,000**. Name it **2.5 Million Loan**. Show the **2.5 Million Loan** scenario, then show the **2 Million Loan** scenario.
15. For all worksheets, add a header that has your name at the left, the date code in the center, and the page number code at the right, and change back to **Normal** view.
16. On the Summary tab, in cell A30, type **as of** and right-align it.
17. In cell A31, insert a function that shows the current date and time.
18. **With your teacher's permission**, print the **Loans** worksheet and the **Net Profit** chart.
19. Save and close the file, and exit Excel.

Illustration 8A

2-Year Total of Expenses		**2-Year Total Expenses by Type**	
Facility Rental	$19,200	Fixed	$48,000
Loan Payment	$28,800	Variable	$6,268,911
Materials	$5,567,857		
Payroll	$694,826	**2018 Expenses by Type**	
Utilities	$6,228	Fixed	$24,000
		Variable	$2,642,102
2018 Expenses			
Facility Rental	$9,600	**2019 Expenses by Type**	
Loan Payment	$14,400	Fixed	$24,000
Materials	$2,344,531	Variable	$3,626,809
Payroll	$294,522		
Utilities	$3,049		
2019 Expenses			
Facility Rental	$9,600		
Loan Payment	$14,400		
Materials	$3,223,326		
Payroll	$400,304		
Utilities	$3,179		

Excel 2016, Windows 10, Microsoft Corporation

➤ Excel Chapter 8—Portfolio Builder

Projecting Business Scenarios

The purchase of the business seems to be a good decision. However, the net profit per month seems to fluctuate quite a bit, making it difficult to predict how much money you can safely borrow to purchase the business. You can be more confident by calculating a moving average of the monthly profits, and by setting up several scenarios with varying degrees of optimism, ranging from worst case to best case.

DIRECTIONS

1. Start Excel, if necessary, and open **EPB08** from the data files for this chapter.
2. Save the file as **EPB08_xx** in the location where your teacher instructs you to store the files for this chapter.
3. On the **Expenses** sheet, insert a new column between columns **B** and **C** and use the DATE function in it to combine the values in **A5: A124** and **B5:B124** into serialized dates in **C5:C124**.

   ✓ *Use **1** for the day argument in the DATE function.*
4. Set the number format for column **C** to match the dates in column **A** on the **Summary** worksheet (Jan-18).
5. Use Paste Values & Number Formatting to copy the values and formatting from **C5:C124** to **A5:A124**, overwriting the existing values there. Then delete columns **B** and **C**, and change the label in cell **A4** to **Date**.
6. On the **Summary** worksheet, in the **F** column, create a 5-interval moving average of the values in the **E** column, and chart the output.

   ✓ *Enable the Analysis Toolpak Add-On, if necessary.*
7. Move the chart to its own sheet. Name the sheet **Profit Moving Average**.
8. On the **Summary** sheet, in the cell range **B29:B40**, use the **GROWTH** function to predict the future monthly gross revenues for 2015. Use the cell ranges for 2014 only in the **GROWTH** function arguments.
9. Copy the formula from cell **E28** to the cell range **E29:E40**.
10. In cell **C29**, enter **$1,500**. Copy that value to the cell range **C30:C40**.
11. In cell **D29**, enter **$370,000**. Copy that value to the cell range **D30:D40**.
12. Use **Format Painter** to copy the formatting from cell **B29** to the cell range **C29:E40**.
13. Type **$1,500** in cell **I29**. Enter **$200,000** in cell **I30**.
14. In cell **C29**, enter a formula that provides an absolute reference to **I29**.
15. In cell **D29**, enter a formula that provides an absolute reference to **I30**.
16. Copy the formulas from the cell range **C29:D29** to the cell range **C30:D40**.
17. Create a scenario called **Best Case** that allows **I29** and **I30** to change, and uses the current values of those cells.
18. Create another scenario called **Most Likely** that sets cell **I29** to **$1750** and cell **I30** to **$300,000**.
19. Create another scenario called **Worst Case** that sets cell **I29** to **$2000** and cell **I30** to **$400,000**.
20. Show the **Most Likely** scenario.
21. For all worksheets, add a header that has your name at the left, the date code in the center, and the page number code at the right, and change back to **Normal** view.
22. **With your instructor's permission**, print the range **A29:E40** on the **Summary** worksheet, and print the **Profit Moving Average** chart.
23. Save and close the file, and exit Excel.

Chapter 9

(Courtesy Goodluz/Shutterstock)

Analyzing Data

Lesson 67
Working with Excel Tables

- Converting Ranges to Tables
- Changing a Table's Name
- Showing a Totals Row in a Table
- Viewing Two Tables Side-by-Side
- Working with Named Ranges and Field Names

Lesson 68
Using Get & Transform

- Understanding Get & Transform
- Creating a Query
- Modifying a Query
- Adding a Calculated Field to a Query
- Merging Data from Different Sources

Lesson 69
Using Advanced Filters and Slicers

- Using Advanced Filters
- Working with Slicers

Lesson 70
Using Database Functions

- Using VLOOKUP and HLOOKUP
- Using MATCH
- Using INDEX
- Using INDEX and MATCH Instead of VLOOKUP

Lesson 71
Using Flash Fill and Data Consolidation

- Working with Flash Fill
- Consolidating Data
- Working with Consolidated Data

Lesson 72
Linking Workbooks

- Linking Workbooks
- Modifying a Linked Workbook

Lesson 73
Using PivotTables

- Working with PivotTables
- Working with PivotTable Fields
- Sorting PivotTable Fields
- Formatting a PivotTable

Lesson 74
Manipulating PivotTable Data

- Adding a Timeline
- Grouping PivotTable Data
- Adding a Calculated Field to a PivotTable
- Referencing PivotTable Data Externally

Lesson 75
Using PivotCharts

- Creating a PivotChart from a PivotTable
- Creating a PivotChart from an External Data Source
- Working with PivotChart Fields
- Formatting a PivotChart

Lesson 76
Using Power Pivot and Power View

- Enabling Data Analysis Add-Ins
- Using Power Pivot to Manage Data
- Creating a Power View Report
- Working with Power View Fields
- Formatting a Power View Report

Lesson 77
Working with the Excel Data Model

- Creating Relationships Between Tables
- Drilling Down in a PivotChart
- Extracting Data with Cube Functions

End-of-Chapter Activities

Lesson 67

Working with Excel Tables

➤ What You Will Learn

Converting Ranges to Tables
Changing a Table's Name
Showing a Totals Row in a Table
Viewing Two Tables Side-by-Side
Working with Named Ranges and Field Names

WORDS TO KNOW

Banded columns
Alternating colors in columns in a table.

Banded rows
Alternating colors in rows in a table.

Field name
The name of a column in a table, as defined by the text entry in the first row of that table in that column.

Filter
To reduce the number of records displayed on the screen by applying one or more criteria.

Range name
A meaningful name assigned to a range of cells.

Structured reference
A reference that uses the cell or range name rather than the row and column address.

Table
In Excel, a range of cells in a datasheet that have been grouped together into a single unit for formatting and data analysis.

Software Skills You can create a table in Excel to sort, filter, and analyze data. A worksheet can have multiple tables, and placing tables side by side is a good way to compare data quickly. Putting the two tables on the same worksheet lets the user filter and compare data on a single sheet. Row and column headings can serve as range names, and you can also create your own range names. Range names can be used in formulas in place of cell addresses.

What You Can Do

Converting Ranges to Tables

- Worksheet ranges can be turned into **tables** for easy analysis. A table can easily be sorted and **filtered** via the drop-down lists associated with each column heading.
- There are two ways to create a table. You can use the Insert > Table command, or you can use the Home > Format as Table command and choose a table format.
- Depending on how it's formatted, a table can also offer visually pleasing formatting with **banded rows** or **banded columns**. The alternating lighter and darker colors make it easy to follow data across a row, or down a column, increasing the accuracy of your work. See Figure 67-1 on the next page.
- Banding is added by default when you create a table out of a data range that does not have previously existing fill applied to it. Several of the table formatting options under Home > Format as Table also include banding.

✓ *The worksheets in the Try It exercises in this lesson already have background fill, so you will not see banding applied when you create the tables.*

- To add or remove banding, use the Banded Rows command on the Table Tools Design tab.
- Multiple ranges in a worksheet can be converted into separate tables.

✓ *When inserting two tables on the same worksheet, there must be at least one row or one column between the data ranges in order for Excel to know that the data will be treated as two tables.*

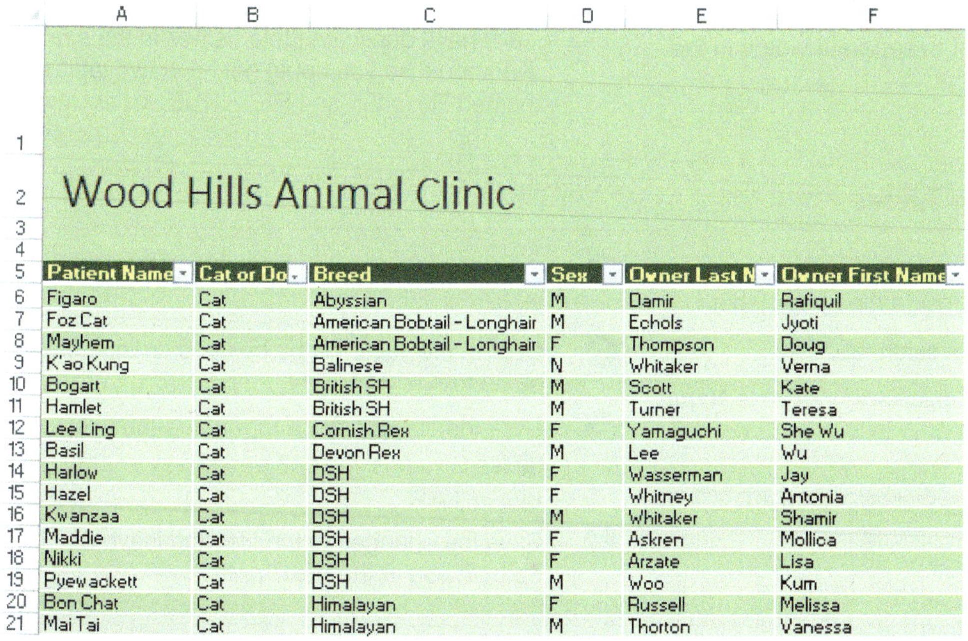

	A	B	C	D	E	F
1						
2	Wood Hills Animal Clinic					
3						
4						
5	Patient Name	Cat or Do	Breed	Sex	Owner Last N	Owner First Name
6	Figaro	Cat	Abyssian	M	Damir	Rafiquil
7	Foz Cat	Cat	American Bobtail - Longhair	M	Echols	Jyoti
8	Mayhem	Cat	American Bobtail - Longhair	F	Thompson	Doug
9	K'ao Kung	Cat	Balinese	N	Whitaker	Verna
10	Bogart	Cat	British SH	M	Scott	Kate
11	Hamlet	Cat	British SH	M	Turner	Teresa
12	Lee Ling	Cat	Cornish Rex	F	Yamaguchi	She Wu
13	Basil	Cat	Devon Rex	M	Lee	Wu
14	Harlow	Cat	DSH	F	Wasserman	Jay
15	Hazel	Cat	DSH	F	Whitney	Antonia
16	Kwanzaa	Cat	DSH	M	Whitaker	Shamir
17	Maddie	Cat	DSH	F	Askren	Mollica
18	Nikki	Cat	DSH	F	Arzate	Lisa
19	Pyewackett	Cat	DSH	M	Woo	Kum
20	Bon Chat	Cat	Himalayan	F	Russell	Melissa
21	Mai Tai	Cat	Himalayan	M	Thorton	Vanessa

Excel 2016, Windows 10, Microsoft Corporation

Figure 67-1

Try It! Converting Ranges to Tables

1. Start Excel, and open **E67Try** from the data files for this lesson.
2. Save the file as **E67Try_xx** in the location where your teacher instructs you to store the files for this lesson.
3. Click the July 22 worksheet tab to select it, if necessary.
4. Select the cell range A6:D23.
5. Click Insert > Table.
6. Click OK to accept the =$A$6:$D$23 range. The range is converted into a table.
7. Select the cell range A29:D46.
8. Click Insert > Table.
9. Click OK to accept the =$A$29:$D$46 range.
10. Save the changes to the file, and leave it open to use in the next Try It.

Changing a Table's Name

- A table has a default name (*Table* plus a number, such as Table1), but you may want to assign it a more memorable name, especially if you plan to use structured references (covered later in this lesson).
- You can change the table's name on the Table Tools Design tab, in the Table Name text box in the Properties group.
- These are the rules for naming a table:
  - A table name can be up to 255 characters long, but short names are easier to manage when referencing the table.

- A table name must be alphanumeric; it cannot contain symbols, except for underscore (_), backslash (\), or period (.).
- A table name must begin with a letter, an underscore character, or a backslash.
- A table name cannot contain spaces, so use an underscore if you want to separate words in the name.
- A table name cannot be the same as a cell reference, whether written in standard notation (like A12) or in row and column notation (like R12C1).
- Table names appear in the case in which they are created, but are not case-sensitive. You can't have duplicate table names in the same workbook, so you could not have two tables named Revenue and REVENUE, for example.

Try It! Renaming Tables

1. In the **E67Try_xx** file, on the July 22 tab, click in cell A6, or anywhere inside the upper table.
2. Click the Table Tools Design tab.
3. In the Properties group, click in the Table Name box and change the name to **South_Bay_722**.

   ✓ *Make sure you use an underscore, not a space, between the words in the name.*
4. Click in cell A29, or anywhere inside the lower table.
5. Click in the Table Name box and change the name to **Mission_Bay_722**.
6. Click the July 23 tab, and rename the two tables **South_Bay_723** and **Mission_Bay_723**, respectively.
7. Save the changes to the file, and leave the file open to use in the next Try It.

Showing a Totals Row in a Table

- Using a Totals row provides a way of summarizing data in the table without having to create formulas or functions for each column. It is one of the many benefits of analyzing data in tabular form in Excel.

Try It! Showing a Totals Row in a Table

1. In the **E67Try_xx** file, on the July 22 tab, click cell A23.
2. Right-click cell A23 and on the shortcut menu that appears, click Table > Totals Row. A totals row appears in the table.
3. Click cell A47.
4. Right-click cell A47 and on the shortcut menu that appears, click Table > Totals Row. A totals row appears in the table.
5. Save the changes to the file, and leave it open to use in the next Try It.

17. On the **Data** worksheet, click any cell in the table. Then on the Table Tools Design tab, click to clear the **Banded Rows** check box.

18. Click to mark the **Banded Columns** check box. The first several rows of the table should look like Figure 67-3.

19. Save the changes to the file and exit Excel.

Figure 67-2

	A	B	C
1	Average Values		
2			
3	Average # of Bedrooms	4	
4	Average # of Baths	3	
5	Average Square Feet	2231	
6			
7			
8			

Excel 2016, Windows 10, Microsoft Corporation

Figure 67-3

	A	B	C	D	E	F	G	H	I	J	K	L
1	Agent	Date Listed	Area	Community	List Price	Bedrooms	Baths	SqFt	Type	Pool	Spa	HOA Fees
2	Hamilton	3/23/2017	Inland	Regent	$ 215,000	3	1.5	2157	Single Family	TRUE	FALSE	TRUE
3	Jeffery	4/10/2017	Inland	Regent	$ 319,000	4	2.5	1690	Condo	FALSE	FALSE	TRUE
4	Kennedy	7/18/2018	Inland	Regent	$ 268,500	4	2.5	1921	Duplex	FALSE	TRUE	TRUE
5	Lam	8/26/2017	Inland	Regent	$ 339,900	4	2	2238	Single Family	FALSE	TRUE	FALSE
6	Langston	9/27/2017	Inland	Regent	$ 250,000	4	3	1943	Single Family	FALSE	FALSE	FALSE
7	Barnes	8/9/2017	Coastal	Linda Vista	$ 345,000	4	3	2388	Single Family	FALSE	FALSE	TRUE

Excel 2016, Windows 10, Microsoft Corporation

Lesson 67—Apply

You work in the sales department for Rural Estates Real Estate. Your manager has asked you to use the table of listings to help a customer find a suitable property.

1. Start Excel, if necessary, and open **E67Apply** from the data files for this lesson.
2. Save the file as **E67Apply_xx** in the location where your teacher instructs you to store the files for this lesson.
3. Click the **Report** worksheet tab, add a header that has your name at the left, the date code in the center, and the page number code at the right, and change back to Normal view.
4. Convert the range **A1:L121** to a table using the **Insert** > **Table** command.
5. On the Table Tools Design tab, change the table's name from Table1 to **Homes**.
6. Click the arrow to the right of the **SqFt** column label, and click Sort Largest to Smallest.
7. Click the arrow to the right of the **Area** column label, click **Select All** to clear that check box, and then click **Coastal**. Click **OK**.
8. Click the arrow to the right of the **Type** column label, click **Select All** to clear that check box, and then click **Single Family**. Click **OK**.
9. Click the arrow to the right of the **HOA Fees** column label, click **TRUE** to clear its check box, and click **OK**.
10. Right-click the table and click **Table** > **Totals Row**.
11. Click cell **L122** and in the Name box, type **Count**.
12. Click **Formulas** > **Name Manager**.
13. Click the **Count** name, and click **Edit**.
14. Change the name to **CountHomes** and click **OK**.
15. On the Summary tab, in cell B3, type **=CountHomes**. Press ENTER.
16. On the Report tab, click in cell **H122**. Click the **down arrow** to the right of the field and click **Min**.
17. On the Summary tab, click in cell **B4**, type **=Report!H122** and press ENTER.
18. On the Report tab, click the arrow to the right of the **Pool** column label, click **FALSE** to clear its check box, and click **OK**.
19. **With your teacher's permission**, print the filtered Report worksheet using Landscape orientation and using the Fit Sheet on One Page scaling option. It should look like Figure 67-4.
20. Save the changes to the file, and exit Excel.

Figure 67-4

Agent	Date Listed	Area	Community	List Price	Bedrooms	Baths	SqFt	Type	Pool	Spa	HOA Fees
Garcia	4/3/2017	Coastal	Mira Mesa	$799,000	6	5	4800	Single Family	TRUE	TRUE	FALSE
Jeffery	8/28/2018	Coastal	Arandale	$1,200,500	5	5	4696	Single Family	TRUE	TRUE	FALSE
Langston	7/21/2017	Coastal	Mira Mesa	$349,000	4	3	3930	Single Family	TRUE	FALSE	FALSE
Conners	6/30/2018	Coastal	Mira Mesa	$229,500	6	3	2700	Single Family	TRUE	TRUE	FALSE
Barnes	3/13/2017	Coastal	Arandale	$264,900	3	2.5	2495	Single Family	TRUE	TRUE	FALSE
Carter	4/6/2017	Coastal	Mono Lake	$309,900	5	3	2447	Single Family	TRUE	TRUE	FALSE
Hamilton	2/23/2017	Coastal	Bend	$425,900	5	3	2414	Single Family	TRUE	TRUE	FALSE
Garcia	8/2/2017	Coastal	Linda Vista	$359,900	3	2	2198	Single Family	TRUE	FALSE	FALSE
Total							**2198**				**8**

Excel 2016, Windows 10, Microsoft Corporation

Lesson 68

Using Get & Transform

➤ What You Will Learn

Understanding Get & Transform
Creating a Query
Modifying a Query
Adding a Calculated Field to a Query
Merging Data from Different Sources

Software Skills Get & Transform is a new feature in Excel 2016 that enables you to gather and analyze data from external data sources. This feature is similar to the Power Query feature in earlier Excel versions.

What You Can Do

Understanding Get & Transform

- Get & Transform enables you to use Excel to create **queries** using data from external data sources, similar to the queries you create in a database program like Microsoft Access. You then **transform** the data by applying different changes to your copy of it, and the save or share the results.
- These are the steps in the Get & Transform process:
  - **Connect**: Make a connection to the data by creating a query.
  - **Transform**: Shape your copy of the data to meet your needs, without affecting the original source.
  - **Combine:** If needed, merge data from multiple data sources into a new query.
  - **Share:** Save the workbook that contains your queries, and share it with others if desired.

Creating a Query

- When you create a new query in Excel, you connect to its data source. Creating a query does not modify the original data.

Words to Know

Calculated Field
A field in a data table that contains a formula or function.

Query
A view of a dataset that can be customized with sorting, filtering, or other transformations.

Transform
To apply changes to a dataset by creating and using a query.

- Data for a query can come from a variety of sources, including local files (like Excel files and plain text files), databases in many different formats, and from most commercial Microsoft tools and platforms like Microsoft Azure, SharePoint, Microsoft CRM, and Active Directory.

✓ *To pull data from two different sources, you create separate queries for each source and then combine the data later in the process. See "Merging Data from Different Sources" later in this lesson.*

Try It! Create a Query

1. Open Excel and start a new blank workbook.
2. On the Data tab, click New Query.
3. Click From Other Sources > From OData Feed.
4. In the URL text box, type **http://services.odata.org/Northwind/Northwind.svc** and click OK.
5. In the Navigator window, click Order_Details.
6. Click Load.
7. On the Data tab, click New Query.
8. Click From Database > From Microsoft Access Database.
9. Browse to the files for this lesson and select **E68TryA.accdb**. Click Import.
10. In the Navigator window, click Products.
11. Click Load.
12. Save the file as **E68TryB_xx** in the location where your teacher instructs you to store the files for this lesson. Leave it open for the next Try It.

✓ *If you had wanted to edit the query right away, you could have clicked Edit instead of load in step 6 or step 11.*

Create a new query from the online database source

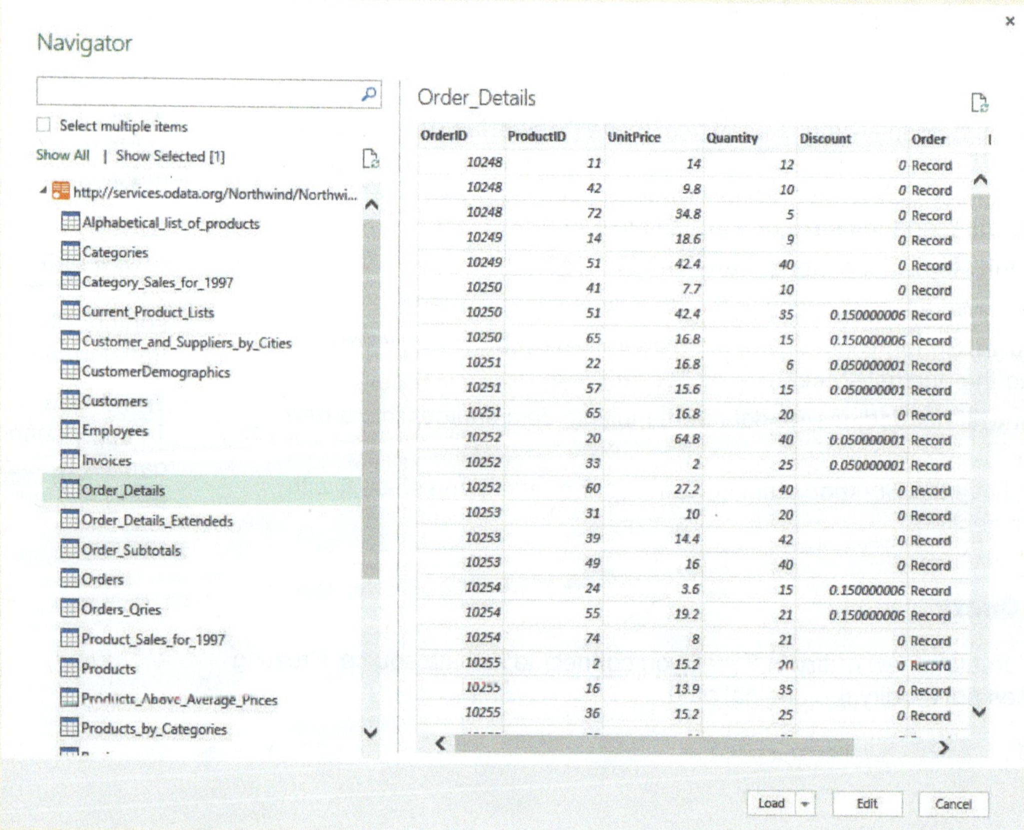

Excel 2016, Windows 10, Microsoft Corporation

Modifying a Query

- The data that you pull when you create the query may not be exactly as you want it. For example, it may contain extra fields you don't want, or records that don't meet your criteria.
- To modify a query, use the Query Editor. You can access the Query Editor from the Query Tools Query tab by clicking Edit.
- In the Query Editor you can remove certain fields (columns) or records (rows), you can sort by a certain column, you can remove duplicates, and more.

Try It! Modify a Query

1. In **E68TryB**, in the Workbook Queries task pane, double-click Products.

   ✓ *If the task pane does not appear, click Data > Show Queries.*

2. In the Query Editor window, Click the Reorder Level column heading to select that column.
3. Hold down the SHIFT key and click the Minimum Reorder Quantity column heading, selecting it and all the columns between them.
4. Press the DEL key to remove those columns.

   ✓ *The columns are removed from the query but not from the original data source.*

5. Click the Description column heading, and then hold down SHIFT and click the Standard Cost heading.
6. Press the DEL key.
7. Click Home > Close & Load.
8. Click the List_Price column heading on the worksheet to select it.
9. Click Home > Accounting Number Format.
10. Double-click the Order Details query to open it in the Query Editor.
11. Click the Discount column heading, and then hold down SHIFT and click the Product column heading.
12. Click Home > Remove Columns. This is an alternate method of removing a column.
13. Click the down arrow to the right of the OrderID field.
14. Click Sort Ascending.
15. Click the Transform tab.
16. Click the UnitPrice column heading, and then open the Data Type drop-down list and click Currency.
17. In the Any Column group, click Rename. Type Unit_Price and press ENTER.
18. Click the Unit_Price column heading, and then drag the column to the right of the Quantity column.
19. Click Home > Close & Load.
20. Save changes to the file and leave it open for the next Try It.

(continued)

Try It! **Modify a Query** *(continued)*

Format and filter the data in the query

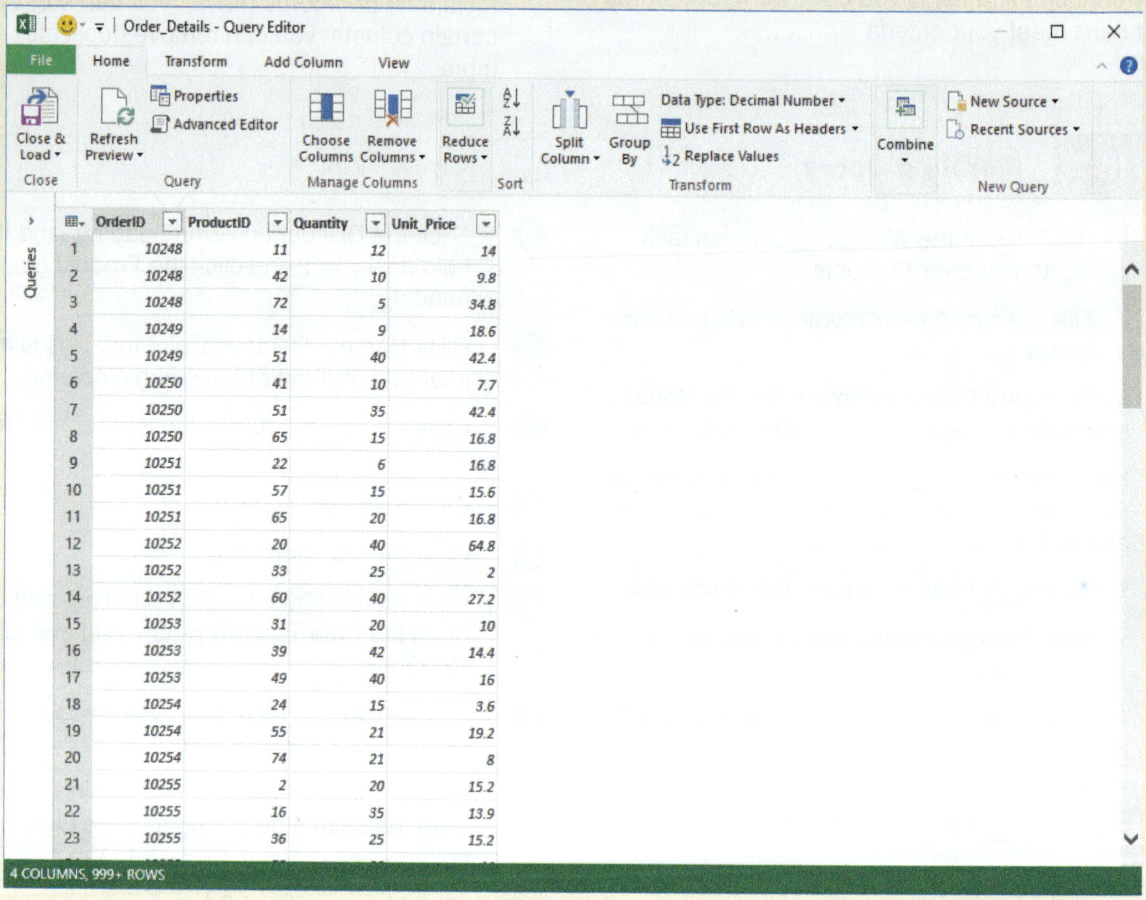

Excel 2016, Windows 10, Microsoft Corporation

Adding a Calculated Field

- A **calculated field** lets you perform operations on the data and show the results in the query worksheet. There are two ways of adding a calculated field to a query.
  - The first way is to type a formula directly into an adjacent blank column in the worksheet (not in the Query Editor). This method does *not* add the field to the query, only to your datasheet that shows the query results.
  - An alternate way is to enter the Query Editor and use the Add Column > Add Custom Column command, and then enter a formula in the Add Custom Column dialog box. This method adds the calculated field to the query itself.

Try It! Add a Calculated Field

1. In **E68TryB**, on the Sheet2 tab (the one that shows the (Order_Details query), click in cell E2.
2. Type **=C2*D2** and press ENTER.

   ✓ *The formula is copied to all other rows automatically.*
3. Click cell E1, type **Total**, and press ENTER. This creates a calculated field on the worksheet only.
4. Select column E and click Home > Delete.
5. In the Workbook Queries pane, double-click Order_Details.
6. Click Add Column > Add Custom Column.
7. Change the name in the New column name text box to Total.
8. Click in the Custom column formula box, after the = sign.
9. In the Available Columns list, click Quantity, and then click << Insert.
10. Type an asterisk (*).
11. In the Available Columns list, click Unit_Price and then click <<Insert.
12. Click OK.
13. Click Home > Close & Load. The new column is added to the table.
14. Save changes to the file and leave it open for the next Try It.

Create a calculated field in a new column

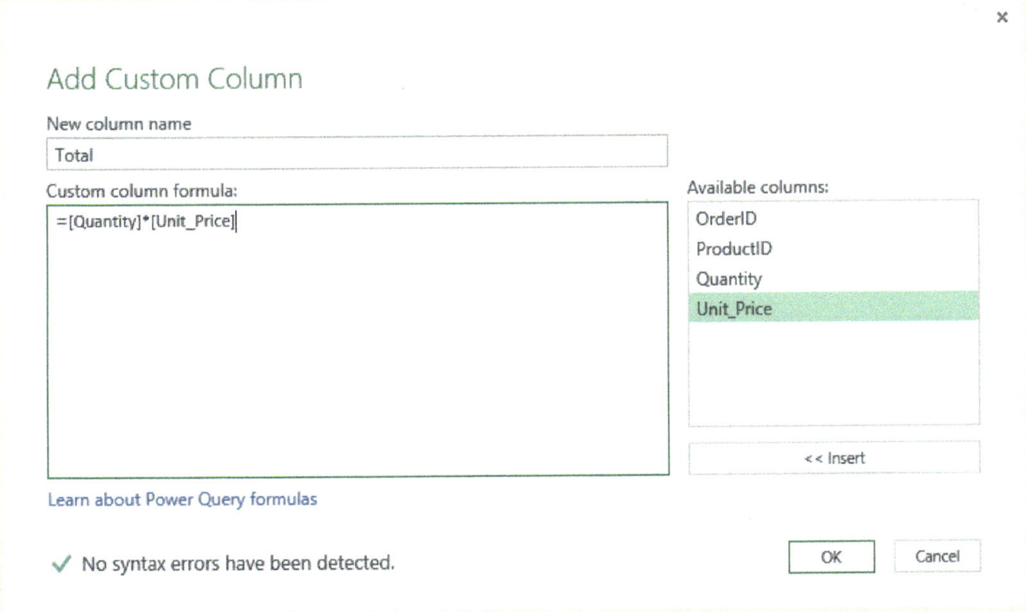

Merging Data from Different Sources

- If the data in two queries are related in some way, you can merge them to create a new query that contains data from both. It doesn't matter that the two data sources are not in the same file, or even on the same computer.
- For example, if both queries refer to the same products by their number, you can join the two queries by the fields that each contain the product number.

Try It! Merging Data from Different Sources

1. In **E68TryB**, click anywhere within the table on Sheet2, and then click Query Tools Query > Merge.
2. In the Merge dialog box, open the lower drop-down list and click Products.
3. In the upper grid, select the ProductID column.
4. In the lower grid, select the ID column.
5. The first time you use these data sources, you are prompted for privacy settings:
   - a. In the Privacy levels dialog box, open the first Select drop-down list and click Private.
   - b. Repeat step 5 for the second Select drop-down list, and then click Save.
6. Click OK.

   ✓ *The merged query opens in the Query Editor. A new column appears called NewColumn, and the entry in every field is Table.*
7. Click the Expand icon on the NewColumn heading.
8. Click (Select All Columns) to clear all checkboxes. Then click Product Name to re-select it.
9. Clear the Use original column name as prefix check box. Then click OK.

   ✓ *Notice that some of the product IDs had no match; they show null in the new column.*
10. Click the down arrow to the right of the Product Name column heading.
11. Click the (null) check box to clear it, and then click OK.
12. Click Home > Close & Load.
13. In the Workbook Queries task pane, right-click Merge1 and click Properties.
14. In the Name box, type **Order_Items_With_Names** and click OK.
15. Select columns D and E on the worksheet, and then click Home > Accounting Number Format.
16. Save changes to the file and exit Excel.

Set up the new column to show the product name

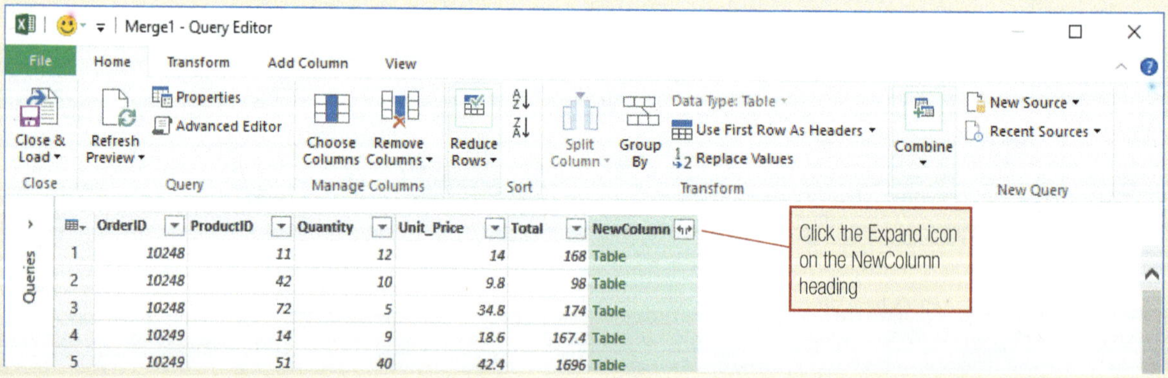

Excel 2016, Windows 10, Microsoft Corporation

Lesson 68—Practice

Rural Estates Real Estate has a database that contains listings, where agents are identified by their number. It has another file that tells the full names associated with each number, but they are in different formats. You will use queries to join this information in a single worksheet using queries.

DIRECTIONS

1. Start Excel, if necessary, and start a new blank workbook.
2. Save the workbook as **E68Practice_xx** in the location where your teacher instructs you to store the files for this lesson.
3. Click **Data** > **New Query** > **From Database** > **From Microsoft Access Database**.
4. Navigate to the location containing the data files for this lesson, select **E68PracticeA**, and click **Import**.
5. Click **RealEstate**, and click **Edit**.
6. In the Query Editor, Click the down arrow to the right of the **Sold** column, and click **Sort Ascending**.
7. Click **Home** > **Remove Rows** > **Remove Top Rows**.
8. In the Remove Top Rows dialog box, type **42** in the Number of Rows box and click **OK**.

   ✓ *The first 42 rows contain TRUE in the Sold field.*
9. Click the down arrow to the right of the **Date Listed** field and click **Sort Ascending**.
10. Click **Transform** > **Data Type** and click **Date**.
11. Click **Home** > **Close & Load**.
12. Click **Data** > **New Query** > **From File** > **From Text**.
13. Navigate to the location containing the data files for this lesson, select **E68PracticeB**, and click **Import**.
14. In the Query Editor, right-click the heading for Column1, click **Rename**, type **ID**, and press **Enter**.
15. Right-click the heading for Column2, click **Rename**, type **First**, and press **Enter**.
16. Right-click the heading for Column3, click **Rename**, type **Last**, and press **Enter**.
17. Click **Home** > **Close & Load**.
18. Right-click **E68PracticeB** in the task pane and click **Properties**. Change the name in the Name box to **Realtors** and click **OK**.
19. Click **Query Tools Query** > **Merge**.
20. In the upper drop-down list, click **RealEstate**. In the lower drop-down list, click **Realtors**.
21. In the upper grid click the **Agent** column. In the lower grid click the **ID** column. Then click **OK**.
22. In the **NewColumn** column, click the **Expand** icon.
23. Clear the **ID** and **First** check boxes.
24. Clear the **Use original column name as prefix** check box. Then click **OK**.
25. Drag the **Agent** field between the Sold field and the Last field.
26. Select the **Sold** field and press **Delete**.
27. Right-click the **Last** column and click **Rename**. Type **Agent Name** and press ENTER.
28. Click **Close & Load**.
29. Select column D and select **Home** > **Accounting Number Format**. Click the **Decrease Decimal** button twice.
30. On the Sheet4 tab, add a header that has your name at the left, the date code in the center, and the page number code at the right.
31. **With your teacher's permission**, print the Sheet4 worksheet in Landscape orientation. The first page should look like the one shown in Figure 68-1 on the next page.
32. Save the changes to the workbook and exit Excel.

Figure 68-1

ID	Date Listed	Area	List Price	Bedrooms	Baths	SqFt	Type	Pool	Agent	Agent Name
4/19/1900	2/9/2018 0:00	Kern	$ 350,499	3	2	2276	Single Family	TRUE	13	Raffa
2/4/1900	2/19/2018 0:00	Kern	$ 354,499	4	2	2088	Single Family	FALSE	4	Hoskins
2/11/1900	2/23/2018 0:00	Ward	$ 425,900	5	3	2414	Single Family	TRUE	15	Schrock
2/26/1900	2/25/2018 0:00	Kern	$ 239,900	2	2	1248	Single Family	FALSE	11	Olson
3/19/1900	2/26/2018 0:00	Imperial	$ 269,900	4	2.5	1911	Single Family	FALSE	16	Simmons
2/20/1900	3/2/2018 0:00	Imperial	$ 338,876	4	2.5	2612	Single Family	FALSE	6	Kemp
1/14/1900	3/6/2018 0:00	Riverside	$ 299,499	3	2	2060	Single Family	FALSE	19	Weiss
2/25/1900	3/7/2018 0:00	Kern	$ 229,900	4	3	2006	Single Family	FALSE	11	Olson
1/13/1900	3/13/2018 0:00	Ward	$ 264,900	3	3	2496	Single Family	FALSE	19	Weiss
3/12/1900	3/13/2018 0:00	Kern	$ 364,900	4	2.5	2607	Single Family	FALSE	10	Mosher
1/16/1900	3/21/2018 0:00	Ward	$ 350,499	3	2.5	1991	Single Family	FALSE	18	Torres
1/28/1900	3/21/2018 0:00	Riverside	$ 205,499	3	2.5	2001	Single Family	TRUE	18	Torres
3/7/1900	3/22/2018 0:00	Yuba	$ 325,499	4	3	2770	Single Family	FALSE	11	Olson
4/28/1900	3/23/2018 0:00	Ward	$ 398,499	4	2.5	2620	Single Family	FALSE	13	Raffa
2/18/1900	3/25/2018 0:00	Yuba	$ 247,500	4	3	2000	Single Family	FALSE	5	Kane
4/13/1900	4/3/2018 0:00	Ward	$ 799,499	6	5	4800	Single Family	FALSE	8	Mason
4/20/1900	4/6/2018 0:00	Kern	$ 365,499	3	2.5	1871	Single Family	FALSE	13	Raffa
3/15/1900	4/6/2018 0:00	Ward	$ 309,900	5	3	2447	Single Family	TRUE	10	Mosher
2/13/1900	4/10/2018 0:00	Kern	$ 319,499	4	2.5	1690	Single Family	TRUE	16	Simmons
1/27/1900	4/20/2018 0:00	Kern	$ 375,499	4	3	2467	Single Family	TRUE	18	Torres
1/22/1900	4/20/2018 0:00	Ward	$ 229,900	3	3	2266	Single Family	FALSE	12	Porter
1/2/1900	4/27/2018 0:00	Kern	$ 265,499	4	3	1906	Single Family	FALSE	2	Ellis
4/9/1900	4/30/2018 0:00	Kern	$ 250,499	3	2	2066	Single Family	FALSE	8	Mason
3/5/1900	5/2/2018 0:00	Imperial	$ 225,911	4	2.5	1908	Single Family	TRUE	16	Simmons
3/4/1900	5/2/2018 0:00	Ward	$ 369,900	3	2.5	2030	Single Family	TRUE	11	Olson
4/21/1900	5/6/2018 0:00	Kern	$ 625,499	6	4	3960	Single Family	TRUE	13	Raffa
1/20/1900	5/8/2018 0:00	Kern	$ 549,499	4	3	1940	Single Family	TRUE	12	Porter
4/17/1900	5/16/2018 0:00	Kern	$ 319,499	3	2.5	2685	Single Family	FALSE	13	Raffa
1/23/1900	5/26/2018 0:00	Ward	$ 229,900	4	3	2041	Single Family	FALSE	2	Ellis
5/4/1900	6/3/2018 0:00	Imperial	$ 574,900	5	4	4700	Single Family	FALSE	13	Raffa
2/23/1900	6/8/2018 0:00	Ward	$ 389,500	4	2	1971	Single Family	FALSE	9	Meyer
3/13/1900	6/17/2018 0:00	Ward	$ 235,990	4	2	1655	Single Family	TRUE	2	Ellis
3/3/1900	6/22/2018 0:00	Ward	$ 359,499	3	2.5	2210	Single Family	FALSE	11	Olson
3/16/1900	6/25/2018 0:00	Imperial	$ 225,499	4	3	2013	Single Family	TRUE	10	Mosher

Lesson 68—Apply

Northwind Traders has asked you to analyze their purchase orders in their database. You will create queries from multiple database tables, including calculated fields, that provide the needed information.

DIRECTIONS

1. Start Excel, if necessary, and start a new blank workbook.
2. Save the workbook as **E68Apply_xx** in the location where your teacher instructs you to store the files for this lesson.
3. Click **Data** > **New Query** > **From Database** > **From Microsoft Access Database**.
4. Navigate to the location containing the data files for this lesson, select **E68ApplyA**, and click **Import**.
5. Click **Purchase Orders**, and click **Load**.
6. Repeat steps 3–5 to create additional queries from the Products and Purchase Order Details objects from the E68ApplyA database.
7. Click **Query Tools Query** > **Merge**.
8. In the upper drop-down list, click **Purchase Order Details**. In the lower drop-down list, click **Products**.
9. In the upper grid click the **Product ID** column. In the lower grid click the **ID** column. Then click **OK**.
10. In the **NewColumn** column, click the **Expand** icon.
11. Click **(Select All Columns)** to clear all check boxes. Then click **Product Name**, and click **OK**.
12. Right-click the **NewColumn.Product Name** column, click **Rename**, edit the name to **Product Name**, and press ENTER.
13. Select columns **Posted To Inventory** and **Inventory ID** and press **Delete**.
14. Select the Date Received column, and drag it between the Product ID and the Quantity fields.
15. Click **Transform** > **Data Type** > **Date**.
16. Click **Add Column** > **Add Custom Column**.
17. In the New column name box, change the name to **Total**.
18. Double-click **Quantity**. Then type an **asterisk (*)** and double-click **Unit Cost**. Click **OK**.
19. Drag the **Total** column to the right of the Unit Cost column.
20. Click **Transform** > **Data Type** > **Currency**.
21. Click **Home** > **Close & Load**.
22. Click **Query Tools** > **Merge**.
23. In the upper drop-down list, click **Merge1**. In the lower drop-down list, click **Purchase Orders**.
24. In the upper grid click the **Purchase Order ID** column. In the lower grid click the **Purchase Order ID** column. Then click **OK**.
25. In the **NewColumn** column, click the **Expand** icon.
26. Click **(Select All Columns)** to clear all check boxes. Then click **Supplier ID**, clear the **Use original column name as prefix** check box, and click **OK**.
27. Click the down arrow to the right of the Supplier ID column.
28. Click **(Select All Columns)** to clear all check boxes. Then click **2**, and click **OK**.
29. Click **Home** > **Close & Load**.
30. Select columns F and G and select **Home** > **Accounting Number Format**. Click the **Decrease Decimal** button twice.
31. On the Sheet6 tab, add a header that has your name at the left, the date code in the center, and the page number code at the right.
32. Select columns A, B, C, and I, and then click **Home** > **Format** > **Hide & Unhide** > **Hide Columns**.
33. **With your teacher's permission**, print the Sheet6 worksheet. It should look like Figure 68-2 on the next page.
34. Save the changes to the workbook and exit Excel.

Figure 68-2

Date Received	Quantity	Unit Cost	Total	Product Name
1/22/2008	100	$ 19.00	$ 1,900.00	Northwind Traders Boysenberry Spread
1/22/2008	40	$ 22.00	$ 880.00	Northwind Traders Dried Pears
1/22/2008	40	$ 30.00	$ 1,200.00	Northwind Traders Curry Sauce
1/22/2008	40	$ 17.00	$ 680.00	Northwind Traders Walnuts
1/22/2008	40	$ 29.00	$ 1,160.00	Northwind Traders Fruit Cocktail
1/22/2008	20	$ 7.00	$ 140.00	Northwind Traders Chocolate Biscuits Mix
1/22/2008	40	$ 61.00	$ 2,440.00	Northwind Traders Marmalade
1/22/2008	20	$ 8.00	$ 160.00	Northwind Traders Scones
1/22/2008	120	$ 14.00	$ 1,680.00	Northwind Traders Crab Meat
1/22/2008	40	$ 7.00	$ 280.00	Northwind Traders Clam Chowder
1/22/2008	100	$ 10.00	$ 1,000.00	Northwind Traders Chocolate
1/22/2008	40	$ 40.00	$ 1,600.00	Northwind Traders Dried Apples
1/22/2008	20	$ 8.00	$ 160.00	Northwind Traders Almonds
1/22/2008	60	$ 10.00	$ 600.00	Northwind Traders Mustard
1/22/2008	30	$ 7.00	$ 210.00	Northwind Traders Chocolate Biscuits Mix
1/22/2008	200	$ 7.00	$ 1,400.00	Northwind Traders Clam Chowder
1/22/2008	100	$ 10.00	$ 1,000.00	Northwind Traders Chocolate
4/17/2008	10	$ 7.00	$ 70.00	Northwind Traders Chocolate Biscuits Mix
4/6/2008	50	$ 7.00	$ 350.00	Northwind Traders Clam Chowder
4/5/2008	25	$ 30.00	$ 750.00	Northwind Traders Curry Sauce
4/5/2008	25	$ 7.00	$ 175.00	Northwind Traders Chocolate Biscuits Mix
	20	$ 7.00	$ 140.00	Northwind Traders Chocolate Biscuits Mix
	40	$ 60.00	$ 2,400.00	Northwind Traders Marmalade
	40	$ 39.00	$ 1,560.00	Northwind Traders Dried Apples

Lesson 69

Using Advanced Filters and Slicers

➤ What You Will Learn

Using Advanced Filters
Working with Slicers

Software Skills When you search for data in a long list of records, you can use Excel's filtering features to display only the records that match criteria you specify. Advanced filters and slicers enable you to set up complex filtering criteria, and to create results that are not possible with standard filtering, such as extracting records to another place in the worksheet.

What You Can Do

Using Advanced Filters

- With an advanced filter you can filter records in a list in one of two ways:
  - You can hide records that do not match the criteria you specify—in much the same way as with a regular filter.
  - You can **extract** records to another place in the worksheet.
- Although an advanced filter can hide records just like a regular filter, it's different in many ways.
  - An advanced filter allows you to enter more complex criteria than a regular filter.
  - Instead of selecting criteria from a drop-down list, you enter it in a special area in the workbook—or even a worksheet by itself—set aside for that purpose.
  - In the marked cells of this criteria range, you enter the items you want to match from the list, or expressions that describe the type of comparison you wish to make.
  - You then open a dialog box in which you specify the range where the list or table is contained, the range containing the criteria, and the range to which you want records copied/extracted (if applicable).

WORDS TO KNOW

Extract
To copy records that match specified criteria to another place in the worksheet.

Slicer
An Excel filtering component that contains a set of buttons to enable you to quickly filter data.

- If you want to compare the values of two fields as part of the filter, create a formula that performs the comparison (beginning with an equals sign) and place it in a cell that has a blank cell directly above it. Then select the blank cell and the cell containing the formula as the criteria range.
- For the comparison operation, refer to the cells in the first data row of the table. Excel will assume that you want to calculate the entire table based on that same pattern.
- Here are some more examples. Each of them assumes that you are evaluating data in a table where the first data row is 7, and that you are using cells M1:M2 (some empty cells away from the main table) as the criteria range. Cell M1 is left blank, and cell M2 contains the value shown in this table.

To find	Place this in cell M2
Records where column F is less than column G	=F7<G7
Records where column F does not equal column G	=F7<>G7
Records where column F is blank	=F7=""
Records where column F equals column G	=F7=G7

Try It! Using an Advanced Filter to Extract Records

1. Start Excel, and open **E69TryA** from the data files for this lesson.
2. Save the file as **E69TryA_xx** in the location where your teacher instructs you to store the files for this lesson.
3. On the Criteria worksheet, create a criterion that includes racers who placed third or better in their qualifying heats:
   a. Click the Criteria worksheet tab.
   b. Click cell E2, type **<=3**, and press ENTER.
4. Apply an advanced filter that finds the matching racers from the July Race worksheet and places it in a blank area of the worksheet:
   a. Click the July Race worksheet tab.
   b. Click Data > Advanced to open the Advanced Filter dialog box.
   c. In the List range box, type **$A$8:$H$44**.
   d. In the Criteria range box, click the Collapse Dialog Box button to collapse the dialog box.
   e. Click the Criteria worksheet tab.
   f. Select the cell range A1:H2, and press ENTER to return to the dialog box.
   g. In the Advanced Filter dialog box, under Action, click Copy to another location. The Copy to box becomes available.
   h. Click in the Copy to box, and click cell J8 on the July Race tab.
   i. Click OK to apply the filter. The matching records appear in range J8:Q33.
   j. Adjust the column widths as needed for columns J through Q.
5. Save the changes to the file, and leave it open to use in the next Try It.

The Advanced Filter dialog box

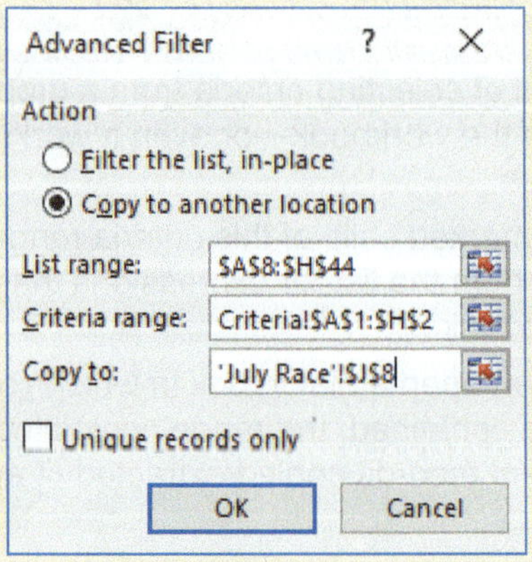

Excel 2016, Windows 10, Microsoft Corporation

Try It! Using an Advanced Filter to Filter In-Place

1. In the **E69TryA_xx** file, click the Criteria worksheet, click cell E2, and press DEL to clear the previous criterion.
2. Click cell D2, type **<=12:01:00 AM**, and press ENTER.

   ✓ *Excel stores all time values as relative to a point on the clock. So an elapsed time of one minute is stored as "12:01 AM," or one minute of elapsed time past midnight—which is Excel's "zero hour."*
3. Apply an advanced filter that finds the matching racers from the June Race worksheet and filters the data in-place:
   a. Click the June Race worksheet tab.
   b. On the Data tab, click Advanced to open the Advanced Filter dialog.
   c. In the List range box, type **$A$8:$H$44**.
   d. In the Criteria range box, click the Collapse Dialog Box button to collapse the dialog box.
   e. Click the Criteria worksheet tab.
   f. Select the cell range A1:H2, and press ENTER.
   g. Click OK. The list is filtered on the June Race worksheet to show only the matching records.
4. Save and close the file, and leave Excel open for the next Try It.

Try It! Using an Advanced Filter with a Comparison Operator

1. Open **E69TryB** from the data files for this lesson.
2. Save the file as **E69TryB_xx** in the location where your teacher instructs you to store the files for this lesson.
3. Click the Criteria worksheet tab, click A2, type **=H7<E7*3**, and press ENTER. The formula result appears as FALSE. This is normal.

   ✓ *This formula checks to see whether the Items Remaining is less than 3 times the Items Per Case. It appears at the moment to refer to cells on the Criteria worksheet tab, but when it is used for the advanced filter's criteria, it will refer to the table on the August Sales worksheet. The fact that it evaluates to FALSE at the moment is irrelevant.*
4. Click the August Sales worksheet tab.
5. Click Data > Advanced to open the Advanced Filter dialog.
6. In the List range box, type **$A$6:$K$93**.
7. In the Criteria range box, click the Collapse Dialog Box button.
8. Click the Criteria worksheet tab, select the cell range A1:A2, and press ENTER to return to the dialog box.
9. Click OK. The filter is applied, and eight records appear.
10. Save the changes to the file, and leave it open to use in the next Try It.

Working with Slicers

- You can use **slicers** to easily view and select the criteria on which you want to filter your data.
- Insert a slicer using the Slicer button in the Filters group on the Insert tab.
- The fields are displayed as column names in the Insert Slicers dialog box. A slicer will be displayed for every field that you select.
- After you create a slicer, it appears on the worksheet alongside the table.
- If you insert more than one slicer, the slicers display in layers.
- You can move slicers within the worksheet to view them more easily.
- Select the item(s) in the slicer on which you want to filter the data.
- To select more than one item in a slicer, hold down the Control key CTRL, and click the items on which you want to filter.
- To remove a filter in the slicer, click the Clear Filter button on the slicer.
- You can change the slicer settings or apply slicer styles from the Slicer Tools Options tab.
- To delete a slicer, click on a slicer to select it, and press DEL. You can also right-click a slicer, and click Remove "Name of slicer."

  ✓ *When you delete a slicer, the filter(s) applied to your data are not removed.*

- You can also use slicers to group records so you can analyze the filtered set of data.

Try It! Inserting Multiple Slicers

1. In the **E69TryB_xx** file, on the August Sales worksheet tab, click any cell in the table.
2. Click Insert > Slicer to display the Insert Slicers dialog box.
3. Click the Drug check box, click the To treat check box, and click OK.
4. Click and drag the To treat slicer so that its upper-left corner is in the upper-left corner of cell O6.
5. Click and drag the Drug slicer so that its upper-left corner is in the upper-left corner of cell M6.
6. In the Drug slicer, scroll down and click Revolution. The table displays the data for the selected drug. Notice that the To treat slicer automatically filters to show the criteria (in this case, Cat, Dog, and Puppy or Kitten) which apply to the Drug criteria (Revolution) that you selected as the filter.
7. In the To Treat slicer, click Dog. The table displays the data for the selected drug and the selected animal it can treat.
8. Click the Drug slicer, and scroll down to view the Revolution criteria. Notice that it is still selected.
9. Save the changes to the file, and leave it open to use in the next Try It.

The Insert Slicers dialog box

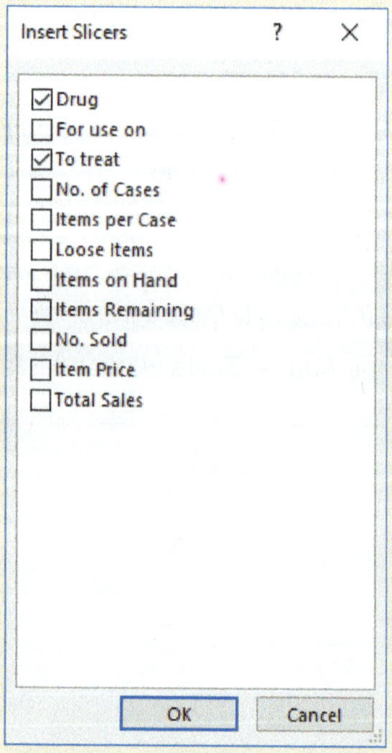

Excel 2016, Windows 10, Microsoft Corporation

Try It! Applying Styles to Slicers

1. In the E69TryB_xx file, on the August Sales worksheet tab, click the Drug slicer.
2. Click the Slicer Tools Options tab.
3. In the Slicer Styles gallery, click Slicer Style Light 2.
4. Click the To treat slicer.
5. In the Slicer Styles gallery, click Slicer Style Light 4.
6. Save the changes to the file, and leave it open to use in the next Try It.

Styles applied to slicers

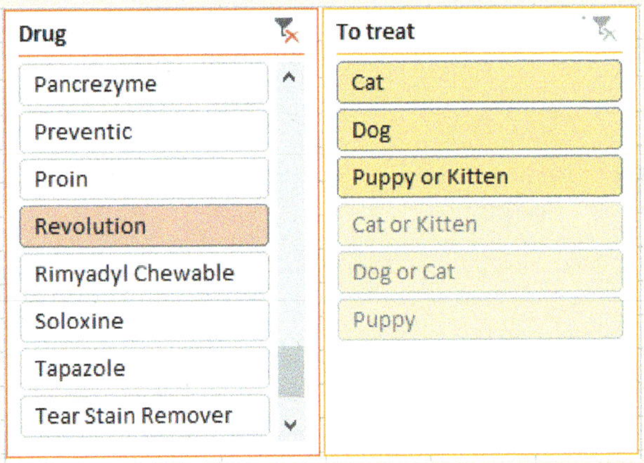

Excel 2016, Windows 10, Microsoft Corporation

Try It! Clearing a Slicer Filter

1. In the E69TryB_xx file, on the August Sales worksheet tab, click the To treat slicer.
2. On the To treat slicer, click the Clear Filter button. The filter clears and resets to the filtered criteria for Revolution.
3. Click the Drug slicer, and scroll down to view the Revolution criteria.
4. Press and hold the Control key CTRL, and click Soloxine. Notice that the table displays the filtered data, and the To treat slicer displays the filtered criteria.
5. On the Drug slicer, click the Clear Filter button. The two filters in the Drug slicer are cleared. Notice that the To treat slicer is also cleared because its criteria depend on the Drug criteria.
6. Save the changes to the file, and leave it open to use in the next Try It.

Try It! **Deleting a Slicer**

1. In the E69TryB_xx file, on the August Sales worksheet tab, click the Drug slicer.
2. In the Drug slicer, scroll down if necessary, and click Revolution. The table displays the filtered data.
3. Right-click the To treat slicer, and click Remove "To treat."
4. Click the Drug slicer, and press DEL. Notice that the table remains filtered on the item you selected in the slicer.
5. Save and close the file, and exit Excel.

Lesson 69—Practice

The owner of Pete's Pets has asked you to help her extract data from the company's databases. The owner wants to use the data to create and process wholesale orders. You will use Excel to examine the company's current database and use advanced filtering, slicers, and database functions to provide the information the owner needs.

DIRECTIONS

1. Start Excel, if necessary, and open **E69Practice** from the data files for this lesson.
2. Save the file as **E69Practice_xx** in the location where your teacher instructs you to store the files for this lesson.
3. For all worksheets, add a header that has your name at the left, the date code in the center, and the page number code at the right, and change back to **Normal** view.
4. Use an advanced filter to create separate (extracted) list of items that need to be reordered.

   ✓ *An item should be reordered if its current inventory is at or below the reorder level.*

   a. On the **Inventory** worksheet, in cell **H2**, type **=D6<=E6**.
   b. Select the cell range **A5:H32**.
   c. Click **Data** > **Advanced** to open the Advanced Filter dialog box. The List range is already filled in.
   d. Click in the Criteria range box, type **=$H$1:$H$2**.
   e. Click **Copy to another location**.
   f. In the Copy to box, type **J5**.
   g. Click **OK** to apply the filter and extract the records.
5. Select cell **H2**, and press DEL.
6. Move the filtered records to the Order Form worksheet.
   a. Select the range **J5:Q20**.
   b. Press CTRL + X.
   c. Click the **Order Form** worksheet tab.
   d. Click cell **A5**.
   e. Press CTRL + V.
7. Adjust the column widths so that all data is displayed.
8. On the **Order Form** worksheet, in cell I5, type **On Order**.
9. Enter the following values in each cell in the ranges:

   I6:I9: **2**

   I10:I12: **4**

   I13:I17: **2**

   I18:I20: **10**
10. In cell **J5**, type **Cost**.
11. In cell **J6**, type **=H6*I6**.
12. Copy the formula from cell **J6** to the range **J7:J20**.
13. Use the Format Painter to copy the formatting from cell **H6** to the cell range **J6:J20**.
14. In cell **I22**, type **Total**.

15. In cell J22, type **=SUM(J6:J20)**.
16. Click **Page Layout** > **Orientation** > **Landscape**. Your worksheet should look like the one shown in Figure 69-1.
17. On the **Inventory** worksheet, convert the data range to a table, and insert a slicer that filters all flavors of Cat's Pride cat food.
    a. Click the **Inventory** worksheet tab.
    b. Select the cell range **A5:H32**.
    c. Click **Insert** > **Table** > **OK**.
    d. Click **Insert** > **Slicer** > **Description** > **OK**.
    e. In the Description slicer, click **Cat's Pride - Beef**, and then press and hold CTRL, and click **Cat's Pride - Salmon**, and **Cat's Pride - Tuna**.
18. Move the Description slicer to below the filtered table. Your worksheet should look like the one shown in Figure 69-2 on the next page.
19. **With your teacher's permission,** print the worksheets.
20. Save and close the file, and exit Excel.

Figure 69-1

	A	B	C	D	E	F	G	H	I	J
1										
2										
3										
4										
5	Product #	Description	Price	Current Inventory	Reorder When	Number per Case	My Cost	Price per Case	On Order	Cost
6	24813	Lg. Collar - Red	$17.50	4	4	12	$ 5.25	$ 63.00	2	$ 126.00
7	24814	Lg. Collar - Black	$17.50	4	4	12	$ 5.25	$ 63.00	2	$ 126.00
8	24815	Lg. Collar - Blue	$17.50	4	4	12	$ 5.25	$ 63.00	2	$ 126.00
9	24816	Lg. Collar - Green	$17.50	4	4	12	$ 5.25	$ 63.00	2	$ 126.00
10	34897	Sm. Bonie	$2.00	22	25	100	$ 0.50	$ 50.00	4	$ 200.00
11	34898	Med. Bonie	$2.75	18	25	100	$ 0.53	$ 53.00	4	$ 212.00
12	34899	Lg. Bonie	$3.50	6	25	100	$ 0.64	$ 64.00	4	$ 256.00
13	44212	Sm. Training Leash	$13.75	9	10	25	$ 7.60	$ 190.00	2	$ 380.00
14	44213	Lg. Training Leash	$15.25	6	10	25	$ 9.80	$ 245.00	2	$ 490.00
15	55123	2 Tier Scratch Post	$22.50	3	5	5	$ 11.75	$ 58.75	2	$ 117.50
16	34897	Chew Toys, asst.	$3.25	27	30	25	$ 0.75	$ 18.75	2	$ 37.50
17	77898	Med. Cedar Chip Bed	$23.50	4	5	5	$ 14.80	$ 74.00	2	$ 148.00
18	83122	Gourmet Delight - Turkey	$2.25	27	30	14	$ 1.80	$ 25.20	10	$ 252.00
19	83123	Gourmet Delight - Chicken	$2.25	24	30	14	$ 1.90	$ 26.60	10	$ 266.00
20	83144	Cat's Pride - Tuna	$3.75	16	18	36	$ 2.20	$ 79.20	10	$ 792.00
21										
22									Total	$ 3,655.00
23										

Figure 69-2

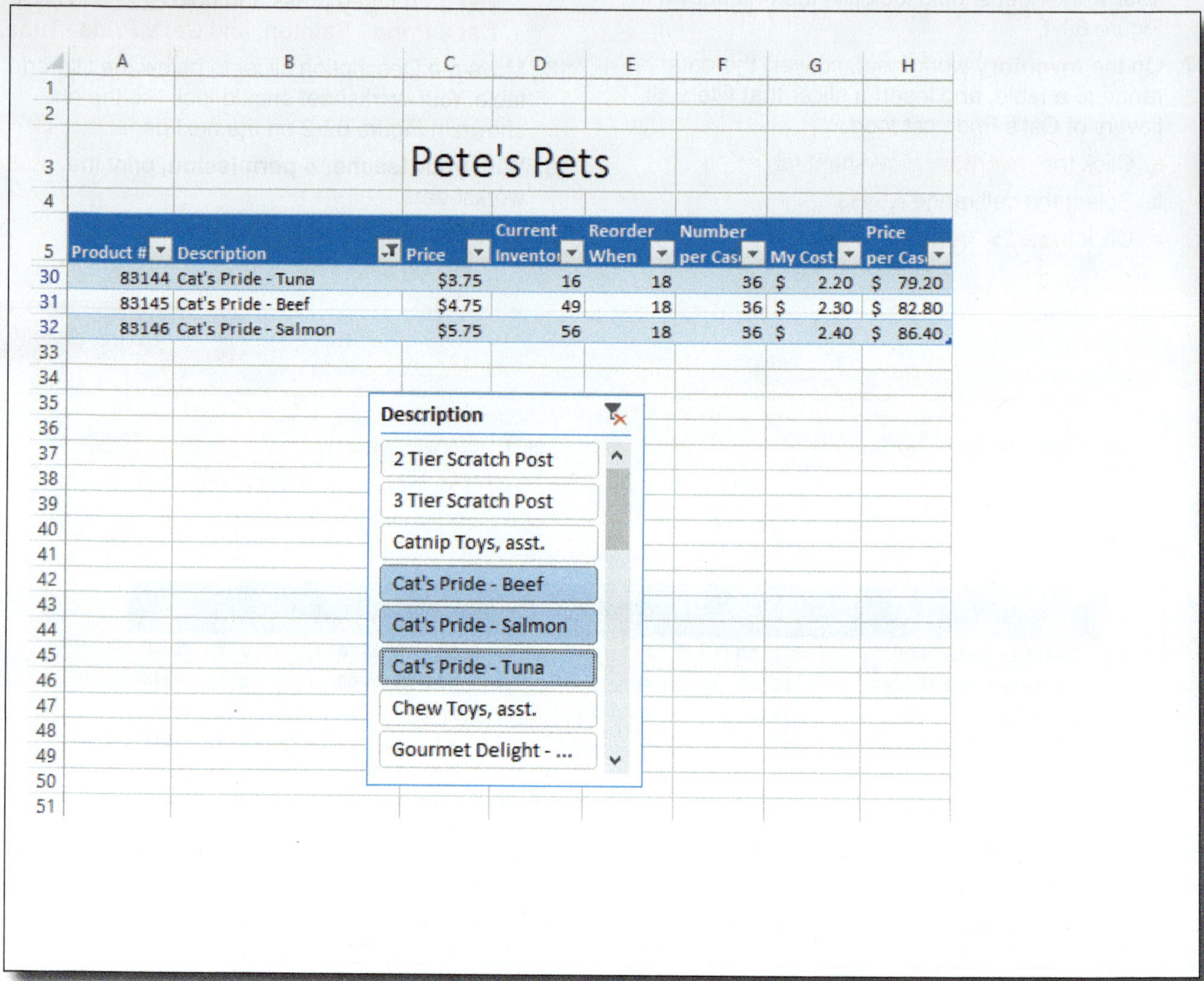
Pete's Pets
Product #
Description
Price
Current Inventory
Reorder When
Number per Case
My Cost
Price per Case
83144 Cat's Pride - Tuna $3.75 16 18 36 $ 2.20 $ 79.20
83145 Cat's Pride - Beef $4.75 49 18 36 $ 2.30 $ 82.80
83146 Cat's Pride - Salmon $5.75 56 18 36 $ 2.40 $ 86.40
Description
2 Tier Scratch Post
3 Tier Scratch Post
Catnip Toys, asst.
Cat's Pride - Beef
Cat's Pride - Salmon
Cat's Pride - Tuna
Chew Toys, asst.
Gourmet Delight - ...

Lesson 69—Apply

The manager for Kat's Catering has received a request from a vendor, Emily's Herbs, for some information about their sales orders. In this project you will use a slicer to pull that information.

DIRECTIONS

1. Start Excel, if necessary, and open **E69Apply** from the data files for this lesson.
2. Save the file as **E69Apply_xx** in the location where your teacher instructs you to store the files for this lesson.
3. Add a header that has your name at the left, the date code in the center, and the page number code at the right, and change back to **Normal** view.
4. Insert slicers to find the name of the product for which Emily's Herbs ordered 7 cases.
   a. Select the cell range **A7:G35**.
   b. Click **Insert** > **Slicer** > **Vendor**, and click **OK**.
   c. In the Vendor slicer, click **Emily's Herbs**.
5. Move the slicer below the filtered table.
6. Change the page orientation to Landscape and then adjust the column widths so that the worksheet will fit on one page. Your worksheet should look like the one shown in Figure 69-3 on the next page.
7. **With your teacher's permission,** print the worksheet.
8. Click the **Clear Filter** button on the slicer to clear the filter.
9. Create a new blank worksheet.
10. On the **Supplies list** tab, copy cells **A7:G7** to the Clipboard.
11. On the new sheet, paste the Clipboard content into **A7:G7**.
12. On the new sheet, in cell **B2**, type **Emily's Herbs**.
13. In cell **A2**, type **Basil**.
14. On the Supplies List tab, click any cell outside the table.
15. Click **Data** > **Advanced**. In the Advanced Filter dialog box, click **Filter the list in-place**.
16. In the List Range box, type **$A$7:$G$35**.
17. In the Criteria Range box, type **Sheet1!$A$1:$G$2**.
18. Click **OK**.
19. **With your teacher's permission**, print the worksheet.
20. Save and close the file, and exit Excel.

Figure 69-3

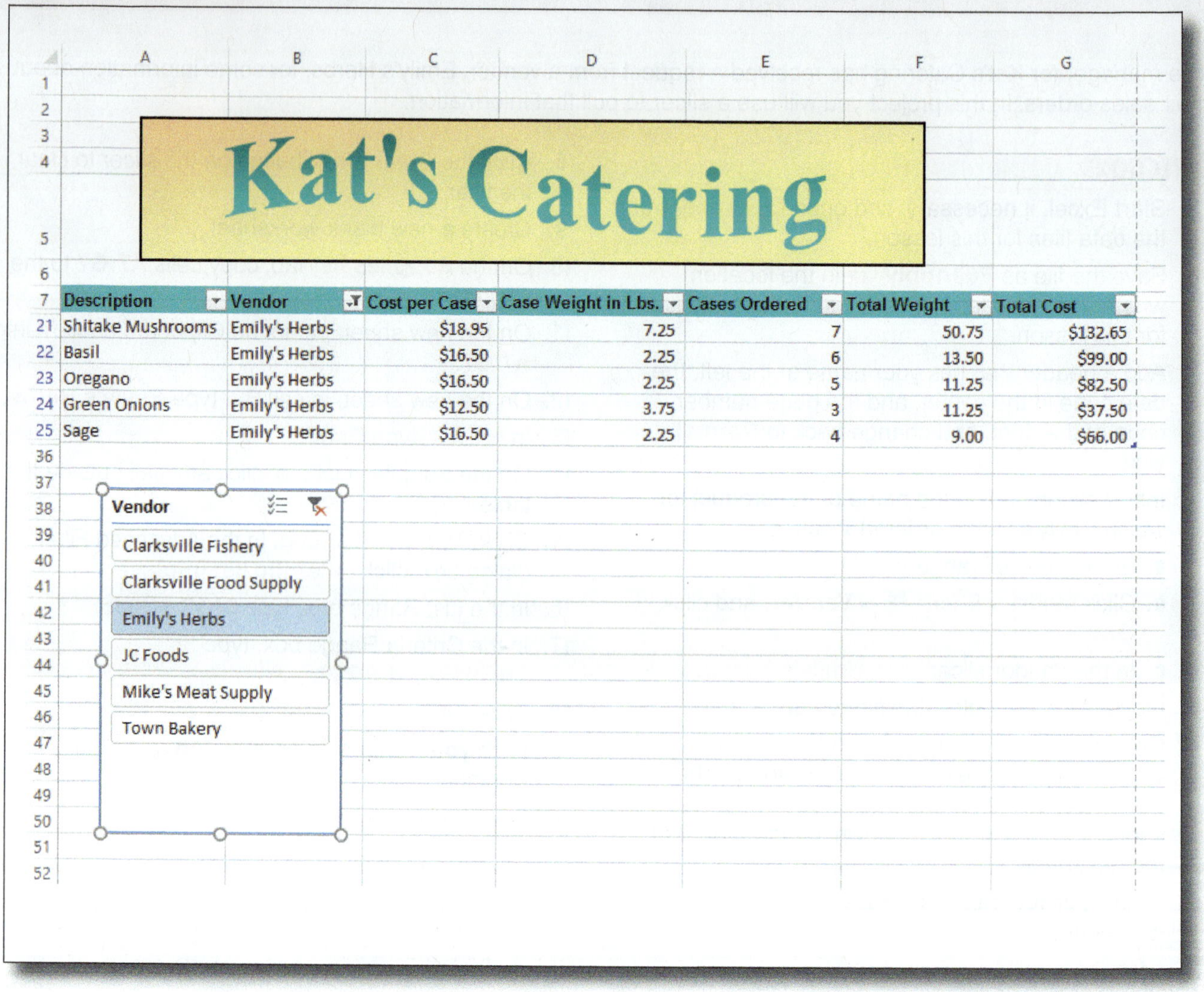

Kat's Catering

Description	Vendor	Cost per Case	Case Weight in Lbs.	Cases Ordered	Total Weight	Total Cost
Shitake Mushrooms	Emily's Herbs	$18.95	7.25	7	50.75	$132.65
Basil	Emily's Herbs	$16.50	2.25	6	13.50	$99.00
Oregano	Emily's Herbs	$16.50	2.25	5	11.25	$82.50
Green Onions	Emily's Herbs	$12.50	3.75	3	11.25	$37.50
Sage	Emily's Herbs	$16.50	2.25	4	9.00	$66.00

Vendor
Clarksville Fishery
Clarksville Food Supply
Emily's Herbs
JC Foods
Mike's Meat Supply
Town Bakery

Excel 2016, Windows 10, Microsoft Corporation

Lesson 70

Using Database Functions

➤ What You Will Learn

Using VLOOKUP and HLOOKUP
Using MATCH
Using INDEX
Using INDEX and MATCH Instead of VLOOKUP

Software Skills The functions covered in this lesson are all database functions used to look up data in a range of cells. VLOOKUP and HLOOKUP are vertical and horizontal versions of the same function, returning the value in a specified position. MATCH returns the relative position of an item in a range, and INDEX returns the value of a cell. MATCH and INDEX can be combined to produce the same type of result as VLOOKUP and HLOOKUP, but with more flexibility.

WORDS TO KNOW

Array
A data range defined as an argument for a function.

HLOOKUP function
A function that searches in one row and returns a value from another row in the same column.

INDEX function
A function that returns the value of a cell or array of cells, or returns a reference to specified cells.

MATCH function
A function that returns the relative position of an item in a range.

VLOOKUP function
A function that searches in one column and returns a value from another column in the same row.

What You Can Do

Using VLOOKUP and HLOOKUP

- **VLOOKUP** looks up data in one column of a range, and provides the value in another column in the same row.
- For example, you might have a list of people's names and their phone extensions. You could use VLOOKUP to enter a person's name and return their extension. In Figure 70-1 on the next page, VLOOKUP is used in cell E7 to look up a name (specified in cell E6) in the range A5:B14 and return that person's extension from column B.
- Here is the syntax for VLOOKUP:
  - **Lookup_value**: The value to look up, or a reference to a cell that contains the value.
  - **Table_array**: The range containing the data.
  - **Col_index_num:** The column containing the data to return.
  - **Range_lookup:** An optional value that can be either TRUE (1, the default) or FALSE (0). If true, it returns the closes match in the first column (provided the column is sorted in ascending order). If false, it finds only an exact match.

- When using VLOOKUP, the column containing the data being looked up (the lookup column) must be the left-most column. In Figure 70-1, this is the person's name.
  - ✓ *The lookup column having to be on the left is one limitation of VLOOKUP that makes some people prefer to use INDEX and MATCH for lookups, as you will learn later in this lesson.*
- If you are using a Range_lookup value of TRUE, the lookup column must be sorted in ascending order.
- **HLOOKUP** is just like VLOOKUP except it assumes you are looking up data by rows rather than by columns. All the arguments and rules are the same.

Figure 70-1

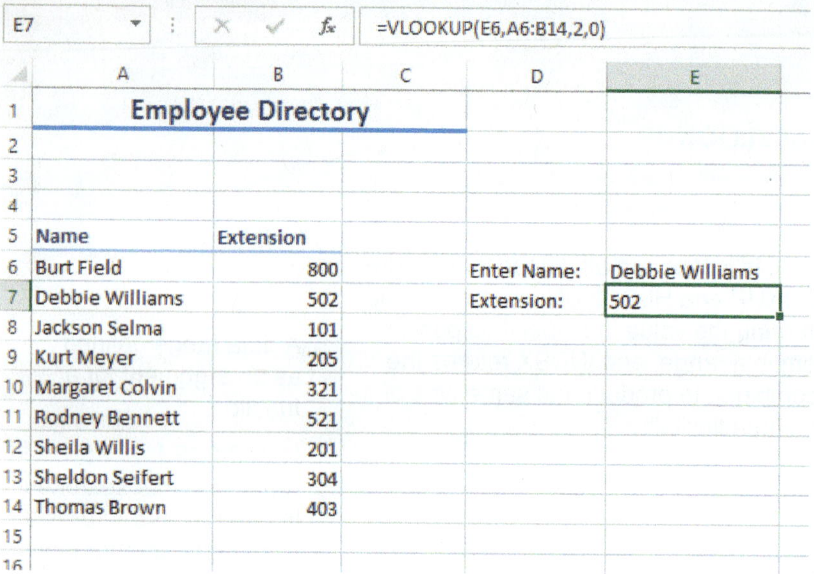
E7 =VLOOKUP(E6,A6:B14,2,0)

	A	B	C	D	E
1	Employee Directory				
2					
3					
4					
5	Name	Extension			
6	Burt Field	800		Enter Name:	Debbie Williams
7	Debbie Williams	502		Extension:	502
8	Jackson Selma	101			
9	Kurt Meyer	205			
10	Margaret Colvin	321			
11	Rodney Bennett	521			
12	Sheila Willis	201			
13	Sheldon Seifert	304			
14	Thomas Brown	403			
15					
16					

Try It! Using VLOOKUP and HLOOKUP

1. Open Excel and open the **E70TryA** file from the data files for this lesson.
2. Save the file as **E70TryA_xx** in the location where your teacher instructs you to store the files for this lesson.
3. On the State Lookup tab, select cell B5.
4. Type **=VLOOKUP(** and then click the Insert Function button *fx* on the formula bar.
5. In the Function Arguments dialog box, in the Lookup_value box, type **B4**.
6. Click the Collapse dialog button for the Table_array box.
7. Drag to select the range E2:51 and press ENTER.
8. Click in the Col_index_num box and type **2**.
9. Click in the Range_lookup box and type **0**.
10. Click OK. #N/A appears in B5. This is expected.
11. In cell B4, enter **Nebraska**. The state's abbreviation appears in cell B5.
12. On the Quantity Lookup tab, select cell B3.
13. Type **=HLOOKUP(B2,B7:I11,5,0)** and press ENTER.
14. In cell B2, type **AC247**. The quantity for that part number appears in B2.
15. Save the changes to the file and close it. Leave Excel open for the next Try It.

(continued)

Try It! Using VLOOKUP and HLOOKUP *(continued)*

Create a VLOOKUP function

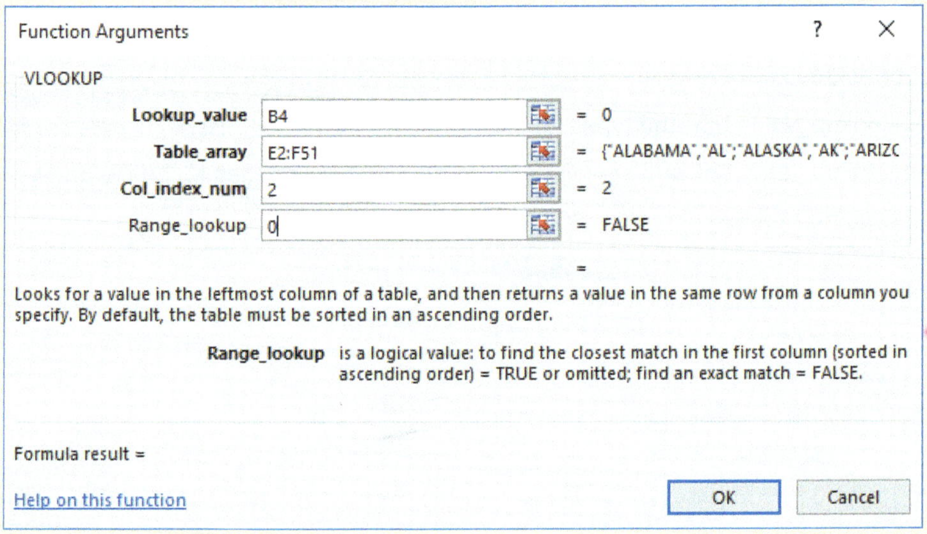

Using MATCH

- The **MATCH** function finds a specified value in a range and returns its relative position. For example, if you have a list in A1:A4 containing the values *Bananas, Peaches*, *Pears, Apples*, the function =MATCH("Pears",A1:A4,0) returns the number 3 because Pears is the third item in the range.

  ✓ *It might not be obvious at first what value such a function could have in practical use, but you will soon see.*

- MATCH is applied to only a single contiguous row or column of values, not to a two-dimensional array. The values need not be sorted in ascending or descending order.

- The arguments for MATCH are as follows:
  - **Lookup_value**: The value to look up, or a reference to a cell that contains the value.
  - **Lookup_array**: The range containing the data. This range must be a range of a single row or single column (or portion thereof)
  - **Match_type:** An optional value that can be either 1 (highest value), 0 (exact value), or -1 (lowest value). The default if omitted is 1. If you use 1, the values must be in ascending order. If you use -1, the values must be in descending order. If you use 0, the values need not be sorted.

Try It! Using Match

1. In **E70TryA**, on the Performance Lookup tab, click in cell F6.
2. Type **=MATCH(** and then click Insert Function *fx* on the formula bar.
3. Click in the Lookup_value box and type **E3**.
4. Click in the Lookup_array box and type **C6:C21**.
5. Click in the Match_type box and type **-1**.
6. Click OK. The number 9 should appear in cell F6 because the lowest value meeting the criteria.

   ✓ *Notice that there are two salespeople with the lowest value (101). It reports the position for the last one.*
7. Save changes to the file and leave it open for the next Try It.

Create a MATCH function

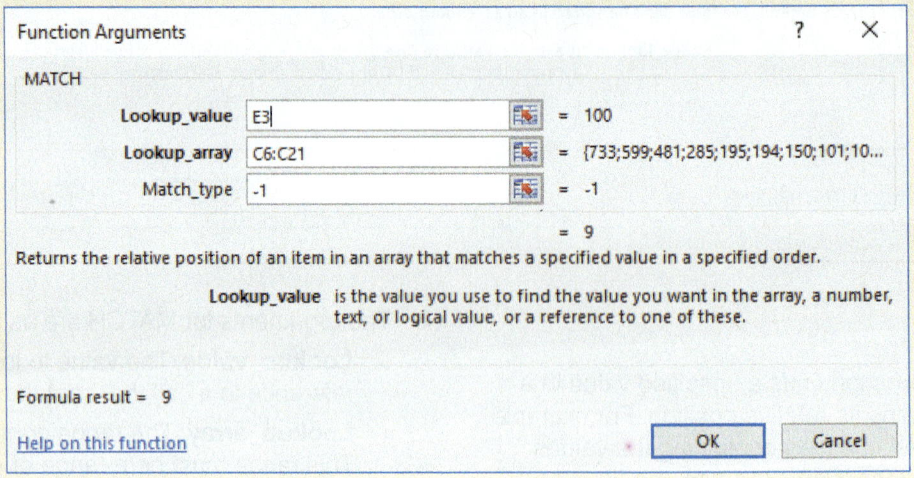

Excel 2016, Windows 10, Microsoft Corporation

Using INDEX

- The INDEX function returns a value from a specified position within the data range. It has two different uses.
  - The **Array** usage returns the value of a specified cell or array of cells.
  - The Reference usage returns a reference to specified cells.
- To distinguish between which use you want, choose the Array or Reference usage when working with the Insert Function feature. Or, if you are typing the function in manually, press CTRL + SHIFT + ENTER when completing the function for an Array usage, or press Enter as you would normally for a Reference usage.

Using Index as an Array

- The arguments for the array form are as follows:
  - **Array**: A range of cells. The array may have multiple rows and multiple columns. If the array contains only one row, or only one column, the corresponding Row_num or Column_num argument becomes optional.
  - **Row_num**: The row in the array from which to return a value. If Row_num is omitted, Column_num is required.
  - **Column_num:** The column in the array from which to return a value. If Column_num is omitted, Row_num is required.
- If both the Row_num and Column_num arguments are used, the function returns the value in the cell at their intersection.
- If you set Row_num or Column_num to 0, the function returns the array of values for the entire column or row, respectively.

Using Index as a Reference

- The arguments for the reference form are as follows:
  - **Reference**: A reference to one or more cell ranges. They can be non-adjacent references, but if so, enclose the reference in parentheses, and separate the ranges with commas within the parentheses.
  - **Row_num**: The row in the array from which to return a value. If Row_num is omitted, Column_num is required.
  - **Column_num:** The column in the array from which to reurn a value. If Column_num is omitted, Row_num is required.
  - **Area_num:** This optional argument selects a range in the reference from which to return the intersection of the specified row and column. This is applicable only if you entered multiple non-adjacent ranges in the Reference argument.
- If omitting a Row_num or Column_num reference, use an extra comma to mark where it would be. For example, if omitting the row number, =INDEX(reference,,column_num).
- If you set Row_num or Column_num to 0, the function returns the reference of values for the entire column or row, respectively.

Try It! Using Index

1. In **E70TryA**, on the Performance Lookup tab, click in cell F7.
2. Type **=INDEX(** and then click Insert Function *fx* on the formula bar.
3. In the Select Arguments dialog box, click *array,row_num,column_num* and click OK.
4. In the Function Arguments dialog box, in the Array box, type **B6:C21**.
5. In the Row_num box type **F6**.
6. In the Column_num box type **2**.
7. Click OK. The value 101 appears in F7.
8. Click in cell F8.
9. Type **=INDEX(** and then click Insert Function *fx* on the formula bar.
10. In the Select Arguments dialog box, click *reference,row_num,column_num;area_num* and click OK.
11. In the Reference box, type **B6:C21**.
12. In the Row_num box, type **1**.
13. In the Column_num box, type **1**.
14. Click OK. The name Colvin appears in cell F8.
15. Edit the formula in F7 to incorporate the MATCH function in it, rather than referring to cell F6:
    a. Click cell F7.
    b. In the formula bar, click Insert Formula *fx*.
    c. In the Select Arguments dialog box, select *array,row_num,column_num* and click OK.
    e. In the Row_num box, delete the current entry and type **MATCH(E3,C6:C21,-1)**.
    f. Click OK.
16. Save changes to the file and close it. Leave Excel open for the next Try It.

Using INDEX and MATCH Instead of VLOOKUP

- By combining MATCH with INDEX, you can create the same results as VLOOKUP. It results in a more complex function, as you saw in the previous Try It (step 15), but you might sometimes want to do it anyway. Here are some reasons:
  - VLOOKUP requires the lookup value to be in the leftmost column of the lookup range. With INDEX MATCH, your lookup column can be anywhere in the range.
  - VLOOKUP can return incorrect results if columns are added or removed from the lookup range because VLOOKUP defines columns by their number within the range. INDEX MATCH specifies the columns directly so it is not subject to this problem.
  - When using VLOOKUP, the total length of your lookup criteria cannot exceed 255 characters. There is no such restriction for INDEX MATCH.

Try It! Combining INDEX and MATCH Functions

1. Open Excel and open the **E70TryB** file from the data files for this lesson.
2. Save the file as **E70TryB_xx** in the location where your teacher instructs you to store the files for this lesson.

   ✓ *Notice that B7 and B8 could be calculated with VLOOKUP, but the data for B9 cannot be gotten through VLOOKUP because the Rank column is to the right of the Country column.*

3. In cell B7, enter the following: **=INDEX(H5:H24,MATCH(B6,F5:F24,0))**.
4. In cell B8, enter the following: **=INDEX(G3:G22,MATCH(B6,F3:F22,0))**.
5. In cell B9, enter the following: **=INDEX(E5:E24,MATCH(B6,F5:F24,0))**.
6. Open the drop-down list in cell B6 and click Japan. The values in B7-B9 change to the ones listed in the table for Japan.
7. Save changes to the file and exit Excel.

   ✓ *The lookup in cell B6 was created with data validation, which you will learn about in Lesson 78.*

Combine INDEX and MATCH functions as an alternative to VLOOKUP

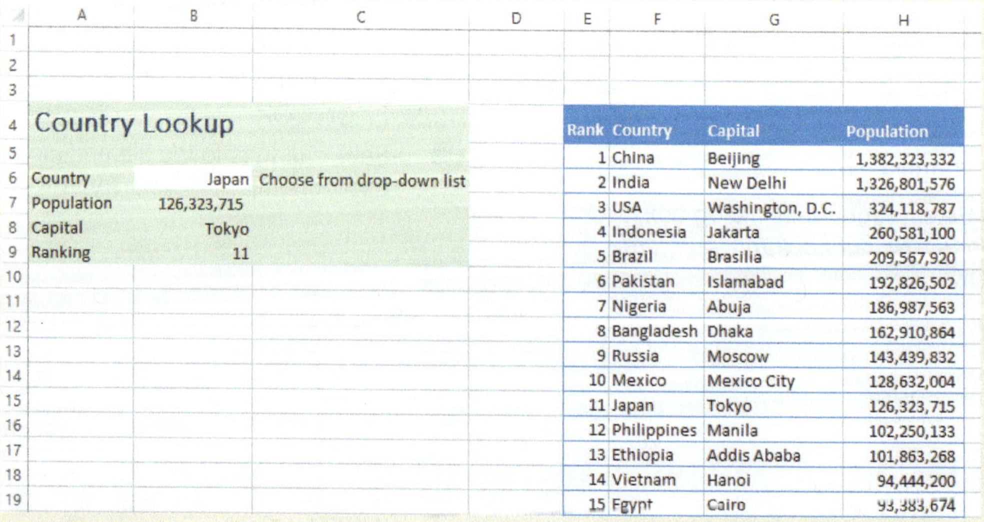

	A	B	C
4	Country Lookup		
6	Country	Japan	Choose from drop-down list
7	Population	126,323,715	
8	Capital	Tokyo	
9	Ranking	11	

Rank	Country	Capital	Population
1	China	Beijing	1,382,323,332
2	India	New Delhi	1,326,801,576
3	USA	Washington, D.C.	324,118,787
4	Indonesia	Jakarta	260,581,100
5	Brazil	Brasilia	209,567,920
6	Pakistan	Islamabad	192,826,502
7	Nigeria	Abuja	186,987,563
8	Bangladesh	Dhaka	162,910,864
9	Russia	Moscow	143,439,832
10	Mexico	Mexico City	128,632,004
11	Japan	Tokyo	126,323,715
12	Philippines	Manila	102,250,133
13	Ethiopia	Addis Ababa	101,863,268
14	Vietnam	Hanoi	94,444,200
15	Egypt	Cairo	93,383,674

Excel 2016, Windows 10, Microsoft Corporation

Lesson 70—Practice

Rural Estates Real Estate's listing table has gotten so large that it's difficult to browse easily. In this project you will use VLOOKUP to create a form that will show the agent, list price, and date listed in response to the user entering the listing ID.

DIRECTIONS

1. Start Excel, if necessary, and open the **E70Practice** file from the data files for this lesson.
2. Save the workbook as **E70Practice_xx** in the location where your teacher instructs you to store the files for this lesson.
3. Add a header that has your name at the left, the date code in the center, and the page number code at the right, and change back to Normal view.
4. Click in cell **C7** and type **=VLOOKUP(** and then click **Insert Function** *fx* on the formula bar.
5. In the Lookup_value box, type C5.
6. Click the **Collapse Dialog** button for the Table_array box, drag to select cells **A12:K88**, and press ENTER.

   ✓ *Because that range is a table, the table's name is filled in, along with [#All] to mean all cells.*

7. In the Col_index_num box, type **11**.
8. In the Range_lookup box, type **0**.
9. Click **OK**.
10. In C5, type **22** and press ENTER. The value in C7 changes to Porter.
11. In cell C8, type **=VLOOKUP(C5,Merge1[#All],4,0)** and press ENTER.
12. In cell C9, type **=VLOOKUP(C5,Merge1[#All],2,0)** and press ENTER.
13. Click cell C8 and click **Home** > **Accounting Number Format**.
14. Click **Home** > **Decrease Decimal** two times.
15. Click cell C9 and click **Home** > **Number Format** > **Short Date**.
16. In cell C5, type **13** and press ENTER.

    ✓ *The values in C7:C9 change to reflect the new listing ID.*

17. **With your teacher's permission**, print the first page of the worksheet in Landscape orientation. It should look like the one shown in Figure 70-2 on the next page.
18. Save the changes to the workbook, and exit Excel.

Figure 70-2

Rural Estates Real Estate

Property Lookup

Enter Listing ID: 13

Agent Simmons
List Price $ 239,900
Date Listed 9/26/2018

ID	Date Listed	Area	List Price	Bedroor	Baths	SqFt	Type	Pool	Agent	Agent Name
1	10/8/2018	Kern	$ 199,499	3	2.5	1510	Single Family	FALSE	16	Simmons
2	8/18/2018	Kern	$ 214,500	4	2.5	1862	Single Family	TRUE	16	Simmons
3	4/27/2018	Kern	$ 265,499	4	3	1906	Single Family	FALSE	2	Ellis
6	7/31/2018	Riverside	$ 309,950	4	3	2800	Single Family	TRUE	14	Rubin
13	9/26/2018	Ward	$ 239,900	4	3	2046	Single Family	FALSE	16	Simmons
14	3/13/2018	Ward	$ 264,900	3	3	2496	Single Family	FALSE	19	Weiss
15	3/6/2018	Riverside	$ 299,499	3	2	2060	Single Family	FALSE	19	Weiss
17	3/21/2018	Ward	$ 350,499	3	2.5	1991	Single Family	FALSE	18	Torres
18	6/25/2018	Ward	$ 355,499	4	2.5	2547	Single Family	TRUE	18	Torres
19	6/25/2018	Imperial	$ 208,750	4	2	1800	Single Family	FALSE	18	Torres
21	5/8/2018	Kern	$ 549,499	4	3	1940	Single Family	TRUE	12	Porter
22	6/30/2018	Ward	$ 229,500	6	3	2700	Single Family	TRUE	12	Porter
23	4/20/2018	Ward	$ 229,900	3	3	2266	Single Family	FALSE	12	Porter
24	5/26/2018	Ward	$ 229,900	4	3	2041	Single Family	FALSE	2	Ellis
25	6/25/2018	Imperial	$ 229,900	3	2.5	1680	Single Family	TRUE	12	Porter
26	7/7/2018	Kern	$ 236,900	3	2	1700	Single Family	FALSE	16	Simmons
27	8/26/2018	Kern	$ 339,900	4	2	2238	Single Family	FALSE	7	Li
28	4/20/2018	Kern	$ 375,499	4	3	2467	Single Family	TRUE	18	Torres
29	3/21/2018	Riverside	$ 205,499	3	2.5	2001	Single Family	TRUE	18	Torres
30	8/2/2018	Riverside	$ 229,500	4	2.5	2284	Single Family	FALSE	20	Williams
31	9/29/2018	Imperial	$ 235,990	5	3	2723	Single Family	FALSE	16	Simmons
32	7/4/2018	Imperial	$ 239,900	4	3	2260	Single Family	FALSE	20	Williams

Excel 2016, Windows 10, Microsoft Corporation

Lesson 70—Apply

In this project you will use INDEX and MATCH functions to look up additional data in the Rural Estates Real Estate listing table. You will take advantage of the INDEX function's ability to show a range of values from a single column when you set the Column_num argument to 0.

DIRECTIONS

1. Start Excel, if necessary, and open the **E70Apply** file from the data files for this lesson.
2. Save the workbook as **E70Apply_xx** in the location where your teacher instructs you to store the files for this lesson.
3. Add a header that has your name at the left, the date code in the center, and the page number code at the right, and change back to Normal view.
4. In cell B8, type **=INDEX(Merge1,MATCH($C$5,Merge1[ID],0),0)** and press ENTER.
5. Select cell **B8** and press CTRL + C to copy the function.
6. Select **C8:K8** and press CTRL + V to paste the function.
7. Widen columns as needed so all data will display in row 8.

   ✓ *Notice that the values in D8:G8 and J8 appear as dates. That happened because the formatting was also copied and pasted in steps 5-6.*

8. Select cells **E8:G8** and then hold down CTRL and click **J8**.
9. Click **Home** > **Number Format** > **Number**, and then click **Decrease Decimal** two times.
10. Select cell **D8** and then click **Home** > **Accounting Number Format**. Then click **Decrease Decimal** two times.
11. In C5, type **1** and press ENTER. Confirm that the values shown in row 8 match those in row 13.
12. **With your teacher's permission**, print the first page only, in Landscape mode. It should look like Figure 70-3 on the next page.
13. Save the changes to the workbook, and exit Excel.

Figure 70-3

Rural Estates Real Estate

Property Lookup

Enter Listing ID: 1

Date Listed	Area	List Price	BR	Baths	SqFt	Type	Pool	Agent	Agent Name
10/8/2018	Kern	$ 199,499.00	3	3	1510	Single Family	FALSE	16	Simmons

ID	Date Listed	Area	List Price	BR	Baths	SqFt	Type	Pool	Agent	Agent Name
1	10/8/2018	Kern	$ 199,499	3	2.5	1510	Single Family	FALSE	16	Simmons
2	8/18/2018	Kern	$ 214,500	4	2.5	1862	Single Family	TRUE	16	Simmons
3	4/27/2018	Kern	$ 265,499	4	3	1906	Single Family	FALSE	2	Ellis
6	7/31/2018	Riverside	$ 309,950	4	3	2800	Single Family	TRUE	14	Rubin
13	9/26/2018	Ward	$ 239,900	4	3	2046	Single Family	FALSE	16	Simmons
14	3/13/2018	Ward	$ 264,900	3	3	2496	Single Family	FALSE	19	Weiss
15	3/6/2018	Riverside	$ 299,499	3	2	2060	Single Family	FALSE	19	Weiss
17	3/21/2018	Ward	$ 350,499	3	2.5	1991	Single Family	FALSE	18	Torres
18	6/25/2018	Ward	$ 355,499	4	2.5	2547	Single Family	TRUE	18	Torres
19	6/25/2018	Imperial	$ 208,750	4	2	1800	Single Family	FALSE	18	Torres
21	5/8/2018	Kern	$ 549,499	4	3	1940	Single Family	TRUE	12	Porter
22	6/30/2018	Ward	$ 229,500	6	3	2700	Single Family	TRUE	12	Porter
23	4/20/2018	Ward	$ 229,900	3	3	2266	Single Family	FALSE	12	Porter
24	5/26/2018	Ward	$ 229,900	4	3	2041	Single Family	FALSE	2	Ellis
25	6/25/2018	Imperial	$ 229,900	3	2.5	1680	Single Family	TRUE	12	Porter
26	7/7/2018	Kern	$ 236,900	3	2	1700	Single Family	FALSE	16	Simmons
27	8/26/2018	Kern	$ 339,900	4	2	2238	Single Family	FALSE	7	Li
28	4/20/2018	Kern	$ 375,499	4	3	2467	Single Family	TRUE	18	Torres
29	3/21/2018	Riverside	$ 205,499	3	2.5	2001	Single Family	TRUE	18	Torres
30	8/2/2018	Riverside	$ 229,500	4	2.5	2284	Single Family	FALSE	20	Williams
31	9/29/2018	Imperial	$ 235,990	5	3	2723	Single Family	FALSE	16	Simmons
32	7/4/2018	Imperial	$ 239,900	4	3	2260	Single Family	FALSE	20	Williams

Excel 2016, Windows 10, Microsoft Corporation

Lesson 71

Using Flash Fill and Data Consolidation

➤ What You Will Learn

Working with Flash Fill
Consolidating Data
Working with Consolidated Data

Software Skills Data that is formatted and organized is easier to work with and analyze. Excel's Flash Fill feature can help you format and organize data. For example, you can combine first, middle, and last names from separate columns into one column. Excel's data consolidation feature allows you to consolidate the data from similar worksheets into a single worksheet. For example, you may have a workbook that contains separate worksheets for three months' worth of sales. After consolidation, you have a single worksheet that contains the totals for the three-month period.

WORDS TO KNOW

Consolidation by category
Data consolidation that can be done from worksheets that are similarly designed into a single worksheet.

Consolidation by position
Data consolidation that can be done from worksheets that aren't organized the same way.

Flash Fill
An Excel feature that fills cells based on a pattern in the data.

What You Can Do

Working with Flash Fill

- The **Flash Fill** feature in Excel can recognize the pattern in the text and change the organization or format of the text for the series.
- You can use Flash Fill to reformat names that have been typed in lowercase to uppercase or change the format of phone numbers to include parentheses for the area code.
- You can use Flash Fill to split data into more than one column or combine data from multiple columns into one column.
- Flash Fill works best when the data labels are consistent. For example, all names have middle initials or all addresses use the same type of postal codes.
- If the data labels are not consistent, Flash Fill may not always format or separate the data elements correctly.
- You can use Flash Fill with data ranges or tables.

Try It! Using Flash Fill to Combine Data Elements

1. Start Excel, and open **E71TryA** from the data files for this lesson.
2. Save the file as **E71TryA_xx** in the location where your teacher instructs you to store the files for this lesson.
3. On the June Race worksheet tab, click the column C heading.
4. On the Home tab, in the Cells group, click Insert.
5. Click cell C8, and type **Racer Full Name**, and press ENTER.
6. In cell C9, type **Carl Allan**, and press ENTER.
7. In cell C10, type **Martin**. Notice that the Flash Fill suggestions fill the rest of the column.
8. Press ENTER. Flash Fill places the suggestions in the column, and the Flash Fill options button appears to the right of the first filled cell.
9. Click the Flash Fill Options button > Accept suggestions.
10. Save the changes to the file, and leave it open to use in the next Try It.

The Flash Fill Options button

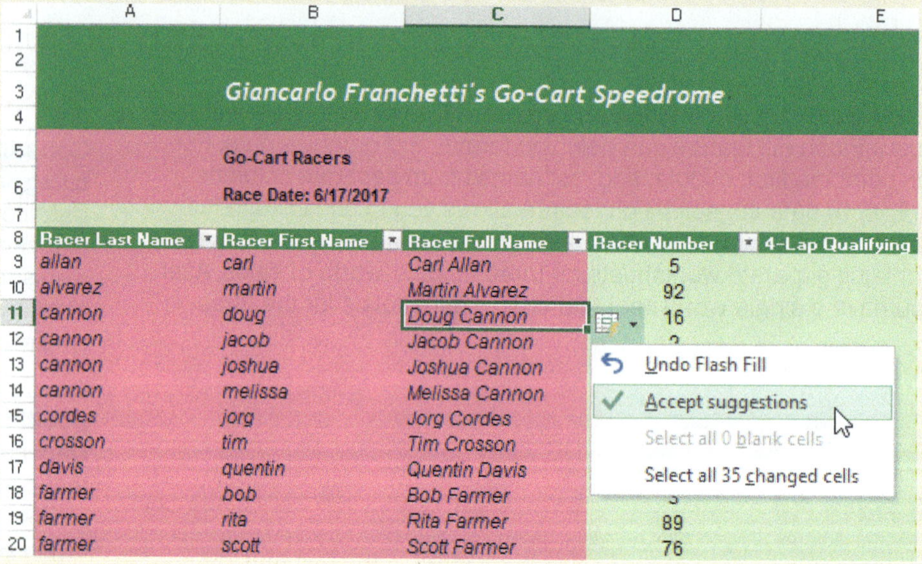

Excel 2016, Windows 10, Microsoft Corporation

Try It! Using Flash Fill to Separate Data Elements

1. In the **E71TryA_xx** file, click the July Race worksheet tab.
2. Click cell B9, type **Carl**, and press ENTER.
3. In cell B10, begin typing **Martin**, and when you see a proposed list appear, press ENTER. Flash Fill completes the column with first name data.
4. Click cell C9, type **Allan**, and press ENTER.
5. In cell C10, begin typing **Alvarez**, when you see a proposed list appear, and press ENTER. Flash Fill completes the column with last name data.
6. Save and close the file. Leave Excel open to use in the next Try It.

Consolidating Data

- With Excel's Consolidate feature, you can consolidate data from separate ranges into a single worksheet.
- You can also consolidate data using 3-D formulas.
- The data can come from the same worksheet, separate worksheets, and even separate workbooks.
- You can consolidate identically structured databases. This is called **consolidation by position**. When you consolidate data by position, you're telling Excel to consolidate the data in the exact same cells on several worksheets.
- You can consolidate data from differently structured databases. This is called **consolidation by category**. When you consolidate data by category, you're telling Excel to consolidate data based on the row and column labels you're using.

✓ *The following Try It uses consolidation by category because the worksheets being consolidated have different data ranges.*

Try It! Consolidating Data

1. Create a new blank workbook.
2. Save the workbook as **E71TryB_xx** in the location where your teacher instructs you to store the files for this lesson.
3. Open the **E71TryC**, **E71TryD**, and **E71TryE** files from the data files for this lesson, and browse the contents of each.

   ✓ *Notice that each one contains product numbers in the A column, but different part numbers appear, and in different orders, in each one. This inconsistency makes consolidation by category appropriate for this job.*
4. In the **E71TryB_xx** file, click Data > Consolidate to open the Consolidate dialog box.
5. Verify that the Function setting is Sum.
6. In the Reference box, click the Collapse Dialog Box button, switch to **E71TryC**, select the cell range A1:D10, and press ENTER.
7. In the Consolidate dialog box, click Add.
8. In the Reference box, select the cell range reference, and click DEL to clear the reference.
9. Click the Collapse Dialog Box button, switch to **E71TryD**, select the cell range A1:D12, and press ENTER to return to the dialog box.
10. In the Consolidate dialog box, click Add.
11. Repeat steps 8–10 to add references to the cell range A1:D11 in **E71TryE**.
12. In the Consolidate dialog box, under Use labels in, click the Top row and Left column check boxes to select them.

    ✓ *If you do not mark these check boxes, Excel considers this a consolidation by position, so in this case it is important to mark them.*
13. Click the Create links to source data check box to select it.
14. Click OK. The consolidated data appears.
15. Save the changes to the **E71TryB_xx** file, and leave it open to use in the next Try It.
16. Close the **E71TryC**, **E71TryD**, and **E71TryE** files without saving changes.

Working with Consolidated Data

- After consolidating data, the results appear in Excel in a special format, containing buttons along the left side for collapsing and expanding the view of the results. See Figure 71-1.
- Click a plus sign to expand a category; click a minus sign to collapse it.

Figure 71-1

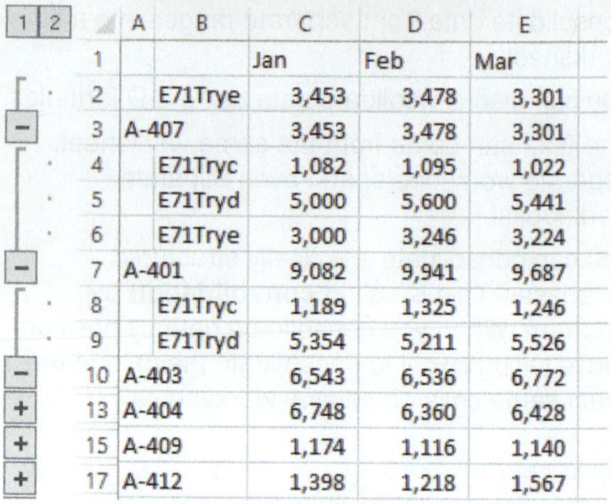

	A	B	C	D	E
1			Jan	Feb	Mar
2		E71Trye	3,453	3,478	3,301
3	A-407		3,453	3,478	3,301
4		E71Tryc	1,082	1,095	1,022
5		E71Tryd	5,000	5,600	5,441
6		E71Trye	3,000	3,246	3,224
7	A-401		9,082	9,941	9,687
8		E71Tryc	1,189	1,325	1,246
9		E71Tryd	5,354	5,211	5,526
10	A-403		6,543	6,536	6,772
13	A-404		6,748	6,360	6,428
15	A-409		1,174	1,116	1,140
17	A-412		1,398	1,218	1,567

Excel 2016, Windows 10, Microsoft Corporation

Try It! Working with Consolidated Data

1. In the E71TryB_xx file, double-click the divider between the columns A and B headers to widen column A.
2. Click the plus sign next to product number A-407 to expand that list.
3. Double-click the divider between the columns B and C headers to widen column B.
4. Click the plus sign next to product number A-401 to expand that list.

   ✓ *Notice that the product number appears at the bottom of the list of expanded records for it, not at the top. For example, row 7, where A-401 appears, contains a summary of the contents of rows 4–6.*

5. Select columns A:E.
6. Click Data > Sort A to Z. The list is sorted by column A (the product numbers).

   ✓ *You might notice the green triangles in the corners of some cells, indicating a possible error. These are not really errors, though; Excel has marked them as errors incorrectly. If you expand more records, you will notice that the rows that have the error indicators on them are the rows for product numbers that appeared in only one of the worksheets that were consolidated.*

   ✓ *The column labels in B through E were moved to the bottom of the list during the sort in step 6. Now you need to move them back to their normal positions.*

7. Select row 1, and click Home > Insert.
8. Select the cell range C53:E53, and press CTRL + X to cut them to the Clipboard.
9. Click cell C1, and press CTRL + V to paste the column labels.
10. Save and close the file, and exit Excel.

Lesson 71—Practice

It's the end of the quarter, and it's time to draw some conclusions about product sales for Holy Habañero, which sells its hot sauces through nine different sales channels. Since the details for each month are stored on separate worksheets, you've decided to use the Consolidate command to bring the data together.

DIRECTIONS

1. Start Excel, if necessary, and open **E71Practice** from the data files for this lesson.
2. Save the file as **E71Practice_xx** in the location where your teacher instructs you to store the files for this lesson.
3. Make a copy of the **March** worksheet to use as a template for the consolidated figures.
   a. Right-click the **March** worksheet tab.
   b. Click **Move or Copy**.
   c. In the Before sheet list, click **(move to end)**.
   d. Click the **Create a copy** check box.
   e. Click **OK**. A March (2) worksheet appears.
   f. Double-click the **March (2)** worksheet tab, type **Totals**, and press ENTER.
4. On the **Totals** worksheet, select the cell range **B8:I16**, and press DEL to clear the cells.
5. Select the cell range **B19:I27**, and press DEL to clear the cells. Then select the cell range B46:I54 and press DEL to clear the cells.
6. Click cell B3, edit the text in to read **Quarterly Sales Breakdown**, and press ENTER.
7. Click cell B4, edit the text to read **Q1 Totals**, and press ENTER.
8. On the **Totals** worksheet, total the Unit sales for the last three months.
   a. Click **B8**.
   b. Click **Data** > **Consolidate**.
   c. Choose **Sum** from the Function list, if necessary.
   d. Click in the **Reference** box, click the **Collapse Dialog Box** button, click the **January** worksheet tab, select the cell range **B8:I16**, and press ENTER.
   e. In the Consolidate dialog box, click **Add**.
   f. In the Reference box, select the cell range reference, and press DEL to clear the reference.
   g. Click the **Collapse Dialog Box** button, click the **February** worksheet tab, select the cell range **B8:I16**, and press ENTER.
   h. Click **Add**.
   i. Repeat steps f–h to add the same range on the **March** worksheet.
   j. Click the **Create links to source data** check box to select it.

      ✓ *Do not mark the Top row or Left column check box.*

   k. Click **OK**. The summarized data appears.

      ✓ *Excel inserts hidden rows that contain links to the selected data. To view hidden rows, click the plus sign next to any row.*

9. Test the automatic updating process by changing cell **H12** in the **January** worksheet to **960**.

   ✓ *Cell J27 in the Totals worksheet should change from 13,339 to 13,371.*

10. Consolidate the data for Gross sales (B19:I27) on the **Totals** worksheet.
    a. On the **Totals** worksheet, click **B46**.
    b. Click **Data** > **Consolidate**.
    c. Choose **Sum** from the Function list, if necessary.
    d. On the All References list, click the entry for the **January** worksheet, and click **Delete**.
    e. Click the entry for the **February** worksheet, and click **Delete**.
    f. Click the entry for the **March** worksheet, and click **Delete**.
    g. Click in the **Reference** box, click the **Collapse Dialog Box** button, click the **January** worksheet tab, select the cell range **B19:I27**, and press ENTER.
    h. In the Consolidate dialog box, click **Add**.
    i. In the Reference box, select the cell range reference, and press DEL to clear the reference.
    j. Click the **Collapse Dialog Box** button, click the **February** worksheet tab, select the cell range **B19:I27**, and press ENTER.
    k. In the Consolidate dialog box, click **Add**.
    l. Repeat steps i–k to add the same range on the **March** worksheet.

m. Click the **Create links to source data** check box to select it, if necessary.

✓ *Do not mark the Top row or Left column check box.*

n. Click **OK**. The summarized data appears.

11. Widen **column J** to accommodate the widest entry, if necessary.

12. On the Totals worksheet, add a header that has your name at the left, the date code in the center, and the page number code at the right, and change back to **Normal** view.

13. **With your teacher's permission,** print the **Totals** worksheet with scaling set to fit sheet on a single page. Your worksheet should look like the one shown in Figure 71-2.

14. Save and close the file, and exit Excel.

Figure 71-2

Holy Habañero

Quarterly Sales Breakdown

Q1 Totals

	Retail				Wholesale				Total
Unit sales	Direct mail catalog	Fundraising catalog	Online	Trade exhibits	Non-profit resellers	For-profit retailers (unit)	For-profit retailers (bulk)	Restaurants (bulk)	
Belly of the Beast	249	182	305	356	323	647	1,632	1,488	5,182
Magma Core	339	173	110	581	295	418	1,760	1,648	5,324
Typhoon Warning	278	155	579	971	891	1,721	3,328	2,528	10,451
Uranium 235	1,564	1,885	1,985	2,744	602	2,474	3,808	3,536	18,598
Szechuan Singe	1,067	1,164	1,240	1,575	1,623	2,142	2,816	1,744	13,371
Wasabi Fusion	282	450	783	1,362	1,983	2,442	3,936	2,736	13,974
Sorrento Serrano	236	350	477	233	447	1,073	1,088	272	4,176
Yucatan Bomb	255	224	270	186	228	1,334	1,472	384	4,353
Toast Jammer	185	379	113	143	336	831	-	-	1,987

Gross sales	Direct mail catalog	Fundraising catalog	Online	Trade exhibits	Non-profit resellers	For-profit retailers (unit)	For-profit retailers (bulk)	Restaurants (bulk)	
Belly of the Beast	$ 1,730.55	$ 1,264.90	$ 2,424.75	$ 2,830.20	$ 1,130.50	$ 3,073.25	$ 6,936.00	$ 5,952.00	$ 25,342.15
Magma Core	$ 2,356.05	$ 1,202.35	$ 874.50	$ 4,618.95	$ 1,032.50	$ 1,985.50	$ 7,480.00	$ 6,592.00	$ 26,141.85
Typhoon Warning	$ 1,932.10	$ 1,077.25	$ 4,603.05	$ 7,719.45	$ 3,118.50	$ 8,174.75	$ 14,144.00	$ 10,112.00	$ 50,881.10
Uranium 235	$ 10,869.80	$ 13,100.75	$ 15,780.75	$ 21,814.80	$ 2,107.00	$ 11,751.50	$ 16,184.00	$ 14,144.00	$ 105,752.60
Szechuan Singe	$ 9,549.65	$ 10,417.80	$ 12,338.00	$ 15,671.25	$ 7,709.25	$ 11,245.50	$ 14,784.00	$ 8,720.00	$ 90,435.45
Wasabi Fusion	$ 2,523.90	$ 4,027.50	$ 7,790.85	$ 13,551.90	$ 9,419.25	$ 12,820.50	$ 20,664.00	$ 13,680.00	$ 84,477.90
Sorrento Serrano	$ 2,112.20	$ 3,132.50	$ 4,746.15	$ 2,318.35	$ 2,123.25	$ 5,633.25	$ 5,712.00	$ 1,360.00	$ 27,137.70
Yucatan Bomb	$ 1,517.25	$ 1,332.80	$ 1,876.50	$ 1,292.70	$ 672.60	$ 4,335.50	$ 5,520.00	$ 1,152.00	$ 17,699.35
Toast Jammer	$ 1,100.75	$ 2,255.05	$ 785.35	$ 993.85	$ 991.20	$ 2,700.75	$ -	$ -	$ 8,826.95
									$ 436,695.05
								Taxes paid	$ 8,753.95
								Sales after taxes	$ 427,941.10

Excel 2016, Windows 10, Microsoft Corporation

Lesson 71—Apply

You are the sales manager of the Brown Street store of the Fulton Appliances chain of stores. The second week of August sales have ended, and you want to provide headquarters with a summary of the week's sales. You want to combine the data from each of the day's sales. You also notice that the names in the spreadsheet are not capitalized, and you need to correct this.

DIRECTIONS

1. Start Excel, if necessary, and open **E71Apply** from the data files for this lesson.
2. Save the file as **E71Apply_xx** in the location where your teacher instructs you to store the files for this lesson.
3. For all worksheets, add a header that has your name at the left, the date code in the center, and the page number code at the right, and change back to **Normal** view.
4. Use Flash Fill to uppercase the names of the salespeople.
   a. On the August Week 2 tab, select the cell range **B10:B13**, and press CTRL + C to copy it.
   b. Click cell **L10**, and press CTRL + V to paste it in the cell range **L:10:L13**.
   c. Click cell **M10**, type **Jack Smithe**, and press ENTER.
   d. In cell M11, type **Joe**, and press ENTER.
   e. Select the cell range **M10:M13**, and press CTRL + C to copy it.
   f. Click cell **B10**, and press CTRL + V to paste it in the cell range **B10:B13**.
   g. Copy and paste the cell range **B10:B13** to the rest of the cell ranges with names of salespeople.
   h. Select the cell range **L10:M13**, and press DEL.
5. Using consolidation by category, insert the **Sum** function to summarize the sales data from the **August Week 2** worksheet into a single table on the **Summary** worksheet in the cell range **C10:J13**. Include the total sales and the commission amounts, or manually re-create them after doing the consolidation by copying the functions from the **August Week 2** worksheet into the appropriate cells on the Summary worksheet.
6. Using consolidation by category, insert the **Average** function to average the sales data from the **August Week 2** worksheet into a single table on the **Summary** worksheet in the cell range **C20:H23**. Do not include total sales or commissions (columns I and J).
7. Format the cells containing the averages with the **Number** format, and show one decimal place.
8. Adjust the column widths as necessary, and format the worksheet as you like.
9. **With your teacher's permission,** print the **Summary** worksheet. Your worksheet should look like the one shown in Figure 71-3 on the next page.
10. Save and close the file, and exit Excel.

Figure 71-3

JJ Fulton Appliances

Brown Street Store

Summary of Sales, Week of August 12th

Totals for the Week

Salesperson	Dishwasher	Oven	Refrigerator	Television	Washer	Dryer	Total Sales	Commission
Jack Smithe	9	8	9	7	8	7	$ 28,006.47	$ 2,030.47
Joe Cooper	7	3	6	9	5	6	$ 22,195.22	$ 1,609.15
Sally Peters	3	6	9	16	6	4	$ 30,684.64	$ 2,224.64
Peter Carter	7	4	3	13	2	2	$ 20,325.26	$ 1,473.58

Averages for the Week

Salesperson	Dishwasher	Oven	Refrigerator	Television	Washer	Dryer
Jack Smithe	1.8	1.6	1.5	2.3	1.6	1.8
Joe Cooper	1.8	1.5	2.0	1.8	1.7	1.2
Sally Peters	1.0	1.2	2.3	2.7	1.5	1.3
Peter Carter	1.4	1.3	1.0	2.2	1.0	1.0

Excel 2016, Windows 10, Microsoft Corporation

Lesson 72

Linking Workbooks

➤ What You Will Learn

Linking Workbooks
Modifying a Linked Workbook

Software Skills In Excel, you can link to data created in another Microsoft program, such as Word or PowerPoint. When you change the Excel data, the data in the source file will update automatically. For example, if you link Excel data to a Word document and then change that data, the changes are automatically updated within the Word document.

What You Can Do

Linking Workbooks

- You can create a **link** between files to create a connection between the data in the files.
- In a linked file, if you change the data in the source file, the data in the destination file changes.
- You can change the link to update manually instead of automatically.
- You can perform other maintenance tasks with the links in your destination file, such as breaking a link and retaining local formatting changes whenever a link is updated.
- Typically, all Microsoft programs support linking, so you can apply the same process to link Excel data in programs other than those of Microsoft Office.

WORDS TO KNOW

Link
A reference to data stored in another file. When that data is changed, the data is updated in the destination file automatically.

Try It! Linking a Workbook to a PowerPoint Presentation

1. Start Excel, and open the **E72TryA** file from the data files for this lesson.
2. Save the file as **E72TryA_xx** in the location where your teacher instructs you to store the files for this lesson.
3. Start PowerPoint, and open the **E72TryB** file from the data files for this lesson.
4. Save the file as **E72TryB_xx** in the location where your teacher instructs you to store the files for this lesson.

   ✓ *For the purposes of this lesson, it is helpful to have the linked files in the same folder. You can link files that are in different file locations, but the files need to stay in their original locations for the files to stay linked.*
5. In the **E72TryA_xx** Excel file, click the January worksheet tab.
6. Select the cell range A6:J16, and on the Home tab, click Copy.
7. Switch to the **E72TryB_xx** PowerPoint presentation, and on the Home tab, click the Paste drop-down arrow > Paste Special.
8. In the Paste Special dialog box, click Paste link.
9. In the As list, click Microsoft Excel Worksheet Object.
10. Click OK. The linked Excel data is placed on the slide.
11. Resize the linked Excel data, and reposition it on the slide as shown in the graphic.
12. Close the **E72TryA_xx** file without saving changes, and exit Excel.
13. Save the changes to the **E72TryB_xx** file, and leave it open to use in the next Try It.

Linked data from an Excel workbook

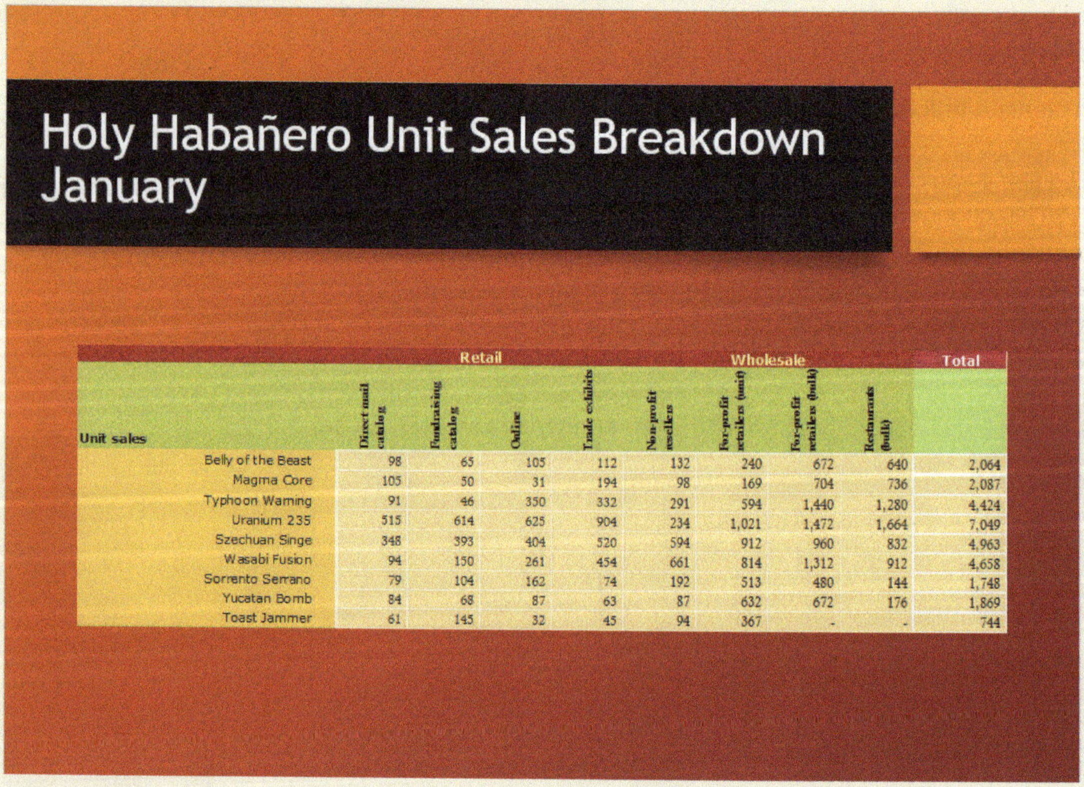

Unit sales	Retail				Wholesale				Total
	Direct mail catalog	Fundraising catalog	Online	Trade exhibits	Non-profit resellers	For-profit retailers (unit)	For-profit retailers (bulk)	Restaurants (bulk)	
Belly of the Beast	98	65	105	112	132	240	672	640	2,064
Magma Core	105	50	31	194	98	169	704	736	2,087
Typhoon Warning	91	46	350	332	291	594	1,440	1,280	4,424
Uranium 235	515	614	625	904	234	1,021	1,472	1,664	7,049
Szechuan Singe	348	393	404	520	594	912	960	832	4,963
Wasabi Fusion	94	150	261	454	661	814	1,312	912	4,658
Sorrento Serrano	79	104	162	74	192	513	480	144	1,748
Yucatan Bomb	84	68	87	63	87	632	672	176	1,869
Toast Jammer	61	145	32	45	94	367	-	-	744

Modifying a Linked Workbook

- You can update data linked to an Excel workbook without having the Excel source file open.
- For example, if you have linked Excel data in a Word document (the destination file), you can open that Word document and double-click the data. Excel automatically starts and opens the linked workbook so you can make changes.
- After you make changes and save them, the changes are automatically updated through the link to the source file.
- If the destination file is not currently open when you make changes in the Excel source file, the changes will be updated when the destination file is opened later.
- Because Excel uses the file path as its location, if the source file is moved from the location where it was originally linked to the destination file, you will need to update the link.

Try It! Modifying a Linked Workbook

1. In the **E72TryB_xx** file, double-click the linked Excel data. Excel opens the **E72TryA_xx** file with the linked data selected.

   ✓ *If a security warning appears, click Enable Content.*
2. Arrange the Excel and PowerPoint windows side by side.
3. In the **E72TryA_xx** file, click cell D10, type **350**, and press ENTER.
4. In the **E72TryB_xx** file, notice the change reflected in the PowerPoint presentation.
5. Save the changes to the **E72TryA_xx** file, and exit Excel.
6. Save the changes to the **E72TryB_xx** file, and close it. Leave PowerPoint open to use in the next Try It.

Try It! Manually Updating a Link

1. In PowerPoint, open the **E72TryB_xx** file from the location where your teacher instructs you to store the files for this lesson.
2. In the security notice dialog box, click Cancel.
3. Click the linked Excel data to select it.
4. Right-click the Excel data, and click Update Link.
5. Save and close the file, and exit PowerPoint.

Manually updating linked data

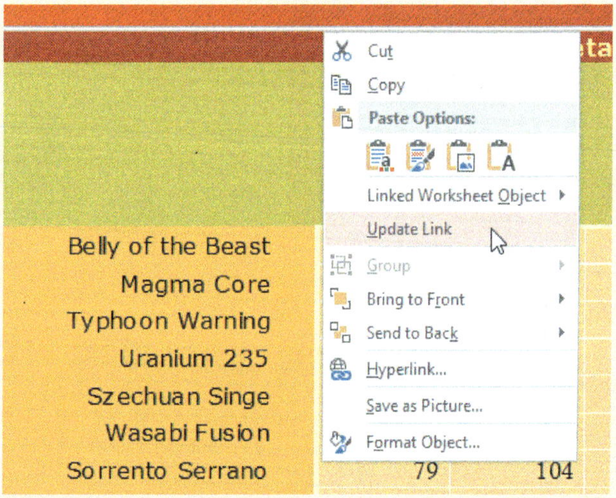

Excel 2016, Windows 10, Microsoft Corporation

Lesson 72—Practice

You are the sales manager for Holy Habañero, which sells hot sauces through nine different sales channels. The owner of the company has asked you create a PowerPoint presentation for the total gross sales figures from the first quarter of the year. You want to create a link to the Excel workbook so that you know the data can be updated if it changes in the future.

DIRECTIONS

1. Start Excel, if necessary, and open **E72PracticeA** from the data files for this lesson.
2. Save the file as **E72PracticeA_xx** in the location where your teacher instructs you to store the files for this lesson.
3. Start PowerPoint, and open the **E72PracticeB** file from the data files for this lesson.
4. Save the file as **E72PracticeB_xx** in the location where your teacher instructs you to store the files for this lesson.

   ✓ *For the purposes of this project, it is helpful to have the linked files in the same folder.*

5. In the **E72PracticeB_xx** file, click in the **Created by:** text box, and type your name.
6. Switch to the **E72PracticeA_xx** file, and click the **Totals** worksheet tab
7. Select the cell range **A45:J84**, and on the Home tab, click **Copy**.
8. Switch to the **E72PracticeB_xx** file, and on the Home tab, click the **Paste** drop-down arrow > **Paste Special**.
9. In the Paste Special dialog box, click **Paste link**.
10. In the As list, click **Microsoft Excel Worksheet Object**.
11. Click **OK** to place the linked Excel data on the slide.
12. Resize the linked object. Your worksheet should look like the one shown in Figure 72-1 on the next page.
13. Close the **E72PracticeA_xx** file without saving changes, and exit Excel.
14. **With your teacher's permission,** print the **E72PracticeB_xx** presentation.
15. Save and close the **E72PracticeB_xx** file, and exit PowerPoint.

Figure 72-1

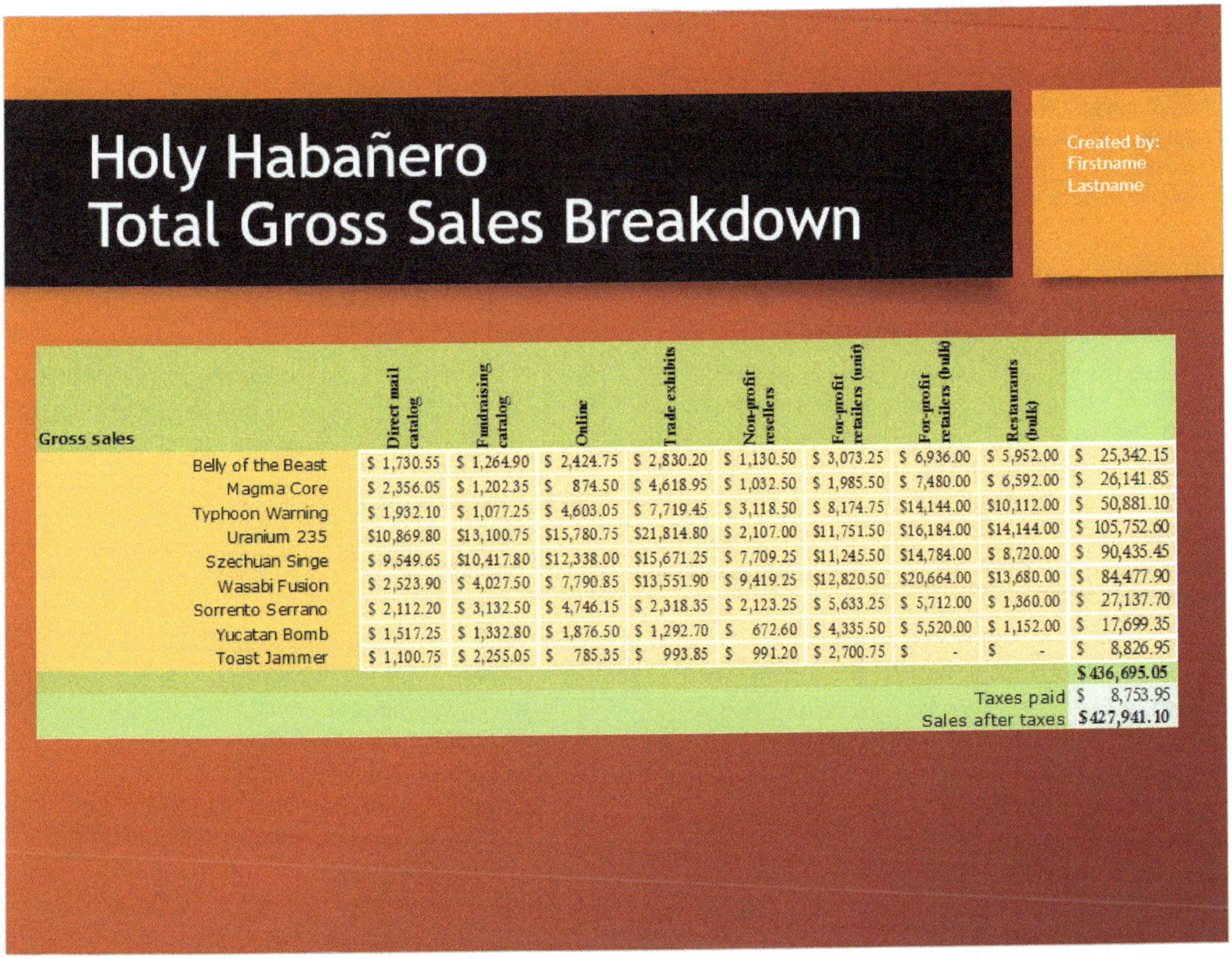

Gross sales	Direct mail catalog	Fundraising catalog	Online	Trade exhibits	Non-profit resellers	For-profit retailers (unit)	For-profit retailers (bulk)	Restaurants (bulk)	
Belly of the Beast	$ 1,730.55	$ 1,264.90	$ 2,424.75	$ 2,830.20	$ 1,130.50	$ 3,073.25	$ 6,936.00	$ 5,952.00	$ 25,342.15
Magma Core	$ 2,356.05	$ 1,202.35	$ 874.50	$ 4,618.95	$ 1,032.50	$ 1,985.50	$ 7,480.00	$ 6,592.00	$ 26,141.85
Typhoon Warning	$ 1,932.10	$ 1,077.25	$ 4,603.05	$ 7,719.45	$ 3,118.50	$ 8,174.75	$14,144.00	$10,112.00	$ 50,881.10
Uranium 235	$10,869.80	$13,100.75	$15,780.75	$21,814.80	$ 2,107.00	$11,751.50	$16,184.00	$14,144.00	$ 105,752.60
Szechuan Singe	$ 9,549.65	$10,417.80	$12,338.00	$15,671.25	$ 7,709.25	$11,245.50	$14,784.00	$ 8,720.00	$ 90,435.45
Wasabi Fusion	$ 2,523.90	$ 4,027.50	$ 7,790.85	$13,551.90	$ 9,419.25	$12,820.50	$20,664.00	$13,680.00	$ 84,477.90
Sorrento Serrano	$ 2,112.20	$ 3,132.50	$ 4,746.15	$ 2,318.35	$ 2,123.25	$ 5,633.25	$ 5,712.00	$ 1,360.00	$ 27,137.70
Yucatan Bomb	$ 1,517.25	$ 1,332.80	$ 1,876.50	$ 1,292.70	$ 672.60	$ 4,335.50	$ 5,520.00	$ 1,152.00	$ 17,699.35
Toast Jammer	$ 1,100.75	$ 2,255.05	$ 785.35	$ 993.85	$ 991.20	$ 2,700.75	$ -	$ -	$ 8,826.95
									$436,695.05
								Taxes paid	$ 8,753.95
								Sales after taxes	**$427,941.10**

Excel 2016, Windows 10, Microsoft Corporation

Lesson 72—Apply

As the sales manager for Holy Habañero, you have been concerned about the unit sales in your inventory. You created several Excel worksheets to show the unit sales for the first three months of the year. The corporate office has asked to review your figures, so you need to prepare a PowerPoint presentation and link Excel data to the presentation. In this project, you will link an Excel workbook to a PowerPoint presentation, update the data, and manually update the link.

DIRECTIONS

1. Start Excel, if necessary, and open **E72ApplyA** from the data files for this lesson.
2. Save the file as **E72Apply_xx** in the location where your teacher instructs you to store the files for this lesson.
3. Start PowerPoint, and open the **E72ApplyB** file from the data files for this lesson.
4. Save the file as **E72ApplyB_xx** in the location where your teacher instructs you to store the files for this lesson

   ✓ *For the purposes of this project, it is helpful to have the linked files in the same folder.*
5. In the **E72Apply B_xx** file, click in the **Created by:** text box, and type your name.
6. In the PowerPoint file, insert a link to the total unit sales data from the Excel worksheet.
   a. Switch to the **E72ApplyA_xx** file, and click the **Totals** worksheet tab
   b. Select the cell range **A6:J44**, and on the Home tab, click **Copy** .
   c. Switch to the **E72ApplyB_xx** file, and on the Home tab, click the **Paste** drop-down arrow > **Paste Special**.
   d. In the Paste Special dialog box, click **Paste link**.
   e. In the As list, click **Microsoft Excel Worksheet Object**.
   f. Click **OK** to place the linked Excel data on the slide.
   g. Resize the linked object, and reposition it on the slide.
7. Close the **E72ApplyA_xx** file without saving changes, and exit Excel.
8. Save the **E72ApplyB_xx** file.
9. Edit the unit sales data in Excel.
   a. Double-click the linked Excel data. Excel opens the **E72ApplyA_xx** file with the linked data selected.
   b. Change the Online value for Magma Core to **185**.
   c. Change the Direct mail catalog value for Toast Jammer to **250**.
   d. Save the **E72ApplyA_xx** Excel file, and exit Excel.
10. In the PowerPoint file, check that the data has been updated.
11. **With your teacher's permission,** print the **E72ApplyB_xx** presentation. Your worksheet should look like the one shown in Figure 72-2 on the next page.
12. Save and close the **E72ApplyB_xx** file, and exit PowerPoint.

Figure 72-2

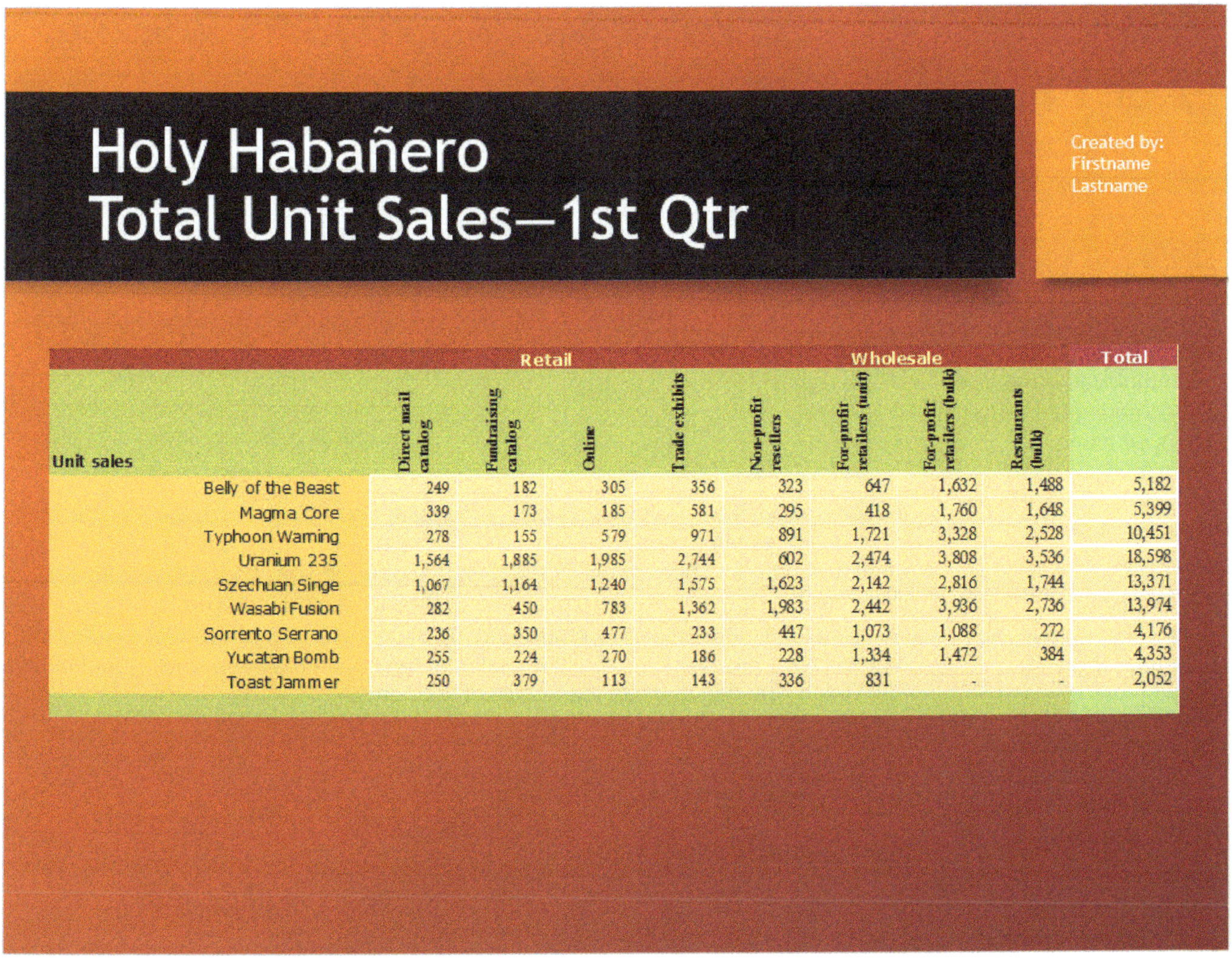

Unit sales	Retail				Wholesale				Total
	Direct mail catalog	Fundraising catalog	Online	Trade exhibits	Non-profit resellers	For-profit retailers (unit)	For-profit retailers (bulk)	Restaurants (bulk)	
Belly of the Beast	249	182	305	356	323	647	1,632	1,488	5,182
Magma Core	339	173	185	581	295	418	1,760	1,648	5,399
Typhoon Warning	278	155	579	971	891	1,721	3,328	2,528	10,451
Uranium 235	1,564	1,885	1,985	2,744	602	2,474	3,808	3,536	18,598
Szechuan Singe	1,067	1,164	1,240	1,575	1,623	2,142	2,816	1,744	13,371
Wasabi Fusion	282	450	783	1,362	1,983	2,442	3,936	2,736	13,974
Sorrento Serrano	236	350	477	233	447	1,073	1,088	272	4,176
Yucatan Bomb	255	224	270	186	228	1,334	1,472	384	4,353
Toast Jammer	250	379	113	143	336	831	-	-	2,052

Excel 2016, Windows 10, Microsoft Corporation

Lesson 73

Using PivotTables

WORDS TO KNOW

Database
An organized collection of records. For example, in an employee database, one record might include:
Employee name
Date of hire
Address
Phone number
Salary rate

Data Model
The linking of elements together in a series.

Data source
The original location of the data. This could be a database, a Web page, a text file, or an XML file.

Field
A single element of a record, such as "Phone number." Multiple related fields, such as one employee's name, address, and phone number, make up one record.

PivotTable
A table that can be rearranged to allow you to analyze complex data in a variety of ways.

Report filter
A field from a database that you can use to filter or limit the data displayed within the PivotTable.

➤ What You Will Learn

Working with PivotTables
Working with PivotTable Fields
Sorting PivotTable Fields
Formatting a PivotTable

Software Skills PivotTables can help you analyze complex data in a variety of ways. For example, you can use a PivotTable to summarize a database with employee data and filter or group the data by name, region, address, or salary. With the PivotTable, you can display information for each employee, or you can rearrange the table to display employees by region. You can use a data model, such as the Excel Data Model, to build a relational data source. With a Data Model-based PivotTable, you can analyze the details of your data.

What You Can Do

Working with PivotTables

- You can more easily summarize and analyze data with a **PivotTable** than you can with a regular table.
- For example, you can use a PivotTable to summarize a **database** with many tables and filter to the exact data elements that you want.
- You can create your own PivotTable, or you can use the recommended PivotTables that Excel provides from the Tables group on the Insert tab or the Tables tab of the Quick Analysis Tool.
- The source data for your PivotTable can be a data range or table in an Excel workbook, or it can be data that is stored outside of Excel, such as a Microsoft Access or Microsoft SQL Server database, or in an Online Analytical Processing (OLAP) cube file.
- When you create a PivotTable from an external data source, you link the data to that source.
- A **Data Model** integrates data from multiple tables to build a relational **data source** inside an Excel workbook. You can use the data model to create and manage the relationships among your data.

- You can choose to add the data to the Excel Data Model when you create a PivotTable.

  ✓ *You will learn more about the Excel Data Model in Excel Lesson 76.*

- As with a regular Excel table, you can insert a slicer or a timeline for a PivotTable.
- If you are using Windows 8 or later, you can publish a PivotTable in an Excel workbook as a Web page.

Try It! Creating a PivotTable from Excel Worksheet Data

1. Start Excel, and open **E73TryA** from the data files for this lesson.
2. Save the file as **E73TryA_xx** in the location where your teacher instructs you to store the files for this lesson.
3. On the August Sales worksheet, click anywhere in the data range.
4. Click Insert > PivotTable to display the Create PivotTable dialog box.
5. Click OK to accept the default placement of the PivotTable on a new worksheet.
6. Double-click on the new worksheet tab, type **Pet Drug Sales**, and press ENTER.
7. Save the changes to the file, and leave it open to use in the next Try It.

Try It! Creating a PivotTable from an Access Database

1. Start Access, and open the **E73TryB** file from the data files for this lesson. Click Enable Content.
2. Save the file as **E73TryB_xx** in the location where your teacher instructs you to store the files for this lesson.

   ✓ *It is helpful to have linked files in the same folder.*

3. Close the **E73TryB_xx** file.
4. In the **E73TryA_xx** file, click the Access worksheet tab.
5. Click cell A1.
6. Click Insert > PivotTable to display the Create PivotTable dialog box.
7. Under Choose the data that you want to analyze, click Use an external data source > Choose Connection. Excel displays the connections that are available.
8. In the Existing Connections dialog box, click **E73TryB_xx** > Open.

   ✓ *If you do not see the appropriate connection, you can click Browse for More and then browse to the location where your teacher instructs you to store the files for this lesson.*

9. In the Create PivotTable dialog box, check that the Existing Worksheet Location is Access!$A$1.
10. Click the Add this data to the Data Model check box to select it.
11. Click OK.
12. Save the changes to the file, and leave it open to use in the next Try It.

Creating a PivotTable from an external data source

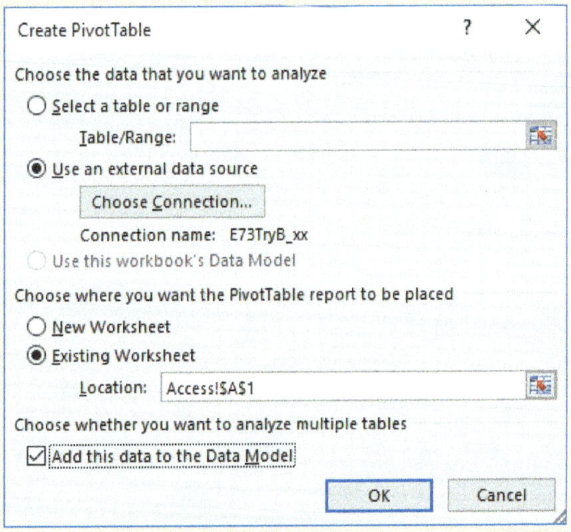

Excel 2016, Windows 10, Microsoft Corporation

Working with PivotTable Fields

- When you create a blank PivotTable, you need to add **fields** to it to show the summarized data.
- When you insert a recommended PivotTable, you can modify the PivotTable fields in the PivotTable Fields task pane.
- To display the PivotTable Fields task pane, use the Field List button in the Show group on the PivotTable Tools Analyze tab.
- The Field List in the PivotTable Fields task pane displays the tables in the Excel Data Model.
- The PivotTable Fields task pane displays the Field Section stacked on top of the Areas Section, by default.
- You can click the Tools button to change the view of the Field Sections and the Areas Section.
- You can drag fields into the four areas of the Areas Section to rearrange the fields.
  - FILTERS: Area fields shown as a **report filter** above the PivotTable. These fields can drill down into the data to show only the items relating to a particular category.
  - COLUMNS: Area fields shown as Column Labels at the top of the PivotTable. These are typically fields that categorize the data, for example, by date, time, or item.
  - ROWS: Area fields shown as Row Labels on the left side of the PivotTable. These are typically text fields that describe the data.
  - VALUES: Area fields that summarize numeric values in the PivotTable, for example, a sum calculating the total sales.
- You can click the drop-down arrow of an area field to access more options. For example, you can change a field in the VALUES area to calculate on an average instead of a sum by choosing Value Field Settings and selecting Average from the Value Field Settings dialog box.
- To remove a field from a PivotTable, deselect the field's check box in the Field List. You can also click the field's down-arrow in the Area Section and click Remove Field, or you can drag it out of the Area Section.

Try It! Adding PivotTable Fields

1. In the **E73TryA_xx** file, click the Pet Drug Sales worksheet tab, and click in the PivotTable box to display the PivotTable Fields task pane.
2. Drag the Drug field into the ROWS area.
3. Drag the For use on field into the FILTERS area.
4. Drag the To treat field into the COLUMNS area.
5. Drag the Total Sales field into the VALUES area.
6. Save the changes to the file, and leave it open to use in the next Try It.

(continued)

Try It! Adding PivotTable Fields *(continued)*

A PivotTable with fields and a filter

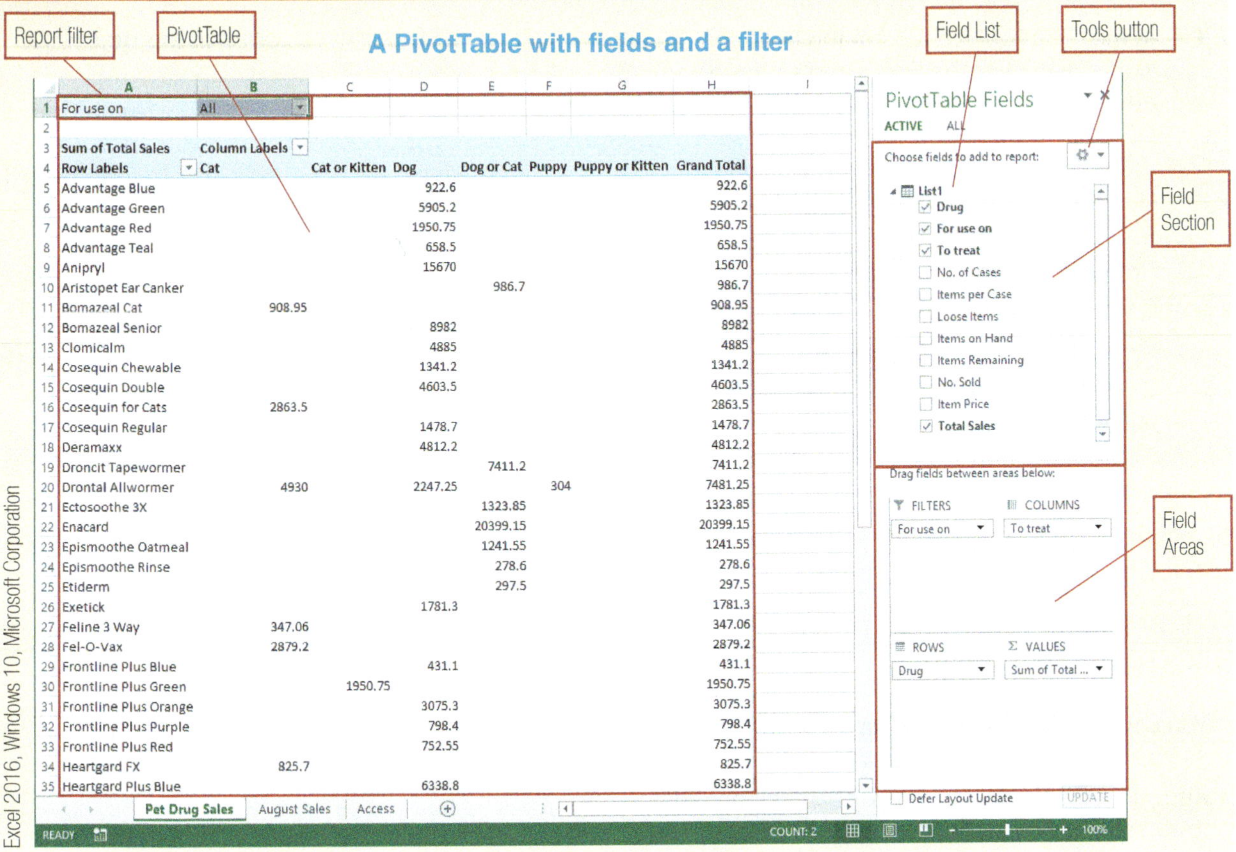

Excel 2016, Windows 10, Microsoft Corporation

Sorting PivotTable Fields

- You can sort PivotTable data so that it's easier to find the items you want to analyze.
- You can sort in alphabetical order or on values, such as from highest to lowest or oldest to newest.
- For the best sort results, be sure that your data doesn't have extra spaces at the front of the data elements.
- Sorting PivotTable data has some limitations.
  - You can't sort case-sensitive text entries.
  - You can't sort data by a format, such as cell or font color, or by conditional formatting indicators, such as icon sets.
- To sort, click the AutoSort drop-drop-down arrow to the left of the field label.
- You can set custom sort options by clicking More Sort Options from the AutoSort menu.

Try It! Sorting PivotTable Fields

1. In the **E73TryA_xx** file, on the Pet Drug Sales worksheet, click the Row Labels drop-down arrow.
2. Click Sort Z to A. The PivotTable is sorted by drug names in reverse alphabetical order.
3. Click the Row Labels drop-down arrow > Sort A to Z. The PivotTable is sorted by drug names in alphabetical order.
4. Save the changes to the file, and leave it open to use in the next Try It.

Try It! Creating a Custom Sort for PivotTable Fields

1. In the E73TryA_xx file, on the Pet Drug Sales worksheet, click the Row Labels drop-down arrow.
2. Click More Sort Options.
3. Under Sort options, click the Ascending (A to Z) by drop-down arrow, and click Sum of Total Sales.
4. Click OK. The PivotTable is sorted by the values of the total sales in ascending order.
5. Save the changes to the file, and leave it open to use in the next Try It.

The custom sort dialog box

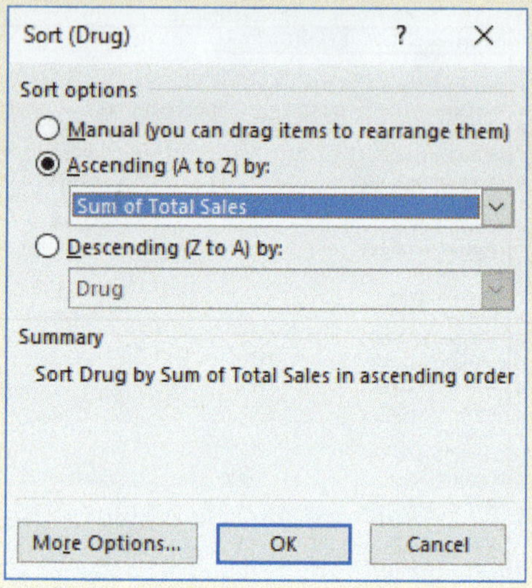

Excel 2016, Windows 10, Microsoft Corporation

Formatting a PivotTable

- You can format a PivotTable with a PivotTable style, as you would a regular Excel table.
- Apply PivotTable style options, such as banded rows or columns, to make it easier to read the data.

Try It! Formatting a PivotTable

1. In the E73TryA_xx file, on the Pet Drug Sales worksheet, click in the PivotTable.
2. Click the PivotTable Tools Design tab.
3. Click the PivotTable Styles More button.
4. In the Dark group, click Pivot Style Dark 2.
5. On the PivotTable Tools Design tab, in the PivotTable Style Options group, click the Banded Rows and Banded Columns check boxes to select them.
6. Save and close the file, and exit Excel.

Lesson 73—Practice

You work in the sales department of Best Sales Real Estate. Your manager has asked you to create a spreadsheet showing the total sales by each salesperson broken out by the areas and communities where the properties were sold. Your manager also wants the spreadsheet to show only single family homes from the Coastal and East County areas. In this project, you will create a PivotTable from the Excel data and filter it so that your manager can easily analyze the data.

DIRECTIONS

1. Start Excel, if necessary, and open **E73Practice** from the data files for this lesson.
2. Save the file as **E73Practice_xx** in the location where your teacher instructs you to store the files for this lesson.
3. Create a PivotTable from the cell range **A1:L121**, and place it on a new worksheet.
   a. On the **Report 1** worksheet, click in the table.
   b. Click **Insert** > **PivotTable**.
   c. Click the **Add this data to the Data Model** check box to select it.
   d. Click **OK**.
4. Double-click the **Sheet1** tab, type **Single Family**, and press ENTER.
5. In the PivotTable, show the total sales of each salesperson by area and community.
   a. On the **Single Family** worksheet, click the PivotTable.
   b. Drag the **Agent** field into the **ROWS** area.
   c. Drag the **Area** field into the **COLUMNS** area.
   d. Drag the **Community** field into the **COLUMNS** area.
   e. Drag the **List Price** field into the **VALUES** area.

      ✓ *Notice that the PivotTable does not include the icon sets from the data table.*

   f. Drag the **Type** field into the **FILTERS** area.
6. Filter the PivotTable to display only Single Family homes.
   a. On the **Single Family** worksheet, click cell **B1**, and click the **All** drop-down arrow.
   b. Click the **All** plus sign to expand the list.
   c. Click **Single Family**.
   d. Click **OK**.
7. Filter the PivotTable to display only Coastal and East County area properties.
   a. On the **Single Family** worksheet, click cell **B3**, and click the **Column Labels** drop-down arrow.
   b. Click to deselect the **Inland** check box.
   c. Click **OK**.
8. Format the cell range **B6:V20** with the **Accounting** format and no decimals.
9. Close the PivotTable Fields task pane.
10. Select the cell range **A1:V20**, and click **View** > **Zoom to Selection**.
11. Adjust the column widths as needed. Your worksheet should look like the one shown in Figure 73-1 on the next page.
12. For all worksheets, add a header that has your name at the left, the date code in the center, and the page number code at the right, and change back to **Normal** view.
13. **With your teacher's permission,** print the **Single Family** worksheet in **Landscape** orientation with the scaling set to **Fit Sheet on One Page**.
14. Save and close the file, and exit Excel.

Figure 73-1

Excel 2016, Windows 10, Microsoft Corporation

Type	Single Family							
Sum of List Price	Column Labels							
	Coastal							
Row Labels	Arandale	Bellevue	Bend	Linda Vista	Marysville	Mira Mesa	Mono Lake	Coastal Total
Barnes	$ 264,900	$ 355,000		$ 345,000				$ 964,900
Carter							$ 309,900	$ 309,900
Conners			$ 229,900			$ 229,500		$ 459,400
Garcia				$ 359,900		$ 799,000		$ 1,158,900
Hamilton			$ 425,900					$ 425,900
Hood					$ 374,900	$ 389,000	$ 369,900	$ 1,133,800
Jeffery	$ 1,550,400						$ 248,500	$ 1,798,900
Kennedy					$ 379,000			$ 379,000
Lam								
Langston			$ 359,000			$ 349,000		$ 708,000
McDonald	$ 398,000							$ 398,000
Severson					$ 379,900		$ 406,900	$ 786,800
Smith			$ 389,500			$ 339,900		$ 729,400
Tyson								
Grand Total	$ 2,213,300	$ 355,000	$ 1,404,300	$ 704,900	$ 1,133,800	$ 2,106,400	$ 1,335,200	$ 9,252,900

Row Labels	East County Bonita	Corona	East Lake	Escondido	Rockville	Santa Fe	Temecula	Tulare	Westood	Westwood	Zion	East County Total	Grand Total
Barnes						$ 208,750						$ 208,750	$ 1,173,650
Carter	$ 365,000	$ 339,900	$ 225,000				$ 297,500	$ 269,900		$ 317,500		$ 1,814,800	$ 2,124,700
Conners	$ 229,900											$ 229,900	$ 689,300
Garcia								$ 229,500				$ 229,500	$ 1,388,400
Hamilton			$ 304,900									$ 304,900	$ 730,800
Hood	$ 249,000	$ 249,900		$ 574,900								$ 1,073,800	$ 2,207,600
Jeffery		$ 338,876				$ 247,500						$ 586,376	$ 2,385,276
Kennedy				$ 208,750								$ 208,750	$ 587,750
Lam	$ 229,500			$ 480,990				$ 205,000	$ 239,900			$ 1,155,390	$ 1,155,390
Langston	$ 685,000				$ 245,000		$ 225,911				$ 325,000	$ 1,480,911	$ 2,188,911
McDonald													$ 398,000
Severson					$ 205,500		$ 349,000					$ 554,500	$ 1,341,300
Smith													$ 729,400
Tyson	$ 289,000				$ 204,900					$ 225,911		$ 719,811	$ 719,811
Grand Total	$ 2,047,400	$ 928,676	$ 529,900	$ 1,264,640	$ 655,400	$ 456,250	$ 872,411	$ 704,400	$ 239,900	$ 543,411	$ 325,000	$ 8,567,388	$ 17,820,288

Lesson 73—Apply

As sales manager of Best Sales Real Estate, you have created a spreadsheet showing the total sales by each salesperson broken out by the areas and communities where the properties were sold. The regional manager has asked you to show him the average list price of each salesperson from one report, as well as the average list price by area from another report. He also wants to see the prices sorted from highest to lowest. In this project, you will modify the data of an existing PivotTable and create a second PivotTable. You will also sort and format the data for both PivotTables.

DIRECTIONS

1. Start Excel, if necessary, and open **E73Apply** from the data files for this lesson.
2. Save the file as **E73Apply_xx** in the location where your teacher instructs you to store the files for this lesson.
3. For all worksheets, add a header that has your name at the left, the date code in the center, and the page number code at the right, and change back to **Normal** view
4. Modify the PivotTable to show the average list price of each salesperson.
   a. On the **PivotTables** worksheet, click **PivotTable Tools Analyze** > **Field List** to display the PivotTable Fields task pane.
   b. Click to deselect the **Area**, **Community**, and **Type** check boxes.
   c. In the **VALUES** area, click the **Sum of List Price** drop-down arrow > **Value Field Settings**.
   d. In the Value Field Settings dialog box, on the Summarize Values By tab, click **Average** > **OK**.
5. In cell **A2**, label the PivotTable **Report 1 PivotTable**. Apply **Bold** to the text, and increase the font size to **14 point**.
6. In cell **A20**, create the label **Report 2 PivotTable**. Apply **Bold** to the text, and increase the font size to **14 point**.
7. Create a PivotTable from the **Report 2** worksheet, and place it on the PivotTables worksheet starting at cell **A21**.
   a. Click the **Report 2** worksheet tab, and click in the table.
   b. Click **Insert** > **PivotTable**.
   c. In the Create PivotTable dialog box, click the **Existing Worksheet** option to select it.
   d. In the Location box, click the **Collapse Dialog Box** button, click the **PivotTables** worksheet tab, click cell **A21**, and press ENTER to return to the dialog box.
   e. Click the **Add this data to the Data Model** check box to select it.
   f. Click **OK**.

8. In the **Report 2 PivotTable**, show the average list price of each area.
   a. Drag the **Area** field to the **ROWS** area.
   b. Drag the **List Price** field to the **VALUES** area.
   c. In the **VALUES** area, click the **Sum of List Price** drop-down arrow > **Value Field Settings**.
   d. In the Value Field Settings dialog box, on the Summarize Values By tab, click **Average** > **OK**.
9. Format the average list prices of both PivotTables with the **Accounting** format.
10. Sort the average list price of the **Report 1 PivotTable** from highest to lowest.
    a. In the **Report 1 PivotTable**, click the **Row Labels** drop-down arrow.
    b. Click **More Sort Options**.
    c. Under Sort Options, click the **Descending (Z to A) by** option.
    d. Click the **Descending (Z to A) by** list > **Average of List Price**.
    e. Click **OK**.
11. Sort the average list price of the **Report 2 PivotTable** from highest to lowest using the same process as in step 10.
12. Format the **Report 1 PivotTable** with the PivotTable Style Dark 3 style.
    a. Click in the **Report 1 PivotTable**.
    b. Click **PivotTable Tools Design**.
    c. Click the PivotTable Styles **More** button > **Pivot Style Dark 3**.
13. Format the **Report 2 PivotTable** with the **Pivot Style Dark 5** style using the same process as in step 12.
14. Close the PivotTable Fields task pane.
15. **With your teacher's permission,** print the **PivotTables** worksheet. Your worksheet should look like the one shown in Figure 73-2.
16. Save and close the file, and exit Excel.

Figure 73-2

	A	B
1		
2	**Report 1 PivotTable**	
3	Row Labels	Average of List Price
4	Jeffery	$ 398,972.00
5	Garcia	$ 351,315.71
6	Hood	$ 349,400.00
7	McDonald	$ 345,383.33
8	Smith	$ 317,741.67
9	Hamilton	$ 301,101.83
10	Severson	$ 296,182.77
11	Langston	$ 295,550.92
12	Tyson	$ 295,535.17
13	Barnes	$ 293,925.00
14	Kennedy	$ 290,950.00
15	Conners	$ 282,950.00
16	Carter	$ 282,349.29
17	Lam	$ 260,959.00
18	Grand Total	$ 308,614.79
19		
20	**Report 2 PivotTable**	
21	Row Labels	Average of List Price
22	Coastal	$ 363,166.41
23	Inland	$ 293,109.93
24	East County	$ 271,850.93
25	Grand Total	$ 308,614.79

Lesson 74

Manipulating PivotTable Data

➤ What You Will Learn

Adding a Timeline
Grouping PivotTable Data
Adding a Calculated Field to a PivotTable
Using the GETPIVOTDATA Function

Software Skills Once you've created a basic PivotTable, there are many actions you can perform with it to view your data in different ways. This lesson covers three of those ways: timelines, grouping, and calculated fields. It also explains how to reference PivotTable data with GETPIVOTDATA.

WORDS TO KNOW

Calculated field
A database field that shows the result of a formula rather than raw data.

Timeline
A floating-box filter you can use to filter data by date, similar to a slicer.

What You Can Do

Adding a Timeline

- A **timeline** is somewhat like a slicer, which you learned about in Lesson 69. When enabled, it floats in a box on your worksheet, and you can use it to filter the data.
- In a PivotTable, you have a choice between using a date field as a regular filter and using a timeline for date filtering. Both work, but you may find the timeline more convenient.

Try It! Using a Timeline

1. Open Excel and open the **E74TryA** file from the data files for this lesson.
2. Save the file as **E74TryA_xx** in the location where your teacher instructs you to store the files for this lesson.
3. On the Averages tab, click anywhere inside the PivotTable to enable the PivotTable Tools tabs on the ribbon.
4. Click PivotTable Tools Analyze > Insert Timeline.
5. In the Insert timelines dialog box, click to select Date Listed.
6. Click OK. A floating timeline appears.
7. Drag the right border of the timeline to expand it enough that the entire timeline shows at once.
8. In the upper right corner of the timeline, click MONTHS.
9. On the menu that appears, click QUARTERS. Now the timeline shows quarters.
10. Click QUARTERS, and on the menu that appears, click MONTHS again.
11. On the timeline, click APR, and then drag to SEP, restricting the timeline to that six-month period.

    ✓ *Restricting the timeline dates applies a corresponding filter to the PivotTable data.*

12. Click the Clear Filter button in the upper-right corner of the timeline.
13. Press CTRL + Z to undo the clearing of the filter.
14. On the Timeline Tools Options tab, in the Timeline Styles group, click the More button and then click Timeline Style Light 2.
15. Save the changes to the file, and leave it open for the next Try It.

Add a timeline

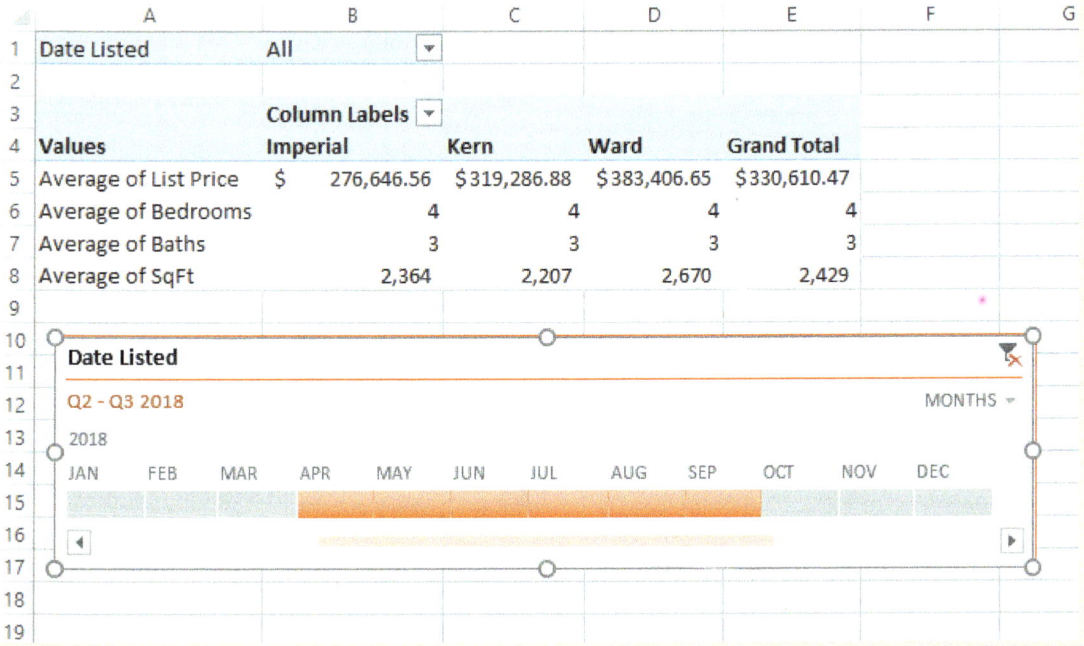

Excel 2016, Windows 10, Microsoft Corporation

Grouping PivotTable Data

- You can group by a numeric or date field in a PivotTable. Grouping summarizes the individual values so you can more easily see the larger trends.
- If the Group controls on the PivotTools Analyze tab are not available, you do not have a field selected by which the report can be grouped.
- To expand or collapse a group, click the minus or plus sign to the left of the group name.

Try It! Grouping PivotTable Data

1. In **E74Try**, on the Highest Prices tab, click in cell A4.
2. Click PivotTable Tools Analyze > Group Field.
3. In the Grouping dialog box, click Months.
4. Click OK. The data becomes grouped.

Group the data by month

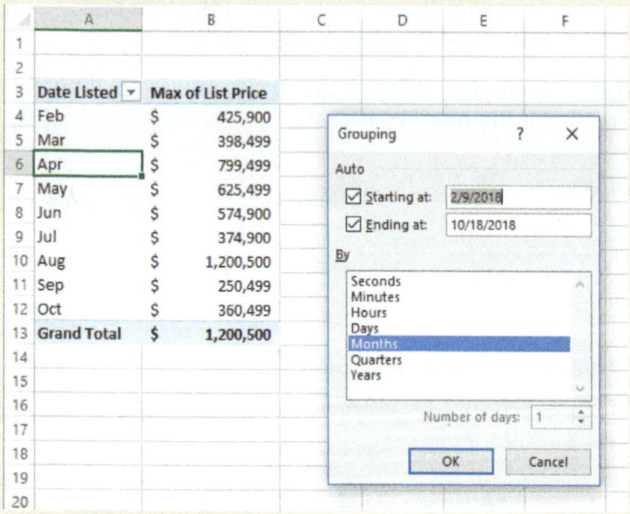

Excel 2016, Windows 10, Microsoft Corporation

5. Click PivotTable Tools Analyze > Ungroup. The grouping is removed.
6. Click PivotTable Tools Analyze > Group Field.
7. Select both Months and Quarters, and then click OK.

✓ *The data is now grouped by quarters and then by months within each quarter.*

8. Right-click the Grand Total line and click Remove Grand Total.

The table should look like this when you finish

Excel 2016, Windows 10, Microsoft Corporation

9. Save the changes to the file, and close it. Leave Excel open for the next Try It.

Adding a Calculated Field to a PivotTable

- PivotTables, by their very nature, are already full of calculated fields. They calculate sums, averages, minimums, maximums, and so on.
- When you add a field to a PivotTable in the VALUES or COLUMNS area, Excel attempts to guess what kind of calculation to use. Sum is its default for numeric values and Count for fields containing text.
- You can change the calculation applied by clicking the item to open its drop-down list and then choosing its Settings command. The exact name of the command depends on the field type; for example, for a numeric field it is Value Field Settings.
- In the dialog box that appears you can choose from among several common calculation types.
- You can also create your own calculated fields manually.

Try It! Adding a Calculated Field to a PivotTable

1. Open Excel and open the **E74TryB** file from the data files for this lesson.
2. Save the file as **E74TryB_xx** in the location where your teacher instructs you to store the files for this lesson.
3. On the Sales tab, in the VALUE pane, click Sum of Sales and click Value Field Settings.
4. On the Summarize Values By tab, click Average.
5. Click OK.
6. In the PivotTable, right-click cell B3, and then click Summarize Values By > Sum.
7. Right-click cell B3 and then click Show Values As > % of Grand Total.
8. Right-click cell B3 and then click Show Values As > No Calculation.
9. Click PivotTable Tools Analyze > Fields, Items, & Sets > Calculated Field.
10. In the Insert Calculated Field dialog box, in the Formula box, type **=Sales*0.02**.
11. In the Name box, type **Bonus**.
12. Click Add, and then click OK.
13. In the PivotTable Fields task pane, drag Bonus to the VALUES area.
14. In cell C3, type **Bonus Amt**, replacing the previous entry.
15. Save changes to the file, and leave it open for the next Try It.

Use the GETPIVOTDATA Function

- The GETPIVOTDATA function enables you to reference data in a PivotTable in other parts of the workbook. This can be useful because the PivotTable often includes calculations, summaries, and other information that the raw data does not readily show.
- An easy way to use this function is to click in the desired cell, type an equals sign (=), and then click the cell in the PivotTable that contains the data you want to reference. The data being referenced must contain a value, not a row or column label.
- The full syntax of GETPIVOTTABLE is as follows:
  - **Data_field**: The name, in quotation marks, for the data field that contains the data to be retrieved.
  - **Pivot_table:** A reference to one or more cells in a PivotTable.
  - **Field1, Item1, Field2, Item2:** You can optionally have 1 to 126 pairs of field names and items names that describe the data to be retrieved. Text must be enclosed in quotation marks.

Try It! Using GETPIVOTDATA to Reference a PivotTable's Data

1. In **E74TryB_xx**, on the Sales tab, right-click cell C3 and click Sort > Largest to Smallest.
2. In cell A19, type **Largest Bonus**.
3. In cell B19, type **=** and then click cell C4 and press Enter.
4. Click in cell C4 and look at the function in the formula bar. It looks like this:
   .. =GETPIVOTDATA("Bonus Amt",$A$3,"Salesperson","Carl Jackson")
5. In cell A20, type **Smallest Bonus**.
6. In cell B20, type **=GETPIVOTDATA(** and then click the Insert Function button on the formula bar.
7. Click in the Data_field box and type **"Bonus Amt"**.
8. Click in the Pivot_table box and type **$A$3**.
9. Click in the Field1 box and type **"Salesperson"**.
10. Click in the Item1 box and type **"Tom Wilson"**.
11. Click OK.
12. Use Format Painter to copy the formatting from C4 to B19:B20.
13. In C19, type **=A4** and press Enter.
14. In C20, type **=A15** and press Enter.
15. Save the changes to the file, and exit Excel.

Use the GETPIVOTDATA function

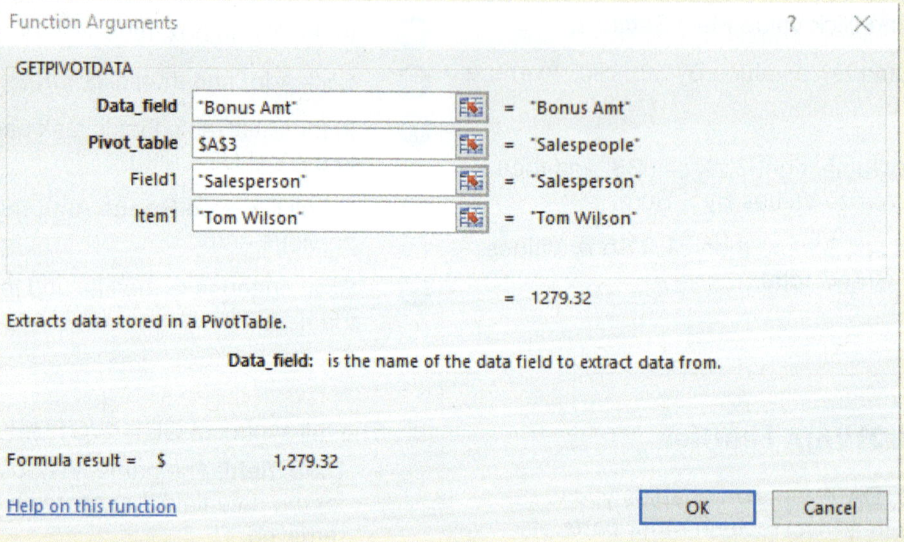

Excel 2016, Windows 10, Microsoft Corporation

Lesson 74—Practice

Holy Habanero's wholesale sales are booming, and they need help analyzing the wholesale data from Q1. A PivotTable report is already created; you will improve the report by adding some features to it.

DIRECTIONS

1. Start Excel, if necessary, and open the **E74Practice** file from the data files for this lesson.
2. Save the workbook as **E74Practice_xx** in the location where your teacher instructs you to store the files for this lesson.
3. On the Wholesale worksheet, add a header that has your name at the left, the date code in the center, and the page number code at the right, and change back to Normal view.
4. Add a timeline to the PivotTable.
   a. Click anywhere within the PivotTable on the Wholesale tab.
   b. Click **PivotTable Tools Analyze** > **Insert Timeline**.
   c. Click **Month**.
   d. Click **OK**.
5. On the slicer, click the blue bar under January to select only that month.
6. Click in the PivotTable and then click **PivotTable Tools Analyze** > **Refresh**.

   ✓ *The PivotTable report updates to show only January values.*
7. Drag the blue bar from January to March so that JAN, FEB, and MAR are all selected on the timeline.
8. Click in the PivotTable and then click **PivotTable Tools Analyze** > **Refresh**.
9. Drag the Timeline box so its upper left corner aligns with cell E18.
10. Create a group consisting of the first 5 products, and then a second group consisting of the remaining products.
    a. Select the range **A4:E23**.
    b. Click **PivotTable Tools Analyze** > **Group Selection**.
    c. Click cell **A4** and type **Product Group 1**.
    d. Select cells **A25:E44**.
    e. Click **PivotTable Tools Analyze** > **Group Selection**.
    f. Click cell **A25** and type **Product Group 2**.
11. Double-click cell **A25** to collapse Product Group 2. Then double-click it again to expand it.
12. Add a calculated field that provides a total for each row.
    a. Click **PivotTable Tools Analyze** > **Fields, Items, & Sets** > **Calculated Field**.
    b. In the Name box, type **Item Total**.
    c. In the Formula box, type **=SUM(**
    d. In the Fields list, double-click **Non-profit resellers**.
    e. Type a comma, and then double-click **For-profit retailers (unit).**
    f. Type a comma, and then double-click **For-profit retailers (bulk).**
    g. Type a comma, and then double-click **Restaurants (bulk).**
    h. Click **Add**.
    i. Click **OK**. The new column is added to the PivotTable.
13. Create a new worksheet named **Summary** and reference the grant total of wholesale units from the PivotTable report.
    a. Click the **New Sheet** icon ⊕ to the right of the existing worksheet tabs.
    b. Double-click the new sheet tab and type **Summary**.
    c. In cell A3 on the Summary sheet, type **Wholesale Units Grand Total**.
    d. Widen column A as needed to fit the text.
    e. Click in cell **B3** and type **=**.
    f. Click the Wholesale tab, and then click cell **F42** and press ENTER.
14. **With your teacher's permission**, print the first page of the Wholesale worksheet in Landscape orientation. It should look like the one shown in Figure 74-1 on the next page.
15. Save the changes to the workbook, and exit Excel.

Figure 74-1

Excel 2016, Windows 10, Microsoft Corporation

Q1 Wholesale Unit Sales

Row Labels	Sum of Non-profit resellers	Sum of For-profit retailers (unit)	Sum of For-profit retailers (bulk)	Sum of Restaurants (bulk)	Sum of Item Total
Product Group 1					
Belly of the Beast	323	647	1632	1488	4,090
January	132	240	672	640	1,684
February	94	201	544	496	1,335
March	97	206	416	352	1,071
Magma Core	295	418	1760	1648	4,121
January	98	169	704	736	1,707
February	92	171	480	496	1,239
March	105	78	576	416	1,175
Sorrento Serrano	447	1073	1088	272	2,880
January	192	513	480	144	1,329
February	134	326	384	96	940
March	121	234	224	32	611
Szechuan Singe	1623	2142	2816	1744	8,325
January	594	912	960		
February	561	765	672		
March	468	465	1184		
Toast Jammer	336	831	0		
January	94	367	0		
February	106	234	0		
March	136	230	0		
Product Group 2					
Typhoon Warning	891	1721	3328	2528	8,468
January	291	594	1440	1280	3,605
February	297	452	960	432	2,141
March	303	675	928	816	2,722
Uranium 235	602	2474	3808	3536	10,420
January	234	1021	1472	1664	4,391
February	234	1021	1472	1664	4,391
March	134	432	864	208	1,638

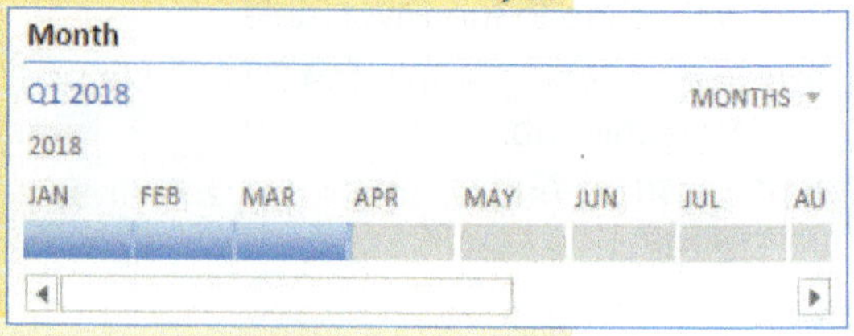

Lesson 74—Apply

Northwind Traders has provided you a workbook with some data about the sales of their private-label gourmet foods. An existing PivotTable summarizes the quantity sold and revenue per item. You will add a calculated field and some grouping to this PivotTable report to glean some additional information.

DIRECTIONS

1. Start Excel, if necessary, and open the **E74Apply** file from the data files for this lesson.
2. Save the workbook as **E74Apply_xx** in the location where your teacher instructs you to store the files for this lesson.
3. On the Analysis worksheet, add a header that has your name at the left, the date code in the center, and the page number code at the right, and change back to Normal view.
4. Create a calculated field that determines the average amount paid per item.
   a. Click anywhere in the PivotTable.

b. Click **PivotTable Tools Analyze** > **Fields, Items, & Sets** > **Calculated Field**.
c. In the Name box, type **Average Price**.
d. In the Formula box, type **=Revenue / Quantity**.
e. Click **Add**.
f. Click OK.
g. In cell D3, change the label to **Avg Price**.
h. Select column D and choose **Home** > **Number Format** > **Currency**.
i. Autofit the width of column D to its content.

5. From the PivotTable Tools Design tab, apply the PivotTable Style Dark 7 style.
6. Change the text in cell A3 to **Product Name**.
7. Right-click the Sum of Revenue column and click **Sort** > **Smallest to Largest**.
8. Group the product with a Sum of Revenue value less than $10,000, and call the group Under $10K.
   a. Select cells **A4:D18**.
   b. Click **PivotTable Tools Analyze** > **Group Selection**.
   c. In cell A4, change the label to **Under $10K**.
9. Group the product with a Sum of Revenue value greater than than $10,000, and call the group Over $10K.
   a. Select cells **A20:D41**.
   b. Click **PivotTable Tools Analyze** > **Group Selection**.
   c. In cell A20, change the label to **Over $10K**.
10. Sort the items within the groups in ascending order.
   a. Click cell **A5**.
   b. Click **Data** > **Sort A to Z**.
11. **With your teacher's permission**, print the first page only. It should look like Figure 74-4.
12. Save the changes to the workbook, and exit Excel.

Product Name	Sum of Quantity	Sum of Revenue	Avg Price
Under $10K			
Northwind Traders Almonds	297	$2,566.00	$8.64
Northwind Traders Beer	506	$6,678.00	$13.20
Northwind Traders Boysenberry Spread	301	$7,345.00	$24.40
Northwind Traders Cajun Seasoning	453	$9,424.80	$20.81
Northwind Traders Chocolate	138	$1,542.75	$11.18
Northwind Traders Chocolate Biscuits Mix	723	$6,159.50	$8.52
Northwind Traders Clam Chowder	981	$9,098.10	$9.27
Northwind Traders Long Grain Rice	500	$3,383.80	$6.77
Northwind Traders Mustard	791	$9,685.00	$12.24
Northwind Traders Olive Oil	298	$5,801.15	$19.47
Northwind Traders Ravioli	434	$7,807.80	$17.99
Northwind Traders Scones	1016	$9,636.00	$9.48
Northwind Traders Syrup	328	$3,080.00	$9.39
Northwind Traders Tomato Sauce	239	$3,519.00	$14.72
Northwind Traders Walnuts	404	$8,630.40	$21.36
Over $10K			
Northwind Traders Chai	828	$14,277.60	$17.24
Northwind Traders Coffee	580	$25,079.20	$43.24
Northwind Traders Crab Meat	1103	$19,048.30	$17.27
Northwind Traders Curry Sauce	372	$13,760.00	$36.99
Northwind Traders Dried Apples	886	$44,742.60	$50.50
Northwind Traders Dried Pears	763	$22,464.00	$29.44
Northwind Traders Fruit Cocktail	978	$35,482.20	$36.28
Northwind Traders Gnocchi	1263	$45,121.20	$35.73
Northwind Traders Hot Pepper Sauce	745	$14,607.00	$19.61
Northwind Traders Marmalade	313	$23,635.80	$75.51
Northwind Traders Mozzarella	806	$25,738.80	$31.93
Grand Total	16046	$378,314.00	$23.58

Figure 74-2

Lesson 75

Using PivotCharts

➤ What You Will Learn

Creating a PivotChart from a PivotTable
Creating a PivotChart from an External Data Source
Working with PivotChart Fields
Formatting a PivotChart

Software Skills PivotCharts can help you summarize and visualize large amounts of data. A PivotChart shows data series, categories, and chart axes in the same way as a standard chart; however, a PivotChart also has interactive filtering controls right on the chart so you can quickly analyze a subset of your data. For example, you can use a PivotChart to summarize a database with many tables and filter to show only the exact data elements that you want.

What You Can Do

Creating a PivotChart from a PivotTable

- You can more easily summarize and analyze data with a **PivotChart** than you can with a regular chart.
- You can create your own PivotChart, or you can use the recommended PivotCharts that Excel provides.
- Use the Recommended Charts command in the Charts group on the Insert tab to insert a recommended PivotChart. Excel indicates a PivotChart with a PivotTable icon in the upper-right corner of the recommended chart.
- When you insert a recommended PivotChart, Excel will automatically create a **coupled** PivotTable as well.
- You can also create a **decoupled** PivotChart from Excel worksheet data without first creating a PivotTable.

WORDS TO KNOW

Coupled
A coupled PivotChart is connected to data from a PivotTable.

Decoupled
A decoupled PivotChart is connected to PivotTable data, but can be displayed on a different worksheet than the data.

PivotChart
A chart based on PivotTable or database data.

Try It! Creating a Coupled PivotChart

1. Start Excel, and open the **E75TryA** file from the data files for this lesson.
2. Save the file as **E75TryA_xx** in the location where your teacher instructs you to store the files for this lesson.
3. On the Nov Sales worksheet, click in the table.
4. Click Insert > Recommended Charts to display the Insert Chart dialog box.
5. On the Recommended Charts tab, click the Sum of Cost by Product Type chart (the third chart from the top).
6. Click OK. The PivotChart is inserted on a new worksheet, along with a new PivotTable..
7. Drag the PivotChart so that its upper-left corner is at the edge of cell E12.
8. Double-click the Sheet1 worksheet tab, type **Excel PivotChart**, and press ENTER.
9. Save the changes to the file, and leave it open to use in the next Try It.

Inserting a Recommended PivotChart

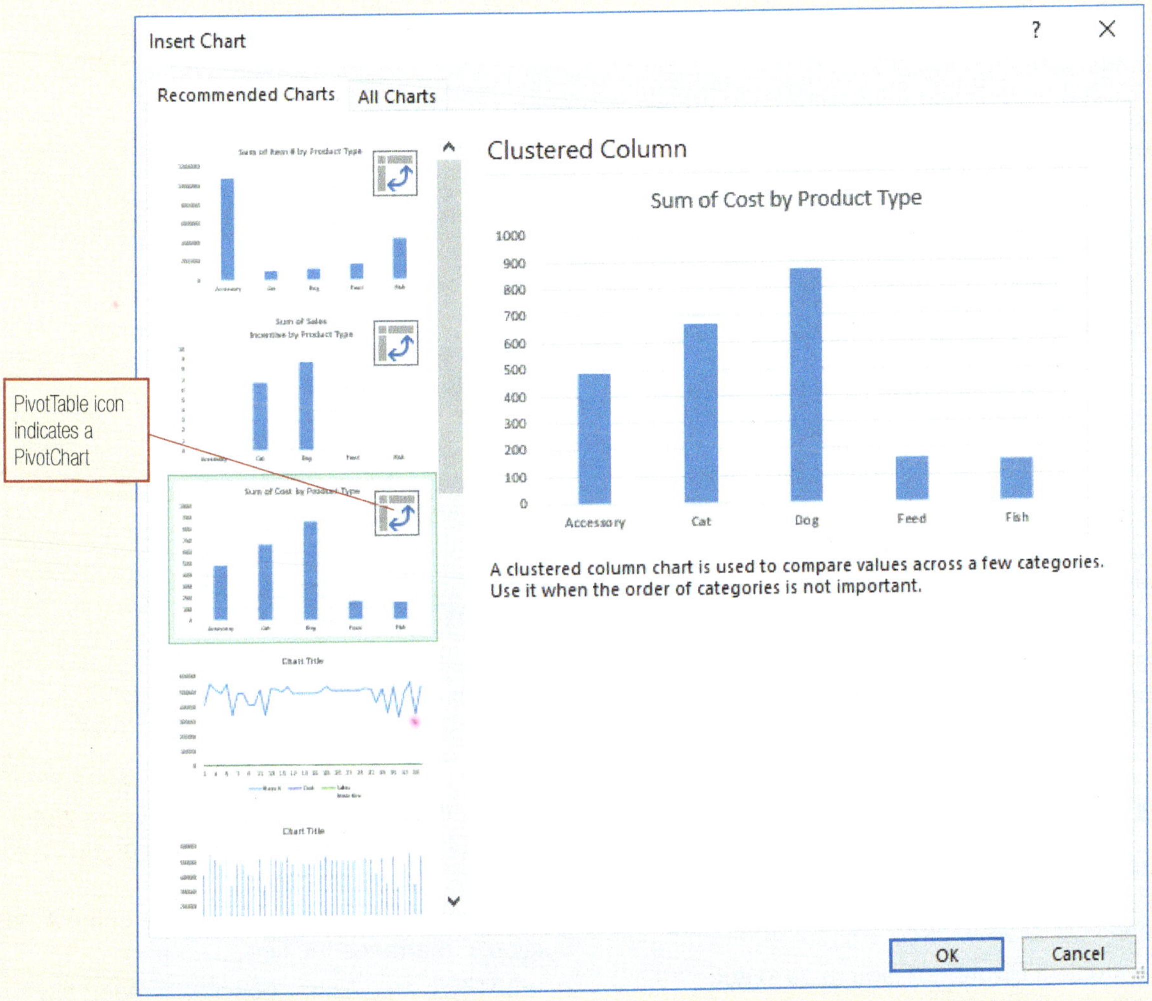

Excel 2016, Windows 10, Microsoft Corporation

Creating a PivotChart from an External Data Source

- The source data for your PivotChart can be a data range or table in an Excel workbook, a PivotTable, or data that is stored outside of Excel, such as data from a Microsoft Access database.
- When you create a PivotChart from an external data source, you link the data to that source.
- You can use the data connections that Excel finds for you, or you can browse to a specific data connection.
- An Excel Data Model is automatically created when you create a recommended PivotChart.

Try It! Creating a PivotChart from an Access Database

1. Start Access, and open the **E75TryB** file from the data files for this lesson. Enable content if necessary.
2. Save the file as **E75TryB_xx** in the location where your teacher instructs you to store the files for this lesson.

   ✓ *It is helpful to have linked files in the same folder.*
3. Close the **E75TryB_xx** file.
4. In the **E75TryA_xx** file, click the Access worksheet tab.
5. Click cell A1.
6. Click Insert > PivotChart to display the Create PivotChart dialog box.
7. Under Choose the data that you want to analyze, click Use an external data source > Choose Connection. Excel displays the connections that are available.
8. In the Existing Connections dialog box, click E75Try_xx > Open.

   ✓ *If you do not see the appropriate connection, you can browse to the location where your teacher instructs you to store the files for this lesson.*
9. In the Create PivotTable dialog box, check that the Existing Worksheet Location is Access!$A$1.
10. Click OK. A PivotTable and a PivotChart are inserted on the worksheet. Both are empty at this point.
11. Drag the PivotChart so that its upper-left corner is at the edge of cell F5.
12. Save the changes to the file, and leave it open to use in the next Try It.

Creating a PivotChart from an external data source

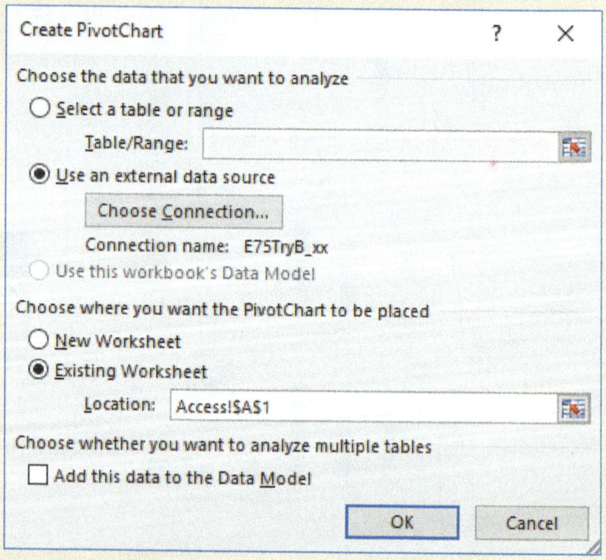

Excel 2016, Windows 10, Microsoft Corporation

Working with PivotChart Fields

- You can customize a PivotChart with the commands on the PivotChart Tools Analyze, Design, and Format tabs.
- When you create a PivotChart, you need to add fields to it to show your data.
- You can modify the PivotChart fields in the PivotChart Fields task pane, which is similar to the PivotTable Fields task pane.
- To display the PivotChart Fields task pane, use the Field List button in the Show/Hide group on the PivotChart Tools Analyze tab.
- You can drag fields into the four areas of the Areas Section to rearrange the fields.
  - FILTERS: Area fields shown as a report filter above the PivotChart. These fields can drill down into the data to show only the items relating to a particular category.

- LEGEND (SERIES): Area fields shown as the legend labels of the PivotChart. These fields are also shown as Column Labels at the top of the PivotTable.
- AXIS (CATEGORIES): Area fields shown as the horizontal (category) axis, or the x-axis, of the PivotChart. These fields are also shown as Row Labels at the top of the PivotTable.
- VALUES: Area fields shown as the vertical (value) axis, or the y-axis, of the PivotChart, for example, the prices of homes.

■ You can click the drop-down arrow of an area field to access more options. For example, you can change a field in the VALUES area to calculate an average instead of a sum by choosing Value Field Settings and selecting Average from the Value Field Settings dialog box.

■ To remove a field from a PivotChart, deselect the field's check box in the Field List. You can also click the field's down-arrow in the Area Section and click Remove Field, or you can drag it out of the Area Section.

■ You can filter and sort the data in a PivotChart the same way you filter and sort data in a PivotTable. Select the items you want to display from the drop-down buttons on the chart.

Try It! Adding PivotChart Fields

1. In the **E75TryA_xx** file, on the Access worksheet tab, click the PivotChart box to display the PivotChart Fields task pane.
2. Drag the Area field into the FILTERS area.
3. Drag the Sold field into the LEGEND (SERIES) area.
4. Drag the Agent field into the AXIS (CATEGORIES) area.
5. Drag the List Price field into the VALUES area.
6. Save the changes to the file, and leave it open to use in the next Try It.

A PivotChart with fields and a filter

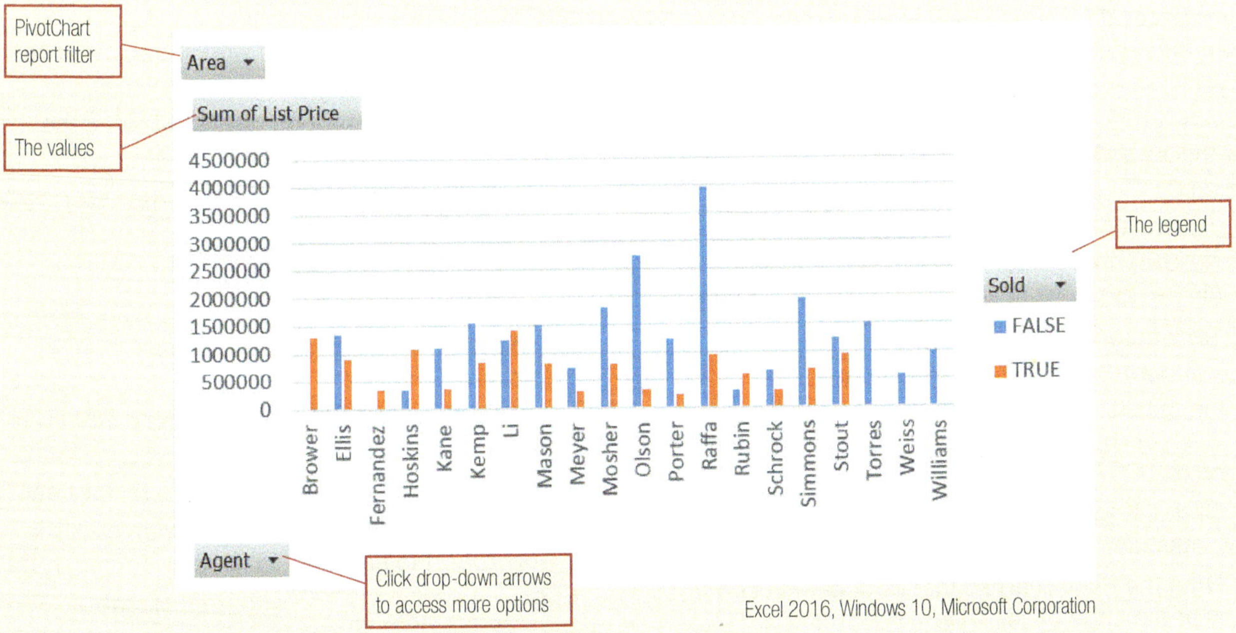

Excel 2016, Windows 10, Microsoft Corporation

Formatting a PivotChart

- You can format a PivotChart as you would a regular Excel chart.
- Apply PivotChart style, color, and layout options from the PivotChart Tools Design tab.
- You can also access style and color options from the Chart Styles shortcut button that appears to the right of the PivotChart.

Try It! Formatting a PivotChart

1. In the **E75TryA_xx** file, on the Access worksheet, click the PivotChart.
2. Click the PivotChart Tools Design tab.
3. In the Chart Styles group, click the PivotChart Styles More button.
4. Click Style 7.
5. Apply the Accounting format to the cell range B5:D25.
6. Close the PivotTable Fields task pane.
7. Save and close the file, and exit Excel.

Lesson 75—Practice

You are the owner of Pete's Pets, a local pet store. Your store has just finished its summer sale, and you want to know how one of your employees performed. You want to chart the data by product type and filter the total sales by salesperson. In this project, you will create a PivotChart from the Excel data and filter it. You will also format the chart so that it can be included in the employee's performance review.

DIRECTIONS

1. Start Excel, if necessary, and open **E75Practice** from the data files for this lesson.
2. Save the file as **E75Practice_xx** in the location where your teacher instructs you to store the files for this lesson.
3. Create a PivotChart from the cell range **B9:G49**, and place it on a new worksheet named **Employee Sales**.
   a. On the **Sales Data** worksheet, click in the table.
   b. Click **Insert** > **Recommended Charts** to display the Insert Chart dialog box.
   c. On the Recommended Charts tab, click the **Sum of Cost by Product Type** chart (the first chart).
   d. Click **OK** to insert the PivotChart on a new worksheet.
   e. Drag the PivotChart so that its upper-left corner is at the edge of cell **D12**.
   f. Rename the worksheet **Employee Sales**.
4. Filter the PivotChart to show the data for Alice Harper.
   a. On the **Employee Sales** worksheet, click the PivotChart to select it.
   b. In the PivotChart Fields task pane, drag the **Salesperson** field to the **Filters** area.
   c. On the PivotChart, click the **Salesperson** report filter drop-down arrow.
   d. Click **Alice Harper** > **OK**.
5. Rename the chart to **Employee Summer Sales**.
   a. On the **Employee Sales** worksheet, double-click the PivotChart title.
   b. Replace the title text with **Employee Summer Sales**.
6. Format the PivotChart with the Style 5 chart style.
   a. On the **Employee Sales** worksheet, click the PivotChart to select it.
   b. Click the **PivotChart Tools Design** tab.
   c. In the Chart Styles group, click the PivotChart Styles **More** button.
   d. Click **Style 5**.

7. Apply the **Accounting** format to the PivotTable cell range **B4:B8**.
8. Close the PivotTable Fields task pane.
9. For all worksheets, add a header that has your name at the left, the date code in the center, and the page number code at the right, and change back to **Normal** view.
10. Change the page orientation to **Landscape**.
11. **With your teacher's permission,** print the **Employee Sales** worksheet. Your worksheet should look like the one shown in Figure 75-1.
12. Save and close the file, and exit Excel.

Figure 75-1

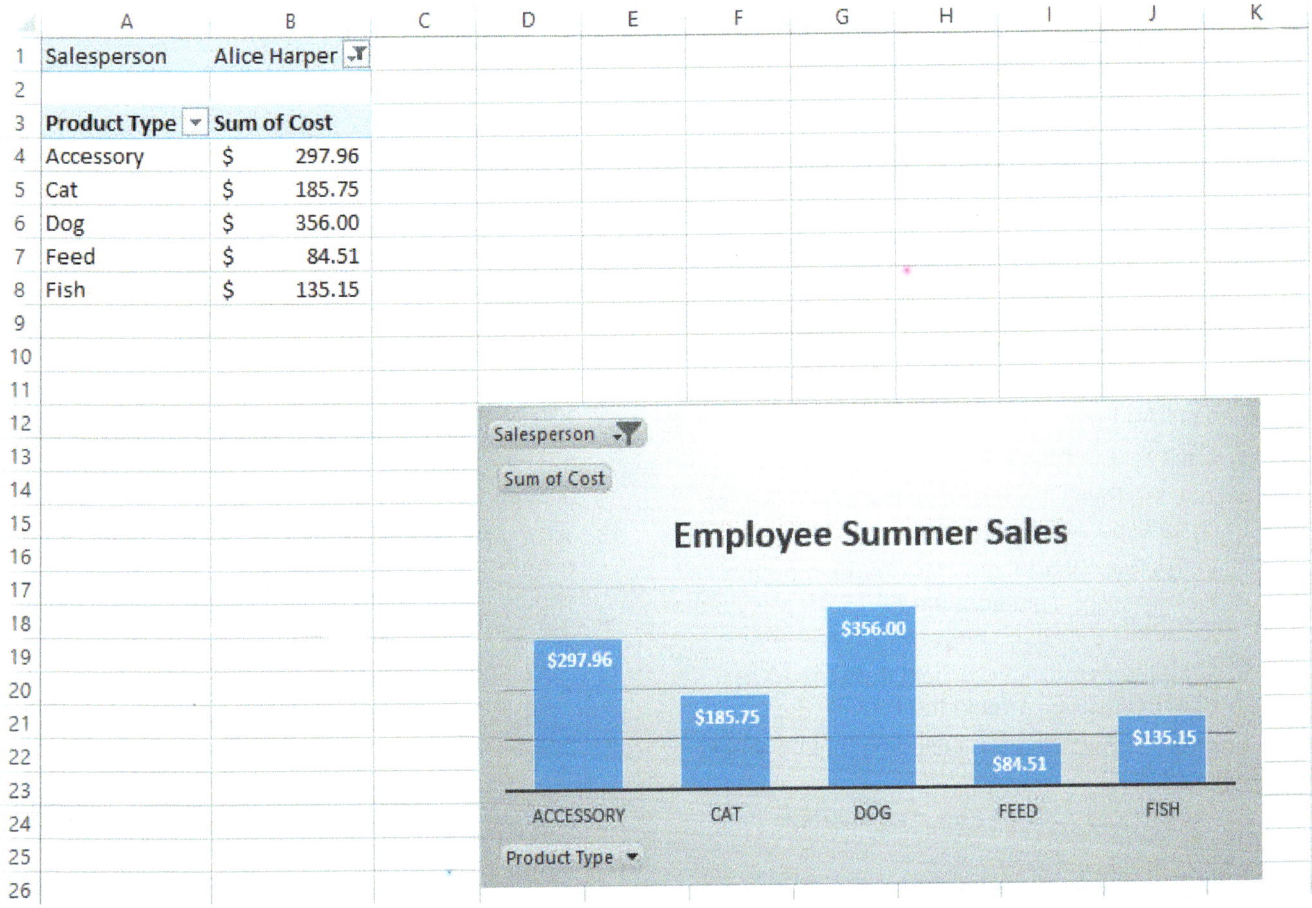

Excel 2016, Windows 10, Microsoft Corporation

Lesson 75—Apply

As the owner of Pete's Pets, a local pet store, you plan to give one of your two employees a raise. Your store has just finished its summer sale, and you want to know which of your salespeople had the best sales for each of your products and overall. You created a PivotChart to show one of your employee's sales data, and you now want to modify the chart so that it shows the product sales for each salesperson. In this project, you will modify a PivotChart and filter the data so that you can easily compare your employee's summer sales. You will also format the charts.

DIRECTIONS

1. Start Excel, if necessary, and open **E75Apply** from the data files for this lesson.
2. Save the file as **E75Apply_xx** in the location where your teacher instructs you to store the files for this lesson.
3. Modify the report filter to show the data for both salespeople.
   a. On the **Employee Sales** worksheet, click the PivotChart to select it.
   b. On the PivotChart, click the **Salesperson** report filter drop-down arrow.
   c. Click **Select All** > **OK**.
4. Modify the PivotChart to show the total sales for each salesperson filtered by product type.
   a. In the PivotChart Fields task pane, drag the **Salesperson** field from the FILTERS area to the **LEGEND (SERIES)** area.
   b. Drag the **Product Type** field from the AXIS (CATEGORIES) area to the **FILTERS** area.
5. Format the PivotChart to include a legend and data labels.
   a. Click the **CHART ELEMENTS** shortcut button [+].
   b. In the CHART ELEMENTS shortcut menu, click the **Legend** check box to select it.
   c. In the CHART ELEMENTS shortcut menu, click the **Data Labels** check box to select it.
6. Format the PivotChart with the Style 6 chart style.
   a. On the **Employee Sales** worksheet, click the PivotChart to select it.
   b. Click the **PivotChart Tools Design** tab.
   c. In the Chart Styles group, click the PivotChart Styles **More** button [▾].
   d. Click **Style 6**.
7. Close the PivotTable Fields task pane.
8. Move and resize the chart so that it fits in the cell range B10:H24.
9. For all worksheets, add a header that has your name at the left, the date code in the center, and the page number code at the right, and change back to **Normal** view.
10. **With your teacher's permission,** print the **Employee Sales** worksheet. Your worksheet should look like the one shown in Figure 75-2 on the next page.
11. Save and close the file, and exit Excel.

Figure 75-2

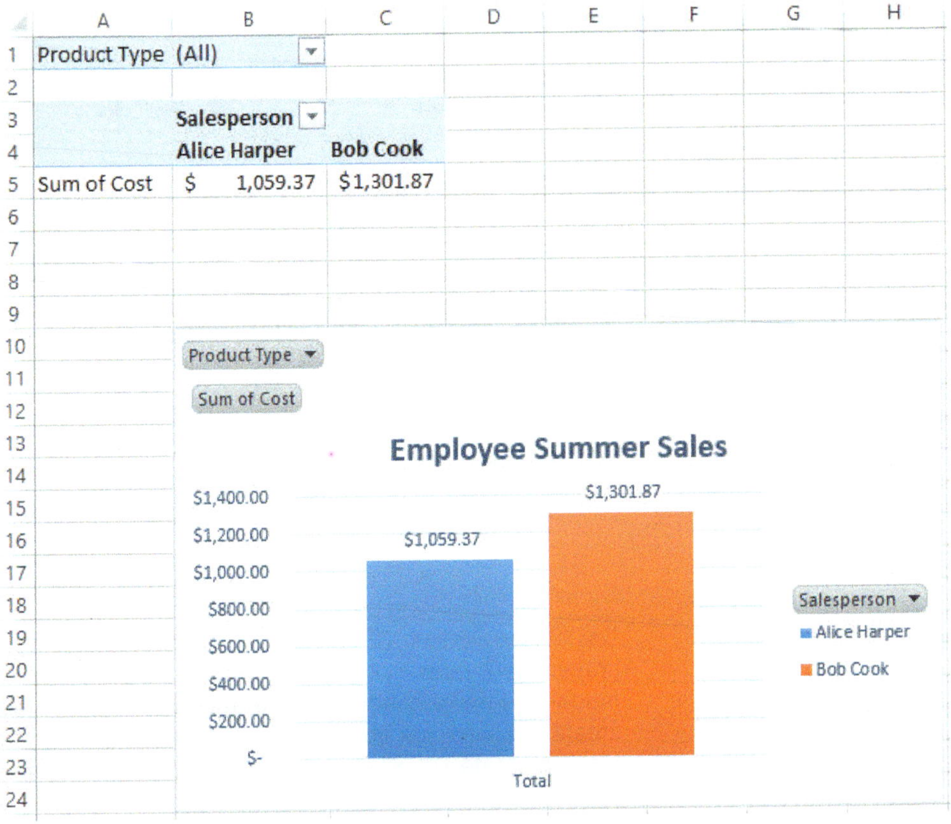
Product Type (All)
Salesperson
Alice Harper
Bob Cook
Sum of Cost
$ 1,059.37
$1,301.87
Product Type
Sum of Cost
Employee Summer Sales
$1,400.00
$1,200.00
$1,000.00
$800.00
$600.00
$400.00
$200.00
$-
$1,059.37
$1,301.87
Total
Salesperson
Alice Harper
Bob Cook

Lesson 76

Using Power Pivot and Power View

➤ What You Will Learn

Using Power Pivot to Manage Data
Creating a Power View Report
Working with Power View Fields
Formatting a Power View Report

WORDS TO KNOW

Data model
A collection of data that can include multiple tables from different sources.

Power Pivot
An Excel add-in that can create and modify the Excel data model.

Power View
A feature in Excel that presents data in an interactive report format.

Software Skills Excel provides powerful data analysis features to work with and present your data. For example, you can use Power Pivot to work directly with a data model and make changes to the data. You can add tables to the data model and create relationships among them. Once the data is prepared, you can use Power View to create an interactive report. With Power View, you can choose the layout and format of the data, present different sets of data, and filter data within the Power View sheet itself.

What You Can Do

Using Power Pivot to Manage Data

- **Power Pivot** is a feature in Excel that comes with Office 2016 Professional Plus and Office 365 Professional Plus.
- Power Pivot allows you to create complex data models and manipulate the data using PivotTables and PivotCharts.
- A **data model** is somewhat like an Access database; it can contain multiple data tables that are related to one another.
- You must first activate the Power Pivot Add-in before you can use Power Pivot.
- You must open a Power Pivot-enabled worksheet from within Excel.
- With Power Pivot, you can add tables to the Excel Data Model, as well as modify and delete them.

- To access the Excel Data Model, use the Manage button in the Data Model group on the Power Pivot tab.
- Tables are organized into individual tabbed pages in the Power Pivot window.
- If the tables are named, the table names appear as the names of the tabs.
- When you add table data to the Excel Data Model, you can use Power Pivot to create a relationship between two tables or among multiple tables.
- You can add a table only once within the Excel Data Model.
- Use Power Pivot to add data from a data range or table in an Excel workbook, or from data that is stored outside of Excel, such as data from a Microsoft Access database.
- You can interact with your data in the Power Pivot window like you can in an Excel worksheet. For example, you can sort the data in the Power Pivot window, and it will sort in the Excel worksheet.

Try It! Enabling the Power Pivot Add-In

1. Start Excel, create a blank workbook, and click File > Options.
2. In the Excel Options dialog box, click Advanced.
3. In the Data section, click to select Enable Data Analysis add-ins: Power Pivot, Power View, and Power Map.
4. Click OK. The Power Pivot tab appears on the ribbon.

Try It! Using Power Pivot to Manage Data

1. In Excel, click File > Open, and open **E76TryA** from the data files for this lesson.

   ✓ *You must first enable the Power Pivot add-in in the Excel Options, then you can open a Power Pivot worksheet from within Excel. Do not use File Explorer to open a Power Pivot worksheet.*

2. Save the file as **E76TryA_xx** in the location where your teacher instructs you to store the files for this lesson.
3. On the Men's Inventory worksheet, click in the PivotTable in the cell range A25:C30.
4. Click Power Pivot > Manage to display the Power Pivot for Excel window. Notice that the Men table is already in the Excel Data Model.
5. In the table, in the Category column, click the Category drop-down arrow > Sort A to Z. The data is sorted in the Power Pivot window and the Excel worksheet.
6. Close the Power Pivot for Excel window.
7. Save the changes to the file, and leave it open to use in the next Try It.

Try It! Adding Data to the Excel Data Model

1. In the **E76TryA_xx** file, click the Women's Inventory worksheet tab, and click in the table in the cell range A8:L14.
2. On the Power Pivot tab, click Add to Data Model. The Women data table is added to the Excel Data Model.

   ✓ *If you get an error at step 2, close and reopen the file, making sure you do so from within Excel, not from File Explorer. After you reopen the file, the worksheet may already be added to the data model.*
3. Close the Power Pivot for Excel window.
4. In the Excel worksheet, click the Teen's Inventory worksheet tab, and click cell A9.
5. Click Insert > PivotTable.
6. In the Create PivotTable dialog box, under Choose where you want the PivotTable report to be placed, click Existing Worksheet.
7. In the Location box, type **A20**.
8. Click the Add this data to the Data Model check box > OK.
9. Click Power Pivot > Manage to display the Power Pivot for Excel window.
10. In the Power Pivot for Excel window, click the Range tab. Notice that the cell range data has been added to the Excel Data Model.
11. Close the Power Pivot for Excel window.
12. Save the changes to the file, and leave it open to use in the next Try It.

Cell range data in the Excel Data Model

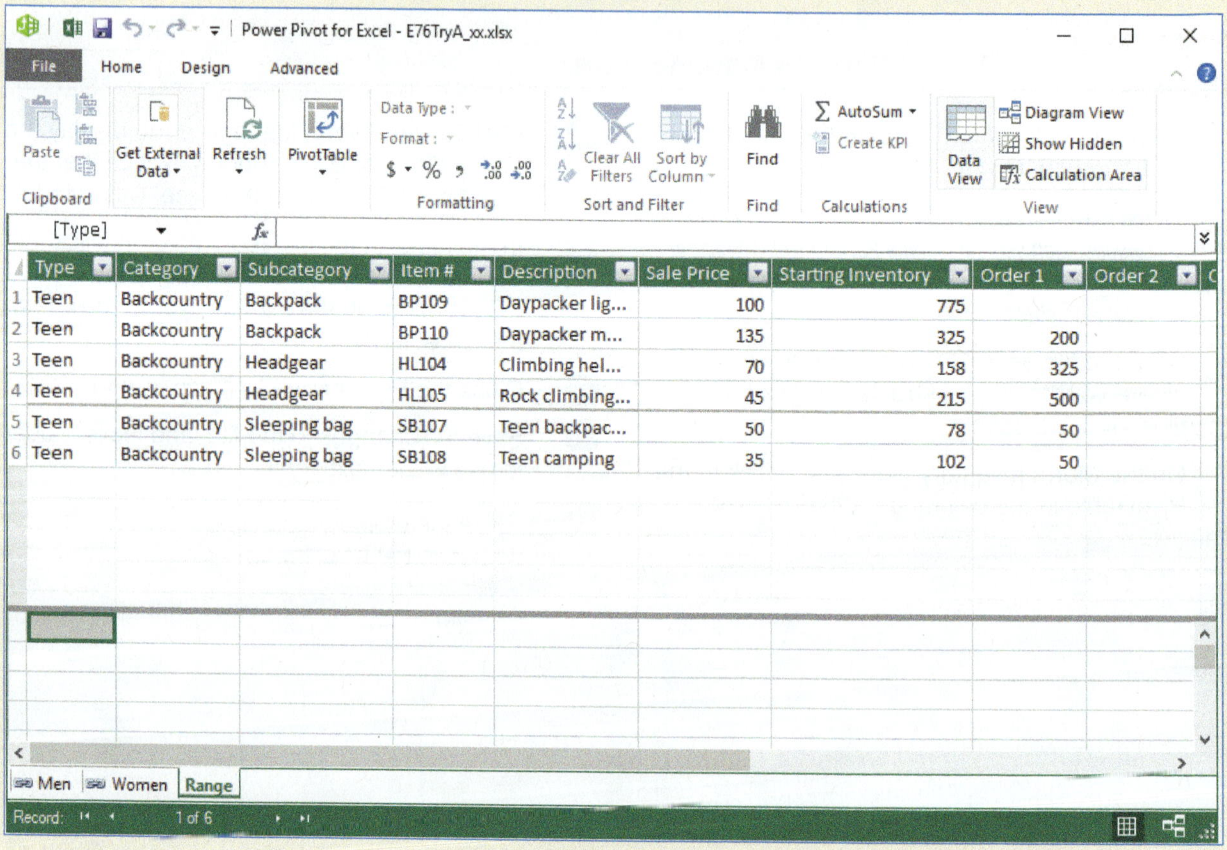

Creating a Power View Report

- **Power View** is a feature in Excel that comes with Office 2016 Professional Plus and Office 365 Professional Plus.
- You can use Power View sheets to present and further analyze your data in an interactive report.
- Power View doesn't appear on the ribbon by default in Excel 2016; you can add it to the ribbon or to the Quick Access Toolbar.
- Power View requires Silverlight, a free plug-in from Microsoft.
- If you don't have Silverlight installed, click Install Silverlight, follow the installation steps, and in Excel click Reload.

✓ *If the Power View Field List displays the message Power View needs data to work with, select the range of cells containing your data, and click Power View on the Insert tab.*

- You can choose to create a new Power View sheet, or add the data to an existing Power View sheet.
- The source data for your Power View sheet can be a data range or table in an Excel workbook, a PivotTable, or data that is stored outside of Excel, such as data from a Microsoft Access database.
- When you add a Power View sheet from data that is not already in the Excel Data Model, Excel automatically adds the data to the Excel Data Model.
- If you insert a Power View sheet by mistake, you can immediately delete the Power View sheet and Excel will automatically delete the data from the Excel Data Model.

✓ *If the data existed in the Excel Data Model before you added the Power View sheet, the data will remain in place.*

✓ *Use Power Pivot to view the current data in the Excel Data Model.*

Try It! Adding Power View to the Ribbon

1. In Excel, click File > Options > Customize Ribbon.
2. In the right pane click Insert and then click New Group.
3. Click Rename, type Power View, and click OK.
4. On the left, open the Choose commands from list and click Commands Not in the Ribbon.
5. Click Insert a Power View Report and click Add >>.
6. Click OK. The button appears on the Quick Access toolbar.

Try It! Creating a Power View Report

1. In the **E76TryA_xx** file, click the Teen's Inventory worksheet tab, and select the cell range A8:L14.
2. Click Insert > Power View.
3. If necessary, click Install Silverlight, follow the installation steps, and in Excel click Reload.
4. Click in the Click here to add a title box, and type **Teen Inventory**.
5. Save the changes to the file, and leave it open to use in the next Try It.

A Power View sheet

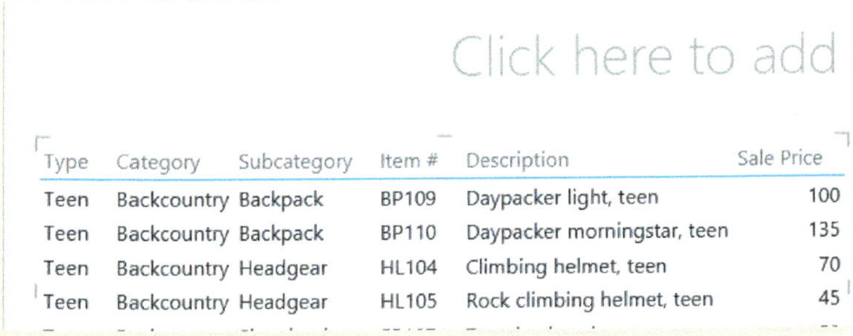

Type	Category	Subcategory	Item #	Description	Sale Price
Teen	Backcountry	Backpack	BP109	Daypacker light, teen	100
Teen	Backcountry	Backpack	BP110	Daypacker morningstar, teen	135
Teen	Backcountry	Headgear	HL104	Climbing helmet, teen	70
Teen	Backcountry	Headgear	HL105	Rock climbing helmet, teen	45

Working with Power View Fields

- You can customize a Power View sheet with the commands on the Power View tab and its contextual tabs on the ribbon. For example, the Design tab will appear on the ribbon next to the Power View tab when you select a data item, and the Text tab will appear when you select the title box.
- The Power View tab has many of the commands found in other tabs on the ribbon. For example, the Power View tab has its own Copy, Paste, and Undo commands.
- You can add objects, such as a table or chart, to a Power View sheet.
- You can add and modify the fields of the object in the Power View Fields task pane.
- To display the Power View Fields task pane, use the Field List button in the View group on the Power View tab.
- Drag fields into the two areas in the Areas Section to rearrange the fields.
  - TILE BY: This area acts as a report filter above the Power View chart or table. Fields in this area can drill down into the data to show only the items relating to a particular category.
  - FIELDS: This area contains the data fields. You can reorder the fields in this area.
- You can filter the data by adding fields to the Filters area on the right side of the Power View sheet.
- To remove a field from the Area Section, deselect the field's check box in the Field List. You can also click the field's down-arrow in the Area Section and click Remove Field, or you can drag it out of the Area Section.
- You can click the drop-down arrow of an area field to access more options. For example, you can choose to show the count of an item.

Try It! Adding and Removing Power View Fields

1. In the E76TryA_xx file, on the Power View1 worksheet tab, click in the table to select it.

   ✓ *The Power View tab may have another number than 1.*

2. In the Power View Fields task pane, click the Category, Item#, Sale Price, and Type check boxes to deselect them.
3. Click the Ending Inventory and Starting Inventory check boxes to select them.
4. In the FIELDS area, click and hold the Starting Inventory field, and drag it above the Ending Inventory field.
5. Save the changes to the file, and leave it open to use in the next Try It.

The Power View Fields task pane

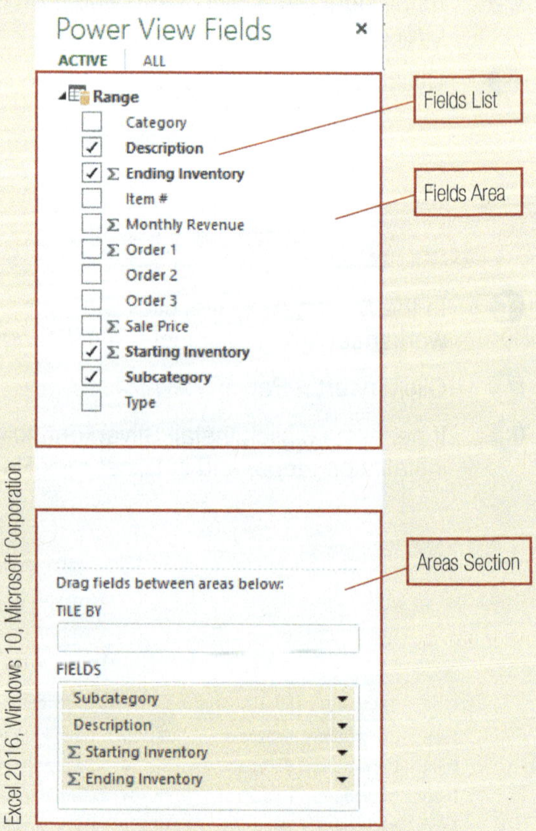

Formatting a Power View Report

- You can use the Power View commands to visualize and present your data in a variety of ways.
- You can change the visualization of a Power View object without having to re-create the object. For example, you can choose to visualize the data as a table, a chart, or a map.
- Use the commands in the Switch Visualization group of the Design tab.
- You can format a Power View sheet with a theme, background, and font set.
- The options in the Themes group on the Power View tab apply to the whole Power View sheet.
- You can enhance your Power View sheet with a background image.
- You can adjust the position and transparency of a background image to make it look like a watermark.

Try It! Formatting a Power View Report

1. In the E76TryA_xx file, on the Power View worksheet, click the first Backpack data element.
2. Click the Design tab.
3. In the Switch Visualization group, click Table > Matrix. The table changes to a matrix with totals.

   ✓ *Resize the table so that all data can be seen, if necessary.*
4. Click the Power View tab.
5. In the Background Image group, click Set Image > Set Image.
6. Browse to the data files for this lesson, click the E76TryB file, and click Open.
7. In the Background Image group, click Image Position > Stretch.
8. Close the Filters area.
9. Close the Power View Fields task pane.
10. Save and close the file, and exit Excel.

Lesson 76—Practice

You work in the sales office of Sydney Crenshaw Realty, a national chain of real estate brokers. You have an Excel spreadsheet of sales data for your local real estate office. You want to create a Power View report to show the commissions of the realtors to analyze which realtors are earning the most commissions.

DIRECTIONS

1. Start Excel, if necessary, and open **E76Practice** from the data files for this lesson.
2. Save the file as **E76Practice_xx** in the location where your teacher instructs you to store the files for this lesson.
3. If the Power Pivot tab does not appear on the ribbon, do the following to add it:
   a. Click **File** > **Options** > **Advanced**.
   b. In the **Data** section, mark the **Enable Data Analysis** add-ins check box.
   c. Click **OK**.
4. Add the data to the Excel Data Model.
   a. On the **Year-to-Date Sales** worksheet, select the cell range **A4:F26**.
   b. Click **Power Pivot** > **Add to Data Model**.
   c. In the Create Table dialog box, click the **My table has headers** check box, and click **OK**.
   d. Close the Power Pivot for Excel window.
5. Create a Power View report with a Stacked Column chart of the commission earned by each realtor.
   a. With the cell range **A4:F26** selected, click **Insert** > **Power View**.

      ✓ *If necessary, add Power View to the Insert tab as you learned earlier in this lesson.*
   b. Click in the *Click to add title* placeholder box, and type **Sydney Crenshaw Realty Local Office**.
   c. Click a data element in the table to select the table.
   d. In the Power View Fields task pane, click the **Date Sold**, **MLS Number**, **Percentage**, and **Sales Price** check boxes to deselect them.
   e. Click **Design** > **Column Chart** > **Stacked Column**.
   f. Resize the Power View object by dragging the lower-right corner down until it fills the sheet.
   g. Click **Layout** > **Data Labels** > **Show**.
6. Change the name of the Power View sheet tab to **Commissions**.
7. Close the Filters area.
8. Close the Power View Fields task pane.
9. **With your teacher's permission,** print the **Commissions** sheet, and write your name on it. Your worksheet should look like the one shown in Figure 76-1.
10. Save and close the file, and exit Excel.

Figure 76-1

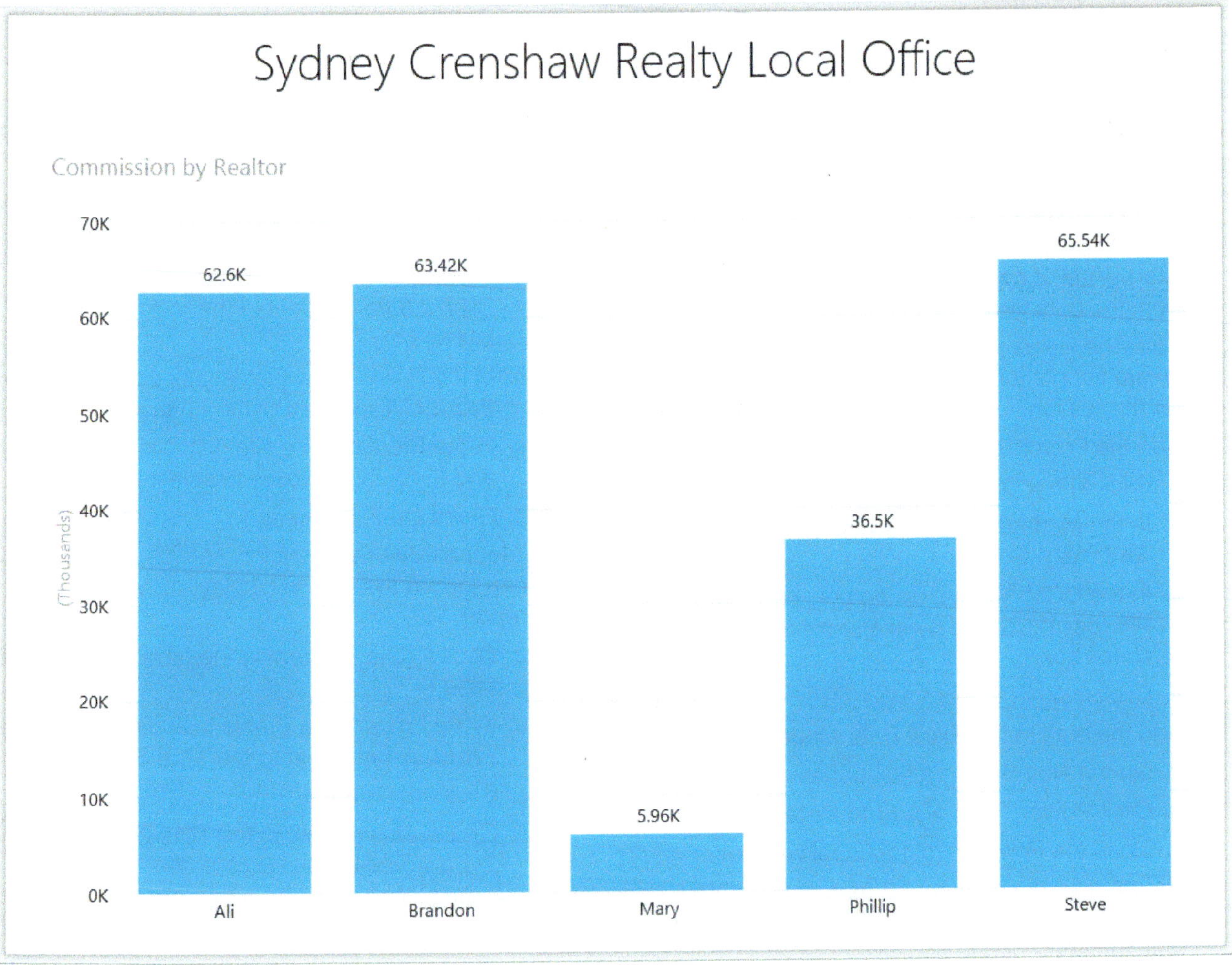

Excel 2016, Windows 10, Microsoft Corporation

Lesson 76—Apply

You are the owner of Pete's Pets, a local pet store, and your store has completed its sales for the month of November. You want to know what type of animal was sold in each of the cats, dogs, and fish categories, and which salesperson sold them. You would like to create and format a Power View report to show at the next employee meeting.

DIRECTIONS

1. Start Excel, if necessary, and open **E76ApplyA** from the data files for this lesson.
2. Save the file as **E76ApplyA_xx** in the location where your teacher instructs you to store the files for this lesson.
3. Add the Power Pivot tab to the ribbon, if necessary.
   a. Click **File** > **Options** > **Add-Ins**.
   b. In the Manage drop-down box, select **COM Add-ins** > **Go**.
   c. In the COM Add-Ins dialog box, click the **Microsoft Office Power Pivot for Excel 2013** check box.
   d. Click **OK**.
4. Add the data to the Excel Data Model.
   a. On the **Nov Sales** worksheet, click in the table.
   b. Click **Power Pivot** > **Add to Data Model**.
   c. Close the Power Pivot for Excel window.
5. Create a Power View report named **November Pet Sales** with a table of the product descriptions, salesperson's name, and cost.
   a. On the **Nov Sales** worksheet, click in the table.
   b. Click **Insert** > **Power View**.

   ✓ *If necessary, install Silverlight, and in Excel click Reload. If the Power View Field List displays the message Power View needs data to work with, select the range of cells containing your data, and click Power View on the Insert tab.*

   c. Click in the title box, and type **November Pet Sales**.
   d. Click a data element in the table to select the table.
   e. In the Power View Fields task pane, click the **Item #**, **Product Type**, and **Sales Incentive** check boxes to deselect them.
   f. Resize the Power View object by dragging the lower-right corner down until it fills the sheet.
6. Filter the Power View report on cats, dogs, and fish.
   a. Click a data element in the table to select the table.
   b. In the Power View Fields task pane, drag the **Product Type** field to the **Filters** area.
   c. In the Product Type filter list, click the **Cat**, **Dog**, and **Fish** check boxes to select them.
   d. Close the Filter area.
7. Tile the Power View report on cats, dogs, and fish, and format the tiles to display at the bottom of the report.
   a. Click a data element in the table to select the table.
   b. In the Power View Fields task pane, drag the **Product Type** field to the **TILE BY** area.
   c. Click the **Dog** tile.
   d. On the Design tab, in the Tiles group, click **Tile Type** > **Tile Flow**.
8. Apply the **Currency** format to the cost data.
   a. Click a cost data element in the table.
   b. On the Design tab, in the Number group, click **Number** drop-down arrow > **Currency**.
9. Add a background image to the Power View report.
   a. Click the **Power View** tab.
   b. In the Background Image group, click **Set Image** > **Set Image**.
   c. Browse to the data files for this lesson, click the **E76ApplyB** file, and click **Open**.
10. Close the Power View Fields task pane.
11. **With your teacher's permission,** print the **Power View1** sheet, and write your name on it.
12. Save and close the file, and exit Excel.

Lesson 77

Working with the Excel Data Model

➤ What You Will Learn

Creating Relationships Between Tables
Creating a PivotTable or PivotChart from the Data Model
Drilling Down in a PivotChart
Extracting Data with Cube Functions

Software Skills The Excel Data Model provides a powerful way of examining data from different sources as a single data source. You can create PivotTables and PivotCharts from its data, and drill down to look at the data that makes up the summary views. You can also use cube functions to refer to data from the Excel Data Model in worksheets.

What You Can Do

Creating Relationships Between Tables

- As you learned in Lesson 76, you to add multiple data sources to the Excel data model via Power Pivot.
- When the Excel data model contains multiple tables that each contain different kinds of information, it is advantageous to create **relationships** between them. For example, an Orders table has a relationship to the Customers table because each order belongs to a certain customer.
- When creating relationships between tables, you link fields in two different tables that contain the same data. The Orders table has a Customer field, for example, that contains the same numeric data as the Customer ID field in the Customers table.
- In the Customers table, the Customer ID field is the **primary key**, meaning it is the unique identifier for each record. In the Orders table, the Customer field is *not* unique for each record. A single customer might have multiple orders. It is the **foreign key** in the relationship.
- The relationship between a primary key and a foreign key is a **one-to-many relationship** because on the primary key side there is only one entry for that value, but on the foreign key side there may be many entries.

WORDS TO KNOW

Cube function
A function designed to work with data in a three-dimensional data model, such as CUBEMEMBER and CUBEVALUE.

Data cube
A multidimensional database containing related tables.

Data Model
A collection of data that can include multiple tables from different sources.

Drill down
To show the details behind a summary value on a PivotTable or PivotChart.

Foreign key
When two tables have a one-to-many relationship, the linked field in the table on the "many" side.

One-to-many relationship
A relationship between two tables where the field being linked is unique for each record in one table (the "one" side) but not in the other table (the "many" side).

Online Analytical Processing (OLAP) Multidimensional database analysis of business data, providing the capability for complex calculations, trend analysis, and sophisticated data modeling.

Primary key When two tables have a one-to-many relationship, the linked field in the table on the "one" side.

Relationship A connection between two tables that have a field in common.

- Relationships are common in a relational database program like Access, but in Excel they are available only via the Excel data model, accessible via Power Pivot.
- When you use Data > Get External Data to get data from an Access database, or some other formats, any existing relationships automatically transfer into the Excel data model.
- You can also manually create relationships.

Try It! Creating Relationships Between Tables

1. Open Excel and open the **E77Try** file from the data files for this lesson. Click Enable Content if needed.

   ✓ *It appears to be a blank workbook, but it has a data model in it.*

2. Save the file as **E77Try_xx** in the location where your teacher instructs you to store the files for this lesson.
3. Make sure that the Power Pivot tab appears on the ribbon.

   ✓ *If it does not, follow the steps in Try It! Enabling the Power Pivot Add-In in Lesson 76.*

4. Click Power Pivot > Manage.
5. Click Home > Diagram View.
6. Click the ID field in the Products table, and then drag-and-drop it onto the Product ID field in the Order Details table.
7. Click the Order ID field in the Orders table, and then drag-and-drop it onto the Order ID field in the Order Details table.
8. (Optional) Drag and resize the field lists for each table to make them appear more orderly, as in the figure below.
9. Double-click the line between the Order Details and Products tables. The Edit Relationship window opens.
10. Confirm that the Product ID field is highlighted for the Order Details table and the ID field is highlighted for the Products table.
11. Click Cancel (or if you made a correction in step 10, click OK).
12. Close the Power Pivot for Excel window.
13. Save the changes to the file and leave it open for the next Try It.

Create relationships between tables

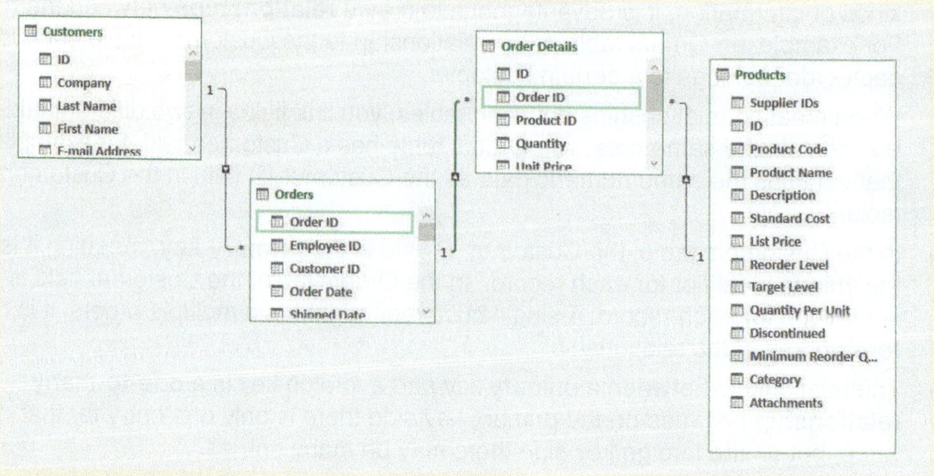

Excel 2016, Windows 10, Microsoft Corporation

Creating a PivotTable or PivotChart from the Data Model

- Normally when you create a PivotTable or PivotChart, you have only one table from which to pull data. However, when you create one from the data model in Power Pivot, you have access to all the fields in all the tables.
- If there are relationships between the tables, Excel automatically uses those relationships to pull related data from the tables.

Try It! Creating a PivotTable and PivotChart from the Data Model

1. In E77Try_xx, click Power Pivot > Manage.
2. Click Home > PivotTable > PivotTable.
3. Click Existing Worksheet.
4. In the Location box, type $A$3.
5. Click OK.
6. On the PivotTable Tools Analyze tab, click Field List if the field list does not already appear.

   ✓ *Each table appears as a collapsed list on the field list.*
7. Click the Products table twice to expand its field list.
8. Drag the Category field to the ROWS area.
9. Expand the Order Details field list.
10. Drag the Quantity field to the VALUES area.
11. Select A3:B17 and then click Insert > PivotChart.
12. In the Insert Chart dialog box, click Pie.
13. Click OK. A PivotChart is created.
14. Drag the PivotChart so its upper left corner aligns with cell D3.
15. Save the changes to the file leave it open for the next Try It.

Create a PivotChart from the data model

	A	B
3	Row Labels	Sum of Quantity
4	Baked Goods & Mixes	105
5	Beverages	1452
6	Candy	200
7	Canned Fruit & Vegetables	40
8	Canned Meat	120
9	Condiments	90
10	Dairy Products	90
11	Dried Fruit & Nuts	175
12	Grains	40
13	Jams, Preserves	140
14	Oil	25
15	Pasta	110
16	Sauces	65
17	Soups	290
18	Grand Total	2942

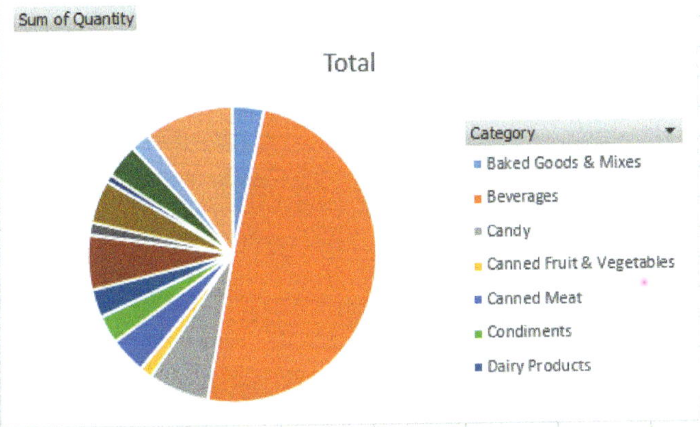

Excel 2016, Windows 10, Microsoft Corporation

Drilling Down in a PivotTable or PivotChart

- **Drilling down** means to see the details behind the summary values represented on a PivotTable or PivotChart. The Excel feature that allows you to drill down is called *Quick Explore*.
- Quick Explore, like Power Pivot, is not available in every edition of Excel—only the professional ones (such as Office 2016 Professional, and Office 365 E3, E4, and ProPlus).

✓ *Quick Explore doesn't work on every PivotTable or PivotChart; there has to be data behind it to drill down to. That's why the feature works best when working with data from multiple tables, such as in the Excel data model where multiple tables have relationships between them.*

- To drill down, hover the mouse pointer over a data point on a PivotChart or over some text or a value in a PivotTable, so a Quick Explore icon appears ; then click the icon. You can also right-click it and choose Quick Explorer.
- If you cannot drill down, a message appears that there are no recommendations.
- If you can drill down, a list of the available tables appears on the left. Click the desired table and then the desired field.
- Drilling down produces a new PivotTable or PivotChart. To return to the previous view, use Undo (CTRL + Z).

Try It! Drilling Down with Quick Explore

1. In E77Try_xx, click Power Pivot > Manage.
2. Click the PivotChart to select it, and then right-click the Beverages line in the chart legend and click Quick Explore.
3. Double-click Products to expand it, and then scroll down and click Product Name.
4. Click Drill to Product Name. A chart appears showing the product names within that category.
5. Press CTRL + Z to undo.
6. In the PivotTable, click cell B5, and then click the Quick Explore icon.
7. Double-click Order Details to expand it. Scroll down and click Quantity. Then click Drill to Quantity.
8. Press CTRL + Z to undo.
9. Double-click cell B5. A table opens showing the details represented by B5's summary value.
10. Click the Sheet1 worksheet tab to return to the original sheet.
11. Save changes to the file and leave it open for the next Try It.

Quick Explore shows background data contributing to the chart

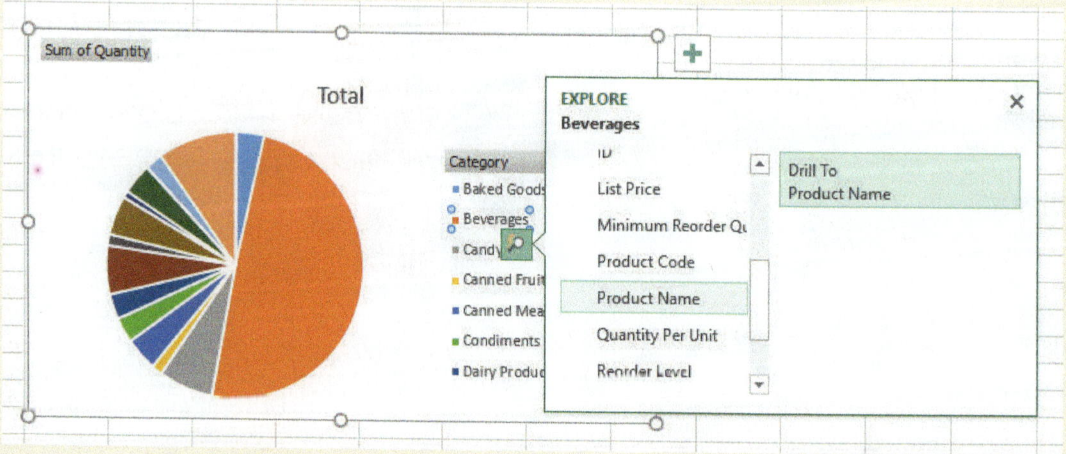

Excel 2016, Windows 10, Microsoft Corporation

Extracting Data with Cube Functions

- Large businesses store data in complex, multi-table databases. Rather than a simple two-dimensional table, these data sources are three-dimensional or more, which is why they are sometimes called **data cubes**. Querying these multi-dimensional databases is called **Online Analytical Processing (OLAP)**.
- The Excel data model is a kind of data cube, although not a large and complex one like the commercial sources you would usually be working with when doing business information analysis. You can use the Excel data model to practice working with cube data.
- One way to extract data from a cube is with a PivotTable or PivotChart. PivotTables and PivotCharts have some limitations, though, even when using Power Pivot.
- An alternative for data extraction is to use cube functions. They are just regular functions, so they can be placed in any cell. That makes them more flexible.
- There are seven cube functions in Excel: CUBEMEMBER, CUBESET, CUBESETCOUNT, CUBERANKEDMEMBER, CUBEVALUE, CUBEKPIMEMBER, and CUBEMEMBERPROPERTY
- Cube functions can be conceptually difficult to understand, but there's a shortcut; click PivotTable Tools Analyze > OLAP Tools > Convert to Formulas. This converts a PivotTable to the equivalent cube functions; you can analyze these to see how cube functions work.

Try It! Converting a PivotTable to Cube Functions

1. In E77Try_xx, on the Sheet1 tab, click any cell in the PivotTable.
2. Click PivotTable Tools Analyze > OLAP Tools > Convert to Formulas.
3. Click the chart.

   ✓ *Notice that the PivotChart tabs do not appear on the ribbon when the chart is selected. That's because this is no longer a PivotChart, because the table on which it is based is no longer a PivotTable.*

4. Click cell A4, and analyze the function in the formula bar:

   =CUBEMEMBER("ThisWorkbookDataModel", "[Products].[Category].&[Baked Goods & Mixes]")

   ✓ *The CUBEMEMBER function pulls data from the data model. In this case it is pulling a particular record from the Category field from the Products table.*

5. Click cell B4, and analyze the function on the formula bar:

   =CUBEVALUE("ThisWorkbookDataModel", $A4,B$3)

   ✓ *The CUBEVALUE function pulls an aggregated value (in other words, a calculated field's data) from the data model. In the preceding example, "ThisWorkbookDataModel" is the name of the cube. The second argument, $A4, refers to Baked Goods & Mixes, and the third argument, B$3, refers to Sum of Quantity.*

6. Click Power Pivot > Manage to open Power Pivot.
7. On the Products tab, sort the Category column in A to Z order. Notice that there are four products with that category.
8. Note the values in the ID column for the four products identified: 19, 21, 85, and 86. This is the data that the second argument in the CUBEVALUE function is referencing.
9. Click the Order Details tab, and on the rows where the product is 19, 21, 85, or 86, look at the number in the Quantity column. This is the data that the third argument in the CUBEVALUE function is referencing.
10. Close the Power Pivot window.
11. Save the changes to the file, and exit Excel.

Lesson 77—Practice

Holy Habanero's sales department is analyzing sales trends to see what products are selling well online and which ones may need more marketing help. You'll work with a data model and some PivotTables to find the information they need.

DIRECTIONS

1. Start Excel, if necessary, and open the **E77Practice** file from the data files for this lesson.
2. Save the workbook as **E77Practice_xx** in the location where your teacher instructs you to store the files for this lesson.
3. Add the table from the Unit Sales tab to the data model.
4. a. Select **A2:J28**.
   b. Click **PowerPivot** > **Add to Data Model**.
5. In the Power Pivot for Excel window, click **Home** > **PivotTable** > **PivotChart**.
6. Click **OK**.
7. Click **Table2** to expand its field list.
8. Drag the **Products** field into the AXIS area.
9. Drag the **Month** field into the LEGEND area.
10. Drag the **Online** field into the VALUES area.
11. Click **PivotChart Tools Design** > **Chart Styles More** > **Style 5.**
12. Drag the bottom-right corner of the chart frame to cell I21.
13. Click **Power Pivot** > **Manage**.
14. Click **Home** > **PivotTable** > **PivotChart**.
15. Click **OK**.
16. Drag the **Products** field into the AXIS area.
17. Drag the **Direct Mail** field into the VALUES area.
18. Drag the **Online** field into the VALUES area.
19. Drill down on the Magma Core product to see its performance by month for Direct Mail compared to Online sales.
    a. Right-click **Magma Core** on the chart.
    b. Click **Quick Explore**.
    c. Click **Month** > **Drill to Month**.
20. On the Sheet1 and Sheet2 worksheets, add a header that has your name at the left, the date code in the center, and the page number code at the right, and change back to Normal view.
21. **With your teacher's permission**, print the charts on Sheet1 and Sheet2. They should look like Figure 77-1 and Figure 77-2 on the next page.
22. Save the changes to the workbook, and exit Excel.

Figure 77-1

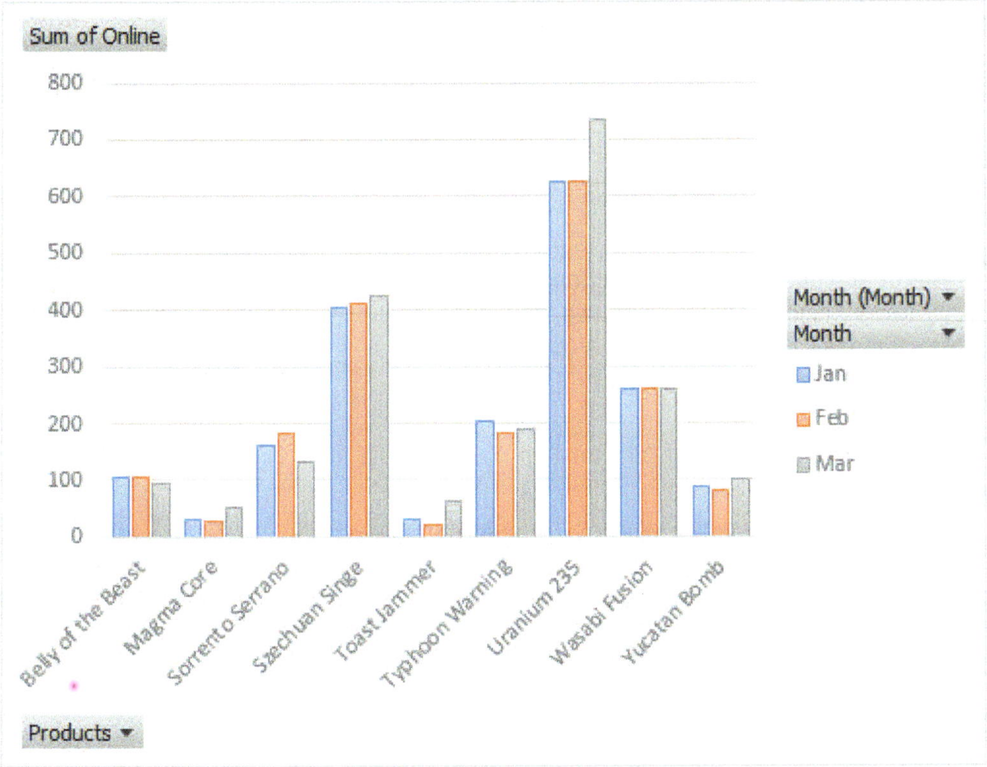

Excel 2016, Windows 10, Microsoft Corporation

Figure 77-2

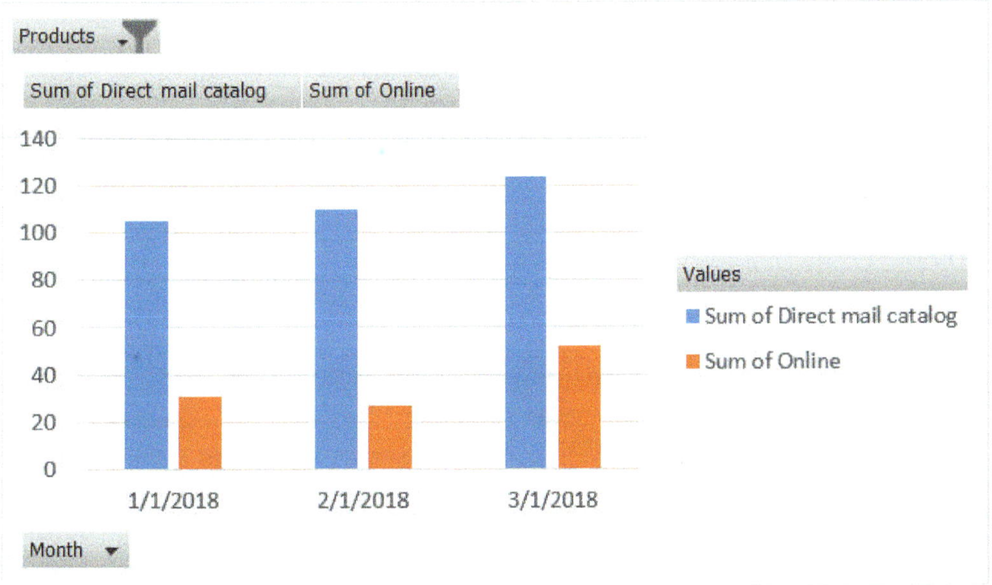

Excel 2016, Windows 10, Microsoft Corporation

Lesson 77—Apply

Northwind Traders managers would like some information about the suppliers from which the company purchases wholesale goods for resale. You will import some additional tables and create relationships between tables, and then create and drill down with a PivotChart created from the data model to get information about a specific supplier.

DIRECTIONS

1. Start Excel, if necessary, and open the **E77ApplyA** file from the data files for this lesson.
2. Save the workbook as **E77ApplyA_xx** in the location where your teacher instructs you to store the files for this lesson.
3. Import the table from the Data tab into the data model.
   a. Click anywhere in the table on the **Data** tab.
   b. Click **Power Pivot** > **Add to Data Model**.
   c. Close the Power Pivot window.
4. Import the Products and Suppliers tables from **E77ApplyB** into the data model and start a new PivotTable.
   a. Click a cell outside the table on the Data worksheet.
   b. Click **Data** > **Get External Data** > **From Access**.
   c. Navigate to the location containing the data files for this lesson, select **E77ApplyB**, and click Open.
   d. Click to mark **Enable selection of multiple tables**.
   e. Click the **Products** table's check box to select it.
   f. Click the **Suppliers** table's check box to select it.
   g. Click **OK**.
   h. Click **Table**.
   i. Click **New worksheet**.
   j. Click **OK**.

   ✓ *Two new sheets are created, one for each imported table. When you import into tables, Excel does not create relationships automatically, unlike when you import into PivotTables or PivotCharts.*
5. Double-click the **Sheet1** tab, type **Products**, and press ENTER .
6. Click the **Sheet2** tab. Then double-click the **Sheet2** tab, type **Suppliers**, and press ENTER .
7. Create relationships between the tables in the data model.
   a. Click **Power Pivot** > **Manage**.
   b. Click **Home** > **Diagram View**.
   c. Drag the **ID** field from the Products table and drop it onto the **ProductID** field in the Order_Items_With_Names table.
   d. Drag the **ID** field from the Suppliers table and drop it onto the **Supplier IDs** field in the Products table.
8. Create a new PivotTable using data from the three tables, starting from the data model.
   a. In the Power Pivot window, click **Home** > **PivotTable**.
   b. Click **OK**.
   c. I the field list doesn't appear, click **PivotTable Tools Analyze** > **Field List**.
   d. From the Order_Items_With_Names table, drag the **Quantity** field and the **Revenue** field to the VALUES area.
   e. From the Products table, drag the **Category** field to the ROWS area.
   f. From the Suppliers table, drag the **Company** field to the ROWS area.
   g. In the VALUES area, drag the **Sum of Quantity** field above the Sum of Revenue field if needed.
   h. In the ROWS area, drag the **Company field** above the Category field if needed.
   i. Click cell B3, type **Suppliers**, and press ENTER .
   j. Select cell B3 and then click **PivotTable Tools Analyze** > **Collapse Field**.
9. Create a new PivotChart from the PivotTable.
   a. Select **B3:D12** and then click **PivotTable Tools Analyze** > **PivotChart**.
   b. In the Insert Chart dialog box, click **Combo**.

c. Open the **Chart Type** drop-down list for the Sum of Revenue field and click **Stacked Line with Markers**.

d. For the Sum of Revenue field, click to mark the **Secondary Axis** check box.

e. Click **OK**.

f. Drag the PivotChart so its upper left corner aligns with cell B16.

10. Drill down in the PivotChart to find out what products are provided by Supplier A.

a. On the PivotChart, right-click **Supplier A** and click **Quick Explore**.

b. Double-click **Products**.

c. Click **Product Name** > **Drill to Product Name**. The PivotChart changes to show the individual products for that supplier only.

11. On the Sheet3 worksheet, add a header that has your name at the left, the date code in the center, and the page number code at the right, and change back to Normal view.

12. Click **Page Layout** > **Orientation** > **Landscape**.

13. **With your teacher's permission**, print one copy of Sheet3. It should look like Figure 77-3.

14. Save the changes to the workbook, and exit Excel.

Figure 77-3

Company	Supplier A	
Suppliers	**Sum of Quantity**	**Sum of Revenue**
Northwind Traders Chocolate Biscuits Mix	723	6159.5
Northwind Traders Gnocchi	1263	45121.2
Northwind Traders Long Grain Rice	500	3383.8
Northwind Traders Ravioli	434	7807.8
Northwind Traders Scones	1016	9636
Grand Total	**3936**	**72108.3**

End-of-Chapter Activities

➤ Excel Chapter 9—Critical Thinking

Chamber of Commerce Presentation

At the Center City Chamber of Commerce, you have been asked to gather, analyze, and present some information at a business meeting with guests who may be interested in relocating their businesses to Center City. You will present information to them about local real estate, schools, and existing businesses that will help them make up their minds. You will convey meaningful information in a concise and attractive format, using the skills you learned in this chapter.

DIRECTIONS

1. Start Excel, if necessary, and open **ECT09A** from the data files for this chapter. Save the workbook as **ECT09A_xx** in the location where your teacher instructs you to store the files for this chapter.
2. Create a new worksheet named **Real Estate Summary**. Place it immediately after the **Real Estate** worksheet.
3. On the **Real Estate Summary** worksheet, create a PivotTable of the areas and their communities, and provide an average price of the homes for sale in each community, as in Illustration 9A. Use any method you like. Format the prices with the **Accounting** format and no decimal places.
4. On the **Real Estate Summary** worksheet, create a Clustered Column PivotChart showing the average list price of the homes for sale in each community. Format the PivotChart with **Style 6**. Resize the chart so that all data is legible.
5. On the **Schools** worksheet, show the high schools with an average SAT score of 1600 in a separate table below the original table.

   ✓ *One way is to copy the table and use a slicer to filter the highest score.*
6. Save the **ECT09A_xx** file, and leave it open for later use.
7. Open the **ECT09B** file from the data files for this project, and save it as **ECT09B_xx** in the location where your teacher instructs you to store the files for this project.

Illustration 9A

	A		B
1	Row Labels	Average of List Price	
2	⊟ **Brent**	**$**	**292,486**
3	Chewton	$	292,486
4	⊟ **Franklin**	**$**	**256,795**
5	Brent	$	241,610
6	Coverdale	$	262,062
7	Edinburg	$	271,728
8	Fayette	$	264,950
9	Nashua	$	234,800
10	Rock Point	$	308,300
11	Rockville	$	218,467
12	⊟ **Hernando**	**$**	**282,138**
13	Pulaski	$	278,480
14	Rockville	$	283,968
15	⊟ **Jefferson**	**$**	**314,537**
16	Hillsville	$	331,667
17	Parkstown	$	319,637
18	Sunnyside	$	287,860
19	⊟ **Lebanon**	**$**	**349,568**
20	Bellevue	$	352,500
21	Coverts	$	389,457
22	Ellicott City	$	327,284
23	Ellport	$	328,050
24	⊟ **Orange**	**$**	**371,205**
25	Duckrun	$	282,795
26	Mayville	$	474,683
27	Wampum	$	311,600
28	⊟ **Pasco**	**$**	**329,562**
29	Marysville	$	336,263
30	Oakwood	$	316,160
31	⊟ **Sumter**	**$**	**268,150**
32	Belmar Park	$	268,150
33	**Grand Total**	**$**	**308,615**

8. Complete the **Sales Summary** worksheet by consolidating the data from each of the month worksheets. Create a link to the source data. Move the label from cell J6 into cell **J7**.
9. On the **Sales Summary** worksheet, convert the cell range **A7:I17** to a table, and then add a **Totals** row to it. Use the drop-down arrow in the Totals row label to show averages for each area, and change the row's label to **Average**.

   ✓ *Hint: Every cell has to have a numeric value for the function to calculate properly.*
10. On the **Sales Summary** worksheet, format the cell range **B8:J18** with the **Accounting** format. Make the font usage consistent by using Format Painter to copy the font settings from cell **B8** to the cell range **H8:J17**. Adjust the column widths as needed.
11. Copy the Sales Summary worksheet from the **ECT09B_xx** workbook to the **ECT09A_xx** workbook, after the **Schools** worksheet.
12. Save and close **ECT09B_xx**.
13. In **ECT09A_xx**, Rename the **Sales Summary** tab **Local Businesses**.
14. Save and close **ECT09A_xx**.
15. Start a new blank workbook, and save it as **ECT09C_xx** in the location where your teacher instructs you to store the files for this chapter.
16. In the new workbook, create a query that pulls data from the Real Estate worksheet in **ECT09A_xx**.
17. Open the query in the Query Editor and delete the first row.
18. Click **Home** > **Use First Row As Headers**.
19. Remove the Pool, Spa, and HOA Fees columns from the query.
20. Close the Query Editor.
21. For all worksheets, add a header that has your name at the left, the date code in the center, and the page number code at the right, and change back to **Normal** view.
22. **With your teacher's permission,** print the **ECT09A_xx** workbook (all sheets).
23. Save and close the file, and exit Excel.

➤ Excel Chapter 9—Portfolio Builder

Basketball Team Data

To promote attendance at professional team sports competitions in the state, the Indiana Visitors Bureau has asked you to collect data about The Indiana Fever, a WNBA team. You will collect statistics and present your findings in an attractively formatted Excel workbook.

DIRECTIONS

1. Start Excel, and open the **EPB09A** file from the data files for this lesson.
2. Save the workbook as **EPB09A_xx** in the location where your teacher instructs you to store the files for this lesson.
3. On the **Stats** worksheet, use the Flash Fill feature to combine the players' first and last names into a single column. Delete the columns containing the individual first and last names, so that column A contains each player's full name. Label this column **PLAYER**.
4. Convert the range **A1:P13** to a table by applying Table Style Medium 1.
5. Sort the table in A to Z order by player name.
6. Use Format Painter to copy the formatting from cell **A1** on the Stats tab to **A4:P4** on the **Summary** tab.
7. In cell A5, set up data validation that pulls names from the list of players on the Stats tab.
   a. Select A5 and then click **Data** > **Data Validation**.
   b. Open the Allow drop-down list and choose List.
   c. In the Source box, type **=Stats!$A$2:$A$13**.
   d. Click **OK**.

8. Open the drop-down list in cell A5 and click **Maggie Lucas**.
9. In cell B5, insert a VLOOKUP function that looks up the G value (column B on the Stats sheet) for the player shown in cell A5 on the Summary sheet.

   ✓ *Tip: Use B5 as the first argument in the VLOOKUP function, use the table on the Stats tab as the second argument, and use the corresponding column number as the third argument.*
10. Create VLOOKUP functions in C5:P5 for each of the corresponding values in the Stats table.

    ✓ *Tip: If you use an absolute reference to A5 in the function in B5, you can copy it into cells C5:P5 and then modify each copy to reflect the differing column number in the third argument.*
11. Open the drop-down list for cell **A5** and choose a different name. The stats also change.
12. Enable the Power Pivot add-in if needed.
13. Change the table name on the **Stats** tab to Data_2016.
14. Add the table to the data model.
15. Open **EPB09B** from the data files for this lesson.
16. Save it as **EPB09B_xx** in the location where your teacher instructs you to store the files for this lesson and then close it.
17. Switch back to **EPB09A** and add the data from the 2014 and 2015 tabs from **EPB09B** to the data model.

    ✓ *From Power Pivot, use the Home > From Other Sources command and choose Excel File. Make sure you use the first row as column headers.*
18. In Power Pivot, sort the 2014 and 2015 tables in A to Z order by the PLAYER field.
19. In Power Pivot, switch to the Diagram view and create relationships between the PLAYER fields in each table.
20. Create a new PivotTable from Power Pivot, and place it on a new worksheet.
21. From the Data_2016 table, drag the PLAYER field into the ROWS area.
22. From the Data_2016 table, drag the **FG%**, **3P%**, and **FT%** fields to the VALUES area.
23. For each of the fields in the VALUES area, change the calculation to **Average**.

    ✓ *To change the calculation, click the field in the VALUES are, click Value Field Settings, and click Average.*
24. Convert the PivotTable to use cube functions.

    ✓ *Use the PivotTable Tools Analyze > OLAP Tools > Convert to Formulas command.*
25. In cell A1, type **Key 2016 Stats**, and apply the Title cell style to it.
26. In cell B3, type **Player Name**, replacing the previous entry.
27. Delete the Grand Total row (row 16).
28. Apply the Heading 3 cell style to the range B3:E3.
29. Rename the sheet **2016 Key Stats**.
30. On the **Summary** and **Key 2016 Stats** worksheets, add a header that has your name at the left, the date code in the center, and the page number code at the right, and change back to Normal view.
31. **With your teacher's permission**, print Key 2016 Stats worksheet (see Illustration 9B on the next page), and print only the first page of the Summary worksheet in Landscape view (see Illustration 9C on the next page).
32. Save your work, and exit Excel.

Illustration 9B

Key 2016 Stats

Player Name	Average of FG%	Average of 3P%	Average of FT%
Brene Moseley	40	50	0
Briann January	0	0	0
Devereaux Peters	50	33.3	62.5
Erica Wheeler	42.1	40	83.3
Erlana Larkins	72.7	0	87.5
Lynetta Kizer	30.8	0	85.7
Maggie Lucas	52.4	20	100
Marissa Coleman	27.8	25	72.7
Natalie Achonwa	83.3	0	71.4
Shenise Johnson	46.7	42.9	80
Tamika Catchings	37.1	22.2	82.4
Tiffany Mitchell	50	33.3	85

Excel 2016, Windows 10, Microsoft Corporation

Illustration 9C

Statistics

PLAYER	G	GS	MPG	PPG	OREB	DREB	RPG	APG	SPG	BPG	FG%
Maggie Lucas	4	0	13.8	7.8	0.3	1.8	2	0.8	0.5	0	52.4

Excel 2016, Windows 10, Microsoft Corporation

Chapter 10

(Courtesy YanLev/Shutterstock)

Collaborating with Others and Preparing a Final Workbook for Distribution

Lesson 78
Tracking Changes

- Creating and Modifying a Shared Workbook
- Tracking Changes in a Shared Workbook
- Managing Comments in a Shared Workbook
- Merging Changes
- Removing Workbook Sharing

Lesson 79
Ensuring Data Integrity

- Turning Off AutoComplete
- Controlling Data Entry with Data Validation
- Circling Invalid Data
- Copying Validation Rules
- Removing Duplicate Data
- Controlling Recalculation

Lesson 80
Protecting Data

- Locking and Unlocking Cells in a Worksheet
- Protecting a Range
- Protecting a Worksheet
- Protecting a Workbook

Lesson 81
Securing a Workbook

- Using Document Inspector
- Encrypting a Workbook
- Identifying Workbooks Using Keywords

Lesson 82
Finalizing a Workbook

- Adding a Digital Signature
- Checking for Accessibility Issues
- Marking a Workbook As Final
- Managing Versions

Lesson 83
Sharing a Workbook

- Setting Precise Margins for Printing
- Uploading a Workbook to OneDrive

End-of-Chapter Activities

Lesson 78

Tracking Changes

➤ What You Will Learn

- Creating and Modifying a Shared Workbook
- Tracking Changes in a Shared Workbook
- Managing Comments in a Shared Workbook
- Merging Changes
- Removing Workbook Sharing

WORDS TO KNOW

Change history
A listing of all changes made in a workbook. You can view the change history in the workbook or on its own worksheet.

Comment
A note attached to a worksheet cell for reference.

Shared workbook
An Excel workbook that you are using collaboratively with other users. When you turn on track changes, the workbook becomes a shared workbook automatically.

Track Changes
A process that keeps track of all changes made to a workbook each time you save it.

Software Skills When you are working on a large worksheet or a major project, you may need to work with other members of your team to complete all the parts of the worksheet that need to be completed. Collaborating successfully in Excel means that you need to be able to create and edit your own sections, add comments to the worksheet, see what changes others are making, merge many changes into one worksheet, and turn off sharing when you no longer need it.

What You Can Do

Creating and Modifying a Shared Workbook

- Sharing a workbook enables you to allow other authors to make changes in the file.
- You can turn a regular workbook into a **shared workbook** by using the Share Workbook command in the Changes group on the Review tab.
- You can restrict the editing of the workbook by removing users from the Share Workbook dialog box.
- On the Advanced tab of the Share Workbook dialog box, you can set sharing options to specify how long changes are kept, when the changes in the file are updated, and how any conflicting changes will be resolved.
- You can tell Excel whether you want to update the file automatically as people work on it or update the file when it is saved.
- You can choose whether you want to see everyone's changes in the file or see only other users' changes.
- If your worksheet contains a table, you will be prompted to convert the table to a range before sharing the file.

- You can save a shared workbook to a network location or your OneDrive account so that others can work with the file.
- You can tell Excel whether you want to be prompted to decide about changes that are in conflict or whether you want the saved changes to be the ones that are preserved in the file.

Try It! Sharing a Workbook

1. Start Excel, and open **E78TryA** from the data files for this lesson.
2. Save the file as **E78TryA_xx** in the location where your teacher instructs you to store the files for this lesson.
3. Click Review > Share Workbook.
4. Click the Allow changes by more than one user at the same time check box.
5. Click OK.
6. If prompted, click OK to save the workbook.
7. Save the changes to the file, and leave it open to use in the next Try It.

Sharing a workbook

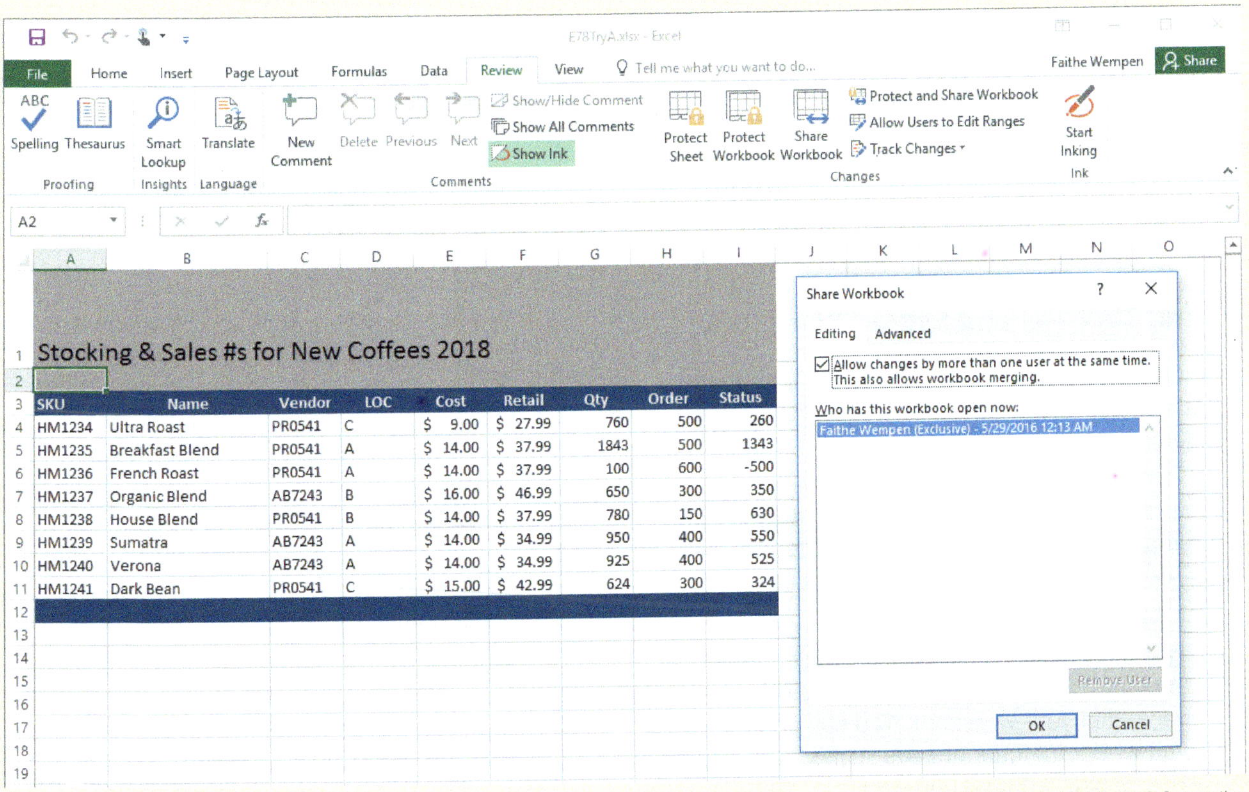

Excel 2016, Windows 10, Microsoft Corporation

Try It! Setting Sharing Options

1. In the **E78TryA_xx** file, click Review > Share Workbook.
2. In the Share Workbook dialog box, click the Advanced tab.
3. Review the Advanced share settings.
4. Under Update changes, click Automatically every.
5. Click OK.
6. Save the changes to the file, and leave it open to use in the next Try It.

Setting sharing options

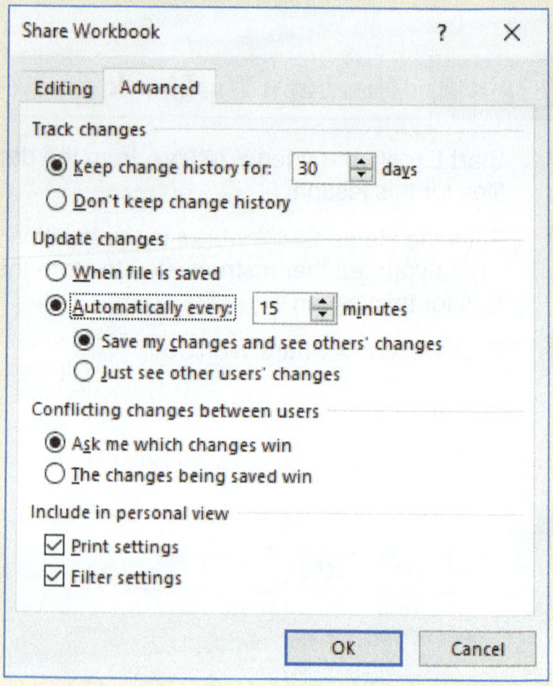

Excel 2016, Windows 10, Microsoft Corporation

Tracking Changes in a Shared Workbook

- Excel makes it easy for you to track the changes that are made in a shared workbook so that you can choose whether to keep, reject, or edit the changes.
- To turn on tracking, use the **Track Changes** command in the Changes group on the Review tab.
- Use the Highlight Changes command to set the tracking options.
  - The Highlight Changes dialog box enables you to make choices about the way changes are tracked in your workbook. You can choose when and where the changes are highlighted. You can also decide whether you want the changes to be highlighted on the sheet or listed on a new worksheet.
  - You can specify when changes are saved in the Highlight Changes dialog box: Since I last saved, All, Not yet reviewed, or Since date.
  - You can choose whose changes you want to review: Everyone, Everyone but Me, or you (as indicated by your username or initials).
  - You can specify where to track changes on a worksheet, for example, within a specific cell or a cell range.
  - When you select the Highlight changes on screen check box, any changes on the worksheet appear in bordered cells with a flag in the upper-left corner.
  - When you click List changes on a new sheet and All is selected in the When setting, a History worksheet is added to the workbook listing all changes made by date, time, user, and location.

    ✓ *The History worksheet is only available until you save the workbook.*
- When you are ready to accept or reject changes, you can choose to do so based on when changes were made, who made the changes, and where the changes are located.

Try It! Turning on Tracking

1. In the **E78TryA_xx** file, click Review > Track Changes.
2. Click Highlight Changes.
3. Click the Track changes while editing check box, if not already marked.
4. Click the When check box if it is not already marked.
5. Click the When drop-down arrow and click All.
6. Click the Who check box if it is not already marked, and make sure it is set to Everyone.
7. Click the Highlight changes on screen check box, if not already marked.
8. Click OK, and if a message box appears, click OK to confirm that no changes were found.
9. Click cell G4, and change the value to **820**. Notice the flag in the upper-left corner of the cell.
10. Click cell H4, and change the value to **550**.
11. Save the changes to the file, and leave it open to use in the next Try It.

Try It! Displaying Change History

1. In the **E78TryA_xx** file, click cell G9, and change the value to **925**.
2. Click cell H9, and change the value to **450**.
3. Save the workbook.
4. On the Review tab, click Track Changes > Highlight Changes.
5. Click List changes on a new sheet.
6. Click OK.
7. Review the History worksheet.
8. Save the changes to the file, and leave it open to use in the next Try It.

The change history

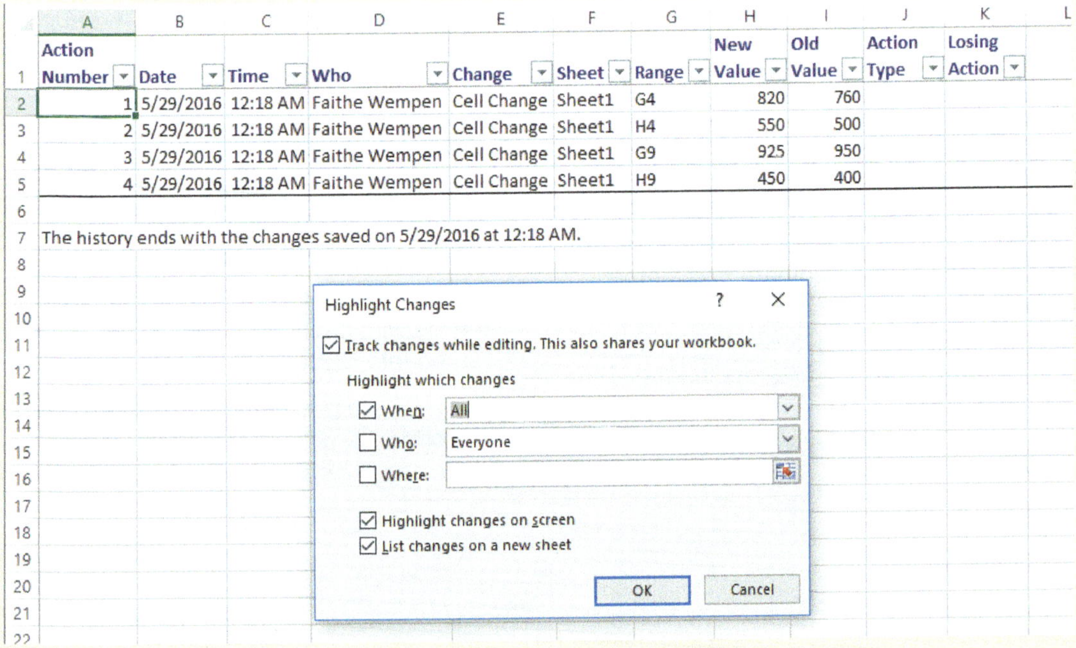

Action Number	Date	Time	Who	Change	Sheet	Range	New Value	Old Value	Action Type	Losing Action
1	5/29/2016	12:18 AM	Faithe Wempen	Cell Change	Sheet1	G4	820	760		
2	5/29/2016	12:18 AM	Faithe Wempen	Cell Change	Sheet1	H4	550	500		
3	5/29/2016	12:18 AM	Faithe Wempen	Cell Change	Sheet1	G9	925	950		
4	5/29/2016	12:18 AM	Faithe Wempen	Cell Change	Sheet1	H9	450	400		

The history ends with the changes saved on 5/29/2016 at 12:18 AM.

Excel 2016, Windows 10, Microsoft Corporation

Managing Comments in a Shared Workbook

- Using **comments** in a shared workbook is the same as doing so in an unshared workbook.
- Use the commands in the Comments group on the Review tab of the ribbon.
- A red triangle appears in the upper-right corner of any cell with an attached comment.
- You can edit the contents of a comment that has been previously inserted.
- Use the Previous and Next commands to navigate among the comments.
- You can choose to show or hide a single comment, or you can show all comments.
- You can delete a single comment, or you can delete all comments in a worksheet.

Try It! Creating and Editing Comments

1. In the **E78TryA_xx** file, on the Sheet1 tab, click cell I6.
2. On the Review tab, click New Comment.
3. In the comment box, type **Order more immediately**.
4. Click cell A1.
5. On the Review tab, in the Comments group, click Next to display the comment.
6. On the Review tab, in the Comments group, click Edit Comment.
7. In the comment, replace the text *Order more immediately* with the text **This has been ordered**.
8. Click outside of the comment.
9. On the Review tab, in the Comments group, click Show All Comments, if necessary.
10. Save the changes to the file, and leave it open to use in the next Try It.

Editing a comment

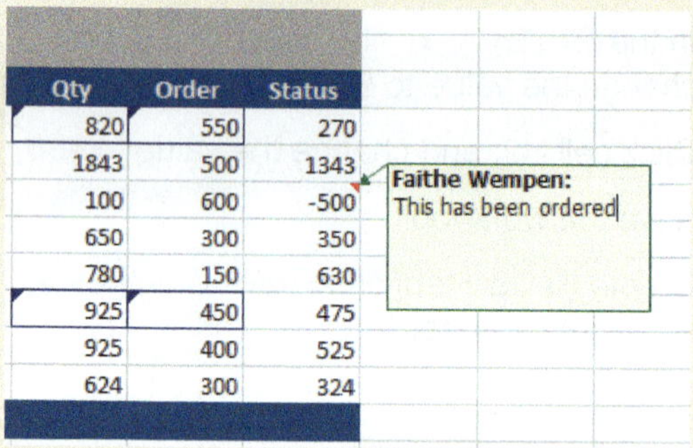

Excel 2016, Windows 10, Microsoft Corporation

Merging Changes

- When you share a workbook and want to compare the changes you and your colleagues have made before combining those changes into one worksheet, you can use the Compare and Merge Workbooks command.
- You can only merge changes that have been made on the same shared workbook, and the workbook must be shared before the Compare and Merge Workbooks command becomes available.
- You can manage workbook versions by selecting which workbooks to merge.
- By default, the Compare and Merge Workbooks command isn't available on the ribbon; you need to add it to the Quick Access Toolbar.
- You can merge the workbook data by selecting the file with changed values in the Select Files to Merge Into Current Workbook dialog box.

✓ *You can open and merge multiple copies of the same workbook by pressing and holding Ctrl while clicking files in the Select Files to Merge Into Current Workbook dialog box.*

Try It! Adding the Compare and Merge Workbooks Command to the QAT

1. In the E78TryA_xx file, click File > Options > Quick Access Toolbar in the left pane.
2. In the Choose commands from list, click All Commands.
3. Scroll down the list, and click Compare and Merge Workbooks > Add.
4. Click OK.
5. Save and close the file. Leave Excel open to use in the next Try It.

Try It! Merging Workbook Data

1. Open the E78TryB file from the data files for this lesson.
2. Save the file as E78TryB_xx in the location where your teacher instructs you to store the files for this lesson.
3. Click Review > Share Workbook.
4. Click the Allow changes by more than one user at the same time check box.
5. Click OK > OK.
6. Save the file as E78TryC_xx in the location where your teacher instructs you to store the files for this lesson.
7. In cell G7, change the value to 400.
8. Save and close the E78TryC_xx file.
9. Open the E78TryB_xx file again.
10. On the Quick Access Toolbar, click Compare and Merge Workbooks.
11. In the Select Files to Merge Into Current Workbook dialog box, browse to the location where your teacher instructs you to store the files for this lesson to, and click E78TryC_xx.
12. Click OK. The new file data is merged with the current file, and the value you changed is flagged on the worksheet.
13. Save the changes to the E78TryB_xx file, and leave it open to use in the next Try It.

Removing Workbook Sharing

- When you are ready to stop sharing the workbook, you can turn the sharing workbook feature off by using the Share Workbook command in the Changes group on the Review tab.
- You can remove other users by clicking the names of colleagues in the Who Has This Workbook Open Now list of the Share Workbook dialog box and clicking Remove User.
- Click to remove the check mark in the Allow changes by more than one user at the same time check box.

✓ *You need to remove workbook protection before sharing or unsharing a workbook. Click Unprotect Shared Workbook in the Changes group of the Review tab to remove protection.*

Try It! Removing Workbook Sharing

1. In the **E78TryB_xx** file, click Review > Share Workbook.
2. In the Share Workbook dialog box, click Allow changes by more than one user at the same time to unselect the check box.
3. Click OK.
4. Click Yes if prompted about the effects the change will have on other users.
5. Save and close the workbook, and exit Excel.

The Share Workbook dialog box

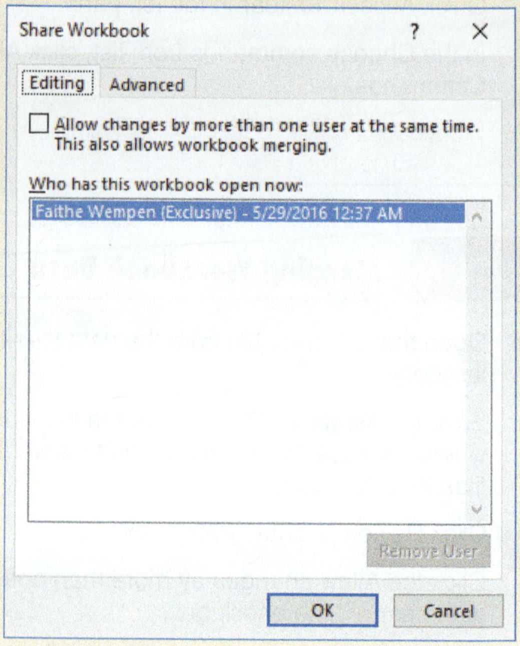

Lesson 78—Practice

You and several friends have decided to go in together to start a great new coffee shop in Portland, Oregon, called Grounds for Thought. You are preparing an expense report worksheet for you and your friends to access and edit. You want to track the changes in the worksheet and update the worksheet with your expenses. You also want to share the workbook. In this project, you will track the changes within the worksheet and view the history of those changes.

DIRECTIONS

1. Start Excel, if necessary, and open **E78Practice** from the data files for this lesson.
2. Save the file as **E78Practice_xx** in the location where your teacher instructs you to store the files for this lesson.
3. Click **Review** > **Share Workbook** > **Allow changes** check box.
4. Click **OK** twice.
5. On the Review tab, click **Track Changes** > **Highlight Changes**.
6. Click the **When** arrow, if necessary, and click **All**.
7. Click the **Who** arrow, and click **Everyone**.
8. Click the **List changes on a new sheet** check box.
9. Click **OK** twice.
10. Enter the following values:

    D11: Santa Fe

    E11: 375.00

    F11: 50.00

    G11: 25.00

    H11: 75.00

    J11: 100.00

    K11: 100.00
11. Save the workbook.

12. Adjust the column widths, as needed.
13. On the Review tab, click **Track Changes** > **Highlight Changes**.
14. Click **List changes on a new sheet** > **OK** to see the **History** worksheet.
15. Turn off sharing by clicking **Share Workbook** > **Allow changes by more than one user at the same time** check box to deselect it > **OK**.
16. Click **Yes** if prompted about the effects the change will have on other users.
17. Add a header that has your name at the left, the date code in the center, and the page number code at the right, and change back to **Normal** view.
18. **With your teacher's permission,** print the worksheet. Your worksheet should look like the one shown in Figure 78-1.
19. Save and close the file, and exit Excel.

Figure 78-1

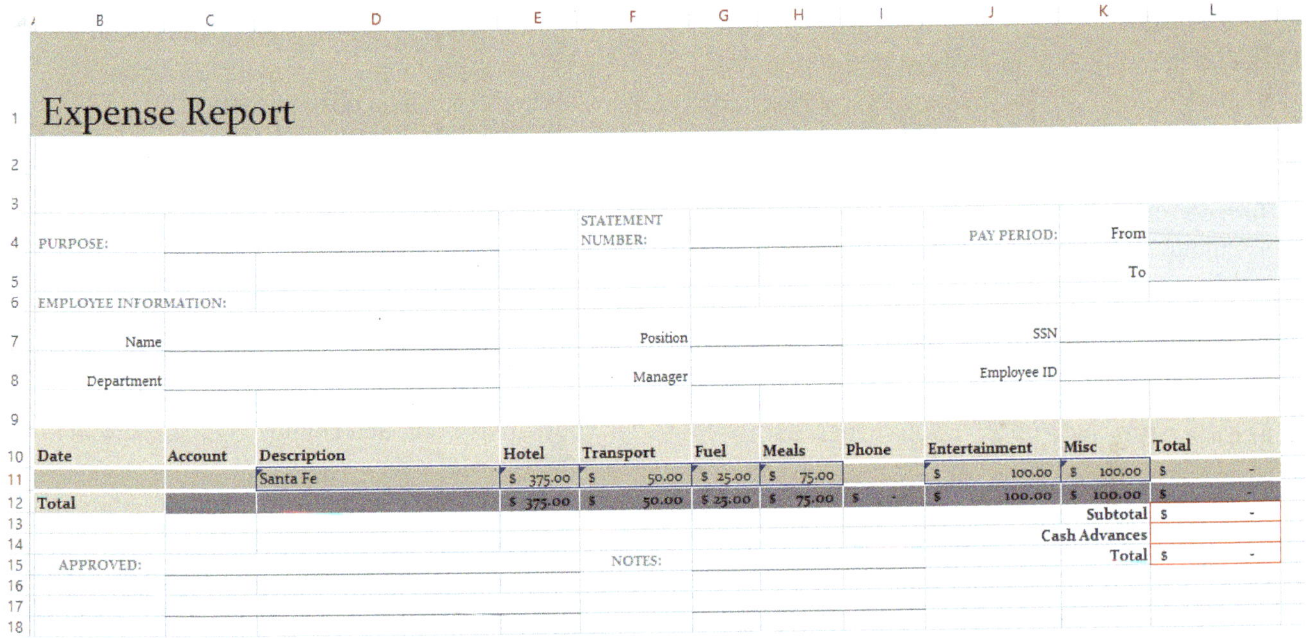

Excel 2016, Windows 10, Microsoft Corporation

Lesson 78—Apply

You and your friends are excited to start your new coffee shop, Grounds for Thought. You are preparing an inventory worksheet and want to apply sharing and track changes. When you last took inventory of the coffee, you noticed that one of the coffees had been overstocked. You want to insert a comment into the worksheet to let your partners know not to order more of that particular coffee.

DIRECTIONS

1. Start Excel, if necessary, and open **E78ApplyA** from the data files for this lesson.
2. Save the file as **E78ApplyA_xx** in the location where your teacher instructs you to store the files for this lesson.
3. Set up the workbook for sharing.
   a. Click **Review** > **Share Workbook** > **Allow changes** check box.
   b. Click **OK** twice.
4. Turn on tracking.
   a. On the Review tab, click **Track Changes** > **Highlight Changes**.
   b. Click the **When** arrow, if necessary, and click **All**.
   c. Click the **Who** arrow, and click **Everyone**.
   d. Click **OK** twice.
5. Save the **E78ApplyA_xx** file.
6. Now save the file as **E78ApplyB_xx** in the location where your teacher instructs you to store the files for this lesson.
7. Make several changes to the values.
8. In cell I5, insert the comment **Do not order any more**.
9. Save and close the **E78ApplyB_xx** workbook.
10. Merge the **E78ApplyA_xx** and **E78ApplyB_xx** workbooks.
    a. Reopen the **E78ApplyA_xx** file.
    b. On the Quick Access Toolbar, click the **Compare and Merge Workbooks** button.
    c. In the Select Files to Merge Into Current Workbook dialog box, navigate to **E78ApplyB_xx**, and click **OK**.
11. Save the workbook.
12. Turn off sharing.
    a. Click **Review** > **Share Workbook** > **Allow changes** check box to deselect it.
    b. Click **OK** , and click **Yes**.
13. Add a header that has your name at the left, the date code in the center, and the page number code at the right, and change back to **Normal** view.
14. Change the page layout orientation to **Landscape**.
15. **With your teacher's permission,** print the **E78ApplyA_xx** workbook. Your workbook should look similar to the one shown in Figure 78-2 on the next page.
16. Save and close the file, and exit Excel.

Figure 78-2

	A	B	C	D	E	F	G	H	I
1	Stocking & Sales #s for New Coffees								
2									
3	SKU	Name	Vendor	LOC	Cost	Retail	Qty	Order	Status
4	HM1234	Ultra Roast	PR0541	C	$ 9.00	$ 27.99	800	500	300
5	HM1235	Breakfast Blend	PR0541	A	$ 14.00	$ 37.99	2100	500	1600
6	HM1236	French Roast	PR0541	A	$ 14.00	$ 37.99	750	600	150
7	HM1237	Organic Blend	AB7243	B	$ 16.00	$ 46.99	800	750	50
8	HM1238	House Blend	PR0541	B	$ 14.00	$ 37.99	600	150	450
9	HM1239	Sumatra	AB7243	A	$ 14.00	$ 34.99	545	300	245
10	HM1240	Verona	AB7243	A	$ 14.00	$ 34.99	256	400	-144
11	HM1241	Dark Bean	PR0541	C	$ 15.00	$ 42.99	744	200	544
12									
13									

Firstname Lastname:
Do not order any more

Excel 2016, Windows 10, Microsoft Corporation

Lesson 79

Ensuring Data Integrity

➤ What You Will Learn

Turning Off AutoComplete
Controlling Data Entry with Data Validation
Circling Invalid Data
Copying Validation Rules
Removing Duplicate Data
Controlling Recalculation

WORDS TO KNOW

Input message
A message that appears when a user clicks in a cell providing information on how to enter valid data.

Paste Special
A variation of the Paste command that allows you to copy part of the data relating to a cell—in this case, the validity rules associated with that cell—and not the data in the cell itself.

Recalculation
The process of computing formulas and displaying the results as values in the cells that contain the formulas.

Validation
A process that enables you to maintain the accuracy of the database by specifying acceptable entries for a particular field.

Software Skills When working with worksheet data, it is all too easy to enter incorrect information. This is especially true when several people maintain a database. Since the accuracy of your data is often critical—especially if the data tells you what to charge for a product or what to pay someone—controlling the validity of the data is paramount. Anything you can do to control data entry and identify errors will contribute to the quality of your work.

What You Can Do

Turning Off AutoComplete

- Excel's AutoComplete feature can complicate data entry in an Excel worksheet, because AutoComplete can alter the case of an entry or complete an entry in a manner the user doesn't intend.
- For example, if a previous entry in the field is Westlane and the user is entering only West, AutoComplete will nonetheless fill in Westlane.

Try It! **Turning Off AutoComplete**

1. Start Excel, and open E79Try from the data files for this lesson.
2. Save the file as E79Try_xx in the location where your teacher instructs you to store the files for this lesson.
3. Click File > Options > Advanced.
4. Under Editing options, click the Enable AutoComplete for cell values check box to deselect it.
5. Click OK
6. Save the changes to the file, and leave it open to use in the next Try It.

Controlling Data Entry with Data Validation

- With data **validation**, you can control the accuracy of the data entered into a worksheet.
- By specifying the type of entries that are acceptable, you can prevent invalid data from being entered. For example, you could create a list of valid department numbers, and prevent someone from entering a department number that wasn't on the list.
- You can set other rules as well, such as whole numbers only; numbers less than or greater than some value; or data of a specific length, such as five characters only.
- After entering the criteria for what constitutes a valid entry, you can also specify a particular error message to appear when an incorrect entry is typed.
- In addition, you can create an **input message** that displays when a user clicks a cell to help that user enter the right type of data.
- The types of validation criteria that are possible are:
  - Any value
  - Whole number
  - Decimal
  - List
  - Date
  - Time
  - Text length—limits the number of characters that can be entered
  - Custom—requires the use of logical formulas

    ✓ *With the Custom option, you can enter a formula that compares the entry value with a value in another column. For example, you could set up a rule that if the Rented column contains the word Yes, then the Number of Occupants field must have a value greater than zero.*
- If you restrict entries to a specified list, a down-arrow button appears when the cell is selected. Clicking the button displays a drop-down list of the acceptable entries, from which you can select.

  ✓ *Entries in a restricted list are case-sensitive. If the list specifies Yes and the user instead types yes, for example, Excel will reject the entry. Whenever possible, use lowercase letters for list entries to prevent case-sensitivity problems and speed up data entry.*
- Data validation is designed to check against data entered directly into cells in the worksheet. Data validation doesn't apply if the cell entry is the result of:
  - Data copied there using the fill handle.
  - Data pasted or moved from another location.
  - Data that is the result of a formula.

Try It! Setting Up a Simple Data Validation Rule

1. In the **E79Try_xx** file, on the Office Items worksheet, select the cell range C4:C15.
2. Click Data > Data Validation to open the Data Validation dialog box.
3. On the Settings tab, click the Allow drop-down arrow, and click Whole number.
4. Click the Data drop-down arrow, and click greater than.
5. Click in the Minimum text box, and type **0**.
6. Click the Error Alert tab, click in the Error message text box, and type **Positive whole numbers only**.
7. Click OK.
8. Click cell C11, type **0**, and press ENTER. The error message appears.
9. Click Cancel to close the error message box.

   ✓ *Clicking Cancel removes the number you entered from cell C11. If you were to click Retry, the number would remain in the cell, highlighted black, and the cell active, waiting for you to retry your entry.*

10. Save the changes to the file, and leave it open to use in the next Try It.

A validation rule that allows positive whole numbers only

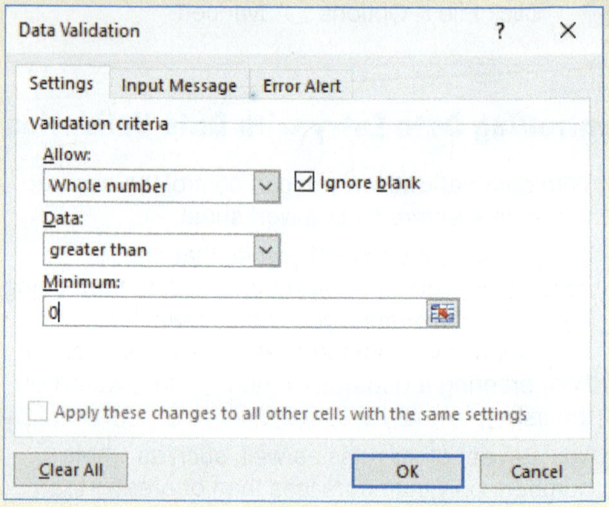

Excel 2016, Windows 10, Microsoft Corporation

Try It! Setting Up Custom Validation

1. In the **E79Try_xx** file, on the Office Items worksheet, select the cell range A4:A15.
2. Click Data > Data Validation to open the Data Validation dialog box.
3. On the Settings tab, click the Allow drop-down arrow, and click Custom.
4. Click in the Formula text box, and type **=ISTEXT(A4)**.

   ✓ *This formula refers to the first cell in the range; the validation formulas for the other cells in the range will be for those cells because Excel considers this a relative reference.*

5. Click the Input Message tab, click in the Title box, and type **Item Name**.
6. Click in the Input message box, and type **Enter only the item name from the catalog.**
7. Click the Error Alert tab, click the Style drop-down arrow, and click Stop, if necessary.
8. Click in the Title text box, and type **Verify Item Name**.
9. Click in the Error message text box, and type **The item name must be text only.**
10. Click OK to close the dialog box. Notice the message that appears.

(continued)

Try It! Setting Up Custom Validation *(continued)*

The Input Message tab

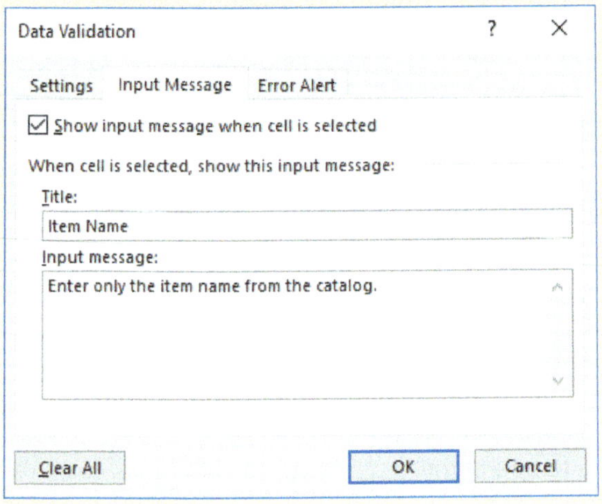

Excel 2016, Windows 10, Microsoft Corporation

11. Click each of the cells in the range A5:A15. Notice the message appears for them too.
12. Click cell B4. No message appears because there is no validation set up for that cell.
13. Click cell A12, type **12345**, and press ENTER. An error message appears.
14. Click Cancel to clear the error message.
15. Save the changes to the file, and leave it open to use in the next Try It.

Try It! Turning Off Notification of Errors

1. In the **E79Try_xx** file, click cell A4.
2. On the Data tab, click Data Validation to open the Data Validation dialog box.
3. Click the Input Message tab, and click the Show input message when cell is selected check box to deselect it.
4. Click the Error Alert tab, and click the Show error alert after invalid data is entered check box to deselect it.
5. Click the Settings tab, click the Apply these changes to all other cells with the same settings check box.
6. Click OK.
7. Click A12, type **12345**, and press ENTER. No warning appears.
8. Save the changes to the file, and leave it open to use in the next Try It.

Circling Invalid Data

- Even with data validation rules in effect, sometimes invalid data can still be recorded. Data entered by copying and pasting, by using the fill handle, or as the result of a formula all bypass Excel's validation rules, for example.
- With the Circle Invalid Data command, data that violates specified validation rules is identified quickly with a red circle.
- As you correct the data, the circle in that cell automatically disappears.
- You can remove any remaining circles (for errors you want to ignore) with the Clear Validation Circles command.

Try It! Circling Invalid Data

1. In the **E79Try_xx** file, on the Data tab, click the Data Validation drop-down arrow > Circle Invalid Data. Cell A12 shows a red circle, indicating the validation rule is violated.
2. Click cell A12, and press DEL. The red circle remains.
3. With cell A12 still selected, type **Product**, and press ENTER. The red circle goes away.
4. Click cell A12, and press DEL.
5. Save the changes to the file, and leave it open to use in the next Try It.

Try It! Turning On Notification of Errors

1. In the **E79Try_xx** file, select the cell range A4:A15.
2. On the Data tab, click Data Validation to open the Data Validation dialog box.
3. Click the Error Alert tab, and click the Show error alert after invalid data is entered check box to select it.
4. Click OK.
5. Save the changes to the file, and leave it open to use in the next Try It.

Copying Validation Rules

- You can copy validation rules between cells using the Clipboard. This enables you to reuse a rule without having to re-create it from scratch.
- To copy a validation rule, use the **Paste Special** feature of the Clipboard. This enables you to specify what aspect of the copied range you want to paste.

Try It! Copying Validation Rules

1. In the **E79Try_xx** file, on the Office Items worksheet, select the cell range A4:A11.
2. Press CTRL + C to copy.
3. Click the Sales Tax worksheet tab.
4. On the Sales Tax worksheet, select the cell range A4:A11.
5. Click CTRL + V to paste. (The two lists are identical, so it's okay to overwrite the content.) The content is copied, and so is the validation rule.
6. Click the Office Items worksheet tab, click cell C4, and press CTRL + C to copy the cell.
7. Click the Sales Tax worksheet tab, and select the cell range B4:B14.
8. Click Home > Paste drop-down arrow > Paste Special.
9. In the Paste Special dialog box, under Paste, click Validation.
10. Click OK. Only the validation rule is copied.
11. Save the changes to the file, and leave it open to use in the next Try It.

Removing Duplicate Data

- Another type of invalid data that might be entered into a worksheet is a duplicate entry.
- Sometimes, duplicates are valid. For example, if two people happen to make $18.45 an hour, that might be perfectly normal. However, if the worksheet contains a database, such as a list of employees or customers, duplicates may indicate an error.
- To remove duplicate entries from a range, use the Remove Duplicates command. When you remove duplicate entries this way, Excel identifies what it considers duplicates, and automatically removes them for you.

✓ *You cannot remove duplicates from data that is outlined or subtotaled. To remove duplicates, remove the outlining/subtotaling.*

Try It! Removing Duplicate Data

1. In the **E79Try_xx** file, click the Office Items worksheet tab and select the range A3:E15.
2. Click Data > Remove Duplicates to open the Remove Duplicates dialog box.
3. Under Columns, click to deselect all the check boxes except Catalog Item Number.
4. Click OK.
5. Click OK to the message that a duplicate has been removed.
6. Save the changes to the file, and leave it open to use in the next Try It.

The Remove Duplicates dialog box

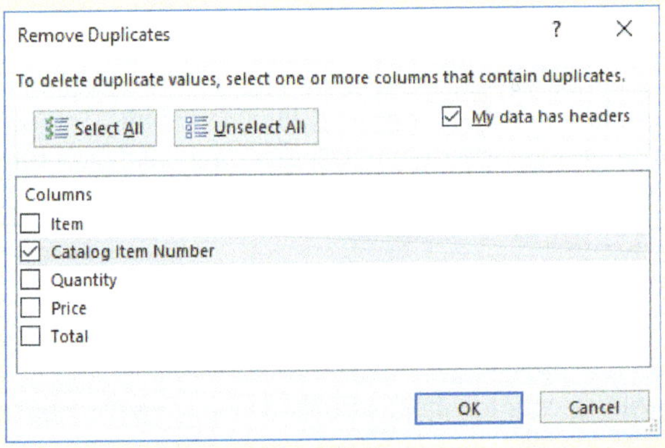

Excel 2016, Windows 10, Microsoft Corporation

Controlling Recalculation

- **Recalculation** options allow you to control the way that Excel recalculates formulas.
- By default, Excel recalculates a worksheet as soon as you make a change to a formula or an element, such as a name, on which your formulas depend.
- If the worksheet is very large and contains tables whose formulas depend on several values, recalculation of those formulas can take a bit of time.
- When you recalculate a worksheet, the pointer changes to an hourglass, and the word "Recalculation" followed by the number of cells left to be recalculated appears on the left side of the formula bar.
- You can manually control when Excel calculates your worksheet.
- Use the commands in the Calculate group on the Formulas tab of the ribbon.
- When manual recalculation is turned on and you make a change in a value, formula, or name, the "Calculate" message displays on the status bar.
- When you want Excel to recalculate a worksheet that has been set to manually calculate, use the Calculate Now command.

Try It! Changing Calculation Options

1. In the E79Try_xx file, on the Office Items worksheet, click the Formulas tab.
2. Click Calculation Options > Manual.
3. Click cell C7, type 7, and press ENTER. Notice that the total in cell E7 did not recalculate.
4. Click Calculate Now. The formulas calculate.
5. Click Calculation Options > Automatic.
6. Save and close the file, and exit Excel.

Lesson 79—Practice

As an employee of PhotoTown, one of your assignments is to make the photo product order form easier to use. Your manager wants the order form to contain only information that matches up with the inventory and product listings. In this project, you will use data validation rules and turn on manual recalculation of formulas.

DIRECTIONS

1. Start Excel, if necessary, and open **E79Practice** from the data files for this lesson.
2. Save the file as **E79Practice_xx** in the location where your teacher instructs you to store the files for this lesson.
3. For all worksheets, add a header that has your name at the left, the date code in the center, and the page number code at the right, and change back to **Normal** view.
4. On the **Order Form** worksheet, test the list-based order form.
   a. Click cell **B12**.
   b. Type **PZ101**, and press TAB. The Description field shows Photo puzzle, and the Size, Color, and Price per Item are filled in.
   c. Click cell **G12**, type **1**, and press ENTER.
5. Add a validation rule for the Item # field that permits only valid item numbers.
   a. Select the cell range **B12:B28**.
   b. Click **Data** > **Data Validation**.
   c. Click the **Settings** tab, click the **Allow** drop-down arrow > **List**.
   d. Click the **Collapse Dialog** button next to the Source box.
   e. Click the **Product Listing** worksheet tab.
   f. Select the cell range **A9:A68**, and press ENTER to return to the dialog box.
   g. Click **OK** to create the rule.
6. Click cell **B13**, click the drop-down arrow that appears to the right, scroll down, and click **GC075**. The information about the product is filled in.
7. Click **Formulas** > **Calculation Options** > **Manual**.
8. Click cell **C13**, and look at the formula in the formula bar to see how the worksheet is constructed.

   ✓ *An IF function evaluates B13 and then looks up data from the Product Listing sheet with VLOOKUP.*
9. Click cell **G13**, type **2**, and press ENTER.
10. On the Formulas tab, click **Calculate Now** to calculate the formula.
11. Click **Formulas** > **Calculation Options** > **Automatic**.
12. **With your teacher's permission,** print the **Order Form** worksheet using **Fit Sheet on One Page**.
13. Save and close the file, and exit Excel.

Lesson 79—Apply

You are working with PhotoTown's photo product order form. Your manager wants you to add data validation messages to make the form easier for the customer to use. He wants the empty order rows to be removed whenever an order contains only a few items. You also need to limit the greeting card text box to a certain number of characters to match the character limit of the database. In this project, you will set data validation rules for the orders and use remove duplicates to remove the extra rows.

DIRECTIONS

1. Start Excel, if necessary, and open **E79Apply** from the data files for this lesson.
2. Save the file as **E79Apply_xx** in the location where your teacher instructs you to store the files for this lesson.
3. For all worksheets, add a header that has your name at the left, the date code in the center, and the page number code at the right, and change back to **Normal** view.
4. On the **Order Form** worksheet, add a validation rule for the Qty field (cell range **G12:G28**) that permits only whole positive numbers and shows a Stop type error message that explains the rule when it is violated.
5. Test the validation rule and make any corrections needed.
6. Add a validation rule for the Greeting card text box (merged cell **G35**) that permits a maximum of 180 characters. Set an input message of **Enter up to 180 characters**. If the rule is violated, an error message should appear: **Please enter a message of no more than 180 characters**.
7. To test the validation rule, attempt to enter the following text into cell **G35**. (Use ALT + ENTER to insert line breaks.) Press ENTER when finished.

   Wheaten's Glenn Apple Orchard
   First Annual Harvest Festival
   September 12th to 28th
   10:00 A.M. to 6:00 P.M.

   Hay rides, apple picking, cider
   tasting, corn maze, and more!
   Take NC-7 to R.R. 12, west 10 miles.

8. When the error message appears, click Retry, and edit the entry to fewer than 180 characters:

   Wheaten's Glenn Apple Orchard
   Harvest Festival
   Sept. 12th to 28th
   10 A.M. to 6 P.M.

   Hay rides, apple picking, cider
   tasting, corn maze, and more!
   NC-7 to R.R. 12, west 10m.

9. Click cell **G35** > **Home** > **Top Align**.
10. Use **Remove Duplicates** to remove any duplicate items in rows **B12:I28**.

    ✓ *This has the effect of removing all of the blank rows from the order form except one. However, it does not completely delete the rows; it only deletes their content and formatting.*

11. Select the unformatted rows (rows 16–28), and click **Home** > **Delete**. Your worksheet should look like the one shown in Figure 79-1 on the next page.
12. **With your teacher's permission,** print the **Order Form** worksheet using **Fit Sheet on One Page**.
13. Save and close the file, and exit Excel.

Figure 79-1

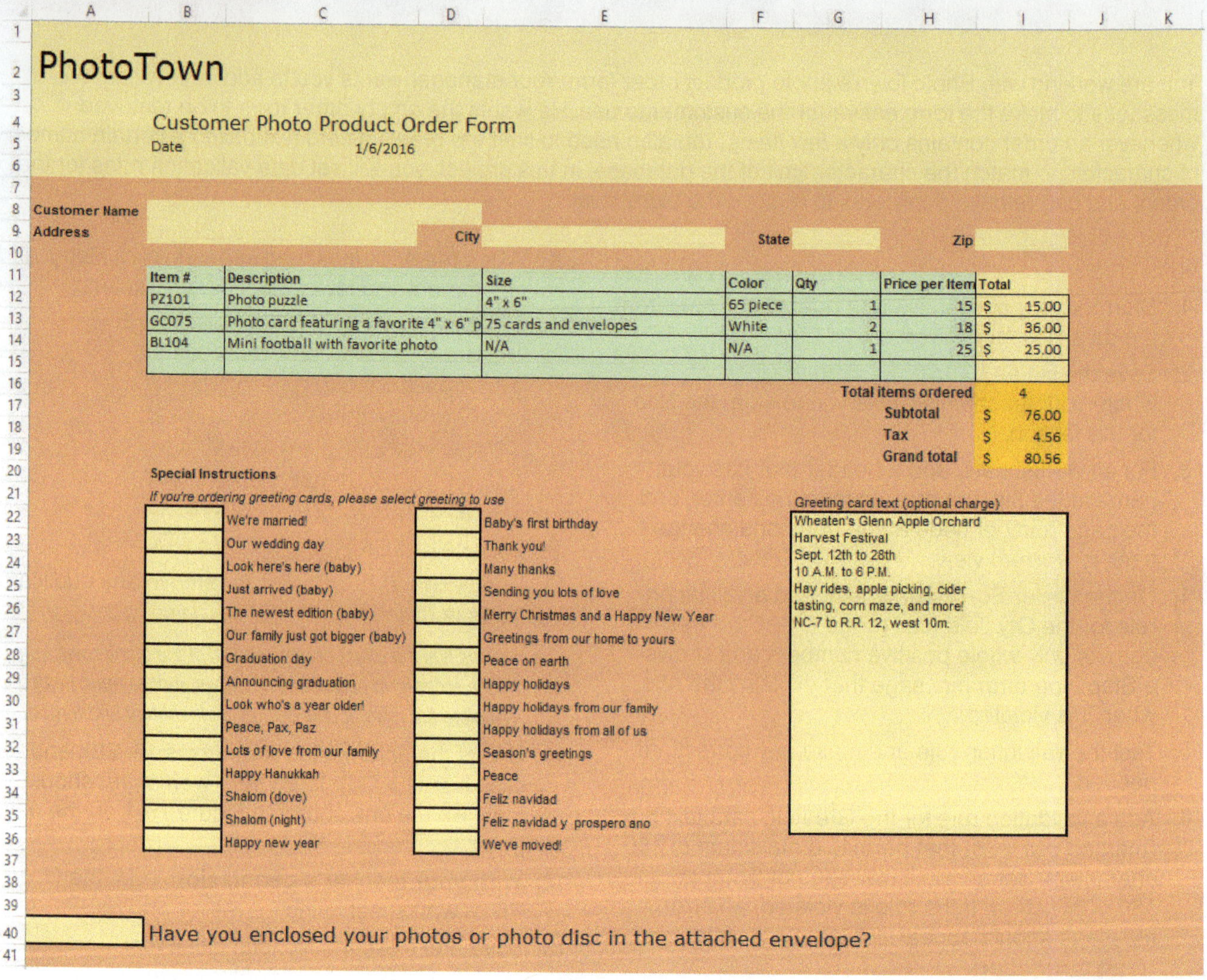
PhotoTown

Customer Photo Product Order Form

Date 1/6/2016

Customer Name

Address City State Zip

Item #	Description	Size	Color	Qty	Price per Item	Total
PZ101	Photo puzzle	4" x 6"	65 piece	1	15	$ 15.00
GC075	Photo card featuring a favorite 4" x 6" p	75 cards and envelopes	White	2	18	$ 36.00
BL104	Mini football with favorite photo	N/A	N/A	1	25	$ 25.00

Total items ordered	4
Subtotal	$ 76.00
Tax	$ 4.56
Grand total	$ 80.56

Special Instructions

If you're ordering greeting cards, please select greeting to use

We're married!	Baby's first birthday
Our wedding day	Thank you!
Look here's here (baby)	Many thanks
Just arrived (baby)	Sending you lots of love
The newest edition (baby)	Merry Christmas and a Happy New Year
Our family just got bigger (baby)	Greetings from our home to yours
Graduation day	Peace on earth
Announcing graduation	Happy holidays
Look who's a year older!	Happy holidays from our family
Peace, Pax, Paz	Happy holidays from all of us
Lots of love from our family	Season's greetings
Happy Hanukkah	Peace
Shalom (dove)	Feliz navidad
Shalom (night)	Feliz navidad y prospero ano
Happy new year	We've moved!

Greeting card text (optional charge)

Wheaten's Glenn Apple Orchard
Harvest Festival
Sept. 12th to 28th
10 A.M. to 6 P.M.
Hay rides, apple picking, cider tasting, corn maze, and more!
NC-7 to R.R. 12, west 10m.

Have you enclosed your photos or photo disc in the attached envelope?

Excel 2016, Windows 10, Microsoft Corporation

Lesson 80

Protecting Data

➤ What You Will Learn

Locking and Unlocking Cells in a Worksheet
Protecting a Range
Protecting a Worksheet
Protecting a Workbook

Software Skills If you design worksheets for others to use, or if you share a lot of workbooks, you may wish to protect certain areas of a worksheet from changes. You can protect any cell you want to prevent it from accepting new data or changes. You can also protect an entire worksheet or workbook so that others may only view its contents and not make changes.

What You Can Do

Locking and Unlocking Cells in a Worksheet

- To prevent changes to selected cells or ranges in a worksheet, you can **protect** the worksheet.
  - All cells in an Excel worksheet are **locked** by default.
  - When you turn on worksheet protection, the locked cells cannot be changed.
  - To allow changes in certain cells or ranges, unlock just those cells before protecting the worksheet.
  - If you **unlock** a cell that contains a formula, an Error Options button appears to remind you that you might not want to allow other people to change your formulas.

    ✓ *You can choose to ignore these errors when they appear, or tell Excel to lock the cell again.*
- If necessary, you can **unprotect** a protected worksheet so that you can change the data in locked cells.
- You can protect charts and other objects in a worksheet by using this same process.

WORDS TO KNOW

Lock
Cells that, if the worksheet is later protected, cannot be changed.

Protect
To prevent changes to locked or protected areas or objects.

Unlock
To enable changes in particular cells of a worksheet you want to later protect.

Unprotect
To remove protection from a worksheet or workbook.

Workbook structure
The worksheets that make up a workbook.

- If someone tries to make a change to a protected cell, a message indicates that the cell is protected and considered read-only.
- You can use TAB to move between the unlocked cells of a protected worksheet.
- You can set the tab order of your worksheet by using locked and unlocked cells. For example, when you have both locked and unlocked cells in a protected worksheet, you can only tab into the unlocked cells.
- The tab order goes from left to right in the first row, then left to right in the second row, and so on. You can change the tab order by changing which cells are locked or unlocked.
- However, if ranges were locked using the Allow Users to Edit Ranges dialog box as explained in the next section, the Tab key does not work.
- Users can copy the data in a locked cell, but they can't move or delete it.
- Data can't be copied to a part of the worksheet that's protected.

Try It! Locking and Unlocking Cells in a Worksheet

1. Start Excel, and open **E80Try** from the data files for this lesson.
2. Save the file as **E80Try_xx** in the location where your teacher instructs you to store the files for this lesson.
3. On the Order Form worksheet, lock the areas of the worksheet that customers will use to enter data:
   a. Select the cell range B8:B9.
   b. On the Home tab, click Format > Lock Cell.
   c. Lock the following cells in the same manner: E9, G9, I9, B12:B28, G12:G28, B35:B49, D35:D49, B53, and G36.
4. Save the changes to the file, and leave it open to use in the next Try It.

The Lock Cell command

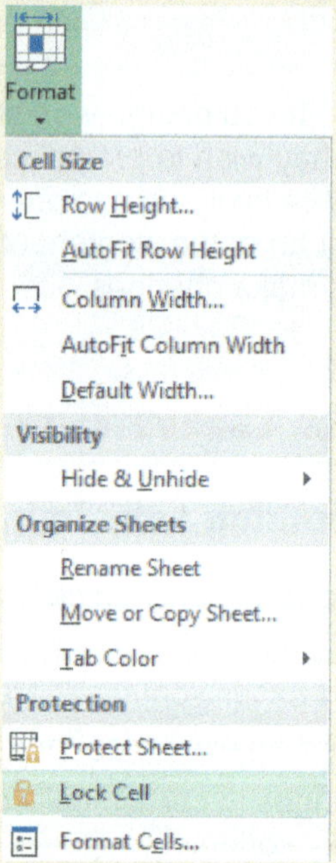

Excel 2016, Windows 10, Microsoft Corporation

Protecting a Range

- When you unlock cells to allow changes, you can tell Excel to allow changes from anyone, or just selected individuals.
- To unlock cells for everyone, remove the Lock Cell protection format.
- To allow changes to selected individuals, use the Allow Users to Edit Ranges dialog box, shown in Figure 80-1 on the next page.
- When protecting ranges within a worksheet, you can tell Excel to create a workbook with the details of the permissions you've granted—the range addresses and passwords you've specified.

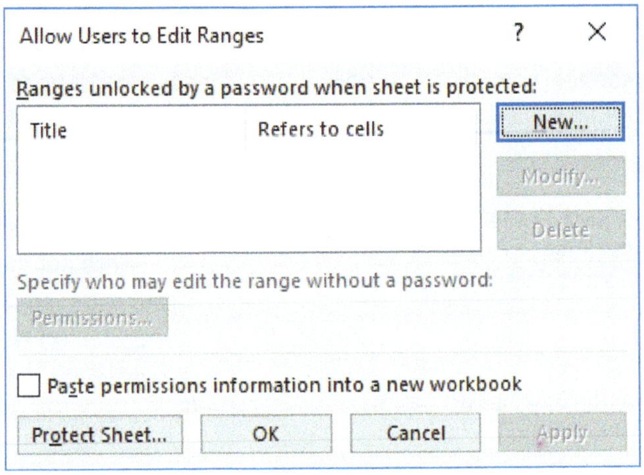

Excel 2016, Windows 10, Microsoft Corporation

Figure 80-1

Try It! Protecting a Range

1. In the **E80Try_xx** file, click the Product Listing worksheet tab.
2. In the Name box, click the drop-down arrow, and click the range name Products, as shown in the figure below.

The Name box

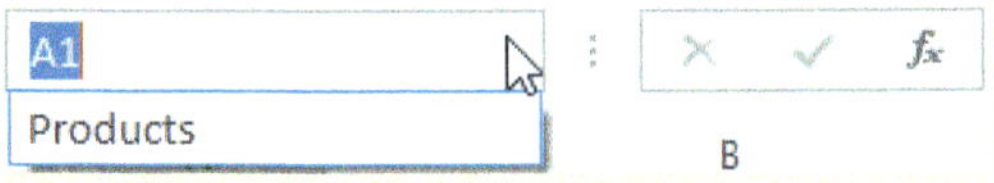

Excel 2016, Windows 10, Microsoft Corporation

3. Click Review > Allow Users to Edit Ranges.
4. In the Allow Users to Edit Ranges dialog box, click New.
5. In the New Range dialog box, in the Title box, type **Product Listing**.
6. In the Range Password box, type **supersecret**, and click OK.
7. In the Confirm Password dialog box, type **supersecret**, and click OK.
8. In the Allow Users to Edit Ranges dialog box, click Protect Sheet.
9. In the Password to unprotect sheet box, type **supersecret**.
10. Check the Select locked cells, Select unlocked cells, Insert rows, and Sort check boxes to select them, and click OK.
11. Confirm the password, and click OK again.
12. Save the changes to the file, and leave it open to use in the next Try It.

The New Range dialog box

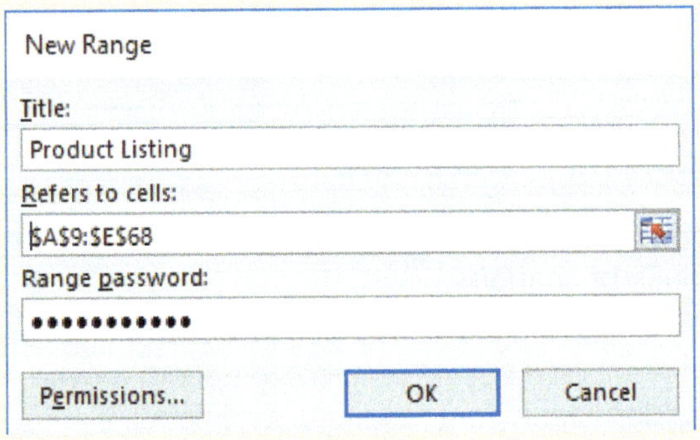

Excel 2016, Windows 10, Microsoft Corporation

Protecting a Worksheet

- Even if you activate worksheet protection, the cells you have unlocked are not protected.

  ✓ *Changes can still be made to those cells.*

- You can also prevent changes to objects, such as clip art or shapes, hyperlinks, PivotTables, and scenarios, which are stored variations of a worksheet.
- Use the options in the Protect Sheet dialog box to prevent certain actions, such as formatting, inserting columns and rows, deleting columns and rows, sorting, and filtering.
- You can password-protect the sheet so that no one can unprotect the worksheet accidentally.
  - If you forget the password, you will not be able to unprotect the worksheet later on.
  - However, you can copy the data to another, unprotected worksheet, to start over.
  - Passwords are case sensitive.

Try It! Protecting a Worksheet

1. In the **E80Try_xx** file, click the Order Form worksheet tab.
2. Click Review > Protect Sheet.
3. In the Password to unprotect sheet box, type **mysecret**.
4. Under Allow all users of this worksheet to, click to deselect all check boxes except the Select unlocked cells checkbox, and click OK.
5. In the Confirm Password dialog box, type **mysecret**, and click OK.
6. Save the changes to the file, and leave it open to use in the next Try It.

Protect Sheet dialog box

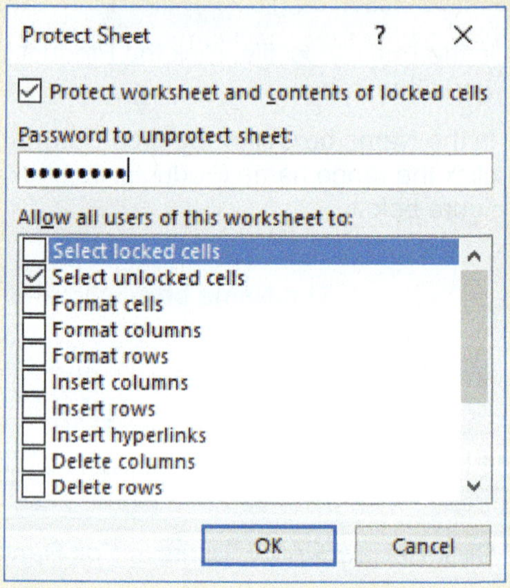

Excel 2016, Windows 10, Microsoft Corporation

Protecting a Workbook

- You can protect an entire workbook against certain kinds of changes.
- By protecting the **workbook structure**, you can prevent worksheets from being added, moved, hidden, unhidden, renamed, or deleted.
- You can also prevent a workbook's window from being resized or repositioned.
- You can add a password from the Protect Structure and Windows dialog box. A password will prevent users from changing the protection level of a workbook.
- If you want to share a workbook with others, and track the changes they make, you can still protect the workbook so that they can't erase the **change history**.

Try It! Protecting a Workbook

1. In the E80Try_xx file, on the Order Form worksheet, on the Review tab, click Protect Workbook.
2. In the Protect Structure and Windows dialog box, click Structure, if necessary.
3. In the Password box, type **secret**, and click OK.
4. In the Confirm Password dialog box, type **secret**, and click OK.
5. Save and close the file, and exit Excel.

Lesson 80—Practice

You are the payroll manager for Marcus Furniture, and you've just created the monthly earnings report used for generating commission checks. You need to have the data checked before the checks can be issued, but you want to ensure that no one can change the data in the file without notifying you. You want to protect certain areas of the worksheet, while still allowing you full access later.

DIRECTIONS

1. Start Excel, if necessary, and open **E80Practice** from the data files for this lesson.
2. Save the file as **E80Practice_xx** in the location where your teacher instructs you to store the files for this lesson.
3. On the **Feb Earnings** worksheet, unlock the areas into which data may be typed.
   a. Click the **Feb Earnings** worksheet tab, and select the cell range **D9:D23**.
   b. Click **Home** > **Format** > **Lock Cell**.
   c. Repeat step b to unlock cell **A5**.
4. Protect the **Feb Earnings** worksheet so that only you can make changes.
   a. Click **Review** > **Protect Sheet**.
   b. In the Password to unprotect sheet box, type **protection**.
   c. In the **Allow all users of this worksheet to** section, verify that the **Select unlocked cells option** is the only check box checked, and click **OK**.
   d. In the Confirm Password dialog box, type **protection**, and click **OK**.
5. Test the worksheet protection.
   a. Click cell **D9**, type **5000**, and press ENTER.
   b. Click cell **A9**, and try to change the name. This cell should be locked and protected.
6. Save and close the file, and exit Excel.

Lesson 80—Apply

As the payroll manager for Marcus Furniture, you have created the monthly earnings report used for generating commission checks. You protected certain areas of the worksheet, and now you need to make some changes.

DIRECTIONS

1. Start Excel, if necessary, and open **E80Apply** from the data files for this lesson.
2. Save the file as **E80Apply_xx** in the location where your teacher instructs you to store the files for this lesson.
3. On the **Feb Earnings** worksheet, unprotect the worksheet.
   a. Click **Review** > **Unprotect Sheet**.
   b. In the Password box, type **protection**, and click **OK**.
4. Edit the worksheet.
   a. Click cell **C11**, and type **$850**.
   b. Click cell **B17**, and type **Mary Williams**.
   c. Click cell **C17**, type **$750**, and press ENTER.
5. Protect the worksheet again; do not set a password.
6. Type the sales amounts in column D that are shown in Figure 80-2 on the next page.
7. Copy the **Feb Earnings** worksheet, place it before the **Comm-Bonus** worksheet, and name it **Mar Earnings**.
8. Change the text in cell **A5** to **March Earnings Report**.
9. Try to make an entry in any cell in the table other than in the Sales column to see if the cells are still locked.
10. Make an entry in the **Sales** column to see if the cells are unlocked, and delete all the entries in the Sales column.
11. For all worksheets, add a header that has your name at the left, the date code in the center, and the page number code at the right, and change back to **Normal** view.
12. **With your teacher's permission**, print the **Feb Earnings** worksheet.
13. Save and close the file, and exit Excel.

Figure 80-2

Marcus Furniture

February Earnings Report

ASSOCIATE	BASE SALARY	SALES	COMM. RATE	COMM. AMT.	BONUS	TOTAL EARNINGS
Bob Walraven	$1,000.00	$14,978.00	11%	$1,647.58	$450.00	$3,097.58
Mike Davis	$1,000.00	$10,254.00	8%	$820.32	$300.00	$2,120.32
Bill Mergenthal	$850.00	$7,521.00	5%	$376.05	$0.00	$1,226.05
Pete Sanger	$850.00	$9,874.00	7%	$691.18	$250.00	$1,791.18
Dorothy Bishop	$750.00	$6,023.00	4%	$240.92	$0.00	$990.92
Mary La Rue	$1,100.00	$13,458.00	11%	$1,480.38	$450.00	$3,030.38
Ernest Dedmon	$1,000.00	$9,141.00	7%	$639.87	$250.00	$1,889.87
Karen Frisch	$750.00	$10,394.00	8%	$831.52	$300.00	$1,881.52
Mary Williams	$750.00	$7,889.00	5%	$394.45	$0.00	$1,144.45
Mike McCutcheon	$750.00	$6,574.00	4%	$262.96	$0.00	$1,012.96
Lorna Myers	$900.00	$10,974.00	8%	$877.92	$300.00	$2,077.92
James Neely	$950.00	$14,958.00	11%	$1,645.38	$450.00	$3,045.38
Scott Gratten	$850.00	$13,425.00	11%	$1,476.75	$450.00	$2,776.75
Betty Miller	$925.00	$10,957.00	8%	$876.56	$300.00	$2,101.56
Fillard Willmore	$1,000.00	$14,958.00	11%	$1,645.38	$450.00	$3,095.38

Lesson 81

Securing a Workbook

➤ What You Will Learn

Using Document Inspector
Encrypting a Workbook
Identifying Workbooks Using Keywords

WORDS TO KNOW

Document Inspector
A tool that evaluates the worksheet to ensure that no hidden or personal information is included in the file.

Encryption
Encryption encodes the content in your workbook so that others cannot access it without having the required password.

Metadata
Data that gives information about other data.

Software Skills As you prepare a workbook to share with others, it's important to know how to secure the file in various ways. Excel enables you to inspect your workbook for hidden properties or personal information you might not want to share. You can also encrypt your workbook and assign a password. You can add tags to the file to help you find it easily later when you search for it.

What You Can Do

Using Document Inspector

- The **Document Inspector** in Excel enables you to check the workbook for information that you don't want to share with others.
- The tool evaluates the workbook for hidden properties or personal information you might not want to share.
- By default, all the check boxes in the Document Inspector are selected. Use the Remove All command to remove any information you don't want to include in the presentation, and then use Reinspect to reinspect the document.

Try It! Using Document Inspector

1. Start Excel, and open **E81Try** from the data files for this lesson.
2. Save the file as **E81Try_xx** in the location where your teacher instructs you to store the files for this lesson.
3. Click File.
4. In the Backstage view, on the Info tab, click Check for Issues.
5. Click Inspect Document > Inspect. Review the inspection results.
6. Click Close to close the Document Inspector.
7. Click the Back button to exit the Backstage view.
8. Save the changes to the file, and leave it open to use in the next Try It.

The Document Inspector inspection results

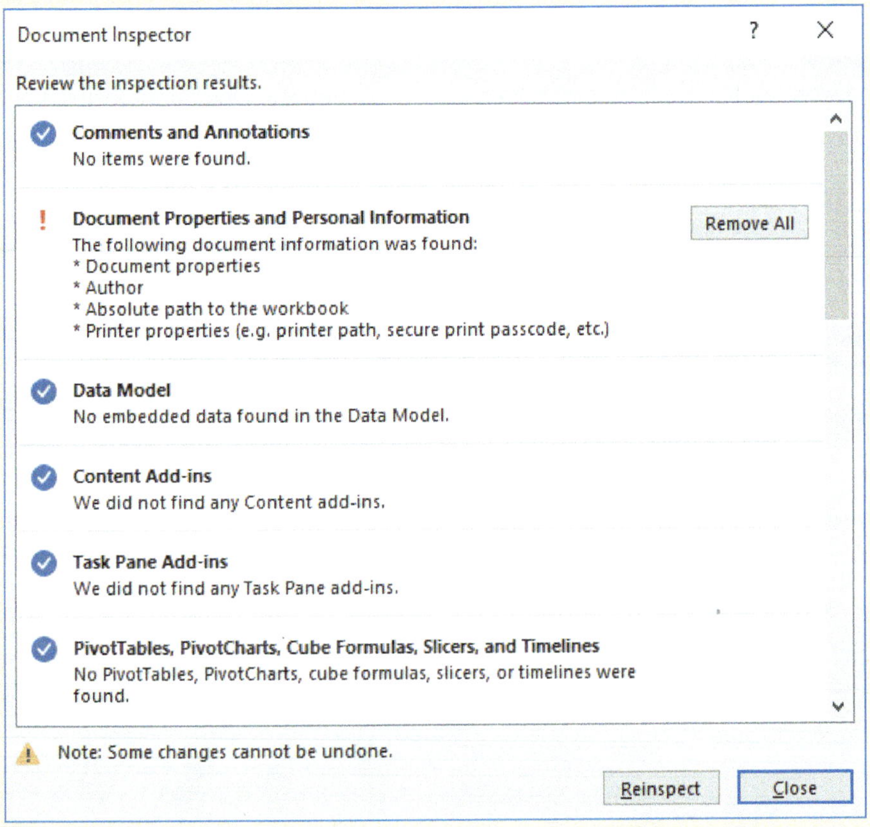

Encrypting a Workbook

- Encrypting a workbook protects the workbook and enables you to assign a password so that others can open the file only if they have the necessary password.
- Excel will prompt you to enter and then re-enter the password.
- Keep the password in a safe place because Excel does not store a copy of the password in a way that you can retrieve it if you forget it later.
- You can remove password **encryption** by displaying the Encrypt Document dialog box, clearing the entry in the Password box, and clicking OK.

Try It! Encrypting with a Password

1. In the E81Try_xx file, click File.
2. In the Backstage view, on the Info tab, click Protect Workbook.
3. Click Encrypt with Password.
4. In the Encrypt Document dialog box, in the Password box, type **newpres34**, and click OK.
5. In the Confirm Password dialog box, in the Reenter password box, type **newpres34**.
6. Click OK.
7. Save the changes to the file, and leave it open to use in the next Try It.

Identifying Workbooks Using Keywords

- You can add keywords to help you identify the workbook in a search.
- Enter tags for the workbook in the Properties area of the Info tab of the Backstage view.
- To enter multiple keywords or key phrases, separate the keywords or key phrases with commas.
- You can remove keywords and other **metadata** using the Document Properties panel.

Try It! Adding Keywords to a Workbook

1. In the E81Try_xx file, click File.
2. In the Backstage view, on the right side of the Info tab, click the Properties button.
3. Click Advanced Properties.
4. In the Properties dialog box, in the Keywords box on the Summary tab, type **gardening, budget**.
5. Click OK to close the dialog box.
6. Save and close the file, and exit Excel.

The Properties dialog box

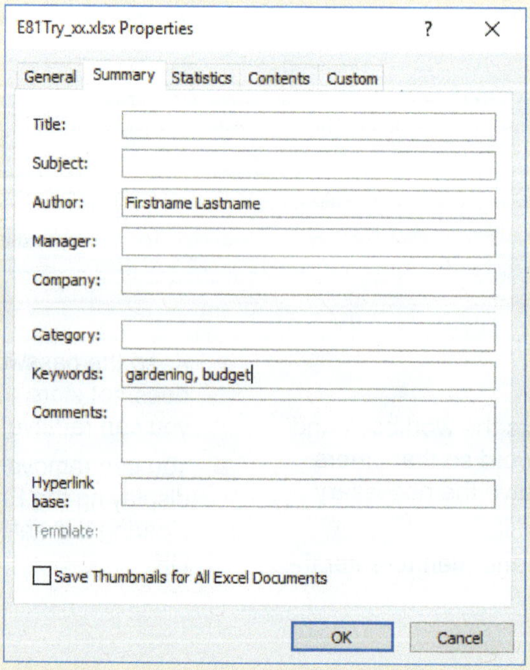

Excel 2016, Windows 10, Microsoft Corporation

Lesson 81—Practice

You are working on a workbook for two clients. You will inspect the workbook for issues, apply passwords, and add keywords to the workbook properties.

DIRECTIONS

1. Start Excel, if necessary, and open **E81Practice** from the data files for this lesson.
2. Save the file as **E81Practice_xx** in the location where your teacher instructs you to store the files for this lesson.
3. Click **File**.
4. In the Backstage view, on the Info tab, click **Check for Issues** > **Inspect Document**.
5. In the Document Inspector, click **Inspect**.
6. Review the results, and click **Close** to close the Document Inspector.
7. In the Backstage view, on the Info tab, click **Protect Workbook** > **Encrypt with Password**.
8. In the Encrypt Document dialog box, in the Password box, type **pass123#**, and click **OK**.
9. In the Confirm Password dialog box, in the Reenter password box, type **pass123#**, and click **OK**.
10. In the Backstage view, on the Info tab, click **Properties** > **Advanced Properties**.
11. In the Properties dialog box, in the Keywords box, type **inventory, reorders**.
12. Click **OK**.
13. Save the file.
14. Click **File**. The Info tab of the Backstage view should look like the one shown in Figure 81-1.
15. Click the Back button to exit the Backstage view.
16. Save and close the file, and exit Excel.

Figure 81-1

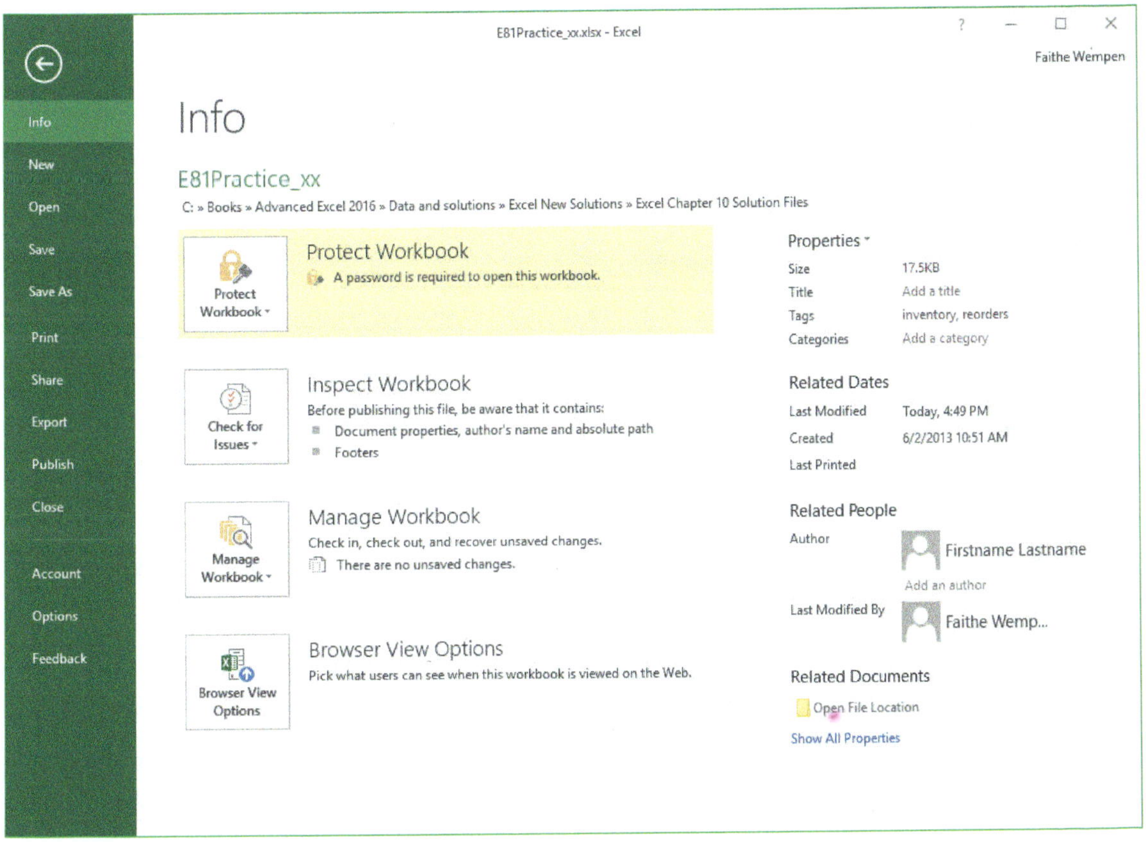

Lesson 81—Apply

You are working on worksheets for two clients. You will inspect the worksheets for issues, apply passwords, and protect the worksheets. You will also add keywords to the properties.

DIRECTIONS

1. Start Excel, if necessary, and open **E81Apply** from the data files for this lesson.
2. Save the file as **E81Apply_xx** in the location where your teacher instructs you to store the files for this lesson.
3. Run the Document Inspector, and remove any found information.
4. Add the password **marketing456&** to the workbook.
5. Add the keywords **marketing, yearly budget** to the workbook, and close the Properties dialog box. Your workbook should look like the one shown in Figure 81-2 in the Backstage view.
6. Save and close the file, and exit Excel.

Figure 81-2

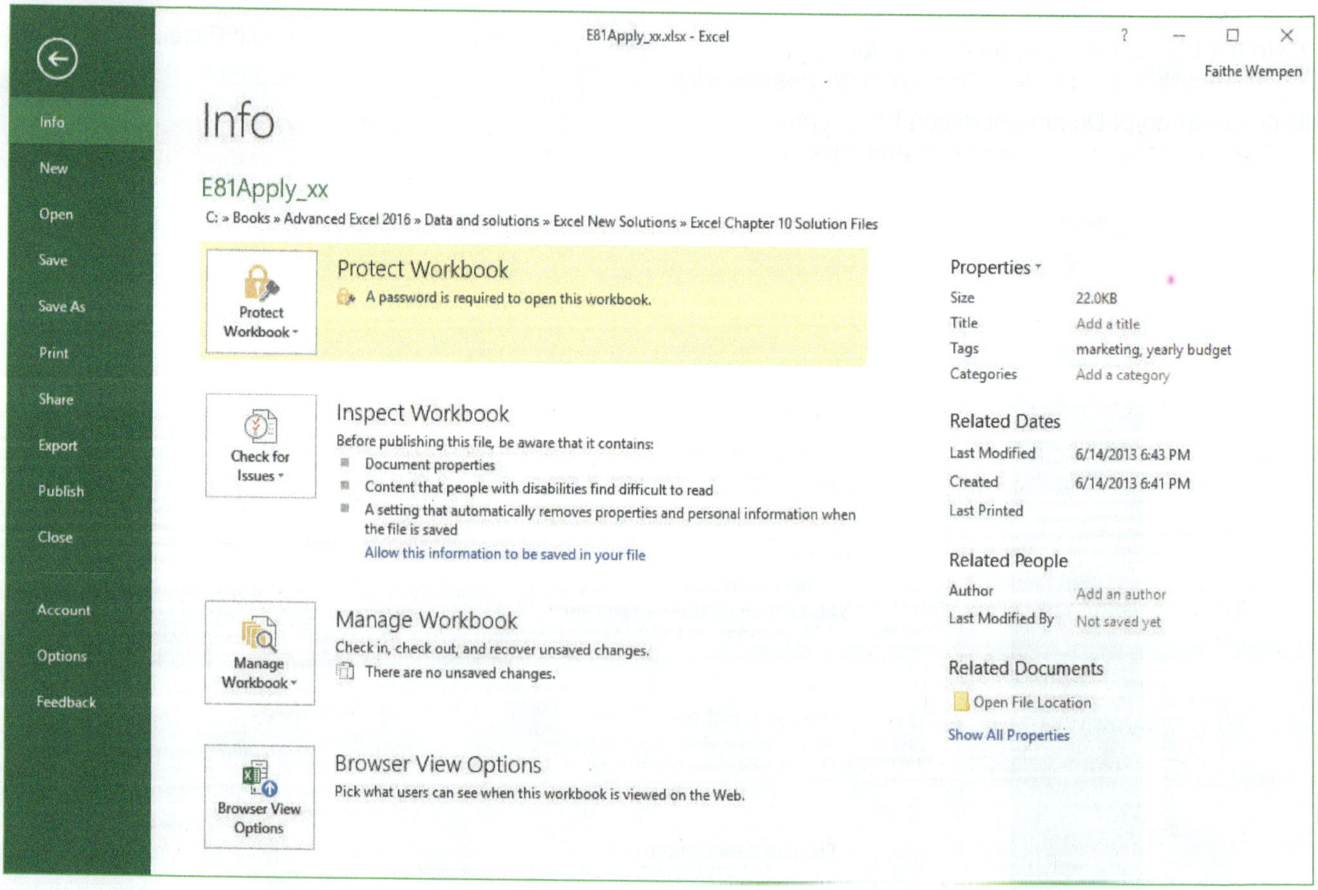

Excel 2016, Windows 10, Microsoft Corporation

Lesson 82

Finalizing a Workbook

➤ What You Will Learn

Adding a Digital Signature
Checking for Accessibility Issues
Marking a Workbook As Final
Managing Versions

Software Skills Especially when you're working with sensitive financial data, you need some way of letting others know a workbook they review is authentically from you. You can digitally sign the workbook to let your colleagues know that they are working with an approved version of the file. Excel offers features to make workbooks easier for users with disabilities to use. You can check the accessibility of your workbook and correct a workbook for possible issues. When you are finished with your workbook, you can mark it as final to show that no further changes should be made to the file. Use Excel's Manage Versions feature to search for an auto-saved version of a file you have not yet manually saved.

What You Can Do

Adding a Digital Signature

- You can apply a **digital signature** to a worksheet or a workbook to indicate that the information is authentically from you.
- To sign the worksheet or workbook with a digital signature, you need a digital ID. You can obtain a digital ID from a Microsoft Partner.

  ✓ *Follow your instructor's instruction on how—or whether—to use digital signatures with Microsoft Excel.*

- You can add a digital signature line to a worksheet by using the Signature Line command in the Text group on the Insert tab.
- To sign a digital signature line, right-click the digital signature line and click Sign.
- You can assign a digital signature to a workbook by clicking File, and using the Protect Workbook command on the Info tab in the Backstage view.
- When you add a digital signature, you can enter a purpose or instructions to the signer.
- A digital signature remains valid as long as the workbook is not changed.
- If you change the workbook at a later time, you will need to sign the file again to make the signature valid.

WORDS TO KNOW

Accessibility
The ability to make documents easier for people with disabilities to use.

Accessibility Checker
A feature in Excel that checks for and displays issues in a document that might be challenging for a user with a disability.

Alternative text (alt text)
Text that appears when you move the mouse pointer over a picture or object.

Digital Signature
An electronic signature that is stored with the workbook to let others know the file is authentic or meets a standard that is important to the group.

Try It! Adding a Digital Signature Line to a Worksheet

1. Start Excel, and open **E82Try** from the data files for this lesson.
2. Save the file as **E82Try_xx** in the location where your teacher instructs you to store the files for this lesson.
3. Click cell F16.
4. Click Insert > Add a Signature Line.
5. In the Signature Setup dialog box, click in the Suggested signer box, and type your name.
6. Click OK. A digital signature line appears.
7. Save the changes to the file, and leave it open to use in the next Try It.

The Signature Setup dialog box

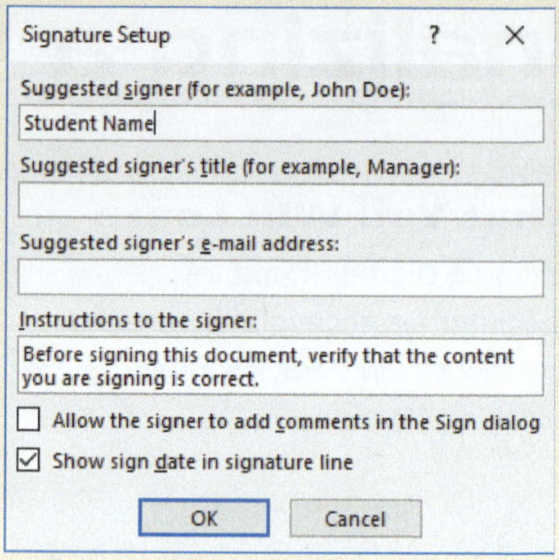

Excel 2016, Windows 10, Microsoft Corporation

Try It! Adding a Digital Signature

1. In the **E82Try_xx** file, click File.
2. In the Backstage view, on the Info tab, click Protect Workbook > Add a Digital Signature.

   ✓ *Follow your instructor's instruction on how—or whether—to use digital signatures with Microsoft Excel.*

3. If so instructed, in the Get a Digital ID dialog box, click No.
4. In the worksheet, right-click the digital signature line, and click Sign.
5. If so instructed, in the Get a Digital ID dialog box, click No.
6. Save the changes to the file, and leave it open to use in the next Try It.

Checking for Accessibility Issues

- You can use **accessibility** features in Excel 2016 to make workbooks more accessible to users with disabilities.
- Use the **Accessibility Checker** to check and correct a workbook for possible issues that might make it hard for a user with a disability to read or interpret the content.
- Access the Accessibility Checker from the Check for Issues button on the Info tab on the File tab in the Backstage view.
- **Alternative text**, or **alt text**, is an accessibility feature that helps people who use screen readers to understand the content of a picture in a workbook.

  ✓ *Alt text may not work with touch-screen or mobile devices.*

- When making a workbook accessible, you should include alt text for objects such as pictures, embedded objects, charts, and tables.
- When you use a screen reader to view a workbook, or save it to a file format such as HTML, alt text appears in most browsers when the picture doesn't display.

  ✓ *You may have to adjust the computer's browser settings to display alt text.*

- You can add alt text from the Size & Properties button on the Format Picture task pane.

Try It! Using the Accessibility Checker

1. In the **E82Try_xx** file, click File.
2. In the Backstage view, on the Info tab, click Check for Issues > Check Accessibility. Notice the Missing Alt Text error.
3. Save the changes to the file, and leave it open to use in the next Try It.

The Accessibility Checker task pane

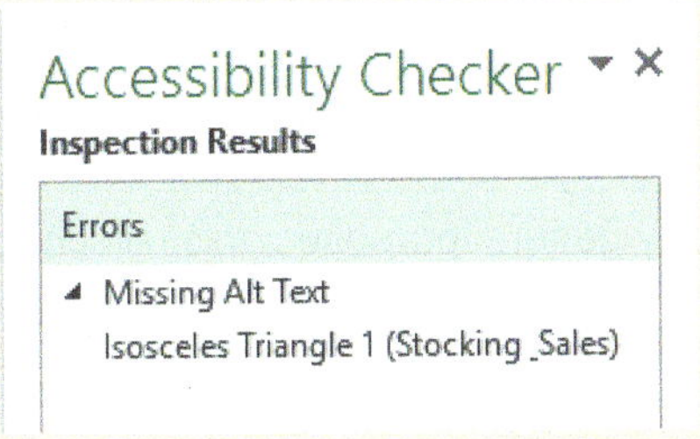

Excel 2016, Windows 10, Microsoft Corporation

Try It! Adding Alternative Text (Alt Text)

1. In the **E82Try_xx** file, right-click the triangle, and click Size and Properties to display the Size and Properties group of the Format Shape task pane.
2. Click Alt Text.
3. Click in the Title box, and type **Triangle**.
4. Click in the Description box, and type **A blue triangle, used as a decorative logo**. The Accessibility Checker Inspection Results now finds no accessibility issues.
5. Close the Format Shape and Accessibility Checker task panes.
6. Save the changes to the file, and leave it open to use in the next Try It.

The Alt Text group of the Format Shape task pane

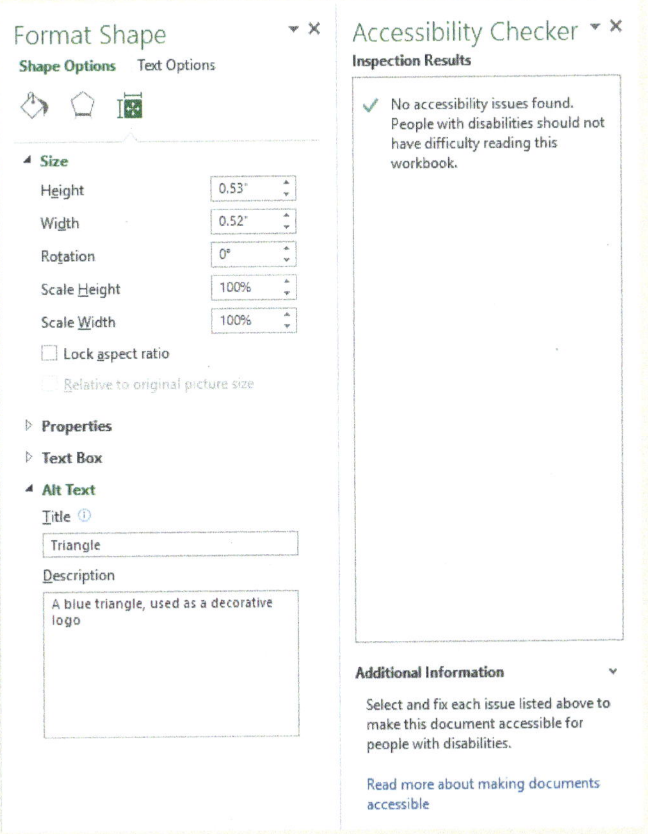

Excel 2016, Windows 10, Microsoft Corporation

Marking a Workbook As Final

- When you mark your workbook as final, colleagues who view the workbook see that it is marked as read-only so no further changes can be made.
- The message bar at the top of the Excel window lets users know that the file has been marked as final.
- For many general purposes, this level of protection may be fine, but users can click Edit Anyway in the message bar to continue to edit the file.
- Users can save the workbook under another name and edit the file as desired.
- If you need stronger security for the workbook, add a password or restrict editing privileges before sharing the file.
- When a file is marked as final, the Marked As Final icon appears in the status bar.
- When you add a digital signature to a file, the file is automatically marked as final.
- Before you can mark a file as final, you must turn off workbook sharing.

Try It! **Marking a Workbook As Final**

1. In the **E82Try_xx** file, click File > Protect Workbook.
2. Click Mark as Final.
3. Click OK.
4. In the information message box, click OK.
5. Close the file, and exit Excel.

Managing Versions

- Excel automatically saves your workbooks to a temporary folder while you are working on them.
- If you forget to save your changes, or if Excel crashes, you can restore the file using AutoRecover.
- If you don't see the file in the AutoRecover list, or if you're looking for an auto-saved version of a file that has no previously saved versions, you can use the Manage Versions feature to search for the file.
- Access the Manage Versions command from the Info tab of the File tab.
- You can recover unsaved workbooks from the default location of the UnsavedFiles folder.
- You can also use the Manage Versions command to delete all unsaved workbooks.

Lesson 82—Practice

You work for the Grounds for Thought Coffee Company, and you need to enhance the company's expense report form. This form will allow employees to get reimbursed by the company. You want to add two digital signature lines to the worksheet, one for the employee and one for the manager. You also want to check for any accessibility issues and correct them.

DIRECTIONS

1. Start Excel, if necessary, and open **E82Practice** from the data files for this lesson.
2. Save the file as **E82Practice_xx** in the location where your teacher instructs you to store the files for this lesson.
3. Add a header that has your name at the left, the date code in the center, and the page number code at the right, and change back to **Normal** view.

4. Add a digital signature for an employee signature in cell C20.
   a. Click cell **C20**.
   b. Click **Insert** > **Signature Line**.
   c. In the Signature Setup dialog box, click in the **Suggested signer** box, and type **Employee Signature**.
   d. Click **OK**.
5. Add a digital signature for a manager in cell F20 using the process in step 4.
6. Check the workbook for accessibility issues.
   a. Click **File**.
   b. In the Backstage view, on the Info tab, click **Check for Issues** > **Check Accessibility**.
7. Close the Accessibility Checker task pane.
8. Change the page layout orientation to **Landscape**.
9. **With your teacher's permission,** print the worksheet using the Fit Sheet on One Page scaling option. Your workbook should look like the one shown in Figure 82-1.
10. Save and close the file, and exit Excel.

Figure 82-1

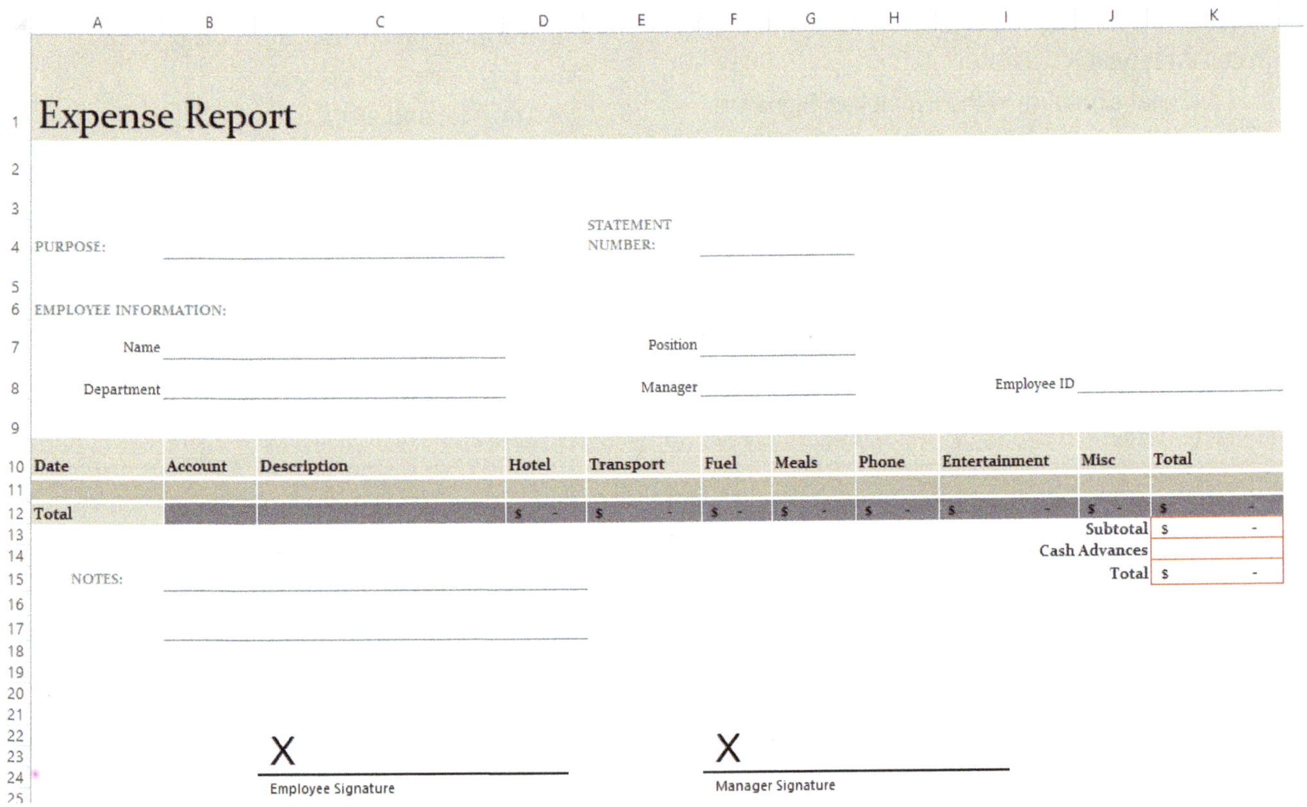

Excel 2016, Windows 10, Microsoft Corporation

Lesson 82—Apply

You have just traveled to a coffee convention for the Grounds for Thought Coffee Company. You now need to complete an expense report to get reimbursed by the company for your travel expenses. You want to complete the worksheet, check for and correct any accessibility issues, and mark the workbook as final before submitting it to your manager.

DIRECTIONS

1. Start Excel, if necessary, and open **E82Apply** from the data files for this lesson.
2. Save the file as **E82Apply_xx** in the location where your teacher instructs you to store the files for this lesson.
3. In cell **C7**, type your name.
4. In cell **A11**, type **=TODAY()**.
5. Add a digital signature to the Employee Signature line.
   a. Right-click the **Employee Signature line**.
   b. Click **Sign**.
   c. Follow your instructor's instruction on how to sign with a digital signature.
6. Check the workbook for accessibility issues. Ignore the Merged Cells errors.
7. Mark the workbook as final.
   a. Click **File** > **Protect Workbook**.
   b. Click **Mark as Final**.
   c. Click **OK**.
   d. In the information message box, click **OK**.
8. Close any open task panes.
9. Close the file, and exit Excel.

Lesson 83

Sharing a Workbook

➤ What You Will Learn

Setting Precise Margins for Printing
Uploading a Workbook to OneDrive

Software Skills After you finish working with workbook content and adding a digital signature, you may be ready to share your file with others. Excel makes it easy to send a worksheet to colleagues. You can make some last-minute choices about the margins for printing the worksheet information and, if you like, you can post the workbook on Windows OneDrive so that you can access and modify it using Excel Online.

WORDS TO KNOW

OneDrive
A free Microsoft offering that enables you to post and share documents in a Web-based library. You can also use OneDrive with Excel Online to co-author workbooks.

Excel Online
The online version of Excel that you can access through OneDrive or Office.com.

What You Can Do

Setting Precise Margins for Printing

- Excel offers a number of ways to control what you want to print.
- You can set a print area by highlighting the range you want to print and clicking Print Area in the Page Layout tab. Use the Set Print Area command to let the program know you want to print the highlighted range.
- You can enter precise measurements for the margins by setting print options:
  - Click File to display the Backstage view, and click Print. Click the Margins arrow toward the bottom of the center column, and click Custom Margins.
  - Enter the values you want to set for each of the page areas: header, right margin, footer, bottom margin, left margin, and top margin.
  - If you want to center the content horizontally or vertically (or both), click the check boxes in the Center on page area of the Page Setup dialog box.

Try It! Setting Precise Margins for Printing

1. Start Excel, and open **E83Try** from the data files for this lesson.
2. Save the file as **E83Try_xx** in the location where your teacher instructs you to store the files for this lesson.
3. Click File > Print.
4. Click Normal Margins > Custom Margins.
5. In the Page Setup dialog box, set the Top margin to 1.0, the Bottom margin to 1.25, and the Left and Right margins to 1.2.
6. Under Center on page, click to select the Horizontally check box.
7. Click OK.
8. Save the changes to the file, and leave it open to use in the next Try It.

Setting precise margins

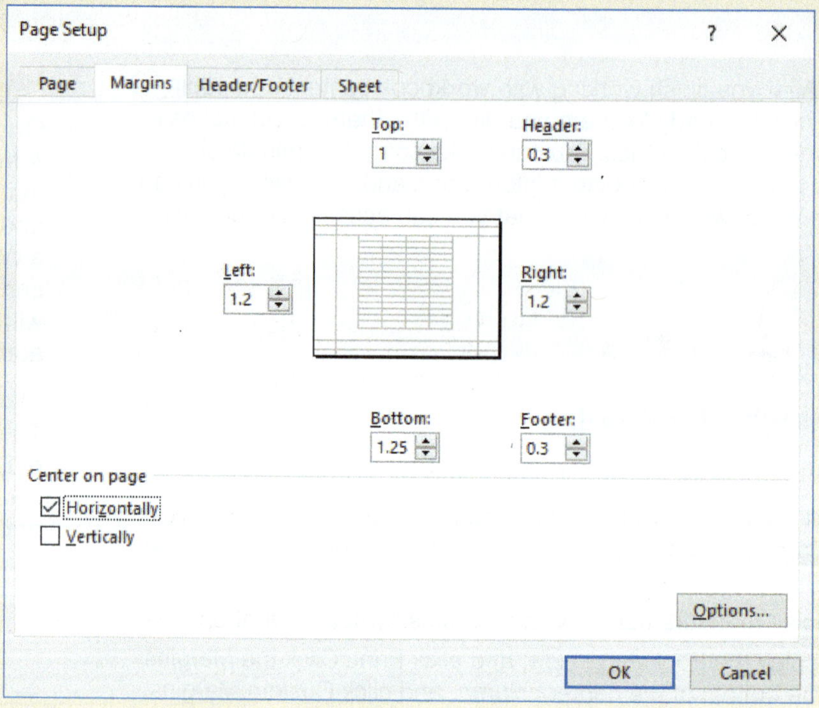

Excel 2016, Windows 10, Microsoft Corporation

Uploading a Workbook to OneDrive

- Excel offers you the ability to save a workbook to your **OneDrive** account so that you can work on it from any point you have Web access.
- If you don't have a OneDrive account, Excel will prompt you to create one when you choose Save To Cloud on the Share tab in the Backstage view.
- You can use OneDrive as your primary storage location for your documents, and access them from any computer at any time.
- You can use **Excel Online** to open, review, and edit your Excel files stored in OneDrive. You might do this when using a PC that does not have Excel installed, for example.
- When you open a workbook in Excel Online, the workbook opens in the Edit in Browser view and automatically displays the ribbon with the tools you need to review, edit, and save the file.
- You can choose to open the workbook in Excel instead of working in it in Excel Online if the PC you are using has Excel installed.
- Your changes to a file in Excel Online are automatically saved to OneDrive.

Try It! Uploading a Workbook to OneDrive

1. In the **E83Try_xx** file, click File > Save As.
2. Double-click OneDrive - Personal .
3. If you don't have a Windows account, click Sign up now.

   ✓ *Your teacher will let you know if you should sign up for an account.*

   OR

   If you already have an account, but are not already signed into it, click Sign In, enter your Windows e-mail address and password, and click Sign in.
4. If a shortcut appears to the desired folder on OneDrive, click it.

   OR

   Click Browse, and then in the navigation pane in the Save As dialog box, click OneDrive and then navigate to the desired folder.

   ✓ *Your teacher will let you know which account and folder to use to store the file.*
5. In the File name box, type **E83Try_online_xx**.
6. Click Save.
7. Close the workbook, and close Excel.

Try It! Working in Excel Online

1. Open your Web browser, and go to **https://onedrive.live.com**.
2. If prompted, sign in with your Microsoft ID.
3. Click the folder in which you saved the workbook file.
4. Click the workbook to display it in the Microsoft Excel Online window. Excel Online automatically displays the ribbon with the tools you need to review, edit, and save the file.
5. In Excel Online, on the Info & Schedule worksheet tab, click cell E4 and type **Jonas Smith**.
6. Click cell E5, and type your name.
7. In Excel Online, click EDIT IN EXCEL.
8. Click Yes to confirm that you want to open the file. Close the information box that lets you know the workbook is opening in Excel. The workbook opens in Excel.
9. Click cell J6, and type today's date.
10. Save the Excel file, and close Excel.
11. Review the workbook in the browser.
12. Close the browser to sign out of OneDrive.

(continued)

Try It! Working in Excel Online *(continued)*

Working in Excel Online

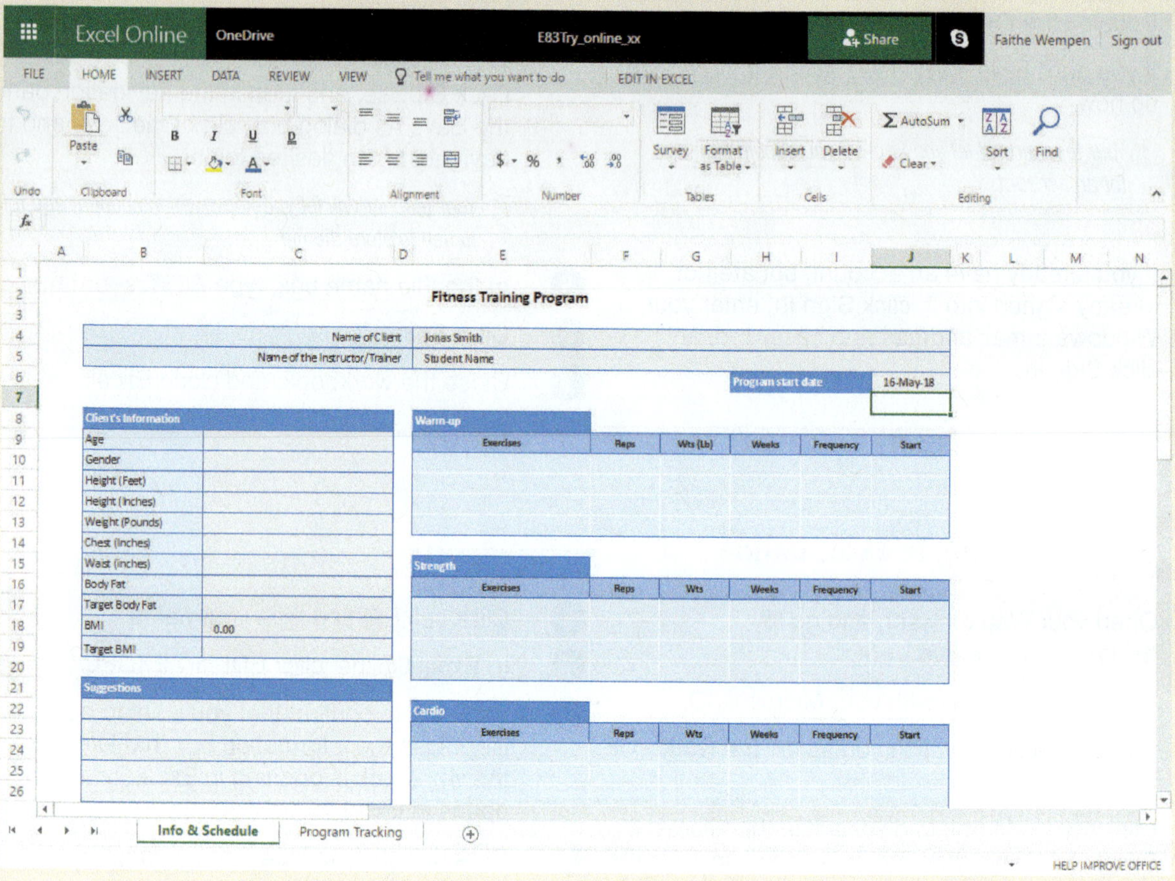

Excel 2016, Windows 10, Microsoft Corporation

Lesson 83—Practice

You and two of your colleagues are collaborating on a research project that requires you to gather field data from a variety of sites around the United States. During the course of your research, you will need to be able to share your workbook with each other online. You want to change the margins of the data tables so that you can print your results to be included in the final research workbook.

DIRECTIONS

1. Start Excel, if necessary, and open **E83Practice** from the data files for this lesson.
2. Save the file as **E83Practice_xx** in the location where your teacher instructs you to store the files for this lesson.
3. Click **File** > **Print**.
4. Click **Normal Margins** > **Custom Margins**.
5. In the Page Setup dialog box, set the **Top** margin to **0.5**, the **Bottom** margin to **0.5**, and the **Left** and **Right** margins to **1.0**.
6. Click **OK**.

7. Click **Scaling** > **Fit Sheet on One Page**.

   ✓ *The wording of the Scaling option depends on previous use of the feature; it may appear as No Scaling or Custom Scaling, for example.*

8. Click Save.
9. Save the file to the OneDrive.

   ✓ *Your instructor will let you know if you should sign up for an account.*

   a. Click **File** > **Save As**.

   b. Double-click **OneDrive - Personal**, and click the folder in which you want to save the file, or click Browse and browse to the desired location.

      ✓ *Your teacher will let you know which account and folder to use to store the file.*

   c. In the Save As dialog box, in the File name box, type **E83Practice_online_xx**.

   d. Click **Save**.

10. Close the workbook in Excel.
11. Open your Web browser, and go to **https://onedrive.live.com**.
12. Sign in if necessary.
13. Click the folder where you saved the workbook, and click the **E83Practice_online_xx** workbook to display it in Excel Online.
14. Edit the file in your browser by changing the dates in the Survey 1 column to the current date. Your file should look like the one shown in Figure 83-1.
15. Close the workbook in Excel Online.
16. Close the browser to sign out of OneDrive.

Figure 83-1

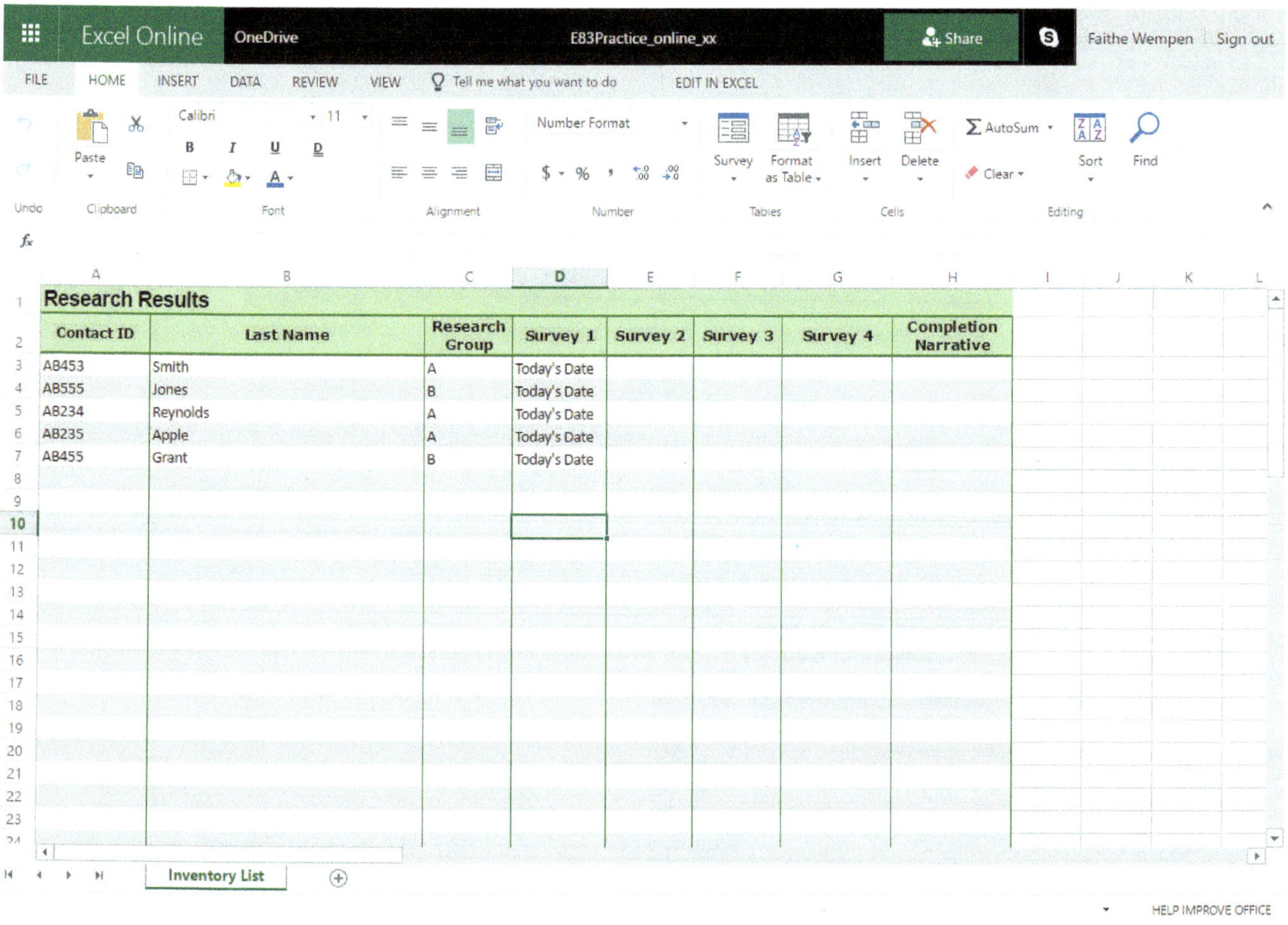

Excel 2016, Windows 10, Microsoft Corporation

Lesson 83—Apply

You are collaborating on a research project with several other people. You need to gather field data from a variety of sites around the United States. During the course of your research, you want to share your workbook online and set custom print margins so that the full report can be printed.

DIRECTIONS

1. Start Excel, if necessary, and open **E83Apply** from the data files for this lesson.
2. Save the file as **E83Apply_xx** in the location where your teacher instructs you to store the files for this lesson.
3. Set the print margins for the worksheet so that the content is centered **vertically** and **horizontally** on the page and the margins are **0.75** all the way around.
4. Save the file to your OneDrive account as **E83Apply_online_xx**, close the Excel workbook, and close Excel.
5. Open your Web browser, and go to **https://onedrive.live.com**.
6. Sign in with your Microsoft ID if prompted.
7. Click the OneDrive folder where you saved the workbook file.
8. Click the **E83Apply_online_xx** workbook to display it in Excel Online.
9. In Excel Online, enter the following data in the cell range A6:D7 as shown in Figure 83-2:

AB235	Apple	A	10/1/2017
AB455	Grant	B	9/30/2017

10. Close the workbook in Excel Online.
11. Close the browser to sign out of OneDrive.

Figure 83-2

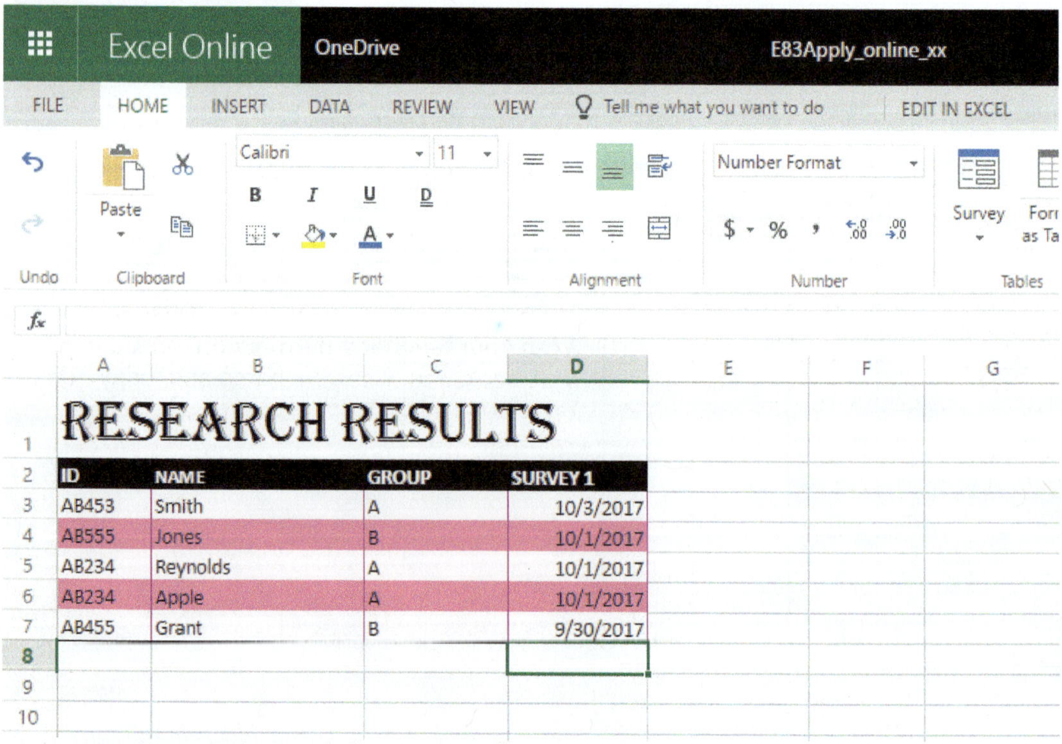

Excel 2016, Windows 10, Microsoft Corporation

End-of-Chapter Activities

➤ Excel Chapter 10—Critical Thinking

Assessing Educational Outcomes

Your school has been working hard to raise test scores in Math and Science, and one of the projects your teachers have undertaken this year involves doing a series of assessments that track a series of results in Math and Science classes.

You have been given a workbook that someone else created, so you want to check the workbook for data integrity and accessibility. Because a variety of teachers will be adding values to the worksheet, you need to set up the file for track changes and sharing. You also want to use data validation rules to circle the failing scores and make them easier to identify. You will encrypt the file and save it to a Windows OneDrive account so all teachers can access the file from home as well as school.

DIRECTIONS

1. Start Excel, if necessary, and open **ECT10** from the data files for this chapter.
2. Save the file as **ECT10_xx** in the location where your teacher has instructed you to save files for this chapter.
3. Inspect the workbook for issues. Do not remove any of the document properties or personal information.
4. Check and correct any accessibility issues.
5. Click **Review**, and turn on the sharing feature.
6. Set Track Changes to highlight all changes that are introduced. In the **When** box, select **All**.
7. Make changes to the values in column E.
8. Save the file, and use Highlight Changes to display the change history on a new sheet.
9. View the change history.
10. Remove sharing from the workbook.
11. In cell **I22**, add a digital signature line, and in the suggested signer box, type **Approver for assessment scores**.
12. For all cells with scores, add data validation for a **whole number** that is **greater than or equal to 25**. Circle the invalid data of failing percentages.
13. Save the file, and then save the file to your OneDrive account as **ECT10_online_xx**. Close the Excel workbook, and close Excel.
14. Open your Web browser, and go to **https://onedrive.live.com**.

    ✓ *Check with your teacher before you access the Web. Depending on the security settings for your computer lab, you may be limited in the types of sites you can access and use.*
15. Log in to your OneDrive account, and open the workbook.
16. Click OK to remove the data validation and digital signature objects from the file.
17. Edit the file in the browser by making changes to the values, and save the file. Your file should look similar to Illustration 10A on the next page.
18. **With your teacher's permission,** print the workbook, and write your name and today's date on the printout.
19. Close the browser to sign out of OneDrive.

Illustration 10A

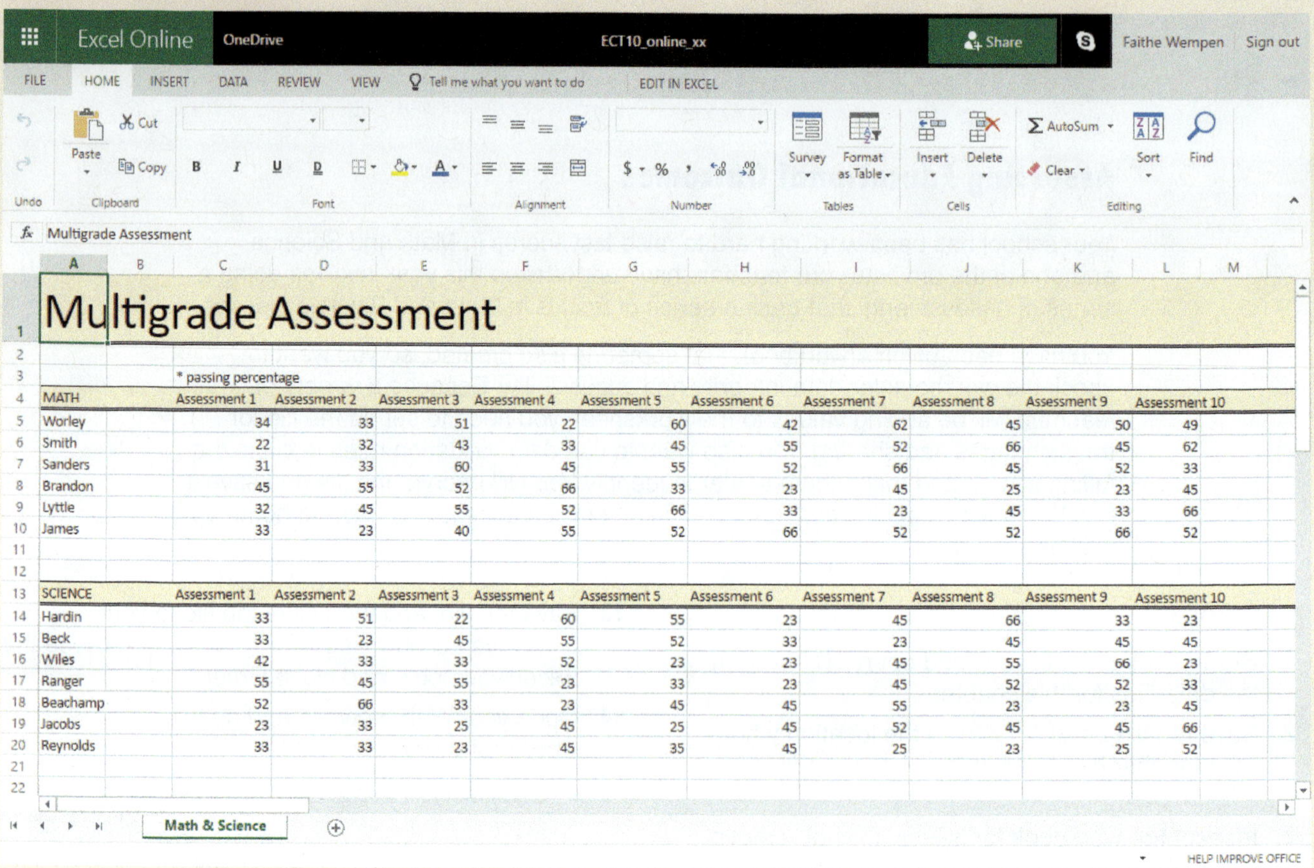

MATH	Assessment 1	Assessment 2	Assessment 3	Assessment 4	Assessment 5	Assessment 6	Assessment 7	Assessment 8	Assessment 9	Assessment 10
Worley	34	33	51	22	60	42	62	45	50	49
Smith	22	32	43	33	45	55	52	66	45	62
Sanders	31	33	60	45	55	52	66	45	52	33
Brandon	45	55	52	66	33	23	45	25	23	45
Lyttle	32	45	55	52	66	33	23	45	33	66
James	33	23	40	55	52	66	52	52	66	52

SCIENCE	Assessment 1	Assessment 2	Assessment 3	Assessment 4	Assessment 5	Assessment 6	Assessment 7	Assessment 8	Assessment 9	Assessment 10
Hardin	33	51	22	60	55	23	45	66	33	23
Beck	33	23	45	55	52	33	23	45	45	45
Wiles	42	33	33	52	23	23	45	55	66	23
Ranger	55	45	55	23	33	23	45	52	52	33
Beachamp	52	66	33	23	45	45	55	23	23	45
Jacobs	23	33	25	45	25	45	52	45	45	66
Reynolds	33	33	23	45	35	45	25	23	25	52

Excel 2016, Windows 10, Microsoft Corporation

➤ Excel Chapter 10—Portfolio Builder

Budgeting a Movie

You've been working with a local video producer to help him put together a treatment for a new film he wants to produce. It's been a fun project, and now some major industry investors are interested in finding out more about the production.

The producer has asked you to create a draft of the budget that you, he, and the director will fine-tune together. You need to create the worksheet, share the file, password protect the worksheet, and save it to OneDrive so that each of you can access the file from any point you have Web access.

DIRECTIONS

1. Start Excel, if necessary, and open **EPB10** from the data files for this chapter.
2. Save the file as **EPB10_xx** in the location where your teacher has instructed you to save files for this chapter.
3. Set up the workbook for sharing.
4. Set the tracking options so all changes are recorded.
5. Enter dollar values in the cell range **E16:21** and the cell range **G16:21**.
6. Save the workbook, and display the change history.
7. On **Sheet1**, set the print margins to **0.5** all around, and center the content on the page.
8. Remove sharing from the workbook.
9. Protect the workbook structure. Do not use a password.
10. Mark the file as final.
11. Edit the file to remove the worksheet protection features.
12. Save the file to OneDrive as **EPB10_online_xx**. Close the Excel workbook, and close Excel.
13. Open the file in Excel Online, and edit the workbook in the browser window.
14. **With your teacher's permission,** print the workbook, and write your name and today's date on the printout.
15. Close the browser to sign out of OneDrive.

Chapter 4

(Courtesy Robert Kneschke/Shutterstock)

Customizing Tables and Databases

Lesson 26
Normalizing and Analyzing Tables

- Copying a Table
- Normalizing Table Structure
- A Normalization Example
- Deleting a Table
- Splitting a Table Using the Table Analyzer
- Identifying Object Dependencies

Lesson 27
Using Advanced Field and Table Properties

- Requiring an Entry and Allowing Zero-Length Entries
- Indexing a Field
- Working with Long Text Fields
- Creating and Using Attachment Fields
- Working with Table Properties
- Adding Hyperlinks

Lesson 28
Formatting and Correcting Tables

- Formatting Tables
- Checking Spelling

Lesson 29
Creating Macros

- Creating and Running a Standalone Macro
- Creating an Embedded Macro
- Printing Macro Details

End-of-Chapter Activities

Lesson 26

Normalizing and Analyzing Tables

➤ What You Will Learn

- Copying a Table
- Normalizing Table Structure
- A Normalization Example
- Deleting a Table
- Splitting a Table Using the Table Analyzer
- Identifying Object Dependencies

WORDS TO KNOW

1NF (First Normal Form)
A normalization standard which dictates that the table must contain no duplicate records.

2NF (Second Normal Form)
A normalization standard which dictates that all other fields must be fully dependent on the primary key.

3NF (Third Normal Form)
A normalization standard which dictates that every field must be directly dependent on the primary or composite key fields, not just indirectly dependent.

Composite key
A key that consists of two or more fields, the unique combination of which forms the key.

Normalized
A table that has been structured so that it conforms to 1NF, 2NF, and 3NF.

Primary key
The unique identifying field for each record, such as an ID number.

Software Skills Databases developed by beginners can sometimes suffer from structural problems that make the database prone to inconsistencies, excess duplication, and so on. By normalizing a database, you can make it both easier to use and less prone to errors.

What You Can Do

Copying a Table

- Often, normalizing a database involves making copies of tables and then modifying the copies.
- To copy a table, you must first close it. Then, you can either use the standard shortcut keys for copying and pasting in Windows (CTRL + C and CTRL + V, respectively) or use the Copy and Paste buttons on the Home tab.
- You have a choice of pasting the structure only, pasting the structure and data, or appending the data to an existing table.

Try It! Copying a Table

1. Start Access, and open **A26Try** from the data files for this lesson.
2. Save the file as **A26Try_xx** in the location where your teacher instructs you to store the files for this lesson. Click Enable Content if the information bar appears.
3. Click the Employees table to select it, but do not open it.
4. Press CTRL + C to copy the table.
5. Press CTRL + V to paste the table. The Paste Table As dialog box opens.
6. Click Cancel. Leave the database open to use in the next Try It.

The Paste Table As dialog box

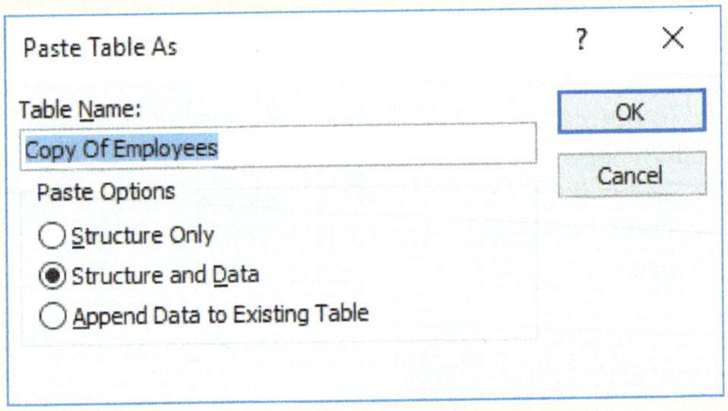

Access 2016, Windows 10, Microsoft Corporation

Normalizing Table Structure

- The choices you make as you design Access tables play a big part in the database's usability and effectiveness.
- In an effective database, tables will:
  - Calculate values when more appropriate than storing the raw data.
  - Link to external sources when required.
  - Use the appropriate field types and formats.
  - Apply data normalization rules to all tables.
- This lesson focuses on the last of those items: applying data normalization rules.
- A database is said to be **normalized** if it follows certain structural rules for avoiding repeated and redundant data.
- Normalization addresses problems such as:
  - Logical inconsistencies from the same information appearing differently in multiple records (such as a customer's address being different in two different orders).
  - Deletion of important data that should be retained when all records of a certain type are deleted (such as tax ID information about an instructor being removed if he is no longer actively teaching).
- Database designers rely on three main criteria for determining a table's degree of vulnerability to logical inconsistencies and abnormalities: **1NF (first normal form)**, **2NF (second normal form)**, and **3NF (third normal form)**.
- A table is in 1NF if it does not allow duplicate rows or null values. A table with a unique **primary key** or **composite key** (either of which, by definition, prevents two records from being complete duplicates of one another) and without any null values is in 1NF.
- A table is in 2NF if it is in 1NF and if all of the other fields are fully dependent on the primary key.
- For example, suppose you have a table with the following fields: Employee ID, Employee Name, Employee Address, and Skill.
- The combination of Employee ID and Skill is the composite key (that is, each record has a unique combination of those two values, but individual records might have the same value as one or the other of those fields).
- The table in Figure 26-1 on the next page is NOT in 2NF because there is the possibility for the same Employee ID to have two different addresses in this table, which would be in error.

Figure 26-1

Employee ID	Employee Name	Employee Address	Skill
1	Bob Smith	123 Main Street	Typing
1	Bob Smith	123 Main Street	Filing
2	Sharon Jones	370 East Warren	Typing
2	Sharon Jones	370 East Warren	Databases

Access 2016, Windows 10, Microsoft Corporation

- To normalize that table, you would need to create two separate tables: one with Employee ID and Skill in it, and another with Employee ID, Employee Name, and Employee Address in it. See Figure 26-2.

Figure 26-2

Employee ID	Skill
1	Typing
1	Filing
2	Typing
2	Databases

Access 2016, Windows 10, Microsoft Corporation

Employee ID	Employee Name	Employee Address
1	Bob Smith	123 Main Street
2	Sharon Jones	370 East Warren

Access 2016, Windows 10, Microsoft Corporation

- A table is in 3NF if it is in 2NF and if every field is directly dependent on the primary or composite key fields, not just indirectly dependent.
- For example, suppose you want to keep track of departments and their managers. Each department has only one manager, and each manager has only one department.
- You have a Departments table with these fields: Department, Manager, and Hire Date. See Figure 26-3.

Figure 26-3

Department	Manager	Hire Date
Sales	Bruce Duncan	12/7/2016
Operations	Jan Roth	5/15/2017
Accounting	Judy Braswell	8/1/2014
Marketing	Riley O'Malley	2/16/2016

Access 2016, Windows 10, Microsoft Corporation

- The Department field is the primary key. The Hire Date is only indirectly related to the Department field. It is directly related to the Manager field. The manager's hire date is irrelevant to the department.
- In this example, these two fields should not be in the same table. You should have separate tables for Managers and Departments. See Figure 26-4.

Figure 26-4

Department	Manager
Sales	Bruce Duncan
Operations	Jan Roth
Accounting	Judy Braswell
Marketing	Riley O'Malley

Access 2016, Windows 10, Microsoft Corporation

Manager	Hire Date
Bruce Duncan	12/7/2016
Jan Roth	5/15/2017
Judy Braswell	8/1/2014
Riley O'Malley	2/16/2016

Access 2016, Windows 10, Microsoft Corporation

- Whenever possible, you should try to use ID numbers for primary keys rather than text, even if it means adding another field to the table. It is much easier to make typos when typing text, so relying on the accuracy of text-based fields to be the primary key can be risky.
- The Managers and Departments tables can further be improved by adding Department ID and Manager ID fields. See Figure 26-5.

Figure 26-5

Department ID	Department	Manager
D01	Sales	M01
D02	Operations	M02
D03	Accounting	M03
D04	Marketing	M04

Access 2016, Windows 10, Microsoft Corporation

Manager ID	Manager	Hire Date
M01	Bruce Duncan	12/7/2016
M02	Jan Roth	5/15/2017
M03	Judy Braswell	8/1/2014
M04	Riley O'Malley	2/16/2016

Access 2016, Windows 10, Microsoft Corporation

A Normalization Example

- Now let's take a look at an example to further reinforce the concepts you just learned.
- The table in Figure 26-6 is not normalized.

Figure 26-6

Access 2016, Windows 10, Microsoft Corporation

Employee ID	First	Last	Position	Department ID	Department Name	Training	Date
1	John	Bell	Accountant	D1	Accounting	Orientation	4/15/2017
1	John	Bell	Accountant	D1	Accounting	Time Cards	4/16/2017
1	John	Bell	Accountant	D1	Accounting	Supervision	4/20/2017
2	Edith	O'Reilly	Assistant	D2	Operations	Orientation	6/1/2017
2	Edith	O'Reilly	Assistant	D2	Operations	Time Cards	6/2/2017

- This table could be problematic to use in the following ways:
  - What if a position is described differently for the same individual? For example, what if Edith's title is entered as Administrative Assistant in some records?
  - What if a person gets promoted into another position?
  - What if there are data-entry errors because of the unnecessary retyping of certain data, like Position, Department Name, and Training?
  - What if an employee quits and you delete his entries, but he was the only person to have taken a particular training class? Does that class's information get deleted from the system entirely?
- To normalize the table to 3NF, it needs to be split into four separate tables. The primary key fields are shown in italics here. Notice that the Training Completed table has a composite key consisting of a unique combination of Class ID and Employee ID.

Employees
Employee ID
First
Last
Position
Department

Departments
Department ID
Department Name

Training Classes
Class ID
Class Name

Training Completed
Class ID
Employee ID
Date

Access 2016, Windows 10, Microsoft Corporation

- You would then need to create relationships between the tables, as in the following illustration:

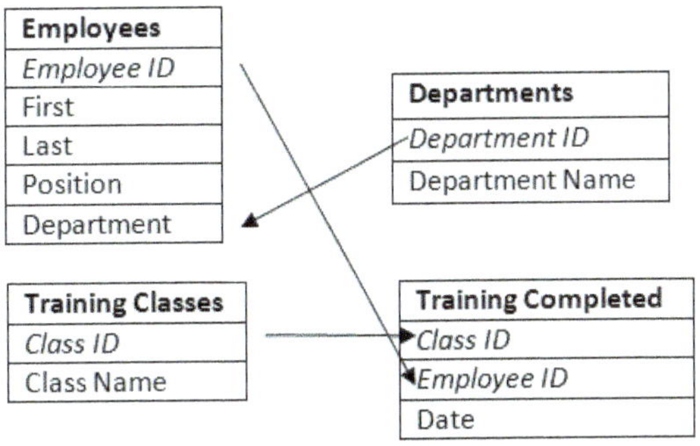

Access 2016, Windows 10, Microsoft Corporation

Try It! Normalizing a Database for First Normal Form (1NF)

1. In **A26Try_xx**, in the Navigation pane, double-click Employees to open it in Datasheet view.

   ✓ *Note that there is no primary key field; this is a violation of 1NF. This table has two records that are exact duplicates (8 and 9); this would not have happened if the table had a primary key field.*

2. In the Navigation pane, right-click the Employees table and click Design View.
3. Click Table Tools Design > Insert Rows. A new row appears at the top of the field list.
4. Type **ID** and press TAB to move to the Data Type column.
5. Open the Data Type drop-down list and click Number.
6. Click Table Tools Design > View. When prompted to save, click Yes.
7. In Datasheet view, select the last record and press DEL, removing the duplicate record. Click Yes to confirm the deletion.
8. In the ID field, number the remaining records consecutively, starting with 1.
9. Right-click the table's tab and click Design View.
10. On the Table Tools Design tab, click Primary Key. The table is now normalized to 1NF.
11. Right-click the table's tab and click Close. Click Yes when prompted to save changes.
12. Leave the database open to use in the next Try It.

Try It! Normalizing a Database for Second Normal Form (2NF)

1. In **A26Try_xx**, double-click the Employees table to open it in Datasheet view.

   ✓ *Notice that there are many records for which almost all the fields are duplicated. This is a violation of 2NF.*

2. Right-click the table's tab and click Close.
3. Make a copy of the Employees table, as you learned in the Copying a Table section. Type the name **Employees Backup** and click OK.
4. Open the Employees table in Datasheet view again, and delete records 2, 3, 5, 6, and 8. One record for each employee remains.
5. Renumber the ID field entries for the remaining records 1, 2, and 3.
6. Switch to Design view and select the Duty field. On the Table Tools Design tab, click Delete Rows and then click Yes to confirm.
7. Switch to Datasheet view to check your work. Then close the table. If prompted, save the changes.

Each Employee has only 1 record now, and the Duty field is gone

ID	First	Last	Address	City	State	ZIP	Phone	Position	Wage
1	Jan	Smith	233 W. 38th Street	Indianapolis	IN	46242	317-555-8822	Custodian	$8.25
2	Tony	Emerson	5211 E. State Street	Noblesville	IN	46060	317-555-1498	Custodian	$7.75
3	Lois	Lowe	720 E. Warren	Macon	IL	62544	217-555-5576	Receptionist	$9.00

Access 2016, Windows 10, Microsoft Corporation

(continued)

Try It! Normalizing a Database for Second Normal Form (2NF) *(continued)*

8. Open the Duties table in Datasheet view, and delete records 4 and 5 so that each remaining record has a unique value in the Duty column.
9. Switch to Design view, and delete all the fields except ID and Duty, the same way you deleted the Duty field in step 6.
10. Change the ID field's Data Type setting to Short Text. Then switch to Datasheet view, saving changes when prompted.
11. Change the entries in the ID column to be consecutively numbered D1 through D6. Then close the table.

Each duty is unique and has a unique ID that begins with D

Duties

ID	Duty
D1	Mop Floors
D2	Wash Windows
D3	Empty Trash
D4	Set Up Lunchroom
D5	Answer Phones
D6	Greet Visitors

Access 2016, Windows 10, Microsoft Corporation

✓ *The ID numbers are changed to include "D" to help avoid confusing the ID numbers in this table with the ID numbers in the Employees table.*

12. Click Create > Table Design to start a new table in Design view. Create the following fields:

Field Name	Data Type
ID	Short Text
Employee	Number
Duty	Short Text

Access 2016, Windows 10, Microsoft Corporation

13. Select the ID field, and click Table Tools Design > Primary Key to set that field as the primary key.
14. Switch to Datasheet view. When prompted to save, click Yes. Type **Assignments** as the table name and click OK.
15. Enter the following records into the Assignments table:

ID	Employee	Duty
A1	1	D1
A2	1	D2
A3	1	D3
A4	2	D3
A5	2	D1
A6	2	D4
A7	3	D5
A8	3	D6

Access 2016, Windows 10, Microsoft Corporation

16. Close all tables, and click Database Tools > Relationships.
17. In the Show Table dialog box, select Assignments, Duties, and Employees and click Add. Then click Close. Move the Assignments table to display it between the other two tables, if necessary.
18. Drag the ID field from the Duties table to the Duty field in the Assignments table. In the Edit Relationships dialog box, mark the Enforce Referential Integrity check box and click Create.
19. Drag the ID field from the Employees table to the Employee field in the Assignments table. In the Edit Relationships dialog box, mark the Enforce Referential Integrity check box and click Create.
20. Click Relationship Tools Design > Close. When prompted to save changes, click Yes.
21. This database is now normalized to 2NF.
22. Leave the database open to use in the next Try It.

Relationships created between the tables connect their data

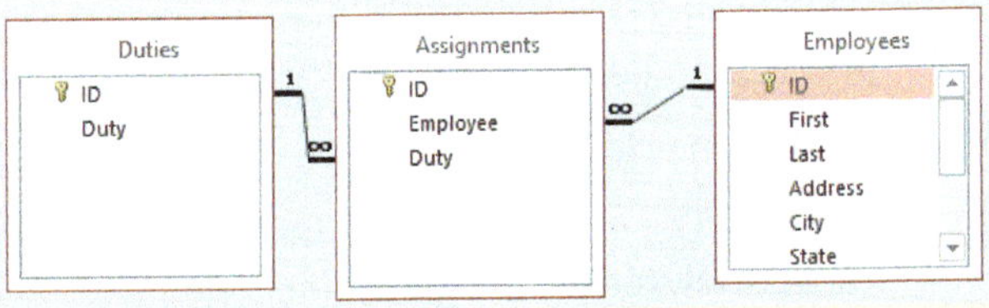

Access 2016, Windows 10, Microsoft Corporation

Deleting a Table

- After manually normalizing a database, as you did in the preceding exercise, you may find yourself with unwanted extra copies of some tables.
- To delete a table, first close it. Then from the Navigation pane, right-click the table and choose Delete, or select it and then press the DEL key on the keyboard. If prompted to confirm, click Yes.

✓ *Deleting a table permanently deletes all the data in it.*

Try It! Deleting a Table

1. In **A26Try_xx**, right-click Employees Backup in the Navigation pane.
2. Click Delete.
3. Click Yes.
4. Click File > Close to close the database file.
5. Leave Access open for the next Try It.

Splitting a Table Using the Table Analyzer

- The Table Analyzer offers a point-and-click interface that looks for normalization problems in your tables. If you are having trouble seeing the normalization issues intuitively, you may find this tool helpful.
- It works by looking at the table to identify repeated data, which could indicate 1NF or 2NF issues, and splits the table to solve the problem. It creates new tables; the original is left alone. You can then delete the original, if desired.

Try It! Running the Table Analyzer

1. Open **A26TryA** from the data files for this lesson.
2. Save the file as **A26TryA_xx** in the location where your teacher instructs you to store the files for this lesson. Click Enable Content if a security warning appears.
3. Click Database Tools > Analyze Table. The Table Analyzer Wizard opens.
4. Read the introductory information and click Next to continue. Then read the additional information and click Next again.
5. In the Tables list, click Employees > Next.
6. Click Yes, let the wizard decide. Click Next.
7. Examine the divisions that the Wizard suggested. Then, click Back to go back to the previous screen.
8. Click No, I want to decide. Click Next.
9. Drag the Duty field out of the Table1 field list. A Table Analyzer Wizard dialog box opens.

   ✓ *(Optional) Drag the field lists to resize or rearrange them if they are difficult to see.*
10. In the Table Name box, replace the default entry with **Duties** and click OK.
11. Click the Table1 field list and click the Add Generated Key button. A Generated Unique ID field appears in that field list.
12. Select all the fields in the Table1 list except Generated Unique Key and Lookup to Duties, and drag them out of the list. The Table Analyzer Wizard dialog box opens.
13. In the Table Name box, replace the default entry with **Employee Info** and click OK.
14. Double-click the Table1 field list heading. The Table Analyzer Wizard dialog box opens.
15. In the Table Name box, replace Table1 with **Assignments** and click OK.
16. In the Assignments table's field list, drag the Lookup to Employee Info field above the Lookup to Duties field.

(continued)

Try It! Running the Table Analyzer *(continued)*

17 Click Next, and then click Finish. The tables are split and a query is created that replicates the original table. The query opens in Datasheet view. The original table's name is changed to Employees_OLD.

✓ *If the Access Help window opens, close it.*

18 Right-click the query's tab and click Close.

19 Open the Assignments, Duties, and Employee Info tables in Datasheet view to examine them; then close them when finished.

20 Delete the Employees_OLD table, as you learned earlier in the lesson.

21 Leave the database open to use in the next Try It.

The finished redesign of the database structure

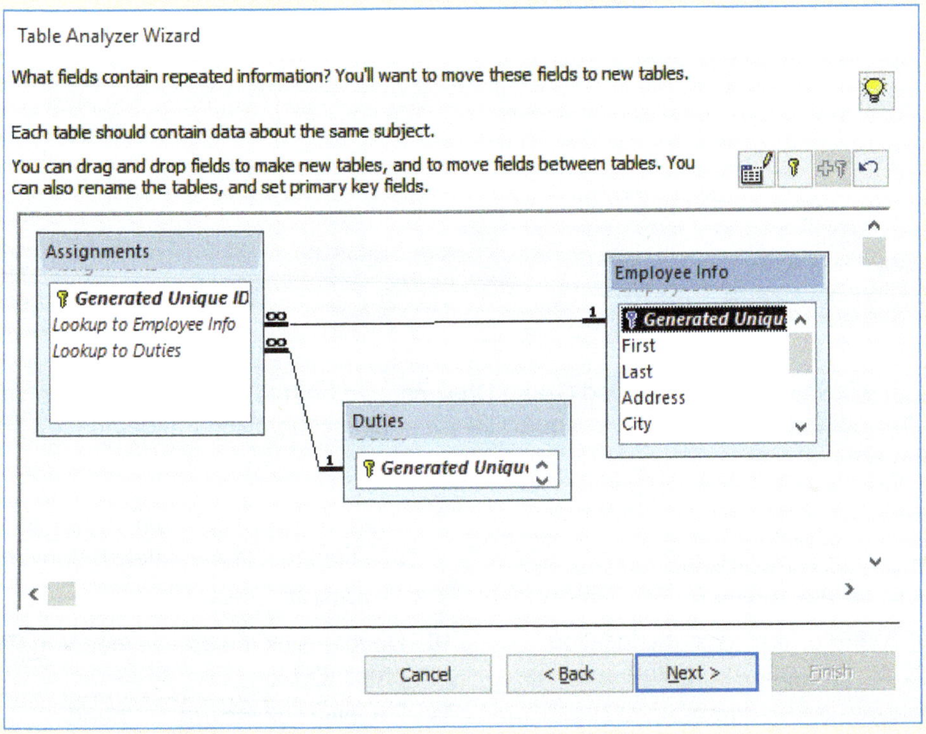

Access 2016, Windows 10, Microsoft Corporation

Identifying Object Dependencies

- Because Access is a relational database system with relationships between objects, many times the changes you make in one object affect another object.
- This is true not only between related tables, but also between tables and the forms, reports, and queries that are based on them. For example, if you change the name of a field in a table design, you might need to edit the label for that field manually on a report.
- In a complex database, it can be difficult to recall what objects rely on what other objects. The Object Dependencies task pane can be used to show these dependencies.
- When the Object Dependencies task pane is open, you can select an object from the Navigation pane and see its dependencies. The Object Dependencies task pane has two buttons: Objects that depend on me, and Objects that I depend on. Click one or the other to see the forward or backward dependencies.
- If you select a different object in the Navigation pane, the Object Dependencies task pane does not immediately update. Click its Refresh button to make it update.

Try It! Identifying Object Dependencies

1. In **A26TryA_xx**, in the Navigation pane, click Assignments.
2. Click Database Tools > Object Dependencies.
3. If a warning appears that information needs to be updated, click OK. If a message appears that objects need to be closed, click Yes. The Object Dependencies task pane opens.
4. Click the Objects that depend on me option button, if it is not already selected. A list of tables that draw data from the Assignments table appears.
5. Click the Objects that I depend on option button. The tables that provide data to the Assignments table appear on the list. (In this case, they are the same as the ones shown before.)
6. Click the arrow next to Duties under the Tables heading. A list of tables from which the Duties table draws data appears. In this case, it is just one table: Assignments.
7. Close the database, and exit Access.

Lesson 26—Practice

A friend is starting up a lawn care service called Green Designs, and he has created a single-table database in Access to hold his business records to date. He would like your help in improving the database's structure before he goes any further.

DIRECTIONS

1. Start Access, if necessary, and open **A26Practice** from the data files for this lesson.
2. Save the file as **A26Practice_xx** in the location where your teacher instructs you to store the files for this lesson.
   ✓ *If a security warning bar appears, click Enable Content.*
3. Double-click the **Business** table to open it in Datasheet view and evaluate its current structure.
   ✓ *Look for violations of 1NF, 2NF, and 3NF.*
4. Right-click the table's tab and click **Close**.
5. Click **Database Tools** > **Analyze Table**. The Table Analyzer Wizard dialog box opens.
6. Click **Next** twice to skip the informational screens.
7. Click **Next** to accept the Business table as the table to analyze.
8. Click **Yes, let the wizard decide.** Click **Next**.
9. Drag the **City** field from **Table4** to **Table2**, positioning it immediately before State.
   ✓ *Table4 disappears.*
10. Double-click the **Table1** heading. Type **Sales** and press ENTER.
11. Double-click the **Table2** heading. Type **Clients** and press ENTER.
12. Double-click the **Table3** heading. Type **Services** and press ENTER. Then click **Next**.
13. Click **Next** to accept the default choices for the primary keys for each table.
14. Click **No, don't create the query**.
15. Click **Finish**.
    ✓ *If you get the message "The command or action 'TileHorizontally' isn't available now," click OK to bypass it.*
16. Close the database, and exit Access. If instructed, submit it to your teacher for grading.

Lesson 26—Apply

In this project, you will modify the table structures in your friend's database.

DIRECTIONS

1. Start Access, if necessary, and open **A26Apply** from the data files for this lesson.
2. Save the file as **A26Apply_xx** in the location where your teacher instructs you to store the files for this lesson.

   ✓ *If a security warning bar appears, click Enable Content.*
3. Create new tables (or copy existing ones) and copy/modify tables to split the information from the **Business** table into the following three tables:

   Services table: **Service ID, Service**

   Sales table: **Sales ID, Client, Service, Service Date**

   Clients table: **Client ID, Client First Name, Client Last Name, Address, City, State, ZIP, Phone**

   ✓ *Set the data type for all fields in all tables to Short Text (except the Service Date field, which should be a Date/Time field).*

   ✓ *Delete duplicate records, as appropriate. Make up ID numbers for the records in each table. Add an S prefix to the Service IDs, an A prefix to the Sales IDs, and a C prefix to the Client IDs.*

   ✓ *Make the first field in each table the primary key.*
4. In the Relationships window, create the relationships between the tables that will enable the database to function. Enforce referential integrity for all relationships.

   Service ID in the **Services** table > **Service** in the **Sales** table

   Client ID in the **Clients** table > **Client** in the **Sales** table
5. Check the relationships using the **Object Dependencies** task pane.
6. After you have copied all the data needed from the Business table, delete the **Business** table.
7. Close the database, and exit Access. If instructed, submit it to your teacher for grading.

Lesson 27

Using Advanced Field and Table Properties

➤ What You Will Learn

Requiring an Entry and Allowing Zero-Length Entries
Indexing a Field
Working with Long Text Fields
Creating and Using Attachment Fields
Working with Table Properties
Adding Hyperlinks

Software Skills After defining the table structures for your database and creating the relationships between them, you may want to tweak the internal properties of one or more tables, including using special field types such as Long Text and Attachment and setting options for the table as a whole. You may also want to insert hyperlinks in fields.

WORDS TO KNOW

Allow Zero Length
A property for a text, hyperlink, or long text field which enables that field to be non-blank but still contain zero characters.

Attachment field
A field type that enables the user to insert and store data files from other programs in the database. The attachments can then be saved to disk outside the database whenever needed, or opened in their native application.

Index
A feature of Access that allows you to speed up searches and sorts and can require that a field contain unique values for each record.

Required
A property for a field that, when set to Yes, forces the user to make an entry in the field for each record.

Rich text formatting
A widely accepted file format for text documents that includes basic character, paragraph, and document formatting.

What You Can Do

Requiring an Entry and Allowing Zero-Length Entries

- Two settings determine whether or not a field must contain data: **Required** and **Allow Zero Length**. They are different in these ways:
  - Required can be set for all field types except AutoNumber (because AutoNumber is by definition a required field). Fields are set to No by default for this property. If you set Yes for the Required property, and then try to save a record that contains no entry for that field, an error message appears.
  - Allow Zero Length is set specifically for short text, long text, or hyperlink fields. It allows you to enter a text string with zero characters in it to indicate that the field does not apply to that record, such as a middle initial entry for someone who has no middle initial. This means you are able to leave a field blank but it will still have a value. This feature is very useful in queries.
- Access allows these two field properties to be set independently, so the possibility exists for having a field that is required and yet that allows zero length. If both of those conditions exist, Access stores a zero-length text string instead of a null value in the field when you leave it blank.

Try It! Setting the Required and Allow Zero Length Properties

1. Start Access, and open **A27Try** from the data files for this lesson.
2. Save the file as **A27Try_xx** in the location where your teacher instructs you to store the files for this lesson. Click Enable Content if the information bar appears.
3. Right-click the Assignments table and click Design View.
4. Click the Employee field.
5. On the General tab at the bottom of the window, set the Required property to Yes.
6. Right-click the table's tab and click Datasheet View. Click Yes when prompted to save changes. Click Yes when prompted that data integrity rules have changed.
7. Try to create a new record that leaves the Employee field blank.
8. When the error message appears, click OK.
9. Press ESC to clear the record you were making.
10. Right-click the table's tab again, and click Design View.
11. Click the Duty field.
12. On the General tab, set Allow Zero Length to Yes.
13. Set the Required property to No.
14. Right-click the table's tab and click Datasheet View. Click Yes when prompted to save changes.
15. Try to create a new record that leaves the Duty field blank.

    ✓ *You will be able to leave the Duty field blank, but the field will have a value.*

16. Delete the record you created in Step 15. Right-click the table's tab and click Design View.
17. Click in the Duty field.
18. On the General tab, set the Required property back to Yes and the Allow Zero Length property back to No.

Set the Duty field to be required and not to allow zero length

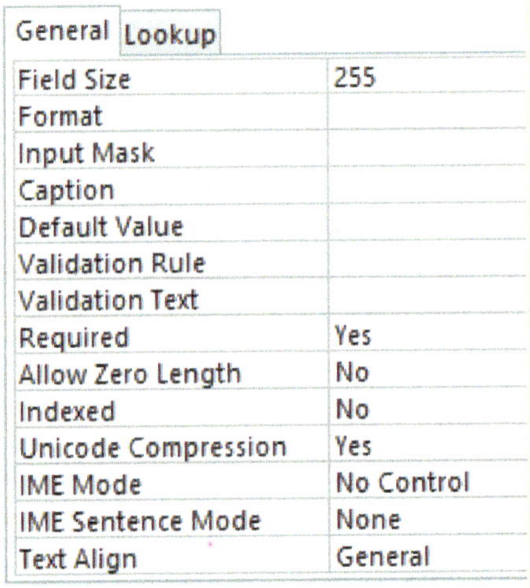

Access 2016, Windows 10, Microsoft Corporation

19. Right-click the table's tab and click Close. Click Yes when prompted to save changes. Click Yes when prompted that data integrity rules have changed.
20. Leave the database open to use in the next Try It.

Indexing a Field

- An **index** makes searching, sorting, and grouping go faster. The speed improves when you use the Find and Sort commands in tables, queries, and forms; the sort and criteria rows in queries; and the sorting and grouping options in reports.
- A minor drawback of indexing comes when you add or delete records. If you are adding one record at a time, you won't see a difference. However, appending many records at once may take longer if you have many indexes.
- When you create a primary key, the field is automatically indexed. You can index other fields by changing the Indexed property of the field to Yes (No Duplicates) or Yes (Duplicates OK).
- Index as many fields as you need, but you cannot index long text, OLE object, attachment, or hyperlink fields.
- Each index has a name, a field (or fields) that makes up the index, a sort order, and three properties:
  - Primary: This identifies which index is the primary key. You can set this by assigning a primary key in Table Design view. Only one index can be the primary index.
  - Unique: When you set the Indexed property to Yes (No Duplicates), this property changes to Yes.
  - Ignore Nulls: If you expect to have lots of blanks, change this to Yes to exclude null values from the index and speed up the searches.

Try It! Indexing a Field

1. In A27Try_xx, in the Navigation pane, right-click Employees and click Design View.
2. Click the ZIP field.
3. On the General tab at the bottom of the window, set the Indexed property to Yes (Duplicates OK).
4. Leave the database and Employees table open to use in the next Try It.

Try It! Viewing and Modifying Indexes

1. In A27Try_xx, with the Employees table open in Design view, click Table Tools Design > Indexes. The Indexes: Employees window opens.
2. Click the ZIP field in the Index Name column.
3. Click in the Ignore Nulls property.
4. Open the drop-down list for Ignore Nulls and click Yes.
5. Click the Close button to close the Indexes: Employees window.
6. Leave the table open in Design view to use in the next Try It.

Working with Long Text Fields

- On the surface, a long text field might appear simply to be a text field with a larger size limit. A long text field can contain up to 65,536 characters (whereas a Short Text field is limited to 255 characters).
- However, the Long Text field type has some other differences as well. For example, you can't index on a long text field.
- You can apply **rich text formatting** to the text in a long text field. For example, you can make certain text bold or underlined, and you can apply different fonts and colors.
- To apply rich text formatting to text in a long text field, you must first set the Text Format property for that field to Rich Text. By default, it is Plain Text.

✓ *The Text Formatting group on the Home tab contains the buttons for formatting text. If you apply formatting to text in some field type other than Long Text, or if you have not yet set the Text Format property for that long text field to Rich Text, the formatting applies to the entire datasheet.*

- Another feature of the Long Text field type is the ability to set a long text field to Append Only. This is one of the field's properties; when it is set to Yes, history will be collected on this field. This enables the Long Text field to be used for ongoing note-taking for records, without worrying that an untrained or careless worker will accidentally delete something that should be retained.
- The phrase "append only" is a bit misleading in that it does not prevent you from deleting or changing the content of the field. Instead, it makes a Show column history command available for that field when you right-click it. When you choose that command, you see a History for Notes dialog box that contains the versions of the field's content over time.
- If you want to clear the history for the field, you must set Append Only to No in the field properties in Table Design view, and then save the table. This clears the history from all records. You can then toggle Append Only to Yes if desired.

Try It! Using Rich Text Formatting in a Long Text Field

1. In **A27Try_xx**, with Employees open in Design view, click the Notes field.
2. On the General tab at the bottom of the window, set the Text Format property to Rich Text.
3. At the confirmation prompt, click Yes.
4. Right-click the table's tab and click Datasheet View. Click Yes when prompted to save changes.
5. Drag the right border of the Notes field's column header to the right to widen the field.

   ✓ *This gives you more room to enter and format text.*
6. Click in the Notes field for the first record and type **Winner of the Staff Performance Award**.
7. Select Staff Performance Award, and press CTRL + I to italicize the text.
8. With Staff Performance Award still selected, on the Home tab, click the down arrow next to the Font Color button, and select the red square.
9. Leave the table open to use in the next Try It.

Try It! Experimenting with Append Only

1. In **A27Try_xx**, right-click the Employees table's tab and click Design View.
2. Click the Notes field.
3. On the General tab, set the Append Only property to Yes.

   ✓ *You may need to scroll down to find that property, depending on your window size and display resolution.*
4. Right-click the table's tab and click Datasheet View. Click Yes when prompted to save changes.
5. In the Notes field for the first record, replace the current entry with **Received Safety Training 9/12** and press ENTER to move away from the field, saving the new entry.
6. Right-click the field and click Show column history. A History for Notes dialog box appears, listing the column history.

   ✓ *Notice that the entry you made earlier in that field is not on the list because you made it prior to turning on the Append Only feature.*
7. Click OK to close the dialog box.
8. Leave the table open to use in the next Try It.

Creating and Using Attachment Fields

- **Attachment fields** enable you to attach data files from word processing programs, spreadsheets, graphics editing programs, and so on. Attachments cannot be edited directly from within Access; the native application launches to edit them.
- Create an attachment field in Table Design view by setting the field type to Attachment. You cannot change a field's type to Attachment; you can select the Attachment type only when you first create the field.
- When you click the paper clip icon for an attachment field in a datasheet or form, the Attachments dialog box opens. From here you can add or remove attachments, open an attachment in its native program, or save an attachment to a separate file.

Try It! Creating and Using Attachment Fields

1. In **A27Try_xx**, right-click the Employees table's tab and click Design View.
2. Click in the first empty row of the field list, and type **Photo** in the Field Name column.
3. Open the Data Type drop-down list and click Attachment.
4. Right-click the table's tab and click Datasheet View. Click Yes when prompted to save changes.
5. Double-click the paperclip icon in the Photo column for the first record. The Attachments dialog box opens.
6. Click Add.
7. Navigate to the folder containing the data files for this lesson, and double-click **JanSmith.jpg**. The file becomes attached, and the file name appears in the Attachments dialog box.
8. Click OK. The dialog box closes and a (1) appears next to the paperclip icon for that record.
9. Leave the database open to use in the next Try It.

Try It! Saving and Removing an Attachment

1. In **A27Try_xx**, in the Employees table, double-click the paperclip icon for the first record. The Attachments dialog box opens. One attachment is listed.
2. Click **JanSmith.jpg** and click Save As.
3. Navigate to the folder where you are storing your completed work for this lesson.
4. Change the file name in the File Name box to **A27Trypic_xx.jpg**.
5. Click Save. The file is saved as a separate file.
6. In the Attachments dialog box, click **JanSmith.jpg**.
7. Click Remove.
8. Click OK to close the dialog box.
9. Right-click the table's tab and click Close.
10. Leave the database open to use in the next Try It.

Working with Table Properties

- Just as each field in a table has field properties, the table itself has properties that apply to the entire table.
- Here are the properties you can set for a table:

✓ *To get more space to enter or edit a property, click in the property and press* SHIFT + F2.

- Read Only When Disconnected: Specifies whether the table can be modified when it is disconnected from its data source. This is applicable only to remotely-stored databases, not to databases created and used on a single PC.
- Subdatasheet Expanded: Specifies whether or not any subdatasheets appear expanded by default when the table opens. If the subdatasheet is not expanded, a plus sign appears next to each record, and you can click that plus sign to expand the subdatasheet manually for a particular record.
- Subdatasheet Height: If the subdatasheet is set to be expanded, this setting controls how large it will be.
- Orientation: Set the view orientation for left-to-right or right-to-left, depending on your language. (English is left-to-right.)
- Description: Text you enter here will appear in tooltips for the table.
- Default View: Set Datasheet, PivotTable, or PivotChart as the default view when the table is opened.
- Validation Rule: You can enter an expression here that must be true whenever you add or change a record. You can also add validation rules to individual fields, of course; this box is mainly for multi-field validation rules, such as for setting up conditions where one field's value must be greater than another (for example, end time must come after start time).
- Validation Text: If you create a validation rule (see above), this specifies the message that is displayed when a record violates the rule.
- Filter: Here you can define criteria so that only rows matching the criteria will appear in the datasheet. This is like creating a query that filters records without actually creating the query.
- Order By: You can select one or more fields by which the data should be sorted by default.
- Subdatasheet Name: Here you can choose which subdatasheet should appear (if any). This is useful if the table has relationships with more than one other table and the wrong one is showing in the subdatasheet.
- Link Child Fields: This lists the fields in the table that are used for the subdatasheet that match the Link Master Fields property (see below).
- Link Master Fields: This lists the fields in the table that match the Link Child Fields property (see above).
- Filter On Load: If you defined criteria in the Filter field, you can set the criteria to be applied or not when the table opens. This is useful to turn the filtering off temporarily without erasing what you have put in the Filter field.
- Order By On Load: If you entered anything in the Order By field, you can turn it on or off here so that the sort order is or is not applied when the table opens.

Try It! Working with Table Properties

1. In A27Try_xx, right-click Employees and click Design View.
2. Click Table Tools Design > Property Sheet.
3. Set the Subdatasheet Expanded property to Yes.
4. Right-click the table's tab and click Datasheet View. Click Yes when prompted to save changes. The table appears with all the subdatasheets expanded.
5. Right-click the table's tab and click Design View.
6. Set the Subdatasheet Expanded property back to No. Close the Property Sheet.
7. Right-click the table's tab and click Close. Click Yes when prompted to save changes.
8. Leave the database open for the next Try It.

Adding Hyperlinks

- Hyperlinks can be added to any field that has been formatted with a Hyperlink data type.
- Using the Hyperlink data type in a form or datasheet automatically activates the hyperlink.
- If you are adding a hyperlink in an object that will not automatically activate it, such as in a report, you can add it using a bound hyperlink control.

Try It! Adding a Hyperlink

1. In A27Try_xx, right-click Employees and click Design View.
2. Click in the first empty row of the field list, and type E-mail in the Field Name column.
3. In the Data Type field, select the drop-down arrow and click Hyperlink.
4. Right-click the Employees tab and click Datasheet View. Click Yes when prompted to save changes.
5. Scroll to the E-mail column, and in the Jan Smith record, enter jansmith@greendesigns.com.
6. Close the database, and exit Access.

Lesson 27—Practice

In this project, you will help Ace Learning with their database. You will add an attachment field and use a table property to sort the records in the table by last name.

DIRECTIONS

1. Start Access, if necessary, and open A27Practice from the data files for this lesson.
2. Save the file as A27Practice_xx in the location where your teacher instructs you to store the files for this lesson.

   ✓ *If a security warning bar appears, click Enable Content.*
3. Right-click tblInstructors and click Design View.
4. Click in the Phone field.
5. On the General tab, set the Required property to Yes and the Allow Zero Length property to No.
6. Click in the ZIP field.
7. On the General tab, set the Indexed property to Yes (Duplicates OK).
8. Click in the first empty row of the field list in the Field Name column and type Documentation.
9. In the Data Type column for the new field, open the drop-down list and click Attachment.
10. Click Table Tools Design > Property Sheet.
11. Set the Order By property to LastName.
12. Click in the next empty row of the field list in the Field Name column and type E-mail.
13. In the Data Type column for the new field, open the drop-down list and click Hyperlink.
14. Right-click the table's tab and click Datasheet View. Click Yes when prompted to save changes. Click Yes when asked to continue with testing the existing data with the new rules.
15. Confirm that instructors are sorted by last name.
16. Go to the E-mail field in the row for Wendy Reynolds and enter wreynolds@yahoo.com.
17. Close the database, and exit Access. If instructed, submit it to your teacher for grading.

Lesson 27—Apply

You continue to work with Ace Learning's database. You will add and modify an attachment and add a long text field where the history is tracked.

DIRECTIONS

1. Start Access, if necessary, and open **A27Apply** from the data files for this lesson.
2. Save the file as **A27Apply_xx** in the location where your teacher instructs you to store the files for this lesson.

   ✓ *If a security warning bar appears, click Enable Content.*
3. Open **tblInstructors** in Datasheet view.
4. For the entry for instructor **Wendy Reynolds**, attach the file **Reynolds.txt** in the **Attachment** field.
5. Open the attachment from within Access, and change the year of her degree from 1990 to **1991**. Close the file, saving your changes.
6. Use **Save As** to save the attachment **Reynolds.txt** in the location where you are storing files for this lesson as **A27ApplyReynolds_xx.txt**.
7. Close **tblInstructors**.
8. Open **tblStudents** in Design view.
9. Add a long text field called **Notes**, and set its **Append Only** property to **Yes**.
10. Set the **Notes** field's **Text Format** property to **Rich Text**.
11. Switch to **Datasheet** view, saving all changes.
12. In the record for **Sean Gartner**, enter the following note into the Notes field:

    10/1/14: Nominated for Student of the Year.

    ✓ *Drag the right border of the Notes field's column header to the right to widen the field.*
13. Format the Words **Student of the Year** in bold and italics.
14. Edit the entry to read:

    10/1/17: Nominated for Student of the Year.
    12/1/17: Dean's List
15. View the field's history.
16. Close the database, and exit Access. If instructed, submit it to your teacher for grading.

Lesson 28

Formatting and Correcting Tables

➤ What You Will Learn

Formatting Tables
Checking Spelling

Software Skills Tables are not the most glamorous vehicle for presenting data to users because they are not usually formatted attractively. The column widths may be too large or small, the fonts may be difficult to read, and so on. You can apply a variety of formatting changes to a table that make it easier and more interesting to read. You can also run a spell check on a table to clean up any errors that may have been made in data entry.

What You Can Do

Formatting Tables

- You can apply most of the same types of formatting to tables that you can apply in a spreadsheet application such as Excel.
- The main difference is that the character formatting you apply to a table applies equally to all entries in the table; you cannot format specific records or fields separately.

  ✓ *The exception to that limitation is the Long Text type field which, as you learned in Lesson 27, can be set to Rich Text format and then the text within it can be separately formatted.*

- Character formatting includes font, font size, attributes such as bold and italic, and font color.
- Paragraph formatting applies to entire columns. For example, you can set a column to be horizontally aligned at the left, center, or right.
- The formatting tools are located on the Home tab.

Try It! Formatting a Table

1. Start Access, and open **A28Try** from the data files for this lesson.
2. Save the file as **A28Try_xx** in the location where your teacher instructs you to store the files for this lesson. Click Enable Content if the information bar appears.
3. Double-click the Employees table to open it in Datasheet view.
4. On the Home tab, click the Font drop-down list, and click Century Schoolbook (or any other font if you do not have that one).
5. Open the Font Size drop-down list and click 10.
6. Click the arrow on the Font Color button and click the dark red square.
7. Click in the ID column and click the Center button.
8. Click the Gridlines button and, on its menu, click Gridlines: None.
9. Click the arrow on the Background Color button and click the yellow square.
10. Click the arrow on the Alternate Row Color button and click an orange square.
11. Right-click the table's tab and click Close. Click No when prompted to save changes.
12. Leave the database open to use in the next Try It.

Checking Spelling

- Access includes a Spell Check feature. It is not as robust as the Spell Check feature included in Word, but it uses the same dictionaries (including any custom dictionaries you have created). See Figure 28-1.
- When a word is found that is not in the dictionary, a list of suggestions appears. Click the word that represents the correct spelling. Or, if none of the suggestions are right, make a correction directly in the Not In Dictionary text box.
- After selecting or typing the correct spelling, you can click Change to change only the found instance of a word or Change All to change all instances of that word in the table with the same misspelling.
- If the word is actually spelled correctly, you can click Ignore to ignore only this instance, Ignore All to ignore all instances in this table, or Add to add the word to the custom dictionary stored on your PC.

Figure 28-1

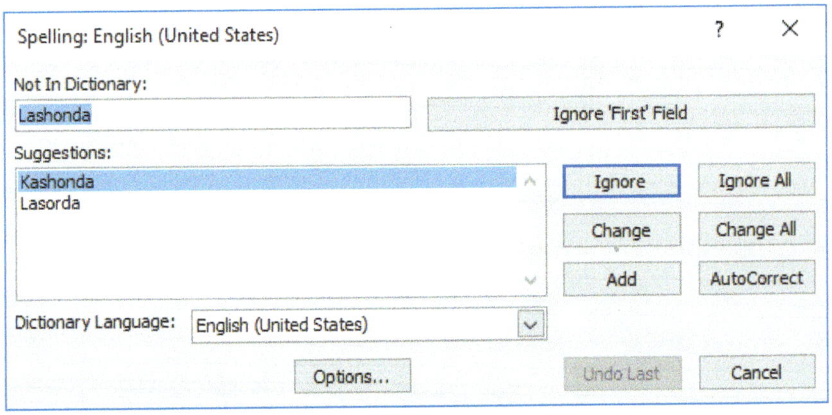

Try It! Checking Spelling

1. In **A28Try_xx**, in the Navigation pane, double-click the Duties table to open it in Datasheet view.
2. Click Home > Spelling. The Spelling dialog box opens.

   ✓ *The first misspelled word found is identified in the Not In Dictionary box. On the Suggestions list, Wash is already selected.*
3. Click Change. The next misspelling appears.
4. Click Change. The word is corrected and a message appears that the spelling check is complete.
5. Click OK.
6. Leave the database open to use in the next Try It.

Try It! Adding a Word to the Dictionary

1. In **A28Try_xx**, double-click the Employees table to open it in Datasheet view.
2. Click Home > Spelling.

   ✓ *A proper name appears as misspelled, but it is actually correct.*
3. Click Add. A message appears that the spell check is complete.
4. Click OK.
5. Close the database, and exit Access.

Lesson 28—Practice

In this project, you will fix spelling errors and change the alignment of the ID field in the Ace Learning database.

DIRECTIONS

1. Start Access, if necessary, and open **A28Practice** from the data files for this lesson.
2. Save the file as **A28Practice_xx** in the location where your teacher instructs you to store the files for this lesson.

   ✓ *If a security warning bar appears, click Enable Content.*

3. In the Navigation pane, double-click **tblClasses** to open it in Datasheet view.
4. Click **Home** > **Spelling**.
5. Click **Change** to change the first misspelled word.
6. Click **Change** to change the second misspelled word.
7. Click **Change** to change the third misspelled word.
8. Click **OK**.
9. Click in the **ID** column.
10. Click the **Align Left** button.
11. Right-click the table's tab and click **Close**. Click **Yes** when prompted to save changes.
12. Close the database, and exit Access. If instructed, submit it to your teacher for grading.

Lesson 28—Apply

The Ace Learning database has been in use for several weeks now, and the staff has been complaining that the datasheet is hard to read and that there are some spelling errors in the data. You will fix these problems.

DIRECTIONS

1. Start Access, if necessary, and open **A28Apply** from the data files for this lesson.
2. Save the file as **A28Apply_xx** in the location where your teacher instructs you to store the files for this lesson.

   ✓ *If a security warning bar appears, click Enable Content.*

3. Open **tblInstructors** and run a spell check. Ignore all possible spelling errors that are found in the Address field. Correct any other errors found.
4. Open **tblStudents** and run a spell check. Ignore all possible spelling errors that are found in the FirstName, LastName, and Address fields. Correct any other spelling errors found.
5. In **tblStudents**, change the alternate row color to **light green**.
6. In **tblStudents**, change the font to **12-point Times New Roman**.
7. In **tblStudents**, widen all the columns as needed so that the content fits (except the Notes field, which can stay truncated).

   ✓ *To widen a column, position the mouse pointer at the right edge of the column header and double-click.*

8. Set the **Gridlines** setting to **Gridlines: Horizontal**.
9. Close the table, saving the changes.
10. Close the database, and exit Access. If instructed, submit it to your teacher for grading.

Lesson 29

Creating Macros

➤ What You Will Learn

Creating and Running a Standalone Macro
Creating an Embedded Macro
Printing Macro Details

WORDS TO KNOW

Embedded macro
A macro that is stored in a database object, such as a table, query, form, or report.

Macro
A sequence of steps that are automatically performed when a specific trigger is activated.

Standalone macro
A macro that exists as a separate object in the database from any other table, query, form, or report.

User Interface (UI) macro
An embedded macro.

Software Skills Macros enable you to automate groups of steps so that they can be executed in a single action, such as pressing a key combination or clicking a button. Writing a simple macro requires no programming experience; the interface for creating a macro is point-and-click. More sophisticated macros can also be written in Visual Basic.

What You Can Do

Creating and Running a Standalone Macro

- A **standalone macro** is a macro that is saved as a separate object. You can run the macro from the Navigation pane, activate it with a shortcut key combination you assign, or start it with a button that you add to the Quick Access Toolbar.
- **Macros** are created in Macro Design view. You select commands from a series of drop-down lists, so no typing of programming code is required.
- You can run macros by double-clicking them in the Navigation pane or by using the Database Tools > Run Macro command. You can also run a macro from Design view, which is useful for testing the macro as you are constructing it.
- If you aren't sure which command to add to the macro, you can browse for an action by category using the Action Catalog, a task pane that appears on the right side of Macro Design view.
- The Action Catalog also includes some Program Flow options that add special sections to the macro (Comment, Group, If, and Submacro).

Try It! Starting a New Macro

1. Start Access, and open **A29Try** from the data files for this lesson.
2. Save the file as **A29Try_xx** in the location where your teacher instructs you to store the files for this lesson. Click Enable Content if the information bar appears.
3. Click Create > Macro. A new Macro object opens, ready for you to enter commands.
4. Open the Add New Action drop-down list, and click OpenTable. Additional drop-down list boxes appear that are specific to that command.
5. Open the Table Name drop-down list and click Assignments.
6. Open the second Add New Action drop-down list, and click OpenTable. A second set of drop-down list boxes appears for the new command.
7. Open the Table Name drop-down list and click Employees.
8. Click the Save button on the Quick Access Toolbar.
9. In the Save As dialog box, type **Open Assignments and Employees** and click OK.
10. Leave the macro open to use in the next Try It.

A command added to the macro

Access 2016, Windows 10, Microsoft Corporation

Try It! Running a Macro (Macro Open)

1. In the **A29Try_xx** database, with the macro open, click Macro Tools Design > Run **!**. Both of the tables referenced in the macro open.
2. Right-click any open object's tab and click Close All.
3. Leave the database open to use in the next Try It.

Try It! Running a Macro (Macro Not Open)

1. In the **A29Try_xx** database, from the Navigation pane, double-click Open Assignments and Employees.
2. Right-click any open object's tab and click Close All.
3. Leave the database open to use in the next Try It.

Try It! Selecting Commands from the Action Catalog

1. In **A29Try_xx**, click Create > Macro. In the Action Catalog, double-click Comment in the Program Flow section.
2. In the comment box that appears, type **This macro closes the current database without exiting Access.**
3. In the Actions section of the Action Catalog pane, click the arrow next to System Commands.
4. Double-click CloseDatabase. The command is added to the macro.
5. Click the Save button on the Quick Access Toolbar. In the Save As dialog box, type **Close Database**. Click OK.
6. Click Macro Tools Design > Run **!**. The macro runs, and the database closes.
7. Reopen the **A29Try_xx** database, and leave it open to use in the next Try It.

Add a command from the Action Catalog

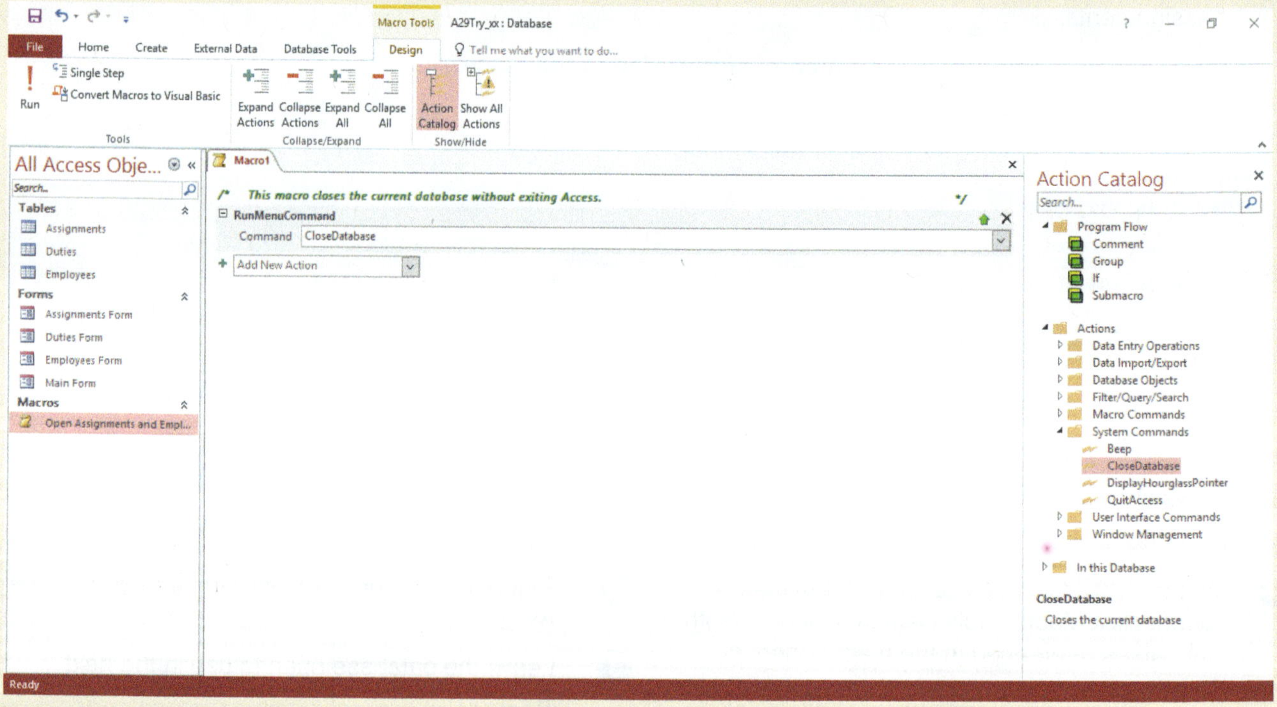

Access 2016, Windows 10, Microsoft Corporation

Creating an Embedded Macro

- An **embedded macro**, also called a **User Interface (UI) macro**, is one that is associated with a particular control. For example, a macro can be assigned to a command button, so that when you click the button, a series of actions execute.
- When you create command buttons, you are creating embedded macros for the buttons through the Command Button Wizard. You can edit these macros to add or change the actions assigned.
- When you are embedding a macro in a form, you need to be sure and select the entire form from the Selection Type drop-down in the Property Sheet.
- You can also embed macros in any database object. For example, you can specify that a certain action occurs when an object opens or closes.

Try It! Editing an Embedded Macro

1. In A29Try_xx, in the Navigation pane, right-click Main Form and click Layout View.
2. Click the Assignments Form button, and click Form Layout Tools Design > Property Sheet.
3. In the Property Sheet, click the Event tab.
4. In the On Click property, click the Build button ... . The macro design interface opens. It is the same interface as with a standalone macro.
5. Open the Add New Action drop-down list and click CloseWindow.
6. Open the Object Type drop-down list and click Form.
7. Open the Object Name drop-down list and click Main Form.
8. Click Macro Tools Design > Close. Click Yes when prompted to save changes.
9. Click the Save button on the Quick Access Toolbar to save the changes to Main Form.
10. Click Form Layout Tools Design > View to switch to Form view.
11. Click the Assignments Form button. If you see a message box, click Yes. The Assignments Form opens and the Main Form closes.
12. Right-click the Assignments Form tab and click Close.
13. Leave the database open to use in the next Try It.

Add another action to the embedded macro

Access 2016, Windows 10, Microsoft Corporation

Try It! Creating an Embedded Macro

1. In A29Try_xx in the Navigation pane, right-click Assignments Form and click Layout View.
2. If the Property Sheet is not already open, click Form Layout Tools Design > Property Sheet.
3. At the top of the Property Sheet, open the Selection Type drop-down list and click Form.
4. In the Property Sheet, click the Event tab.
5. Click in the On Close property box.
6. Click the Build button.
7. Click Macro Builder and click OK.
8. Open the Add New Action drop-down list and click OpenForm.
9. Open the Form Name drop-down list and click Main Form.
10. Click Macro Tools Design > Close. Click Yes when prompted to save changes.
11. Click Save on the Quick Access Toolbar to save the changes to the Assignments Form.
12. Right-click the form's tab and click Close. The Main Form opens.
13. Right-click the Main Form tab and click Close.
14. Leave the database open to use in the next Try It.

Printing Macro Details

- To keep track of the macros in your database, you may wish to document each macro in printed form.
- When you print a macro, a variety of information about it also prints in addition to the macro commands.

Try It! Printing Macro Details

1. In A29Try_xx, in the Navigation pane, right-click the Open Assignments and Employees macro and click Design View.
2. Click File > Print > Print Preview. The Print Macro Definition dialog box opens.
3. Click OK to accept all the additional information to print.

   ✓ *The report appears in Print Preview. Click the report to zoom in, if necessary to read the report data.*
4. Click Close Print Preview.
5. Close the database, and exit Access.

Lesson 29—Practice

You continue to work with the Ace Learning database. In this project, you will create a macro to open the frmClasses form when the frmMenu form closes, and a macro to open the frmMenu form when the frmClasses form closes.

DIRECTIONS

1. Start Access, if necessary, and open **A29Practice** from the data files for this lesson.
2. Save the file as **A29Practice_xx** in the location where your teacher instructs you to store the files for this lesson.

   ✓ *If a security warning bar appears, click Enable Content.*

   ✓ *Enabling all content is especially important when working with macros, as macros are one of the content types that are otherwise blocked.*
3. Right-click **frmClasses** and click **Layout View**.
4. If the Property Sheet is not already displayed, click **Form Layout Tools Design** > **Property Sheet**.
5. Open the **Selection Type** drop-down list in the **Property Sheet** pane and click **Form**.
6. Click in the **On Open** property box.
7. Click the **Build button**.
8. Click **Macro Builder** and click **OK**.
9. Open the **Add New Action** drop-down list and click **CloseWindow**.
10. Open the **Object Type** drop-down list and click **Form**.
11. Open the **Object Name** drop-down list and click **frmMenu**.
12. Click **Macro Tools Design** > **Close**. Click **Yes** when prompted to save changes.
13. Click in the **On Close** property box.
14. Click the **Build button**.
15. Click **Macro Builder** and click **OK**.
16. Open the **Add New Action** drop-down list and click **OpenForm**.
17. Open the **Form Name** drop-down list and click **frmMenu**.
18. Click **Macro Tools Design** > **Close**. Click **Yes** when prompted to save changes.
19. Right-click the **frmClasses** tab and click **Close**. Click **Yes** when prompted to save changes.
20. On the **frmMenu** form in Form view, click the **Classes** button. The **frmClasses** form opens, and the **frmMenu** form closes.
21. Right-click the **frmClasses** tab and click **Close**. The **frmClasses** form closes, and the **frmMenu** form opens.
22. Close the database, and exit Access. If instructed, submit it to your teacher for grading.

Lesson 29—Apply

You will create macros to help users navigate the Ace Learning database in a more efficient manner.

DIRECTIONS

1. Start Access, if necessary, and open **A29Apply** from the data files for this lesson.
2. Save the file as **A29Apply_xx** in the location where your teacher instructs you to store the files for this lesson.

   ✓ *If a security warning bar appears, click Enable Content.*
3. Open **frmVolunteers** in Layout view and set its **On Open** property so that **frmMenu** closes when **frmVolunteers** opens.
4. Set the **On Close** property so that **frmMenu** opens when **frmVolunteers** closes.
5. Save and close **frmVolunteers**. The **frmMenu** form opens automatically.
6. Test each of the buttons on **frmMenu** to confirm that each button opens a form and closes **frmMenu**, and that closing each of the opened forms causes **frmMenu** to reappear.
7. Create a new macro that opens all the tables in the database. Name it **mcrOpenAll**.
8. Run **mcrOpenAll** to test it, and then close all tabs.

   ✓ *Right-click any tab and click* **Close All**.
9. Open the **frmClasses** form in Layout view and select the **Notes** text box.
10. Open the **Property Sheet** for the Notes text box and click in the **On Got Focus** property.
11. Open the **Macro Builder**, and create a **MessageBox** action with the following properties:
    Message: **Please enter notes about classes whenever possible**

    Beep: **No**

    Type: **Information**

    Title: **Notes Requested**
12. Save and close the macro.
13. Test the new macro by viewing the **frmClasses** form in Form view and clicking the **Notes** field for a record.
14. Close the database, and exit Access. If instructed, submit it to your teacher for grading.

End-of-Chapter Activities

➤ Access Chapter 4—Critical Thinking

Creating a Multi-table Database

Bugs Be Gone, a pest control company, is not satisfied with their current database. They have a lot of data that they want to organize in a way that will improve their business operations. You have been hired to design a new database that will help them solve problems such as inconsistent customer and client records and scheduling concerns. The initial meeting with the general manager resulted in the notes shown in Illustration 4A.

Your job is to develop a working, multi-table database that accomplishes the key goals identified in the notes.

DIRECTIONS

1. Referring to the notes in Illustration 4A on the next page, make a list (on paper or in a word processing program) of the tables you will create, the fields in each table, the primary key field for each table, and how the tables will be related.

   ✓ *Make sure that your tables are normalized to 3NF.*

2. Start Access, if necessary, and create a new blank database called **ACT04_xx**.
3. Create the needed tables. Use Rich Text for the Notes fields in each table.

   ✓ *When creating fields that will have relationships to the primary key values in other tables, make sure you use the right data type. For example, if the Badge Number field in Employees is Number, make sure that the Employee field in the Schedule table is also set to Number. Otherwise you won't be able to create the relationships.*

4. Create the needed relationships between the tables, and enforce referential integrity where it is helpful to do so.
5. Arrange and size the field lists in the Relationships window so that they are all fully visible and the relationship lines are clear.
6. **With your teacher's permission**, print a Relationships report showing the relationship window.
7. Create reports that deliver the information described in the *Most important information retrieval goals* in Illustration 4A on the next page.
8. Enter one record in each table, for example purposes. (Make up the data.) Check your spelling in each table to make sure you have not made any typos.
9. Close the database, and exit Access. If instructed, submit it to your teacher for grading.

Illustration 4A

Notes from Meeting

Data to include, at a minimum:

- About the customers: contact information (mailing address, phone number, e-mail), notes
- About the services we offer: name, description, cost, time interval between treatments, notes
- About the employees: Badge number, name, job title, hire date, notes
- The service schedule: date, time, customer, service being performed, employee performing the service, whether or not the service has been performed yet, notes

Most important information retrieval goals:

- A list of services that have been scheduled but not yet performed, sorted by date
- A list of services scheduled for a particular day, grouped by employee

➤ Access Chapter 4—Portfolio Builder

Improving a Database

Marketing Concepts, Inc. has started a database in Access, but they would like you to help them improve its functionality. You will help them by creating forms, adjusting properties, and creating a macro.

DIRECTIONS

1. Start Access, if necessary, and open **APB04** from the data files for this chapter.
2. Save the file as **APB04_xx** in the location where your teacher instructs you to store the files for this chapter.

   ✓ *If a security warning bar appears, click Enable Content.*
3. Open the **Staff** table in Datasheet view, and change its font to **10-point Arial**. Do the same for the **Clients** and **Promotions** tables.
4. Create a form for each of the tables by doing the following:
   a. Click the table name in the Navigation pane.
   b. Click **Create** > **Form**.
   c. Save the form with the same name as the table name, but with frm at the beginning. For example, the form for **Clients** would be **frmClients**.
5. Open the **Clients** table in Design view.
6. Change the Indexed property of the **ZIP** field to **Yes (Duplicates OK)**.
7. Create a standalone macro that opens all three tables.
8. Save the macro as **Open All Tables**.
9. Close all open tabs and then test the macro.
10. Close the database, and exit Access. If instructed, submit it to your teacher for grading.

Chapter 5

(Courtesy Konstantin Chagin/Shutterstock)

Developing Advanced Queries

Lesson 30
Creating Crosstab Queries

- Using the Crosstab Query Wizard
- Creating a Crosstab Query in Design View

Lesson 31
Creating Queries That Find Unmatched or Duplicate Records

- Using the Find Unmatched Query Wizard
- Using the Find Duplicates Query Wizard

Lesson 32
Creating Queries That Prompt for Input

- Understanding Parameter Queries
- Creating Criteria-Based Prompts
- Showing All Records If No Parameter Is Entered
- Creating a Field Prompt

Lesson 33
Creating Action Queries

- Understanding Action Queries
- Creating an Update Query
- Creating a Delete Query

Lesson 34
Working with Advanced Query Options

- Changing the Join Type in an Ad-Hoc Query
- Changing Field Properties in Query Design View
- Showing Top Values

End-of-Chapter Activities

Lesson 30

Creating Crosstab Queries

➤ What You Will Learn

Using the Crosstab Query Wizard

Creating a Crosstab Query in Design View

WORDS TO KNOW

Column heading
The field that provides labels for the columns in a Crosstab query.

Crosstab query
A query that summarizes one field by two or more other category fields. The category fields display in row and column headings. At the intersection of each row and column is a summary (sum, average, count) of the value.

Row heading
One or more fields that label each row of a Crosstab query.

Value
The field that provides the data to summarize for the intersection of each column and row of a Crosstab query.

Software Skills Crosstab queries are a rather "special purpose" item. Instead of presenting just summary data, or just detail data, they allow you to combine summary and detail in specific ways to deliver information you need. In this way, they are somewhat like PivotTables in Excel.

What You Can Do

Using the Crosstab Query Wizard

- A **Crosstab query** summarizes data in a very specific way that allows you to customize it to answer a specific need.
- For example, in Figure 30-1 on the next page, each product is listed along with its price per unit, and a sum of the quantity of that product ordered appears, first totaled (Total Of Quantity), and then broken out by salesperson's last name.

  ✓ *If the fields that you want to summarize are in more than one table, you must create a query that joins those tables before you use the Crosstab Query Wizard and then base the Crosstab query on that query.*

- The Crosstab Query Wizard leads you through the steps to create a Crosstab query.
- The Wizard first asks for a table or query on which to base the new query. Then it asks you to choose which field will be the source for **row headings** in the left column of the query. All like **values** from the row heading field are grouped together, and each unique value in the row heading field becomes a heading for each row of the query. You can choose up to three fields for row headings.
- The Wizard then asks you to choose which field will be the source for **column headings** along the top of the query. All like values from the column heading field are grouped together and each unique value in the column heading field becomes a heading for the data columns of the query. You can choose only one field for a column heading.

  ✓ *If you choose a field that is a Date data type for a row or column heading, you will be asked how you want to group the dates on the next step of the wizard. You can choose Year, Month, or another date category.*

Figure 30-1

Access 2016, Windows 10, Microsoft Corporation

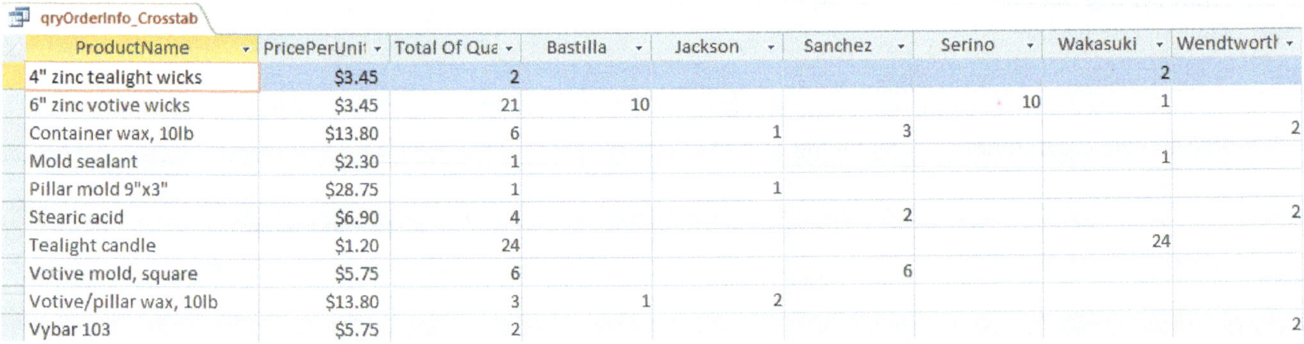
qryOrderInfo_Crosstab

ProductName	PricePerUni	Total Of Qua	Bastilla	Jackson	Sanchez	Serino	Wakasuki	Wendtwortl
4" zinc tealight wicks	$3.45	2					2	
6" zinc votive wicks	$3.45	21	10			10	1	
Container wax, 10lb	$13.80	6		1	3			2
Mold sealant	$2.30	1					1	
Pillar mold 9"x3"	$28.75	1		1				
Stearic acid	$6.90	4			2			2
Tealight candle	$1.20	24					24	
Votive mold, square	$5.75	6			6			
Votive/pillar wax, 10lb	$13.80	3	1	2				
Vybar 103	$5.75	2						2

- The next step of the Wizard enables you to choose which field you are going to summarize. Generally, this field is a number that you can sum. Sometimes this field is a text or other type of field that you may want to count. You choose both the field and the function you want to perform on it.
- Table 30-1 summarizes the functions you can use. The available functions change depending on whether the value data field is a number or other data type. In this step of the wizard, you can also choose if you want a total for each row. (This will total all column values for each row.)

Table 30-1 Functions in the Crosstab Query Wizard

Function	Description
Avg	Sum the numeric values and divide by the number of values.
Count	Count the number of records.
First	Show the field value for the first record.
Last	Show the field value for the last record.
Max	Show the highest value (if a number), the last alphabetic value (if a text string), or the latest date (if a date).
Min	Show the lowest value (if a number), the first alphabetic value (if a text string), or the earliest date (if a date).
StDev	Calculate the standard deviation, which is used to see how close all values are to the average.
Sum	Sum numeric values.
Var	Calculate the variance of the number, which is another way to see how close values are to the average.

Try It! Using the Crosstab Query Wizard

1. Start Access, and open **A30Try** from the data files for this lesson.
2. Save the file as **A30Try_xx** in the location where your teacher instructs you to store the files for this lesson. Click Enable Content if the security warning bar appears.
3. Click Create > Query Wizard. The New Query dialog box opens.
4. Click Crosstab Query Wizard and click OK.
5. In the Crosstab Query Wizard dialog box, click the Queries option button.
6. Click qryOrderInfo on the list of queries.
7. Click Next.

Select the qryOrderInfo query as the basis for the Crosstab query

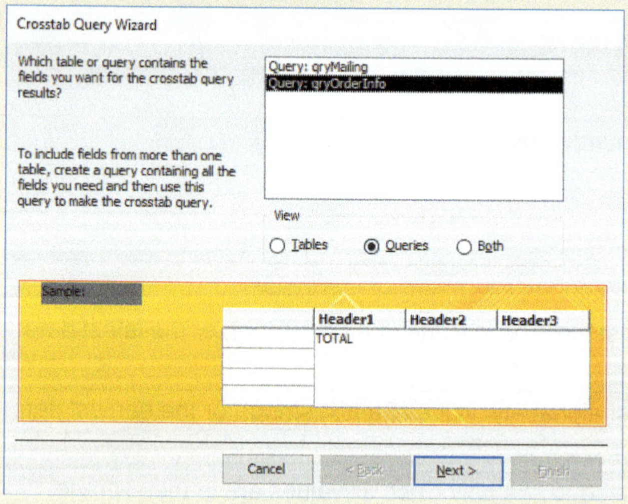

Access 2016, Windows 10, Microsoft Corporation

8. Click ProductName and click Add >.
9. Click PricePerUnit and click Add >.
10. Click Next.

Choose ProductName and PricePerUnit as the rows

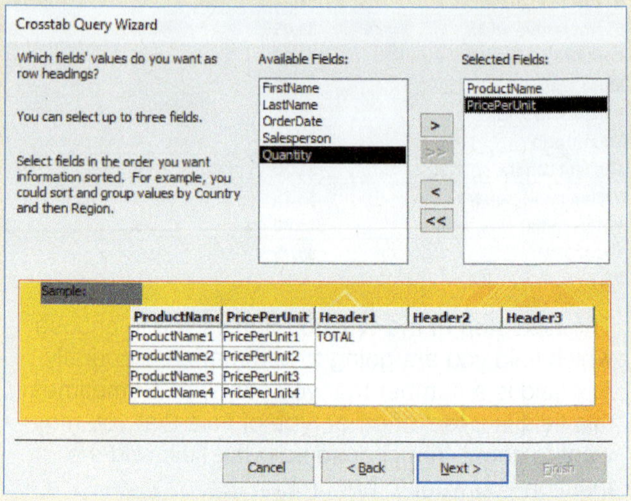

Access 2016, Windows 10, Microsoft Corporation

11. Click LastName to select it for a column heading and click Next.
12. On the Fields list, click Quantity.
13. On the Functions list, click Sum.

Choose to sum the Quantity field

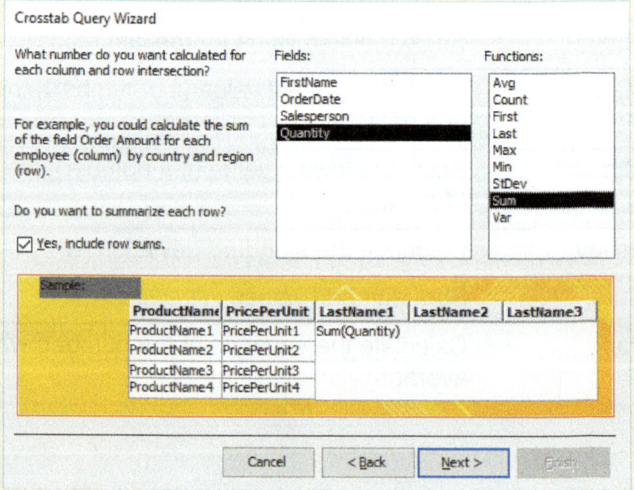

Access 2016, Windows 10, Microsoft Corporation

14. Click Next.
15. Leave the default name and click Finish. The query results appear. Leave the database open for the next Try It.

Creating a Crosstab Query in Design View

- In a Crosstab query, a Crosstab row appears in the query design grid. Figure 30-2 shows the query design grid for the query you created in the last Try It. You can switch to Datasheet view or click the Run button to see the results of the Crosstab query.
- The choices in the Crosstab row are Row Heading, Column Heading, and Value. You must have at least one of each.

  ✓ *You can make any query into a Crosstab query by clicking the Crosstab button on the Query Tools Design tab.*

- You can have more than one Row Heading field, but not more than one Column Heading or Value field.
- The Total row for the Row Heading and Column Heading fields shows Group By.
- If you choose to display row totals, the Crosstab row also shows Row Heading, but the Total row shows the Sum (or other) function.
- The Total row for the Value field shows the function you want to apply, such as Sum.
- If you want to include only certain records, choose Where in the Total row and type the filtering criteria in the Criteria row.

Figure 30-2

Field:	[ProductName]	[PricePerUnit]	[LastName]	[Quantity]	Total Of Quantity: [Qu		
Table:	qryOrderInfo	qryOrderInfo	qryOrderInfo	qryOrderInfo	qryOrderInfo		
Total:	Group By	Group By	Group By	Sum	Sum		
Crosstab:	Row Heading	Row Heading	Column Heading	Value	Row Heading		
Sort:							
Criteria:							
or:							

Access 2016, Windows 10, Microsoft Corporation

Try It! Creating a Crosstab Query in Design View

1. In the **A30Try_xx** file, click Create > Query Design.
2. In the Show Table dialog box, click the tblCustomers table. Hold down the CTRL key and click the tblOrderDetails, tblOrders, and tblProducts tables, too.
3. Click Add to add the tables to the query grid. Then click Close to close the Show Table dialog box.

   ✓ *You can drag the query field lists to arrange them so they are more readable if desired.*

4. Double-click the LastName field in tblCustomers to add it to the query grid.
5. Double-click the ProductName field in tblProducts.
6. Double-click the Quantity field in tblOrderDetails.

   ✓ *You needed to add the tblOrders table to the query in step 2 to get the linkage between the other tables; however, none of its fields are used directly in this query.*

7. Click Query Tools Design > Crosstab.
8. A Crosstab row appears in the grid.
9. In the LastName column, open the Crosstab drop-down list and click Column Heading.
10. In the ProductName column, open the Crosstab drop-down list and click Row Heading.
11. In the Quantity column, open the Crosstab drop-down list and click Value.
12. In the Quantity column, open the Total drop-down list and click Sum.

(continued)

Try It! Creating a Crosstab Query in Design View *(continued)*

13. Right-click the Query1 tab and click Save.
14. In the Save As dialog box, type **Products Crosstab** and click OK.
15. Click Query Tools Design > Run ! to see the results.
16. Close the database, and exit Access.

Create a Crosstab query from scratch in Query Design view

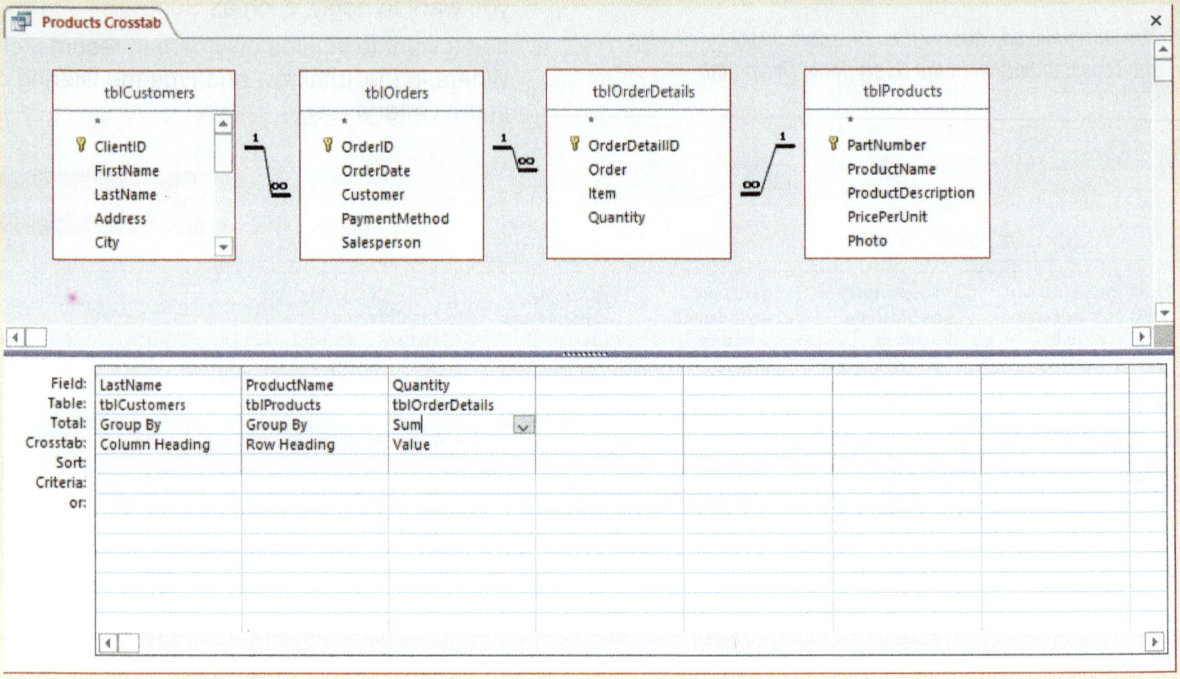

Lesson 30—Practice

You are helping a company called Bookseller Source that offers large quantities of textbooks to bookstores at 50 percent off retail prices. They have already set up the database for this business, and they have three days' worth of sales data entered. Now the owners would like to look at the data for these first few days to evaluate what items are selling well and which salespeople are performing the best. You will use Crosstab queries to produce this data.

DIRECTIONS

1. Start Access, if necessary, and open **A30Practice** from the data files for this lesson.
2. Save the file as **A30Practice_xx** in the location where your teacher instructs you to store the files for this lesson.

   ✓ *If a security warning bar appears, click Enable Content.*
3. Click **Create** > **Query Wizard**.
4. Click **Crosstab Query Wizard** and click **OK**.
5. Click the **Queries** option button.
6. Click **Next**.
7. Click the **Salesperson** field, and click the **Add** > button to move it to the Selected Fields list. Then click **Next**.
8. Click the **OrderDate** field and click **Next**.
9. Click **Date** and click **Next**.
10. In the **Fields** column, click **Total**.
11. In the Functions column, click **Sum**. Make sure the **Yes, include row sums** check box is marked.
12. Click **Next**.
13. Replace the default name with **qrySalesValuePerDay-Crosstab**, and click **Finish**.
14. In the query results, double-click the dividers between each set of column headers, expanding the column widths as needed to fit the contents, as shown in Figure 30-3.
15. **With your teacher's permission**, print the query results.
16. Save and close the database, and exit Access. If instructed, submit this database to your teacher for grading.

Figure 30-3

qrySalesValuePerDay-Crosstab

Salesperson	Total Of Total	1/15/2017	1/16/2017	1/17/2017
Christine Cutler	$12,338.00	$7,498.50		$4,839.50
Julie Burrow	$80,291.38	$61,109.00	$14,184.38	$4,998.00
Marjorie Hopper	$108,652.00	$74,420.00	$29,607.50	$4,624.50
Melissa Louks	$53,493.00	$21,495.50		$31,997.50

Access 2016, Windows 10, Microsoft Corporation

Lesson 30—Apply

In this project, you will take the Bookseller Source queries and create Crosstab queries to help them navigate their database more efficiently.

DIRECTIONS

1. Start Access, if necessary, and open **A30Apply** from the data files for this lesson.
2. Save the file as **A30Apply_xx** in the location where your teacher instructs you to store the files for this lesson.

   ✓ *If a security warning bar appears, click Enable Content.*
3. Open the **qrySalesValuePerDay-Crosstab** query in Design view.
4. Change the column name of the Total Of Total column to **Total All Days**.

   ✓ *To do this, edit the text in the Field row to read Total All Days:Total.*
5. Run the query. Then save and close it.
6. Make a copy of the qrySalesValuePerDay-Crosstab query, and name the copy **qrySalesQuantityPerDay-Crosstab**.

   ✓ *To do this from the Navigation pane, select the query, press* CTRL *+* C*, and then press* CTRL *+* V*. You will be prompted for the new name.*
7. Open the **qrySalesQuantityPerDay-Crosstab** query in Design view, and edit the query so that it shows the total number of books sold, rather than the value of the books sold, per salesperson per day.

   ✓ *To do this, in the Field row, change the references from the Total field to the Quantity field in the last two columns of the query grid.*
8. Save and run the query. It should look like Figure 30-4. Close the query.
9. Start a new Crosstab query in Design view that is based on **qryOrdersWithDetails**,
10. Enter the appropriate fields and settings to produce the results shown in Figure 30-5.
    - The order dates are the row headings.
    - The salespeople are the column headings.
    - The average price of the books sold (Our Price field) is the value.
11. Run the query, and widen the columns as needed so that no text is truncated.
12. Save the new query as **qryAvgPricePerDay-Crosstab**.
13. **With your teacher's permission**, print the results for all three queries used in this exercise.
14. Close the database, and exit Access. If instructed, submit this database to your teacher for grading.

Figure 30-4

qrySalesQuantityPerDay-Crosstab

Salesperson	Total All Days	1/15/2017	1/16/2017	1/17/2017
Christine Cutler	600	300		300
Julie Burrow	2675	1600	675	400
Marjorie Hopper	2875	2050	675	150
Melissa Louks	2000	1000		1000

Access 2016, Windows 10, Microsoft Corporation

Figure 30-5

qryAvgPricePerDay-Crosstab

Order Date	Christine Cutler	Julie Burrow	Marjorie Hopper	Melissa Louks
1/15/2017	$27.50	$36.71	$32.92	$20.00
1/16/2017		$18.50	$31.93	
1/17/2017	$17.10	$12.50	$35.00	$32.00

Access 2016, Windows 10, Microsoft Corporation

Lesson 31

Creating Queries That Find Unmatched or Duplicate Records

➤ What You Will Learn

Using the Find Unmatched Query Wizard
Using the Find Duplicates Query Wizard

Software Skills The Find Unmatched Query Wizard and the Find Duplicates Query Wizard are two special-purpose query types for specific tasks. They do just what their names suggest. The Find Unmatched Query Wizard compares two tables and reports records from one that do not have a corresponding entry in the other. The Find Duplicates query lists records that have the same value for one or more specified fields.

WORDS TO KNOW

Duplicate
Two or more records that contain the same data in a field that ought to be unique for each record.

Unmatched
Records that should have a corresponding reference in another table but do not.

What You Can Do

Using the Find Unmatched Query Wizard

- The Find Unmatched Query Wizard leads you through the steps needed to create a query that will show records that do not match up with corresponding values in another table.
- Suppose, for example, that you have separate tables for Orders and OrderDetails. Every record in OrderDetails should refer to a valid order number in the Orders table. If there are detail records that do not, they are **unmatched**.

  ✓ *This type of error would not occur if you were enforcing referential integrity in the relationship between the two tables. This illustrates the importance of referential integrity.*

- The results appear in a datasheet, just like a select query. You can print it to use as a reference when fixing the problems.
- You can also use this type of query in cases where there aren't any errors, but you just want information. For example, in the following steps, you'll use it to find payment methods that no customers have used.

Try It! Using the Find Unmatched Query Wizard

1. Start Access, and open **A31Try** from the data files for this lesson.
2. Save the file as **A31Try_xx** in the location where your teacher instructs you to store the files for this lesson. Click Enable Content if the security warning bar appears.
3. Click Create > Query Wizard.
4. Select Find Unmatched Query Wizard and click OK.
5. Click Table: tblPaymentMethods and click Next.

Select the table from which to display unmatched records

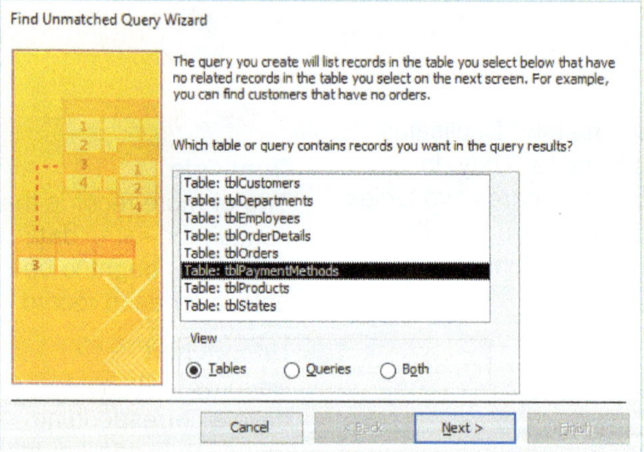

Access 2016, Windows 10, Microsoft Corporation

6. Click Table: tblOrders and click Next.
7. The field matching should already be set correctly, as shown in the next figure. Click Next to accept it.

Access guesses the field matching correctly in this case

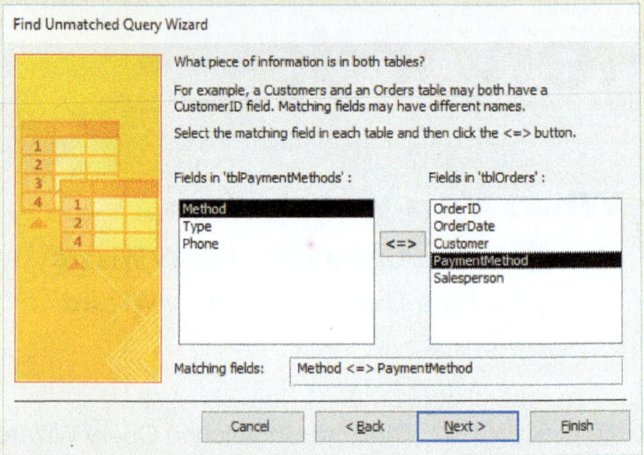

Access 2016, Windows 10, Microsoft Corporation

8. Click the All Fields button >> to select all the fields to include in the query results. Then click Next.
9. Replace the default query name with **qryUnusedPaymentMethods**.
10. Click Finish. Access finds four unmatched records.
11. Right-click the query's tab, and click Close.
12. Leave the database open to use in the next Try It.

Using the Find Duplicates Query Wizard

- The Find Duplicates Query Wizard is like a super "search" that helps flush out duplication in your data.
- For example, suppose you want a single record in your Customers table for each business, but you have ended up with some businesses entered multiple times with different contact people in each record. You could find the **duplicates** with the Find Duplicates Query Wizard.

✓ *This error would not occur if you set up the business name field to not allow duplicates. Setting its Indexed property to Yes (No Duplicates) would prevent the problem from happening in the future.*

- In the following Try It, you will find products that have the same name in a product table. You can then examine the duplicate products to make sure they are indeed different products and, if they are not, you can delete or combine the duplicates.

Try It! Using the Find Duplicates Query Wizard

1. In the **A31Try_xx** file, click Create > Query Wizard.
2. Click Find Duplicates Query Wizard, and click OK.
3. Click Table: tblProducts and click Next.
4. Click the ProductName field, and click the Add button >. Then click Next.
5. Click the ProductDescription field, and click the Add button >.
6. Click Next.
7. Replace the default query name with **qryProductDuplicates**.
8. Click Finish. Query results appear showing products with duplicate names.

   ✓ *Note that even though products have the same name, they have different descriptions and so do not need to be deleted or combined.*
9. Right-click the query's tab, and click Close.
10. Close the database, and exit Access.

Lesson 31—Practice

To help enhance the Bookseller Source database, you will create an unmatched query based on tblOrderDetails and tblOrders.

DIRECTIONS

1. Start Access, if necessary, and open **A31Practice** from the data files for this lesson.
2. Save the file as **A31Practice_xx** in the location where your teacher instructs you to store the files for this lesson.

   ✓ *If a security warning bar appears, click Enable Content.*
3. Click **Create** > **Query Wizard**.
4. Click **Find Unmatched Query Wizard** and click **OK**.
5. Click **Table: tblOrderDetails** and click **Next**.
6. Click **Table: tblOrders** and click **Next**.
7. The field matching should already be set correctly. Click **Next** to accept it.
8. Click the **All Fields** button >> to select all the fields to include in the query results, and then click **Next**.
9. Replace the default query name with **qryUnmatchedOrders**.
10. Click **Finish**. Access finds five unmatched records.
11. **With your teacher's permission**, print the query results. See Figure 31-1.
12. Close the database, and exit Access. If instructed, submit this database to your teacher for grading.

qryUnmatchedOrders

OrderDetailID	Order	ISBN	Quantity
12	7	Computer Networks, 4th Edition	650
13	7	Computer Science: An Overview 7th Edition	700
32	19	The Web Wizard's Guide to Freeware and Shareware	200
33	19	Authentication: From Passwords to Public Keys	100
34	19	Internet Visual Reference Basics	100
(New)			

Figure 31-1

Access 2016, Windows 10, Microsoft Corporation

Lesson 31—Apply

You are doing work for Bookseller Source, and you just learned that they have not set up referential integrity in the relationships between their tables; this means there may be some errors in the database. You will fix these errors by creating a Find Duplicates query, fix the Indexed properties in tblCustomers, and enforce referential integrity between tblOrders and tblOrderDetails.

DIRECTIONS

1. Start Access, if necessary, and open **A31Apply** from the data files for this lesson.
2. Save the file as **A31Apply_xx** in the location where your teacher instructs you to store the files for this lesson.

   ✓ *If a security warning bar appears, click Enable Content.*
3. Create a Find Duplicates query that locates all records in the **tblCustomers** table with a duplicate value in either **Store** or **Phone**. Include all fields in the query results and name the query **qryDuplicateCustomers**.
4. Fix the records in the table so that each store exists only once. You can delete either of the duplicate records in the query results to achieve this.
5. Close the query, and then reopen it in Datasheet view to run it again. This time it should produce no results. Close the query window.
6. Open **tblCustomers** in Design view and set the **Store** and **Phone** fields' Indexed properties to **Yes (No Duplicates)** so the problem will not happen again. Save and close the table.
7. Run the **qryUnmatchedOrders** query. In the query results, change all references to order 7 to **8**. Change all references to order 19 to **18**.
8. Close the query and then reopen it to confirm that there are no more unmatched orders. Close the query.
9. Open the Relationships window for the database, and enforce referential integrity between the **tblOrders** and **tblOrderDetails** tables.
10. **With your teacher's permission**, print the database relationships.

    ✓ *To do this you will need to create a relationship report. With the Relationships tab still open, click Relationship Tools Design > Relationship Report. Click Print and then click OK.*
11. Close the report without saving changes, and then save and close the Relationships window.
12. Close the database, and exit Access. If instructed, submit this database to your teacher for grading.

Lesson 32

Creating Queries That Prompt for Input

What You Will Learn

Understanding Parameter Queries
Creating Criteria-Based Prompts
Showing All Records If No Parameter Is Entered
Creating a Field Prompt

Software Skills Instead of creating many similar queries, you can create one query that will prompt you for different possibilities. For example, if you use a query to look up addresses in different states, rather than create a version of the query for each state, you can create a single query that prompts you for the state each time you run it.

WORDS TO KNOW

Parameter
A value that is required to run a query (or other object). The parameter is entered in a dialog box.

SQL (Structured Query Language)
A computer language common to database programs that is generally used for selecting or managing data.

What You Can Do

Understanding Parameter Queries

- Parameter queries allow you to use the same query to extract data that meets different criteria.
- For example, suppose you need to show all customers from a specific city. Rather than create a query for each city in the database table, you can place a prompt in the Criteria row of the City field in the query design. When you run the query, you are prompted to enter the desired city. The city name you enter is the **parameter** needed to run the query and show only the records that meet that criteria.
- You can run a parameter query as a select query or change the query type to an action query. For example, you could prompt the user for which records to delete every month.

  ✓ *Action queries are covered in a later lesson.*

- A parameter query can also be the source for a report or form. For example, you could request a date range for a report or choose a state for printing mailing labels.
- The parameter can be in a stand-alone query or can be part of the **SQL** statement in the Record Source property for a form or report.

Creating Criteria-Based Prompts

- Perhaps the most common type of parameter occurs in the Criteria row of a query's design.
- Place the message you want for the prompt in square brackets. In Figure 32-1, the Criteria row shows [What state?]
- When you run the query, a dialog box displays with the message and a text box for your input, as shown here:

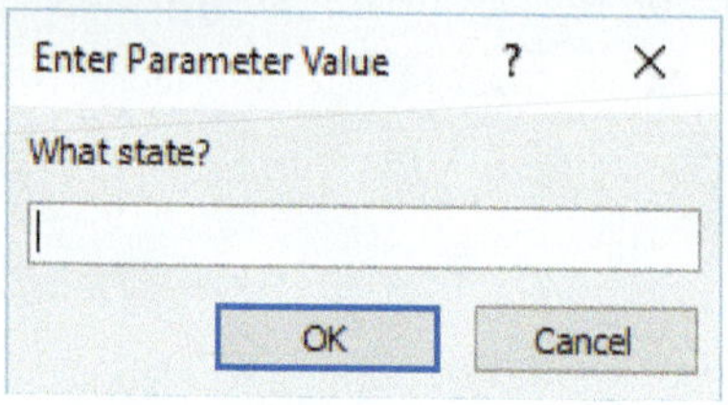

Access 2016, Windows 10, Microsoft Corporation

- Access takes the value the user types in the message box and places it in the Criteria row in place of the prompt to select the records.
- If you want to re-run the prompt from Datasheet view without returning to Design view, press SHIFT + F9.

- The prompt can be combined with other criteria to permit a variety of responses. Suppose, for example, you were prompting for a particular state:

Entry in Criteria	Permissible Responses
[What state?]	Entire state abbreviation
Like [What state?]	Entire state abbreviation Any portion of field contents with a wildcard; for example, c* displays CA, CO, CT *A displays CA, IA, PA, WA
Like [What state?] or Is Not Null	Entire state abbreviation Any portion of field contents with a wildcard Nothing (press Enter or click OK) displays all records
Like [What state?] &***	Same as above except wildcard displays all entries with the letter in any position; for example, *A displays AR, CA, and so on.

- You can have multiple prompts in one query, or even in one box within one query.
- For example, if you have an invoice date, you could type **Between [Enter Start Date] and [Enter End Date]** to create two prompts to give you a date range to select specific invoices.

Figure 32-1

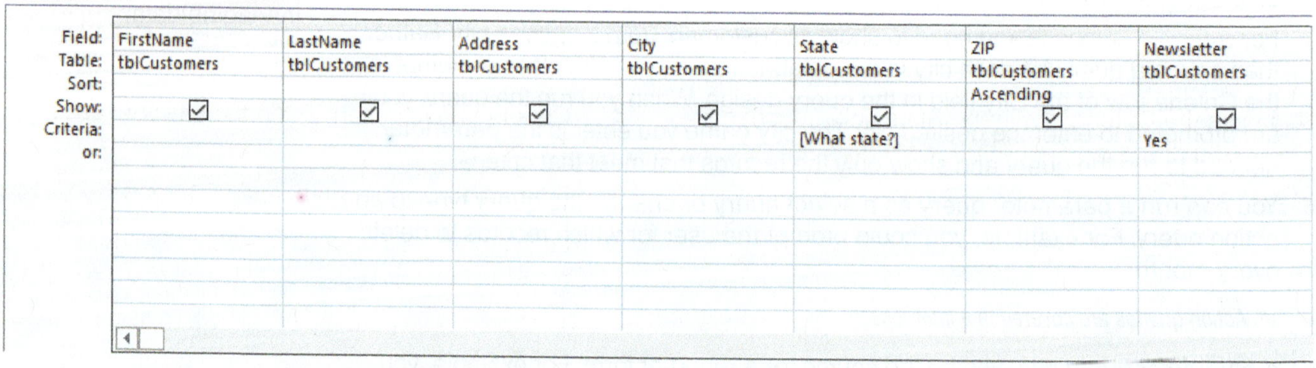

Access 2016, Windows 10, Microsoft Corporation

Try It! Creating Criteria-Based Prompts

1. Start Access, and open A32Try from the data files for this lesson.
2. Save the file as A32Try_xx in the location where your teacher instructs you to store the files for this lesson. Click Enable Content if the security warning bar appears.
3. In the Navigation pane, right-click qryMailing and click Design View.
4. In the State column in the Criteria row, type [What state?].
5. Click Query Tools Design > Run !. The prompt appears.
6. Type IN and click OK. The query results display only customers who live in Indiana.
7. Click the Save button on the Quick Access Toolbar.
8. Press SHIFT + F9 to redisplay the prompt.
9. Type NJ and click OK. The results display the one customer who lives in New Jersey.
10. Right-click the query's tab and click Close.
11. Leave the database open to use in the next Try It.

Showing All Records If No Parameter Is Entered

- One minor issue with parameter queries is that if the user does not enter anything for the parameter, no records will show.
- In fact, what you probably want is for ALL records to show if the user doesn't enter a parameter.
- To accomplish this, add &"*" at the end of the parameter, and if it is a text field, add Like at the beginning. (Do not add Like if it is a numeric field.)
- This extra code allows all records to show if the parameter returns a null value.

Try It! Showing All Records If No Parameter Is Entered

1. In A32Try_xx, in the Navigation pane, double-click qryMailing. In the Enter Parameter Value dialog box, click OK without entering a value.

   ✓ *The query results show no records.*
2. Right-click the query's tab, and click Design View.
3. In the Criteria row in the State column, change the entry to: Like [What state?]&"*"
4. Click Run !. The Enter Parameter Value dialog box opens.
5. Click OK without entering a parameter. The query results show all records.
6. Press SHIFT + F9 to reopen the Enter Parameter Value dialog box.
7. Type IN and click OK. Only the records from Indiana appear.
8. Click the Save button on the Quick Access Toolbar.
9. Right-click the query tab, and click Close.
10. Leave the database open to use in the next Try It.

Creating a Field Prompt

- You can also place a parameter in the Field row of the query design, creating a new field column in the query results.
- Generally, the purpose of a field parameter is to create a calculation using the same value in every record.
- For example, you may want to see the value of a variable price decrease for every record:
  New Price: [Asking Price]-([Asking Price]*[Percentage Decrease?]/100)

  ✓ *Note that running this query does not actually change the prices in the database; to do that, you would need to run an action query, as described in a later lesson.*

- Here's an explanation of that example:
  - [Asking Price] is a field name. For example, suppose a record's asking price was $30.
  - The rest of the expression is in parentheses, indicating that it should be performed first, before being subtracted from the [Asking Price] amount.
  - [Percentage Decrease?] is a prompt, not a field name.
  - [Percentage Decrease?] is divided by 100 to create a percentage (such as 0.10) when a whole number is entered (such as 10). If you wanted to make that clearer to avoid entry errors, you could include a more verbose instruction, such as:
    New Price: [AskingPrice]-([AskingPrice]*[Enter the desired percentage of decrease as a whole number]/100)

Try It! Creating a Field Prompt

1. In **A32Try_xx**, click Create > Query Design.
2. In the Show Table dialog box, double-click tblProducts and then click Close.
3. Double-click ProductName and PricePerUnit to add those fields to the query grid.
4. In the first empty column in the Field row, type **New Price: [PricePerUnit]+([PricePerUnit]*[Enter the markup percentage as a whole number]/100)**.
5. If the Property Sheet is not open, right-click the text you just entered and click Properties.
6. In the Property Sheet, open the Format drop-down list and click Currency.
7. Click Query Tools Design > Run **!**. A prompt appears.
8. Type **20** and click OK. New prices in the query results show with a 20% markup.

Part of the query results

Query1

ProductName	PricePerUnit	New Price
Votive mold, round	$1.00	$1.20
Votive mold, square	$5.00	$6.00
Pillar mold 9"x3"	$25.00	$30.00
Pillar mold 6"x6"	$32.00	$38.40
Mold sealant	$2.00	$2.40
Votive/pillar wax, 10lb	$12.00	$14.40
Container wax, 10lb	$12.00	$14.40
Stearic acid	$6.00	$7.20
Vybar 103	$5.00	$6.00

Access 2016, Windows 10, Microsoft Corporation

9. Right-click the query tab and click Save.
10. In the Save As dialog box, type **qryMarkup** and click OK.
11. Right-click the query tab, and click Close.
12. Close the database, and exit Access.

Lesson 32—Practice

You are working for a company called The Textbook Exchange, which buys and sells individual copies of textbooks. The company managers would like to be able to target people and books in the database that have specific properties, but the desired properties may change each time they run the query. For example, they might want to see all of the people in a certain state or city. In this project, you will create a parameter query for this database.

DIRECTIONS

1. Start Access, if necessary, and open **A32Practice** from the data files for this lesson.
2. Save the file as **A32Practice_xx** in the location where your teacher instructs you to store the files for this lesson.

   ✓ *If a security warning bar appears, click Enable Content.*
3. In the Navigation pane, select **qryBooksForSale**.
4. Press CTRL + C to copy it, and then CTRL + V to paste the copy.
5. In the Paste As dialog box, type **qryBooksByDiscount** and click **OK**.
6. Right-click **qryBooksByDiscount** and click **Design View**.
7. In the Criteria row for the Discount field, enter the following: **>([Minimum discount?]/100)**

   ✓ *You may need to scroll to the Discount field.*

   ✓ *This parameter enables the user to enter a whole number for the minimum percentage of discount to show.*
8. Click **Query Tools Design** > **Run** !. A prompt appears.
9. Type **60** and click **OK**.

   ✓ *Only records with at least 60% discount appear.*
10. **With your teacher's permission**, print the query results.
11. Click **Home** > **View** to return to Design view.
12. In the Criteria row for the Discount field, change the parameter so that leaving the parameter value empty will display all records: **>([Minimum discount?]/100)&"*"**
13. Click **Query Tools Design** > **Run** !. A prompt appears.
14. Click **OK** to bypass the prompt. All the records appear.
15. Click **Save** on the Quick Access Toolbar.
16. Close the database, and exit Access. If instructed, submit this database to your teacher for grading.

Lesson 32—Apply

In this project, you will continue working on The Textbook Exchange's database. You will create a parameter query, using wildcards, that is based on tblBooks.

DIRECTIONS

1. Start Access, if necessary, and open **A32Apply** from the data files for this lesson.
2. Save the file as **A32Apply_xx** in the location where your teacher instructs you to store the files for this lesson.

   ✓ *If a security warning bar appears, click Enable Content.*

3. Create a query based on **tblBooks** (all fields) that will show only the books that begin with a certain string of numbers in their ISBN field. Name the query **qryBooksByISBN**.

   ✓ *For example, you might use this parameter:* **Like [ISBN begins with:]&"*"**

4. Test the query using **1** as the parameter value.
5. **With your teacher's permission**, print one copy of the result in Landscape orientation.
6. Retest the query (SHIFT + F9) using **02** as the parameter value.
7. Retest the query by leaving the parameter value prompt blank.

   ✓ *Leaving the parameter prompt blank should display all records.*

8. Save and close the query.
9. Create a new query called **qryCustomersByLocation** that uses all the fields from **tblCustomers**.
10. Use wildcards to add parameter criteria for both the **City** and **State** fields that prompt the user to enter the desired city or state.

    ✓ *Don't forget to add Like at the beginning and &"*" at the end of the parameter statements so that if the user enters nothing, all records will be included. For example, for the city, you might use* **Like [What city?]&"*"**

11. Run the query, specifying **Macon** as the city name and not entering a state name.
12. **With your teacher's permission**, print one copy of the results in Landscape orientation.
13. Save the query.
14. Close the database, and exit Access. If instructed, submit this database to your teacher for grading.

Lesson 33

Creating Action Queries

➤ What You Will Learn

Software Skills Action queries can save a significant amount of time if you need to change a number of records at once. You may want to delete or update records based on criteria.

WORDS TO KNOW

Action query
A query that changes the value of one or more records.

Delete query
A query that removes records from a table.

Update query
A query that changes the entry in one or more fields in multiple records at once.

What You Can Do

Understanding Action Queries

- **Action queries** modify records based on what criteria is added.
- A good starting point for an action query is to begin with a regular Select query, and to view the datasheet to make sure the selection is what you want to change. Then modify the query in Design view to apply the action functionality.
- Be careful with action queries. Each time you run them, they make permanent changes to the table.
- There are four kinds of action queries: Make Table query, **Update query**, Append query, and **Delete query**. In this lesson, you will learn how to use an Update query and a Delete query. Make Table and Append queries operate in much the same way.

✓ *Any of these queries can optionally have parameters in the Criteria, Field, or Update To rows.*

Creating an Update Query

- An Update query enables you to change the value of one or more fields in the records you select.
- Create a select query, and then, in Query Design view, switch it to an Update query. An Update To row is added to the query grid. In the Update To row for the field to be modified, type an expression that describes the updated data. For example, to decrease the value in the [Price] field by 20%, you might use **=[Price]*.8**.
- To preview the records to be changed by the update, switch to Datasheet view. Showing the query in Datasheet view lets you make sure the query is correctly identifying the records you want to change. Then, when the query is run, the records show this change. You can switch to Datasheet view for an action query to review results without changing the database objects. To actually update the records, click Run.

Try It! Creating an Update Query

1. Start Access, and open **A33Try** from the data files for this lesson.
2. Save the file as **A33Try_xx** in the location where your teacher instructs you to store the files for this lesson. Click Enable Content if the security warning bar appears.
3. Make a backup copy of the tblProducts table. Name it **tblProducts Backup**.
4. Click Create > Query Design.
5. Double-click tblProducts to add the table to the query, and then click Close.
6. Double-click the ProductName and PricePerUnit fields to add them to the grid.
7. In the Criteria row for the ProductName field, type **Like "Tealight candle"**.
8. Click Query Tools Design > Run ! to view the results. The results should show only Tealight candles.
9. Click Home > View to return to Design view.
10. Click Query Tools Design > Update !. An Update To row appears in the grid.
11. In the Update To row for the PricePerUnit field, type **$2.00**.
12. Click Query Tools Design > Run !. A confirmation message appears.
13. Click Yes. The query is run. You will not see the results onscreen.
14. Click the Save button on the Quick Access Toolbar.
15. In the Save As dialog box, type **qryUpdateTealightPrices** and click OK.
16. Right-click the query tab and click Close.
17. In the Navigation pane, double-click tblProducts and check that the Tealight prices were updated.
18. Right-click the table tab and click Close.
19. Leave the database open to use in the next Try It.

Creating a Delete Query

- An Append query and a Delete query are often run together. For example, first you append old records to an archive table for storage, and then you delete them from the current table.
- If you receive a message about key violation when you are deleting records with a Delete query, check the relationships. If referential integrity is enforced between two tables, such that deleting records will cause a violation of the rules, Access won't let you run the Delete query until you turn off referential integrity for the relationship.

Try It! Creating a Delete Query

1. In A33Try_xx, click Create > Query Design.
2. Double-click tblProducts and then click Close.
3. Double-click the ProductName field to add it to the query grid.
4. Click Query Tools Design > Delete.
5. In the Criteria row, type Like "Tealight" & "*".
6. Right-click the query tab and click Datasheet View to switch to Datasheet view and preview the results. Nine records should appear.
7. Click Home > View to return to Design view.
8. Right-click the query tab and click Save. In the Save As dialog box, type qryDeleteProducts and click OK.
9. Click Query Tools Design > Run !. A confirmation message appears.
10. Click Yes.
11. Right-click the query tab and click Close.
12. In the Navigation pane, double-click tblProducts and confirm that the Tealight records have been deleted.
13. Close the database, and exit Access.

Lesson 33—Practice

In this project, you will create an Action query in The Textbook Exchange database.

DIRECTIONS

1. Start Access, if necessary, and open **A33Practice** from the data files for this lesson.
2. Save the file as **A33Practice_xx** in the location where your teacher instructs you to store the files for this lesson.

   ✓ *If a security warning bar appears, click Enable Content.*

3. In the Navigation pane, select **tblBooks** and press CTRL + C to copy it.
4. Press CTRL + V to paste the copy. Type **tblBooksBackup** as the new table name, and click **OK**.
5. Click **Create** > **Query Design** to start a new query. Double-click **tblMoreBooks**, and click **Close**.
6. Select all the fields except OutOfPrint from the **tblMoreBooks** field list and drag them to the grid, adding them to the query.
7. Click **Query Tools Design** > **Append**.
8. In the Table Name box, type **tblBooks**. Click **OK**. An Append To row appears in the query grid.

   ✓ *Notice that there is no entry in the Append To row for the RetailPrice column.*

9. In the RetailPrice column, open the **Append To** row's drop-down list and click **Retail Price**.
10. Click **Query Tools Design** > **Run** !.
11. Click **Yes** to confirm.
12. Click the **Save** button on the Quick Access Toolbar.
13. Type **qryAppendBooks** and click **OK**. View the query in Datasheet view, and then close the query.
14. Close the database, and exit Access. If instructed, submit this database to your teacher for grading.

Lesson 33—Apply

The owners of The Textbook Exchange have decided to start a new spin-off company called The Textbook Place that will sell only new books, but at 20% off retail prices. They have started a new database file with some of the old data plus some new data. You will use action queries to further prepare this data for use.

DIRECTIONS

1. Start Access, if necessary, and open **A33Apply** from the data files for this lesson.
2. Save the file as **A33Apply_xx** in the location where your teacher instructs you to store the files for this lesson.

   ✓ *If a security warning bar appears, click Enable Content.*
3. Start a select query based on **tblBooks** using all the fields.
4. Enter criteria that will include only books that were published prior to 01/01/2010.
5. Test the query by running it, and return to Design view.
6. Change the query to a Make Table query that creates a new table called **tblOldBooks** based on the criteria entered earlier. Run the query to make the new table.
7. Save the query as **qryPre2010** and close it.
8. Open **tblOldBooks** in Datasheet view to confirm that it contains five records, and then close it.
9. Copy and paste **qryPre2010**. Name the new query **qryDeletePre2010** and open it in Design view.
10. Change the query to a Delete query that deletes the records that have dates before 01/01/2010.
11. Run the query. Click Yes to confirm the deletion.
12. Save the query, and close it.
13. Open **tblBooks** in Datasheet view to confirm that it contains no records with dates before 01/01/2010. Widen the column if necessary to display all dates.
14. Open **tblBooks** in Design view, and add a new field called **Our Price**. Set its data type to **Currency**.
15. Save and close the table.
16. Create a select query based on **tblBooks**. Include only the ISBN, Retail Price, and Our Price fields.
17. Change the query to an Update query that sets the value in the Our Price field to 80% of the Retail Price field's value.
18. Run the query and save it as **qryOurPrice**.
19. Modify **qryOurPrice** so instead of multiplying the Retail Price by 80%, it multiplies it by a percentage that the user enters when prompted. Use a parameter for this, as you learned earlier in this chapter.
20. Run the query, and when prompted, specify **50** as the percentage of discount.
21. Save and close the query.
22. Open **tblBooks** and confirm that the values in Our Price are 50% of the values in Retail Price.
23. Close the database, and exit Access. If instructed, submit this database to your teacher for grading.

Lesson 34

Working with Advanced Query Options

➤ What You Will Learn

Changing the Join Type in an Ad-Hoc Query
Changing Field Properties in Query Design View
Showing Top Values

Software Skills A query is a great way of tying multiple tables together for use as a single data source on which to base other objects such as forms or reports. In this lesson, you will learn how to create ad-hoc joins that establish temporary relationships within a query and manage the join types for those relationships. You will also learn how to format fields in a query design and how to show top values in a summary query.

What You Can Do

Changing the Join Type in an Ad-Hoc Query

- When you create queries that pull fields from multiple related tables, join type becomes important. Join type determines which records will be included when compiling a list of records by pulling information from both tables. For example, you might want to allow records from one table to be included in the results only if they have a valid corresponding record in the other table.
- You can force each table to contain only records for which there is a corresponding record in the other table. This is called an **inner join**.
- You can allow all records to appear from one table, even if there isn't a match in the joined table. This is called an **outer join**.
- You can change the join type either for an **ad-hoc join**, or for a regular (permanent) relationship between two tables in the Relationships window.
- You cannot change the join type for a relationship that has enforced referential integrity unless it is a one-to-one relationship. That is not an issue for an ad-hoc join because you can't have enforced referential integrity for an ad-hoc join.

WORDS TO KNOW

Ad-hoc join
A relationship between two tables that exists only within the query in which it is created.

Inner join
A join that includes only records that have corresponding matches in a related table.

Outer join
A join that includes all the records in one table, but only the records in a related table that have a corresponding record in the original table.

Top values
Property of a query that shows the first set number of records in a query. When sorted descending, the query shows the top values in the list. When sorted ascending, the query shows the bottom values in the list.

Try It! Changing the Join Type

1. Start Access, and open **A34Try** from the data files for this lesson.
2. Save the file as **A34Try_xx** in the location where your teacher instructs you to store the files for this lesson. Click Enable Content if the security warning bar appears.
3. Open qryIndianaOrders in Datasheet view, and take note of the query results.
4. Right-click the query tab and click Design view. Double-click the join line between the two tables. The Join Properties dialog box opens.
5. Click the third join option. This will create an outer join.

Select a join type for an ad hoc join

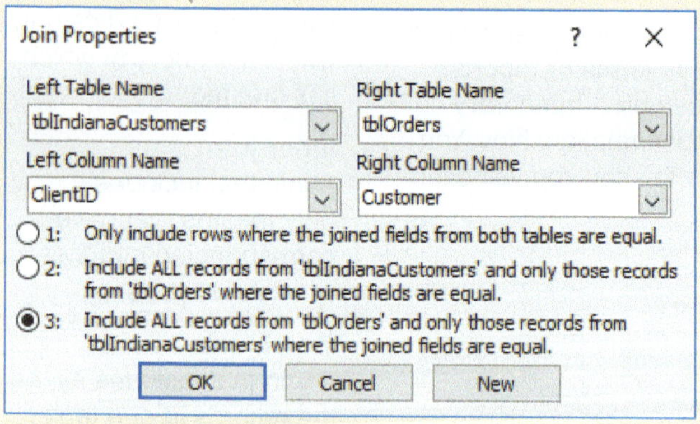

Access 2016, Windows 10, Microsoft Corporation

6. Click OK.
7. Click Query Tools Design > Run ! to see the query results.

   ✓ *Notice that the results have changed since you checked them in step 3.*

8. Click Home > View to return to Design view.
9. Double-click the join line between the two tables.
10. Click the first join option. This will create an inner join.
11. Click OK.
12. Click Query Tools Design > Run ! to see the query results.

    ✓ *Notice that the results are different because of the different join type.*

13. Click the Save button on the Quick Access Toolbar.
14. Right-click the query tab, and click Close.
15. Leave the database open to use in the next Try It.

Try It! Changing the Join Type for a Relationship

1. In **A34Try_xx**, click Database Tools > Relationships.
2. Double-click the line between tblProducts and tblOrderDetails.
3. Click Join Type.
4. In the Join Properties dialog box, click the first option.
5. Click OK.
6. In the Edit Relationships dialog box, click OK.
7. Click Relationship Tools Design > Close.
8. Leave the database open to use in the next Try It.

Changing Field Properties in Query Design View

- You can change the way a field looks in the query results by changing its field properties in Query Design view in the Property Sheet.
- In the Property Sheet, the Format property displays options in the drop-down list depending on the data type. Text fields do not have any drop-down choices in the Format property.
- You can type a custom format in the Format property, such as m/d/yyyy to display the four-digit year along with the month and day. For more details on custom formats, click in the Format property and press F1.
- Type > (greater than) in the Format property to force a text field to be all uppercase or < (less than) to force the field to display in lowercase.
- The Description property allows you to add a note to help you remember what the field does. The description will appear on the status bar in Datasheet and Form views when you are in the field.
- The Input Mask property validates each character as you type it in the field and displays parentheses, dashes, or other characters. Click the Build button to the right of the field and choose a build option in the Input Mask Wizard, just as you do when working in a table's Design view.
- By default, Yes/No fields appear as check boxes. If you want them to display Yes or No, click on the Lookup tab in the Property Sheet and change the Display Control property from Check Box to Text Box.

Try It! Changing Field Properties in Query Design View

1. In **A34Try_xx**, in the Navigation pane, double-click qryOrderInfoSummary. Notice that the amounts in the Total field are formatted as plain numbers.
2. Right-click the query's tab, and click Design View.
3. Click in the Total field's column.
4. If the Property Sheet is not displayed, click Query Tools Design > Property Sheet.
5. In the Property Sheet pane, click in the Format text box. A drop-down list arrow appears.
6. Open the Format drop-down list and click Currency.
7. Click in the Decimal Places field. Open its drop-down list, and click 2.
8. Click Query Tools Design > Run !. The query results appear. Notice that the amounts are formatted as currency.
9. Click the Save button on the Quick Access Toolbar to save the query.
10. Right-click the query's tab, and click Close.
11. Leave the database open to use in the next Try It.

Choose Currency as the field format

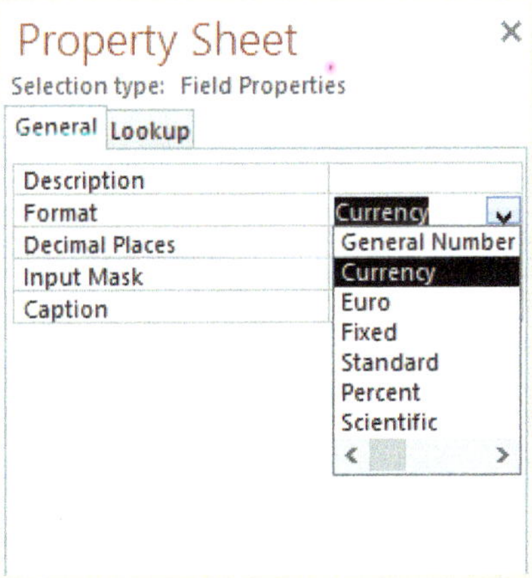

Access 2016, Windows 10, Microsoft Corporation

Showing Top Values

- The **top values** property of a query allows you to see the top (or bottom) values of your list.
- You can use top values in conjunction with a summary query to see a summary of the highest categories, or use it without Totals turned on to see the individual records with the lowest or highest values.
- The top values depend on the sort order of the records. If you want to see the highest values, first sort the field in descending order. If you want to see the lowest values, first sort the field in ascending order.
- Choose a value in the Top Values box (labeled Return), or type a value or percent.
- If you choose or type a percent, the number of values depends on the total number of records. If there are 50 records, 10% will show 5 records.
- If there is a tie on the last record, the query will show all ties. For example, if the 10th, 11th, and 12th records had the same value, you would see all 12 records even if 10 was input in Top Values.

Try It! Showing Top Values

1. In A34Try_xx, in the Navigation pane, right-click qryTopProducts and click Design View.
2. In the Quantity field's column, open the Sort drop-down list and click Descending.
3. On the Query Tools Design tab, open the Return drop-down list and click 5.
4. Click Query Tools Design > Run ! to see the top five products.
5. Click Home > View to return to Design view.
6. Open the Return drop-down list and click 25%.
7. Click Query Tools Design > Run ! to see the top 25% of products.
8. Click Home > View to return to Design view.
9. Click in the Return drop-down list's text box and type 4.
10. Click Query Tools Design > Run ! to see the top 4 products.
11. Right-click the query tab, and click Close. Click Yes to confirm saving your work.
12. Close the database, and exit Access.

Lesson 34—Practice

The Textbook Exchange would like to get some additional information from the database, but the information needed is scattered among several unconnected tables. You will create some queries that bring the needed data together to answer some specific questions they have.

DIRECTIONS

1. Start Access, if necessary, and open **A34Practice** from the data files for this lesson.
2. Save the file as **A34Practice_xx** in the location where your teacher instructs you to store the files for this lesson.

   ✓ *If a security warning bar appears, click Enable Content.*
3. Click **Create** > **Query Design**.
4. Double-click **tblBooks** and **tblMoreBooks** to add them to the query. Then click **Close**.
5. Drag the **ISBN** field in **tblBooks** to the **ISBN** field in **tblMoreBooks**, creating an ad-hoc join.
6. Double-click the join line between the two tables, opening the Join Properties dialog box.
7. Click option **3 (Include ALL records from 'tblMoreBooks' and only those records from 'tblBooks' where the joined fields are equal)**.
8. Click **OK**.
9. Double-click the following fields to add them to the query grid:

   From **tblBooks: ISBN, Title, Our Price**

   From **tblMoreBooks: OutOfPrint**
10. Open the **Table** drop-down list for the **ISBN** column in the query grid and click **tblMoreBooks**.
11. Click **Query Tools Design** > **Run** ! to check the query results. See Figure 34-1. Then click **Home** > **View** to return to Query Design view.
12. Right-click the query's tab and click **Close**. Click **Yes** when prompted to save.
13. In the Save As dialog box, type **qryCrossCheckBooks** and click **OK**.
14. Close the database, and exit Access. If instructed, submit this database to your teacher for grading.

Figure 34-1

Query1

ISBN	Title	Our Price	OOP
020133466X			☐
0201741244	Introduction To Data Security	$21.00	☐
0805346332	Lectures in Design Technique	$37.00	☐
201237368	Understanding Web Publishing	$20.00	☐
201402894			☐
201615993	Public Key Encryption	$25.00	☐
201700028			☐
201702733	Network Administration for All	$27.50	☐
201730598	The HTML Companion	$22.50	☐
201736279	Understanding Broadband Technologies	$20.00	☐
201746717	The Web Wizard's Guide to PHP	$14.20	☐
201751686	Visual Basic from the Ground Up	$35.00	☐
201758791	Nitty Gritty HTML	$15.00	☐
*			▣

Access 2016, Windows 10, Microsoft Corporation

Lesson 34—Apply

In this project, you will continue working on The Textbook Exchange's database. You will add queries that will allow them to access the information they need in a more efficient manner.

DIRECTIONS

1. Start Access, if necessary, and open **A34Apply** from the data files for this lesson.
2. Save the file as **A34Apply_xx** in the location where your teacher instructs you to store the files for this lesson.

   ✓ *If a security warning bar appears, click Enable Content.*
3. Create a new query in Design view. Add **qryBooksForSale** and **tblMoreBooks** as the data sources.
4. Add the following fields to the query grid:

   From **tblMoreBooks**: **ISBN**, **Author**

   From **qryBooksForSale**: **Condition**, **AskingPrice**, **Retail Price**
5. If **qryBooksForSale** and **tblMoreBooks** are not already joined by their ISBN fields, join them.
6. Edit the join type for the relationship so that all books from **tblMoreBooks** appear in the results and only the records from **qryBooksForSale** where the joined fields are equal.
7. Save the query as **qryMoreBooksForSale** and run it to check your work. See Figure 34-2. Then close the query.
8. Open **qryBooksByDiscount** in Design view.
9. Using the Property Sheet, set the format for the **Discount** column to **Percent**.
10. Run the query to confirm that the Discounts show up as percentages. Then save and exit the query.
11. Copy **qryBooksByDiscount** and name the copy **qryTopBargains**.
12. Open **qryTopBargains** in Design view. Set it up to be sorted in **Descending** order by the **Discount** column.
13. Set up the query to show only the top **10** records.
14. Run the query to confirm that only 10 records show. Then save and close the query.
15. Close the database, and exit Access. If instructed, submit this database to your teacher for grading.

Figure 34-2

qryMoreBooksForSale

ISBN	Author	Condition	Asking Price	Retail Price
020133466X	Cheswick			
0201741244	Roeger			
0805346332	Crane			
1562438115	Ashford	Good	$10.00	$30.00
1562438115	Ashford	Like New	$15.00	$30.00
1585770884	Stevenson	Good	$22.00	$30.00
1585770884	Stevenson	Like New	$21.00	$30.00
201237368	Robertson			
201402894	Salvage			
201615993	Smith			
201700028	Budd			
201702733	Limoncelli			
201730598	Bradley			
201736279	Smith			
201746717	Lehnert			
201751686	Skansholm			
201758791	Stein			
*				

End-of-Chapter Activities

➤ Access Chapter 5—Critical Thinking

Cleaning Up a Database

A friend who is trying to organize her collection of vintage CDs has asked for your help with her database. She has created several tables, but because she did not enforce referential integrity, there are some problems with inconsistencies between them. In addition, the database still contains records for some CDs that she has given away or sold. You will help her out by using queries to tidy up her database.

DIRECTIONS

1. Start Access, if necessary, and open **ACT05** from the data files for this chapter.
2. Save the file as **ACT05_xx** in the location where your teacher instructs you to store the files for this chapter.

   ✓ *If a security warning bar appears, click Enable Content.*
3. Using a Find Unmatched query, find any recordings from **tblRecordings** that have no tracks listed in **tblTracks**.
4. Keep the query; name it **qryFindUnmatchedRecordings**.
5. Delete the track from **tblRecordings**.
6. Enforce referential integrity between **tblRecordings** and **tblTracks** so the problem will not occur in the future.
7. Create a query called **qryMinimumPrice** that prompts the user to enter a minimum purchase price to display, and then displays a list of all recordings that cost at least that amount. Show all available fields from the **tblRecordings** table for each recording. Test the query to ensure that the results are accurate.
8. Use an Append query to add the records from **tblMoreArtists** to **tblArtists**. Save the Append query as **qryAppendArtists**. Run the query to append the records to tblArtists.
9. Create a query that shows the last 5 recordings purchased using Top Values. Name the query **qryLastFive**. Run the query to check the results.
10. Close the database, and exit Access. If instructed, submit this database to your teacher for grading.

➤ Access Chapter 5—Portfolio Builder

Creating Queries in a Database

You are a consultant for The Tutoring Center, a company that offers academic test preparation and tutoring. You will create some queries that will help the office staff get information from their database.

DIRECTIONS

1. Start Access, if necessary, and open **APB05** from the data files for this chapter.
2. Save the file as **APB05_xx** in the location where your teacher instructs you to store the files for this chapter.

   ✓ *If a security warning bar appears, click Enable Content.*

3. Using the Crosstab Query Wizard, create a new query based on **qryEnrollment** that counts the number of enrollments for each course offered, with separate columns for each year as in Illustration 5A. Name the query **qryEnrollmentSummary**.
4. Make a copy of **qryEnrollment**, and name the copy **qryFutureEnrollment**.
5. Modify **qryFutureEnrollment** to create a parameter prompt that asks the user for today's date and then shows enrollments only for classes that begin after the current date. Test it by entering several different dates before and after the start dates in the unfiltered query results.
6. Create a query that deletes the inactive records from the **tblClasses** table and run it. Save the query as **qryDeleteInactiveClasses**.
7. In **qryClassesAndInstructors**, format the **ClassName** field so that all class names appear in all uppercase. Run the query to test it.
8. Using any method, create a query that lists the names of the top 3 most expensive courses offered and their prices. Name it **qryTop3Prices**.
9. Close the database, and exit Access. If instructed, submit this database to your teacher for grading.

Illustration 5A

qryEnrollmentSummary

Class	Total Of EnrollmentID	2016	2017
ACT Prep	11	11	
Algebra I	6		6
SAT Prep	6		6

Access 2016, Windows 10, Microsoft Corporation

Chapter 6

(Courtesy auremar/Shutterstock)

Customizing Forms and Reports

Lesson 35
Working with Report Layouts

- Viewing a Report in Layout View
- Switching Between Layout Types
- Adjusting Control Margins and Control Padding
- Adding, Deleting, and Reordering Fields
- Inserting a Title
- Changing the Page Setup
- Adding Statistics

Lesson 36
Working with Controls

- Understanding Controls
- Inserting Text Box Controls
- Binding a Record Source to a Form
- Binding and Unbinding Fields to Controls
- Inserting List Boxes and Combo Boxes
- Inserting Labels
- Renaming a Control
- Inserting Check Boxes
- Inserting Option Button Groups

Lesson 37
Formatting Controls

- Formatting Controls on Forms and Reports
- Using Conditional Formatting
- Concatenating Fields

Lesson 38
Creating Special Forms

- Using Multi-Item Forms
- Creating a Split Form Using the Split Form Tool
- Setting a Form's Default View

Lesson 39
Working with Subforms and Subreports

- Understanding Subforms and Subreports
- Creating a Form and Subform with the Form Wizard
- Creating a Subform with the Subform Wizard
- Creating a Subreport with Drag-and-Drop
- Editing a Subform or Subreport

Lesson 40
Working with Charts

- Inserting a Chart in a Report
- Editing a Chart
- Changing the Chart Type
- Changing Chart Options

Lesson 41
Creating Switchboards

- Opening the Switchboard Manager
- Managing Switchboard Pages
- Editing a Switchboard Page's Content
- Formatting the Switchboard
- Activating or Deactivating the Switchboard

Lesson 42
Creating Navigation Forms

- Creating a Navigation Form
- Adding Command Buttons to a Form
- Tying a Navigation Form into the Switchboard

End-of-Chapter Activities

Lesson 35

Working with Report Layouts

➤ What You Will Learn

Viewing a Report in Layout View
Switching Between Layout Types
Adjusting Control Margins and Control Padding
Adding, Deleting, and Reordering Fields
Inserting a Title
Changing the Page Setup
Adding Statistics

WORDS TO KNOW

Print layout
The placement of fields on a report page.

Stacked report
A report that arranges data in rows with each field for each record on a separate row.

Tabular report
A report that arranges data in columns with each column representing a field.

Totals
Statistics that summarize report data, such as sum, count, or average.

Software Skills The default reports that Access creates are fine for some circumstances, but in many cases you can improve them with a few simple tweaks. For example, you can control the print layout and change the margins or you can change the orientation.

What You Can Do

Viewing a Report in Layout View

- **Print layout** refers to the placement of fields on a report page. It can include margin settings, field sizes, spaces between fields, placement of text labels, page orientation, and more.
- You can change the print layout either in Design view or Layout view.
- Layout view enables you to move, resize, and arrange fields in a what-you-see-is-what-you-get environment, unlike in Design view. This lesson focuses on Layout view.
- When you are working in Layout view, four additional tabs appear on the ribbon:
  - Report Layout Tools Design: Contains buttons and commands for grouping controls and for adding more controls to the report. You will learn more about these options in a later lesson.
  - Report Layout Tools Arrange: Enables you to change the overall layout of the report fields and the positioning of individual objects quickly.
  - Report Layout Tools Format: Contains buttons and commands for formatting controls and text on the report.
  - Report Layout Tools Page Setup: Provides settings that govern the page size and orientation, margins, and number of columns.

Try It! Viewing a Report in Layout View

1. Start Access, and open **A35Try** from the data files for this lesson.
2. Save the file as **A35Try_xx** in the location where your teacher instructs you to store the files for this lesson. Click Enable Content if the security warning bar appears.
3. Right-click rptCustomerMailing and click Layout View.
4. Leave the report open to use in the next Try It.

Switching Between Layout Types

- A report can be laid out either in Tabular or Stacked mode.
- A **tabular report** arranges data in columns with each column representing a field. Figure 35-1 shows an example of a tabular report.
- A **stacked report** arranges data in rows with each field for each record in a separate row, as shown in Figure 35-2 on the next page.
- You can select all of the fields at once by clicking the Layout Selector icon in the upper-left corner of the layout grid.
- To switch between the two modes, select the fields you wish to change and select either Tabular or Stacked on the Report Layout Tools Arrange tab.
- Fields must be selected before changing the layout, so that it is possible to have a combination report, using tabular layout for some fields and stacked layout for others. If you do not select fields before the layout change, then the entire report layout will be changed.
- The Remove command takes a field out of the layout grid, making it a free-floating object on the report. This might be useful to position a field in a precise location, for example.

Figure 35-1

Access 2016, Windows 10, Microsoft Corporation

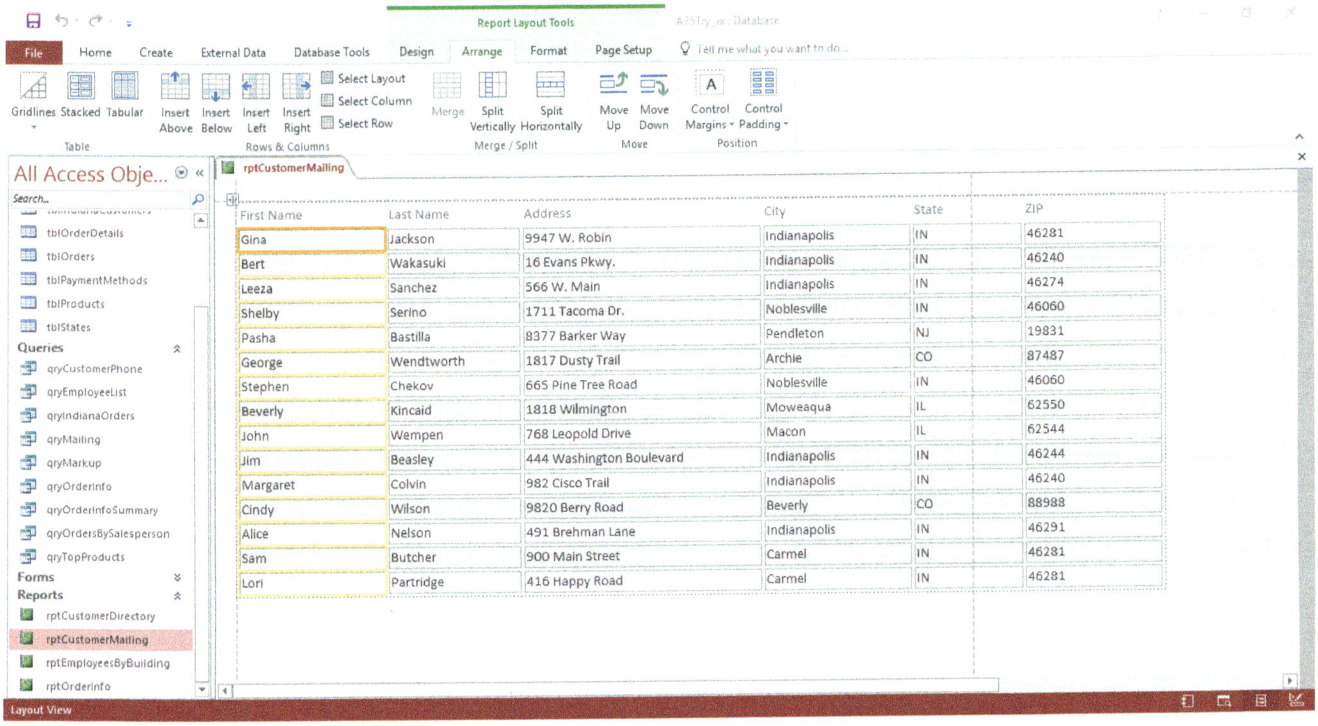

Figure 35-2

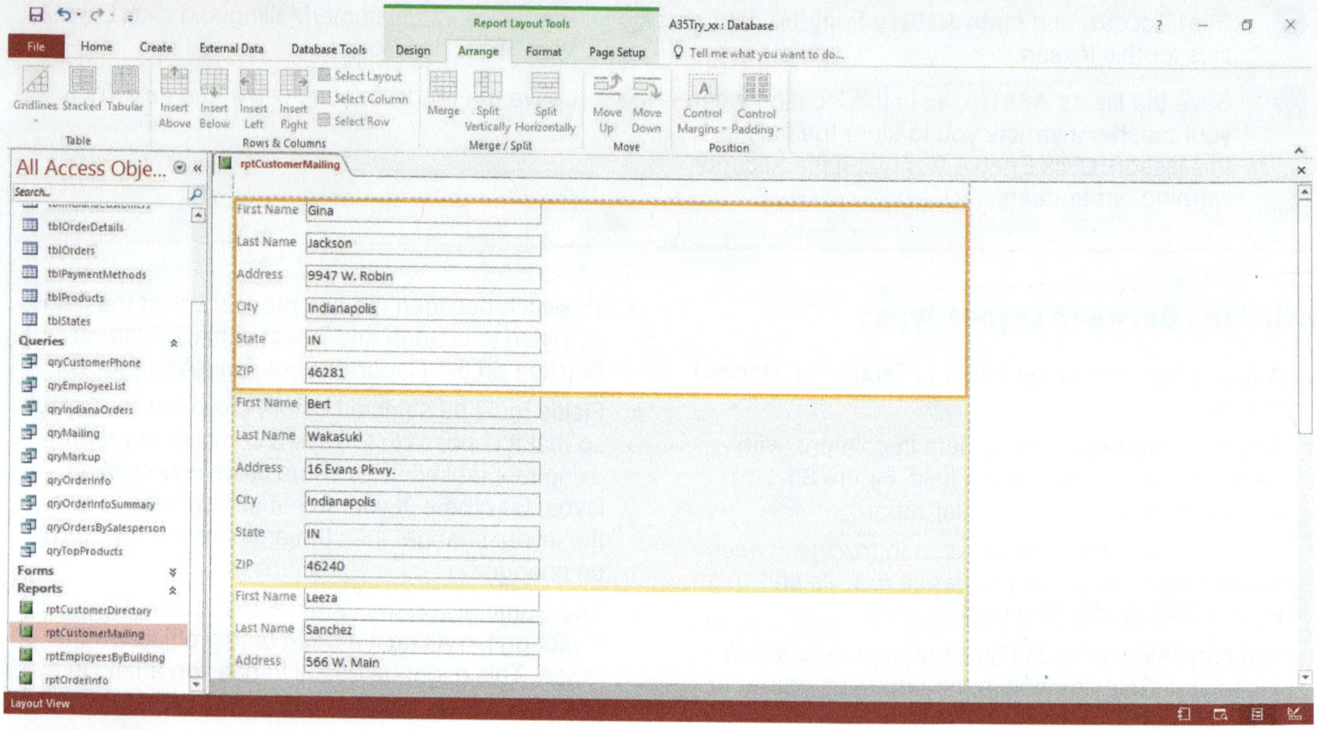

Access 2016, Windows 10, Microsoft Corporation

Try It! Switching Between Layout Types

1. In the A35Try_xx file, in rptCustomerMailing click the Layout Selector Icon in the upper-left corner of the table. All fields appear with an orange border around them indicating that they are selected.
2. Click Report Layout Tools Arrange > Stacked. The layout changes to a stacked layout, as seen in Figure 35-2.
3. Press CTRL + Z to undo the last action, returning the report to a Tabular layout.
4. Leave the report open for the next Try It.

Click the Layout Selector icon to select all fields

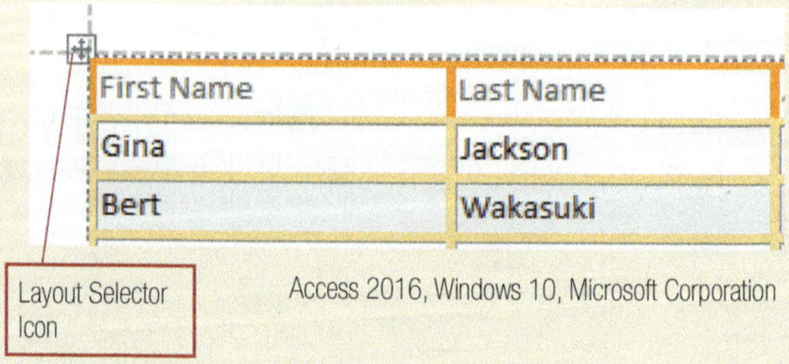

Access 2016, Windows 10, Microsoft Corporation

Adjusting Control Margins and Control Padding

- Each field and its data appear in a separate tabular cell on the layout. Each of these cells can have its margins and paddings set individually.
- The Control Margins drop-down list on the Arrange tab refers to the internal margins within the cells of the layout, not to the margins for the entire page. The margin setting here determines how much blank space there will be between the inner edge of a cell and the text within it.

✓ *If you want to change the margins for the entire report, use the Margins button on the Page Setup tab.*

- The Control Padding drop-down list sets the space between the outer edge of a cell and the outer edge of an adjacent cell in the layout grid.

Try It! Adjusting Control Margins and Control Padding

1. In the A35Try_xx file, open rptCustomerMailing in Layout view, if it isn't already open.
2. Click the first entry in the First Name column.
3. Click Report Layout Tools Arrange > Control Padding > Medium. The padding between the cells increases.
4. Click Report Layout Tools Arrange > Control Margins > Wide. The internal margins in each cell increases so much that the text is no longer fully visible.
5. Click Report Layout Tools Arrange > Control Margins > Narrow. The text appears readable in the cell.
6. Leave the report open for the next Try It.

Adding, Deleting, and Reordering Fields

- To add a field to the layout, click Add Existing Fields on the Report Layout Tools Design tab. A Field List task pane appears. From there you can view a list of fields in the available tables and drag-and-drop a field onto the layout grid.
- You can change the order of the fields by dragging the field to the left or right (in a tabular layout) or up or down (in a stacked layout).
- To remove a field from the layout, select it and press DEL.

Try It! Adding, Deleting, and Reordering Fields

1. In the A35Try_xx file, with rptCustomerMailing open in Layout view, click in the First Name column.
2. Click Report Layout Tools Arrange > Select Column.

   ✓ *Step 2 is necessary to select the entire column, not just the content in it. If you don't do this, you'll be left with an empty but still-present column when you delete.*

3. Press DEL.
4. In Report Layout Tools Design click Add Existing Fields.
5. Drag the FirstName field from the Field List to the report layout, and drop it between the Last Name and Address fields. Close the Field List pane.
6. Click in the First Name column.
7. Click Report Layout Tools Arrange > Select Column.
8. Drag the First Name column to the left and drop it to the left of the Last Name column.
9. Leave the report open to use in the next Try It.

Inserting a Title

- If the report does not already have a label at the top that functions as a title, you can add one by clicking the Title button on the Report Layout Tools Design tab.
- If the report already has a title, this command moves the insertion point into the title box, so that you can change the title if needed.

Try It! Inserting a Title

1. In the **A35Try_xx** file, with rptCustomerMailing open in Layout view, click Report Layout Tools Design > Title. A placeholder title appears.
2. Type **Customer Mailing Information**, replacing the placeholder text.
3. Click the blank cell to the left of the title.
4. Press DEL.
5. Leave the report open to use in the next Try It.

Changing the Page Setup

- Page setup includes the paper size, page orientation, page margins, and number of columns. All of these are controlled from the Report Layout Tools Page Setup tab.
- On the Report Layout Tools Page Setup tab, you can:
  - Select a paper size from the Size button's list.
  - Select a margin preset from the Margins button's list.
  - Mark or clear the Show Margins check box to show margins in Layout view or not.
  - Mark or clear the Print Data Only check box to print data only or not. You might do this, for example, if filling out a preprinted form. You would want to see the preprinted labels and headings onscreen, but not on the hard copy.
  - Click Portrait or Landscape to change page orientation.
  - Click the Columns button to open the Columns tab in the Page Setup dialog box.
  - Click Page Setup to open a Page Setup dialog box in which you have greater control over many of these settings, such as the ability to specify exact margin amounts.

Try It! Changing the Page Setup

1. In the **A35Try_xx** file, with rptCustomerMailing open in Layout view, click Report Layout Tools Page Setup > Margins > Normal.
2. Click Size > Letter 8.5"x11".
3. Click Landscape.
4. Click Page Setup. The Page Setup dialog box opens.
5. On the Print Options tab, enter **0.45** in the Left text box, replacing the current value.
6. Enter **0.45** in the Right text box, replacing the current value.
7. Click OK.
8. Close the report, saving changes.

Adding Statistics

- Report statistics are called **totals** in Access.
- After clicking More for a grouping, you can click with no totals for a Totals box in which you can specify the statistics you want to display for each group. You can choose the field on which to total the function to use (such as Sum or Average), whether or not to show grand totals, and whether to show totals in the group header or group footer.
- When you specify totals, the expressions needed to create them are inserted automatically in the proper section(s).
- You can also manually enter your own expressions in placed text boxes in any section. Click the Text Box tool on the Report Layout Tools Design tab, and then click in a footer or header section and type in any of the following:
  - =SUM([fieldname]) to total the values in the fieldname field.
  - =AVG([fieldname]) to average the values in the fieldname field.
  - =COUNT([fieldname]) to return the number of items in the fieldname field.
  - =MAX([fieldname]) to return the largest value in the fieldname field.
  - =MIN([fieldname]) to return the smallest value in the fieldname field.

✓ *If you just want to show the statistics and not the records themselves, click the Hide Details button on the Report Layout Tools Design tab.*

Try It! Adding Statistics with the Totals Pane

1. In the **A35Try_xx** file, right-click the rptEmployeesByBuilding report and click Layout View.
2. On the Report Layout Tools Design tab, click Group & Sort. Click More on the Group on Building bar.
3. Click the down arrow to the right of with no totals. A Totals panel opens.
4. Open the Total On drop-down list and click Building.
5. Click the Show subtotal in group footer check box. The Totals panel closes, and the report now shows the number of values in each group. Close the Group, Sort, and Total pane.
6. Right-click the report's tab and click Close. Click Yes when prompted to save your changes.
7. Leave the database open to use in the next Try It.

Add a subtotal by group

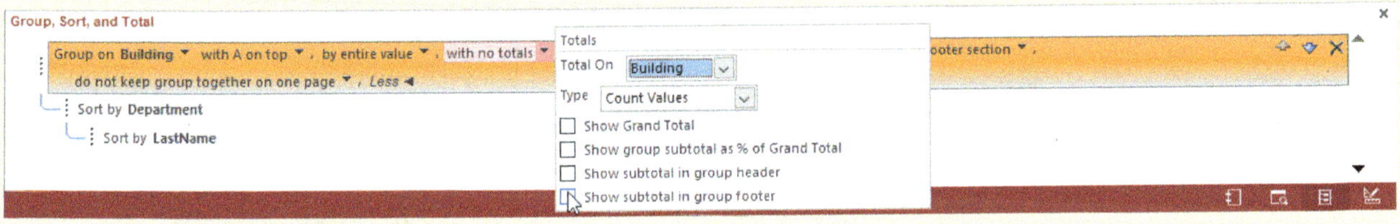

Access 2016, Windows 10, Microsoft Corporation

Try It! Adding Statistics with a Function

1. In the A35Try_xx file, right-click rptOrderInfo and click Design View.
2. Click Report Layout Tools Design > Text Box.
3. Click in the Salesperson Footer section, approximately 1.5" from the right edge. An unbound text box appears. Drag the text box to make its right edge align with the right edge of the Quantity text box above it.
4. Click in the text box and type =SUM([Quantity]).
5. Double-click the text in the label associated with the text box to select the label text and type Total:.
6. Click the Total: label to select it, and then drag it (by its upper-left corner selection handle) closer to the text box.

   ✓ *Dragging a label by its upper-left corner selection handle enables you to move the label separately from its associated text box.*
7. Right-click the report's tab, and click Report View to preview your work.
8. Right-click the report's tab and click Close. Click Yes when prompted to save your work.
9. Close the database, and exit Access.

Lesson 35—Practice

In this project, you will create a new report in the Michigan Avenue Athletic Club's database that shows instructor's teaching assignments. You will edit the report's set up to look more professional.

DIRECTIONS

1. Start Access, if necessary, and open **A35Practice** from the data files for this lesson.
2. Save the file as **A35Practice_xx** in the location where your teacher instructs you to store the files for this lesson.

   ✓ *If a security warning bar appears, click Enable Content.*
3. Open **rptEnrollment** in Layout view.
4. Click **Report Layout Tools Design** and click **Group & Sort**.
5. Click **More** in the Group, Sort, and Total pane.
6. Click the down arrow to the right of with ClassName totaled. A Totals panel opens.
7. Uncheck the **Show Grand Total** check box.
8. Click **More** again.
9. Then, click the down arrow to the right of with no totals.
10. Click the **Show subtotal in group footer** check box.
11. Resize the subtotal box if necessary to display the data, and then save and close **rptEnrollment**.

    ✓ *The subtotal box will appear at the end of each section.*
12. In the Navigation pane, click **qryTeachingAssignments** once to select it.
13. Click **Create** > **Report**. A new report appears in Layout view.
14. Double-click the report title to select it. Type **Teaching Assignments**, replacing the default title.
15. Select one of the fields in the report, then click the **Layout Selector** icon to select all fields and records.
16. Click **Report Layout Tools Arrange** > **Stacked**.
17. Click **Report Layout Tools Page Setup** > **Margins** > **Wide**.
18. On the **Report Layout Tools Page Setup** tab, click **Landscape**.
19. Click **Report Layout Tools Arrange** > **Control Padding** > **None**.

20. **With your teacher's permission**, print the report.
21. Press CTRL + S to save the report.
22. In the Save As dialog box, type **rptTeachingAssignments** and click **OK**.
23. Close the database, and exit Access.

Lesson 35—Apply

The Michigan Avenue Athletic Club would like you to improve on a report in their database that lists class enrollments. You will set up a print layout for this report that makes it as attractive as possible.

DIRECTIONS

1. Start Access, if necessary, and open **A35Apply** from the data files for this lesson.
2. Save the file as **A35Apply_xx** in the location where your teacher instructs you to store the files for this lesson.

   ✓ *If a security warning bar appears, click Enable Content.*
3. Open **rptEnrollment** in Layout view.
4. Add a title to the top of the report. Title it **Enrollment Information**.

   ✓ *Be sure and remove the cell to the left of the title.*
5. Use Page Setup to change the report margins to **0.5"** on all sides.
6. Set the control padding for the entire report to **Medium**.
7. Adjust the column widths for all columns so that all the fields fit across one page horizontally.
8. At the bottom left of the report, delete the record count field (37).
9. At the bottom right of the report, delete the **Page 1 of 1** text.
10. **With your teacher's permission**, print the report.
11. Save and close the report.
12. Close the database, and exit Access. If instructed, submit this database to your teacher for grading.

Lesson 36

Working with Controls

➤ What You Will Learn

Understanding Controls
Inserting Text Box Controls
Binding a Record Source to a Form
Binding and Unbinding Fields to Controls
Inserting List Boxes and Combo Boxes
Inserting Labels
Renaming a Control
Inserting Check Boxes
Inserting Option Button Groups

WORDS TO KNOW

Bound control
A control that is connected to a field from a table or query.

Combo box
A text box with an associated drop-down list. Users may enter their own values or select from the list.

Control
Any object on a form or report, including fields, text labels, pictures, and so on.

List box
A control that consists of a drop-down list. Users are restricted to the values on the list; they cannot enter other values.

Unbound control
A control that has no connection to a field from a table or query.

Software Skills For more control over a form or report's appearance, you can create it in Design view. In Design view, you can insert various types of controls such as check boxes, option buttons, and drop-down lists that enhance the form or report's appearance and functionality.

What You Can Do

Understanding Controls

- A **control** is any object on a form or report. Controls can include text boxes, labels, drop-down list boxes, hyperlinks, and many other object types.
- Some types of controls display data from a table or query. For example, fields can appear as text boxes, list boxes, check boxes, or other control types.
- Other types of controls provide visual aids that make the form or report easier to understand, such as labels that identify the title of the report or a tab or grouping that provides a logical structure in which you place fields.
- Some text boxes and labels can be placed in Layout view, but most work involving controls is typically done in Design view. In Design view, you can move, format, insert, and delete all types of controls.

  ✓ *Most controls can be used on either forms or reports, but many of them make more sense on a form. For example, a list box on a report would not be very useful because it would show only one value when printed; it would not be, functionally, any different from a text box.*

- Figure 36-1 shows some of the most common types of controls you can use.

Figure 36-1

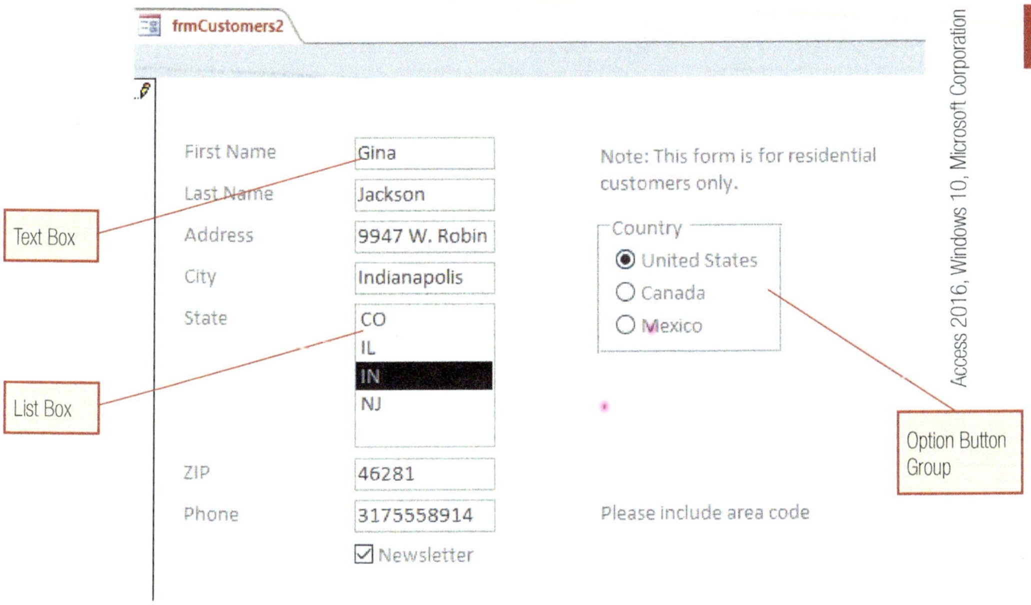

Inserting Text Box Controls

- Text boxes can be placed on forms and reports in either of two ways, based on whether or not they are bound or unbound. A **bound control** is connected to a field in a table or query. For example, when you place a field on a form, you are actually placing a bound text box on that form.
- An **unbound control** is not linked to one particular field. You might place an unbound text box on a form and then type a formula in it that calculates values from multiple fields, for example.

Try It! Inserting a Bound Text Box and Label on a Form

1. Start Access, and open **A36Try** from the data files for this lesson.
2. Save the file as **A36Try_xx** in the location where your teacher instructs you to store the files for this lesson. Click Enable Content if the security warning bar appears.
3. Click Create > Form Design. A blank form opens.
4. If the Field List pane does not appear, click Form Design Tools Design > Add Existing Fields.
5. If a list of tables does not appear in the field list, click Show all tables.
6. Click the plus sign next to tblCustomers, if the list of its fields is not already expanded.
7. Double-click the FirstName field. A text box (for the field itself) and a label (containing the field's caption) appear on the form.
8. Double-click the LastName, Address, City, State, and ZIP fields to add them to the form.
9. Click the Save button on the Quick Access Toolbar.
10. In the Save As dialog box, type **frmCustomers2** and click OK.
11. Leave the form open to use in the next Try It.

Try It! Inserting an Unbound Text Box and Label on a Form

1. In the frmCustomers2 form in the **A36Try_xx** file, right-click the Detail section bar, and click Form Header/Footer. The form header and footer areas open up.
2. Scroll down to the Form Footer area, and drag the bottom border of the footer down, enlarging the footer by 0.5".
3. On the Form Design Tools Design tab, in the Controls group, click the Text Box button [ab|]. The mouse pointer changes to a text box button symbol.
4. Click in the Form Footer section, near the 4" mark on the horizontal ruler. A new unbound text box is placed in the form footer.
5. Click the label associated with the new text box and press [DEL]. The label is deleted; the text box remains.
6. Drag the left edge of the text box to the left to enlarge the text box so it is at least 1.5" in width.
7. Click in the text box and type **=now( )**.
8. Click Form Design Tools Design > View to check the text box. Today's date and time should appear in it.

   ✓ *If #### appears in the text box, you did not widen it enough in step 6.*

9. Right-click the form's tab, and click Design View to return to Design view.
10. Press [CTRL] + [S] to save the changes to the form.
11. Leave the form open to use in the next Try It.

Place a new unbound text box in the footer of the form

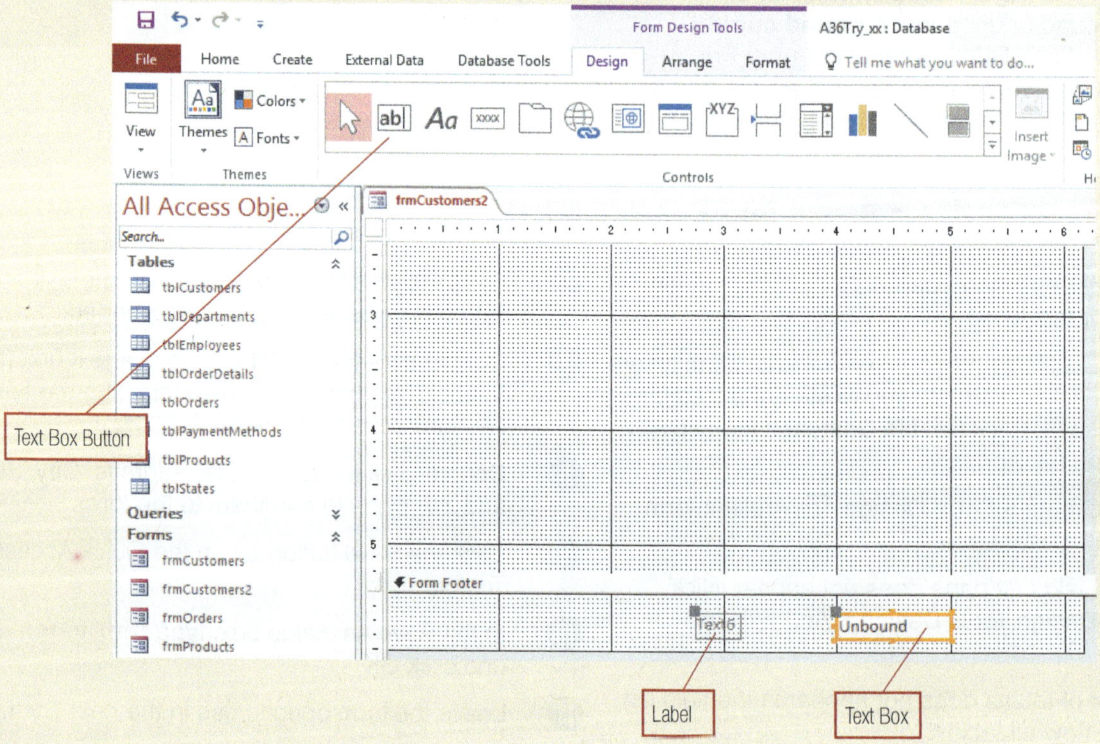

Access 2016, Windows 10, Microsoft Corporation

Binding a Record Source to a Form

- A form that you create from scratch using the Create > Form Design command does not have a record source assigned. In other words, the form is not associated with a table or query, by default.
- As you add fields to the form, those individual fields become part of its record source. However, any fields from that same table/query that are not added to the form are not part of the record source and therefore are not available for binding to controls that you manually insert.
- For this reason, it may be useful to bind a table or query to the report before you start adding controls other than field text boxes. Additional individual fields can be bound as well as an entire table or query.

Try It! Editing the Record Source for the Form

1. In the **A36Try_xx** file, click the Form Selector button in the upper-left corner of the form to select the frmCustomers2 form itself (not any specific section or object).

   ✓ *The Form Selector button selects the entire form, but it does not appear highlighted.*

2. If the Property Sheet pane does not already appear, click Form Design Tools Design > Property Sheet.
3. In the Property Sheet, on the Data tab, click the Build button for the Record Source property. A Query Builder interface appears, similar to Query Design view.
4. Scroll the query grid to the left, if necessary, to see which fields are currently included. Only the fields you added to the form earlier in the lesson are included.
5. On the field list, double-click InputDate to add it to the query, and then double-click each of the other fields following InputDate.
6. Click Query Tools Design > Close. A confirmation appears.
7. Click Yes.
8. Leave the form open to use in the next Try It.

Click the form selector to select the entire form

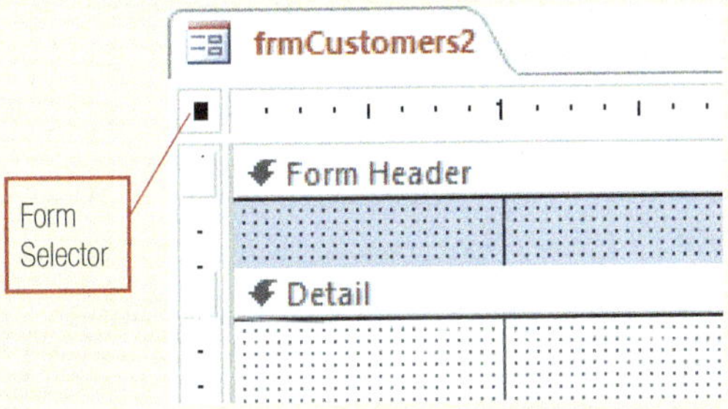

Access 2016, Windows 10, Microsoft Corporation

Try It! Assigning an Entire Table As a Record Source

1. In the **A36Try_xx** file, click the Form Selector button in the upper-left corner of the form to select the frmCustomers2 form itself (not any specific section or object).
2. In the Property Sheet, on the Data tab, open the drop-down list for the Record Source property.
3. Click tblCustomers.
4. Leave the form open to use in the next Try It.

Binding and Unbinding Fields to Controls

- You can create an unbound control and then bind a field to it later if you prefer.
- A control's binding is controlled from the Control Source property in its Property Sheet. The Control Source property can be found on both the Data and the All tabs.
- When you click in the Control Source box, a drop-down list of the fields in the currently selected data source (table or query) appears. You can select one of these to avoid potential typing errors from manually typing the field name.
- If you know the exact names of the table and field you want to reference in the control, you can manually type them as an expression; you do not have to go through the Expression Builder. If the field is from the same table or query as the primary record source for the form, you can type its name directly into the text box in Design view.
- If you want to reference a field from a different (related) table or query, you can write an expression that references the table name and the field name, like this: **=[tblEmployees]![Notes]**.

  ✓ *Alternatively, you can click the Build button ... to open the Expression Builder. From here, you can pick fields from other data sources or you can create more complex expressions.*
- To unbind a control from the data source, clear the value in the Control Source box.

Try It! Binding a Control to a Field

1. In the **A36Try_xx** file, with frmCustomers2 open in Design view, insert an unbound text box immediately below the ZIP field's text box.

   ✓ *Refer to the steps provided earlier in the lesson.*
2. If the Property Sheet is not already displayed, click Form Design Tools Design > Property Sheet.
3. Click the Data tab in the Property Sheet pane.
4. Open the Control Source property's drop-down list and click Phone.
5. Edit the Phone field's label to display Phone.
6. Insert another unbound text box immediately below the Phone field's text box.
7. Click in the new text box, and type **InputDate**. Change the new text box's label to Input Date.
8. Right-click the form's tab, and click Form View to preview the form and confirm that the Phone and Input Date fields appear correctly.
9. Right-click the form's tab, and click Design View to return to Design view.
10. Leave the form open to use in the next Try It.

Try It! Unbinding a Control

1. In the **A36Try_xx** file, with frmCustomers2 open in Design view, click in the InputDate text box to select it.
2. In the Property Sheet pane, clear the Control Source text box. Unbound appears in the text box.
3. Select the text box and press DEL, removing it from the form.
4. Press CTRL + S to save the changes to the form.
5. Leave the form open to use in the next Try It.

Inserting List Boxes and Combo Boxes

- **List boxes** and **combo boxes** are alternatives to text boxes for entering and displaying data. Both are text boxes with drop-down list capability, and both are used to allow users to select a value from a list rather than having to type a value.
- A list box restricts users to only the values you present on the list. A combo box allows users to also enter their own values (for example, if none of the list's values are appropriate).

Try It! Inserting a List Box on a Form

1. In the **A36Try_xx** file, with frmCustomers2 open in Design view, on the Form Design Tools Design tab, in the Controls group, click the More button to open a palette of available controls.
2. Click the List Box button. The mouse pointer changes to a crosshair.

Click the List Box button in the Controls palette

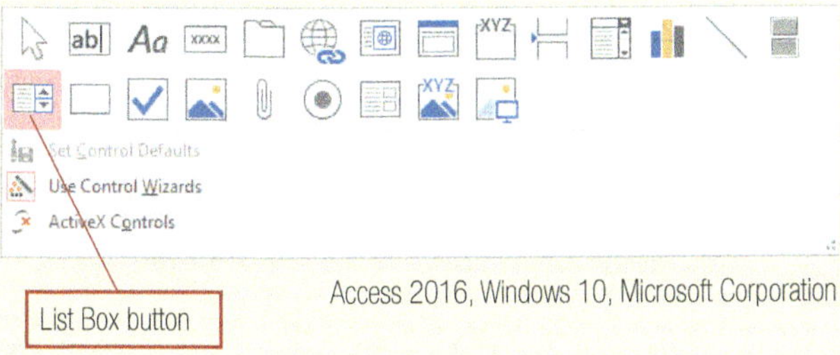

Access 2016, Windows 10, Microsoft Corporation

Select State as the field in which to store the values

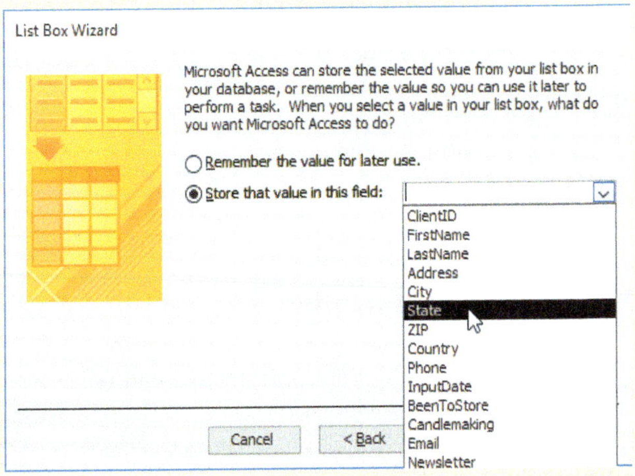

Access 2016, Windows 10, Microsoft Corporation

3. Position the crosshair about 2" to the right of the right edge of the State field's text box, and click. The List Box Wizard appears.
4. Click Next to accept the default value (I want the list box to get the values from another table or query).
5. Click Table: tblStates and click Next.
6. Click the > button to move the State field to the Selected Fields list. Then, click Next.
7. When prompted for sorting, open the drop-down list and click State. Then, click Next.
8. Click Next to accept the default width of the list column.
9. Click the Store that value in this field option button.
10. Open the drop-down list and click State. Then, click Next.
11. Type **State** in the text box, replacing the default label for the control.
12. Click Finish.
13. Click the original State field (not the list box you just created) and press DEL.
14. Drag the ZIP and Phone fields down on the form to make enough space that the new State list box fits in the space formerly occupied by the old State text box.
15. Drag the State list box into the spot formerly occupied by the deleted State field.
16. Click Form Design Tools Design > View to view the form. Look at the State list and confirm that it is working.
17. Click the Save button on the Quick Access Toolbar.
18. Right-click the form's tab, and click Design View to return to Design view.
19. Leave the form open to use in the next Try It.

Inserting Labels

- When you add bound controls to a field, such as a field text box, the associated caption for it automatically appears in a label.
- You can also create unbound labels for titles or explanatory notes.
- If you click on the form after selecting the Label button, a label box appears that automatically expands as you type. To create line breaks, press SHIFT + ENTER.
- If you drag on the form after selecting the Label button, a label box appears that is the size and shape of the area you dragged. Text automatically wraps to the next line as needed as you type in it.

Try It! Inserting a Label on a Form

1. In the **A36Try_xx** file, with frmCustomers2 open in Design view, on the Form Design Tools Design tab, in the Controls group, click the Label button *Aa*.
2. Click in the empty area to the right of the form fields in the Detail section.
3. Type the following: **Note: This form is for residential**.
4. Press SHIFT + ENTER to start a new line.
5. Type the following: **customers only.**
6. Leave the form open to use in the next Try It.

Try It! Associating a Label with a Control

1. In the **A36Try_xx** file, with frmCustomers2 open in Design view, on the Form Design Tools Design tab, in the Controls group, click the Label button.
2. Click on the form to the right of the Phone text box.
3. Type **Please include area code**.
4. Click outside of the control and then click the control to select it. Then, click the warning icon to the left of the new label. A menu appears.
5. Click Associate Label with a Control.
6. Click Text8 and click OK.

   ✓ *The number following Text may be something other than 8. There should only be one item that starts with Text on the list.*

7. Press CTRL + S to save the form.
8. Leave the form open to use in the next Try It.

The warning icon opens a menu

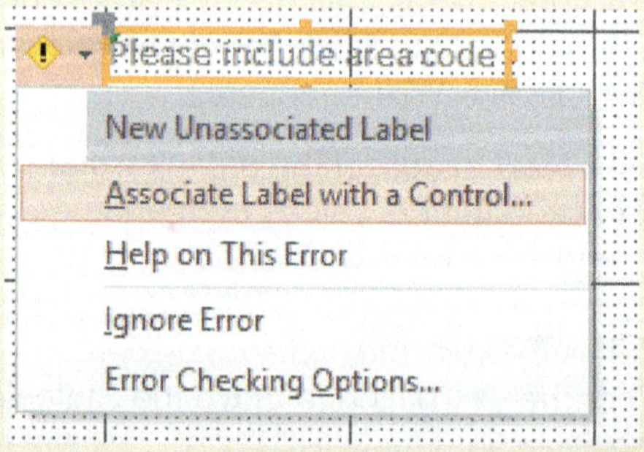

Access 2016, Windows 10, Microsoft Corporation

Renaming a Control

- In the preceding exercise, the text box for the Phone field had a generic name, such as Text8, because it was originally an unbound text box when created. Text boxes that start out bound to fields have names assigned that match the field names automatically.
- You can rename a control on its Property Sheet.

Try It! Renaming a Control

1. In the **A36Try_xx** file, with frmCustomers2 open in Design view, select the Phone text box.
2. If the Property Sheet pane is not open, click Form Design Tools Design > Property Sheet.
3. Click the Other tab.
4. In the Name property, change the name to **Phone**.
5. Leave the form open to use in the next Try It.

Inserting Check Boxes

- When you place a Yes/No field on a form, it automatically appears as a check box control with an associated label.
- You can also place an unbound check box on a form and then bind it to a field as you learned earlier in the lesson.

Try It! Inserting Check Boxes

1. In the **A36Try_xx** file, with frmCustomers2 open in Design view, on the Form Design Tools Design tab, in the Controls group, click the More button to open a palette of available controls.
2. Click the Check Box button. The mouse pointer changes to a crosshair.
3. Click on the form, immediately beneath the Phone field text box. A check box and generic label appear.
4. On the Property Sheet, on the Data tab, open the Control Source property's drop-down list and click Newsletter.
5. Click in the label associated with the check box and type **Newsletter**, replacing the placeholder.
6. Leave the form open to use in the next Try It.

Inserting Option Button Groups

- Option button groups are used as an alternative to a list box when there are only a few valid values that a field can have.
- In an option button group, when one button is selected, the previously-selected button becomes deselected. This exclusivity is what distinguishes option buttons from check boxes, which can each, individually, have their own on/off state.

Try It! Inserting Option Button Groups

1. In the **A36Try_xx** file, with frmCustomers2 open in Design view, on the Form Design Tools Design tab, in the Controls group, click the More button to open a palette of available controls.
2. Click the Option Group button.
3. Click in the blank area to the right of the Address text box on the form. The Option Group Wizard opens.
4. Type the following label names, each on their own row:

   United States

   Canada

   Mexico
5. Click Next.
6. Click Next to accept the default choice of United States.
7. Click Next to accept the default number assignments for the options.
8. Click Store the value in this field.
9. Open the drop-down list and click Country. Then, click Next.
10. Click Next to accept the default button type.
11. Type **Country**, replacing the default caption text.
12. Click Finish.
13. Press CTRL + S to save the form.
14. Right-click the form's tab and click Form View to display the form in Form view.
15. Save and close the form.
16. Close the database, and exit Access.

Enter the values for the option buttons

Access 2016, Windows 10, Microsoft Corporation

Lesson 36—Practice

In this project, you will create a form with the Combo Box control type for the Michigan Avenue Athletic Club's database.

DIRECTIONS

1. Start Access, if necessary, and open **A36Practice** from the data files for this lesson.
2. Save the file as **A36Practice_xx** in the location where your teacher instructs you to store the files for this lesson.

   ✓ *If a security warning bar appears, click Enable Content.*

3. Click **Create** > **Form Design**. A new form appears in Design view.
4. If the Property Sheet does not appear, click **Form Design Tools Design** > **Property Sheet**.
5. Select the Data tab. In the Record Source property, open the drop-down list and click **tblClassOfferings**.
6. Click ✕ to close the Property Sheet.
7. Click **Form Design Tools Design** > **Add Existing Fields**. A list of fields in tblClassOfferings appears.
8. Double-click the **ClassOfferingID** field. It is added to the form.
9. On the Form Design Tools Design tab, in the Controls group, click the **More** button, opening a palette of control types.
10. Click the **Combo Box** button.
11. Click on the form, immediately below the ClassOfferingID field. The Combo Box Wizard appears.
12. Leave the default option selected (I want the combo box to get the values from another table or query) and click **Next**.
13. Click **Table: tblClasses** and click **Next**.
14. Click the **ClassName** field and click > to move it to the Selected Fields list. Then, click **Next**.
15. Open the drop-down list and click **ClassName** to set the sort field. Then, click **Next**.
16. Double-click the right edge of the **Class** heading in the dialog box to auto-widen the column to fit the longest entry. Then, click **Next**.
17. Click **Store that value in this field**.
18. Open the drop-down list, and click **Class**. Then, click **Next**.
19. Type **Class**, replacing the default label for the control. Then, click **Finish**.
20. Drag the right edge of the new control to the right to increase its width to **2"**.
21. Click the **Save** button on the Quick Access Toolbar.
22. Type **frmClassOfferings** and click **OK**.
23. Right-click the form's tab and click **Form View** to display the form in Form View. See Figure 36-2.
24. **With your teacher's permission**, print the form.
25. Close the database, and exit Access. If instructed, submit this database to your teacher for grading.

Figure 36-2

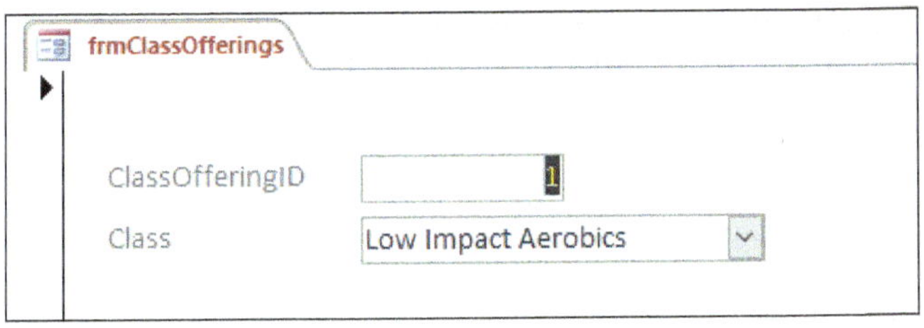

Access 2016, Windows 10, Microsoft Corporation

Lesson 36—Apply

Michigan Avenue Athletic Club would like for you to create a form that the office manager can use to enter and look up class offerings. You will create this form using a variety of control types and enter a record for him.

DIRECTIONS

1. Start Access, if necessary, and open **A36Apply** from the data files for this lesson.
2. Save the file as **A36Apply_xx** in the location where your teacher instructs you to store the files for this lesson.

   ✓ *If a security warning bar appears, click Enable Content.*
3. Open **frmClassOfferings** in Design view.
4. Delete the **Notes** field.
5. Beneath the Size Limit field, add a combo box for the **Instructor** field.
   a. Set it to look up the first and last names from **tblInstructors**.
   b. Sort the list by **Last Name**.
   c. Store the value in the **Instructor** field.
   d. Name the combo box **Instructor**.
6. Below the Instructor combo box, add an option group that provides buttons for selecting a location:
   a. Use the following list: **Gym, Pool, Upstairs Studio**.
   b. Do not set a default choice.
   c. Use the default values for each option.
   d. Store the value in **Location**.
   e. Use **Option buttons**.
   f. Use **Shadowed** as the group style.
   g. Name the group **Location**.
7. Move the option group's label to the left, to align with the other labels on the form.
8. Save the form, and view it in Form View.
9. In Form View, enter a new record:

   Class: **Low Impact Aerobics**

   Start: **11/27/2017 08:00 AM**

   Days: **MWF**

   Duration: **6 weeks**

   Size Limit: **20**

   Instructor: **Carrie Anderson**

   Location: **Upstairs Studio**
10. In Design view, to the right of the Start fields, create a new label with the following text:

    Enter a date and time. You can use the Calendar button to select a date, if desired.
11. Associate the label with the **StartTime** control.

    ✓ *Click the icon to the left of the unbound label, and on the menu that appears, click Associate Label with a Control, and click StartTime.*
12. **With your teacher's permission**, print one copy of the form with the new record displayed. See Figure 36-3.
13. Open the frmClasses form in Design view and create a calculated field, with a currency format, in the Form Footer section that calculates the total price for all of the sessions. Label the field as **Total Price for All Sessions.**

    ✓ *You will need to add a text box field. You will need to build the =[NumberOfSessions]*[Price] formula.*

    ✓ *Go to the Format tab to change the calculation to currency.*
14. Close the database, and exit Access. If instructed, submit this database to your teacher for grading.

Figure 36-3

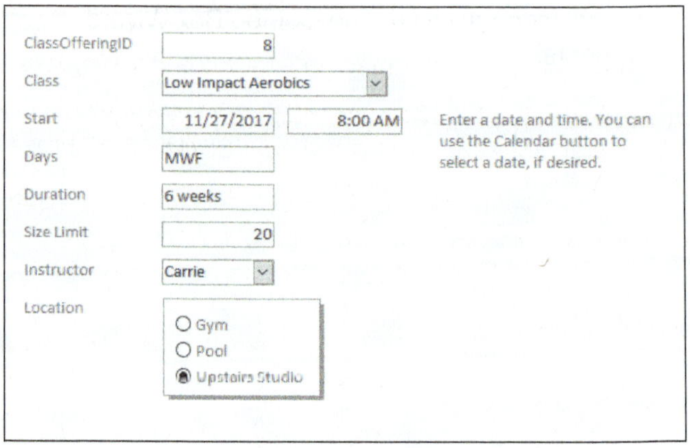

Access 2016, Windows 10, Microsoft Corporation

Lesson 37

Formatting Controls

➤ What You Will Learn

Formatting Controls on Forms and Reports
Using Conditional Formatting
Concatenating Fields

Software Skills Forms and reports are very similar in terms of the formatting you can apply to them. Both enable you to position fields and labels for optimal viewing; the main difference is that a form is designed for onscreen use whereas a report is designed to be printed. In this lesson, you will learn some tips and tricks for formatting and concatenating controls on forms and reports.

WORDS TO KNOW

Concatenate
To join two separate entities into a single one, such as combining a first and last name to form a full name.

Conditional formatting
Formatting that is applied only when a condition is met.

Expression
A logical condition including comparison operators such as greater than (>), less than (<), or equals (=).

What You Can Do

Formatting Controls on Forms and Reports

- You can apply the same types of formatting to controls on forms and reports that you would apply in any word processing program. For example, you can change the font, font size, font color, attributes such as bold and italics, and text alignment (left, right, or center).
- You can also apply a background fill to the control that applies color behind the text in that control's frame.
- To copy formatting between controls, use the Format Painter. Select the control that is already formatted correctly, and then click the Format Painter button. Then, click the control to receive the formatting.

  ✓ *To paint the formatting onto multiple destinations without having to reselect the source each time, double-click instead of single-clicking the Format Painter button.*

- All of these formatting features are found on the Format tab when in Layout or Design view. See Figure 37-1 on the next page.

Figure 37-1

Access 2016, Windows 10, Microsoft Corporation

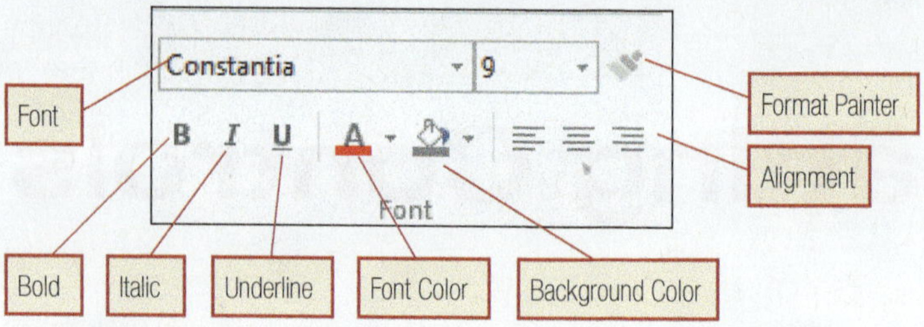

Try It! Formatting Controls on a Report

1. Start Access, and open **A37Try** from the data files for this lesson.
2. Save the file as **A37Try_xx** in the location where your teacher instructs you to store the files for this lesson. Click Enable Content if the security warning bar appears.
3. In the Navigation pane, right-click rptEmployeesByBuilding and click Layout View.
4. Click the Building column heading to select it.
5. Hold down CTRL and click the Department column heading.
6. Click Report Layout Tools Format > Bold **B**.
7. Open the Font Size drop-down list and click 11.
8. Open the Font Color button's menu and click Yellow.
9. Click the Building column heading so that only that heading is selected.

   ✓ *Format Painter is available only when a single object is selected.*
10. Double-click the Format Painter button.
11. Click the Last Name and First Name headings.
12. Press ESC to cancel Format Painter.
13. Right-click the report's tab and click Close. Click Yes when asked to save changes.
14. Leave the database open to use in the next Try It.

Using Conditional Formatting

- **Conditional formatting** sets up special formatting conditions that should apply if the value in a field or other control meets certain criteria.
- Some examples: You could color items with low sales (under a certain dollar amount) in red to indicate a problem, or you could underline the names of students who have not yet paid for a class.
- Conditional formatting can be applied to both forms and reports, in both Design and Layout views.
- Conditional formatting conditions can be set either by the field's value or by an expression. An **expression** is a formula. It can reference field names (enclosed in square brackets).
- [Quantity] * [Unit Price] > 1000 is an example of an expression. In this case, the conditional formatting would apply if multiplying the values from the Quantity and Unit Price fields resulted in a value of more than 1,000.
- You must use an expression if you want to format a control (or multiple controls) based on the value of another control, or based on the result of a calculation.
- You must also use an expression to apply conditional formatting to an unbound control (that is, a control that is not connected to a field in an underlying table, query, or SQL statement). The date in a report's footer is an example of an unbound control.
- You do not have to type an equals sign at the beginning of a function in the Conditional Formatting dialog box.

- You can use almost all of the functions from Microsoft Excel in expressions in Access.
- For example, suppose you want the date at the bottom of the report to print in bold if the report is being printed on a Monday because it is the first report of the week.
- Access has a WEEKDAY function that converts a date to a number representing the day of the week (starting with Sunday as 1). Access also has a NOW function that returns today's date and time. You can combine these to make an expression for conditional formatting: WEEKDAY(NOW)=2.

Try It! Using Conditional Formatting

1. In the **A37Try_xx** file, in the Navigation pane, right-click frmOrders and click Layout View.
2. Click the Payment Method text box (not its label) to select it.
3. Click Form Layout Tools Format > Conditional Formatting. The Conditional Formatting Rules Manager dialog box opens.
4. Click New Rule. The New Formatting Rule dialog box opens.
5. Open the second drop-down list (currently showing as between) and click equal to.
6. In the text box to the right of the drop-down list, type **Cash**.
7. Click the Bold button **B** in the dialog box.
8. Open the Font Color button's menu in the dialog box and click a green square.
9. Click OK.
10. Click OK to close the Conditional Formatting Rules Manager dialog box.
11. Click the Next Record button to move to record 2, which has Cash as the payment type. Note the formatting applied.
12. Click the Save button on the Quick Access Toolbar to save the changes. Then, right-click the form's tab and click Close.
13. Leave the database open to use in the next Try It.

Set up the new formatting condition

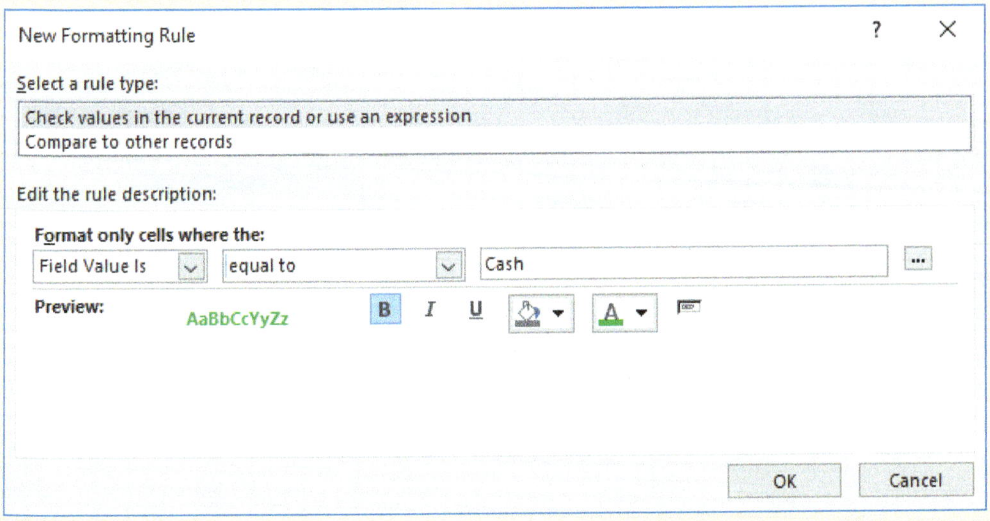

Access 2016, Windows 10, Microsoft Corporation

Try It! Using an Expression in Conditional Formatting

1. In the A37Try_xx file, in the Navigation pane, right-click rptOrderInfo and click Layout View.
2. Click the first entry in the Quantity column.
3. Click Report Layout Tools Format > Conditional Formatting.
4. Click New Rule.
5. Open the first drop-down list (currently set to Field Value Is) and click Expression Is.
6. Click the Build button to open the Expression Builder.
7. In the middle pane (Expression Categories), double-click Quantity. It appears in the text box at the top of the dialog box.
8. Type **>1**.
9. Click OK.

✓ *You can type the expression directly into the New Formatting Rule dialog box if you prefer; the Expression Builder's use is optional. When typing field names, enclose them in square brackets, like this: [Quantity].*

10. Open the Font color button's drop-down list and click Automatic.
11. Open the Background color button's drop-down list and click a light blue square.
12. Click OK.
13. Click OK to close the Conditional Formatting Rules Manager. In all records where the Quantity is more than 1, the quantity now appears with a light blue background.
14. Right-click the report's tab and click Close. When prompted to save changes, click Yes.
15. Leave the database open to use in the next Try It.

Create an expression with the Expression Builder

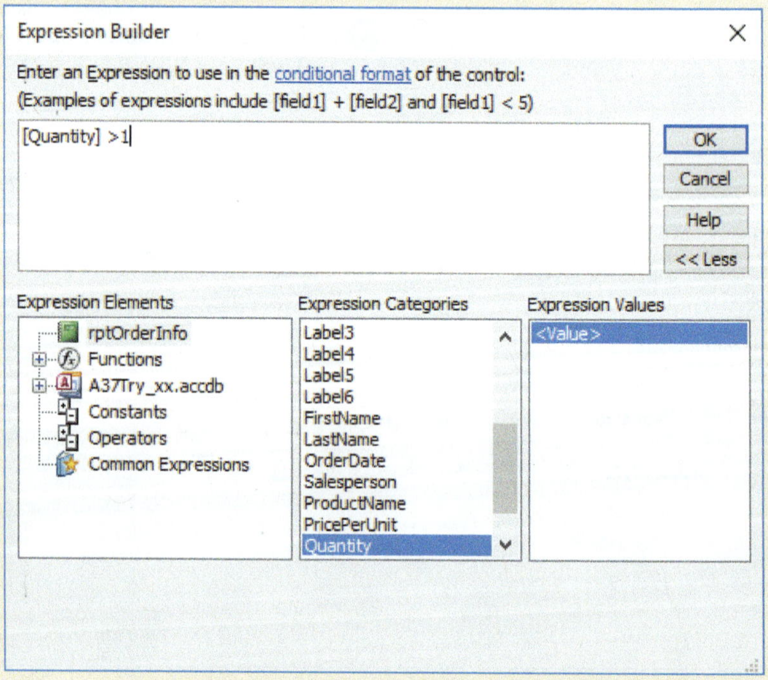

Access 2016, Windows 10, Microsoft Corporation

Concatenating Fields

- Some reports may look better if multiple fields are combined in a single control, such as first and last name.
- To **concatenate** (combine) fields, first delete their original individual fields from the report. Then, in Design view, add a new text box with the Text Box tool. (You cannot do this from Layout view.) In the new text box, type an expression that begins with an equals sign and then contains the field names in square brackets, separated by ampersand signs (&).
- To include spaces or fixed text or punctuation between the fields, enclose it in quotation marks.
- For example, to combine FirstName and LastName fields:
  =[FirstName]&" "&[LastName]
- To combine City, State, and ZIP fields:
  =[City]&", "&[State]&" "&[ZIP]

Try It! Concatenating Fields

1. In the **A37Try_xx** file, in the Navigation pane, right-click rptCustomerDirectory and click Design View.
2. In the Detail section, select LastName and press DEL.
3. In the Detail section, select FirstName and press DEL.
4. On the Report Design Tools Design tab, in the Controls group, click the Text Box button ab|.
5. Click in the Detail area in the blank spot. A new blank text box appears.
6. Type **=[FirstName]&" "&[LastName]**.
7. Click away from the text box to deselect it.
8. Click the label to the left of the new text box and press DEL to remove it.
9. Drag the right border of the new text box to the right to widen it to fill the available space.

   ✓ *The expression you typed in the text box will appear truncated; that's okay. It will still work.*
10. In the Page Header section, select the First Name label and press DEL.
11. In the Page Header section, in the Last Name label, delete Last so the label reads Name.
12. Click Report Design Tools Design > View to switch to Report view so you can check your work.
13. Right-click the report's tab and click Close. Click Yes when prompted to save changes.
14. Close the database, and exit Access.

Create an expression that concatenates the values of two fields

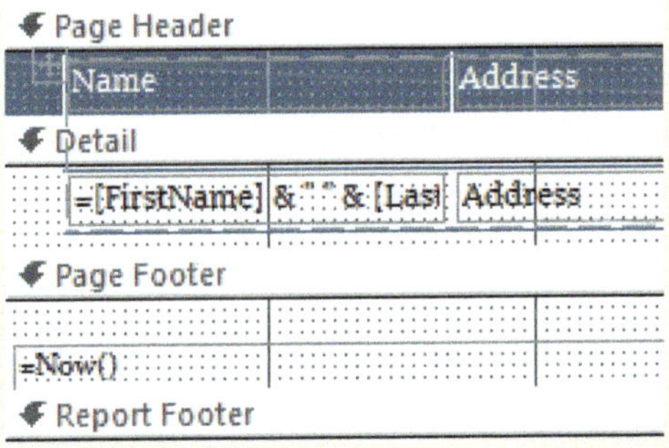

Access 2016, Windows 10, Microsoft Corporation

Lesson 37—Practice

In this project, you will edit a report and format the report's controls for the Michigan Avenue Athletic Club.

DIRECTIONS

1. Start Access, if necessary, and open **A37Practice** from the data files for this lesson.
2. Save the file as **A37Practice_xx** in the location where your teacher instructs you to store the files for this lesson.

   ✓ *If a security warning bar appears, click Enable Content.*
3. In the Navigation pane, right-click **rptTeachingAssignments** and click **Layout View**.
4. Click the **Class** label for the first record if it is not already selected.
5. Click **Report Layout Tools Format** > **Bold** B.
6. Right-click the report's tab and click **Design View**.
7. Click the **FirstName** text box and press DEL.
8. Click the **LastName** text box and press DEL.
9. Click **Report Design Tools Design** > **Text Box** ab|.
10. Click in the space formerly taken by the FirstName field to place an unbound text box there.
11. Click in the text box and type **=[FirstName] &" "& [LastName]**.
12. Click the label associated with the new text box and change its text to **Instructor**.
13. Drag the text box and label to align with the other text boxes and labels on the form.

    ✓ *Because the form uses a layout, you can make the text box and label snap to the layout. Drag the text around slightly until an orange box lights up behind it, indicating that if you drop it, it will drop into the layout. Then, release the mouse button. Doing this not only positions it in the layout but also automatically adjusts its width to match the other fields. Figure 37-2 shows the completed design.*
14. Right-click the report's tab, and click **Report View**.
15. **With your teacher's permission**, print the report.
16. Right-click the report's tab and click **Close**. When prompted, click **Yes** to save your work
17. Close the database, and exit Access. If instructed, submit this database to your teacher for grading.

Figure 37-2

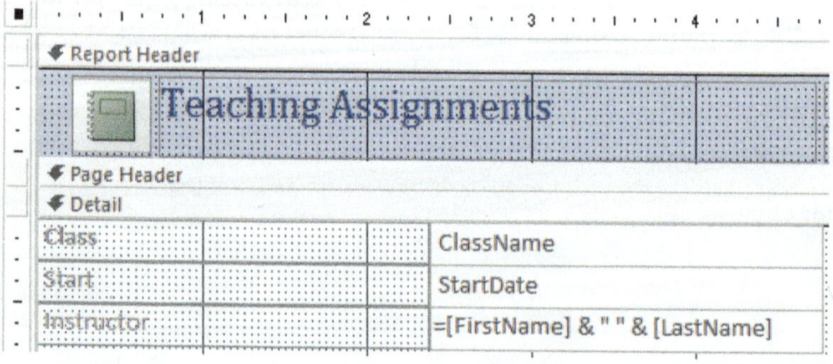

Access 2016, Windows 10, Microsoft Corporation

Lesson 37—Apply

Michigan Avenue Athletic Club would like you to modify a form that shows class offerings such that if a particular class is on sale, the sale price is reflected onscreen and is marked with special formatting.

DIRECTIONS

1. Start Access, if necessary, and open **A37Apply** from the data files for this lesson.
2. Save the file as **A37Apply_xx** in the location where your teacher instructs you to store the files for this lesson.

   ✓ *If a security warning bar appears, click Enable Content.*
3. Open **frmClassOfferings** in Layout view.
4. Create a conditional formatting rule that makes the price of the class appear in red if the Sale check box is marked.
5. Using the Text Box tool, place a new text box below the Sale check box.
6. In the new text box, enter **="On Sale Now"**.
7. Delete the label associated with the new text box.
8. Format the new text box to use pale gray font color, so the text disappears into the background.
9. Click **Form Design Tools Format** > **Shape Outline** and click **Transparent** to remove the border from the new text box. If the text box has a white fill, click **Form Design Tools Format** > **Shape Fill** and click **Transparent** to remove the fill color.
10. Check your work in Form view to make sure that there is gray text that blends into the background.
11. Set up a conditional format for the new text box so that if the Sale check box is marked, the text in it appears in bright red.
12. Check your work in Form view, viewing several records, to make sure the *On Sale Now* text appears only when the class is on sale. See Figure 37-3.
13. Close the database, and exit Access. If instructed, submit this database to your teacher for grading.

Figure 37-3

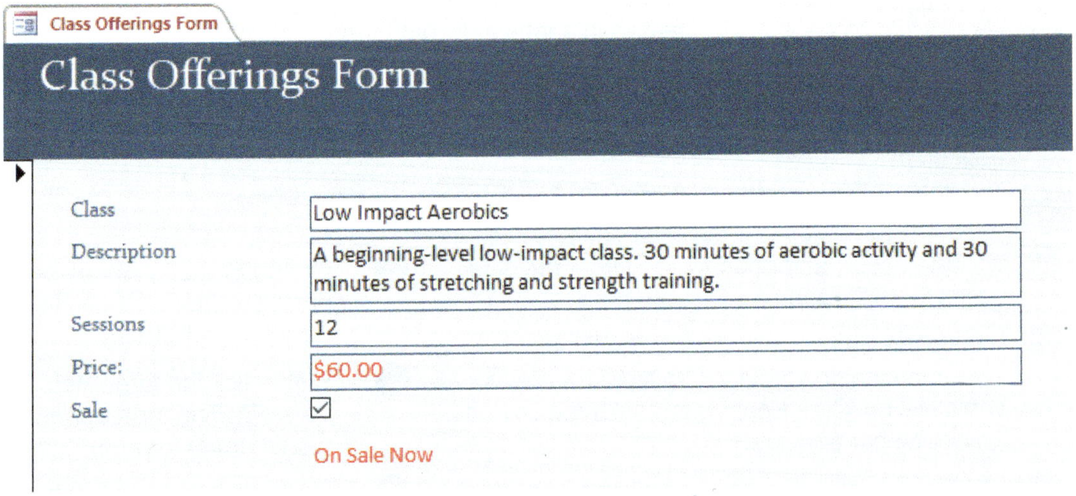

Access 2016, Windows 10, Microsoft Corporation

Lesson 38

Creating Special Forms

➤ What You Will Learn

Using Multi-Item Forms
Creating a Split Form Using the Split Form Tool
Setting a Form's Default View

WORDS TO KNOW

Multi-item form
A form that shows more than one record at the same time.

Split form
A form view that shows Datasheet view in half the window and Form view fields in the other half.

View
A formatting filter through which an object can be seen. Different views arrange fields and records differently onscreen without changing the underlying structure.

Software Skills Access offers a variety of form views. In this lesson, you will try your hand at using several types of form views that differ from the traditional default layout.

What You Can Do

Using Multi-Item Forms

- A **multi-item form** is not actually a form type, but rather a **view** of a form (also called Continuous Forms view). In this view, multiple records are displayed at once. The form can use any arrangement (tabular or stacked). Figure 38-1 on the next page shows a multi-item form.
- You can also create a new multi-item form from any table, query, or form. This results in a tabular layout form.

Try It! **Displaying a Form in Continuous Forms View**

1. Start Access, and open **A38Try** from the data files for this lesson.
2. Save the file as **A38Try_xx** in the location where your teacher instructs you to store the files for this lesson. Click Enable Content if the security warning bar appears.
3. In the Navigation pane, right-click frmCustomerContact and click Design View.
4. If the Property Sheet is not already open, click Form Design Tools Design > Property Sheet.
5. On the Property Sheet, on the Format tab, open the Default View drop-down list and click Continuous Forms.
6. Right-click the form's tab, and click Form View. The form appears as a multi-item (continuous) form.
7. Right-click the form's tab and click Close. Click No when prompted to save changes.
8. Leave the database open for the next Try It.

Figure 38-1

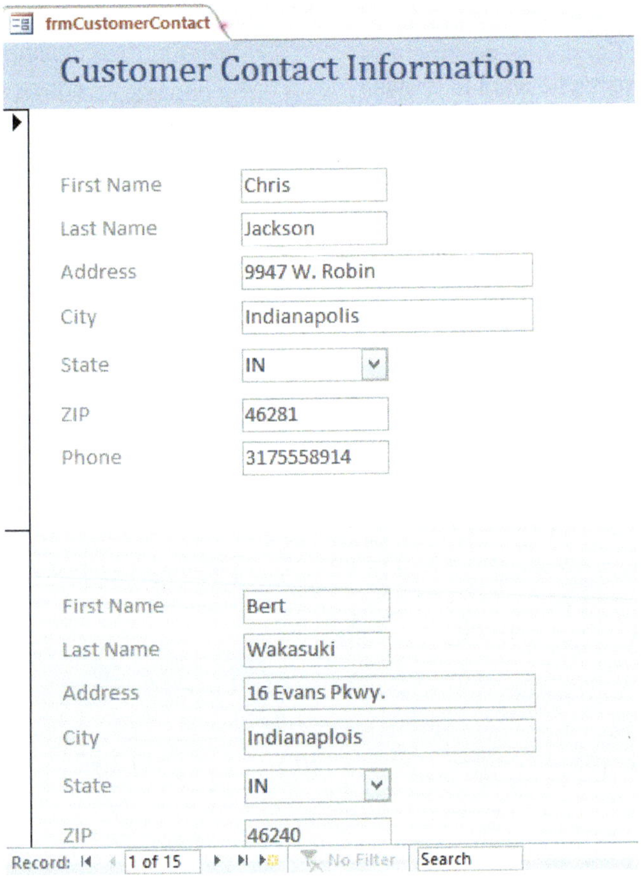

Try It! Creating a New Multi-Item Form

1. In the **A38Try_xx** file, in the Navigation pane, click tblDepartments to select it.
2. Click Create > More Forms > Multiple Items. A multi-item form appears based on the selected table.
3. Right-click the form's tab and click Close. Click No when prompted to save changes.
4. Leave the database open to use in the next Try It.

Creating a Split Form Using the Split Form Tool

- A **split form** is one that displays a Datasheet view on half of the screen and a Form view on the other half. It is useful in cases where you want to browse the data records easily, as with a datasheet, but you also want the ease of data entry that Form view provides. Figure 38-2 shows an example.
- As with the other views discussed so far in this lesson, Split view is just a view, not an actual type of form. Any form can be viewed as a Split form by setting its Default View to Split Form (in Design view) and then closing and reopening the form.
- You can also create a new split form from a table, query, or form.

Figure 38-2

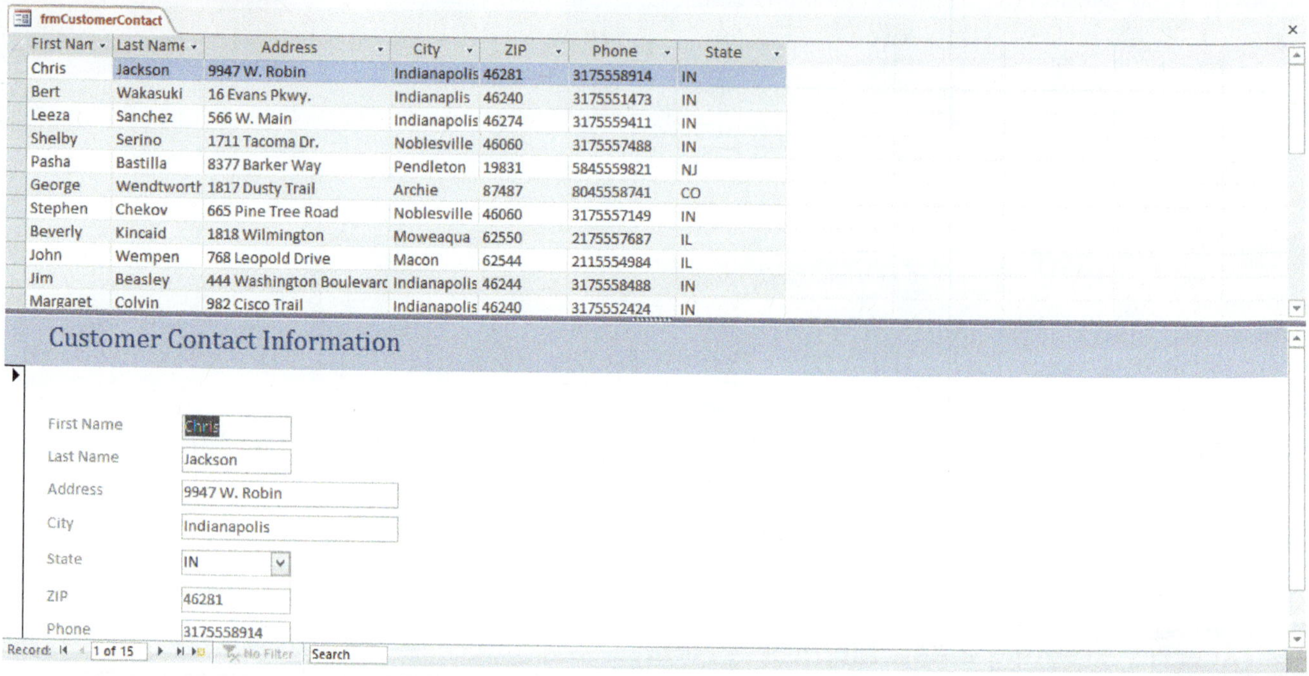

Access 2016, Windows 10, Microsoft Corporation

Try It! Displaying a Form in Split View

1. In the **A38Try_xx** file, in the Navigation pane, right-click frmCustomerContact and click Design View.
2. If the Property Sheet is not already open, click Form Design Tools Design > Property Sheet.
3. On the Property Sheet, on the Format tab, open the Default View property's list and click Split Form.
4. Right-click the report's tab, and click Form View. The form appears as a split form.
5. Right-click the form's tab and click Close. Click Yes when prompted to save changes.
6. Leave the database open for the next Try It.

Try It! Creating a New Split Form

1. In the A38Try_xx file, in the Navigation pane, click tblOrders to select it.
2. Click Create > More Forms > Split Form. A split form appears based on the selected table.
3. Right-click the form's tab and click Close. Click No when prompted to save changes.
4. Leave the database open to use in the next Try It.

Setting a Form's Default View

- If you decide later that you want a form to default to a different view than you chose when you created it, you can edit its properties to make that happen. Change the Default View property to the desired view.

Try It! Setting a Form's Default View

1. In the A38Try_xx file, in the Navigation pane, right-click frmCustomers and click Design View.
2. If the Property Sheet pane does not appear, click Form Design Tools Design > Property Sheet.
3. On the Property Sheet, on the Format tab, set the Default View property to Datasheet.
4. Right-click the form's tab and click Close. Click Yes when prompted to save changes.
5. In the Navigation pane, double-click frmCustomers. It opens in Datasheet view.
6. Right-click the form's tab, and click Design View.
7. On the Property Sheet, set the Default View property to Single Form.
8. Right-click the form's tab and click Close. Click Yes when prompted to save changes.
9. Close the database, and exit Access.

Lesson 38—Practice

You have been asked by a friend who works at Sycamore Knoll Bed and Breakfast for suggestions on improving their database. You will set up their database's forms to use a new view that demonstrates the power of forms in Access.

DIRECTIONS

1. Start Access, if necessary, and open **A38Practice** from the data files for this lesson.
2. Save the file as **A38Practice_xx** in the location where your teacher instructs you to store the files for this lesson.

   ✓ *If a security warning bar appears, click Enable Content.*
3. In the Navigation pane, click **frmReservations** and press CTRL + C to copy it.
4. Press CTRL + V to paste it. In the Paste As dialog box, type **frmReservationsDatasheet** and click **OK**.
5. Right-click **frmReservationsDatasheet** and click **Design View**.
6. If the Property Sheet pane does not appear, click **Form Design Tools Design** > **Property Sheet**.
7. On the Format tab in the Property Sheet pane, open the drop-down list for the **Default View** property and click **Datasheet**.
8. Right-click the form's tab and click **Close**. Click **Yes** when prompted to save changes.
9. In the Navigation pane, double-click **frmReservationsDatasheet**. It opens in Datasheet view.
10. **With your teacher's permission**, print one copy of the form.
11. Close the database, and exit Access. If instructed, submit this database to your teacher for grading.

Lesson 38—Apply

In this project, you will change the view of a form and split a form for the Sycamore Knoll Bed and Breakfasts database.

DIRECTIONS

1. Start Access, if necessary, and open **A38Apply** from the data files for this lesson.
2. Save the file as **A38Apply_xx** in the location where your teacher instructs you to store the files for this lesson.

   ✓ *If a security warning bar appears, click Enable Content.*
3. Change the default view of the **frmEmployees** form to a Continuous Forms view and save it as **frmEmployeesContinuous**.
4. Create a new split form based on **frmReservations** and save it as **frmReservationsSplit**.
5. Close the database, and exit Access. If instructed, submit this database to your teacher for grading.

Lesson 39

Working with Subforms and Subreports

➤ What You Will Learn

Understanding Subforms and Subreports
Creating a Form and Subform with the Form Wizard
Creating a Subform with the Subform Wizard
Creating a Subreport with Drag-and-Drop
Editing a Subform or Subreport

Software Skills When you have one set of records that is related to another, it is much easier to input new records when you can see the main record and the records that are related to it. For example, if you have an order record that could be related to one or more order detail items, the top half of the form might show the order information in general and the bottom half might show the items within the order.

WORDS TO KNOW

Main form
A form that contains a subform or several subforms.

Subform
A form that is enclosed inside another form.

Subreport
Similar to a subform. A report can have a subreport that is the child side of a parent-to-child relationship.

What You Can Do

Understanding Subforms and Subreports

- **Subforms** and **subreports** allow you to see values related to a main record.
- You can go ten levels deep with a subform within a subform within the **main form**. However, one subform level deep is probably plenty in most circumstances; otherwise your forms get too complicated.
- A subform can be displayed in any view (Form view, Datasheet view, and so on). However, most subforms are displayed in Datasheet view by default because it is the most efficient view for packing a lot of information into a small space, and subforms are usually limited in the amount of space they occupy.

✓ *There must be a relationship between the table or query that comprises the main form and the one that comprises the subform. You must create that relationship before creating the form.*

- In a form with a subform, there are two sets of record-navigation controls. The subform has its own set, as does the main form. Figure 39-1 shows a main form and subform.

  ✓ *Once created, a subform also exists outside of the main form, as a separate form in the object list for your database. You can open and use it as a separate form whenever you like. It is customary to include "subform" in the names you assign to subforms so that you will remember what they were created for.*

- To create a subform, you can do any of the following:
  - Use the Form Wizard to create both the main form and the subform at the same time.
  - Create the main form and then use the Subform wizard to build the subform.
  - Drag-and-drop another form onto an existing form in Design view to place it there as a subform.
- A subreport is much like a subform, except there isn't a wizard for creating subreports; you must set them up manually.

Figure 39-1

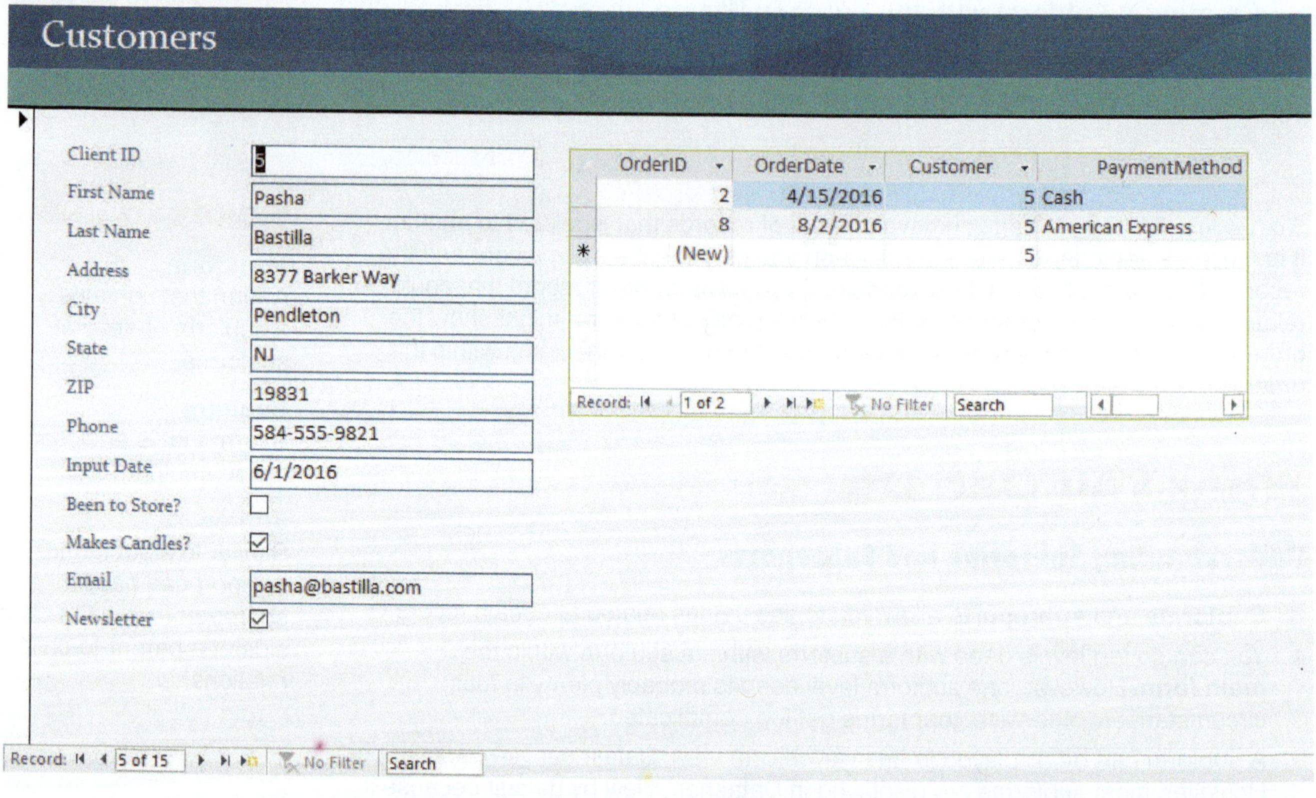

Access 2016, Windows 10, Microsoft Corporation

Creating a Form and Subform with the Form Wizard

- If you create the form and subform at the same time using the Wizard, Access does all the work for you.
- When you select fields from more than one table or query, the Wizard automatically offers to set up the subform.

Try It! Creating a Form and Subform with the Form Wizard

1. Start Access, and open **A39Try** from the data files for this lesson.
2. Save the file as **A39Try_xx** in the location where your teacher instructs you to store the files for this lesson. Click Enable Content if the security warning bar appears.
3. Click Create > Form Wizard. The Form Wizard opens.
4. Open the Tables/Queries drop-down list and click Table: tblOrders.
5. Click the >> button to add all the fields to the form.
6. Open the Tables/Queries drop-down list and click Table: tblOrderDetails.
7. Click the >> button to add all the fields to the form. Then, click Next.
8. When prompted for how you want to view your data, click Next to accept the default of by tblOrders.

   ✓ *The Linked forms option places a button on the main form instead of displaying the subform there. Users can click the button to open the subform separately.*

9. Click Next to accept the default of Datasheet for the subform layout. In the Form text box, replace the default name with **frmOrderForm**.
10. In the Subform text box, replace the default name with **frmOrderDetailsSubform**.
11. Click Finish. The new form and subform appear.
12. Right-click the form tab and click Close. You are not prompted to save changes because the Wizard saved the forms.
13. Leave the database open for the next Try It.

Specify that the main form will be tblOrders

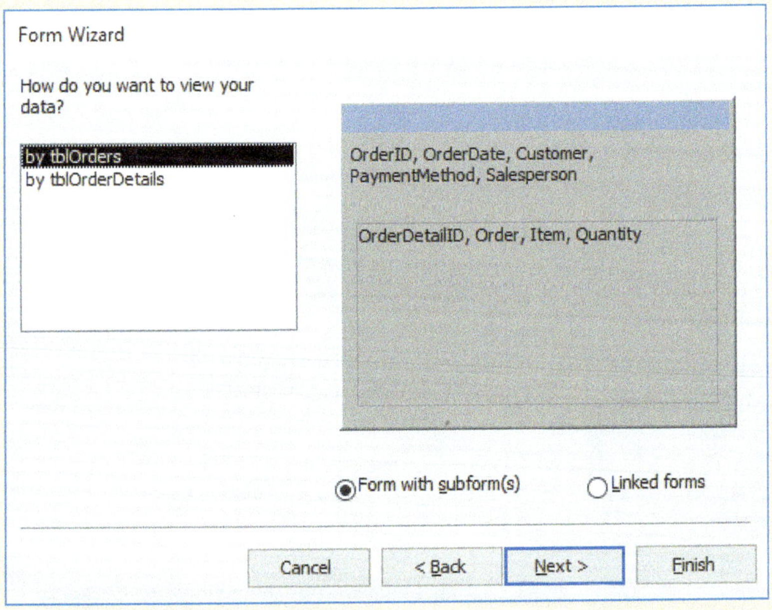

Access 2016, Windows 10, Microsoft Corporation

Try It! Creating a Subform with the Subform Wizard

1. In the **A39Try_xx** file, right-click frmCustomers and click Design View.
2. Drag the right border of the form to the 9.0" mark on the horizontal ruler, expanding the form width.
3. On the Form Design Tools Design tab, click the More button for the Controls group.
4. Make sure Use Control Wizards is selected. If it's not, click it to select it, and then repeat step 3.
5. In the Controls group, select the Subform/Subreport icon.
6. Click on the blank area of the form, at approximately the 4" mark on the horizontal ruler and aligned vertically with the top of the ClientID text box. The Subform Wizard opens.
7. Click Next to accept the default of Use existing Tables and Queries.
8. Open the Tables/Queries drop-down list, and click Table: tblOrders.
9. Click the >> button to select all the fields. Then, click Next.
10. When prompted to define which fields link the forms, click Next to accept the default.
11. Replace the default name with **frmOrdersSubform** and click Finish. The subform appears on the form.
12. Click the subform's label to select it, and press DEL to delete the label.

    ✓ *Do not worry that the subform appears in Single Item form view rather than Datasheet view. It will appear correctly in Layout and Form views.*

13. Right-click the form's tab and click Form View to view your work. Click Next Record a few times to move through the records in the main form and confirm that the records shown in the subform change.
14. Right-click the form's tab and click Close. Click Yes when prompted to save changes.
15. Leave the database open for the next Try It.

Click the Subform/Subreport button

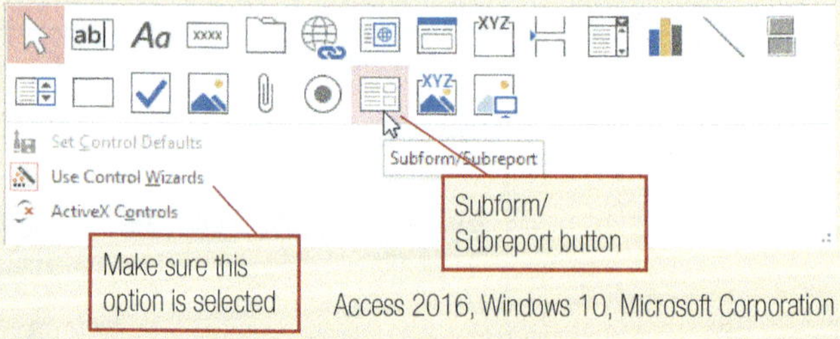

Access 2016, Windows 10, Microsoft Corporation

Define which fields link the forms

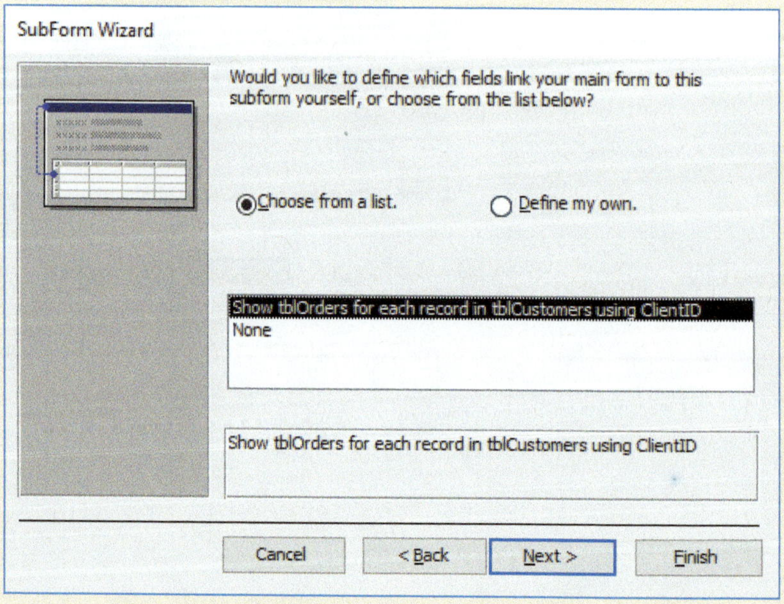

Access 2016, Windows 10, Microsoft Corporation

Creating a Subreport with Drag-and-Drop

- The easiest way to create a subform on a form, or a subreport on a report, is if you have already created both of them separately. You can then drag the subform or subreport onto the main one in Design view from the Navigation pane.
- You can also drag a table directly onto a form or report in Design view, and a wizard will ask you to verify the relationship.

Try It! Creating a Subreport with Drag-and-Drop

1. In the A39Try_xx file, in the Navigation pane, right-click rptMailerMain and click Design View.
2. From the Navigation pane, drag rptMailerSub to the report layout grid, below the existing fields.
3. Click the subreport's label (rptMailerSub) on the report design grid and press DEL.
4. Click the Save button on the Quick Access Toolbar.
5. Right-click the report's tab, and click Report View to check your work.
6. Right-click the report's tab and click Close. Click Yes, if prompted to save.
7. Leave the database open for the next Try It.

Drag the subreport onto the main report directly from the Navigation pane

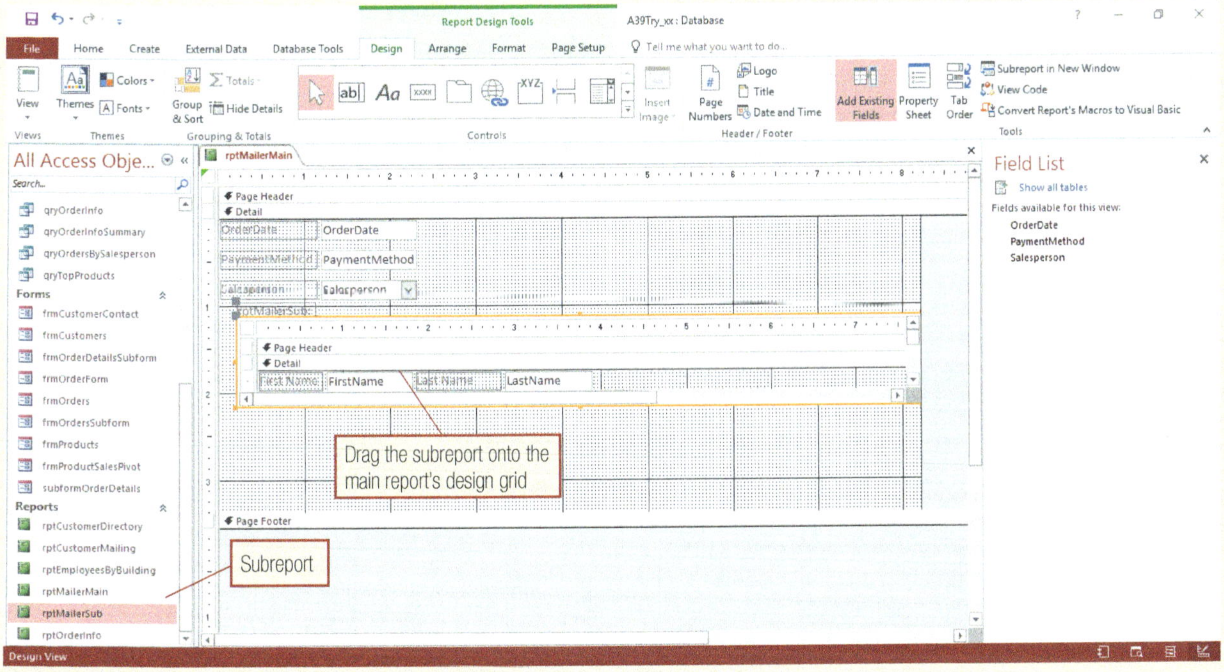

Editing a Subform or Subreport

- You can change the size of the subform or subreport like any other object by selecting it and then dragging its borders.
- When you save the form, both the main form and the subform are saved (or the main report and subreport).
- When using a preexisting form or report as your subform or subreport, there may be fields that you do not want to include on the subform. You can hide them from Layout view by right-clicking the unwanted field and choosing Hide Fields.

Try It! Editing a Subform

1. In the **A39Try_xx** file, right-click the rptMailerMain report and click Design View.
2. Drag the right border of the subreport to the left until it does not overlap the page margin line.
3. Right-click the report's tab and click Close. Click Yes when prompted to save changes.
4. In the Navigation pane, right-click frmOrderForm and click Design View.
5. Click the subform's label and press DEL to remove it.
6. Drag the subform to the left to align with the left edges of the labels on the main form.
7. Drag the right edge of the subform to the 5.25" mark on the horizontal ruler.
8. On the subform, click the OrderDetailID text box and DEL.
9. Right-click the main form's tab and click Form View.

   ✓ *Note that OrderDetailID does not appear in the subform.*
10. Right-click the form's tab and click Close. Click Yes when prompted to save changes.
11. Close the database, and exit Access.

Adjust the position of the subform in Design view

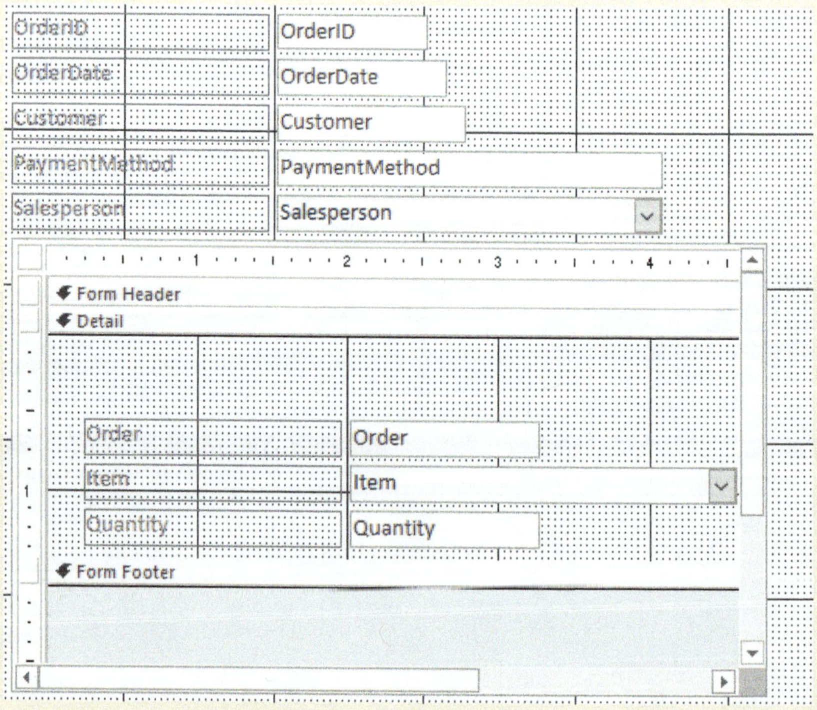

Access 2016, Windows 10, Microsoft Corporation

Lesson 39—Practice

In this project, you will add a subform to a form and modify it to make the Textbook Exchange's database look more professional.

DIRECTIONS

1. Start Access, if necessary, and open **A39Practice** from the data files for this lesson.
2. Save the file as **A39Practice_xx** in the location where your teacher instructs you to store the files for this lesson.

   ✓ *If a security warning bar appears, click Enable Content.*
3. In the Navigation pane, right-click **frmMembers** and click Design View.
4. Drag **frmForSale** from the Navigation pane to the empty area at the bottom of the **frmMembers** form, making it a subform.
5. Right-click the main form's tab, and click **Form View**.
6. Notice that this does not look very good because of the large form header on the frmForSale form. It is clear that a new subform should be created, rather than trying to use an existing form as a subform.
7. Right-click the main form's tab, and click **Design View**.
8. Select the subform, and press DEL to remove it.
9. Click **Form Design Tools Design** > **More** to open the palette of controls you can insert.
10. Click **Subform/Subreport**.
11. Click on the main form, below the Phone label. The Subform Wizard opens.
12. Click **Next** to accept the default (Use existing Tables and Queries).
13. Open the **Tables/Queries** drop-down list and click **Table: tblForSale**.
14. Click the **ListingDate** field and click > to add it to the form. Do the same for **Book, Condition**, and **Asking Price**. Then, click **Next**.
15. Click **Next** to accept the default field associations.
16. Replace the default name with **frmForSaleSubform** and click **Finish**.
17. Click the **frmForSaleSubform** label on the form and press DEL.
18. Switch to Layout view and resize the subform and its columns so that all data is visible. See Figure 39-2.
19. Right-click the form's tab and click **Form View**.
20. Right-click the form's tab and click **Close**. When prompted to save changes, click **Yes**.
21. Close the database, and exit Access. If instructed, submit this database to your teacher for grading.

Figure 39-2

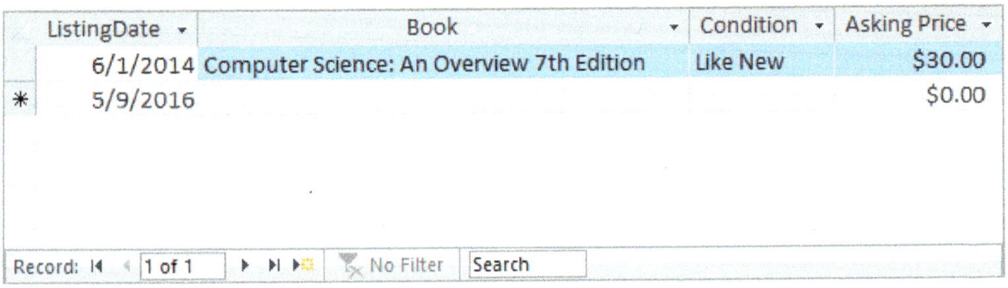

Access 2016, Windows 10, Microsoft Corporation

Lesson 39—Apply

Working for the Textbook Exchange, you will set up a form with a subform that helps salespeople see at a glance the details of each book being offered for sale.

DIRECTIONS

1. Start Access, if necessary, and open **A39Apply** from the data files for this lesson.
2. Save the file as **A39Apply_xx** in the location where your teacher instructs you to store the files for this lesson.

   ✓ *If a security warning bar appears, click Enable Content.*

3. Open **frmBookInformation** in Design view and add a subform to it showing which members are selling each book. Name the subform **frmSaleSubform**.

   ✓ *Use any method and settings you wish, but make sure that for each book, the user viewing the form will be able to see who is selling a copy (the member number) and what is the condition and asking price of each book. Check your work in Layout view and make adjustments to the subform's columns and overall width as needed.*

4. Save and close all forms.
5. Use the Form Wizard to create a new form/subform combo called **frmBooks2**. The main form should use all the fields from **tblBooks** and the subform should show all fields from **tblForSale** and should open in a linked form. The subform should be named **frmSaleSubform2**.
6. Try out the button for the linked form in Form view. It doesn't work because the form title is covering it.
7. In Design view, move the form's title (in the Form Header) to the right so it does not overlap the button.
8. Switch to Form view, and try the button again. This time it works. The subform opens in a separate tab.
9. Close the subform. Return to Design view and make the following changes:
   a. Change the text on the button to **Copies for Sale**.
   b. Change the form title label to **Books**.
10. Close the form, saving changes.
11. Display **frmSaleSubform2** in Layout view, and delete the form title.
12. Resize columns as needed so all text fits.
13. Save your changes, and close the form.
14. Open **frmBooks2** in Form view again, and test the button.

    ✓ *The subform opens showing only the records that are associated with the record that was showing in the main form.*

15. Close the database, and exit Access. If instructed, submit this database to your teacher for grading.

Lesson 40

Working with Charts

➤ What You Will Learn

Inserting a Chart in a Report
Editing a Chart
Changing the Chart Type
Changing Chart Options

Software Skills Although Access is not known for the kind of powerful charting capabilities Excel has, you can still produce attractive and useful charts using Access data.

WORDS TO KNOW

Legend
A color-coded key that tells what each color in a chart represents.

Microsoft Graph
A charting tool that creates embedded charts in applications such as Access.

What You Can Do

Inserting a Chart in a Report

- To create a chart in Access, you can place a Microsoft Graph chart on a report or form.
- **Microsoft Graph** charts use a somewhat awkward user interface from earlier versions of Microsoft Office, but can be placed on any report or form.
- To create a chart report, first create a blank report using the Blank Report button on the Create tab. Then, in Design view, use the Chart button on the Design tab to start a new chart.
- The Chart Wizard runs, prompting you to select the table or query from which you want to pull data.

✓ *After selecting the chart options, the Chart Wizard has a layout section where you can decide how the chart should be formatted. You can also change how the information is to be summarized and preview the chart in this section. Do not be alarmed that the chart does not show the data from your selected data source in Design view. This is one of the quirks of Microsoft Graph. It does not show the actual chart data in Design view. Switch to Layout view or Report view to see your data.*

Try It! Inserting a Chart in a Report

1. Start Access, and open **A40Try** from the data files for this lesson.
2. Save the file as **A40Try_xx** in the location where your teacher instructs you to store the files for this lesson. Click Enable Content if the security warning bar appears.
3. Click Create > Blank Report. A blank report appears in Layout view.
4. Right-click the report's tab, and click Design View.

   ✓ *Some controls can be inserted from Layout view, but a chart is not one of them.*
5. On the Report Design Tools Design tab, in the Controls group, click the More button to display a palette of available tools.
6. Click the Chart button, and click on the report in the Detail section. The Chart Wizard opens.
7. Click Table: tblOrderDetails and click Next.
8. Click Customers and click > to select it.
9. Click Quantity and click > to select it. Then, click Next.
10. Click Pie Chart (the first chart type in the bottom row of the dialog box) and click Next.
11. Double-click SumOfQuantity. The Summarize dialog box opens.
12. Click None and OK.
13. Click Preview Chart. Click Close.

    ✓ *The chart will look strange at this point, but we will fix that later.*
14. Click Next.
15. Replace the default name with **chtOrderDetails** and click Finish. The chart appears on the report layout. The actual data does not appear at this point.
16. Right-click the report's tab, and click Report View to see the actual chart.
17. Click the Save button on the Quick Access Toolbar.
18. In the Save As dialog box, type **rptOrderChart** and click OK.
19. Leave the report open to use in the next Try It.

Editing a Chart

- If the chart is the wrong size, you can drag the chart object's border to resize it. You can do this in either Design or Layout view.
- To edit the chart's content, you must return to Design view and double-click the chart. This opens Microsoft Graph. Notice that Microsoft Graph uses a traditional menu and toolbar. See Figure 40-1 on the next page.
- When you are working in Microsoft Graph, the chart displays dummy data, except for the chart title. You can format the labels, **legends**, axes, and so on, and those formatting settings will be passed on to the actual chart that is generated when you are in Layout or Report view.
- The small floating spreadsheet is called the datasheet. You can close it or reopen it by clicking the View Datasheet button on the toolbar. It does not contain the actual data for the chart; it is only for the sample chart.

✓ *The Standard and Formatting toolbars in Microsoft Graph appear on a single line, which means both are truncated. You can access hidden buttons on a toolbar by clicking the More button at the right end, or you can click More and then click Show Buttons on Two Rows to separate them so all buttons are visible.*

Figure 40-1

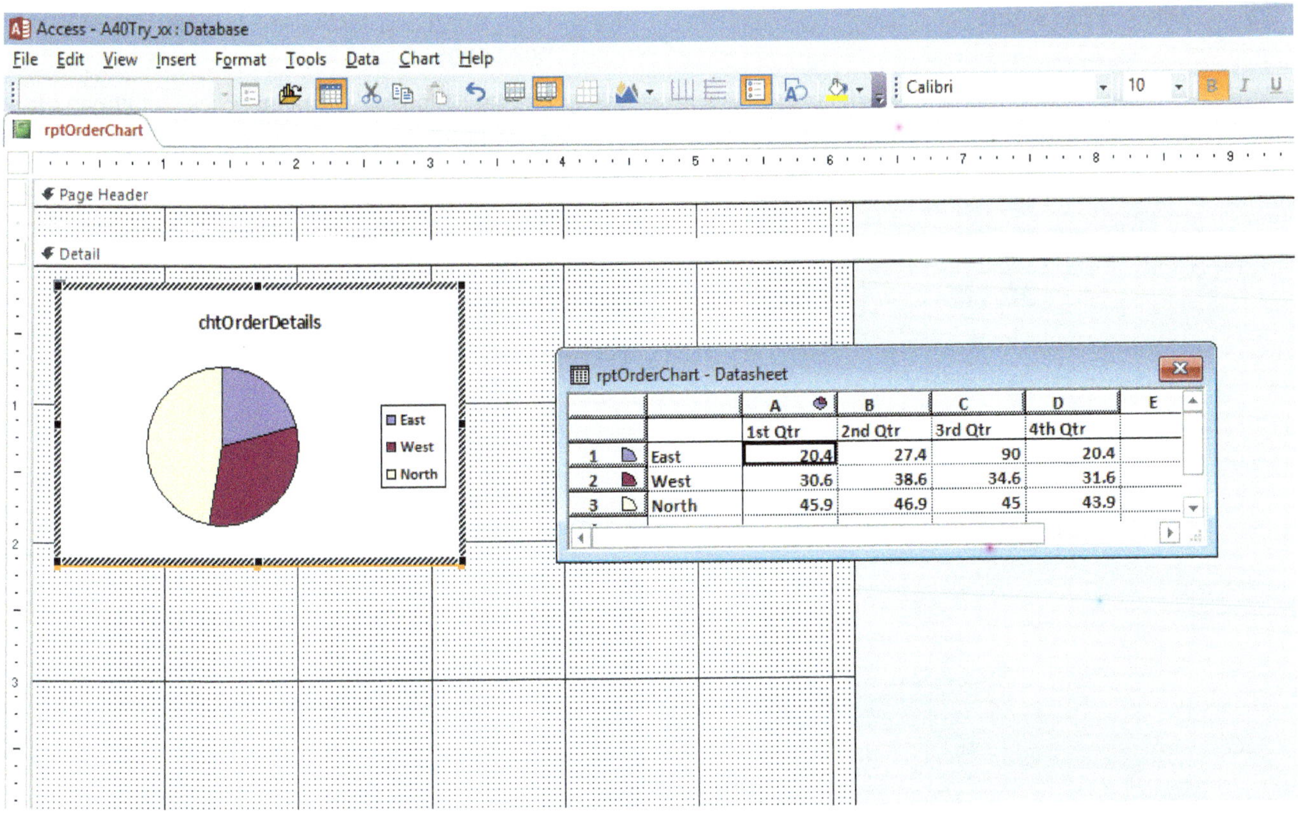

Access 2016, Windows 10, Microsoft Corporation

Changing the Chart Type

- You can change the chart's type without having to recreate it entirely.
- To change the chart's type, open it in Microsoft Graph and then click the drop-down arrow next to the Chart Type button. From the palette of types, click the one you want.

✓ *If you have a chart that uses three fields, such as a bar chart, and you switch to a chart that uses only two fields, such as a pie chart, only the first series will show (that is , the first color of the bar from the legend).*

- For additional chart types, open the Chart menu and click Chart Type. From the Chart Type dialog box, you can select a type and subtype. There is also a Custom Types tab that has some interesting preset formatting types on it.

Try It! Editing a Chart

1. In the **A40Try_xx** file, right-click the rptOrderChart tab and click Design View.
2. Double-click the chart to open Microsoft Graph.
3. Click the drop-down arrow on the Chart Type button to open a palette of chart types.

(continued)

Try It! Editing a Chart *(continued)*

4. Click 3-D Bar Chart.

Select a different chart type

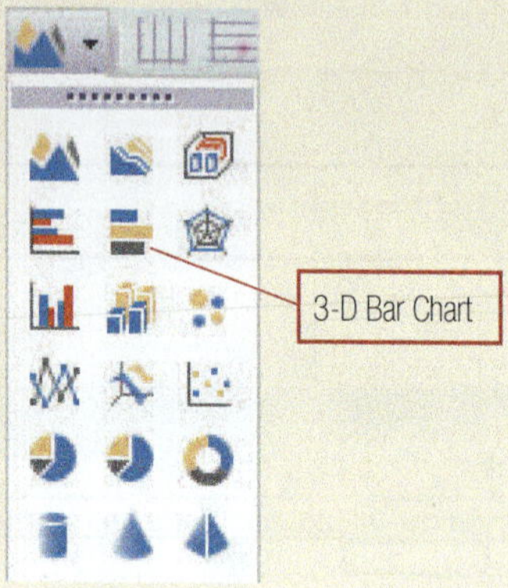

Access 2016, Windows 10, Microsoft Corporation

5. Click Chart > Chart Type. The Chart Type dialog box opens.
6. On the Standard Types tab, click Column in the list of chart types.
7. Click the Clustered Column subtype (first sample in the top row).
8. Click OK.
9. Press CTRL + S to save your work.
10. Leave the chart open for the next Try It.

The Chart Type dialog box contains more chart subtype options

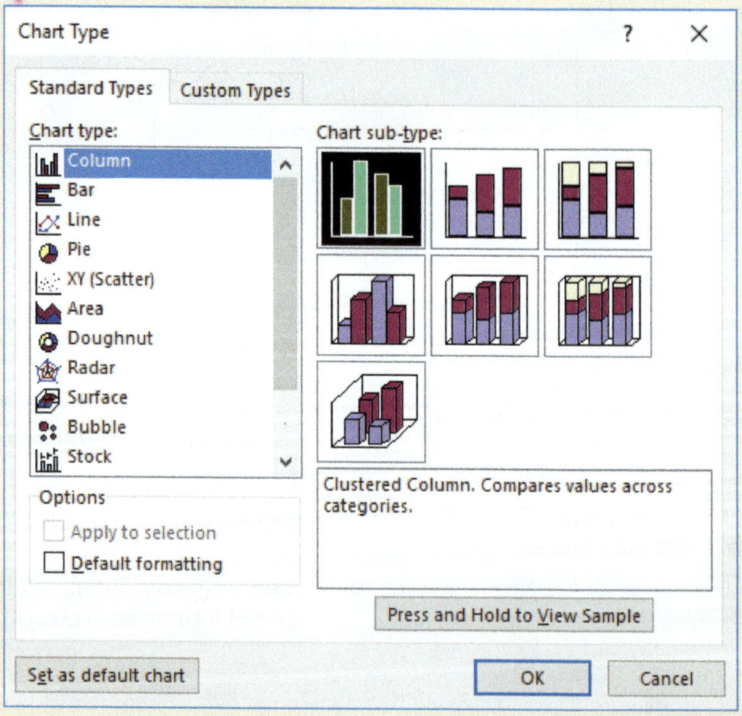

Access 2016, Windows 10, Microsoft Corporation

Changing Chart Options

- Sometimes a chart can convey a different message if you display its data by row versus by column. To switch between the two on a two-axis chart such as a bar, line, column, or area chart, use the By Row and By Column buttons on the Standard toolbar.

  ✓ *This option is not applicable to pie charts.*

- You can toggle certain optional elements on/off the chart by clicking the buttons on the Standard toolbar. Some of these buttons are available only for certain chart types. See Figure 40-2 on the next page.

Figure 40-2

Access 2016, Windows 10, Microsoft Corporation

- Many other chart features can be controlled from the Chart Options dialog box. You can control the axis scale, legend, gridlines, titles, data labels, and data table from here. See Figure 40-3.

Figure 40-3

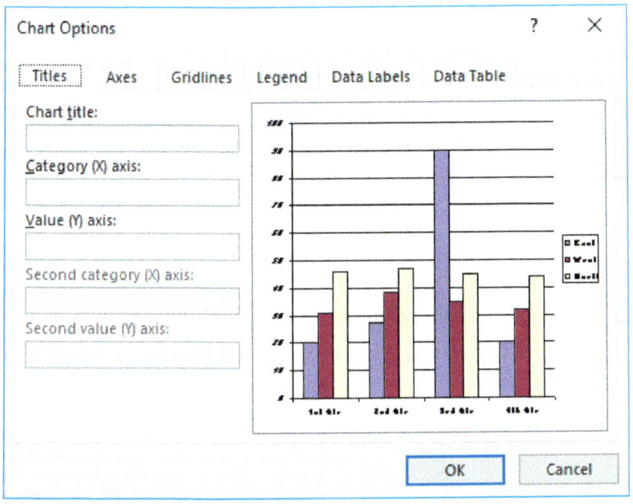

Access 2016, Windows 10, Microsoft Corporation

- You can use the character formatting buttons on the Formatting toolbar to format any of the text objects on the chart, such as the title, legend, and axes. Select any of these and then choose a different font, font size, attribute (such as bold and italic), and so on. These work just like they do in any other Office application. See Figure 40-4.
- There are also buttons on the Formatting toolbar for applying formatting to numbers, such as making numbers appear as currency or percentages and changing the number of decimal places. These work just like in Excel. See Figure 40-5.
- There are also buttons on the Formatting toolbar for aligning the text horizontally within its text box and slanting the text diagonally. See Figure 40-5.

Figure 40-4

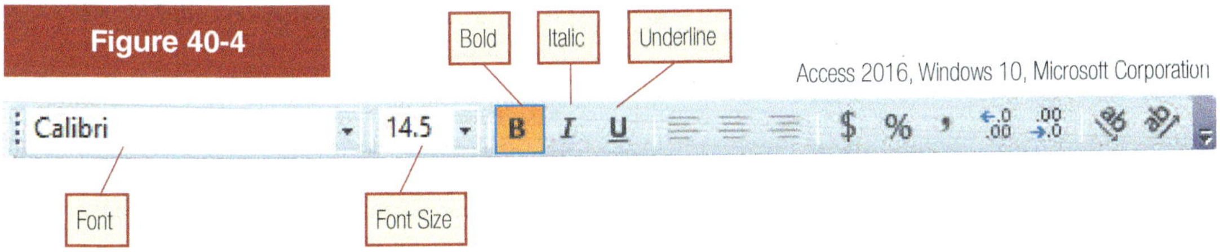

Access 2016, Windows 10, Microsoft Corporation

Figure 40-5

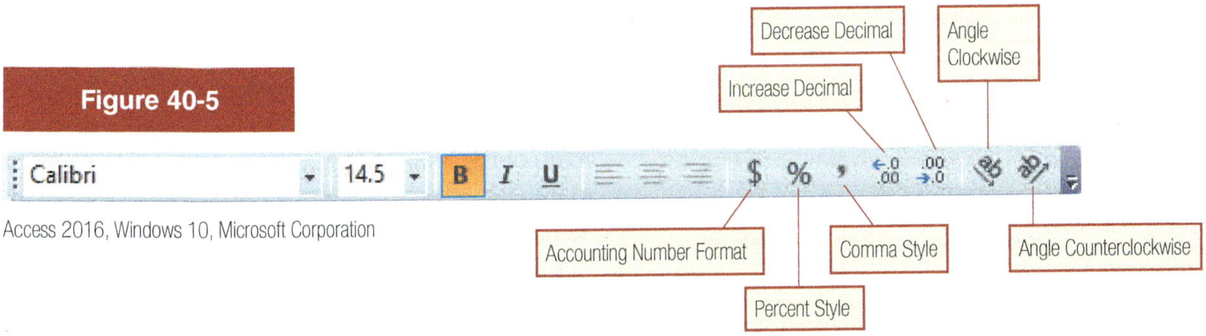

Access 2016, Windows 10, Microsoft Corporation

Try It! Changing Chart Options

1. In the **A40Try_xx** file, in Microsoft Graph, select the chart title (chtOrderDetails) on the chart, and press DEL. The chart title is removed.
2. Click the By Row button.
3. Click the Value Axis Gridlines button.
4. Click the vertical axis (vertical line along the left edge of the chart) to select it.
5. Click the Italic button *I*.
6. Click the report background, away from the chart, to exit from Microsoft Graph.
7. Drag the lower-right corner of the chart frame to enlarge the chart by 2" in each direction.
8. Right-click the report tab, and click Report View to check your work.
9. Right-click the report tab and click Close. Click Yes when prompted to save changes.
10. Close the database, and exit Access.

Lesson 40—Practice

In this project, you will create a chart based on a query for The Textbook Exchange's database.

DIRECTIONS

1. Start Access, if necessary, and open **A40Practice** from the data files for this lesson.
2. Save the file as **A40Practice_xx** in the location where your teacher instructs you to store the files for this lesson.

   ✓ *If a security warning bar appears, click Enable Content.*
3. Click **Create** > **Blank Report**.
4. Right-click the report's tab, and click **Design View**.
5. Click **Report Design Tools Design** > **More** (in the Controls group).
6. Click the **Chart** button.
7. Click in the Detail area of the report layout. The Chart Wizard opens.
8. Click the **Queries** button.
9. Click **Query: qryTopFiveExtended** and click **Next**.
10. Click **Last** and click >.
11. Click **Condition** and click >.
12. Click **AskingPrice** and click >. Then, click **Next**.
13. Click **3-D Column Chart** and click **Next**.
14. Click the **Preview Chart** button. A preview appears in its own window. Close the preview window.
15. In the Preview area, swap the positions of the **Condition** and **Last** fields. To do this:
    a. Drag the **Condition** field from the sample area to the list at the right. It is removed from the sample.
    b. Drag the **Last** field from the sample area to the list at the right.
    c. Drag the **Condition** field from the list to the **Axis** placeholder.
    d. Drag the **Last** field from the list to the **Series** placeholder.
16. Click the **Preview Chart** button. A preview appears in its own window. Close the preview window.
17. Click **Next**.
18. Replace the default name with **chtTop5ByCondition** and click **Finish**.
19. Drag the lower-right selection handle on the chart frame to approximately double the height and width of the chart.
20. Right-click the report tab and click **Save**. In the Save As dialog box, type **rptTop5Chart** and click **OK**.
21. Right-click the report tab, and click **Report View** to check your work. It should look like Figure 40-6 on the next page.
22. Close the database, and exit Access. If instructed, submit this database to your teacher for grading.

Figure 40-6

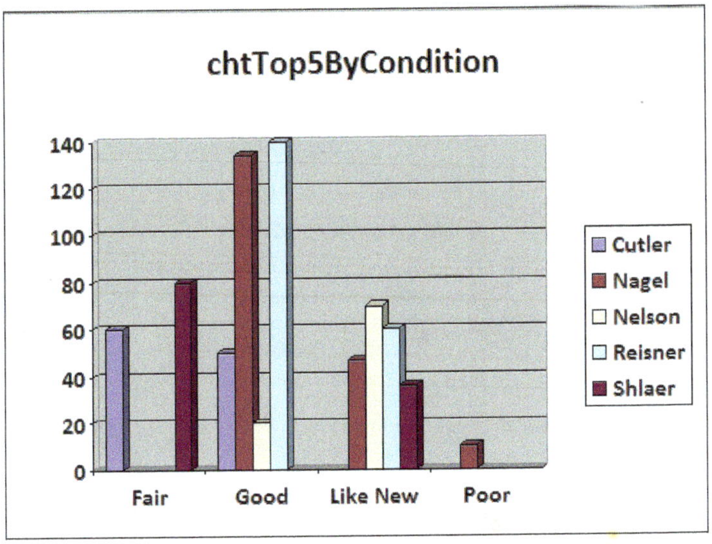

Lesson 40—Apply

The manager of The Textbook Exchange has asked about charting in Access and would like to see some examples of what can be created. You will take one of The Textbook Exchange's charts and edit it.

DIRECTIONS

1. Start Access, if necessary, and open **A40Apply** from the data files for this lesson.
2. Save the file as **A40Apply_xx** in the location where your teacher instructs you to store the files for this lesson.

   ✓ *If a security warning bar appears, click Enable Content.*
3. Open **rptTop5Chart** in Design view. Change the width of the report area to 8 inches and change the chart width to 7 inches and the height to 5 inches.

   ✓ *You may need to increase the height of the Detail section to increase the height of the chart.*
4. Open the chart in Microsoft Graph and make the following edits:
   a. Remove the chart title.
   b. Change to a **By Row** layout.
   c. Change the chart type to **3-D Bar Chart**.
   d. Add a data table.
   e. Change the font size in the chart to **10**.
5. View the chart in Report view to check your work. See Figure 40-7 on the next page.
6. Close the report, saving your changes.
7. Close the database, and exit Access. If instructed, submit this database to your teacher for grading.

Figure 40-7

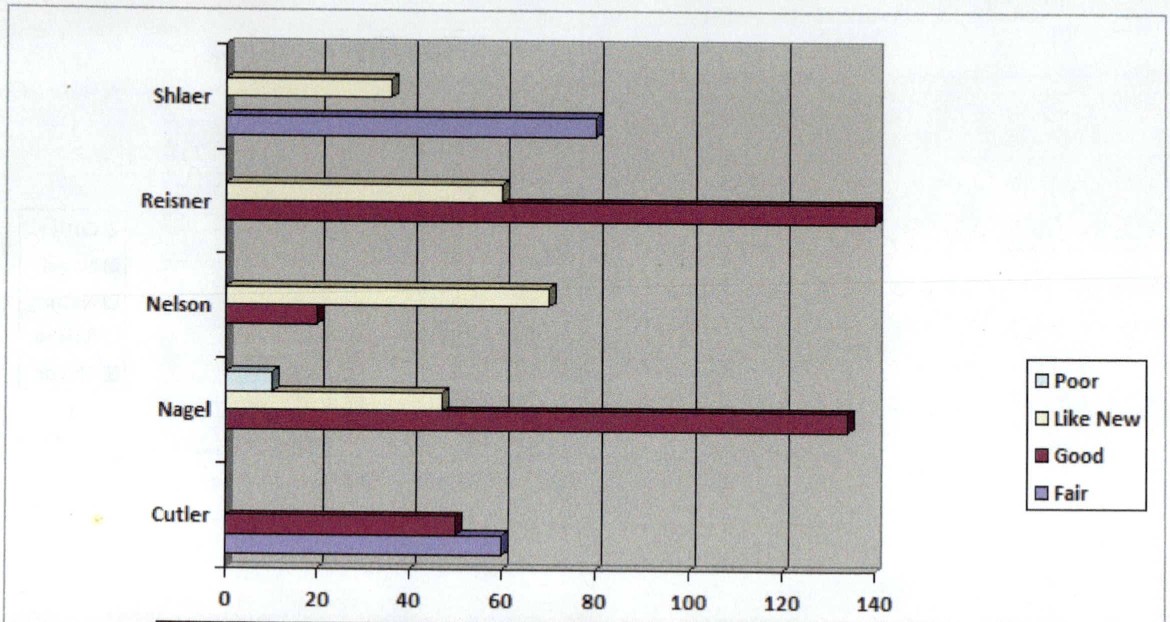

	Cutler	Nagel	Nelson	Reisner	Shlaer
Poor		10			
Like New		47	70	60	36
Good	50	134	20	140	
Fair	60				80

Access 2016, Windows 10, Microsoft Corporation

Lesson 41

Creating Switchboards

➤ What You Will Learn

Opening the Switchboard Manager
Managing Switchboard Pages
Editing a Switchboard Page's Content
Formatting the Switchboard
Activating or Deactivating the Switchboard

Software Skills All the powerful queries, reports, and other objects you create are perhaps a little intimidating for a beginner. If you are going to allow other people to access the database, it might be a good idea to create a friendlier interface than the standard Navigation pane. Access has a built-in system for this purpose called the Switchboard.

WORDS TO KNOW

Switchboard
A set of system-generated forms that help less-experienced users access database objects.

What You Can Do

Opening the Switchboard Manager

- The **Switchboard** is a set of forms that Access generates for navigation among database objects.
- The Switchboard is not just a single form, but a whole system of interconnected forms. The menu buttons in Figure 41-1 open other forms, which are also part of the Switchboard.
- The Switchboard Manager command is not available on the ribbon by default. You can add it to the ribbon, or you can add it to the Quick Access Toolbar.

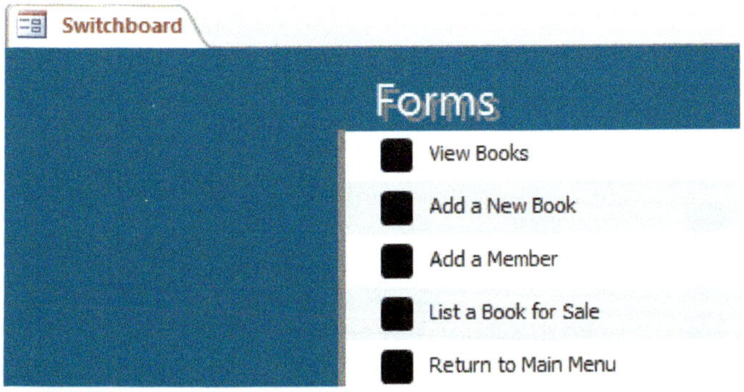

Figure 41-1

Access 2016, Windows 10, Microsoft Corporation

- Clicking the Switchboard Manager button opens the Switchboard if one has already been created. The Switchboard Manager lists each page of the switchboard. By default, there is just one Main page.
- If the database does not yet have a Switchboard, Switchboard Manager offers to create one.
- Once you have created the Switchboard, the Main Switchboard page always exists; you cannot delete it.

✓ *However, you can change its content.*

Try It! Adding the Switchboard Manager to the Quick Access Toolbar

1. Start Access, and open **A41Try** from the data files for this lesson.
2. Save the file as **A41Try_xx** in the location where your teacher instructs you to store the files for this lesson. Click Enable Content if the security warning bar appears.
3. Click File > Options.
4. Click Quick Access Toolbar.
5. Open the Choose commands from drop-down list and click Commands Not in the Ribbon.
6. On the list of commands that appears, click Switchboard Manager.
7. Click Add to add the command to the Quick Access Toolbar.
8. Click OK. A button for the Switchboard Manager appears on the Quick Access Toolbar.
9. Leave the database open to use in the next Try It.

Try It! Creating the Switchboard

1. In the **A41Try_xx** file, click the Switchboard Manager button on the Quick Access Toolbar.
2. When prompted to create a switchboard, click Yes. The Switchboard Manager dialog box opens.
3. Leave the database open to use in the next Try It.

Managing Switchboard Pages

- Add a new Switchboard page if you want additional pages to be available from the Main page.
- You can change which page appears first by clicking the desired page in the Switchboard Manager and then clicking Make Default.
- To delete a Switchboard page, select the page in the Switchboard Manager dialog box and click Delete. Click Yes.

Try It! Adding a Switchboard Page

1. In the **A41Try_xx** file, in the Switchboard Manager dialog box, click New.
2. In the Create New dialog box, type **Forms** and click OK.
3. Click New.
4. Type **Reports** and click OK.
5. Click New.
6. Type **Master** and click OK.
7. Leave the database open to use in the next Try It.

Try It! Changing the Default Switchboard Page

1. In the **A41Try_xx** file, in the Switchboard Manager dialog box, click Master.
2. Click Make Default. The Master page moves to the top of the list, and (Default) appears next to it.
3. Leave the database open to use in the next Try It.

Try It! Deleting a Switchboard Page

1. In the **A41Try_xx** file, in the Switchboard Manager dialog box, click Main Switchboard.
2. Click Delete.
3. Click Yes.
4. Leave the database open to use in the next Try It.

Editing a Switchboard Page's Content

- By default, a Switchboard page is empty. You add entries that correspond to an action that the user will be able to select, such as opening a form or a report.
- The list of items on each level of the Switchboard is stored in a table called Switchboard items. You can edit the records in this table to edit the item names on the Switchboard menus.
- When at least one Switchboard page exists, a Switchboard form appears in the list of database forms in the Navigation pane.

Try It! Adding a Link to Another Page

1. In the **A41Try_xx** file, in the Switchboard Manager dialog box, if necessary, click Master (Default).
2. Click Edit. The Edit Switchboard Page dialog box opens.
3. Click New.
4. In the Text box, type **Forms Page**.
5. Open the Switchboard drop-down list and click Forms.
6. Click OK.
7. Click Close.
8. Leave the database open to use in the next Try It.

Create a link to the Forms switchboard page off of the main (Master) page

Access 2016, Windows 10, Microsoft Corporation

Try It! Adding a Link to a Form

1. In the **A41Try_xx** file, in the Switchboard Manager dialog box, click Forms.
2. Click Edit.
3. Click New.
4. In the Text box, type **Customer Form**.
5. Open the Command drop-down list and click Open Form in Edit Mode.

✓ *When working with form-based commands, you have a choice of Open Form in Edit Mode or Open Form in Add Mode. Edit Mode starts on the first record, whereas Add Mode starts with a new blank record.*

6. Open the Form drop-down list and click frmCustomers.
7. Click OK.
8. Leave the Forms switchboard open for the next Try It.

Try It! Adding a Link That Returns to the Main Switchboard

1. In the **A41Try_xx** file, on the Forms switchboard page, click New. The Edit Switchboard Item dialog box opens.
2. In the Text box, type **Return to Main Form**.
3. Open the Switchboard drop-down list and click Master.
4. Click OK.
5. Click Close.
6. Click Close to close the Switchboard Manager.
7. Leave the database open to use in the next Try It.

Try It! Testing the Switchboard

1. In the **A41Try_xx** file, in the Navigation pane, in the Forms section, double-click Switchboard.
2. Click the Forms Page button.
3. Click the Return to Main Form button.
4. Right-click the form's tab and click Close.
5. Leave the database open to use in the next Try It.

Formatting the Switchboard

- You can open the Switchboard form in Design or Layout view and edit it, much the same as you would edit any other form, including changing the background color.
- One thing that is very different, however, is that in Design view you will see placeholders labeled as ItemText with buttons next to them. These generically represent the text that will appear on each page.
- You can change the font used for the Switchboard text by formatting these ItemText placeholder boxes.
- The Switchboard is formatted in one entire unit; this keeps its formatting consistent across all pages.
- Each page appears as a separate form when you are working with the Switchboard, but you see only a single form for the Switchboard in the Navigation pane. Part of the benefit of the Switchboard system is that it keeps certain formatting features constant among all pages of the Switchboard.

Try It! Formatting the Switchboard

1. In the A41Try_xx file, in the Navigation pane, right-click Switchboard and click Design View.
2. In the Form Header, click the turquoise rectangle.
3. On the Form Design Tools Format tab, click the Shape Fill button's drop-down list.
4. Click the dark blue square in the top row of the Standard Colors area.
5. In the Detail section, click the turquoise rectangle.
6. On the Form Design Tools Format tab, click the Shape Fill button's drop-down list.
7. Click the dark blue square in the top row of the Standard Colors area.
8. In the Detail area, click ItemText.
9. On the Form Design Tools Format tab, open the Font Size drop-down list and click 10.
10. Increase the height of the Detail section and the ItemText placeholder to accommodate the new font size.
11. Right-click the form's tab, and click Form View to check your work.
12. Right-click the form's tab and click Close. Click Yes when prompted to save changes.
13. Leave the database open to use in the next Try It.

Activating or Deactivating the Switchboard

- To make the Switchboard load automatically when the database is opened, set it up as the default display form.
- To do this, set the Display Form value to Switchboard in the Current Database category in the Access Options dialog box.
- You might also want to hide the Navigation pane so that users are limited to the commands provided on the Switchboard.

Try It! Activating the Switchboard

1. In the A41Try_xx file, click File > Options.
2. Click Current Database.
3. Click the Display Form drop-down list and click Switchboard.
4. Click OK.
5. Click OK.
6. Close and reopen the database file. The Switchboard loads automatically.
7. Leave the database open to use in the next Try It.

Try It! Deactivating the Switchboard

1. In A41Try_xx, click File > Options.
2. Click Current Database.
3. Click the Display Form drop-down list and click (none).
4. Click OK.
5. Close the database, and exit Access.

Lesson 41—Practice

In this project, you will begin creating a Switchboard system for The Textbook Exchange's database.

DIRECTIONS

1. Start Access, if necessary, and open **A41Practice** from the data files for this lesson.
2. Save the file as **A41Practice_xx** in the location where your teacher instructs you to store the files for this lesson.

   ✓ *If a security warning bar appears, click Enable Content.*
3. Click the **Switchboard Manager** button on the Quick Access Toolbar.

   ✓ *If you did not already put the Switchboard Manager button on the Quick Access Toolbar earlier in this lesson, go back and do so now by completing the first Try It exercise in this lesson.*
4. Click **Yes** to create a new switchboard. The Switchboard Manager opens.
5. Click **New**. In the Create New dialog box, type **Reports** and click **OK**.
6. Click **New**. In the Create New dialog box, type **Forms** and click **OK**.
7. Click **Main Switchboard (Default)** and click **Edit**. The Edit Switchboard Page dialog box opens.
8. Click **New**. In the Edit Switchboard Item dialog box, in the Text box, type **Forms**.
9. Open the **Switchboard** drop-down list and click **Forms**. Then, click **OK**.
10. Click **New**. In the Edit Switchboard Item dialog box, in the Text box, type **Reports**.
11. Open the **Switchboard** drop-down list and click **Reports**. Then, click **OK**.
12. Click **Close**.
13. Click **Close**.
14. Close the database, and exit Access. If instructed, submit this database to your teacher for grading.

Lesson 41—Apply

The Textbook Exchange has asked you to create a user-friendly interface from which employees can access the database's objects. You will create a Switchboard system that does so.

DIRECTIONS

1. Start Access, if necessary, and open **A41Apply** from the data files for this lesson.
2. Save the file as **A41Apply_xx** in the location where your teacher instructs you to store the files for this lesson.

   ✓ *If a security warning bar appears, click Enable Content.*
3. Open the Switchboard Manager.
4. On the Main Switchboard page, create a **Close the Database** option that calls the **Exit Application** command.
5. On the Reports page, create the following items:

Text	Command	Object
Books Report	Open Report	rptBooks
Members Report	Open Report	rptMembers
Return to Main Menu	Go to Switchboard	Main Switchboard

6. On the Forms page, create the following items:

Text	Command	Object
View Books	Open Form in Edit Mode	frmBooks
Add a New Book	Open Form in Add Mode	frmBooks
Add a Member	Open Form in Add Mode	frmMembers
List a Book for Sale	Open Form in Add Mode	frmForSale
Return to Main Menu	Go to Switchboard	Main Switchboard

7. Close the Switchboard Manager, and view the Switchboard in Form view. Then, close it.
8. Open the Switchboard Items table and change Main Switchboard in record 1 to **The Textbook Exchange**.
9. Reopen the Switchboard form in Layout view, and format the text next to the buttons as **10 pt Arial**.
10. Switch to Form view, and check each button to make sure you can navigate between all three Switchboard pages using the buttons and that each form or report button opens the appropriate object.
11. Close the database, and exit Access. If instructed, submit this database to your teacher for grading.

Lesson 42

Creating Navigation Forms

➤ What You Will Learn

Creating a Navigation Form
Adding Command Buttons to a Form
Tying a Navigation Form into the Switchboard

WORDS TO KNOW

Command button
A button on a form that, when clicked, performs some action or command, such as opening a form or report.

Navigation form
An unbound form that exists to provide command buttons that move the user between other objects in a database.

Unbound form
A form that is not associated with any specific table or query.

Software Skills The Switchboard is the easiest way of creating user navigation forms, but there are some limitations. Each page of the Switchboard is formatted the same way, for example. Although it's a lot more work, you might want to create your own user navigation forms and tie them together into a Switchboard-like system that you develop yourself.

What You Can Do

Creating a Navigation Form

- To create a **navigation form**, start a new form without specifying a table or query on which it should be based.
- An **unbound form** is a form that has no data source (no table or query providing records to it). An unbound form can serve a variety of purposes, including creating your own dialog boxes and menus.
- A navigation form is a special type of unbound form that serves the same purpose as a Switchboard page. It displays various options for opening and editing data in forms and reports and contains command buttons for selecting those options.

Try It! Creating a Navigation Form

1. Start Access, and open **A42Try** from the data files for this lesson.
2. Save the file as **A42Try_xx** in the location where your teacher instructs you to store the files for this lesson. Click Enable Content if the security warning bar appears.
3. Click Create > Blank Form. The form opens in Layout view.
4. Close the Field List pane.
5. Click the Save button on the Quick Access Toolbar.
6. In the Save As dialog box, type **Custom Menu** and click OK.
7. Leave the form open for the next Try It.

Adding Command Buttons to a Form

- The heart of a navigation form is a set of **command buttons**—buttons that the user will click to open objects.
- When you place a command button on a form in Design view, the Command Button Wizard runs, prompting you with step-by-step instructions to set up the button.
- If you are creating a command button that will open another form, you must create that form before setting up that command button.

Try It! Adding a Command Button to a Form

1. In the **A42Try_xx** file, with the Custom Menu form open in Layout view, click the Form Layout Tools Design tab, if necessary.
2. On the Controls group's palette of buttons, click the Button button.
3. Click on the form. The Command Button Wizard opens.
4. Click Form Operations.
5. Click Open Form and click Next.
6. Click frmOrders and click Next.
7. Click Next.
8. Click Text.
9. Replace the default label (Open Form) with **Order Form**. Click Next.
10. Replace the default button name (Command0) with **cmdOpenOrderForm**.
11. Click Finish. The Order Form button appears on the form.
12. Right-click the Custom Menu form tab, and click Form View.
13. Click the button to test it. The Orders form opens.
14. Right-click the Orders form tab and click Close.
15. Right-click the Custom Menu tab, and click Layout View.
16. Leave the form open for the next Try It.

Use the Command Button Wizard to set up the button

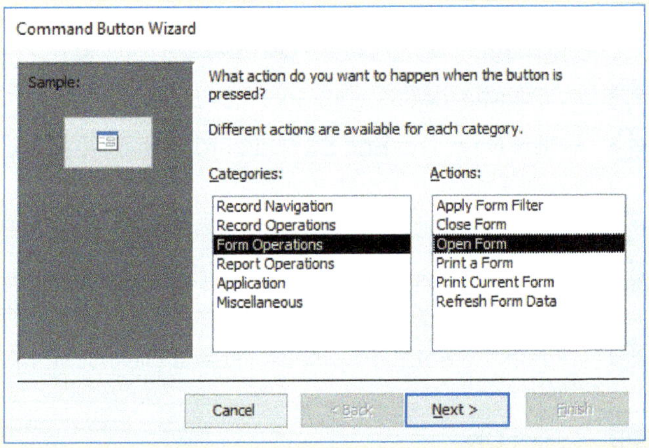

Access 2016, Windows 10, Microsoft Corporation

Tying a Navigation Form into the Switchboard

- You can use your own navigation forms as part of the Switchboard by creating an item on the Main Switchboard or any of the subordinate switchboards that opens the desired form.
- Set up the Switchboard item as if you were opening a form in Edit mode, and specify the navigation form's name as the form to open.

✓ *If you want to use your own navigation form instead of the Switchboard, use the Display Form drop-down list in the Access Options dialog box to select your navigation form.*

- Make sure you include an item on your custom form that links back to the Switchboard so the user can return to it. The following exercise shows how to do that; it's just the same as creating an item for any other form on the Switchboard.

Try It! Creating a Button That Links Back to the Switchboard

1. In the **A42Try_xx** file, with the Custom Menu form open in Layout view, click the Form Layout Tools Design tab, if necessary.
2. On the Controls group's palette of buttons, click the Button [xxxx].
3. Click on the form, immediately below the Order Form button. The Command Button Wizard opens.
4. Click Form Operations.
5. Click Open Form. Then, click Next.
6. Click Switchboard and click Next.
7. Click Next to accept the default of Open the form and show all the records.
8. Click Text, and replace the default label (Open Form) with **Return to Main Menu**. Then, click Next.
9. Replace the default button name with **cmdSwitchboard**.
10. Click Finish. The button appears, but the text in it is truncated.
11. Drag the right edge of the button to the right to enlarge the button so the text fits.

    ✓ *Both buttons will enlarge.*
12. Right-click the form's tab and click Close. Click Yes when prompted to save changes.
13. Leave the database open to use in the next Try It.

Try It! Adding a Custom Navigation Form to the Switchboard

1. In the **A42Try_xx** file, click the Switchboard Manager button on the Quick Access Toolbar.
2. Click Master (Default) and click Edit.
3. Click New. The Edit Switchboard Item dialog box opens.
4. In the Text box, type **Custom Page**.
5. Open the Command drop-down list, and click Open Form in Edit Mode.
6. Open the Form drop-down list and click Custom Menu.
7. Click OK.
8. Click Close.
9. Click Close.
10. In the Navigation pane, double-click Custom Menu.
11. Click Order Form. The Orders form opens.
12. Close the Orders form.
13. In the Custom Menu form, click Return to Main Menu. The Switchboard form opens.
14. Close the Switchboard and Custom Menu forms.
15. Close the database, and exit Access.

Lesson 42—Practice

The Switchboard that you created for The Textbook Exchange earlier is working well, but since some features they want to use aren't possible with the Switchboard, you will create a navigation form for them.

DIRECTIONS

1. Start Access, if necessary, and open **A42Practice** from the data files for this lesson.
2. Save the file as **A42Practice_xx** in the location where your teacher instructs you to store the files for this lesson.

   ✓ *If a security warning bar appears, click Enable Content.*
3. Click **Create** > **Blank Form**.
4. On the Form Layout Tools Design tab, click the **Button** button.
5. Click on the blank form. The Command Button Wizard runs.
6. Click **Report Operations**.
7. Click **Open Report**. Then, click **Next**.
8. Click **rptBooks** and click **Next**.
9. Click the **Text** button.
10. Replace the default text (Open Report) with **Books Report**. Then, click **Next**.
11. Replace the default button name with **cmdBooksReport**.
12. Click **Finish**.
13. On the Form Layout Tools Design tab, click the **Button** button.
14. Click on the blank form. The Command Button Wizard runs.
15. Click **Application**.
16. Click **Quit Application**. Then, click **Next**.
17. Click the **Text** button.
18. Replace the default text (Quit App) with **Exit Access**. Then, click **Next**.
19. Replace the default button name with **cmdExit**.
20. Click **Finish**.
21. Click the **Save** button on the Quick Access Toolbar. Type **Reports Form** as the name, and click **OK**.
22. Test the form by viewing it in Form view and clicking the Books Report button.
23. Close the database, and exit Access. If instructed, submit this database to your teacher for grading.

Lesson 42—Apply

The Navigation form you created in the practice is working great. The Textbook Exchange would like you to make more. In this project you will make another Navigation form.

DIRECTIONS

1. Start Access, if necessary, and open **A42Apply** from the data files for this lesson.
2. Save the file as **A42Apply_xx** in the location where your teacher instructs you to store the files for this lesson.

   ✓ *If a security warning bar appears, click Enable Content.*

3. Open the **Forms Form** in Layout view, and add the following command buttons to it:
   a. Add a **Members Form** button that opens **frmMembers**.
   b. Add a **Return to Main** button that opens the **Main Form**.
   c. Add an **Exit Access** button that exits the application.
4. Format the three forms as desired (**Main Form**, **Forms Form**, and **Reports Form**). At the minimum, change the background color and the font used on the buttons. Make all forms and buttons identical in design. See Figure 42-1 for an example.
5. Delete the **Forms** and **Reports** pages from the Switchboard, and edit the default page of the Switchboard so that your new navigation forms can be accessed from it.

   ✓ *You will need to add the Main Form, Forms Form, and Reports Form to the Default page.*

6. Save your work, and try all the options in the Switchboard to make sure everything works.
7. Close the database, and exit Access. If instructed, submit this database to your teacher for grading.

Figure 42-1

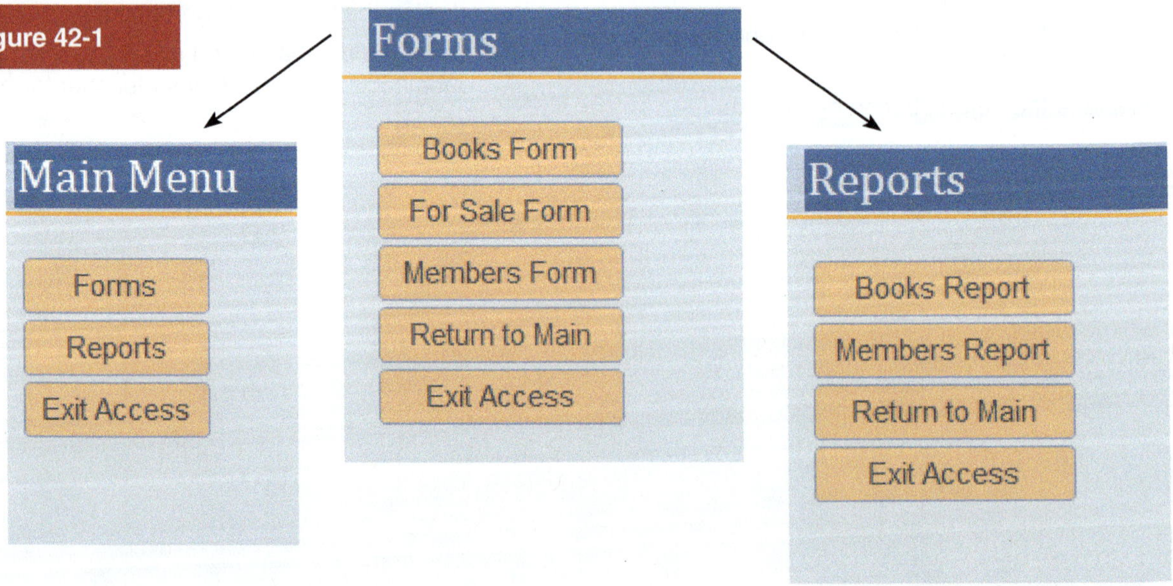

Access 2016, Windows 10, Microsoft Corporation

End-of-Chapter Activities

➤ Access Chapter 6—Critical Thinking

Creating Forms and Reports

In Biology class, you are learning how to analyze data samples collected from field research. You have a database that contains a table of data collected about frog activity in Vermont from 2015 through 2017, and you will create some forms and reports that summarize the data.

DIRECTIONS

1. Start Access, if necessary, and open **ACT06** from the data files for this chapter
2. Save the file as **ACT06_xx** in the location where your teacher instructs you to store the files for this chapter.

   ✓ *If a security warning bar appears, click Enable Content.*
3. Open the Frog Activity Form and create a conditional formatting rule that makes the Average Intensity number bold and red if it is above 2. Then, split the form.

   ✓ *To split the form you will need to select the whole form.*
4. Open the Frog Activity Report in Layout view and set the control padding to medium.
5. Switch to Design view and then create a Subreport to the right side of the Detail section. The subreport should include all of the fields from the Activity by Month query. Replace the default name with **Activity by Month Subreport** and click Finish. Delete the label associated with the subreport.
6. Click in the Forms section and create a Switchboard Manager.
7. Under Main Switchboard (Default), create a new switchboard item called **Frog Activity Form** that opens the Frog Activity Form in edit mode.
8. Create a new switchboard item called **Activity by Month Subreport** that opens the Activity by Month Subreport.
9. Create another switchboard item called **Frog Activity Report** that opens the Frog Activity Report.
10. Close the database, and exit Access. If instructed, submit this database to your teacher for grading.

➤ Access Chapter 6—Portfolio Builder

Organizing a Database with Forms and Reports

The Computers for Seniors donation program has a basic database in which donors and donations are being tracked. You will improve this database by adding some additional forms and reports to it, so that the organization's management can analyze and use the data more effectively.

DIRECTIONS

1. Start Access, if necessary, and open **APB06** from the data files for this chapter.
2. Save the file as **APB06_xx** in the location where your teacher instructs you to store the files for this chapter.

   ✓ *If a security warning bar appears, click Enable Content.*
3. Copy **frmDonors** and name the copy **frmDonorsAndDonations**.
4. Place the **frmDonations** form as a subform at the bottom of **frmDonorsAndDonations** that shows the individual donations in Datasheet view. Resize the column widths to display all data in the subform.
5. Change the default view of **frmDonors** to **Continuous Forms**.
6. In **frmDonations**, set up conditional formatting so that if no thank-you note has been sent, the donor name appears in bright red.

   ✓ *Hint: Use the expression ThankYouNote Is Null.*
7. Create a new query called **qryDonorsAndDonations** that combines all the fields from **tblDonations** and **tblDonors**.
8. Create a pie chart on a report called **rptDonationPieChart** that shows each donor's last name and the total value of what they have donated. Use the query you just created as the data source.
9. Format the chart attractively, using whatever chart options you think are appropriate. Use data labels for category name and value, and do not use a legend. Format the numbers as currency.

   ✓ *Add the Category name and Value data labels from the Chart Options dialog box.*
10. Set up a Switchboard that accesses all forms and reports.
11. Close the database, and exit Access. If instructed, submit this database to your teacher for grading.

Chapter 7

(Courtesy Yuri Arcurs/Shutterstock)

Securing, Integrating, and Maintaining Data

Lesson 43
Converting and Securing Data

- Backing Up a Database
- Compacting and Repairing a Database
- Converting to a Different Database Format
- Adding File Locations to Trusted Locations

Lesson 44
Sharing Data with Word and Other Text Applications

- Merging an Access Table with a Word Document
- Importing Data from a Word Table
- Exporting Data to a Text File
- Exporting Data to a Word Document
- Publishing in PDF or XPS Format

Lesson 45
Sharing Data with Excel and Access

- Inserting an Excel Chart into an Access Report
- Exporting Data to Excel
- Copying Selected Records to Excel
- Importing Data from Another Access Database
- Exporting Data to Another Access Database
- Saving and Running Export Specifications

Lesson 46
Linking to Data Sources

- Linking to a Table in Another Database
- Removing a Linked Table
- Refreshing or Updating a Link

Lesson 47
Customizing Access

- Setting Database Properties
- Documenting a Database
- Modifying Access Options
- Customizing the Quick Access Toolbar
- Customizing the Navigation Pane

End-of-Chapter Activities

Lesson 43

Converting and Securing Data

➤ What You Will Learn

Backing Up a Database
Compacting and Repairing a Database
Converting to a Different Database Format
Adding File Locations to Trusted Locations

WORDS TO KNOW

Legacy
An earlier version or format.

Software Skills When working with databases, the data stored is often more valuable than the software and hardware that is used to access it. Therefore, it is critical to back up your database frequently and to pay attention to any security warning messages that may appear. You can also convert databases to different formats (for example, for use by people using earlier versions of Access), and repair any errors that might cause a database to malfunction.

What You Can Do

Backing Up a Database

- You have been backing up databases throughout this book. Every time you save a database with a different name, which nearly every exercise has asked you to do, you are backing it up.
- There is also a Back Up Database command available that saves a copy of the database. The difference is that the Back Up Database command leaves the original database open, whereas Save As closes the original database and opens the copy.

Try It! Backing Up a Database

1. Start Access, and open **A43Try** from the data files for this lesson. Click Enable Content if the security warning bar appears.
2. Click File > Save As.
3. Click Save Database As.
4. Click Back Up Database.
5. Click Save As.
6. Navigate to the location where your teacher instructs you to store the files for this lesson.
7. In the File name text box, type **A43Try_xx**.
8. Click Save. The new file is created, and **A43Try** remains open.
9. Click File > Open > This PC > Browse. Navigate to the location where you saved the file.
10. Click **A43Try_xx** and click Open. Click Enable Content if a security warning appears.
11. Leave the database open to use in the next Try It.

Select the Back Up Database command

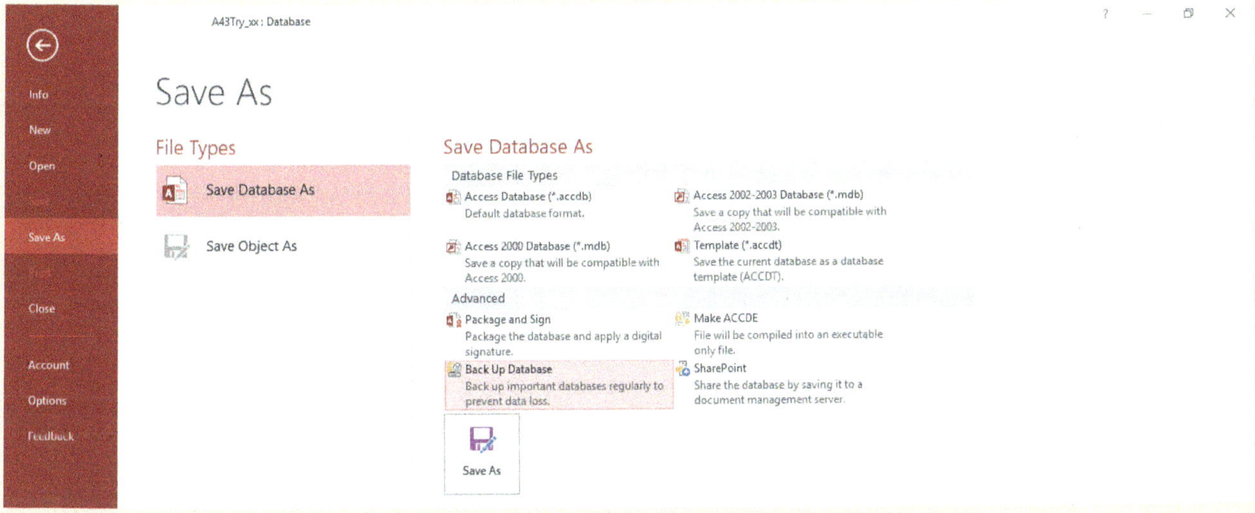

Compacting and Repairing a Database

- The Compact and Repair feature in Access serves two purposes:
  - Compact removes excess space in the data file. Excess space can develop when you delete records and objects, and it can make the file size larger than it needs to be.
  - Repair corrects any errors in the file's structure, solving or preventing data access problems.
- You can compact and repair a database at any time, but it is especially useful before you send the file to someone else (because it will be smaller after compacting) or when you are experiencing errors in reading or writing to the database file.

Try It! Compacting and Repairing a Database

1. In the **A43Try_xx** file, click File > Info > Compact & Repair Database.

   ✓ *The operation executes in the background; there is no confirmation message.*

2. Leave the database open to use in the next Try It.

Converting to a Different Database Format

- Whenever possible, you should use the latest data format in Access: Microsoft Access Database (.accdb). This format allows you to use some of the special features in Access that may not be available in earlier versions, such as multi-valued fields and Rich Text Formatting in Long Text fields.
- However, sometimes you may need to save a database or table in a **legacy** format in order to share it with others who do not have the latest version of Access.
- Some incompatible features will hinder you from saving the database. Some incompatible features will still allow you to save the database in an earlier version of Access, but these incompatible features will not carry over to the new database.

Try It! Saving in Access 2003 Format

1. With **A43Try_xx** open, click File > Save As.
2. Click Save Database As > Access 2002-2003 Database (.mdb).
3. Click Save As. A warning appears.
4. Click OK to close the warning box.
5. On the Home tab, in the Navigation pane, right-click the Employees table and click Design View.
6. Select the Notes field and press DEL. Click Yes to confirm.
7. Select the Photo field and press DEL. Click Yes to confirm.
8. Right-click the table's tab and click Close. Click Yes when prompted to save changes.
9. Click File > Save As.
10. Click Save Database As > Access 2002-2003 Database (.mdb).
11. Click Save As. The Save As dialog box opens.
12. Navigate to the location where your files are saved.
13. In the File Name box, type **A43TryA_xx**.
14. Click Save. If a dialog box opens saying the collated sequence isn't supported with this file format, click OK.

✓ *Only the tables have been saved in this file format.*

15. Click File > Close.

This warning appears because one of the objects contains features that are not backward compatible

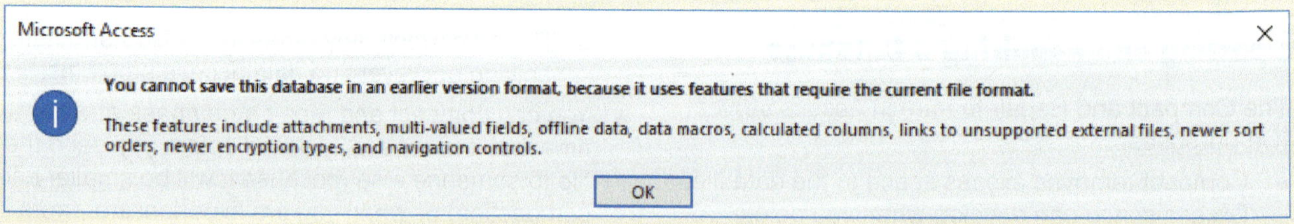

Access 2016, Windows 10, Microsoft Corporation

Try It! Exporting a Word Table to a Delimited Text File

1. In Word, open **A44TryB.docx** from the data files for this lesson.
2. Select the entire table.
3. Click Table Tools Layout > Convert to Text. Click OK to accept the default delimiter character (Tabs).
4. Click File > Save As > This PC > Browse.
5. Open the Save as type drop-down list and click Plain Text.
6. Navigate to the location where your teacher instructs you to store the files for this lesson.
7. In the File name text box, type **A44TryB_xx**.

   ✓ *If you do not add the .txt extension, Word adds it for you when you save.*
8. Click Save.
9. Click OK to accept the default export settings.
10. Exit Word.

Try It! Importing a Delimited Text File to Access

1. Start Access, if necessary, and open **A44TryA** from the data files for this lesson.
2. Save the file as **A44TryA_xx** in the location where your teacher instructs you to store the files for this lesson. Click Enable Content if the security warning bar appears.
3. Click External Data > Text File. The Get External Data – Text File dialog box opens.
4. Click Browse. Browse to the location where you stored the text file in the previous exercise.
5. Click **A44TryB_xx** and click Open.
6. Click OK. The Import Text Wizard runs.
7. Click Next to accept Delimited as the data type.
8. Click the First Row Contains Field Names check box. Then, click Next.
9. Click Next to accept the default field data types.
10. Click Choose my own primary key. Accept the default of Part # that appears.
11. Click Next.
12. In the Import to Table text box, replace the default name with **Parts**.
13. Click Finish.
14. Click OK to bypass the message that the index or primary key cannot contain a null value. (We'll fix this next.)
15. Click Close to close the Wizard.
16. Double-click the Parts table to open it in Datasheet view.
17. Select the blank record (or records) at the bottom of the table and press DEL to remove it. Click Yes to confirm.
18. Right-click the Parts tab and click Close.
19. Leave the database open to use in the next Try It.

Exporting Data to a Text File

- You can export data from any table or query to a delimited text file. This file can then be imported into almost any database program, regardless of its native format.

Try It! Exporting Data to a Text File

1. In Access, with the **A44TryA_xx** file open, click the Duties table in the Navigation pane.
2. Click the External Data tab. In the Export group, click Text File. The Export – Text File dialog box opens.
3. Click Browse and navigate to the location where your teacher instructs you to store the files for this lesson.
4. Change the file name to **A44TryC_xx**.
5. Click Save to accept the location.
6. Click OK. The Export Text Wizard dialog box opens.
7. Click Next to accept Delimited as the export type.
8. Click Tab as the delimiter character to use. Then, click Next.
9. Click Finish. The export completes.
10. Click Close.
11. Close the Duties table, if necessary, and leave the database open to use in the next Try It.

Exporting Data to a Word Document

- You can export from Access to a Word document in Rich Text Format (RTF). Unlike exporting to plain text, exporting to Word in RTF allows you to keep any formatting that has been applied to the data.
- An RTF file is not really a Word document in that it is not in Word's native format. However, Word easily opens an RTF file—as easily as it does native Word files. Other word processing programs can also open RTF files.

Try It! Exporting Data to a Word Document

1. In Access, with the **A44TryA_xx** file open, click the Employees table in the Navigation pane.
2. Click the External Data tab. In the Export group, click More > Word. The Export – RTF File dialog box opens.
3. Click Browse and navigate to the location where your teacher instructs you to store the files for this lesson.
4. Change the file name to **A44TryD_xx**.
5. Click Save to accept the location.
6. Click OK. The Export – RTF File dialog box appears.

   ✓ *There are no options you can set for the export.*
7. Click Close.
8. Leave the database open to use in the next Try It.

Publishing in PDF or XPS Format

- If you want to export data in a format that the recipients cannot easily edit, PDF and XPS are both excellent choices.
- Both are page description languages, which are encoding schemes that result in pages that look the same when viewed and printed on any computer system, regardless of the operating system or hardware.
- PDF is a format created by Adobe. It has been around for many years and is very popular. To read PDF files you need a free program called Adobe Reader or some other application that reads PDF files, such as Adobe Acrobat.
- XPS is the Microsoft equivalent of PDF. XPS files can be read using a built-in reader in newer Windows versions, and a free reader is available for download for versions prior to Windows 7.

Try It! **Publishing a Table in XPS Format**

1. In Access, with the **A44TryA_xx** file open, double-click the Employees table in the Navigation pane. It opens in Datasheet view.
2. Click File > Save As.
3. Click Save Object As.
4. Under Save the current database object, click PDF or XPS.
5. Click Save As. The Publish as PDF or XPS dialog box opens.
6. Open the Save as type drop-down list and click XPS Document.
7. Navigate to the folder where your teacher has instructed you to store the files for this lesson.
8. In the File name box, type **A44TryE_xx**.
9. Click Publish. The XPS file opens in the XPS Viewer, or in a Web browser, depending on your system settings.

   ✓ *You may need to execute additional steps to get to the XPS Viewer, depending on your system settings.*
10. Close the XPS Viewer window.
11. Return to Access. Close the database, and exit Access.

Lesson 44—Practice

The owner of Green Designs wants to reward clients with a gift certificate. You can use a table in Access as the data source for a mailing to clients. In this project, you will merge the Access table into a Word document. You will then add merge fields to the document and complete the merge.

DIRECTIONS

1. Start Access, if necessary, and open **A44Practice** from the data files for this lesson.
2. Save the file as **A44Practice_xx** in the location where your teacher instructs you to store the files for this lesson.

   ✓ *If a security warning bar appears, click Enable Content.*
3. Click the Clients table in the Navigation pane, and then click **External Data** > **Word Merge**. Click **OK** to accept the default setting in the Mail Merge Wizard (Link your data to an existing Microsoft Word document).
4. Navigate to the folder where the data files are stored for this lesson, select **A44PracticeA.docx**, and click **Open**. Microsoft Word opens the specified document, with your Access database as the merge data source.
5. In Word, click **File** > **Save As** and save the file as **A44Practice_xx** in the folder where your teacher instructs you to store the files for this lesson.
6. Click immediately before the colon (:) in the greeting line to move the insertion point there.
7. On the **Mailings** tab, click the down arrow under **Insert Merge Field**. and click **Client_First_Name**.
8. Click two lines above the greeting line to move the insertion point there.
9. Click **Address Block**. The Insert Address Block dialog box opens.
10. Click **Match Fields** and match the **Client First Name** and **Client Last Name** fields with the **First Name** and **Last Name** fields, respectively. Then, click **OK** to close the Match Fields dialog box.
11. Click **OK** to close the Insert Address Block dialog box.
12. Click **Mailings** > **Finish & Merge** > **Edit Individual Documents**.
13. Click **OK** to accept the default of All.
14. Save the new document as **A44PracticeB_xx**.
15. Save and close both documents, and exit Word.
16. In Access, close the database, and exit Access. If instructed, submit this database to your teacher for grading.

Lesson 44—Apply

One of the workers at Green Designs has created a couple of files that he wants to convert to different file formats. First you will help him save a query as a PDF file and export the Clients table to a text file. Then, you will convert a Word file into a text file and import it into the Access database.

DIRECTIONS

1. Start Access, if necessary, and open **A44Apply** from the data files for this lesson.
2. Save the file as **A44Apply_xx** in the location where your teacher instructs you to store the files for this lesson.

   ✓ *If a security warning bar appears, click Enable Content.*
3. Save the **Service Summary** query as a PDF file called **A44ApplyA_xx**.
4. Export the Clients table to a comma-delimited text file called **A44ApplyB_xx.**
5. Open **A44ApplyC** in Word, and convert the table to tab-delimited text.
6. Save the document as a text file called **A44ApplyC_xx.txt**. Then, exit Word.
7. Switch back to Access, and import **A44ApplyC_xx.txt** into a new table called **Products**.

   ✓ *Make sure you mark the First Row Contains Field Names check box, so the field names will import properly. Use the Product# field as the primary key.*
8. Delete the blank record(s) from the **Products** table.
9. Close the database, and exit Access. If instructed, submit this database to your teacher for grading.

Lesson 45

Sharing Data with Excel and Access

➤ What You Will Learn

Inserting an Excel Chart into an Access Report
Exporting Data to Excel
Copying Selected Records to Excel
Importing Data from Another Access Database
Exporting Data to Another Access Database
Saving and Running Export Specifications

Software Skills Excel and Access are closely related; often data that is created in one application needs to be shared with the other. In this lesson, you will learn how to use Excel charts within Access and how to export Access records to Excel. You'll also learn how to share data with other Access databases and how to save your export specifications for later reuse.

WORDS TO KNOW

Import
To take data from one file and place the information in another file.

What You Can Do

Inserting an Excel Chart into an Access Report

- Because Access's charting features are not as robust as those in Excel, you may sometimes want to create a chart in Excel and then **import** it into Access for use in a report.
- Because the chart has no relationship to any of the data in the Access database, it is not affected by any changes made to any of the tables in Access.
- If you want to edit the chart later, you can double-click it in Report Design view and use the Excel charting tools.

Try It! Importing an Excel Chart into Access

1. Start Access, and open **A45Try** from the data files for this lesson.
2. Save the database as **A45Try_xx** in the location where your teacher instructs you to store the files for this lesson. Click Enable Content if the security warning bar appears.
3. Click Create > Blank Report.
4. Right-click the report's tab, and click Design View.
5. Open **A45TryA.xlsx** in Excel from the data files for this lesson.
6. Click the chart to select it.
7. Press CTRL + C to copy the chart to the Clipboard.
8. Switch to Access, and click the Detail section header on the report.
9. Press CTRL + V to paste the chart into the Detail area of the report.
10. Click Report Design Tools Design > View to view the report in Report view.
11. Click the Save button on the Quick Access Toolbar.
12. In the Save As dialog box, type **Imported Chart** and click OK. Close and save changes to the Excel document.
13. Close the Imported Chart report. Leave the database open to use in the next Try It.

Place the chart in the Detail area of the report

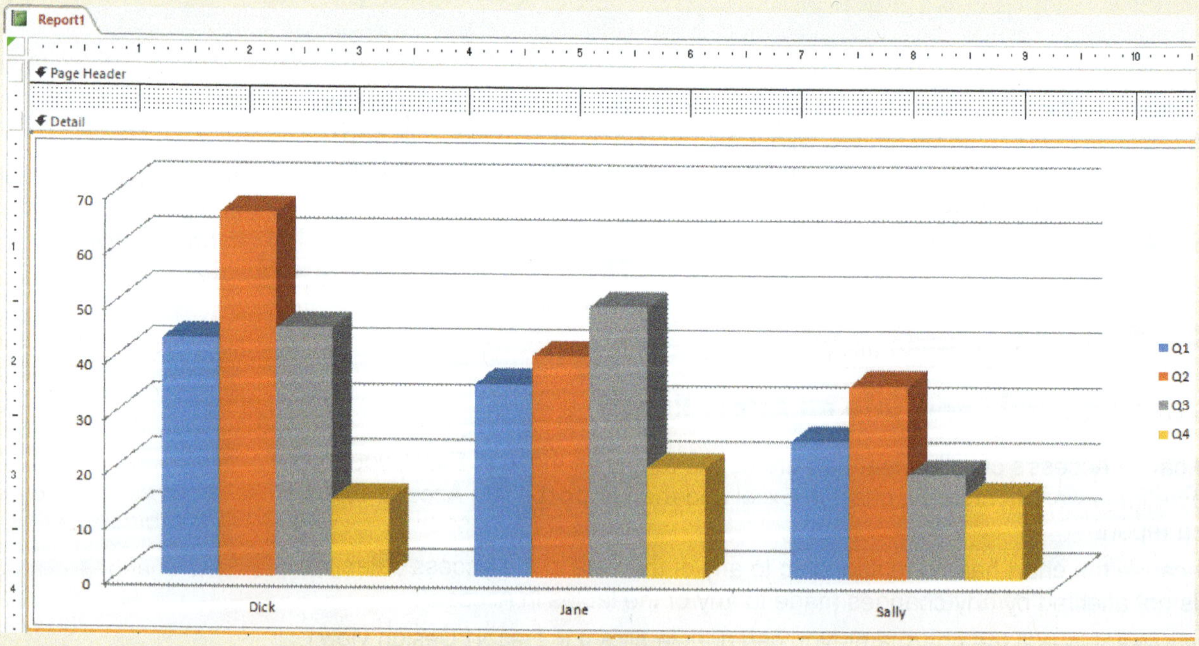

Exporting Data to Excel

- You can move data from Access to Excel. This may be useful when you want to perform more complex calculations on data, for example, because Excel's number-manipulating functions are more robust than those in Access.
- You can export an entire table to Excel, or you can export selected records only.
- You can use the Export feature to export to a new Excel file, or you can simply copy and paste into Excel from Datasheet view in an existing Excel file.
- To export an entire table, use the Export Spreadsheet Wizard. When you use this method, you are prompted to specify a name for a new Excel workbook into which to place the data.

Try It! Exporting an Entire Table to Excel

1. In the A45Try_xx file, in the Navigation pane, click Employees.
2. On the External Data tab, click the Excel button in the Export group.
3. Click the Browse button, and navigate to the location where your teacher has instructed you to store the files for this lesson.
4. In the File name box, type A45TryA_xx.
5. Click Save.
6. Click OK.
7. Click Close.
8. Leave the database open to use in the next Try It.

Copying Selected Records to Excel

- When you copy records to Excel, you don't have to go through a Wizard; you can use the Clipboard, which is faster and easier.
- You must already have an Excel workbook open into which you can paste. This can be a blank workbook or one that already contains data.

Try It! Copying Records to Excel

1. Start Excel, and open a new blank workbook.
2. Switch to Access.
3. In the A45Try_xx file, in the Navigation pane, double-click Employees. The table opens in Datasheet view.
4. Select the three records in the table.

   ✓ *To select a record, click the record selector to the left of the first field. Drag across multiple record selectors to select multiple records.*
5. Press CTRL + C to copy the records to the Clipboard.
6. Switch to Excel.
7. Click in cell A1.
8. Press CTRL + V to paste the records.
9. Exit Excel without saving the changes.
10. Close the Employees table.
11. Leave the database open to use in the next Try It.

(continued)

Try It! Copying Records to Excel *(continued)*

Select the records to copy

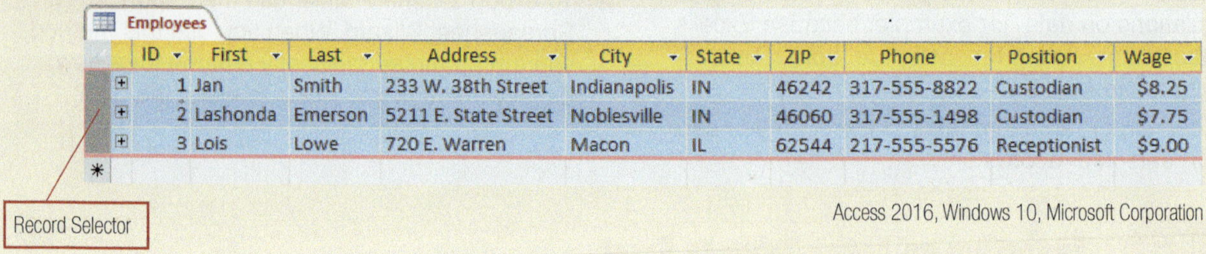

Access 2016, Windows 10, Microsoft Corporation

Importing Data from Another Access Database

- You can copy tables from other Access databases. This can save a lot of development time if you need the same table structures in multiple databases.
- You aren't limited to copying tables; you can copy any object type from any other Access database. However, only tables carry data with them when copied.
- Copying a report, for example, copies only the report definition; if the destination database does not have a table by the same name as the one referenced in the report, the report will not work.

Try It! Importing Data from Another Access Database

1. In the **A45Try_xx** file, on the External Data tab, click the Access button in the Import & Link group.
2. Click the Browse button, and navigate to the location of the data files for this lesson.
3. Click **A45TryB** and click Open.
4. Click OK. The Import Objects dialog box opens, listing all the objects in the database by type.

   ✓ *Each type is on a different tab. The Tables tab appears by default.*
5. Click tblMembershipType and click OK.
6. Click Close. The table appears in the Navigation pane.
7. Leave the database open to use in the next Try It.

Select the table to be imported

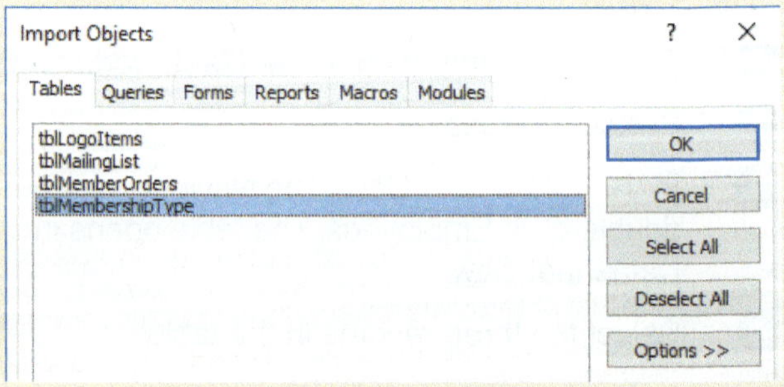

Access 2016, Windows 10, Microsoft Corporation

Exporting Data to Another Access Database

- You can export objects to other Access databases.
- To share objects between databases, you can initiate the process from either side, importing from one or exporting from the other. The result is the same.

Try It! Exporting Data to Another Access Database

1. Open A45TryB from the data files for this lesson.
2. Save the database as A45TryB_xx in the location where your teacher instructs you to store the files for this lesson.
3. Close A45TryB_xx, and reopen A45Try_xx, if necessary.
4. In the Navigation pane, click Parts.
5. Click the External Data tab.
6. In the Export group, click Access.
7. Click the Browse button, and navigate to the location where you stored the database file in step 2.
8. Click A45TryB_xx and click Save.
9. Click OK. The Export dialog box opens.
10. Click OK to accept the defaults.
11. Click Close.
12. Leave the database open to use in the next Try It.

Saving and Running Export Specifications

- If you frequently repeat the same import or export operation on the same data files, you may want to save the specifications so that you can re-run the import or export quickly without having to work through the Wizard each time.
- The following Try Its show how to save an export; saving an import works the same way when performing an import.

Try It! Saving Export Specifications

1. In the A45Try_xx file, in the Navigation pane, click the Assignments table.
2. On the External Data tab, in the Export group, click Excel.
3. Click the Browse button, and navigate to the location where your teacher instructs you to store the files for this lesson.
4. In the File name box, type A45TryC_xx and click Save.
5. Click OK.
6. Click the Save export steps check box. Additional options appear in the dialog box.
7. Click Save Export. The export is saved.
8. Leave the database open to use in the next Try It.

(continued)

Try It! Saving Export Specifications *(continued)*

Click the Save export steps check box

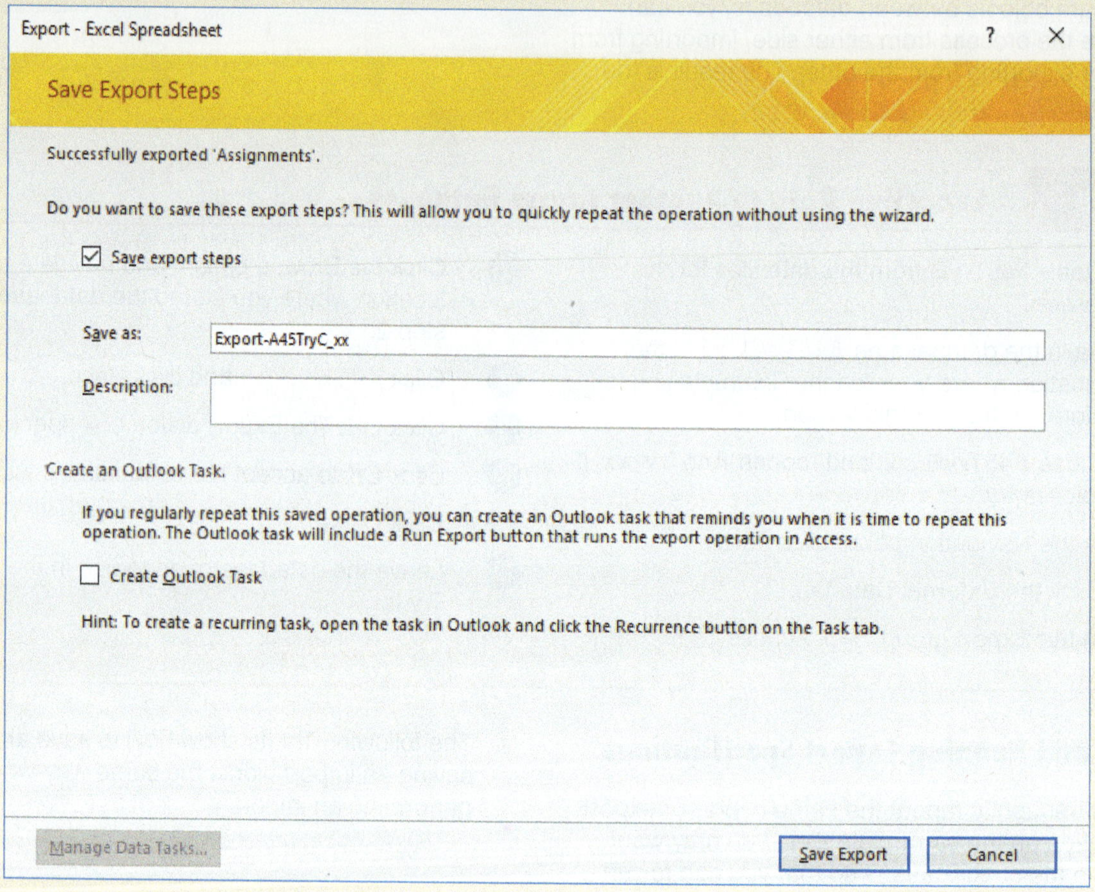

Try It! Re-Running a Saved Export

1. In the **A45Try_xx** file, click External Data > Saved Exports.
2. Click the **Export-A45TryC_xx** export specification.
3. Click Run. A message appears that the file already exists.
4. Click Yes. A confirmation appears.
5. Click OK.
6. Click Close.
7. Close the database, and exit Access.

Lesson 45—Practice

In this project, you will create a new database and import a table from another Access database.

DIRECTIONS

1. Start Access, if necessary, and click **Blank desktop database**.
2. In the File name box, type **A45Practice_xx**.
3. Click the **Browse for a location to put your database** icon and navigate to the location where your teacher instructs you to store the files for this lesson.
4. Click **OK**.
5. Click **Create**. A new database opens, and a new table opens in Datasheet view.
6. Right-click the table's tab and click **Close**.
7. Click the **External Data** tab.
8. In the **Import & Link** group, click **Access**.
9. Click **Browse**, and navigate to the location of the data files for this lesson.
10. Click **A45Practice** and click **Open**.
11. Click **OK**. The Import Objects dialog box opens.
12. Click **tblStates** and click **OK**.
13. Click **Close**.
14. Close the database, and exit Access. If instructed, submit this database to your teacher for grading.

Lesson 45—Apply

The manager at Ace Learning would like to use Excel to create a chart for an enrollment report because of Excel's enhanced formatting options. You will export a table from the database to Excel, make a chart, and import the chart into an Access report.

DIRECTIONS

1. Start Access, if necessary, and open **A45Apply** from the data files for this lesson.
2. Save the file as **A45Apply_xx** in the location where your teacher instructs you to store the files for this lesson.

   ✓ *If a security warning bar appears, click Enable Content.*
3. Export the **qryEnrollmentSummary** query to a new Excel workbook. Name the workbook **A45ApplyA_xx.xlsx**. Save the export steps as **A45ApplyA_Export_xx**.
4. Open **A45ApplyA_xx** in Excel.
5. Change the entry in B1 to **Enrollment**.
6. Select A1:B4.
7. Click **Insert** > **Insert Pie or Doughnut Chart** in the Charts group and click the first sample. A pie chart appears.
8. Click the **Chart Tools Design** tab, and click **Style 1** in the Chart Styles box.
9. Copy the chart to the Clipboard.
10. Save your work, and close Excel.
11. Switch back to the Access database and start a new blank report. Display the report in Design view.
12. Paste the chart from the Clipboard to the Detail area of the report.
13. Save the report as **rptEnrollmentChart**, and close the report.
14. Close the database, and exit Access. If instructed, submit this database to your teacher for grading.

Lesson 46

Linking to Data Sources

➤ What You Will Learn

Linking to a Table in Another Database
Removing a Linked Table
Refreshing or Updating a Link

WORDS TO KNOW

Link
To create a path in one file to data in another file. When you update data in either file, updates appear in both files.

Software Skills When an independent data source changes frequently, it may not be enough to synchronize it manually by importing or exporting. You may find it more effective to create a link that automatically synchronizes the data.

What You Can Do

Linking to a Table in Another Database

- Tables in different databases can be **linked**, just as you can import tables from other databases.
- Changes you make in one place will be reflected in the other, and vice-versa. This allows two or more database files to make use of the same data source and have it always be up-to-date.

Try It! **Linking to a Table in Another Database**

1. Start Access, and open A46TryA from the data files for this lesson.
2. Save the database as A46TryA_xx in the location where your teacher instructs you to store the files for this lesson and close the database.
3. Open A46Try from the data files for this lesson.
4. Save the database as A46Try_xx in the location where your teacher instructs you to store the files for this lesson. Click Enable Content if the security warning bar appears.
5. Click the External Data tab.
6. In the Import & Link group, click Access.
7. Click Browse and navigate to the location where you saved your file in step 2.
8. Click A46TryA_xx and click Open.
9. Click the Link to the data source by creating a linked table button.
10. Click OK. The Link Tables dialog box opens.
11. Click tblStates and click OK. The linked table appears in the Tables list in the Navigation pane.
12. Leave the database open to use in the next Try It.

Try It! Changing a Linked Table

1. In the A46Try_xx file, in the Navigation pane, double-click the tblStates table to open it.
2. In the State field, change ILL to IL and close the table.
3. Open A46TryA_xx and double-click the tblStates table to open it.
4. Observe that the ILL field has automatically been changed to IL.
5. Close A46TryA_xx.
6. Leave the A46Try_xx database open to use in the next Try It.

Removing a Linked Table

- Removing a linked table deletes the link but does not affect the original data source. You can recreate the link any time you want it.
- If you decide you want the data imported rather than linked, the easiest way is to delete the link and then import the data from scratch, as you would from any other data source. There is no command for converting a link to an import.

Try It! Removing a Linked Table

1. In the A46Try_xx file, in the Navigation pane, click tblStates and press DEL.
2. Click Yes to confirm.
3. Click Undo in the Quick Access Toolbar to restore the deleted table. You will use this table in the next Try It.
4. Leave the database open to use in the next Try It.

Refreshing or Updating a Link

- If the location of the source data file changes, you might need to update the link.
- You can check your links and update them if needed by opening the Linked Table Manager. To do that, right-click any linked table and choose Linked Table Manager.

  ✓ *You can also open the Linked Table Manager from the External Data tab.*

- From within the Linked Table Manager, place a check mark next to each link to update, and then click OK.
- If any data sources are not in their expected locations, you are prompted to re-select them. You can also force the Linked Table Manager to prompt a new location by marking the Always prompt for new location check box.

Try It! Refreshing a Link

1. In the A46Try_xx file, click External Data > Linked Table Manager.
2. Click to place a check mark next to the linked tblStates table.
3. Click OK. The links are checked.

   ✓ *If prompted, navigate to the appropriate location of the linked file.*

4. Click OK to confirm that the tables are up to date.
5. Click the Always prompt for new location check box.
6. Click to place a check mark next to the linked tblStates table.
7. Click OK. The Select New Location of tblStates dialog box opens.
8. Click Cancel to close the dialog box. (You do not need to select a new location because the old one is still accurate.)
9. Click Close to close the Linked Table Manager.
10. Close the database, and exit Access.

Lesson 46—Practice

In this project, you will update an outdated link in the Ace Learning database that no longer points to a valid source and you will link and change a table.

DIRECTIONS

1. Start Access, if necessary, and open **A46PracticeB** from the data files for this lesson.
2. Save the file as **A46PracticeB_xx** in the location where your teacher instructs you to store the files for this lesson. Close the database.
3. Open **A46Practice** from the data files for this lesson.
4. Save the file as **A46Practice_xx** in the location where your teacher instructs you to store the files for this lesson.

   ✓ *If a security warning bar appears, click Enable Content.*
5. Double-click **tblDonations**.

   ✓ *An error message appears because the table is no longer linked to the data source.*
6. Click **OK**.
7. Click **External Data** > **Linked Table Manager**.
8. Click the check box next to **tblDonations**.
9. Click **OK**. The Select New Location of tblDonations dialog box opens.
10. Navigate to the location of the data files for this lesson and click **A46PracticeA.xlsx**.
11. Click **Open**.
12. Click **OK**.
13. Click **Close**.
14. Double-click **tblDonations** in the Navigation pane. It opens in Datasheet view.
15. Close the table.
16. On the External Data tab, in the Import & Link group, click **Access**.
17. In the File Name field, click **Browse** and navigate to the location where you saved your file in step 2.
18. Click **A46PracticeB_xx** and click Open.
19. Click the Link to the data source by creating a linked table button.
20. Click **OK**. The Link Tables dialog box opens.
21. Click **tblStates** and click **OK**. The linked table appears in the Tables list in the Navigation pane.
22. Double-click the **tblStates** table.
23. In record 15, change **ILL** to **IL** and close the database.
24. Open **A46PracticeB_xx.**
25. Double-click the **tblStates** table. Observe that record 15 has automatically changed.
26. Close the database, and exit Access. If instructed, submit this database to your teacher for grading.

Lesson 46—Apply

At Ace Learning, the office manager has been keeping an inventory of property in Excel. You will link it into the main database.

DIRECTIONS

1. Start Access, if necessary, and open **A46ApplyA** from the data files for this lesson.
2. Save the file as **A46ApplyA_xx** in the location where your teacher instructs you to store the files for this lesson and close the database.
3. Open **A46Apply** from the data files for this lesson.
4. Save the file as **A46Apply_xx** in the location where your teacher instructs you to store the files for this lesson.

   ✓ *If a security warning bar appears, click Enable Content.*
5. Delete the **tblDonations** linked table.
6. Link the **tblInventory** table from the file **A46ApplyA_xx** into the database.
7. Open the **tblInventory** table. Change the location in row 6 to **Classroom A**.

   ✓ *Be sure and save the table before moving on.*
8. Check **A46ApplyA_xx** to make sure the changes have been made.
9. Close both databases, and exit Access. If instructed, submit the **A46Apply_xx** database to your teacher for grading.

Lesson 47

Customizing Access

➤ What You Will Learn

Setting Database Properties
Documenting a Database
Modifying Access Options
Customizing the Quick Access Toolbar
Customizing the Navigation Pane

WORDS TO KNOW

Metadata
Information about a data file, independent from the data file's content. Metadata can include file size, creation date, and author name.

Software Skills Like other Office programs, Access is very customizable. You can change properties not only for the current database, but for Access in general. You can change settings that govern how Access behaves and how controls and objects appear in the Quick Access Toolbar and the Navigation pane.

What You Can Do

Setting Database Properties

- The properties for a database file consist of **metadata**—that is, data about the data file itself. Properties include read-only statistics that describe the file, such as its size and creation date, and editable information about the file, such as author name and keywords.
- To view and edit a database's properties, you can display the Properties dialog box for it.
- You can view the file's properties from Windows, as with any other file. However, when you view the Properties dialog box that way, some of the editable properties are not available, such as author and keywords.
- You can view the file's properties from within Access also. This method grants you full access to all editable properties.

Try It! Viewing Properties from Windows

1. In Windows, navigate to the folder containing the data files for this lesson.
2. Right-click **A47Try.accdb** and click Properties. The Properties dialog box appears.
3. On the General tab, examine the general properties of the file.
4. Click the Security tab. This tab controls who may access the file according to Windows permissions.
5. Click the Details tab. This tab shows you the file details and allows you to remove properties and personal information.
6. Close the Properties window.

The Properties dialog box for a file, accessed via File Explorer

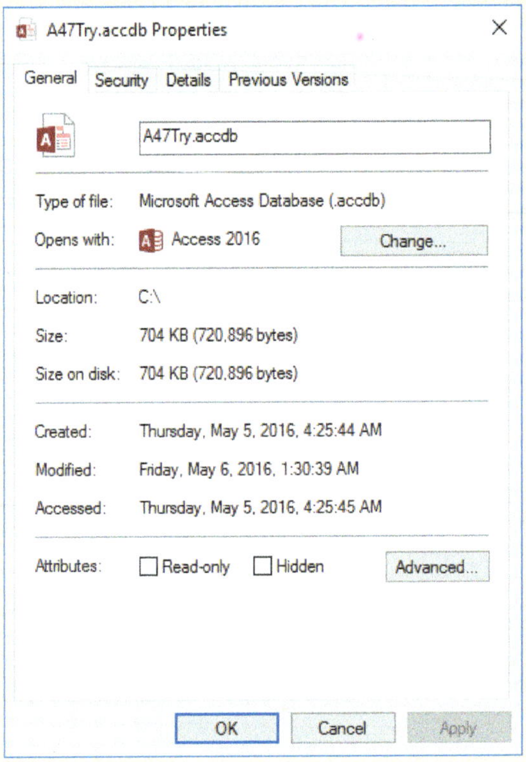

Access 2016, Windows 10, Microsoft Corporation

Try It! Viewing Properties from Access

1. Start Access, and open the file **A47Try** from the data files for this lesson.
2. Save the database as **A47Try_xx** in the location where your teacher has instructed you to save your work. Click Enable Content if the security warning bar appears.
3. Click File > Info.
4. Click View and edit database properties.
5. Click the General tab. This tab contains the same information as the General tab did in the previous Try It.
6. Click the Summary tab. This tab contains a set of editable properties for the file.
7. Delete the text in the Title field and type **Practice Database**.
8. Delete the text in the Author field and type your own name.
9. Click the Statistics tab and review the statistics.
10. Click the Contents tab. This tab shows a list of the objects in the database.
11. Click the Custom tab. On this tab you can create your own properties.
12. Click OK to close the Properties dialog box.
13. Navigate to the Home tab.
14. Leave the database open to use in the next Try It.

(continued)

Try It! Viewing Properties from Access *(continued)*

The Properties dialog box for a file, accessed via Access

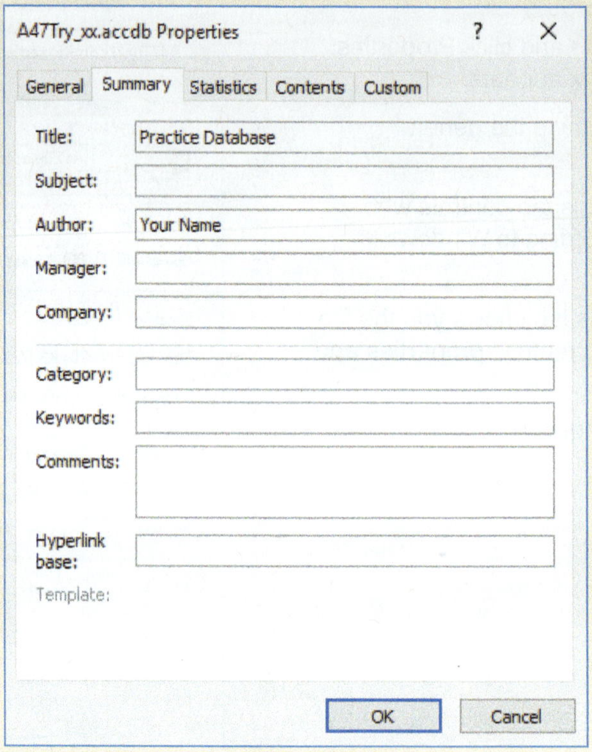

Access 2016, Windows 10, Microsoft Corporation

Documenting a Database

- Documenting a database involves creating a detailed report of its structure, dependencies, properties for every object and every field, and so on. The complete documentation of a database can be used to rebuild it in the event of loss or corruption of the data file.
- To document a database, use the Database Documenter feature. Access generates a report called Object Definition. You can print that report as full documentation of your database, and you should keep it in a safe location.
- You cannot save the report in the database as you would a regular report; the Save command is unavailable. However, you can export it in any of a variety of formats, including Word, plain text, PDF, or XPS.

✓ *The export buttons are found in the Data group on the Print Preview tab.*

Try It! Documenting a Database

1. In the A47Try_xx file, click Database Tools > Database Documenter.
2. Click the Tables tab.
3. Select the Assignments check box.
4. Click Options. The Print Table Definition dialog box opens.
5. Clear the Permissions by User and Group check box. Then, click OK.
6. Click OK to generate the report.
7. Examine the report in Preview.
8. Click Print Preview > PDF or XPS.
9. Navigate to the location where your teacher has instructed you to save your work.
10. Open the Save as type drop-down list and click PDF.
11. In the File name box, type A47TryA_xx.
12. Click Publish. The report opens in a PDF Viewer or a Web browser.
13. Close the PDF Viewer or Web browser window.
14. Switch to Access and click Close.
15. Right-click the report tab and click Close.
16. Leave the database open to use in the next Try It.

Modifying Access Options

- There are also many Access options that refer to the application itself, and not to any specific data file.
- Over a hundred options and settings are available, organized into several categories, such as Datasheet, Object Designers, Proofing, and Client Settings.

Try It! Modifying Access Options

1. Click File > Options. The Access Options dialog box opens with the General options displayed.
2. Open the Default file format for Blank Database drop-down list and examine the options.
3. Click the Datasheet tab.
4. In the Default font area, open the Size drop-down list and examine the choices. This setting controls the default font size for text in a datasheet. Set it to 11 if it is not already set to this size.
5. Click the Object Designers tab.

   ✓ *This tab contains options for each of the various Design views (Table design, Query design, and so on).*
6. Click the Proofing tab.

   ✓ *This tab contains spell-check and AutoCorrect options.*
7. Click the Client Settings tab.

   ✓ *This tab contains settings that control how Access behaves when a user interacts with it.*
8. Scroll down through the options on the Client Settings tab and examine what's available.
9. Click OK to close the Access Options dialog box.
10. Leave the database open to use in the next Try It.

Customizing the Quick Access Toolbar

- The Quick Access Toolbar appears at the upper-left corner of the Access window. As the name implies, it provides quick access to any tools that you choose to place on it.
- By default, it contains three buttons: Save, Undo, and Redo. You may also have a Switchboard Manager button there from a previous lesson.
- You can add any button from any tab to the Quick Access Toolbar by right-clicking it and clicking Add to Quick Access Toolbar.
- You can remove any button from the Quick Access Toolbar by right-clicking it and choosing Remove from Quick Access Toolbar.
- You can also add buttons to the Quick Access Toolbar that do not exist on any tab of the ribbon by default using the Quick Access Toolbar section of the Access Options dialog box.

Try It! Customizing the Quick Access Toolbar

1. Click File > Options. The Access Options dialog box opens.
2. Click Quick Access Toolbar.
3. Open the Choose commands from drop-down list and click Commands Not in the Ribbon.
4. On the list of commands, click Help.
5. Click Add to add the Help command to the list of commands on the toolbar.
6. Click OK.
7. Right-click the Help button on the Quick Access Toolbar, and click Remove from Quick Access Toolbar.
8. Leave the database open to use in the next Try It.

Customizing the Navigation Pane

- The Navigation pane is probably very familiar to you by now. It lists the objects in the current database.
- You can arrange and filter the Navigation pane's object list in several ways:
  - You can sort the list by date or by object type.
  - You can filter the list to show only certain types of objects.

Try It! Customizing the Navigation Pane

1. In the A47Try_xx file, examine the list of objects in the Navigation pane.
2. Click the All Access Objects button in the upper-right corner of the Navigation pane. A menu opens.
3. Click Tables and Related Views. The listing changes so that objects are grouped by table. A table and its related objects appear together.
4. Click the down arrow again and click Object Type. The list returns to being sorted by type.
5. Click the down arrow again and click Tables. The list is filtered to show only tables.
6. Click the down arrow again and click All Access Objects. The filter is removed.
7. Close the database, and exit Access.

Click the down arrow to open the Navigation pane's menu

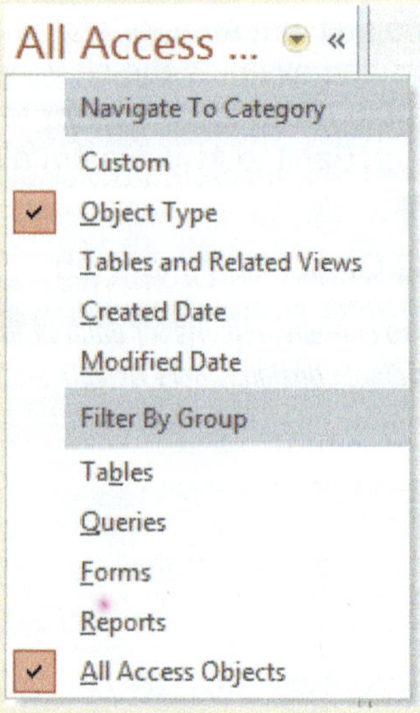

Access 2016, Windows 10, Microsoft Corporation

Lesson 47—Practice

In this project, you will customize the database.

DIRECTIONS

1. Start Access, if necessary, and open **A47Practice** from the data files for this lesson.
2. Save the database as **A47Practice_xx** in the location where your teacher instructs you to store the files for this lesson.

   ✓ *If a security warning bar appears, click Enable Content.*
3. Click **File** > **Info** > **View and edit database properties**.
4. On the **Summary** tab, in the Title box, type **Ace Learning**.
5. In the **Author** box, type your full name.
6. In the **Manager** box, type your teacher's name.
7. In the **Company** box, type your school's name.
8. Click **OK** to close the Properties dialog box.
9. Navigate to the **Home** tab.
10. Close the database, and exit Access.
11. In Windows, navigate to the location where **A47Practice_xx** is stored.
12. Right-click **A47Practice_xx** and click **Properties**.
13. On the **General** tab, click **Read-only**.
14. Click **OK**.
15. Close File Explorer.

Lesson 47—Apply

Your friend at Ace Learning has asked you to change the properties of their database. You will customize the properties for one of their main databases.

DIRECTIONS

1. Start Access, if necessary, and open **A47Apply** from the data files for this lesson.
2. Save the file as **A47Apply_xx** in the location where your teacher instructs you to store the files for this lesson.

   ✓ *If a security warning bar appears, click Enable Content.*
3. In the Access Options dialog box, set the following options for the Current Database:
   a. Set the Application Title to **Ace Learning**.
   b. Turn off the display of the status bar.
   c. Turn on the **Compact on Close** option.
   d. Set the Display Form to **frmMenu**.
4. Set the following options on the Datasheet tab of the Access Options dialog box:
   a. Turn off the display of both horizontal and vertical gridlines.
   b. Set the default column width to **1.25"**.
5. Set the following options on the Client Settings tab:
   a. Set the default print margins to **0.5"** on all sides.
   b. Set the default Open mode to **Exclusive**.
6. On the Quick Access Toolbar tab, add the following buttons:

   AutoFormat

   Insert Chart

   Run Macro
7. Close the Access Options dialog box. Click **OK** in the message box.
8. Change the Navigation pane so that it shows objects grouped by Tables and Related Views.
9. Remove the **AutoFormat**, **Insert Chart**, and **Run Macro** buttons from the Quick Access Toolbar.
10. Close the database, and exit Access.

End-of-Chapter Activities

➤ Access Chapter 7—Critical Thinking

Maintaining and Manipulating a Database

Clown Brigade, a nonprofit organization, is raising funds by selling logo items. Several people in the organization maintain records, and now it is time to pull all the information together into an Access database. You will create a new database and then import tables into it from various sources. You will then compact and repair the database.

DIRECTIONS

1. Start Access, if necessary, and create a new blank database called **ACT07_xx**.
2. Import **ACT07A.txt** into the database as a new table called **Items**:
   a. The first row contains the field names.
   b. Ensure that the field titles have the proper spacing.
   c. Format the **Price** field as **Currency**.
   d. Use **Item Number** as the primary key field.
   e. Save the import steps with the default information.
3. Import the **ACT07B.xlsx** Excel file into the database as a new table called **Members**:
   a. The first row contains the field names.
   b. Use **ID** as the primary key field.
4. Import the table from **ACT07C.accdb** into the database as a new table called **Member Orders**.

   ✓ *You don't have a choice of what to call the table while importing it, so you will need to rename it after import. The same is true for the XML file in the next step.*
5. Import **ACT07D.xsd** into the database as a new table called **Membership Types**.

   ✓ *Click OK in the Import XML dialog box.*
6. Open the **Members** table in Design view and change the field size for the **ID** field to **Long Integer**. Close the table, saving your changes.

   ✓ *This is necessary in order to create a relationship between the Members and Member Orders fields in the next step. Ignore any warnings you might see.*
7. Open the **Relationships** window, and create the relationships shown in Illustration 7A.
8. In the database Properties dialog box (from within Access), set the following:

   Title: **Clown Brigade**.

   Author: **Your Name**.
9. Compact and repair the database.
10. Document the **Items** table in the database, and save the documentation report as an XPS file called **ACT07E_xx.xps**.
11. In the options for this database, set the Application Title to **Clown Brigade**.
12. Save a copy of the database as an ACCDE file. Name the copy **ACT07F_xx.accde**.
13. Close the database, and exit Access. If instructed, submit this database to your teacher for grading.

Illustration 7A

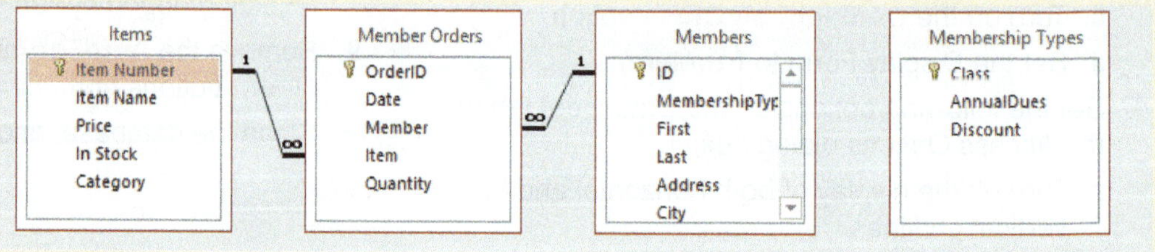

Access 2016, Windows 10, Microsoft Corporation

➤ Access Chapter 7—Portfolio Builder

Improving Data Safety and Security

The Computers for Seniors database is nearly complete, but the program manager has some concerns about data safety and security. He worries that inexperienced users will poke around in Access and delete data that they shouldn't, and that there won't be a backup of that data from which to restore the database. In this project, you will back up the database and then make some changes to the database's user interface options that will make it more difficult for an inexperienced user to wander off the path.

DIRECTIONS

1. Start Access, if necessary, and open **APB07** from the data files for this chapter.
2. Save the file as **APB07_xx** in the location where your teacher instructs you to store the files for this chapter.
3. Make a backup copy of the database. Name the copy **APB07_backup_xx**. If necessary, close the backup database and reopen **APB07_xx**.
4. In the Access Options dialog box, for the Current Database, set the following options:

   Application Title: **Computers for Seniors**

   Display Form: **frmMain**

   Document Window Options: **Overlapping Windows**
5. In the Access Options dialog box, for the Current Database, clear the following check boxes:

   Display Status Bar

   Enable Layout View

   Enable design changes for tables in Datasheet view
6. Close and reopen the database to see the changes in effect.
7. Test all the buttons on the form to make sure they work correctly. Use the **Return to Main Menu** button at the bottom of each form or report to return to the main menu when finished, or close the form or report.

   ✓ *The main menu reopens automatically when a form or report is closed. This is set up with macros.*
8. Right-click the **Main Menu** window's title bar and click **Design View**.
9. Display the **Property Sheet** for the form, and set the **Navigation Buttons** and **Record Selectors** properties to **No**.
10. Set the **Close Button** property to **No**.
11. Set the **Min Max Buttons** property to **Max Enabled**.
12. Switch to Form View to check the effect of the changes you have made.

    ✓ *Now the form is more difficult to close or minimize accidentally. The Close (X) button still appears on its title bar, but is inactive.*
13. Compact and repair the database.
14. Export the data from the **tblDonors** table to a Delimited TXT file with commas and Windows coding. Name the file **APB07B_xx.txt**.
15. Reopen the **Access Options** dialog box. For the Current Database, clear the **Display Navigation Pane** check box.
16. Close and reopen the database to confirm that the Navigation pane does not appear.
17. Close the database, and exit Access. If instructed, submit this database to your teacher for grading.

Chapter 5

(Courtesy Monkey Business Images/Shutterstock)

Working with Masters, Handouts, and Text

Lesson 32
Working with Advanced Slide Master Features

- Adding Graphics to Slide Master Layouts
- Customizing a Slide Master Background
- Customizing Placeholders on Slide Layouts

Lesson 33
Customizing Themes and Effects

- Applying a Theme to Selected Slides
- Customizing Effects
- Using the Design Ideas Feature

Lesson 34
Working with Notes and Handouts

- Using Advanced Notes and Handout Master Formats
- Working with Linked Notes (OneNote 2016)

Lesson 35
Integrating PowerPoint with Word

- Exporting Handouts to Word
- Linking Presentations to Word
- Communicating with Others

Lesson 36
Fine-Tuning Text Formats

- Applying Paragraph and Special Indents
- Setting Tab Stops
- Controlling Text Box Margins
- Applying Advanced Text Formats

Lesson 37
Using Research Tools

- Using Smart Lookup
- Translating Text

End-of-Chapter Activities

Lesson 32

Working with Advanced Slide Master Features

➤ What You Will Learn

Adding Graphics to Slide Master Layouts
Customizing a Slide Master Background
Customizing Placeholders on Slide Layouts

WORDS TO KNOW

Gradient
A fill option that uses gradations of one or more colors.

Gradient stop
Point at which a gradient changes from one color to another color.

Transparency
Amount of light that can pass through an object.

Software Skills You can customize slide masters by adding a shape or picture, by creating a custom background, or by modifying the placeholder arrangement.

What You Can Do

Adding Graphics to Slide Master Layouts

- Graphics such as shapes, lines, and pictures can be added to slide master layouts. These graphics appear on every slide to which that layout is applied.
- Use the shapes on the Home tab or Insert tab to draw basic objects, such as lines, rectangles, and circles, as well as more complex shapes such as stars, banners, and block arrows, on a slide master layout.

  ✓ *You can also create your own custom objects by merging shapes.*

- Use the Pictures or Online Pictures command on the Insert tab to locate a picture to display on a slide master layout.

Try It! Adding Graphics to Slide Master Layouts

1. Start PowerPoint, and open **P32Try** from the data files for this lesson.
2. Save the presentation as **P32Try_xx** in the location where your teacher instructs you to store the files for this lesson.
3. Click View > Slide Master.
4. Display the Title Slide layout, if necessary.
5. Click Insert > Shapes.
6. Select the Rectangle shape.
7. Draw a shape 0.5" high by 2.5" wide and position it at the bottom center of the gray rectangle at the right side of the slide.
8. Right-click the shape, select Edit Text, and type **Helping Hands**.
9. Click Insert > Pictures.
10. Navigate to the data files for this lesson, select the **P32Try_picture.jpg** image, and click Insert.
11. Adjust the width of the picture to 2.5" and position it on top of the shape, as shown in the figure.
12. Click the Close Master View button.
13. Save the **P32Try_xx** file, and leave it open to use in the next Try It.

Picture and shape placed on a slide master

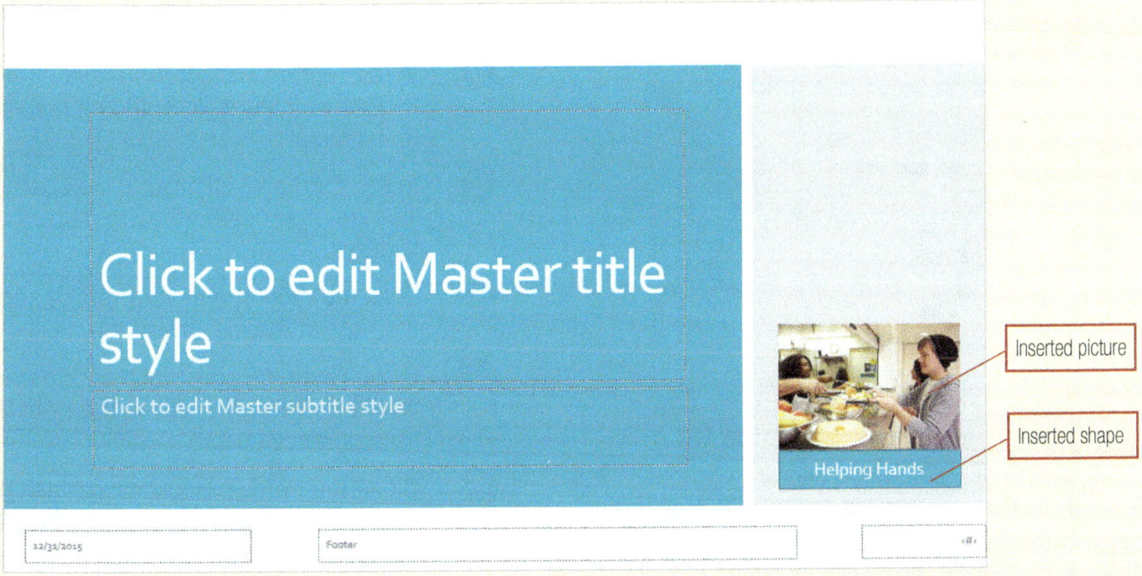

PowerPoint 2016, Windows 10, Microsoft Corporation

Customizing a Slide Master Background

- As you know, backgrounds on slide masters are controlled by the applied theme. You can, however, customize one or more slide master layouts by applying a **gradient**, a texture, or a picture as a background.
- PowerPoint includes preset gradients you can apply at the click of a button, but you can also create your own custom gradient using options on the Format Background task pane. You can use the same process to create a gradient for any object, such as a placeholder, text box, shape, or even text.
- Create a gradient by selecting **gradient stops** and then choosing a color for each stop. You can also choose the direction and the angle for the gradient to control how color flows.

- Add gradient stops to add additional colors to the gradient. Drag gradient stops along the gradient color bar to change where the color starts. Remove gradient stops to simplify the gradient.
- PowerPoint includes a gallery of textures you can choose among to give a slide layout an interesting background appearance.
- When you apply a texture, you may want to adjust the **transparency** setting so that text can easily be read against the texture. The same holds true if you insert a picture as a slide background.
- You can adjust the transparency of textures and pictures in the Format Background task pane.

Try It! Customizing a Slide Master Background

1. In the **P32Try_xx** file, click View > Slide Master.
2. In Slide Master view, click the Blank layout that is currently used by slide 2.
3. Click Slide Master > Background Styles > Format Background.
4. In the Format Background task pane, click Gradient fill. A default gradient is applied to the slide master.

Apply a color to a gradient stop

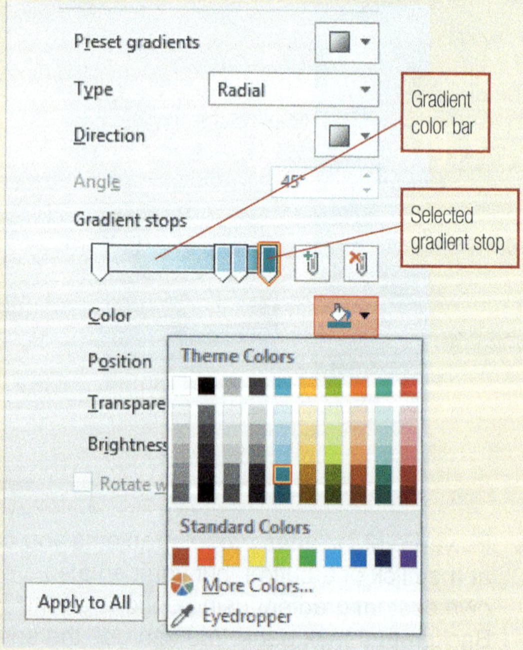

PowerPoint 2016, Windows 10, Microsoft Corporation

5. Click the Type drop-down arrow and select Radial.
6. Click the Direction drop-down arrow and select From Top Left Corner.
7. Click the far-right gradient stop on the gradient color bar, click the Color button below, and select Turquoise, Accent 1, Darker 25%.
8. In the Thumbnail pane, click the Content with Caption layout that is currently used by slide 8.
9. In the Format Background task pane, click Picture or texture fill. A default texture is applied to the slide.
10. In the Format Background task pane, click the Texture drop-down arrow to display a gallery of textures.
11. Click the Woven mat texture, the second from the right in the top row of the gallery.
12. In the Format Background task pane, drag the Transparency slider to the right until the transparency setting is 65%.
13. Close the Format Background task pane, and close Slide Master view to see the texture on the slide in Normal view. Scroll up to see the custom gradient on slide 2.
14. Save the **P32Try_xx** file, and leave it open to use in the next Try It.

Customizing Placeholders on Slide Layouts

- When a slide layout is selected (rather than the slide master), the Title and Footers check boxes are active in the Master Layout group on the Slide Master tab.
- Deselect the Title check box to remove the title placeholder from the layout. Deselect the Footer check box to remove the date, footer, and slide number placeholders from the layout. Display these placeholders again by selecting the appropriate check box.
- You can also select and delete any default placeholder on a layout.
- You can restore deleted placeholders using the Master Layout dialog box. This command is active when the slide master is selected.
- The dialog box shows all placeholders with check boxes selected to show which are active on the slide. To restore a placeholder you have deleted, simply click the appropriate check box.

Try It! Customizing Placeholders on Slide Layouts

1. In the P32Try_xx file, click View > Slide Master.
2. Scroll down in the Thumbnail pane and select the Two Content layout, currently used by no slides.
3. In the Master Layout group, click the Title check box to remove the title placeholder.
4. Click the Title check box to restore the placeholder.
5. Select the slide master at the top of the Thumbnail pane.
6. Click the border of the slide number placeholder.
7. Press DEL.
8. Click Slide Master > Master Layout.
9. Select the Slide number check box to restore the placeholder.
10. Click OK.
11. Close Slide Master view.
12. In Normal view, click Insert > Header & Footer, select Slide number, if necessary, and click Apply to All to display the slide number on all slides.
13. Close the P32Try_xx file, saving changes, and exit PowerPoint.

The Master Layout dialog box

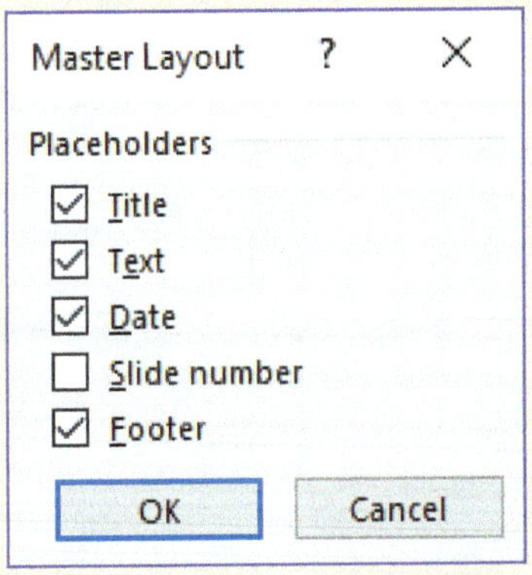

Lesson 32—Practice

In this project, you work on a presentation for Yesterday's Playthings. You customize and add graphic elements to the slide master.

DIRECTIONS

1. Start PowerPoint, if necessary, and open **P32Practice** from the data files for this lesson.
2. Save the presentation as **P32Practice_xx** in the location where your teacher instructs you to store the files for this lesson.
3. Click **View** > **Slide Master**.
4. Click the **Title Slide** layout.
5. Click the aqua rectangle and press DEL to remove it.
6. Click **Slide Master** > **Background Styles** > **Format Background**.
7. On the Format Background task pane, click **Picture or texture fill**.
8. Click the **Texture** drop-down arrow and click the **Recycled paper** texture. Then drag the Transparency slider until the transparency is **30%**. Close the Format Background task pane.
9. Scroll up to click the slide master.
10. On the slide master, draw a Rectangle shape that is **1.1"** wide and **7.5"** high.
11. Remove the shape outline and fill the shape with **Aqua, Accent 2, Darker 25%**.
12. Move the shape to the far right side of the slide, as shown in Figure 32-1.
13. Draw a Right Triangle shape that is **2"** wide and **7.5"** high.
14. Click **Drawing Tools Format** > **Rotate** > **Flip Horizontal**.
15. Remove the shape outline and use the same fill as for the rectangle.
16. Move the triangle shape to align at the right side with the rectangle shape, as shown in Figure 32-1. (Both shapes should align at the right with the right edge of the slide.)
17. Select both shapes and then click **Drawing Tools Format** > **Send Backward** > **Send to Back** to move the shapes behind the footer and the slide number placeholders.
18. Select the slide number placeholder and press DEL to remove it.
19. Click **Slide Master** > **Close Master View**.
20. Preview the slides to see the new formats in place.
21. Close the presentation, saving changes, and exit PowerPoint.

Figure 32-1

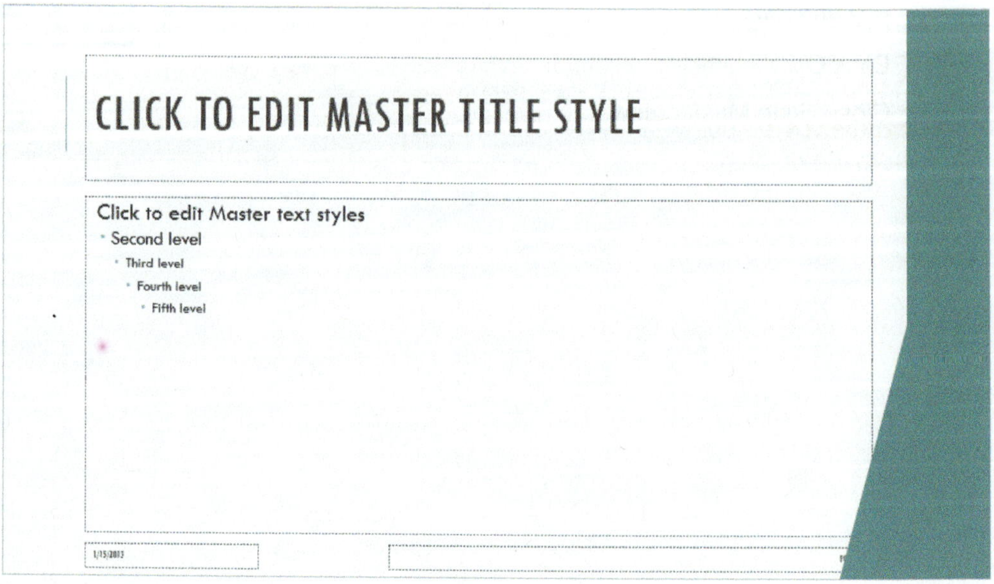

PowerPoint 2016, Windows 10, Microsoft Corporation

Lesson 32—Apply

You continue to work on the presentation for Yesterday's Playthings. In this project, you return to the slide master to adjust the appearance of the shapes you added in the practice exercise, create a gradient background, and insert a picture to appear on all slides.

DIRECTIONS

1. Start PowerPoint, if necessary, and open **P32Apply** from the data files for this lesson.
2. Save the presentation as **P32Apply_xx** in the location where your teacher instructs you to store the files for this lesson.
3. Switch to Slide Master view and display the slide master.
4. Display the Format Background task pane, select the rectangle shape, and change the transparency to **40%**.
5. Select the triangle shape and change the transparency to **35%**.
6. Create a gradient on the slide master as follows:
   a. With the Format Background task pane displayed and no shape selected, choose to create a gradient fill.
   b. Select the **Light Gradient – Accent 2** preset gradient.
   c. Change the direction of the gradient to **Linear Diagonal – Bottom Left to Top Right**.
   d. With the first gradient stop selected, click the **Color** button and select **White, Background 1**. Then drag the gradient stop to the right until the Position box reads **25%**.
   e. Click the gradient stop at the far right of the gradient color bar and then click the **Remove gradient stop** button to remove the color from the gradient.
   f. Click the right-most gradient stop, and change its color to **Aqua, Accent 2, Lighter 40%**.
   g. Click the center gradient stop, change its color to **Gold, Accent 3, Lighter 80%**, and drag it to the left until its position is **55%**. Close the Format Background task pane.
7. Remove the Date placeholder from the slide master.
8. Search for an online picture using the keyword **toys** and then insert a picture of a toy such as the car shown in Figure 32-2.
9. Crop the picture to remove as much of the background as possible. Then resize the image to be **1.8"** wide.
10. Reposition the image in the lower-left corner of the slide, as shown in Figure 32-2 on the next page.
11. Close Slide Master view.
12. Insert a footer with your full name on all slides.
13. Preview the presentation to see the new formats in place.
14. **With your teacher's permission,** print slide 2. It should look similar to Figure 32-2.
15. Close the presentation, saving changes, and exit PowerPoint.

Figure 32-2

PowerPoint 2016, Windows 10, Microsoft Corporation

Lesson 33

Customizing Themes and Effects

➤ What You Will Learn

Applying a Theme to Selected Slides
Customizing Effects
Using the Design Ideas Feature

Software Skills To add visual interest to a presentation using themes, you can apply a theme to selected slides. Choose the slides to which you want to apply the theme, or apply a theme to an entire section. Choose a different set of effects to customize the appearance of graphics in a presentation. If you have an Office 365 subscription, you can use the Design Ideas feature to customize a slide to which you have added a picture.

What You Can Do

Applying a Theme to Selected Slides

- One way to add visual interest to a presentation is to add a second slide master so that you have a number of different layouts to choose among when formatting slides.
- If you want to apply a different theme to only a few slides, however, you can do so in Normal view using one of these options:
  - Select the slides you want to format with a different theme and then use the Apply to Selected Slides command to apply the new theme only to those slides.
  - Select a section in the presentation and then apply a theme. The theme will automatically apply only to the slides in the section.
- When applying a different theme to selected slides in a presentation, try to make sure that the new theme coordinates with the existing theme, and do not apply more than two or three themes to avoid a loss of consistency among the presentation's slides.

Try It! Applying a Theme to Selected Slides

1. Start PowerPoint, and open **P33Try** from the data files for this lesson.
2. Save the presentation as **P33Try_xx** in the location where your teacher instructs you to store the files for this lesson.
3. Click slide 2.
4. Click Design > Themes More button and right-click the Basis theme.
5. Click Apply to Selected Slides.
6. Click the second variant from the right, the variant with the orange border.
7. Click the Who Needs Help section name to select the three slides in this section.
8. Click Design > Themes More button and click the Metropolitan theme. The theme is applied only to the slides in the selected section.
9. Save the **P33Try_xx** file, and leave it open to use in the next Try It.

Customizing Effects

- When you customize a theme for a particular presentation, you can change colors, fonts, and background styles, either in Normal view or on the slide master.
- You can also choose a different scheme of effects. Effects control the appearance of objects to which you have applied Quick Styles, such as placeholders, text boxes, or shapes.
- Each theme supplies a set of effects that you can see applied to sample shapes in the Shape Styles gallery.
- To further customize a theme, you can select a different effects scheme by clicking Effects on the Variants drop-down menu. Choosing a different scheme applies that scheme to the current presentation.
- You can also apply a different group of effects in Slide Master view to customize a shape or placeholder on the slide master.

Try It! Customizing Effects

1. In the **P33Try_xx** file, display slide 1.
2. Click Design > Variants More button > Effects to display the Effects gallery. The default effects scheme for the current theme is Subtle Solids.
3. Watch the two shapes on the slide as you move the pointer over some of the different effects schemes.
4. Click the Top Shadow effects scheme.
5. Click View > Slide Master and select the slide master at the top of the Thumbnail pane.
6. Click the turquoise rectangle behind the Master title style placeholder to select it.
7. Click Drawing Tools Format > Shape Styles More button and then select the Moderate Effect – Turquoise, Accent 1 style.
8. Click Slide Master > Effects and then click the Inset effect.
9. Click Slide Master > Close Master View .
10. Display slide 6 to see the change in effects to the placeholder rectangle as well as the shapes on the slide.

    ✓ *Because you applied the Inset effects scheme in Slide Master view, the effects are applied globally throughout the presentation.*

11. Save the **P33Try_xx** file, and leave it open to use in the next Try It.

Using the Design Ideas Feature

- If you have a subscription to Office 365, you have access to several interesting features that are not available in standard PowerPoint installations.
- One of these bonus features is Design Ideas, which appears on the PowerPoint Design tab.
- After you have added a picture to a slide, you can click Design Ideas and allow the online designer to suggest several layouts that will incorporate existing slide content and the picture you added.
- Click an option in the Design Ideas task pane to apply the new design to the slide.

✓ *You must have an active Internet connection to use Design Ideas.*

Try It! Using the Design Ideas Feature

1. In the **P33Try_xx** file, display slide 2.
2. Click Insert > Pictures.
3. Navigate to the data files for this lesson, select the **P33Try_picture.jpg** image, and click Insert.
4. Click Design > Design Ideas, and then click Let's Go to enable the Design Ideas feature. PowerPoint opens the Design Ideas task pane and displays a number of design ideas for the current slide.

   ✓ *It may take some time for PowerPoint to contact Office 365 and display design ideas.*
5. Click several of the design ideas to see how they look on the slide, and then choose the option that sets the picture as a light grayscale background for the slide.
6. Close the Design Ideas task pane.
7. Close the **P33Try_xx** file, saving changes, and exit PowerPoint.

Lesson 33—Practice

Restoration Architecture wants you to customize the appearance of a presentation to give it a bit more visual interest. You begin that task in this project by creating a simplified version of the presentation from a Word outline. You apply and modify a theme by changing colors, background styles, and effects. You then save the theme so that you can apply it to Restoration Architecture's presentation in the next exercise.

DIRECTIONS

1. Start PowerPoint, and click **Open Other Presentations** to display the Open tab in Backstage view.
2. Navigate to the location where the data files for this lesson are stored, and choose to display All Files.
3. Select **P33Practice.docx** and click **Open**.
4. Save the presentation as **P33Practice_xx** in the location where your teacher instructs you to store the files for this lesson.
5. Click **View** > **Outline View** to display the Outline pane.
6. Right-click *Design for Life—Design That Lasts* and click **Demote** to move this slide title back to slide 1 as a subtitle.
7. Click **View** > **Normal** to return to Normal view.
8. Display each slide and click **Home** > **Reset** to reset the slide formats. Apply the **Title Slide** layout to slide 1 and **Title and Content** to the remaining slides.
9. On slide 4, click the **Insert a SmartArt Graphic** icon in the content placeholder, click **Hierarchy**, and click the **Organization Chart** layout. Click **OK**.

10. Click **SmartArt Tools Design** > **Change Colors** and select **Colorful Range – Accent Colors 5 to 6**. Then click the **Intense Effect** in the SmartArt Styles gallery.

    ✓ *You have now set up a simplified version of the presentation you intend to modify so that you can check appearance as you format.*

11. With slide 4 still displayed, click **Design** > **Themes** More button and select the **View** theme.
12. Click the **Variants** More button, click **Colors**, and click **Median**.
13. Click the **Variants** More button, click **Effects**, and click **Smoky Glass**.
14. Click **View** > **Slide Master**, and select the **Title Slide** layout.
15. Click the light blue rectangle at the left side of the slide and press DEL to remove it.
16. Click **Slide Master** > **Background Styles** > **Format Background**.
17. In the Format Background task pane, click **Gradient fill**, click the **Preset gradients** button, and click **Radial Gradient – Accent 2**.
18. Click the slide master in the Thumbnail pane, click the brown rectangle at the right side of the slide, click the **Color** button in the Format Shape task pane, and select **Orange, Accent 2, Darker 25%**.
19. Click **Slide Master** > **Close Master View**.
20. Click **Design** > **Themes** More button > **Save Current Theme**, and type the file name **P33Practice_xx_theme**. Click **Save**.
21. Insert a footer on all slides with your name and the date.
22. **With your teacher's permission**, print slide 4. It should look similar to Figure 33-1.
23. Close the presentation, saving changes, and exit PowerPoint.

Figure 33-1

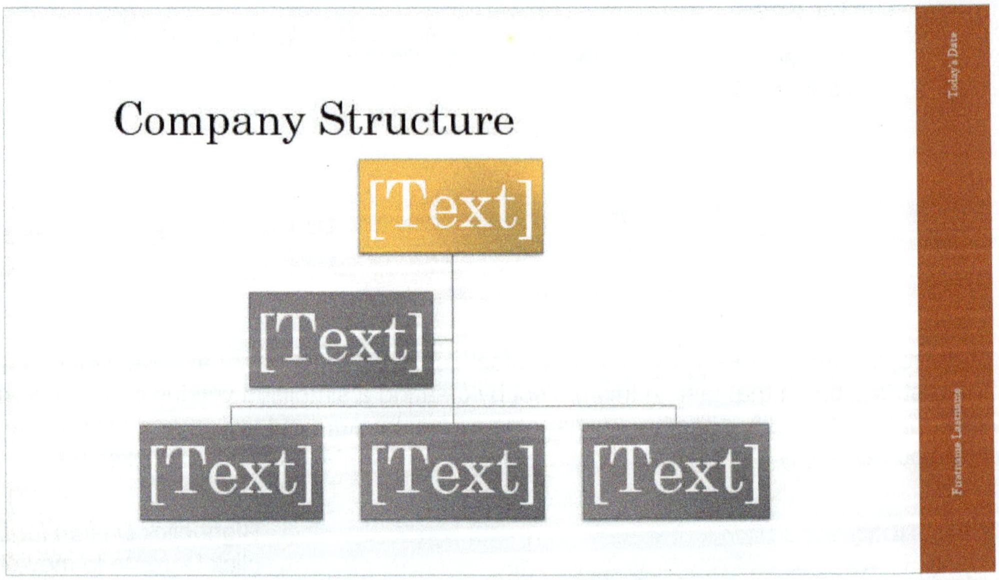

PowerPoint 2016, Windows 10, Microsoft Corporation

Lesson 33—Apply

In this project, you apply the theme you created in the practice exercise to selected portions of the existing Restoration Architecture presentation.

DIRECTIONS

1. Start PowerPoint, if necessary, and open **P33Apply** from the data files for this lesson.
2. Save the presentation as **P33Apply_xx** in the location where your teacher instructs you to store the files for this lesson.
3. With slide 1 displayed, on the Design tab, right-click the custom theme you created in the practice exercise, **P33Practice_xx_theme**, and apply the theme to the selected slide.
4. Click the Company Graphics section name and apply **P33Practice_xx_theme** to the slides in that section. Note the change in colors and effects for the SmartArt diagrams and the charts.
5. Display slide 4 and click the text box to the right of the picture.
6. Apply the **Smoky Glass** effects scheme so this object will match the effect appearance of the other objects in the presentation.
7. Preview the entire presentation to see the changes you have made.
8. Insert a footer with your name and the date on all slides.
9. **With your teacher's permission,** print slide 5. It should look similar to Figure 33-2.
10. Save changes, close the file, and exit PowerPoint.

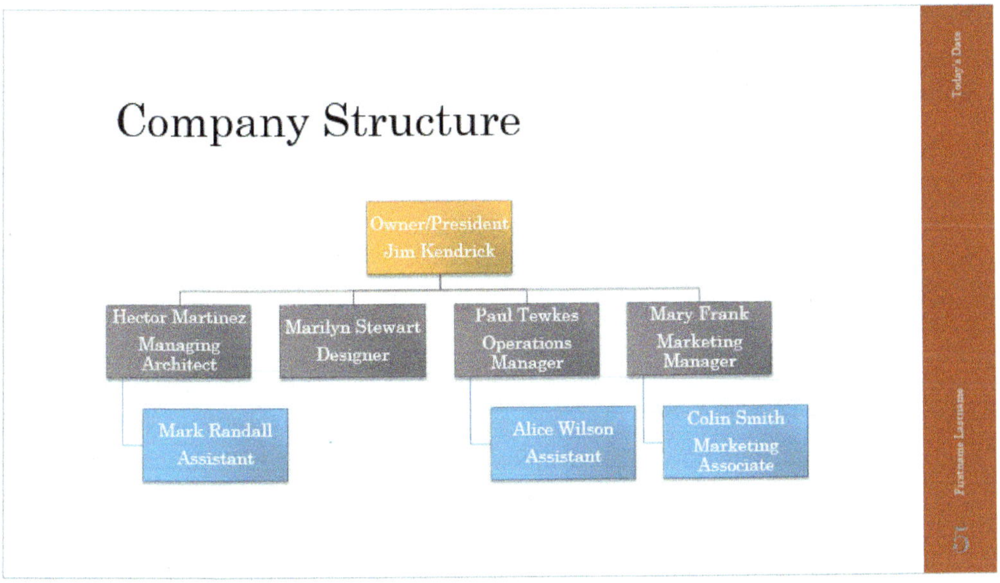

PowerPoint 2016, Windows 10, Microsoft Corporation

Figure 33-2

Lesson 34

Working with Notes and Handouts

➤ What You Will Learn

Using Advanced Notes and Handout Master Formats

Working with Linked Notes (OneNote 2016)

Software Skills You can customize your notes and handouts by making changes to the notes and handout masters. You can also use the Linked Notes feature to take notes on a presentation and share your notes with others.

What You Can Do

Using Advanced Notes and Handout Master Formats

- You can customize the notes and handout masters to improve the visual appearance of printed notes pages and handouts.
- By default, the notes and handout masters use the Office theme colors, fonts, and effects, no matter what theme is applied to the slides in the presentation.
- You can, however, use the Colors, Fonts, and Effects buttons to apply theme formatting to your masters.

  ✓ *Although the Themes button appears on the Notes Master tab and the Handout Master tab, you cannot use it to apply a theme.*

- Changing fonts and colors to match the current theme can give your notes pages and handouts consistency with the slides, enhancing the value of your support materials.
- You can apply graphic formats such as Quick Styles or fills, borders, and effects to any placeholder on the notes or handout master.
- Use the Background Styles option in the Background group to apply a background that fills the entire notes page or handout. Background colors are controlled by the theme colors you have applied to the master.
- You can also add content, such as a new text box or a graphic, to the handout master. The content will appear on all pages.

- When adding content such as a text box to the handout master, be sure to position the content so it doesn't interfere with slide image placeholders for other layouts.
- If you insert a text box above the slide image on the one-slide-per-page layout, for example, it will obscure the slide images for other handout layouts.

Try It! Applying Notes Master Formats

1. Start PowerPoint, and open **P34Try** from the data files for this lesson.
2. Save the presentation as **P34Try_xx** in the location where your teacher instructs you to store the files for this lesson.
3. Click slide 10.
4. Click View > Notes Master.
5. Click Notes Master > Fonts and select the Corbel font scheme to match the fonts used on the slides.
6. Click the Notes placeholder, then click Drawing Tools Format > Shape Styles > Colored Outline – Blue, Accent 1.
7. Click Notes Master > Background Styles and select Style 6.
8. Click Notes Master > Close Master View.
9. Click View > Notes Page to display the presentation in Notes Page view. Scroll through the pages to see the formats you added to the master.
10. Click View > Normal to return to Normal view.
11. Save the **P34Try_xx** file, and leave it open to use in the next Try It.

Applying custom formats to the notes master

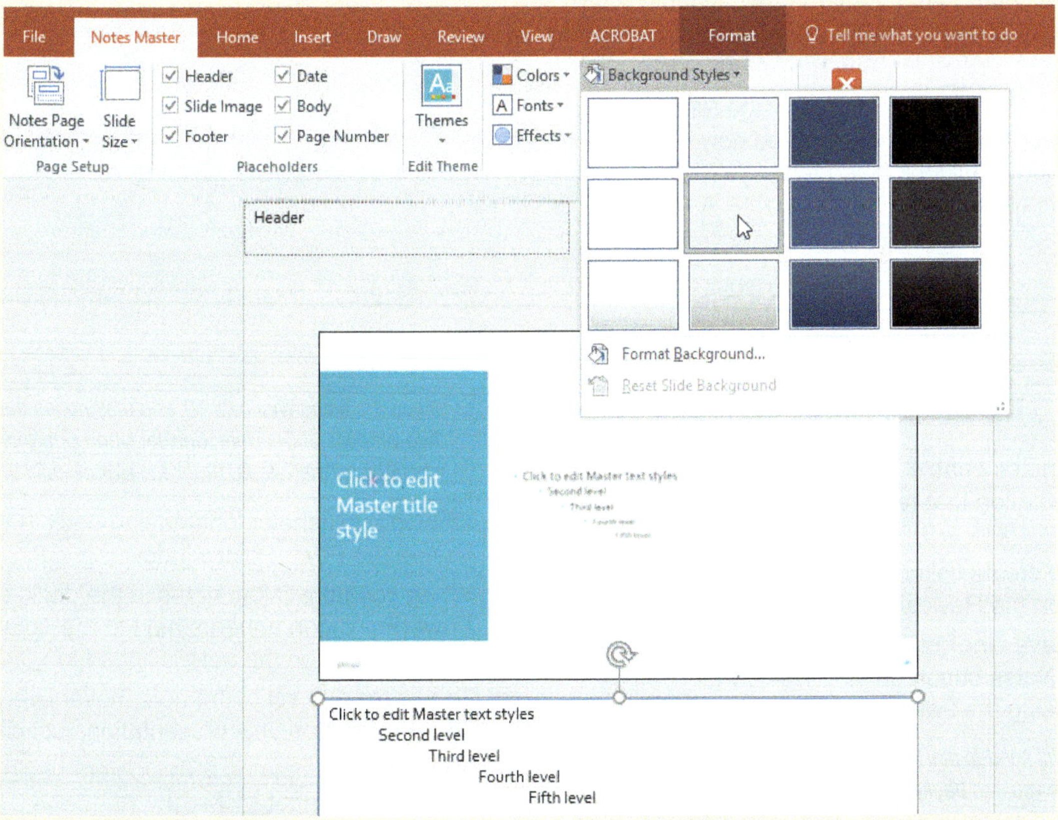

PowerPoint 2016, Windows 10, Microsoft Corporation

Try It! **Applying Handout Master Formats**

1. In the P34Try_xx file, click View > Handout Master.
2. Click Handout Master > Theme Colors.
3. Select the Blue Green theme colors.
4. Click Handout Master > Background Styles and select Style 9.
5. Click Insert > Shapes > Rectangle.
6. Draw a rectangle that covers the top of the page, as shown in the figure.
7. Right-click the shape, click the Outline shortcut button, and click No Outline.
8. Right-click the shape and select Send to Back.
9. Select the Header and Date placeholders, then click Home > Font Color and select White.
10. Click Handout Master > Close Master View.
11. Click Insert > Header & Footer. On the Notes and Handouts tab, choose to display the date and time and the page number. In the Header box, type your full name. In the Footer box, type The Power of Giving. Click Apply to All.
12. Click File > Print, click Full Page Slides and select 1 Slide Handout to see how the new handout will look. Then return to Normal view without printing.
13. Save the P34Try_xx file, and leave it open to use in the next Try It.

A formatted handout

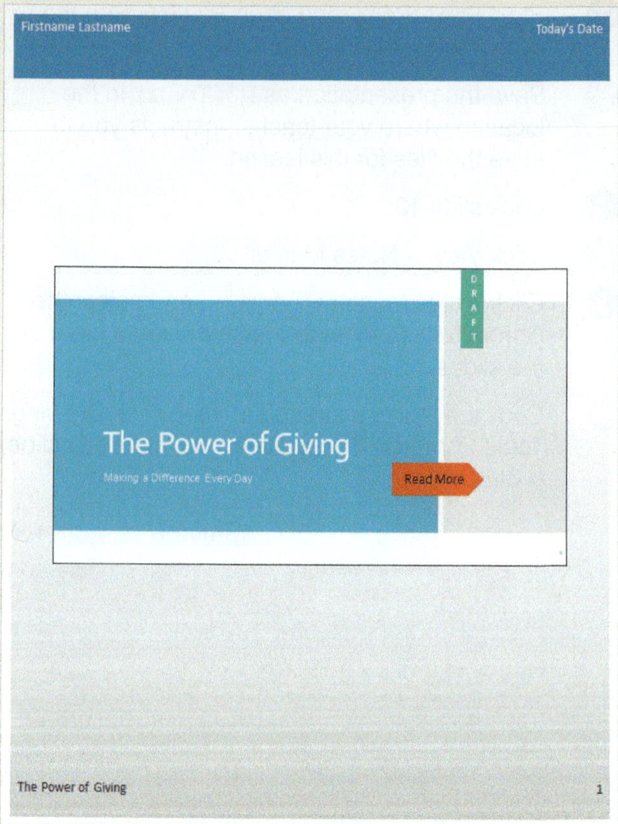

PowerPoint 2016, Windows 10, Microsoft Corporation

Working with Linked Notes (OneNote 2016)

- Linked notes enable you to keep a set of notes on a presentation that retain the context of the original slides.
- You can create linked notes using the Linked Notes button on the Review tab.
- If you have OneNote installed, but don't see the Linked Notes button on your Review tab, you can add it using the PowerPoint Options dialog box.

✓ *You will need to start OneNote to set up the application before you can begin working with it. You may also need to dock a OneNote window to your desktop before the Linked Notes button can be added to the Review tab.*

✓ *If you are using Windows 10, you may notice that you have two versions of OneNote: OneNote, and OneNote 2016. You should use OneNote 2016 for the exercises in this lesson.*

- OneNote attaches a note-taking dock to the desktop beside the PowerPoint window.
- When you take linked notes in the dock, a PowerPoint icon appears next to the note to show what application the note is linked to.
- To see the subject of the note, hover over the icon. To review the original presentation, just click the icon.
- You can tag a note as a To Do item using the keyboard shortcut CTRL + 1.
- When you use shared OneNote notebooks to store your Linked Notes, team members can see and respond to each other's notes.

Try It! Adding the Linked Notes Button to the Ribbon

1. In the **P34Try_xx** file, click File > Options > Customize Ribbon.

   ✓ *Remember that OneNote 2016 must be installed on your computer in order to use this feature.*

2. On the Customize Ribbon page, select Main Tabs in the Choose commands from drop-down menu.
3. Click the button next to Review in the Main Tabs list on the left to expand the Review tab options and select OneNote.

   ✓ *If you do not see the OneNote option on the Review tab, start OneNote, choose Dock to Desktop on the View tab, close OneNote, and close PowerPoint. After you restart PowerPoint, you should then see the OneNote option on the Review tab.*

4. Select the Review tab in the Main Tabs list on the right as the location for the button.
5. Click the Add button and click OK.
6. Save the **P34Try_xx** file, and leave it open to use in the next Try It.

Try It! Working with Linked Notes (OneNote 2016)

1. In the **P34Try_xx** file, select slide 8.
2. Click Review > Linked Notes.
3. Select any section or page, such as Quick Notes under your notebook, in the All Notebooks area and click OK.

   ✓ *If OneNote docks to the desktop above the PowerPoint window, you may want to click the Normal View double-headed arrow at the upper-right corner of the docked pane to display OneNote in Normal view.*

   ✓ *Click the three dots at the top of the docked OneNote pane, if necessary, to display the Ribbon, and click New Page on the Pages tab.*

4. In the header area above the date, type your name and press ENTER.
5. In the note area, type **Find out when the MS Walk and AIDS Awareness Week will take place.**

   ✓ *If you receive a message about the linked note, click OK.*

6. Display slide 10.
7. In the docked OneNote panel, click on the note box to select it. Hover your mouse over the PowerPoint icon next to the note box to see the original slide.
8. Close the OneNote dock. Close the **P34Try_xx** file, saving changes, and exit PowerPoint.

Select Location in OneNote dialog box

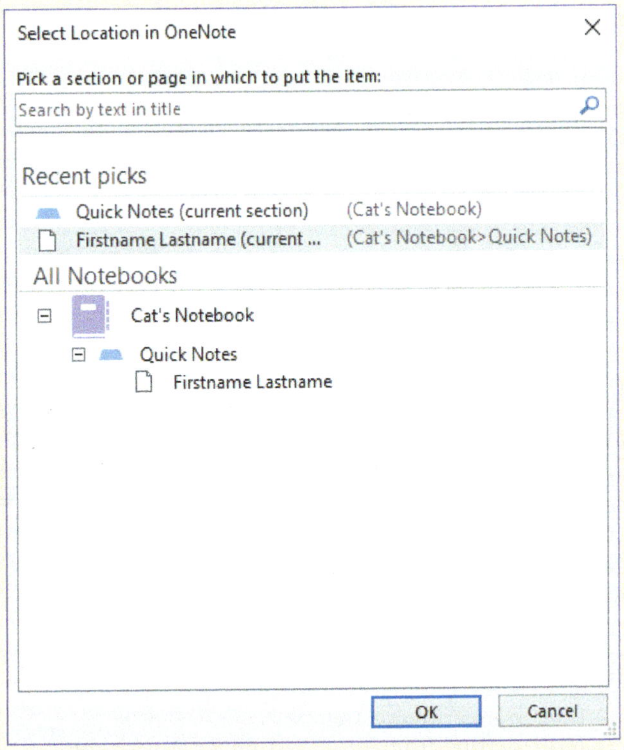

PowerPoint 2016, Windows 10, Microsoft Corporation

(continued)

Try It! Working with Linked Notes (OneNote 2016) *(continued)*

A linked note

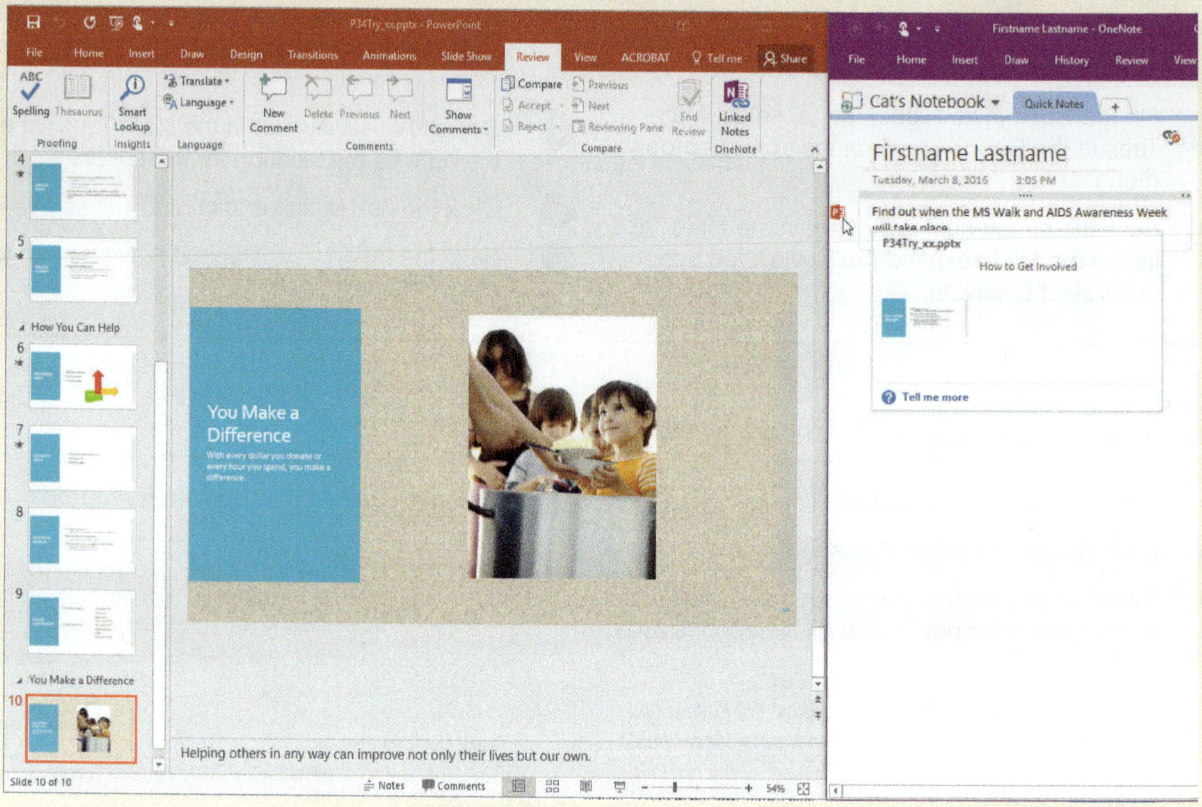

PowerPoint 2016, Windows 10, Microsoft Corporation

Lesson 34—Practice

Planet Earth, a local environmental action group, has asked you to prepare a presentation that can be shown at your civic garden center to inspire residents to go green. In this project, you customize the notes master.

DIRECTIONS

1. Start PowerPoint, if necessary, and open **P34Practice** from the data files for this lesson.
2. Save the presentation as **P34Practice_xx** in the location where your teacher instructs you to store the files for this lesson.
3. Click **View** > **Notes Master**.
4. Click **Notes Master** > **Colors** and select **Green**.
5. Click **Notes Master** > **Background Styles** > **Format Background** to open the Format Background task pane.
6. In the Format Background task pane, click **Gradient fill**.
7. Click the **Preset gradients** button and click **Top Spotlight – Accent 2**. Close the Format Background task pane.

8. Click **Notes Master** > **Close Master View** .
9. Click **Insert** > **Header & Footer** and insert a header on the Notes and Handouts tab that includes your full name and today's date.
10. Click **View** > **Notes Page** to see the formats you added to the notes master. Your notes page should look similar to Figure 34-1.
11. Close the presentation, saving changes, and exit PowerPoint.

Figure 34-1

PowerPoint 2016, Windows 10, Microsoft Corporation

Lesson 34—Apply

In this project, you continue to work on the Planet Earth presentation. You complete the formatting of the notes pages and apply custom formatting to the handout master.

DIRECTIONS

1. Start PowerPoint, if necessary, and open **P34Apply** from the data files for this lesson.
2. Save the presentation as **P34Apply_xx** in the location where your teacher instructs you to store the files for this lesson.
3. Display the presentation in Notes Master view.
4. Draw a rectangle that covers the top of the page; make the rectangle the same height as the header and date placeholders.
5. Use the Shape Styles gallery to apply **Intense Effect – Green, Accent 1** to the rectangle, and send the rectangle to the back.
6. Change the size of the header and date text to 14 point, apply bold, and change the color if desired to contrast better with the shape behind the text.
7. Select the notes placeholder and apply the **Colored Outline – Lime, Accent 3** shape style.
8. Change the fonts to the **Gill Sans MT** scheme.
9. Close the Notes Master view and switch to the Notes Page view. Display slide 1.
10. In the notes placeholder, type **Going green can help save the planet, but it is also a great way to save you real green in your wallet!**
11. Insert your full name in the header, today's date, and an appropriate footer.
12. Display the handout master, choose to format the background, and choose to insert an online image as the page background.
13. Search for an image using the keyword **Earth**, and select an appropriate image.
14. Adjust the transparency to make the picture light enough that the slides will be easy to see on the handout.
15. Preview the handout pages to make sure your inserted picture is formatted correctly. Figure 34-2 on the next page shows one way that your page might look.
16. Preview the notes page for slide 1. It should look similar to Figure 34-3.
17. **With your teacher's permission**, print the notes page for slide 1.
18. Close the presentation, saving changes, and exit PowerPoint.

Figure 34-2

PowerPoint 2016, Windows 10, Microsoft Corporation

Figure 34-3

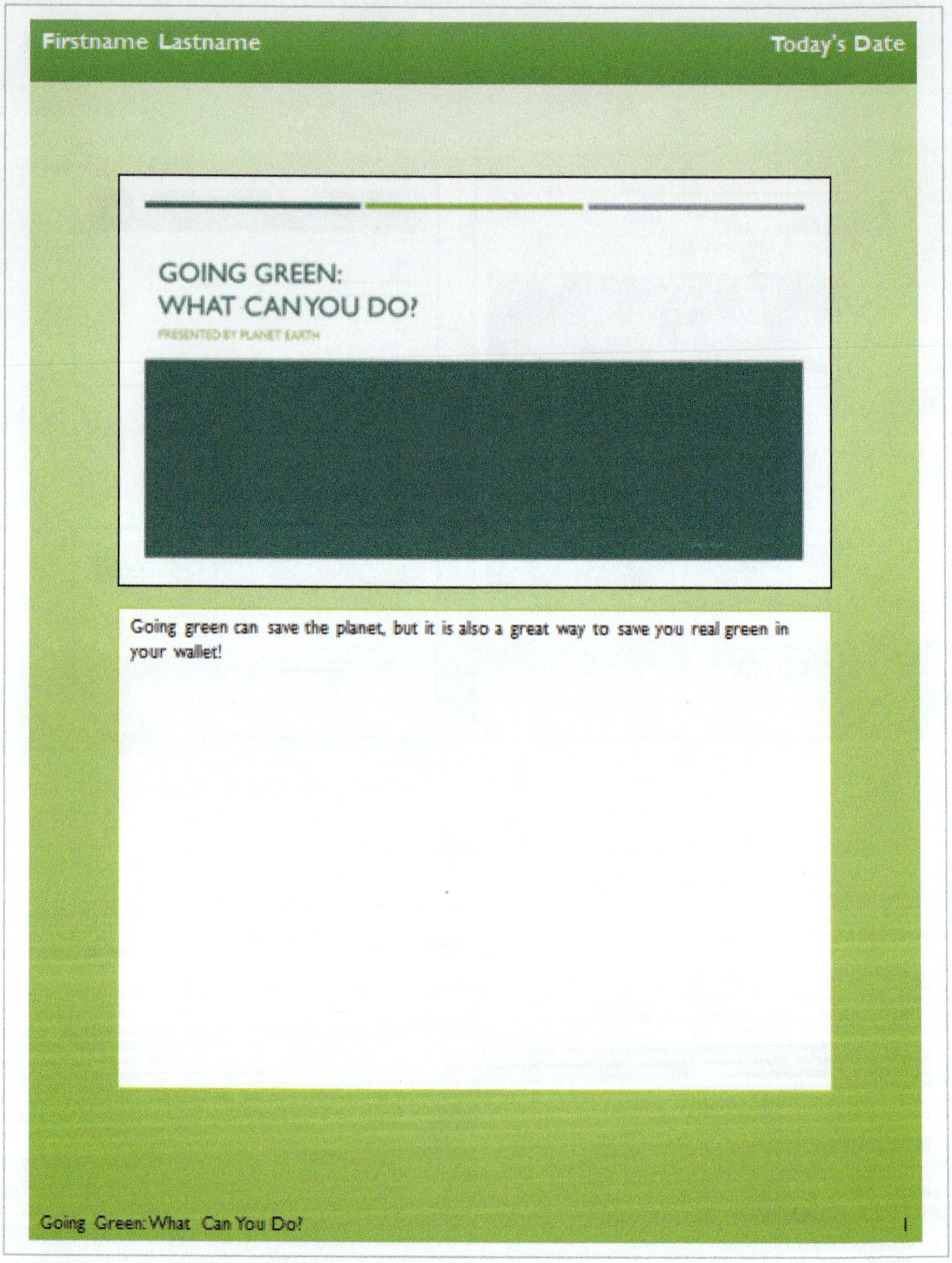
Firstname Lastname
Today's Date
GOING GREEN:
WHAT CAN YOU DO?
PRESENTED BY PLANET EARTH
Going green can save the planet, but it is also a great way to save you real green in your wallet!
Going Green: What Can You Do?
1

Lesson 35

Integrating PowerPoint with Word

➤ What You Will Learn

Exporting Handouts to Word
Linking Presentations to Word
Communicating with Others

Software Skills Send presentation materials to Microsoft Word to take advantage of Word's formatting options. You can also choose to link the presentation materials to a Word document. Handouts linked to a presentation will change automatically when the presentation is updated.

What You Can Do

Exporting Handouts to Word

- When you are preparing a presentation, one aspect you should consider carefully is identifying and creating supporting materials that will enhance the presentation for your audience.
- Having handouts that include thumbnails of each slide will help your audience stay focused on and engaged with your presentation.
- Besides simply printing handouts from PowerPoint, you can send presentation data to Microsoft Word to create handouts or an outline. Exporting a presentation to Microsoft Word gives you the option of using Word's tools to format the handouts.
- You can modify the size of the slide images, format text, and add new text as desired to customize your handouts.
- Use the Create Handouts command on the Export tab in Backstage view to begin the process of sending materials to Word.
- The Send to Microsoft Word dialog box opens to allow you to select an export option.
- You have two options for positioning slide notes relative to the slide pictures and two options for placing blank lines that your audience can use to take their own notes.

WORDS TO KNOW

Active listening
Paying attention to a message, hearing it, and interpreting it correctly.

Communication
The exchange of information between a sender and a receiver.

Nonverbal communication
The exchange of information without using words.

Verbal communication
The exchange of information by speaking or writing.

- Slide thumbnails in the Word document usually display a border on three sides. You can delete this partial border, if desired, using the Borders tab in the Borders dialog box.
- You can also choose to send only the outline. The exported outline retains the font used in the presentation and displays at a large point size. You can then, if desired, apply Word heading styles to create a more useful document.

Try It! **Exporting Handouts to Word**

1. Start PowerPoint, and open **P35Try** from the data files for this lesson.
2. Save the presentation as **P35TryA_xx** in the location where your teacher instructs you to store the files for this lesson.
3. Click File > Export.
4. Click Create Handouts in the Export list, and click Create Handouts in the right pane.
5. Select Blank lines next to slides and Paste under Add slides to Microsoft Word document.
6. Click OK.
7. Click the Word icon on the taskbar to display the newly created Word document to see how the handouts look. Close Microsoft Word without saving changes.
8. Save the **P35TryA_xx** file, and leave it open to use in the next Try It.

The Send to Microsoft Word dialog box

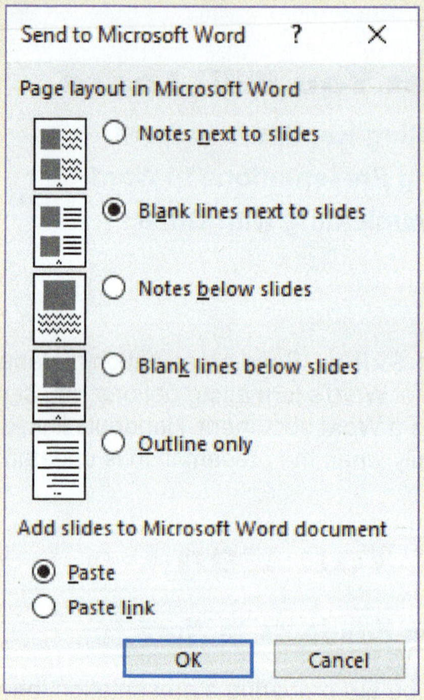

Linking Presentations to Word

- If the presentation might change over time, the best option is to maintain a link between the handouts in Word and the material displayed on a slide.
- When you choose the Paste link option in the Send to Microsoft Word dialog box, you create a link between the Word document and the PowerPoint presentation. Any changes you save to the slides in PowerPoint will appear in the Word document.

✓ *You do not have the paste/paste link options when exporting an outline.*

Try It! Linking Presentations to Word

1. In the **P35TryA_xx** file, click File > Export.
2. Click Create Handouts under Export, and click Create Handouts in the right pane.
3. Select Notes next to slides, if necessary, and Paste link under Add slides to Microsoft Word document.
4. Click OK.
5. View the newly created Microsoft Word document to see how the handouts look.
6. Return to **P35TryA_xx**, click Design, and change the variant to the second variant from the right.
7. Save the changes, close **P35TryA_xx**, and exit PowerPoint.
8. Return to the Microsoft Word document and note that the slide thumbnails show the new variant you applied in PowerPoint.
9. Save the file as **P35TryB_xx** in the location where your teacher instructs you to store the files for this lesson.
10. Close the document, and exit Microsoft Word.

Updated linked handouts

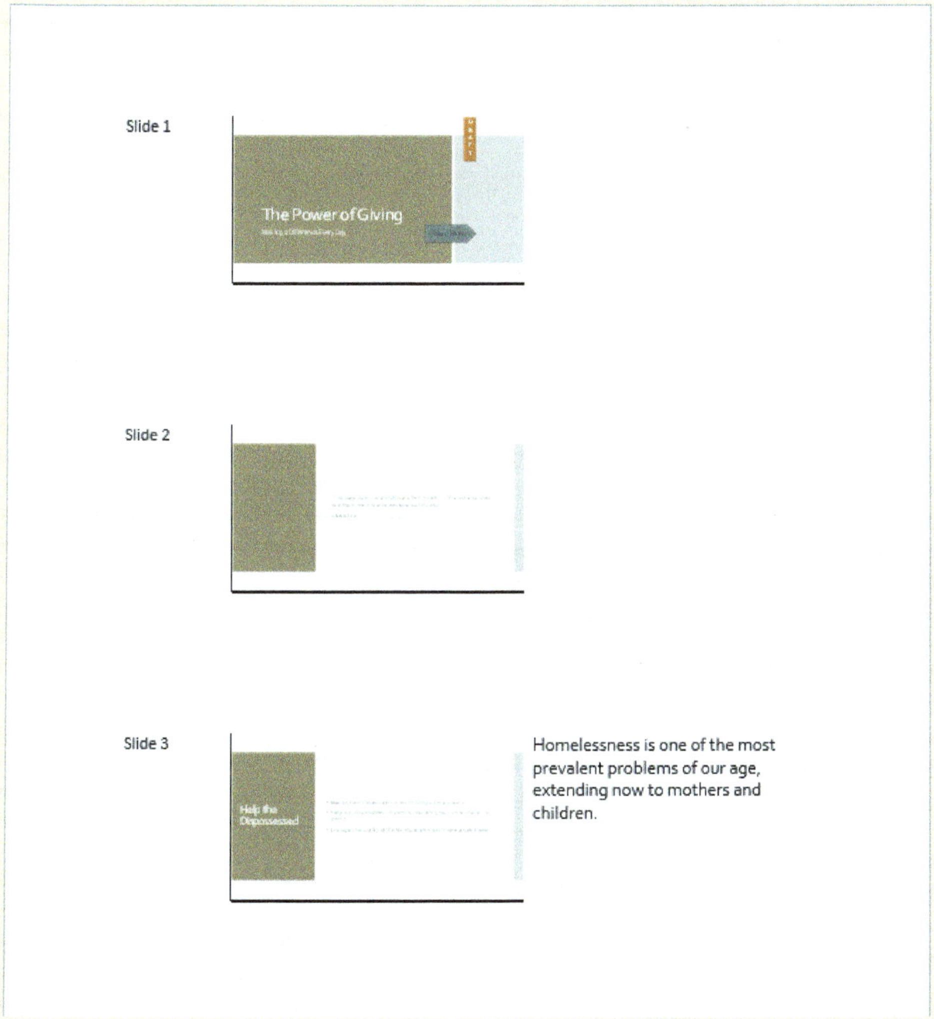

Communicating with Others

- When you prepare a presentation, you should always remember that the presentation is a form of **communication** and you should strive to make it as effective as possible.
- You communicate effectively when your audience interprets the information in the presentation in the way you intended it to be interpreted.
- As you prepare the presentation and its supporting materials, choose options that contribute to effective communication:
  - Make sure the slides are visually interesting.
  - Make sure text is easy to read and understand.
  - Use charts and tables to organize information for improved comprehension.
- A presentation's effectiveness also depends on how it is delivered.
- If you are presenting the slides yourself or using narration on slides, use good **verbal communication** skills:
  - Speak slowly and clearly, allowing plenty of time for your audience to view each slide.
  - Avoid speaking in a monotone or reading the slide text verbatim.
  - Ask the audience if they have questions or encourage them to participate in the discussion, if appropriate, to foster communication between audience members and the speaker.
- Remember that you also deliver a message using **nonverbal communication** cues. Being at ease on the podium, smiling, and making eye contact with your audience are nonverbal ways to foster effective communication with others.
- You can ensure effective communication with your audience even if you are setting up a presentation to be browsed by an individual. Make sure the slides are displayed long enough that the content can be viewed and absorbed by people with all levels of reading skills.
- If the presentation does not loop automatically, make sure a viewer can easily navigate the presentation by including action buttons, links, and other prompts.
- As a presenter, you want to do everything you can to encourage active listening. **Active listening** is a sign of respect from your audience. It shows that they are engaged in the presentation, willing to communicate with you, and interested in you and your message.

Lesson 35—Practice

Surgeons from Wynnedale Medical Center want you to prepare handouts to accompany a presentation they will be making at a health fair. In this project, you send the presentation data to Microsoft Word to create handouts. You use some Word table formatting options to improve the appearance of the handouts.

DIRECTIONS

1. Start PowerPoint, if necessary, and open **P35Practice** from the data files for this lesson.
2. Click **File** > **Export**.
3. Click **Create Handouts** under Export and click **Create Handouts** in the right pane.
4. Select **Notes next to slides**, if necessary.
5. Make sure **Paste** is selected under Add slides to Microsoft Word document and click **OK**.
6. Close **P35Practice** without saving any changes.
7. View the newly created Microsoft Word document, and save it as **P35Practice_xx**.
8. Make the following changes to the table in which the slide information is stored:
   a. Select the table and apply the **Grid Table 1 Light – Accent 1** table style.
   b. In the Table Style Options group, click **First Column** to apply bold to the first column of the table.
   c. Select the center and right columns and click **Table Tools Layout** > **Align Center Left**.

9. Insert a header with your name and today's date.
10. **With your teacher's permission,** print the document. It should look similar to Figure 35-1.
11. Close the document, saving changes, and exit Word.

Figure 35-1

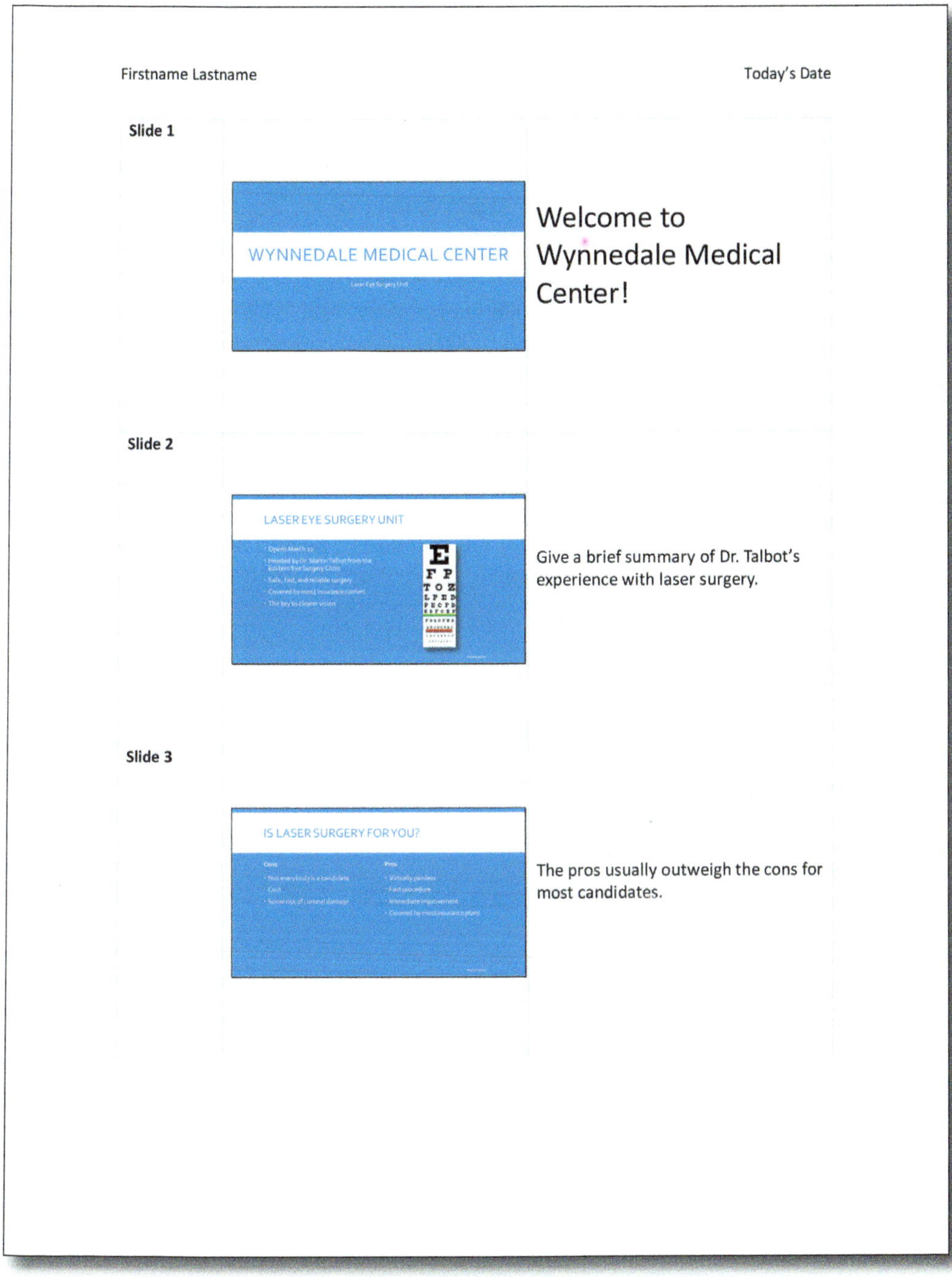

Lesson 35—Apply

The surgeons at Wynnedale Medical Center plan to make changes to their presentation to suit particular audiences. They have asked you to link the slides to handouts so that they can easily print handouts that will reflect changed content in the presentation. In this project, you link the presentation to a Word document.

DIRECTIONS

1. Start PowerPoint, if necessary, and open **P35Apply** from the data files for this lesson.
2. Save the presentation as **P35ApplyA_xx** in the location where your teacher instructs you to store the files for this lesson.
3. Export the presentation as handouts. Select the Paste link option and Notes below slides.
4. Save the Word document as **P35ApplyB_xx**.
5. In PowerPoint, apply the **Slice** theme to the presentation. Adjust the positions of pictures as necessary. Save your changes and close the presentation.
6. Return to the Word document. If necessary, right-click each slide thumbnail and click **Update Link**.
7. Right-click each slide thumbnail and click **Borders and Shading**. In the Borders dialog box, click **None** to remove the border from the slide thumbnail.
8. Click **Insert** > **Header** and choose **Slice 2** from the list of built-in header styles.
9. Click **Insert** > **Footer** and choose **Slice**. Your name should be inserted automatically in the footer.
10. **With your teacher's permission,** print the document. Page 1 should look similar to Figure 35-2 on the next page.
11. Close the document, saving changes, and exit Word.

Figure 35-2

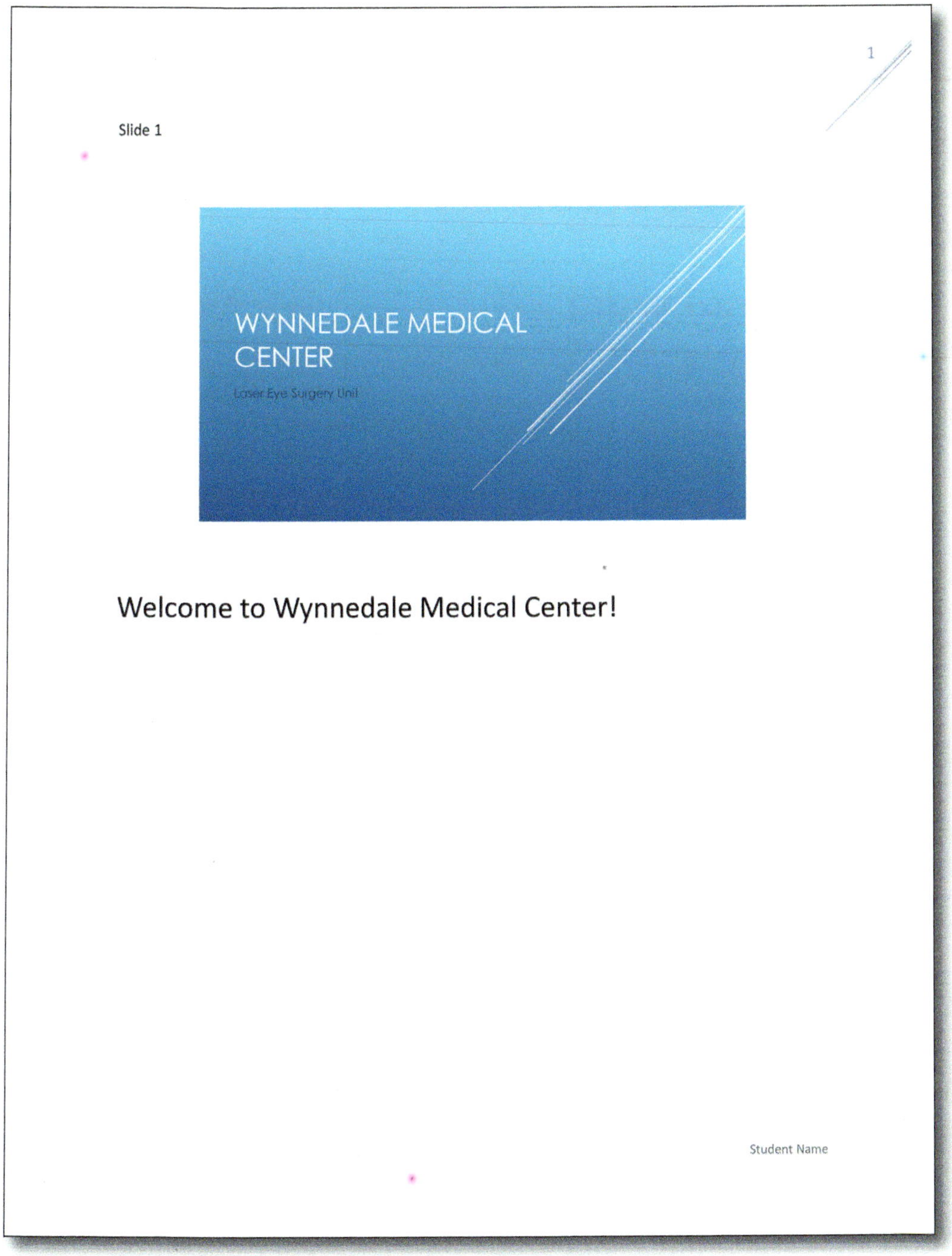

PowerPoint 2016, Windows 10, Microsoft Corporation

Lesson 36

Fine-Tuning Text Formats

➤ What You Will Learn

Applying Paragraph and Special Indents
Setting Tab Stops
Controlling Text Box Margins
Applying Advanced Text Formats

WORDS TO KNOW

First-line indent
The first line of a paragraph moves to the right so there is a space between the margin and the first word.

Hanging indent
The first line of the paragraph aligns at the left margin, and all other lines of the paragraph are indented.

Indents
Indents enable you to control the amount of space between the text and the edges of the text box or placeholder.

Tab stops
Tab stops, also called tabs, enable you to align text according to settings you specify. You can choose to create left, center, right, or decimal tabs.

Software Skills Fine-tune the placement of text on your slides by adjusting indents and inserting tab stops to control tabular text. Change default margins in text boxes to allow more text to fit. To add visual interest to text, you can apply fill and outline formats.

What You Can Do

Applying Paragraph and Special Indents

- **Indents** can help you format your text so that your audience will be able to read it easily.
- Each level of bulleted text has a different indent, so that you can easily see how some items are subordinate to others.
- The first level of text is aligned with the left margin; the second level of text is indented to the right. Each additional level is indented further to the right.
- You can easily indent your slide text by clicking and dragging the indent markers in the PowerPoint ruler or by displaying the Paragraph dialog box and choosing an indent setting there.
- Use the Before text box in the Indentation area of the Paragraph dialog box to specify an exact measurement for the current paragraph's indent.
- Use the Special settings to apply a first-line or hanging indent.
  - A **first-line indent** moves the first line of a paragraph to the right; remaining lines of the paragraph align at the left margin.
  - A **hanging indent** aligns the first line of a paragraph with the left margin; remaining lines of the paragraph are indented.

Try It! Adjusting an Indent on the Ruler

1. Start PowerPoint, and open **P36Try** from the data files for this lesson.
2. Save the presentation as **P36Try_xx** in the location where your teacher instructs you to store the files for this lesson.
3. If the rulers are not currently displayed, click View > Ruler to display them.
4. Display slide 2.
5. Click in the second paragraph in the text box and then drag the first-line indent marker to the 0.5" mark on the ruler. The text indents.
6. Display slide 5 and click in the second paragraph in the content area.
7. Drag the left indent marker to the 1" mark on the ruler.
8. Save the **P36Try_xx** file, and leave it open for the next Try It.

Drag an indent marker to create an indent

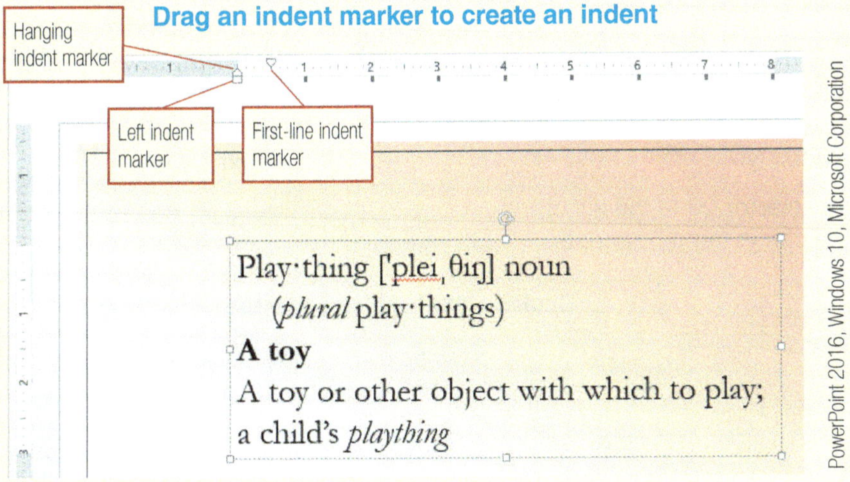

Try It! Setting Indents in the Paragraph Dialog Box

1. In the **P36Try_xx** file, click in the third paragraph on slide 5.
2. On the Home tab, click the Paragraph dialog box launcher to open the Paragraph dialog box.
3. In the Indentation section, click in the Before text box and type **2**.
4. Click OK. The third paragraph is indented 2 inches.
5. Display slide 2.
6. Click in the last paragraph in the text box (*A toy or other object . . .*).
7. Click Home > Paragraph dialog box launcher.
8. In the Special area of the Indentation section, click the drop-down arrow to the right of (none) and click First line.
9. Click OK. A first-line indent is applied to the paragraph.
10. Click the Paragraph dialog box launcher.
11. In the Before text box in the Indentation section, click the up arrow until 0.5" appears. In the Special section, click the drop-down arrow to the right of First line and click Hanging.
12. Click OK. The first-line indent changes to a hanging indent.
13. Save the **P36Try_xx** file, and leave it open for the next Try It.

Setting Tab Stops

- **Tab stops** enable you to create tabular text on your PowerPoint slides. You can choose to insert four different types of tabs: Left, Right, Center, and Decimal.
- You can set tabs by selecting the tab stop style you want to create and clicking the PowerPoint ruler, or you can display the Paragraph dialog box, click the Tabs button, and enter the settings for the tab in the Tabs dialog box.
- Adjust a tab by dragging it on the ruler. Removing a tab is equally simple—just drag it off the ruler.
- You can also clear all tabs at once by clicking the Clear All button in the Tabs dialog box.

Try It! Setting Tab Stops on the Ruler

1. In the **P36Try_xx** file, display slide 7.
2. Click in the first paragraph in the content placeholder, and click on the ruler at the 3" mark to set a left tab.
3. Click the tab selector to the left of the ruler until the center tab appears.
4. Click at the 5.5" mark on the ruler to set a center tab.
5. Save the **P36Try_xx** file, and leave it open for the next Try It.

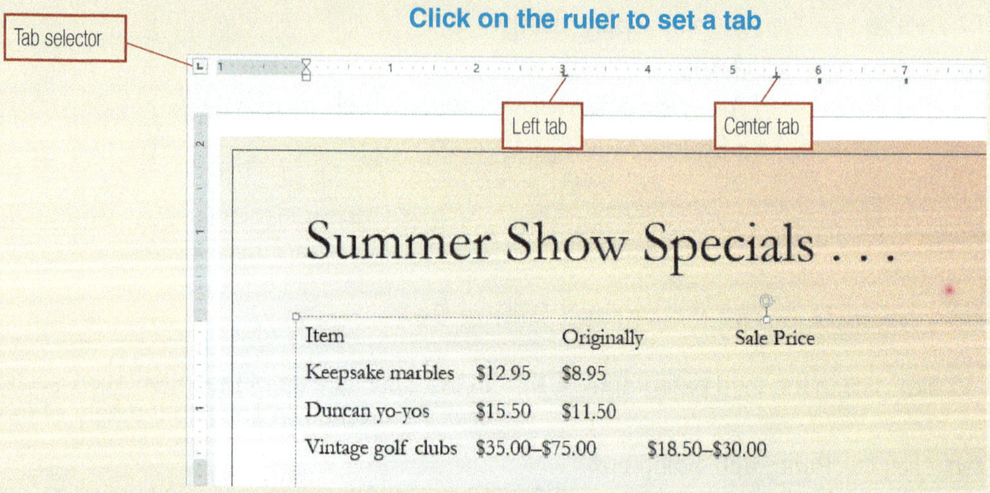

PowerPoint 2016, Windows 10, Microsoft Corporation

Try It! Setting Tab Stops in the Tabs Dialog Box

1. In the **P36Try_xx** file, with slide 7 displayed, select the second, third, and fourth paragraphs in the content placeholder.
2. Click Home > Paragraph dialog box launcher.
3. Click the Tabs button.
4. In the Tabs dialog box, click in the Tab stop position box, type **3**, click the Decimal option button, and click Set.
5. In the Tab stop position box, type **5.5**, click the Center option button, and click Set.
6. Click OK, and then click OK again to close the Paragraph dialog box.
7. Save the **P36Try_xx** file, and leave it open for the next Try It.

Try It! Adjusting a Tab Stop on the Ruler

1. In the **P36Try_xx** file, with slide 7 displayed, note that the original prices for marbles and yo-yos are not lined up correctly under the column heading.
2. Select the second and third paragraphs in the content placeholder.
3. Drag the decimal tab on the ruler to the 3.4" mark.
4. Save the **P36Try_xx** file, and leave it open for the next Try It.

Controlling Text Box Margins

- Text boxes are designed to fit closely around text, with default margins of 0.1" at the left and right sides and 0.05" at the top and bottom.
- If you need to enter several sentences in a text box that you have formatted with a fill, these default margins can make the text look crowded in the box.
- You can use the Textbox settings in the Format Shape task pane to adjust text box margins. You can also choose options for wrapping and fitting text in the text box.

Try It! Controlling Text Box Margins

1. In the **P36Try_xx** file, display slide 6.
2. Click Insert > Text Box and draw a text box 3" wide on the slide near the bottom of the slide between the two content placeholders.
3. Type the following text: **We are always adding events to our calendar. To find out when we are coming to a location near you, visit our Web site.**
4. Click Drawing Tools Format > Shape Styles More button and apply the Moderate Effect – Ice Blue, Accent 1 shape style.
5. Right-click the text box and click Format Shape on the shortcut menu.
6. In the Format Shape task pane, click Text Options and then click Textbox.
7. In the Left margin box, click the up increment arrow to change the margin to 0.2".
8. In the Top margin box, click the up increment arrow to change the margin to 0.1".
9. In the Bottom margin box, click the up increment arrow to change the margin to 0.1".
10. Close the Format Shape task pane.
11. Save the **P36Try_xx** file, and leave it open for the next Try It.

Applying Advanced Text Formats

- One way to add visual interest to text is to create a WordArt graphic or apply WordArt styles directly to selected text.
- If you do not find a WordArt style that complements your presentation, however, you can use the Text Fill, Text Outline, and Text Effects options on the Drawing Tools Format tab or Format Shape task pane to apply custom formats to any text on a slide.
- When you are applying text fill and outline formats, your formats will have more impact if you use a heavy, wide font at a large point size to display the fill and outlines clearly. Applying these formats to smaller text can make the text harder to read.

Try It! Applying Advanced Text Formats

1. In the **P36Try_xx** file, display slide 1.
2. Select the title text *Yesterday's Playthings*.
3. Click Drawing Tools Format > Text Fill and then click Orange, Accent 2.
4. Click Drawing Tools Format > Text Fill and then click Gradient.
5. Under Dark Variations, click the Linear Down gradient.
6. With the text still selected, click Drawing Tools Format > Text Outline and then click Eyedropper.
7. Use the Eyedropper to sample a dark brown color from the checkerboard picture.

   ✓ *To sample the color, click with the eyedropper on the location where you want to pick up the color.*

8. With the text still selected, right-click and select Format Text Effects. The Format Shape task pane opens with Text Effects active.
9. Click Shadow to expand the shadow options.
10. Click the Presets button and select Offset Bottom in the Outer section.
11. Close the Format Shape task pane.
12. Close the **P36Try_xx** file, saving changes, and exit PowerPoint.

Lesson 36—Practice

Whole Grains Bread is branching out into a new market: donuts that are made fresh several times a day in select mall locations. As part of this venture, the company plans to offer delivery of fresh donuts to corporate clients. In this project, you create a new presentation that incorporates existing slides from another presentation and then adjust indents, tabs, and text formats.

DIRECTIONS

1. Start PowerPoint, if necessary, and open **P36PracticeA** from the data files for this lesson.
2. Save the presentation as **P36PracticeA_xx** in the location where your teacher instructs you to store the files for this lesson.
3. Click **Home** > **New Slide** down arrow, and click **Reuse Slides**.
4. In the Reuse Slides task pane, click **Browse** and then click **Browse File**.
5. Navigate to the location where data files are stored, select **P36PracticeB**, and click **Open**.
6. Insert slides from the Reuse Slides task pane as follows:
   a. Click the first slide in the task pane to insert it in the presentation. In the Thumbnail pane, move the new slide so that it is the first slide in the presentation.
   b. Insert the fourth slide from the task pane.
   c. Click slide 5 in the Thumbnail pane, then insert the last slide from the task pane.
   d. Close the Reuse Slides task pane.
7. Display slide 3.
8. Click in the second *Donuts* paragraph and then drag the left indent marker on the ruler to the **3"** mark.
9. Click in the third Donuts paragraph and then drag the left indent marker on the ruler to the **7"** mark.
10. Make the following changes in the text box on slide 3:
    a. Click in the text, click the Paragraph dialog box launcher, and change the Special indent to **(none)**, if necessary. Click **OK**.
    b. Right-click anywhere in the text, click **Format Text Effects**, and click the **Textbox** icon in the Format Shape task pane.
    c. Change the text box margins to **0.2"** on all sides and then close the task pane.
    d. Click **Home** > **Justify** to justify the text in the text box.
11. Display slide 4.
12. Click in the first paragraph and set tabs as follows:
    a. Set center tabs at the **4.5"** and the **6"** marks on the ruler.
    b. Set a left tab at the **7"** mark on the ruler.
13. Select the remaining four paragraphs in the content placeholder, click the Paragraph dialog box launcher, and click **Tabs**.
14. In the Tabs dialog box, set tabs as follows:
    a. Type **3.4** in the Tab stop position box, click **Right**, and click **Set**.
    b. Type **4.5** in the Tab stop position box, click **Center**, and click **Set**.
    c. Type **6** in the Tab stop position box, click **Decimal**, and click **Set**.
    d. Type **7** in the Tab stop position box, click **Left**, and click **Set**.
    e. Click **OK** twice.
15. Insert a footer with your name and today's date on all slides.
16. **With your teacher's permission,** print slide 4. It should look similar to Figure 36-1 on the next page.
17. Close the presentation, saving changes, and exit PowerPoint.

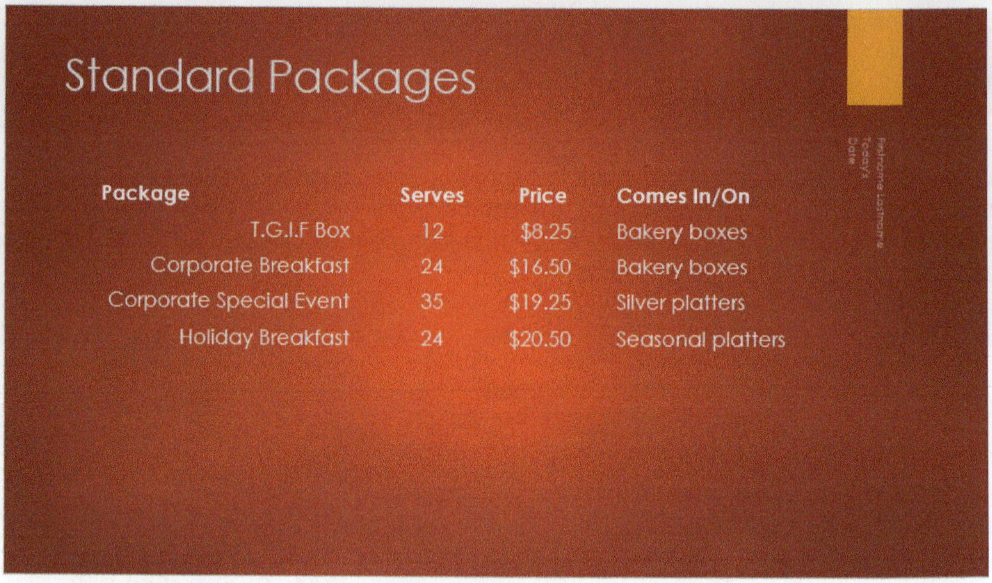

Figure 36-1

PowerPoint 2016, Windows 10, Microsoft Corporation

Lesson 36—Apply

In this project, you continue to work on the Whole Grains Bread presentation. You adjust tabs and indents, apply more interesting text formats for the presentation title, and finally replace several of the figures to customize the presentation for the new donut venture.

DIRECTIONS

1. Start PowerPoint, if necessary, and open **P36Apply** from the data files for this lesson.
2. Save the presentation as **P36Apply_xx** in the location where your teacher instructs you to store the files for this lesson.
3. On slide 1, select the slide title and change the font to **Bauhaus 93**. Reduce the font size until the title fits on one line in the placeholder.

   ✓ *If you do not have Bauhaus, choose another heavy, wide font.*
4. Apply a gradient fill to the text and then adjust the gradient as desired. Apply an outline and a text effect such as a shadow, glow, or reflection.
5. On slide 4, insert a center tab to center the heading *Package* over the packages in the table below. Then click to the left of the word *Package* and press TAB to tab the heading to the new tab stop.
6. On slide 6, select all paragraphs and insert a left tab stop on the ruler at the **1.5"** mark. Press TAB after the boldfaced word at the beginning of each paragraph to move the explanatory text to the tab. Then apply a hanging indent of **1.5"** to all paragraphs to align the second lines of text with the first word following the tab.
7. On slide 5, draw a text box to the right of the bulleted text and type the text shown in Figure 36-2 on the next page. (Use Wingding star symbols for the ratings.) Use indents and tabs to align the text as shown.
8. Apply a shape style to the text box and then adjust the text box margins as desired to improve appearance.
9. Display slide 1, right-click the picture, and click **Change Picture**. In the Insert Pictures dialog box, type **donuts** in the Bing Image Search box and press ENTER. Choose an appropriate donut picture.
10. Repeat step 9 to replace the picture on slide 7 with a different bread, bagel, or donut picture.

11. Insert a footer with your full name and the current date on all slides.
12. Preview the presentation. Make any adjustments necessary.
13. **With your teacher's permission,** print the slides as handouts with 4 slides per page.
14. Close the presentation, saving changes, and exit PowerPoint.

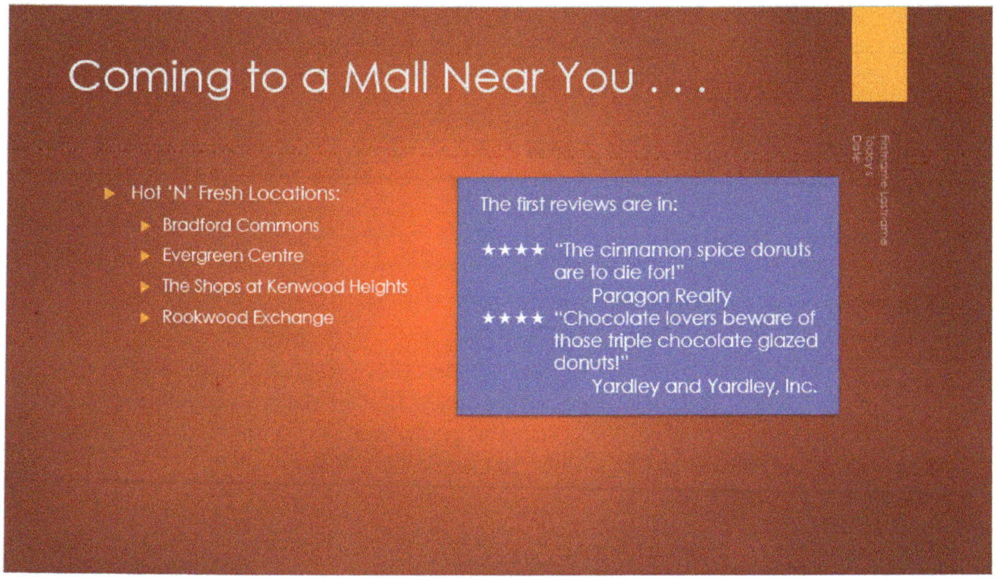

Figure 36-2

Lesson 37

Using Research Tools

➤ What You Will Learn

Using Smart Lookup
Translating Text

Software Skills If you want to add to the content of your presentation—including the latest information on a particular subject—you can use the research tools built right into PowerPoint to find what you need. These tools include options for searching the Web and translating text into different languages.

What You Can Do

Using Smart Lookup

- You can research more about your topic from within PowerPoint.
- Select text about which you wish to know more, display the Review tab, and click Smart Lookup in the Insights group.
- PowerPoint opens the Smart Lookup task pane, displaying information on two tabs, Explore and Define.
- The Explore tab shows information from sources such as Wikipedia and Bing. Information might include articles on a topic or images relating to the topic. Click a link in the task pane results to open a browser window showing the complete article.
- The Define tab provides a dictionary definition of the selected word or words.

Try It! Using Smart Lookup

1. Start PowerPoint, and open **P37Try** from the data files for this lesson.
2. Save the presentation as **P37Try_xx** in the location where your teacher instructs you to store the files for this lesson.
3. Display slide 5 and select the text *Rain gardens*.
4. Click Review > Smart Lookup to open the Smart Lookup task pane.
5. Click the Wikipedia "Rain garden" entry to open your browser to this Web site.
6. Read the article to find out what a rain garden is and how it can be useful in an urban landscape.
7. Select the first sentence of text in the Wikipedia article, right-click, and click Copy.
8. On slide 5, type **according to Wikipedia:** at the end of the first bulleted item and then press ENTER and TAB.
9. Press CTRL + V to paste the text you copied.
10. Return to the Web page, click in the address bar, click CTRL + C to copy the URL, and then paste it at the end of the Wikipedia text on the slide.
11. Save the **P37Try_xx** file, and leave it open to use in the next Try It.

Use the Smart Lookup task pane to find information

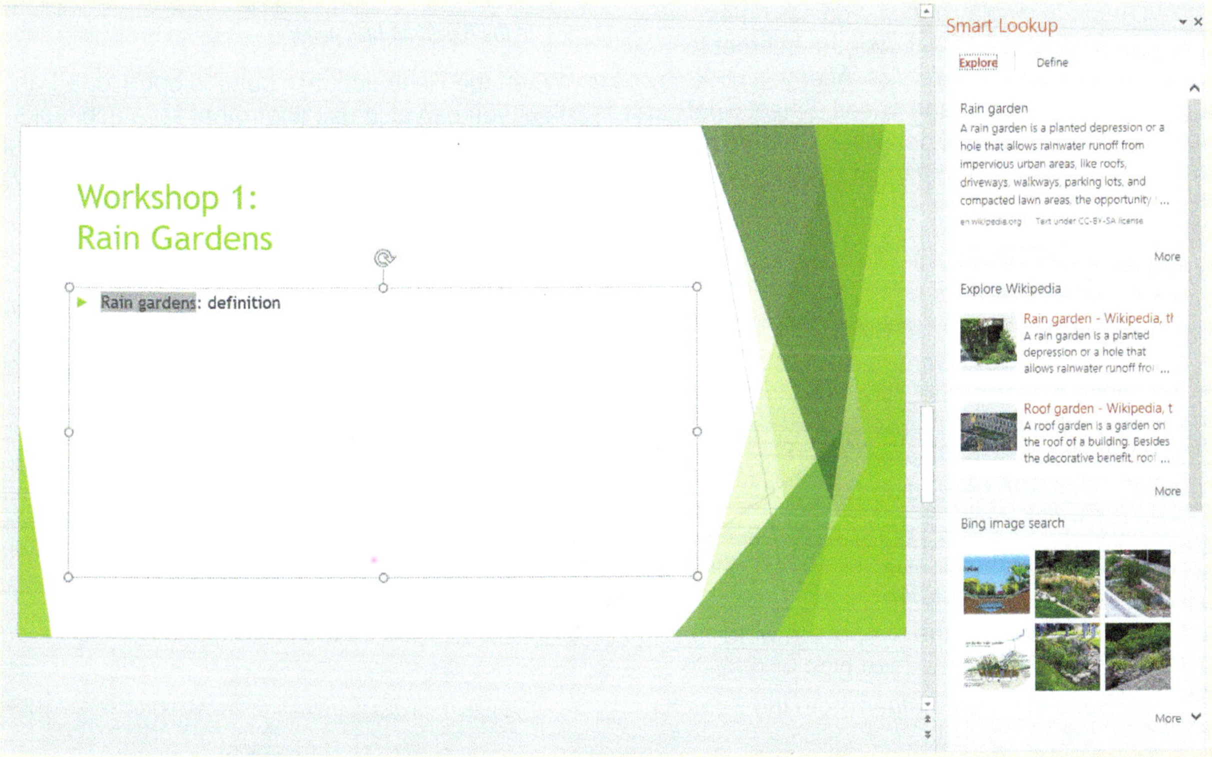

PowerPoint 2016, Windows 10, Microsoft Corporation

Try It! Using a Dictionary in the Smart Lookup Task Pane

1. In the **P37Try_xx** file, display slide 6.
2. Select the word *compost* in the first bullet item.
3. Click Review > Smart Lookup to refresh the Smart Lookup task pane.
4. Click Define at the top of the task pane, and under the heading *noun: compost*, drag the pointer over the definition, and press CTRL + C.
5. On the slide, click at the end of the bulleted item, press ENTER, and then press TAB.
6. Type **According to the dictionary, compost is** and then press CTRL + V to paste the definition.
7. Insert quotation marks before and after the definition you pasted.
8. Close the Smart Lookup task pane.
9. Save the **P37Try_xx** file, and leave it open to use in the next Try It.

Translating Text

- PowerPoint offers you the option of translating slide text without your having to leave the program to open a translator.
- Right-click a word and click Translate on the shortcut menu to display a message asking if you want your text to be sent over the Internet to Microsoft or a translation service. After you click yes, the Research task pane opens. Select what language to translate to, if necessary, and you will then see the translation appear in the task pane.
- If PowerPoint can find the word in an installed bilingual dictionary, it displays the translation from that source. Otherwise, PowerPoint uses an online translation program such as Microsoft Translator.

✓ *If the word you want to translate is capitalized, the translation service may not find a translation. Try lowercasing the word in the Research task pane.*

- When the Research task pane is open for a translation, you can also use it for other research tasks. Click the drop-down arrow to the right of Translation and choose a research tool such as a dictionary or thesaurus, or click Bing to research on the Web.

Try It! Translating Text

1. In the **P37Try_xx** file, display slide 7.
2. Right-click the word *Garden* and click Translate. If a dialog box displays telling you information will be sent over the Internet to a translation service, click Yes to proceed. The Research task pane opens with translation options active.
3. Click the To box's down arrow and select French (France). The translation is shown from the Bilingual Dictionary, *jardin*.
4. On the slide, click to the right of the word *Garden*, press TAB, and then type **jardin**.
5. In the Research task pane, click in the Search for box and type **truck**.
6. Click the To box's down arrow and select Spanish (Spain). The translation is shown from the Bilingual Dictionary, *camión*.
7. On the slide, position the insertion point in the Spanish column for the *Truck* paragraph and type **camión**.

   ✓ *Use the Symbol dialog box to find the letter o with the correct accent.*

8. Close the Research task pane.
9. Close the **P37Try_xx** file, saving changes, and exit PowerPoint.

Use the Research task pane to translate text

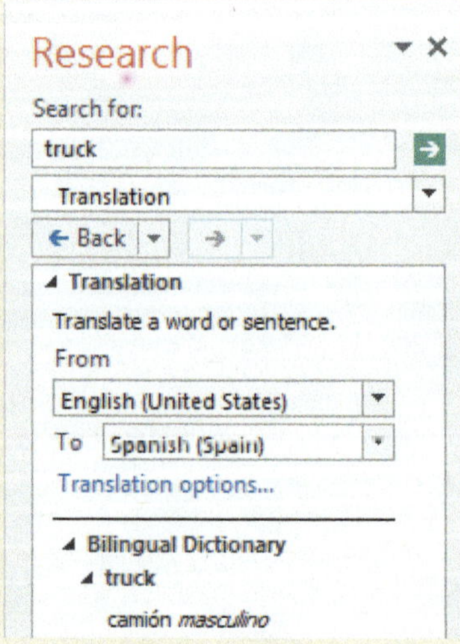

PowerPoint 2016, Windows 10, Microsoft Corporation

Lesson 37—Practice

The Clifton Community Center (CCC) runs a presentation on a screen in the lobby to keep community members up to date with the latest events in the community and at the center for a given month. The CCC is committed to serving a diverse population with information for and about different cultures. In this project, you begin work on the November presentation. You use the Translator and the Smart Lookup task pane to locate information about a November event and define a word.

DIRECTIONS

1. Start PowerPoint, if necessary, and open **P37Practice** from the data files for this lesson.
2. Save the presentation as **P37Practice_xx** in the location where your teacher instructs you to store the files for this lesson.
3. Display slide 2.
4. Click at the end of the bullet item, press ENTER, and type **The dictionary defines mincemeat as follows:**
5. Double-click the word *mincemeat* that you just typed, and then click **Review** > **Smart Lookup** to open the Smart Lookup task pane.
6. Click **Define** near the top of the task pane.
7. Under the heading *noun: mincemeat*, drag over the definition (*a mixture of spiced . . .*), and press CTRL + C.
8. On the slide, press ENTER at the end of the second bullet item, press TAB, and then press CTRL + V to paste the definition.
9. Remove the bullet formatting from the definition, change the first letter to a capital *A*, and then drag the left indent marker on the ruler to create a **1"** left indent. Your slide should look similar to Figure 37-1.

Figure 37-1

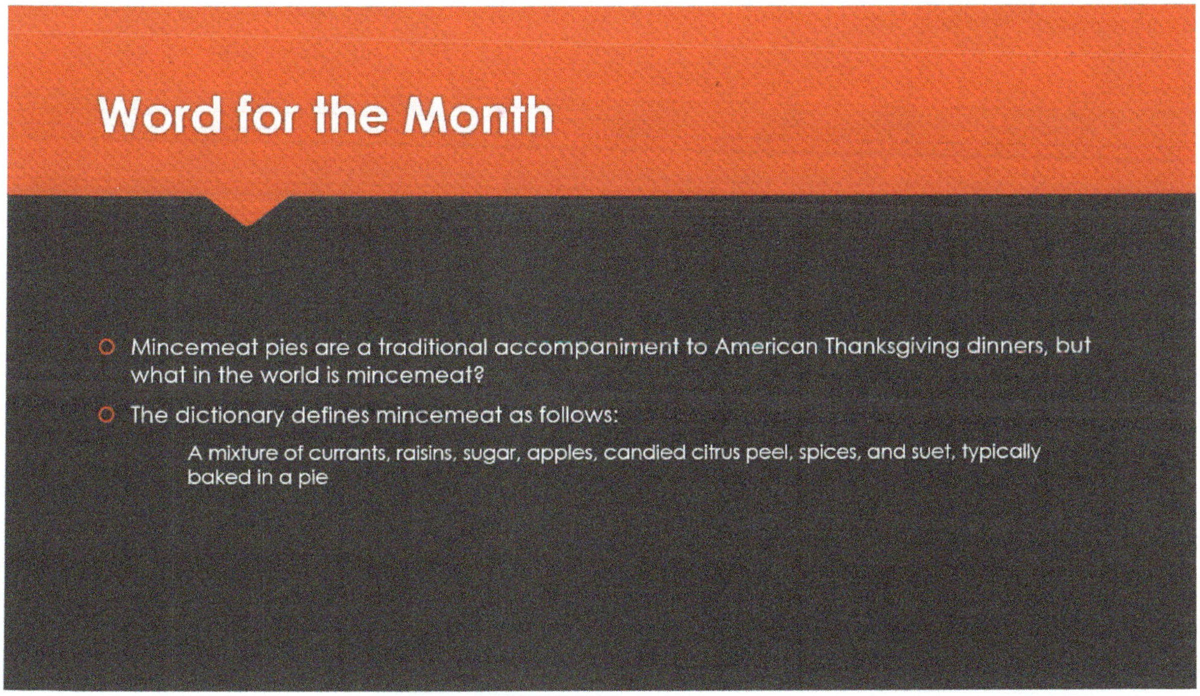

PowerPoint 2016, Windows 10, Microsoft Corporation

10. Create a new Two Content slide at the end of the presentation and insert the title **CCC Explores the World**.
11. Click the **Online Pictures** icon in the right content placeholder and search for a map of Mexico. Adjust size as desired, and apply a picture style of your choice.
12. In the left content placeholder, type the following text:

    Our focus this month is on Mexican holidays

    One of the most important is the day of the dead
13. Select the phrase *day of the dead*, and click **Review** > **Translate** > **Translate Selected Text**. Click Yes, if necessary.
14. In the Research task pane, change the Translation settings to translate from English to Spanish, if necessary.
15. Under Microsoft Translator, note the translation, and then click **Insert** to replace the selected phrase with its proper Spanish wording.
16. With *day of the dead* still displayed in the Search for box in the Research task pane, click the Translation down arrow and select Bing for research on this phrase. Click the Wikipedia article for more information on this holiday.
17. Notice in the article that *Día* and *Muertos* should be capitalized. Make this change on slide 3.
18. Select the phrase *Día de los Muertos*, and press CTRL + C to copy it.
19. Insert a new Two Content slide, and press CTRL + V to paste the copied phrase in the title placeholder.
20. In the left content placeholder, insert several bullet items to explain the holiday, using the information you find from one of the references in the Research task pane. Close the Research task pane.
21. Select the slide title, click Review > Smart Lookup, and choose an image in the Smart Lookup task pane that relates to the information you inserted on the slide. Adjust the size of the text placeholder, as necessary, to contain all text.
22. Preview the presentation and make any necessary adjustments.
23. Insert a footer with your name and today's date on all slides.
24. **With your teacher's permission,** print the presentation as handouts with 4 slides per page.
25. Close the presentation, saving changes, and exit PowerPoint.

Lesson 37—Apply

In this project, you continue working for the Clifton Community Center to create the December presentation. You research a topic, translate a word, and use a dictionary to find a definition.

DIRECTIONS

1. Start PowerPoint, if necessary, and open **P37Apply** from the data files for this lesson.
2. Save the presentation as **P37Apply_xx** in the location where your teacher instructs you to store the files for this lesson.
3. Change the theme colors to a scheme more appropriate for winter.
4. On slide 2, use any research tool to look up Boxing Day, and paste the definition in a new text box below the last bullet. Format the text box attractively. Figure 37-2 shows one option.

   ✓ *You may want to align the text in the content placeholder at the top of the placeholder, as shown in Figure 37-2.*

5. On slide 3, add the following text:

   Have you ever heard the Christmas carol *O Tannenbaum*?

   ***Tannenbaum* is German for**

6. Use the translator to translate *tannenbaum* from German to English, and then add the translation to the end of the second bullet.
7. On the slide, insert a picture that has to do with Germany, such as a map or flag.
8. Insert a new slide and add the slide title **O Christmas Tree**.
9. Use the Smart Lookup or Research task pane to research the custom of decorating a tree at Christmas. Insert the most important points you learn on slide 4, and then add an appropriate picture.
10. Preview the presentation and make any necessary adjustments.
11. Insert a footer with your name and today's date on all slides.
12. **With your teacher's permission,** print the presentation as handouts with 4 slides per page.
13. Close the presentation, saving changes, and exit PowerPoint.

Figure 37-2

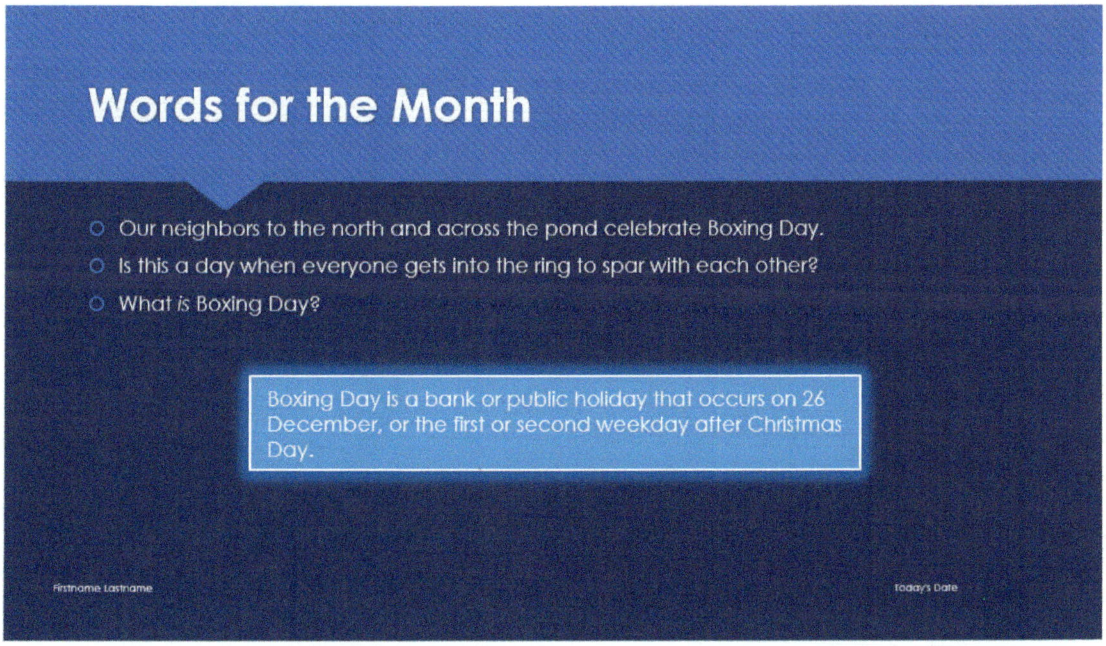

PowerPoint 2016, Windows 10, Microsoft Corporation

End-of-Chapter Activities

➤ PowerPoint Chapter 5—Critical Thinking

Communicating with Coworkers and Clients

You and your colleagues at Restoration Architecture work with clients every day. Some recent misunderstandings and miscommunications have convinced you that the staff could benefit from a presentation that reviews how to communicate effectively not only with clients but also with coworkers.

In this project, working alone or in teams, you will research effective workplace communication. Your research should cover the following topics:

- Communicating effectively with colleagues and clients.
- Recognizing the difference between verbal and nonverbal forms of communication.
- Understanding how both verbal and nonverbal behaviors help you communicate with coworkers and clients.
- Employing active listening to help you understand issues.
- Employing strategies that will help you communicate with clients and colleagues from diverse backgrounds.
- Understanding how to resolve conflicts that might arise within a diverse workforce and client base.
- Avoiding behaviors that could be considered sexual harassment.

As part of this project, you should prepare support materials that will enhance the presentation.

DIRECTIONS

1. Start a new presentation, and save it as **PCT05A_xx** in the location where your teacher instructs you to store the files for this chapter.
2. Insert the title **Effective Workplace Communication**. In the subtitle placeholder, type **A Presentation by** and then insert your first and last name.
3. Apply a theme and variant of your choice. In Slide Master view, customize the background of at least one slide layout with a gradient, picture, or texture.
4. Change the font on the title slide to a heavy, bold font and apply advanced text formatting such as a fill, outline, and effect.
5. Add a slide to the presentation with the title **Sources**. Use this slide to record the Web addresses of sites you use to find information for this presentation.
6. **With your teacher's permission,** use the Smart Lookup task pane to research the topics listed above. Use valid and reputable sites for your research, and copy site information to your Sources slide.
7. When your research is complete, organize your material into topics and plan how to use the material in your presentation. You may use a storyboard, if desired. Select slide layouts suitable for the type of information you find. Add illustrations as desired, using online pictures or other graphics.
8. Use at least one slide for each topic. Use additional slides to expand the topic as necessary.
9. On one slide, define the word *communication* using a source from the Smart Lookup task pane. Adjust indents as desired to present the definition clearly.
10. Check spelling.
11. Apply transitions to enhance the presentation's effectiveness.

12. Preview the presentation and then make any necessary corrections and adjustments.
13. Deliver the presentation to your class. Ask for comments on how the presentation could be improved.
14. Export the presentation to Word as handouts with blank lines beneath slides. Apply the same theme to the handouts that you applied to the slides.
15. Insert a Motion (Odd Page) header to the Word document with your name as the title. Save the Word document as **PCT05B_xx**.
16. **With your teacher's permission**, print the handout document.
17. Close the document, saving changes, and exit Word. Close the presentation, saving changes, and exit PowerPoint.

➤ PowerPoint Chapter 5—Portfolio Builder

Creating a Kiosk Presentation

Peterson Home Health Care has asked you to create a presentation that can be used at local health fairs to give viewers information about the company's home health care options. You will start work on that presentation in this project.

DIRECTIONS

1. Start PowerPoint, if necessary, and open **PPB05** from the data files for this chapter.
2. Save the presentation as **PPB05_xx** in the location where your teacher instructs you to store the files for this project.
3. Click **View** > **Slide Master**.
4. On the slide master, make the following changes.
   a. Select the Date placeholder and use **Drawing Tools Format** > **Align** > **Align Center** to move it to the horizontal center of the slide.
   b. Use **Insert** > **Online Pictures** to insert a medical symbol. Position the symbol in the lower-right corner of the slide master and resize as shown in Illustration 5A. Recolor the symbol if necessary using **Picture Tools Format** > **Color** to match the current theme.
5. On the Two Content layout, insert a narrow rectangle shape along the bottom edge of the right-hand content placeholder. Apply a Quick Style of your choice to the rectangle shape.
6. Select an Effects scheme of your choice.
7. Close Slide Master view and insert your name, slide numbers, and the current date on all slides. Slide 4 should look similar to Illustration 5A.

Illustration 5A

8. Display slide 7, and adjust the tabs in the content placeholder to organize the information into a table.
9. On slide 7, apply a new shape style to the text box and then adjust margins to improve appearance. Move the text box as necessary on the slide to avoid crowding the table.
10. On slide 2, indent the second paragraph 1" from the left margin, and then indent the third paragraph an additional 1".
11. Display the notes master and make the following changes to the master.
    a. Apply theme fonts that are the same as those used on the slides.
    b. Apply theme colors that complement those in the slides.
    c. Insert a picture background that uses the same symbol you used on the slide master, and adjust transparency as necessary so notes text can easily be read.
    d. Change the size of the text in the notes placeholder to 14 point.
12. On notes pages and handouts, insert a header with your full name and the date. Your notes pages should look similar to the one shown in Illustration 5B.
13. Preview the presentation and then make any necessary corrections and adjustments.
14. Deliver the presentation to your class. Ask for comments on how the presentation could be improved.
15. **With your teacher's permission,** print the presentation.
16. Close the presentation, saving changes, and exit PowerPoint.

Illustration 5B

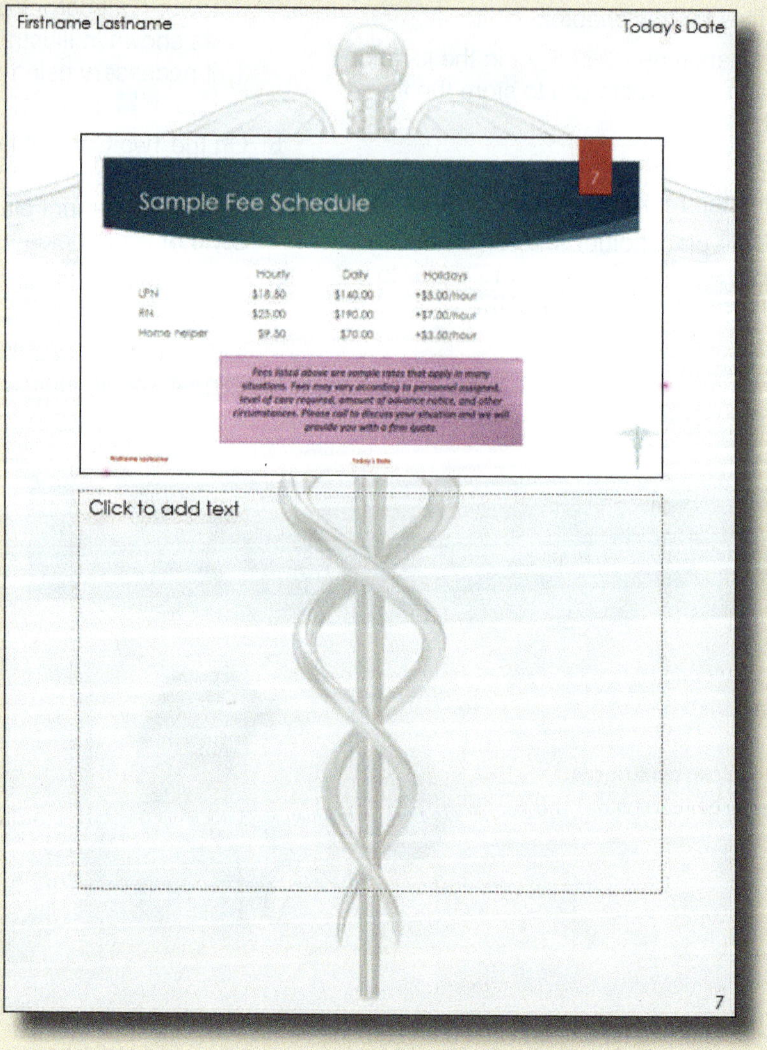

PowerPoint 2016, Windows 10, Microsoft Corporation

Chapter 6

(Courtesy Yuri Arcurs/Shutterstock)

Working with Graphic Objects and Media

Lesson 38
Applying Advanced Picture Formatting

- Understanding Picture Formats
- Formatting Different Types of Pictures
- Using a Picture As a Fill
- Using Advanced Cropping Techniques

Lesson 39
Working with Advanced Multimedia Features

- Understanding Multimedia Presentations
- Setting Advanced Video Options
- Setting Advanced Audio Options
- Recording Screen Actions
- Embedding a Flash Animation

Lesson 40
Applying Advanced Animations

- Applying More Than One Animation to an Object
- Adjusting a Motion Path Animation
- Applying Advanced Effect Options
- Controlling an Animation with a Trigger
- Working with the Animation Timeline

Lesson 41
Drawing and Adjusting Tables

- Drawing a Table
- Using the Eraser to Merge Cells
- Adjusting Column Width and Row Height
- Adjusting Cell and Table Size
- Changing Text Alignment and Direction

Lesson 42
Formatting Tables

- Customizing a Table Style
- Modifying Cell Fill, Borders, and Effects
- Adding an Image to a Table

Lesson 43
Formatting Charts

- Adding Trendlines and Error Bars
- Formatting Chart Text
- Fine-Tuning Chart Appearance

End-of-Chapter Activities

Lesson 38

Applying Advanced Picture Formatting

➤ What You Will Learn

Understanding Picture Formats
Formatting Different Types of Pictures
Using a Picture As a Fill
Using Advanced Cropping Techniques

WORDS TO KNOW

Bitmap image
Graphic created from arrangements of small squares called **pixels**. Also called raster images.

Lossless compression
Compression accomplished without loss of data.

Lossy compression
Compression in which part of a file's data is discarded to reduce file size.

Pixel
Term that stands for picture element, a single point on a computer monitor screen.

Vector image
Drawing made up of lines and curves defined by vectors, which describe an object mathematically according to its geometric characteristics.

Software Skills Understanding picture formats helps you select an appropriate file type for your presentation. Different types of pictures can be formatted in different ways. Use a picture to fill any shape for a more sophisticated presentation. Advanced cropping options enable you to crop to a shape or a specific aspect ratio and choose how a picture will fill an area.

What You Can Do

Understanding Picture Formats

- PowerPoint 2016 accepts a number of picture formats, including **bitmap** and **vector images**.
- Understanding the advantages and disadvantages of these common graphic file formats can help you choose pictures for your presentations.
- Table 38-1 on the next page lists some of the more common formats that PowerPoint supports, with their file extensions.
- When selecting pictures, consider the following:
  - If you plan on displaying the picture only on a screen, GIF and JPEG files will provide a good-quality appearance.
  - If you plan to print your slide materials, you may want to use TIFF images for a better-quality printed appearance.
  - For small graphics with a limited number of colors, a picture in GIF or PNG format will be perfectly adequate.
  - Photographs, on the other hand, should be saved in JPEG or TIFF format.
  - Remember that the higher the picture quality, the larger the presentation's file size.
  - You can decrease the file size by compressing pictures you have inserted in the presentation.

Table 38-1 Supported File Types for PowerPoint

Format	Extension	Characteristics
WMF	.wmf	Windows Metafile. Contains both bitmap and vector information and is optimized for use in Windows applications.
PNG	.png	Portable Network Graphics. A bitmap format that supports **lossless compression** and allows transparency; no color limitations.
BMP	.bmp	Windows Bitmap. Does not support file compression so files may be large; widely compatible with Windows programs.
GIF	.gif	Graphics Interchange Format. A widely supported bitmap format that uses lossless compression; maximum of 256 colors; allows transparency.
JPEG	.jpg	Joint Photographic Experts Group. A bitmap format that allows a tradeoff of **lossy compression** and quality; best option for photographs and used by most digital cameras.
TIFF	.tif	Tagged Image File Format. Can be compressed or uncompressed; uncompressed file sizes may be very large. Most widely used format for print publishing; not supported by Web browsers.

Formatting Different Types of Pictures

- The Picture Tools Format tab offers a number of options for working with pictures of various formats.
- For any type of picture, use the tools in the Adjust group to remove the picture background, correct brightness and contrast, sharpen or soften an image, adjust color saturation and tone, recolor an image using the current theme colors or any other color, apply artistic effects, or compress the image.
- Use the tools in the Picture Styles group to apply a picture style, a border, or an effect such as Shadow, Reflection, Glow, or 3-D Rotation.
- If you have inserted a PNG or GIF image, both of which support transparency, you can use Set Transparent Color on the Color menu to remove any color in the image to make that area transparent.
- Use the Format Picture task pane to make more detailed adjustments to images.

Try It! Formatting Different Types of Pictures

1. Start PowerPoint, and open **P38TryA** from the data files for this lesson.
2. Save the presentation as **P38TryA_xx** in the location where your teacher instructs you to store the files for this lesson.
3. With slide 1 displayed, click Insert > Pictures and navigate to the data files for this lesson.
4. Click **P38TryB_picture.png** and then click Insert.

   ✓ *If the Design ideas task pane opens after you insert the picture, close the task pane.*
5. With the picture selected, click Picture Tools Format > Color > Set Transparent Color, and then click the white area surrounding the picture of Earth to make that area transparent.
6. With the picture still selected, click Picture Tools Format > Color and then click the Dark Teal, Accent color 1 Light option in the bottom row of the Recolor options.
7. Move the image to the right side of the teal color bar on slide 1.

(continued)

Try It! Formatting Different Types of Pictures *(continued)*

8. Display slide 2.
9. Click Insert > Pictures and navigate to the data files for this lesson.
10. Click **P38TryC_picture.jpg** and then click Insert.

    ✓ *Don't worry about the size of the picture; you will adjust the size in a later exercise.*
11. With the picture selected, click Picture Tools Format > Corrections and then click Sharpen: 25% in the Sharpen/Soften gallery.
12. With the picture still selected, click Picture Tools Format > Corrections. In the Brightness/Contrast area, click Brightness: +20% Contrast: -20%.
13. With the picture still selected, click Picture Tools Format > Color > Temperature: 8800 K in the Color Tone gallery.
14. Display slide 4 and select the picture.
15. Click Picture Tools Format > Picture Border > Eyedropper. Use the Eyedropper to sample a dark red color from the red pepper near the center of the picture.
16. With the picture still selected, click Picture Tools Format > Picture Border > Weight > 4½ pt.
17. Save the **P38TryA_xx** file, and leave it open to use in the next Try It.

Reformatted PNG image

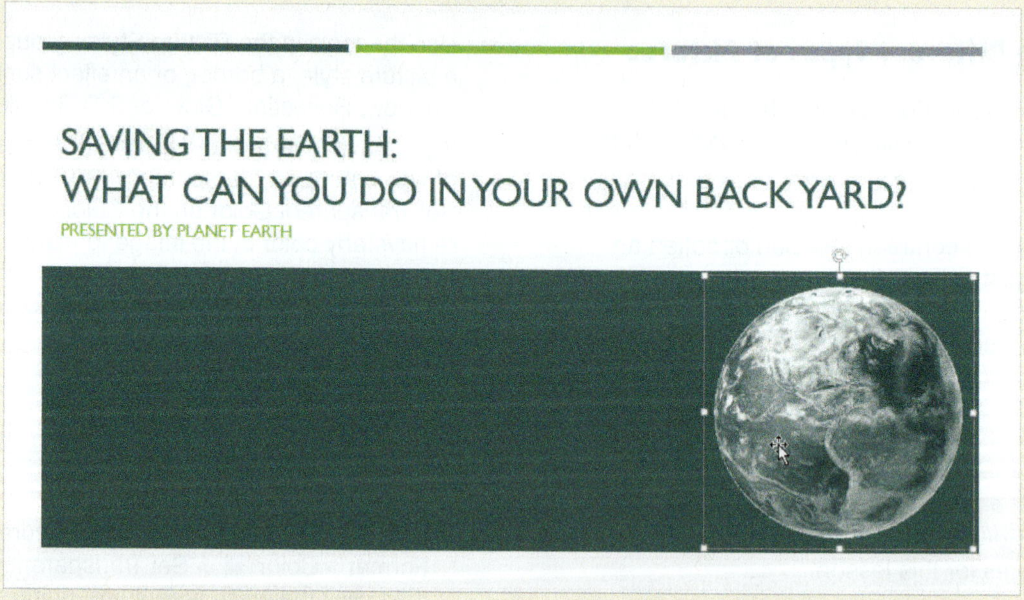

Using a Picture As a Fill

- You can use a picture to provide a fill for any object such as a shape or placeholder.
- Use the Picture option on the Shape Fill gallery to insert a picture fill. In the Insert Picture dialog box, you can choose to browse to a file, search for clip art, do an image search with Bing, or find a picture on your OneDrive.
- The picture you select will completely fill the selected shape, like any solid color or gradient fill, but you can still format the picture using tools on the Picture Tools Format tab.

Try It! Using a Picture As a Fill

1. In the **P38TryA_xx** file, display slide 3.
2. Select the shape at the right side of the slide, right-click, and click the Fill shortcut button.
3. Click Picture on the Shape Fill gallery.
4. Click in the Bing Image Search box, type **garden**, and click the Search button.
5. Click a picture in landscape format (such as the one shown below) and then click Insert.
6. With the shape still selected, click Drawing Tools Format > Shape Outline > No Outline.
7. With the shape still selected, click Picture Tools Format > Artistic Effects > Paint Brush.
8. With the shape still selected, click Picture Tools Format > Picture Effects > Shadow > Perspective Diagonal Upper Left.
9. Save the **P38TryA_xx** file, and leave it open to use in the next Try It.

Picture used as a fill for a shape

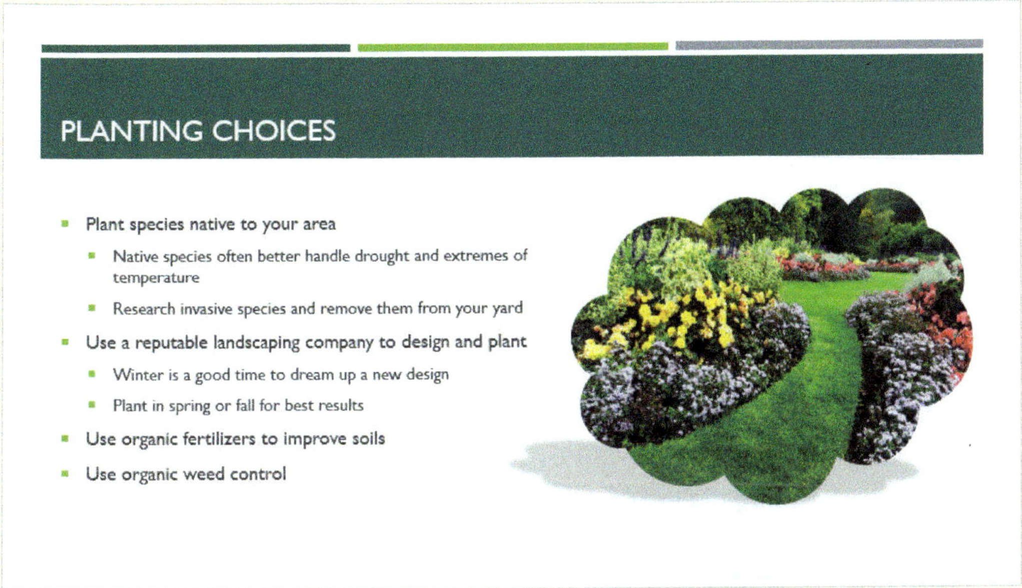

Using Advanced Cropping Techniques

- Clicking the Crop button on the Picture Tools Format tab displays crop handles at the outside edges of a picture. You can drag a handle to remove a portion of the image on that side.

✓ *Hold down CTRL while you drag a side to crop the opposite side at the same time.*

- Clicking the Crop button's down arrow displays a gallery of other options you can use to achieve a specific effect with the crop.
  - Use Crop to Shape to crop an image to any shape in the Shapes gallery.
  - Select an option from the Aspect Ratio menu to crop the image in a square or in a portrait or landscape aspect ratio.
- When you crop to a shape, the shape will be as wide and as high as the original image, and the image fills the shape. Areas outside the shape border are cropped but not removed entirely.

✓ *When you compress an image, the cropped areas are removed.*

- If you resize the shape to which you have cropped, you can select whether the image will fill the shape at its original aspect ratio or will fit entirely in the shape.
- If the image is larger than the shape, you can move the image to display the desired part of it in the shape.

Try It! Using Advanced Cropping Techniques

1. In the **P38TryA_xx** file, display slide 2 and select the picture.
2. On the Picture Tools Format tab, click the Crop button down arrow, point to Aspect Ratio, and click 1:1 in the Square section. The crop handles appear to show how the image would be cropped into a shape that is as wide as it is high.
3. Click Undo on the Quick Access Toolbar to undo the crop.
4. Click the Crop button's down arrow and point to Crop to Shape.
5. In the Shapes gallery that pops out, click Oval in the Basic Shapes section. The image is cropped to an oval shape as wide and high as the original image.
6. Drag the left center sizing handle on the oval to the right until the shape fits into the right side of the slide area. It should be about 5.4" wide.
7. Drag the top center sizing handle downward until the shape is about 4" high. Note that resizing the shape has distorted the image within the shape.
8. Click the Crop button's down arrow and click Fit to fit the entire image in the resized shape. Note that the image does not completely fill the shape.
9. Click the Crop button's down arrow and click Fill to completely fill the resized shape.
10. Click on the image in the center of the shape and drag it to the left until the right edge of the image aligns with the right side of the shape.
11. Click the Crop button to complete the crop.
12. With the image still selected, click the Beveled Oval, Black picture style on the Picture Tools Format tab.
13. Close the **P38TryA_xx** file, saving changes, and exit PowerPoint.

Drag the image to reposition it within the shape

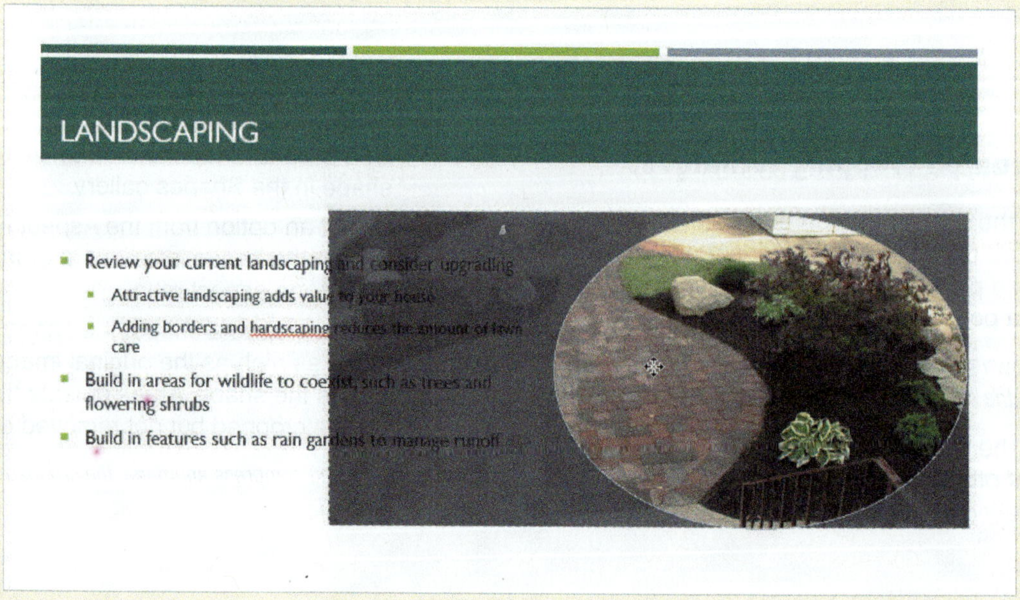

Lesson 38—Practice

Thorn Hill Gardens wants to run a presentation on a kiosk at the main entrance to advertise the annual Butterfly Show. In this project, you add several pictures to a presentation, apply various formatting options, and use image correction options to improve the appearance of the pictures.

DIRECTIONS

1. Start PowerPoint, if necessary, and open **P38PracticeA** from the data files for this lesson.
2. Save the presentation as **P38PracticeA_xx** in the location where your teacher instructs you to store the files for this lesson.
3. On slide 1, click **Insert** > **Pictures** and navigate to the data files.
4. Select **P38PracticeB_picture.jpg** and click **Insert**.
5. With the picture still selected, click **Picture Tools Format** > **Crop** drop-down arrow > **Crop to Shape** and select **Oval** from the Shapes gallery.
6. Click **Picture Tools Format** > **Crop** drop-down arrow > **Aspect Ratio** and select **1:1** from the Square section.
7. Click on the image in the center of the shape and drag to the left until the right edge of the image aligns with the right side of the circle. Then click **Crop** to complete the crop.
8. Resize the picture to be **4"** square and move the picture to the lower-right side of the slide.
9. With the picture still selected, click **Picture Tools Format** > **Picture Border** , and select **Lime, Accent 1** from the Theme Colors palette. Click **Picture Border** again, point to **Weight**, and click **4½ pt**.
10. Display slide 2 and click the butterfly shape to select it.
11. Click **Drawing Tools Format** > **Shape Fill** > **Picture**.
12. In the Insert Pictures dialog box, click in the Bing Image Search box, type **flowers**, and click **Search** .
13. Scroll down the search results to find a red flower similar to the one shown in Figure 38-1 on the next page, select it, and click **Insert**.

   ✓ *If you cannot find a red flower, look for any flower that will fill the shape attractively.*

14. With the shape still selected, click **Picture Tools Format** > **Picture Effects** > **Reflection** > **Half Reflection, 4 pt offset**.
15. Display slide 5 and click the **Pictures** icon in the content placeholder.
16. Navigate to the data files, if necessary, click **P38PracticeC_picture.jpg**, and click **Insert**.
17. With the picture still selected, click **Picture Tools Format** > **Corrections** and click **Sharpen 50%** in the Sharpen/Soften gallery.
18. With the picture still selected, click **Picture Tools Format** > **Artistic Effects** and click **Paint Brush** in the effects gallery.
19. Preview the slides to see the images in place. Then insert your full name and the date on all slides.
20. **With your teacher's permission**, print the presentation as handouts.
21. Close the presentation, saving changes, and exit PowerPoint.

Figure 38-1

PowerPoint 2016, Windows 10, Microsoft Corporation

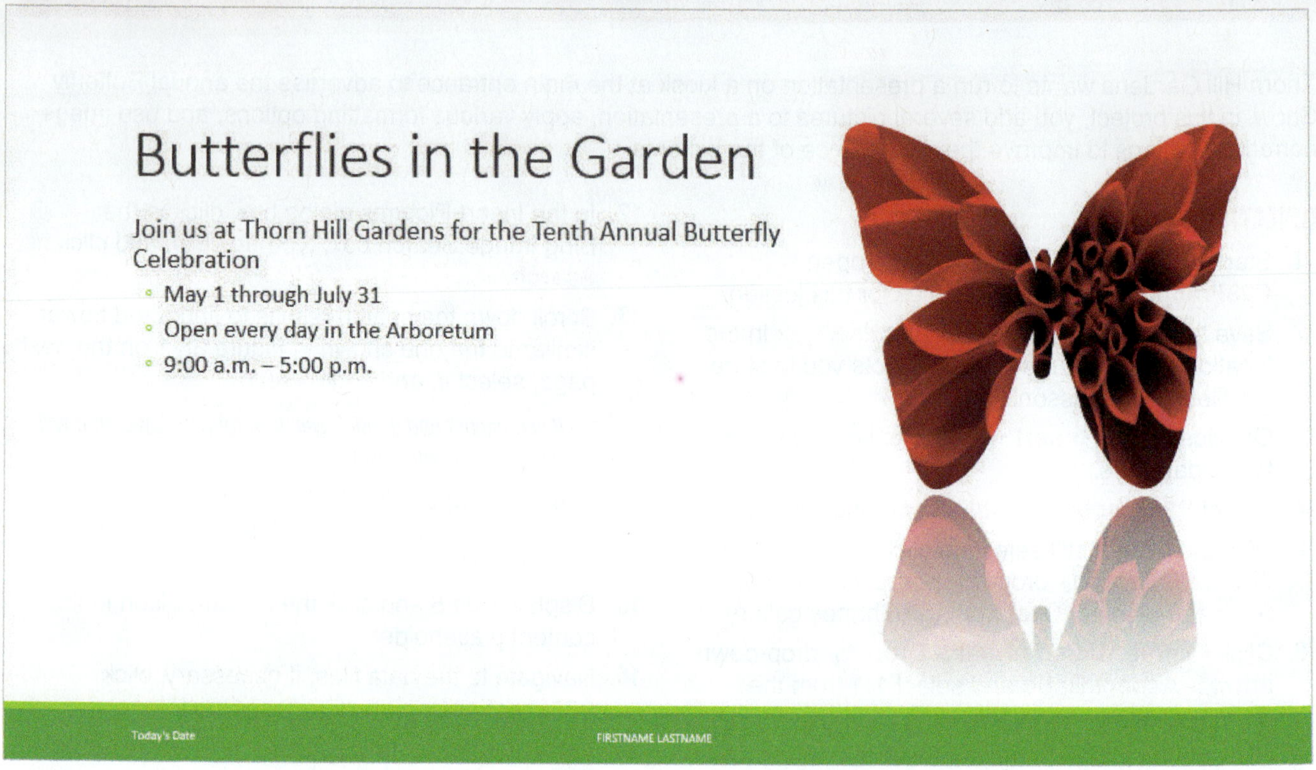

Lesson 38—Apply

In this project, you continue to work on the presentation for Thorn Hill Gardens. You insert and format a GIF image, add another picture, and do some corrections on existing images. You also crop a picture to a shape for a final touch.

DIRECTIONS

1. Start PowerPoint, if necessary, and open **P38ApplyA** from the data files for this lesson.
2. Save the presentation as **P38ApplyA_xx** in the location where your teacher instructs you to store the files for this lesson.
3. On slide 1, select the picture and adjust its color by selecting **Color** on the **Picture Tools Format** tab and then choosing **Saturation: 200%** from the Color Saturation gallery.
4. Display slide 3 and then insert **P38ApplyB_picture.gif** from the data files. Modify the picture as follows:
   a. Make the yellow background color around the butterfly transparent.
   b. Display the Color gallery, click **More Variations** at the bottom of the gallery, and then click **Light Green** from the Standard Colors palette.
   c. Resize the image to be about **4.3"** wide and rotate it to the left. Position the image attractively at the right side of the slide.
   d. Apply the **Plastic Wrap** artistic effect.

5. On slide 4, insert **P38ApplyC_picture.jpg** in the content placeholder. Adjust the image as follows:
   a. Right-click the image and select **Format Picture** to display the Format Picture task pane.
   b. Click the **Picture** icon, expand **Picture Corrections**, and then adjust Brightness to **20%** and Contrast to **25%**. Close the task pane.
   c. Apply the **Drop Shadow Rectangle** picture style.
6. On slide 6, insert **P38ApplyD_picture.jpg** and format the image as follows:
   a. Crop the image to the **Oval Callout** shape.
   b. Resize the shape by dragging handles to be about **4"** high by **5.5"** wide.
   c. Select the **Fit** cropping option to make sure the entire image width is included, and then adjust the crop oval so that there are no blank areas at the top of the oval or at the point of the callout arrow. The final image should be about 3.6" high. Complete the crop.
   d. Select the image, if necessary, and move it to the right side of the slide. Drag the yellow adjustment handle on the callout arrow to point to the text in the left placeholder.
   e. Apply a picture border using the Eyedropper to sample a color from the image. Change the border weight as desired.
   f. Apply a picture effect such as a reflection or shadow. Figure 38-2 shows one way the image could be formatted.
7. Preview the presentation to see the formatted images. Then insert your full name and the date on all slides.
8. **With your teacher's permission,** print the presentation as handouts.
9. Close the presentation, saving changes, and exit PowerPoint.

Figure 38-2

PowerPoint 2016, Windows 10, Microsoft Corporation

Lesson 39

Working with Advanced Multimedia Features

➤ What You Will Learn

Understanding Multimedia Presentations
Setting Advanced Video Options
Setting Advanced Audio Options
Recording Screen Actions
Embedding a Flash Animation

Software Skills Media clips can add considerable impact to a presentation as well as convey information in ways that other graphic objects cannot. You can insert video from a file and use formatting options to fine-tune the video appearance and playback. Use audio options to customize sounds in a presentation. Two features new to PowerPoint 2016, Screen Recording and Embed Flash, give you other ways to add multimedia to your slides.

What You Can Do

Understanding Multimedia Presentations

- Multimedia presentations display information in a variety of media, including text, pictures, videos, animations, and sounds.
- Multimedia content not only adds visual and audible interest to slides but also presents information in ways that plain text cannot.
- A simple picture can convey an image that would take many words to describe; likewise, a video can show a process or sequence of events that might take many pictures to convey.
- You can choose how much or how little multimedia content to include in a presentation.
- When deciding on multimedia options for a presentation, you must consider the tradeoff between multimedia impact and the presentation's file size. Multimedia files such as videos and sounds can be quite large.
- You also need appropriate computer resources, such as speakers and video or sound cards, to play media files successfully.

- Use good research standards when locating multimedia content. Always request permission to use materials you find on the Internet, or follow directives for crediting persons or agencies.
- When creating a presentation for personal use, you can use CD music tracks for background sound, but do not use such copyrighted materials if you plan to sell your presentation or post it to a location such as a public OneDrive folder.
- If you decide to include multimedia content in a presentation, PowerPoint offers a number of options for playing both videos and sounds.

Setting Advanced Video Options

- You need to understand video formats to determine the quality of video clips you intend to insert.
- A file in MPEG-1 format, for example, is not likely to display with the same quality as an MPEG-2 file, but it will be smaller in size. An MPEG-4 file will have the best appearance and allows for more efficient compression than MPEG-2.
- Table 39-1 shows the video formats that PowerPoint supports. Note that PowerPoint does not support some popular video formats, such as QuickTime and RealMedia files.
- Use the tools on the Video Tools Playback tab to work with a video.
  - Insert a bookmark so you can jump to a specific point in the video.
  - Trim a video to remove portions of it that you don't need.
  - Apply Fade settings to fade a video in or out.
  - Choose options such as Play Full Screen or Hide While Not Playing to control the appearance of the video on the slide during the presentation.
  - You can also choose to loop a video until you stop it, or return the movie to its first frame after it has finished playing.
- Use the Volume button to control the sound of the individual video clip within the overall presentation.

Table 39-1 Supported Video Formats for PowerPoint

Format	Extension	Characteristics
ASF	.asf	Advanced Systems Format. Microsoft's streaming format that can contain video, audio, slide shows, and other synchronized content.
AVI	.avi	Audio Video Interleave. A file format that stores alternating (interleaved) sections of audio and video content; widely used for playing video with sound on Windows systems; AVI is a container (a format that stores different types of data), not a form of compression.
MPEG	.mpg, .mpeg, .mp4, .m4v, .mov	Moving Picture Experts Group. A standard format for lossy audio and visual compression that comes in several formats, such as MPEG-1 (CD quality), MPEG-2 (DVD quality), and MPEG-4 (broadcast quality).
SWF	.swf	Adobe Flash Media. Flash uses vector and bitmap objects to create animations that can include text, graphics, and audio.
WMV	.wmv	Windows Media Video. Microsoft's lossy compression format for motion video; it results in files that take up little room on a system.

Try It! Setting Advanced Video Options

1. Start PowerPoint, if necessary, and open **P39TryA** from the data files for this lesson.
2. Save the presentation as **P39TryA_xx** in the location where your teacher instructs you to store the files for this lesson.
3. Display slide 3 and click the video to select it.
4. Add a timed fade to the beginning of the video: on the Video Tools Playback tab, click the up arrow to increase the Fade In time to 00.50.
5. Click the Play button below the video and let it run for about 10 seconds, then pause it.
6. Click Video Tools Playback > Add Bookmark to add a bookmark at the current location on the video timeline.

Bookmark in a video

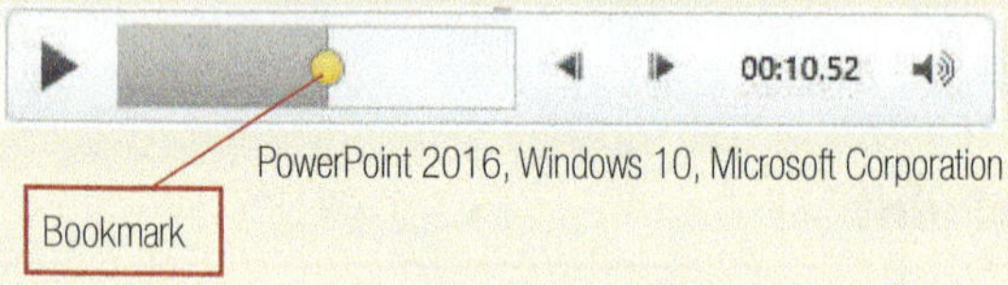

PowerPoint 2016, Windows 10, Microsoft Corporation

7. Click Video Tools Playback > Trim Video.
8. In the Trim Video dialog box, drag the red End Time indicator to the left until the End Time box shows about 00:20:00.
9. Click OK.
10. Click Video Tools Playback > Rewind after Playing.
11. Click Slide Show on the status bar and click the video to play it, noting the fade-in and the rewind when finished.
12. Move the pointer over the video after it has finished and click the bookmark to jump to that location. Click the play button to play the remainder of the video.
13. Press ESC to end the presentation.
14. Save the **P39TryA_xx** file, and leave it open for the next Try It.

Setting Advanced Audio Options

- Options on the Audio Tools Playback tab are very similar to those on the Video Tools Playback tab.
- As for a video, you can add a bookmark to an audio file, trim it, and fade it in or out.
- You can adjust the volume and choose to play the sound across slides or loop it.
- Use the Hide During Show option to prevent the audio file icon from appearing during the presentation.
- Selecting the Play in Background option sets the audio file to start automatically, play across slides, and loop until stopped.

Try It! Setting Advanced Audio Options

1. In the **P39TryA_xx** file, display slide 1 and click the audio object in the lower-right corner of the slide.
2. Click Audio Tools Playback and click the Fade In up arrow until 01.00 appears.
3. Click Volume and click Medium.
4. Click Hide During Show.
5. Click Play in Background.
6. Click Slide Show on the status bar to play the presentation. Notice that the audio object is hidden; the music plays automatically and continues to play as you view each slide.
7. Save the **P39TryA_xx** file, and leave it open for the next Try It.

Recording Screen Actions

- A new feature in PowerPoint 2016 allows you to record actions and embed the resulting recording on a slide.
- Use a screen recording to show a viewer or audience how to complete a task, such as conduct a Web search or create an equation.
- To record a screen, display in a presentation the slide on which you want the screen recording to be embedded. Then click Insert > Screen Recording to begin the process of capturing a process.
- A small toolbar appears at the top of the screen. Use the Select Area button to drag a marquee around an area that contains the application you want to record. When the screen shows what you want to record, begin recording.
- As for recording a macro, take the steps you want to record. When you have finished, stop the recording.
- You can choose to add audio to your recording and show or hide the pointer during the recording.

Try It! Recording Screen Actions

✓ *In this exercise, you will record the steps necessary to insert a new Two-Content slide and add content to it.*

1. In the **P39TryA_xx** file, display slide 3.
2. Click the Home > New Slide drop-down arrow and select the Blank slide layout.

   ✓ *Your screen recording will be embedded on this slide.*
3. Click Insert > Screen Recording. The Screen Recording toolbar appears at the top of the window.
4. Minimize any open applications to display your desktop.
5. Click the Select Area button on the Screen Recording toolbar and drag over an area of your desktop that includes the PowerPoint icon on the taskbar.
6. Click the PowerPoint icon to open the PowerPoint window.
7. Read the following steps so you are familiar with what you are going to record. When you are ready to record them, click the Record ● button on the Screen Recording toolbar.

   ✓ *You will see a countdown screen. Begin recording after the 1 message disappears.*

   a. Click the Home > New Slide drop-down arrow and select the Two Content slide layout.

   b. Click in the slide title placeholder and type **WE ONLY HAVE ONE . . .**

   c. Click in the left content placeholder and type the following bullet entries:

   We only have one Planet Earth

   Help us keep Planet Earth beautiful

   d. Select the outside border of the right content placeholder and press DEL to remove the placeholder.
8. Move the pointer near the top of the screen to redisplay the Screen Recording toolbar, and click the Stop ■ button.
9. Click the Play/Pause ▶ button at the bottom of the screen recording to review your screen recording. If you are not happy with it, delete the recording and start over.
10. With the recording selected, click Video Tools Playback > Trim Video and trim the video to remove parts of the recording that show the Screen Recording toolbar at the beginning and end of the recording.
11. Resize the recording to fit attractively on slide 4. If desired, crop the recording to remove the title bar and the taskbar.
12. Apply a video style such as Drop Shadow Rectangle.
13. Save the **P39TryA_xx** file, and leave it open for the next Try It.

(continued)

Try It! **Recording Screen Actions** *(continued)*

Completed screen recording on slide 4

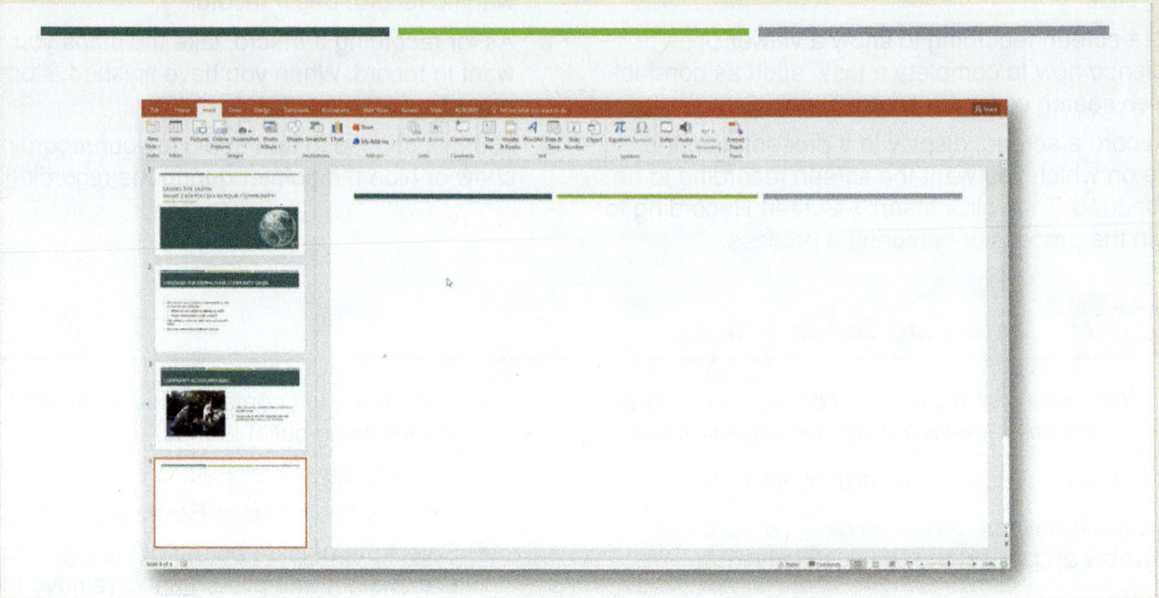

PowerPoint 2016, Windows 10, Microsoft Corporation

Embedding a Flash Animation

- Another way to add multimedia interest to a presentation is by adding animations such as those that can be created with Adobe Flash (now referred to as Adobe Animate).
- Embedding a Flash file has been possible in previous versions of PowerPoint, using an ActiveX control that had to be inserted from the Developer tab.
- PowerPoint 2016 offers the Embed Flash command on the Insert tab to make it easier to insert a Flash animation.
- After selecting the command, you navigate to the location of the SWF file to insert it.
- You can modify properties of the animation if desired by displaying the object's Property Sheet.

✓ *You'll notice when you view the PowerPoint file in File Explorer that it has been saved as a folder containing an Assets folder with the animation file in it.*

Try It! **Embedding a Flash Animation**

1. In the **P39TryA_xx** file, display slide 5.

   ✓ *This is the slide you created when recording in the last Try It.*

2. Click Insert > Embed Flash. The Insert Flash dialog box displays.
3. Click Browse, navigate to the data files, click **P39TryB_flash.swf**, and click Open.
4. A preview of the animation displays in the Insert Flash dialog box. Click OK.

   ✓ *The Flash object displays on the slide as a black rectangle. No matter what color the background of the animation was when created in Flash, it will appear black when embedded on the slide.*

5. Move the Flash object to the right side of the slide, where the right content placeholder was.

   ✓ *If desired, right-click the Flash object, select Property Sheet, and adjust the following settings: Change BgColor to 003366; change Width to 300. Make sure Playing is set to True. Click the close button in the property sheet to apply the changes.*

(continued)

Try It! Embedding a Flash Animation *(continued)*

6. Click Slide Show in the status bar to view the slide. The animation should start automatically. To replay the animation, right-click the Flash object and select Play.
7. Press Esc to end the slide show.
8. Close the **P39TryA_xx** file, saving changes, and exit PowerPoint.

Embedded Flash animation on the slide

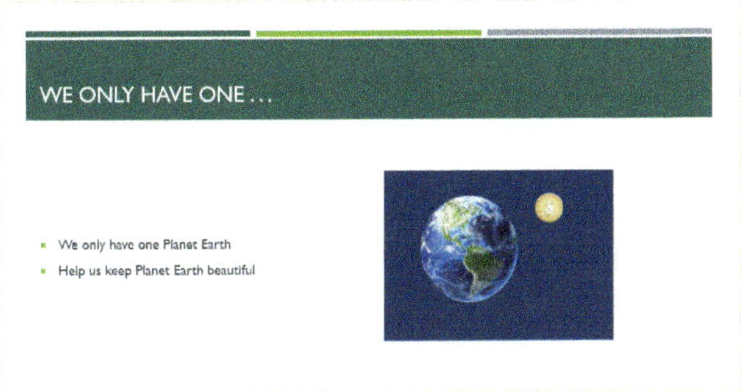

PowerPoint 2016, Windows 10, Microsoft Corporation

Lesson 39—Practice

Voyager Adventure Travel is beginning the task of adding a new hiking package to its list of adventures. The decision-making process requires consideration of both pros and cons for each suggested venue, and you have been asked to prepare a slide show to present the information. In this project, you begin work on the presentation with pros and cons for Glacier National Park.

DIRECTIONS

1. Start PowerPoint, if necessary, and open **P39PracticeA** from the data files for this lesson.
2. Save the presentation as **P39PracticeA_xx** in the location where your teacher instructs you to store the files for this lesson.
3. Display slide 5 and click **Insert** > **Video** > **Video on My PC**. The Insert Video dialog box opens.
4. Navigate to the data files for this lesson and select **P39PracticeB_video.mpg**.
5. Click **Insert**. The video will be upgraded before being inserted.
6. Center the video in the content area.
7. Point to the timeline beneath the video to display a counter that moves as you move the pointer, and click when the counter reaches **00:02.30**.
8. Click **Video Tools Playback** > **Add Bookmark** to bookmark this location in the video.
9. Click the **Fade In** up arrow to set the beginning fade to **01.00**.
10. Click the **Start** down arrow and select **Automatically**.
11. Display slide 6 and click **Insert** > **Audio** > **Audio on My PC**.
12. Navigate to the data files for this lesson and select **P39PracticeC_audio.wav**. Then click **Insert**.
13. With the audio clip selected on slide 6, on the Audio Tools Playback tab, change the **Fade In** setting to **00.50**, the **Fade Out** setting to **00.50**, and the Volume to **Medium**.
14. On the Audio Tools Playback tab, click **Play Across Slides**, and then click the **Start** down arrow and select **Automatically**.
15. On the Audio Tools Playback tab, click **Hide During Show**.
16. Preview the presentation from the beginning. On slide 5, play the entire video, then select the bookmark and play the video from that location.
17. Play the remaining slides, noting how the sound fades in and out and plays through the remaining slides.
18. Close the presentation, saving changes, and exit PowerPoint.

Lesson 39—Apply

In this project, you continue working with the Voyager Adventure Travel presentation. You adjust video and audio settings, add another video from the Web, and insert a picture to add a final touch to this multimedia presentation.

DIRECTIONS

1. Start PowerPoint, if necessary, and open **P39ApplyA** from the data files for this lesson.
2. Save the file as **P39ApplyA_xx** in the location where your teacher instructs you to store the files for this lesson.
3. Display slide 5 and select the video.
4. Remove the Fade In setting and then trim the video so it starts at approximately **00:01.00**.
5. On the Video Tools Format tab, select the **Drop Shadow Rectangle** video style.
6. On slide 7, insert the **P39ApplyB_picture.jpg** file in the right content placeholder and then apply the **Drop Shadow Rectangle** picture style. Your slide should look like Figure 39-1.
7. View the slide show to view changes.
8. Insert your name and the date on all slides.
9. **With your teacher's permission,** print the presentation as handouts with 4 slides per page.
10. Close the presentation, saving changes, and exit PowerPoint.

Figure 39-1

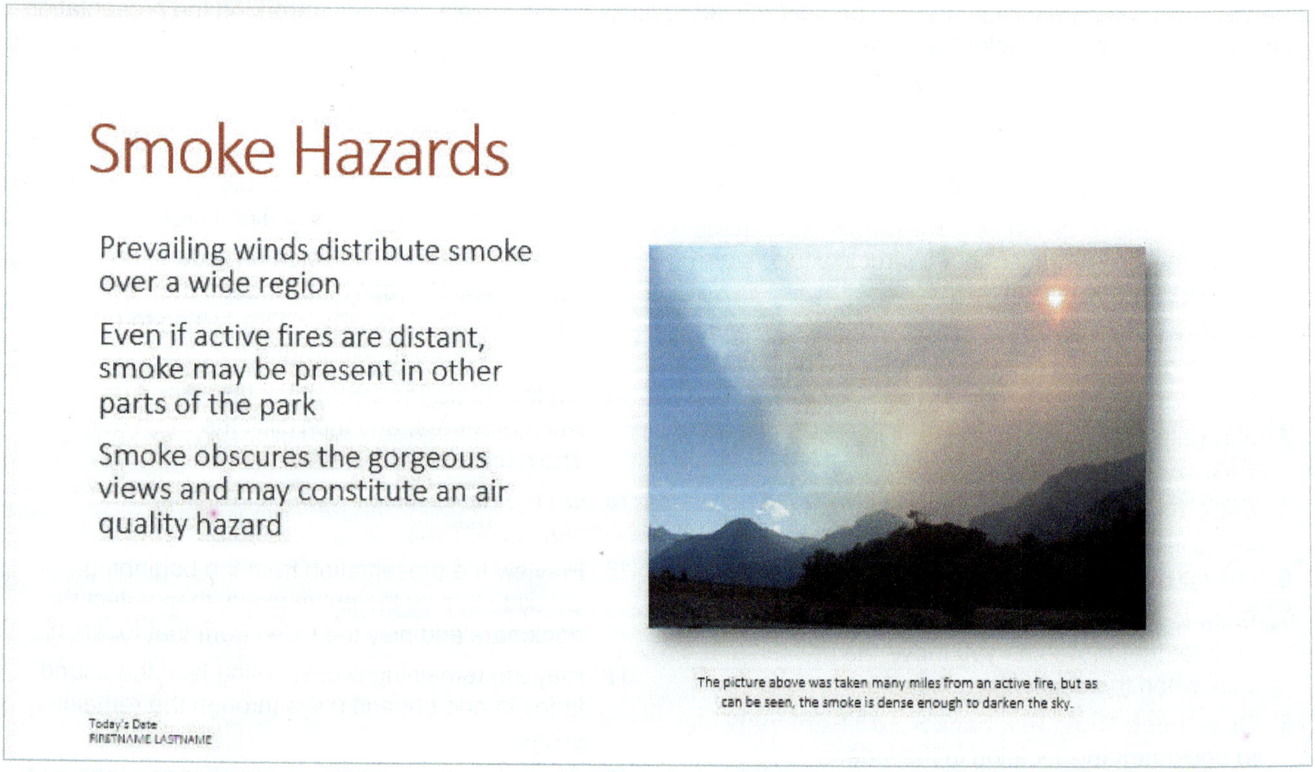

PowerPoint 2016, Windows 10, Microsoft Corporation

Lesson 40

Applying Advanced Animations

➤ What You Will Learn

Applying More Than One Animation to an Object
Adjusting a Motion Path Animation
Applying Advanced Effect Options
Controlling an Animation with a Trigger
Working with the Animation Timeline

Software Skills Using custom animation options, you can fine-tune the way objects enter, exit, and move on slides. Use advanced features to trigger animations, and use the timeline to control when animations start and how long they last.

What You Can Do

Applying More Than One Animation to an Object

- You can apply more than one animation effect to any object on a slide.
- For example, apply an entrance effect to display an object and then an exit effect to remove the object from the slide.
- Use the Add Animation button on the Animations tab to add another animation to an object.

WORDS TO KNOW

Trigger
An object you click to start the animation of another object.

Try It! Applying More Than One Animation to an Object

1. Start PowerPoint, and open **P40Try** from the data files for this lesson.
2. Save the presentation as **P40Try_xx** in the location where your teacher instructs you to store the files for this lesson.
3. Display slide 7 and click the Profit text box to select it.
4. Click the Animations tab and select Fly In from the Entrance gallery.
5. With the Profit text box still selected, click Animations > Add Animation to display a gallery of animation effects.
6. In the Emphasis section of the gallery, click Pulse.
7. Click Animations > Preview to view the added animation on the Profit text box.
8. Display slide 8 and click the pointing arrow shape to select it.
9. Click Animations > Add Animation and select Wipe.
10. Click Animations > Effect Options > From Right.
11. Click Animations > Add Animation and select Shrink & Turn from the Exit gallery.
12. Click Animations > Preview to view the animations on the arrow.
13. Save the **P40Try_xx** file, and leave it open to use in the next Try It.

Choose an Exit effect for an object

Adjusting a Motion Path Animation

- PowerPoint offers many options for setting objects in motion on your slides. You can choose among lines, turns, arcs, and special shapes.
- If you cannot find a default motion path that suits your needs, you can adjust any motion path to specify exactly where you want an object to be at the beginning and the end of the animation.
- A green handle or pointer marks the beginning of a motion path, and a red handle or pointer marks the end of the path. You can drag these handles as desired to reposition the path.
- You will see a shaded version of the object at the end of the motion path to help you position it correctly at the end of the path.
- You may also want to edit curve points along the path or use the Effect Options gallery to change the direction of the motion.

Try It! Adjusting a Motion Path Animation

1. In the **P40Try_xx** file, display slide 1 and click the Planet Earth object in the upper-right corner. (Click the outside border to select the entire group.)
2. Click Animations > Add Animation and scroll down to display the Motion Paths effects.
3. Click Lines to apply a straight-line motion path to the object.
4. Click the red handle in the center of the shaded object as shown in the illustration and drag to the lower-left of the slide to position the end of the path below the words *Planet Earth*.
5. Release the mouse button when you are satisfied with the position of the object.
6. Click the Start down arrow and select After Previous. Set the Duration to 3:00.
7. Click Animations > Preview to view the adjusted motion path.
8. Save the **P40Try_xx** file, and leave it open to use in the next Try It.

Drag the handle at the end of the path to adjust the path

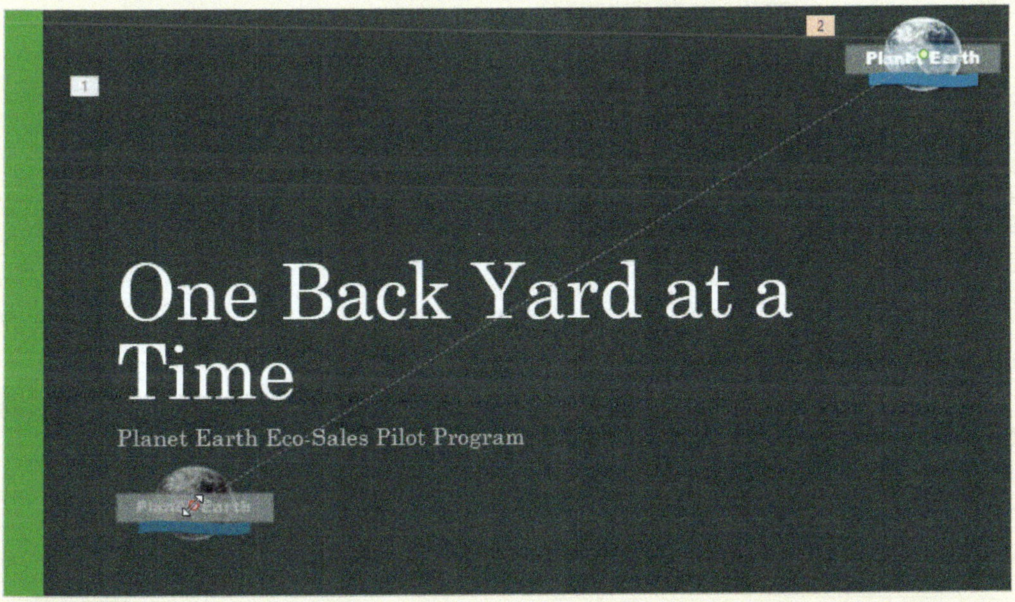

PowerPoint 2016, Windows 10, Microsoft Corporation

Applying Advanced Effect Options

- When you select an animation in the Animation Pane, a down arrow appears containing a number of options that you can use to modify an effect.
- Selecting Effect Options from the content list opens a dialog box for the currently selected effect. The Effect tab offers a number of special effects that you can apply to an object, depending on the type of object being animated.
- You can adjust the direction of the animation and choose Smooth start and Smooth end to control how the object starts and stops during the animation.
- All animation types enable you to select a sound effect from the Sound list to accompany the effect.

✓ *Use sound effects sparingly; it can be distracting to hear the same sound effect over and over when multiple parts of an object are animated.*

- The After animation menu gives you a number of options for emphasizing or deemphasizing an object after the animation ends. You can hide the object after the animation, hide it the next time you click the mouse, or change its color.
- If the animated object contains text, the Animate text settings become active, enabling you to animate the text all at once, by word, or by letter, and set the delay between words or letters.

Try It! Applying Advanced Effect Options

1. In the **P40Try_xx** file, display slide 9.
2. Click Animations > Animation Pane to display the Animation Pane.
3. Select the Title 1 animation and then click Fade in the Animation gallery to change the animation effect from Split to Fade.
4. Select the Title 1 animation again in the Animation Pane, if necessary, and click the down arrow to the right of the animation title.
5. Click Effect Options to open the Fade options dialog box.
6. Click the Animate text down arrow and click By word.
7. Click the Timing tab in the Fade dialog box, click the Start down arrow, and select With Previous. Click the Duration down arrow and select 5 seconds (Very Slow).
8. Click OK to apply the animation effects.
9. Click the subtitle on the slide, and apply the Fly In animation.
10. With the subtitle animation selected in the Animation Pane, click the animation's down arrow and click Effect Options.
11. Click the Direction down arrow and select From Right; click the Bounce end up arrow to apply a 0.5 sec bounce; click the After animation down arrow and select Hide After Animation.
12. Click the Timing tab, set the Start to After Previous and the Duration to 5 seconds (Very Slow).
13. Click OK to apply the animation effects.
14. Preview the effects on the slide.
15. Save the **P40Try_xx** file, and leave it open to use in the next Try It.

Advanced effect options for the Fly In animation

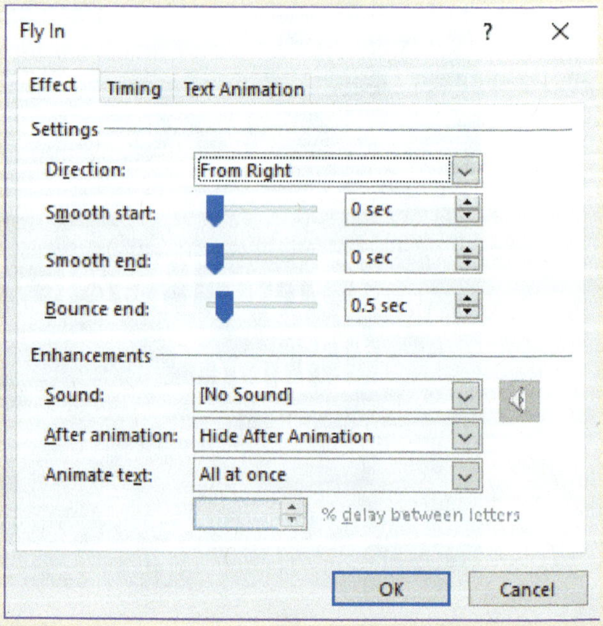

PowerPoint 2016, Windows 10, Microsoft Corporation

Controlling an Animation with a Trigger

- You can specify that an animation will begin when you click an object called a **trigger**.
- Using triggers is one way to make a slide show interactive. A presenter can click one object during the presentation to start the animation of another object.
- Use the Trigger button in the Advanced Animation group to set the trigger that will start an animation sequence. You can also set a trigger from within an effect's options dialog box.

Try It! Controlling an Animation with a Trigger

1. In the P40Try_xx file, display slide 7.
2. Select the chart and the three text boxes at the bottom of slide 7.

   ✓ *Hint: Press CTRL to enable you to select multiple objects.*
3. Click Animations > Float In.
4. Click Animations > Trigger > On Click of > TextBox 7.
5. Click Slide Show on the status bar to display the current slide in Slide Show view. The first two text boxes animate automatically. Click the slide to display the Profit box. Click to display the Pulse animation effect.
6. Point to the Profit box, which is the trigger for the next animation. Click the Profit box to display the chart and the remaining text boxes.
7. Click ESC to end the slide show.
8. Save the P40Try_xx file, and leave it open to use in the next Try It.

Working with the Animation Timeline

- The easiest way to fine-tune animation timing is to use the timeline feature in the Animation Pane.
- The bar next to an effect in the Animation Pane indicates the duration of the effect and when it starts relative to other effects.
- The timeline includes a seconds gauge at the bottom of the Animation Pane. You can use this gauge to see the duration of each effect as well as the overall duration of all animations on the slide.
- You can use the timeline to set a delay or adjust the length of an effect.
- You can double-click a timeline bar to open the Timing dialog box for further adjustments.
- Before you use the timeline to adjust animations, you may need to change the order in which the animations play. You can drag animations in the Animation Pane to change their order or use the Reorder Animation buttons Move Earlier and Move Later to change animation order.

Try It! Working with the Animation Timeline

1. In the **P40Try_xx** file, display slide 6.
2. Click Animations > Preview to see how the objects are currently animated.
3. In the Animation Pane, click the Title 2 animation, which has a green star indicating an entrance effect.
4. In the Timing group, click the Move Earlier button to move the animation to the top of the Animation Pane.
5. Click the Group 12 animation, which has a red star indicating an exit effect, and then click the Move Later button twice to move the animation to the bottom of the list.
6. Click the Seconds down arrow at the bottom of the Animation Pane and select Zoom Out.
7. Click the Picture 11 animation in the Animation Pane, and position the pointer on the right edge of the green timeline box until the pointer changes to a double-headed arrow pointer. A ScreenTip indicates the start time and end time.
8. Drag the right edge of the timeline box to the right until the ScreenTip indicates 2.5s.

   ✓ *To make it easier to adjust the timeline, you can increase the width of the Animation Pane by dragging its left border to the left.*

9. Click the expand contents arrow below the Content Placeholder effect in the Animation Pane to see both list items.
10. Use the left and right edges of the first effect's timeline box to adjust the timing on the first paragraph to Start 2s, End 3s.

Using the timeline to change the duration of an effect

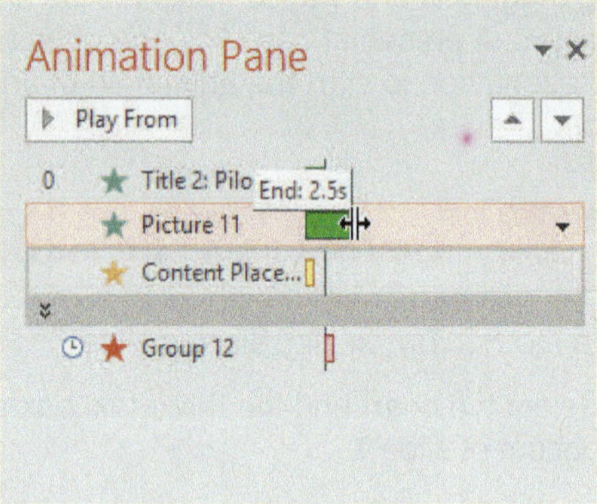

PowerPoint 2016, Windows 10, Microsoft Corporation

11. Adjust the timing of the second paragraph to Start 3s, End 4s.
12. Click the Seconds down arrow and click Zoom In.
13. Position the pointer on the Group 12 exit effect's timeline so that it becomes a horizontal two-headed arrow. Click and drag the entire timeline box to the right until the ScreenTip shows Start: 4.5s.

Setting a delay by dragging a timeline box

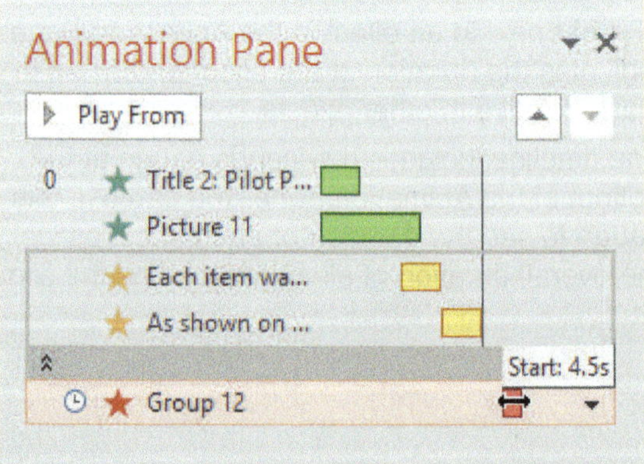

PowerPoint 2016, Windows 10, Microsoft Corporation

14. Preview the animations on the slide to see how timeline adjustments have changed duration and delay.
15. Close the **P40Try_xx** file, saving changes, and exit PowerPoint.

Lesson 40—Practice

Natural Light has asked you to add animations to a presentation that will be available in the showroom for visitors to browse. In this project, you work with a number of custom animation options.

DIRECTIONS

1. Start PowerPoint, if necessary, and open **P40Practice** from the data files for this lesson.
2. Save the file as **P40Practice_xx** in the location where your teacher instructs you to store the files for this lesson.
3. On slide 1, select the Star object.
4. Click **Animations** > **Add Animation** > **Color Pulse** in the Emphasis section of the gallery.
5. Click **Animations** > **Effect Options** and select the last color on the top row.
6. Click **Animations** > **Start** > **After Previous**.
7. Click **Animations** > **Animation Pane** .
8. In the Animation Pane, click the Star animation's down arrow and select **Timing** from the menu.
9. In the dialog box, click the **Repeat** down arrow and select **Until Next Click**. Click **OK**.
10. Select the title and subtitle placeholders on slide 1 and click **Animations** > **Add Animation** > **More Entrance Effects**.
11. Select **Dissolve In** and click **OK**.
12. Select the subtitle placeholder and click **Animations** > **Start** > **After Previous**.
13. In the Animation Pane, click the title animation down arrow and select **Effect Options**.
14. On the Effect tab, click the **After animation** down arrow and select the pale yellow-green square at the far right.
15. Click the **Animate text** down arrow and select **By word**.
16. On the Timing tab, click the **Start** down arrow and select **With Previous**.
17. Click **OK**.
18. Select the timeline box for the title animation and drag the right edge to the right until the ScreenTip reads **By Word: 4.0s**.
19. Drag the right edge of the subtitle animation to end the animation at **7.0s**.
20. Close the Animation Pane and click the **Slide Show** button on the status bar to view your animations in Slide Show view. Click ESC to end the slide show.
21. Insert a footer with your name and the date on all slides except the first slide.
22. Close the presentation, saving changes, and exit PowerPoint.

Lesson 40—Apply

In this project, you continue to work on the Natural Light presentation. You add and adjust animations to complete the presentation.

DIRECTIONS

1. Start PowerPoint, if necessary, and open **P40Apply** from the data files for this lesson.
2. Save the presentation as **P40Apply_xx** in the location where your teacher instructs you to store the files for this lesson.
3. Display slide 4 and apply animation effects as follows:
   a. Set the **Sales** placeholder to **Fade**, **After Previous**, **Fast**.
   b. Select the content placeholder below the Sales object and fade the text into view **After Previous**.
   c. Select the **Sales** placeholder and then click **Animations** > **Animation Painter**.
   d. Click the **Service** placeholder to apply the same settings to the Service placeholder that you applied to the Sales placeholder.
   e. Delay the start of the Service placeholder by 1.5 seconds.
   f. Use the Animation Painter to apply the settings from the left content placeholder to the right one under Service. (You may need to reapply After Previous timing to the second bullet in this placeholder.)
4. Display slide 5 and apply a **Fly In** entrance animation to the SmartArt graphic, **After Previous**, **Fast From Left**. Then modify the animation effects as follows:
   a. Change the SmartArt Animation option in the Effect Options dialog box to **One by one**, then expand the effect to see all the shapes that make up the diagram. (You may need to apply After Previous timing to shapes after the first one.)
   b. Using the timeline, adjust the duration and delay of each shape so that a viewer has time to read the Step 1 shape before the first list shape appears, read the text in this shape before the Step 2 shape appears, and so on.
   c. Use the **Play From** button in the Animation Pane and the **Slide Show** button to test your delays until you are satisfied with the results.
5. On slide 6, set a trigger to animate the picture with a **Wipe** entrance effect, **From Top**, **Fast**, when the slide title is clicked. Then animate the picture description with a **Fade** effect so it appears after the picture.

   ✓ *Hint: You might need to reorder the effects to get the animation right.*
6. On slide 7, apply to the WordArt object the **Fade** entrance effect, the **Grow/Shrink** emphasis effect, and the **Fade** exit effect. Apply the following settings:
   a. Apply **After Previous** to all of the effects.
   b. Change the timing of the entrance effect to **Slow**.
   c. Make sure the timing of the emphasis effect is **Medium**.
   d. Change the timing of the exit effect to **Slow**.
7. On slide 7, add a motion path to the Star object so that it moves to the center of the slide after the WordArt object exits. Then apply a **Grow/Shrink** emphasis effect and use the Effect Options dialog box to increase the size of the object **200%**. Apply **After Previous** to both effects. The motion path should look similar to Figure 40-1.
8. View the slide show to see the effects. Make any adjustments necessary.
9. Insert your name and the date in a footer on all slides except the first slide.
10. Close the presentation, saving changes, and exit PowerPoint.

Figure 40-1

PowerPoint 2016, Windows 10, Microsoft Corporation

Lesson 41

Drawing and Adjusting Tables

➤ What You Will Learn

Drawing a Table
Using the Eraser to Merge Cells
Adjusting Column Width and Row Height
Adjusting Cell and Table Size
Changing Text Alignment and Direction

Software Skills Tables can help you present information clearly and succinctly by displaying information in a column-and-row format. You can customize tables by drawing the structure and adjusting the size of rows and columns, cells, and the table itself. Change the text direction and alignment for a final, expert touch.

What You Can Do

Drawing a Table

- You can create a new table using the Insert Table dialog box to specify the number of columns or rows. Or, you can click the Table button on the Insert tab and then drag the pointer over the table grid to select rows and columns.
- To create a table that may not consist of a regular column-and-row grid, you can use the Draw Table option on the Table menu.
- After you click Draw Table, the pointer changes to a pencil, indicating that you can draw the table you want on the screen.
- Click and drag the outline of the table. Then select Draw Table in the Draw Borders group on the Table Tools Design tab to activate the Draw Table pointer so you can create the table's columns and rows.
- You can change the color, style, and thickness of the lines you draw by using the Pen Style, Pen Weight, and Pen Color tools, also in the Draw Borders group.
- You can also use the Draw Table tool to change border formats on existing tables. Just choose the desired formats (pen style, pen weight, and pen color) and then drag the Draw Table pointer over existing borders to apply the new formats.

Try It! Drawing a Table

1. Start PowerPoint, and begin a new presentation using the Retrospect design.
2. Save the presentation as **P41Try_xx** in the location where your teacher instructs you to store the files for this lesson.
3. Click Home > Layout and select Title Only.
4. Click Insert > Table.
5. Click Draw Table.
6. Drag the pencil to draw the table outline in the content area of the slide. Release the mouse button when the outline is as large as you want it.
7. Save the **P41Try_xx** file, and leave it open to use in the next Try It.

Drag the pencil to draw the outline of the table

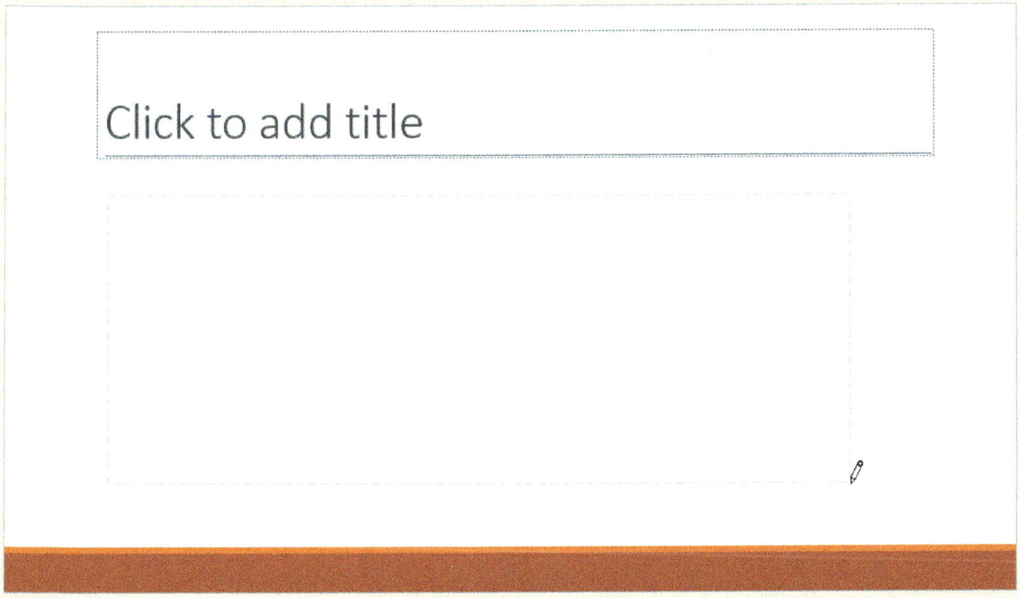

PowerPoint 2016, Windows 10, Microsoft Corporation

Try It! Adding Rows and Columns

1. In the **P41Try_xx** file, click Table Tools Design > Draw Table.
2. Click on the left side of the new table about one-quarter of the way down from the top border and drag the pencil to the right border.

   ✓ *Click slightly inside the border of the table to begin drawing; otherwise, PowerPoint may create a table within a table. If you accidentally insert a new table by clicking in the wrong place, simply press CTRL + Z to undo the error and try again.*
3. Repeat until you have created four rows.
4. Click just inside the top border about halfway across the table and drag the pencil down to the bottom border.
5. Repeat to create a third column.
6. Save the **P41Try_xx** file, and leave it open to use in the next Try It.

Try It! **Changing Border Formats As You Draw**

1. In the **P41Try_xx** file, click Table Tools Design > Pen Style down arrow. Select one of the dotted line styles.
2. Click Table Tools Design > Pen Weight down arrow and select 3 pt.
3. Click Table Tools Design > Pen Color and select Blue from the Standard Colors palette.
4. Click just inside the top table border to the right of the existing column lines, and draw a new line in the new style, weight, and color that extends to the bottom table border.
5. Choose a new Pen Style, Weight, and Color and draw a fourth line, similar to the third.
6. Save the **P41Try_xx** file, and leave it open to use in the next Try It.

Drawing new table lines with various styles

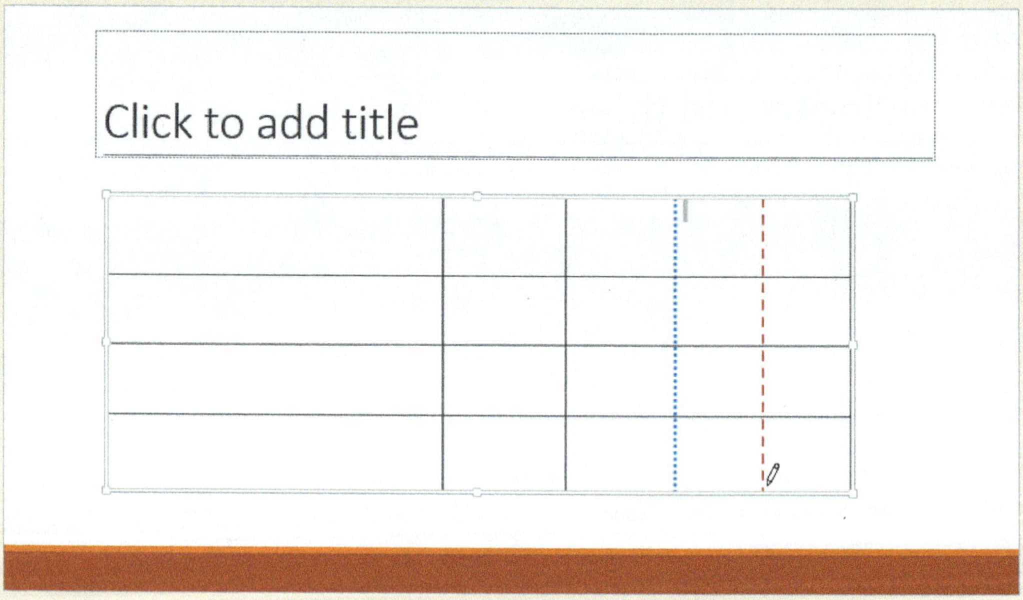

PowerPoint 2016, Windows 10, Microsoft Corporation

Using the Eraser to Merge Cells

- In some cases, you may want to merge cells to create a larger area.
- You might do this, for example, when you want to create a table heading that spans the width of the table, or when you want to create one cell for a column header that spans two subheads.
- One way to combine cells is to use the Merge Cells button on the Table Tools Layout tab. Another way is to use the Eraser tool to remove cell borders.
- The Eraser tool is available in the Draw Borders group of the Table Tools Design tab.
- To erase a line, select the Eraser tool and then click the line segment you want to erase. You can also drag the eraser over the line to erase several segments.
- When you erase a row or column line, the cells in the affected row or column merge to make a larger cell.
- The Eraser tool remains selected until you click Eraser again or click a different tool.

Try It! Using the Eraser to Merge Cells

1. In the **P41Try_xx** file, click the table, if necessary, to select it.
2. Click Table Tools Design > Eraser.
3. Click the first vertical segment in row 1 of your table.
4. Click the remaining vertical segments in row 1.
5. Click Table Tools Design > Eraser again to turn off the tool.
6. Click in the merged row 1 and type **New Courses**.
7. Click outside the table to deselect it.
8. Save the **P41Try_xx** file, and leave it open to use in the next Try It.

Adjusting Column Width and Row Height

- PowerPoint makes it simple for you to adjust the column widths in your table.
- Simply position the mouse pointer over the column border you want to adjust. When the pointer changes to double vertical lines with right- and left-pointing arrows, click and drag the column border to increase or decrease the column width.
- Similarly, to adjust the row height, hover the mouse pointer over the row you want to change.
- The mouse pointer changes to double horizontal lines with up- and down-pointing arrows. Click and drag the row border to increase or reduce the height.

Try It! Adjusting Column Width and Row Height

1. In the **P41Try_xx** file, position the mouse pointer over the leftmost column divider.
2. When the pointer changes, click and drag the column divider to the left, enlarging the second column.
3. Release the mouse button to complete the move.
4. Adjust the three columns on the right by dragging the column dividers until the columns appear to be of equal width.

Drag column and row dividers to adjust the table layout

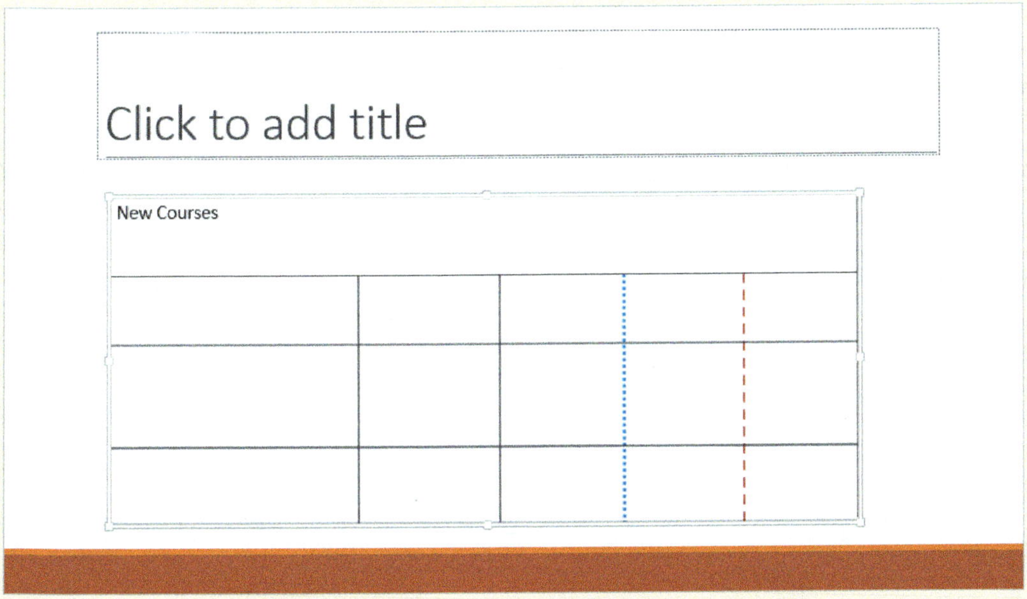

PowerPoint 2016, Windows 10, Microsoft Corporation

(continued)

Try It! Adjusting Column Width and Row Height *(continued)*

5. Position the mouse pointer over the row divider above the bottom row of the table.
6. When the pointer changes, drag the row divider downward, enlarging the height of the middle row and making the table a little taller.
7. Release the mouse button to complete the operation.
8. Save the **P41Try_xx** file, and leave it open to use in the next Try It.

Adjusting Cell and Table Size

- The tools in the Table Tools Layout tab enable you to adjust cell and table size.
- Use the Table Column Width and Table Row Height boxes in the Cell Size group to set specific column widths or row heights.
- To space the rows or columns evenly throughout the table, use the Distribute Rows or Distribute Columns tool.
- In the Table Size group, you can enter size values for the Height and Width of the table.
- You can also drag a table handle or border to change the size of the table on the slide.
- Click the Lock Aspect Ratio check box if you want to preserve the shape of the current table no matter how you may resize it.

Try It! Changing Cell Size

1. In the **P41Try_xx** file, click in the second row in the table.
2. Click Table Tools Layout, click in the Row Height box, and type **0.75**.
3. Click Table Tools Layout, click in the Column Width box, and type **1.5**. Press ENTER.

✓ *Notice that the new column or row value is applied only to the current selection. To apply the new value to more than one column or row, select the additional columns or rows you want to change before entering the new value.*

4. Save the **P41Try_xx** file, and leave it open to use in the next Try It.

Try It! Distributing Rows and Columns

1. In the **P41Try_xx** file, click in column 2 in the table.
2. Click Table Tools Layout > Distribute Rows ⊞. All rows in the table are now the same height.
3. Click Table Tools Layout > Distribute Columns ⊞. All columns in the table are now the same width.
4. Save the **P41Try_xx** file, and leave it open to use in the next Try It.

Try It! Resizing the Table

1. In the **P41Try_xx** file, select the table.
2. Click the Lock Aspect Ratio check box on the Table Tools Layout tab.
3. Click in the Height box and type **4**.
4. Click the lower-right corner of the table and change the size of the table by dragging to the right until the Width shows **8.5**.
5. Release the mouse button. Because aspect ratio is locked, the height may also change as you adjust the width.
6. Save the **P41Try_xx** file, and leave it open to use in the next Try It.

Resize the table with Lock Aspect Ratio selected

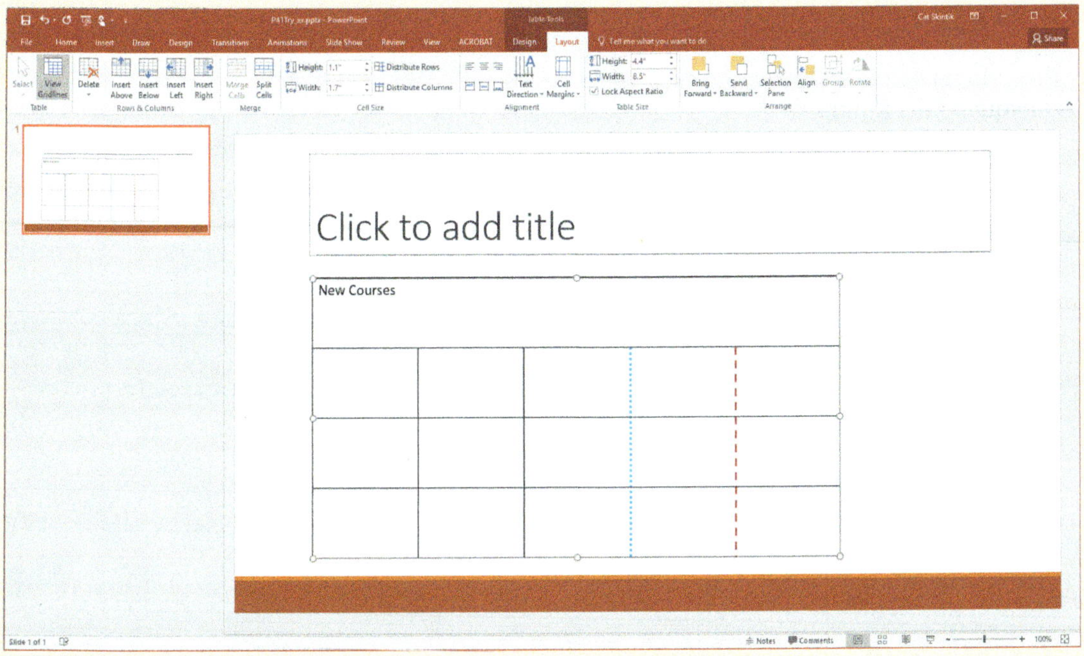

PowerPoint 2016, Windows 10, Microsoft Corporation

Changing Text Alignment and Direction

- The way you align your text can help readers make sense of the information you're presenting.
- You can align text horizontally at the left, center, or right, or vertically at the top, middle, or bottom of a table cell.
- You can also change text direction so that text appears vertically in a cell. This is sometimes helpful when you have long column titles but don't want to use wide columns.
- When changing text direction, you can choose Horizontal, Rotate all text 90°, Rotate all text 270°, or Stacked.
- You can also choose More Options in the Text Direction list to further control cell margins, alignment, and spacing options.

Try It! Changing Text Alignment and Direction

1. In the **P41Try_xx** file, click in the second row of the table, and type the following in each of the cells:

   No.
   Course Title
   Instructor
   Days Offered
   Features

2. Select the row of text you just entered and click Table Tools Layout > Center.
3. Click Table Tools Layout > Center Vertically.
4. With the column labels still selected, click Table Tools Layout > Text Direction.
5. Click Rotate all text 270°.
6. Click Table Tools Layout > Text Direction, then click More Options. The Format Shape task pane appears.
7. Click the Vertical alignment down arrow and select Center Middle.
8. Close the task pane.
9. Adjust the row height as needed to accommodate the text.
10. Close the **P41Try_xx** file, saving changes, and exit PowerPoint.

New text alignment

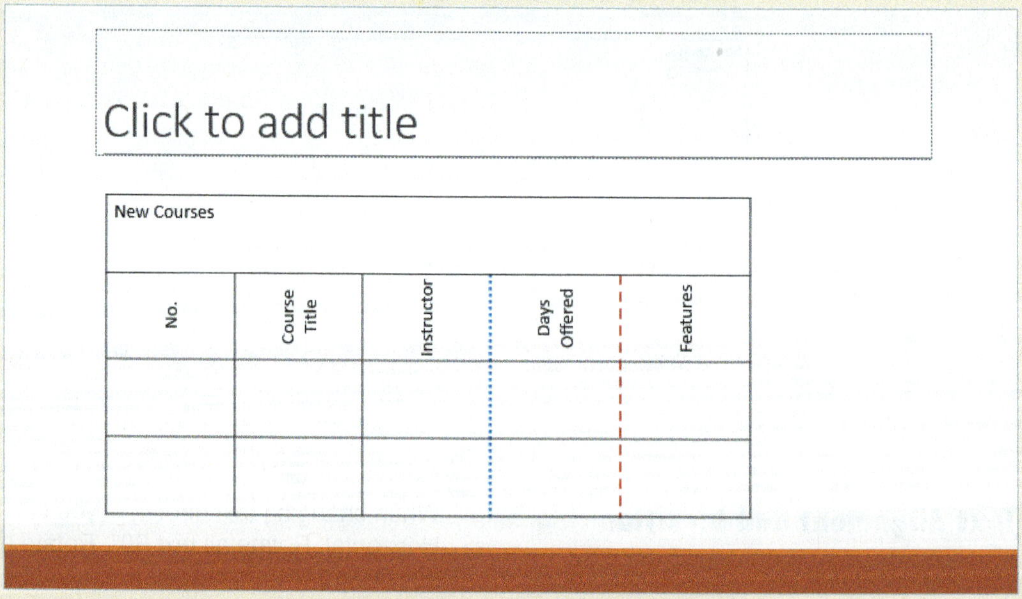

PowerPoint 2016, Windows 10, Microsoft Corporation

Lesson 41—Practice

Your local community college is offering a series of summer classes that give students a range of experiences in different fields. One of the professors has asked you to create a PowerPoint presentation that tells a bit about each class. At the end of the presentation, you want to include a table that shows the features in each class so that students can easily decide among the course offerings. In this project, you begin by drawing the table and aligning text.

DIRECTIONS

1. Start PowerPoint, if necessary, and open **P41Practice** from the data files for this lesson.
2. Save the presentation as **P41Practice_xx** in the location where your teacher instructs you to store the files for this lesson.
3. Display slide 2 and click in the title placeholder. Type **Course Offerings**.
4. Click **Insert** > **Table** > **Draw Table**, and move the pointer to the content area.
5. Click and drag the pencil to draw a table about **4"** high by **10"** wide.

   ✓ *Don't worry if the table border uses the same formats you applied earlier in the Try It exercise.*
6. On the Table Tools Design tab, click the **Pen Style** down arrow and choose the solid line, if necessary.
7. Click the **Pen Weight** down arrow and click **2¼ pt**.
8. Click **Pen Color** and choose a dark orange color.
9. Click just below the top border of the table and drag the mouse down to the bottom to create a column divider.
10. Repeat the previous step three times so that you create five columns.
11. Click at the left side of the table and draw a line to the right side of the table to create a new row.
12. Repeat the previous step four times so that you have a total of six rows in your table.
13. Click **Table Tools Design** > **Eraser** and erase all the column segments in row 1. Click the Eraser button a second time to turn off the tool.
14. Merge the last two columns by highlighting all cells in the last two columns of the table and then clicking **Table Tools Layout** > **Merge Cells**.
15. Resize the column on the right to about **3"** by dragging the rightmost column divider to the right.
16. Add the table title and column labels as shown in Figure 41-1 on the next page.
17. Select the column labels and click **Table Tools Layout** > **Center**.
18. With the labels still selected, click **Table Tools Layout** > **Center Vertically**.
19. Insert your name and the date on all slides.
20. **With your teacher's permission,** print slide 2. It should look similar to Figure 41-1.
21. Close the presentation, saving changes, and exit PowerPoint.

Figure 41-1

PowerPoint 2016, Windows 10, Microsoft Corporation

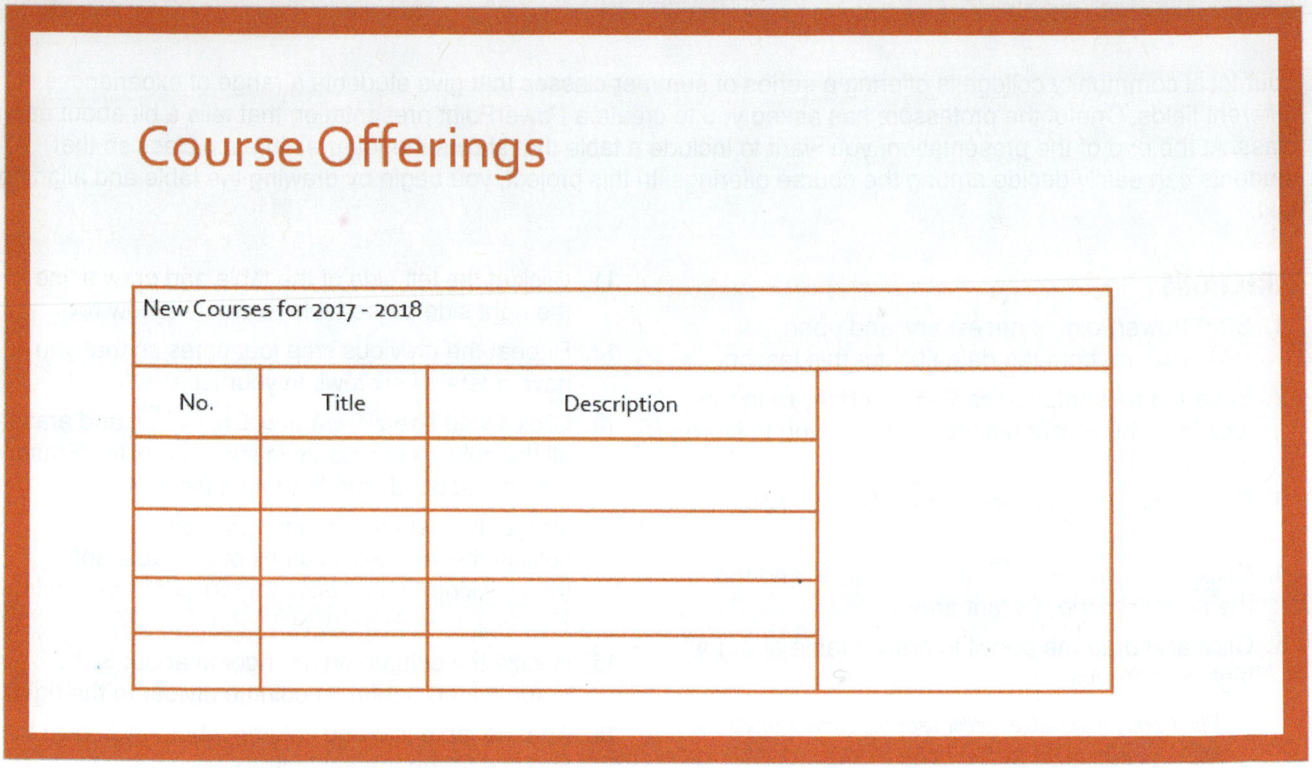

Lesson 41—Apply

In this project, you continue working with the Sinclair College presentation. You adjust cell sizes, change alignments and text direction, and use the Draw Table tool and Eraser to change the table layout.

DIRECTIONS

1. Start PowerPoint, if necessary, and open **P41Apply** from the data files for this lesson.
2. Save the presentation as **P41Apply_xx** in the location where your teacher instructs you to store the files for this lesson.
3. Display slide 2 and use **Distribute Rows** to make all rows the same height.
4. Use **Distribute Columns** to make all columns the same width.
5. Use the **Draw Table** tool to draw a diagonal line in the last, empty column, as shown in Figure 41-2 on the next page.
6. Click at the top of the divided column and type **300 and above for**, press ENTER, and type **Full-Time students**.
7. Press ENTER eight times and then change to right alignment. Type **299 and below for**, press ENTER, and type **Part-Time students**.
8. Insert a new column at the far left of the table, and use the Eraser tool to erase all row borders in the new column.
9. Change the column width to **1"** and type **2017 - 2018**.
10. Change the text direction to rotate all text 270°, and then center the text vertically and horizontally. Change the font size to **36 points**.

11. Delete the text *for 2017 - 2018* from the first row of the table.
12. Change the width of the No. column to **1.5"**, the Description column to **3"**, and the divided column to **2.6"**.
13. Insert your name and the date on all slides.
14. **With your teacher's permission,** print slide 2. It should look similar to Figure 41-2.
15. Close the presentation, saving changes, and exit PowerPoint.

Figure 41-2

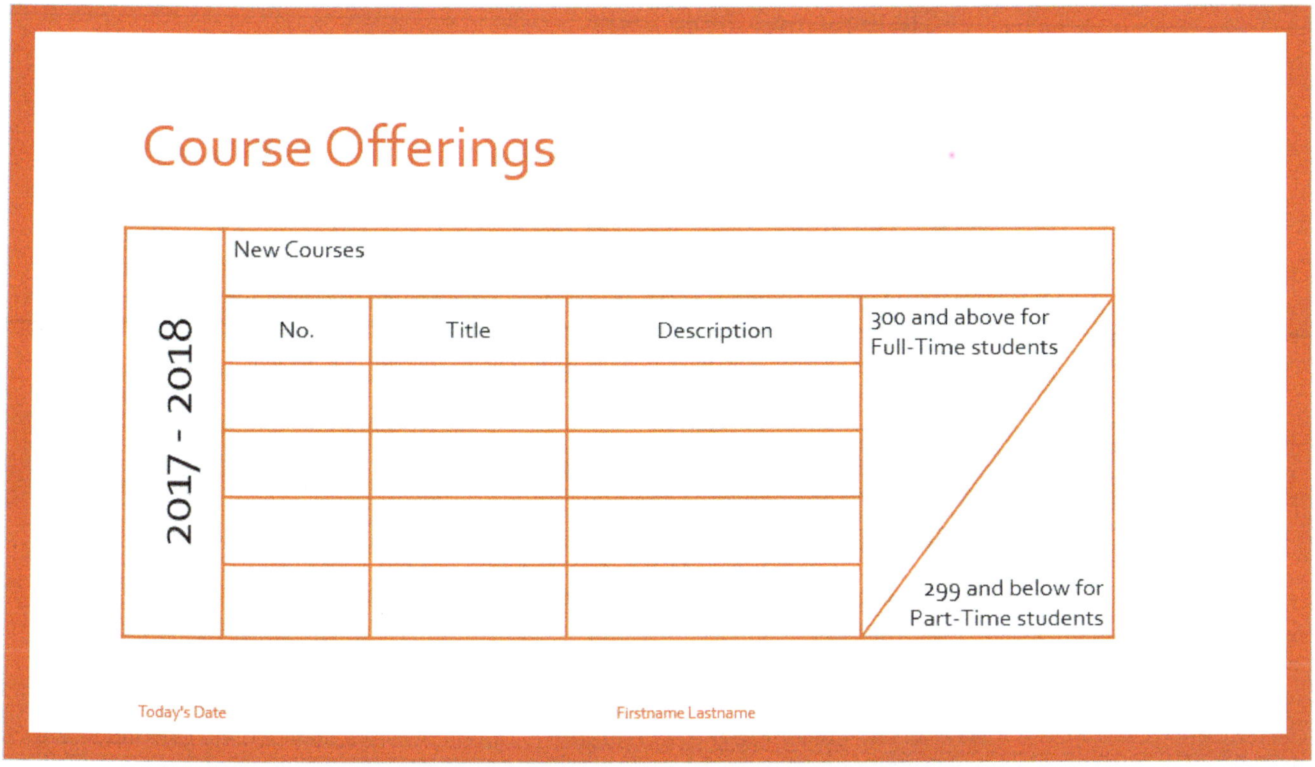

PowerPoint 2016, Windows 10, Microsoft Corporation

Lesson 42

Formatting Tables

➤ What You Will Learn

Customizing a Table Style
Modifying Cell Fill, Borders, and Effects
Adding an Image to a Table

Software Skills You can modify the way a table style looks by selecting and deselecting formatting options. If a table style does not provide the formats you want, you can apply shading, borders, and effects to customize the table appearance. You can add images to a table as either fill or background for a special touch.

What You Can Do

Customizing a Table Style

- The easiest way to format a table is to apply a table style from the Table Styles gallery on the Table Tools Design tab.
- A table style applies shading, border, and font formatting to a table using the color scheme for the current theme.
- You can customize the appearance of the table style by selecting options in the Table Style Options group on the Table Tools Design tab.
- Click the check boxes in the Table Style Options group to add specific elements to your table, such as emphasis on the header row or first column, or banded rows or columns.
- These options control how shading and borders are used in your table style.
- As you select or deselect these options, the table styles shown in the Table Styles gallery change to reflect your choices.

Try It! **Customizing a Table Style**

1. Start PowerPoint, and open **P42TryA** from the data files for this lesson.
2. Save the presentation as **P42TryA_xx** in the location where your teacher instructs you to store the files for this lesson.
3. Click in the table to select it and display the Table Tools Design tab.
4. In the Table Styles gallery, click the More button and then select the Medium Style 1 – Accent 1 table style to apply it.
5. In the Table Style Options group, click Total Row to add formatting for a total row—a double-line border above the last row in the table.
6. Deselect Total Row and select First Column. Bold formatting is added to the entries in the first column.
7. Select Banded Rows to apply shading on alternate rows of the table.
8. Save the **P42TryA_xx** file, and leave it open for the next Try It.

Customize a table style

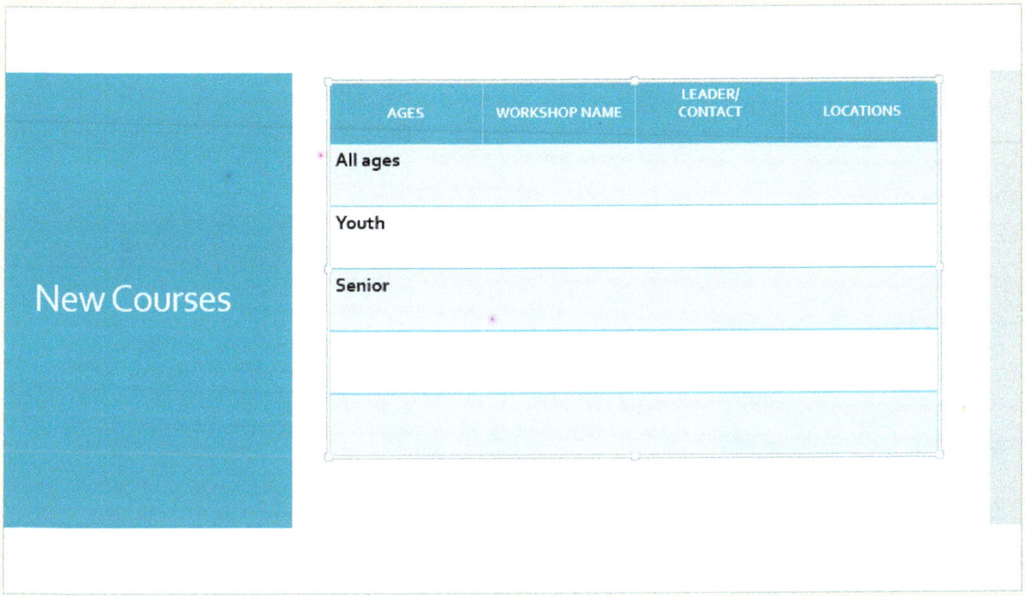

PowerPoint 2016, Windows 10, Microsoft Corporation

Modifying Cell Fill, Borders, and Effects

- After you apply a table style to your table, you can fine-tune the look by changing the appearance of selected cells, rows, or columns using shading, borders, or effects available on the Table Tools Design tab.
- For example, you can make a section of a table stand out by changing the shading of the section.
- Shading options include solid colors, pictures, gradients, and textures.
- You can also use borders to give a section of cells a special look.
- Adjust Pen Style, Pen Weight, and Pen Color options and then apply those formats to cell or table borders.
- You can apply the Cell Bevel effect to emphasize cells, or apply shadow or reflection effects to the table as a whole.
- You can also use the Format Shape task pane to apply formatting to the table or its cells.

Try It! Modifying Cell Fill, Borders, and Effects

1. In the P42TryA_xx file, select the cells under the column header *Workshop Name*.
2. Click Table Tools Design > Shading.
3. Click Gold, Accent 2 in the Theme Colors palette.
4. With the cells still selected, click Table Tools Design > Shading > Gradient > More Gradients. The Format Shape task pane appears.
5. In the Format Shape task pane, click the Gradient fill option button. The cells fill with a default gradient. Close the Format Shape task pane.
6. Select the cells under *Ages*.
7. On the Table Tools Design tab, click Pen Style and select the dashed line style. Click Pen Weight and click 2¼ pt. Click Pen Color and click Red, Accent 6.
8. Click Table Tools Design > Borders drop-down arrow.
9. Click All Borders.
10. Select all the cells in the row containing the column labels.
11. Click Table Tools Design > Effects.
12. Click Cell Bevel and click the Cool Slant bevel style.
13. Click outside the table to see the effect of the beveling.
14. Save the P42TryA_xx file, and leave it open for the next Try It.

Add a border to cells

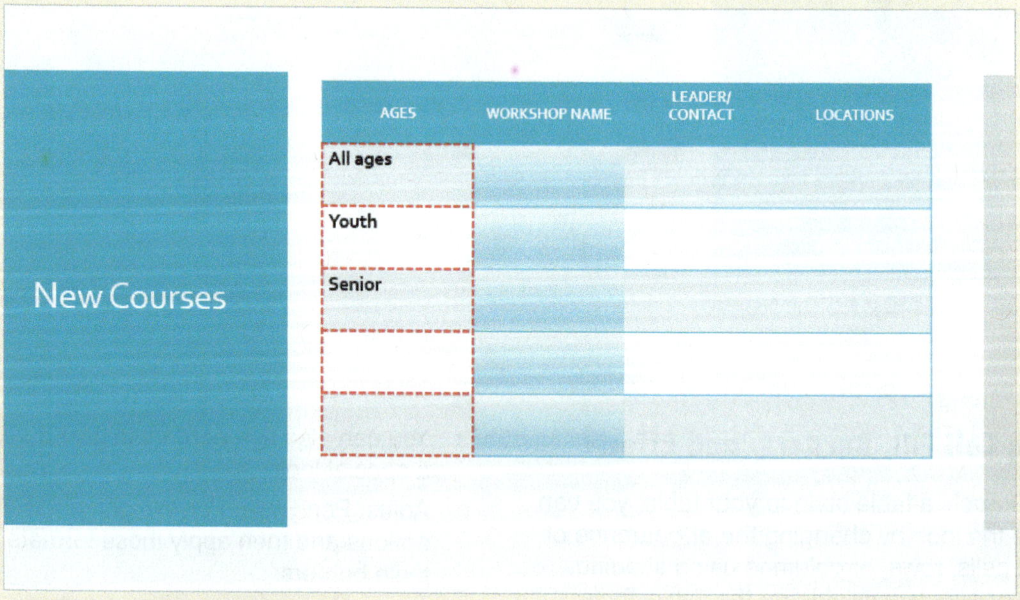

Adding an Image to a Table

- You can add a special touch to your tables by including pictures or textures.
- You might add pictures of products you're introducing, company logos, or images that represent particular programs or people.
- You cannot insert a picture as an object in a table cell; you must instead insert the picture as a fill by using the Picture option on the Shading palette.
- After you select the Picture option, you can browse to a file on your computer, choose a picture from your OneDrive site, or search the Web for an image.
- If you choose an image that is not large enough to fill the selected area, PowerPoint will tile the image so the amount of space you selected is covered.
- Pictures may be distorted when they are inserted in table cells that have a height and width different from the picture. The cell will not automatically resize to fit the picture. You may need to adjust row height and column width to display the picture correctly.
- You can add an image to an individual cell or apply the image to the entire table background.
- An image added to the table background may be obscured by table style formatting you have already applied to the table. To see a table background, you may need to remove shading or other fills from the table cells.
- If you add an image to the table background, be sure to preview your slides to ensure that the text shows up against the image you have added.

Try It! Adding an Image to a Cell

1. In the **P42TryA_xx** file, click the first cell in column 3 beneath the column label.
2. Click Table Tools Design > Shading > Picture.
3. Click Browse in the From a file area, navigate to the data files for this lesson, click **P42TryB_picture.jpg**, and click Insert.
4. Resize the row height and column width to display the photo without distortion.
5. In the rows below, insert two additional photos in the data files folder, **P42TryC_picture.jpg** and **P42TryD_picture.jpg**. Adjust row height as necessary.
6. Remove the unused table rows by right-clicking each row and choosing Delete Rows on the Mini toolbar.
7. Save the **P42Try_xx** file, and leave it open for the next Try It.

Add pictures to cells

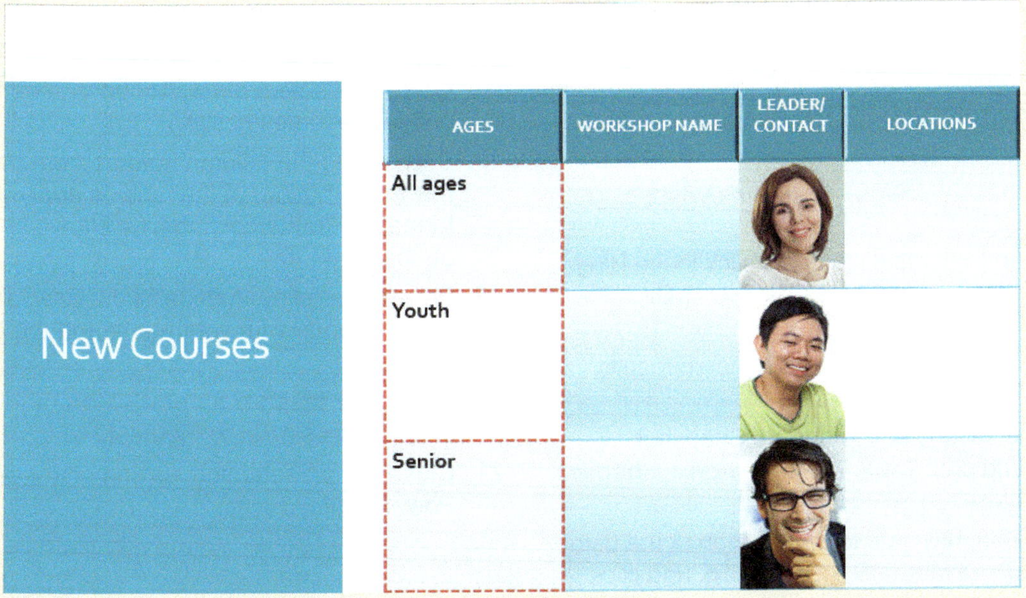

PowerPoint 2016, Windows 10, Microsoft Corporation

Try It! **Adding an Image to the Table Background**

1. In the P42TryA_xx file, click Table Tools Design > Shading > Table Background > Picture.
2. Click Browse, navigate to the data files for this lesson, and choose P42TryE_picture.jpg.
3. Click Insert. You will not see the background because of the table style shading.
4. Select all cells and click Table Tools Design > Shading > No Fill. The background image appears.
5. Close the P42TryA_xx file, saving changes, and exit PowerPoint.

Lesson 42—Practice

Thorn Hill Gardens wants you to work on several tables in a new presentation on the organization's events and workshops. In this project, you customize formats and add pictures to one of the tables.

DIRECTIONS

1. Start PowerPoint, if necessary, and open **P42PracticeA** from the data files for this lesson.
2. Save the presentation as **P42PracticeA_xx** in the location where your teacher instructs you to store the files for this lesson.
3. Display slide 2 and select the table.
4. On the Table Tools Design tab, in the Table Style Options group, select **Header Row**, if necessary, and then select **First Column**.
5. In the Table Styles gallery, click the **Medium Style 1 – Accent 1** table style.
6. Adjust the table style by applying **Banded Columns**.
7. Click in the first cell under the Snapshot column heading.
8. Click **Table Tools Design** > **Shading** > **Picture**.
9. In the Insert Pictures dialog box, click in the Bing Image Search box and type **poinsettia**. Click **Search**.
10. Choose a picture or photo in the search results and click **Insert**.
11. Click in the second cell under the Snapshot heading, and click **Table Tools Design** > **Shading** > **Picture**.
12. Click **Browse**, navigate to the location of the data files, click **P42PracticeB_picture.jpg**, and click **Insert**.
13. Repeat steps 11 and 12 to insert the **P42PracticeC_picture.jpg** file in the third cell under the Snapshot heading.
14. Adjust the height of the rows that contain pictures to **1.3"**.
15. Adjust the height of the column header row to **0.6"** and apply Center Vertically alignment.
16. With the column header row selected, click **Table Tools Design** > **Effects** > **Cell Bevel**. Click the **Angle** bevel option.
17. On the Table Tools Design tab, in the Draw Borders group, click **Pen Style** and select the single line, click **Pen Weight** and select **¾ pt**, and click **Pen Color** and select **Lime, Accent 1**. The Draw Table pointer becomes active.
18. Draw along the column borders from the header row to the bottom of the table to apply green border formatting to the columns, as shown in Figure 42-1 on the next page.
19. Preview the slide in Slide Show view, and then insert a footer with your name and the date on all slides.
20. **With your teacher's permission,** print slide 2. It should look similar to Figure 42-1.
21. Close the presentation, saving changes, and exit PowerPoint.

Figure 42-1

PowerPoint 2016, Windows 10, Microsoft Corporation

Lesson 42—Apply

In this project, you continue to work with the Thorn Hill presentation. You concentrate on the workshop table and improve its appearance by adding a picture background and customizing shading and border options.

DIRECTIONS

1. Start PowerPoint, if necessary, and open **P42ApplyA** from the data files for this lesson.
2. Save the presentation as **P42ApplyA_xx** in the location where your teacher instructs you to store the files for this lesson.
3. Display slide 3, select the table, and insert **P42ApplyB_picture.jpg** as the table background.
4. Select row 1 and apply shading of **Lime, Accent 1**. Then apply the **Linear Left** gradient from the Dark Variations gallery.
5. Select the cells in the first column below the *Program* heading.
6. Right-click the selected cells and click **Format Shape**.
7. In the Format Shape task pane, expand the **FILL** settings and click **Picture or texture fill**. Click the **Texture** down arrow and select the **Stationery** texture. Adjust transparency to **30%**.
8. To make it easier to read the text in the rest of the table, select the remaining unformatted cells, apply a **Solid fill** of **White, Background 1**, and adjust transparency to **70%**.
9. Change all borders in the table to a dotted or dashed line format with a weight and color of your choice.

10. Apply a Shadow effect of your choice to the table.
11. Insert your name and the date on all slides.
12. **With your teacher's permission,** print slide 3. It should look similar to Figure 42-2.
13. Close the presentation, saving changes, and exit PowerPoint.

Figure 42-2

PowerPoint 2016, Windows 10, Microsoft Corporation

Lesson 43

Formatting Charts

➤ What You Will Learn

Adding Trendlines and Error Bars
Formatting Chart Text
Fine-Tuning Chart Appearance

Software Skills You can customize a chart by changing a wide variety of formatting options. Insert trendlines and error bars to make chart analysis easier. Apply font formatting to emphasize the chart text. Format any part of the chart to make it stand out on the slide.

WORDS TO KNOW

Error bars
A chart feature available for some chart types that enables you to display the amount of error that may be present in a graphed quantity.

Trendlines
A chart feature that displays a line showing the progression of value change over time.

What You Can Do

Adding Trendlines and Error Bars

- PowerPoint includes a number of features you can use to add advanced formatting to your chart elements. You will explore some of those features in this lesson. Not all advanced formatting options are available for all types of charts.
- Two advanced tools that can help you analyze and present your data are **trendlines** and **error bars**.
- Trendlines show the progression of your data over time, and error bars show the amount of uncertainty that may be possible for the given data item.
- You cannot add trendlines to 3-D, radar, pie, doughnut, or surface charts.
- You can customize trendlines and error bars by changing the line color, style, regression type, and format.

Try It! Adding and Modifying Trendlines

1. Start PowerPoint, and open **P43Try** from the data files for this lesson.
2. Save the presentation as **P43Try_xx** in the location where your teacher instructs you to store the files for this lesson.
3. Click slide 3 and click in the chart to select it.
4. Click the Chart Elements button + to display the pop-out menu of chart elements.
5. Click the Trendline check box to display the trendline. A default linear trendline appears on the chart, as shown in the figure below.
6. With the Chart Elements menu still displayed, move the pointer to the right of Trendline to display the right-pointing arrow, and then click the arrow to display a menu of further options.
7. Click More Options to open the Format Trendline task pane.
8. In the Format Trendline task pane, click the Trendline Options heading to expand options, then click Moving Average.
9. Click the Fill & Line icon and select Solid Line.
10. Click the Color down arrow and choose Gold, Accent 5.
11. Click the Width up arrow until 3 pt appears.
12. Click the Begin Arrow type down arrow and select Diamond Arrow.
13. Click the End Arrow type down arrow and select Diamond Arrow.
14. On the chart, click the original linear trendline and press DEL to remove it.
15. Save the **P43Try_xx** file, and leave it open to use in the next Try It.

A trendline in a chart

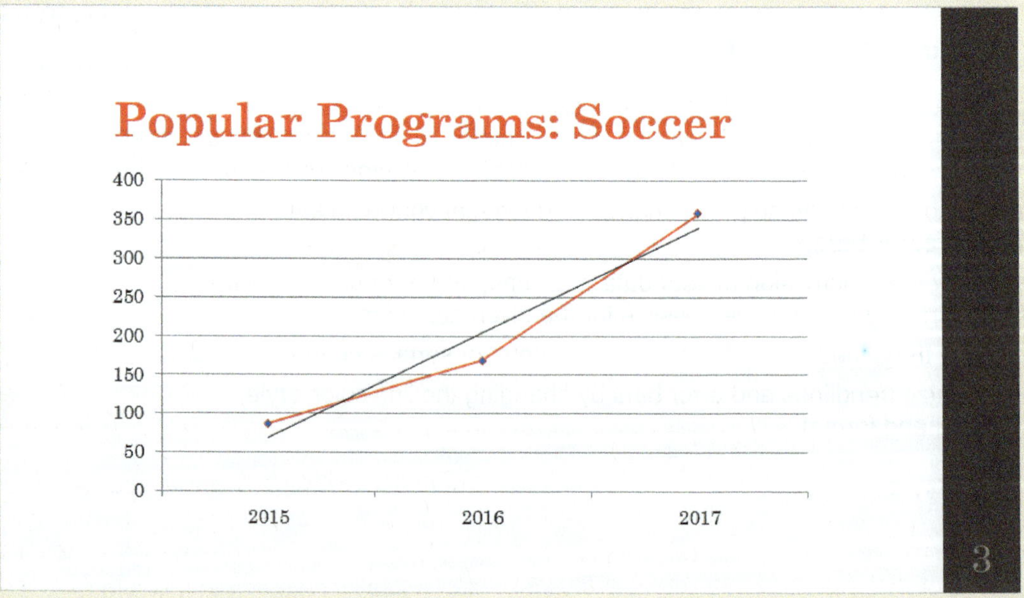

PowerPoint 2016, Windows 10, Microsoft Corporation

Try It! Adding Error Bars

1. In the P43Try_xx file, click slide 4 and select the chart.
2. Click the Chart Elements button to display the menu of chart elements, and then click the Error Bars check box.
3. Click the right-pointing arrow to the right of Error Bars and then click More Options.
4. In the Add Error Bars dialog box, make sure 2015 is selected, and then click OK.

   ✓ *If the Add Error Bars dialog box does not appear, you have added error bars to only one series. Click Undo, select the outside border of the chart, and repeat steps 2 and 3.*
5. In the Format Error Bars task pane, click the Fill & Line icon and then click Gradient line.
6. Click the Preset gradients down arrow and select Medium Gradient – Accent 6.
7. Click the Width up arrow until 2.5 pt appears.

   ✓ *Note that the changes are applied only to the data series currently selected. To modify another set of error bars, choose the data series by clicking on the chart.*
8. Close the Format Error Bars task pane.
9. Save the P43Try_xx file, and leave it open to use in the next Try It.

The chart with formatted error bars

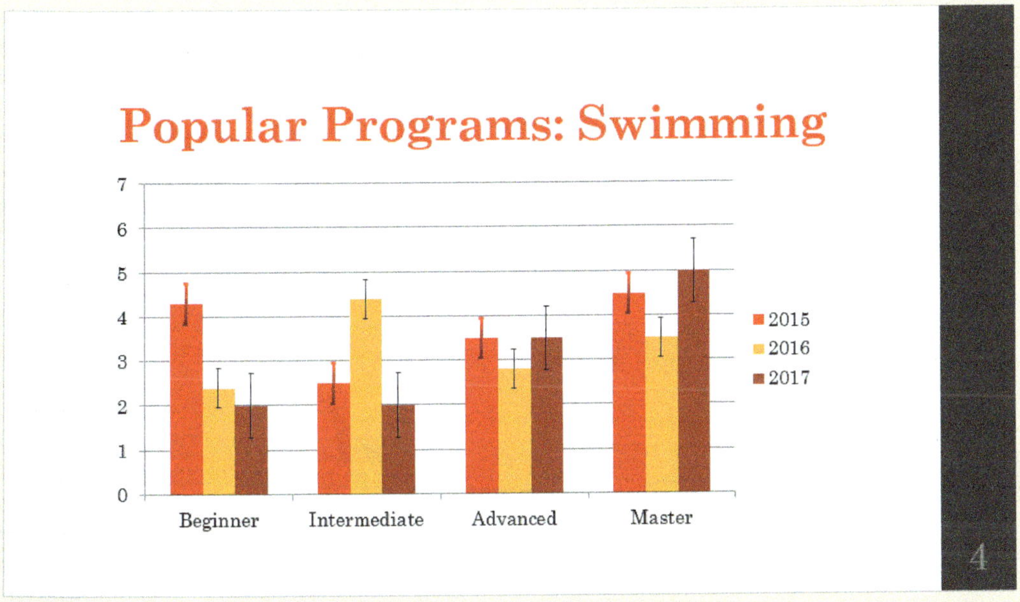

Formatting Chart Text

- You can change formats for any text that appears on a chart. Adjust font, font size, font style, or font color to emphasize text.
- By default, numbers that appear on chart axes use the General number style, unless you have applied number formatting in the data sheet used to create the chart.
- In the Format task pane, you can adjust number formatting for the specific chart element.
- To fine-tune the appearance of axis labels, you can adjust alignment and text direction. You can also specify an angle on which to set labels, which can be helpful when you have a number of axis labels that would otherwise crowd each other.

Try It! **Formatting Chart Text**

1. In the **P43Try_xx** file, display slide 2.
2. Click the legend to select it.
3. Click Home > Font Size > 14, and then click Bold **B**.
4. Click the Chart Elements button [+], point to Data Labels, click the right-pointing arrow, and select More Options.
5. In the Format Data Labels task pane, with Label Options selected, click Inside End in the Label Position options.
6. Click Number to expand those options.
7. Click the Category down arrow and click Currency.
8. In the Decimal places box, type **0**.
9. Click Text Options. In the Text Fill area, click the Color down arrow and select Black, Text 1.
10. Display slide 4 and click the horizontal axis to select it.
11. In the Format Axis task pane, click Text Options and then click the Textbox icon.
12. Click the Custom angle box and type **-20**.
13. Close the Format Axis task pane.
14. Save the **P43Try_xx** file, and leave it open for the next Try It.

Changing font and number formats on a chart

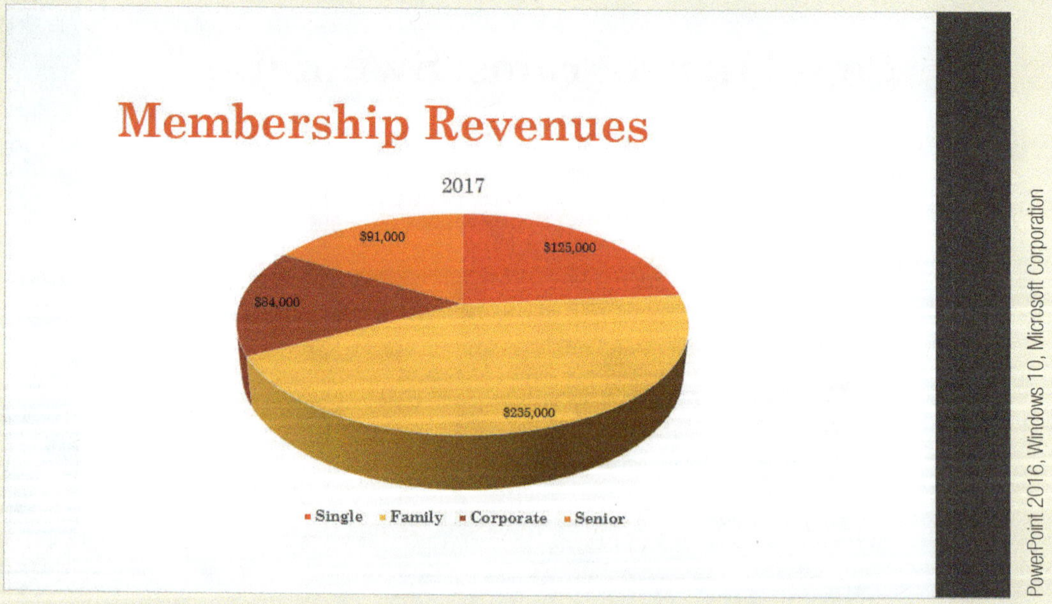

Fine-Tuning Chart Appearance

- PowerPoint offers many ways to customize the appearance of charts.
  - You can choose to start numbering on an axis from a particular value, and select numbering intervals.
  - You can add axis labels to provide more information about the data.
  - For column and bar charts, you can adjust the gap and overlap of series columns and bars.
  - You can change the appearance of a specific data series with a new fill. For a line chart, you can format the markers to make them stand out more.
  - You can customize the plot or chart background to improve appearance.

- When applying a number of different formats to a chart, you can save time in selecting the element to format by clicking the down arrow next to the currently selected element in the Format task pane to display a drop-down list of other elements.
- Clicking an element in this list displays the task pane options for that element.

Try It! Changing Axis Formats

1. In the **P43Try_xx** file, display slide 3 and click the chart to select it.
2. Click the Chart Elements button + and point to Gridlines. Click the right-pointing arrow and then click Primary Major Vertical to add vertical gridlines to the chart.
3. With the Chart Elements menu still displayed, click the Axis Titles check box, click the right-pointing arrow, and deselect Primary Horizontal.
4. With the default axis title displayed on the vertical axis, type **Participants**.
5. Right-click the vertical axis and click Format Axis to display the Format Axis task pane.
6. Under Units, change Major to 25.0.
7. Under Bounds, change Minimum to 75.0 and press ENTER.
8. Save the **P43Try_xx** file, and leave it open for the next Try It.

Try It! Changing the Appearance of Data Series

1. In the **P43Try_xx** file, click the orange data series line on the chart, right-click, and select Format Data Series to display the Format Data Series task pane.
2. Click the Fill & Line icon. In the Line settings, click the Width up arrow until 4 pt appears.
3. Click Marker to display the settings for the data markers, and then click Marker Options to expand those settings.
4. Click Built-in, click the Type down arrow, and click one of the large square shapes. Then click the Size up arrow until 16 appears.

Line chart formats

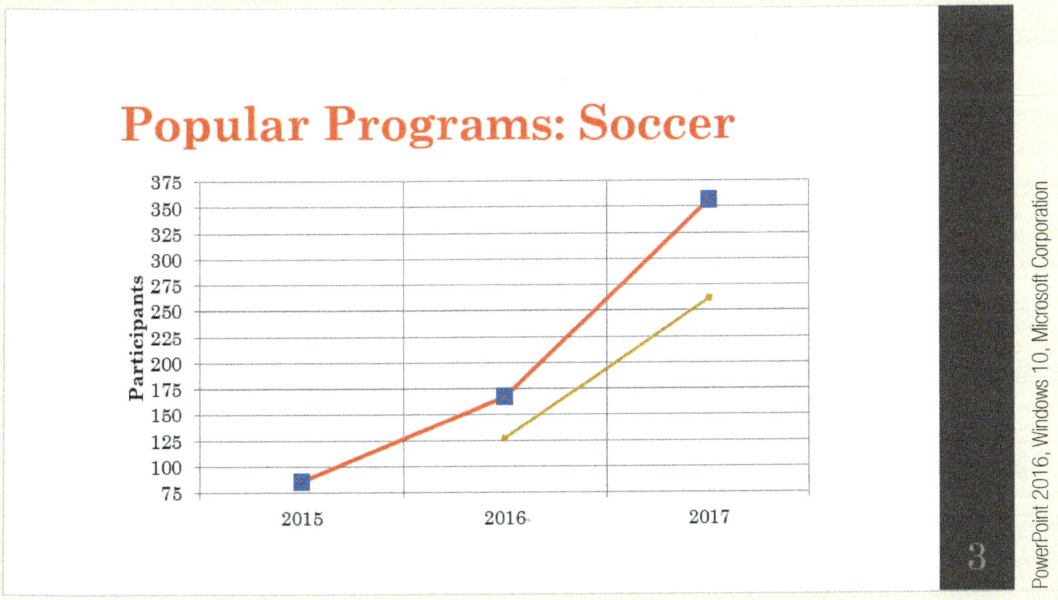

(continued)

Try It! Changing the Appearance of Data Series *(continued)*

5. Display slide 4 and select the chart by clicking its outside border. The task pane should be Format Chart Area.
6. In the task pane, click the down arrow to the right of Chart Options to see a list of chart elements.
7. Click Series "2016" to select that data series on the chart and display series options in the task pane.
8. In the Fill settings, click Gradient fill and then apply the Bottom Spotlight – Accent 2 preset gradient.
9. Click the Series Options icon.
10. Click the Series Overlap down arrow until -10% appears.
11. Save the **P43Try_xx** file, and leave it open for the next Try It.

Try It! Formatting a Chart Background

1. In the **P43Try_xx** file, click the down arrow next to Series Options in the task pane and click Chart Area.
2. Click the Fill & Line icon, and then click Picture or texture fill in the Fill settings.
3. Click the Texture down arrow and then click the Water droplets texture.
4. Change the transparency setting to 30%, if necessary.
5. Scroll down in the task pane to display the Border settings.
6. In the Border settings:
   a. Click Solid line.
   b. Click the Color down arrow and click Blue from Standard Colors.
   c. Click the Width up arrow until 3 pt appears.
7. Click the Rounded corners check box at the bottom of the task pane, and then close the task pane.
8. Close the **P43Try_xx** file, saving changes, and exit PowerPoint.

Column chart formats

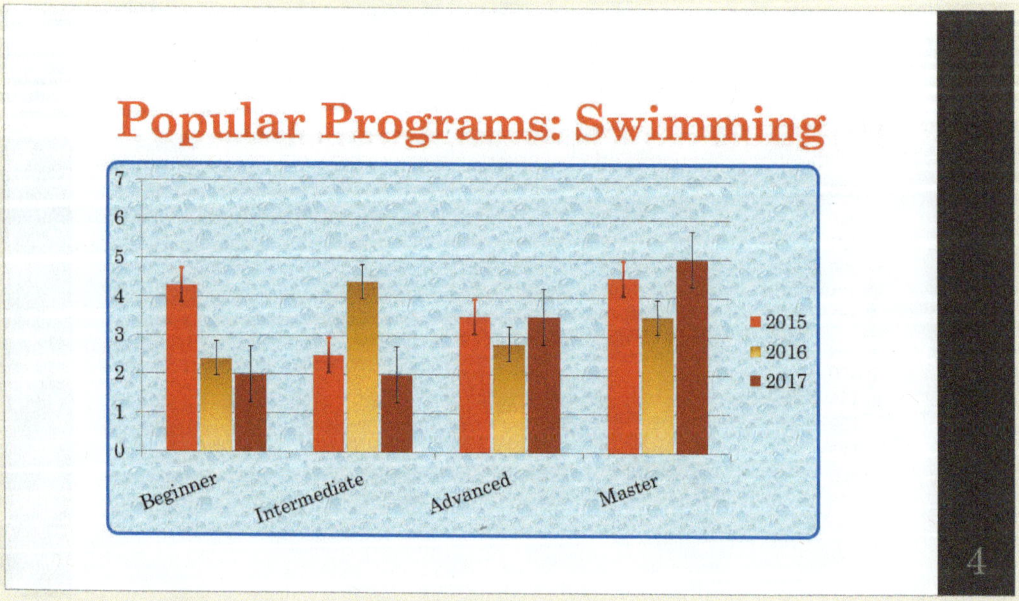

PowerPoint 2016, Windows 10, Microsoft Corporation

Lesson 43—Practice

Jones & Madden Realty is preparing a presentation on housing sales and trends in a city neighborhood. In this project, you work on the charts included in the presentation to improve their usefulness and appearance.

DIRECTIONS

1. Start PowerPoint, if necessary, and open **P43Practice** from the data files for this lesson.
2. Save the presentation as **P43Practice_xx** in the location where your teacher instructs you to store the files for this lesson.
3. Display slide 3.
4. Click one of the **Single-Family** bars to select that data series.
5. Click the **Chart Elements** button + and then click **Trendline** to add a trendline for the Single-Family series.
6. Right-click the trendline and select **Format Trendline**.
7. Click the **Fill & Line** icon, click the Color down arrow and select **Tan, Accent 6**, click the **Width** up arrow until **3 pt** appears, and apply the **Oval Arrow** beginning and ending arrows.
8. Click the down arrow next to Trendline Options in the Format Trendline task pane and click **Horizontal (Value) Axis**.
9. Click the Axis Options icon. In the Axis Options settings, click the Display units down arrow and select **Millions**.
10. Click **Number** to expand those settings. Click the **Category** down arrow and select **Number**, and then click in the Decimal places box and type **1**.
11. Display slide 5 and click the chart title to select it.
12. Click **Home** > **Font Size** > **20**, and then click **Bold** B.
13. In the Format Chart Title task pane, click the down arrow to the right of Title Options and select **Plot Area**.
14. Click **Gradient fill**, then click the **Preset gradients** down arrow and select **Medium Gradient – Accent 6**.
15. Click the **Direction** down arrow and click **Linear Diagonal – Bottom Right to Top Left**. Your slide should look similar to Figure 43-1 on the next page.
16. Preview the presentation to see your chart formats. Then insert your name, slide numbers, and the date on all slides.
17. **With your teacher's permission,** print the presentation as handouts with 6 slides per page.
18. Close the presentation, saving changes, and exit PowerPoint.

Figure 43-1

PowerPoint 2016, Windows 10, Microsoft Corporation

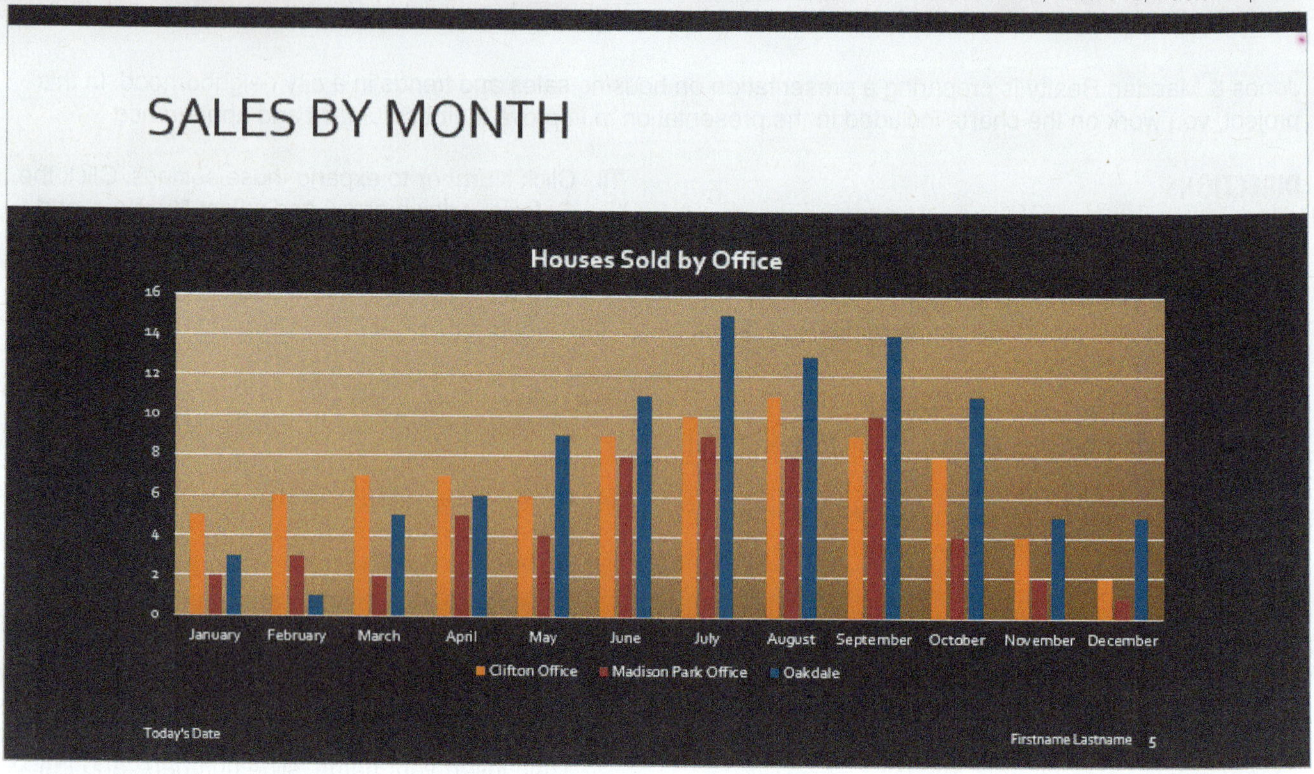

Lesson 43—Apply

[illegible] Madden to customize charts for the sales presentation.

[illegible]

2. Save the presentation as [illegible] the location where your teacher instructs you to store the files for this lesson.
3. Display slide 3. Right-click the trendline and click **Delete** to remove it.
4. Add error bars to the chart on slide 3. On the submenu, choose **Percentage**.
5. Choose to format the error bars for the Single-Family series. Change the color to **Tan, Text 2** and the width to **2.5 pt**.
6. Display slide 4. Display the primary major vertical gridlines.
7. Change the units of display for the vertical axis to **Thousands**, then apply **Number** formatting with **1** decimal place.
8. Change the Minimum under Bounds to **6.0**.
9. Increase the font size of the text for both axes to **16**.
10. Apply different line markers for each line on the line chart and adjust the line weight to show up more clearly.
11. Add a fill of your choice to the chart's plot area. Your slide might look similar to Figure 43-2 on the next page.
12. Display slide 5. Click any column for the Oakdale series. In the Format Data Series task pane, change Series Overlap to 0%. Change Gap Width to 100%.

13. Preview the presentation and make any necessary adjustments. Then insert your name, slide numbers, and the date on all slides.

14. **With your teacher's permission,** print the presentation as handouts with 6 slides per page.

15. Close the presentation, saving changes, and exit PowerPoint.

Figure 43-2

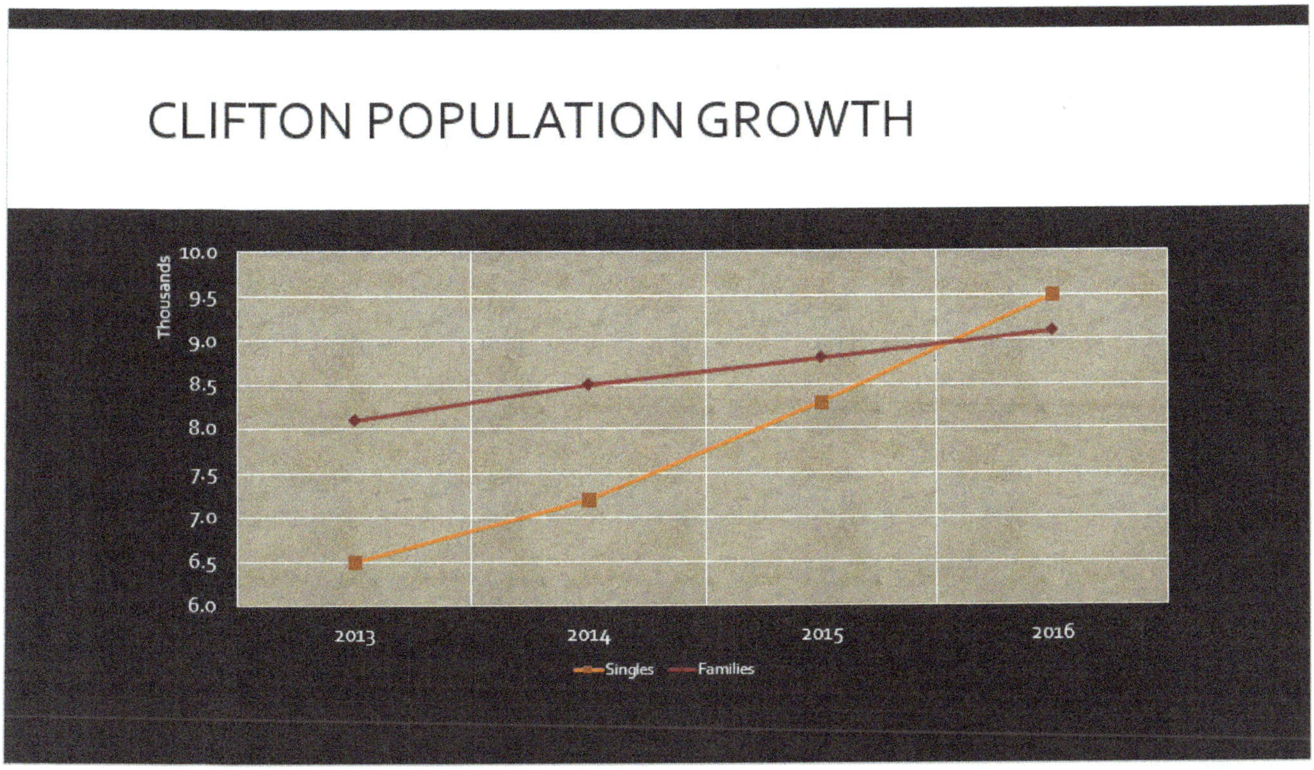

PowerPoint 2016, Windows 10, Microsoft Corporation

End-of-Chapter Activities

➤ PowerPoint Chapter 6—Critical Thinking

Analyzing Data and Preparing a Multimedia Presentation

You work for Harris Inc., a marketing firm that has been hired by your local chamber of commerce to prepare a presentation on tourism in your city. The chamber of commerce wants to see some information on top attractions in your area and has asked Harris to focus on the most popular destination.

In this project, working alone or in teams, you will research on the Internet to find information on what attractions in your area are considered the most popular by travelers and travel guide Web sites. (If you live in a small community, research attractions in a nearby city or in a city you would like to visit.) You will use a table to list the top five attractions and a chart to rank them by popularity. You will use several slides to concentrate on the most popular attraction, giving information about the attraction and including pictures. You will apply advanced animation effects to give the presentation additional visual interest.

DIRECTIONS

1. Start a new presentation, and save it as **PCT06_xx** in the location where your teacher instructs you to store the files for this chapter.
2. Insert the title **Top Attractions in** and add the name of your city or the city you would like to research. In the subtitle placeholder, type **A Presentation by** and then insert your first name and last name.
3. Apply a theme and variant of your choice.
4. Add a slide that gives some basic information about your chosen city.
5. **With your teacher's permission**, use the Web to research the topics listed above. Use valid and reputable sites for your research and make a rough table of the most popular attractions in your city. You should try to find information from at least three travel information sites, and you should try to rank the sites according to how often they are mentioned first, second, third, and so on.
6. Add a new slide and draw a table to organize the information on which attractions in your area are listed most often by travel writers. In the first column, list as many attractions as you have room for on the slide. In the other columns, type the names of the Web sites as the column headers. Use a simple X to indicate which Web site mentioned each location.
7. Apply advanced table formatting to improve the appearance of the table: apply and adjust a table style, apply additional shading and border formats, and adjust cell widths and table size to present the information clearly. If you have an appropriate image of your city, you may want to use it as a background image for the table. Or, you may search for an image online.

   ✓ *Be sure to supply a credit line for the location where you find the image.*
8. Work out a system you can use to create number values for each attraction; for example, each instance where an attraction is ranked first is 5, each instance where it is ranked second is 4, and so on. Add up all of the rankings for each attraction.

9. Add a slide and create a column chart that shows the rankings of the top destinations. You may not want to use all the attractions listed in the table on slide 4—only the most popular.
10. Apply advanced chart formatting to improve the appearance of the chart: add or remove chart elements, adjust text formatting, change the appearance of the data series, apply a plot or chart background, and so on.
11. Add a slide that lists the top destination, as determined by your chart. If you have pictures of the attraction, add them to this slide, or search online for suitable pictures.

    ✓ *If you find pictures online, be sure to supply a credit line for each image.*
12. Use advanced picture formatting to improve the images on the slide: apply corrections and effects, crop to a shape, or use a picture as a fill for a shape.
13. Check spelling.
14. Animate the chart to have each column fly in separately. Then add an emphasis effect to only the column of the most popular attraction. Using the timeline, adjust timing to allow viewers enough time to understand the importance of each column before the next one appears.
15. Animate the pictures you inserted, using a variety of animation effects. Insert a text box with text such as *Click here* that will act as a trigger to animate the images. At least one animation should use a motion path.
16. Preview the presentation and then make any necessary corrections and adjustments. Insert your name and the date on all slides.
17. Deliver the presentation orally to your class in a manner that sustains the listeners' attention. Ask for comments on how the presentation could be improved.
18. **With your teacher's permission**, print the presentation as handouts. Then compress and optimize all media in the presentation.
19. Close the presentation, saving changes, and exit PowerPoint.

➤ PowerPoint Chapter 6—Portfolio Builder

Glacier National Park Presentation

Voyager Travel Adventures is finalizing a presentation on its newest adventure location, Glacier National Park. In this project, you complete some final tasks on the presentation, including applying advanced image formats, improving the appearance of a chart, creating and formatting a table, and adding animations.

DIRECTIONS

1. Start PowerPoint, if necessary, and open **PPB06A** from the data files for this chapter.
2. Save the presentation as **PPB06A_xx** in the location where your teacher instructs you to store the files for this chapter.
3. On slide 1, insert **PPB06B_picture.jpg** as a fill for the mountain shape. Adjust the saturation of the picture to **200%**.
4. Animate the title to **Fade** in by word, with a **35%** delay between words. Set the animation to occur **After Previous**.
5. Animate the subtitle to **Float In** and then change color to black. Set the animation to occur **After Previous**.
6. On slide 3, modify the chart as follows:
   a. Change the display units for the vertical axis to **Millions**. Change the Minimum under Bounds to **1500000.0**.
   b. Insert a Linear trendline and format it to stand out on the chart.
   c. Change the title to **Visitors per Year**, and remove the legend.
   d. Format all chart text as boldface, except for the *Millions* label. Format *Millions* in italic.
   e. Apply a fill of your choice to the chart area, and then change the color of gridlines if necessary to show up well.
7. On slide 4, apply the **Float In** animation effect to the SmartArt diagram. Use the **After Previous** start option, and animate each element of the graphic so that the picture and the description appear at the same time. Use the timeline to create **2.5** second delays to adjust the appearance of each element.
8. On slide 7, select the leftmost image in the top row and use the Corrections button to increase sharpness by **25%** and contrast by **20%**.
9. Select all of the images on the slide and apply the **Simple Frame, White** picture style. Then use the Picture Border button to change the border color to **Olive Green, Accent 3, Lighter 40%**.
10. Animate the images by using the **Zoom** effect, from **Slide Center**, **After Previous**. Use the Animation Painter to apply the same effect settings to each image in whatever order you wish. Use the timeline to adjust timing. Adjust the rotation of the images to make a more interesting display.
11. On slide 8, make the following changes:
    a. Apply one of the soft edge picture formats to each image and change the size of each image to approximately 3.0 wide.
    b. Stack the images so they are centered on each other in the middle of the slide.
    c. Use motion path settings to move each picture to a new location on the slide. Make sure each starts **After Previous**.
12. Add a new Title Only slide at the end of the presentation and insert the title **Adventure Packages**.
13. Draw a table on slide 10 into which you can copy the information from the content area of slide 9. Format the material as follows. (See Illustration 6A on the next page.)
    a. Place the text *Short Tours* and *Full Tours* in a column to the left of the tabular information and change text rotation to **270°**.
    b. Center the rotated text vertically and horizontally, and center the remaining table text vertically.

c. Apply shading colors and fills to make it easy to differentiate the short tour and full tour information.

d. Apply formatting such as gradients to improve the visual appearance.

e. Apply an effect such as Shadow to the table.

14. Delete slide 9.

15. Insert the date, slide number, and a footer with your full name on all slides.

16. Preview the presentation and then make any necessary corrections and adjustments to transitions and other effects.

17. Deliver the presentation orally to your class in a manner that sustains the listeners' attention. Ask for comments on how the presentation could be improved.

18. **With your teacher's permission,** print the presentation.

19. Close the presentation, saving changes, and exit PowerPoint.

Illustration 6A

Adventure Packages

	Days	Lodging	Meals Provided
Short Tours	4	Glacier Park Lodge	Breakfast, Dinner
	4	Village Inn at Apgar	None
	4	Rising Sun Cabin	Breakfast
Full Tours	Days	Lodging	Meals Provided
	6	Swiftcurrent Inn, Lake McDonald Lodge	Breakfast, Dinner
	6	Many Glacier Hotel, St. Mary Lodge	Breakfast, Dinner

Today's Date
FIRSTNAME LASTNAME

9

PowerPoint 2016, Windows 10, Microsoft Corporation

Chapter 7

(Courtesy Konstantin Chagin/Shutterstock)

Finalizing and Sharing a Presentation

Lesson 44
Making a Presentation Accessible to Everyone

- Adding Narration to a Presentation
- Working with Advanced Accessibility Options

Lesson 45
Saving a Presentation in Other Formats

- Saving Slides As Pictures
- Creating a Picture Presentation
- Saving a Presentation in PDF or XPS Format
- Sharing a Presentation with Others

Lesson 46
Working with Links and Actions

- Using Advanced Link Settings
- Working with Advanced Action Settings

Lesson 47
Working with Online Presentations

- Working in the OneDrive
- Editing a Presentation in PowerPoint Online
- Sharing Online Files
- Working with Co-authors
- Supporting and Maintaining Web-Based Presentations

End-of-Chapter Activities

Lesson 44

Making a Presentation Accessible to Everyone

➤ What You Will Learn

Adding Narration to a Presentation
Working with Advanced Accessibility Options

WORDS TO KNOW

Alternative text
Text associated with a picture or other object that conveys in words what can be seen in the object.

Software Skills Add narration to a presentation to allow people with visual challenges to hear your content. Supplying accessibility information such as alternative text descriptions of pictures and other objects can also help a viewer to understand your presentation.

What You Can Do

Adding Narration to a Presentation

- One way to ensure that your presentation is accessible is to add narration to the presentation. Narration can help those who have visual impairments to understand your points.
- Narration can also be helpful in a self-running slide show to explain or emphasize your points to viewers. Narration takes precedence over all other sounds on a slide.
- To record narration, your computer must have a microphone, speakers, and sound card.
- Before you begin adding narration to slides, make sure your microphone is working correctly.
- To record narration, use the Record Slide Show button on the Slide Show tab.
- When you select whether to start at the beginning of the presentation or at the current slide, the presentation begins in Slide Show view so you can match your narration to each slide.
- You also have the option to record timings and narration or just narration.

- You will see that each slide to which you added narration has a sound icon displayed in the lower-right corner. Viewers can click the icons to hear your narration, or you can use the Audio Tools Playback tab to specify that the narration will play automatically.
- Before you begin, remember these tips.
  - Click through the entire presentation at least once, reading each slide's content.
  - Don't begin reading until the timer indicates 0:00:01.
  - If you make a mistake, keep reading (especially if you're also recording timings). Remember you can always go back and redo a single slide.

Try It! Adding Narration to a Presentation

1. Start PowerPoint, and open **P44Try** from the data files for this lesson.
2. Save the presentation as **P44Try_xx** in the location where your teacher instructs you to store the files for this lesson.
3. On the Slide Show tab, click the Record Slide Show down arrow.
4. Click Start Recording from Beginning.
5. If you have a microphone attached to your computer, select both options in the Record Slide Show box. If you don't have a microphone set up, you may not have the option of selecting Narrations and laser pointer. Click Start Recording.
6. When the slide show opens, read the text on the slide as clearly as possible. Be sure to time your reading with the way the text appears on screen.
7. When you've finished with slide 1, click the screen to move to the next slide.
8. Continue recording the slide text until the end of the presentation.
9. Save the **P44Try_xx** file, and leave it open to use in the next Try It.

Record Slide Show dialog box

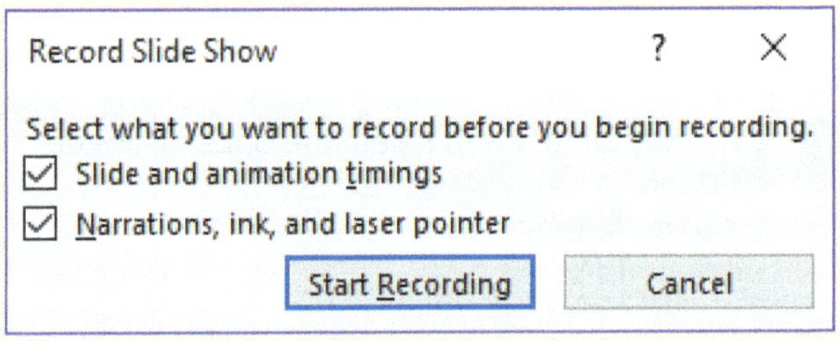

PowerPoint 2016, Windows 10, Microsoft Corporation

Working with Advanced Accessibility Options

- Ensuring that presentations are accessible to all viewers can require you to do some behind-the-scenes work.
- Use the Accessibility Checker to identify issues that could make the presentation difficult to understand for persons with disabilities.
- You will remember that the Accessibility Checker task pane divides issues into three categories.
  - Errors are issues you should definitely fix if you want all viewers to be able to understand content.
  - Warnings are issues you do not necessarily have to fix but could fix for best comprehension by all viewers.
  - Tips give you suggestions for ways to improve content.
- Use the instructions in the Accessibility Checker task pane to help you make the necessary corrections.
- Missing Alt Text is a very common accessibility error, especially in presentations that contain pictures and other graphics. You provide **alternative text** to describe images for viewers who cannot see them.
- The Accessibility Checker will also always prompt you to check reading order—to make sure a screen reader will read content in the order you want. You will usually want the slide title to be read first, followed by text in the content placeholder.
- If you have added sounds or narration to a presentation, you may also be prompted to supply captions for the audio content to meet the needs of those with hearing challenges.

Try It! Working with Advanced Accessibility Options

1. In the **P44Try_xx** file, display slide 1.
2. Click File > Check for Issues > Check Accessibility. The Accessibility Checker task pane opens with a list of issues to check and correct.
3. View the Missing Alt Text errors. You do not need to supply alternative text for the Audio objects, but you should supply alternative text for the images and the table.
4. On slide 3, right-click the butterfly image, and then click Format Picture. In the Format Picture task pane, click the Size & Properties icon.
5. Scroll down, if necessary, and expand the Alt Text heading.
6. In the Title box, type **Butterfly Image 1**. In the Description box, type **Butterfly shape filled with a picture of a red flower**.

   ✓ *Notice that as you supply alternative text, the error is removed from the Accessibility Checker list.*

7. Display slide 4 and select the butterfly image. Supply the alternative text title **Butterfly Image 2** and the description **Butterfly shape with a green floral fill**.
8. Display slide 5 and select the table. Supply the alternative text title **Thorn Hill Workshops** and the description **Information about workshops at Thorn Hill Gardens, including programs for water features, perennial gardening, annuals, pruning, and shrubs and trees**.
9. In the Accessibility Checker task pane, view the suggestions under TIPS. You do not need to supply captions for the audio files, because they consist of narration you read directly from the slides. Under Check Reading Order, click Slide 1 to go to that slide.
10. To check reading order, click Home > Select > Selection Pane. Objects are read from the bottom of this pane to the top. Content on slide 1 is in the correct order, with the title at the bottom, the subtitle next, and then the narration audio object.
11. Check the reading order for the remaining slides. On slide 4, move the TextBox 4 object to be the third object from the bottom of the list. Then close the Selection and the Accessibility Checker task panes.
12. Close the **P44Try_xx** file, saving changes, and exit PowerPoint.

Checking reading order for slide content

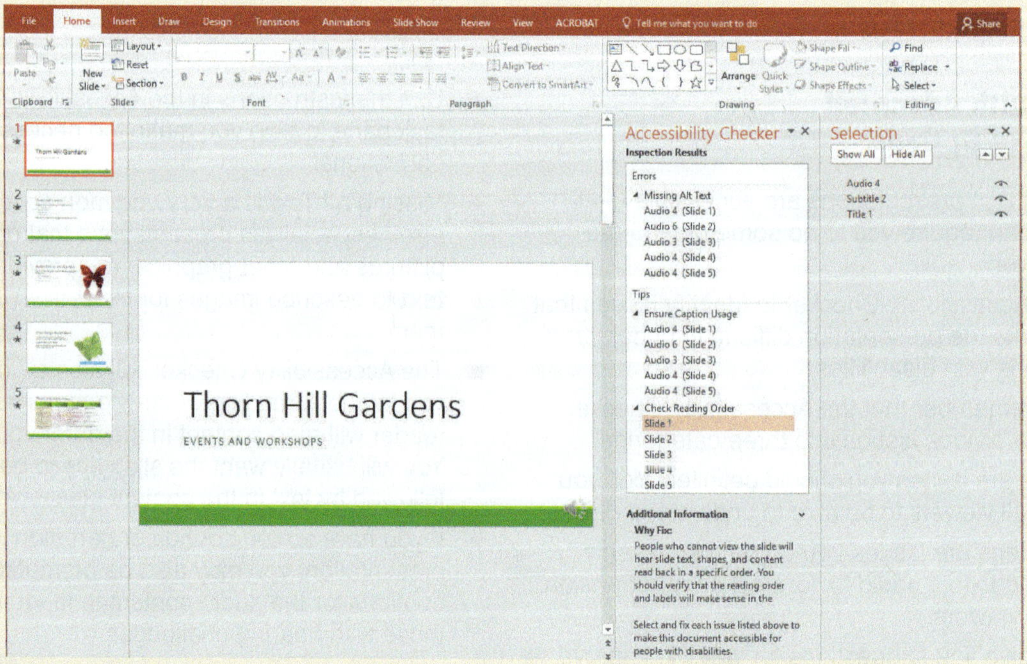

PowerPoint 2016, Windows 10, Microsoft Corporation

Lesson 44—Practice

Peterson Home Healthcare is preparing information for its annual board meeting. Several of the board members have physical challenges that you need to address as you are preparing presentations. In this project, you add narration to a presentation about options for upgrading IT equipment throughout the company.

DIRECTIONS

1. Start PowerPoint, if necessary, and open **P44Practice** from the data files for this lesson.
2. Save the presentation as **P44Practice_xx** in the location where your teacher instructs you to store the files for this lesson.
3. Create a footer with your name in it.
4. Click **Slide Show** > **Record Slide Show** down arrow > **Start Recording from Beginning**.
5. If you have a microphone attached to your computer, select both options in the Record Slide Show box.
6. Click **Start Recording** to begin.
7. Read the contents of each slide until you reach the end of the presentation.
8. Click **Slide Show** > **From Beginning** to listen to your narration.
9. Select slide 4 and in the Stage 2 box, place the insertion point at the beginning of the bullet point. Type **Hire a contractor** and press ENTER .
10. Click **Slide Show** > **Record Slide Show** down arrow > **Start Recording from Current Slide**.
11. Select the same options in the Record Slide Show box that you chose for the initial recording and click **Start Recording**.
12. Read the entire slide and then close the recording box.
13. **With your teacher's permission**, print slide 4. It should look like Figure 44-1.
14. Close the presentation, saving changes, and exit PowerPoint.

Figure 44-1

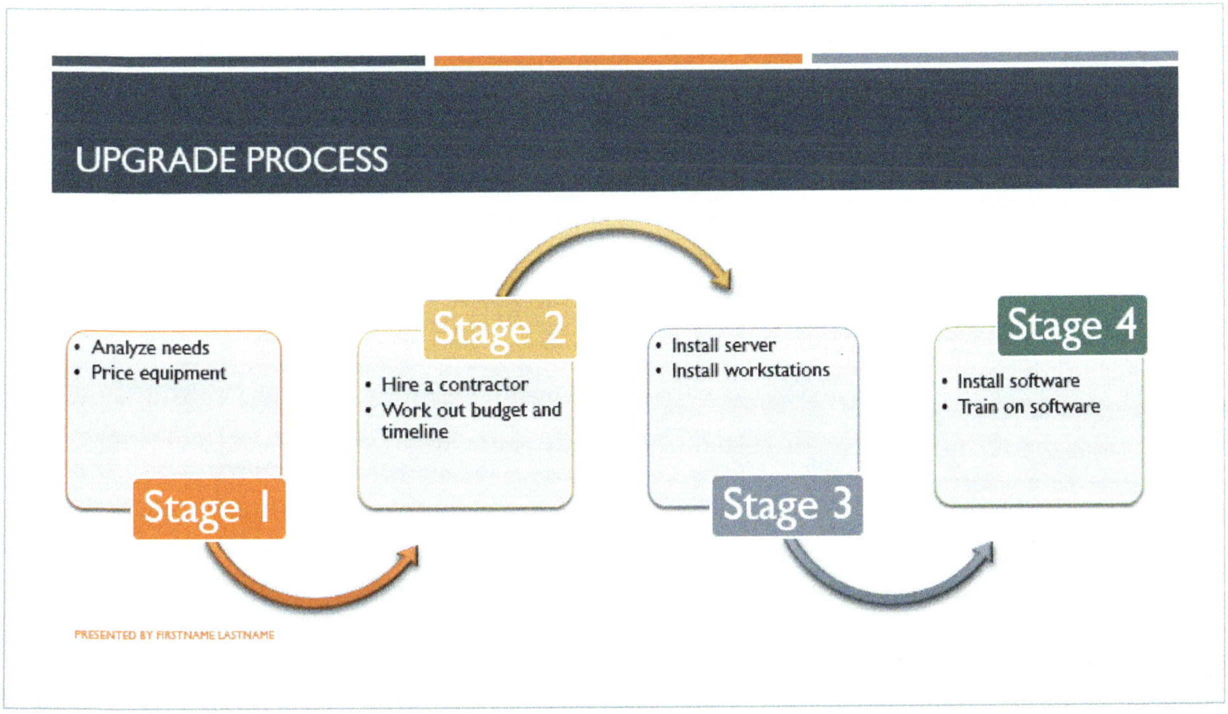

PowerPoint 2016, Windows 10, Microsoft Corporation

Lesson 44—Apply

In this project, you continue to work on the presentation for Peterson Home Healthcare. You check accessibility for the slides and make the necessary corrections to ensure that all viewers will be able to understand the presentation.

DIRECTIONS

1. Start PowerPoint, if necessary, and open **P44Apply** from the data files for this lesson.
2. Save the presentation as **P44Apply_xx** in the location where your teacher instructs you to store the files for this lesson.
3. Create a footer with your name in it.
4. Run the Accessibility Checker, and review the errors and tips listed in the Accessibility Checker task pane.
5. On slide 1, provide alternative text for the clip art image, supplying both a title and a description.
6. On slide 2, provide alternative text for the photo, supplying both a title and a description.
7. On slides 3 and 4, provide alternative text for the SmartArt diagrams.
8. Check the reading order on each slide and correct the order if necessary. Make sure the narration always appears just below the footer placeholder in the list of items that will be read.
9. Close the presentation, saving changes, and exit PowerPoint.

Lesson 45

Saving a Presentation in Other Formats

➤ What You Will Learn

Saving Slides As Pictures
Creating a Picture Presentation
Saving a Presentation in PDF or XPS Format
Sharing a Presentation with Others

Software Skills Save slides or a presentation in a picture format so the slides can be used in other applications. You can save a presentation in other formats that make it easy to share the presentation with colleagues or clients. Use the Share feature to streamline the sharing process.

What You Can Do

Saving Slides As Pictures

- You can save a single slide or an entire presentation in a graphic file format that allows you to insert the slides as pictures in other applications, such as Word documents.
- By saving a slide or presentation as a picture, you can ensure that it is viewable by anyone with a computer regardless of whether they have a Mac or PC computer or what version of software they are using.
- Use the Change File Type option on the Export tab in Backstage view to save a slide or presentation as a picture.
- You can choose among four picture file formats.
  - PNG and JPEG are listed on the Change File Type tab.
  - If you prefer GIF or TIFF, you can use the Save As button at the bottom of the tab and choose either option in the Save as type list.
- Once you have provided a name for the new file, selected a format, and issued the Save command, PowerPoint displays a dialog box to ask if you want to save only the current slide or every slide in the current presentation.
- The resulting files can be used just like any other picture file.

Try It! Saving Slides As Pictures

1. Start PowerPoint, and open **P45TryA** from the data files for this lesson.
2. Save the presentation as **P45TryA_xx** in the location where your teacher instructs you to store the files for this lesson.
3. Display slide 3.
4. Click File > Export > Change File Type.
5. Click JPEG File Interchange Format and then click Save As.
6. Change the file name to **P45TryB_xx** and make sure the file location is the folder where you are storing files for this lesson.
7. Click Save.
8. Select Just This One at the prompt.
9. In Word, open **P45TryC** from the data files for this lesson.
10. Position the insertion point on the blank line following the first paragraph of the memo, and then click Insert > Pictures.
11. Navigate to the location where you are storing files for this lesson, click **P45TryB_xx.jpg**, and click Insert.
12. Resize the inserted picture to 5" wide, center it, and use Picture Tools Format > Picture Border to apply a Lime, Accent 1 border.
13. Save the document as **P45TryC_xx** in the location where your teacher instructs you to store the files for this lesson.
14. Close the document and Word. Leave the **P45TryA_xx** file open in PowerPoint for the next Try It.

A slide used as an illustration in a document

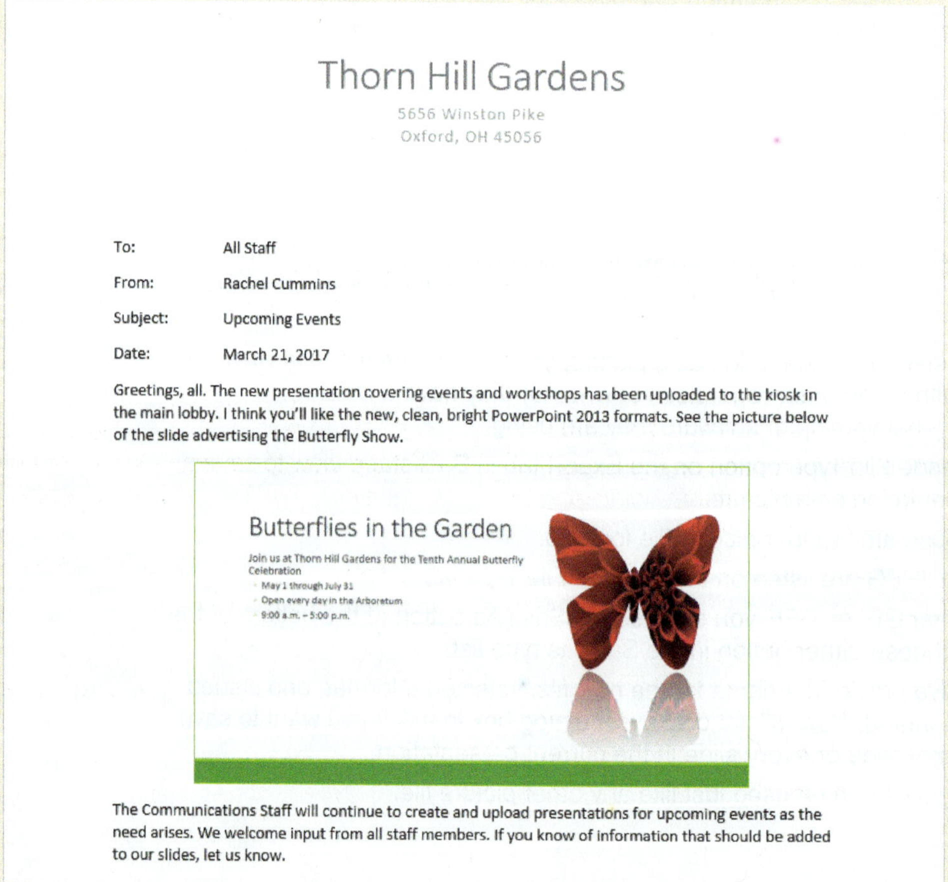
Thorn Hill Gardens
5656 Winston Pike
Oxford, OH 45056

To: All Staff
From: Rachel Cummins
Subject: Upcoming Events
Date: March 21, 2017

Greetings, all. The new presentation covering events and workshops has been uploaded to the kiosk in the main lobby. I think you'll like the new, clean, bright PowerPoint 2013 formats. See the picture below of the slide advertising the Butterfly Show.

The Communications Staff will continue to create and upload presentations for upcoming events as the need arises. We welcome input from all staff members. If you know of information that should be added to our slides, let us know.

Creating a Picture Presentation

- When you save slides as pictures using a picture file type, you create separate graphic files. This is the option to use if you need to insert a picture of a slide in a standard graphic format.
- You have another option for saving a presentation so that its slides become pictures.
- The PowerPoint Picture Presentation format, which can be selected from the Save as type list, transforms each slide in the presentation to a picture.
- You might use this option if you want to share a presentation but you do not want the recipient to be able to edit the presentation.
- Because all objects on a slide become part of a single picture, the presentation's file size may be smaller than the presentation from which it was created. This is often helpful when you are sharing a presentation via e-mail.
- A picture presentation uses the same .pptx extension as a default PowerPoint presentation.

Try It! Creating a Picture Presentation

1. In the **P45TryA_xx** file, click File > Export > Change File Type > Save as Another File Type, and then click Save As.
2. Change the file name to **P45TryD_xx**.
3. Click the Save as type down arrow and select PowerPoint Picture Presentation.
4. Click Save, and then click OK when you see the information box about how the presentation has been saved.
5. In File Explorer, navigate to the location where you are saving files for this lesson.
6. Position the pointer over the **P45TryA_xx** file to see a ScreenTip with properties, including the file size.
7. Now point to the **P45TryD_xx** file and compare the size of the file to that of the original PowerPoint presentation.
8. Double-click **P45TryD_xx** to open it.
9. Click on the first slide to see the selection box that surrounds the entire slide, indicating that it is a single picture.
10. Close the **P45TryD_xx** file. Leave the **P45TryA_xx** file open to use in the next Try It.

Saving a Presentation in PDF or XPS Format

- Another way you can prepare a presentation for sharing with others is to save it in PDF or XPS format.
- PDF, or Portable Document Format, is a format that preserves the look of a page or a slide so that a viewer can see the content without being able to edit it.
- XPS, or XML Paper Specification, is a Microsoft document format that preserves page content as PDF does.
- When you choose to save as PDF or XPS, by default PowerPoint will save the presentation as slides, with the slides proceeding one after another in the document.
- If you choose the Options button in the Publish as PDF or XPS dialog box, you can choose to save the presentation as handouts or notes pages, or in outline view. You can choose which slides to publish and choose among other options such as whether to apply a frame to slides or include comments and markup.
- Your PDF or XPS reader opens by default after you publish the presentation to enable you to review the presentation in its new format.

Try It! Saving a Presentation in PDF or XPS Format

1. In the **P45TryA_xx** file, click File > Export > Create PDF/XPS Document, and then click the Create PDF/XPS button.
2. In the Publish as PDF or XPS dialog box, change the file name to **P45TryE_xx**, and then click the Options button.
3. In the Options dialog box, in the Publish options area, click the Publish what down arrow and select Handouts. Then click the Frame slides check box.
4. Click OK, and then click Publish.
5. Your PDF or XPS reader opens to display the published handouts.
6. Navigate back to the presentation.
7. Leave the **P45TryA_xx** file open to use in the next Try it.

Handouts published to PDF

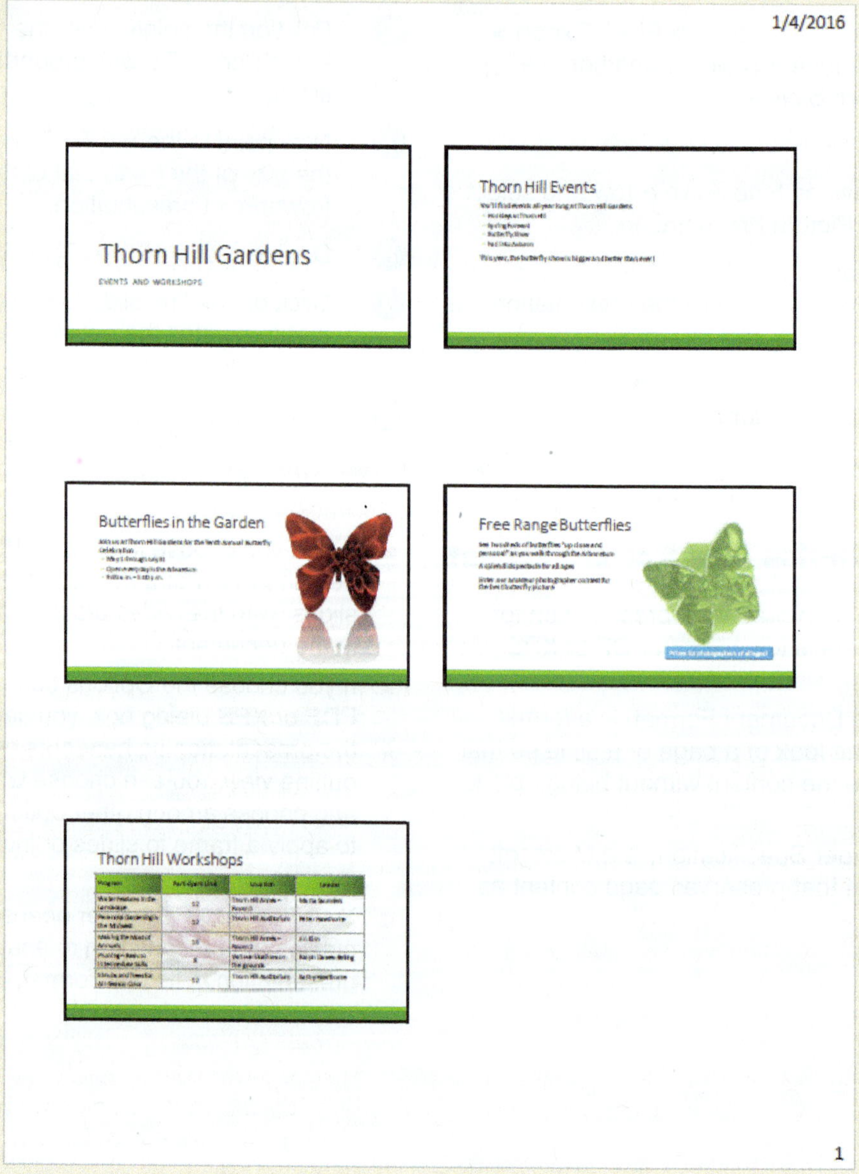

Sharing a Presentation with Others

- PowerPoint 2016 streamlines the sharing process with the Share button at the upper-right corner of the PowerPoint window.
- Click the Share button to see options in the Share task pane for sharing the current presentation, including saving the presentation to a cloud location and sending the presentation as an attachment to an email message.
- Clicking the Save to Cloud button displays the Save As settings in Backstage view. Choose OneDrive or another online location and the desired folder in which to save the presentation.

✓ *You will learn more about sharing presentations online in Lesson 47.*

- Clicking Send as attachment in the Share task pane displays options for attaching the current presentation either in PowerPoint format or as a PDF file.

Try It! Sharing a Presentation with Others

✓ *You will need to have an e-mail application configured to complete the steps in this exercise.*

1. In the **P45TryA_xx** file, click the Share button near the upper-right corner of the application window. The Share task pane displays.
2. Click Send as attachment near the bottom of the task pane.
3. Click Send as PDF. The presentation will be published as a PDF file and your default email application will open a new message with the PDF attached.
4. Type the e-mail address of a classmate or your teacher, as directed by your teacher, and then click Send.
5. Close the **P45TryA_xx** file, saving changes, and exit PowerPoint.

Lesson 45—Practice

Planet Earth is preparing materials for a presentation at the Civic Garden Center on what every homeowner can do to promote a healthy natural environment. In this project, you save a slide as a picture and then insert it in an Excel worksheet. Then you save the presentation in picture format to archive the presentation in a smaller file size.

DIRECTIONS

1. Start PowerPoint, if necessary, and open **P45PracticeA** from the data files for this lesson.
2. Save the presentation as **P45PracticeA_xx** in the location where your teacher instructs you to store the files for this lesson.
3. Display slide 4.
4. Click **File** > **Export** > **Change File Type** > **JPEG File Interchange Format**, and then click **Save As**.
5. Navigate to the location where you are storing files for this lesson, and change the file name to **P45PracticeB_xx**.
6. Click **Save**.
7. Click **Just This One**.
8. Start Excel, and open **P45PracticeC** from the data files for this lesson.
9. Save the worksheet as **P45PracticeC_xx** in the location where your teacher instructs you to store the files for this lesson.
10. Click cell A3, and then click **Insert** > **Pictures**.
11. Navigate to the location where you are storing files for this lesson, click **P45PracticeB_xx**, and then click **Insert**.
12. Resize the picture to **5"** wide, and adjust its position to fit in the blank rows between the *Compost Initiative* heading and the worksheet data.

13. With the picture still selected, click **Picture Tools Format** > **Picture Border** and select **Green, Accent 1**.
14. **With your teacher's permission,** print the worksheet. Your printout should look similar to Figure 45-1.
15. Close the **P45PracticeC_xx** file, saving changes, and exit Excel.
16. In the **P45PracticeA_xx** file, click **File** > **Export** > **Change File Type** > **Save as Another File Type**, and then click **Save As**.
17. Change the file name to **P45PracticeD_xx**, click the **Save as type** down arrow, and click **PowerPoint Picture Presentation**.
18. Click **Save**, and then click **OK**.
19. Close the presentation, saving changes, and exit PowerPoint.

Figure 45-1

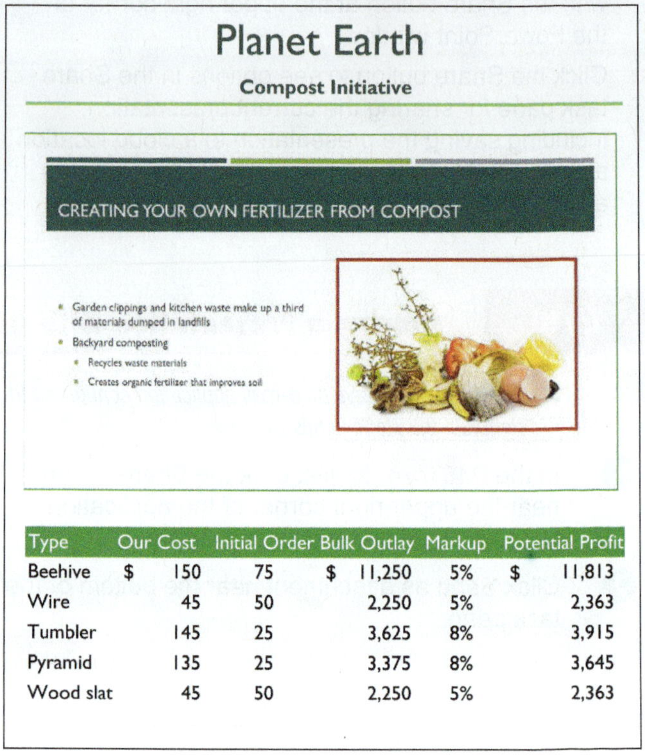
Planet Earth

Compost Initiative

CREATING YOUR OWN FERTILIZER FROM COMPOST

- Garden clippings and kitchen waste make up a third of materials dumped in landfills
- Backyard composting
  - Recycles waste materials
  - Creates organic fertilizer that improves soil

Type	Our Cost	Initial Order	Bulk Outlay	Markup	Potential Profit
Beehive	$ 150	75	$ 11,250	5%	$ 11,813
Wire	45	50	2,250	5%	2,363
Tumbler	145	25	3,625	8%	3,915
Pyramid	135	25	3,375	8%	3,645
Wood slat	45	50	2,250	5%	2,363

PowerPoint 2016, Windows 10, Microsoft Corporation

Lesson 45—Apply

In this project, you continue working with the Planet Earth presentation. You save all slides as pictures so that you can insert them in a Word document you have prepared to help you deliver the presentation. Then you save the presentation as a PDF so that you can easily e-mail it to the Planet Earth communications coordinator for approval.

DIRECTIONS

1. Start PowerPoint, if necessary, and open **P45ApplyA** from the data files for this lesson.
2. Save the presentation as **P45ApplyA_xx** in the location where your teacher instructs you to store the files for this lesson.
3. Insert your name and the date on all slides. For notes and handouts, insert your name and the date in the header.
4. Export all slides in the presentation in JPEG format with the file name **P45ApplyB_xx**, storing the resulting folder with your files for this lesson.
5. Start Word, if necessary, and open **P45ApplyC** from the data files for this lesson.
6. Save the document as **P45ApplyC_xx** in the location where your teacher instructs you to store the files for this lesson.
7. Click in the first cell under the Image heading, and then choose to insert pictures and navigate to the **P45ApplyB_xx** folder. Open the folder and select **Slide1.JPG**.
8. Resize the picture to **3.5"** wide.
9. Insert the remaining three slides in the appropriate table cells.

10. **With your teacher's permission,** print the Word document. The first page should look similar to Figure 45-2.
11. Close the **P45ApplyC_xx** document, saving changes, and exit Word.
12. In the **P45ApplyA_xx** file, save the presentation in PDF format with the name **P45ApplyD_xx** as handouts with 4 slides per page, and frames around the slides.
13. Share the presentation with a classmate or your teacher by attaching a PDF version of the presentation to an e-mail message.
14. Close the presentation, saving changes, and exit PowerPoint.

Figure 45-2

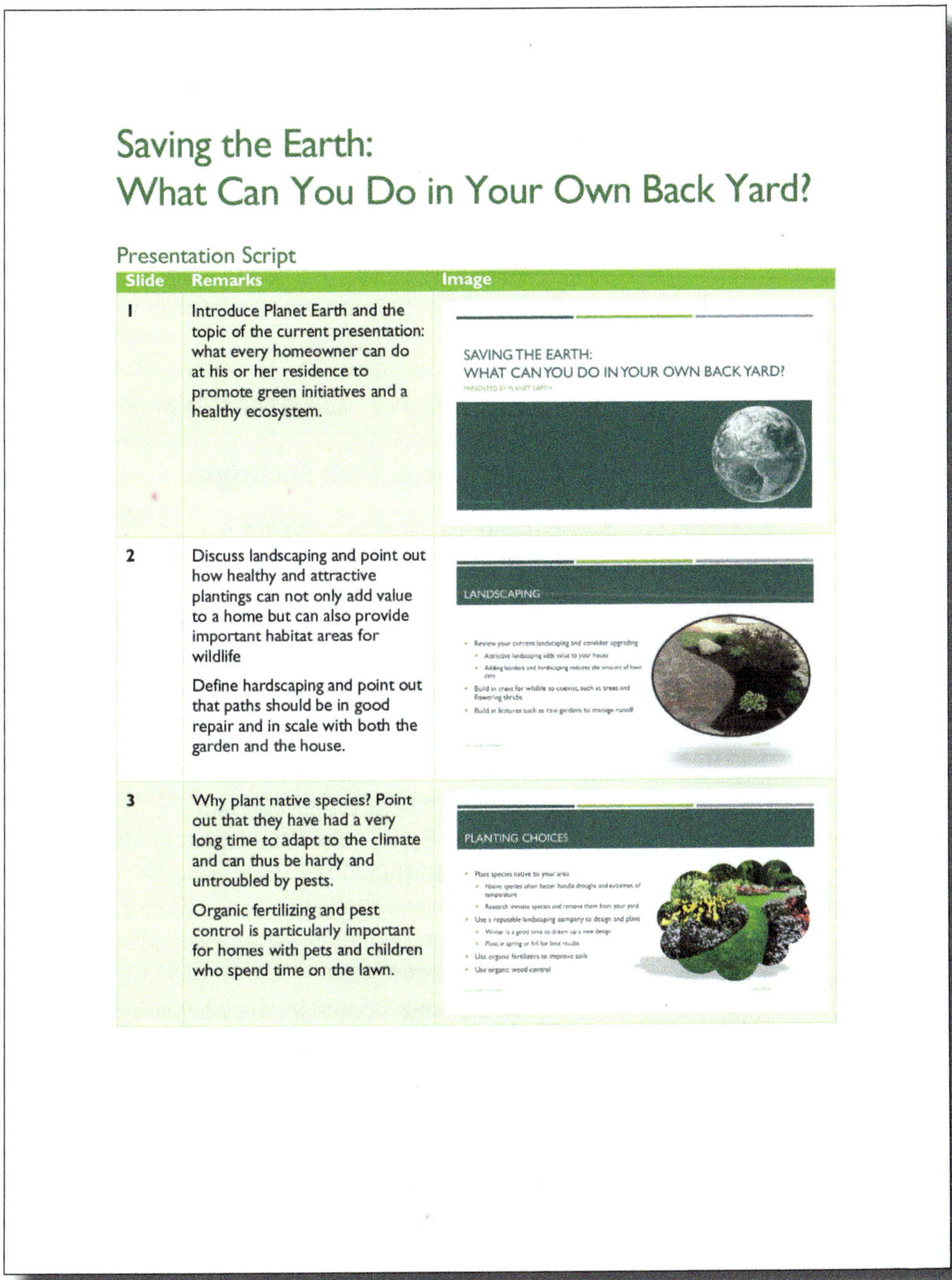

Saving the Earth:
What Can You Do in Your Own Back Yard?

Presentation Script

Slide	Remarks	Image
1	Introduce Planet Earth and the topic of the current presentation: what every homeowner can do at his or her residence to promote green initiatives and a healthy ecosystem.	SAVING THE EARTH: WHAT CAN YOU DO IN YOUR OWN BACK YARD?
2	Discuss landscaping and point out how healthy and attractive plantings can not only add value to a home but can also provide important habitat areas for wildlife Define hardscaping and point out that paths should be in good repair and in scale with both the garden and the house.	LANDSCAPING
3	Why plant native species? Point out that they have had a very long time to adapt to the climate and can thus be hardy and untroubled by pests. Organic fertilizing and pest control is particularly important for homes with pets and children who spend time on the lawn.	PLANTING CHOICES

Lesson 46

Working with Links and Actions

➤ What You Will Learn

Using Advanced Link Settings
Working with Advanced Action Settings

WORDS TO KNOW

Target
The slide, show, file, or page that appears when you click a link on a slide.

Software Skills Links and action settings can be used to create interactive presentations that allow viewers to jump to different locations in the presentation, open other files, run programs, or interact with objects on the slide.

What You Can Do

Using Advanced Link Settings

- You can use links to move from a presentation to another application to view data in that application. For example, you could link to a Microsoft Excel worksheet during a presentation.
- If the computer on which you are presenting the slides has an active Internet connection, you can also use a link to jump from a slide to any site on the Web.
- You can set up a link using text from a text placeholder or any object on the slide, such as a shape or picture.
- You have four **target** options to choose from.
  - Existing File or Web Page lets you locate a file on your system or network. Use the Browse the Web button to start your browser so you can locate the page you want to use as a target.
  - Place in This Document lets you select a slide or custom show from the current presentation. When you click a slide for the target, it appears in the Slide preview area.
  - Create New Document allows you to specify the name of a new document and link to it at the same time. If you create a file with the name Results.xlsx, for example, Excel opens so you can enter data in the Results workbook.
  - E-mail Address lets you set up a link that will open a new e-mail message to send to the address you specify.
- If you want to provide a little extra help to a viewer about what will happen when a link is clicked, you can provide a ScreenTip. The ScreenTip will appear when the presenter or viewer moves the mouse pointer over the link.

Try It! Creating Links to External Documents

1. Start PowerPoint, and open **P46TryA** from the data files for this lesson.
2. Save the presentation as **P46TryA_xx** in the location where your teacher instructs you to store the files for this lesson.
3. Start Word, and open **P46TryB** from the data files for this lesson.
4. Save the document as **P46TryB_xx** in the location where your teacher instructs you to store the files for this lesson. Close the document and exit Word.
5. Start Excel, and open **P46TryC** from the data files for this lesson.
6. Save the workbook as **P46TryC_xx** in the location where your teacher instructs you to store the files for this lesson. Close the workbook, and exit Excel.
7. On slide 1, click the earth in the Planet Earth logo.
8. Click Insert > Hyperlink.
9. In the Insert Hyperlink dialog box, make sure Existing File or Web Page is selected.
10. In the Look in box, navigate to the location where you are storing files for this lesson, select **P46TryB_xx**, and click OK.
11. Display slide 10 and click the Discussion shape to select it.
12. Click Insert > Hyperlink.
13. In the Current Folder list, scroll down and select **P46TryC_xx**, then click OK.
14. Save the **P46TryA_xx** file, and leave it open to use in the next Try It.

Insert Hyperlink dialog box

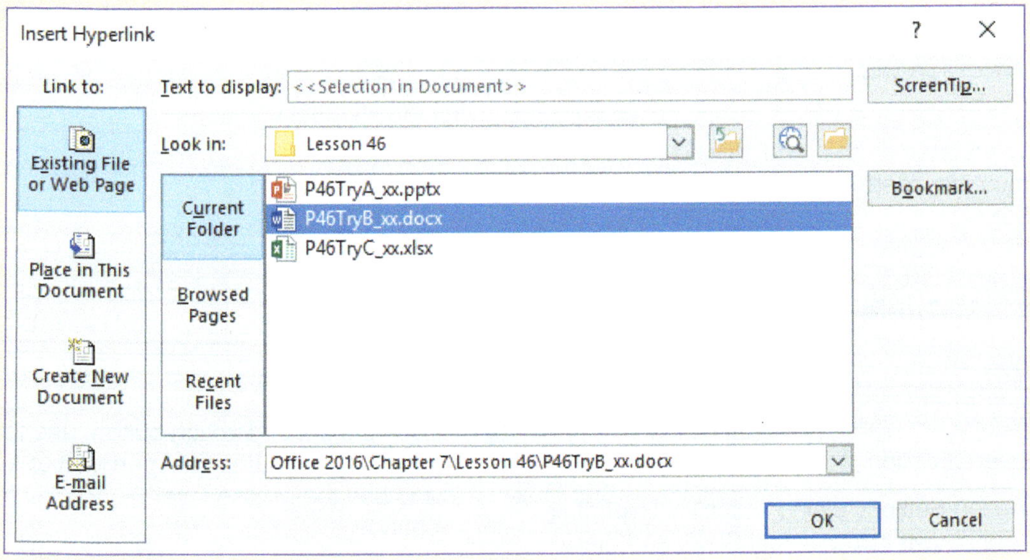

Try It! Creating a ScreenTip for a Link

1. In the **P46TryA_xx** file, display slide 1 and right-click the earth in the Planet Earth logo.
2. Click Edit Hyperlink to open the Edit Hyperlink dialog box.
3. Click the ScreenTip button.
4. In the Set Hyperlink ScreenTip dialog box, click in the ScreenTip text box and type **Click here to learn more about Planet Earth**.
5. Click OK twice.
6. Save the **P46TryA_xx** file, and leave it open to use in the next Try It.

Working with Advanced Action Settings

- Like links, actions allow you to link to a slide in the current presentation, a custom show, another presentation, a Web page URL, or another file.
- Actions are most commonly associated with action buttons, shapes you select from the Shapes gallery and draw on a slide to perform specific tasks.
- You have a number of other options for applying actions, however.
  - You can use an action to run a program, such as Excel, or a macro.

    ✓ *You may have to respond to a security warning the first time you run a program.*

  - You can also use an action to control an object you have inserted on the slide; however, the object must be inserted using the Insert Object dialog box.

    ✓ *If you use an existing file, you can choose in the Insert Object dialog box to display the object as an icon on the slide.*

  - You can use an action setting to play a sound effect or sound file.
- Use the action options, such as Hyperlink to, Run program, or Play sound, in the Action Settings dialog box to set the target for the action.
- By default, you set actions on the Mouse Click tab, which means that the action takes place when you click on the action object during the presentation.
- The Mouse Over tab contains the same options as the Mouse Click tab. Actions you set on this tab will take place when you hover the mouse pointer over the action object.

Try It! Working with Advanced Action Settings

1. In the **P46TryA_xx** file, display slide 2 and click the first action button on the slide.
2. Click Insert > Action ★.
3. In the Action Settings dialog box, click Hyperlink to, click the down arrow, select Slide, and then select 3. Project Overview.
4. Click OK.
5. In the Action Settings dialog box, click the Mouse Over tab, click the Play sound check box, click the down arrow, and click Chime.
6. Click OK.
7. Click the second action button, use the Action Settings dialog box to hyperlink it to slide 7, and use the Mouse Over tab to play the Chime sound.
8. Continue setting actions for the next two buttons, linking to slide 12 and slide 16, and playing the Chime sound.
9. Display slide 9 and click the action button in the lower-right corner.

(continued)

Try It! Working with Advanced Action Settings *(continued)*

Specify actions in the Action Settings dialog box

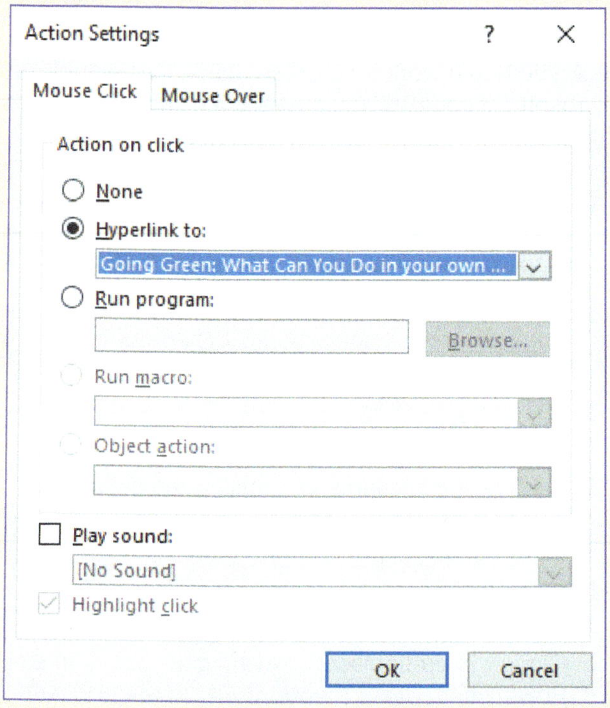

PowerPoint 2016, Windows 10, Microsoft Corporation

10. Click Insert > Action.
11. Click Run program and then click Browse.
12. Click Desktop in the left pane and select one of the shortcuts on the Desktop.
13. Click OK twice.
14. Click Slide Show > From Beginning and watch the slide show, clicking all the links and action buttons as they appear. On slide 2, move the mouse pointer over the action buttons to hear the chimes and then click the button to jump to a new slide. When you jump to an external document, view the content, then close the document and its application and return to the presentation.

    ✓ *If you receive a security warning when you click the action button on slide 9 to run a program, click Enable.*

15. Close the **P46TryA_xx** file, saving changes, and exit PowerPoint.

Lesson 46—Practice

Peterson Home Healthcare is starting the process of training employees on Microsoft Office 2016 after the installation of the new network and workstations. In this project, you begin work on a presentation that employees can access from their own computers to learn more about Microsoft Office 2016. You create links and action items to make it easy for employees to interact with the training materials.

DIRECTIONS

1. Start PowerPoint, if necessary, and open **P46PracticeA** from the data files for this lesson.
2. Save the presentation as **P46PracticeA_xx** in the location where your teacher instructs you to store the files for this lesson.
3. Start Word, if necessary, and open **P46PracticeB** from the data files for this lesson.
4. Save the file as **P46PracticeB_xx** in the location where your teacher instructs you to store the files for this lesson.
5. Display slide 2 and select the first bullet item.
6. Click **Insert** > **Hyperlink** > **Place in This Document** and select the **Introduction** slide. Click **OK**.
7. Repeat this process for each of the other bullet items on slide 2, linking them to the corresponding slide.
8. Select the *Test Your Knowledge* object on slide 6. Click **Insert** > **Hyperlink** > **Existing File or Web Page**.
9. Select the file **P46PracticeB_xx** from the solution files for this lesson. Click **OK**.
10. Preview the presentation, testing the links you inserted on slides 2 and 6. Then insert your name, the date, and slide numbers on all slides.
11. **With your teacher's permission,** print slide 2. It should look similar to Figure 46-1.
12. Close the presentation, saving changes, and exit PowerPoint. Close the Word document and exit Word.

Figure 46-1

Lesson 46—Apply

In this project, you continue to work on the Peterson Home Healthcare interactive presentation. You add action settings to allow viewers to open other applications and links to make it easy to navigate the materials.

DIRECTIONS

1. Start PowerPoint, if necessary, and open **P46ApplyA** from the data files for this lesson.
2. Save the presentation as **P46ApplyA_xx** in the location where your teacher instructs you to store the files for this lesson.
3. Insert your name, slide numbers, and the date on all slides.
4. Open **P46ApplyB** from the data files for this lesson.
5. Save the presentation as **P46ApplyB_xx** in the location where your teacher instructs you to store the files for this lesson.
6. Select the shape at the upper-right corner of the first slide in **P46ApplyB_xx** and create a hyperlink to **P46ApplyA_xx**. Then save and close **P46ApplyB_xx**.
7. Select the word *here* in the last bullet item on slide 8 and link it to **P46ApplyB_xx**.
8. Open Slide Master view. On the Title and Content layout (not the slide master), select the **Questions** text box and create a link to an e-mail address. Use the following address: **jpeterson@petersonhomehealth.com**

   ✓ *This e-mail address is a dummy for setup purposes only.*
9. Select the **More Info** box and create a link to the Office Online home page at **https://products.office.com/en-us/home**.
10. Add the following ScreenTip to the More Info link: **View Microsoft Office Products**.
11. Insert a rounded rectangle from the Shapes gallery below the More Info box and use Action settings to link the button to slide 2. Type **Contents** on the action button, and format the button with the same Quick Style as the text boxes but a different color, as shown in Figure 46-2 on the next page.
12. Make sure all three boxes are the same shape, width, and height. Align left and distribute the three boxes vertically. Then select the boxes, copy them, and paste them on all slide layouts except the title layout, section header layout, and picture layouts. Exit Slide Master view.
13. Display slide 4 and select the *Open Word* shape. Apply an action setting that will run Microsoft Word: In the Action Settings dialog box, select **Run** and then click **Browse**. Navigate to the location where the Office 16 program files are stored.

    ✓ *On a Windows 10 computer, your path may be similar to C:\Program Files\Microsoft Office 15\root\office16\WINWORD.EXE.*
14. Select the *Open Excel* shape and browse to the same location, but select **EXCEL.EXE** in the Office 2016 folder.
15. You are ready to test your interactive presentation. Follow these steps in Slide Show view:
    a. On slide 2, test each of the links to slides, using the **Contents** action button to return each time to slide 2.
    b. Test the **Questions** and **More Info** buttons. Close the e-mail message window without creating a message, and close the Web page after you are done viewing it.
    c. On slide 4, click the **Open Word** shape, and then click **Enable** when alerted to the potential security risk. Close Word. Click the **Open Excel** shape, click **Enable** if necessary, and close Excel.
    d. On slide 6, click the **Test Your Knowledge** object to open the Word document with three questions. For extra credit, answer the questions and then save the document with a new name such as **P46ApplyC_xx**. Close the document to return to the presentation.

       ✓ *If you get an error message when you click this link, adjust the link target in Normal view and then return to the slide show.*
    e. On slide 8, click the link that takes you to **P46ApplyB_xx**. Use the link to navigate to the information on customizing the Quick Access Toolbar, then use the action button to return to the first slide. Use the button at the upper-right corner of the slide to return to **P46ApplyA_xx**.
16. **With your teacher's permission,** print slide 8. It should look similar to Figure 46-2 on the next page.
17. Close the presentation, saving changes, and exit PowerPoint.

Figure 46-2

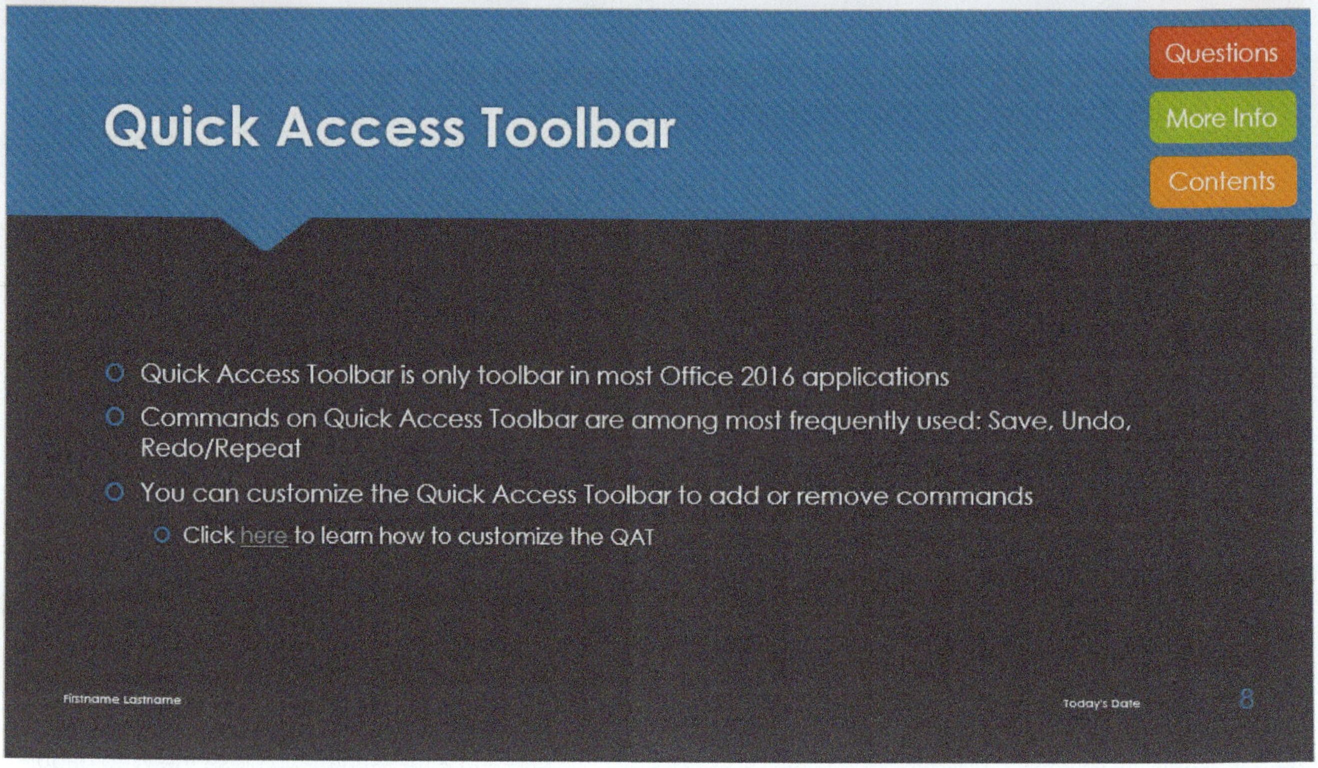

PowerPoint 2016, Windows 10, Microsoft Corporation

Lesson 47

Working with Online Presentations

➤ What You Will Learn

Working in the OneDrive
Editing a Presentation in PowerPoint Online
Sharing Online Files
Working with Co-authors
Supporting and Maintaining Web-Based Presentations

Software Skills Teamwork really is the name of the game for many people who work on presentations today. Often more than one person is responsible for content, another works on the design, another prepares the photos, and someone else gathers the video and audio clips. PowerPoint Online enables a team to work together on a presentation that is stored on the OneDrive. You can set options to share documents so that your team members can easily participate in a joint project.

WORDS TO KNOW

Co-authoring
A form of teamwork when more than one author can work on a file at the same time.

What You Can Do

Working in the OneDrive

- Working on a presentation with a team can be a simple process when you post a file to an online location such as a SharePoint team site or your Windows OneDrive account.
- A presentation stored on your OneDrive is accessible from any location where you have Web access.
- The OneDrive offers several default folders, such as Documents and Pictures, in which you can store your files. You can also create your own folders.
- Creating your own folders makes it easy to share some files without giving others access to all of your documents.
- You can save files to the OneDrive from within any Office 2016 application. The files can then be accessed not only from your desktop but also from the OneDrive

- You can also upload files from your computer to the OneDrive using the OneDrive's Upload option.
- In the OneDrive, folders are represented by tiles. You can select folders by clicking check boxes and open them by clicking or tapping on a touch screen.
- You can change the OneDrive display to see folders in a hierarchy.
- Use the Information pane to see more information about a folder.

Try It! Creating a OneDrive Folder and Saving a File to the OneDrive

1. Start PowerPoint, and open **P47Try** from the data files for this lesson.
2. Click File > Save As, and then click your OneDrive in the Save As list.
3. Click More options beneath the save boxes in the right pane. The Save As dialog box opens.
4. Click the New folder button in the menu bar and then type **Presentations** as the new folder name. Press ENTER.
5. Double-click the Presentations folder to open it.
6. Change the file name to **P47TryA_xx** and then click Save. Notice that the renamed file is now open on your desktop, and the Save button in the Quick Access Toolbar has changed to show the link symbol that means you can refresh the file to show any changes others have made to the file.
7. Close the **P47TryA_xx** file, and leave PowerPoint open to use in the next Try It.

Try It! Working with Folders in the OneDrive

1. Start your Web browser, and type **https://onedrive.live.com** in the address bar.
2. If necessary, sign in with your Microsoft account name and password. Your OneDrive appears with default folders such as Documents and Pictures and the Presentations folder you created in the last Try It.
3. Click in the upper-right corner of the Presentations folder tile to display a check box, and then click the check box to select the folder.
4. Click the Details icon to open the Information pane and display the sharing status and other information for the Presentations folder.
5. Click the Details icon to close the Information pane.
6. Click the check box on the Presentations folder to deselect it, then click the Presentations folder to open it and display the tile for the **P47TryA_xx** file you saved to the OneDrive.
7. Click the **P47TryA_xx** tile to open the presentation in PowerPoint Online.
8. Leave the **P47TryA_xx** file open in the OneDrive to use in the next Try It.

(continued)

Try It! Working with Folders in the OneDrive *(continued)*

Viewing information for a OneDrive folder

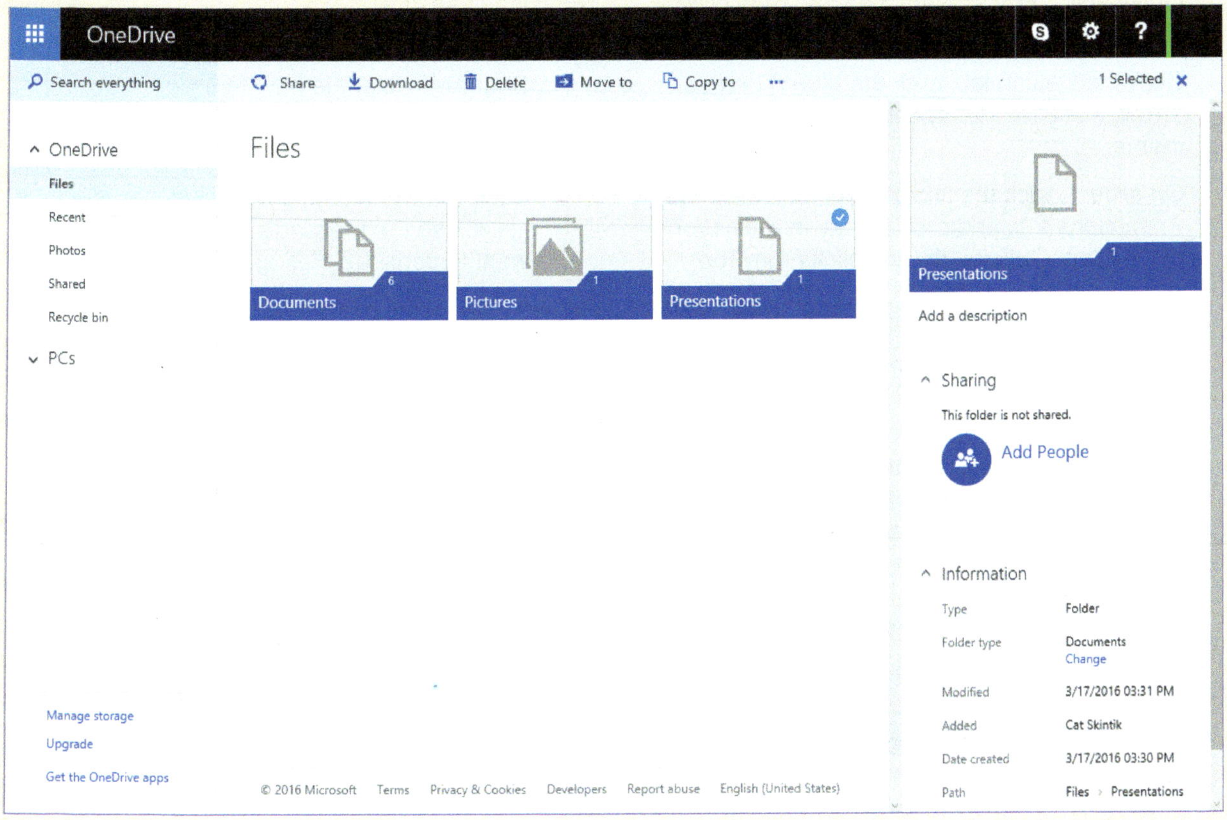

Windows 10, Microsoft Corporation

Editing a Presentation in PowerPoint Online

- You have two options for editing a presentation stored on the OneDrive. You can edit it in PowerPoint Online, or you can open the file in your desktop version of PowerPoint.
- PowerPoint Online offers many of the same commands you find in your desktop PowerPoint.
- You can modify text; insert objects such as pictures, shapes, or SmartArt diagrams; change the theme or variant; apply some animation and transition effects; and view the presentation in Reading or Slide Show view.
- You can also insert and work with comments, a valuable tool when you are working on a presentation with a team.
- You can click OPEN IN POWERPOINT at any time to open the presentation in your desktop version of PowerPoint. You might do this to use tools or features that aren't available in PowerPoint Online.
- Microsoft presents a warning about opening the online version. If you are not sure about the security of the OneDrive site or the file you want to open, you may not want to open it on your desktop.
- Whenever you open and edit the online version in PowerPoint, saving your changes updates the version stored on the OneDrive.

Try It! Editing a Presentation in PowerPoint Online

1. With the **P47TryA_xx** file open in PowerPoint Online, click Edit Presentation and then click Edit in PowerPoint Online.
2. Click the Design tab, click the More Themes arrow, and click Metropolitan to change the theme.
3. On slide 1, click the title placeholder, click the Animations tab, and click the Fly In animation. Click Effect Options and click From Top.
4. Click the subtitle placeholder, click the Animations tab, and click the Fly In animation. Click Effect Options and click From Bottom.
5. Display slide 5.
6. Click Insert > Online Pictures. In the Insert Pictures dialog box, type **soccer** in the search box and then click Search.
7. Click a search result that relates to soccer. Click Insert.
8. Move the picture to the lower-right corner and increase its size.
9. On the Picture Tools Format tab, click the Drop Shadow Rectangle picture style.
10. Click OPEN IN POWERPOINT to save changes and open the file in your desktop PowerPoint. Click Yes when asked if you want to open the file. Close the message box that asks if you want to continue editing in PowerPoint Online or get PowerPoint.

    ✓ *If you do not see the changes you made in PowerPoint Online, click the Save button on the Quick Access Toolbar.*
11. Click the Animations tab and display the Animation Pane. Set both animations to occur After Previous.
12. On the Design tab, click the Variants More button, click Colors, and change the color scheme to Red Orange.

Applying an animation to a slide in PowerPoint Online

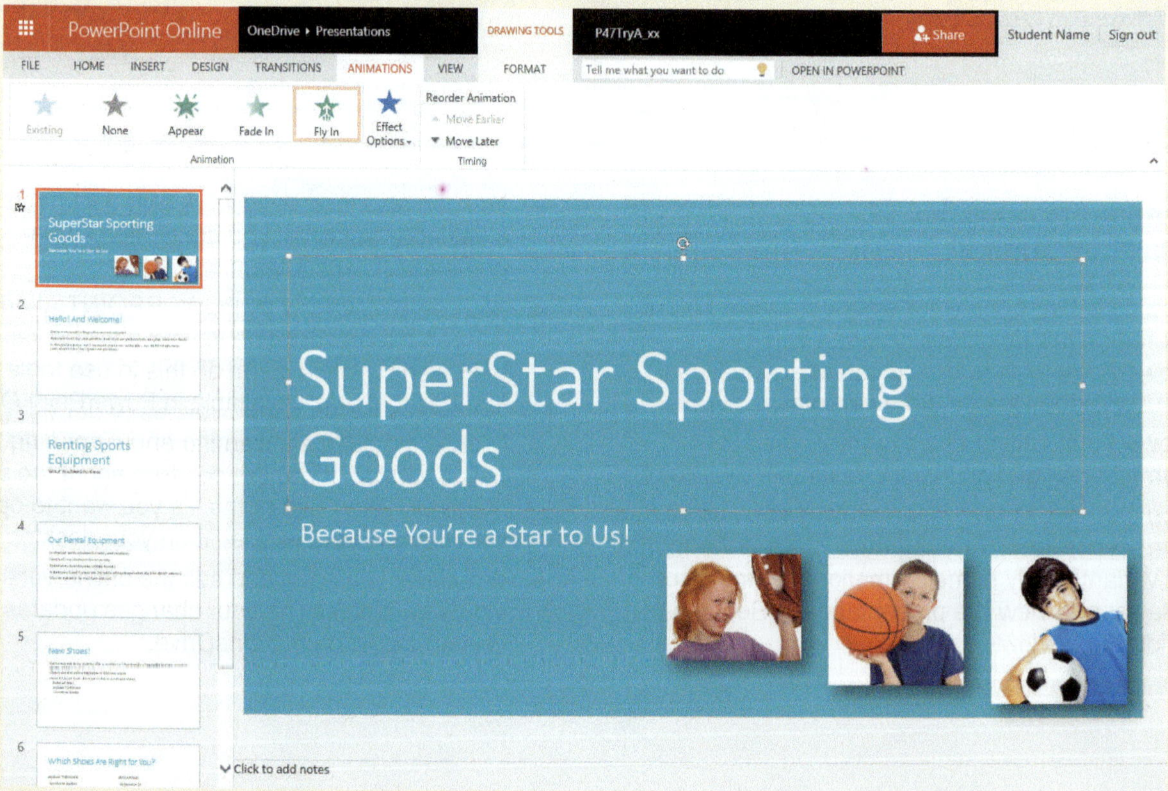

(continued)

Try It! Editing a Presentation in PowerPoint Online *(continued)*

13. Click Save on the Quick Access Toolbar to save changes and update the presentation on the OneDrive.
14. Click File > Save As, and then save the presentation with the same name in the location where your teacher instructs you to store the files for this lesson.
15. Close the presentation in PowerPoint, make the Web browser active, and open the **P47TryA_xx** file in PowerPoint Online.
16. Click Start Slide Show to view the presentation as a slide show. Notice that the changes you made in PowerPoint to animations and colors are present in the online presentation.
17. Close the **P47TryA_xx** presentation, and leave the OneDrive open for the next Try It.

Sharing Online Files

- When you are working with PowerPoint Online, you can share the presentation and work in the same file with other editors at the same time. This feature is known as **co-authoring**.
- If you have stored your files in the default Documents folder, you can choose to make this folder public, allowing anyone with a Microsoft account to access the folder. You would not want to share files in this way if they contained sensitive information.
- A much safer option is to create your own folders and then choose who can share the files in those folders.
- You set sharing options by selecting the folder or file you want to share and then sending a link to the folder or file via e-mail to your colleagues.
- You can choose whether team members can edit the file and whether anyone with access to the folder has to first sign in.

Try It! Sharing Online Files

1. In the OneDrive, select the Presentations folder. (Select the folder, do not open it.)
2. In the OneDrive toolbar, click Share and then click Email.
3. In the To box, type the e-mail address of a fellow student or your teacher.

   ✓ *If you have another e-mail account, you can send the sharing invitation to yourself and play the role of team member in the next Try It.*
4. In the *Include a personal message (optional)* box, type **Please view the P47TryA_xx file in this folder.**
5. Click Share. A sharing icon displays in the lower-right corner of the Presentations folder.
6. Have your teammate open his or her e-mail account. Your teammate should see a new message with a link to the file.
7. Leave your browser open to use in the next Try It.

(continued)

Try It! Sharing Online Files *(continued)*

Invite a colleague to share a OneDrive folder

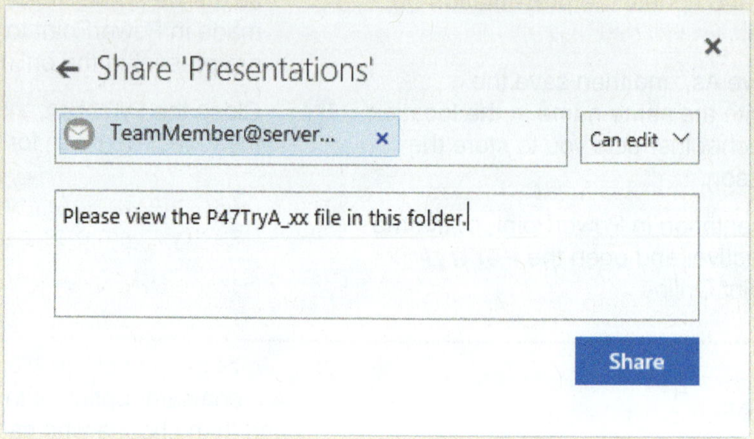

Windows 10, Microsoft Corporation

Working with Co-authors

- When you're working in PowerPoint Online, you can work with co-authors on the same file at the same time.
- While you're working in the file, your co-authors have the option of opening a read-only copy or editing the file and then synchronizing the file with the presentation on the OneDrive.
- If a co-author makes a change to the presentation, the changes will be added to the presentation when you close the file.
- To avoid confusion when several authors are working on the same file at the same time, co-authors should make a point of using positive communication skills.
  - When a group is working on a single project, they should appoint a team leader who can be responsible for establishing procedures that all group members can understand and follow.
  - Communication pathways should be established so that all participants know the best ways to contact each other to obtain and convey information. A team with good communication skills is better able to identify and resolve issues that would otherwise become problems.
  - Objectives for the project should be clarified so that all participants know the scope of work and the kinds of changes they can make. For a presentation, team members should also understand what audience the presentation is intended to reach.
- One issue that should be resolved when co-authoring is how changes are to be made. Can each reviewer make changes independent of others, or should reviewers use comments to suggest changes?
- In the latter case, one team member or the team leader would then be designated to respond to all changes and reconcile edits.

Try It! Working with Co-authors

✓ *The first five steps are instructions for your teammate. If you are using an alternate e-mail account to act as a co-author, perform these steps yourself.*

1. Your teammate should click View in OneDrive. The Presentations folder opens in the OneDrive. Click the presentation to open it.
2. Click Edit Presentation > Edit in PowerPoint Online.
3. Display slide 5. Notice the second subbullet below the last bullet item refers to Adidas TS Bound. The shoe name should be TS Bounce.
4. Click Insert > Comment. Click in the box with your login name in the Comments pane and type: **Notice name of Adidas TS shoe is wrong. It should be Bounce.**
5. At the upper-right side of the PowerPoint Online window, click Sign Out. The Online window reappears, with an option to sign in.
6. Sign in as yourself.
7. Click **Edit Presentation** > **Edit in PowerPoint Online**. Display slide 5 and click the comment marker at the upper-left corner of the slide to read the comment from your co-author.
8. In the Reply box, type **Oops!**
9. Correct the word *Bound* to **Bounce**, and then close the Comments pane.
10. Click the OPEN IN POWERPOINT tab and click Yes.
11. Save the presentation as **P47TryB_xx** in the location where your teacher instructs you to store the files for this lesson.
12. Close the **P47TryB_xx** file, and exit PowerPoint. Exit your browser.

Comments in PowerPoint Online

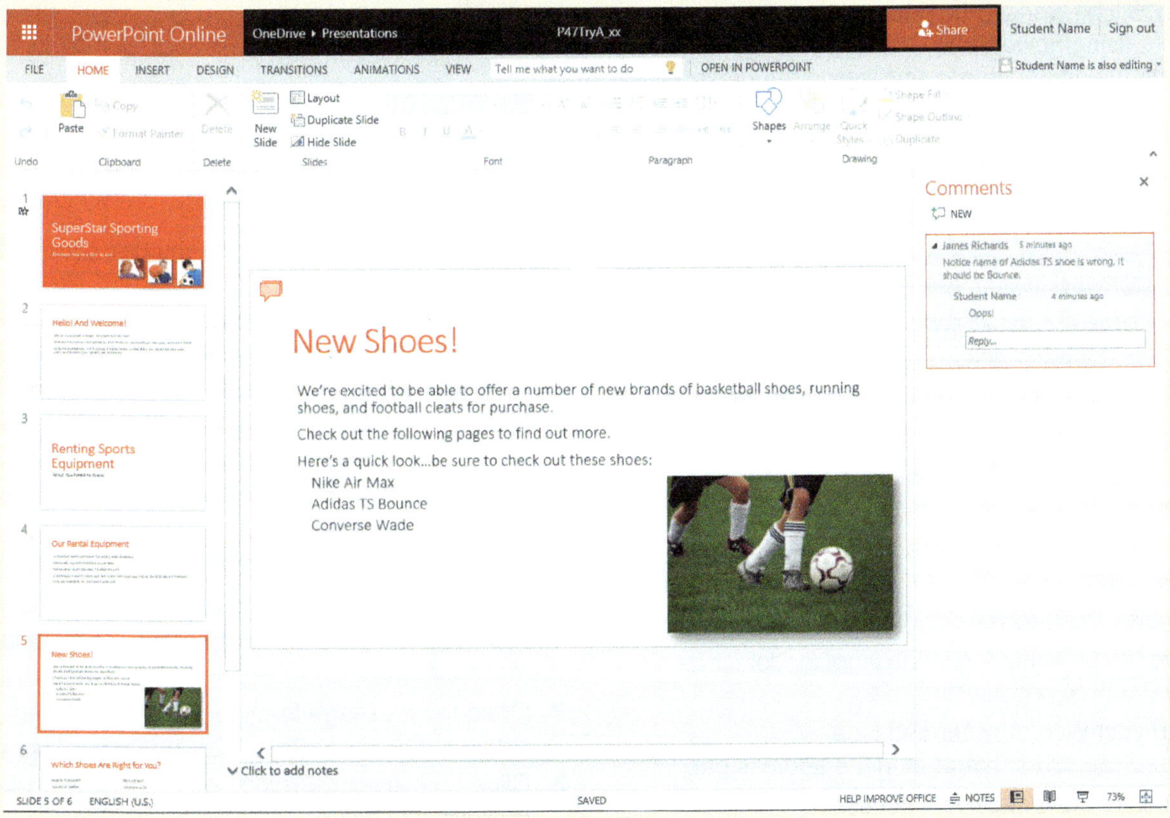

Supporting and Maintaining Web-Based Presentations

- When you upload presentations to an online environment in the expectation that others will share those files, you have a responsibility to maintain those files so that the presentations can be properly accessed and viewed.
- If a presentation contains multimedia objects, for instance, it is your responsibility to make sure that all objects play correctly on the slides when viewed. If supporting files are necessary, such as video or audio files that are linked to slides rather than embedded on them, you must make sure those linked files are available in the same folder with the presentation.
- It may also be necessary to check for new versions of multimedia objects and to update links to objects and other Web pages on a regular basis.
- Over the course of a project, online materials may go through a number of versions. If site maintenance is your job, you will need to work out a file-naming system that all users can follow to make clear which files are the most recent.
- It will also be helpful to maintain a folder of archive materials, in case it is necessary to consult a previous version.

Lesson 47—Practice

You are working with your local humane society to put together a presentation that showcases some of the animals currently available for adoption. Several of the other people working on the presentation are volunteers, and they will be working from home. You need to post the presentation to the OneDrive, so that you can all work on it using PowerPoint Online. In this project, you post the file, invite a teammate to share it, and allow the teammate to edit and add comments to the presentation.

DIRECTIONS

✓ *Work with a teammate on this exercise, or use two e-mail accounts to do all steps yourself. Steps that should be done by your teammate are in the Teammate Actions section. You will perform these steps if you are someone else's teammate or if you are doing all steps yourself.*

1. Start PowerPoint, if necessary, and open **P47Practice** from the data files for this lesson.
2. Click **File** > **Save As** > **OneDrive - Personal**
3. Click the **More options** link in the right pane to open the Save As dialog box.
4. Click **New folder** and type **Humane** as the new folder name.
5. Double-click the **Humane** folder to open it.
6. Save the presentation in the Humane folder as **P47Practice_xx**.
7. Start your Web browser and type **https://onedrive.live.com** in the address bar.
8. Sign in to the OneDrive if necessary.
9. Open the Humane folder to display the **P47Practice_xx** file, and then click the file to open it in PowerPoint Online.
10. On the PowerPoint Online menu bar, click **Share with people**.
11. In the To box, type the e-mail address of your teammate. Then in the *Include a personal message* box, type **Please review and add comments as necessary.**
12. Click **Share**, and then click **Close**.
13. Close your Web browser. Close the **P47Practice** file, and exit PowerPoint.

Teammate Actions

1. Start your e-mail program and choose to receive messages.
2. Open the message from your teammate that contains the link to the **P47Practice_xx** file.
3. Click **View in OneDrive** to open the file in PowerPoint Online.

4. Sign in with your account name and password if necessary.
5. Click **Edit Presentation** > **Edit in PowerPoint Online**.
6. With slide 1 displayed in PowerPoint Online, click **Insert** > **Comment**, and then type the following comment: **I like the theme but not the colors. Can we change color scheme?**
7. Add a second comment to slide 1: **I've animated pictures for more visual interest. Please check settings.**
8. Select the left picture, click **Animations** > **Fly In**, and then click **Effect Options** and click **From Left**.
9. Animate the center picture to **Fly In From Top**, and the right picture to **Fly In From Right**.
10. Display slide 5 and insert the following comment: **Let's change this content to a SmartArt diagram for visual variety.**
11. Click **Sign out** and then sign back in with your own account.

Update the Presentation

1. In your OneDrive, with the **P47Practice_xx** file open, click **Edit Presentation** > **Edit in PowerPoint**.
2. Click **Yes**. The presentation should show the comments added by your teammate. (If it doesn't, click the **Save** button in the Quick Access Toolbar to refresh the presentation.)
3. Save the presentation with the same name in the location where your teacher instructs you to store the files for this lesson.
4. Close the presentation, and exit PowerPoint.

Lesson 47—Apply

In this project, you continue working with the humane society presentation. You work in PowerPoint Online and in PowerPoint on your desktop to respond to your teammate's comments and finalize the presentation.

DIRECTIONS

1. Start PowerPoint, if necessary, and open **P47Apply** from the data files for this lesson.
2. Save the presentation as **P47Apply_xx** in the Humane folder on your OneDrive.
3. Open your browser and navigate to the OneDrive site. Sign in if necessary.
4. Open the **P47Apply_xx** presentation in the OneDrive and choose to edit it in PowerPoint Online.
5. On slide 1, view the comments by your teammate. Both of these issues need to be handled in the desktop version of PowerPoint, so you cannot address them now.
6. Display slide 5 and view the comment. Then close the Comments task pane.
7. On the Home tab, click **New Slide**. In the New Slide dialog box, click **Title and Content**. Click **Add Slide**.
8. Insert the title **The Adoption Process**.
9. Click in the content placeholder and then click **Insert** > **SmartArt** and select the **Vertical Chevron List** layout.
10. Insert the SmartArt content as follows:
    a. Click in the first chevron shape to select it. When the diagram changes to a text pane, type **Step 1** in the first bullet item.
    b. Click next to the first subordinate bullet and type **Come to the shelter or visit our Web site**.
    c. Click in the second subordinate bullet and then click the **Promote** button on the SMARTART TOOLS Design tab.
    d. Type **Step 2**, press ENTER, click the **Demote** button, and type **Find your special friend**.
    e. Continue adding steps as shown in Figure 47-1.
11. Click outside the diagram and wait a few seconds for it to update. Then select it and change colors to the **Colorful – Accent Colors** option.

Figure 47-1

PowerPoint 2016, Windows 10, Microsoft Corporation

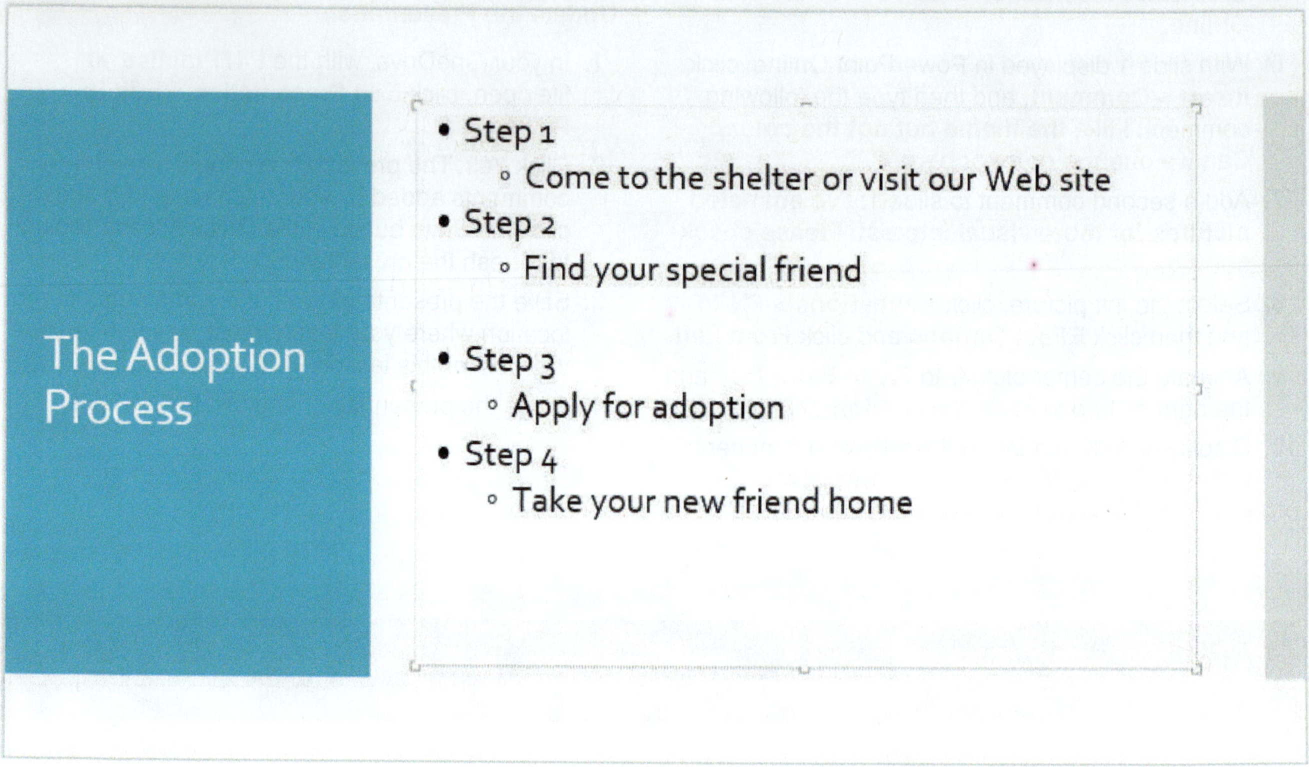

12. You no longer need slide 5, so click it and then click **Home** > **Delete**.
13. Open the presentation in PowerPoint. If you do not see the new slide 5, click **Save** in the Quick Access Toolbar to refresh the presentation.
14. Address the first comment on slide 1 by changing the color scheme to **Paper**.
15. Address the second comment on slide 1 by previewing the animations, and then change the Start option to **After Previous** for each picture. Change the Duration to **01:00** for each picture. Apply a Delay of **00.50** to the center and right pictures.
16. Delete both comments on slide 1.
17. Preview the presentation and then save changes to update the OneDrive version.
18. Save the presentation with the same name to the location where your teacher instructs you to store the files for this lesson. Then insert your name and the date on all slides.
19. **With your teacher's permission,** print slide 5. It should look similar to Figure 47-2.
20. Close the presentation, saving changes, and exit PowerPoint. Close your browser.

Figure 47-2

PowerPoint 2016, Windows 10, Microsoft Corporation

End-of-Chapter Activities

➤ PowerPoint Chapter 7—Critical Thinking

Developing a Professional Digital Portfolio

You work for Sinclair College in the Student Affairs office. Sinclair encourages students to develop a professional digital portfolio that they can present to graduate schools and prospective employers.

The Dean of Student Affairs has asked you to take on the responsibility of managing a project to educate students on how to develop their portfolios. In this project, you start, execute, control, and close the project. You will execute the project by creating a sample digital portfolio to help students design their own. You control the project by setting a deadline of two weeks and outlining the research. You research on the Web to determine what kinds of content a digital portfolio should contain, and then you develop some of that content in the form of *artifacts* such as descriptions of technical skills that have been attained, certifications, awards, community service projects, membership in organizations, a resume, sample professional documents such as application and follow-up letters, samples of project work, and evaluations of work. You create the presentation and deliver it to your classmates, closing the project efficiently and on time. The Dean of Student Affairs is very pleased with your monitoring of the project through the use of regular updates and feedback. She considers the project closed.

DIRECTIONS

1. Start a new presentation, and save it as **PCT07A_xx** in the location where your teacher instructs you to store the files for this chapter.
2. Apply a theme and variant of your choice. You may also want to change the orientation to Portrait and change the slide size to Letter Paper.
3. On slide 1, insert the title **Digital Portfolio** and use your name as the subtitle.
4. **With your teacher's permission,** research online what a digital portfolio is. View samples of digital portfolios and identify the categories of content a professional digital portfolio should include.
5. On slide 2, create a table of contents for your presentation. The contents entries should be the types of content included in a digital portfolio, as listed above.
6. Create one or more slides for each contents item. For each category of portfolio information, provide specifics of your achievement in that category. For a category such as Awards and Scholarships, for example, list awards and scholarships you have received in your educational career, or make up representative content.
7. For categories that require external documents, such as a resume or samples of application or follow-up letters, use documents you have prepared for this course or create sample documents. Save copies with appropriate names in the location where your teacher instructs you to store the files for this chapter.
8. Provide links or action buttons from the slide to those documents. Provide action buttons to return to the portfolio presentation from all external files.
9. For the project work category, select one of the Critical Thinking projects you have completed for this course. Save the title slide as a picture and use it on your portfolio slide as a link to the Critical Thinking file.
10. After you have created all the slides for the categories of the portfolio, return to slide 2 and create links from each contents item to the relevant slide.
11. For all slides except the title and the contents slide, insert a Return action button that links back to the contents slide.
12. Check the spelling and grammar in the presentation and correct errors.

13. Preview the slides and check all links and action buttons. Insert your name, slide numbers, and the date on all slides.
14. Deliver the presentation orally to your class in a manner that sustains the listeners' attention. As part of your presentation, discuss the importance of digital portfolios and why a person would want to develop one. Ask for comments on how the presentation could be improved.
15. **With your teacher's permission**, print the presentation as handouts.
16. Close the presentation, saving changes, and exit PowerPoint.

➤ PowerPoint Chapter 7—Portfolio Builder

Glacier National Park Presentation

In this project, you do the final work on Voyager's Glacier presentation. You save a slide as a picture to use in a Word document, check and address accessibility issues, add links and action buttons to external content, and finally save the presentation in PDF format.

DIRECTIONS

1. Start PowerPoint, if necessary, and open **PPB07A** from the data files for this chapter.
2. Save the presentation as **PPB07A_xx** in the location where your teacher instructs you to store the files for this chapter.
3. Start Word and open **PPB07B** from the data files for this chapter.
4. Save the document as **PPB07B_xx** in the location where your teacher instructs you to store the files for this chapter.
5. In PowerPoint, open **PPB07C** from the data files for this chapter.
6. Save the presentation as **PPB07C_xx** in the location where your teacher instructs you to store the files for this chapter.
7. In the **PPB07A_xx** file, display slide 1 if necessary, and export only the current slide as a JPEG file with the name **PPB07A_slide 1**. Save the picture in the location where your teacher instructs you to store the files for this chapter.
8. Switch to the **PPB07B_xx** Word document, and insert the **PPB07A_slide 1** picture in the first blank paragraph.
9. Save the Word document and close it.
10. Check accessibility for the presentation. Address issues as follows:
    a. Supply alternative text for the shape on slide 1, for the chart on slide 3, for the SmartArt diagram on slide 4, and for all pictures in the presentation, including the pictures in the SmartArt diagram.

       ✓ *For the pictures on slide 8, display the Selection pane and hide all pictures except Picture 2, create the Alt Text entry, and then display each additional picture to add Alt Text.*

    b. Notice the warning about merged cells in the table on slide 9. Fix this issue by deleting the first column of the table (the one with the rotated text).
    c. Read the information on how to fix the No Header Row Specified error. Delete the third row from the bottom of the table and then fix the header row error as directed in the task pane.
    d. Add alternative text for the table.
11. Display slide 2 and create a link from the phrase *Web cams* in the last bullet item to **http://www.nps.gov/glac/photosmultimedia/webcams.htm**.

12. Still on slide 2, insert actions as follows:
    a. Create a text box in the lower-left corner with the text **A brief look at . . .** . Add an action setting to the text box that links to the **PPB07B_xx** file in your solution folder.
    b. Draw a Custom action button about the same size as the text box and use the Mouse Over tab in the Action Settings dialog box to link to the first slide in the **PPB07C_xx** presentation.
    c. Format the text button and action button as desired, and position the action button behind and slightly below the text box, so that you can easily rest the mouse pointer on it during the presentation.
13. Check the reading order for all slides.
14. Insert a footer with the date and your full name on all slides.
15. Run the presentation to test your links and actions. Close the browser after testing the Web cams link; close Word after viewing the packages document; play the album slide show all the way through and then end it to return to your main presentation. Save your changes.
16. Deliver the presentation to your class. Ask for comments on how the presentation could be improved. Make any necessary changes.
17. Export the presentation in PDF format with the name **PPB07D_xx**. Select the Handouts option with 6 slides per page and frame the slides.
18. **With your teacher's permission,** print the PDF presentation.
19. Close the presentation, saving changes, and exit PowerPoint.

Illustration 7A

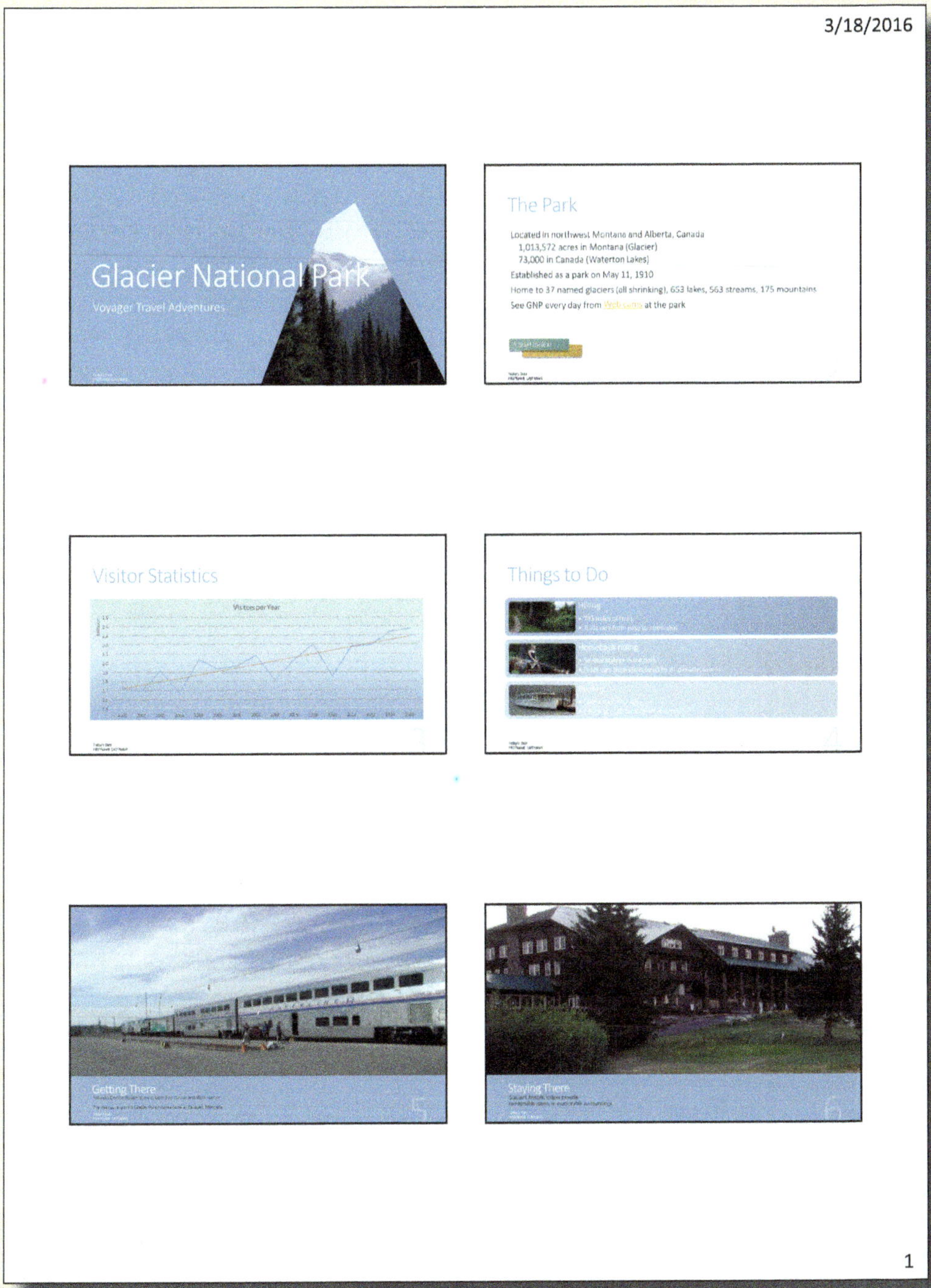

Illustration 7B

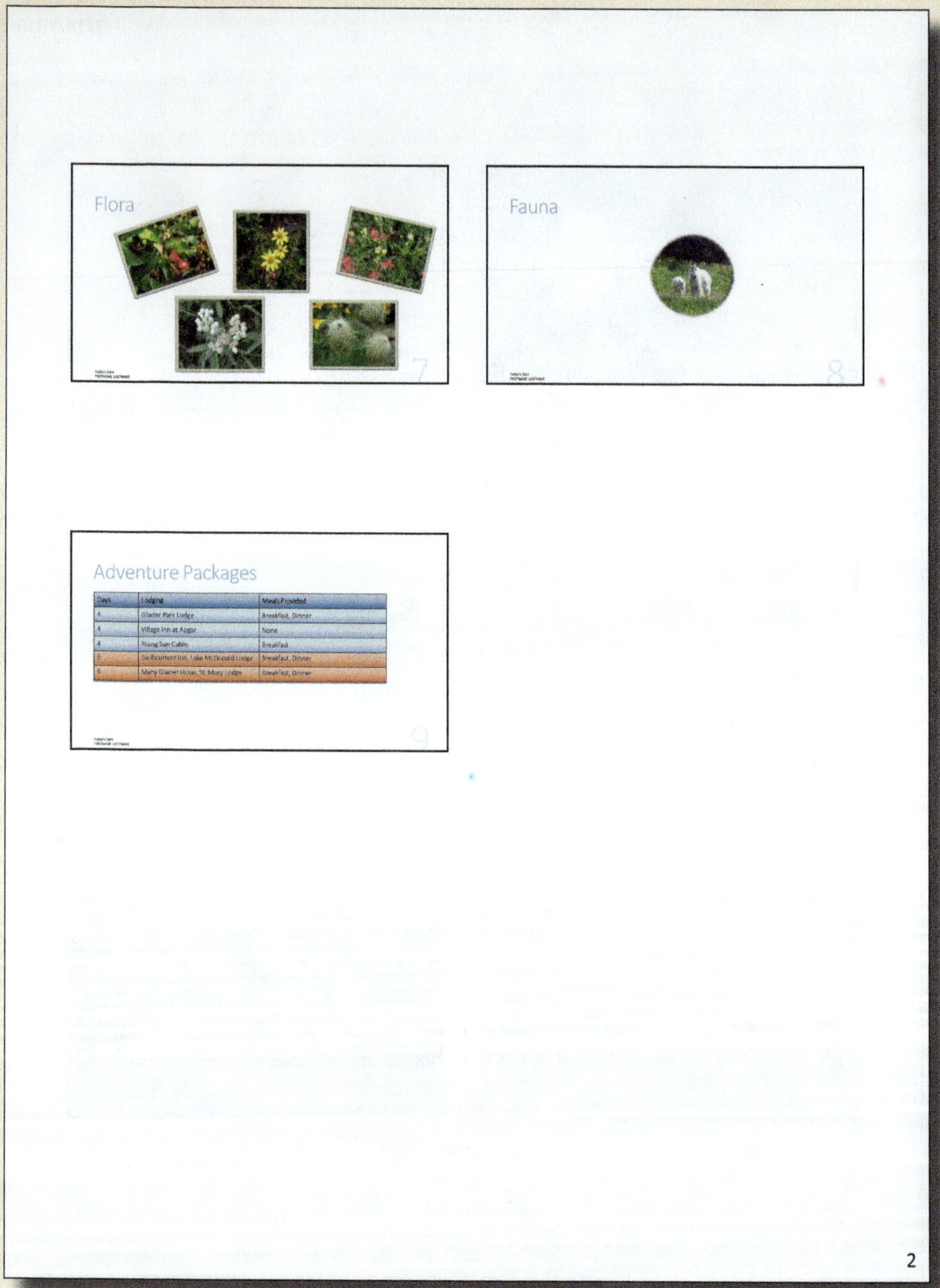

Index

D

F

X